W9-AFR-952

HANDBOOK OF BUDGETING
Fourth Edition

HANDBOOK OF BUDGETING
Fourth Edition

Robert Rachlin

Editor

JOHN WILEY & SONS, INC.

New York • Chichester • Weinheim • Brisbane • Singapore • Toronto

This book is printed on acid-free paper. ∞

Published simultaneously in Canada.

Library of Congress Cataloging-in-Publication Data:

Handbook of budgeting / [edited by] Robert Rachlin.—4th ed.
p. cm.
Includes bibliographical references and index.
ISBN 0-471-18350-4
1. Budget in business. I. Rachlin, Robert, 1937- .
HG4028.B8H36 1998
658.15′4—dc21 98-2520
CIP

Printed in the United States of America.

10 9 8 7 6 5 4 3 2 1

ABOUT THE EDITOR

Robert Rachlin, B.B.A., M.B.A., is President of Robert Rachlin Associates, and is an internationally known author, lecturer, and consultant in the area of financial management. He has spent over 40 years in planning and budgeting positions with such companies as Texaco, Gulf + Western, General Foods, SCM, and other well-known organizations.

During those years, Mr. Rachlin developed policies and procedures, financial reviews, board of directors reports, pricing strategies, mergers and acquisitions, budgeting, planning, and overall financial assignments. Such financial topics presented to executives around the world include strategic budgeting, return on investment, capital-expenditure evaluation, inventory-control techniques, sales evaluation, basic financial management, and strategic management and have earned Mr. Rachlin a worldwide reputation.

He has traveled around the world and is an internationally known consultant, educating home-based and multinational companies on such topics as strategic budgeting, profit and cash-flow management for operating managers, a management approach to capital expenditure analysis and budgets, and return-on-investment techniques and practices.

He has also served as an Adjunct Associate Professor of Management at New York University, New York Institute of Technology, and currently at Hofstra University.

He was the recipient of the ''Fellow'' Award for outstanding service to the planning profession by the Planning Executives Institute, an organization for which he served as New York Chapter President.

Mr. Rachlin is the author and/or co-editor of *Successful Techniques for Higher Profits, Return on Investment—Strategies for Decision-Making, Handbook of Strategic Planning, Total Business Budgeting: A Step-by-Step Guide with Forms, Managing Cash Flow and Capital During Inflation,* and *Return on Investment Manual: Tools and Applications for Managing Results.*

CONTRIBUTORS

George Adams, C.P.A., M.B.A., is a Managing Associate in the Financial Management Services practice of PricewaterhouseCoopers L.L.P. in Chicago. He has over 15 years experience in the industry and consulting sectors, providing expertise in the areas of cash and working capital management, shared services, financial processes, materials management, performance measurement, financial analysis, and business strategy. He has an M.B.A. from the University of Chicago, a B.S. in Accounting from the University of Illinois, and is a C.P.A.

John Antos, M.B.A., is a management consultant specializing in activity-based management, quality costs, acquisitions, planning, and modern cost systems. He consults and lectures around the world to major companies and is a recognized professional in his field. He has been a Chief Financial Officer, Director, and Controller within industry and has turned around a company on the verge of bankruptcy. He has consulted on such topics as ABM, ABC, ABB, accounting systems, strategic planning, plant expansion studies, acquisitions, and marketing. Mr. Antos has an M.B.A. in Accounting and Marketing from the University of Chicago and a B.S. in Business Administration from the University of Illinois–Urbana. He is also a Certified Management Accountant and a Certified Financial Planner.

Robert Dale Apgood, C.P.A., Ph.D., M.B.A., is a leasing and financial consultant, specializing in international leasing, accounting, and finance. Dr. Apgood has served as Chairman of the Accounting Standards Committee for the broadcast industry, as Vice-President of Finance for a broadcasting and telecommunications conglomerate, and as a full professor of accounting. In addition to his consulting practice, he is currently Vice-President of Canterbury Group, a high-tech bioremediation firm.

James A. Brimson, M.B.A., is President of IPM, Inc., an international confederation of consulting, training, and software companies who specialize in activity-based management. Prior to IPM, Inc., Mr. Brimson served as partner-in-charge of PricewaterhouseCoopers L.L.P., Deloitte's worldwide activity-based management consulting practice in London, England. He also served as director of CAM-I (an international consortium) with over 13 years of industry experience concentrating in cost management and systems development activities primarily in the manufacturing industry. Mr. Brimson is the author of *Activity Accounting: An Activity-Based Costing Approach,* published by John Wiley & Sons, Inc., and co-editor of *Cost Management for Today's Advanced Manufacturing, The CAM-I Conceptual Design,* published by Harvard Business School Press. He has a B.S. from Auburn University and an M.B.A. in quantitative science from Arizona State University.

George Cassidy is President of SC Management Services Corporation, an international business consulting firm. He has been associated for over 20 years with multinational businesses in a number of industries.

Gyan Chandra, Ph.D., is C. Rollin Niswonger Professor of Accountancy at The Richard T. Farmer School of Business Administration, Miami University, Oxford, Ohio. His principal areas of teaching and research interest are financial and managerial accounting.

Mohammad Ali Chaudry, Ph.D., was formerly Chief Financial Officer for Productivity–Cost Control of AT&T where he was responsible for developing and managing the annual budget. During his career at AT&T, he has worked on the economics of competition in the telecommunications industry, building econometric planning models, instrumental in instituting econometric demand analysis in the Bell System companies, developed quarterly and annual macroeconomic forecasts, and led the measurement of total factor productivity for the Bell System and its extension to a model linking productivity to budgeting and analyzing net income. His publications include *An Econometric Planning Model for AT&T,* Productivity Brief 18 on ''Projecting Productivity to the Bottom Line'' for the American Productivity Center, and *Net Income and Productivity Analysis (NIPA) as a Planning Model.* He received his Bachelor of Economics and Econometrics (Honors) degree from the London School of Economics and his Ph.D. from Tufts University. He also taught econometrics at the New School for Social Research, economics at Fairleigh Dickinson University and Rutgers University.

Graef S. Crystal has many years' business experience including Vice-President and member of the board of directors of Towers Perrin where he headed the firm's compensation consulting practices. He served personally as an executive compensation consultant to the senior management and their boards of more than 30 multibillion dollar companies. He also held management positions at Booz, Allen & Hamilton, Pfizer International, and General Dynamics. He has written several hundred articles on executive compensation topics, and is a frequent contributor to major publications. He is currently a columnist for *Pensions & Investments* and *The New York Observer.* He is the author of six books including *In Search of Excess: The Overcompensation of American Executives* and *What Are You Worth?.* In addition, he has contributed chapters to 11 other books.

Michael W. Curran is President and Principal Consultant of Decision Sciences Corporation, a St. Louis–based consulting and software development firm he formed in 1968. He is the developer of the theories of Bracket Budgeting and Range Estimating. He is listed in *Who's Who in Consulting, Who's Who in Industry and Finance, Who's Who in America, Who's Who in the World,* and other biographical references. He has chaired or appeared as a guest speaker at over two hundred courses and conducts seminars for top managers in many foreign countries.

Ronald A. Follet is currently a Principal in the RF Group, a consulting and advisory organization catering primarily to small and medium sized companies. Prior to his consulting activities, he held senior staff positions with several high-tech companies. He consults, lectures, and writes articles for technical and industry periodicals, and has developed specialized TQM programs for specific industry implementation. He has worked with recognized leaders in the quality field, and was a contributor/collorator on the customer quality chapter in the *Quality Handbook.* Mr. Follet has a B.S. degree in electronics engineering from the University of Rhode Island.

Albert A. Fried is an expert in the practical applications of the strategic planning process.

Leonard A. Haug is the U.S. Payroll Manager for Digital Equipment Corporation. He has held other positions within Digital and has worked for Xerox Corporation and United Airlines before joining Digital. Mr. Haug is a recognized leader in the application of TQM and EFT within the discipline of payroll. He is both an author and frequent speaker at major conferences. Under his direction, the Digital Payroll team has become one of the premier payroll organizations among U.S. industries, and has been recognized as best-in-class by multiple independent consulting organizations and publications. Mr. Haug is an active member of the American Payroll Association (APA) and serves as the chairman of the Automated Clearing House (ACH) Committee and is a member of both the APA Board of Advisors and Board of Contributing Writers. In April 1994, he was recognized by the APA as ''The Payroll Man of the Year'' for his contributions to the profession and to the association. He has a B.A. degree from North Central College and is a Certified Payroll Professional (CPP) and a Certified Six Sigma instructor.

William B. Iwaskow, M.B.A., J.D., is a consultant, business executive, and adjunct professor of management. He was formerly an Executive Vice-President at Hoffman-La Roche; a Division President and General Manager of Allied Chemical; a Director of Business Development and Planning for the International Division of American Cyanamid; and a principal at Korn Ferry International. Mr. Iwaskow is currently an Adjunct Professor of Management at William Paterson College; previously, he served in the same capacity at Pace University. In addition, he has conducted many management seminars and developed a variety of multimedia products for several trade associations. He has a broad education with degrees in engineering, business (M.B.A.), and law. He has also received President Reagan's citation for ''Private Sector Initiatives'' at the White House for raising $7 million for New Jersey doctoral engineering scholarships.

Mike Kaufman is President of Management Advisory Group, a New York consulting firm specializing in business planning and profitability improvement. His previous experience includes the New York Director of Corporate Finance Associates, a financial consulting consortium; Corporate Director of Operations Improvement for Lever Brothers Company, where he was responsible for capital planning and analysis, and held a similar position with the Sperry Corporation. Mr. Kaufman teaches corporate finance at the graduate school of Pace University and has authored a book on capital budgeting. He also lectures on financial and general management topics and conducts ongoing research regarding corporate practices in areas of finance, including cost of capital determination and other capital budgeting criteria.

Malcolm M. Knapp, M.B.A., is President of Malcolm M. Knapp, Inc., a leading consultancy to the foodservice industry. He is an advisor to many CEOs of major companies, frequently addresses trade associations, and is often quoted in the national and trade press. Mr. Knapp received a B.A. from Columbia University and an M.B.A. from Harvard University's School of Business.

Eugene H. Kramer, C.P.A., was previously a Principal in the firm of E.H. Kramer and Company.

James E. Kristy is an internationally known lecturer, writer, and consultant specializing in financial management. His background comprises an active career in business and advanced degrees in management. He was a former Senior Vice-President and Chief Financial Officer of a statewide California bank. He has practiced financial management for over 25 years in such diverse settings as the cement, motion picture, computer industries, and commercial banking. He is the creator of the Commercial Credit Matrix, a rating system for measuring a firm's financial strength. His booklet, *Analyzing Financial Statements: Quick and Clean,* describes the system, and there is a software version for personal computers. Other writings include *A Guide to Financial Planning, Finance Without Fear,* and a computer tutorial, *Analyzing Financial Statements With Electronic Spreadsheets.* He is listed in *Who's Who in Finance and Industry* and *Who's Who in the World.*

Jay H. Loevy, C.P.A., C.F.E., is a retired Partner of KPMG Peat Marwick. His present practice includes management consulting, litigation support, and forensic accounting. Mr. Loevy is also Chairman of the MCS Technical and Industry Consulting Practices Subcommittee of the AICPA.

Maria Theresa Mateo, M.B.A., is a managing associate in the Manufacturing Industrial Practice of PricewaterhouseCooper Consulting. Ms. Mateo has over eight years of consulting experience in strategic planning, business re-engineering, cost reduction, operations management, supply-chain management, in-controls risk management, and organizational analysis. Prior to consulting, Ms. Mateo capitalized on fad and established a company to domestically manufacture and distribute novelty boxer shorts. She has a B.S. degree in biology, an M.B.A. from Columbia Business School, and a psychology and economics degree from the University of Michigan.

Robert F. McElroy is a Managing Associate in PricewaterhouseCoopers L.L.P.'s Consulting Division, in the Financial Management & Business Analysis (FMBA) group, located in the New York metropolitan area. He has over six years of consulting experience in a variety of industries, including telecommunications and chemical manufacturing. He specializes in financial process redesign work, as well as activity-based management projects.

C. Eugene Moore is Principal of C. Eugene Moore & Associates. For over 25 years, he has been a manufacturing executive with profit and loss responsibility as well as a lecturer and seminar leader. In his executive capacities, he has participated in and directed notable profit improvement and growth processes for E.M.D., Crown Cork and Seal Company, Mack Truck, Crompton and Knowles, Singer, and Littell Machine Company. Mr. Moore has completely planned, contracted, and managed the construction and occupancy of manufacturing plants in the United States, Europe, and South America.

Donald R. Moscato, Ph.D., M.B.A., is a Professor in the Department of Management Science and Systems of the John G. Hagan Graduate School of Business Administration of Iona College. He holds a Ph.D. degree from the Graduate School of Business of Columbia University and has a B.A. degree in economics and an M.B.A. in management science from Iona College. He has authored numerous articles, consulted, and is a frequent speaker at professional seminars. He was awarded a Certificate in Data Processing by the Institute for the Certification of Computer Professionals.

Athar Murtuza, Ph.D., C.M.A., is an Associate Professor of Accounting at Seton Hall University. His teaching interest is in the areas of managerial and cost accounting, and his research and consulting interests include effective communication of accounting information, activity-based costing, and process design. Dr. Murtuza has published articles in a number of professional and academic journals and is a Certified Management Accountant.

Thomas F. Norris is a Managing Associate in the consumer and industrial manufacturing practice of the New York metro consulting office of PricewaterhouseCoopers L.L.P. Mr. Norris has over 20 years' experience in operations, materials management, accounting, and information technology. His experience also includes both centralized and decentralized management in global environments. He has a B.B.A. from Siena College in Accounting and has both CPIM and CIRM designations from the American Production and Inventory Control Society.

Thomas Pollina, M.B.A., C.P.A., is an Associate Professor of Accounting at Iona College. He is a former member of the accounting firm of Ernst & Ernst and currently owns his own accounting practice, specializing in computer applications in accounting.

Peter A. Pyhrr is chairman of three specialty printing companies in Dallas, Texas (Hospital Forms & Systems Corporation, Magnetic Ticket & Label Corporation, and Inkless Image Corporation). He was formerly president of his own consulting company and controller of two divisions of Texas Instruments. He is invariably identified as developing the concept of ''zero-based budgeting.'' He served as a consultant to then Georgia Governor Jimmy Carter for the first government implementation. He has many years of consulting experience in both industry and government, specializing in long-range planning, operational planning, budgeting, and control. He has lectured and written extensively on the subject of zero-based budgeting.

Donniel S. Schulman is the lead partner of PricewaterhouseCoopers L.L.P., New York Financial Management practice. Mr. Schulman has over 15 years of industry and consulting experience in the areas of business process re-engineering, shared services, world-class finance, cash, and working capital management. He is the leading expert in assisting companies to manage their accounts receivables and working capital. His principal focus is to help the client's finance function forge a partnership with the businesses. He has worked across industries including manufacturing, consumer products, telecommunications, chemicals, publishing, and P&C, and group health insurance. Mr. Schulman has frequently been quoted as an expert in financial management processes in *CFO* magazine, *Chemical Weekly,* and other trade publications.

Gert Schumann is an independent business consultant. He was formerly the officer in charge of international operations for a major paper and forest products company.

R. Malcolm Schwartz is a Partner with PricewaterhouseCoopers L.L.P. and responsible for the delivery of financial management consulting services in the eastern region. He also led the firmwide development of the activity-based management practice and was a principal author of *Internal Control—Integrated Framework.* He currently focuses on the consumer products industry and has clients in the public and private sectors. He has held senior management roles in finance and control, distribution, industrial engineering, and division and general management. Prior to his association with PricewaterhouseCoopers L.L.P., he was a senior partner and chief financial officer of a major worldwide management consulting firm.

Surendra S. Singhvi, Ph.D., C.P.A., C.M.A., is President of Singhvi and Associates Inc., a consulting firm offering a broad spectrum of services in the fields of business strategy and financial management. He has served the industry in numerous positions including General Manager–Financial Management at Armco, Inc., and Vice-President and Treasurer of Edison Brothers Stores, Inc. With a doctorate in finance from Columbia University, Mr. Singhvi has taught at Xavier University, Miami University, and the University of New Hampshire. He is co-editor of *Frontiers of Financial Management* and *Global Finance 2000.* He has published about 100 articles and monographs in finance and planning.

Francoise Soares-Kemp, C.F.P., was a Director with Swiss Bank Corporation and previously served as a member of senior management at Credit Suisse Private Banking. Mrs. Soares-Kemp has been a foreign exchange analyst for over 20 years and is a prolific contributor to major magazines and textbooks. She is widely and frequently quoted in the financial press as well as appearances on television on subjects dealing with foreign exchange markets. She earned her M.A. degree in economics at New York University and has continued to teach foreign exchange markets as an adjunct associate professor for over a decade. She was awarded the Award for Teaching Excellence by the same university in 1990.

Christopher S. Spence, M.B.A., is a Consulting Manager in the Hartford, Connecticut, office of Ernest & Young. He serves as a national resource for preparing and reviewing health-care budgets and markets, and sells and supports health-care budgeting software packages. He also consults with hospitals and other health-care providers on budgeting, cost management, and other financial and operational issues.

Ronald K. Tucker, B.B.A., C.P.C.U., A.R.M., is a Vice President with Hagedorn & Company and was previously Vice-President in the Johnson & Higgins Middle Market Division where he was responsible for new business sales activities. Mr. Tucker has served in various sales and management roles with another national broker; was responsible for wholesale and retail sales at the Rhulen Organization; has owned his own insurance agency; and worked for two large insurers, Reliance Insurance Company and American International Group.

Vicki L. Tucker, M.S., A.R.M., is a risk consultant. She has developed risk-management systems within the health-care industry. Her prior experience includes President, Risk Management & Quality Assurance Consulting Services, Inc.; Administrator for Professional Services for the Lake County Health Care Systems, Inc.; and Director of Medical Staff Services/Risk Management/Quality Assurance. Ms. Tucker is currently an administrator with the Center for Rehabilitation.

Frederick J. Turk, C.P.A., M.B.A., is President of Campus Services, a division of Aramark Corporation which specializes in providing a broad range of managed services to over 400 institutions of higher education in the United States. Prior to joining Aramark, Mr. Turk was a Partner with KPMG Peat Marwick L.L.P., where he served as National Director of the Higher Education, Research, and Other Not-For-Profits line of business and directed the firm's accounting and auditing, consulting, and tax services to colleges and universities. Mr. Turk is on the faculty of the College Business Management Institute at the University of Kentucky. He is a frequent speaker at workshops and seminars focusing on the business of higher education and has written numerous articles on subjects pertaining to resourcing, planning, organization restructuring, information systems management, costing, and financial analysis. Mr. Turk is a member of the Advisory Board of the Graduate School of Management at the College of William and Mary in Williamsburg, Virginia. He is also a member of the University of Delaware's Hotel, Restaurant, and Institutional Management Advisory Board.

Paul D. Warner, C.P.A., LL.M., Ph.D., is Chairperson and Professor of Accounting and Business Law, Frank G. Zarb School of Business, Hofstra University. Dr. Warner was also active in public accounting, holding various positions, the most recent as the National Director of Auditing at BDO Seidman, L.L.P., and previously was director of management services as well as a tax and an audit partner in other regional and national CPA firms. Dr. Warner is currently a member of the New York Society of Certified Public Accountants' Auditing Standards and Procedures Committee, its General Committee on Higher Education and Entry to the Profession, and the Scope of Practice Task Force. He recently completed a three-year term as a member of the American Institute of Certified Public Accountants' Computer Audit Committee of the Auditing Standards Board. Dr. Warner received his Ph.D. in accounting and computer applications and information systems and an M.B.A. in Accounting from the Graduate School of Business Administration, New York University. He also received J.D. and LL.M. (taxation) degrees from the New York University School of Law. He is a C.P.A., a member of the New York and federal bars, and holds a Certificate in Data Processing.

Richard S. Wasch is Partner in the New York Office of Andersen Consulting. He has specialized in the financial information systems area of their practice, primarily for the service industries. He has had extensive experience with nonprofit organizations in the design and implementation of management accounting and reporting systems for project, program, and grant management in numerous fields. He frequently lectures on planning and budgeting techniques for various associations. He is a graduate of Lehigh University with a B.A. in industrial engineering and an M.A. in management science.

R. Layne Weggeland was formerly Vice-President of Business Operations and Planning for UNIX International Inc. He also served as President of Maple Business Consultants, Inc.; President of Royal Worcester Spode, Inc.; and Vice-President of Finance for Estee Lauder International, Inc. He has served as Director of the Internal Audit Department for Estee Lauder. Mr. Weggeland received his B.A. from Drew University and attended New York University's Graduate School of Business.

Glenn A. White is a Senior Manager in PricewaterhouseCoopers L.L.P.'s Consulting Division, in the Integrated Health Care Services Consulting group, located in Philadelphia. He works with pharmaceutical and biotechnology manufacturers to provide value-adding solutions in the areas of materials management, production operations, sales, marketing, financial operations, and other corporate support functions. His background includes activity-based cost management; business-process re-engineering; systems requirements analysis, definition, selection, and implementation; financial analysis; and operations and cost improvement.

Serge L. Wind, Ph.D., is Special Project and Analysis Director at Lucent Technologies, with responsibility for identifying and targeting financial measures, monitoring the capital and investment program, establishing financial targeting via competitor analogs, generating financial models, overseeing transfer pricing, and performing special analytical studies (including analyzing corporate mergers and acquisitions). Mr. Wind holds Ph.D. and B.A. degrees in statistics and economics from Columbia University.

Maurice I. Zeldman is President of Emzee Associates of Pittsburgh, PA. His technical consulting group works in all of the interface activities associated with product or process development, including research and development, engineering, marketing, production, and transfer of technology. His prior experience includes Director of Technical Development for Rockwell International, where he planned, staffed, and operated a development center that was responsible for developing new products and a new business. He was also responsible for technological planning for 14 industrial divisions. Mr. Zeldman has written several books, is a frequent lecturer, and is a licensed professional engineer in the state of New York.

PREFACE

A budget has generally been defined as the formal expression of the plans and objectives of management that covers all phases of operations for a specific period of time. No other management tool can provide the operational direction that a well-planned and meaningful budget can, as well as provide the link between the short- and long-term plans of an organization. It allows and encourages participation from all parts of the organization and focuses on longer-term strategies, and most importantly, it enhances the planning of organizational goals and objectives.

The budgeting process also establishes guidelines for acceptable organizational performance in the future and provides a mechanism to allocate human resources, facilities, and other resources, rationally and economically. In summary, budgets help any organization identify opportunities, define problems, and intelligently allocate resources.

In addition, budgeting aids the decision-making process and helps coordinate the efforts of the various groups within the organization. As a final note, the budget process provides objective measures of organizational performance targets.

The fourth edition of the *Handbook of Budgeting* has been completely revised and restructured to bring together in one volume all facets of budget preparation and presentation for both profit and nonprofit organizations. Additional chapters have been added to reflect unique budgeting processes within specific industries such as educational institutions, health care, nonprofit organizations, and biotech companies.

Every effort has been made to enlist the contributions of leading experts in the field of budgeting. Each author brings to this book his or her expertise in each of their respective areas. All of these contributors have been and/or continue to be practitioners in one or more fields of budgeting, and some have combined their practical experience into the educational arena. Their views are current and timely, and they are approached from many different levels within an organization. They indeed reflect the state-of-the-art in the field of budgeting. To maintain this state-of-the-art, periodic updates and supplements will be issued to buyers of the book from time to time.

The fourth edition of the *Handbook* is structured by dividing the book into major segments, which includes the following parts:

1. **Introduction to the Budgeting Process.** A comprehensive review of the relationships between the managerial process, strategic and other plans, and the economic environment. This part will also address internal control.
2. **Tools and Techniques.** Examines the many tools and techniques needed in the budgeting process and the relationship of cost behavior. Such tools and techniques as breakeven, cost of capital, performance compensation, and scheduling shareholder value are fully explored.
3. **Preparation of Specific Budgets.** Details the comprehensive preparation of such

specific budgets as sales and marketing, manufacturing, research and development, payroll, foreign exchange, leasing, administrative, capital investments, cash, the balance sheet, international operations, and property and liability insurance requirements.

4. **Budgeting Applications.** Focuses on various applications used in the budgeting process such as zero-base, quality control, activity based techniques, fuzzy logic, bracket, and program budgeting. Both the applications of computers in budgeting and the behavioral aspects of budgeting are explored in detail.
5. **Industry Budgets.** A comprehensive review of the budgeting process within such industries as, nonprofit organizations, higher education, the health care industry and biotech industry.

Within the 38 chapters, over 42 experts discuss the concepts that are basic to the budgeting process and time tested as well as some of the most modern budgeting concepts and applications.

Practical working examples of forms, techniques, reports, and so on, are also included. Thus, we believe that in its entirety, this *Handbook* is one of the most current, comprehensive, and authoritative works on the subject of budgeting.

The fourth edition features complete reviews and updates on all original chapters as well as the eight new chapters. These new chapters address important issues of budgeting. They include ''Budgeting Shareholder Value,'' ''Budgeting Payroll Costs,'' ''Budgeting the Purchasing Department and Tax Purchasing Power,'' ''Leasing,'' ''Understanding Foreign Exchange Transactions,'' ''Budgeting for Total Quality Control,'' ''Activity-Based Budgeting,'' and ''Fuzzy Logic Applied to Budgeting: An Intuitive Approach to Coping with Uncertainty.''

The authors have updated most chapters to reflect changes in budgeting and other related environments, with major rewrites in ''Profitability and the Cost of Capital,'' ''Sales and Marketing Budget,'' ''Administrative Expense Budget,'' ''Cash Budgeting,'' ''Bracket Budgeting,'' ''Program Budgeting: Planning, Programming, Budgeting,'' and ''Techniques of Scheduling Budgets.''

The fourth edition is the latest update on the most complete, practical ''how to'' book of budgeting preparation, presentation, analysis, and uses ever published for today's modern manager.

The cooperation and contribution of all the authors have been instrumental in the final product and to each of them we give a sincere thanks for another job well done. As usual, we are particularly grateful to the staff of John Wiley & Sons for their individual assistance and guidance in preparing the content on this most important subject.

ROBERT RACHLIN
Editor

Plainview, New York

CONTENTS

PART 1

INTRODUCTION TO THE BUDGETING PROCESS

CHAPTER 1
Budgeting and the Managerial Process

CHAPTER 2
Budgeting and the Strategic Planning Process

CHAPTER 3
Budgeting and Its Relation to the Economic Environment

CHAPTER 4
The Budget: An Integral Element of Internal Control

CHAPTER 1

BUDGETING AND THE MANAGERIAL PROCESS*

Athar Murtuza

Associate Professor of Accounting, Seton Hall University

1.1 FUNCTIONS PERFORMED BY THE BUDGETING PROCESS. The budgeting or planning process serves a number of functions. The performance of such functions depends largely on management itself. Manager's needs and expectations, and the use they make of budgeting, are influenced heavily by a number of factors related to management background and the business system. These will be discussed in the following section, after considering what management expects from the budget activity.

Ideally, management wants its budgeting function to provide some or all of the following (the list does not include all possible uses/benefits associated with budgets):

- An accurate, timely analytical tool
- The ability to predict performance
- Assistance in allocating resources
- The ability to control ongoing (current) performance
- Early warnings of departure from forecasts
- Early signals of oncoming opportunities or threats
- As an organizational learning device
- Leads to organizational consensus
- Promotes understanding among members of management of their co-workers' problems
- Forces the firm to examine itself
- A means of communicating
- Reduces uncertainties
- Frees managers from day-to-day operational problems through the formulation of plans, procedures, and policies
- Forces managers to think in concrete terms

* Original chapter in the second edition of the *Handbook of Budgeting* was written by Hugh W. Schwartz, president of Penzance Associates, Inc.

If the budget process is to serve the above-mentioned functions, there must be a good linkage to the company chart of accounts and an equally good linkage to the planning system.

Often, a budget is equated with a map. The analogy is only partially correct. Geography is relatively unchanging, and road maps retain their relevance for long stretches of time. However, there is nothing constant when it involves the working of an organization. In normal corporate life, the ideal is seldom attained. Rapidly changing environments, legislative change, and/or unexpected business events (e.g., strikes, accidents) can disrupt the process. Management spends more of its time in ''fire fighting''—that is, in handling crises—than in running the business. Despite the lack of certainty that can make budgets lose their relevance, there is no denying the usefulness of the budget. Such usefulness extends to not just the document itself, but benefits can accrue to an organization on account of the entire process.

1.2 OVERVIEW OF THE BUDGETING PROCESS. Budgets should be a product of strategical planning on the part of an alert, informed management. Through the budget-planning process, management can organize and effectively deploy organizational resources. With the help of budgets, management can evaluate organizational performance and make necessary changes when external or internal variables warrant correction. While formulating budgets and then using them to evaluate and/or correct organizational performance, managers must by necessity make decisions and choose among a wide range of options. Budgets can help narrow the range of options and improve the quality of decisions made.

Budgeting cannot displace good management. It is only a tool whose use depends on the skills managers bring to their jobs. Even though there is much more to management than the budget, the fact remains that management and budget are inextricable. The relationship between them is identical to the one visualized by the poet W. B. Yeats concerning inseparability of dancers from their dances. You may see the relationship between an organization and its budget as being symbiotic. The technical, quantitative elements of the budget and its organizational aspects enjoy a mutually supportive relationship; the two help shape each other. Budget implementation reflects management, and although management is responsible for helping to develop the budget, it in turn is shaped by it. The process and its product are a means of making managers more effective.

Budgets are shortchanged when they are seen as only quantitative expressions of plans of action. To be fully appreciated, budgets must not be seen merely as end products described in monetary and quantitative terms. Instead, the appreciation of budgets can be enhanced if one focuses on the entire budgetary process and not just on the budget document itself. Budget, or rather the budget document, is one of the elements and not the entire process.

Exhibit 1.1 illustrates the budgeting process. This diagram depicts the managerial activity that leads to budget preparation in a business organized by profit centers. The horizontal arrow labeled ''Time'' is a representation of the time span (typically several months) during which the process occurs. Although companies may not follow these steps exactly, in one way or another they pass through them. A centralized, integrated firm would have cost centers instead of profit centers, and the budget would be prepared at the top level, but similar information would be handled and a set of analogous steps followed.

Each component of the process is dependent on the components that precede it; in turn, each component helps to formulate those that follow it. The process is cyclical, repeating

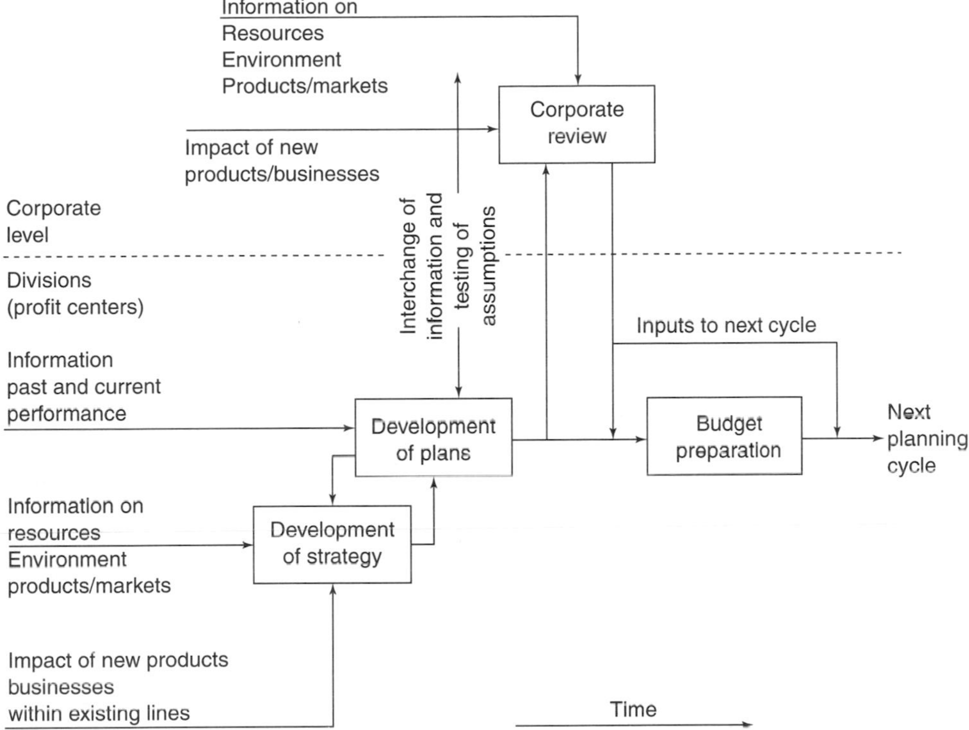

Exhibit 1.1. Strategy/plans/budgets

itself constantly, subject to modification based on the lessons learned throughout the process. The process is recurrent and continuous with one cycle leading to the next. In the ideal situation, there is a constant interaction of strategies, plans, and budgets. New products or processes are phased in, old ones are dropped, and the budget is revised to reflect the changes. Real life is hardly ever that tidy, but the budget is still the principal control exercised by management. In the following pages, different components of the budgeting process are discussed.

The budgeting process for a firm building large commercial airplanes will be quite different from that used for budgeting in a consumer goods (retail) business. Although the concepts of budgeting are the same, the airplane producer is apt to be integrated, to be set up by cost centers, and to have a product cycle, from inception to delivery, of several years. The final product is a complex assembly put together from tens of thousands of different parts. In contrast, the consumer goods business may be divided into product or product-line profit centers, and its product cycle can be a matter of months. The key factors in the two businesses may be quite different. The airframe and engine activity depends heavily on engineering and production expertise; the design and production costs will be key elements. In the consumer goods business, the marketing costs and especially the elusive activity of merchandising may be the critical sectors. Although the end result—having a usable, accurate budgeting process—is the same, the elements examined and the way they are put together will be quite different.

The role of the chief executive officer (CEO) in the budgeting process is also a key component. The part he or she elects to play depends on his or her background, skills, and personal inclinations. Some CEOs take an intense and detailed interest; others may make only a final review or leave the whole process up to other officers, merely accepting or rejecting the final report. Experience indicates that better results are obtained when CEOs are fully involved at all important decision points so that they understand what lies behind the figures. Many CEOs believe that they must be an integral part of both the design and the use of the budgeting system.

Managers are generally fairly rational, so there is a natural effort to build a base of goals, assumptions, and strategies on which the budget can be established. In some companies, the process is highly developed, with substantial interchange of information and a clear statement of goals, objectives, and strategies. Product and product-line performance expectations are developed, and the budget emerges from well-defined guidelines. Budgets then become useful tools for resource allocation, staffing changes, production schedules, and, in short, the operation of the enterprise.

In most budgeting systems, there is a close relationship to the chart of accounts—in many systems the budget is based on this—so that actual performance will be very close to budget if none of the assumptions change. As other chapters in this handbook illustrate, there are many ways to analyze budget variances, to identify the causes, and to take corrective action. It is this practice of budget reviews that represents one of management's best uses of the budgeting process—or certainly one that is most sought. Exhibit 1.2 restructures the process depicted in Exhibit 1.1 and adds some detail to show more of the steps involved in producing a budget. The planning phase appears on the left-hand side, with budgeting in the center and on the right. The review and control activity is along the left at the bottom.

1.3 BUDGET DOCUMENTATION. A typical textbook definition of budget will refer to it as a quantitative or financial expression of a plan of action prepared annually. A previous edition of this chapter defined budgeting as "the orderly presentation of the anticipated results of a plan, project, or strategy." Such a definition circumscribes the budget much too narrowly. It focuses on what and when but says nothing about the "who" and "why" of budgeting. Such a narrow definition gives the budget an independent identity and by so doing, it ignores the managers and the organization. It may be that managers, because of their indoctrination, have themselves come to see the definition as sufficient, which may explain why they forget that *they are responsible for managing.* Instead of managing, they abdicate their responsibility and "manage by the budget." Unfortunately, the budget (being time bound) does not anticipate the future and does not provide ready-made answers to managerial questions that subsequently arise.

Planning information is brought together in the revenue and cost forecasts, which form the starting point of an operating budget. In most businesses, such information takes the form of income (profit and loss) statements. There are, of course, all of the supporting schedules such as funds flow, capital projects, human resources, and so forth, none of which are indicated in Exhibit 1.2. The format is (or may be) also repeated for each profit or cost center, department, division, or management unit for which budgets are to be used as a management tool.

Depending on their background and viewpoint, managers will emphasize different steps in the budget preparation process as crucial. For example, the chief financial officer (CFO) is apt to feel that the preparation of the financial schedules is of paramount importance, whereas the marketing executive will focus on the key role(s) of product strategies, compet-

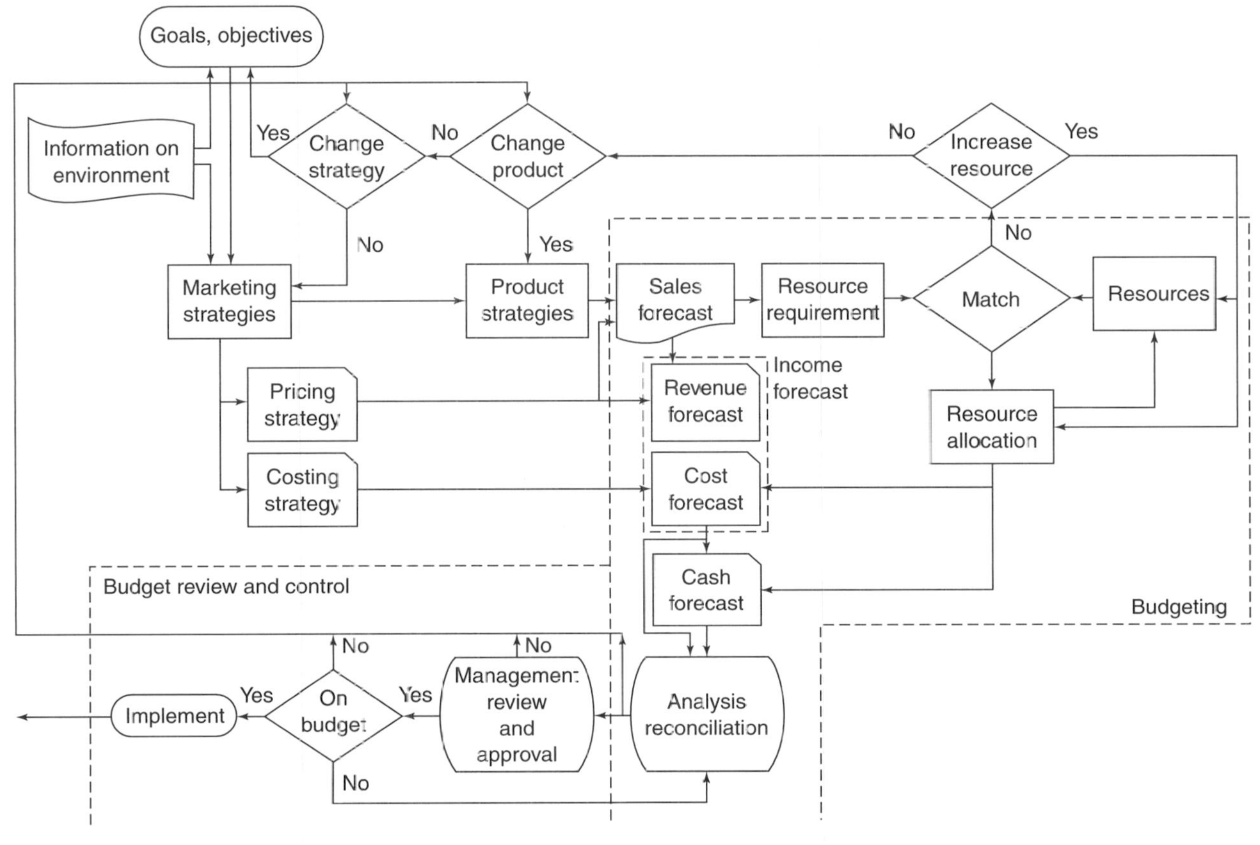

Exhibit 1.2. Planning/budgeting process

itive environment, and the sales forecast. The cash budget may be of chief interest to a different department of the firm.

In Exhibit 1.2, two of the more crucial points in the managerial process are readily visible. Failure to handle them properly will undermine the entire budgeting process. One of these is the step of matching (Match) resource requirements to resource availability; the other (Analysis Reconciliation) is the step in which the budget is compared with the expected outcome. In this latter step, the budget is compared to company goals and objectives if these have been stated. However, these may be informal, and the budget either meets or does not meet management expectations. The reconciliation step may be repeated several times before an acceptable budget is obtained, and, as indicated previously, the process can be abrasive.

Depending on production and product life cycles, problems of resource matching step may be (initially) skirted. However, a budget that is based on a mismatch of requirements and availability will eventually require substantial or complete revision. If resources are unavailable, inventories and eventually markets will run dry. If excess resources are available, price levels may be eroded or inventories increased to uneconomic levels. The budgeting process, if executed properly, embodies all management functions, and the difficulty of harmonizing all of the conflicting pressures is apparent. Any of the reasons mentioned in the following section as to why budgeting is not more successful—or at least easier to perform—can throw a serious kink into the overall process. With this in mind, the distinctly different viewpoints that managers bring to the budgeting operation become significant.

1.4 IMPEDIMENTS TO EFFECTIVE BUDGETING. Barriers to effective budgeting and planning include the following:

- Management's failure to understand its business system. Managers become concerned with details or try to control the wrong factors.
- Lack of management support for the budgeting system. Top management does not support or participate meaningfully in the activity.
- Failure to understand the critical role of budgeting in the management process.
- Overcommitment to, or undue reliance on, the budget process—that is, trying to substitute "following the budget" for judgment. Blind adherence to a budget can place excessive restraint on a business, choking innovation.
- Misunderstanding or mismatching of products and markets.
- Managers sometimes engage in "games" to "protect their turf" or protect their budget against anticipated reductions.

It could be said that competent managers will not allow any of the preceding situations to occur; nevertheless, anyone who has experienced an annual budget review understands the difficulties. Even if the budget process is working properly, the final preparation and/or review of an annual budget is a rigorous test of management. There are usually hard decisions regarding trade-offs of resources allocated to new products versus existing ones, between various market areas, and between research and production. Staffing levels, employee benefits, and changes needed to comply with government regulations compete with corporate profits. Meeting the test makes a management team effective.

1.5 WHAT IS EFFECTIVE MANAGEMENT? An organization cannot function in isolation of its environment; as a result, managers must constantly scan their environments.

Additionally, an organization cannot function in an ad hoc fashion; it must anticipate and plan. An organization needs resources to function, and these resources must be obtained, organized, and led. Along the way, managers need to monitor and adjust the deployment of organizational resources. Through it all, they must make decisions that involve choosing among alternatives. The effectiveness of managers is directly related to the decisions they make as they scan, plan, organize, lead, and control. The quality of the decisions they make is directly related to how well informed managers are and how well they communicate.

Information communicated to managers and information that they subsequently disseminate have a lot to do with the decisions they make and how they are implemented. Informed managers with a talent for communicating, we assume, are better managers than those who, afflicted with communicational myopia, can only shoot in the dark—which they must do without appropriate information. Budgets are a major form of communication within a firm. Throughout the budgetary process, communication of information is taking place.

1.6 BUDGETS AS A CONTROL TOOL. Management must ensure that plans and policies are being implemented. Seeing to it that the plans are being implemented requires effective control. Properly used, budgets are the principal means of control available to managers. Budgets become instruments of control by helping to set in motion the setting of standards and variance analysis.

1.7 BUDGETS, STANDARD COSTS, AND VARIANCE ANALYSIS. Strategic plans, budgets, standard costs, and variance analysis, distinct yet interrelated, help managers plan and control organizational activity. Strategic plans are the starting point. Budgets are derived from the strategic plans and usually cover a year's activity. A budget may be the first year of a three- to five-year plan. Standards translate budget to the operational level, and variance analysis helps one with performance measurement, to plan subsequent budgetary goals, and directs managers to areas that need attention. Without variance analysis, budgets and standards have the potential of turning into mere good intentions (and everybody knows that the road to hell is paved with good intentions).

Budgets help to define performance standards, which then provide operational managers with guidelines about what is expected. They are the foundation of responsibility accounting, which measures managers' performances on the basis of what they actually control.

Even though standards and standard costs are often spoken of as being identical, it is worth noting that there is a difference between standards and standard costs. Standard costs may be seen as a translation of standards into an accounting framework or monetary terms.

From the perspective of the budgetary process, there are two activities that often cause great difficulty. The first is the handling of standards or objectives that differ from the budget—for example, sales targets or quotas that are set higher than the budget. When these are properly used, they can be incentives for superior performance. There is, however, a tendency for management to incorporate them into the budget. They then become a commitment, which management uses as a club, thus destroying their effectiveness.

The second activity is closely related and concerns the so-called budget game. Here, department or division heads submit a budget whose performance level is scaled down from what they feel capable of doing. They do this because they know that management is going to push for higher performance levels.

1.8 WHAT DO VARIANCES REVEAL? Variances are the differences between what happened and what was expected. The failure to realize the budget or the expectations can be a result of assorted problems. Variance, therefore, can be seen as symptoms that alert managers to potential and/or actual problems that may be affecting the production. By following up these symptoms, managers can take corrective steps. Not every symptom can or should be followed up, only those that suggest the presence of a problem of significant magnitude.

1.9 ATTRIBUTES OF EFFECTIVE STANDARDS. Standards and variances reported back should have the following six characteristics:

1. The reporting of variances should allow management to know as early as possible when the costs are getting out of hand. Management can then take steps to address the problem and control it as soon as possible. Reporting variances once a month may not be fast enough—a month is too late to know about potential problems and to take corrective steps.
2. The variances reported should be itemized, that is, broken down, so that individual variances do not cancel or offset each other, and the source(s) of variances can be more easily pinpointed.
3. Standards must be based on current work environment and not on past historical figures alone. Workers may have grown more experienced, material may be more expensive, or machines may be more advanced. Factors such as these can render the standards obsolete.
4. They must be developed as a cooperative effort between all those involved (e.g., engineers, purchasing departments, and accountants as well as the production people). The standard setting should also involve those line personnel directly involved. Accounting's role is to translate the standards into dollars—dollarize them—and to report the variances. Those impacted by the standards are more likely to strive to meet them if they were involved in setting them.
5. The reporting associated with standards should be cost effective. It should not take more resources to operate than what it will save.
6. Its reports should be relevant and understandable, in terms that different levels within an organization can understand. All too often it is described in terms that concern only accountants.

In summary, standards are derived from budgets, and they help reveal if the budget is being implemented as planned. They are a necessary tool of management control and a crucial element of the budgetary process.

1.10 EFFECTIVENESS OF BUDGETS AS A CONTROL TOOL. The variables that affect the design of the budgeting system will influence its use as a control tool. The following are a few of the factors that bear on both how the budget is used and how often it is revised:

- Selling seasons
- Product turnover
- Borrowing needs

- Raw material cycles
- Production cycles
- Labor availability
- Environment (degree of impact, amount of change)

It can be seen that, although financial news is commonly couched in terms of this year versus last year, the actual conduct of the business will vary due to many forces not linked in a linear fashion to the passage of time.

The close relationship between budget format and charts of accounts was mentioned previously. The closer the relationship, the easier it is to compare budget to actual figures. However, from the standpoint of the management process, a balance has to be struck between the amount of detail and the ability to control. This is where an understanding of the critical factors affecting the business becomes extremely valuable.

The frequency of budget reviews also varies, depending on the business and management factors. Usually, managers will review their own performance on a monthly basis, even if, as is common, full-scale company-wide reviews are done on a quarterly, semiannual, or annual schedule. The size of the enterprise is a key influence on the frequency and procedures followed in the reviews.

In any review covering several sectors of a business, it is important that the heads of all the responsible departments or profit centers be present. This allows full discussion of the relevant factors, ensures that evenhanded corrective action is taken, and avoids the "handing-off" process, in which various groups in the business chain can blame others. It is also important that the tenor of the review be positive with a focus on constructive feedback rather than assessing blame.

1.11 ENVIRONMENT. Up to this point, the managerial process has been portrayed as a largely rational activity, with a primary focus on the business. Exhibits 1.1 and 1.2 refer to the term *environment,* but the significance of the environment to management and the budget process has not been discussed.

An organization is part of the world in which it operates, and it will naturally be influenced by what happens in the environment. Effective management will keep itself informed of the changes occurring in their competitive environment. The changes may be general, involving economic, technological, sociocultural, political, legal, and international factors. Alternatively, the changes may be task related—more specific to the organization and those with a stake in it, such as shareholders, customers, competitors, suppliers, workers, and/or government regulators.

Until the 1960s, business in the United States operated almost independently of cultural trends. To be sure, the trends affected consumer goods markets, but economic and technical factors were more important. We have only to consider the status of the automobile industry to realize how much the situation has changed. The first recognition of the changed environment was in strategic planning. Companies began scanning their environment(s) and considering the likely impact(s) of the changes. Earlier, the business world was not blind to society's needs, but it spent more time monitoring the legislative and financial sectors. Now, firms are concerned with all significant trends bearing on their industry. Exhibits 1.3 and 1.4 summarize the relationship between organizational planning and the environment.

In theory, environmental scanning is a complex operation. Depending on its size and complexity, a company may undertake the scanning operation itself or may utilize some of the voluminous published material. The following are the principal tasks:

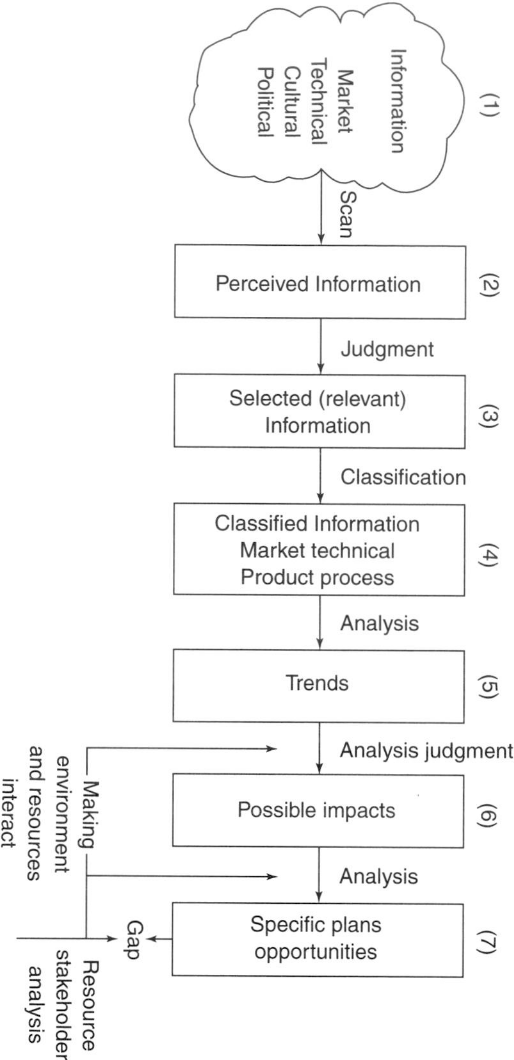

Exhibit 1.3. Linking environmental analysis to planning

- Finding the information
- Selecting that which is relevant
- Relating it to the business in a meaningful way—deciding what the probable impact will be
- Incorporating the information into the decision process

Several sophisticated techniques are available for peering into the future, and many companies are spending considerable time and money on the process. Long-term scans are used to prepare more sharply focused near-term estimates of events that may occur during the current and subsequent years. These become part of the background information used in preparing the strategic plans and budgets.

A. Business Issues
   1. Future of business system
      - How much (if any) will it change (authority and discipline versus consensus and bureaucracy)
      - Industrial survival/divestiture
   2. Business–government relationships
      - Implications for business in political trends
      - Public problems with private sector solutions
      - Government–corporate combinations
   3. Corporate governance
      - Disclosure/accountability
      - Decision making/disclosure
B. U.S./World Economic Issues
   1. Economic interdependence
      - Economic control versus free trade
      - East–west, north–south conflicts
      - International monetary system
      - Role of MNCs
   2. Inflation
   3. Energy
   4. World food problem
   5. Growth
C. Political Issues
D. Cultural/Demographic Issues
E. Technological Issues
F. Health/Human Resources Issues
G. Recognition of Limits on World Resources

Exhibit 1.4. Issues affecting planning

This activity may seem rather nebulous, but many companies have developed techniques for connecting the generalized environmental issues directly to operating decisions for their industry and firm. Some of these techniques are sophisticated and take considerable time and money. Included in this category would be Delphi studies, probability analyses, and dynamic modeling. Another approach is to use simpler devices, blending management judgment with some analytical procedures. All of the methods depend on reducing the number of issues of potential impact to a manageable set—fewer than 20 and often fewer than 10. These are reviewed by management, and assessments of the potential impact are made.

In today's complex and interdependent world, environmental pressures can impinge on a business in a variety of ways. Some of these pressures may be so widespread in their effect as to call for a variety of solutions. Companies may have to rethink product lines, products, or even their overall corporate strategy. For example, concern for consumer safety may indicate that a product will come under increasing government regulation. The company has a choice of (1) proving that the product is safe, (2) changing the product, (3) withdrawing the product, or (4) finding a substitute/replacement product. It may elect to pursue all or several of these paths simultaneously. By scanning the environment and identifying issues, management is able to decide what can be done, by whom, and when.

1.12 STRATEGIC PLANNING/ORGANIZATIONAL SCANNING. While getting to know how the world around it is changing, an organization must also know itself. Such an effort is an important part of strategic planning. The strategic planning literature is comprehensive in its treatment of this need and alternative methods of meeting the need. Perhaps the best-known writer/contributors to the literature are Michael Porter of Harvard and the Boston Consulting Group. One of the best-known models/approaches is the SWOT (strengths, weaknesses, opportunities, and threats) analysis, which provides an orderly procedure for assessing the firm's products and their strengths and weaknesses.

The attraction of such techniques is that they help management test strategies before they are implemented. In the past, companies could test products or policies in real life; depending on the circumstances, this procedure was not too expensive. With increasing costs, shorter life cycles, and more aggressive competition, management is searching for comprehensive, rapid, and inexpensive ways to ask "what if" questions. Exhibit 1.3 reminds us that strategy and plans underlie the detailed figures reflected in the budgets. As strategies (and the related information) are changed, corresponding changes will appear in the various (revised) budget schedules and pro formas. Managers have to be careful to keep the variables with which they are working in front of them so they know which changes produce a given result. Large quantities of data are often needed, and talented analysts are a key ingredient.

As a simple example of the kind of challenge involved, consider a company developing budgets for two products (among many others). One product is growing slowly in a stable market, has good margins, and generates substantial profits. The other is a new product growing rapidly in a market judged to be potentially large. The margins are excellent, but some reduction in the forecast is needed as competition grows. Start-up costs (assumed to be nonrecurring) have offset most of the profit thus far. Both products use some of the same raw materials and are produced in some of the same plants, but they have divergent distribution patterns.

A strategic decision might be made to go for a larger market share for the new product, using aggressive pricing and marketing programs. To offset the overall impact of these costs, volume of the new product is expected to grow, and a policy decision that raises the price on the older product will be tested. Although the overall strategic changes seem to be limited to price, volume, and marketing costs, there may be hundreds of line-item changes in the budget. The products may come in various sizes, colors, and qualities. There will be changes in plant schedules and costs, in inbound and outbound freight, and in many other items. Five years of actual performance or assumed values may be needed for the strategic models, and several runs may have to be made before the forecasts are accepted.

1.13 SUMMARY. If the budget-planning process is performing well, the annual budget decision making of goals versus performance provides management with a rigorous challenge. If the process is not performing well, it can be a painful and humbling experience. Much has been written about the games budgetary managers can play. It may be hard to understand how a somewhat mundane business activity such as the annual budget review can sometimes cause such havoc. The reasons are embedded in the following five issues:

1. Uncertainty about future events
2. Different interpretations of available information
3. Different goals of principal managers

4. Character of principal managers
5. Difficulty in addressing differences of opinion, differences of style, and difficulty in resolving differences in opinion

Budgeting can be a difficult and sometimes frustrating task, but when it is done well, the rewards far outweigh the penalties. The chapters that follow should make the budget process more effective and easier to perform.

Managers with a total system linked from strategy through to budgets are in the challenging position of knowing a great deal about the way in which strategy changes will affect performance. They have the ability to trace the linkages quantitatively and therefore must cope with the conflicts and inconsistencies that the process supposes. This requires good understanding of the analytical techniques and managers capable of dealing objectively with the points of controversy.

Finally, it must be remembered that the answers being generated by the analytic processes are no better than the judgment underlying the original assumptions. This is sometimes hard to remember when you are surrounded by sophisticated output. This same warning is voiced by all competent system analysts and modelers, but is too seldom heeded.

SOURCES AND SUGGESTED REFERENCES

Certo, Samuel C., and J. Paul Peter, *Strategic Management: A Focus on Process.* 2nd ed., Homewood, IL: Richard D. Irwin, 1993.

Cooper, R., and R. S. Kaplan, *The Design of Cost Management Systems: Text, Cases, and Readings.* Englewood Cliffs, NJ: Prentice-Hall, 1991.

Drucker, Peter F., "The Emerging Theory of Manufacturing," *Harvard Business Review,* May/June 1990.

Drucker, Peter F., *The New Realties.* New York: Harper & Row, 1989.

Finney, Robert G., *The Basics of Budgeting.* New York: AMACOM, 1993.

Mintzberg, Henry, "The Effective Organization: Forces and Forms," *Sloan Management Review,* Winter 1991.

Naisbitt, John, *Megatrends.* New York: Warner Books, 1984.

Ramsey, Jackson Eugene, and Inez L. Ramsey, *Budgeting Basics: How to Survive the Budgeting Process.* New York: Franklin Watts, 1985.

Senge, Peter M., *The Fifth Discipline: The Art and Practice of the Learning Organization.* New York: Doubleday, 1990.

Shank, John K., and Vijay Govindarajan, *Strategic Cost Analysis: The Evolution from Managerial to Strategic Accounting.* Homewood, IL: Richard D. Irwin, 1989.

Shim, Jae K., and Joel G. Siegel, *Budgeting Basics & Beyond: A Complete Step-by-Step Guide for Nonfinancial Managers.* Englewood Cliffs, NJ: Prentice-Hall, 1994.

Shim, Jae K., and Joel G. Siegel, *Complete Budgeting Workbook and Guide.* Englewood Cliffs, NJ: Prentice-Hall, 1994.

Stewart, Thomas A., "Why Budgets are Bad for Business," *Fortune,* June 4, 1990.

Thomsett, Michael, *The Little Black Book of Budgets and Forecasts.* New York: AMACOM, 1988.

Tracy, John, *Budgeting a la Carte: Essential Tools for Harried Business Managers.* New York: John Wiley & Sons, 1995.

Umapathy, Srinivasan, "How Successful Firms Budget," *Management Accounting,* vol. LXVIII, no. 8, February 1987.

CHAPTER 2

BUDGETING AND THE STRATEGIC PLANNING PROCESS

Albert A. Fried

2.1 DEFINITION OF STRATEGIC PLANNING. *Strategic planning* is actually a simple, familiar concept. *Webster's New Collegiate Dictionary* defines planning as the "devising of a method for making or doing something to attain an end." Planning is thus a daily, almost unconscious activity for everyone. The unique aspect of strategic planning as currently applied in sophisticated business management stems from the connotations of the word *strategic*—that is, important, clever, and skillful.

Strategic planning as applied to business management is characterized by the following attributes:

- It is directed at accomplishment of a specific, defined set of objectives.
- It examines alternate ways of doing the job and provides an estimate of resources required.
- It provides a yardstick to measure how much has been done.

Even in this sense, strategic planning per se is not new. Caesar, Hannibal, Napoleon, and all other great generals were superb strategists. Carnegie and Ford devised very effective strategic plans for their businesses, based largely on brilliant intuitive insight. The use of *formal* strategic planning systems in business management is a relatively recent phenomenon, however, which has developed because an increasingly complex and rapidly changing environment has made decision making too difficult to rely solely on intuitive judgment. (Even intuitive geniuses such as Ford blundered when they failed to assess and react to environmental and competitive change.)

It is important to note that long-range forecasting and strategic planning are not synonymous. Forecasting, regardless of whether it is of long or short range, is an attempt to predict future events and conditions. Strategic planning devises a set of actions and programs that should be implemented *now* (or at least within the next year). Environmental analysis and forecasting are very important inputs into the planning process. A good plan provides actions that are responsive to the opportunities and threats identified as a consequence of the environmental analysis and forecast.

2.2 PLANNING CYCLE. Exhibit 2.1 illustrates the typical progression of planning and budgeting through a corporation. (For clarity, only one business unit is shown below the dotted line. Most corporations consist of multiple business units; for purposes of this illustration, unit A should be considered representative of a number of units.)

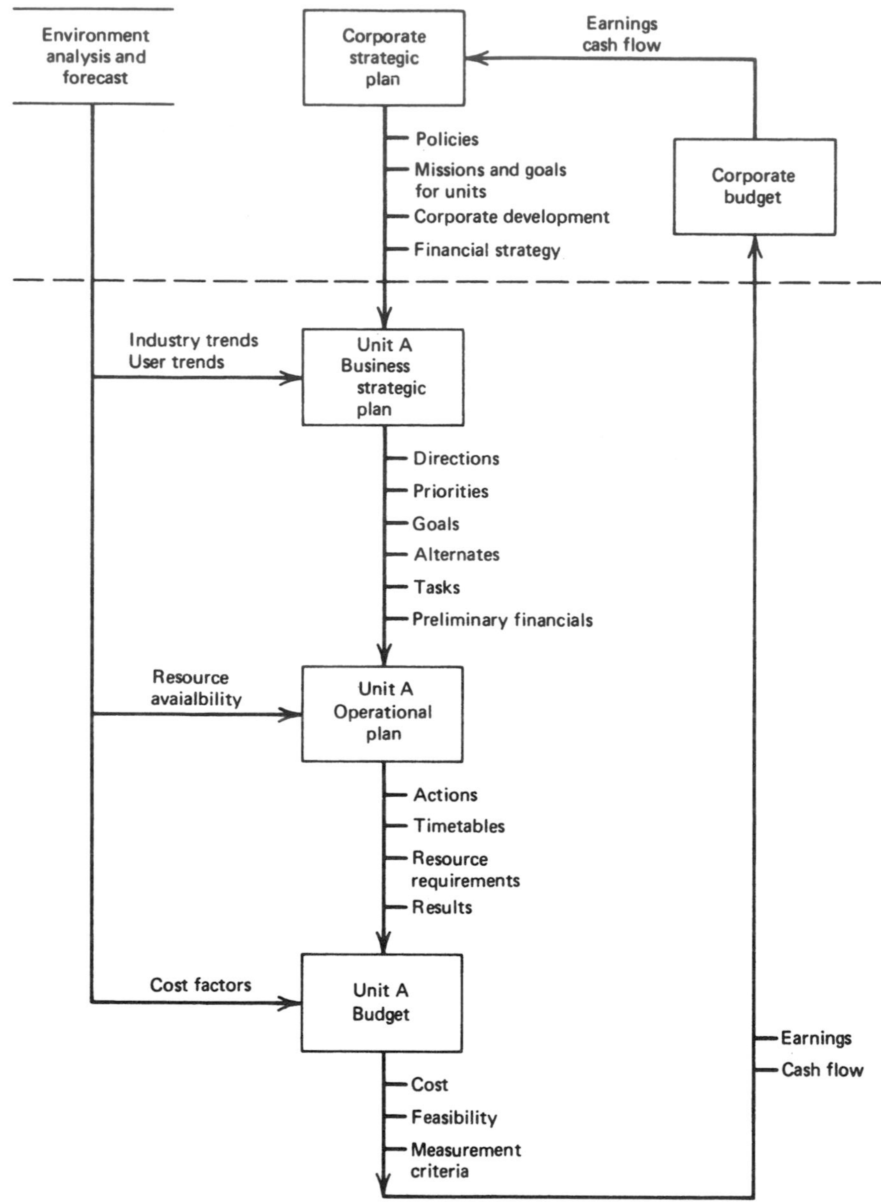

Exhibit 2.1. The planning cycle

At the top of the exhibit, representing the corporate level—that is, the chief executive officer (CEO) and his or her staff—is the corporate strategic plan. This is the CEO's plan for the company. It sets corporate policy; defines the business units and their individual missions and goals; establishes guidelines for corporate development activities, particularly with regard to major acquisitions and divestitures; and determines the financial policies, including dividend policy and debt structure.

Details of corporate strategic planning processes are beyond the scope of this chapter. There are, however, several points regarding this process that should be mentioned.

1. Many companies, especially loosely tied conglomerates, have no formal corporate strategic plan. All companies have policies and goals, however, even if they have not been reduced to writing. It is important that these be understood by the unit manager. If the corporate strategy is not clear and reasonably explicit, the planning cycle will be considerably less efficient because the plans are likely to be inconsistent with the corporate objectives.
2. The corporate strategic plan does not have to be formulated each year, nor does it need to be tied to an annual planning and budgeting cycle. It must be updated, however, when inputs from environment analysis, forecasts, and/or budgets indicate that significant changes are occuring.

The next elements of the planning cycle are the business unit's strategic plan and operation plan. These two closely linked processes are the first steps in an effective budgeting process and are the principal subjects of this chapter. It is important to prepare and review these plans *before* starting to develop a detailed budget because they will determine the directions the business will follow and the tasks it intends to undertake. If the annual budgeting cycle is designed to allow for such development, review, and management approval before preparation of the budget, much unnecessary effort will be eliminated. If the budget is not prepared *after* agreement on the strategic plan, the following problems can occur:

- The budget must be redone—often under tight time constraints and stress, with considerable wasted effort—as a result of a revision in the direction of the plans.
- An unrealistic set of goals and measurements are established for the business because of insufficient time or resources to redo the budget.

The strategic planning process uses inputs of the environmental analysis, the forecasts (particularly of industry and user trends), and the corporate objectives for the business. The strategic plan provides direction, priorities, a set of goals, alternatives (including the preferred alternative), an outline of the tasks to be undertaken, and a first approximation of the financial implications. The operational plan uses the output of the strategic plan to develop the detailed actions and timetable for the budget period. This plan serves as the guideline for the various segments of the business and provides a means of integrating the activities to reach a common goal. The next step is the preparation of the budget, in which the financial implications of the operational plan are determined.

As a business proceeds through this cycle, the level of detail becomes progressively greater. Thus, the strategic plan must contain some description of the tasks and a preliminary indication of the financial implications in order to permit a meaningful assessment of the plan. A preliminary operating plan is often prepared together with the strategic plan to allow better assessment of the proposed strategies. It is important, however, to retain flexibility during the strategic planning process; therefore, operational plans and budgets should not be prepared in great detail at this stage of the cycle.

The planning cycle shown in Exhibit 2.1 also contains two important feedback loops. The first loop feeds the results of the budget back to strategic planning. This permits reassessment of the strategy selected, based on more detailed and up-to-date information. (The strategic plan, as we shall see later in this chapter, is a dynamic concept rather than a fixed, permanent manifesto. It should be adjusted and revised as new information becomes available.)

The second loop takes the sum of the unit budgets up to a total corporate budget, which then determines the corporate earnings, cash flow, and related financial parameters. This must be fed back to the corporate strategic plan to permit a reassessment of its feasibility.

In many companies with a formal planning cycle, the strategic plan and a preliminary operation plan are prepared and reviewed with management during the second quarter of the year to ensure that there is substantial agreement and understanding on the business direction before work starts on the detailed operational plan and annual budget. The detailed operational plan is then prepared during the third quarter of the year, and the annual budget during the fourth quarter.

2.3 STRATEGIC PLANNING PROCESS: A DYNAMIC CYCLE. The strategic planning process has been shown to be part of the total corporate planning cycle. It is also a cycle within itself, as indicated in Exhibit 2.2.

For convenience in describing the process, each part of the cycle is described as a discrete ''step.'' Actually, a good planning process has continual interaction and reiteration among the parts, so that there is less distinction among the parts of the process than this illustration might imply.

The first step in the process is the *situation analysis.* In this step, the business is broken down into appropriate segments for planning; the environmental analysis, including competitor and industry assessments, are integrated; and the critical issues facing the business are defined.

The second step is the *business direction/concept,* where the leverage points (i.e., the situations or elements that have the highest payoff potential) are identified, and a concept for the business is developed that will enable it to exploit its unique advantages.

The third step is the development of *alternate approaches* for moving the business in the proposed direction. This step provides an ''envelope'' of realistic possibilities from which a decision can be made.

The fourth step is the *operational plan,* which sets out the action programs and the timetable required to achieve the desired goals. This plan is included as an integral part of the strategic plan in this review. In practice, however, where the strategic planning is done well in advance of the budget preparation, the operational plan is usually done in two stages—first, a preliminary plan, which is integral to the strategic plan, and second, a detailed plan, which is prepared just prior to preparing the annual budget. The difference between the two is in the level of detail. The preliminary plan lists major actions and their timing and provides an estimate of the resource requirements. The detailed plan lists actions, timing, and resources for each function of the business. It serves as an integrating tool for the business as well as a planning tool.

The fifth step in the cycle is *measurement.* This involves the establishment of criteria against which the effectiveness of the actions can be measured and a monitoring system to permit timely assessments. Strictly speaking, this is not a formal part of strategic planning, but it is a vital adjunct. The monitoring system should be designed so as to be a part of the regular financial reporting system for the business. The data obtained provide the basis for the last step in the cycle, the *feedback.*

This step is critical to making the entire strategic planning process a useful management

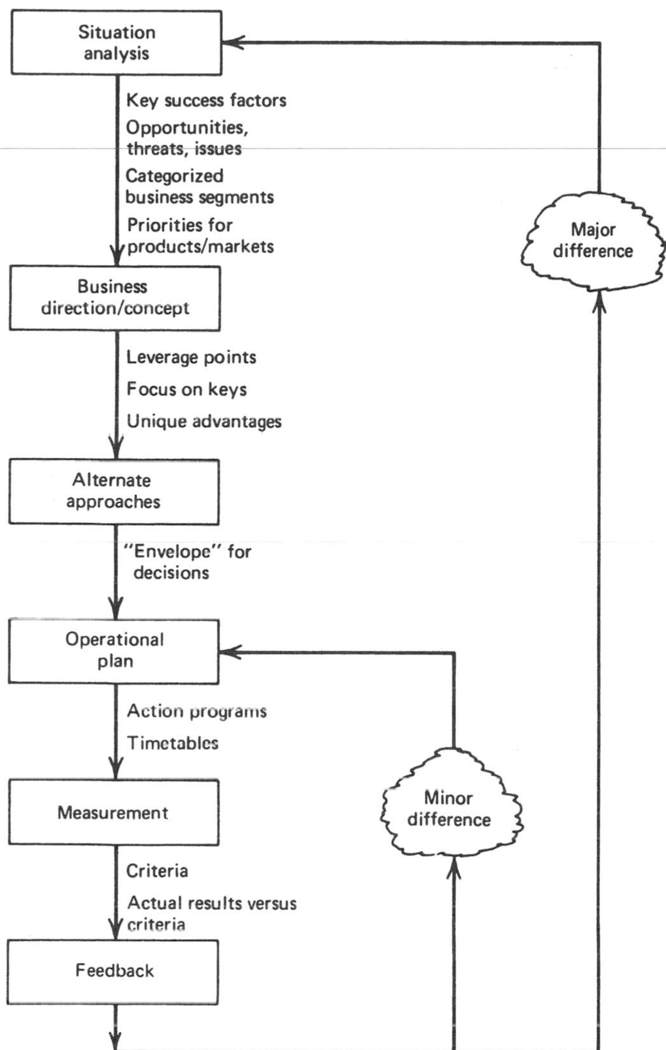

Exhibit 2.2. The strategic planning cycle

tool rather than a set of documents sitting on the shelf collecting dust. Most businesses operate in a rapidly changing environment, and the only way to keep the plan up to date and therefore usable is to adjust it continually according to the feedback of the actual results. The type of modifications made depend of course on the extent of the difference between the actual results and the plan. Minor differences may require only some adjustment in the timetable or in the sequence of actions. A major difference should precipitate a re-examination of the assumptions used in the situation analysis and possibly even a change in business direction.

2.4 SITUATION ANALYSIS. This step in the planning process (which is also called the environmental assessment) consists of three interrelated parts: (a) describing the environment, (b) positioning the business(es), and (c) defining the opportunities, threats, and critical issues. For clarity, each will be discussed separately.

(a) Describing the Environment

(i) Use of Forecasts. The environmental forecast and analysis are important inputs. In many larger companies, forecasts of the economy and of specific industries are prepared by a corporate staff. Smaller companies use a variety of external forecasts, ranging from subscription services offered by consulting organizations, financial institutions, and universities, to special studies done for groups of companies or for individual companies, to published documents issued by government agencies, industry associations, and trade publications. The collection and analysis of such data is an important activity, this aspect will be discussed further in Chapter 3. (Some references have been included at the end of this chapter.) For an example of how one large company uses this concept, see Exhibit 2.3.

(ii) Identifying Key Success Factors. An effective way of identifying success factors in a particular business is to compare the "winners" and the "losers" in that industry. The attributes that the successful businesses have in common and that the unsuccessful ones lack are the key success factors.

Development of an explicit understanding of these factors has ramifications far beyond the efficiency of the strategic planning process. Use of key success factors will be shown in a subsequent section of this chapter to be a vital element in the business positioning process and, in turn, in the development of strategies. Even more important, however, is the application of these factors in the ongoing management and control of a business. Executives who understand the key success factors and who develop their priorities accordingly are likely to be more effective than those who do not have this focus.

(iii) Segmenting the Business. Selection of the proper business segments is also critical in the planning process and deserves careful attention. The segment or business unit used for planning does *not* have to correspond to the existing organization unit. That particular organization may be efficient for management and control, but it is not necessarily the most relevant division of the business for planning. In a business that produces a family of products, such as thermometers, it may be efficient to have a broad range of products within one management organization, but there are sufficient differences among product application, customer type, specifications, and marketing channels to warrant different plans.

Following are some guidelines for selecting appropriate segments for planning:

- Use the smallest practical segment. For example, "imported beer" is more meaningful than "beer," which in turn is more precise than "alcoholic beverages." On the other hand, the segment should be large enough to have some available industry data.
- Use segments only if there is a meaningful difference between them. (A meaningful difference is one that allows for different actions, especially where they have an effect upon the key success factors.) Typical differences are product characteristics, users, competitors, and geography.
- A segment should contain *all* of the direct competitors. For example, imported automobiles were once considered in a different segment than domestic automobiles. Yet

Product Line: ______ Country: U.S.A.

Description of Expected Event/Change	Timing	Significance to Business	Management Reaction
Increasing price inflation will lead to user demand for "high yield" product. Competitors "A" and "B" believed to have product in test	Competitor "A" market introduction 4Q 1980	$X million of sales threatened by lower price/unit usage	1. Get complete tests on competitive products: develop "quality campaign" by Dec. 1980 2. Develop offset product by IQ 1981
Growth of generic products	Continuing over next 3 years	Could affect up to 20% of segment sales	1. Start Research and Development program for differentiated product—target introduction by 4Q 1982.

Product Line: Overall Country Country: Brazil

Description of Expected Event/Change	Timing	Significance to Business	Management Reaction
Brazil agrees to Tokyo Round of General Agreement on Tariffs and Trade (GATT) reduced import tariffs and removes *all* export subsidies	July 1, 1981	1. Aggressive import competition in ______ and ______ products 2. $X millions of export sales threatened 3. Items 1 and 2 above combine to produce excess capacity in Brazil 4. Availability of lower cost packaging materials	1. Increase efforts on cost reduction project 2. Determine which export products are competitive without subsidy and focus efforts in 1980–1981 on reinforcing their position 3. Delay expansion to 1983? 4. Start development and testing of new packages for ______ and ______ products

Exhibit 2.3. Examples of the use of environmental analysis by a large company

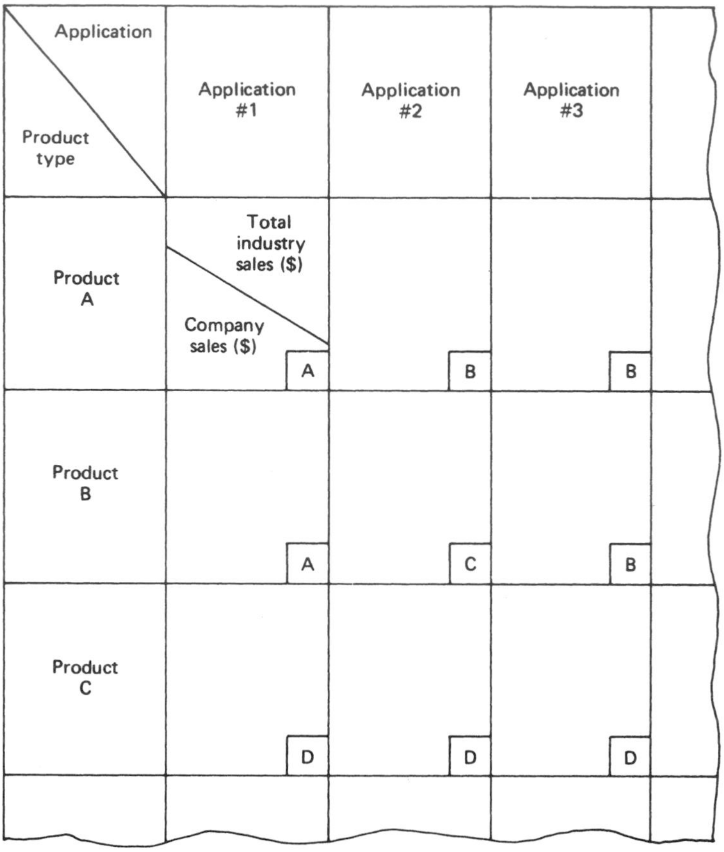

Application / Product type	Application #1	Application #2	Application #3	
Product A	Total industry sales ($) / Company sales ($) A	B	B	
Product B	A	C	B	
Product C	D	D	D	

[a] Leading competitors (shown in lower right corners) are keyed; A. —— company, B —— Inc., C. —— Ltd., and D. —— Inc.

Exhibit 2.4. Example of product/application matrix

the competition between a Mercedes and a Cadillac Seville, or between a Honda and a Chevette, is more meaningful than the competition between a Honda and a Mercedes. In this case, the meaningful difference is price rather than country of origin.

A product/application matrix such as that illustrated in Exhibit 2.4 is sometimes used as a guide for developing appropriate segments. By entering dollar or unit volume numbers, the relative importance of specific products—both current and potential—can easily be identified. The example also is keyed to allow the identification of the strongest competitor in each product/application box. This display can also be useful as an initial guide to market opportunities that might be exploited and to potential competitive threats.

(b) Positioning the Business(es)

(i) Business Gridding. The concept of business gridding was designed as an aid to developing different strategies and actions for responding to different business environments. The premises behind this approach are as follows:

- It is easier to generate profits from a business operating in a favorable environment. (Oil companies usually have better returns than tanneries.)
- The strongest competitors in an industry are usually more profitable. (Compare General Motors with Chrysler or AMC.)
- It is usually easier and less costly to maintain and build upon existing strength than to attempt to overtake a competitor.

The strategic position of a business (or, more appropriately, a business segment) thus is a primary input to development of an effective strategy. The business grid provides a means of identifying this position based on an assessment of the industry's attractiveness and of the competitive strength of the company.

There are several different versions of this grid in use. Two of the most popular are the 2 × 2 matrix, developed by the Boston Consulting Group, and the 3 × 3 matrix, developed by McKinsey and the General Electric Company.

In the Boston Consulting Group's matrix, industry growth rate is used as a proxy for industry attractiveness, and market share as a proxy for competitive strength. Using this grid, businesses are positioned as shown in Exhibit 2.5, with different strategies for each position:

- *Star (high share, high growth).* Maintain or increase market strength
- *Cash cow (high share, low growth).* Slow growth minimizes investment needs; use business to generate cash for investment in "wildcat" below

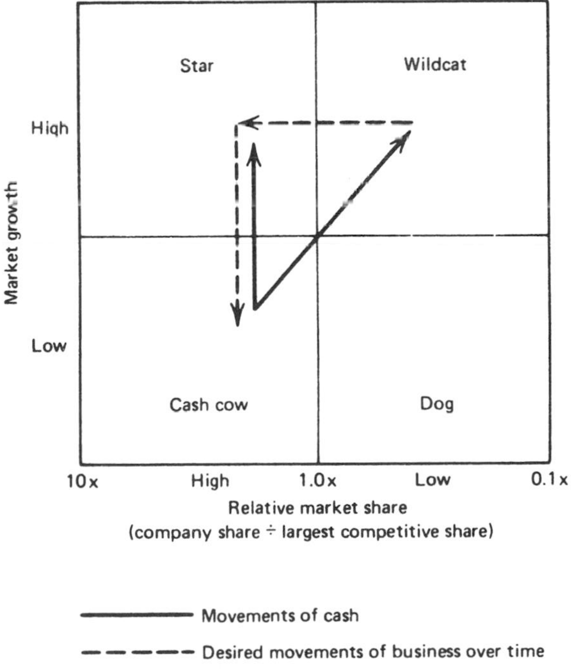

Exhibit 2.5. The Boston consulting group's 2 × 2 matrix

	(1) High	(2) Medium	(3) Low
(A) High	1	2	3
(B) Medium	4	5	6
(c) Low	7	8	9

Industry attractiveness (of segment) — columns; Company strength (in business segment) — rows

Exhibit 2.6. The McKinsey/General Electric Company 3 × 3 matrix

- *Wildcat (low share, high growth).* Investment and effective strategies to fulfill their potential; move into "star" category
- *Dog (low share, low growth).* No future; exit from the business

The 3 × 3 matrix system developed by McKinsey and General Electric, shown in Exhibit 2.6, provides for a more inclusive assessment of the strategic position of the business by using a combination of factors (which can be tailored to individual businesses) rather than the single measurements of industry growth and market share. Industry attractiveness is rated high, medium, or low and is assigned to the appropriate column. Company strength is also rated high, medium, or low.

(ii) Rating Industry Attractiveness. There is no valid cookbook approach for evaluating industry attractiveness for a specific business segment. There are, however, some common characteristics, such as market size and industry growth, that are usually important for all business segments. In addition, there may be some unique characteristics that are especially significant for a particular business and not for others. For example, government regulations are much more significant for the medical equipment business than for the plastic film business.

Following are some guidelines:

- The evaluation of attractiveness should not be based on just one or two characteristics. A large, growing market does not automatically result in an attractive industry for all participants—witness the sad experience of General Electric and RCA in computers, for example.
- The number of characteristics should be limited to the five or six most important ones. Use of more tends to complicate and confuse the analysis, without adding much insight. Use of the key success factors described previously will aid in selection.
- Hard factual information should be used, and an effort to collect such information should be made *before* undertaking this analysis. However, some useful analysis can be done even if the information base is incomplete by using informal guesswork.
- The process should be considered a repetitive one. As the analysis proceeds, data gaps will be identified; some of these can be filled, and the analysis can be modified.

The following characteristics are usually among the most important:

- Market size and growth potential
- Industry profitability (average margins)
- Competitive structure
- User attitude shifts/opportunities for differentiation
- Legislative impacts

Exhibit 2.7 is an example of a format used in one company to assess industry attractiveness. In this example, the company actually used a numerical rating system by assigning an importance weighting to each of the factors. Each factor in the business was given a rating of 1, 2, or 3, based upon benchmarks related to company objectives, as indicated in an Industry Attractiveness Worksheet, shown in Exhibit 2.8. Returning to Exhibit 2.7, note that the format for assessing industry attractiveness includes entries for trends in each factor and implications for action of the ratings in each factor.

(iii) Rating Company Strengths. Again, there is no valid cookbook approach. In rating company strengths, two aspects should be considered:

- Company performance in key success factors. How well does the company do in *each* of the factors that make the difference between success and failure?
- Defendable competitive strengths. What strengths does the company have compared to its competitors, and can those strengths be defended and maintained? For example, a patent is a strength, provided that (a) it will not expire shortly and (b) it cannot be circumvented.

The general guidelines mentioned in the comments on rating industry attractiveness are also applicable here. The following factors are usually among the most important:

- Share
- Product quality
- Unique/proprietary product features
- Relative manufacturing costs
- Distribution
- Patent position

Exhibit 2.9 gives an example of a format used by one company to rate company strengths. As in the illustration in Exhibit 2.7, the company used a numerical rating by assigning an importance weighting to each factor. It then ranked itself on a scale of 1 to 3 against its two most important competitors for each factor. The format in Exhibit 2.9 also requires entry of supporting data, comments on the company's advantages and disadvantages related to each factor, and the implications of the ratings for each factor for future action.

(c) Defining Opportunities, Threats, and Critical Issues

(i) Opportunities and Threats. An *opportunity* is a combination of time, place, and circumstances that offers potentially favorable results for the business. It usually results

Product Line/Category ____________

Division ____________

Factor	Importance 1998	Importance 1999	Trends	Implications for Opportunities, Threats, and Issues	Rating 1998	Rating 1999
Market Size and Growth Market Definition:			Compound Growth Rate: 1997 / 1998 / 1999 / 1997–1999 / 1995–1996 Total $ Total units			
Industry Profitability Ability to pass on cost increases Gross margin levels						
Competitive Structure Ease of entry/technological barriers Ease of share acquisition Competitive stability Dominant competitors Extent of industry overcapacity						
Customer/User Outlook Key user segment growth trend Changing consumer attitudes and/or legislation/regulation						
Opportunity Chance to gain franchise or pre-emptive position with unique product, positioning, or appeal						
Other						
Other						

Exhibit 2.7. Example of format for rating industry attractiveness

BPU ____________
Year ____________

Factor	Importance	Ratings and Benchmarks 3	2	1	Final Rating (Weighted)
Market Size and Growth					
Size: $ value of the market in 1998–1999 or 2001 as measured by manufacturer's shipments		Less than $50MM	$50–$150MM	More than $150MM	
Growth: Compound annual growth projected on *real* $ for 1997–1999		Less than 2%	2%–5%	More than 5%	
Industry Profitability					
Ability to pass on cost increases in higher prices		Difficult	Sometimes possible	Relatively easy	
Industry gross margin levels		Less than 20%	20%–40%	More than 40%	
Competitive Structure					
Ease of entry (existence of technological or other barriers)		Easy (low barriers to entry)	Moderately difficult (some barriers)	Difficult (high barriers to entry)	
Ease of share acquisition		New competitor can easily pick up share	Moderately difficult	Very difficult to acquire share	
Competitive stability		Several new competitors in market	Some new entrants	Few or no new market entrants of consequence	
Dominant competitor		Major competitor holds 50% or higher share of market	Major competitor holds 30%-50% share	Major competitor holds less than 30% share	
Extent of industry overcapacity		High	Medium	Low	
Customer/User Outlook					
Key user segment growth trend (see date package)		Little growth or decline in key user/customer segment	Some growth in key user segment	Major growth in key user/customer segment forecast	
Changing consumer attitudes or legislation/regulation		Negative impact	Little or no impact	Positive impact	
Opportunity					
Chance to gain franchise or preemptive position with unique product, positioning, or appeal		None identified	Some potential	Clearly exists	
Others					

Exhibit 2.8. Industry attractiveness worksheet

Product Line Category ______
Country ______

Factor	Importance	Relative Rating *	Relative Rating A	Relative Rating B	Relevant Data/Support	Comments on Company's Advantages/Disadvantages	Action
Share (enter below) Company share ____ Competitor A ____ Company + Competitor A ____					Segment % Total Co. A B		
Product quality/perception of quality							
Unique or proprietary product features					Product features	Ability to defend against competitors	
Pricing					Company Leader or follower ____ ____		
Relative manufacturing cost							
Distribution/coverage					Company % National Distribution 1996 1997 1998 ____ ____		
Sales force effectiveness (direct; indirect)							
Advertising and consumer promotion					Total $ Exp. 1996 1997 1998 ____		
Trade promotion					____		

Exhibit 2.9. Company/competitor strength evaluation format: Product line review

from an ongoing or potential change in government, market, or competitive environment. It is a potential short- and/or long-term competitive edge for the business that can be exploited by undertaking an appropriate action. If no action is required to attain the benefit, then the change should be considered part of the forecast rather than an opportunity. If the action required to take advantage of the potential benefits is not feasible, then there is no real opportunity.

A *threat* is a combination of time, place, and circumstances that could have a negative impact on the future performance of the business. A threat usually results from an ongoing or potential change in the government, market, or competitive environment and provides some advantage to a competitor, which can result in a decline in share, earnings, and so forth, unless an appropriate action is undertaken.

Opportunities and threats have been treated together because, in a sense, they are two sides of a coin. An opportunity can become a threat if a competitor seizes it first. A threat can become an opportunity if it forces a response that has side benefits. A business is likely to be faced with a multitude of opportunities and threats. For planning purposes, it is important to set priorities and to focus upon the most important ones. There are three factors to consider in establishing priorities:

1. *Probability.* Likelihood that the event or condition will occur
2. *Impact.* The probable change in the business result if action is taken
3. *Timing.* How urgently an action is required

Use of an array such as that shown in Exhibit 2.10 can help in sorting priorities. It may be useful to use several such displays (e.g., separate ones for opportunities and threats and for the long range and the short range).

(ii) Critical Issues. The opportunities and threats that have the highest priority are *critical issues* for the strategic plan. Additional critical issues may emerge from examination of internal situations. For example: Should we add additional capacity? How much? Should we move the operation to a lower labor cost area?

The purpose of defining issues is to indicate the principal decisions that need to be made, and where feasible, to identify the alternate choices that should be considered. Where the specific decision and options are not yet clear, the issue should carefully frame the question which, when resolved, will lead to action. Therefore, issues will typically be of three types:

1. *Position issues.* Issues related to the current and future grid position, which, in turn, will determine the basic strategic direction. Examples: How large is the potential market? How will new technology affect our competitive position—can we use it to develop a proprietary position? How will entry of competitor X affect our share and/or profitability, considering potential effect on prices, advertising, and promotion?
2. *Decision issues.* Issues related to specific near-term decisions, which have a significant impact on the conduct of the business during the next several years. Examples: Should we exit the business? Should we expand our production capacity in Canada?
3. *Tactical issues.* Issues related to the programs to implement a particular strategy. Examples: Pricing strategy and tactics for _____; evaluate desirability of using _____

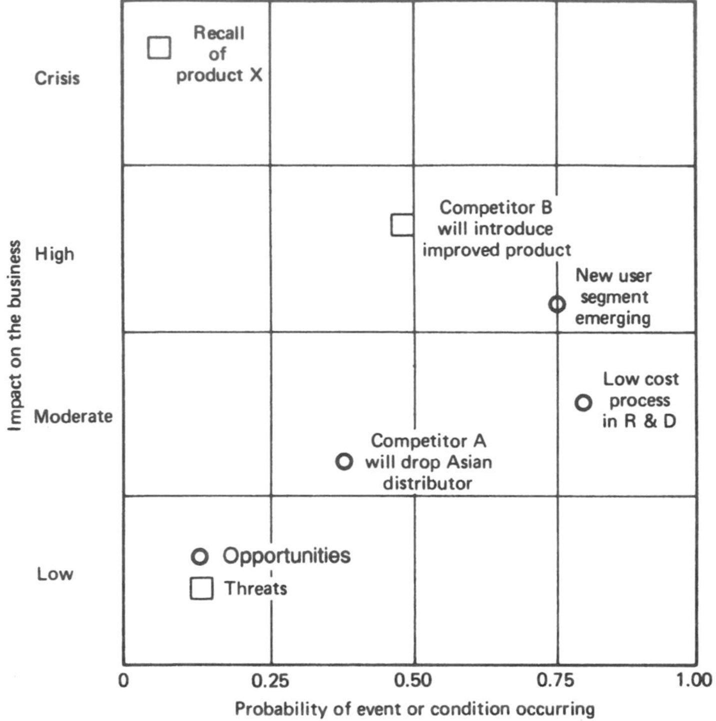

Exhibit 2.10. Priority assessment array for opportunities and threats

name on our new premium product versus a new brand name umbrella that conveys premium quality.

A list of critical issues for the business should be agreed to by all levels of management involved in the planning and budgeting process before the strategic plan is completed. A consensus as to which items will be addressed, and as to the degree of detail with which they will be treated, facilitates a more efficient and more useful planning effort.

2.5 BUSINESS DIRECTION/CONCEPT

(a) Setting Differentiated Objectives. Different matrix positions will have different characteristics and different problems. Using the McKinsey/General Electric matrix shown in Exhibit 2.6, for example, four broad business classifications can be defined. Each classification has different characteristics and problems and should have different objectives. This is illustrated in Exhibit 2.11.

Use of the matrix approach to differentiating business segments facilitates the establishment of priorities among businesses. It allows a rational approach to making basic decisions regarding the setting of objectives for each business and the determination of which priority decisions to resolve first. This, in turn, will provide a basis for allocating resources among the different businesses and for resolving conflicts between the short and the long term.

(b) Identifying Leverage Points and Unique Advantages. The business direction or concept is developed by first identifying the important economic leverage points of

Box Numbers	1, 2, 3	4, 5, 6	7, 8	9
Business Class	Invest/Grow	Selectivity/Earnings	Harvest	Divest
Characteristics	Long-term growth Worldwide Changes coming rapidly Uses cash	Plateaued or weakening Limited long-term opportunities Short-term profits Self-financing	Declining profits High-risk opportunities with questionable future Special situations	''Dogs''
Typical problems	Digestion Containing risk	Protecting position without excessive resource commitment	Keeping position from eroding too fast Avoiding unrealistic ''rebuilds''	Stemming operating losses
Principal objective	Build market position for long-term profit	Self-financing with high short-term earnings	Maximize cash flow	Exit with minimum loss

Exhibit 2.11. Matrix approach to differentiating business segments

the business and then devising a means for building and/or preserving a unique advantage against the competitors. This is not an easy task, because it requires a combination of rigorous analysis (of the company's strengths and weaknesses) and creative insights. There are, however, some useful guidelines that may facilitate the process:

- The key success factors described previously are good indicators of the critical economic leverage points and in some instances may in fact be identical.
- Leverage points must be measurable and related to the economic outcome in the business. It is useful to undertake a sensitivity analysis for each proposed leverage point to verify that it is really significant to the business.
- The unique advantage must also be economically measurable. Although there are many intangibles that can reinforce a business, the basic concepts of the strategy must be developed around advantages that can be translated into economic benefits; otherwise, the plan will be fuzzy and will contain generalities that do not provide useful direction. For example, a plastics producer's concept directed at "enhancing the company's reputation as a high-quality supplier" is not as explicit as a concept directed at "maintaining product leadership through the introduction of a family of products that provide greater strength and lower density." The more explicit concept permits evaluation to determine: (a) Is it feasible, considering the relative strengths of the company? (b) What is the advantage worth in terms of price and/or market share? (c) Are there offsetting advantages (e.g., product service, ease of use) that might be more important?
- The unique advantage must be preservable. In the preceding example, if competitors respond quickly with comparable or better products, the concept will not result in a winning strategy. The company must have some unique capability to maintain the proposed product leadership (e.g., patents, special know-how, long-term production, and cost advantage) for this to be the foundation of a viable strategy.

(c) Use of the Matrix Position as a Guide. The position of the business or business segments often suggests appropriate directions for development of concepts, as indicated in Exhibit 2.12. It should be recognized, however, that the elements used to determine the matrix position are dynamic and that a position will change with time. In developing the concept, both the current matrix position and the anticipated future direction (especially with regard to the industry attractiveness) should be considered.

2.6 ALTERNATE APPROACHES. This stage of planning addresses, over a broad spectrum, the basic choices available for running the business. It produces an envelope of possibilities for decision making. Each strategy alternate must be a realistic possibility, not merely set up to prove that the preferred alternate is the best.

The selection of alternates poses a problem for the planning team in that a complete range of alternates must be included to ensure that a significantly better choice is not overlooked. Yet there must be a limited number (usually no more than five), or else the planning effort will get bogged down.

Some organizations find it helpful to have the planning team review the proposed alternates with the next higher level of management before starting to undertake a detailed evaluation. This is a good juncture in the planning process at which to conduct a preliminary review because it allows top managers to participate at the conceptual stage, when they can provide input to make the process more effective. Such a review will eliminate alter-

Industry attractiveness ←

Business strengths ↑

	High	Medium	Low
High	Maximum investment Diversify worldwide Consolidate position Accept moderate near-term profits	Investment in selected segments Earnings where share ceiling Seek attractive new segments to apply strength	Defend strengths Focus on attractive subsegments Evaluate opportunities for market revitalization Monitor for H/D timing
Medium	Build selectively on strengths Define implications of leadership challenge Avoid vulnerability—fill out weaknesses	Segment business further to develop differentiated product strategies	No essential commitment Position to divest or to shift to more attractive segments
Low	Ride market Seek niches, specialization Increase strength opportunistically (e.g., acquisition)	Action to preserve/ increase cash flow Opportunistic sale or Opportunistic rationalization to increase strength	Exit/prune Timing to maximize return

Exhibit 2.12. Matrix position as a guide to concept development

nates that are inconsistent with other corporate objectives before much evaluation effort is expended. Also, additional alternates may surface, which can be addressed more efficiently at this stage than after the completion of the total planning cycle.

(a) Evaluation of Alternatives. The first step in the evaluation of a proposed alternate is to test it for completeness and usefulness to the development of the plan.

- *Critical issues.* The proposed concept must provide an answer to the major issues and/or choices identified in the situation analysis.
- *Benefits and risks.* The benefits and the risks must be identified and cross-checked against the conclusions reached in the situation analysis. Specifically, do they exploit the identified opportunities and/or meet the threats? What is the probable impact on competitors and their likely reaction? How much do the uncertainties in the forecast increase the potential benefit or risk?
- *Competitive advantage.* A successful strategy develops or maintains a significant advantage over competitors. An alternate should describe how this will be accomplished.
- *Program oriented.* The alternate must be explicit enough to permit a set of operating plans to be readily derived from it.

- *Differentiated.* There must be a meaningful difference in the strategic approach between alternates; otherwise, too much effort will be expended on analysis of minor variations. For a meaningful difference to exist, there must be a significant difference in some of the key actions in each alternate.

The next step in the evaluation of alternates is to itemize the principal actions, the timing, and the resources required to implement the proposed alternate. This is, in essence, a "preliminary" operating plan, different from the "final" operating plan only in its level of detail. In the preliminary plan, activities are defined in sufficient detail to permit an economic assessment of each alternate, whereas in the final plan, programs and related tasks should be defined in sufficient detail to permit development of budgets and measurements for each function in each business unit.

If the alternates are truly differentiated, the financial forecasts, based on the cost/benefits implications, will usually be sufficiently different to permit approximations based on estimates rather than on a detailed account-by-account buildup. For example, if one of the key programs in an alternate were product development to achieve improved product properties, it would probably be sufficient to estimate the number of man-years required in each year and to multiply it by a representative average cost/man-year. In development of the final plan, more specific programs, manpower, description, and associated cost would be developed.

2.7 OPERATIONAL PLAN.

Previously in this chapter, in describing the overall strategic planning cycle shown in Exhibit 2.2, the point was made that the operational plan is usually done in two stages, especially when the strategic plan is prepared well in advance of the budget. The preliminary plan, which is integral to the strategic plan, serves to define and refine the strategy alternates and to provide a basis for selecting between them, as described in the preceding section of this chapter. The final operational plan is much more detailed and serves as the basis for establishing annual budgets, business measurements, and individual performance measurement. It is also an effective device for integrating and communicating between the functions in a business.

(a) Contents of Operational Plan.

The operation plan is essentially a summary of the principal action programs. The plan should contain the following information for each of these programs:

- Description of program and how it relates to the strategy objective
- Resource requirements, including manpower and costs
- Expected results
- Time schedule to reach key decision points
- Assignment of responsibilities
- Support or input required from other organizations within the company

The amount of detail included will differ considerably between new developmental activities and those that are part of an ongoing program.

The presentation of the operational plan to management requires careful abstracting and highlighting in order to keep the volume of material down to manageable proportions. Most companies use simplified formats for summarizing and presenting the operational plan. An example of one such format is shown in Exhibit 2.13. (This is actually a highly condensed version of a two-page format.)

(b) Consistency of Actions with Strategic Approach. The actions outlined in the operational plan should be a logical extension of the selected strategic alternate. Previously in this chapter, it was demonstrated how the business position in a 3 × 3 matrix can be used as a guide for concept development. This technique can also be carried a step further, using the four basic business classes to develop appropriate differentiated actions for elements of the operational plan. Exhibit 2.14 provides an array for testing the consistency of the operational plans and actions with the business position as determined in the situation analysis.

(c) Successive Commitments. An operational plan must balance the need to commit to a strategy with the need to maintain sufficient flexibility—that is, to allow for changes or shifts as new information becomes available in order to resolve uncertainties that were present at the time the plan was prepared. This can be accomplished by adopting a progressive approach in which only those commitments that are necessary are made at the onset. The following elements are essential for developing a plan with successive commitments:

- Identification of the key decision points
- Timetable to trigger key decisions
- Level of resource investment (money, people, etc.) at each decision point
- Criteria and measurements by which key decisions are to be made

In this way, it is possible to step up the level of commitment to a program as results are obtained and as the degree of risk is reduced.

The following example illustrates this approach: Consider a business in which unit sales volume has grown at a compound annual rate of 12% per year for the past five years. The environmental analysis and forecast indicate that the market will continue to grow at approximately 12% per year. An aggressive new marketing plan is being activated, and, as a result, unit sales volume is forecast to increase at a compound annual rate of 14% per year for the next five years. If this were achieved, the production facility would be beyond capacity, with no room to expand in the present site in three years. If the marketing plan were more successful than forecast, growth could be as high as 20% per year, which would result in an out-of-capacity condition in two years. However, the sales growth rate might be as low as 5% per year if foreign competitors successfully entered the market. If this occurred, present facilities would be adequate for at least five years. The three forecasts and their relation to the current capacity are summarized in Exhibit 2.15.

A new plant involves a major investment, with the amount heavily dependent on the size of the facility. Exhibit 2.16 is representative of the timing and the level of commitment at various stages. Since the entire process would take at least 24 months, the program would have to be started immediately in order to avoid an out-of-capacity condition if the high-case forecast were achieved. (This is a serious risk for the business, because it provides an opportunity for foreign competitors to establish a position in the market.) However, if growth were slowed to the 5% per year rate, the company might have a substantial investment tied up in a facility that would not be used for four or five more years. It is possible in this case, however, to avoid delay, and yet not take an imprudent risk, by using successive commitments.

Strategy and Programs Summary								
Product Group ______				Division ______				
Recommended strategies				Opportunities/threats/issues addressed by strategy				
Second best alternate strategy				Reasons for not recommending alternate				
Key programs								
Description				How does it implement strategy				
Level of effort $	Manpower	Investment	Milestones Description	Date	Responsibility		Benefits $ Income before taxes	$ Cash
1990						1991		
1991						1992		
1992						1993		

Exhibit 2.13. Illustration of format for summarizing and presenting the operational plan

	Objective			
Plan elements	Build market position for long-term profit	High short-term earnings Medium cash flow	Maximize cash generation	Exit
Financial commitment	Maximum digestible	Selective/high-return segments	Minimum	Dispose
Risk	Accept/contain	Limit	Avoid	No new risk
Markets	Expand into new segments	Concentrate on core	Withdraw from marginal segments	Maintain if possible
Products	Lead, diversify new categories	Differentiate Specialization Line extensions Value/cost	Prune	Maintain where needed for sale of business
Share	Build, create preservable competitive advantage	Target growth/protect position	Forgo share for profit	Forgo share
Pricing/promotion	Aggressively heavy merchandising	Stabilize for maximum contribution	Up, even at expense of volume	Pricing up, no promotion
Advertising	Heavy creativity	Limit creativity	Cut	Minimize
Distribution	Build coverage, performance	Protect coverage	Pull out of marginal regions	Isolate if practical from other businesses
Purchasing	Ensure adequate forward coverage	Protect cost competitiveness	Limit extended commitments	No long-term commitment
Cost/capacity	Utilize scale, not thrift, capacity ahead of demand	Aggressive reduction of variable, economize on fixed balance capacity	"Variabilize" by cutting consolidation	Major effort to reduce overhead
Management	Entrepreneurs—high variable compensation	Skeptical—balanced	Disciplined—strong cost control, high base salary	Entrepreneurs—high variable, commitment after exit

Exhibit 2.14. Specific actions based on matrix position

	Year	Plan (14%/year)	High (20%/year)	Low (5%/year)
	Current	7000/month	7000/month	7000/month
	1	8,000	8,499	7,350
Current capacity 10,000/ month	2	9,100	10,080	7,720
	3	10,400	12,100	8,100
	4	11,800	14,500	8,500
	5	13,500	17,400	8,930

Exhibit 2.15. Sales volume at three forecast levels for illustrative case

Exhibit 2.16 illustrates that a considerable amount of the preliminary program work (which is time consuming) can be done without making a major commitment. The first step—selection of a new site—can be started immediately, with a very small investment commitment and low risk. The next decision point and step up in level of commitment would come in the ninth month with a decision on whether to proceed with detailed engineering design. At this time, the results of the first year of the new marketing plan, the imminence of the foreign competitive threat, and the likelihood of achieving the high

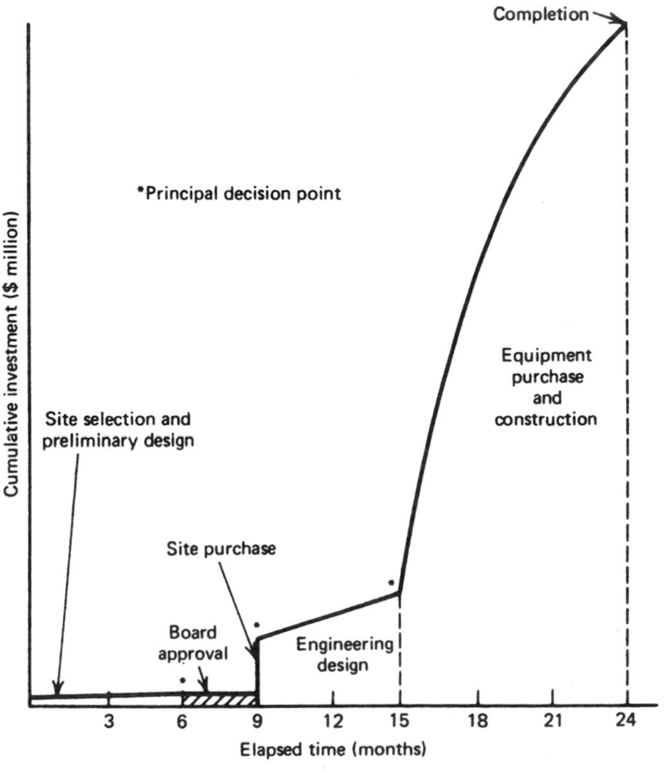

Exhibit 2.16. Example of program timing and commitment level for new facility

forecast would all be much better defined. A decision on the major commitment, however, still does not have to be made until the 15th month.

Use of successive, progressive commitments enables rapid action to exploit opportunities that might develop faster and be larger than planned, yet it contains the risk at a level consistent with the level of certainty. It is not just "buying time" or a way of avoiding decisions that should be made. In fact, as the previously described example illustrates, it can facilitate a more aggressive action plan.

2.8 MEASUREMENT. The concept of a dynamic strategic plan, where actual results are compared to expectations and revisions are made to accommodate the plan to the real world, is essential to using such a plan as a management tool in running the business. Each program in the operational plan must have a finite, quantifiable result as an objective. The result must also be time dependent. The plan should specify interim results, not just a final objective, especially if the program is of relatively long duration. Examples of some usable program objectives are as follows:

Program	Objective	Time
Develop high-strength product	Demonstrate feasibility or Polymer X with laboratory samples	Month 2
(Polymer X)	Achieve consistent test results on five laboratory batches—impact strength—density	Month 4
	Complete detailed economic evaluation with price below 85¢/pound	Month 6
Improve distribution to hospitals	Identify 10 qualified distributors	Month 1
	Sign three distributors	Month 3
	Obtain $100,000/month sales in hospital through new distributors	Month 9

These examples were selected to illustrate the type of results that are not normally reported in the monthly or other periodic financial reports. It is just as important to track these results as it is to measure the usual financial parameters in the business. In many instances, the nonroutinely reported results will provide early warning signals that the financial objectives will not be met or will be greatly exceeded and that the plans should be modified.

2.9 FEEDBACK. There is nothing worse in planning than an irrevocable commitment to an unworkable strategy. A feedback system will help avoid such a situation.

All planning processes, whether they are formal or informal, are built upon a series of assumptions regarding the internal and external environment and the principal changes that are likely to occur. A major benefit of a formal planning process is that it compels an explicit statement of the underlying assumptions. It also provides a direct link between these assumptions and the business positioning, the business direction, and, eventually, the action plans.

The strategic plan can be used effectively as a day-to-day management guide only if objective measurements are established for the action plans and the results are compared to these objectives periodically. This enables revisions in the plan based on the latest information. Maintaining an ability to shift and modify keeps the plan realistic and, provided that the changes are consistent with the strategy, still allows an orderly approach to managing a complex business in the face of uncertainty.

In some companies with sophisticated planning systems, detailed monthly financial reports are prepared that are tied to the annual financial budget, but there are no regular reports on those program objectives that are not directly measured in the financial results. Without regular reports on those results, however, the plan cannot be kept current. If the plan is outdated before it is printed, it loses credibility, and the business management will tend to regard the strategic planning effort as an exercise done primarily to satisfy higher management whims, considering it to be a diversion from the ''real'' job of running the business.

It is possible, however, to develop regular reporting systems that compare actual results to the plan objectives. If there are minor differences, it may require only revision of the timetables in the operational plan. Major differences should provoke a re-examination of the situation analysis and the assumed business position, which, in turn, may lead to change in the business direction and strategic concept for the business. If the plan is prepared with a feedback system as an integral element, necessary changes are likely to be made in a more timely manner and with less resistance.

2.10 CONTINGENCY PLANNING. The preceeding discussion on feedback focused on detecting changes in the environment or differences between results and plan expectations and on adjusting the plan to accommodate changes and/or differences. In some companies, an attempt is made to anticipate unexpected situations by preparing a responding course of action in advance. This can help avoid surprise and enable an intelligent, rapid response to crises. If the response is ready when an emergency arises, presumably a more well-thought-out decision can be made without scrambling. Contingency planning can also help sharpen planning skills by forcing managers to ''stretch'' their look at the environment and to identify possibilities that might have been overlooked in preparing the strategic plan.

Contingency planning systems usually consist of a three-step process:

1. Identifying the possible event
2. Determining the trigger points
3. Developing responses to the event

(a) Identifying the Possible Event. This step lists the possible events that might be important to the business and that have not been forecast in the base plan. The potential impact of each event on the business is determined, and the probability of its occurring is estimated. An array, similar to the one shown in Exhibit 2.10, is useful for assessing priorities and selecting the most important events for further work.

(b) Determining the Trigger Points. In this step, the indicators that alert us to the impending occurrence are identified, and individuals are assigned to track these indicators and warn when the event appears imminent.

(c) Developing Responses to the Event. To develop an appropriate response, it is assumed that the event will occur and that it will produce a result significantly different than what was assumed in the base plan. Thus, the approach is the same as previously described in the section on feedback. The difference from the base case assumption is evaluated to determine its impact on the assessment of the business situation and the business position. The necessary changes in business direction, and the consequent operational plan to exploit the new opportunities or to respond to the threats, are then determined, and a standby plan is developed.

Although the preceding description implies a formal, structured system comparable to the one employed for the base case, this is not the actual practice in most companies. Contingency planning is often done on an informal basis, with only verbalization or skeleton outlines. Emphasis is placed in many cases on the thought process, and it becomes part of the discussion in the review process rather than a documented plan.

There are several reasons for this. Many of the contingencies contemplated are radical. The development of a written plan and its inevitable dissemination may cause problems through exposure and discussion of unlikely events with highly negative connotations (e.g., plant shutdown or sale of business). In some cases, contingency actions have also created more damage than they tried to correct by causing managers to anticipate the contingency (especially a negative one) and to start cutting back even in advance of the triggers. Other problems with contingency planning are the added burden of managerial time and energy required to prepare additional plans and the possibility that contingency plans will be used as "escape hatches" for poor performance on the base plan.

Although contingency planning is a useful exercise, the need for formal contingency plans is considerably reduced if the initial plan is designed with flexibility, using a progressive commitment approach and employing measurement and feedback on a regular basis.

2.11 PROBLEMS IN IMPLEMENTING FORMAL STRATEGIC PLANNING SYSTEMS. G. A. Steiner surveyed 215 corporations in diverse industries[1] to identify the most common problems encountered in organizing and implementing formal long-range and strategic planning systems. His study, which has been supported by other investigations, found that the following were the 10 most important pitfalls to avoid:

1. Top management's assumption that it can delegate the planning function to the planner
2. Top management's becoming so engrossed in current problems that it spends insufficient time on long-range planning with the result that the process becomes discredited among other managers and staff
3. Failure to develop company goals suitable as a basis for formulating long-range plans
4. Failure to assure the necessary involvement in the planning process of major line personnel
5. Failing to use plans as standards for measuring managerial performance
6. Failure to create a climate in the company that is congenial and not resistant to planning
7. Assuming that corporate comprehensive planning is something separate from the entire management process
8. Injecting so much formality into the system that it lacks flexibility, looseness, and simplicity, thereby restraining creativity
9. Failure of top management to review with departmental and divisional heads the long-range plans that they have developed
10. Top management's consistently rejecting the formal planning mechanism by making intuitive decisions which conflict with the formal plans

[1] G. A. Steiner, *Pitfalls in Comprehensive Long-Range Planning* (Oxford, OH: The Planning Executive Institute, 1972), pp. 52–54.

Some of these problems have been addressed in the preceding section. It is important, however, to recognize that these are real dangers to successful implementation. Most of these problems can be overcome if the CEO is committed to a formal planning system. In the final analysis, the success of a formal planning system depends on three factors:

1. The involvement, dedication, and support of the CEO
2. The degree of practical business insight, experience, and credibility of the individuals responsible for designing and administering the system
3. The degree to which the planning system is tailored to the particular needs of the business (rather than fitting into a standardized planning package)

2.12 SUMMARY. Formal strategic planning systems are useful management tools that should serve as a day-to-day guide, not just as an annual exercise. The following characteristics distinguish a useful strategic plan:

- It is *oriented toward decision making,* not just a set of objectives or written plans.
- It is an *operational* tool, not just a long-term forecast. It is the foundation for the annual budget, all major programs, short-term actions, performance measurement, and so forth.
- It is *competitor oriented,* aimed at developing economic, preservable advantages.
- It is *factual and analytical:* it avoids ''motherhood'' statements, using objectivity and detail where necessary to resolve issues.
- It is *selective,* focusing on the priorities of the business and on the most critical issues.
- It is *continuing and dynamic* providing a framework for decisions rather than an excuse for indecision.

SOURCES AND SUGGESTED REFERENCES

Agababian, Haig K., ''Strategic Budgetary Planning,'' *Retail Control,* vol. 57, no. 5, May/June 1989.

Freeman, Eva, ''Turn Your Budgeting Operation into a Profit Center.'' *Datamation,* vol. 43, no. 1, January 1997, pp. 90–93.

Gray, Daniel H., ''Uses and Misuses of Strategic Planning,'' *Harvard Business Review,* January–February 1986.

Johnson, Hazel J., *Strategic Capital Budgeting: Developing and Implementing the Corporate Capital Allocation,* Homewood, IL: Irwin Professional Publishing, 1993.

Kovacevic, Antonio, and Nicholas Majluf. *Six States of IT Strategic Management.* Sloan Management Review, Summer 1993, pp. 77–87.

Perry, Lee Tom. *Real-Time Strategy: Improvising Team-Based Planning for a Fast-Changing World.* New York: John Wiley & Sons, 1993.

Rugman, Alan M., and Alain Verbeke, ''Strategic Capital Budgeting Decisions and the Theory of Internalisation,'' *Managerial Finance (UK),* vol. 16, no. 2, 1990.

Skok, James E., ''Strategic Budgeting: Reviewing the Literature of an Emerging Theory,'' *International Journal of Public Administration,* vol. 14, no. 5, September 1991.

Suutari, Raymond K., ''Rethinking Budgeting,'' *CA Magazine,* vol. 124, no. 10, October 1991.

West, Robert N., and Amy M. Snyder, ''How to Set up a Budgeting and Planning System,'' *Management Accounting,* vol. 78, no. 7, January 1997, pp. 20–26.

CHAPTER 3

BUDGETING AND ITS RELATIONSHIP TO THE ECONOMIC ENVIRONMENT

Mohammad Ali Chaudry

AT&T and Seton Hall University

3.1 INTRODUCTION. Managers of all varieties of enterprises recognize the importance of external events in planning and budgeting. A recession, a depression, an interest rate advance, the dollar's decline, an internal monetary crisis, an environmental regulation, a new invention, antitrust legislation, distant revolution, a merger or acquisition, crop failure or a natural disaster, a competitor's action, a supplier's capacity limitation or a strike, a customer's market collapse—all occurrences outside a manager's control can upset plans and budgets.

Recognition of the potential impact of external developments has led to the inclusion of environmental considerations in the planning and budgeting process. It has also led to the inclusion in this handbook of this chapter on the relationship of the economic environment to budgeting.

3.2 SIGNIFICANCE OF ECONOMIC FACTORS. Why is the economic environment singled out for special attention? Surely domestic and international political developments have been as threatening to a world without surprises, and social attitudes have shown their power in stopping wars and in limiting pollution and discrimination. Should we not consider all environmental factors that affect budgets directly or indirectly? That is the attitude expressed in this response to a questionnaire that we sent to the controller of a major materials handling equipment firm:

> Rather than dealing with *economic* inputs to the *budgeting* process we approach this from the viewpoint of environmental inputs to the *planning* process, incorporating data regarding the competitive, political/social, and commercial environment into the process of arriving at and implementing a *business strategy* which fully reflects the external environment.

In the assessment of a business environment, many factors that are not narrowly economic are included as follows:

- U.S. political climate
- Economics
- Market competition

- International climate
- Acquisitions and mergers
- Technological impact
- Operations requirements
- Human resources outlook
- Information services needs
- Financial markets
- Legal issues
- Contracting considerations
- Accounting and tax issues

Noneconomic factors are clearly important, but the emphasis here and elsewhere is often on the economic environment. This can be explained by the importance of economic factors to all kinds of activities. Inflation rates are universally incorporated in private and public budgets. Similarly, economic growth rates have effects on most markets and budgets. It is also true that the economic environment is more consistently structured and more readily applied than other environmental influences. Finally, noneconomic events often translate into economic effects such as prices, costs, productivity, and availability.

In the early 1970s, the planning department at AT&T developed a comprehensive model (Davis, Caccappolo, and Chaudry) that incorporated the linkages between the economy and the internal planning process. As Exhibit 3.1 illustrates, it consisted of an Environmental Model, a Corporate Model, and a Management Model. The National Economy module of the Environmental Model was driven by the McGraw Hill–Data Resources, Inc.'s (DRI) macroeconometric model of the U.S. economy, along with internal forecasts of relevant economic variables, such as gross national product (GNP), personal disposable income, consumer price index (CPI), the GNP implicit deflator, and the implicit deflator for personal consumption, among others. These variables were used in the product demand equations of the Demand module, which, when coupled with product prices, yielded revenues for planning purposes.

The level of total demand for products and services was used in the Production Module to estimate capital and labor requirements. Adding in a forecast of materials and services purchased from others yielded an estimate of total costs for budgeting purposes. Built as a recursive model, FORECYT could be used to simulate the impact of changes in economic variables assumed by planners or produced by the DRI macroeconometric model simulations of alternative scenarios for the national economy. The functional schematic in Exhibit 3.2 shows these relationships.

Most large companies generate internal forecasts that are shared with operating divisions during the budgeting cycle. Following are some of the key variables that play a role, directly or indirectly, in developing budget forecasts: real and nominal GNP, real and nominal gross domestic product (GDP), CPI, final sales, industrial production, capacity utilization, civilian unemployment rate, auto sales, housing starts, personal disposable income, exchange rates, and after-tax corporate profits.

In a communications and computer company, demand forecasts utilize a variety of these variables, depending on the scope of markets being analyzed. For example, real disposable personal income per household is one of the explanatory variables in an econometric demand equation that includes relative price and other relevant factors. These demand forecasts, in turn, form the basis of budgets at various levels in the planning cycle.

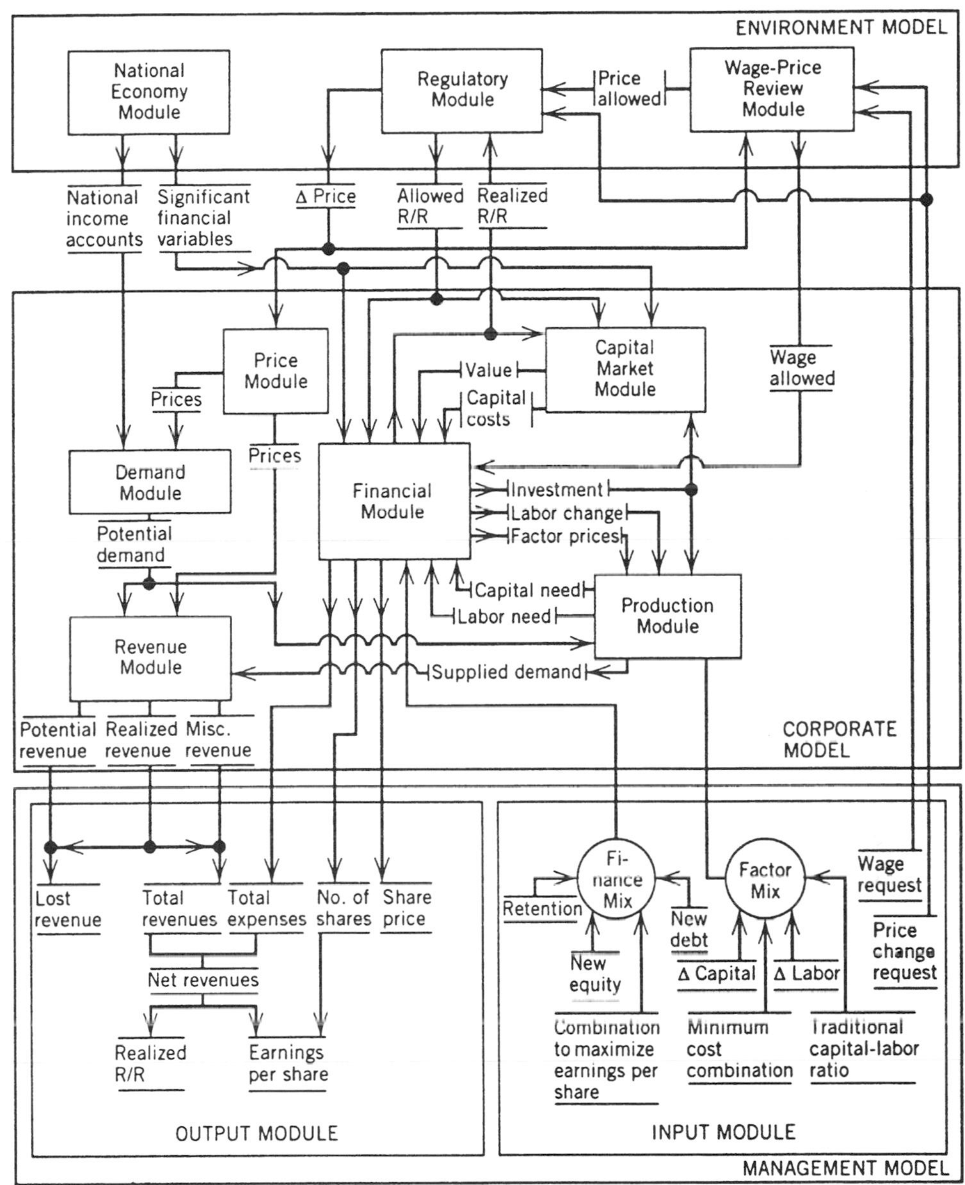

Exhibit 3.1. Linkages between the economy and the internal planning process—FORECYT model

In Lowe's companies, as in others, a sales budget is key to the entire budgeting process. Company controllers develop accurate sales forecasts on the basis of historical trends, market research, competitive assessment, and, last, but not least, general economic conditions and movements of economic indicators (Howell).

Inflation and the level of economic activity are obvious economic influences on budgets. What are others? To answer this, a questionnaire was sent in mid-1979 to more than 700

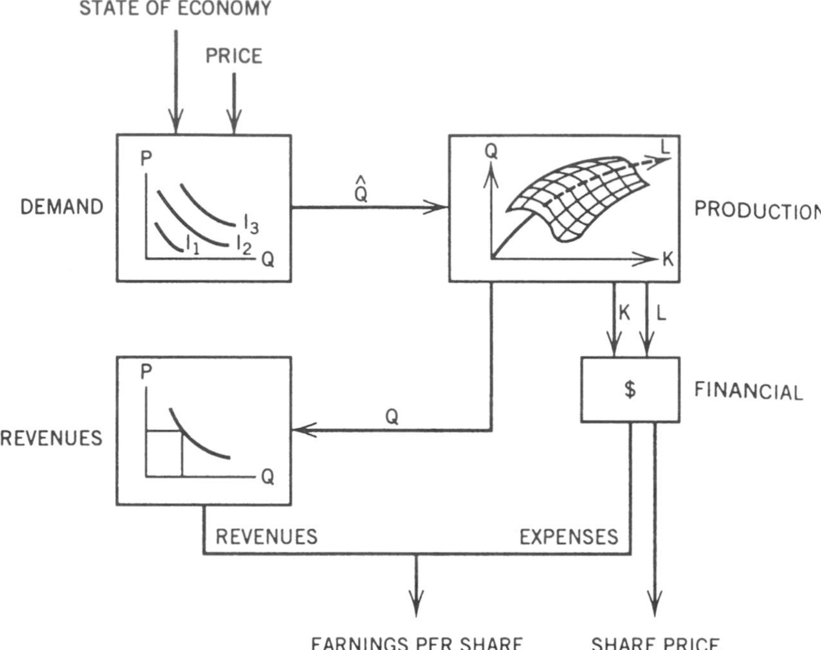

Exhibit 3.2. Functional schematic

controllers who were members of the Financial Executives Institute. This yielded 130 replies from executives in financial and nonfinancial businesses in the United States and somewhat fewer such replies from Canada. There were also replies from several universities and nonprofit institutions.

Exhibits 3.3 and 3.4 are excerpts of the survey letter and the answer sheet. Although examples of economic variables were mentioned in the letter, it is important to note that there was no checklist on the answer sheet. Respondents replied in their own words.

The results of the survey are summarized in Exhibit 3.5. Inflation led the responses by a wide margin, and, if there had been a checklist, it would probably have been scored in the high 90s. Gross national product ranked second, and it was not surprising to find this widespread sensitivity to the level of overall economic activity. The GNP was closely

---

May I request your professional help on three points? (An answer sheet is attached.)

1. Economic inputs important to your budgeting.
2. Diagrams of your budgeting process. Information flows would help me identify economic premises (market growth, inflation, exchange rates, interest rates, etc.) needed to make budget projections.
3. Instances in which economic developments had a major impact on your budget and the company's performance.

Exhibit 3.3. Portion of survey letter

1. (*a*) Most needed direct and indirect economic inputs in budgeting:
   (*b*) Economic inputs that are somewhat specialized because of the nature of our industry or firm:
2. Budget flow charts ( ) are attached.
   ( ) will be mailed separately
   ( ) are not available.
3. Instance(s) in which an economic development greatly affected our firm and budget:

Exhibit 3.4. Portion of survey answer sheet: Budgeting/economy survey

Top 10 Replies and Frequency (%)	
Inflation	68
GNP	48
Interest rates	47
Labor costs and strikes	32
Industry growth	30
Regulations	28
Exchange rates	27
Energy	26
Housing and other construction	25
Material costs	18

Other Inputs Identified in 7 to 14% of Replies (Declining Order)

Taxes
Capital spending plans and appropriations
Industrial production index and capacity utilization
Controls—wage and price
Competitors' actions
Regional data
Stock market data
Disposable income
Employment and unemployment
Automobile and truck sales
Money supply
Population
Material shortages
Foreign data
Product outlook
Government spending
Market share

Exhibit 3.5. Summary of survey results: Most needed direct and indirect economic inputs in budgeting

followed by interest rates. These three factors—inflation, GNP, and interest rates—significantly outdistanced the rest of the field.

Labor costs and strikes were considered a single item in the tabulation of results and ranked fourth. Material costs were mentioned less frequently, but still scored among the top 10 inputs to budgets. Two specific industries appeared often enough to be included in Exhibit 3.5. Housing and other construction ranked ninth, and automotive 20th.

The nearly identical scores of regulations, exchange rates, and energy would have been hard to predict. Each promises to be a persistent feature of the economic environment. The importance of exchange rates has increased as the investment of enterprises in international banking, trade, and production has grown.

Energy is, of course, not exclusively an economic environmental factor—political overtones are often involved. The economic effects of energy have been felt through both higher costs and limited supply. For example, in response to our survey, a cement manufacturer emphasized the cost effects, whereas a recreational center was more affected by the uncertain availability of gasoline during one period.

The high rank of regulations is particularly noteworthy because some might say that it is a social or governmental, rather than an economic, variable. It was regarded as an economic variable by no less an authority than Adam Smith, who wrote the following:

> Even the regulations by which each nation endeavors to secure to itself the exclusive trade of its own colonies are frequently more hurtful to the countries in favor of which they are established than to those against which they are established.[1]

Regulations might have ranked even higher if a checklist had included it for all to consider. Still, it was mentioned by representatives of a wide range of industries—for example, metals, tobacco, telephone, gas, oil, transportation, and financial.

Regarding noneconomic or quasi-economic variables in the responses to our survey, the foreign data of interest included, but were not limited to, economic statistics. Military and political developments were referenced in a number of the replies.

Competitor's actions are clearly ''economic'' in that much of microeconomics is concerned with the behavior of competitors in various kinds of markets. Some may not have thought of that, however, in the context of the economic environment; again, a checklist might have raised competitors' actions in the standings.

Items that were identified, but not often enough to be listed in Exhibit 3.5, included the following: construction costs, customers' forecasts, inventories, labor availability, loan demand, retail sales, technology, and transportation costs. In addition, there were numerous references to economic measures specific to certain industries.

The remainder of the chapter relies heavily on the results of this survey. Those results have been buttressed by interviews, studies by others, and experience in preparing environmental analyses for plans and budgets. From these sources have emerged the three topics of this chapter:

1. The process of incorporating the external environment into plans and budgets
2. Forecasting the environment
3. Specialized industry and functional economic inputs to budgeting

3.3 PROCESS

(a) Capital versus Operating Budgets and Budgets versus Plans. Within a week of mailing the survey letters, there were calls asking whether our interest was in capital or operating budgets. Some callers also asked about budgeting as opposed to long-range planning. Later, some written responses made the same distinctions. Those telephoning about capital versus operating budgets were urged to include economic inputs to both.

[1] Adam Smith, *The Wealth of Nations* (New York: Modern Library, Random House, 1937), p. 592.

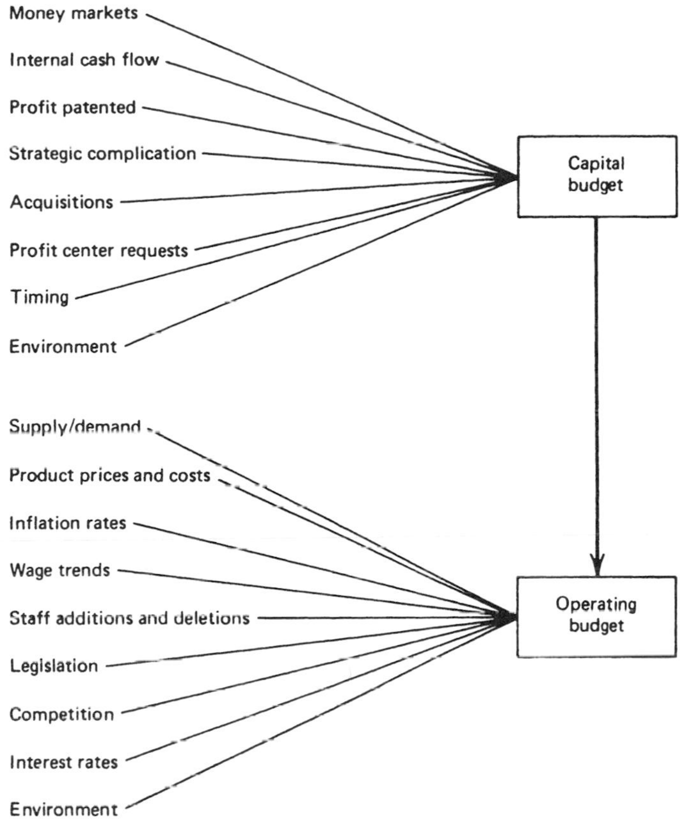

Source: Northern Natural Gas Company, Omaha.

Exhibit 3.6. Budget flow chart

Similarly, we suggested including economic inputs to plans that led to budgets as well as direct inputs to budgets. A gas utility emphasized the distinction between capital and operating budgets through the chart reproduced in Exhibit 3.6.

On the planning-versus-budget question, the director of business and economic research of a textile firm wrote:

> Our experience has been that economic inputs have played a far more important part in our longer term planning than they have in our budgeting process (which normally has a one-year time horizon). It is obvious that the needs are very different given the different time frames. . . .

Exhibit 3.7, submitted by a steel company, presents a particularly clear picture of the relationship among all of these concepts—strategic planning, capital budgeting, and operating budgets. In fact, the three horizontal elements of the chart are labeled "strategic plan," "capital budget," and "program of operations." On the chart, "assumption review" covers economic inputs. These were detailed in an accompanying list, shown in Exhibit 3.8.

Exhibit 3.7 is so beautifully simplified that it may make the processes of planning and

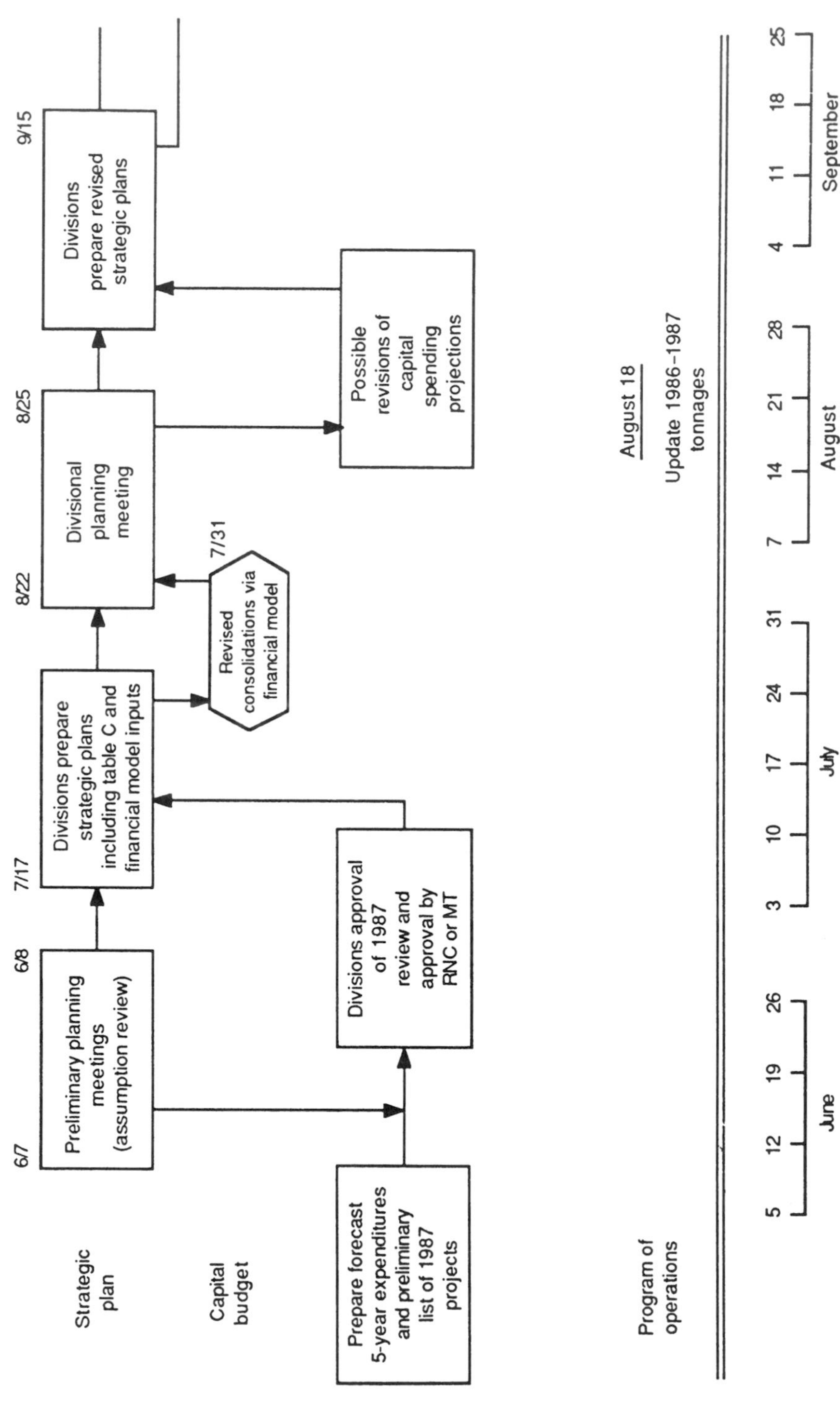

Exhibit 3.7. Planning calendar for a steel firm

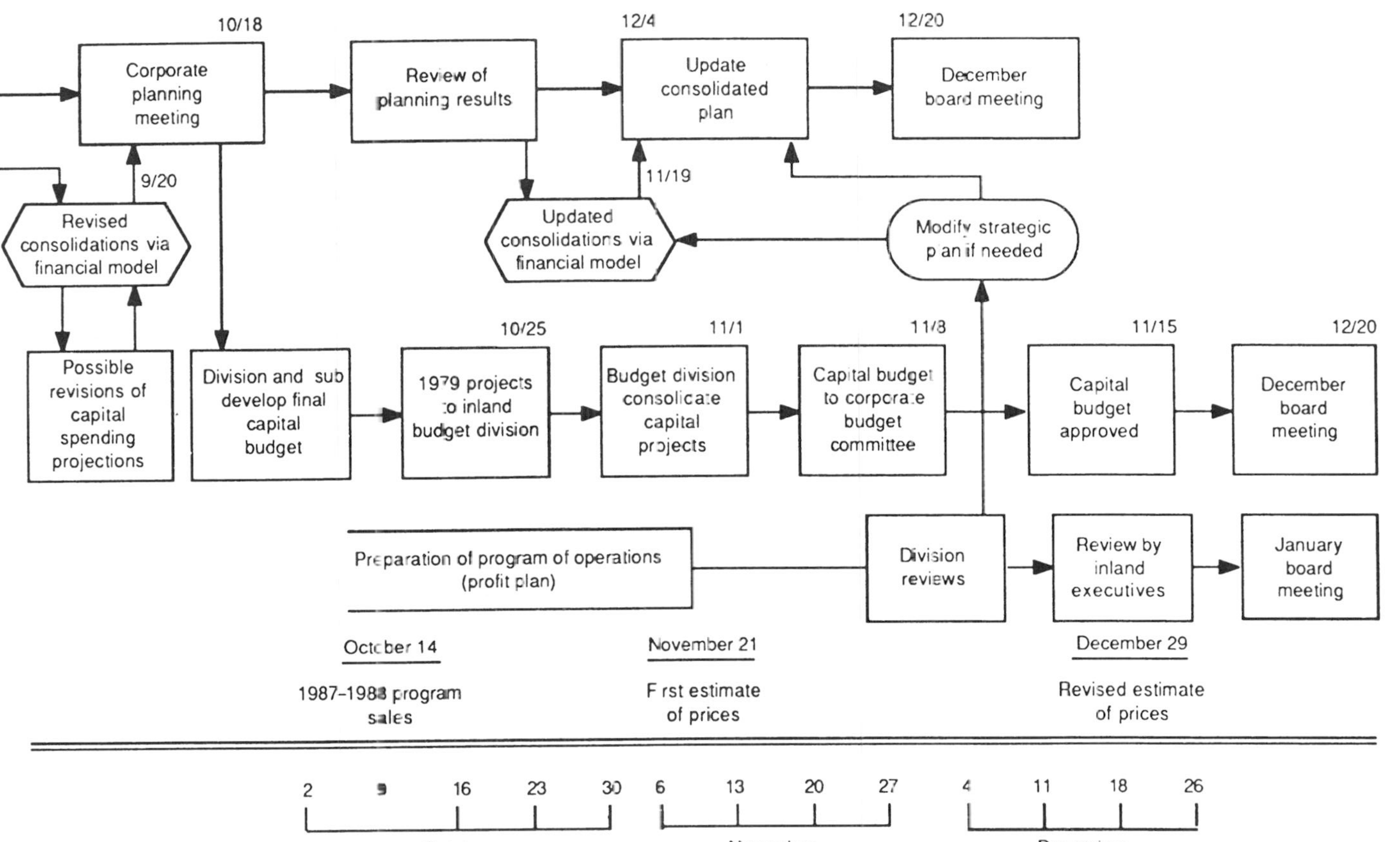

Exhibit 3.7. *(Continued)*

U.S. and foreign economies
Industry
Competitor reactions
Market share
Energy costs, availability, and alternative sources
Raw materials
EPA requirements and other government regulations
Foreign steel imports—trigger prices
Transportation of raw material and finished steel
Tax policy and legislation

Exhibit 3.8. Economic inputs in budgeting for a steel firm

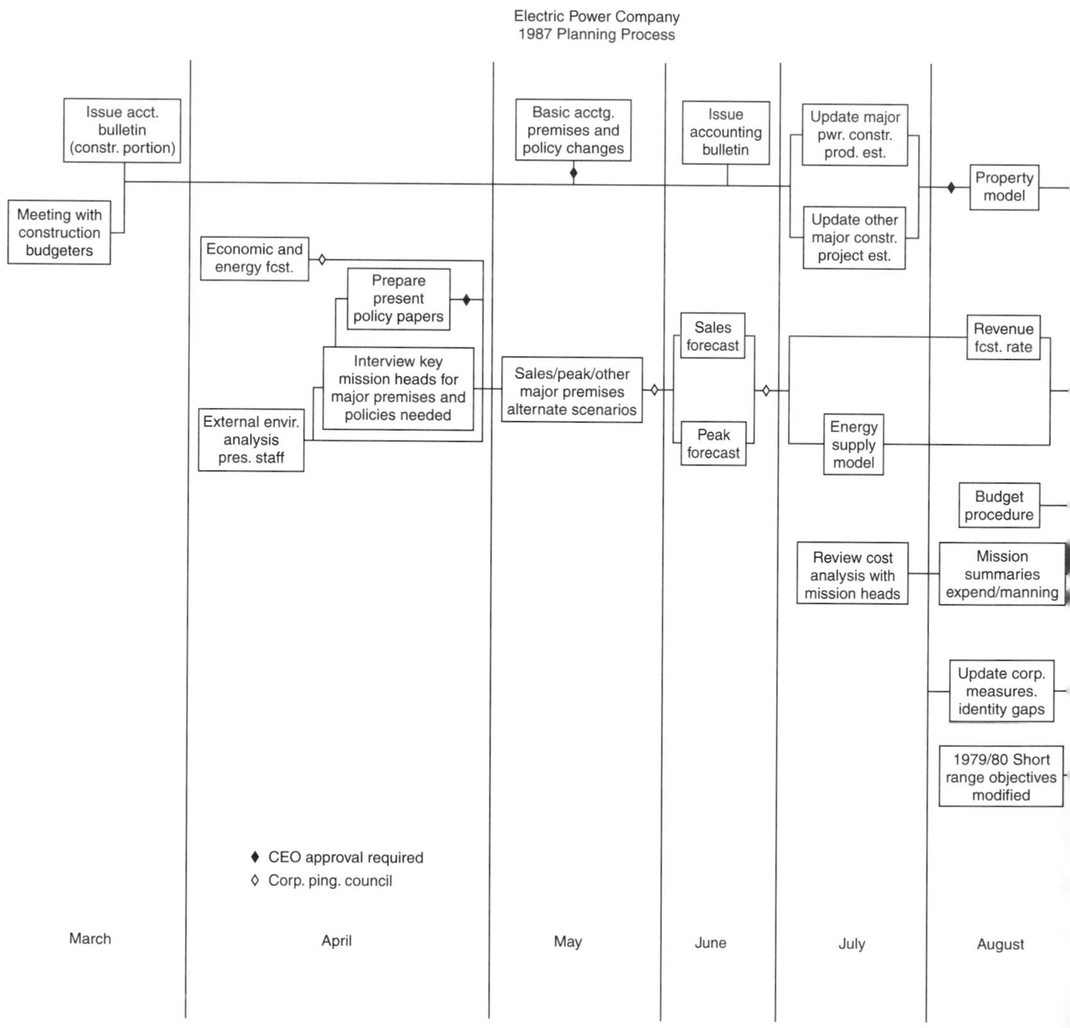

Exhibit 3.9. Planning calendar for an electric utility

budgeting seem routine. Exhibit 3.9, which is from an electric utility, is similar to Exhibit 3.7 but includes more complexities. It shows—most clearly through a magnifying glass—careful tracking of economic developments, the use of scenarios, and the identification of long- and short-range objectives. Economic and energy forecasts appear first in April, as does an external environmental analysis. The alternate scenarios are considered in May. Note the re-appearance of economics and energy in August, as work on the corporate long-range strategic plan is updated. Short-range objectives also receive attention at that point. Early in September the preliminary 10-year forecast is prepared. The whole process culminates in operating and construction budgets before year's end.

(b) Direct Environmental Inputs to Budgets. Not all of the replies to the survey followed the pattern shown in Exhibits 3.7 and 3.9, which relate budgeting to strategic planning. It is possible, of course, to have an annual operating budget without directly

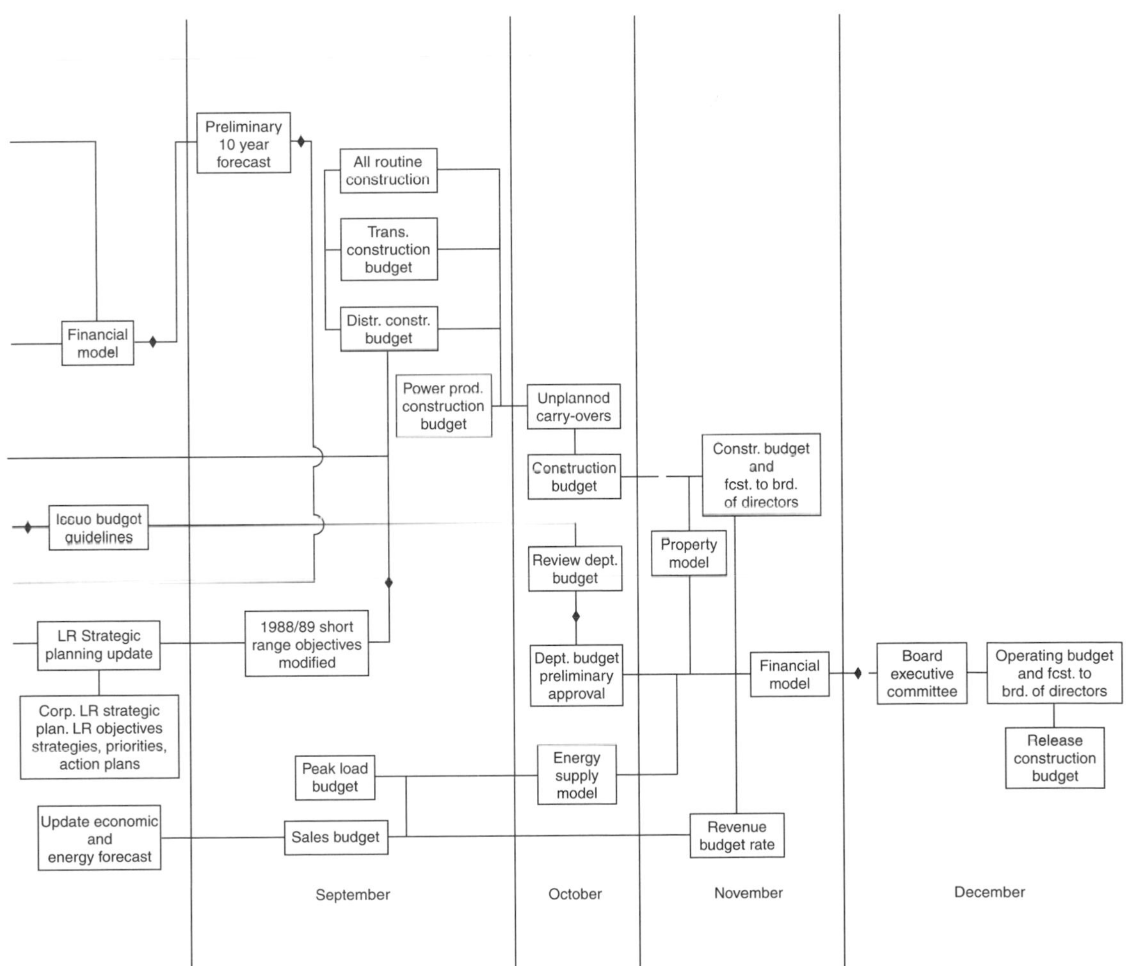

Exhibit 3.9. *(Continued)*

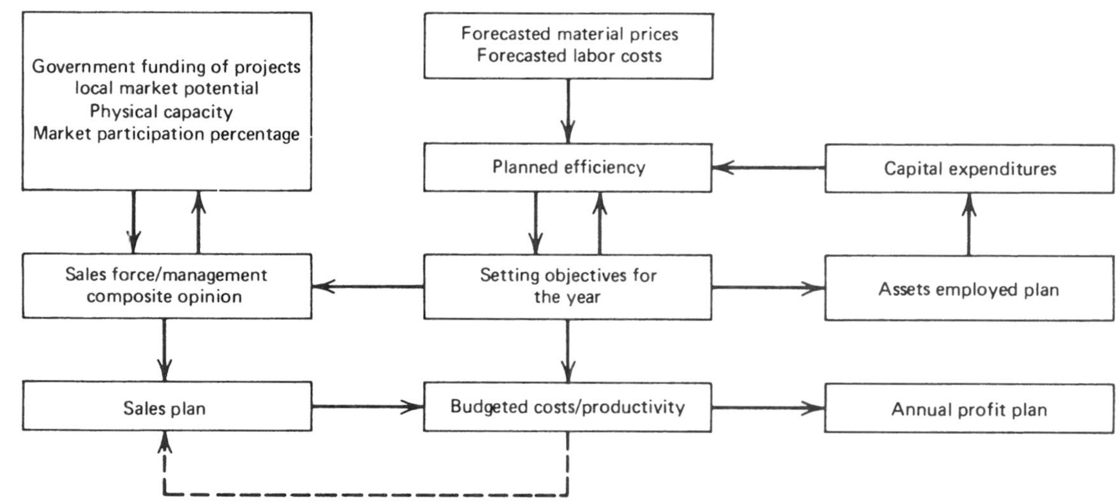

Exhibit 3.10. Annual budgeting process for a construction firm

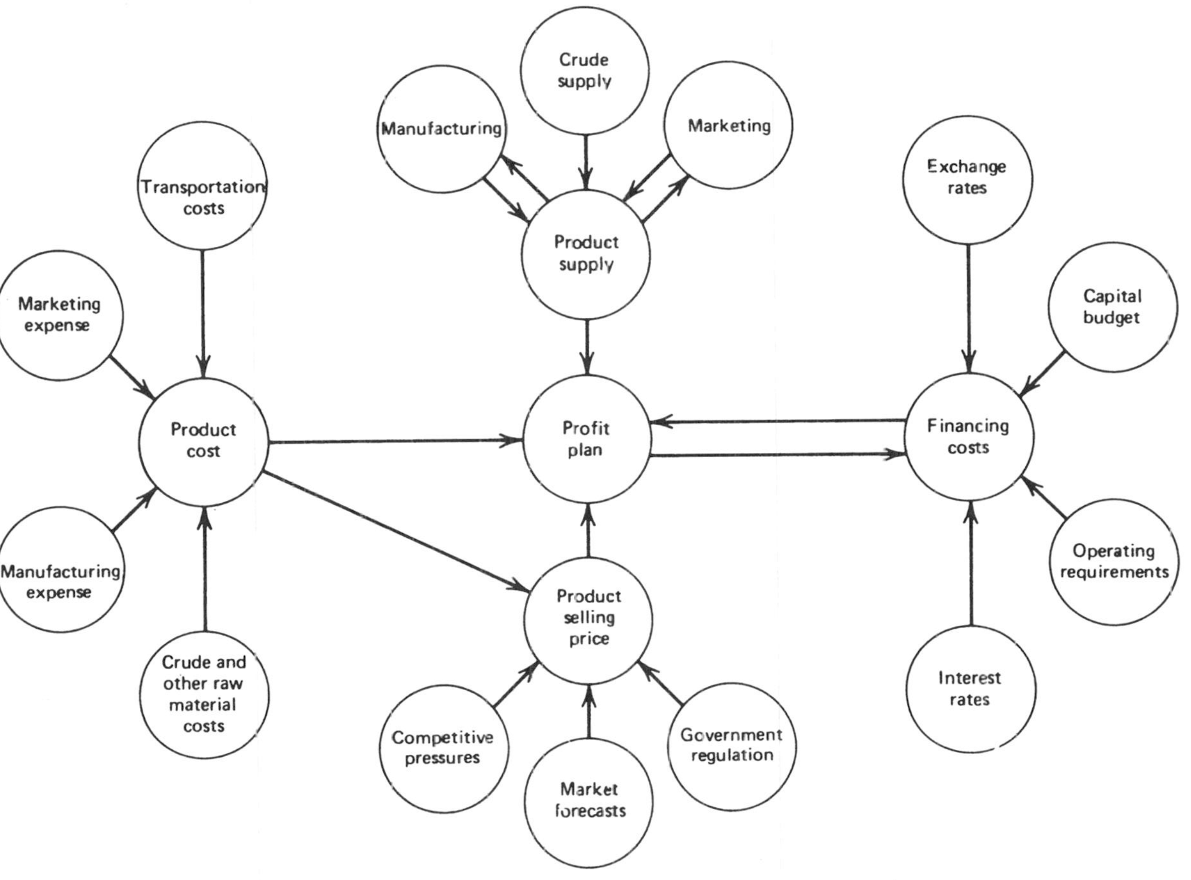

Exhibit 3.11. **Profit planning process for an oil company**

relating it to a strategic plan. For example, the strategic plan may not exist or may not be updated annually, in which cases there would be no annual coupling of the strategic plan to an operating budget. With or without a strategic plan, certain items—for example, inflation rates and interest rates—necessarily affect the budget directly.

An example of such direct ties between environmental factors and the budget was contained in the response to our survey by a firm providing security services. Their answer to the most needed direct and indirect economic inputs in budgeting was simply "wage rates and payroll taxes."

Only a few lists were that limited. A more inclusive reply is shown in Exhibit 3.10, submitted by a construction firm. In addition to labor and material costs, the firm's budgeted sales require estimates of government funding, local market potential, and measures of production capacity and market penetration.

A still more elaborate set of inputs is depicted in Exhibit 3.11, submitted by an oil company. The scope is limited to the one-year budget or profit plan, and yet inputs include a number of economic and noneconomic projections from the external environment: crude oil supply, transportation costs, raw material costs, competitive pressures, government regulations, market forecasts, exchange rates, and interest rates.

In summary, there are two basic processes for bringing economic and other environmental factors to bear on budgeting. As noted in Chapter 2, some factors may be introduced in strategic planning, whereas others are almost certain to be applied directly in establishing operating and capital budgets. In both cases, the environmental inputs attempt to describe a set of conditions during a future period. This brings us to the subject of forecasting.

3.4 FORECASTING. Economic forecasting has advanced greatly in the 1980s and 1990s, thanks primarily to the commercial application of econometrics. Thousands of forecasts of individual series are made monthly or quarterly by econometric services. The forecasts are used by clients because they are objective, detailed, internally consistent, and as accurate as most other forecasts. Furthermore, they are as close as a personal computer (PC) at an analyst's desk. Software to facilitate analysis and plotting of the data is also part of the system and is now available on CD-ROM from most of the forecasting services. Moreover, the Internet provides instant access to those forecasts and many other resources. For instance, the WEFA Group (http://www.Wefa.com) offers its forecasts and econometric modeling services to its subscribers through the World Wide Web.

Although thousands of series are forecast using elaborate models, that number is small compared to the millions—more than five million in one case—of historic series kept current in data banks and accessible on a remote terminal. Hundreds of simultaneous equations and millions of historical series do not, however, constitute an infallible forecasting record. Many examples of inaccurate and noneconometric forecasts could be cited. Here is one true story. It is told in a softened fable form, because we are all fallible.

Once upon a time (it may have been a month ago) in a kingdom by the sea (not far from Santa Monica) the chief seer (sometimes referred to as the seer's overseer) from the distant Temple of Econometrica replied to a question from one of the devout. He revealed that the second-quarter GNP growth would not be at the 3% rate that he had foretold a week earlier. It would be 1% to 2% instead. That second quarter was just ending, and many breathed a sigh of relief. The long-predicted plague of recession had not yet afflicted the land. Alas, they sighed too soon! The chief seer was destined to see yet again. With only days left in that fateful quarter, he sent forth a new proclamation (it came over the terminal): GNP not up; GNP *down* 2% in that ending second quarter. How right he was to cop another look. Why? Why indeed! Only weeks later the kingdom's high statistician announced that GNP in fact had fallen 3.3% that quarter. Some skeptics asked, "How can you trust one who sees something different with every glance?" Believers replied, "He was looking at what was mostly past. His 900 equations aren't for forecasting the past, they are for forecasting the future!"

The moral of this fable is that despite great strides in forecasting the future—or even the recent past—it is still hard to predict turning points.

Econometric models are built on theoretical relationships that are quantified by statistical analyses. The validity of these relationships is checked continuously and adjustments are made. The adjustment may be to add or to multiply by some constant amount. At times the basic theoretical equations and statistical estimation of constants are re-evaluated. In addition, judgment is used to override results given by the model if they seem unrealistic.

In a statistical process there is, of course, an assumption that past relationships will continue in the future. For example, if inflation led to a higher savings rate once, it will lead to higher savings rates again—maybe. At times the economy seems as nonrepetitive as that fascinating madam in the film version of *The Seven Percent Solution.* She proclaims in a haunting Sondheim lyric:

> Once, yes, once is a lark.
> Twice though loses the spark.
> Once, yes, once is delicious.
> But twice would be vicious or just repetitious . . .
> Still no matter what the price,
> I never do anything twice!

Fortunately, the economy does do some things twice, or forecasts would be worse than they are.

The record of econometric forecasts may be better than our narrative has suggested. Exhibit 3.12 shows a comparison among forecasts for 1991 made by McGraw Hill–DRI, WEFA Group, and an internal corporate forecast made by the chief economist of a large

Comparison of Average Absolute Errors of Annual Forecasts
Prepared by The WEFA Group, Data Resources, Inc., and Internal Corporate Economists

	Average of Four Forecasts for 1991 Made in 1990			Average of Four Forecasts for 1991 Made in 1991		
Economic Series Forecast	DRI	WEFA	Internal	DRI	WEFA	Internal
Real GDP (% change)	2.3	2.3	2.3	0.5	1.0	0.3
CPI (% change)	0.3	0.6	0.8	0.1	0.2	0.1
Industrial production (% change)	3.4	3.9	4.0	0.3	1.0	0.3
Unemployment rate (%)	0.9	0.8	0.8	0.1	0.2	0.1
Housing starts (mil units)	0.32	0.23	0.28	0.04	0.05	0.02
Treasury bill rate (%)	2.0	2.3	1.9	0.3	0.4	0.1
Yield on 30-year T bonds (%)	0.7	0.5	0.4	0.1	0.1	0.2

Exhibit 3.12. An evaluation of forecasts for the U.S. economy, 1991.

corporation. The first set of comparisons shows average absolute error in the forecasts for a number of key variables made in 1990 and second set for those made in 1991. Exhibit 3.13 shows a longer-term performance from 1980 to 1991 of the Blue Chip Consensus (BCC) forecasts, reflecting input from more than 50 well-known forecasters, and that of the internal corporate forecasts for real GNP and the CPI. These results show that the closer we get to the event, the more accurate the forecast. A review of the forecasting record of a large number of forecasters also reveals that it is very difficult to do consistently better than the consensus forecast. Thus, the budget planner needs to scan a number of forecasts to ensure that all relevant economic information is brought to bear on the budget projection.

Many models are now readily accessible on desktop PCs, and as Professor Gerard Adams demonstrates in his book, *The Business Forecasting Revolution,* many of the forecasting techniques can be integrated into the diverse forecasting needs of firms. The need for forecasts and simulations is likely to grow in coming years with the evolving structure of the U.S. economy; growing importance of international trade; formation of regional trade pacts, such as the North American Free Trade Agreement; and changes in government regulations. This demand will further increase with the rapid globalization of business enterprises in the 1990s, which will necessitate evaluation of key foreign economies and their impact on the corporate plans and budgets. There is reassurance in the fairly accurate forecasts of all four groups in most years.

Not all macroeconomic forecasts are made using econometric models. There are still individual forecasters, but their work is seldom wholly independent of that of the econometricians. Lawrence Klein, who heads the econometric forecasting at the Wharton School, emphasized the support given forecasters by econometric models in an article in the February 1979 issue of *Across the Board.* To buttress the argument, he quoted Paul Samuelson of the Massachusetts Institute of Technology (MIT) as follows:

> I would no more dream of tackling the back of an envelope before I had looked at the Wharton, and Michigan, and St. Louis models than I would dream of doing so on the basis of tea leaves or re-reading Alfred Marshall's *Principles.* In other words, we dwarfs of judgment see as far as we do because we stand on the shoulders of computer giants.[2]

(a) Sources of Economic Data. This is not the place for an exhaustive treatment of methods of forecasting. (Some bibliographic items at the end of this chapter are helpful on that subject.) However, we should identify sources of economic inputs into plans and budgets. One source is, of course, the econometric services we have been discussing. There are probably 2,000 firms that subscribe to one or more of these services, and in our survey a number of respondents referred to them. The United States and foreign government and international agency reports are a major source for both individual forecasters and services. Firms also referred to the business press, trade associations, and banks as sources of environmental inputs.

Respondents to our survey frequently noted that the corporate economist or economics group provided the economic assumptions for subsidiaries or divisions. The corporate economist's office, in turn, often makes use of econometric services and/or consultants in arriving at guidelines. The following description is from a subsidiary of a publishing firm:

---

[2] L. Klein, ''Econometrics,'' *Across the Board,* February 1979, vol. 16, no. 2, p. 57.

An Internal Corporate Forecast versus
The Blue Chip Consensus (BCC) of Thirty Forecasts
Real GNP
Percent Change from Prior Year

		Forecasts†		Absolute Forecast Error	
	Actual	Internal*	BCC	Internal*	BCC
1980	−.02	−.04	− 1.0	0.2	0.8
1981	1.9	2.3	1.1	0.4	0.8
1982	− 2.5	0.9	1.2	3.4	3.7
1983	3.6	2.5	3.1	1.1	0.5
1984	6.4	5.4	5.3	1.0	1.1
1985	2.7	3.4	3.3	0.7	0.6
1986	2.5	2.9	3.1	0.4	0.6
1987	2.9	2.6	2.6	0.3	0.3
1988	3.8	1.8	1.9	2.0	1.9
1989	2.9	2.9	2.5	0.0	0.4
1990	0.9	2.2	1.7	1.3	0.8
1991	− 0.5	0.0	1.1	0.5	0.9
Average Absolute Error				0.9	1.1

Consumer Price Index
Percent Change from Prior Year

		Forecasts†		Absolute Forecast Error	
	Actual	Internal*	BCC	Internal*	BCC
1980	13.5	10.4	10.3	3.1	3,2
1981	10.4	10.5	10.2	0.1	0.2
1982	6.1	8.7	8.3	2.6	2.2
1983	3.2	5.0	5.3	1.8	2.1
1984	4.3	5.0	5.0	0.7	0.7
1985	3.6	5.3	4.6	1.7	1.0
1986	1.9	3.6	3.8	1.7	1.9
1987	3.7	3.5	3.2	0.2	0.5
1988	4.1	4.3	4.2	0.2	0.1
1989	4.8	4.7	4.7	0.1	0.1
1990	5.3	4.2	4.2	1.1	1.1
1991	4.0	6.0	5.5	2.0	1.5
Average Absolute Error				1.3	1.2

*Initial GNP estimate as reported in January of following year.
†Forecasts made in November of preceding year.

Exhibit 3.13. Average forecast error in real GNP and CPI, 1980–1991.

> Each year at the inception of the planning program, the ''X'' Corporate Economics Department prepares an environmental statement which covers the years included in the planning cycle. . . . The environmental statement is approximately 20 pages of statistics and brief narrative covering the environment that ''X'' and its divisions do business in, and the general and specific economic indicators used are growth as measured by the changes in the real GNP, inflationary rates, labor force, interest rates, corporate profits, capital investment and the identification of the risks that could develop over the forecast period such as recessions and the impact of international activities.

A chemical firm provides equally detailed background information to its product organizations. This reply includes some noneconomic variables:

> In the fall of each year, various staff departments within the company present perspectives that should be considered by the industrial departments in preparing their forecasts.
>
> - Chief Economist presents his five-year economic forecast for the U.S. and for the other major countries in which . . . does business. Domestic discussion includes comments on outlook for real GNP, chemical industry, inflation, productivity and demographics; international discussion includes comments, by country, on real GNP, inflation, and general expectations re exchange rates, as well as timely international issues.
> - Energy and Materials, Central Research & Development, and Engineering Departments present the five-year outlook for oil, natural gas, and key raw material prices.
> - Engineering, Legal, and Transportation and Distribution Departments and the Environmental Quality Committee present the outlook for various environmental issues.
> - Employment Relations Department presents views on personnel matters (e.g., delayed retirement, labor relations environment, compensation, etc.).
> - Legal Department discusses implications in areas such as antitrust, tax, labor law, international trade.
>
> The five-year forecasts generated by the industrial departments are used for business planning purposes. A separate financial forecast is prepared by Finance Department, with assistance from the Chief Economist and Corporate Plans Department for various financial planning purposes (e.g., debt planning, dividend decisions, capital budgeting, etc.).

A number of the respondents to the survey pointed out that a major external input to their budget is their customers' level of business. The question as to whether this source was relevant was raised most directly in this abstract of a response from a division of an electrical manufacturing firm:

> First of all, I am not sure that we have a meeting of minds in the terms you are using in your request. In our company, a budget relates to anticipated future expenditures. A sales forecast is just that, a forecast of future or anticipated sales. At ''Y,'' the budgeting process follows after the sales forecast, and as such relies pretty much on whatever economic input went into the sales forecast. No specific economic data is gathered for the budgetary process.
>
> Our entire forecasting procedure starts with an assessment of the economy, which is developed largely from material that is prepared by our corporate economic unit. This material is supplemented with our own data that are compiled by us internally. The specific things that we look for in the economy that most noticeably affect our business would be consumer spending patterns, both for durables and nondurables.
>
> Against the broad economic backdrop, we then try to develop a forecast for each of the industries that we serve. This is for general information only and is used primarily to test the validity of some of the forecasts of sales that we do develop.

> Our principal method of forecasting sales is to try to track, in as fine a detail as possible, the anticipated sales performance that we will experience over the next 12 months with the relatively few companies who represent approximately 90% of our business. Our field sales personnel, in concert with sales management and our marketing staff, develop by-customer, by-product forecasts of what each customer is expected to purchase from us over a 12-month period.

In the following reply from a chemical division, the economic analysis slips a little further into the background:

> Normally, detailed information available from customers is used as a basis for sales budgets. Economic data, particularly those related to Energy and Automobiles, are used for five-year forecasts. Therefore economic developments would have an *indirect impact* by affecting input received from customers. (Italics added for emphasis.)

Doubtless, there are firms that rely entirely on customer plans for sales estimates in their budgets, but it was encouraging (to an economist) to find in our survey that those stressing the importance of analysis of sales to customers usually had access to an appraisal of the economic outlook as well.

(b) The Impact of Uncertainty in the Economic Environment. That even the most elaborate modeling cannot always be depended upon to predict the future of the economy has been demonstrated to most observers' dissatisfaction. The last question on our survey inquired about economic developments that greatly affected a firm and its budget. Many factors were mentioned, but two outdistanced all others—recession and energy. For once, inflation was not number one; it ranked third with 19 respondents mentioning inflation and well below 35 respondents each for recession and energy (oil prices or availability).

Other shocks to firms mentioned with above average frequency were interest rates, strikes, exchange rates, wage and price guidelines/controls, and other forms of government regulation. Items that also appeared, although less frequently, included food prices, labor and material costs, demographic developments, regional shifts in population, movement of major customers, nationalization of foreign industries, changing energy-consumption patterns, imports, weather, the rate of growth abroad, tax changes, mortgage rates, material shortages, and specific regulations that affected various industries.

Here are some specific examples of the effects that unexpected developments had on budgets:

> Fall 1974. The sudden recession caused us to revise our 1975 sales forecast downward by 30% from the original figure developed at midyear.
>
> *A wire manufacturer*
>
> We use a nonflexible budget. However, any economic developments that significantly differ from our budget forecast may result in large variances from plan. For instance, in 1978 . . . rapidly changing prime (interest rates and) inflation rates that were not consistent with our forecast resulted in large variances from plan in certain categories.
>
> *A bank*
>
> Strikes—where employee benefits are suspended.
>
> *A medical insurer*
>
> Foreign exchange conversion rate change required higher payback on Swiss franc borrowing.

Sharp increases in interest rates resulted in increased earnings from surplus cash.

OPEC [Organization of Petroleum Exporting Countries] crude oil price changes caused significant effects on cost and availability of crude oil, selling prices of our U.S. production, price and supply/demand of refined products—and more.

An oil company

Rapid expansion of the leisure industry coupled with the scarcity of automobile fuel has made the Hawaii tourist destination attractive. This has created significant business opportunities for construction, transportation, and retailing in this area.

A diversified firm

The gasoline shortage created by the 1973 oil crisis had a significant impact on the occupancies of several of the inns, particularly those located on major highways.

A hotel operator

During 1974–1975 period, material and labor costs escalated more rapidly than anticipated. Excess demand was the basic cause. Unfortunately, the Marketing personnel continued to accept firm selling price orders. The inevitable result was rapid deterioration of profit margins as production lead times became abnormally extended and costs continued to escalate.

A machinery manufacturer

In 1975, the Company's budget was set too high, and the severeness of the recession that year was not expected. Consequently, sales dropped to 5% below budget levels and operating income plummeted to nearly 20% below budget.

A rubber company

A fall in the exchange rate made our principal export product competitive in foreign markets.

An aerospace firm

Proposed changes in tax legislation will have a significant impact on our cash budget.

A durable equipment producer

(c) Scenario Answer to Uncertainty. The preceding statements reinforce the conviction that the environment does affect performance and sometimes defies prediction. How should the uncertainty be dealt with in planning and budgeting?

Recognition that the future holds alternate possibilities is widespread. Jerry Pohlman, the economist for California Federal Savings, began one of his speeches by saying that economists no longer revise their forecasts; instead, they change the probabilities assigned to alternate scenarios. That is a slight exaggeration; probabilities for basic scenarios are changed as events unfold, but the basic scenarios are updated and changed, too.

Scenarios are outlines of hypothesized chains of events; alternate scenarios are developed by changing some of the critical assumptions from case to case. A great deal or a relatively modest amount of effort may go into formulating scenarios.

Econometric services typically provide at least three forecasts at any time. They assign probabilities to each of the forecasts, and the one considered most likely—it may be judged less than 50% probable—is their standard forecast. Alternative forecasts—scenarios—are either more or less pessimistic with regard to consumption, food, energy, strikes, or other variables.

Equitable Life included a description of its current scenarios as part of an article, ''Five-Year Economic Forecasting,'' by its economics department in the Fall 1978 issue of Equitable's *Basis Point* publication (pp. 7–10). Here is an abstract of the article:

> Management cannot make crucial planning assumptions regarding business growth, cash flow, and the average new money rate without an assessment of the economic environment in which the company is likely to be operating, nor can vital strategies such as portfolio mix, investment timing, and product pricing be developed without a calculated appraisal of the future.
>
> Judgments are made about prospective economic policy . . . the likely outcome interpreted through study of the building blocks of demographics and labor force, productivity, inflation, and interest rates. In effect, the five-year forecast is converted into a schematic economic and political scenario. The associated set of internally consistent illustrative numbers paints a broad picture of a future that is less than crystal-clear.
>
> The pitfalls in a five-year forecast are numerous. The unpredictable has a way of occurring especially in international politics and economics. . . .
>
> The first scenario portrays a reasonably healthy economy for 1979–1983, with five-year real growth about on long-term trend, and a modest and gradual improvement in inflation. A moderate cyclical correction is foreseen in 1979, but no major recession is predicted in any of the five years. This forecast is assigned a 70% probability.
>
> The second postulates intensified inflation followed by a severe correction. This forccast is assigned a 30% probability.

	Five-Year Annual Averages	
	Scenario I	Scenario II
Real GNP	3.6	2.6
GNP price deflator	6.4	7.1
Unemployment rate	6.0	6.4
Profits before taxes	10.5	7.0
Bank prime rate	7.8	8.6

An oil company that is a sophisticated user of these econometric model services made it clear that it does not believe forecasts but does work with alternative environments:

> *We hold the philosophy that it is impossible to predict the future.* In-depth analysis of the leveraging (of the) most consequential factors is, however, a fruitful approach to testing alternative future events. We look at planning as a useful process for analyzing the consequence of alternative actions against a background of alternative environments. Decisions on financial and operating strategies, project selection, and capital allocations may then be made on the basis of those which best *survive a range of possible environments.*

This firm carefully develops those alternative scenarios through corporate planning staff and divisional interaction. However, in the end, the planning and budgeting of the operating divisions are done against a single scenario:

> The key scenario choices along with their associated effects are presented to top corporate management from which they choose a set of useful "assumptions" for promulgating to the operating divisions for tactical plan development.

A forceful reply relating to alternative scenarios was received from a stock brokerage firm. Here is an excerpt from the instructions for the firm's profit plan:

> The problem in achieving these objectives has always been that the Profit Plans have been based on an overall economic scenario which is always different from the actual for the year.

This, in turn, makes the revenue projections virtually worthless and results in the plan being filed away as being no longer relevant.

To change this, the following will be our approach to this year's Profit Plan:

1. Each manager will be given a reasonable negative environment and positive environment pre-tax contribution which his area must achieve under the applicable economic conditions (see Exhibit 3.14).
2. The job of the manager is to establish an Operating Plan which will be flexible enough to produce the required result within the environment that develops.
3. If the manager feels the given environments are not appropriate, he should define those he feels are.

Basic strategic objectives for this year are:

	Environment	
	Positive	Negative
Return on equity (after tax)	12%	5%
Earnings per share	$.90	$.35
Liquidity	+ $5 mil.	Flat
Acquisitions	One	None

No other reply to our survey was as direct as this one. The brokerage firm stated alternative scenarios and assigned objectives for its budget depending on how the environment actually developed over the year.

The use of alternate scenarios fits comfortably into the idea of strategic planning. Appreciation of different possible futures should affect behavior, and effort directed toward identifying some of these futures seems a natural enough part of planning. Alternate futures should lead to strategies that would try to take into account the various possibilities. However, carrying alternate futures into *budget* instructions is less likely. It is possible to set objectives and budgets for alternate environments, as was illustrated by the brokerage firm example given. However, one can easily imagine a departure of actual developments from any number of specified environments. No single environment can be forecast with certainty, but neither can any two or three. A single set of budgeting instructions or premises is surely the most common practice, but those instructions may take advantage of insights from—and may make provisions for—alternative futures.

Another approach is to be relaxed about the whole thing and to try to pick a single reasonable environment without struggling with alternative scenarios. A chemical company wrote:

> Economic inputs do not play a great part in the preparation of our short- and long-range plans. We have found in the past that we have had a great deal of conversation about the effects of the economy, but generally, we have prepared our plans assuming an economic mid-range.

A reply from the fragrance division of a cosmetics firm made it clear that debates on scenarios would not be very useful:

> I have tried to relate the historical results of our Division with various subsets of the gross national product, such as disposable income, total income, etc., but no correlation could be found. . . . However, we utilize the current and projected inflation rates and general wage

	Last Year's Actual				Current Year											
					Positive View*				Negative View*				Your View			
	1Q	2Q	3Q (Est.)	4Q (Est.)	1Q	2Q	3Q	4Q	1Q	2Q	3Q	4Q	1Q	2Q	3Q	4Q
I. Economic Variables (%)																
CPI	8.0	10.9	9.3	7.5	6.1	6.6	6.5	6.4	7.6	8.3	8.3	8.6				
Prime rate	8.0	8.3	9.0	9.0	8.5	8.1	8.1	8.3	9.0	8.8	9.0	9.3				
Federal Funds	6.8	7.3	7.9	7.8	7.0	6.5	6.7	7.0	7.8	7.5	7.8	8.2				
Yield on new high-grade corporates	8.6	8.9	9.1	9.0	8.7	8.5	8.7	8.9	9.0	9.0	9.2	9.4				
II. Equity Market																
Price level Dow Jones Industrial Average	760	830	900	900	925	950	950	900	850	800	750	800				
Average daily volume (millions)																
NYSE	20	34	30	30	30	35	25	35	25	22	20	25				
All other	13	21	19	19	20	22	18	22	18	16	15	18				
Total	33	56	49	49	50	57	43	57	43	38	35	43				
III. Underwriting Volume (billions)																
Corporates	6.3	6.6	7.0	7.0	7.7	7.7	7.7	7.7	6.3	6.3	6.6	6.3				
Municipals	10.1	12.7	12.5	12.5	14.0	14.0	14.0	14.0	11.0	11.0	11.0	11.0				
Equities	1.1	2.7	2.3	2.5	2.7	2.7	2.3	2.7	2.7	2.0	1.8	2.0				

*These data are a guideline. It is not necessary that each area accept them, but note your assumptions should they differ. The market judgments are ▮▮▮▮▮▮▮▮
The economic variables for the positive and negative view come from DRI (September).

Exhibit 3.14. Economic and capital market guidelines

> and salary increases that are occurring and projected to occur in both union and nonunion sectors of our economy.

As hinted here, an appreciation of uncertainties and of their potential impact can lead not only to planning strategy changes but also to provisions for contingencies in the budget. Contingency plans were identified in several responses to our survey. There can be reserves for hazards or the retention of capabilities on the chance that opportunities can be better exploited if those resources are retained, though at a cost. Insurance and hedging can cover quantifiable risks. Scenarios can help identify and quantify uncertainties. Thus, the budget can be influenced by alternate scenarios even if only one specific set of assumptions is specified for budgeting.

To summarize, there is value in studying alternate scenarios in order to better understand hazards and opportunities. Although the scenarios seem more at home in deriving strategies in long-range plans than in budgets, they can also improve budgets if they lead to better provisions for contingencies.

That delightful economist, Kenneth Boulding, from the University of Colorado at Boulder deserves the last word on this subject:

> Although there is no necessary harm in writing scenarios, . . . there is great danger in believing them. The way to prepare for the future should rather enable us to recognize and take advantage of good luck and to anticipate bad luck so that we are not destroyed by it. Any strategy which assumes a known future involves delusions of uncertainty which can lead to catastrophic decisions.
>
> Science has been extraordinarily successful in finding out what there is to know. All the science in the world will not find out what is not there to know. Accordingly, we should give far more attention to the study of how to make decisions under conditions of irreducible ignorance and uncertainty.[3]

3.5 SPECIALIZED ECONOMIC INPUTS. One section of the survey asked for economic inputs that are somewhat specialized because of the nature of the industry or firm. This brought forth some of the most interesting and varied answers. For example, weather, not one of the most orthodox economic variables, appeared as an environmental factor important to industries as diverse as gas utilities, recreation centers, hotels, and steel production. Vinters doubtless also had weather in mind when they listed crop yield for grapes.

Here are some of the specialized variables listed by firms from selected industries:

- *Oil companies.* Worldwide energy supply/demand balance; government intervention in prices, facilities construction, lease sales, storage, drilling, and environmental requirements generally; foreign government and OPEC actions; prices of coal, butane, propane, ethane, and so forth; housing starts; and automobile sales.
- *Universities.* Demographics related to enrollment; and legislation on state aid to education, payroll taxes, and insurance coverage.
- *Telecommunications companies.* Per capita income; retail sales; housing starts; population; households; postage rates; construction costs; detailed development plans for

[3] Kenneth E. Boulding, "Sciences and Uncertain Futures," *Technology Review,* vol. 81, no. 7, June–July 1979, pp. 8–9.

residential areas, shopping centers, and industrial centers; university enrollments; capital investment by other telecommunications companies; return permitted by utilities commissions; technology change in communications; investment tax credit; telecommunications and durable goods manufacturing. If the survey was done in 1998, we would see the impact of changes in attitudes toward voice mail, fax, and the Internet explosion on demand for telecommunications services. Moreover, the 1996 Telecommunications Act has opened these markets to intense competition among carriers offering customers real choices.

- *Steel companies.* Environmental Protection Agency (EPA) and other government regulations and resulting nondiscretionary environmental protection expenditures; steel imports; trigger prices; transportation costs; seasonal patterns of orders; weather patterns; availability and prices of coal, ore, and raw materials; markets for total steel, stainless steel, and welding consumables; pipeline projects; railroad car building and refurbishing; machinery orders; titanium ingots availability; and labor contracts.
- *Tire industry.* Vehicle, hose, and conveyor belt markets; automobile and transportation regulations; and United Rubber Workers' settlements with competitors.

Other industries could be added to the list, but it may be more useful to look within a particular industry at some of the functions other than planning and budgeting that are affected by economic environment. There are budgets at all levels within organizations, and environmental effects on budgets anywhere find their way into a consolidated budget.

To illustrate, let us look at the aerospace industry. The commercial aircraft marketing function is supported by a strong marketing planning function. Analysts there are concerned with both domestic and international economic developments at the macro levels of GNP, with population growth and distribution by age groups, and with disposable personal income. The economic analysis becomes more detailed as they examine the characteristics of city pairs that are important transportation centers. Fares are a key variable, and deregulation has had important effects. The financial conditions of airlines and aircraft producers are financial data of importance. Government financing has become a critical consideration. Specific aircraft types and their performance characteristics include economic dimensions such as fuel costs per seat mile. Exhibit 3.15 depicts economic and noneconomic environmental effects on airline aircraft markets.

The military market analyst is concerned ultimately with tracking individual programs but recognizes that this is in a context of a government budget constrained by social values and domestic political considerations. It is also shaped by international political and military relationships. Even here, inflation is influential, since the defense budget may not expand to accommodate higher personnel, operating, and hardware costs. Military and commercial programs are both concerned with providing for inflation. This often involves economic adjustment clauses to index prices to inflation. Measures that are used to adjust contracts are economic statistics found in the Bureau of Labor Statistics (BLS) such as detailed producer price indexes, average hourly earnings, and the CPI.

The contracting and industrial relations functions were responsible twice in the 1970s for dealing with government wage and price controls and guidelines. Compliance has involved such aspects of the economic environment as inflation rates, profit rates, productivity, pricing, and costs. For those companies with cost-of-living adjustment clauses in labor contracts, adjustments based on the CPI have added more to wages in some periods than the directly negotiated increases. Low rates of inflation in the 1980s and 1990s have made inflation less important, but pressures to reduce costs have increased.

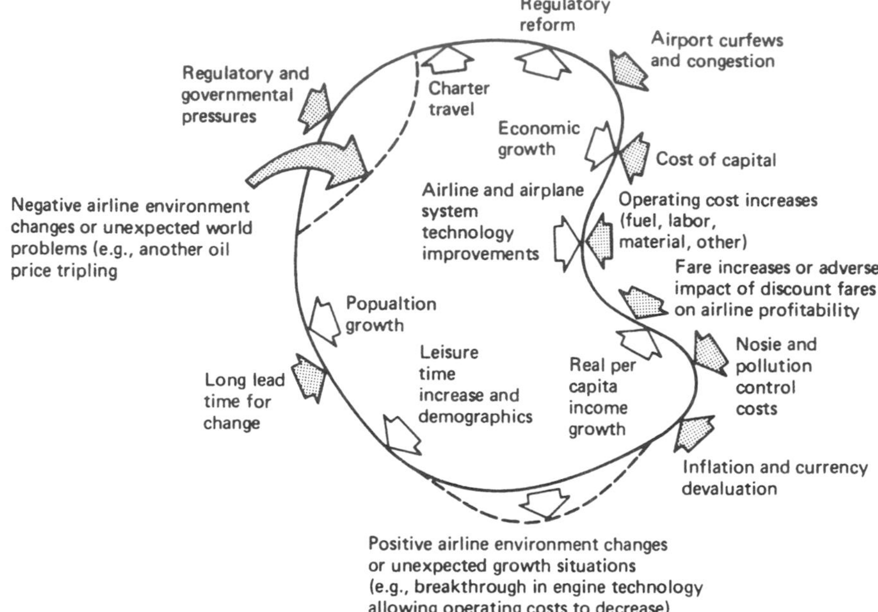

Exhibit 3.15. Pressures and constraints for airline growth

Source: Boeing Commercial Airplane Company, Dimensions of Airline Growth, February 1979.

The materiel function is also greatly affected by economic variables. If capacity utilization increases, lead times will extend and bottlenecks will appear. Costs and prices will increase. The buyers in the materiel function find their jobs ever more difficult, and so do those in materiel planning, forecasting, and budgeting. Contracts with escalation clauses are negotiated with some suppliers; paying the price at the time of delivery becomes a more common practice.

Foreign markets, lendable funds, candidates for mergers and acquisition, branch operations, and even foreign investment of employee benefit funds—all add to the importance of the international economic environment. The international political environment is important not only to defense firms but also to others, as energy crises have demonstrated.

Back home, retirement funding is complicated by inflation and stock market performance. Domestic acquisition and merger efforts are avid consumers of economic data that relate the performance of firms and industries to the economy. Public relations professionals are good customers for economic data and issues, because they prepare speeches for executives and press releases.

In the finance area, inflation, interest rates, and money supply matter, whether the problem is structuring a firm's own finances or arranging financing for a customer.

As accounting principles and tax provisions change, budgeting and performance measures are impacted.

3.6 SUMMARY. The influence of economic and other environmental developments on enterprises of all types has been illustrated in this review of the experience of some 130 U.S. and Canadian businesses and other institutions. Our survey has also documented the inclusion of many environmental factors in the plans and budgets of those enterprises.

Uncertainty has emerged as a dominant perplexity. Even that most sophisticated forecasting approach, the econometric model, cannot be depended upon to predict the future accurately at turning points.

The environment is a force that cannot be ignored or consistently predicted. How should it be included in planning and budgeting? Some firms have been discouraged by past attempts to predict the future and have decided to use a consensus forecast without searching for alternative futures. The delineation of alternate scenarios is another approach. Plans will usually be better if they are tested against a number of possible futures for key variables. Although only one set of environmental assumptions may be carried into budgeting, the budget can provide for flexibility and allow for contingencies. Budgeting should be done in light of a likely future and yet make provisions for key uncertainties in the external environment.

The final word is one of thanks to those managers who made the effort to respond so generously to our survey. It is self-evident how indebted this chapter is to them.

SOURCES AND SUGGESTED REFERENCES

Adams, F. Gerard, *The Business Forecasting Revolution.* New York: Oxford University Press, 1986.

DeAngelo, David J., "The Business Economist at Work: Pennsylvania Power and Light Co.," *Business Economist,* vol. XXI, no. 2, April 1986.

Handler, Douglas P., "The PC Corner: Confession of a Forecaster," *Business Economist,* vol. XXIII, no. 2, April 1986.

Herman, T., "Analysts Predict a Barely Noticeable Recovery," *The Wall Street Journal,* July 6, 1992.

Howell, Keith A., "Lowe's Companies' Statistical "Approach to Sales Forecasting," *Corporate Controller,* vol. 3, no. 5, May/June 1991.

Jorgenson, Dale W., Daniel T. Slesnick, and Thomas M. Stoker, "Two-Stage Budgeting and Exact Aggregation," *Journal of Business & Economic Statistics,* vol. 6, no. 3, July 1988.

Marcus, Alfred A., and Baruch Mevorach, "Planning for the U.S. Political Cycle," *Long Range Planning,* vol. 21, no. 4, August 1988, pp. 50–56.

McMillan, Robert A., "The Business Economist at Work: The BF Goodrich Company," *Business Economist,* vol. XXI, no. 1, January 1986.

CHAPTER 4

THE BUDGET: AN INTEGRAL ELEMENT OF INTERNAL CONTROL

Jay H. Loevy

4.1 INTRODUCTION. It is abundantly evident from the body of technical literature (this book included) that the *raison d'etre* of budgeting is its use as a control tool by management. The whole process—setting goals and objectives, establishing standards of performance, and analyzing and acting on results—is almost synonymous with the term *management control.* It is the way management is assured that "people in the organization do what they are supposed to do."[1]

Yet the subject of this chapter deals with *internal control* rather than management control. The difference in terms lies with its use. Internal control appears to be used exclusively in the field of auditing. In its "Statement on Auditing Standards, Number 55," the American Institute of Certified Public Accountants (AICPA) states that

> Although the internal control structure may include a wide variety of objectives and related policies and procedures, only some of these may be relevant to an audit of the entity's financial statements. Generally, the policies and procedures that are relevant to an audit pertain to the entity's ability to record, process, summarize, and report financial data consistent with the assertions embodied in the financial statements.[2]

Thus, staying with the more narrow definition of internal control, this chapter will focus on those controls relevant to financial records and reports, but which exist within the total control framework of the company.

The "output" of an internal control system results from comparing actual results of operations with the results expected from the planning process. Through use of reports comparing planned with actual results, management could identify such problems as the following:

- Inaccurate information reported in the company's financial records
- Unauthorized operations, such as overextending credit or entering into higher-risk transactions

[1] Robert N. Anthony, John Deardon, and Norton M. Bedford, *Management Control Systems* (Homewood, IL: Richard C. Irwin, 1984), p. 5.

[2] American Institute of Certified Public Accountants (AICPA), *Statement on Auditing Standards 55, Consideration of the Internal Control Structure in a Financial Audit* (New York: AICPA, 1988), p. 4.

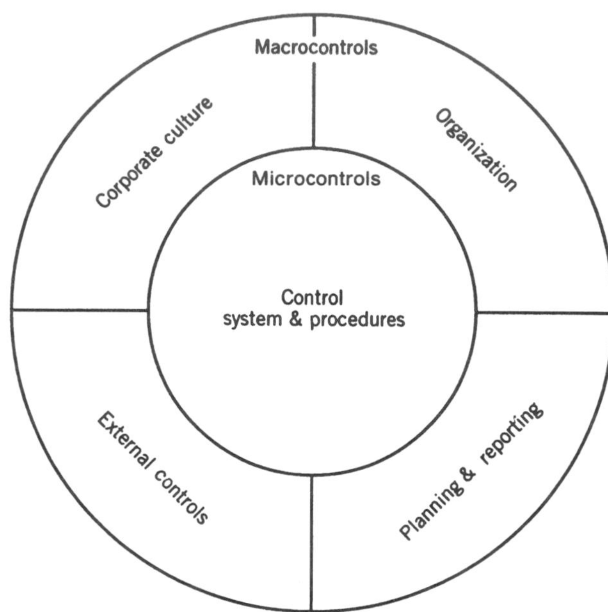

Exhibit 4.1. The control environment

- Defalcations, such as conversion of company receipts, diversion of inventories, or unauthorized disbursements
- Reduction in planned profit for any number of reasons

The planning process as an integral element of internal control and its relationship to the control environment will be described in the following sections.

4.2 THE CONTROL ENVIRONMENT. Exhibit 4.1 illustrates the control environment and shows how this environment is divided between *macrocontrols* and *microcontrols.* The former are the framework for the control environment, while the latter systems and procedures put them into action.

(a) Macrocontrols. The four macrocontrol elements—corporate culture, organization, planning and reporting, and external controls—are interrelated, and management should ensure that all four exist within their company.

For example, companies that rely solely on the integrity and conscientiousness of their employees (organization) without planning systems and outside controls are imprudent. Likewise, planning and reporting systems that are not made a part of the corporate culture will likely be ineffective in guiding the way employees think and act.

(i) Corporate Culture. This segment could be the most important of the four, yet it is the most difficult to define. Company culture is that unique combination of ideas, mission, policies, goals, and ways of personal interaction that are created by top management and echoed by other personnel. Control policies and procedures can become a code to live by in the company, or they can be given only lip service. Employees are very quick to discern

the *real* control environment by the way management reacts to procedural and/or policy infractions or other operating problems. Thus, corporate culture sets the tone for the whole company, including its commitment to exercising control over its operations.

One of the ways management exercises this control and exhibits its commitment to a controlled environment is through the use of an internal audit section. Internal auditors are company employees, as differentiated from external auditors, who are independents, such as certified public accountants. While both internal and external auditors are concerned with controls, they approach the subject from a somewhat different perspective. The internal auditor's primary objective is to ascertain that the company's policies and procedures are being followed; the external auditor's primary objective is to express an opinion on the fairness of the company's financial statements.

(ii) Organization. In order for an internal control system to operate, there must be persons to whom management can assign authority and responsibility, a structure to define reporting relationships, and a means to communicate with others. This is accomplished by establishing an organization having a formal, well-defined structure in which the incumbents of all positions operate within the scope of their assigned authority and responsibility.

(iii) Planning and Reporting. This set of macrocontrols provides the means by which management can define the company's mission, set forth company goals and operating objectives, set performance standards, monitor performance of its operating units, and evaluate and control the managers who are responsible for such performance. As we will see from the following sections, planning and reporting are formal and structured methods, as differentiated from the corporate culture, which tends to be more anecdotal and unstructured.

(iv) External Controls. A company relies on certain controls exercised by organizations and persons external to the management of the company. They may include external auditors, the board of directors and committees thereof, regulatory agencies (especially in regulated industries), and the body of customers and suppliers who can be expected to complain of unfair or illegal treatment.

(b) Microcontrols. In order to carry out the goals and objectives of management, a *system* must exist that governs the procedures for control over all relevant transactions. Such controls will encompass the processes known as "management information systems," "management control systems," "operating policies and procedures," and other such descriptive titles.

Microcontrols differ from macrocontrols in that they are more *procedural* in nature. Consider, for example, how the subject of product pricing might be handled within the control environment.

During strategic planning sessions, it is determined that product pricing will be competitive with national companies. Product division heads are given the authority to adjust prices within certain limits without higher-level approval. In order to carry out these macrocontrol decisions, certain control procedures are instituted. These require the division head to document the existence of national company pricing, determine that such pricing is not due only to short-term promotions, and document the actions taken to adjust and communicate revised pricing in the field.

The existence of microcontrol procedures in the above example "closes the loop," in that top management is able to review and analyze the actions taken by subordinates in carrying out policies that they had approved. This is further described in Section 4.4.

4.3 PLANNING SYSTEMS. Certified public accountants, in conducting financial audits, rely on the effectiveness of a company's planning and reporting system in forming an opinion on the company's financial statements. The AICPA's Statement 55 delineates the following management methods, which should be present in a properly controlled environment:

> Establishing planning and reporting systems that set forth management's plans and the results of actual performance. Such systems may include business planning; budgeting, forecasting, and profit planning; and responsibility accounting.
>
> Establishing methods that identify the status of actual performance and exceptions from planned performance, as well as communicating them to the appropriate levels of management.
>
> Using such methods at appropriate management levels to investigate variances from expectations and to take appropriate and timely corrective action. . . .[3]

Budgeting policy and procedures are termed the foundation of the discipline of budgeting. The term *discipline* is apt. Internal control depends on discipline, and thus the origination of the company's plans must be done in a controlled, disciplined manner. The first step in this procedure is the setting of goals and objectives.

(a) Goals and Objectives. In a well-controlled environment, all personnel are supposed to work toward common goals, using prescribed, authorized procedures. Management cannot expect employees to act effectively if they are unaware of, or do not fully subscribe to, the goals set forth by company policy.

In a military analogy, a battlefield commander can exercise control over his troops only if his subordinates understand the battlefield objectives and follow out his orders accordingly. A platoon leader, who is expected to render surveillance but instead attacks an enemy position, could put the whole operation in jeopardy. Control within a company operates in a similar fashion, although it is not lives that are at stake, but instead, it is money, jobs, and eventually the entity itself.

The importance of goal setting as a control element is directly proportional to the size and complexity of the organization. In a small, one-location organization, the company's goals are discussed frequently in one form or another. Even the morning coffee break can be a forum for reinforcing such goals. Conversely, if operating chiefs are thousands of miles away and do not communicate often with their superiors, company goals tend to become "fuzzy," and can eventually disappear.

Consider what happens in a football game. In the huddle, the players are close together and understand what the play will be and what will be expected of them. However, if the quarterback decides to call an "audible" at the line of scrimmage, his teammates behind him and at the far ends may not be able to hear over the crowd noise. Such lack of communication can result in a busted play.

---

[3] *See* footnote 2. p. 26.

Thus, the consequences of inadequate goal setting and the attendant communication of same is at best a dilution of company-wide effectiveness; at worst it is a forerunner of the eventual collapse of the organization.

(b) Assigning Responsibility for Performance. Plans will remain plans unless they are carried out. The assignment of responsibility for putting the goals and objectives into practice is an important link in the chain of controls. This should be done in a formal manner and should include the following:

- An organization chart showing at least the key operating personnel and the reporting relationship among and between them. In multidivision companies, there would normally be charts of the organization at different levels: operating unit, division, and total corporation, for example.
- Job descriptions for all positions, which should include title, reporting relationship, limits of authority, primary job responsibilities, and qualifications for the job.
- A written statement of the goals and objectives for the organization unit, including a profit plan or budget and narrative description of the problems and opportunities faced by the unit.

Anthony, Deardon, and Bedford use the term *responsibility center* to denote any organization unit headed by a responsible manager. They further categorize such responsibility centers as: revenue centers, expense centers, profit centers, and investment centers.[4] (Investment centers are also profit centers and for this chapter's purpose need not be separated.) The other three categories could be illustrated as follows:

1. *Revenue centers.* Sales offices and marketing and sales promotion units
2. *Expense centers.* Administrative departments and units servicing other units, such as engineering or quality control
3. *Profit centers.* Manufacturing plants, retail operations, and operating companies

Budgets developed for responsibility centers should be both *relevant* to the type of center and *controllable* by it. There must be a clear and demonstratable relationship between the goals and objectives of the unit and the opportunity of the responsible manager to control results. For example, it would not be meaningful to a manufacturing department head to be responsible for profits if he or she had no opportunity to control sales or selling price. One would need to go higher in the organization, say to the vice-president of manufacturing or the head of a product division, to properly assign profit responsibility.

The meaning of assigning responsibility within the internal control framework should be obvious: Only people can bear responsibility for budgetary results. (Thankfully, we have not yet assigned such responsibility to computers!) These people, the managerial group, form a required element in the internal control system. They are measured and controlled in comparison to the expectations developed in the goal-setting stage of planning.

The means by which top management exercises this control is the subject of Section 4.4.

---

[4] *See* footnote 1, pp. 194–210.

4.4 REPORTING SYSTEMS.

In exercising their job responsibilities, company personnel make decisions, which collectively influence the conduct of the company as a whole. Some individual decisions will have only a minor effect, such as selecting a forms vendor, while some will have more significance, such as the hiring of a key executive. According to Ackoff,

> Control is the evaluation of decisions, including decisions to do nothing, once they have been implemented. The process of control involves four steps:
> 1. Predicting the outcomes of decisions in the form of performance measures.
> 2. Collecting information on actual performance.
> 3. Comparing actual with predicted performance.
> 4. When a decision is shown to have been deficient, correcting the procedure that produced it and correcting its consequences where possible.[5]

The first item was discussed in Section 4.3 (a). In this section, we will cover the collection, reporting, and analysis of information in order to close the control loop.

Decision making depends on reliable, accurate information. The more significant the decision, the more important it is to have confidence in the information on which the decision is based. Take the example of a manager who must decide on shutting down a division because it is unprofitable. He must be certain that profitability, as reported on division income statements, is accurate. The manager may be confident that the company's computer programs operate as intended, since no problems have arisen in this regard, but he or she may not be so sanguine about the control over input data.

(a) Control over Input.

All information begins with input of data to the management information system. Obviously, the output of the system is only as reliable as its input. The following are some of the considerations the manager might have regarding the accuracy of input to these reports:

Area of concern	Possible control procedures by management or auditors
Have all sales been recorded?	Reconciliation of shipping and billing data
	Inventory verification, such as cycle counting
Has proper credit been given to intracompany sales?	Review and reconciliation of intracompany sales
Has unit pricing been applied correctly?	Periodic reporting and review of unit pricing tables in the billing program
Have unauthorized sales allowances been granted	Separation of duties involving approval and recording of sales allowances
	Comparison of sales allowances to gross sales by customer
Have incorrect methods been used to calculate cost of goods sold?	Review and analysis of cost variances

[5] Russell L. Ackoff, *A Concept of Corporate Planning* (New York: John Wiley & Sons, 1970), p. 112.

Have there been defalcations or errors affecting:	
—Cost of materials?	Independent matching of purchase, receiving, and payment data
	Rotation of duties and mandatory vacations of purchasing personnel
	Cycle counting of inventory
—Cost of labor?	Surprise inspections of payroll check issuance procedures
	Rotation of duties and mandatory vacations of accounting personnel
Was the budget data entered correctly?	Review printout of budget after data entry

(b) Reporting, Review, and Response. The last phases of the budgetary control process close the loop. This loop, which is illustrated in Exhibit 4.2, starts with the planning phase, then records actual transactions, and finally reports against the plan and generates management response.

Usually, one or more documents are produced in each phase of the control loop: the budget after the planning phase; reports comparing budget with actual after the execution phase; memos or reports analyzing results after evaluation; and action-type documents, containing management directives, in the response phase. The results of such actions are then included in the next period's planning.

Evaluation is based on reports of actual results for a responsibility center in comparison to budget and a calculation of the difference, or variance, therefrom. A very useful report

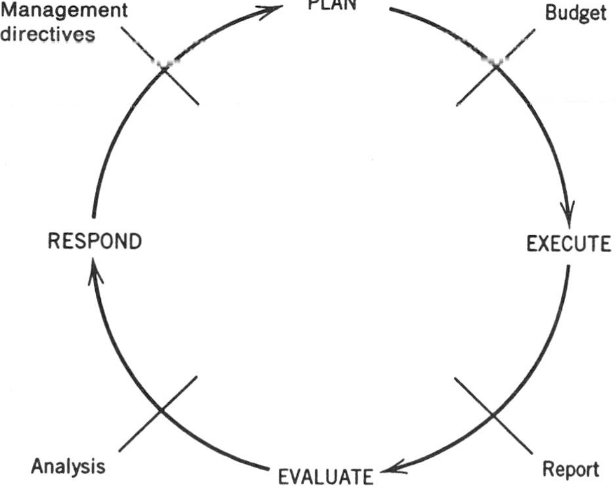

Exhibit 4.2. The control loop

format would include both current period and year to date, such as the following abbreviated example:

Current Period				Year to Date		
Budget	Actual	Variance		Budget	Actual	Variance
1,000	980	[20]	Sales	25,500	26,300	800
850	820	30	Expenses	23,000	22,500	500
150	160	10	Net income	2,500	3,800	1,300

Note that unfavorable variances are bracketed, regardless of whether they are revenue or expense.

The most effective reports are those that deliver the message clearly and succinctly. What the message should be is determined by the circumstances, including the scope of responsibility of the recipient, the relevance and usefulness of detailed information, and the frequency of reporting. In any case, reports should be designed to highlight the most important parts of the message, so that the recipient does not have to waste time getting to the heart of the matter.

Interpretation and analysis of these reports is a vital control step, because budget variances, by themselves, will not necessarily provide guidance to the organization. For example, the fact that gross sales were lower than plan does not indicate what, if any, action should be taken. Was the difference caused by the number of units, the selling price per unit, the mix of products, or some combination thereof? The manager must go behind the top-level numbers to properly analyze cause and effect.

Often, there are so many variables that it is extremely difficult to isolate the major cause or causes of variances. For example, in a multiproduct environment, some products' sales may be up, some down; some gross margins may be affected by special sales promotions and/or purchasing discounts; and all sales may have been affected by adverse weather conditions. Thus, without corroboration of these variables, the manager would be ill advised to take corrective action.

Instead, the manager should track one or more of the seemingly significant variables for a period of months to see if he or she can isolate the major causes for a degradation of gross profit. This might necessitate creating specialized data input, processing, and reporting, such as separating all sales that resulted from special promotions or other such circumstances. When it appears that the cause or causes have been found, the manager should take steps to ameliorate the situation.

In a well-controlled environment, top management would be figuratively ''looking over the shoulder'' of the manager, since they would be receiving either the same reports or those at a higher level. In either case, any significant change in responsibility center gross profit should be noticeable. It is incumbent on management to see that the problem is being studied and that corrective action is taken or recommended.

4.5 SUMMARY. In order to express an opinion on the fairness of financial statements, the auditor must examine and evaluate the company's system of internal control. This system operates within the internal control structure, composed of macrocontrols and microcontrols. One of the four macrocontrol elements is planning and reporting.

Planning involves the establishment of goals and objectives for the company as a whole, as well as its components, which, for control purposes, are termed *responsibility centers.*

Reporting involves the comparison of actual results with plan. It is the manager's responsibility to analyze such results and develop action plans to try to correct any situations causing unfavorable variances from plan.

The proper conduct of such a system of internal controls provides assurance to the auditor that data has entered the accounting system in a controlled fashion and that any transactions that were materially inaccurate or unauthorized would be identified and corrected.

SOURCES AND SUGGESTED REFERENCES

Booth, Rupert, *Control Your Overheads: A Practical Program to Improve Performance and Reduce Costs.* New York: Pitman Publishing, 1994.

Cox, Raymond, *Financial Administration & Control.* Williston, VT: Blackwell Publishing, 1993.

Green, L. C., Jr., *Financial Control.* Lakewood, CA: Executive Business Services, 1993.

Kutz, Douglas W., and Dawn K. Rhodes, *Policies and Procedures Manual for Accounting and Financial Control.* Englewood Cliffs, NJ: Prentice Hall, 1992.

Walsh, Ciaran, *Key Management Ratios: How to Analyze, Compare and Control the Figures That Drive Company Value.* New York: Pitman Publishing, 1993.

PART 2

TOOLS AND TECHNIQUES

CHAPTER 5

COST BEHAVIOR AND THE RELATIONSHIP TO THE BUDGETING PROCESS

Eugene H. Kramer

5.1 INTRODUCTION. Management is always faced with uncertainty about the future. Unless managers can forecast cost and revenue trends reasonably well, their decisions may yield unfavorable results. Forecasts concerning cost–volume–profit relationships are necessary to make accurate decisions about such matters as how many units should be manufactured, should price be changed, should advertising be increased, or should plant and equipment be expanded.

5.2 COST BEHAVIOR. Cost–volume–profit relationships depend on accurate descriptions of cost behavior. Cost behavior is affected by a number of factors, including volume, price, efficiency, sales mix, and production changes. Therefore, any analysis must be made with regard to its limitations. The benefit of cost–volume–profit relationships is in understanding the interrelationships affecting profits.

To be analyzed, all costs must be broken down into their fixed and variable portions. This is essential in determining what a cost will be at a certain point (usually defined as production or sales volume). Otherwise, management will not be able to regulate the costs properly, which is vital for efficient budgeting or for making any plans or decisions. Various alternatives as to how costs will be allocated may be utilized, and accurate cost estimates should be prepared for each alternative in determining the best decisions.

(a) Fixed Costs. Costs that remain constant over the entire range of output are referred to as *fixed costs.* These costs are incurred simply because of the passage of time and do not change as a direct result of changes in volume. Exhibit 5.1 depicts the relationship of fixed costs on a graph.

Depreciation, property insurance, property taxes, and administrative salaries are all examples of fixed costs.

(b) Variable Costs. Costs that vary directly with changes in volume are referred to as *variable costs.* Exhibit 5.2 depicts the relationship of variable costs on a graph.

Variable cost equals unit cost multiplied by the volume. A good example is the direct materials used in making a product. Every automobile has one steering wheel. If steering wheels cost $10 each, then the steering wheel cost of one automobile is $10, of two automobiles $20, of 100 automobiles $1,000, and so on. Other examples include direct

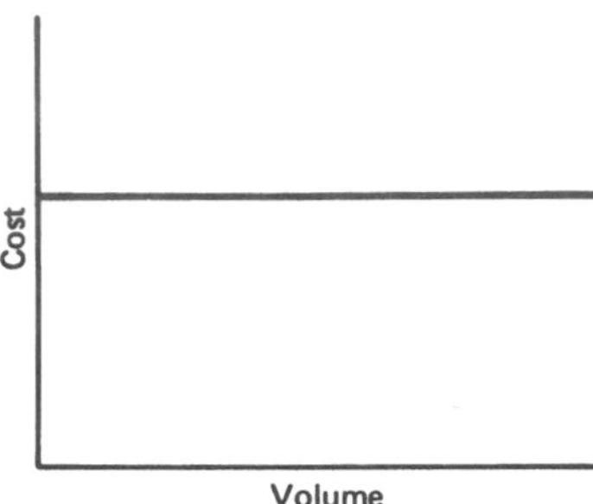

Exhibit 5.1. Relationship of fixed costs

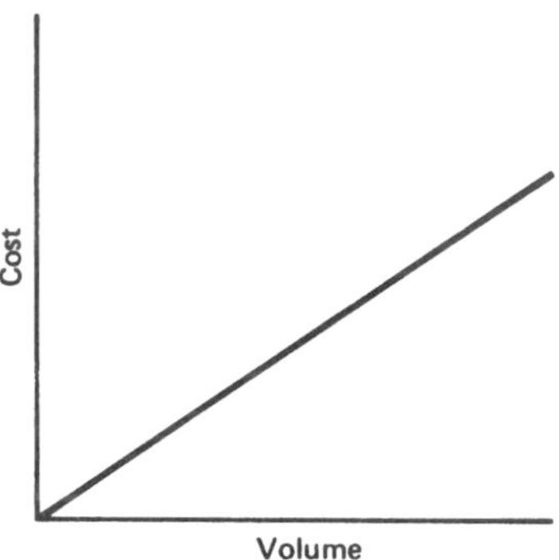

Exhibit 5.2. Relationship of variable costs

labor in variation with production volume and sales commissions and cost of goods sold in variation with sales volume.

(c) Semivariable Costs. *Semivariable costs* are those costs that have traits similar to both fixed and variable costs. These types of costs can be seen in various forms. For example, while a manufacturing plant is idle, certain maintenance costs will be incurred. Once production is underway, though, additional maintenance costs vary with production volume. Exhibit 5.3 depicts these costs, separating them into their fixed and variable portions.

Some semivariable costs will not fit into a straight-line pattern. They may begin at a certain point and rise at an increasing or decreasing rate. For cost analysis, however, they are assumed to have straight-line relationships (see Exhibits 5.4 and 5.5.)

Sometimes a cost will function as a fixed cost for a segment of the range, jump to a different cost level for another segment of the range, and then jump to yet another level. Clerical costs may fit this pattern. The clerical staff may be able to handle the work at a certain range of production, but once production moves into another range, additional staff will be required. These types of costs may be handled in one of two ways. The first is to assume that a straight-line relationship exists, as depicted in Exhibit 5.6.

When there are only one or two steps, the costs are sometimes treated solely as fixed costs. Thus, for one step, total fixed costs would change for the two different ranges (see Exhibit 5.7).

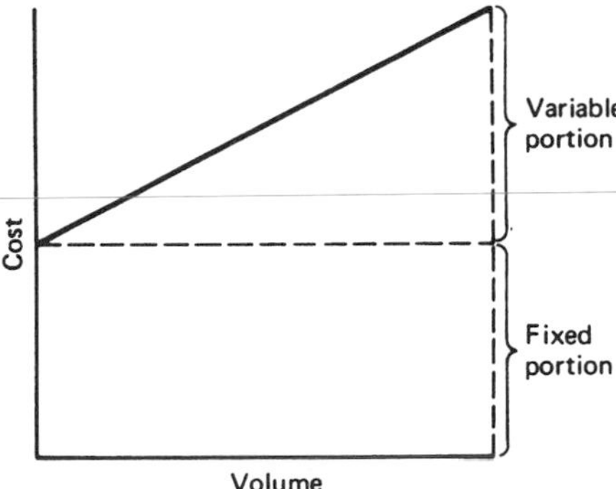

Exhibit 5.3. Relationship of semivariable costs

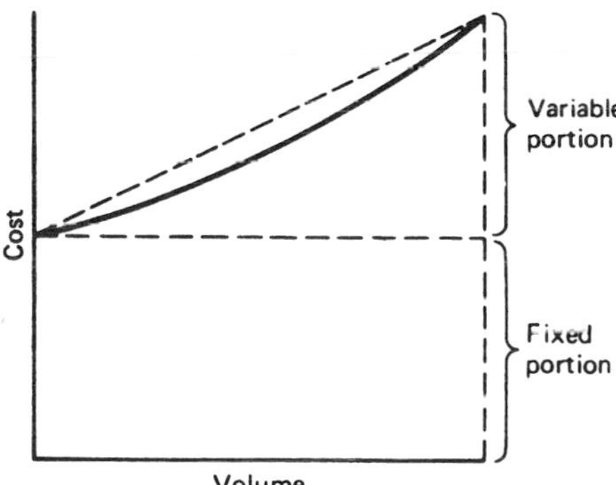

Exhibit 5.4. Relationship of semivariable costs not fitting into a straight-line pattern

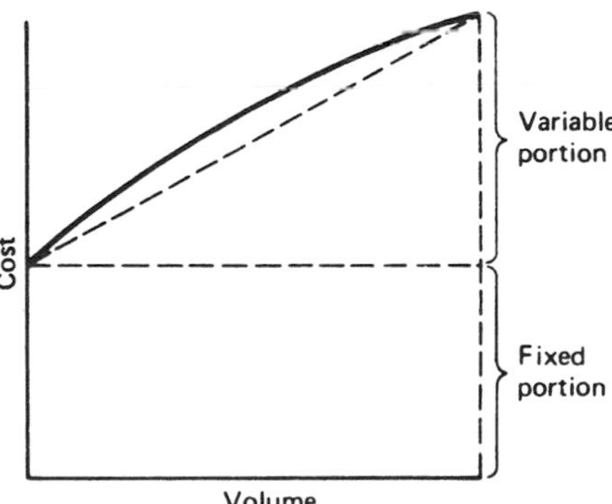

Exhibit 5.5. Relationship of semivariable costs not fitting into a straight-line pattern

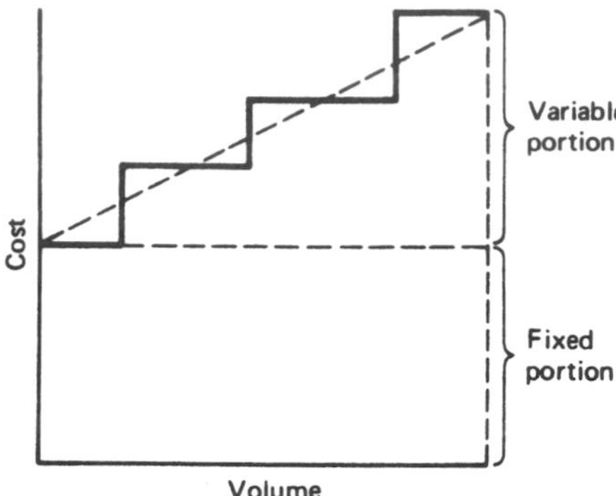

Exhibit 5.6. Example of step costs

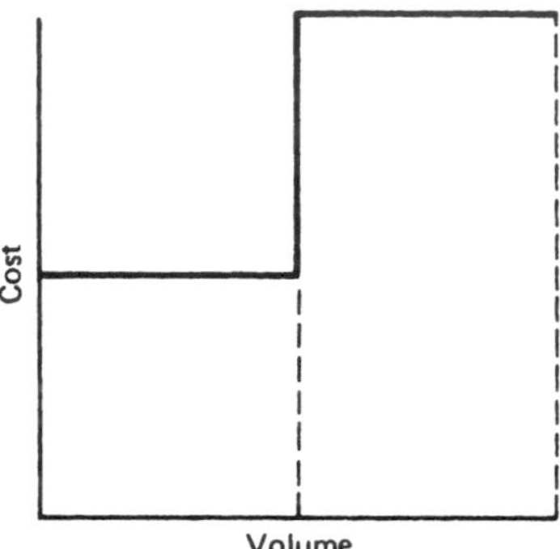

Exhibit 5.7. Example of step costs, assuming only one or two steps

5.3 BREAK-EVEN ANALYSIS. The effects of cost behavior can be seen quite clearly in cost–volume–profit relationships when using a break-even chart. With break-even analysis, we can see the effect upon net income of various decisions that affect sales and costs (see Exhibit 5.8).

The *break-even point* is that point of output at which total revenues and total costs are equal. The ability of management to control costs accurately can be greatly enhanced by forecasts of the effect on the break-even point. To keep management informed of the effect of major and minor changes in cost and revenue patterns, the management accountant must continually analyze cost behavior and update break-even points periodically.

Break-even charts enable managers to glance over potential profits. The use of preliminary budget figures as a basis for the break-even chart can give management a chance to make changes in the budget if the forecast is not satisfactory.

(a) Variable Cost and the Contribution Margin. In break-even analysis, variable cost is an important determinant in establishing the optimum level of activity. When the variable cost ratio (total variable costs divided by total sales) is known, the total variable costs at any level of activity can be determined.

The *contribution margin* is that portion of the sales dollar available to cover fixed costs and to attain profits. It is a complement of variable costs and is computed by subtracting

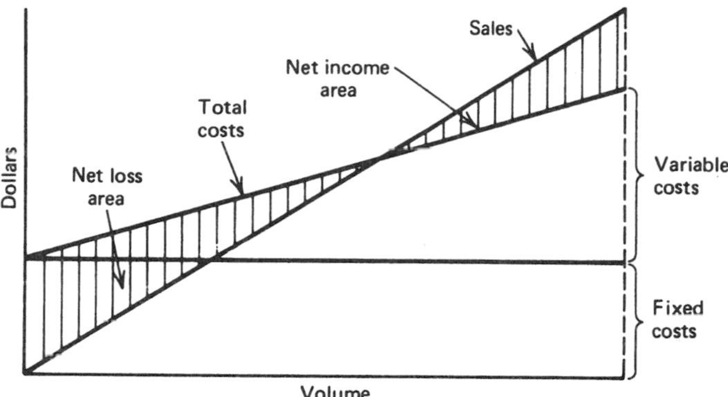

Exhibit 5.8. Example of break-even analysis

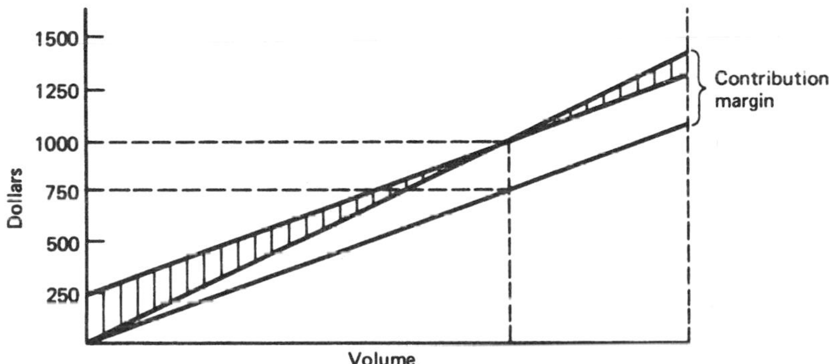

Exhibit 5.9. Break-even chart showing contribution margin

variable costs from sales. When using the contribution margin technique, the break-even chart will take the form that is depicted in Exhibit 5.9.

When the contribution margin is presented as a ratio of sales, the effect on profits is easily computed with respect to prospective changes in volume. Using the data presented in Exhibit 5.9, Exhibit 5.10 gives an example of this computation.

Because the total fixed costs do not change over the volume range, they are not relevant. Thus, the contribution margin ratio will give the results for any contemplated change in activity.

Knowledge of the contribution margin ratio can benefit management in a variety of useful ways. The ratio indicates how much profits will either diminish or increase with each dollar change in volume. A high ratio will cause greater profits as volume increases above the break-even point, whereas it will cause greater losses as volume decreases below the break-even point. A low contribution margin ratio will require greater increases of volume to create noticeable increases in profits. Basically, the greater the ratio, the larger the change in profits as volume changes.

(b) Changes in Fixed Costs. It has been seen that changes in variable costs will affect the contribution margin, which directly influences earnings. Fixed costs are not stable

	Given Volume	Percentage	Increase in Volume	Decrease in Volume
Sales	$1000	100	$100	$200
Variable costs	750	75	75	150
Contribution margin	$250	25	$25	$50
Fixed costs	250			
Net income	$0		$25	$50

Exhibit 5.10. Example of computing contribution margin using changing volumes

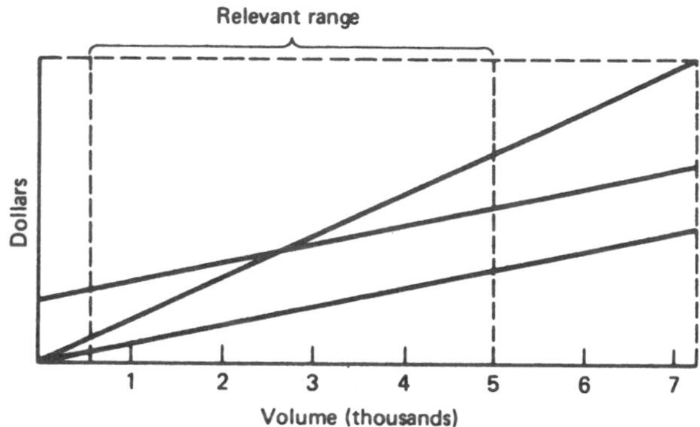

Exhibit 5.11. Example of relevant range

year after year either. They must be budgeted for as accurately as possible because of their long- and short-term effects on the profits of a business.

Fixed costs are not independent of the other two major profit determinants: revenue and variable costs. A manufacturer may decide to create a new department in order to sell directly to retailers instead of selling through intermediaries and thereby create a greater per unit sales price. Management may also be contemplating purchasing more efficient machinery, which would result in lower variable costs per unit. Thus, when a major change in fixed costs is proposed, determining the effects on the break-even point and the contribution margin is vital for wise management decisions.

(c) Relevant Range. Each cost analysis is assumed valid only for a specified relevant range of volumes. Outside of this range, the intrusion of different costs will alter the assumed relationship. In a manufacturing company, variable costs would be quite high if only a few units of a product were produced. However, producing more than the capacity of the plant will permit would require additional fixed costs to cover expansion or additional costs to cover overtime and other inefficiencies not taken into account under normal production.

Exhibit 5.11 depicts on a graph an example of relevant range. In this case, the figures are relevant for output from 500 to 5,000 units. All other data are irrelevant.

(d) Short-Run Budgeting. Although an analysis of cost–volume–profit relationships by itself is insufficient for proper decision making, knowledge of the relationships can be

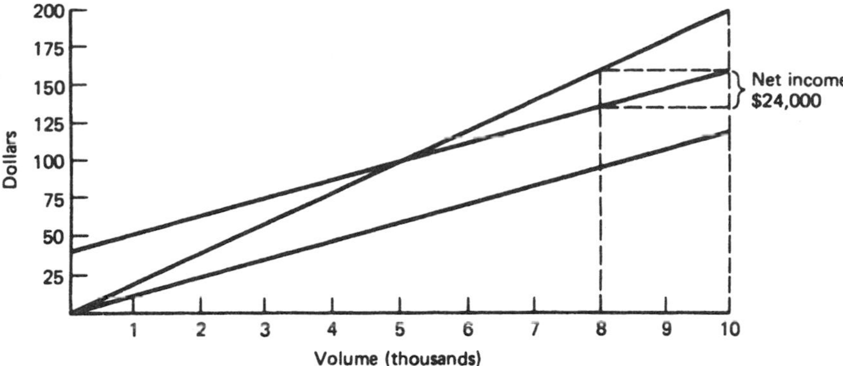

Exhibit 5.12. Illustration of use of break-even in budgeting

valuable for many short-run budgeting decisions. Such decisions as whether to increase sales promotion costs in order to increase sales volume, whether to make or buy a part, or whether to eliminate a product can be enhanced by the knowledge of how these additional or remaining costs will affect net income. The differences in costs are compared with the differences in revenue for various alternative actions in order to form a sound basis for decision making. Planning, in general, is made easier by careful evaluation of break-even charts.

Assume that data for a company are as follows:

1. *Sales price.* $20 per unit
2. *Variable costs.* $12 per unit
3. *Fixed costs.* $40,000

If management wished to collect $24,000 net earnings, then that sales volume must be 8,000 units, as shown in Exhibit 5.12.

Management now learns that if it invests $10,000 of fixed costs in sales promotion, it will be able to operate at 100% of capacity, or at a sales volume of 10,000 units. By making a new chart, it can be seen whether this investment would be profitable. Exhibit 5.13 shows the effects of the change, with earnings increasing to $30,000, provided the cost and revenue estimates are correct.

The validity of using break-even analysis in decisions such as these depends on the facts in each case. In the preceding example, if peak operating capacity was 8,000 units, then, in order to increase the volume, even more fixed costs would be required, and probably new data computations would be necessary to determine the cost behavior.

The size of the contribution margin would also affect decision making. A low percentage margin would require a greater change in volume in order to increase the total contribution margin enough to cover any increases in fixed costs.

Decisions must also take into account any long-term effects. It is possible that profits may increase in a short-run situation, but over the long run they may suffer because of the disordered use of such a technique.

(e) Long-Run Budgeting. Knowledge of cost behavior patterns is often useful in long-run planning. Studying fixed and variable costs, and relating these costs to prospective

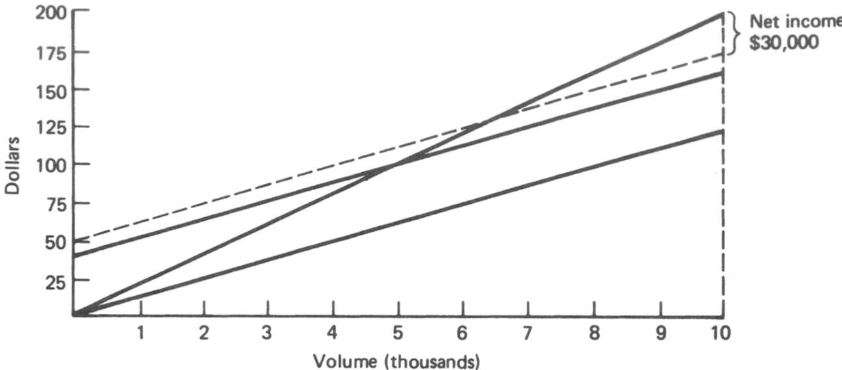

Exhibit 5.13. Illustration of the effects of investments in additional fixed costs

Profit goal	$10,000
Expected fixed costs	10,000
Contribution margin	$20,000
Gross profit per unit ($20,000/5,000 units)	$4
Variable costs	1
Selling price	$5

Exhibit 5.14. Using selling price to meet expected profit goals

sales and profit goals, will give management additional information to use in making an initial budget or in revising plans as deemed necessary.

One method of planning is to determine the profit goal that management would like to attain. This profit goal plus the expected fixed costs will equal the contribution margin needed to cover the fixed costs and the desired profit. By determining the expected operating volume, gross profit per unit can then be computed. Adding expected variable cost per unit to the gross profit will determine the net sales figure that must be attained.

As an example, assume that management requires a $10,000 net income each year and that expected costs are $10,000 of fixed costs and $1 per unit of variable costs at a normal operating level of 5,000 units. Exhibit 5.14 gives the computations for determining the net sales figure per unit that must be attained in order to meet the profit goal.

If the selling price of $5 per unit is not a competitive figure, then managers must revise their plans in order to achieve the profit goal. The break-even point could be lowered, possibly by reducing fixed costs or variable costs. Studies may show that, by increasing volume over the normal level, the necessary profit goal may be attained. Alternatively, managers may decide to alter the products, add or delete products, or improve methods of production in order to increase the contribution margin per unit. Nevertheless, several studies and break-even charts may be necessary for surveying the various alternatives in order to reach the best decision.

5.4 ADDITIONAL COST CONCEPTS. To meet the needs of managers, costs are classified in many ways. The behavior patterns of fixed, variable, and semivariable costs, and their importance to the budgeting process, have already been discussed. The ability of managers to plan and budget costs also must be taken into account in any analysis of cost–volume–profit relationships. In this regard, a number of questions must be answered: Can costs be controlled? How do costs relate to a certain cost objective? Is an individual department profiting the company? If not, can it be eliminated?

(a) Committed versus Discretionary Costs. Fixed costs can be divided into two types: committed and discretionary. The distinction between these two types is important to managers in their budgeting decisions.

Committed fixed costs are those costs that relate to the basic framework of the company. They are based on top management decisions that will affect the business for several years. Depreciation on buildings, equipment, and salaries to executives are examples of such costs.

Discretionary fixed costs are those costs that fall under management control from one period to another. Managers are not committed to a certain level of expenses and may increase or decrease the level as seems warranted. Advertising, reasearch and development, and training programs fall into this area.

Distinguishing between committed and discretionary costs has relevance to the cost–volume–profit analysis. As an example, in a recessionary period a company whose fixed costs are almost all committed will have trouble reducing the break-even point and probably will experience some losses, whereas a company with substantial discretionary fixed costs may be able to cut costs enough without disrupting operations so that it can show some earnings.

(b) Controllable versus Noncontrollable Costs. In determining the efficiency of a company or in planning the budget, responsibility reports must be made by the managers. These evaluations of costs are necessary at each level of management, so that in the case of an undesirable situation, corrective action can be taken at the point at which it is necessary. For example, if direct labor is excessively high, the problem area can be seen and proper steps can be taken to alleviate the problem. This type of reporting is essential for controlling costs and for proper budgeting.

In preparing cost evaluations, it is necessary to separate the costs of a segment into controllable and noncontrollable costs, because not all costs in a given segment are control lable at that managerial level and therefore the manager cannot be held responsible for them. Controllability must therefore be defined with reference to a specific management level for proper evaluation.

A cost is controllable at a given managerial level if the manager has the authority to significantly influence its amount. For example, a supervisor may have control over maintenance, equipment, and overtime costs, but the department's depreciation and overhead, as well as the supervisor's salary, are noncontrollable costs at this managerial level. Exhibit 5.15 illustrates the use of responsibility reporting with regard to controllable costs and the budget.

(c) Direct versus Indirect Costs. Costs are frequently classified as direct or indirect. Such classification has nothing to do with the nature or behavior of these costs, but rather it indicates the objective against which the costs are being measured. *Direct costs* are those costs that can be clearly identified with the cost objective. All variable costs therefore are direct costs. *Indirect costs* are costs that cannot be clearly identified with a single cost objective and therefore must be allocated among the various cost objectives to which they apply. For example, the wages of employees working in a single department are direct

Controllable Expenses	Amount	Over or (Under) Budget
Supervisor, Shop #1		
Maintenance	$200	$10
Supplies	100	20
Tools	50	(30)
Overtime	100	50
Total	$450	$50
Plant Manager		
Office expense	$250	$(10)
Shop #1 costs	450	50
Shop # 2 costs	600	20
Supervisor salaries	5,000	0
Total	$6,300	$60
Manufacturing V.P.		
Office expense	$500	$0
Plant costs	6,300	60
Purchasing	500	200
Receiving	700	0
Plant management salaries	7,000	0
Total	$15,000	$260
President		
Office expense	$1,000	$100
V.P., manufacturing	15,000	260
V.P., sales	8,700	400
V.P., finance	4,000	(100)
V.P. salaries	9,000	0
Total	$37,700	$660

Exhibit 5.15. Illustration of responsibility reporting using controllable costs

costs of that department, but the cost of heating the building where they work would have to be allocated among all the departments in the building, and so it would be an indirect cost to the department.

Direct costs are sometimes defined as those costs that would be dropped if their cost objective were eliminated. Although there are exceptions, this concept can be important in evaluating performance and in deciding whether to keep a segment of a company. Even if the segment were eliminated, many or all of the indirect costs would not be eliminated and would have to be allocated among the remaining segments of the company. This situation can be illustrated as follows.

Suppose that sales, direct costs, indirect costs, and net income are reported for three segments as seen in Exhibit 5.16.

Management is trying to determine whether to eliminate Segment C because of its continuing losses. It can be seen that, if the segment is eliminated, the company will lose a contribution to indirect expenses of $10,000 ($20,000 − $10,000). Segment C's indirect costs will have to be allocated among the remaining segments. Exhibit 5.17 shows the effects of the elimination, assuming these costs are allocated evenly.

5.5 DIFFERENTIAL COST CONCEPTS. Many budgeting decisions made by managers are short-run decisions that involve differential analysis. These short-run decisions

	Segment A	Segment B	Segment C	Total
Sales	$20,000	$25,000	$20,000	$65,000
Direct costs	5,000	10,000	10,000	25,000
Indirect costs	5,000	10,000	15,000	30,000
Net income	$10,000	$5,000	($5,000)	$10,000

Exhibit 5.16. Impact of costs on business segments

	Segment A	Segment B	Total
Sales	$20,000	$25,000	$45,000
Direct costs	5,000	10,000	15,000
Indirect costs	12,500	17,500	30,000
Net income	$2,500	($2,500)	0

Exhibit 5.17. Impact of allocating costs evenly

may involve such matters as whether to change the price of a product, to manufacture a product instead of buying it, to add or drop a product, or to process joint products and by-products.

(a) Relevant Costs. *Relevant costs* are future costs that differ between alternatives. Past costs, or *sunk costs,* are not relevant because there is nothing management can do about them since they have already been incurred. Future costs that are the same for two alternatives are not relevant either since they will affect both alternatives equally. The amount by which the relevant costs of two alternatives differ is called the *differential cost.*

To illustrate relevant costs, assume that management has been working on Project A, which has incurred costs of $10,000. To finish the project, it is estimated that $10,000 of fixed costs and $20,000 of variable costs will be incurred. A new proposal, Project B, has been introduced, which would require $10,000 of fixed costs and $15,000 of variable costs. Exhibit 5.18 shows the differential cost between the two alternatives, assuming that total revenues for both projects would be the same and that only one project can be attempted.

The $10,000 already incurred in conducting Project A is a sunk cost, and the future fixed costs of $10,000 do not differ between the alternatives; therefore, the only relevant costs are the future variable costs of $20,000 and $15,000 for Projects A and B, respectively. Thus, Project B should be chosen by management because of the savings of $5,000.

(b) Incremental (Marginal) Costs. *Marginal cost* is a term used to describe the increase in total cost resulting from the production or sale of one more unit. Decisions usually involve levels of operation of hundreds or thousands of units. The difference of total cost between the levels of operation in this case is called *incremental* (or differential) cost.

The incremental cost concept can be described as follows: Suppose normal production is set at 10,000 units, with price, fixed costs, and variable costs set at $10 per unit, $50,000, and $4 per unit, respectively. An order has been received for an additional 5,000 units at $5 per unit. This is half the regular selling price and less than the average cost per unit at normal production. An analysis of relevant costs and revenues is seen in Exhibit 5.19.

	Project A	Project B	Differential
Revenues	0	0	0
Costs	$20,000	$15,000	$5,000
Net benefit in favor of choosing Project B			$5,000

Exhibit 5.18. Illustration of the differential cost between two alternatives

	Accept Order	Reject Order	Differential
Revenue	$125,000	$100,000	$25,000
Variable costs	60,000	40,000	20,000
Net benefit in favor of accepting order			$5,000

Exhibit 5.19. Analysis of relevant costs and revenues

Product	Selling Price at Separation	Cost of Processing	Selling Price After Processing
A	$5	$6	$10
B	4	3	8

Exhibit 5.20. Illustration of joint products

Because the selling price of the additional units was greater than the variable cost per unit, additional net income could be received. Usually, it is the variable costs that set a floor for the selling price in marginal and incremental analysis, because a price only slightly higher than variable costs will bring a contribution to earnings. The exception is in the case of semivariable costs when a different level of production will cause an increase in fixed costs. This type of analysis, however, is used only for short-run decisions. In the long run, full costs must be covered, and any incremental analysis should be appraised in light of the long-run effects on the company.

(c) Joint Product and By-product Costs. Several products are sometimes manufactured from raw materials or from a manufacturing process. These are called *joint products.* Examples are the meat and hide processed from livestock. The costs incurred until the products are separated from each other are called *joint-product costs.* These are sunk costs when determining whether to process or sell a joint product once it is separated. This concept is the same in deciding whether to discard or to further process and sell low-value (or waste) products resulting from the manufacturing process. These low-value products are called *by-products.*

Assume that the data in Exhibit 5.20 concern joint products A and B.

The differential revenues and costs of further processing the two products are seen in Exhibit 5.21.

Based on this joint-product analysis, Product B should be further processed because

Product	Differential Revenue	Differential Cost	Net Advantage (Disadvantage)
A	$5	$6	($1)
B	4	3	1

Exhibit 5.21. Impact of differential revenues and costs on joint products

	Product A	Product B	Product C
Units produced	2,000	2,000	2,000
Sales price per unit	$2.00	$1.00	$1.50
Variable cost per unit	1.00	0.50	1.00
Contribution margin per unit	1.00	0.50	0.50
Fixed costs	$1,000	$ 500	$1,000
Net earnings	1,000	500	0

Exhibit 5.22. Relevant data for the production of three products

of a net increase in earnings of $1, whereas Product A should not be further processed because of a decrease in net earnings of $1.

5.6 MAXIMIZING RESOURCES. In budgeting, managers need to determine the most efficient method of allocating costs in order to provide maximum profits. This is most important in a multidepartment or multiproduct company. It has been seen that several cost analysis techniques can provide management with assistance in deciding whether to eliminate or add products and departments and whether to increase or decrease production in order to establish profit goals. These techniques usually determine whether an alternative contributes to fixed expenses or whether the incremental revenue is greater than the incremental cost. These methods may be incomplete, though, and may overlook other facts, such as the operating capacity of a firm, when determining production of various products.

Exhibit 5.22 presents relevant data for a company producing three products.

The break-even chart for the company realizing the product mix in Exhibit 8.22 is shown in Exhibit 5.23.

By analyzing the data in Exhibit 5.23, it is seen that all three products should be retained because of positive contribution margins in all departments. This analysis is incomplete, however, because it is possible that the production schedules are being utilized inefficiently for maximum profit.

Suppose that plant operating capacity is 1,700 hours. If the full resources of the plant are devoted to only one product, it is computed that 4 units of Product A can be produced per hour, 3 units of Product B per hour, and 10 units of Product C per hour. Also, maximum production is limited to 6,400 units for Product A, 3,000 units for Product B, and 5,000 units for Product C.

Instead of contribution margin per unit of sales, contribution margin per hour of operating capacity is used to determine maximum rates. Exhibit 5.24 illustrates this point with the three products using the data given.

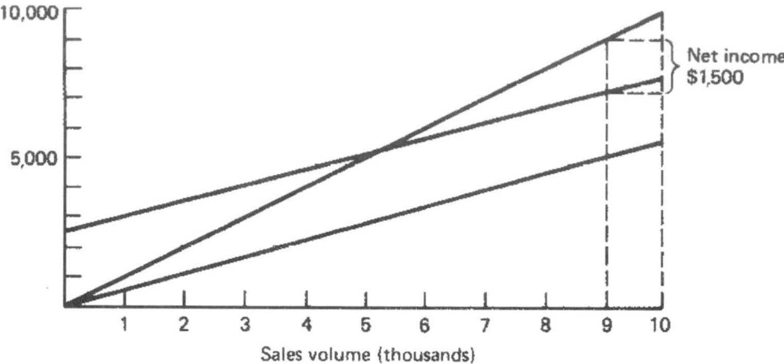

Exhibit 5.23. Example of break-even

Product	Contribution Margin per Unit	Units Produced per Hour	Contribution Margin per Hour
A	$1.00	4	$4.00
B	0.50	2	1.00
C	0.50	10	5.00

Exhibit 5.24. Computation of contribution margin per hour

Based on these figures, Product C is the most profitable to produce, and Product A is the next best alternative. Exhibit 5.25 shows the determination of the production rates of the three products, taking into account the limitation on producing the three.

According to this analysis, Product B should be eliminated. Exhibit 5.26 shows the effect of this product mix on the break-even point. It is seen that net earnings have increased over $1,000 by allocating production in this fashion.

This type of analysis should also take into account other factors. Switching to other products may cause an increase in fixed costs. Also, the long-run objectives of a company could prevent the elimination of a product.

Other methods of determining the cost allocation within a company can also be used. These include quantitative decision models such as economic order quantity (EOQ), which determines ordering cost and carrying cost behavior for inventory control; linear programming, used in various phases of decision making; and statistical analysis, used when decision variables are not deterministic but are probabilistic.

5.7 ESTIMATING COSTS. As stated previously, it is necessary to identify costs as fixed or variable. With semivariable costs, it is sometimes difficult to do this, and methods of estimating these costs must be used. The fixed portion represents the cost of having a service available for use. The variable portion is the cost associated with various levels of activity.

Product	Contribution Margin per Hour	Maximum Production	Units to Produce	Time to Produce
A	$4.00	6,400	4,800	200
B	1.00	3,000	0	0
C	5.00	5,000	5,000	500
				1,700

Exhibit 5.25. Computing production rates

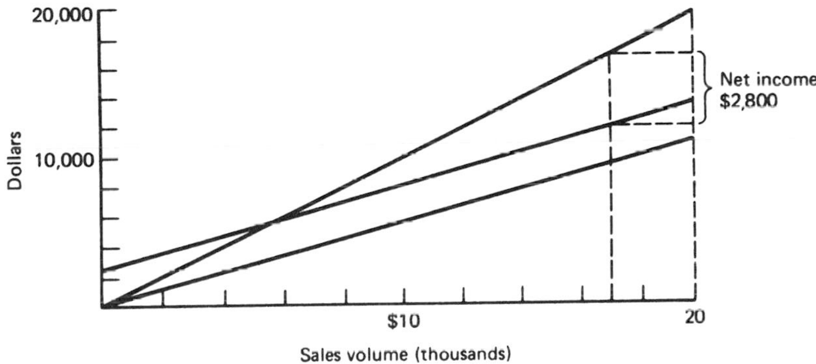

Exhibit 5.26. Break-even analysis

(a) The Scatter Diagram. One method of estimating semivariable costs is to use a scatter diagram. With this method, actual incurred costs at varying levels of activity are plotted on a graph. A line (called the *regression line*) is then drawn through what appears to be the center of the pattern (see Exhibit 5.27). In Exhibit 5.27, the fixed portion would be \$18,000, and the variable portion would be figured as follows:

$$\frac{\$51{,}000 - \$18{,}000}{10{,}000 \text{ units}} = \$3.30 \text{ per unit}$$

(b) The Least Squares Method. A more accurate method of obtaining the regression line is called the *least squares method.* This method makes use of statistical analysis and requires the solving of two simultaneous equations:

$$\Sigma XY = a(\Sigma X) + b(\Sigma X^2)$$

and

$$\Sigma Y = Na + b(\Sigma X)$$

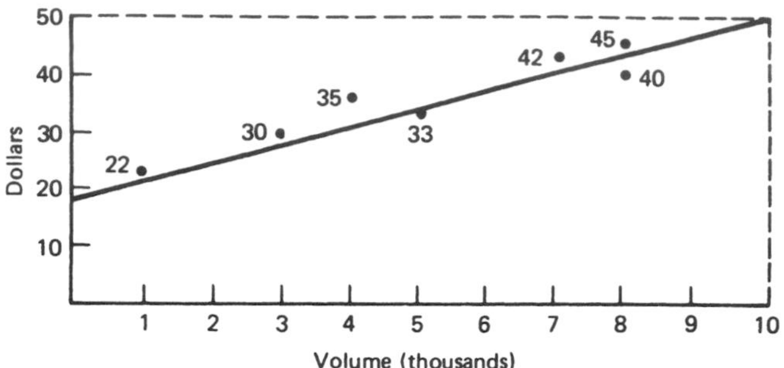

Exhibit 5.27. Scatter diagram

where N = number of observations

X = units of volume

Y = total costs

a = total fixed costs

b = variable cost per unit

The following data were developed from Exhibit 5.27:

X-axis	Y-axis
1	22
3	30
4	35
5	33
7	42
8	45
8	40

EX	EX2	EY	EXY
1	1	22	22
3	9	30	90
4	16	35	140
5	25	33	165
7	49	42	294
8	64	45	360
8	64	40	320
36	228	247	1391

Using the above data and substituting them into the equations, we get

$$\$1{,}391 = 36a + 228b$$

and

$$\$\ 247 = 7a + 36b$$

Solving the equations, we have fixed costs of $15,300 and variable cost of $3.69 per unit.

(c) High–Low Method. Another widely used, but less precise, method of identifying the behavior of semivariable costs is called the *high–low method.* This method uses only the highest and lowest plots on the scatter diagram for the analysis.

Again using the values in Exhibit 5.27, the amount of variable cost is found as follows:

$$\frac{\text{Change in cost}}{\text{Change in volume}} = \frac{\$45{,}000 - \$22{,}000}{8{,}000 - 1{,}000 \text{ units}} = \$3.29 \text{ per unit}$$

The amount of fixed costs is then found as follows, using the highest plotted output:

Total cost at 8,000 units	$45,000
Less variable cost (8,000) × $3.29	26,320
Fixed cost at all levels	$18,680

5.8 SUMMARY. For purposes of cost–volume–profit analysis, costs must be divided into their fixed and variable portions. Various techniques, including scatter diagrams and statistical analyses, are used to separate semivariable costs.

Computation of the break-even point is an important aspect of cost–volume–profit analysis. The modern multiproduct company is influenced by so many factors that it would be quite tedious, if not impossible, to portray all of them on a single break-even chart. Therefore, assumptions must be made and several charts must be devised in order to give management full information on the various factors. When properly used, cost–volume–profit analysis offers an overview of costs and sales in relation to profit planning.

In preparing budgets, costs are sometimes classified in different ways in order to determine the effectiveness of different phases of the company. These classifications assist management in determining which costs can be controlled and which costs are influenced by a certain objective and in making various short-run decisions, such as eliminating a department or a product.

It is imperative that managers know the behavior patterns of costs for their company. Proper decision making and budgeting depends on the knowledge of how costs will react in a set of circumstances, how costs will affect profits, and what changes can be made to produce greater profits.

SOURCES AND SUGGESTED REFERENCES

Bell, Jan E., James H. Cypher, and Patric Dears, *Target Costing: The Next Frontier in Strategic Cost Management.* Ansari, Shahid L., ed., Burr Ridge, IL: Irwin Professional Publishing, 1996.

Cascio, Wayne F., *Costing Human Resources: The Financial Impact of Behavior in Organizations* (Kent Series in Human Resource Management). Boston, MA: PWS, 1991.

Drury, C., *Costing: An Introduction* (2nd ed.). New York: Routledge, 1992.

Hansen, Don R., and Maryanne M. Mowen, *Cost Management: Accounting and Control.* Cincinnati, OH: South-Western, 1995.

Kaplan, Robert S., and Robin Cooper, *Cost and Effect: Using Integrated Cost Systems to Drive Profitability and Performance.* New York: McGraw-Hill, 1997.

Reeve, James M., *Readings and Issues in Cost Management.* Cincinnati, OH: South-Western, 1994.

Welsch, Glenn A., Ronald W. Hilton, and Paul N. Gordon, *Profit Planning and Control* (5th ed.). Englewood Cliffs, NJ: Prentice Hall, 1990.

Wright, David, *A Practical Foundation in Costing.* New York: Routledge, 1994.

CHAPTER 6

COST-ACCOUNTING SYSTEMS: INTEGRATION WITH MANUFACTURING BUDGETING

Paul D. Warner, Ph.D., LL.M., C.P.A.

Hofstra University

6.1 INTRODUCTION. The purpose of this chapter is to identify the basic cost-accounting system options available for accounting for the manufacturing costs of a company. A cost system is necessary for reliable product costing and pricing, the execution of plans and budgets, and timely management reporting of operations that permit cost control and the identification of cost-reduction opportunities. The various cost-accounting systems described in this chapter do not represent discrete alternatives; the cost-accounting system selected by a company frequently combines features of the various options.

A properly designed cost-accounting system should be integrated with the organization's structure and budgeting system. Budgets are structured according to area of responsibility and represent the financial implications of a plan; the cost-accounting system provides a system for reporting against the plan as well as for cost control over manufacturing operations.

Although this chapter will not discuss the other information systems within a manufacturing environment, the cost-accounting system must function in harmony with the systems depicted in Exhibit 6.1. Information needs and data collection required to maintain the cost-accounting system are dependent upon and interact with other information systems.

The basic cost-accounting concepts addressed in this chapter relate to the control of costs associated with manufacturing a product. The costs of manufacturing a product are those costs used to measure inventory value on the balance sheet and the costs of goods sold on the income statement. The total product cost includes the direct material and direct labor, and may include indirect manufacturing overhead costs.

By definition, *direct material* is material that is used directly in the product. *Direct labor* is the labor directly identified with producing a product. *Manufacturing overhead costs* are those indirect manufacturing costs necessary to the manufacturing process but not necessarily directly identified with a specific product or process. The manufacturing overhead costs associated with a product involve different conceptual considerations (variable [direct] versus full [absorption] costing) as well as the nature of the manufacturing process, the organization's structure, and the financial reporting system.

Exhibit 6.1. Manufacturing information systems

6.2 DECISION FACTORS IN THE SELECTION PROCESS. In order to obtain the benefits of the cost-accounting system selected, the following factors should be evaluated before the cost system is designed and implemented:

- Management philosophy and information requirements
- The organization's structure
- Control objectives of the company
- Accounting system and accounting personnel capabilities
- Detailed information available or required from the shop floor
- Integration of detailed reporting for budgeting and cost control with other information requirements such as sales, production scheduling, inventory control, and purchasing
- External financial reporting requirements
- Nature of the manufacturing process
- Type of industry
- Costs benefits of the various cost-accounting options

6.3 COST-ACCOUNTING SYSTEM OPTIONS. A cost-accounting system can be represented as a three-tier option tree, as depicted in Exhibit 6.2.

The first option is to determine the manufacturing costs to be included in product costing (variable versus full).[1] The second option is to determine the system to use in collecting the costs and in monitoring the flow of production (process versus job order).

[1] Internal Revenue Regulation 1.471–11 imposes other rules regarding the accumulation of product costs.

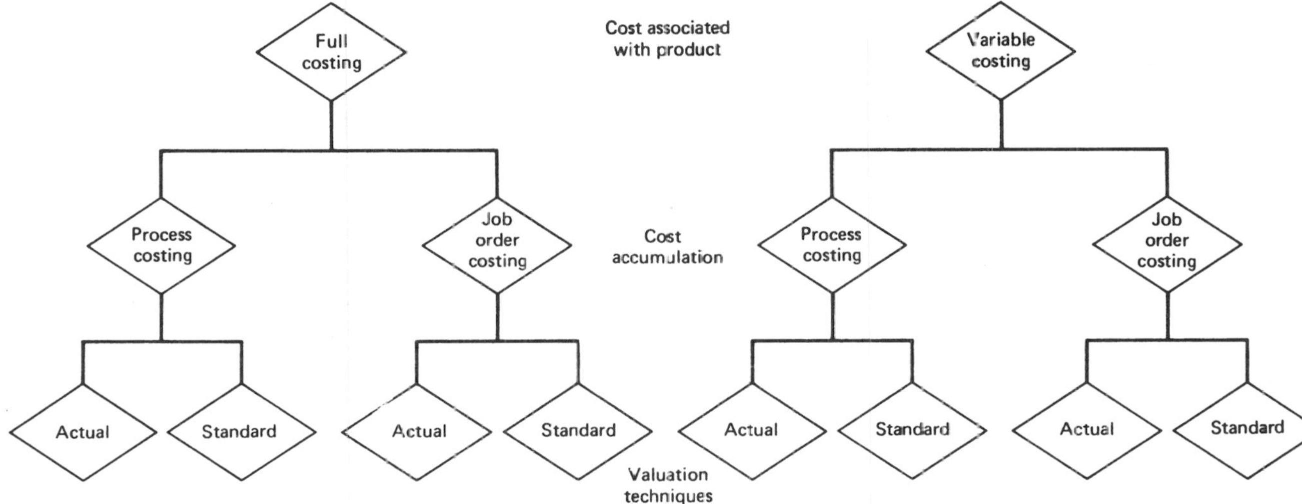

Exhibit 6.2. Cost-accounting system options

The last option to be selected is the valuation technique selected (actual versus standard). This chapter will discuss each component of the cost accounting selection process—the options, purpose, advantages, disadvantages, and interrelationship with the budget process.

6.4 COSTS ASSOCIATED WITH A PRODUCT. The distinction between full (absorption) manufacturing costing and variable (direct) manufacturing costing is in the treatment of fixed manufacturing overhead. *Fixed costs* are defined as those costs that do not change over a substantial range of operations and/or for a given time span. For budgeting purposes, items such as property taxes, managers' salaries, and building depreciation normally constitute fixed costs. These items are essential and directly related to manufacturing operations; therefore, proponents of full costing believe that these costs should be included in the cost of the product. They tend to be related to capacity to produce rather than to the products.

Variable costing is based on the concept that costs identified with a product should be only those costs that vary with the production activity. As in full costing, the cost of product includes direct material, direct manufacturing labor, and variable manufacturing overhead. (Variable manufacturing overhead normally includes employee fringe benefits, payroll taxes, supplies, machine maintenance, and other costs that vary in proportion with the level of operations.) Proponents of variable costing believe that fixed costs should be excluded from the product cost because they interfere with certain decision-making procedures.

6.5 VARIABLE COSTING AND BUDGETING. Full costing and variable costing have a direct impact on the budgeting process. Using variable costing, the budget process must distinguish between fixed and variable costs so that capacity variances do not affect product costs.

The responsibility for control over manufacturing variable costs and fixed costs may rest with different functional areas within an organization. A responsibility budgeting system using variable costing must distinguish among variable costs, discretionary fixed costs, and committed costs.

Manufacturers' *variable costs* may be defined as those costs directly associated with producing an item as well as those costs that vary with the level of production activity. The common components are the direct material and direct labor required to produce an item and those manufacturing overhead costs that vary with the level of activity. *Discretionary fixed costs* are costs reflecting periodic appropriations by management as determined during the budgeting process. These costs may include lease commitments and employee training programs.

Committed costs are those costs that are required to maintain the operating facilities of the company. Committed costs normally reflect capital budgeting decisions. For budgeting purposes, these items are represented by depreciation, property taxes, insurance, and top-level management salaries.

Variable costing is a logical extension of a responsibility and flexible budgeting and reporting system. Top management is responsible for profitability and therefore is ultimately responsible for all variable, committed, and discretionary costs incurred. In the short run, the department operating managers must control variable costs based on activity (production) levels.

(a) Variable Overhead Manufacturing Costs and the Accounting Records. To maintain the distinction between variable and fixed costs, the chart of accounts must include two expense classifications—one for variable costs and one for fixed costs. Additionally, a department code is necessary to identify the department responsible for and/or controlling the cost.

Variable overhead manufacturing costs are charged directly to the department and expense classification. The source for the actual postings to the department account may be purchase register, material requisition, labor distribution, or journal entries.

Fixed costs are re-allocated from the department, or cost center, that incurred them. Frequently, department activity ledgers are maintained as subsidiary ledgers to a manufacturing overhead control account(s) in the general ledger. The credit to the overhead control account is the application of overhead to work in process, based on a predetermined rate(s). The difference between actual charges and the applied amount represents overapplied or underapplied overhead. The concept of overhead and the procedures for applying overhead to product costing will be discussed later in this chapter. Although there are various alternative procedures for integrating responsibility budgeting with product costing, the basic objectives for accumulating manufacturing overhead are (1) reporting costs to the appropriate responsibility center; (2) comparing actual cost to budgeted amounts and determining causes, if any, for variations; and (3) assigning manufacturing cost to the product (inventory).

Because fixed manufacturing costs are not charged to a product using a variable-costing system, they are reflected in the income statement as period expenses (i.e., they are charged off fully in the period incurred) during the accounting period. No determination of applied overhead is required.

(b) Variable (Direct) Costing as a Management Tool. Variable (direct) costing is considered by many authorities as most useful for short-range planning. Application areas include short-term profitability planning and break-even analysis. Variable costing provides relevant management data regarding the effect of changes in production or sales mix, the effect of changes in pricing, the impact of volume on profitability, and the impact of variable-cost reductions brought about by increasing capacity costs (fixed) or vice versa.

Management asks such questions as what happens to profit if we increase the sale of B and this reduces the sale of A? Should we accept the order at a reduced price during a period of less than full capacity operations? At full capacity, management needs variable-costing data in order to determine which product makes the largest contribution to profits. These orders normally should be given sales priority.

Additionally, variable costing can be used to compare actual profits to budgeted profit goals. There are four main conditions that contribute to the overall profitability of a manufacturing organization: sales volume, product mix, pricing level, and expense control.

(c) Illustration of Product Profitability Analysis. The illustrations used in the exhibits in this section of the chapter depict the various profitability evaluation techniques available that use variable budgeting and costing techniques. The amount of detail used in the analysis depends on its intended use. For instance, the accuracy of product cost data necessary for strategic planning would not need to be as accurate or detailed as it would for cost estimating.

The mathematics of these analyses are relatively simple; however, the analytic process should be a continuous effort in which management constantly evaluates the potential for cost reduction or other procedures necessary for improving profitability. Additionally, the cost data should be constantly reviewed for reliability. Changes in the product structure, the manufacturing process, activity levels, costs, and cost relationships must be included in the analysis. Outside factors such as competitive forces and financial, market, production, and manpower constraints must also be considered.

The following analysis should be performed during each phase of the profit-planning and budgeting cycle, as depicted in Exhibit 6.3. During the profit-planning period, top management requires preliminary estimates to determine whether profitability will be in the range of established corporate goals, based on current or expected financial conditions.[2]

During the detailed budgeting process, the product cost information should be a logical and necessary extension of the process. Detailed product cost data developed during this period should provide data required for pricing decisions.

During the budgeting reporting period, actual results should be compared to budgeted product cost data. Any significant variation from budgets should be investigated, and, if necessary, product cost data must be adjusted to reflect current operating and economic conditions.

In evaluating the results of operations for the budget period, the cost-accounting system must provide data that will allow comparison of the budget to the actual results of operations. The product cost variances must also be analyzed. The information in Exhibit 6.4 is used to illustrate the various evaluation techniques using variable costing.

Based on the budget data provided in Exhibit 6.4, budgeted income from operations is determined as shown in Exhibit 6.5.

The profit goal, as established during the planning or budgeting period, depends on volume, sales price, product mix, and cost. Any variance from planned operations will have an immediate impact on income from operations.

The original budget, shown in Exhibit 6.5, indicates that, with a sales volume of 3,500 units of product A and 2,000 units of product B, the contribution to period expenses will be approximately $9,900. Exhibit 6.6 shows what the actual results of operations are assumed to be.

A comparative operating statement, as illustrated in Exhibit 6.7, indicates that income from operations has declined, based on volume, price, and cost variances from budget.

The decline in income from operations is composed of the variations from budget, as shown in Exhibit 6.8.

The causes for these variations should be analyzed, and corrective management actions, if appropriate, can be made based on the analyses provided.

(d) Other Uses of Variable Costing. Variable costing is an excellent tool for evaluating results of current operations in terms of comparison of actual results to budgets or plans. In addition, variable costing provides valuable information required for other management decisions. Selected uses for variable costing include the following:

- Appraising alternative pricing or marketing strategies. These decisions require knowledge of the change in the contribution margin as compared to the increase in sales volume.

[2] Variable product cost data constitute one component of product cost considered during the profit-planning and budgeting process; however, some additional cost concepts also affect the profit-planning decision. Other costs useful for profit planning include the following: current or future investments in facilities, machinery, and equipment (out-of-pocket costs); the amount invested in tangible, productive assets or an intangible asset (sunk costs); costs that are directly associated with a product or product line (traceable), which can be variable, semivariable, or fixed; costs associated with replacing current facilities, machinery, or equipment (replacement cost); the cost of alternative courses of action (opportunity costs); and costs that can be saved by selecting an alternative method (avoided) or postponed.

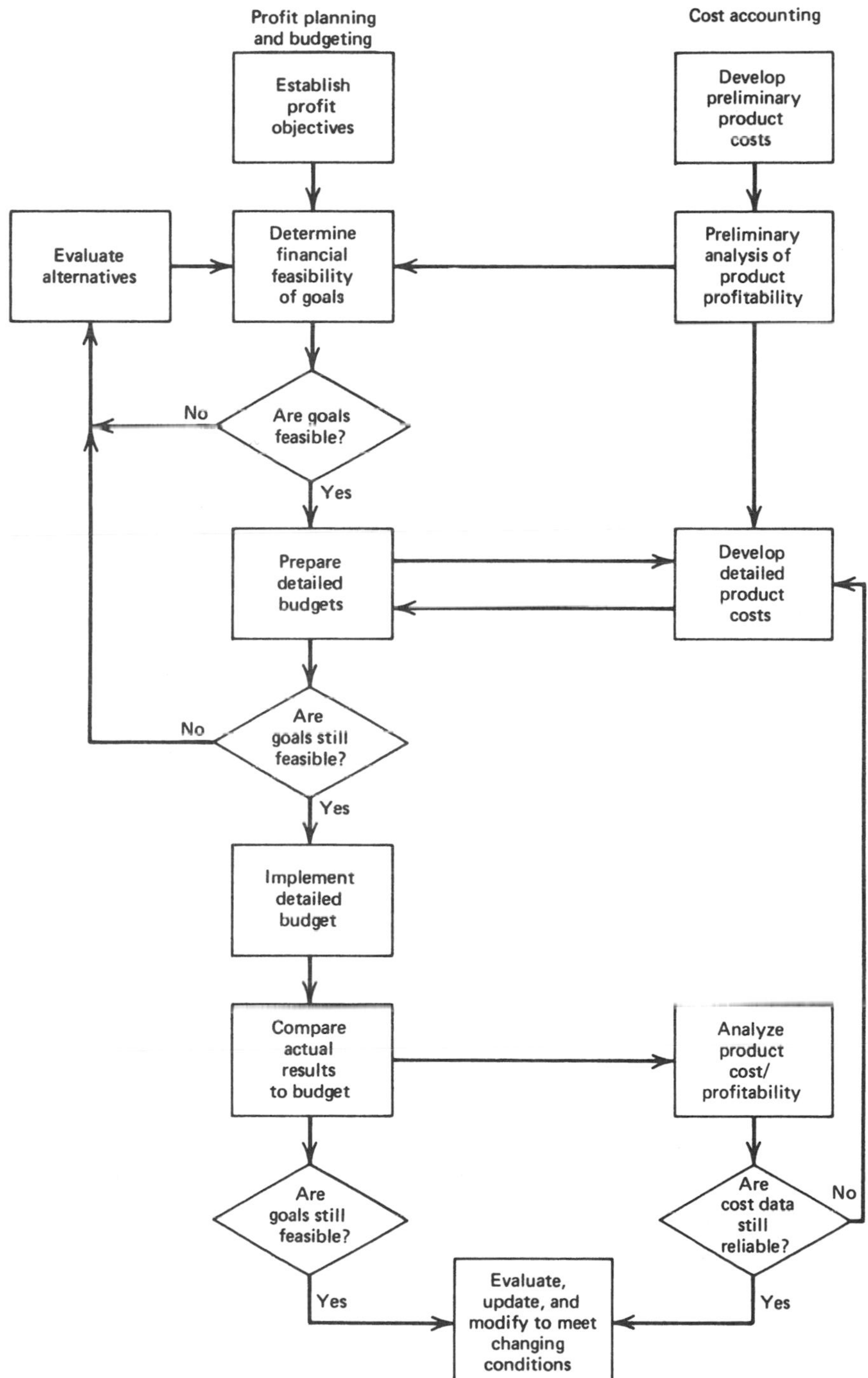

Exhibit 6.3. Cost-accounting, profit-planning, and budget overview

Evaluation Technique	Product A		Product B
Sales			
Price per unit	$3.50		$8.25
Sales volume (units)	3,500		2,000
Cost per Unit			
Direct material	$0.75		$2.80
Direct labor	0.50		0.85
Variable manufacturing overhead	1.05		1.75
Total cost per unit	$2.30		$5.40
Other Budget Data			
Fixed manufacturing overhead		$3000	
Selling, general and administrative		$2200	
Production Statistics			
Practical capacity (units)	5,000		2,400
Budgeted volume (units)	3,800		2,100

Exhibit 6.4. Budget data

Item	Amount
Sales	$28,750
Variable Manufacturing Costs	
Direct material	8,225
Direct labor	3,450
Variable overhead	7,175
	18,850
Contribution margin	9,900
Period Expenses	
Fixed manufacturing	3,000
Selling, general and administrative	2,200
	5,200
Income from Operations	$ 4,700

Exhibit 6.5. Budgeted results of operations

	Product A		Product B
Sales			
Price per unit	$3.40		$8.50
Sales volume (units)	4,125		1,390
Cost per Unit			
Direct material	$0.80		$3.00
Direct labor	0.50		0.90
Variable manufacturing overhead	1.10		1.60
	$2.40		$5.50
Period Expenses			
Fixed manufacturing		$3,400	
Selling, general and administrative		2,320	

Exhibit 6.6. Actual results of operations

	Budget		Actual		Over (Under) Budget	
	Amount	%	Amount	%	Amount	%
Sales	$28,750	100.0	$25,840	100.0	($2,910)	(10.1)
Cost of Goods Sold						
Direct material	8,225	28.6	7,470	28.9	(755)	(9.2)
Direct labor	3,450	12.0	3,314	12.8	(136)	(3.9)
Variable overhead	7,175	25.0	6,761	26.2	(414)	(5.8)
	18,850	65.6	17,545	67.9	(1,305)	(6.9)
Contribution margin	9,900	34.4	8,295	32.1	(1,605)	(16.2)
Period Expenses						
Manufacturing	3,000	10.4	3,400	13.2	400	13.3
Selling, general and	2,200	7.6	2,320	8.9	120	5.5
administrative	5,200	18.0	5,720	22.1	520	10.0
Income from Operations	$4,700	16.4	$2,575	10.0	(2,125)	(45.2)

Exhibit 6.7. Comparative income statement

- Prioritizing customer orders or product orders when a company is at capacity. Variable costing can assist in determining the product that makes the greatest contribution to profit. The greatest contribution to profit is determined by the unit contribution margin and the number of units that can be produced based on the available resources (i.e., operating hours).
- Evaluating plant or production-line expansion or reduction programs. Variable costing can assist in determining the affect of changes in volume on contribution to fixed operating costs.
- Establishing market or sales strategies and/or determining sales commission rates. Variable costing provides contribution margins necessary to ranking products by a profitability index. Those products with the largest unit dollar-contribution margin are normally ranked highest. Limited resources, such as operating capacity or market demand constraints, must also be considered.
- Make versus buy decisions. Management must be able to determine the variable and incremental costs associated with producing an item.
- Short-run cost-control purposes. Variable costs are considered controllable at the departmental operating levels. Variable-costing budget statements highlight variances from currently controllable costs.

(e) Identifying Fixed Manufacturing Costs. There are problems encountered in determining which expenses are fixed and which are direct. Some expenses are easily recognized as fixed (e.g., real estate taxes); others as direct (e.g., direct materials); many, however, are mixed (e.g., plant heat and power). The simplest solution is to classify those that are product related as direct and those that are capacity dependent as fixed. Techniques are available for segregating the direct and fixed components of an expense. The effort involved is usally unwarranted.

The relationship between fixed and direct costs is best shown by the following problem:

	Product A	Product B	Total
A. Sales Volume			
Actual unit sales	4,125	1,390	
Budgeted unit sales	3,500	2,000[a]	
	625	(610)	
× Budgeted unit price	3.50	8.25	
	$2,188	$(5,032)	
B. Sales Price			
Actual unit price	$3.40	$8.50	
Budgeted unit price	3.50	8.25	
	(.10)	.25	
× Actual unit sales	4,125	1,390	
	$(413)	$347	
C. Unit Cost			
Budgeted unit cost	$2.30	$5.40	
Actual unit cost	2.40	5.50	
	(.10)	(.10)	
× Actual unit sales	4,125	1,390	
	$(412)	$(139)	
D. Product Mix			
Budgeted unit sales	3,500	2,000	
Actual unit sales	4,125	1,390	
	(625)	(610)	
× Budgeted unit cost	2.30	5.40	
	$(1,438)	$3,294	
E. Summary			
Sales volume	$2,188	($5,032)	($2,844)
Sales price	(413)	347	(66)
Unit cost	(412)	(139)	(551)
Product mix	(1,438)	3,294	1,856
Decrease in contribution margin	($75)	($1,530)	($1,605)
Fixed expenses over budget			(520)
Total decrease in income from operations			($2,125)

[a] Decrease in income from operations is in parentheses.

Exhibit 6.8. Profitability analyses

The XYZ Company sells 100 units in April at a price of $10.00 per unit. Unit and total costs for the month are:

	Per Unit	*Total for Month*
Sales	$10.00	$1,000.00
Direct costs	6.00	600.00
Fixed costs	2.00	200.00
Total costs	8.00	800.00
Operating profit	$2.00	$200.00

How much would profits have increased in April if one additional unit had been sold? It depends on whether the fixed costs have been completely absorbed in the first 100 units sold.

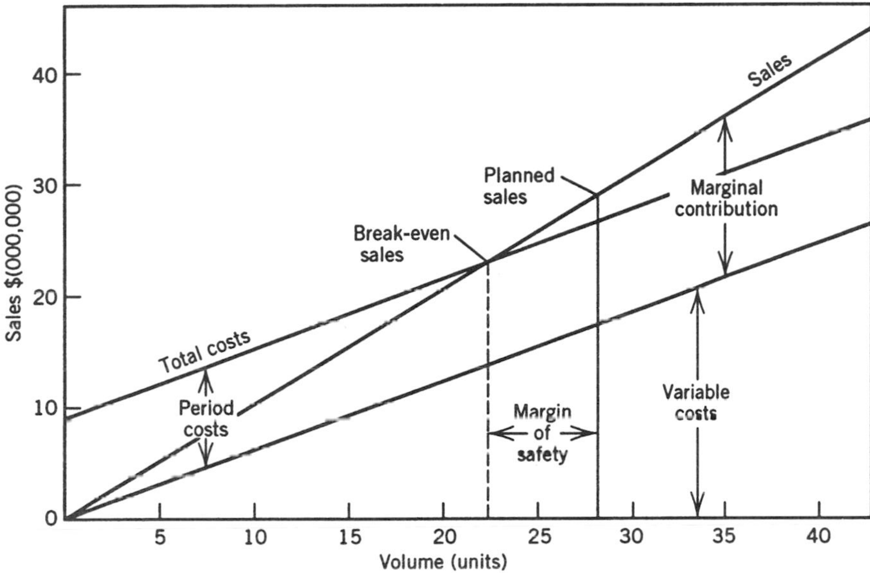

Exhibit 6.9. Break-even chart

(f) Break-Even Relationship. One of the major benefits of direct costing is its ability to provide break-even analysis data for decision-making purposes. Although break-even data and the information below are available from absorption costing, the effect of the absorbed fixed costs must be taken into consideration. The use of direct costing avoids this unnecessary work.

- Product decisions relative to sales mix and the establishment of our selling prices
- Procurement decisions relative to make versus buy decisions and plant capacity changes
- Marketing decisions relative to sales efforts, sales commissions, and other marketing matters
- Responsibility reporting based on controllable cost information

The following definitions are required in order to examine how the break-even relationship functions (break-even analyses are graphically presented in Exhibits 6.9 and 6.10):

- The break-even (BE) point is reached when sales (S) covers just the sum of the direct costs (DC) and fixed costs (FC). Thus, at the BE point, there is no profit (P). The algebraic form is:

$$S = DC + FC + P, \text{ but since } P = 0 \text{ at the break-even point,}$$

$$\text{then } S_{(BE)} = DC + FC$$

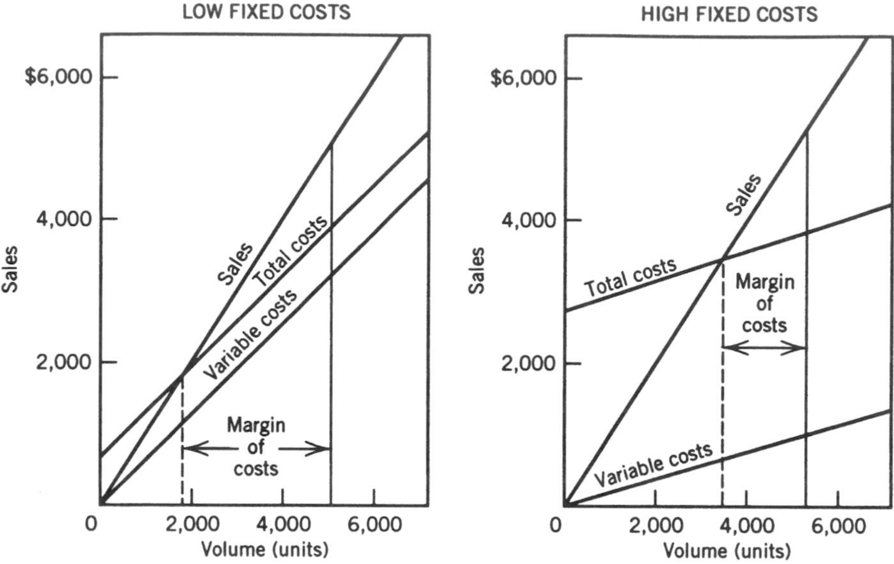

Exhibit 6.10. Break-even charts—low fixed costs and high fixed costs

- The contribution margin (CM) is defined as:

$$CM = S - DC = FC + P$$

- The profit–volume (P/V) relationship is defined as:

$$P/V = \frac{SP - VC}{SP}$$, where SP is defined as the selling price.

- Gross profit (GP) is defined as:

$$GP = \frac{SP - (VC + FC)}{SP}$$

- The margin of safety (MS) is the difference between the average sales and the sales at break-even but only if the average sales is greater than the break-even sales, thus

$$MS = \frac{\text{Av. Sales} - \text{BEP Sales}}{\text{Av. Sales}}$$

- The profit contribution (PC) is defined as:

$$PC = \frac{CM}{\text{Sales}}$$

- The profit-contribution ratio (PCR) is defined as:

$$\text{PCR} = \frac{\text{PC}}{\text{Sales}}$$

- Break-even sales in dollars $= \dfrac{\text{FC}}{\text{PCR}}$

Exhibit 6.10 shows the impact of fixed costs on the break-even point.

- Break-even sales in units $= \dfrac{\text{FC}}{\text{PC/unit}}$

The following shows the type of information available when direct costing is used (refer to Exhibits 6-11 to 6-14):

Tentative Profit Plan
($000 omitted)

	Total	Product Line A	Product Line B	Product Line C
Forecast sales	$ 70,000	$ 10,000	$ 20,000	$ 40,000
Variable cost of sales	53,000	5,000	14,000	34,000
Margin	$ 17,000	$ 5,000	$ 6,000	$ 6,000
P/V	24.3%	50%	30%	15%
Planned period				
Specific	$ 5,000	$ 1,500	$ 1,000	$ 2,500
Nonspecific	7,000	1,000	3,000	3,000
Total planned period	$ 12,000	$ 2,500	$ 4,000	$ 5,500
Operating profit	$ 5,000	$ 2,500	$ 2,000	500
% of Sales	7.4%	25%	10%	1.3%
Capital employed	$ 32,000	$ 10,000	$ 12,000	$ 10,000
% Return	15.6%	25%	16.7%	5%

Exhibit 6.11. ABC Company—tentative profit plan

Tentative Profit Plan—Revision 1
($000 omitted)

	Total	Product Line A	Product Line B	Product Line C
Forecast sales	$ 70,500	$ 13,500	$ 17,000	$ 40,000
Variable cost of sales	52,650	6,750	11,900	34,000
Margin	$ 17,850	$ 6,750	$ 5,100	$ 6,000
P/V	25%	50%	30%	15%
Planned period expense	$ 12,000			
Operating profit	$ 5,850			
% of Sales	8.3%			
Capital employed	$ 32,000			
% Return	18%			

Exhibit 6.12. ABC Company—tentative profit plan (revision 1)

Tentative Profit Plan—Revision 2
($000 omitted)

	Total	Product Line			
		Regular A	DEF A	B	C
Forecast sales	$ 72,100	$ 13,500	$ 1,600	$ 17,000	$ 40,000
Variable cost of sales	53,570	6,750	920	11,900	34,000
Margin	$ 18,530	$ 6,750	$ 680	$ 5,100	$ 6,000
P/V	25.7%	50%	42.5%	30%	15%
Planned period expense	$ 12,000				
Net operating profit	$ 6,530				
% of Sales	8.8%				
Capital employed	$ 32,000				
% Return	20.4%				

Exhibit 6.13. ABC Company—tentative profit plan (revision 2)

Tentative Profit Plan—Revision 3
($000 omitted)

	Total	Product Line			
		Regular A	DEF A	B	C
Forecast sales	$ 72,100	$ 13,500	$ 1,6000	$ 17,000	$ 40,000
Variable cost of sales	53,570	6,750	920	11,900	34,000
Margin	$ 18,530	$ 6,750	$ 680	$ 5,100	$ 6,000
P/V	25.7%	50%	42.5%	30%	15%
Planned period expense	$ 11,722				
Operating profit	$ 6,808				
% of Sales	9.4%				
Capital employed	$ 32,000				
% Return	21.3%				

Exhibit 6.14. ABC Company—tentative profit plan (revision 3)

A. The tentative profit plan (Exhibit 6.11) shows a proposed P/V of 24.3% and a return on investment (ROI) of 15.6%. (Operating profit + capital employed − 5,000/ 32,000 = 15.6%.) Plans are usually set up on this basis.

B. The tentative profit plan also shows planned period costs (planned fixed costs) broken into specific and nonspecific categories.

1. Specific planned period costs are fixed costs applicable to a given product line.

2. Nonspecific planned period costs are fixed costs not applicable to any specific product line (e.g., corporate manufacturing expenses). These are allocated to product lines on some predetermined basis (e.g., estimated sales).

C. There are numerous changes possible once the basic plan is formulated. The basic plan (Exhibit 6.11) shows an ROI of 15.6%. Suppose the desired ROI is 20% (an operating profit of $6,400,000). What can be done?

1. One possibility is to shift sales from product lines B and C to product line A.

Such shifts would be explored by marketing. Exhibit 6.12 shows the effect of shifting sales from product line B (reduction of $3,000,000) to product line A (increase of $3,500,000). The net effect is to increase both the margin and the operating profits by $850,000, thereby increasing the ROI to 18%. The improvement results from two factors:

(a) Increased profit margin –	
20% × $3,000,000 =	$600,000
(b) Additional sales	250,000
50% × $500,000 =	$850,000

2. When capacity permits, special orders may be appropriate. Suppose customer DEF offered to buy $1,600,000 per annum of product line A if 24-hour delivery could be guaranteed. Suppose this could be achieved, but at an increase in the variable cost of sales. The results of this offer can be seen in Exhibit 6.13. The P/V has decreased to 42.5%, but both the margin and the net operating profit have increased by $680,000 with the result that the ROI has now increased to 20.4%. The desired ROI of 20% has been achieved.

3. Other possibilities for improvement exist. For example, a review of the planned period expense might reveal a potential savings in plant maintenance of $278,000 (Exhibit 6.14). Such an item is included as part of the fixed factory overhead, which is absorbed into the product costs under an absorption system. It tends to be lost unless it is isolated. Direct costing highlights such items by keeping them isolated.

The central issue in the absorption costing versus direct costing controversy is really a question of timing. The central question is, ''What is the proper timing for the release of fixed factory overhead as an expense: when incurred, or at the time the finished units to which the fixed overhead relates are sold?''

The affect of this timing difference can be seen in Exhibit 6.15.

- When sales and production are in balance, direct- and absorption-costing methods yield the same profit. Under both methods, the amount of fixed cost incurred during the period is charged against revenue of the period. (See the first year in Exhibit 6.15.)
- When the production exceeds sales (that is, when in-process and finished inventories are increasing), absorption costing shows a higher profit than does direct costing. The reason is that, in absorption costing, a portion of the fixed manufacturing cost of the period is charged to inventory and thereby deferred to future periods. The total fixed cost charged against revenue of the period, therefore, is less than the amount of fixed cost incurred during the period. (See the second year in Exhibit 6.15.)
- When sales exceed production (that is, when in-process and finished inventories are decreasing), absorption costing shows a lower profit than does direct costing. Under absorption costing, fixed costs previously deferred in inventory are charged against revenue in the period in which the goods are sold. Total fixed costs charged against revenue, therefore, exceed the amount of fixed cost incurred during the period. (See the third and fourth years in Exhibit 6.15.)

Annual Statements

Basic production date at standard cost:					
Direct materials			$ 1.30		
Direct labor			1.50		
Variable overhead			.20	$ 3.00	
Fixed overhead ($150,000 ÷ 150,000 unit denominator volume)				1.00	
Total				$ 4.00	
Sales price, $5.00 per unit					
Selling and administrative expense, assumed for simplicity as being all fixed, $100,000 per year					

	First Year	Second Year	Third Year	Fourth Year	Four Years Combined
Opening inventory in units	—	—	30,000	10,000	—
Production	150,000	170,000	140,000	150,000	610,000
Sales	150,000	140,000	160,000	160,000	610,000
Closing inventory in units	—	30,000	10,000	—	—
Direct costing:					
Sales	$ 750,000	$ 700,000	$ 800,000	$ 800,000	$ 3,050,000
Cost of goods manufactured	$ 450,000	$ 510,000	$ 420,000	$ 450,000	$ 1,830,000
Add opening inventory @ $3	—	—	90,000	30,000	—
Available for sale	$ 450,000	$ 510,000	$ 510,000	$ 480,000	$ 1,830,000
Deduct ending inventory @ $3	—	90,000	30,000	—	—
Cost of goods sold	$ 450,000	$ 420,000	$ 480,000	$ 480,000	$ 1,830,000
Contribution margin	$ 300,000	$ 280,000	$ 320,000	$ 320,000	$ 1,220,000
Fixed factory overhead	(150,000)	(150,000)	(150,000)	(150,000)	(600,000)
Selling and administrative expense	(100,000)	(100,000)	(100,000)	(100,000)	(400,000)
Net operating income	$ 50,000	$ 30,000	$ 70,000	$ 70,000	$ 220,000
Absorption costing:					
Sales	$ 750,000	$ 700,000	$ 800,000	$ 800,000	$ 3,050,000
Cost of goods manufactured	$ 600,000	$ 680,000	$ 560,000	$ 600,000	$ 2,440,000
Add opening inventory @ $4	—	—	120,000	40,000	—
Available for sale	$ 600,000	$ 680,000	$ 680,000	$ 640,000	$ 2,440,000
Deduct ending inventory @ $4	—	120,000	40,000	—	—
Cost of goods sold	$ 600,000	$ 560,000	$ 640,000	$ 640,000	$ 2,440,000
Volume variance*	—	(20,000)	10,000	—	(10,000)
Adjusted cost of goods sold	$ 600,000	$ 540,000	$ 650,000	$ 640,000	$ 2,430,000
Gross margin	$ 150,000	$ 160,000	$ 150,000	$ 160,000	$ 620,000
Selling and administrative expense	100,000	100,000	100,000	100,000	400,000
Net operating income	$ 50,000	$ 60,000	$ 50,000	$ 60,000	$ 220,000

*Computation of volume variance based on denominator volume of 150,000 units:
Second year $20,000 overapplied: (170,000 − 150,000) × $1.00
Third year 10,000 underapplied: (150,000 − 140,000) × $1.00
Four years combined $10,000 overapplied: (610,000 − 600,000) × $1.00

Exhibit 6.15. Comparison of direct costing and absorption costing

- When sales volume is constant but production volume fluctuates, direct costing yields a constant profit figure, because profit is not affected by inventory changes. Under the same circumstances, absorption costing yields a fluctuating profit figure, which will be directly affected by the direction and amount of the changes in inventories. (See the third and fourth year in Exhibit 6.15.)
- If production volume is constant, profit moves in harmony with sales under either direct or absorption costing. The profit figures will move in the same direction but will not necessarily be the same in amount, because inventory costs that are carried over from period to period will be greater under absorption costing. (See the first and fourth years in Exhibit 6.15.)
- The divergence between period profit figures computed by direct- and absorption-costing methods tends to be smaller for long periods than for short periods, because production and sales volume tend to approach equality over a long period. Thus, the difference between total profit figures computed by the two methods is usually smaller for a few years (taken together) than the difference between year-to-year profit figures. Over a period of years, the methods should give substantially the same result, because sales cannot continuously exceed production, nor can production continuously exceed sales.
- Direct costing excludes fixed factory overhead from inventory. In formula form, the difference between net incomes of absorption and direct costing may be shown as follows:

$$\text{Profit computed by absorption costing} - \text{Profit computed by direct costing} = \frac{\text{Total fixed factory overhead}}{\text{Volume used for unitizing fixed overhead}} \times \text{(Volume produced minus volume sold)}$$

or

$$\text{Difference in profits} = \text{Fixed factory overhead per unit} \times \text{Change in inventory units}$$

Application of this formula to Exhibit 6.15 is shown as follows:

- Note that the difference in profit between the absorption-costing and the direct-costing methods is due to the changes in inventory position.

(g) Disadvantages of Variable Costing. In the long run, both variable and fixed costs must be recovered through the pricing structure. No company could stay in business without its sales price covering fixed costs to include a reasonable profit. Any pricing decision must include full recovery of all costs over the expected sales life of the product.

The following six problems are considered by some to be major deterrents to implementing a variable cost-accounting system:

1. The determination of a causal relationship between a cost and a unit of activity is often difficult, and therefore management is reluctant to implement flexible budgeting procedures necessary for an effective variable-costing system.

2. It is believed that variable costing will lead to underpricing of products. However, variable costing is an effective tool for ensuring that long-run profitability is considered in the decision process.
3. The Securities and Exchange Commission, the Internal Revenue Service, and the American Institute of Certified Public Accountants do not recognize variable costing as a generally accepted procedure for inventory valuation.
4. Variable-cost data as used for product profitability analysis are inappropriate whenever capital investment requirements for various products or product lines vary significantly.
5. The use of absorption costing appears to be the preferable method since direct costing excludes fixed factory overhead from the cost of the product. Therefore, sufficient data may not be available with which to properly establish minimum selling prices. That is, the product cost is incomplete.
6. Other problems may result from the use of direct costs, such as:
   - Valuation of inventories for insurance, merger, and so on.
   - Seasonal distortions due to changes in inventory levels.
   - Inability to compare operating results with other companies.
   - The requirement of absorption-cost data in order to comply with the requirements of:
     a. The Robinson–Patman Act
     b. Cost-plus contracts
     c. Government contracts
     d. Litigation

(h) The Direct/Absorption Alternative. The solution to the above problems is to have a system that provides both direct- and absorption-costing data. Such a cost system would provide direct-cost information for:

- Product decisions
- Procurement decisions
- Plant capacity decisions
- Marketing decisions
- Profit planning

and would provide absorption-cost information for:

- Full-cost inventory
- Full-cost sales price evaluations
- Conventional financial statements
- Income tax reporting purposes
- Comparability with other companies
- Elimination of seasonal distortions

The only mechanical difference between direct and absorption costing is the level at which fixed factory overhead is allocated to the product. Direct costing does not allocate the fixed factory overhead below the product level, and then it does so only on a total level,

The Direct-Absorption Cost Co.
For the Year Ended December 31, 19XX

Net sales—at standard (Schedule I)	$ 32,250,000		
Direct cost of sales—at standard	21,000,000		
Contribution at standard	11,250,000		
Variances—sales (Schedule I)	198,000		
—direct costs (Schedule II)	462,000		
—contractor costs (Schedule II)	74,000		
Total variances	734,000		
Contribution at actual	10,516,000		
	Actual	Variance	Budget
Period Costs			
Factory overhead (Schedule III)	4,125,000	$ (125,000)	$ 4,000,000
Selling expenses	2,726,000	(26,000)	2,700,000
General and administrative	1,205,000	(55,000)	1,150,000
Total period costs	8,056,000	$ (206,000)	$ 7,850,000
Net profit before allocation of factory overhead to inventories	2,460,000		
Allocation of factory overhead to inventories (Schedule IV)	268,000		
Net profit absorption-cost method	2,728,000		
Other income and expenses	(31,000)		
Net profit before taxes	2,679,000		
Income taxes	1,300,000		
Net profit	$ 1,379,000		
Net increase in inventories during period (Schedule IV)—at standard	$ 1,500,000		

Exhibit 6.16. Managerial cost statement

without adjustment for the amount absorbable into inventory. Absorption costing utilizes the fixed factory overhead into the individual product or job.

Exhibits 6.16 through 6.20 depict a direct/absorption-costing system report.

6.6 FULL COSTING AND BUDGETING.

For budgeting purposes, full costing is often associated with fixed budgeting. This means that once the level of activity is established during the budget process, the budget remains fixed regardless of the level of activity (volume). This is not always true; a company may use flexible budget techniques that adjust budgeted costs to changes in activity, yet may use full costing for inventory valuation and cost of sales determination. Some companies combine flexible budgeting and variable costing for internal management reporting and use full costing for external reporting.

(a) Comparison of Full Costing and Variable Costing.

Both full costing and variable costing will provide identical operating income when there is no change in the inventory level of manufactured goods. When production is greater than sales during a period, net income normally will be higher using full costing because fixed manufacturing costs are deferred (included in inventory); using variable costing they are charged against current sales. Net income will normally be lower with full costing in a period when sales are

The Direct-Absorption Cost Co.
For the Year Ended December 31, 19XX
Schedule I

	Standard	Actual	Variance
Sales—regular merchandise	$ 40,500,000	$ 40,300,000	$ (200,000)
Less returns and allowances	3,200,000	3,180,000	20,000
Net	37,300,000	37,120,000	(180,000)
—irregular and other	—	—	—
Total sales	37,300,000	37,120,000	(180,000)
Less: trade discounts	2,700,000	2,690,000	10,000
Salesmen's commissions	2,350,000	2,378,000	(28,000)
	5,050,000	5,068,000	18,000
Net sales	$ 32,250,000	$ 32,052,000	$ (198,000)

Exhibit 6.17. Net sales schedule

The Direct-Absorption Cost Co.
For the Year Ended December 31, 19XX
Schedule II

	Total		
	Standard	Actual	Variance
Direct labor			
Cutters	$ 600,000	$ 612,000	$ 12,000
Bundlers	18,000	18,000	—
Operators	2,800,000	2,913,000	113,000
Belt department	48,000	49,000	1,000
Button/slides	15,000	14,000	(1,000)
Pleaters	26,000	27,000	1,000
Examiners	94,000	99,000	5,000
Finishers	15,000	14,000	(1,000)
Pressers	324,000	321,000	(3,000)
Bonus	200,000	200,000	—
Total	4,140,000	4,267,000	(127,000)
Pension and health insurance	190,000	197,000	(7,000)
Payroll taxes	590,000	600,000	(10,000)
Total direct labor	4,920,000	5,064,000	(144,000)
Direct material			
Piece goods and trim—purchases	14,682,000	14,960,000	(278,000)
Freight and trucking	410,000	454,000	(44,000)
Discounts and anticipation	(12,000)	(16,000)	4,000
Total direct materials	15,080,000	15,398,000	(318,000)
Total direct costs	$ 20,000,000	$ 20,462,000	$ (462,000)
Contractor costs	$ 2,500,000	$ 2,574,000	$ (74,000)

Exhibit 6.18. Direct-cost schedule

The Direct-Absorption Cost Co.
For the Year Ended December 31, 19XX
Schedule III

	Actual	Total Variance	Budget
Buildup	$ 189,000	$ 6,000	$ 183,000
Overtime (premium portion)	295,000	22,000	273,000
Holiday and vacation	453,000	4,000	449,000
Truck drivers	39,000	1,000	38,000
Supervisors	977,000	20,000	957,000
Pattern makers	246,000	2,000	244,000
Shippers	309,000	5,000	304,000
Receiving department	159,000	2,000	157,000
Repairs (garments)	46,000	4,000	42,000
Sewing office	7,000	—	7,000
Factory maintenance	146,000	4,000	142,000
Nonproduction	210,000	—	210,000
Vice President Production (partial)	26,000	—	26,000
Pension—salaried persons	97,000	—	97,000
Severance pay	25,000	3,000	22,000
Rent	51,000	—	51,000
Cutting room expenses	74,000	3,000	71,000
Heat, light and power	86,000	22,000	64,000
General factory expense	129,000	3,000	126,000
General maintenance expense	70,000	6,000	64,000
Depreciation	124,000	—	124,000
General insurance	182,000	2,000	180,000
Vice President Engineering (partial)	15,000	—	15,000
Travel factory	20,000	6,000	14,000
Telephone	4,000	1,000	3,000
Buying expenses	11,000	1,000	10,000
Trim buyers	24,000	1,000	23,000
Factory office	64,000	3,000	61,000
Machine repairs and parts	47,000	4,000	43,000
Total factory overhead	$ 4,125,000	$ 125,000	$ 4,000,000

Exhibit 6.19 Factory overhead schedule

greater than production because fixed costs previously included in inventory are now being charged against current sales via cost of goods sold.

Using the data given in Exhibit 6.21, a comparative income statement using the two cost-accounting options is demonstrated in Exhibit 6.22.

Regardless of the option selected, the cost-accounting concept (variable or full costing) must be fully understood by users of the data. Careful investigation and interpretation by the accountant or budget director are essential to acceptance by operating managers.

(b) A Final Word on Variable and Full Costing. In the long run, a company must sell a product at a price that recovers both variable and fixed costs and that contributes

Lifo Basis
The Direct-Absorption Cost Co.
For the Year Ended December 31, 19XX

	Standard Cost	%	Overhead	Totals Absorption
Opening inventory	$ 6,000,000	(A)	$ 200,000	$ 6,200,000
Total direct costs (Schedule II)	20,000,000		4,000,000	24,000,000
Contractor costs	2,500,000		—	2,500,000
Total	22,500,000	100.0	4,000,000	26,500,000
Direct cost of sales	21,000,000	93.3	3,732,000(B)	24,732,000
Increase in inventory	1,500,000	6.7	268,000(B)	1,768,000
Closing inventory	$ 7,500,000		$ 468,000(C)	$ 7,968,000

Notes
(A) % computed as follows: 21,000,000 + 22,500,000 = 93.3%
(B) Computed as follows: 93.3% and 6.7% of $4,000,000
(C) Opening balance ($200,000) plus increase applicable to increase in inventory ($268,000)

Exhibit 6.20. Changes in inventories and proration of factory overhead

Budgeted Production (units)	12,000
Budgeted Sales	11,200
Sales Price per Unit	$25.00
Budgeted Variable Cost per Unit	
Material	$8.00
Labor	2.00
Manufacturing overhead	2.00
	12.00
Fixed Manufacturing Overhead	2.50
	$14.50
Budgeted Fixed (Period) Costs	
Manufacturing	$30,000
Selling	28,600
Administration	32,500
	$91,100
Beginning Finished Goods Inventory	
Units	4,000
Material	$7.50
Labor	1.75
Variable manufacturing overhead	1.50
Fixed manufacturing overhead	2.00
	$12.75

Exhibit 6.21. Variable versus full costing

	Variable Costing		Full Costing
Sales	$280,000		$280,000
Cost of Goods Sold			
Beginning inventory	43,000		51,000
Production	144,000		174,000
Less ending inventory	(57,600)		(69,600)
	129,400		155,400
Contribution margin—gross profit	150,600		124,600
Period Expenses			
Manufacturing	30,000		NA[a]
Selling	28,600		28,600
Administration	32,500		32,500
	91,100		61,100
Income from Operations	59,500		63,500
The difference can be reconciled as follows:			
Full costing income from operations		$63,500	
Less fixed manufacturing costs included in ending inventory (4,800 units × $2.50)		(12,000)	
Plus fixed manufacturing costs deferred (inventoried) from the prior period and charged against sales in the current period (4,000 units × $2.00)		8,000	
Variable-costing income from operations		$59,500	

Exhibit 6.22. Comparative income statement

to net income. The system selected must be able not only to provide data required for short-term decisions but also to convey the long-term implications of the decision.

In many industries we are witnessing increased automation, government environmental requirements, and so forth, all of which require increasing investments in plant and equipment. The cost of these assets must be recovered over their useful life.

The key to a properly designed direct-costing system is the inclusion of fixed manufacturing overhead in the product cost. In an absorption-costing system, this is done at the product level; in a variable-costing system, it should be done at the product-line level.

6.7 COST-ACCUMULATION PROCEDURES. Regardless of which manufacturing costs are associated with a product, the cost-accounting option selected must be able to accumulate and monitor the selected costs. With a job order–costing system, material, direct labor, and manufacturing overhead are charged to a specific job, shop, or customer order (a discrete order). As a result of this accumulation procedure, work-in-process inventory can be computed as the sum of all open orders at the end of an accounting period. Upon order completion, the cost of the order is transferred to finished goods or to cost of sales, using either standard or actual cost as discussed later in this chapter. With a process-costing system, manufacturing costs are charged to specific work centers or departments. This work-in-process inventory can be computed as the sum of all production costs charged to each department plus transfers in from other departments or finished goods inventory.

A comparison of the production and cost flow of a job costing and a process costing is illustrated in Exhibit 6.23.

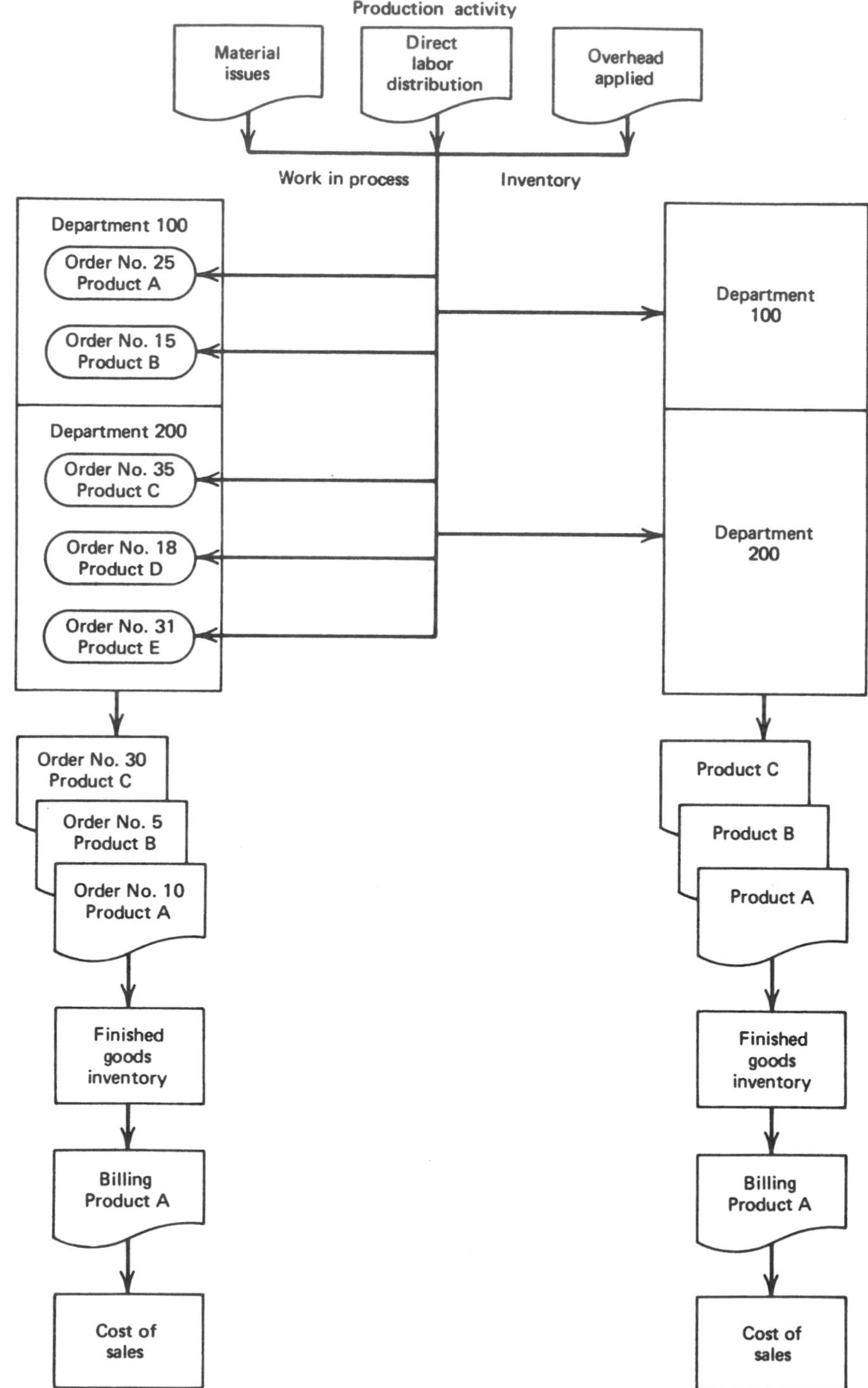

Exhibit 6.23. Job versus process cost accounting

(a) Impact on Budgeting. Although the main purpose of job and process cost accounting is in determining product cost, the properly designed cost-accumulation system should be readily integrated with a responsibility budgeting system. Production reports indicating only unit costs would not be satisfactory for controlling costs. The system must be able to identify each element of cost (material, labor, and overhead) for each department. The production data, such as direct labor utilization, material usage, scrap, and budget control over manufacturing overhead costs, must also be reported.

(b) Selection of the Cost-Accumulation Procedure. Each cost-accumulation procedure has several advantages and disadvantages. A process-costing system is normally associated with industries requiring mass production or continuous processing operations, and a job order–costing system with companies that control manufacturing operation by issuing specific production orders for defined quantities of a specific product. The production order can be for stock replenishment (finished goods) or for a specific customer order. However, many manufacturing companies have all the requirements necessary for a job order–costing system but select process-accumulation techniques. The reasons vary, but it appears that the major reason for not selecting job-accumulation procedures is the reluctance to implement the detailed shop floor reporting and accounting procedures necessary for a successful job order–costing system.

Although job order–costing procedures require detailed shop floor reporting and detailed postings to the accounting records, the system has some distinct advantages over process costing in that:

- It provides details of costs incurred on each order.
- It theoretically provides more reliable product costing because costs are reported against a specific order and product.
- It facilitates comparison of actual costs with cost estimates or standards. Additionally, product profitability via gross margin analysis can be calculated on each order.
- It can be readily incorporated into most computerized manufacturing product cost systems.

A properly designed and installed system also facilitates responsibility budgeting by associating costs (and cost variances) with specific areas of responsibility, such as department, work center, or operation.

Process costing has certain advantages and disadvantages. The main advantage is that it identifies costs by responsibility area. (However, a properly designed job order–costing system can also provide costs by responsibility area). Additionally, the system does not require the detailed record keeping as required for job order costing. The major disadvantages of process costing are that there may be less reliable product costing because of averaging units of production during the accounting period and that gross margins on each customer order are not available.

6.8 VALUATION: ACTUAL VERSUS STANDARD. The final cost-accounting system option to be selected is the identification of costs associated with the product, or *valuation.* The selection of variable or full costing was the first valuation option selected; however, within these two options, the cost-accounting system can be either an actual or a standard cost system. The term *actual cost* should not be constructed as the true cost but as the actual quantity required to produce an item times the computed actual unit cost.

The key concept is that an actual-cost system uses an actual quantity, such as material and labor, times an actual unit cost. In using actual costs, there is no predetermined material usage or predetermined labor time for each operation in the manufacturing process.

With standard costs, actual costs not only are identified and monitored but also are compared to predetermined standards to determine variances from the standard. The identification of variances is the distinguishing feature of standard costing and is considered indispensable to cost control. The establishment of standard costs is a logical extension of the budgeting system. Standard costs allow management to report against budgets as well as to provide input into the development of budgets.

The various valuation techniques are depicted in Exhibit 6.24.

6.9 ACTUAL COSTING.

In considering actual costing, each distinct transaction must be considered. Various transactions of the manufacturing process include the following:

- Purchase of materials
- Issues of material to production
- Labor operations performed
- Application of manufacturing overhead
- Production completion and transfer to finished goods
- Shipment (sale) of finished goods

Although this is an oversimplified depiction of the manufacturing process, these transactions represent the essential production control points of a cost-accounting system and are useful in analyzing valuation alternatives.

(a) Purchase of Materials.

With an actual-cost system, material purchases are recorded at the actual unit cost. The purchase price per unit includes the vendor's invoice price plus freight-in charges. Purchase discounts may be deducted from the computation of unit cost; however, many companies record the material purchase at the gross invoice amount and separately record the discount in a separate account.

As a practical matter, freight-in may be charged to a separate freight-in account. As material is issued to production, freight-in is charged to production at an applied rate. At the end of an accounting period, the balance in the freight-in account (actual less applied) is closed to work-in-process inventory or prorated between work-in-process inventory and materials inventory.

(b) Issues of Material to Production.

Three of the four procedures for computing actual material cost are compared in Exhibit 6.25. The specific invoice method is not really practical unless it is material that can be assigned to a specific product and/or customer order. The other three methods of costing material to production can be adopted to most actual-cost systems.

Weighted average actual cost is usually determined at the end of an accounting period where the records are maintained manually.[3] It is determined by adding the beginning inventory value plus receipts during the period to obtain the total available for production.

---

[3] Computer-based accounting systems typically recompute the weighted average cost after each purchase.

Actual	Standard
Material Cost	
Weighted average	Price of most economical supplier
First-in–first-out (FIFO)	
Last-in–first-out (LIFO)	Weighted average of several suppliers
Specific vendor invoice	Price for the quantity usually purchased
	Most economical quantity size
Labor Rate	
Employee	Operation
Operation	Work center
Work center	Department
Department	Plant-wide
Plant-wide	
Manufacturing Overhead	
Budget Technique	
Flexible (variable)	Flexible (variable)
Fixed	Fixed
Combined	Combined
Types of Rates	
Plant-wide	Plant-wide
Department	Department
Work center	Work center
Operations	Operations
Overhead Allocation Procedures	
Direct	Direct
Sequential	Sequential
Cross allocation	Cross allocation
Bases for Applying Overhead	
Direct labor hours	Direct labor hours
Direct labor dollars	Direct labor dollars
Machine hours	Machine hours
Material value	Material value
Units produced	Units produced
Other	Other
Activity Level	
Theoretical	Theoretical
Practical	Practical
Normal	Normal
Expected (budgeted)	Expected (budgeted)

Exhibit 6.24. Valuation techniques

The total available ($10,460) is divided by the total available units (19,000) to determine the weighted average cost per unit ($0.55). All issues to production during the period are charged to production based on the computed average cost. A company using a job order system would charge each job for the actual material issued to the job at the actual computed average cost ($0.55). With a process system, each department (or work center) would be charged at $0.55 per unit.

	Units	Unit Cost	Weighted Average	FIFO	LIFO
Beginning inventory	5,000	$0.50[a]	$2,500	$2,500	$2,500
Purchases					
First	3,000	0.52	1,560	1,560	1,560
Second	4,000	0.55	2,200	2,200	2,200
Third	7,000	0.60	4,200	4,200	4,200
Total receipts	14,000		7,960	7,960	7,960
Total available	19,000		10,460	10,460	10,460
Issues					
First	(7,000)		(3,850)	(3,540)	(4,200)
Second	(6,000)		(3,300)	(3,320)	(3,240)
Total issues	(13,000)		(7,150)	(6,860)	(7,440)
Ending inventory	6,000		$3,310	$3,600	$3,020

[a] For illustration purposes, all beginning inventory unit costs are assumed to be the same. This would normally not be true in a dynamic environment.

Exhibit 6.25. Actual material valuation procedures

Using first-in–first-out (FIFO) cost, issues would be charged to production based on the order of receipt. In this example, the first issue of 7,000 units to production is valued as follows:

Beginning inventory	5,000 × $0.50 =	2,500
First receipt	2,000 × $0.52 =	1,040
	7,000	$3,540

Ending inventory is to be composed of the most current receipts valued—in this example, at $0.60/unit, or $3600.

Using last-in–first-out (LIFO) costs, the flow of inventory is the last purchased and the first to be issued to production. In this example, the first issue to production of 7,000 units is valued as the third receipt (last purchase) of 7,000 × $.060 = $4,200.

The ending inventory is composed of the units included in beginning inventory of 5,000 units valued at $2,500 plus the increase in ending inventory of 1,000 units first purchased during the period at $0.52 per unit, or $520.

As a practical matter, LIFO is not used to charge material to production on a day-to-day basis. Computations of LIFO reserves, the adjustment to state FIFO, and weighted-average or standard-cost inventories at FIFO values are normally maintained in a separate LIFO adjustment to the inventory accounts.

(c) Labor Operations Performed. The next component of a product is the direct labor required to fabricate, assemble, machine, and so forth the product. The *actual cost of labor* is defined as actual hours charged to a job, a product, or a department multiplied by the actual rate. The actual rate, as illustrated in Exhibit 6.24, may be the employee, operation, work center, department, or plant-wide rate. The actual selection of the rate would be based on (1) the variation in skill levels and wage rates, (2) the control objectives of the company, and (3) the budget system used. The greater the variation in skill level and wage rate and the greater the need to identify and measure performance by responsibility center, the greater the need to establish the labor rate by the smallest control unit, such as an operation.

Regardless of the rate selected, the procedure for reporting actual labor must be consistent with the procedures used to develop the budget. If direct labor budgets are prepared by department, then direct labor hours and dollars must be determined based on the department wage rate.

(d) Application of Manufacturing Overhead. In an actual-cost system, predetermined overhead rates are determined during the budgeting process. The amount charged to production (job, product, or department) would be determined as the actual overhead base, such as labor hours, times the predetermined rate. The difference between actual manufacturing costs and the amount applied to production would be considered an overabsorption or underabsorption of overhead costs. The procedures for developing overhead rates and the accounting and budgeting procedures related to the cost-accounting system are discussed in the section on manufacturing overhead in this chapter.

(e) Production Completion and Transfer to Finished Goods. The actual cost of a completed product is the sum of all actual material, labor, and overhead costs "rolled up" through the final operations performed. The actual product cost is determined in the same manner as the cost of purchased material. However, it is important that the material, labor, and overhead actual costs be separately identified. The data from the actual product cost will provide input into cost estimating, budgeting direct labor and materials, requirements, current cost control, and budget review.

(f) Shipment of Finished Goods. The actual cost of sales or transfer of finished goods is determined in the same manner used to value issues of material to production, as illustrated in Exhibit 6.26. The weighted average, FIFO, and LIFO valuation techniques are acceptable procedures for valuing sale or transfer of finished goods.

6.10 ACTUAL COSTING, BUDGETING, AND COST CONTROL.

Actual costing has several inherent deficiencies that make it incompatible with budgeting and cost control. The basic requirements of a manufacturing budget include the ability to:

- Determine cost control responsibilities within the manufacturing organization
- Compare actual results of operations to predetermined (budgets) results
- Identify variations from budgets in a timely manner

An actual-cost system provides no predetermined measurement standards. As a result, the actual cost of a product may include excess material usage and labor and machine inefficiencies, which are not easily identifiable. To determine if the "actual" cost represents the real or true cost necessary to produce an item, the actual-cost data must be analyzed. Additionally, the credibility of the cost-accounting system may be impaired because actual costing often means varying cost for the same product within the same business cycle.

Actual costing cannot be effectively used for product profitability analysis if it is out of line with what the product should cost based on engineered standards, production capabilities, and economic purchasing and production quantities.

6.11 STANDARD COSTING.

Standard costing is considered an indispensable extension of the manufacturing budget process. Standards provide the ability to compare actual

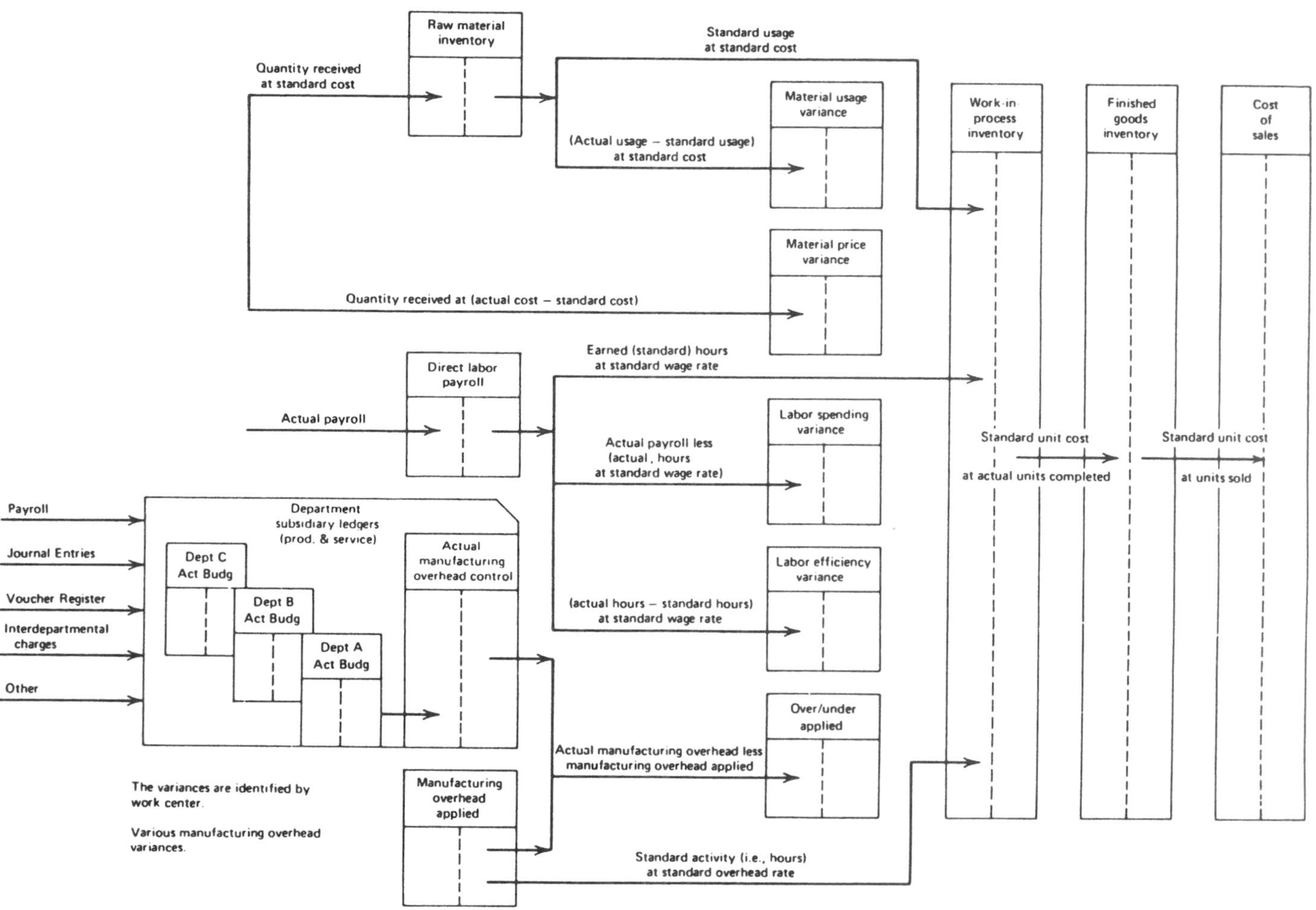

Exhibit 6.26. Standard-cost system—accounting transaction overview

to predetermined results and the cost data that identify the variance from budgeted results in a timely manner. The difference between an operating budget and standard costing is that a budget represents a summary of standard costs at the budgeted level of operations and production mix, whereas standard costs represent what product costs should be based on measurement standards (performance objectives).

(a) Definition. *Standard costs* are defined as the measure of what a product should cost. As with an actual-cost system, the standard-cost system collects the actual-cost data, but it charges the product only for the standard quantity at the standard unit cost. The difference between the amount charged to a product (costs that can be inventoried) and the amount actually incurred is considered a variance.

The standard cost comprises a standard unit of measure (hours, quantity, etc.) and a standard unit cost. With a properly structured standard-cost system, management can make timely evaluations manufacturing options on both a quantitative and a financial basis.

The accounting transaction flow is graphically displayed in Exhibit 6.14.

(b) Standard Costs and Budgets. If standards are based on current operating and business levels as defined during the budget process, then the budget represents the sum of standard costs. In this chapter, we assume that standards represent reasonable performance measurements that are currently attainable and that are accepted by operating managers as being reasonable goals.

(c) Purpose of Standard Costs

(i) Cost Control. The main purpose of a standard-cost system is to control costs. Actual costs can be compared with predetermined standards to determine variance from planned (budgeted) results. Variances from standards represent ''red flags'' to management. The properly structured standard-cost system should also provide the ability to identify the operation and the product or products incurring the variance. The variance will indicate a deviation from plans; management analysis of the cause for the variance is necessary to determine why the variance occurred and to identify actions to prevent variances from occurring in the future.

(ii) Preparation of Budgets. Raw material, purchased parts, and direct labor requirements to meet budgeted production schedules require predetermined usage and/or operation times as well as procedures to translate production and inventory data into financial terms necessary for the budget. Standard costs, which are composed of two components (a standard measurement unit and a unit cost), can be used in determining the production and inventory quantity requirements and in costing the requirements. The department overhead budgets are essential to the development and evaluation of manufacturing overhead rates as discussed in the section of this chapter on manufacturing overhead.

(iii) Measurement of Production Capabilities. A summary of operation requirements based on standard operating hours can assist in identifying production capabilities and/or constraints. The identification of potential production constraints will directly affect the capital investment budgeting process (see Chapter 19); the identification of excess capacity may affect management decisions to add a new product or product line or to increase marketing efforts for an existing product line.

(iv) Valuing Inventory and Determining the Cost of Sales. Generally accepted accounting principles (GAAP) recognize the acceptance of the FIFO, average, LIFO, and reverse mark-up procedure (normally associated with retail accounting) of inventory costing. However, the accounting profession recognizes that standard costs are acceptable (for inventory costing) if adjusted at reasonable intervals so that at the balance sheet date standard costs reasonably approximate costs computed under one of the recognized bases.

(v) Cost Estimating. Standard costs are often used for cost estimating subject to the following revisions:

- Standard material costs are adjusted to expected or current purchase price.
- Standard labor costs are adjusted for expected wage increases.
- Manufacturing overhead rates are adjusted to meet the production volume at levels greater or less than budgeted (expected).
- Depreciation included in the overhead rate utilized for cost-estimating purposes may be based on replacement cost.

The standard quantities identified on the bill of material and the operation times (machine or labor) can be used for cost estimating for existing products or for products with slight modifications or enhancements.

(d) Successful Standard-Cost Systems. The major elements of a successful standard-cost system can be judged using these six criteria:

1. Standards must reflect current economic, production, and product-design (structure) considerations.
2. Standards should be attainable.
3. Operating managers should be responsible only for those costs that they control. Managers must believe that the cost-accounting system is providing reliable and relevant data.
4. Significant variances from standards should be reported in a timely manner and properly investigated as to the reason for the variances.
5. The system should not overburden production personnel with cumbersome paperwork.
6. The standard-cost system should be integrated with the manufacturing budget process.

Although these concepts are fairly self-evident, they are presented to stress their importance. The exclusion of any of these elements could make the system ineffective.

(e) Setting Standard Costs. Standard costs are composed of two components: a standard measurement unit and a unit cost. The components of a standard cost, the means of documenting the standards, and the source for developing the information are illustrated in Exhibit 6.27.

(i) Material. The bill of material identifying the product structure (quantity requirements) should include acceptable levels of waste, spoilage, shrinkage, and so forth. The

Component	Document	Source
Quantity of material	Bill of material	Engineering specifications
Material unit cost	Purchasing records	Vendor/purchasing analysis
Operation times	Process routings	Industrial engineering studies
Wage rate	Payroll records	Labor agreements
Overhead rate	Overhead rate determination process	Budget system

Exhibit 6.27. Standard-cost components

standard material unit cost should be the expected purchase price reflecting economic volume purchases from vendors who will fulfill delivery schedules and quality requirements. Normally, the cost includes inbound freight, if significant.

The standard material unit cost is normally set for a prescribed period, such as one year. As such, the price should reflect anticipated price increases or decreases during the period under consideration.

(ii) Labor/Machine Operating Times. Operating standards can be determined based on nonengineered or engineered work-measurement techniques. The various alternative procedures are illustrated in Exhibit 6.28.

(iii) Wage Rates. Standard wage rates are established during the budget process. The procedures for determining the standard wage rate are identical to the procedures used to determine the actual wage rate, as illustrated in Exhibit 6.24. The rate should include adjustments for any incentive pay based on contracted efficiencies. For effective cost control, the standard wage rate should indicate the skill level required to perform the operation. It would be expected that the greater the fluctuation in skill (and pay) levels within a manufacturing organization, the greater the need to develop wage rates for each specific operation type or work center.

(iv) Overhead Rates. Manufacturing overhead rates are predetermined rates usually established during the budget process. The procedures for setting overhead are discussed in the section of this chapter on manufacturing overhead. These rates are applied to product cost based on the standard bases of manufacturing activity, such as labor hours or machine hours.

6.12 VARIANCE REPORTING.

A key difference between an actual cost-accounting system and a standard cost-accounting system is the recognition of variances from standards. The ability to distinguish between what should occur (standards) and what actually occurred by way of variance reporting is essential to cost control. There are several major variances; some of the more common ones are illustrated in Exhibit 6.29. The computations of the more common variances are identified in Exhibit 6.30.

(a) Material Variances.

The *material price variance* is normally recorded at the time of purchase (alternatively, it may be recorded when the materials are used); all subsequent inventory transactions are recorded at the standard unit cost. If the actual unit price paid for an inventory item is greater than or less than the standard cost, a price variance occurs. Significant price variances should be investigated. (This is why the price variance should

A. Nonengineered work-measurement techniques

1. One-man standard. A person is timed by wristwatch while performing a job on several occasions. This technique is useful when trying new methods, improvement ideas, and work-flow alterations.
2. Time ladders. This method accounts for a person's time during the day and is most useful on long-cycle, relatively low-volume tasks, where interruptions are likely to occur and confuse other methods of establishing standards. This method is frequently used for establishing office clerical standards.
3. Historical standard data. This method bases standards on results previously achieved. It shows how long it actually took to perform specific jobs, but not how long it should have taken.

B. Engineered work-measurement techniques

1. Work sampling. This is a statistical technique using random sampling of what a person is doing and when he or she is idle. The output is divided by the active time to establish a labor standard. This process is not recommended for specific task elements in which relatively precise measurement of task elemental time is required.
2. Time (stopwatch) study. Time standards applicable to any form of human or mechanical effort may be established by either of two methods using a stopwatch:
   - **a.** Job study consists of measuring the time required to perform an operation and using this operation time plus a standard allowance for delays and personal needs as the standard time for that job.
   - **b.** Elemental standards development consists of measuring the time required for each work element contained in an operation on a part or a product, collecting and tabulating similar information for other parts and operations, deriving a time value for each element from these data, and establishing an operation or job standard by adding together the element times so developed. Additionally, an allowance for delays and personal needs is provided.
3. Predetermined time standards. Methods–time measurement (MTM) is the most widely accepted of the predetermined time systems. It is well suited to measurement of highly repetitive short-cycle operations because it demands close analysis of work motions. The time required to establish standards, however, may be longer and more costly than with time study.
4. Standard data for determining various types of machine cycles are available from published engineering guides and textbooks. Standard data also can be prepared for operations unique to a plant by using time study, MTM, or some other method. This method's advantage is the relative ease of applying standard data.

Exhibit 6.28. Procedures for setting labor/machine time standards

be generated at the time of purchase). Although it is the normal procedure to hold the purchasing department responsible for price variances, the underlying reason for the variance could be attributable to a multitude of factors. For instance, a rush order or abnormal expediting by production scheduling may affect the purchasing function. Purchasing may have to expedite materials delivery, thereby incurring excess freight costs and/or loss of quantity discounts. The price variance may be only a manifestation of problems occurring in other manufacturing departments.

The *material usage variance* represents the difference between the actual quantity of material issued to production for a specified product, order, or operation and the standard quantity specified. Often, material is issued to a production order or to a work center based on the standard quantity requirements indicated on the bill of material (or prior production records). Any material in excess of the original issue is often requisitioned on a separate requisition card and is specifically identified as "excess" usage. A periodic summary of excess usage provides the total of the usage variance. To be an effective cost-

Variance	Purpose	Recorded
Material		
Price	Impact of price increases or decreases on profitability	Purchase
Usage	Effective direct use of material in production	Issue to production
Substitution	Substitution of alternative material(s)	Issue to production
Labor		
Rate	Skill-level utilization	Operation performed
Efficiency	Relative productivity	Operation completed
Manufacturing Overhead		
Spending	Control over spending level based on actual activity	End of an accounting (budget) period
Variable efficiency	Efficient use of production facilities	End of an accounting (budget) period
Fixed efficiency	Effective employment of available capacity	End of an accounting (budget) period
Idle capacity	Cost of not operating at capacity	End of an accounting (budget) period

Exhibit 6.29. Standard-cost variances

Variance	Computation
Material	
Price	(Actual unit cost less standard unit cost) × actual units
Usage	(Actual quantity less standard quantity) × standard unit cost
Labor	
Rate	(Actual rate less standard rate) × actual hours worked
Efficiency	(Actual hours less standard hours) × standard rate
Overhead	
Spending	Actual manufacturing overhead less budgeted expenses based on actual hours
Variable efficiency	Budgeted overhead (based on actual hours) less budgeted overhead (based on standard hours)
Fixed efficiency	(Actual hours × predetermined fixed overhead rate) less (standard hours × predetermined fixed overhead rate)
Idle capacity	(Budgeted capacity hours × predetermined fixed overhead rate) less (actual hours × predetermined fixed overhead rate)

Exhibit 6.30. Common variance computation methods

control document, the usage variance should identify the product or process and the area or individual responsible for the variance.

(b) Labor Variances. Direct labor is charged to production based on standard hours multiplied by the standard wage rate. The difference between the actual dollars paid for direct labor operations performed and the amount charged to production is composed of two major variances: wage rate and efficiency (productivity).

(c) Wage Rate Variances. Since wage rates are normally based on contractual or prior agreements, wage rate variances would not be frequent in nature. However, if standard rates have been established for skill levels, such as operation or work center, rate variances would occur under the following conditions:

- The operation(s) is performed by an employee with a different skill (and play) level than required (standard).
- The skill rating is changed for specified operations without a change in the standard rate.
- Wage rate increases made during the period exceed or are less than rates used to establish standards.

(i) Efficiency (Productivity) Variances. The determination of the productivity variance is based on a comparison of actual direct labor hours reported and the standard hours required to perform the operation. An effective standard-cost system records the productivity variance upon operation completion and provides daily and weekly departmental variance reports. The hourly productivity variance is then summarized at the end of the reporting (accounting) period.

The productivity variance indicates the relative efficiency of labor production efforts. The cause of the variance may be the result of actions and/or problems beyond the control of the operator or department incurring the variance. Potential causes of variance could be as follows:

- Expediting activities are interfering with planned operations.
- Defective material is causing unusual manufacturing operations, assembly, and other problems.
- Personnel are being trained, do not have the appropriate skills, and/or are not properly supervised.
- Actual production operations as performed are not as documented (as used to determine standard operating hours).

The productivity variance indicates that production efforts are not being performed efficiently; appropriate investigation is necessary to determine why the variance occurred.

(d) Manufacturing Overhead Variances. Regardless of whether a standard- or actual-cost system is selected, manufacturing overhead is applied to product cost based on a predetermined rate. The predetermined overhead rate times the actual production level is applied to product cost with an actual-cost system; a standard-cost system applies overhead based on earned (standard) production levels.[4]

The following data are used to illustrate the computation techniques for analyzing the difference (variance) between actual manufacturing overhead costs and the amount applied to product cost during an accounting period:

---

[4] It should be noted that fixed manufacturing overhead is not applied when direct costing is used. It is charged off as a current period expense.

The *overapplied/underapplied manufacturing overhead* is the difference between the total of all costs charged to manufacturing overhead accounts and the amount applied to production, computed as follows:

Total manufacturing overhead (actual)	$20,480
Less manufacturing overhead applied	
(5,000 earned hours × $4.00)	20,000
Overhead variance (debit)	$ 480

The accounting entry to apply overhead to production would be:

Work-in-process inventory	20,000	
Manufacturing overhead applied		20,000

To close out the remaining balance (credit) in the manufacturing overhead control account, a classification and identification of the variance must be made using the techniques described in the paragraphs to follow. For practical purposes, many companies group all variances in the overapplied/underapplied overhead account. A separate analysis of the types of variances is provided to management as a supplemental report to the operating statements.

The *spending variance* is the difference between the actual overhead costs and the budgeted amount based on the actual hours reported. As a practical matter, the spending variance is composed of differences in the budget variable application rate and the actual application rate. Before any judgment is made regarding the spending variance, a careful review should be made of the reliability of the variable overhead rate.

Spending variance is computed as follows:

Actual manufacturing overhead		$20,480
Less budgeted at actual hours		
Fixed cost	10,500	
Variable cost (5,200 reported hours × $2.25 variable rate)	11,700	22,200
Spending variance (credit)		$1,720

The spending variance can be further identified as a budget that is $2,500 under in fixed cost and $780 over in variable cost. The variable spending variance is normally considered the responsibility of the department supervisor; the fixed spending variance is the responsibility of the supervisor or manager having control over discretionary and committed costs.

The *variable efficiency variance* is a relative indication of the cost of not maintaining efficient operations. It is computed as follows:

Variable budget allowance based on actual reported hours	$11,700
Less variable costs applied to production	
(5,000 earned hours × $2.25 variable rate)	11,250
Variable efficiency variance (debit)	$ 450

The *fixed efficiency variance* is a measure of the effective use of plant and equipment. It is computed as follows:

5,200 actual hours × \$1.75 fixed rate	\$9,100
Less 5,000 earned hours × \$1.75 fixed rate	8,750
Fixed efficiency variance (debit)	\$ 350

The *idle capacity variance* represents the cost of unused capacity based on the budgeted level of operations. For budgeting and accounting purposes, the idle capacity variance represents the difference between the budgeted activity base used in establishing the fixed rate and the actual hours reported. It is computed as follows:

6,000 expected hours × \$1.75 fixed rate	\$10,500
5,200 reported hours × \$1.75 fixed rate	9,100
Idle capacity variance (debit)	\$ 1,400

The excess of actual manufacturing overhead to applied overhead can be summarized as follows:

Spending (credit)	\$(1,720)
Variable efficiency	450
Fixed efficiency	350
Idle capacity	1,400
Underapplied manufacturing overhead	\$480

6.13 VARIANCES AND BUDGETING. Variances represent exceptions from standards and budgeted manufacturing costs. To control manufacturing operations and costs effectively, variances must be analyzed. The computation techniques provided in this chapter identify the type of variance; however, it is necessary to determine why the variance occurred, what functional area or department could have controlled the variance, and what actions are necessary to prevent the variance from occurring in the future.

A properly designed standard-cost system will collect the cost-accounting information from the lowest control level and provide the data required for summary reporting of actual results to budget. Significant variances at the summary level can be investigated by determining the applicable department(s) or product(s) responsible for the variance. If further information is required, the cost-accounting system should be able to provide the specific control point, such as an operation or work center. The depth of the analysis would be contingent on the relative magnitude of the problem as well as the level within the organization responsible for control. A schematic of the variance identification and analysis is depicted in Exhibit 6.31.

6.14 MANUFACTURING OVERHEAD. Both standard- and actual-cost systems require the determination of a manufacturing overhead rate to apply to product cost. The key difference is that an actual-cost system applies the rate to product cost based on actual activity; standard cost applies overhead based on the standard (earned) activity level.

The 14 steps and decisions required in determining and analyzing overhead rates are as follows:

1. Determine variable- and fixed-cost categories.
2. Select departments to include in manufacturing costs. (For discussion purposes,

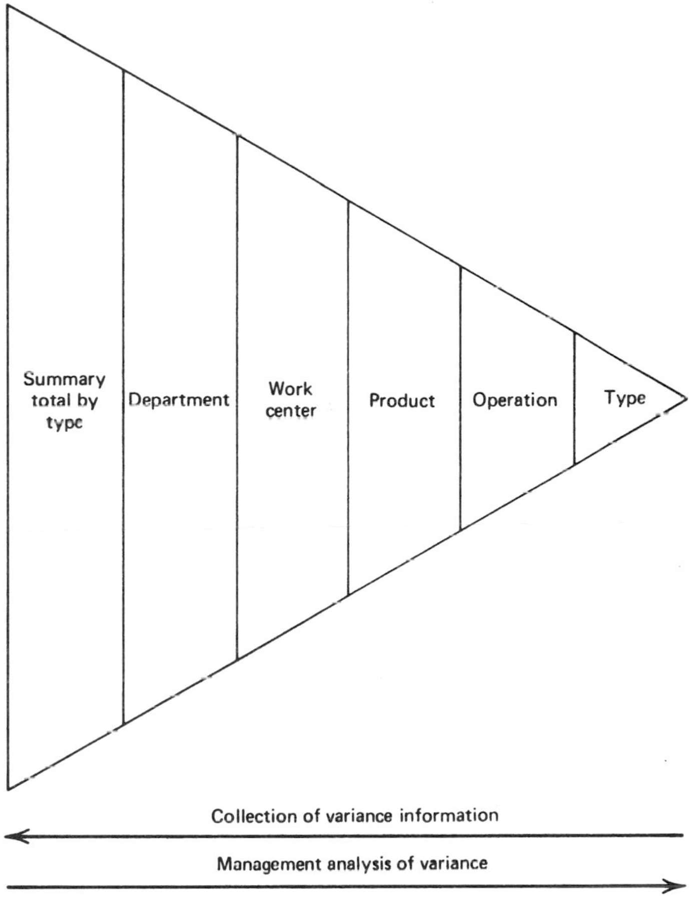

Exhibit 6.31. Variance identification and analysis

a *department* represents the lowest operating level with budget and operational responsibilities.)

3. Budget controllable expenses by department.
4. Budget indirect expenses.
5. Develop and collect statistics to allocate indirect expenses to departments based on causal relationships.
6. Allocate indirect expenses to manufacturing departments.
7. Redistribute service department costs to production departments.
8. Select appropriate base to assign overhead to product cost.
9. Determine activity level.
10. Calculate overhead rates.
11. Assign overhead to product cost.
12. Compare actual manufacturing overhead to budgets and to manufacturing applied.
13. Analyze overhead variances.

14. Provide variance analyses data to management.

Steps 1 through 6 are normally performed during the budget process; steps 7 through 10 are necessary for converting budget data to predetermined overhead rates. Steps 11 through 14 are completed at the end of each accounting period. The various overhead rate options available are depicted in Exhibit 6.24. The options selected may have a significant impact on overhead rates and therefore on product cost.

The steps necessary to convert department budgets to a manufacturing overhead rate are not necessary for responsibility budgeting; the procedures are necessary only so that (1) indirect manufacturing costs can be charged to a product and (2) the analyses of overhead variances provide management with summary information on the manufacturing operation.

(a) Converting Budgets to Overhead Rates

(i) Steps 1–6. The manufacturing overhead budget identifies the expenses that are directly controlled (or influenced) by the appropriate operating level of the organization (steps 1–3), as discussed in other chapters. Costs such as payroll fringe benefits, building depreciation, and utilities cannot be directly assigned to a department; however, they can be assigned to each department based on either benefits received or a causal relationship. The various procedures for allocating indirect expenses are numerous and can be grouped into the following general classifications:

- Payroll/labor
- Consumption level
- Space
- Investment value
- Activity level

For instance, payroll fringe benefits are normally allocated on the basis of payroll dollars or hours[5]; building depreciation is often allocated on the basis of department size (square feet). In practice, the selection of the appropriate allocation statistic must be based on the ability to obtain the appropriate statistic as well as on the materiality of the expense to be allocated.

(ii) Step 7. The manufacturing operation is usually organized along functional lines. Departments responsible for direct production are organized according to similarity and/or location; departments providing service to the direct production departments are normally organized according to functional responsibilities. The actual department classifications do not have to adhere to the classifications used for budgeting. The departments used for setting overhead rates may be larger or smaller than the number required for budgeting. The reliability of the overhead rate(s) and the effort required to evaluate actual results of operations should be the determining factors in the final selection process.

Since manufacturing overhead rates are calculated for production departments only,

[5] Where payroll fringe benefits are substantial in regard to payroll, they are frequently considered to be part of the direct payroll cost rather than as an overhead item.

service department costs must be redistributed to production departments based on a causal relationship or on measurable benefits received. There are three redistribution methods available: direct, sequential, and cross-allocation.

Using the direct allocation method, the direct costs of a service department are allocated directly to production departments only, with no allocations made to other service departments. No redistribution of total service department costs are required. This is the simplest method, but it is the least accurate; it does not recognize the interdependence among service departments.

Sequential allocation methods recognize the interdependence of service departments. The sequential allocation begins with the service department's providing the most universally used services being redistributed to all other departments. The total costs (direct and redistributed) of the service department next most widely used are redistributed next and so on. This method is demonstrated in Exhibit 6.32.

The cross-allocation method recognizes the interdependence of service departments. Each service department is charged with a portion of the costs of each of the other service departments from which it receives benefits. The redistributions are determined simultaneously. This is the most accurate method, but it may require the use of special "multiple apportionment" computer programs.

(iii) Step 8. The selection of the base for activity depends on the activity that determines (measures) production effort and cost relationships.

Several bases may be used by way of supplementary rate procedures. For example, payroll fringe benefits may be computed based on direct labor dollars or hours; indirect material costs on material usage and machine-related costs such as depreciation, machine maintenance, and so forth can be allocated to production based on machine hours. The degree of cost accuracy and the significance of total product cost differences using supplementary rates should be weighed against the cost and time required to develop and monitor the rates. Various alternative bases for applying overhead rates are detailed in Exhibit 6.24.

(iv) Step 9. There are four levels that may be used for estimating production activity levels: theoretical, practical, normal, and expected (budgeted).

Theoretical capacity represents maximum efficiency with no allowance for normal downtime. Using this procedure, the applied overhead will always be less than actual overhead. Use of this activity level implies that any production at less than "100%" utilization represents idle capacity costs and should be charged against current income.

Practical capacity is a measure of manufacturing activity that includes an allowance for normal machine setup, maintenance, and idle time. Practical capacity is a more realistic appraisal of maximum production capabilities.

Normal capacity considers the utilization of plant and equipment required to meet average production demands over a period long enough to level out the production peaks and valleys. Often, normal capacity is used in the determination of the fixed overhead rates.

Expected capacity represents the capacity required to meet current production levels based on budgeted sales and inventory levels. The expected level is used in establishing variable overhead rates.

The capacity level used to set overhead rate(s) must be considered in the analysis of the overapplied/underapplied overhead.

Description	Fixed (F) or Variable (V)	Total Manufacturing Budget	Production Departments: Special Assembly	General Assembly	Machining	Service Departments: Manufacturing Administration	Maintenance	Industrial Engineering	Production/ Inventory Control	Budget Bases
Indirect Labor										
Supervision	F	$ 317,840	$ 16,400	$ 51,350	$ 47,100	$100,890	$ 40,700	$ 18,300	$ 43,100	Direct charge
Other indirect	F	202,300	19,800	45,600	29,300	—	39,400	53,400	14,800	Direct charge
Rework	V	28,950	6,640	12,450	9,860	—	—	—	—	Direct charge
		549,090	42,840	109,400	86,260	100,890	80,100	71,700	57,900	
Payroll-Related Costs										
Vacation and holiday	V	93,405	19,320	36,240	28,695	—	3,350	4,540	1,260	Direct charge
Overtime premium	V	27,325	5,680	10,655	8,440	—	1,180	1,070	300	Direct charge
Pension plan	V	83,410	14,146	29,175	24,755	7,073	5,304	4,421	3,536	Total salaries and wages
Group insurance	V	142,145	27,008	51,172	41,222	5,686	7,107	5,686	4,264	Number of employees
Workers compensation	V	34,205	5,473	11,288	9,577	2,736	2,053	1,710	1,368	Total salaries and wages
Payroll taxes	V	127,200	20,352	41,976	35,616	10,176	7,632	6,360	5,088	Total salaries and wages
		$512,690	91,979	180,506	148,305	25,671	26,626	23,787	15,816	

Other Variable Costs										
Power	V	78,800	18,124	33,884	26,792	—	—	—	—	Rated machine consumption
Supplies	V	8,930	2,050	3,840	3,040	—	—	—	—	Direct charge
Perishable tools	V	131,370	30,360	56,375	44,635	—	—	—	—	Direct charge
		219,100	50,534	94,099	74,467	—	—	—	—	
Fixed Discretionary Costs										
Employee education	F	12,400	900	250	550	3,400	350	5,150	1,800	Direct charge
Equipment rental	F	6,900	3,820	90	2,120	70	—	800	—	Direct charge
		19,300	4,720	340	2,670	3,470	350	5,950	1,800	
Fixed Committed Costs										
Building depreciation	F	20,330	2,440	5,896	7,929	1,830	1,218	610	407	Building square feet
Machine depreciation	F	46,000	10,000	13,000	23,000	—	—	—	—	Direct charge
Property taxes	F	68,500	15,070	19,865	33,565	—	—	—	—	Material charge
General insurance	F	67,700	8,124	19,633	26,403	6,093	4,062	2,031	1,354	Building square feet
		202,530	35,634	58,394	90,897	7,923	5,280	2,641	1,761	
Total		$1,502,710	$225,707	$442,739	$402,599	$137,954	$112,356	$104,078	$77,277	

Exhibit 6.32. ABC Manufacturing Company manufacturing expense budget (December 31, 19XX)

(v) Step 10. The procedure for determining the overhead rates is illustrated in Exhibits 6.32 through 6.34.

(vi) Steps 11–14. These are completed at the end of the accounting period. Examples of the worksheets required to determine overapplied/underapplied overhead and the accounting entries are provided in the ABC Manufacturing Company. ABC Manufacturing has three production departments—special assembly, general assembly, and machining—and four service departments—manufacturing administration, maintenance, industrial engineering, and production/inventory control. The department classification corresponds to the organization chart of the company. Based on an analysis of indirect costs, the company has decided to allocate these costs to each department based on the data collected during the budget process. ABC Manufacturing Company uses the sequential allocation method of redistributing service department costs to production departments. The company uses full costing for inventory valuation (overhead rates); however, flexible budgeting is used in evaluating department performance. Additionally, variable data are monitored and provided to management. Direct labor hours and machine hours are used to recover overhead costs (and therefore are used to set overhead rates).

(b) Actual Manufacturing Overhead. Direct manufacturing expenses are charged to the department responsible for the expense; indirect expenses such as fringe benefits are initially recorded in a pooled/indirect expense category. At the end of an accounting period, these indirect expenses are allocated to both production and service departments based on the actual statistics accumulated during the period. Additionally, the service department actual expenses are redistributed to the production departments.

For illustration purposes, the ABC Manufacturing Company maintains the following:

- Subsidiary activity ledgers for each production and service department
- Separate subsidiary ledger for each pooled/indirect expense
- Control accounts in the pooled/indirect expenses subsidiary ledger for allocations to production and service departments
- Control accounts in the general ledger to post summary totals of production department expenses to include allocations of pooled/indirect and service department reallocations
- Control accounts in the general ledger to apply manufacturing overhead to the cost of production (work-in-process inventory)

Exhibit 6.35 illustrates the procedures for determining the overapplied/underapplied manufacturing overhead. Although not illustrated in this example, a manufacturing expense report comparing year-to-date actual results of operations to operating budgets is prepared for each department. The actual statistics accumulated during the period are illustrated in Exhibit 6.36.

(c) Accounting Procedures. During an accounting period, the manufacturing overhead rate is applied to production (work in process) based on the data supplied by a production report, labor-machine report, or customer-factory order. Regardless of the procedure(s) used to accumulate the base to apply overhead, the amounts must be periodically

Description	Total Manufacturing Budget	Production: Special Assembly	Production: General Assembly	Production: Machining	Service: Manufacturing Administration	Service: Maintenance	Service: Industrial Engineering	Service: Production/ Inventory Control	Budget Basis
Total overhead manufacturing budget before redistribution	$ 1,502.710	$ 225,707	$ 442,739	$ 402,599	$ 137,954	$ 112,356	$ 104,078	$ 77,277	
Redistributions: manufacturing administration		26,211	52,423	42,766	$(137,954)	6,897	5,518	4,139	Number of employees
Maintenance		16,695	41,739	54,856		$(119,253)	3,578	2,385	Building square feet
Industrial engineering		26,030	48,665	38,479			$(113,174)	—	Direct labor hours
Production/inventory control		18,436	24,302	41,063				$(83,801)	Material usage
Total service department redistributions		87,372	167,129	177,164					
Total	$ 1,502,710	313.079	609,868	579.763					
Bases									
Direct labor hours		33.030	61,950						
Machine hours				25,000					
		$ 9.48	$ 9.85	$ 23.19					

Exhibit 6.33. ABC Manufacturing Company calculation of manufacturing overhead rates

	Direct Labor		Direct Labor		Total Salaries and Wages[a]		Employees		Materials		Building Square Feet		Rated Machine Consumption[b]		Machine Hours	
Departments	Hours	%	Dollars	%	Dollars	%	Number	%	Usage[b]	%	Feet	%	Units	%	Hours	%
Production																
Special assembly	33,030	23%	$168,453	21%	$ 211,293	16%	23	19%	$1,875,000	22%	4,406	12%	9,640	23%	—	—
General assembly	61,950	43	328,335	42	437,735	33	45	36	2,540,000	29	10,885	29	18,085	43	—	—
Machining	49,050	34	291,848	37	378,108	28	36	29	4,290,000	49	14,292	39	14,313	34	25,000	100%
Service																
Manufacturing administration	—	—	—	—	100,890	8	5	4	—	—	3,369	9	—	—	—	—
Maintenance	—	—	—	—	80,100	6	6	5	—	—	2,258	6	—	—	—	—
Industrial engineering	—	—	—	—	71,700	5	5	4	—	—	963	3	—	—	—	—
Production/inventory control	—	—	—	—	57,900	4	4	3	—	—	852	2	—	—	—	—
Total	144,030	100%	$788,636	100%	$1,337,726	100%	124	100%	$8,705,000	100%	37,025	100%	42,038	100%	25,000	100%

[a] Total of indirect and direct labor.
[b] Based on production budget.

Exhibit 6.34. ABC Manufacturing Company budget statistics (December 31, 19XX)

Description	Total Manufacturing Expense	Production: Special Assembly	Production: General Assembly	Production: Machining	Service: Manufacturing Administration	Service: Maintenance	Service: Industrial Engineering	Service: Production/ Inventory Control	Budget Bases
Total manufacturing expense before redistribution	$ 136,070	$ 20,520	$ 41,400	$ 36,800	$ 11,550	$ 10,300	$ 9,050	$ 6,450	Direct and allocated pooled/indirect expenses
Redistributions									
Manufacturing administration	—	2,030	4,330	3,660	(11,550)	580	580	370	Number of employees
Maintenance	—	1,525	3,770	4,950		(10,880)	330	305	Building square feet
Industrial engineering	—	2,285	4,275	3,400			(9,960)	—	Direct labor hours
Production/inventory control	—	1,515	2,045	3,565				$(7,125)	Material usage
Total service department redistributions		7,355	14,420	15,575					
Total	$ 136,070	$ 27,875	$ 55,820	$ 52,375					
Total applied manufacturing overhead	$ 133,849	$ 28,535	$ 55,456	$ 49,858					
Overapplied/(Underapplied) manufacturing overhead	$ (2,221)	$ 660	$ (364)	$ (2,517)					

Exhibit 6.35. ABC Manufacturing Company redistributions of actual service department costs and calculation of overapplied/(underapplied) manufacturing overhead (period ended January 31, 19XX)

	Employees		Building Square Feet		Earned Direct Labor		Standard Material Usage		Machine Hours	
	Number	%	Feet	%	Hours	%	Unit	%	Hours	%
Production										
Special assembly	22	18%	4,406	12%	3,010	23%	170,900	21%	—	—
General assembly	45	36	10,885	29	5,630	43	230,900	29	—	—
Machining	38	30	14,292	39	4,480	34	402,000	50	2,150	100%
Service										
Manufacturing administration	5	4	3,369	9	—	—	—	—	—	—
Maintenance	6	5	2,258	6	—	—	—	—	—	—
Industrial engineering	5	4	963	3	—	—	—	—	—	—
Production/inventory control	4	3	852	2	—	—	—	—	—	—
	125	100%	37,025	100%	13,120	100%	803,800	100%	2,150	100%

[a] Statistics required for redistribution of support departments only.

Exhibit 6.36. ABC Manufacturing Company manufacturing statistics (January 31, 19XX)

summarized and entered into the general ledger. The entry to record the applied manufacturing overhead for the ABC Manufacturing Company would be as follows:

Work in process	$133,849	
Manufacturing overhead applied—special assembly (3,010 earned hours at $9.48 per hour)		$28,535
Manufacturing overhead applied—general assembly (5,630 earned hours at $9.85 per hour)		$55,456
Manufacturing overhead applied—machining (2,150 machine hours at $23.19 per hour)		$49,858

The control account balances for the manufacturing departments would be as follows:

Special assembly—control	$27,875
General assembly—control	$55,820
Machining—control	$52,375
Total	$136,070

A comparison of actual manufacturing expenses incurred and the amount applied to production results in an underapplied overhead (actual manufacturing overhead in excess of amount applied) of $2,221. The variance between actual and applied should be categorized, using computations illustrated in the section on manufacturing overhead variance in this chapter.

6.15 MANUFACTURING OVERHEAD, BUDGETING, AND COST CONTROL.

Overhead rates are necessary for product costing, product profitability evaluation, and evaluation of gross variances from budgets. An effective cost-accounting system depends upon effective budgeting and cost-control systems. Manufacturing overhead variances (spending and efficiency) provide gross measurements of how well manufacturing supervisors are controlling costs. Additionally, the fixed efficiency and idle capacity variances, as discussed previously, provide management with an analytical tool in measuring the effective use of plant and equipment. The activity level of operations as measured by these variances provides management with data necessary for directing marketing efforts, introducing new products or product lines, scheduling existing orders through production, identifying work-center bottlenecks, and so forth.

For instance, underutilized capacity in a certain department or product line, as measured by an idle capacity ''unfavorable'' variance, would affect the decision to search for products or additional orders to utilize excess capacity. A ''favorable'' idle capacity variance (actual production in excess of normal or practical capacity) may indicate that additional equipment or additional shifts are required.

A well-designed cost-accounting system not only will provide product cost data necessary for inventory valuation and cost of sales determination but also will incorporate responsibility budgeting and reporting and affect profit-planning strategies.

SOURCES AND SUGGESTED REFERENCES

Cokins, Gary, *Activity-Based Cost Management Making It Work: A Manager's Guide to Implementing and Sustaining an Effective ABC System.* Irwin Professional Publications, 1996.

Forrest, Edward, *Activity-Based Management: A Comprehensive Implementation Guide.* Irwin Professional Publications, 1996.

Horngren, Charles T., et al., *Cost Accounting: A Managerial Emphasis* (9th ed.). Prentice Hall Series, 1996.

Lewis, Ronald J., *Activity-Based Models for Cost Management Systems.* Westport, CT: Quorum Books, 1994.

Mellman, Martin, et al., *Accounting for Effective Decision Making: A Manager's Guide to Corporate, Financial, and Cost Reporting.* Irwin Professional Publications, 1994.

Polimeni, Ralph S., et al., *Product Costing Concepts and Applications* (2nd ed.). McGraw-Hill Companies, Inc., 1998.

Reeve, James M., *Readings and Issues in Cost Management.* South-Western Publications, 1995.

Shank, John K., *Cases in Cost Management: A Strategic Emphasis.* South-Western Publications, 1996.

CHAPTER 7

BREAK-EVEN AND CONTRIBUTION ANALYSIS AS A TOOL IN BUDGETING

Jay H. Loevy

7.1 INTRODUCTION. The budgeting process is the manager's primary tool for dealing with future uncertainty. In developing a period budget, managers must make certain assumptions of cause and effect: "Unit sales will increase 10% because of overall demand for the product, assuming that sales prices can be held to a 5% increase." "Gross profit percentage can be maintained despite a 6% increase in purchase costs." "Sales demand will hold steady unless there is a war in Abyssinia."

Although they cannot do anything about Abyssinian affairs, managers can, to some degree, influence purchase costs, sales volume, and selling prices. How well they understand their relationship and the effect on the enterprise will largely determine the effectiveness of the business plan. This chapter describes the relationship of cost, volume, and price as well as certain techniques for integrating these considerations into the budgeting process.

7.2 BREAK-EVEN ANALYSIS. Perhaps the best way to understand the cost–volume–price relationship is to examine the technique commonly referred to as *break-even analysis.* The name is unfortunate. Except for certain situations, such as the start-up of a new business or the determination of when to pull the plug on losing operations, managers are not particularly interested in pinpointing break-even volume. The planning effort is directed toward maximizing profit, and where the break-even point happens to fall is academic. Nevertheless, the techniques used to determine break-even are useful, because they help us understand the interplay of cost, price, and volume.

There are two cost elements in break-even analysis: fixed costs and variable costs. These are illustrated in Exhibit 7.1. In this example, the fixed cost of $100 remains the same regardless of volume. The minute the doors are opened, $100 is incurred. Thus, at zero volume the chart indicates $100 of cost. The variable cost is $0.10 per unit. At a volume of 1,000 units, the total cost is $200, calculated as follows:

Fixed cost	$100
Variable cost: 1000 at $0.10 per unit	100
Total cost	$200

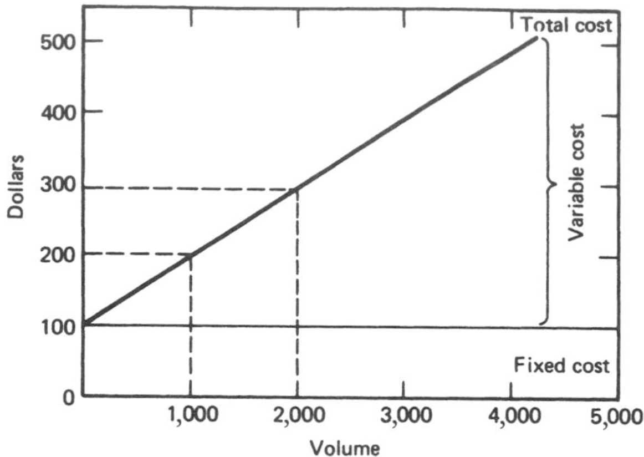

Exhibit 7.1. Break-even analysis

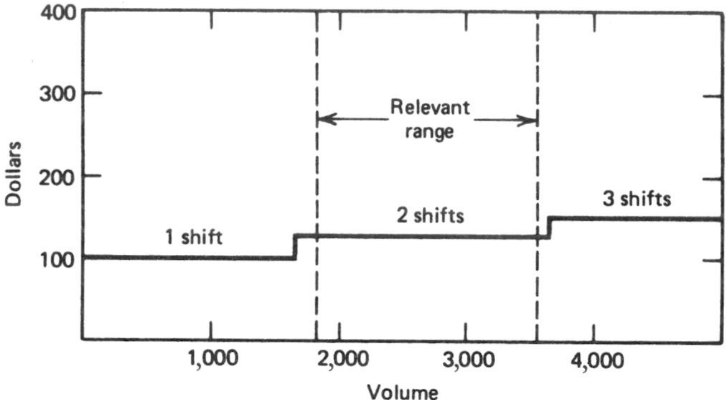

Exhibit 7.2. Relevant range

Doubling the volume to 2,000 units will add only $100 to total cost, since the fixed cost remains at $100.

This calculation, simple though it is, illustrates the basic functioning of costs. It lies at the heart of break-even analysis and contribution analysis.

Since the treatment of costs as fixed or variable is critical to the analysis, it will be useful to define and illustrate these terms.

(a) Fixed Costs. *Fixed costs* are those cost elements that are expected to remain at a constant level regardless of the volume of business. In reality, no cost is fixed forever. It is considered fixed only under a given set of conditions. For example, the fixed cost connected with a one-shift manufacturing operation would change if the company were to go to a two- or three-shift facility, since there would be added fixed costs for production-control personnel, plant management, foremen, certain utilities, and so forth. A fixed-cost line for each condition might appear as in Exhibit 7.2.

For planning purposes, it is necessary to deal only with those costs that are *relevant* to the planning horizon. In Exhibit 7.2, it is assumed that a two-shift operation will be used and that the expected production would be in the range of 1,850 to 3,500 units. This is termed the *relevant range.* The planner can normally ignore conditions outside that range.

In judging what costs are fixed, the planner must look beyond traditional labels. For example, direct labor is normally considered a variable cost. However, there is a printing plant that operates three shifts, six days per week, with a mandatory crew size on each press. The plant always has sufficient orders to operate at capacity. In this company, direct labor is considered a fixed element. The same could be true of a company that, as a matter of policy, does not lay off employees even if production is down. Within the relevant range, such costs are fixed.

These conditions notwithstanding, costs that are normally considered fixed in a manufacturing company would include rent, property taxes, building maintenance and insurance, administrative and supervisory salaries, depreciation, and so on.

(b) Variable Costs. Variable costs are those cost elements that are expected to vary in direct proportion to a volume indicator (e.g., units produced, service calls made, applicants processed). Variable costs are usually more difficult to identify than fixed costs, because there is often not a true linear relationship between volume and cost. Some costs tend to be variable over long periods but may not vary directly within one year. For example, it is not unusual to find that the cost of hand tools did not change appreciably from the prior year, even though there was a drop in annual production volume. This happened because there was a fixed element in the cost of hand tools: affected employees needed a full array of tools to do their jobs, regardless of the production volume processed at their station. That tools did not wear out as fast had less of an impact on the annual cost. Costs of this nature—and there are many of them—are actually *semivariable,* in that they are composed of both fixed and variable elements.

Since these elements usually cannot be identified with any great precision, and since such precision is not usually required in financial planning, it is common to classify as variable those costs that are more variable than fixed over the long term. Costs that are normally considered variable include direct labor, direct materials, sales commissions, freight, packing supplies, and so on.

(c) The Break-Even Chart. Exhibit 7.3 illustrates a break-even chart. It is composed of the fixed and variable cost lines shown on Exhibit 7.1 plus a sales line, which represents the linear relationship of units sold and the resulting sales dollars. The point at which the total cost and sales lines intersect (1,800 units/\$270) is the break-even point. Additional sales will produce a profit, whereas fewer sales will result in a loss. The difference between the expected sales volume of 2,500 units and the break-even volume of 1,800 units is termed the *margin of safety*. It is that number of units under the expected volume at which a profit could still be expected.

The break-even point can also be calculated by the following equation:

$$\text{Break-even sales} = \frac{\text{Total fixed costs}}{1 - \dfrac{\text{Total variable costs}}{\text{Total sales}}}$$

Using the figures from Exhibit 7.3, we have

$$\text{Break-even sales} = \frac{100}{1 - \dfrac{240}{380}}$$

$$= \frac{100}{0.37}$$

$$= \$270$$

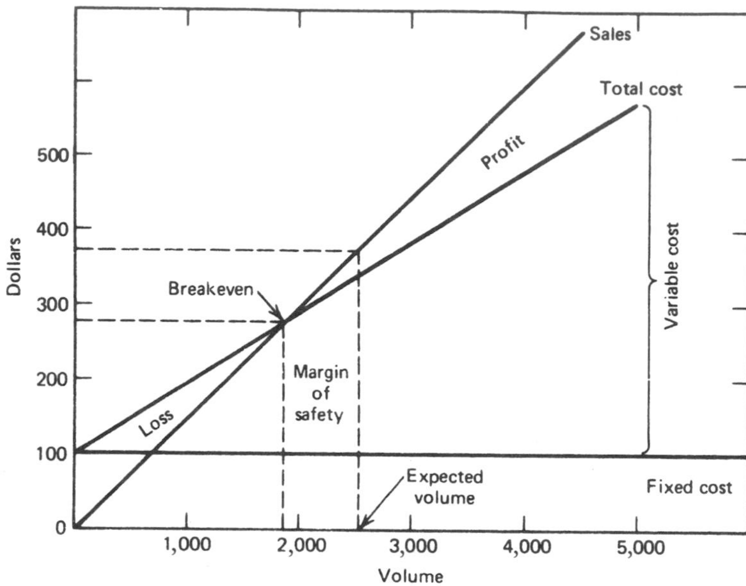

Exhibit 7.3. Break-even chart

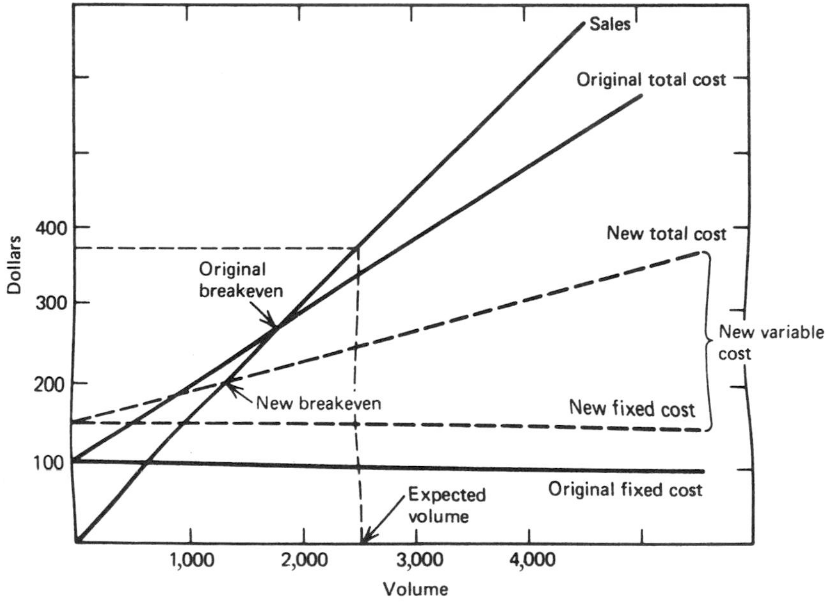

Exhibit 7.4. Change in break-even

Consider the effect on break-even of a company that wishes to modernize its plant. In so doing, the fixed costs are expected to rise 50% to $150 to cover additional depreciation and amortization of plant improvements. However, production throughput should also rise, causing a 20%, or $54, decrease in unit variable costs, primarily attributable to a reduction in direct labor per unit. The change in break-even is illustrated in Exhibit 7.4.

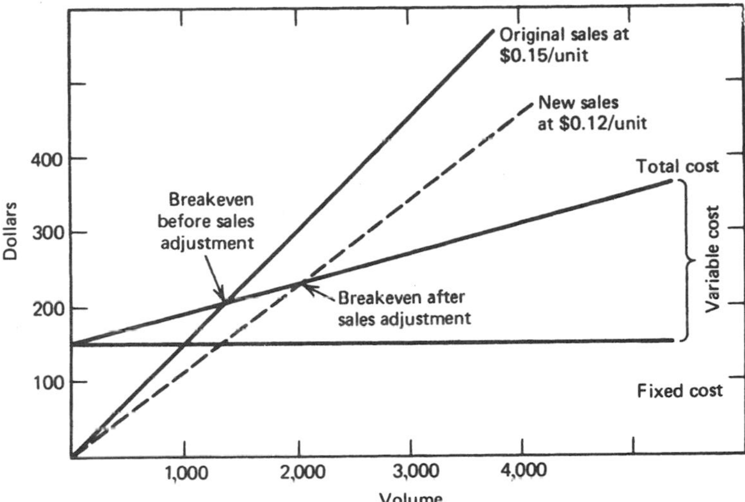

Exhibit 7.5. Anticipated pricing

The calculation of the new break-even is:

$$\text{Break-even sales} = \frac{150}{1 - \dfrac{100}{380}}$$

$$= \frac{150}{0.74}$$

$$= \$202$$

Further, because of advances in technology, the unit selling price in the company's industry is expected to decrease. Thus, to properly reflect anticipated pricing after the plant modernization, an adjustment is made to the slope of the sales line, as shown in Exhibit 7.5.

7.3 PRICE/VOLUME CHART. The manager is primarily interested in profits—the "bottom line." In the break-even charts that have been illustrated, profit is indicated by the gap between the sales and cost lines. A clearer presentation of profit is achieved by the price/volume chart, which is illustrated in Exhibit 7.6.

Here, the relationship of the fixed and variable cost and the sales lines are combined into a profit line. The starting point on the vertical axis indicates the amount of fixed costs ($100 and $150 in the examples). The slope of the line is determined by the amount of profit per unit of sales. The steeper the slope, the more profitable the sales. The three conditions of the break-even chart example are charted to illustrate the change in slope and profit using the price/volume chart.

7.4 CONTRIBUTION ANALYSIS. The preceding charts illustrate that each additional unit of sales reduces the loss until the break-even point is reached. Profits increase thereafter. Another way of looking at it is that the direct, or variable, profit on each unit of

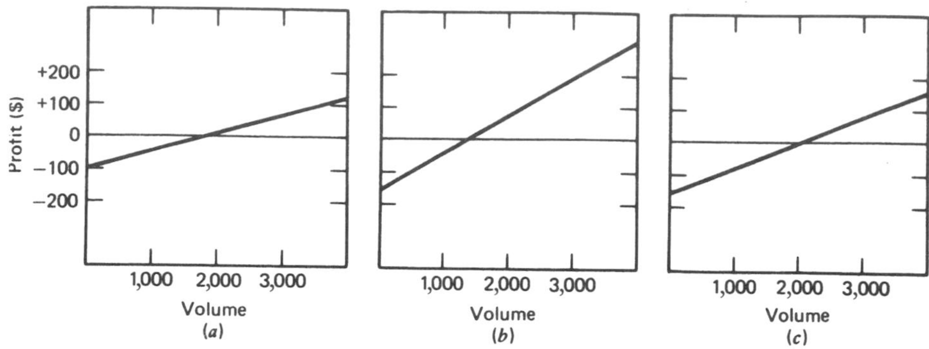

Exhibit 7.6. Price/volume charts

Traditional Method		
Sales		$1,000,000
Cost of sales		500,000
Gross profit		500,000
Selling expense	$250,000	
General and administrative expense	100,000	350,000
Income before tax		$150,000
Contribution Method		
Sales		$1,000,000
Variable costs		
Manufacturing	$200,000	
Selling	150,000	350,000
Contribution to fixed cost		650,000
Fixed manufacturing cost		300,000
Operating profit		350,000
Selling, general and administrative expense		200,000
Income before tax		$ 150,000

Exhibit 7.7. Comparison of methods presenting period income

sales "contributes" to the payment of fixed expenses. That is, the sales price less the variable cost yields a profit, the cumulative effect of which will, it is hoped, exceed the total fixed cost by a desired amount.

Such an approach was used to present period income in Exhibit 7.7. The "traditional" method presents manufacturing costs as one amount, whereas the contribution method separates fixed and variable components. Further, selling expense, traditionally shown below gross profit, is shown as a variable cost above the line on the contribution statement. Although income before tax remains the same, the effect of the contribution statement can be quite different. The fixed expenses represent a commitment on the part of company management. Operating managers have little control over such costs as depreciation, rent, insurance, and so forth, and thus their performance should usually not be measured by the levels of fixed costs. However, managers do have direct control over the variable manufacturing costs and should be measured by the effective use of such costs in the

	Current Policy	Raise Price 10%	Lower Price 5%	Lower Price 10%
Sales price per unit	$1.00	$1.10	$0.95	$0.90
Expected volume	1,000,000	900,000	1,100,000	1,250,000
Sales	$1,000,000	$990,000	$1,045,000	$1,125,000
Variable cost at $0.35	350,000	315,000	385,000	437,500
Contribution to fixed cost	$650,000	$675,000	$660,000	$687,500

Exhibit 7.8. Alternative pricing policies

manufacture of product. Likewise, sales managers control variable costs, such as commissions and travel expense, and their performance can be evaluated on the basis of cost per unit of sale. The identification of such variable costs as separate statement items permits such evaluation.

The contribution approach has great significance to budget managers as well, because it permits them to derive an optimum plan in which, for instance, alternative pricing policies are possible. It is axiomatic that in a normal market (i.e., one that is not heavily skewed to either buyers or sellers), volume will vary inversely with selling price. Increasing prices above the market level will normally reduce volume. A decrease in price should increase volume. Being able to quantify the effect on profits for alternate pricing policies enables budget managers to reach the optimum level. Contribution analysis is a tool to make this happen.

Consider the examples shown in Exhibit 7.8. Through market analysis or perhaps merely by "guesstimate," the budget manager determines the sales volume that would result from four alternative pricing policies. By applying variable costs per unit, the manager finds that lowering prices by 10% will yield the greater contribution and thus the greater net income, assuming fixed costs will remain fixed. (If fixed costs must be increased to produce the additional volume, the calculation must be extended to the operating profit line.)

The preceding example, although illustrative of a basic technique, does not reflect the typical company. Most business enterprises deal in many variations of a product—differing sizes, qualities, packaging—or even entirely different products manufactured at a common site. (One enterprise, for example, manufactures missile parts and furniture in the same plant.) In such situations, the determination of cost by product line and the resulting profitability become more difficult to calculate with accuracy. Normally, variable costs can be determined either through identification of materials and labor specifically used by product line or through the use of "engineered assumptions," or standards, to identify the variable costs that should be borne by a product or product line. However, there remains the problem of identifying the portion of fixed cost that a particular product or product line should bear.

Exhibit 7.9 illustrates how a different method of apportionment affects the conceived profit by product. The amounts shown as "direct fixed cost" are those that are identifiable by product line, such as depreciation on equipment, supervisory salaries, amortization of leasehold improvements, and so forth. All other fixed costs are allocated to product lines on some rational basis.

In method 1, fixed costs were allocated on the basis of square footage occupied by the equipment used in each product line. The rationale for this method was that fixed costs

	Allocation Method #1				Allocation Method #2			
	Jiffy Spread	Hot Sauce	Chili Mix	Total	Jiffy Spread	Hot Sauce	Chili Mix	Total
Sales	$500,000	$150,000	$350,000	$1,000,000	$500,000	$150,000	$350,000	$1,000,000
Variable cost	160,000	75,000	115,000	350,000	160,000	75,000	115,000	350,000
Contribution to fixed cost	340,000	75,000	235,000	650,000	340,000	75,000	235,000	650,000
Direct fixed cost	40,000	15,000	40,000	95,000	40,000	15,000	40,000	95,000
Allocated fixed cost	65,000	25,000	115,000	205,000	97,000	49,000	59,000	205,000
Total fixed cost	105,000	40,000	155,000	300,000	137,000	64,000	99,000	300,000
Operating profit	$235,000	$35,000	$80,000	$350,000	$203,000	$11,000	$136,000	$350,000
Operating profit (%)	47.0	23.3	29.9	35.0	40.6	7.3	38.9	35.0

Exhibit 7.9. Impact of allocating fixed costs

Cost	Alternatives for Allocation Basis
Building costs—depreciation, maintenance, insurance, taxes, and so forth	Square footage occupied
Heat, light, and power	Square footage occupied
Production control department	Number of direct labor employees Amount of direct labor Total direct cost
Shipping and receiving, purchasing	Number of items Cost of material
Stores	Number of requisitions Cost of material
Personnel department	Number of employees Hours worked

Exhibit 7.10. Some typical bases for allocating fixed cost

were related primarily to supporting the costs of operating the building and equipment. In method 2, fixed costs were allocated on the basis of variable costs, because it was felt that fixed costs were related more to supporting direct labor and the acquisition, storage, and handling of direct materials. From the standpoint of product profitability, the results are strikingly different. In method 2, for example, hot sauce appears to be a marginally profitable item, whereas in method 1, the profit margin is respectable. The consequences of making decisions regarding the retention, expansion, or elimination of product lines on the basis of such calculations are apparent—such decisions must be made with caution.

Unfortunately, there is no "right" or "wrong" method to guide us. Most cost-accounting literature speaks of the doctrine of "fairness" in the allocation of fixed costs. That is, each product or product line should bear its fair share of fixed costs, allocated on some logical basis. Exhibit 7.10 provides a somewhat conventional approach to allocation. It is a good starting point for determining a fair allocation, but it must, of course, be tailored to fit the circumstances found in a particular business.

An effective test of any allocation method is to develop a *pro forma* operating cost budget based on the total elimination of a product line from the operation. In so doing, it should be possible to estimate the costs that would not be incurred under such circumstances. For example, the production-control section might be reduced from eight to five employees, or the electricity bill might be lowered by 20%, and so on. The total so eliminated should approximate the total being allocated under present methods.

7.5 COST–VOLUME–PRICE AND THE BUDGETING PROCESS. In the foregoing sections, the elements of cost, volume, and price have been discussed separately so as to illustrate the effects of each on business profits. In actual business situations, however, the three elements co-exist. Because they are interrelated, any budgeting effort must consider the total effect on profit of these interrelated variables. Attempting to do this manually in the normal multiproduct environment is almost impossible because of the amount of "pencil pushing" required to develop alternate strategies. The only effective method for dealing with a great number of variables is through computer modeling techniques.

Several software programs are available that allow the user to quickly obtain profit calculations resulting from the simultaneous input of a number of variables. For example, the marketing manager may wish to test the profit effect of several pricing plans. Each plan could involve a change in volume, sales mix, distribution costs, commissions, cash discounts, and so on. Further, within each plan, it might be necessary to input various distribution cost arrangements or commission structures. Thus, perhaps 20 or 30 different *pro forma* income statements might be produced before the marketing manager is satisfied with the results.

The chief financial officer, on the other hand, would want to determine the effect on cash flow of the various marketing plans, plus certain other variables, such as inventory levels required to support the plans. Thus, the computer software should be able to produce cash flow analyses as well as income statements.

In fact, many packaged programs are integrated to the extent that the effect of any input would be reflected in *pro forma* balance sheets, income statements, cash flow analyses, and any number of subsidiary schedules. The bases upon which such computer programs are constructed are definitions of fixed costs and a number of defined relationships between volume and variable costs.

Obviously, the results of this method of budgeting are directly proportional to the validity of the underlying data. The definition of fixed and variable costs, and the interrelationship of cost, volume, and price upon which the program's algorithms are based, are critical to the success in using this automated tool. The more knowledgeable managers are about the effect of these elements on the business, the better they will budget and the more effective the budgets will be.

SOURCES AND SUGGESTED REFERENCES

Gitman, Lawrence J, *Principles of Managerial Finance,* (6th ed.). New York: Harper Collins, 1991, pp. 482–486.

Kim, Ji Soo and Jin Wook Kim, ''A Breakeven Procedure for a Multi-Period Project.'' *Engineering Economist (EEC),* vol. 41, no. 2, Winter 1996, pp. 95–104.

Moyer, Charles R., James R. McGuigan, and William J. Kretlow, *Contemporary Financial Management* (5th ed.). St. Paul, MN: West Publishing Company, 1992, pp. 308–316.

Worm, Mark, ''Breakeven Analysis and the Commercial Loan Decision.'' *Journal of Lending & Credit Risk Management (CBC),* vol. 80, no. 3, November 1997, pp. 38–45.

CHAPTER 8

PROFITABILITY AND THE COST OF CAPITAL

Mike Kaufman

Management Advisory Group

8.1 INTRODUCTION. Developments over several decades have focused attention on the cost of capital as a management decision factor.

- Our loss of international competitive position, although largely regained, has been partially blamed on a relatively high cost of capital.
- Choices among emerging technologies with different cash flow profiles may depend on the cost of capital used for discounting.
- The rise of multibusiness corporations has led to the need to estimate divisional cost of capital.
- The desire to measure and improve performance has caused many corporations to link costs of capital to executive profit goals and executive compensation plans.

International position and technological choices reflect the quality of new capital investment. However, performance evaluation standards and divisional costs of capital should also consider capital already committed.

This chapter considers that question of how to manage existing investments over a normal planning horizon. In that context, it is important to address the question of determining the cost of capital, at both corporate and division levels.

Traditionally, companies have relied on computations of earnings and earnings growth to gauge the performance of a division and its managers. More recently, firms have realized that price/earnings ratios do not reflect shareholder's required returns. This has led to increased popularity of certain accounting measures (e.g., return on assets employed). Unfortunately, this approach often creates more problems than it solves.

For example, many companies try adding a computation of return on assets employed to the management reports, perhaps on a divisional or group basis. It can be guaranteed that in short order the manager of group A will be complaining that he has newer (or older) capital goods than group B and that therefore his performance is distorted, or he will be making some other seemingly valid objection. The manager of group B will soon follow with similar complaints, but on the other side of the issue.

This sort of situation can quickly convince senior management that return on assets is useless as a guide to action. More insidiously, it can also foster the fallacy of "the higher the better," in which good performance is equated with ever higher rates of return. Obviously, what is important is to improve future profits, not percentage returns, and they are emphatically not the same thing. To take an extreme example, a manager can become a hero in a rate environment by converting his or her $1 million asset division earning $175,000 (17.5% return) into a $500,000 division earning $100,000 (20%). Excess emphasis on high rates of return is an implicit command to limit the growth of the enterprise and perhaps even endanger its future health by failure to commit capital at more modest, but still attractive, rates.

Most companies say that they avoid such problems by controlling more than just rate of return. One company controls financial performance on 17 key variables, which reminds one of the cartoon showing a harried secretary asking her boss, "Should I rush this job before I rush the rush job I'm rushing now?" Inevitably, the question of priorities among financial objectives arises, prompting some firms to resort to increasingly complex and bizarre bonus systems, wherein profit targets count so much, inventory targets so much, and on and on.

Obviously, no single measure applied in a single year can totally describe a manager's performance. Market position and personnel development are important, and a myriad of other factors can come into play. In the financial area, however, performance factors are too often treated as discrete variables rather than as elements in the accomplishment of the one paramount financial objective: maximizing future economic profit, which is dollar profit after deducting the dollar cost of all the capital employed.

Capital employed can be managed within an integrated system of financial controls focusing on profitability. In fact, such a system is the only sensible way to manage either capital or profits. To appreciate this, it helps to recall that there are only three ways by which to increase profitability:

1. Add new profit-making investment in either fixed or working capital.
2. Improve the rate of return on existing investment either by increasing the amount of profit per dollar of sales or by decreasing the amount of capital needed to produce each sales dollar.
3. Increase the use of debt leverage by escalating the percentage of capital supplied by relatively inexpensive debt.

Only the first method is consistently available to management as a means of improving profitability. Profit margins cannot be infinitely improved, nor can the productivity of capital employed, although there is often more room for improvement in the latter because of a lack of systematic attention to it in the past. Similarly, there is an obvious limit to the increased use of leverage. Investment of capital, however, is a means of profit improvement available to management day in and day out, year after year.

The focus here is not on major new capital projects, which presumably get their fair share of attention, but on managing the employment of working capital and existing fixed assets to ensure that they are being committed wisely. Portions of working capital are being liquidated and re-invested every day. Is the re-investment truly profitable? Underutilized plant and equipment represent a most costly investment. Operating managers should be made aware that the assets they control are in no sense free, simply because they are already owned by the company. As noted previously, profit and return on investment are not independent measures of performance but are inextricably intertwined.

If profitability and capital investment are so interrelated, one cannot be effectively managed without the others being so. This chapter will discuss a system of capital management and performance control that brings these two together while avoiding some of the horrendous problems that have plagued control systems. No performance control system, however, is any better than its standard of measurement. Let us turn, then, to the problem of developing a standard that can evaluate the ongoing performance of committed capital as well as new capital investments.

8.2 A MARKET GAUGE FOR PERFORMANCE. It is a rule of science that any measure be objective and independent of the thing being measured. Where can one find an objective measure of financial performance? Certainly not by taking last year's performance and aiming to improve on it. How good was last year's performance anyway? We cannot reliably take a comparison with the rest of our industry group. It is a strange definition of performance indeed to equate it with being perhaps the least wretched example in a crowd of ne'er-do-wells.

Look everywhere. The only objective performance evaluator is the market. The product market gives us an objective answer as to the quality of our products. The financial market provides an objective answer as to the quality of our performance. The financial market, however, cannot be as tightly circumscribed as the product market. The buyer in the financial market is not limited to buying the securities of Acme Widgets or Beta Widgets. The whole panoply of financial instruments offers options, from venture capital to Treasury bills. It is not that the individual buyers are considering all of these, but rather that all buyers are trying to acquire the same thing: a dollar return on the funds they invest. This permits the market to arbitrage among investments, based on the relative risk/return tradeoff each one offers.

The price the market will pay for a company's securities is a function of the returns it promises in relation to the risks it offers. Since the cost of anything can be defined as the price one must pay to get it, the cost of capital is the return a company must promise in order to get capital from the market, either debt or equity. A company does not set its own cost of capital; it must go into the market to discover it. Yet, meeting this cost is the financial market's one basic yardstick for determining whether a company's performance is adequate.

The cost of debt capital is unmistakable. It is there for all to see in the form of an effective interest rate. The cost of equity capital is another matter entirely. Does equity have a cost? If so, does the company bear sole responsibility for meeting it? How is it determined?

8.3 COPING WITH THE COST OF EQUITY. Does equity capital have a cost? Unless one asserts that stock certificates are bought simply as collector's items, equities must be bought in anticipation of a dollar return (yield, if any, plus appreciation), which will be a cost to whomever pays it. The problem is that the consequences of not meeting that cost are unclear. If a customer pays for 12 light bulbs and finds only 10 in the package, there is certain to be some commotion. However, if he or she buys a stock anticipating a 12% return and gets only 10%, the consequences to the company are not immediately obvious. Of course, in economic substance, an owner of the business is being shortchanged. Moreover, no company can build a viable long-run business by systematically and continually shorting its customers, either product or securities customers. No company of substance would plan to do so.

Is the company solely responsible for meeting the cost of equity capital? Shareholders buy their stock in the market. Should they not have to look to the market for at least a substantial portion of their return? The argument seems persuasive. Unfortunately, on an overall basis, the market itself is unable to provide any return whatsoever. Were it not for company earnings, gains for some shareholders in the market would be precisely offset by the losses of others. Yet, over time, stocks do provide a positive return.

In the most extensive study of this nature, the return (yield plus appreciation) on a portfolio consisting of all the common stocks on the New York Stock Exchange was calculated for 51 years (January 1926 through December 1976). The average return was 9.9% for the series of 42 10-year holding periods beginning in each year from 1926. In a similar study, the same return on the Standard & Poor's (S&P) 500 was reviewed from January 1926 through December 1985. For this series of 51 10-year holding periods, the average return was 9.8%. Returns in recent years have moved higher with the current extended bull market. The 10-year period ending December 1995 shows a shareholder return around 15%. Current in-year values approaching 20% will likely push future 10-year returns beyond 15%. However, so far, these values continue to be close to the aggregate value of corporate returns on equity (ROEs) for the same periods. Thus, over time, what shareholders as a group get is what companies earn.

(a) Cost of Equity. Determining the cost of equity is the hardest question of all. This question cannot be answered with great mathematical precision, which is very disturbing to many people. Executives who are quite willing to stake vast sums based on some readings of the product market can become very tense when told that assessing the cost of equity capital depends on some readings of the securities market. We are all required to make judgments based on limited information, and in judging the cost of equity capital, we can at least be assured that we are asking the right question in developing an objective performance standard.

The outlook for finding a good answer is not all that bleak. We can rather quickly dismiss some approaches that are clearly wrong. First, the cost of common equity does not equal dividends paid. If this were so, we could reduce the cost (i.e., the investors' demand) to zero by eliminating the dividend, which flies in the face of reason. Second, the cost of common equity does not equal the reciprocal price/earnings of the ratio. If a stock earning $5 sells at $100, its cost of capital is not 5%. Who would buy a stock expecting to earn 5% when Treasury bills will pay as much or more?

No amount of lead/lag analysis of historical earnings and stock prices is likely to be productive, because the relevant earnings are expected future earnings, not historical earnings. The relationship between those expected earnings and the market price defines the cost of common equity. The relationship is expressed as a percentage, and the size of that percentage is a function of the perceived risk.

Any reasoned attempt to judge the cost of equity capital must give some consideration to relative risk. A four-step process is suggested.

First, one can observe the strong central tendency of returns in the area of 10% over long periods for large groups of equities. In recent periods, that average has drifted up to about 15%. Companies, of course, do not have the market value of their stocks to work with in the form of earning assets. However, if we could look instead at returns on book value, studies indicate that ROE also tends to be around 15% for the same period.

Over a period spanning more than a decade, several hundred senior financial officers were asked to assume the role of manager of their companies' pension funds and to indicate what rate of return on the equity portion of their funds over the next several years would satisfy them. Through the early 1980s, their answers averaged around 12% to 13%. Since investors in the aggregate can receive only what companies earn, these demands will be met only if the companies they invest in earn at that rate. As a second step, one can observe the logical bounds for equity costs on either side of the central tendencies that have been mentioned. At the upper end of the scale, the returns sought by venture capitalists for very high-risk deals begin somewhere around 25%. No well-managed company with a decent track record should need to offer consistent returns above 20%. Common stock, the ultimate residual security, would have to offer more return to the investor than the bonds of investment grade issuers, which suggests a lower limit of around 10%. Thus, we can have a logical range, with an observed strong mean value toward the lower end.

Third, one can look at risk directly. What is risk to investors? Basically, it is uncertainty concerning the amount of their return. If corporate earnings followed a smooth, fully predictable trend line, there would be no uncertainty. Thus, risk for the investor can be associated with variability of returns, which can be measured. For example, earlier studies of ROE had coefficients of variation around 0.150. This, or some other standard, can be the basis for estimating relative risk for a sector or industry, and thus the premium to be added to a return standard.

Finally, one can apply a judgmental overlay to these statistics. In what direction are overall market returns moving? What factors would suggest that this industry will become relatively more or less risky in the future? What factors in regard to the particular company being studied would tend to suggest that it will display more or less risk than the industry average?

As mentioned earlier, the process does not produce great mathematical precision. It does, however, permit one to zero in on the probable cost with enough accuracy for the purpose of developing an overall profit standard, derived from objective market information.

(b) Combining Capital Costs. Surveys show that weighted average cost of capital (WACC) is the reigning method among leading corporations. However, variation in the calculation of key elements leads to disparate results. Therefore, in computing the WACC for the firm, the following caveats are in order:

- Common equity must include both common stock issues and retained earnings.
- Proportions should be calculated using market-value rather than book-value weights, since market value reflects the true cost of each financing component.
- Logically, marginal weights should be employed in the case of new projects. However, a case can be made for using current or target aggregate weights for capital already commited.
- Marginal costs of debt and equity should be based on forecasts of future market expectations.

8.4 BUILDING COMPANY-WIDE PROFIT GOALS.

With an informed judgment of the company's cost of debt and equity in hand, there remains the matter of blending these into a WACC, based on the planned use of each:

	Planned Percentage		Cost Rate (%)		Cost of Capital (%)
Long-term debt	25	×	8	=	2
Common equity	75	×	12	=	9
Total capital	100				11%

In this illustration, a WACC of 11% has been calculated, assuming a pretax average future debt rate of 8% and an aftertax future common equity cost (including all paid-in capital and retained earnings) of 12%. If there were an existing or planned use of preferred stock, that would be included on an aftertax basis as well, and all convertible issues would be treated as equity for this purpose. The combining of pretax and aftertax rates is deliberate, since the cost of capital reflects the market's requirements, which are set irrespective of the company's tax position.

Developing a numerical profit goal from the WACC is a simple matter of translating to an aftertax equivalent rate. For example, if the tax rate were 50%, the aftertax cost of debt would be reduced to 4%, and the profit goal would be 10% overall: (25% × 4% = 1%) + (75% × 12% = 9%).

Setting the profit goal equal to the overall aftertax cost of capital permits evaluation of ongoing performance and new investment without regard to the source of the capital being employed. Without it, one would have to read across the balance sheet, appraising each asset investment based on the source of its financing. This can lead to some rather absurd results. For example, one might be able to justify a new plant because it could be debt financed but unable to justify the net investment in receivables and inventory that it would generate, since these might have to be financed out of retained earnings.

In our example, requiring all asset investments to earn 10% before consideration of financing charges will provide for meeting the individual costs of both debt and equity. To illustrate, for $100 of capital:

Profit goal	$10
Add back taxes at 50%	10
Pretax equivalent	$20

This pretax equivalent is composed of the following:

Net income before interest and taxes	$20
Less interest ($25 at 8%)	2
Income before tax	$18
Taxes at 50%	9
Net income ($75 at 12%)	$ 9

A profit goal established in the preceding manner is the most effective way to bring home to operating management the standards of performance being set by the financial markets. New profit-making capital should not be deliberately committed below such a rate; existing capital should be managed so that it achieves or betters that rate.

Three rates of return are of interest in evaluating the performance of a business: (1) the cost of capital, (2) current corporate return on today's stock prices, and (3) management's forecast of the corporate rate of return. A premium, based on market expectations, explains the difference between the cost of capital and current corporate return.

The central question is which standard to use for evaluating managers. Paying managers for returns above the firm's cost of capital justly rewards them for creating shareholder value. However, such a standard falls short of what shareholders need to realize their required return at current share prices.

Using market price return to evaluate managers is an alternative; however, management may not believe that market expectations are reasonable. Using management's forecast of corporate return invokes the problem of using a standard different from that required to create shareholder value.

In making the choice of an appropriate standard, one may again wish to distinguish new projects from capital that is already committed. For example, use cost of capital or market expectations for committed funds and management's forecast for new projects.

8.5 BUILDING DIVISIONAL PROFIT GOALS. The appropriate profit goal for the whole company should at least equal the aftertax equivalent of its cost of capital. To illustrate, if a firm determines that (1) its proper capitalization should be 25% debt and 75% equity; (2) its future cost of debt and equity should be 8% (pretax) and 12%, respectively; and (3) its future effective tax rate on income should be 50%; then its profit goal would be 10%, as follows:

(% of debt × cost)	+ (% of equity × cost)	= Cost of debt and equity	= Profit goal
(0.25 × (8% × 0.50)) +	(0.75 × 12%)	= (1% + 9%)	= 10%

Let us see what happens when this concept is applied to the multidivisional firm. Suppose there was a large company, half of whose business was manufacturing computer equipment and half commercial financing. (Any resemblance to a company you may think of is purely coincidental.) A well-capitalized manufacturer might well opt for a 25/75 debt/equity mix, whereas a solid commercial finance business could easily carry a 75/25 mix. For simplicity, assume that each division has the same capital investment and that the market cost of debt and equity would be the same for both divisions. We would then have the profit goals that are outlined in Exhibit 8.1.

Consider what would happen if decisions were based strictly on the overall corporate goal rate. Capital would flow easily to the computer division. The required rate for investment is only 8%, but they should be able to average 10% or more in competition with other computer equipment firms.

	Proportion	×	Cost		
Computer Division					
Debt	25	×	(0.08 × 0.50)	=	1.00
Equity	75	×	0.12		9.00
Capital	100				10.00
Profit goal					10%
Finance Division					
Debt	75	×	(0.08 × 0.50)	=	3.00
Equity	25	×	0.12	=	3.00
Capital	100				6.00
Profit goal					6%
Corporate					
Debt	100	×	(0.08 × 0.50)	=	4.00
Equity	100	×	(0.12)	=	12.00
Capital	200				16.00
Profit goal					8%

Exhibit 8.1. Divisional versus corporate profit goals

However, the finance division management would be hard pressed to justify even its current investment, since 8% is still the standard, whereas 6% is a legitimate expectation in the business. Of course, management may indeed decide that it wants to emphasize one division at the expense of the others, but this is no way to do it. If, over time, the company became 75% manufacturing and 25% finance, the corporate profit goal itself would have shifted to 9%, while investments were still being judged at 8%.

Profit goals must be developed and applied to each of the company's identifiable lines of business. It will not do to look at the company overall or to lump the several units, divisions, or subsidiaries together and take an average. What is an identifiable line of business? There is no easy answer. Certainly, 8-ounce cans are not one line and 12-ounce cans another. However, drilling for oil overseas and refining and marketing it in the United States may well be two distinct lines, with different risks and capitalization standards as recognized by the financial markets.

The key is just that—what is the market's perception of the company? Does it view the company as being in one business or several? In general, the market tends to accept management's implicit judgment on the point, as revealed by the extent of divisionalization of the firm.

A universal problem for divisional goal setters is selecting a basis for division standards. One common approach is the so-called pure play, employing an independent proxy corporation as standard. The imputed capital structure model proposed earlier would draw on the structure of such a proxy. The pure-play method has its own shortcomings, a primary one being the frequent failure to identify a public proxy. Of course, this is yet another reason to rely on the logical methodology suggested here, drawing on management's experience and intuition.

(a) A Problem for Divisional Goals: Overhead. Divisional profit goals introduce at least two other sources of complication. The first is what to do with the capital and expenses of central service departments (research and development [R&D], purchasing, etc.) and the home office itself. Some of this may be chargeable to the divisions based on their actual use of these departments or units. One convenient solution establishes such departments as internal profit centers, charging user divisions at cost plus a mark-up percentage designed to produce a return on the internal center's capital equal to the weighted average corporate profit-goal rate.

However this is handled, there will almost always be a block of capital and expense that cannot logically be associated with any division. At this point, one may make a gross allocation of the balance to the divisions (which is a practical answer if the amounts are relatively small) or leave it undistributed, viewing the divisional goal rates as, in effect, contributed and the divisional returns as, in effect, contribution margins—that is, available to cover both overhead and profit. In general, the contribution margin method seems preferable, since profit independence is vital to any good system of evaluation and control, and since it heads off pointless grousing about the fairness of what is definitionally an irrational allocation of corporate overhead.

(b) Another Problem: Portfolio Effect. The second complication concerns the theory of portfolio effect. Portfolio theory says that, by combining two or more businesses within one company, we may decrease (or increase) the cost of capital for the firm overall, beyond what would be the weighted average for the component lines of business. Statistics and logic would both suggest that this is at least a possibility for any multidivisional company. The real issue, however, is whether the benefit of any such portfolio effect should go to reduce the profit goal of the several divisions below the appropriate goal for an independent company in the same line of business. One would think not.

In any event, it must be recognized that any company has but one cost of capital, in that investments in the divisions separately are not available to the market. The company must meet or better that overall cost. If portfolio effects have decreased the indicated overall profit goal below the weighted average of the several divisions, the company should consistently sell at a premium in the market. Potential diversifications should be weighed carefully, lest the premium potential be destroyed by adding other elements to the business mix.

If, on the other hand, the company's apparent cost of capital far exceeds what a weighted average of the divisional profit goals can produce, management should consider the composition of the business and possible divestitures.

(c) Use of Hurdle Rates. Why do we spend so much time and effort agonizing over a rather precise profit-goal estimate? Why not just pick a hurdle rate that we know is above any reasonable estimate of our cost of capital? Management could, if necessary, set different hurdle rates for various divisions, to reflect their judgment of relative risk or to force allocations of capital in line with their strategic plans. This approach has particular appeal when the company has traditionally earned a high rate of return. Why let a manager "get away with" a 12% standard when the company has consistently earned 18% or more on total permanent capital? Perhaps we should even set a "stretch target" of 20% to get division managers really producing.

The hurdle rate approach to goal setting is widely applied, but it has a number of very serious problems. First, the hurdle rate approach constitutes a retreat from objective standards. Lacking a demonstrable anchor in market evidence, hurdles become matters of management fiat, fit subjects for argumentation, dispute, and perhaps even evasion. To operating managers, such hurdles become "rules of the game" rather than hard tests of performance.

Second, the purpose of market-determined profit goals is to recognize costs, not to soak up all economic value from investments. No imminent ruin looms over managements that refuse to invest in all opportunities down to the point at which costs (including capital costs) and revenues are exactly equal, that is, the profit-goal rate. If a division has traditionally earned 18%, and management expects that such performance can continue, it may justifiably require that performance for planning purposes and establish a new investment cutoff at that level through a profitability-index system of evaluation. By using a market-determined profit goal to charge for both existing and new capital, however, management avoids deluding itself into thinking that it cannot afford to accept investments with lower returns.

This is a very important concept, yet it is not widely appreciated. The cost of capital measures the risk of committing funds to a particular line of business. If we insist that all of our investments in that business be at rates appreciably above that cost, sooner or later our risk-adjusted cost will likely rise above the old nominal cost, since we will take only the riskiest investments offered and not make the cost reduction or other risk-reducing investments that will keep us in line with the general risk parameters of the business.

Finally, if the cost of capital is a reasonable measure of our future financing costs (as it is meant to be), the company is demonstrably better off using the equivalent profit goals for evaluation rather than higher hurdle rates. For example, consider a company with a profit goal derived from market evidence of 10%, yet showing a consistent ability to earn

Year		Investment	
		A	B
0		$ (1,000)	$ (1,000)
1		—	291
2		—	291
3		—	291
4		—	291
5		1,925	291
	Total return	$ 1,925	$ 1,455
	Future value, using 14% hurdle rate	$ 1,925	$ 1,925

Exhibit 8.2. Comparison using a hurdle rate: investment A versus investment B

14% in its business. It is evaluating two investments, A and B, of $1 million each, as described in Exhibit 8.2. If investments A and B were evaluated at a 14% hurdle rate, the company would see equal value and be indifferent between the two. Obviously, since $291,000 × 5 is not arithmetically equal to $1,925,000, the equivalence must reflect an implicit assumption that the annual $291,000 can be reinvested at some rate to produce a future value of $1,925,000 in total. It should come as no surprise that the rate is 14%.

Stated another way, the problem with investment A is that it throws off no cash until year 5 and thus funds no other interim investments, whereas B is funding such 14% return investments in years 1, 2, 3, and 4. That is, using the hurdle rate implies that the interim investments of $291,000 per year would not be made under investment A.

To make a fair comparison, assume that we make the same $291,000 re-investments under both alternatives. Because investment A provides no interim returns, the re-investments with new capital will be financed at our cost of capital rate (see Exhibit 8.3). The other investments will add their $470,000 return to the value of investment A, minus the $326,000 cost of the additional capital. Investment A's net worth is now $146,000 more than investment B and is clearly preferable. If this evaluation had used the 10% profit-goal rate from the start, the conclusion would have been immediately apparent. Do profit goals or hurdle rates exert a better influence on managerial behavior? Do profit goals set at the cost of capital discourage managers from seeking outstanding but risky investments? Do hurdle rates above the cost of capital exclude value-creating projects essential to the firm's future? Or do hurdle rates above the cost of capital encourage optimistic forecasts for low-return projects?

For new investments, the answer may depend on the culture of the firm, its competitive standing, and its economic cycle position. For managing committed funds in the form of existing investments, profit goals based on divisional cost of capital appropriately address the needs of the capital market, not the economics of the product market.

There are, of course, other approaches to developing the cost of equity capital. All have their advocates in academic circles and among financial analysts. Some begin with the microeconomic concept of the risk-free rate of return, analyzing its components in terms of a basic cost of deferred consumption, plus a factor for inflation. From these data, one would then attempt to derive a risk premium for various classes of securities, up through the common equities of untried, aggressive new companies. Others implicitly abandon the idea of equity investors' being the true "owners" of a business. Under this

		Investment A						Investment B		
		Reinvestment at 14%			Financing at 10%					
Year	Project	Amount ×	FV[a] Factor =	FV	Amount ×	FV Factor =	FV	Amount ×	FV Factor =	FV
Now	($1,000)	—	—	—	—	—	—	($1,000)	—	
1	—	(291)	1.689	$ 492	$291	1.464	($ 426)	291	1.689	$ 492
2	—	(291)	1.482	431	291	1.331	(388)	291	1.482	431
3	—	(291)	1.300	378	291	1.210	(352)	291	1.300	379
4	—	(291)	1.140	332	291	1.100	(321)	291	1.140	332
5	1,925	—	—	—	—	—	—	291		291
	$1,925			$1,633			($1487)			$1,925
		Future value of A					$1,925 + $1,633 − ($1,487) =	$2,071		
		Future value of B						1,925		
		Net advantage to A						$146		

[a] FV = future value

Exhibit 8.3. Revised comparison of investment A versus B ($ thousands)

approach, one would assent that the only real costs to a business can be measured by the cash that flows out of it. Thus, the ''cost'' of equity capital is equal to the minimum dividend that it must pay (presumably to keep management incumbent).

By far the most popular variation, however, begins with the idea that the earnings of a stock can be divided by its market price to derive its cost. In other words, the reciprocal of the price/earnings ratio yields a percentage that is the cost of equity capital. Of course, as an abstract principle, this is absolutely correct: the discount rate, which equates the summation of all future earnings to the market price, is mathematically the cost of capital. The difficulty is in deriving an accurate summation of all those future earnings. Even if such an objectively accurate summation could be developed, there is no certainty that the market's subjective opinion would be the same. Furthermore, real-world evidence suggests that there is very little market pricing of stocks being done this way. In fact, there is some evidence to suggest that the market changes its pricing judgments mainly by shortening or lengthening the future period over which it is even willing to consider potential earnings. Thus, in the real world, the discount rate (or cost of capital) stays relatively constant, and the discounting period changes most.

Many companies employing mathematical models for calculating the cost of equity now use a dividend growth model and/or the *capital asset pricing model (CAPM).* Consider that the first only makes intuitive sense for companies that pay a dividend and are able to forecast growth. Second, the CAPM may provide low-quality results. The well-known beta coefficient yielded by the CAPM is often statistically insignificant, being poorly correlated with market behavior.

Many corporations using these models find themselves forced to introduce subjective preference factors to rationalize their results. Why not eliminate spurious number crunching and adopt the largely intuitive, but logically appealing model described above?

Future research may provide financial analysts with a more rigorous mathematical approach to estimating the cost of capital. Such an approach would have to provide a means of developing the utility function (risk profile) of the financial markets and a way of identifying the earnings horizon being evaluated, as well as a means of dealing with the statistical ''noise'' being generated by current economic conditions and short-term expectations of dividend increases, stock splits, and so on. Until that day, we are left, as we so often are in business dealings, making decisions based on reasonable, but incomplete, information. As always, when one is in that position, it is at least comforting to know that one has asked the right questions.

8.6 INFORMATION PROBLEMS AND COST OF CAPITAL. Information quality affects the cost of capital in the form of ''agency costs.'' Since investors have imperfect knowledge of their agent managers' actions and expectations, managers must be motivated to act in investors' interests.

(a) Agency Cost of Debt. Managers can increase shareholder wealth at the expense of lenders by creating a riskier portfolio of assets. This hazard, plus the cost of monitoring and ensuring against it, constitute the agency cost of debt. Lenders will want an interest rate that includes these costs.

(b) Agency Cost of Equity. Managers may not act responsibly on behalf of shareholders, thereby increasing expenses and reducing investment quality. The smaller the percentage of management ownership, the more likely managers are to act in their own self-interest, and the greater the agency cost of equity.

(c) Communicating with the Market. Managers have more information about their firms than do their shareholders; management's credibility in communicating news to the market obviously affects the company's share price. Communication can be enhanced by using changes in capital structure to signal investors about management's expectations: a debt ratio increase is a signal of good prospects, and vice versa. For these signals to be credible, managers must be time-restricted as to buying or selling company shares; they must be seriously penalized in the event of bankruptcy.

8.7 SUMMARY. Determining the cost of capital is one of the many controversial issues of corporate finance. Financial authors often disagree among themselves, and more often with corporate practitioners, as to relevant capital structures and cost of capital models. However, the WACC model advocated here continues to be widely accepted among authors and practitioners.

Division-level standards for performance evaluation assume a fair level of homogeneity among project types within a division. If division projects run a gamut of categories, then project specific hurdle rates may be useful.

Also worth consideration is the more generalized concept of opportunity cost, defined as the rate of return on the best alternative investment available. As an investment-standard concept, opportunity cost is quite flexible, allowing for project-specific, divisional, or corporate investment alternatives as a basis. Distinctions may also be made between strategic and tactical opportunities or between monitoring committed capital and evaluating new investments. As with other investment standard methods, care must be taken that weighted average divisional returns recover the corporate cost of capital.

Economic value added (EVA, see Chapter 9), is a recently popular measurement for determining whether a business is earning more than its true cost of capital. It has its own ways of measuring capital employed and linking performance to management compensation; however, its practitioners tend to accept a company's assessment of the true cost of capital.

SOURCES AND SUGGESTED REFERENCES

Hergert, Michael, ''Strategic Resource Allocation Using Divisional Hurdle Rates,'' *Planning Review,* January–February 1987.

Kester, W. Carl, and Robert A. Taggart, Jr., ''Capital Allocation—Hurdle Rates, Budgets, or Both?,'' *Sloan Management Review,* vol. 30, no. 3, Spring 1989.

Kincheloe, Stephen C., ''The Weighted Average Cost of Capital—The Correct Discount Rate,'' *Appraisal Journal,* vol. 58, no. 1, January 1990.

Rachlin, Robert, *Return on Investment Manual: Tools and Applications for Managing Financial Results.* Armonk, NY: M. E. Sharpe, 1997.

Stanley, Marjorie T., ''Cost of Capital in Capital Budgeting for Foreign Direct Investment,'' *Managerial Finance* (UK), vol. 16, no. 2, 1990.

Taggart, Robert A., Jr., ''Allocating Capital Among a Firm's Divisions: Hurdle Rates vs. Budgets,'' *Journal of Financial Research,* vol. 10, no. 3, Fall 1987.

CHAPTER 9

BUDGETING SHAREHOLDER VALUE

Serge L. Wind

Lucent Technologies

9.1 INTRODUCTION. Businesses that want to grow their market shares, or at least to be competitive in their markets, must improve productivity, foster innovation, and strive toward enhanced customer satisfaction. Businesses that want to grow, as manifested by these objectives, must increase investment now for the future.

As the source of much of this required funding, shareholders assess the potential increase in ''value'' of their investments in a business when deciding whether to invest. This assessment is based on their anticipated return and the risk they associate with it.

It is vital, then, for firms to focus on shareholder satisfaction by understanding what is important to this stakeholder. In this manner, the drivers of intrinsic value (or *shareholder value*) of the firm can be discerned and its value managed.

(a) Purposes. Shareholder value provides the valuation of a business. The principal purposes of implementing (period) performance measurement of shareholder value are as follows:

- To provide an economic measurement of business performance from the perspective of the shareholder
- To supplement traditional accounting-based measures of business performance with cash flow valuation
- To provide proper vehicles for achieving management objectives and decisions—including the planning process, resource utilization, and employee compensation—that drive creation of value
- To provide a link between period performance metrics and shareholder value

(b) What Is Shareholder Value? Return to the shareholder is in the form of cash dividends and share price appreciation. Aside from psychic and other nonfinancial attributes of an investment, these are the only returns available to common stockholders.

The value of the shareholder investment emanates from the cash flow generated over the life of the business, assessed with the associated business risk. Thus, shareholder value—the economic measure of the value of a business—is expressed as the sum of future cash flows in today's dollars.

The cash flows are aftertax cash generated each period from the operations of the business, available to all providers of company capital. For a proper analysis of the true worth of cash flows over time, they must be expressed in terms of today's dollars. [See Section 9.2(b) on the time value of money.]

(c) Why Focus on Cash Flow? The concept of shareholder value is expressed in terms of cash flows and is based on current and future cash outflows and inflows from now out to the future. We are adopting an economic perspective in which cash outlays are delineated as the underlying components of an economic model of valuation. This framework was laid out by Rappaport and others (see Sources and Suggested References).

The emphasis on the discounted cash flow (DCF) approach versus the standard, accounting-based approach also manifests itself in the types of financial measures that are most expressive of economic performance in which investors are interested. Traditional measures, such as earnings per share, returns on equity (ROE) and operating assets, do not capture all aspects of value creation, including the following:

- Business risk
- Investor expectations
- Time value of money

They also often reflect the effects of leverage or the debt ratio, which is the total debt of the firm divided by total capital. Finally, they are single-period, short-term measures. We need to start concentrating on measures, such as the two value-based indicators delineated in the next section, which (unlike accounting earnings) have been found by studies to be highly correlated with stock price, an external indicator of company value.

In their book on valuation, Copeland et al. sum it up accurately: ''Managers who use the DCF approach to valuation, focusing on long-term cash flow, ultimately will be rewarded by higher share prices. The evidence from the market is conclusive. Naive attention to accounting earnings will lead to value-destroying decisions.''[1]

(d) Two Complementary Value-Based Measures. Two measures of shareholder value will be discussed, because they are related in important ways. Both are value-based measures.

Shareholder value, based on discounted cash flows, measures total long-term value. Long-term valuation is used for the following:

- Evaluation of investment decisions (both capital projects and acquisitions)
- Assessment of long-term plans and projects
- Economic decision making

As we have seen, this measure—the investors' perception of the total worth of a company—is based on all the cash flows to be generated, in order to include all future benefits or returns, as well as costs of all current and future investments and added assets.

For both short-term planning and tracking, *Economic Value Added* (EVA), developed by Stern and Stewart, captures the value created (or depleted) during a period of business

[1] Tom Copeland, Tim Koller, and Jack Murrin, *Valuation—Measuring and Managing the Value of Companies* (New York: John Wiley & Sons, 1990), p. 94.

activity.[2] (A *period* is a finite time interval, like a year.) Because of its importance to planning and budgeting, EVA is more fully explained in Section 9.3.

Both measures share another key property: They distinguish between operations and financing and measure the effects of only the former in valuation. Inclusion of financing effects (such as interest and number of shares), along with traditional accounting, introduces misleading non–cash-based information in measures like ROE and earnings per share (EPS).

The critical assertion to be developed for budgeting purposes is that EVA is particularly useful in tracking a plan's contribution to the total shareholder value. The nature of cash flows and their inherent difficulty for budgeting, coupled with the observation that the period cash-flow component does not reveal the state of incremental value, combine to favor an added role for EVA. Thus, EVA, apparently relegated to a period measure of value added, takes on an important new role: short-term budget tracker of total value.

9.2 LONG-TERM VALUATION.

In the last section, we introduced two measures: shareholder value and EVA. Shareholder value is the long-term valuation of a company, whereas EVA is a measure of short-term value creation for a period of business activity. Total value, or shareholder value, is always quantified at a point in time (e.g., as of this year), and value is a function of all future time periods.

(a) Shareholder Value Recapitulation.

Long-term valuation is the best approach to linking shareholder value creation to investment decisions. We have defined *value* as the summation of all projected free cash flows for a business or project, expressed in the equivalent of today's dollars.

Free cash flow represents the aftertax cash generated each period after re-investment from the operations—not financing—of the business. Re-investment, from the firm's perspective, consists of net plant adds (or capital expenditures for plant and equipment), changes in operating capital (or changes in receivables and inventory less payables), and investments (or acquisitions, mergers, etc.).

In Exhibit 9.1, an example is shown of free cash flow, forecasted in terms of future dollars, which must be subsequently "discounted" back to today's dollars.

(b) Time Value of Money.

The reference to "today's dollars" in Section 9.1(c) is to the economic tenet that "most people prefer to have cash now rather than later," because the cash can now be invested to produce returns unavailable if the cash flow is delayed. The time value of money derives from the cost of foregone opportunities.[3] With the cash flows forecasted in terms of future dollars, the time-value-of-money concept dictates that they must be discounted to equate them to today's dollars, thus providing an estimate of the present value of the business from each period. We will see later that risk as reflected in the cost of capital determines the discount rate.

(c) Cost of Capital.

The rate used to discount future cash flows back to the present for valuation is called the *cost of capital,* or *discount rate* [See Chapter 8 for further discussion on the subject; capital itself is defined in Section 9.3(f).]

---

[2] Joel Stern and Bennett Stewart defined a form of residual income or *Economic Value Added* (EVA) in two publications: G. Bennett Stewart III, *The Quest for Value* (New York: HarperCollins, 1990); and G. Bennett Stewart III, *Stern Stewart Corporate Finance Handbook* (New York: Stern Stewart Management Services, 1986).

[3] *See* footnote 1, p. 94.

Example of a Statement of Funds Flow		
Operating income (before interest and taxes)	$895	
+ Other income (operating)	112	
− Cash operating taxes paid	(189)	
Income after cash taxes (before interest)	818	$818
− Additions to plant net of depreciation	(98)	
− Additions to operating capital	(34)	
− Additions to investments	—	
Re-investment	$(132)	$(132)
Free cash flow		$686
= Income after cash taxes (before interest) less re-investment		

Exhibit 9.1. Definition of free cash flow

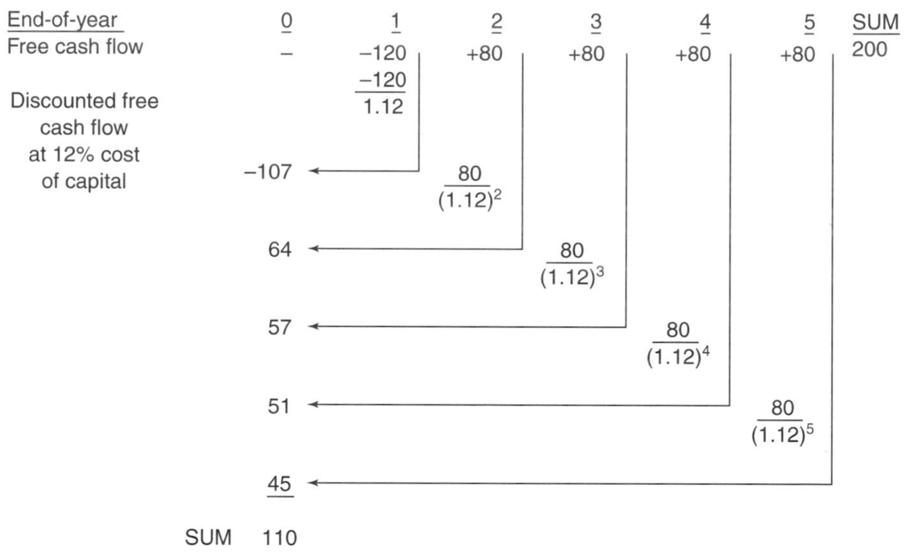

Exhibit 9.2. Discounted free cash flow: an example

The numerical example of discounting assumes negative cash flow of $120 in the first year for an initial project investment, and positive cash flows of $80 in each of the next four years. Although the total of the five years added up to $200 in absolute dollars, that $200 is only equivalent to $110 in today's dollars. The $110 is the *present value.* Exhibit 9.2 illustrates the end-of-year free cash flows using discounted cash flow techniques at a 12% cost of capital.

The cost of capital is the risk-adjusted opportunity cost for investors, or the minimum required return. The cost of capital represents the average rate of return that investors expect when they decide to invest in a company of a certain risk.

The cost of capital is the weighted average cost of debt capital supplied by bondholders and equity capital supplied by the shareholders.

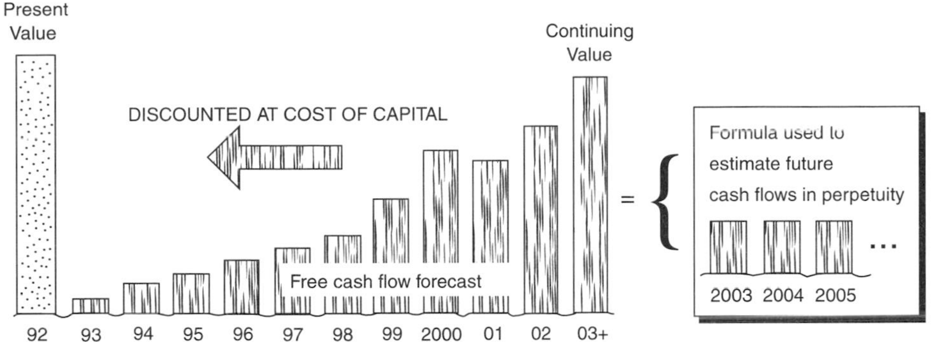

Exhibit 9.3. Long-term value: an illustration

$$\text{Cost of capital} = (\text{Aftertax cost of debt} \times \%\text{ of debt in capital ratio}) + (\text{Cost of equity} \times \%\text{ of equity in capital ratio})$$

For debt, with interest tax deductible, the aftertax cost of debt is based on the prevailing interest rates (and the effective income tax rate). For equity, the more complicated methods described in Stewart's book[4] are needed to estimate the cost of equity of different companies. Finally, the weights are determined by the corporate objective (or sometimes the actual) debt ratio, usually determined by the treasurer of the company. The cost of equity, in essence, is an estimate of the return required by shareholders for investing in the company's common stock, based on an assessment of the level of risk in the company and other investment alternatives in the marketplace.

(d) Continuing Value. As shown in the graphical representations of a long-term value calculation (see Exhibit 9.3), *shareholder value* is the present value of all future free cash flows. For time beyond the explicit planning period (usually 5 or 10 years), a term called *continuing value* captures the remaining future cash flows forecasted into perpetuity. Formulas for continuing value, or residual value, can be found in the valuation book by Copeland, Koller, and Murrin.[5]

Continuing value, absolutely necessary to compute discounted cash flows, often accounts for more than 70%, and sometimes more than 100%, of total value. Moreover, with even near-term forecasts often hard to estimate, the long-term–based continuing value is often difficult to estimate reliably. However, it does represent the premium that investors are expecting beyond the explicit planning period.

(e) Budgeting Implications. With the most important decisions made by company managers involving value of a pending project or business unit, accountability based on successful implementation is vital. A business plan and budget for the company must

[4] *See* footnote 2, *The Quest for Value,* pp. 431–475.
[5] *See* footnote 1, pp. 207–230.

reflect the benefits and costs of those projects and business units for which value has been altered.

However, we have seen that valuation is a complex procedure, depending on multi-years' continuing value, which is determined by imprecise parameters and accounts for the majority portion of value, and cash flow projections with start-up problems that reverberate throughout the DCF. Budget practitioners responsible for cash flow items know that actual end-of-year (or start-up) balance sheet items (known only after the budget has been approved) must be taken into account in re-estimating budget-year cash flows (like payables, receivables, additions to plant, and free cash flow).

The complexity and reliability of budgeting and tracking discounted cash flows for even the first few years leaves us amenable to other budgeting notions.

9.3 ECONOMIC VALUE ADDED. We have seen why shareholder value is vital in assessing a company's value over the long term. An ongoing firm must be able to check progress as well, and measure increases in value with a short-term measure. Economic value added, depicted as the most important period measure of value added (or depleted),[6] will also be seen to provide a means for effective budgeting for the DCF measure of shareholder value.

(a) Economic Value-Added Overview. Rather than estimating total value via multi-year cash flows, economic value added measures period value added to or depleted from shareholder value. It relates income statement and balance sheet activity to shareholder expectations and uses traditional accounting information as a surrogate for cash flows. It is more highly correlated with stock price than are traditional measures, according to empirical studies by Stern Stewart.

The EVA formula incorporates earnings, cash income taxes, balance-sheet capital, and the cost of capital so that value created is measured (positive value is created when the return on invested capital exceeds the cost of capital). Operating returns in excess of (or below) the cost of capital are measured by EVA. (Financing impacts, such as the tax deductibility of interest expense, are excluded.)

(b) Example of Value-Added Concept. If you borrow $100 from a bank at a 10% rate for one year, and you earn 12% return on the money through investment or the race track, you have created value for yourself. Your return exceeds the bank's cost to you by two percentage points.

If, however, with the bank cost fixed at 10%, you manage only an 8% return, you have lost money and value by two percentage points.

In an analogous fashion, if the return on invested capital (ROIC) exceeds the cost of capital, value is added. Value is depleted for the period when ROIC is less than the weighted average cost of capital (WACC).

We have already referred to the cost-of-capital component; it is more complex (e.g., two dimensions) than the cost of debt in the example, but plays a role analogous to the hurdle rate. (A *hurdle rate* is a threshold value for determining economic acceptance of a project: The return must exceed the hurdle rate.)

We now need to be a bit more precise in defining the return on capital and an explicit EVA equation.

---

[6] *See* footnote 2, *Stern Stewart Corporate Finance,* pp. 3–14.

(c) Economic Value-Added Formula. Building into the formula the feature that EVA is positive only when the return exceeds the cost of capital, the EVA formula[7] can be written as follows:

$$\text{EVA} = (\text{Return on invested capital} - \text{Cost of capital}) \times \text{Average invested capital}$$

Note that EVA is an actual dollar figure, not a percentage. Its sign indeed depends on the sign of the *spread,* the difference between return and cost of capital (both percentages). Its magnitude or size depends, in large part, on average capital, which is also dollar denominated. [*Capital* is defined in Section 9.3(f).]

(d) Implications for Value Creation. There are three basic means of securing an increase in EVA for the company, as pointed out by Stewart.[8] An increase in EVA will result:

- If operating efficiency is enhanced (rate of return on existing capital base improves)
- If value-added new investments are undertaken (additional capital invested returns more than cost of capital)
- If capital is withdrawn from uneconomic activities (capital withdrawn where returns are below cost of capital)

(e) Components of Economic Value Added—Return on Invested Capital. Return on invested capital in the EVA formula must exceed the cost of capital, the hurdle rate which was defined in Section 9.2(c). Also a percentage, ROIC is defined as follows:

$$\text{ROIC} = \frac{\text{Net operating profit after taxes (NOPAT)}}{\text{Average invested capital}}$$

Net operating profit after taxes represents posttax earnings before payment of capital costs (i.e., interest and dividends). Essentially, NOPAT includes all revenues and sales net of costs and expenses, plus other operational income, less cash income taxes paid (except for the deductibility of financing-related interest). As such, NOPAT is the right measure to compare pre–capital-cost earnings with investors' costs. Cash taxes are more consistent with cash flow valuation and serve as an appropriate operating driver of EVA, because of comprehensive income taxation employed in accounting.

(f) Components of Economic Value-Added—Invested Capital. The third component of the EVA formula is average *invested capital;* it also forms the denominator of ROIC. Invested capital represents the cumulative cash invested in the company over time. Exhibit 9.4 illustrates how EVA is calculated.

Economic value-added capital is defined as the difference between assets and EVA liabilities (excluding debt and deferred taxes), or, equivalently, in terms of the right-hand side of the balance sheet, equity plus equity equivalents (e.g., deferred taxes), plus debt.

In both capital and NOPAT, some corresponding adjustments to each term are required

---

[7] Joel Stern and Bennett Stewart defined economic value added and its concept and are responsible for its development into an important model for creating and managing value; the description of EVA in this chapter is based on the value-based framework they generated (see note 2).

[8] *See* footnote 2, *The Quest for Value,* p. 138.

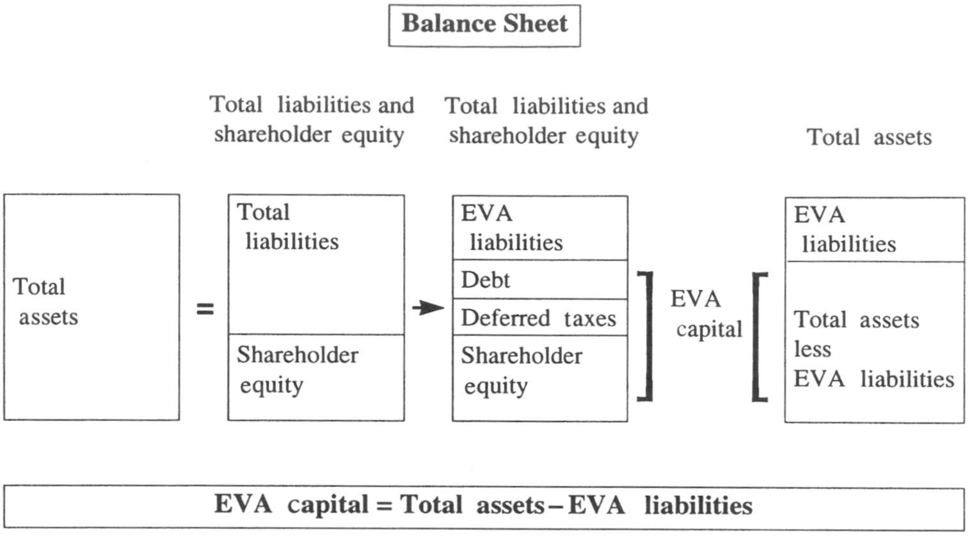

Balance Sheet

		Total liabilities and shareholder equity		Total liabilities and shareholder equity		Total assets
Total assets	=	Total liabilities	→	EVA liabilities		EVA liabilities
				Debt	EVA capital	Total assets less EVA liabilities
				Deferred taxes		
		Shareholder equity		Shareholder equity		

EVA capital = Total assets − EVA liabilities

Exhibit 9.4. EVA capital

to fit in the EVA formula in Section 9.3(c). Basically, as defined by Stewart,[9] most of these adjustments involve replacing book accounting value with terms that are more cash-flow or economic based. Economic value-added capital, including the adjustments contained in equity equivalents (e.g., deferred taxes), which convert the standard accounting book value to a form of economic book value, is a truer measure of the cash invested.

(g) Operating Drivers of Value. Key value drivers can be used effectively to include a detailed analysis of the EVA sensitivity to changes in input parameters. Operating drivers include revenue growth, NOPAT margin (i.e., NOPAT divided by revenues), capital turnover (revenues divided by average capital), and some of the other variables from the income statement and balance sheet as depicted in Exhibit 9.5. For example, inventory turnovers and receivables turnover (or days outstanding) are operating drivers of EVA via capital.

Most of these drivers are related to ROIC via duPont decomposition, or *ROIC tree.*[10] For example, NOPAT margin times capital turnover times the tax factor equals ROIC.

Financing drivers, distinct from operating drivers, include debt ratio and amounts and costs of capital but are not controlled by business units or profit centers.

Sensitivity analysis can be applied to valuation and associated decision making once the key drivers with the greatest impact on value are identified. For budgeting, the drivers can identify the source of any variance and can be used for unit trend comparison.

(h) Economic Value-Added Attributes. In describing EVA, its principal attribute in short-term planning is that it is "the single most important indicator of value creation. . . . EVA measures not only management's ability to manage capital efficiently, but takes into account the magnitude of capital investment as well."[11]

[9] See footnote 2, *Stern Stewart Corporate Finance Handbook,* pp. 8–13.
[10] See footnote 1, p. 125.
[11] See footnote 2, *Stern Stewart Corporate Finance Handbook,* pp. 3–14.

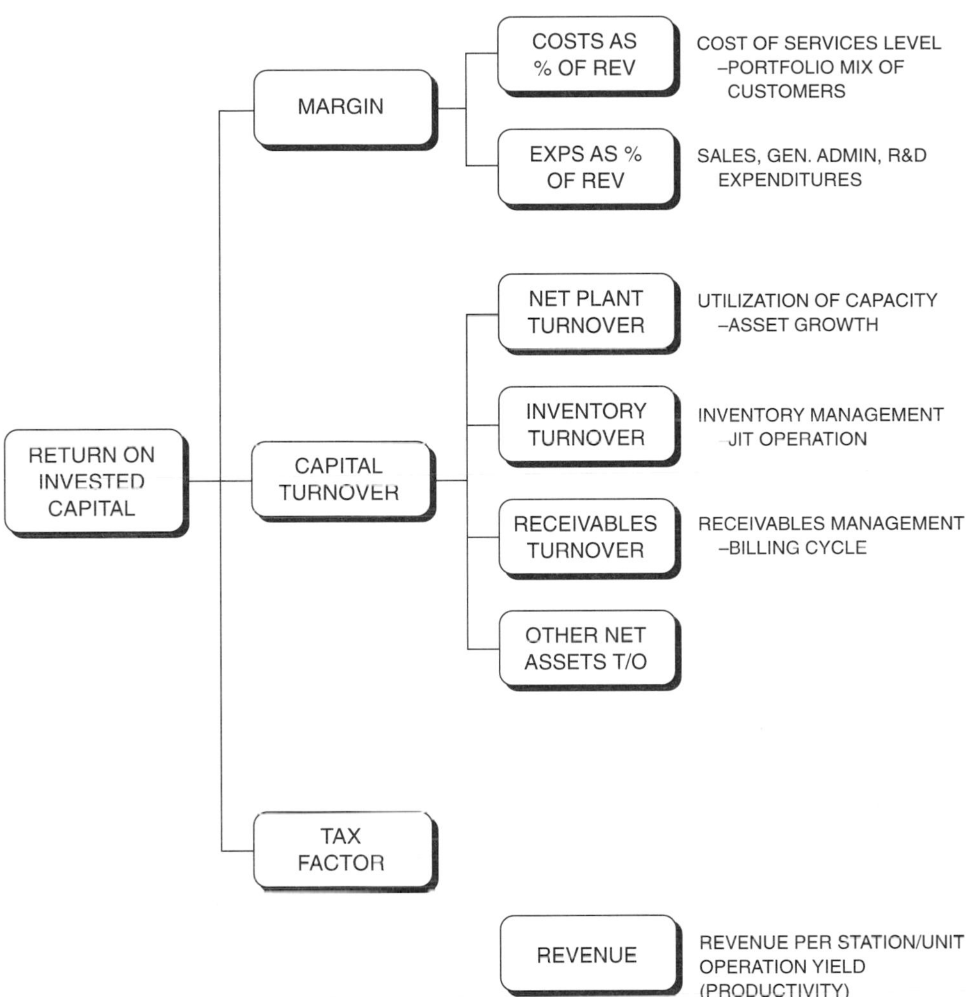

Exhibit 9.5. Value drivers

In addition, EVA is an indicator of the company's productivity. We usually think of a firm or industry as competing in a market for products and/or services. The conceptual approach of shareholder value suggests that there is another market—the market for investor capital—in which all publicly owned companies must compete simultaneously with their other markets. (Section 9.1 begins with a discussion of the need of companies to be competitive in securing funding.)

As indicated in Exhibit 9.6 (generated by Deo[12]), the firm strives to attain a sustainable competitive advantage in its markets for its products and services, through product differentiation, cost minimization, and so forth, to satisfy its customers. Simultaneously, via profit-

[12] Adapted from Prakash Deo's unpublished AT&T paper, ''Resource Alignment'' (1991).

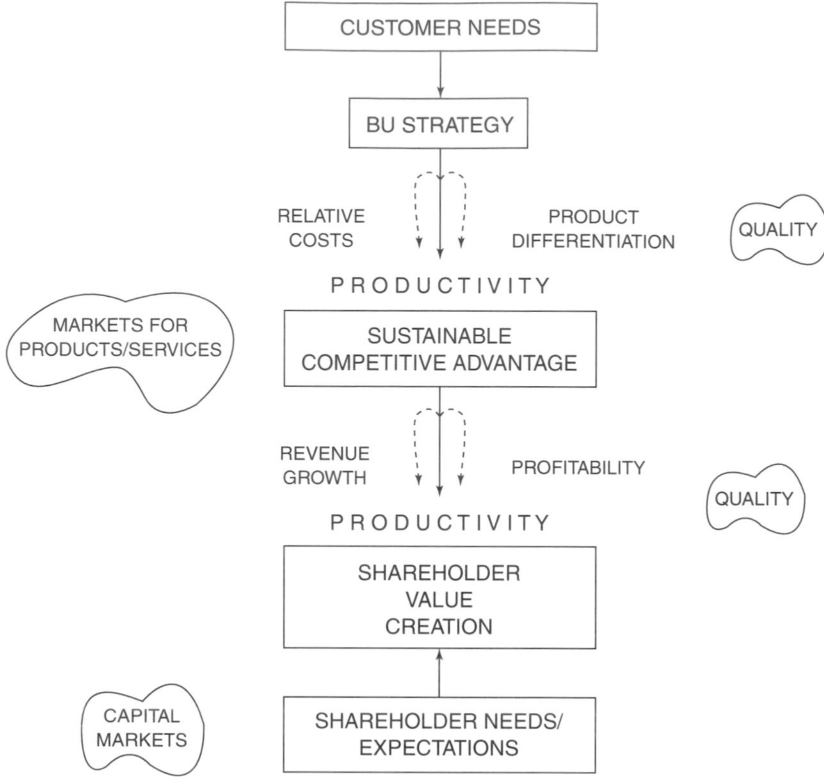

Exhibit 9.6. Linking customer and shareholder needs

ability and revenue growth drivers, the firm satisfies its shareholders' expectations by value creation emanating from its products and services.

Productivity is foremost a measure of ability to create value (or output) in excess of the cost (input) of generating it. Two complementary productivity measures are suggested:

1. *Operating margin.* For expense productivity and income statement efficiency (pretax NOPAT divided by total revenues)
2. *Capital turnover.* For capital productivity and balance sheet efficiency (revenue per average capital)

Productivity improvement is year-over-year percentage change in either measure.

Return on invested capital is the joint measure of operating margin and capital productivity; it reveals the company's productivity, as determined by the spread between return on capital and cost of capital, in competition for investor capital.[13]

Economic value added can also be decomposed by disaggregating financial results to delineate the impact of key operating drivers, such as revenue growth; pretax profit margin per sale; cash tax rate; net operating capital (NOC) charge; and plant, property, and equip-

[13] See footnote 2, *Stern Stewart Corporate Finance Handbook,* pp. 3–14.

ment (PPE) charge. These last two drivers, proposed by Stern Stewart, represent the normalized variable (NOC/sales and PPE/sales) times the cost of capital (COC) (before taxes), and are derived from viewing EVA as residual income (of earnings in excess of capital charges); that is, EVA = NOPAT − COC × average invested capital.

In the 1992 AT&T Annual Report, chief financial officer Alex Mandl wrote that: "EVA is truly a system of measurement. It supplements traditional accounting measures of performance, giving us additional insight into our business and helping us to identify the factors that affect our performance. We have made it the centerpiece of our 'value-based planning' process. And we are linking a portion of our managers' incentive compensation to performance against EVA targets in 1993."

Moreover, EVA has the important facility of connecting forward-looking valuation to performance evaluation (via actual operating performance) over discrete periods. Economic value added thereby enables consistent tracking of valuation. However, first, we need to explore in more depth the relationship between the two measures, EVA and shareholder value.

9.4 COMPLEMENTARY MEASURES OF VALUATION.

(a) Economic Value Added and Valuation. *Shareholder value* was defined in Section 9.2 as the multiperiod, long-term valuation of a company (as of a point in time), whereas we have just seen that EVA measures value added to a shareholder's investment for a period (e.g., a year or quarter).

To determine the economic value of an enterprise, operating unit, or project requires a valuation—or all-period analysis—of all future cash flows. Generally, the entity value is the future expected cash flows discounted at a rate (or cost of capital) that reflects the riskiness of the operating cash flow. In particular:

$$\text{VALUE} = \text{PV(FCF)} = \frac{\text{FCF 1}}{1 + \text{COC}} + \frac{\text{FCF 2}}{(1 + \text{COC})^2} + \cdots$$

where FCF 1, stands for the free cash flow in period 1 and PV denotes present value or discounted sum.

It is, however, true (only under some conditions) that VALUE also equals the present value of the EVAs plus initial capital CAP:

$$\text{VALUE} = \text{PV(EVA)} + \text{CAP}$$

where

$$\text{PV(EVA)} = \frac{\text{EVA 1}}{1 + \text{COC}} + \frac{\text{EVA 2}}{(1 + \text{COC})^2} + \cdots$$

Capital, defined in Section 9.3(f), is not equal to the book value of traditional accounting but represents economic book value, where adjustments, such as the deferred tax reserve, are added to book debt and equity to allow capital to reflect a more economic and accurate base on which to earn. In Exhibit 9.7, an example of valuation is shown.

Although individual-period EVA is usually different from FCF for the same period, under a specific set of assumptions, the two approaches generally yield the same value, that is,

$$\text{PV (FCF)} = \text{PV (EVA)} + \text{CAP} = \text{VALUE},$$

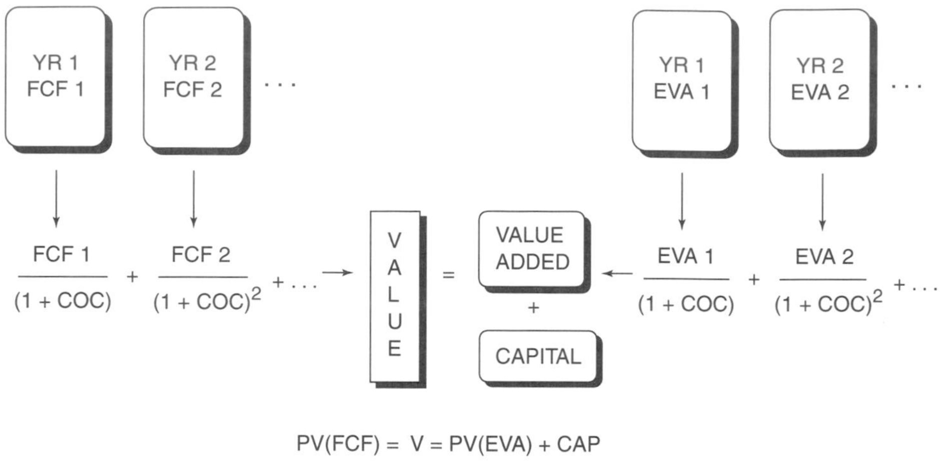

YR 1 FCF 1 | YR 2 FCF 2 | . . .

$$\frac{FCF\ 1}{(1 + COC)} + \frac{FCF\ 2}{(1 + COC)^2} + \ldots \rightarrow \text{VALUE} = \text{VALUE ADDED} + \text{CAPITAL} \leftarrow \frac{EVA\ 1}{(1 + COC)} + \frac{EVA\ 2}{(1 + COC)^2} + \ldots$$

YR 1 EVA 1 | YR 2 EVA 2 | . . .

PV(FCF) = V = PV(EVA) + CAP

Exhibit 9.7. Valuation

when the amount of initial capital of the firm is added to the discounted EVA (or value-added) sum.

This result is important, because it suggests that VALUE may, under certain assumptions, be calculated using EVA components (in place of cash flow) and that the definition of EVA as a period measure of value added yields the same VALUE when a discounted sum of EVA terms is taken. Shareholder value can be expressed in terms of EVA components, too.

For initial implementation, using VALUE (EVA) for valuation is not always recommended, because the set of assumptions for value equality may not be valid in all cases, and FCF-based routines are well established for project valuation in business cases in most firms. The specialized circumstances and assumptions for VALUE equality may not be applicable to the majority of projects and investments of a firm without an adjustment.

Identification and correction of any systematic difference in the VALUE determined by EVA and FCF (usually a function of project timing and start-up assumptions) may be viewed as a transition issue. As implementation takes root, the advantages of consistency—of using EVA as one common measure with a common language and framework, with operating drivers for all planning and budgeting, for both period and total value estimation—may dominate the discomfort of any needed adjustments. In addition, as shown by Worthington,[14] the contribution (as a percentage of total value) from EVA continuing value will be less than the percent value attributed to the FCF continuing value; part of this effect is attributable to the role of initial capital in the EVA net present value (NPV) formulation. Even with reliance on the cash flow approach to calculating value, it would be useful to complement it with the EVA approach to get a different perspective on the components of total value, specifically the value added in the early years and the continuing value.

What is interesting, however, is that the period component of PV (FCF) does not yield

[14] Adapted from Mac Worthington's unpublished AT&T presentation, "Terminal Value Computation in Cash Flow Valuation of Business Opportunities" (1994).

any information about value added for the period—but EVA does, by definition. Instead, FCF merely indicates the dependence on parent or external financing.

(b) Tracking by Economic Value Added. We have already touched upon some difficulties associated with budgeting and tracking valuation by cash flows: the dependence on an intractable continuing value, the impossibility of tracking all years, the shifts in cash flows in the budget year caused by actual prior year-end balance sheet variances, and the lack of information inherent in component cash flows.

A few years of EVA data, on the other hand, indicate how much value has been created by management, and thereby evaluate progress toward shareholder value. When all-period valuation is appropriate, it is recommended that EVA period measures be generated for the first three to five years of analysis, along with the multi-year valuation to supplement the FCF valuation approach and to provide a basis for meaningful budgeting and tracking. As a period performance measure, EVA connects forward-looking valuation to performance evaluation. Because EVA is not a cash-flow measure, and because its period interpretation is value oriented, it greatly facilitates period tracking of value, thereby adding "memory" to the planning process.

(c) Guide to Appropriate Uses of Economic Value Added. Economic value added is the best internal, single-period measure of value creation. However, single-period values of EVA are not to be used for critical asset or investment and project evaluation decisions, which are based on long-term value creation potential. Instead, discounted cash-flow valuation utilizing NPV is mandated for decisions involving multiperiod benefits, such as business unit evaluation, lease/buy decisions, mergers and acquisitions, and strategic options assessment. (Subject to the conditions raised in Section 9.4(a), NPV based on EVA could be utilized.)

As discussed in the previous section, EVA, in addition to its primary role, can serve as a complement to discounted cash-flow valuation, particularly to gauge the initial impact of the project or investment, and to track.

9.5 BUDGETING SHAREHOLDER VALUE.

Critical investment decisions, based on long-term valuation, come in several different forms in a typical corporation. Budgeting of these investments is often spotty, partly because it is difficult to isolate the effects of an investment project embedded in an operating unit's returns.

(a) Business Cases. Business cases are the fundamental support analysis for business decisions involving resource utilization. The business-case process, while dealing with periodic projects and investments, must be an integral part of budgeting and planning.

Business cases for research and development (R&D) and capital (additions to plant, property, and equipment) also serve as the basis for subsequent measurement and tracking actions.

As part of the financial analysis of the project, business-case output should exhibit the net present value and other standard measures, as well as the EVA forecasts for the first three to five years. The latter will be compared to actuals to determine whether initial additions (or depletions) from value are on schedule. Incremental cash-flow effects of investment are represented, along with risks, uncertainty, and alternatives.

Review and approval procedures are usually specified by corporate governance. For example, it is a Lucent corporate requirement that a rigorous business-case process drive business investment decisions. Capital investments are further discussed in Chapters 19 and 20.

(b) Capital and Investment Programs. Potential mergers and acquisitions, divestitures, investments, and joint ventures are included in these programs, along with additions to capital and additions to finance assets; the latter two categories are included in the program at a more aggregate level.

Consummated ventures should be tracked quarterly, comparing budget and actual values for revenues, EVA, funding, and the like.

Part of the investment analysis is an evaluation of the expected impact on the parent's reported EVA earnings after the acquisition. This assessment is usually more important than the EVA expected from the new entity itself.

Review of major investments will be based on a comparison of original enabling business case expectations with actuals. Again, comparison of the first few years' actuals versus plan EVA values is strongly recommended.

A clear understanding should exist as to the circumstances under which a potential acquisition should be included in the company and entity budgets, rather than merely covered by a separate investment program or business case. Generally, large magnitudes combined with a high degree of uncertainty result in omission of the investment from the budget, or statement of the budget with and without the investment. ''Ready for approval'' investments are usually reflected in the budget.

(c) Business Plans. As a part of the annual planning process, each business unit is expected to generate a business plan, consisting mainly of a strategic plan and a financial plan. The first year of the financial plan usually becomes next year's budget. Its monitoring and tracking are discussed in Section 9.5(e).

However, budgeting and tracking should also play a role in subsequent assessments of the business plan. To curtail undue optimism in the late years of the plan (the ''hockey stick effect''), financial projections, particularly EVA and revenue, should be monitored and compared to actuals, from the second through tenth years. Such an assessment would conceivably contribute to a greater degree of comfort or discomfort for the attainability of the immediate budget year.

(d) Resource Allocation. Based on resource requirements expressed in the business plans to achieve business strategies and long-term economic profits, senior management makes resource allocation decisions as a step in arriving at a budget for next year and beyond. Strategic considerations are paramount, or at least share equal billing with economic considerations in all resource-allocation decisions. A business-case analysis of the life-cycle cash flows indicates the economic value of a project.

Economic considerations generally can be assessed by two broad categories: benefit and efficiency measures.[15] Benefit measures reveal the cash benefit from investing in a particular proposal, expressed in dollar terms: measures include shareholder value, NPV, and discounted cash flows. Efficiency measures, expressed as a percentage, indicate how productive a project is in generating cash, relative to resource costs. A ratio of shareholder value or NPV to the present value of all cash outflows (resource expenditures) is used, as is an internal rate of return. Long-term attractiveness tends to dominate decisions, and capital projects and investments could be ranked by total value (or by value per resource input).

Translation of the consequences of resource allocation must be included in the budget.

[15] Adapted from Harish Chandra's unpublished AT&T memo, ''Resource Allocation'' (1993).

Economic impact should include impact on EVA and total value. Considerations of cash affordability for the firm must also be evaluated.

(e) Operating Budget Review. Once major resource allocation decisions are made, attention falls on the commitment budget. Now, period measures such as EVA and FCF are more important as indicators of value added and current cash flow than total valuation. The year-to-year change in unit EVA is as important a measure as the current level of EVA (and its sign).

The budget should pose a challenge that is achievable. If each operating unit makes its EVA level, and that EVA level is viewed as a stepping stone toward maximizing shareholder value over time, the enterprise will be successful.

A budget (by year; quarter; and, usually, month) consists of parts or all of an income statement, balance sheet, funds flow, and measures (particularly, the explicit commitment measures to which compensation is tied). In this budgeting mode, EVA is the best measure.

(f) Monthly Actuals Reporting. Key measures compared by unit and month for budget versus actual and budget versus last year's period should include EVA, FCF, and revenue. Economic value added can be decomposed into its operating drivers—revenue growth, NOPAT margin, and capital turnover—and the respective variances compared, to better understand shortfalls. As EVA is implemented in the company, additional critical information can be shown, such as variance in the EVA operating drivers, discussed in Section 9.3(g).

Exhibit 9.8 displays useful information for management of budget/actual differences in EVA, underlying data, and drivers. Consolidated EVA is also shown in internal company reports as a sum of entity EVAs for actual and budget, enabling identification of entity shortfalls. A modified tree diagram (see Exhibit 9.5) displays more value drivers, to assess the principal source of actual/budget variance.

9.6 SUMMARY. Effectively managing and measuring value calls for different, although complementary, techniques depending on the intended use and the associated time

($)	Actual	Budget	Difference
Operating income	133	139	(6)
EVA adjustments	(11)	(9)	(2)
Adjusted operating income	122	130	(8)
Cash taxes paid	(35)	(37)	2
	—	—	—
NOPAT	87	93	(6)
Average invested capital	579	599	(20)
EVA	20	24	(4)
EVA Drivers Impact			
Change in NOPAT			(6)
Change in adjusted operating income		(8)	
Change in cash taxes paid		2	
Change in average capital @ 11.5% cost of capital			2
Change in EVA			(4)

Exhibit 9.8. EVA year-to-date results

period required. For decisions involving long-term value creation potential, the all-period FCF valuation should be utilized to estimate shareholder value. However, for budgeting purposes, the EVA annual component is particularly valuable in budgeting as a measure of value created in a period. It indicates how much value is to be created from capital by management, and thereby evaluates progress toward the all-period shareholder value.

For a single period, EVA is the best measure of value creation, and EVA should be monitored and tracked for budgeting.

Valuation must be closely linked to single-period measures of value created. When all-period valuation is required (e.g., business cases), it is recommended that EVA period measures be generated for the first three to five years of analysis to provide a basis for meaningful budgeting and tracking.

We have seen that EVA is particularly well suited to discern the drivers of EVA budget variances, especially to determine whether the income statement or balance sheet is variance causative.

Adding measures such as EVA to budget and planning processes has some practical consequences, which have been very positive. In particular, attention must be paid to balance sheets, as well as just income statements.

The use of EVA has also aided the establishment of market-facing business units and strategic business units by prescribing a meaningful sufficient set of financials and an associated measure of value added that enables close scrutiny of the true financial performance of these discrete entities. Thus, adoption of EVA is seen as a boon to driving financials to the smallest revenue-generating units, because cash taxes and capital on the balance sheet, in addition to standard profitability, are required components at a business unit or strategic business unit level (usually characterized by separate markets, customers, products/services, competitors, and so on).

SOURCES AND SUGGESTED REFERENCES

Copeland, Tom, Tim, Koller, and Jack, Murrin, *Valuation—Measuring and Managing the Value of Companies.* New York: John Wiley & Sons, 1990.

Rachlin, Robert, *Return on Investment Manual: Tools and Applications for Managing Financial Results.* Armonk, New York: M. E. Sharpe, 1997.

Rappaport, Alfred, *Creating Shareholder Value.* New York: The Free Press, 1986.

Stewart, G. Bennett III, *The Quest for Value.* New York: HarperCollins, 1990.

Stewart, G. Bennett III, *Stern Stewart Corporate Finance Handbook.* New York: Stern Stewart Management Services, 1986.

CHAPTER 10

APPLYING THE BUDGET SYSTEM

R. Layne Weggeland
Malcolm M. Knapp

Malcolm M. Knapp Inc.

10.1 INTRODUCTION. This chapter discusses the considerations and techniques involved in the analysis, review, presentation, and approval of the budget.

Earlier chapters have described the need for the budget manager to issue both a comprehensive planning calendar and the chief executive's statement of overall corporate and divisional goals and objectives for the next planning period. The budget manager should also prepare a clear and concise planning manual containing completed examples of all forms that must be used by the divisions. Care must be taken to ensure that the forms are simple in format and easy to use.

The manager responsible for the review, presentation, and approval process must accomplish several tasks early in the budget planning and review cycle. First, in establishing an effective budgetary control system, the budget manager of any organization must create a system within his or her department that will provide for the careful analysis and review of the data submitted as part of a budget proposal. The manager must then present the budget, after appropriate review and discussion with lower-level management and departmental groups, in a clear and concise format for senior management review, discussion, and eventual approval. Second, the budget manager should try to convince the chief executive officer (CEO) of the need for a clear relationship of the line-division executive's performance review, compensation, and career-path development with the budgeting process. When this linkage is established, the divisional operating executives are involved thoroughly in the budgeting process and follow, with great care and commitment, the analysis, review, and approval of their individual budgets. Third, the budget manager should be sure that the budgetary planning system reflects both the artificial time constraints proposed by the need for annual financial reporting and tax filing and the real-world, longer-term business patterns of various corporate projects, that is, major marketing plans, capital improvements, and research and development activities, which frequently extend over a two- to five-year time span.

Before detailed analyses and reviews are made of individual divisional budget plans, it is important that the budget manager identify and keep clearly in mind the key variables in his or her own corporation, its industry, and the economy. These variables include the following:

- The rate of new product introduction by the company and its competitors
- Market share and relationship to competitors

- Marketing and sales policies
- Financial ratios
- The degree of capital intensity
- Raw material and manufacturing capacity limitations
- Governmental restrictions
- Economic factors

There might be other key variables that are carefully monitored by senior management and that must be considered by the budget manager in the review.

Budget managers must be very knowledgeable about the degree of accuracy that their organizations have attained in their accounting and reporting systems and sales forecasts and about the organization's historical ability to achieve marketing and cost-control programs and goals.

Before beginning any analysis, the budget manager also must be very clear about the budget-year goals of the company as stated by senior management early in the planning-cycle year. Ideally, the budget officer would have been involved in discussions with senior management in formulating the goals of the company that must be incorporated in the budget period to be reviewed.

Each division or appropriate operating group prepares as part of its budget package (where appropriate and as requested by the budget manager) the following items:

- Detailed sales and marketing plans
- Manufacturing and operating expense plans
- Manpower budgets
- Capital expenditure plan
- Financial budgets (balance sheet, profit and loss statement, sources, and application of funds)

The budget manager, depending on the circumstances and the degree of detail that is needed, may request the preparation of a variety of additional budget forms to provide details under the broad categories just listed. Each operating group's budget package could possibly contain a combination of the following detailed schedules:

- Gross/net sales by product line
- Analysis of gross sales growth
- Sales forecasts by product line
- Manufacturing expense analysis
- Monthly departmental expense plan
- Personnel compensation analysis
- Summary of operating group net income
- Cost of sales plan
- Operating expense analysis
- General administrative expense analysis
- Capital projects summary

- Capital projects listing of new projects
- Capital projects listing of carry-over projects
- Balance sheet
- Cash-flow forecast plan
- Inventory forecast plan

Accompanying each operating group's budget submission should be a general manager's commentary on the plan's assumptions, profit objectives, primary programs, and required investment and profit potential that would result from the acceptance by senior management of the operating group's budget plan.

10.2 INITIAL BUDGET DEPARTMENT REVIEW OF DIVISIONAL BUDGET PACKAGES. Following the receipt of the divisional budget packages, the budget-planning group starts a series of reviews of each budget submission, as shown in Exhibits 10.1 and 10.2.

The initial review includes the following steps:

1. **Data Verification**
   a. Review of the mathematical calculations within the plans
   b. Confirmation that the sales and marketing estimates are integrated correctly into all operating budgets within each division
2. **Analysis of Previous Forecast Reliability.** A comparison should be made between the forecasts of past years, that of the current year, and the proposed performance in the next planning year. The reasons for the current year variances should be carefully evaluated, and then a comparison should be made with the proposed budget year to see that corrective action has been built into the plan in order to avoid significant variances in the following year.
3. **Analysis of Divisional Budget Assumptions and Goals.** The assumptions and goals incorporated into each division's budget plans must be tested for validity in the following areas:
   a. Correlation to CEO's planning objectives and goals
   b. Relation to general economic conditions and forecasts of possible economic changes within the forthcoming planning year
   c. Impact of specific economic issues affecting that operating division's interest rates, cost of capital, and so forth
   d. Competitive analysis
   e. Technological change
   f. Raw material cost and availability
   g. Other assumptions incorporated into the budget submission, such as sales and marketing goals

10.3 DIVISIONAL REVIEW MEETINGS. After the budget department's initial review of each division's budget-plan submissions, the budget manager should hold a series of review meetings at the divisional staff level. These meetings should involve discussion and resolution of the issues that developed from the initial budget department staff review. The outcome of these meetings should be a revised budget that is free from obvious errors and omissions.

BUDGET REVIEW PROCESS

BUDGET DEPARTMENT
INITIAL REVIEW

DIVISION
K

DIVISION
O

DIVISION
W

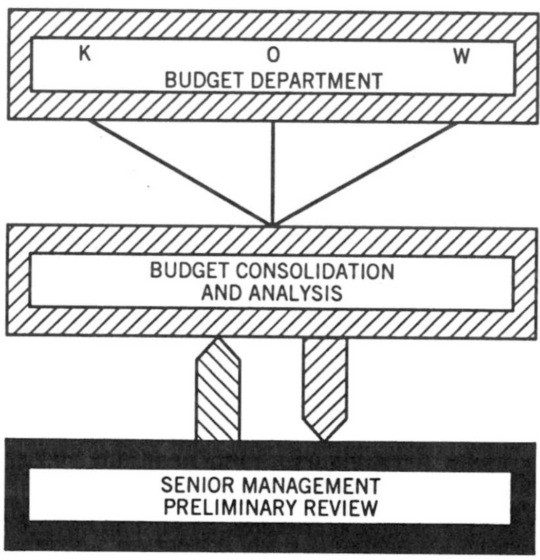

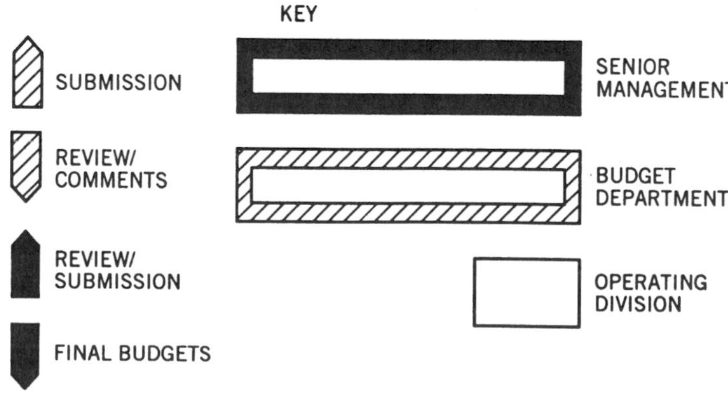

Exhibit 10.1. Budget review process—initial review

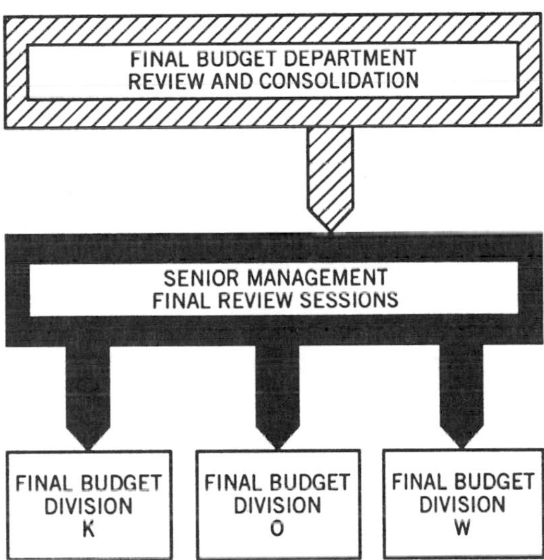

Exhibit 10.2. Budget review process—final revision of division operating plans

Following the divisional group staff-level reviews, the budget manager should hold a private review meeting with the division's general manager. During this meeting, the budget manager should identify and attempt to resolve those items that surfaced during the staff-level review meetings and to be certain that the division's general manager will make a total commitment to the revised budget plan that has resulted from the review meetings at the divisional staff level. Since, ideally, the division's general manager's compensation would, in part, be related to his or her division's performance in the next planning cycle, it is important that all areas of dispute be clearly resolved and that the general manager and his or her staff be in total agreement and fully accept and support the revised budget plan.

During these review meetings, the budget manager must be very alert to the possibility of reserves being incorporated into the division's plans in order to provide a cushion and to protect performance-oriented compensation payments for the division's general manager and his or her senior management group. This type of reserve must be clearly identified and eliminated at the divisional level prior to the final presentation of each plan to senior management.

10.4 BUDGET CONSOLIDATION AND ANALYSIS. Following its review of the divisional plans, the budget department staff prepares a consolidation of the various divisional budgets. Ideally, budget managers and their staffs would have access to one of the various computerized budget-control systems now available. These computerized systems permit rapid and accurate consolidation of the divisional group budgets and provide easy intercompany eliminations.

At this point, budget managers would have their first indication of the total corporate profit that would result from the consolidation of the individual budget plans. They must then test the total corporate budget against the previously stated senior management goals and objectives for the next planning period. Typical goals might be the following:

- A certain level of sales for the corporation
- Specific earning targets
- A specific return on asset targets
- Manpower levels
- Inventory levels

The budget manager should form a comprehensive opinion as to whether the total corporation will be within or will fail to obtain the original objectives that were set forth by the CEO.

10.5 PRELIMINARY SENIOR MANAGEMENT REVIEW. After the first corporate consolidated budgets are reviewed and analyzed, the budget manager and his or her staff should prepare a summary written review and analysis for the CEO, the chief financial officer (CFO), and the executive vice-president. The budget manager then would meet with the senior executive management of the company and review in broad terms the total corporation's consolidated budget summaries, discussing whether each operating division has, in its budget plan, satisfactorily met the CEO's planning objectives.

If, during the planning cycle, external events and internal evaluation provided by the divisional managers create the need for a critical reassessment of the CEO's original goals and objectives, then the budget manager must raise this question with senior management. Possibly, modifications may be required in the corporation's goals and objectives.

If senior management gives a general acceptance of the division's plans and the overall corporate plan, then the budget manager goes back to each division and indicates senior management's acceptance of the division's plans or identifies specific areas that must be changed prior to senior management's final review and approval.

10.6 FINAL REVISION OF OPERATING GROUP PLANS. The operating division's general manager and his or her management would revise their budget to conform with any comments, suggestions, and criticisms expressed by senior management during its initial review.

10.7 SECOND BUDGET STAFF REVIEW OF OPERATING GROUP PLANS. Following revisions, the budget manager and his or her staff would again test the revised budgets against the stated objectives and the specific comments raised during the initial senior management review. The divisions would again be contacted, and any further modifications would be discussed and accepted by the operating groups.

10.8 REVISED CONSOLIDATED BUDGET PREPARATIONS. When the budget department is satisfied that the divisional revised plans are in accord with the planning goals and that they are properly prepared, the budget department would prepare a new consolidated corporate budget summary. The summary would be prepared in various levels of detail, to reflect the particular interests and needs of senior management and divisional management.

Also, the budget department, where appropriate, could prepare a variety of visual aids to be used during the senior management planning review sessions. The budget manager and his or her staff should be very careful to preview visual aids with the division's general manager and staff prior to using them in the senior management review sessions.

10.9 FINAL SENIOR MANAGEMENT BUDGET REVIEW SESSIONS. At least a week before the senior management final budget review meeting, the budget manager should distribute the divisional and consolidated budgets, with appropriate commentary, to all managers scheduled to attend these meetings. It is very important that the commentary and any additional data prepared by the planning department for use during senior management review meetings be reviewed in advance with each divisional manager and his or her staff.

The final senior management review should ideally be scheduled in a location away from the normal work environment. In this way, all levels of management can concentrate totally on the divisional and consolidated budget plans without being distracted by other activities.

During the review meetings, the budget manager should take careful and detailed notes of all decisions and changes made during the review process. In addition, the planning manager should promptly issue minutes of each planning session so that there will be a clear understanding of all agreed-upon changes and/or additions within each divisional plan.

10.10 OPERATING GROUPS' MONTHLY SUBMISSIONS. Following the final review and revision of group and corporate plans, the budget manager should request monthly divisional budgets. These budgets should then be quickly incorporated into the financial reporting system of the company, and the monthly financial reporting should accurately reflect variances from previously budgeted performance and cost levels. In addition, the budget manager and his or her staff should prepare at least quarterly performance analyses and reviews of all operating groups. Review meetings should be held with all divisional and senior management groups.

The budget manager should be satisfied that the financial reporting system of the company can provide enough detail to permit each operational unit within the divisions to identify promptly the reasons for a variance from previously forecasted budget performance and to take corrective action in order to maintain budgeted performance levels.

10.11 EFFECTIVE USE OF COMPUTER-BASED SPREADSHEETS AND GRAPHICS PROGRAMS. In recent years, computerized spreadsheets, quality graphics programs, and low-cost laser printers have become available to all budget managers. One must use them or become obsolete.

The great value of spreadsheet programs such as Lotus 1-2-3™ is that they save an enormous amount of time, and, because of this happy fact, one is able to test and analyze many more possible variations. This leads to better estimates, because one does not have the barrier of time to limit the ability to experiment and explore a series of scenarios. The resulting series of possible projections shows the consequences, both positive and negative, of a variety of assumptions and can serve to focus attention on the truly key variables that can dramatically affect the attainment of the organization's budget goals and objectives.

The budget manager must also either thoroughly understand one or more graphics programs or have several key subordinates who have the necessary skills, because effective graphical presentation of data is a requirement of senior management. The best presentation will often win the day. One should not limit the acceptance of his or her ideas because of inadequate graphical presentations.

10.12 SUMMARY. The most important element in applying the budget system effectively is the appropriateness of the system to the culture of the company, its internal workings, and the external environment. The CEO must believe in the system and promote its use and must insist on the clear linkage of line-division executives' performance reviews, compensation, and career-path development to the budgeting system. Finally, the system must be mechanically good, clear, easy to use, and well executed.

SOURCES AND SUGGESTED REFERENCES

Finch, Gerald L., and William Mihal, ''Spend It or Lose It?,'' *Management Accounting (NAA),* vol. LXX, no. 9, March 1989.

Hirst, M. K., ''The Effects of Setting Budget Goals and Task Uncertainty on Performance: A Theoretical Analysis,'' *Accounting Review,* vol. 62, October 1987.

Merchant, Kenneth A., and Jean F. Manzoni, ''The Achievability of Budget Targets in Profit Centers: A Field Study,'' *Accounting Review,* vol. 64, July 1989.

Olenick, Arnold J., *Managing to Have Profits: The Art of Hitting Your Target Profit.* New York: McGraw-Hill, 1989.

Pasewark, William R., and Ronald L. Clark, ''Understanding What Went Wrong With the Budget,'' *Corporate Accounting,* vol. 6, no. 1, Winter 1988.

Rachlin, Robert, *Return on Investment Manual: Tools and Applications for Managing Financial Results.* Armonk, New York: M. E. Sharpe, 1997.

CHAPTER 11

BUDGETS AND PERFORMANCE COMPENSATION

Graef S. Crystal

11.1 INTRODUCTION. "You didn't make your budget, so there's not going to be any bonus this year." Or: "If you exceed your budget by 20%, you will receive twice your normal bonus."

Statements like these reverberate through "mahogany row" as companies come to grips with the difficult issue of rewarding their executive cadre. The top managers of these companies know that before performance can be rewarded, it must first be measured. Therefore, they frequently seize on the company's already established budgeting process as the yardstick by which some people will receive a lot, others a little, and still others nothing. Interestingly, they do this notwithstanding that at other times, and perhaps even on the very same day, they are holding their sides and rolling on the floor after first viewing the ludicrous budget figures submitted by their operating unit managers.

The purpose of this chapter is to view the budget as a tool for measuring and rewarding executive performance. Its uses and abuses will be explored first concerning the area of short-term incentive compensation plans and later, longer-term incentive plans. Short-term incentives are aimed at rewarding performance in a single fiscal year, whereas longer-term incentives (e.g., stock options) are geared toward rewarding performance over a series of years.

11.2 MEASURES OF EXECUTIVE PERFORMANCE. By definition, incentive plans are supposed to "incent" something. So, before we begin to talk about budgets per se, we must first briefly explore the various profit measures that different companies use for incentive compensation purposes.

(a) Net Income After Everything. Let us start by mentally evoking a picture of a company's income statement and focusing on its bottom line, the one labeled "net income after taxes and after extraordinary items." There is an instinctive appeal for this measure of corporate performance. Shareholders, after all, take their rewards from the bottom line, and, so the argument goes, why should executives not do the same?

Few companies, however, see it this way in practice. They believe that extraordinary items, as the name implies, are truly extraordinary and that executives should not be held accountable for what might be termed the "UFOs of the income statement." Besides, changes in accounting rules have made extraordinary items really extraordinary as opposed to the looser interpretations of the past. Also, an extraordinary item might be the result of actions taken years ago and by a different management team.

(b) Exclusion of Taxes. This being the case, let us move up a line on the income statement and look at "net income before extraordinary items." Surely, this ought to be a winner for incentive-compensation purposes. Once again, however, some companies are contrary minded. They note that this measure includes the effects of income taxes, and they point out, seemingly quite properly, that executives have no control over income taxes.

Lately, a growing number of companies have begun to reject this line of reasoning. They note that the government is, most of the time, also in the incentive business, offering reductions in taxes for investing in new capital equipment, drilling for oil, and the like. (To be sure, the comprehensive tax law passed in 1986 is designed to take the government out of the incentive business, but tax incentives nonetheless remain. If history is any guide, more tax incentives will, like barnacles on a ship, attach themselves as time passes.) They reason that executives should not be insulated from these governmental inducements, or else they just might decide not to build a new plant because the pretax return on capital in contrast to the aftertax return looks marginal. These companies are also of the more generalized view that, in the final analysis, many facets of business life (not just taxes) are inherently uncontrollable. Take the case of a supermarket chain in which the supplier of shopping bags raises prices. If you are managing the supermarket chain, what are you going to do? Presumably, you will first ascertain whether you can get a better deal from another supplier; but suppose you cannot. Well, you can stop giving shoppers any bags at all or you can charge them for bags, but in either case, your assumption that you will lose market share will likely be borne out—and quite quickly. Alternatively, you can look for some other costs to cut—for example, paring inventories or decreasing the number of checkers—these strategies may also prove counterproductive. As a last resort, you may be forced to raise prices to cover the costs of the shopping bags, or you may simply have to live with a lower bottom line. The point here is that income taxes, like shopping bags, are a cost of doing business and cannot be conveniently ignored just because they are uncontrollable.

(c) Exclusion of Incentive-Plan Costs. Nonetheless, for the sake of discussion, let us grant the pretax school its point of view. Do we stop here with net income before income taxes and before extraordinary items? Most likely not, for we have yet to confront a cost that is "upstream" to this measure of performance; namely, the cost of the incentive plan itself. Consider this hypothetical conversation between a chief executive officer (CEO) and his or her controller.

Controller: Well, Chief, it looks like our pretax profits this year will be an even $1 million.

CEO: That's great. Since our incentive plan gives us 20% of pretax profits, we'll have a $200,000 bonus fund to play around with.

Controller: Well, not quite. If we spend $200,000 on bonuses, our pretax profits will be only $800,000.

CEO: Oh, I see. So I guess we'll have to be content with a fund of only $160,000, or 20% of the $800,000 of profits.

Controller: Well, that's still not quite right, Chief. If we spend only $160,000 on bonuses, our pretax profits will be $840,000!

And so it goes. If the dialogue were carried far enough, the CEO and the controller would finally hit on the correct bonus fund amount; or if they still remembered their algebra, they could have employed simultaneous equations to determine the answer. However, given that most top managers seemingly have little patience and sometimes even less mathematical ability, it usually makes sense to utilize a profit measure for incentive purposes that excludes any accruals already made for the incentive plan itself. Thus, if we are dealing with a pretax profit measure, we simply add back to pretax profits any amounts already charged for the incentive plan. If we are dealing with an aftertax profit measure, we add back a sum equal to the increase in aftertax profits that would have occurred had no bonuses been payable. This involves not only the reversal of the bonus accrual itself, but also the related reduction in provision for income taxes.

Thus far, several alternative corporate performance measures have been discussed, all of them drawn from the company's income statements. There are pros and cons for each of these measures, and one cannot axiomatically state that a given measure is better under all circumstances than other measures.

(d) Taking Account of the Cost of Capital. In a sort of ''pox on all your houses'' perspective, one can at least question whether any of these measures is really right for most companies. This is because the cost of raising capital has not yet been taken into full account.

Remember that the philosophical view underlying most incentive plans is that executives will not instinctively do what is right for the company. Rather, they will do what is right for themselves, and if that happens by chance to benefit the company, so much the better. Accordingly, the primary purpose of most incentive plans is to align executives' economic interests with those of the company, permitting them to maximize their income while doing the same for the shareholders.

Let us assume that net income after taxes has been tentatively adopted as the measure of corporate performance that we wish to ''incent.'' How are we going to get into any real trouble? Well, for example, the executive group decides to sell another 1 million shares of stock to the public. At a price of $100 each, the company gains $100 million in cash. For want of a better alternative, this $100 million can be invested in short-term securities to yield another $6 million in pretax profits, another $4 million in aftertax profits, and *voilà,* some extra bonus money as well.

Do we really want to give this executive group extra rewards for earning a paltry 4% aftertax return on incremental capital at a time when the shareholders could earn essentially twice as much by investing their funds in high-grade corporate bonds?

(e) Earnings per Share. We can, of course, remedy this problem by changing our performance measure from net income after taxes to net income per share. That way, our executive group will presumably steer clear of further share issuances unless it can earn a decent return on incremental capital.

However, net income per share still allows the executives a free ride on incremental retained earnings. If the company produces $100 million of aftertax income for the year, and you are the CEO, why not try to keep the dividends as low as possible or, better yet, eliminate them entirely? That way, the entire $100 million will be available for investment. Since there are neither interest costs nor extra share issuances associated with this capital, any positive return, no matter how minuscule, will drop to the bottom line and enhance the company's bonus fund.

(f) Return on Shareholders' Equity. For this reason, many companies adopt as their measure of performance net income after taxes as a percentage of shareholders' equity, or more simply, return on equity (ROE). Now, for the first time, the executives will have to pay the freight on all sources of capital. If they take on extra debt, the numerator of the ROE fraction will be lowered by the interest costs involved. If they sell more shares to the public, the denominator of the fraction—equity—will be increased and ROE will drop unless some productive use can be made of the incremental capital. If some of the earnings are not paid out in dividends but are retained in the business, the denominator of the fraction will rise again and hit executives in their pocketbooks unless that capital can be made to earn its keep.

It can be seen, therefore, that an earnings per share (EPS) performance measure has the implicit effect of "disincenting" dividends, whereas an ROE performance measure sometimes has the opposite effect. Both the EPS and the ROE performance measures, however, have the seeming effect of "incenting" the creation of debt over equity as the preferred method of financing and business. For example, a company has earned $200 million of pretax profits and has $1 billion of equity. On that basis, it has a pretax ROE of 20%. The company wishes to raise $300 million of new capital for purposes of building a plant with a targeted pretax rate of return of 15%. One alternative is to sell another $300 million of equity to the public. By so doing, pretax profits will rise $45 million (15% of the $300 million of incremental equity) to $245 million, and the equity will rise from $1 billion to $1.3 billion. However, ROE will drop from 20% to 18.8%. Alternatively, the executives can visit their friendly bankers and come away with a loan of $300 million at an interest rate of 10%. In this case, pretax profits will rise by only $15 million ($45 million return on the new plant less $30 million in interest), but equity will remain unchanged at $1 billion. The result is an increase in ROE from 20% to 21.5%. If you were being "incented" for ROE, which alternative would you take?

(g) Return on Capital Employed. Of course, executives do not have a totally free hand in deciding whether they will finance the business through debt or equity. If they get too piggish regarding the assumption of additional debt, they will find their interest costs rising and eventually may be denied access to the credit markets altogether. Then, the board of directors has to give final approval to the proposed course of financing, and outside directors will presumably not accede to unlimited leveraging.

Nonetheless, many boards of directors do not wish to police this area themselves. Rather, they wish to let the incentive plan do it for them. In such a situation, they are likely to reject both EPS and ROE as measures of performance, preferring instead to utilize what is often termed *return on capital employed* (ROCE). Here, the numerator of the fraction starts with the company's basic profit measure for incentive purposes. For example, pretax profits plus any charges already accrued against pretax profits for the incentive plan itself. To this basic profit measure are then added interest costs for long-term debt. (If the basic profit measure is stated in aftertax terms, aftertax interest costs rather than pretax interest costs are added.) The denominator of the ROCE equation is the sum of equity and long-term debt.

The ROCE has the effect of making the executive group indifferent as to the utilization of debt or of equity for financing the business. The numerator of the fraction—profits—

remains the same in either instance, inasmuch as any interest costs on long-term debt are reversed out of profits. The denominator of the fraction—equity plus debt—also remains the same.

No wonder drug is without its side effects, and this is the case here. Although the executive group has been rendered indifferent as to use of debt or equity, it has also been rendered indifferent as to the costs of debt. In the somewhat unreal world of ROCE, it matters not what the interest rate on long-term debt is, because all interest costs on such debt have been reversed out of profits. Rather, it matters only what the incremental return before interest costs is; if the interest costs turn out to exceed this incremental return, well no one is perfect.

Highly capital-intensive companies nevertheless tend to prefer an ROCE measure over either an ROE or an EPS measure. Indeed, a few of these companies go even further and use a return-on-assets measure. In this case, they reverse all interest costs out of the numerator of the fraction, including those on both short- and long-term debt. The denominator then becomes the total assets of the company.

It seems appropriate here to introduce the concept of ''shareholder value.'' Ultimately, a shareholder benefits only from increased dividends and/or increased stock price appreciation. Any other performance, such as great growth in EPS, is interesting, but it does not put bread on the shareholder's table by itself.

In a sense, anyone designing an incentive plan (unless he or she is out to lunch) is making an implicit but highly critical assumption, namely, that the performance measure being used is somehow linked to shareholder value creation. To put it another way, unless you are being paid off by the competition, why do you want to design an incentive plan that hands out goodly sums of the shareholders' money and yet does not increase shareholder value?

For some years, many experts asserted a strong linkage between EPS and EPS growth on the one hand, and stock prices on the other. Hence, it was supposed that the higher a company's EPS, the higher its stock price would be. Moreover, it was also thought even more strongly that the higher the growth rate in EPS, the higher the price would be earnings multiple.

More recent studies have shown that there is some linkage between EPS and shareholder value, but the linkage is nowhere as strong as has been previously asserted. Indeed, the studies show that if you really want to account for what drives stock prices, at least over the longer term, you must pay attention to the following three factors:

1. The book value per share
2. The growth in book value per share
3. The ''true'' return on equity

If a company is exhibiting only normal growth and is earning only a normal return, then its stock price is apt to be about equal to its book value. In other words, its market: book ratio is apt to be 1.00. However, if the company is increasing its earnings at a higher-than-average rate and is also earning a higher-than-average ROE, its market:book ratio is apt to be higher than 1.00. (By the same token, lower-than-average growth coupled with lower-than-average returns will likely produce a market:book ratio lower than 1.00.)

The concept of ROE traces from the so-called capital assets pricing model. This model tells us the following:

- When the late Maurice Chevalier celebrated his 80th birthday, a correspondent asked him how he felt to be 80 years old. His reply: Consider the alternative! By the same token, you, as an investor, also have to consider the alternative—or, more correctly, alternatives. One such alternative is to put your money in riskless 90-day Treasury bills. The interest rate may only be 5.5%, but you can at least sleep at night secure in the knowledge that your principal is protected.
- If you are going to invest in anything more risky than T-bills, you are going to want to earn a higher return to compensate for the risk. Studies show that, over long time periods, an investment in your average stock will earn you a return that is about seven percentage points above the riskless return rate. Therefore, if the riskless return rate is 5.5%, then investing in a stock with normal risk characteristics should earn you a return of around 12.5%.
- Of course, if you invest in a highly risky stock, you are going to want more than just an average return. Here, risk is measured by the so-called beta. The beta gauges the degree to which a particular stock's price movements are more or less volatile than the price movements of the market as a whole. Thus, if the entire market changes its price, on average, by 10% (up or down), and the price of your company's stock also changes, on average, by 10%, we speak of your beta as being 1.00. However, if the entire market changes its prices by 10% while your company's prices change by 20%, then we consider your beta to be 2.00. In this case, your stock is twice as volatile as the average stock.

  In this example, the capital asset pricing model tells us that an investor will demand a return equal to the sum of the riskless return rate and a risk premium, with the latter determined by multiplying the average risk premium (e.g., 7%) by the beta of the stock in question. If the riskless return rate is 5.5% and if the stock has normal volatility (beta of 1.00), then investors will demand a return of 5.5% + 7.0%, or 12.5%. If the riskless return rate is 5.5% and the stock's beta is 2.00, then investors will demand a return of 5.5% + (7.0% × 2.00), or 19.5%.

How does an investor get the return he or she desires? If investors demand a 12.5% return and the company obliges by producing a 12.5% aftertax ROE level, things are pretty easy. If the stock trades at its book value and continues to trade at its book value, then investors will get the 12.5% return they demand. What if the company is not so obliging? What if the return, instead of being 12.5%, is half of that, at 6.25%. Investors can still get their 12.5% return, provided they let the stock price drop until it is worth only half its book value per share. In that case, even though the company is telling its shareholders that they earned only 6.25% on book value in a particular year, those shareholders who were wise enough to buy when the stock price was trading at only half its book value are nonetheless receiving their desired 12.5% return. By the same token, if our hypothetical company is earning not a 12.5% return, but a whopping 25.0% return, it is not unreasonable to suppose that investors will bid up the price of the stock until it is trading at around 2.00 times its book value per share. In that manner, investors will continue to receive their desired 12.5% return.

What the capital asset pricing model tells us is that returns and growth are the stuff out of which smiling shareholders are created. Growth and return alone, however, are not going to do the trick. Moreover, performance cannot be considered in a vacuum but must be evaluated against the many alternatives that are always available to investors. Therefore, if inflation kicks up and that in turn triggers an increase in interest rates, your company had better start finding a way to earn an even greater return on its equity. Otherwise, its "true return on equity," which we now see is the amount by which its actual return on equity exceeds the return level demanded by investors will fall. Does all this mean, then, that ROE is all that matters? No, it does not and for the following reasons:

- Return on equity is very important in determining shareholder value. In fact, it is the single most important variable, but it is not the only variable.
- Return on equity can be measured directly or through proxies. Over the long run, there is a very high correlation between ROE levels and levels of ROCE or return on assets. These two measures can be viewed as surrogates, or proxies, for ROE in most instances. After all, like ROE, they too emphasize the maximization of returns on capital resources.
- Years ago, when I directed the compensation programs of General Dynamics Corporation, a senior executive, who was reviewing the return on investment (ROI) levels of the company's various divisions, was brought up short when he discovered that the Fort Worth division (which is appropriately located in Fort Worth, Texas) had suffered a staggering decline in its ROI levels—from 48,000% to 24,000%. A call to the president of that division revealed the source of the problem. It seems that the government owned all the assets in the entire division, except for the furnishings in the office of the division president. It also seems that the division president had recently bought new furniture, thereby doubling General Dynamics' investment in the division from around $5,000 to around $10,000!

In reality, there are some types of business, but not many, where capital is not a major consideration (i.e., advertising agencies and management consulting firms). In such cases, the use of ROE measures makes no sense at all. With this digression behind us, let us continue to scan the various performance measures that can be linked to incentives.

(h) Operating Unit Performance Measures. Until now, we have been discussing corporate-wide measures of performance. But what about the performance of an operating unit (division, group, etc.)?

We must start with all the same thought processes concerning the preferred measure of raw profits—that is, the inclusion or exclusion of extraordinary items, income taxes, and the costs of the incentive plan itself. We must also go a step further and consider what to do with charges for corporate overhead.

(i) Exclusion of Corporate Overhead. Virtually all operating unit managers consider charges for corporate overhead to be anathema. They cannot control such charges and do not see why they should be penalized by the profligacy of the corporate staff. Although it is true that they will, in theory, be the beneficiaries of any economies achieved by the corporate headquarters, they are quick to underscore the phrase "in theory."

However, a number of CEOs see a certain virtue in allocating charges for corporate overhead. They have a hard time controlling the growth of the corporate bureaucracy, and they figure that all the screaming on the part of the operating unit managers, who have to bear the charges, will stiffen their spines in dealing with their own corporate department heads. At the same time, they know that if they do not charge out corporate overhead, their operating unit managers will not only be seemingly indifferent to the costs involved but will try to transfer some of their own staff to the corporate headquarters. Apropos of all this, I am reminded of a conversation some years ago between the head of a major operating unit and his CEO.

Operating unit manager: You give me these ridiculous profit budgets to meet, and at the same time you charge my budget with the actual costs of corporate overhead. I'm having a hard enough time meeting my own part of the budget, but I'm finding it nearly impossible to achieve the bottom line after having to eat all the costs you're incurring in this puzzle palace you're running out of New York.

CEO: Listen, you ought to consider yourself lucky you're not getting all the service you're paying for!

Operating unit manager (upon reflection): You know, you're right. I'll just keep taking those charges as long as you keep your goons in New York!

(j) Use of a Capital Charge. No matter how the question concerning charging out or not charging out corporate overhead is resolved, one must still confront the issue, discussed previously, concerning the fact that raw profits do not fully reflect the costs of capital. This is more so here, since a few companies do not allocate the costs of debt, much less the costs of equity, to their operating units.

Some companies think they have the problem licked by defining operating unit performance in terms of contribution to EPS. By this, they mean the operating unit's profits divided by the number of shares outstanding. Their reasoning is, of course, fallacious in that the current number of shares outstanding, or accretions to the number of shares outstanding, is not necessarily correlated with the capital utilization patterns of any particular operating unit.

It would be theoretically possible to utilize an ROE measure, but most companies employ only truncated balance sheets for their operating units. These companies have developed the assets side of the balance sheet in full, but they show only current liabilities on the liabilities side. The reason lies in their inability to come up with any rational, defensible rules for determining the allocation between debt and equity with respect to a particular operating unit.

This problem can perhaps be seen more clearly in the case of a true subsidiary as opposed to a division of a company. In this instance, there is a full balance sheet probably containing some debt as well as some equity. What really is ''debt'' in the context of a wholly owned subsidiary? In the final analysis, debt is whatever the parent wants it to be (and so is equity) given the parent's ability to decree any dividend policy it wishes. Thus, the only thing that really matters in the case of an operating unit—whether that unit is a true subsidiary or a division—is its level of capital employed: its total assets minus its current liabilities.

In working with ROCE for an operating unit, one first has to learn whether the parent allocates to its operating units the costs of debt, particularly long-term debt. (Strangely, some companies do not allocate long-term debt on an operating unit's balance sheet, but they blithely charge the operating unit's profit-and-loss statement with some portion of the parent's long-term debt.) If such costs are allocated, they will have to be reversed out of profits.

In their place is usually levied a ''capital charge'' for some or all of the capital employed by the operating unit. This capital charge comes in two basic flavors. In some companies, a charge is made for all capital employed by the operating unit, including the capital the unit has had in place for a long time. If this method is utilized, then the operating unit's profit-and-loss budget will have to reflect the contemplated charge. For example, the operating unit starts out the year with $100 million of capital employed (again, total assets less current liabilities), and the parent imposes a 10% capital charge. The unit's business plans call for it to utilize a further $10 million of capital during the year. In that case, the unit's budget (at least for incentive purposes) should reflect a capital charge item of $11 million, thereby lowering budgeted profits by a like sum.

Other companies prefer not to use this approach, since the resulting budget figures are perceived to be too low. These companies will establish a targeted level of capital employed for the operating unit for the particular year, but they will make no capital charge for the targeted level itself. Hence, the operating unit's budget does not have to reflect any capital charge. However, actual profits are debited (or credited) by applying the capital charge factor (10% in the earlier example) to the amount by which actual capital employed during the year exceeds (or is less than) the targeted level of capital employed. From an incentive compensation standpoint, it really makes no difference which way a company chooses to proceed.

11.3 STRUCTURING REWARD OPPORTUNITIES. Before looking at budgets per se, let us consider how companies structure their reward opportunities. Compensation levels can never be set in a vacuum. Rather, they are set relative to what other companies are offering. That being the case, the typical company goes through a number of steps in structuring compensation opportunities for its executive corps.

First, the company selects a number of other companies against which it wishes to test its compensation levels. Sometimes, this group of other companies is engaged in the same industry as the company undertaking the examination. Sometimes, this group is more or less the same size (e.g., all companies with $1 to $3 billion of sales, regardless of industry). In still other cases, this group of companies consists simply of all the companies participating in some national survey conducted by a third party (e.g., a survey conducted by the Conference Board).

Next, the company attempts to determine the going rates of base salary and total cash compensation being paid to selected executive positions by the group of companies chosen. In this context, the term *going rate* usually means the average or the median rate of pay. Total cash compensation means the sum of base salary and the average or median short-term incentive award being offered. For example, let us assume that a company has determined that the going rate of base salary for one of the company's operating unit heads, taking into account the responsibilities of that executive and the size of the unit, is $200,000. Let us also assume that the going rate of total cash compensation for the same position is $280,000.

The company has to integrate the findings from its survey into its own internal compensation structure. If our hypothetical company is like most companies, it will assign the operating unit head to a base salary range carrying a midpoint of approximately $200,000 and will go on to offer a norm bonus of $80,000, or 40% of salary.

What does norm bonus mean here? In most cases, a norm bonus is what executives will receive if their corporation performs in an average manner, if the operating unit of which they are a part performs in an average manner, and if they personally perform in an average manner. This definition should be kept in mind because it can present serious problems in trying to link performance against budget to incentive compensation awards.

Finally, our hypothetical company will have to determine how much swing it will permit around the norm bonuses it has structured and the conditions under which the bonuses will in fact swing. For example, the company might decide that bonuses can range all the way from 0 to 200% of the norm award, or, in the case of our example, from 0 to $160,000. It might further decide the following:

- The operating unit head's bonus will be zero in the event that the unit achieves less than 85% of its budget for the year (''budget'' being the item[s] on the overall budget that conform to the company's definition of profitability for incentive compensation purposes).
- The bonus will be equal to the norm award of $80,000 in the event that actual profits exactly equal budget.
- The bonus will be twice the norm award, $160,000, in the event that actual profits are equal to 120% of budget or more.

This is a rather neat arrangement at first glance. However, first glances are often deceptive, and this could well be the case here.

11.4 PITFALLS OF LINKING INCENTIVES TO BUDGETS

(a) Corporate-Level Pitfalls. If you were the executive involved, would you not want to submit the lowest budget you thought you could get away with? By so doing, you would minimize the possibilities of receiving anything less than your norm award and you would maximize the possibilities of receiving your maximum award.

This is one fundamental lesson of using budgets to determine incentive awards—namely, if there is already ''game playing'' in the budget-setting process, the game playing will be exacerbated; if there was no game playing previously (an unlikely prospect!), there will shortly be some as soon as the players get a handle on the new rules.

Of course, one can assume that CEOs are no slouches at playing games themselves, or else they would not have made it that far in the organization. They can spot a phony budget a mile away, or they can at least spot a phony budget submitted by one of their operating unit heads. Perhaps their own corporate budget is another matter, inasmuch as they are also the beneficiaries of a low budget. Let us assume here, however, that the CEO has a board of directors that exercises more than the usual amount of scrutiny over budget figures or that he or she is capable of exhibiting more ''Satan, get thee behind me'' behavior than the usual CEO. That being the case, let us go on to assume that the CEO prepares a ''realistic'' corporate budget that is neither terribly demanding nor terribly easy.

If all these good things happen, are we then in good shape? Well, not exactly. Assume our hypothetical company is very high performing. In years past, it has consistently returned 20% after taxes on its equity. Given what he or she knows now, there is no reason for the CEO to assume that the company will not pull the rabbit out of the hat yet again this forthcoming year. Therefore, the CEO submits to the board of directors a budget calling for a continued 20% ROE.

Under the ground rules discussed previously, the CEO and the other senior executives with corporate-wide responsibilities will receive their norm bonuses if they meet budget—in this case, a 20% ROE. On the surface, this looks to be reasonable, inasmuch as a 20% ROE is believed to be a realistic budget for that company in that particular year.

How does a 20% ROE stack up against the ROE performance of the group of companies on which the base salary, norm bonus, and total cash compensation levels were predicted? For example, suppose an examination of the financial performance of these other companies revealed that the median company's ROE was only 14%. In this case, our hypothetical company would be paying only the going rate of total cash compensation for performance that, though usual for the company itself, was considerably above the average of the group used for comparison. In this instance, the concept of pay for performance would have a rather hollow ring.

To make matters worse, many CEOs (acting on the empirical observation that if you put the carrot right next to the horse's nose, it will disappear and the horse will not move) demand that their budgets contain a lot of the elusive term known as *stretch.* In our example, the CEO might well give the board a budget calling for a 22% ROE, thereby demanding even more performance for no more than median pay.

What about a company that has heretofore been performing at median levels in relation to other companies but now believes that the year in question will likely prove a disaster? Carrying its convictions onto paper, it adopts a budget calling for only a 5% ROE level. Ironically, that 5% ROE level may well contain plenty of stretch, given all the bad things the company expects to happen. Nonetheless, are we to pay out norm bonuses to that company's executives because they achieved a 5% ROE level and thereby "made budget"? If we do, we will be offering the same levels of total cash compensation for 5% ROE as the median company is offering for 14% ROE. Previously, we had a case of no extra pay for high performance; we now have a case of extra pay for nonperformance. In this situation, we are unwittingly rewarding executives for being the first to run in with the news that "the sky is falling."

(b) Pitfalls at the Operating Unit Level. The problems described for the corporate level are often magnified at the operating unit level. The fundamental question here is: How do we know we have achieved equal stretch among the budgets of the various operating units? For example, some CEOs think they have achieved equal stretch simply by demanding the same absolute performance level from each of their operating unit as they have budgeted for the company as a whole. Thus, if the corporate budget calls for a 10% aftertax ROCE, they demand the same 10% ROCE level from each operating unit. They do this notwithstanding that one operating unit has comfortably achieved a 16% ROCE level for years and shows every expectation of continuing to do so, while another operating unit is struggling to cut its losses because it is either in the very early or very late stages of its product life cycle.

Other CEOs avoid this pitfall and properly demand "realistic" budgets from each operating unit based on the environment in which the operating unit then finds itself. They assign the first unit an ROCE budget of 16%, while insisting that the second unit cut its losses to only $5 million the next year. Having done so, however, they may not be able to bring themselves to give norm bonuses to the executives of the second unit.

As if all this were not enough, there are often problems surrounding the swing in bonuses as a function of the swing in actual versus budgeted performance. Earlier, we talked about paying no bonus at all if actual performance fell below 85% of budget and about doubling the norm bonus if actual performance rose to 120% of budget or more. Perhaps that is a good range of performance for incentive compensation purposes as far as the parent corporation is concerned. It does not necessarily follow, however, that the range will prove optimal for each and every one of the corporation's various operating units.

For example, contrast the following two units: The first operates from an order backlog that stretches beyond one year. It buys little in the way of raw materials, and what it does buy is not subject to wild price swings. The unit has also signed a recent three-year agreement with its unions and can look forward to identified labor costs for the next several years. In that case, would it not be reasonable to assume that an achievement of even 90% against budget would nonetheless represent an abysmal performance? Also, would it not be reasonable to assume that the operating unit was, in retrospect, lying through its teeth if it ended up achieving 120% of budget?

The second operating unit has little in the way of order backlog from which to work. A good part of every sales dollar is used to buy highly price-volatile raw materials, and it is just ending a three-year labor agreement with a highly militant union. In that case, would it not be reasonable to assume that an achievement of 80% of budget, though not satisfactory, might not be considered abysmal either under the circumstances? Also, would it not be reasonable to assume that an achievement of 120% of budget, though reasonably good, might not connote outstanding performance under the same circumstances?

Finally, there is a problem described by the ancient Chinese adage, "Victory has a thousand fathers; defeat has none." For example, a particular operating unit badly misses its budget. Just as it is about to be passed over at bonus distribution time, the operating unit head points to the fact that oil price increases, pushed through by a resurgent Organization of Petroleum Exporting Countries (OPEC), were the culprit. Some top managements, besides recalling the preceding Chinese adage, will also recall another adage, "You live by the sword, you die by the sword." On that basis, the operating unit executives would still receive nothing. Others in top management, however, acting from the theory that executives should not be held accountable for things they cannot control might be inclined to grant the operating unit some bonus relief. They would do so either by decreasing the unit's original budget figures or by constructing a *pro forma* income statement showing what the unit would have earned that year had OPEC not instituted its price rise, and then comparing the *pro forma* results to the original budget numbers. In either event, the task would be difficult unless the assumptions underlying the original budget had been made explicit.

It should go without saying that a budget document is essentially worthless unless one understands and accepts its major underlying assumptions. All too often, budget figures are based on the inspiration of the operating unit head after heeding the exhortation of the CEO. In truth, there are no underlying assumptions except inchoate desires to please the CEO and, if possible, to save back some profit for a rainy day.

11.5 AN OPTIMAL APPROACH. The reader will have to be forgiven if he or she has come to this point with the belief that only the most benighted company would ever try to use its budgeting process as a means of determining the rewards its executives should receive. Clearly, there are many pitfalls involved in linking budgets to pay, but to a large degree, these pitfalls can be avoided by using the budgeting process in an indirect fashion rather than directly.

Most budget experts agree that a truly viable budgeting process is at heart an iterative process. Someone—whether the corporate top manager or an operating unit head—starts the ball rolling with a tentative budget figure. This figure is then responded to with the result that it may be changed. The changed figure is then responded to again, and once again some further change may be made. This continues until all the parties agree on a final budget. This being the case, let us start the iterative process at the bottom of the organization—with the company's various operating units.

(a) Preparation of Operating Unit Budgets. If budgets are going to play an optimal role in the determination of incentive awards, it would be desirable for each operating unit head to submit not a single budget but rather three different budgets.

The first of these budgets might be termed the worst-case budget. Having identified the major variables affecting profits for the operating unit (e.g., raw material prices, wage rates, staffing levels, volume in physical units, product prices, etc.), the operating unit head would start by assuming that things really go wrong during the year under consideration. For example, if economic projections indicate that it is highly unlikely that oil will cost less than $14.50 per barrel or more than $17.00 per barrel, the operating unit head would use $17.00 as the assumption for the price of oil in determining the worst-case budget.

The second budget is termed the best-case budget. Here, the operating unit head will assume that things really go right. Thus, in the case of oil, a $14.50 per barrel assumption will be used.

Finally, the operating unit head will prepare a likely budget. In some situations, this may be merely the midpoint of the range between the worst-case and best-case budgets, but in other situations, the likely budget may lie somewhere other than in the exact middle of the range.

Once these three budgets are prepared by each operating unit head, it will be up to top management to ensure that the principle of equal stretch has been achieved among the various operating units. Here, we are dealing not with the question of whether the particular operating unit is delivering sufficient profits, but rather with the fundamental assumptions underlying each of the three budgets. For example, suppose an operating unit is about to negotiate a new labor agreement with its principal union. Wage rates are currently averaging $8.00 per hour. Given that other recent settlements by the same union have been running around a 10% annual increase level, is it reasonable to assume (as the operating manager has assumed in the likely budget) that wage rates during the first year of the new contract will average $9.25, or 15.6% higher than the current wage levels? Also, is it reasonable to assume (as the operating manager has assumed in the worst-case budget) that wage rates will average $10.50 per hour during the first year of the new contract? Finally, is it reasonable to assume (as the operating manager has assumed in the best-case budget) that wage rates will rise only about 1% to $8.10 per hour?

(b) Setting Corporate Performance Targets. Having critically examined the major assumptions underlying each operating unit's worst-case, likely, and best-case budgets, and having made such changes as are necessary to ensure that the probabilities of attainment are reasonably the same among the operating units top management will then be in a position to set some incentive compensation targets for the corporation as a whole.

It might seem that the company need only consolidate the likely budgets of its operating units to derive a likely budget for the corporation as a whole. This budget would then trigger the payment of norm awards. Similarly, it might seem that the company need only consolidate the worst- and best-case corporate budgets of the operating units to derive worst- and best-case corporate budgets for the purposes of paying, respectively, no bonuses and maximum bonuses.

However, such thinking could well prove wrong for the reasons discussed previously. Once again, why should a corporation deliver only norm awards when its ''likely'' performance can be considered superlative in relation to the performance of other companies utilized for pay-determination purposes? On the other hand, why should a corporation deliver as much as norm awards when its likely performance can be considered poor in relation to the performance of other companies?

The next step involves not the consolidation of the three budgets from each operating unit, but rather the determination of corporate incentive compensation performance targets based on the performance of the same companies utilized for pay-determination purposes. Let us assume that our hypothetical company has adopted aftertax ROE as its measure of corporate performance for incentive compensation purposes. It then determines the ROE levels of the companies in its survey group and tentatively picks the median level as the level it will demand for payment of norm bonuses. Since norm bonuses, as used here, are median bonuses, it follows thus far that the company is offering median incentive compensation for median ROE performance.

Next, the company has to decide on a tentative outstanding ROE level. It could, if it wished, peg this level to the highest ROE level attained by any of the survey companies, but to do so would put it at the mercy of the extremes of the ROE distribution. More likely, the company would adopt some percentile criterion—for example, outstanding performance is equal to the 85th percentile of the ROE distribution.

The next step involves the determination of a tentative minimal ROE level. Our company could use the same reasoning as was used with respect to the determination of an outstanding ROE level; that is, minimum ROE performance is equal to the 15th percentile of the ROE distribution of the companies under study. Alternatively, the company might post an ''alternative investment'' test—one using the tenets of the capital asset pricing model. Here, the minimum ROE performance might be assumed to be a rate 60% as high as the rate mandated by the capital assets pricing model. Hence, if the model shows that investors are demanding a 15% ROE level, then the minimum ROE level built into the incentive plan would be 15% × 60%, or 9%.

For the sake of discussion, assume that our hypothetical company has tentatively identified the following ROE targets:

- Minimal—9% (modeled generally after the alternative investment theory)
- Norm—14% (equal to the median ROE of the survey group)
- Outstanding—18% (equal to the 85th percentile ROE of the survey group)

Presumably, these tentative targets would be locked in place as final targets for the particular year if our company were already achieving an ROE level of approximately 14% or more. However, suppose the company has not been performing well in the past and has been delivering an ROE level of only 10%. In such a case, it would likely prove unreasonable to demand a huge surge in ROE—from 10% to 14%—before norm bonuses would become payable.

This, in turn, raises a philosophical question as to the reasons for paying bonuses. Clearly, a company that is already delivering median performance (compared to other companies) and continues to deliver median performance should pay bonuses that, when added to base salaries, yield median total cash compensation levels. Obviously, a company that is already delivering median performance and then goes on to deliver outstanding performance should pay bonuses that, when added to base salaries, yield outstanding total cash compensation levels. Does it necessarily follow, however, that a company that is delivering poor performance and still cannot perform up to median levels should pay bonuses that, when added to base salaries, yield something less than median total cash compensation? The answer is yes, except when the company is demonstrating disproportionate progress in raising its performance from its current levels to median levels. It is this exception that must now be addressed.

Assume that our hypothetical company has been achieving only a 10% ROE (with equity calculated as of the beginning of the particular year) and that it has a policy of paying out 40% of its earnings in dividends. Were the company to increase its aftertax earnings by 6% per year, to continue paying out 40% of earnings in dividends, and to raise no new equity capital from outside sources, it would continue to produce a steady 10% ROE year after year. In this case, a 6% growth in earnings would be indicative of continued poor performance. Alternatively, were the company to increase its aftertax earnings by 8.4% per year, to continue paying out 40% of earnings in dividends, and to raise no new equity capital from outside sources, its ROE level would begin to rise above 10% until it reached 14% (the median ROE level of the survey group). At that point, the ROE level would remain at 14% as long as the preceding assumptions held true.

The only problem here, however, is that it will take 59 years before a 14% ROE level is finally achieved! (In year 1, the ROE rises from 10% to 10.2%. In year 2, it rises from 10.2% to 10.4%. In year 5, it reaches 11%. In year 11, it reaches 12%; in year 20, 13%; and in year 29, 13.5%. During the next 30 years, it crawls slowly from 13.5% to 14%.)

Therefore, although an 8.4% annual growth in earnings represents progress toward a 14% ROE level, and will actually maintain a 14% ROE level once the company gets there, one can hardly think of such performance as representing "disproportionate progress."

Accordingly, our hypothetical company will probably have to select a time frame shorter than 59 years to reach median levels of ROE performance if it still wishes to pay out norm bonuses. For example, the company decided that "disproportionate progress" would be achieved by reaching a 14% ROE level in five years.

Starting with a 10% ROE level and continuing to pay out 40% of earnings in dividends, the company would have to increase its earnings 15% per year. In such a case, the ROE pattern would be as follows:

Year	ROE (%)
Base	10.0
1	10.8
2	11.7
3	12.6
4	13.5
5	14.3

By way of further illustration, suppose our company decided that it really should reach a 14% ROE level in only three years. In that case, the growth in earnings would have to average 20% per year, and the ROE pattern would be as follows:

Year	ROE (%)
Base	10.0
1	11.3
2	12.7
3	14.2

Here, the company would adopt an 11.3% ROE level as indicative of norm performance for the particular year under discussion. Subsequently, it would have adopted 10.8% as the norm ROE level had it decided to reach for a 14% ROE level over five years instead of three.

Having adopted an 11.3% ROE level as its norm performance level for the particular year, would the company then go on to scale down its tentative outstanding ROE target of 18% and its tentative minimal ROE target of 9%? Presumably, it would scale down the former target; perhaps in a *pro rata* fashion. (Thus, an 11.3% ROE level represents 81% of a 14% ROE level. Applying this 81% factor to the tentative outstanding ROE level of 18% yields a 14.6% final outstanding ROE level for the particular year.) It is questionable, however, whether the company would touch its minimal ROE target of 9%. That minimal target, by definition, is pretty minimal. To pay any bonuses at all for performance below this point would seemingly be a travesty, no matter how much "progress" might or might not have been made in relation to years past.

11.6 ADJUSTING OPERATING UNIT TARGETS. For the sake of further discussion, assume that our hypothetical company has finally settled on the following ROE targets for the particular year:

- Minimal—9%
- Norm—11.3%
- Outstanding—14.6%

These targets have been modeled not on the corporate budget for the year in question, but rather on the ROE level of the survey group and on the past ROE levels of the company itself. Hence, we may well have a discontinuity between these ROE targets and the three consolidated budget figures (worst case, likely, and best case) submitted by the various operating units. This discontinuity will now have to be reconciled.

Initially, the company must restate its aftertax, corporate ROE targets in terms that match the performance measure adopted for the operating units. For example, the operating units are to be judged on net income before taxes, before interest charges on long-term debt, before corporate overhead, and before the costs of the incentive plan itself. In that case, the company would start with its minimal ROE target of 9% and would follow these eight steps:

1. Multiply beginning equity by 9% to determine the aftertax earnings represented by a 9% ROE (e.g., assume that the beginning equity is $1 billion. Therefore, aftertax earnings at a 9% ROE level will be $90 million).

2. Reverse out of the figure in step 1 the provision for income taxes to produce net income before taxes. (Assuming that the company anticipates a 36% effective tax rate at a $90 million aftertax profit level, the resulting figure for net income before taxes will be $141 million.)
3. Reverse out of the figure in step 2 the anticipated charges for interest on long-term debt to produce net income before taxes and before interest charges on long-term debt. (Assuming that the company has long-term debt of $500 million and is paying an average interest rate of 8%, the resulting interest charges will be $40 million. Hence, net income before taxes and before interest charges on long-term debt will be $181 million.)
4. Reverse out of the figure in step 3 the anticipated charges for corporate overhead to produce net income before taxes, before interest charges on long-term debt, and before corporate overhead. (Assuming that the company anticipates corporate overhead of $15 million, the resulting figure will be $196 million.)
5. Reverse out of the figure in step 4 the anticipated charges for incentive compensation payable at a 9% ROE level. (Given that a 9% ROE level is the minimal target, no bonuses will be payable, and the $196 million figure developed through step 4 will remain unchanged here.)
6. Add together the worst-case budgets of all the operating units. (Assume that the figure is $175 million.)
7. Divide the figure obtained in step 5 by the figure obtained in step 6. ($196 million divided by $175 million equals 1.12.)
8. Multiply the worst-case budget of each operating unit by the factor obtained in step 7 to derive the minimal incentive compensation performance level for that operating unit. (Assuming that operating unit A submitted a worst-case budget of $40 million, the minimal incentive compensation performance level will be increased by 12% to $44.8 million.)

These same eight steps will then be repeated twice more, first starting with the norm ROE level of the corporation (11.3%), and then with the outstanding ROE level (14.6%).

It is possible at this point to end up with two different sets of budgets. The first are the original worst-case, likely, and best-case budgets developed under realistic sets of assumptions. These original budgets will likely remain unchanged for financial-control purposes. The second set consists of the revised budgets developed through integration with the incentive compensation performance targets adopted for the corporation as a whole. This second set of budgets will be used only for incentive compensation purposes.

(a) Advantages of the Suggested Approach. In my view, the approach suggested here has a number of advantages compared to simply predicating bonus awards on actual performance versus budget. First, the company has avoided the trap of always offering median total cash compensation for making budget, whether the budgeted results compare to the achievements of other companies or are abysmal, average, or superior. Hence, the pay-for-performance principle that many companies espouse has been preserved intact.

Second, bonus payments will be in line with those offered by comparable companies and not simply in line with those offered in the past by the company itself. This should be reassuring news for the shareholders who, it may be suspected, are every bit as interested in paying for performance as the executives themselves.

Third, the temptation to play games with budgets will be minimized. If all operating unit managers submit "low-ball" budgets, each will end up having his or her figures increased through the eight-step process described previously. Granted, it is possible for one operating unit manager, or a couple of managers, to low ball their budgets and end up having only a portion of the decrement laid at their doorstep (the remainder being assigned to the other operating unit managers). However, given a critical examination of each operating unit budget on the part of top corporate management, and a concomitant striving to achieve roughly equal stretch among all the operating unit budgets, the likelihood of this happening should be fairly remote.

Fourth, the budgeting process can continue to play a useful role in the proceedings. In effect, though every operating unit manager's budget may get changed in the reconciliation of operating unit budgets to corporate incentive compensation performance targets, the relativities will still have been preserved. Presumably, rough justice also will still have been done.

Fifth, the temptation to assume that a given percentage achievement above or below budget represents the same relative performance for each operating unit will be eliminated. The preparation of thoughtful worst-case, likely, and best-case budgets will underscore the volatility of different operating units to changes in key, and often uncontrollable, factors.

Finally, the explicit identification of major assumptions underlying the worst-case, likely, and best-case budgets will go a long way in resolving after-the-fact disputes as to whether a particular operating unit performed poorly because of events outside its control or just simply performed poorly.

11.7 BUDGETS AND LONG-TERM INCENTIVE PLANS. The great bulk of this chapter has been devoted to the role that budgets can play in the determination of incentive compensation for annual results. Virtually all companies, however, have more than a single incentive plan with which to reward their management teams.

Most readers will likely be aware, if only slightly, that there are numerous strategies for maximizing the annual results of a firm or an operating unit thereof. Some of these strategies are productive (e.g., increasing market share). Others are hardly productive, at least viewed over the longer term. These include cutting expenses for research and development, for management training and equipment maintenance, reducing product quality, and the like. Eventually, these latter strategies will result in lowered profits (and perhaps bankruptcy), and the managers who used them will "get theirs" in the form of zero annual incentive awards—if they are still with the company or the particular operating unit. If they are not, they will have received the best of both worlds; higher bonuses during the good years and an enhanced reputation later. ("When Joe was running the division, the profits were tremendous. Now Joe has left and things are in deplorable shape. I tell you, that Joe is a miracle worker!").

To minimize the adoption of counterproductive long-term strategies, most companies offer their executives an annual incentive opportunity as well as a further incentive opportunity based on results not in a single year but over a series of years. Thus, the executive who neglects the long-term aspects of the business will end up being penalized even if he or she has left the company or moved to another operating unit. (In effect, he or she will receive maximum bonuses under the short-term plan but nothing under the long-term plan.)

Approximately 20 years ago, virtually every long-term incentive plan consisted of a stock option. However, for a number of reasons (e.g., a plunge in the stock market during the 1970s, changes in tax laws, and increases in interest rates), many companies decided to downplay and, in a few cases, even eliminate the role of the market price of their stock in the determination of long-term incentive awards. Instead, they have predicated part, or sometimes all, of their long-term incentive opportunities on such things as growth in earnings per share over a series of years and/or the achievement of pre-established ROE or ROCE levels.

Having decided to move away from the market price, which is impersonally set, these companies had to face the task of deciding how much growth in earnings per share should be required for a given payout and/or what level of ROE or ROCE should be attained.

At first, there was a tendency to look to the company's long-term business plans as the yardstick of executive long-term performance. However, most companies shortly discovered that their long-term plans could not take much weight. In effect, they began to perceive that the relationship between the long-term forecast for a particular year and reality was inversely proportional to the square of the number of years between the current year and the year under consideration. To put it another way, they began to perceive that their long-term plans, while providing a useful demonstration to the board of directors that professional management was behaving professionally, were basically exercises in extrapolation.

Accordingly, long-term budgets really are not allowed to play much of a role in the establishment of performance targets under most companies' long-term incentive compensation plans. Rather, the reasoning goes something like this:

- A survey of other companies shows that, on average, the typical chief financial officer (CFO) receives annual options on stock carrying a purchase price of 1.0 times base salary.
- Given that the median competitive base salary for a CFO in a company our size is \$200,000, this means an average annual option grant of \$200,000 would be in order, or 4,000 shares at our current market price of \$50 per share.
- We think it is unlikely that our long-term earnings per share growth will be any greater than 15% per year, and, indeed, it may well be somewhat less.
- If EPS growth did turn out to be 15% per year and if our stock traded at a constant price/earnings multiple, then the price of our stock would also advance 15% per year.
- If the CFO were to exercise his 4,000-share option halfway through its 10-year term (a Solomonic assumption), the market price of the stock would have risen from \$50 per share to \$100.57 per share, yielding him a pretax gain of \$50.57 per share, or \$202,300 on all 4,000 shares.
- We wish to reward the CFO purely for EPS growth, while simultaneously insulating him from the vagaries of the price/earnings multiple.
- Accordingly, under our new long-term incentive plan, we will offer him \$202,300 in cash at the end of a five-year performance cycle, provided our EPS has increased an average of 15% per year during the period.
- If EPS growth turns out to be less than 15% per year, we will, of course, give the CFO a lesser payment, with such payment derived by applying the very same methodology.
- If EPS growth averages less than 6% per year, we will give him no payment at all.

It is granted that a 6% EPS growth rate when combined with a constant price/earnings multiple does produce a 34% appreciation in stock over five years. Given an inflation rate that is running around 5%, however, we cannot fail to take account of the fact that 6% nominal EPS growth really translates into very little real EPS growth. To put it another way, we cannot continue to assume that the price/earnings multiple of our stock would indeed remain constant in the face of a 6% nominal EPS growth rate and a 5% inflation rate.

11.8 SUMMARY. A company's budgeting process can, if carefully handled, play a useful role in determining incentive compensation for annual results (while playing little or no role in the determination of incentive compensation for longer-term results). However, unless the handling is indeed careful, there is the risk that executives will end up being either undercompensated or overcompensated for their performance achievements, and there is the even greater risk that the budgeting process will become so subverted as to render it useless for even its traditional financial role.

SOURCES AND SUGGESTED REFERENCES

Chalos, Peter, and Susan Haka, ''Participative Budgeting and Managerial Performance,'' *Decision Sciences,* vol. 20, no. 2, Spring 1989.

Chenhall, Robert H., and Peter Brownell. ''The Effect of Participative Budgeting on Job Satisfaction and Performance: Role Ambiguity as an Intervening Variable,'' *Accounting, Organizations & Society* (UK), vol. 13, no. 3, 1988.

Chow, Chee W., Jean C. Cooper, and William S. Waller, ''Participative Budgeting: Effects of a Truth-Inducing Pay Scheme and Information Asymmetry on Slack and Performance,'' *Accounting Review,* vol. 63, no. 1, January 1988.

Dunk, Alan S., ''Budget Emphasis, Budgetary Participation and Managerial Performance: A Note,'' *Accounting, Organizations & Society* (UK), vol. 14, no. 4, 1989.

Finch, Gerald L., ''Improving the Bottom Line with Budget Incentive Programs,'' *Management Accounting,* vol. 69, no. 4, October 1987.

Imoisili, Olumhense A., ''The Role of Budget Data in the Evaluation of Managerial Performance,'' *Accounting, Organizations & Society* (UK), vol. 14, no. 4, 1989.

LaForge, Ann E., ''Why Are Incentive Programs So Hard to Budget?,'' *Successful Meetings,* vol. 37, no. 12, November 1988.

LaForge, Ann E., Bruce Bolger, and Todd Englander, ''Build Your Budget,'' *Incentive* (Section 2), vol. 165, no. 5, May 1991.

Lawler, Edward E, *Strategic Pay: Aligning Organizational Strategies and Pay Systems.* San Francisco, CA: Jossey-Bass, 1990.

Liesse, Julie, ''Pay for Performance Picking Up Speed,'' *Advertising Age,* vol. 64, no. 33, August 9, 1993, pp. 19–21.

Mann, Gary J., ''Reducing Budget Slack,'' *Journal of Accountancy,* vol. 166, no. 2, August 1988.

Mia, Lokman, ''The Impact of Participation in Budgeting and Job Difficulty on Managerial Performance and Work Motivation: A Research Note,'' *Accounting, Organizations & Society* (UK), vol. 14, no. 4, 1989.

Tanner, L. D., ''Seeking a Pay Formula,'' *Monthly Labor Review,* vol. 115, no. 3, March 1992, p. 42.

CHAPTER 12

TECHNIQUES OF SCHEDULING BUDGETS

Donald R. Moscato

Iona College

12.1 INTRODUCTION. Whenever a manager must pull together a diverse and complex network of resources, as in the budgeting process, there is a natural tendency to try to organize the task in an orderly way. To accomplish the task of budgeting, some type of scheduling effort must be followed if all of the necessary information is to be gathered, analyzed, and reviewed in sufficient time to be presented to management.

The degree of formality of the scheduling activity depends largely on the managerial style of the individual coordinating the process. The budgeting director must establish a timetable that clearly sets forth "hit dates" for various plans from the operating departments. The creation of a timetable takes into account the realities of the budgeting cycle within the context of each individual organization and the specific attention that is devoted to particular areas of concern. The timetable is but a plan, which, if followed, will yield the completed budget on time.

Controlling the budgeting process requires a continuous monitoring of events against the plan in order to ensure that the entire process will be completed within the designated period allocated to the effort. This fact is the principal function of the scheduling activity within the budgetary process.

The purpose of this chapter is to present several methods of scheduling activities that are applicable to the budgeting function. After exposure to each technique, the reader should be able to select an approach to scheduling that would be compatible with his or her managerial style while consistent with the specific budgeting needs of the particular organization.

12.2 GANTT CHARTS. The budget director must isolate specific activities that must be accomplished for completion of the budget. Once this task has been accomplished, the activities are arranged in the natural order that they will take place in the budgeting process. At this point, the planner must make certain judgments as to the time it will take to complete each of the component steps of the budget. This information could come from past experience as well as from an understanding of existing resources within each of the feeder areas. Regardless of the degree of knowledge that the planner has about the departmental capabilities, he or she must make an estimate as to how much time it will take to complete the given tasks. Obviously, the more accurate the estimate, the more likely the schedule will represent the true timetable for the budgeting activity.

After the budgeting tasks have been identified and the completion times have been estimated, the planner determines a sequence for scheduling them. Certain tasks might overlap, which means that they could be carried out concurrently. At this point, the budget director is prepared to develop the scheduling chart that forms the basis for the budget preparation activity.

The technique can be illustrated by the use of a dramatically reduced scenario for the creation of a departmental budget. The steps are identified as follows:

Consider company goals	2 days
Evaluate existing operations	4 days
Evaluate new business opportunities	5 days
Derive sales forecast	3 days
Departmental managers review sales forecast	4 days
Prepare departmental budget proposals	7 days
Develop implementation strategies	2 days
Present budget to management	1 day

Exhibit 12.1 shows a plausible Gantt chart created in Microsoft Project™ for our example. Each step is represented as a bar on the chart. The left column shows the number of the tasks. The next column depicts the finish times. The next column identifies those tasks that have predecessor requirements. The final column highlights the daily schedule. Note that the analysis shows that no work is scheduled for weekends. Exhibit 12.2 presents the task sequence in the form of a more familiar calendar schedule.

As each step is completed, the budget director visually conveys this fact by making a darkened impression in the designated area of the completed process. This operation can be accomplished in a number of different ways and is left to the preferences of the person who is tracking the budget activity. Along the top of the calendar portion of the chart, a movable indicator is used to identify the current period. In this way, a snapshot of the process exists for the purpose of managerial review. If, for one reason or another, a stage is behind schedule, this fact is readily conveyed by the chart. Once a serious out-of-schedule situation is discovered, effort can be concentrated on revising the schedule of the remaining events so that the impact on the final target date can be assessed. With this approach, the budget director has a continuous picture of the budget schedule as it is unfolding.

The reader will quickly recognize that, if this tracking procedure is maintained manually, then there can be a formidable task in keeping the chart current even with a relatively uncomplicated budgeting procedure. There are various methods in use, ranging from computer programs to magnetic boards, that simplify the task of updating the chart.

The reader should appreciate the simplicity of the approach and the ease with which it can be understood. The major shortcoming of the approach is the drudgery of updating the progress of events to reflect the current status of the budget process. In addition, no reason for the delays is identified directly on the chart, although this information is quite critical to controlling the budget activity.

In conclusion, the simplicity of Gantt-type charts is appealing, and they might prove to be appropriate in relatively simple budgeting environments provided that the organization can accept the shortcomings of the approach.

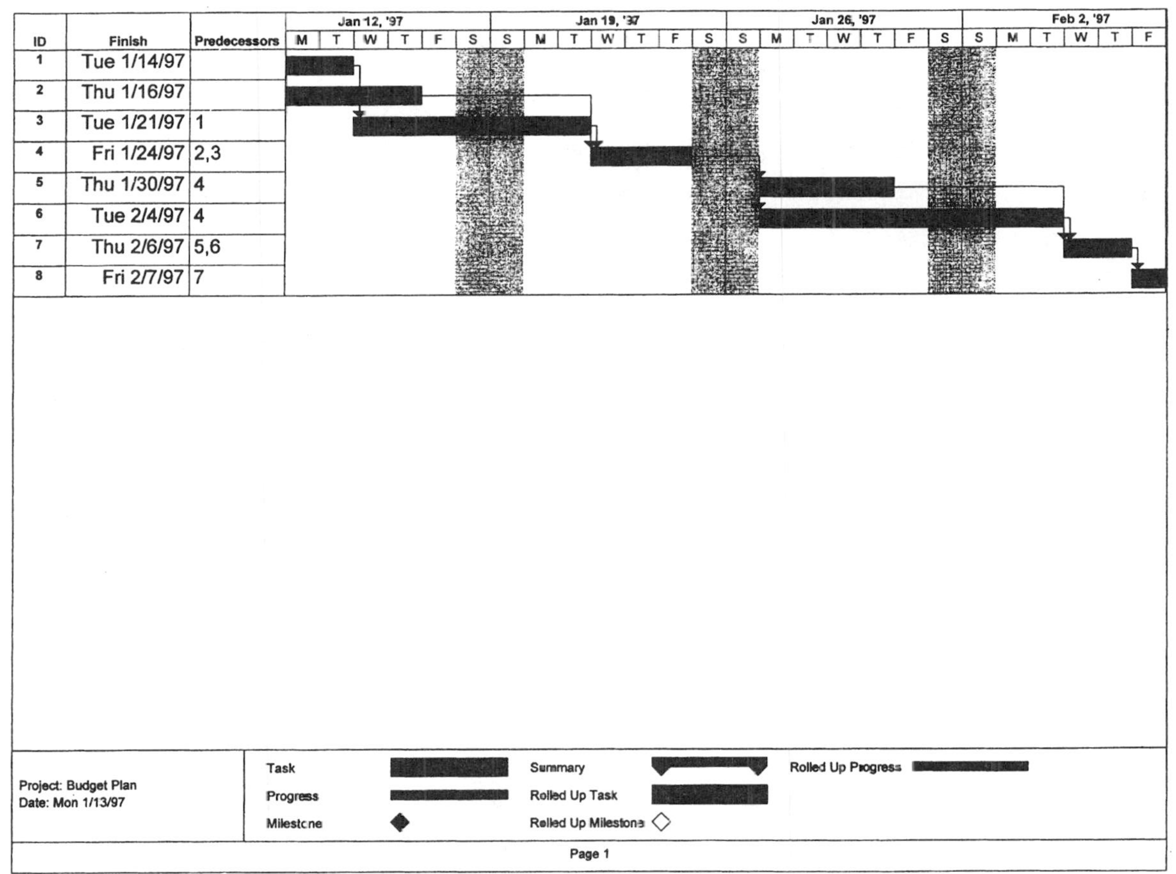

Exhibit 12.1. Gantt chart

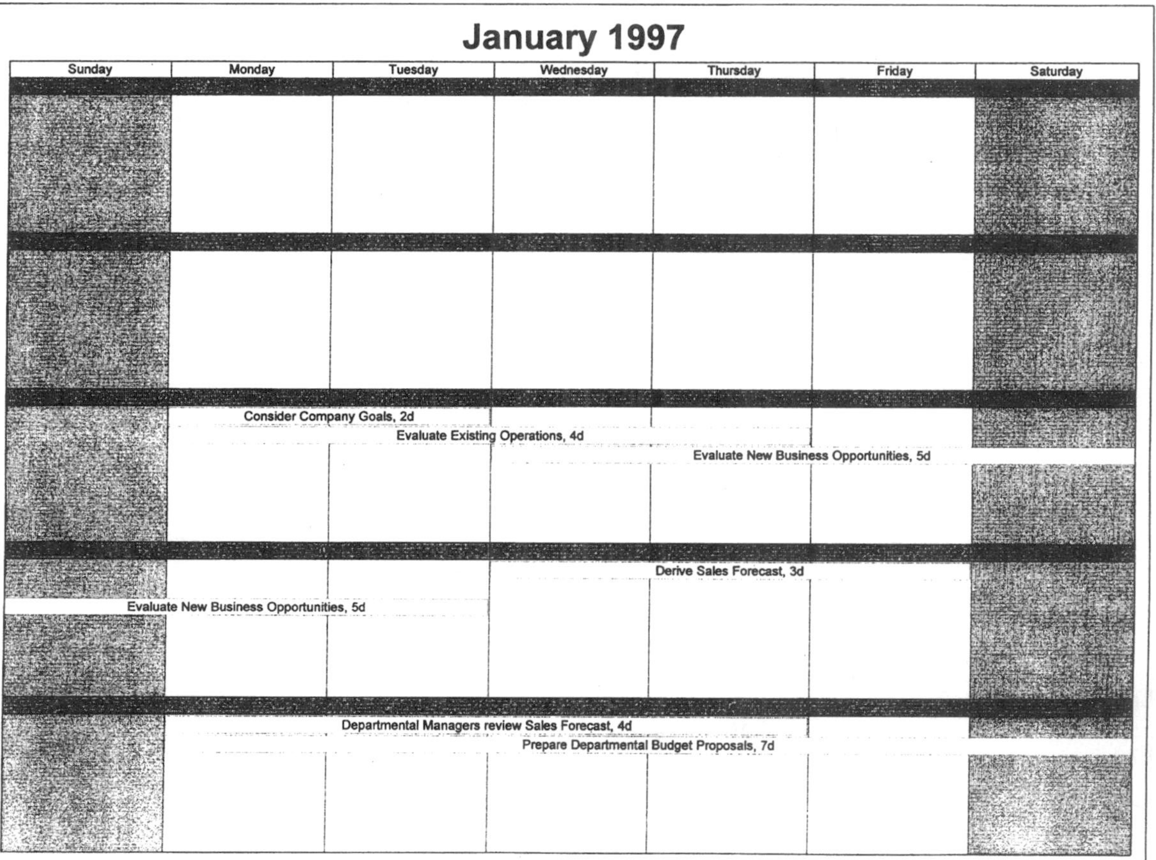

Exhibit 12.2. Budget calendar

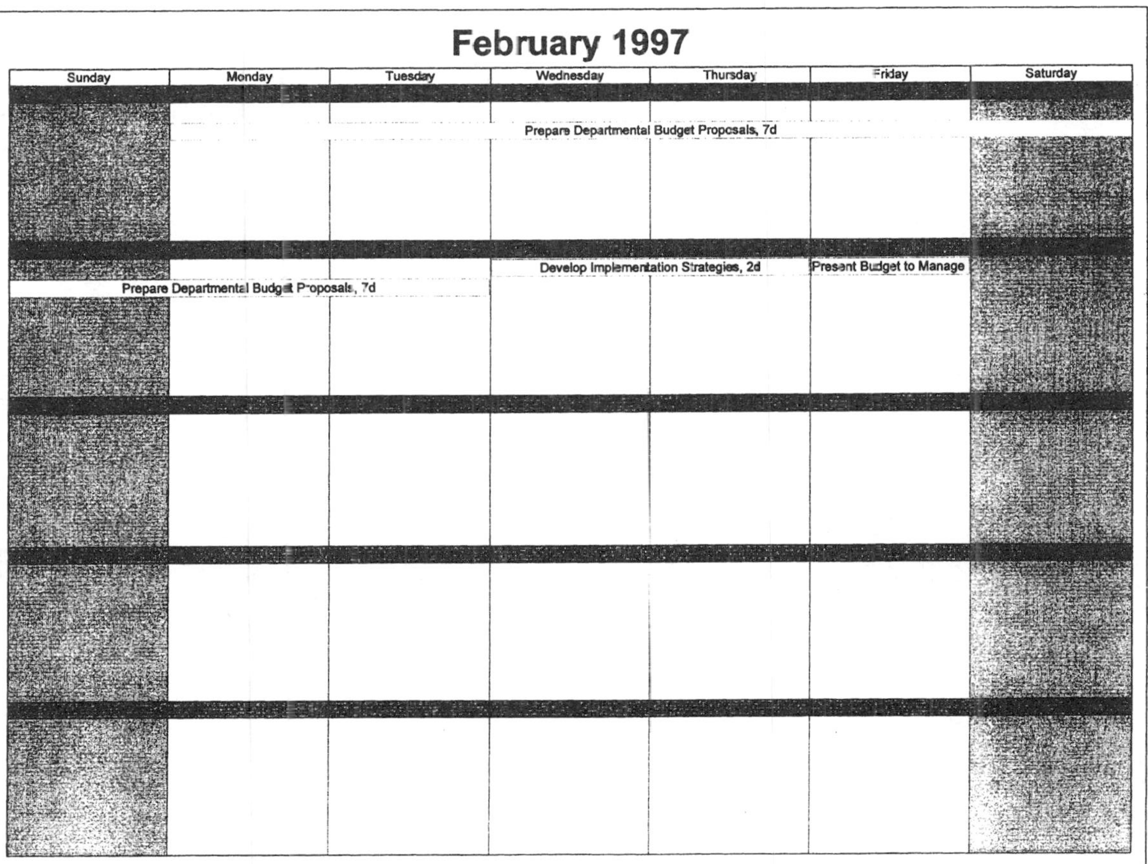

Exhibit 12.2. Budget calendar

12.3 PLANNING CHARTS. Often, the major value of composing a scheduling chart is to clarify the interrelated steps that make up the budgetary process of an organization. Control, although desirable, is not explicitly of concern. In a situation of this type, one can construct a milestone chart of the type discussed in the previous section and refrain from updating it on a regular basis. In this approach, the chart merely serves as a master schedule with target dates for the completion of the necessary subtasks. This approach, though ignoring the explicit control information of the Gantt-type chart, is a more informal aid to facilitating the budget scheduling activity. As was stated previously, not all organizations need to exercise the same degree of control in ensuring that the budgeting activity will be completed on time and in the most efficient manner.

It should be noted that the degree of detail depicted by the tasks in these methods should be as aggregated as desired by the budget director. As a general rule, one should not go into unnecessary detail in a master planning chart. if the budget director needs additional detail, then the individual departments can establish charts at a more specific level. At all times the value derived from the effort expended on the elaboration of the budget schedule should exceed the costs incurred in generating and monitoring the additional schedules.

12.4 CRITICAL-PATH METHOD. Since the late 1950s, the techniques based on the critical path method have been in considerable use. The two principal techniques in this category are the critical-path method (CPM) and the program evaluation and review technique (PERT). Both techniques have given birth to derivatives that retain the essential common structure of computing a critical path or route through a network.

These techniques were developed independently to assist in the planning, monitoring, and controlling of complex activities in organizations. Although based on the same mathematical structure, the two approaches have different application areas as their targets. Of the two, PERT has been demonstrated to be more effective in nonrepetitive situations in which there is a considerable degree of uncertainty regarding the estimation of completion times for the tasks under consideration.

However, CPM has been used successfully in project planning in which, because of the repetitive nature of the process, events can be estimated with a greater degree of certainty. Its primary area of application has been in the planning and scheduling of projects in the construction area.

Throughout the years since the introduction of these techniques, various nuances have been added that necessitate the use of a computer for applications of any real significance, as is the case with budgeting. Packaged software programs are available for use on most general-purpose computers being marketed today. The existence of computer-based systems allows the tedious calculations required by the techniques to be accomplished with little difficulty. However, there still remain the requirements to collect data periodically from the departmental managers and to update the project network so that effective control over the budgetary process is maintained. Two factors are important in this area. The first is the number of tasks in the budgeting process and the complexity of their interrelationships. The second factor is the frequency of updating the network. Both factors can prove significant in terms of cost and administrative burden. As a practical matter, these have been the principal criticisms of network-based planning models.

For purposes of illustrating this family of techniques, discussion will be limited to CPM. Where appropriate, comments will be made to indicate how PERT might treat a situation differently.

Project management methods consist of five distinct stages. These stages will be identified now and elaborated on later in the chapter. The stages are as follows:

1. Logical analysis of required activities
2. Establishment of precedence relationships among activities
3. Timing analysis of activities
4. Computation of longest path (critical path)
5. Project control

The first step is to identify a series of activities that must be performed in order for the completed budget documents to be prepared. Project-planning techniques have traditionally used the following terms to describe the scheduling process:

- *Event.* A milestone, typically the starting date or finishing date for some activity. It involves no expenditure of resources. (An event is represented as a circle on the network diagrams in this chapter.)
- *Activity.* An action or task that takes place over time, for example, forecast sales for next year. Activities involve expenditures of resources to accomplish their tasks. (An activity is represented as an arrow or arc on the network diagrams in this chapter.)

The next step in creating a critical-path network model for scheduling the budgeting activity is to establish clear precedence relationships among the activities and events. This requirement forces the budget director to identify the subtasks at whatever level of detail is desired. Recall the previous discussion about the appropriate level of aggregation, which meets the goals of the particular organization without encumbering the process with needless reporting requirements.

For purposes of illustration, the same example described in the previous section will be applied to the current situation.

Description of Activity	Arc	Label
Consider company goals	1–2	A
Evaluate existing operations	1–3	B
Evaluate new business opportunities	2–3	C
Derive sales forecast	3–4	D
Departmental managers review sales forecast	4–5	E1
Prepare departmental budget proposals	4–5	E2
Develop implementation strategies	5–6	F
Present budget to management	6–7	G

These precedence relationships can be converted into a network diagram, which forms the basis for the calculations required by the critical-path technique. It should be noted that, although we are working with a diagram here, the actual computer program works on tables or other, more convenient forms. The diagram appears as Exhibit 12.3.

Before the critical path in the diagram can be solved, an additional concept must be considered. While developing the precedence diagram, one might find that there are two activities that possess identical starting and finishing events. In the illustration in Exhibit 12.3, note that both the activities, "departmental managers review sales forecast" and

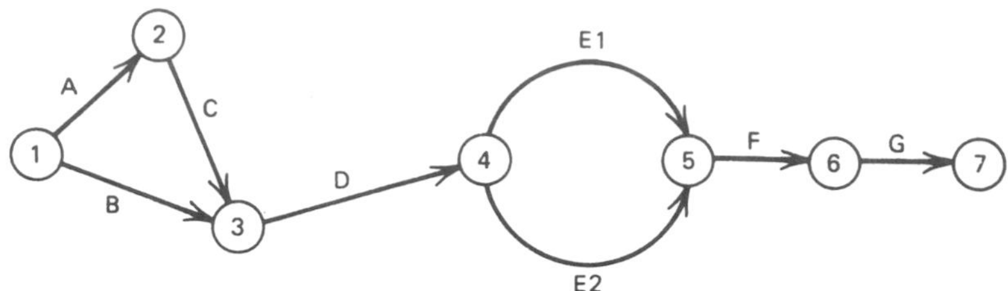

Exhibit 12.3. Precedence diagram

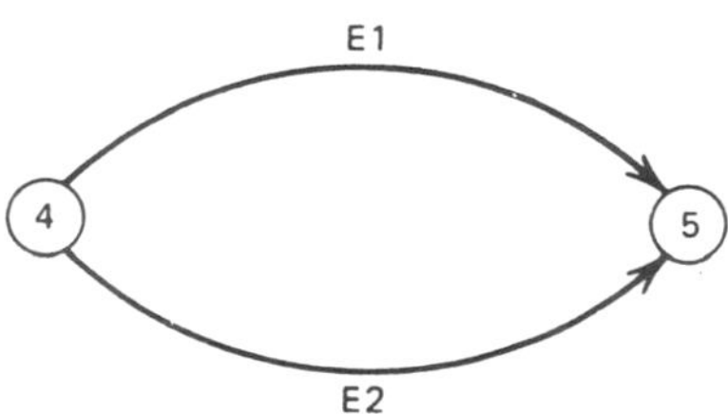

Exhibit 12.4. Precedence diagram

"prepare departmental budget proposals," fall into this category (the two arcs going from 4 to 5, E1 and E2).

To resolve this situation, a "dummy" activity is created. This activity has no real impact on the final solution. It merely serves as a computational device so that standard solution procedures can be employed by the computer software. On occasion, it can act as a device to clarify a precedence relationship.

To illustrate the use of a dummy activity, let us assume that event 5 has two predecessor activities, namely, (1) departmental managers review sales forecast and (2) prepare departmental budget proposals (see Exhibit 12.4).

Exhibit 12.4 is not an acceptable representation for depicting the precedence relationship. A corrected version using the dummy activity concept is illustrated in Exhibit 12.5.

Exhibit 12.6 shows the revised network diagram for the departmental budgeting process with the dummy activity included.

As soon as a completed precedence diagram has been agreed upon, the task of estimating completion times for the activities must be initiated. In the case of CPM, only a single best estimate for each completion time is required. In the PERT technique, a total of three estimates must be generated by the budget analyst. The three estimates represent the following factors:

1. a—The optimistic time to complete the activity
2. b—The pessimistic time to complete the activity
3. m—The most likely time to complete the activity

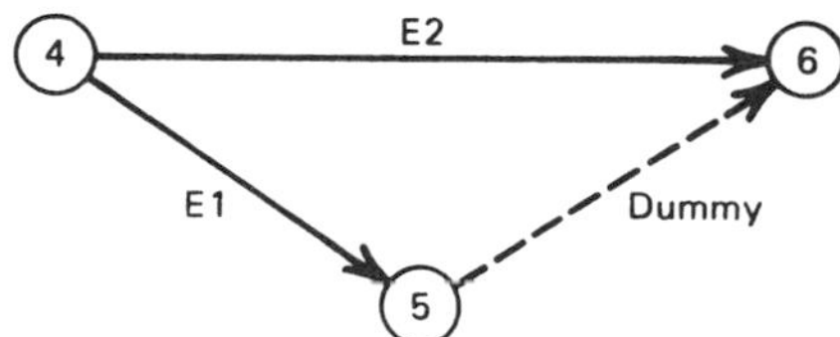

Exhibit 12.5. Dummy activity concept

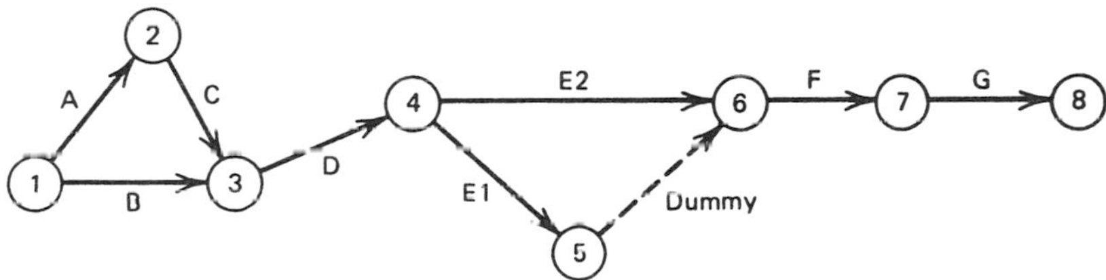

Exhibit 12.6. Revised network diagram

These three estimates are combined in the PERT technique to derive an expected time of completion for each of the activities in the network. The following is the appropriate formula for the expected time:

$$t_e = \frac{a + 4m + b}{6}$$

There has been much discussion on the appropriateness of using this equation to estimate the expected completion time for an activity. The controversy has centered around the assumptions underlying its derivation; the estimation procedures used for obtaining values for a, m, and b: and the utility of the probabilistic estimates that are eventually derived in the PERT solution procedure. The interested reader should consult the Sources and Selected References at the end of the chapter for a more technical discussion of the issues raised.

Since the CPM procedure requires providing a single estimate for activity completion times, care must be taken to ensure that values are used that represent the best assessment of each task's time. It should be obvious that, no matter how valuable a given scheduling technique might be, it is only as good as the data that drive the model. If casual and slipshod attention is given to this area of the scheduling process, then the results are almost certainly going to be disappointing, and any effort expended on the process will have been wasted.

Exhibit 12.7 shows the completed network diagram for our example, with the estimated activity times inserted. Note that the value for arc 5–6 is zero. This value reflects the fact that we have created a dummy activity. Recall that there will not be any penalty incurred because the dummy convention is being used in the formulation.

(a) Computation. We are now ready to begin the computational phase of the critical-path analysis. To start the process, a quantity must be defined for the earliest start time

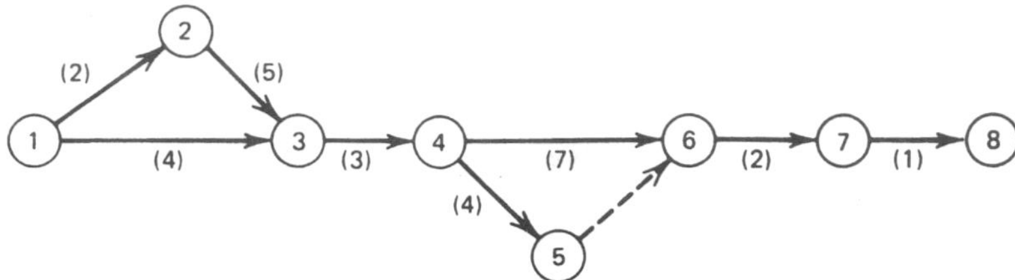

Exhibit 12.7. Budget network with activity times

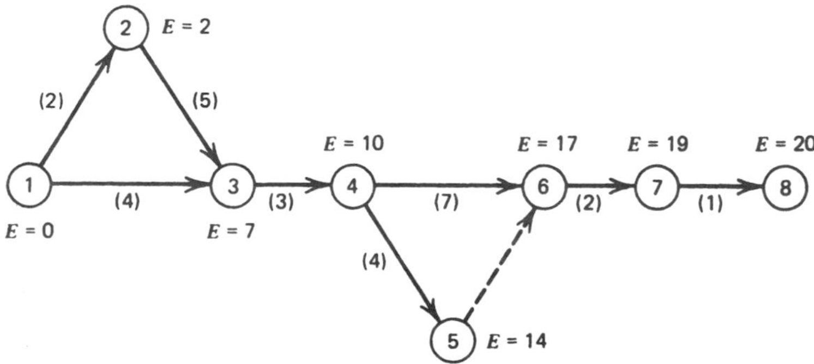

Exhibit 12.8. Network diagram with earliest event times

for an activity. This expression is referred to as E, and every node will have an associated value of E. It should be noted that before any activity is begun, all activities preceding it in the precedence diagram must have been completed.

We compute E for each event in the network, starting at the beginning and working our way to the end or terminal node. Whenever a situation is encountered in which there is more than one way to reach a given node, the largest time value is always selected. This is consistent with the previous statement that all preceding activities must be finished before the current activity can start. To reiterate, t is added to the largest value of E of the preceding activities. Exhibit 12.8 shows the completed network diagram, with the computed values for E inserted at each node.

(i) Forwards Phase. Using Exhibit 12.8, we can illustrate the "forwards" phase of the computational procedure. The first node is given a value for E of zero, since it is the start of the budget process. In order to compute the value of E for each succeeding node, the value of E is taken for each immediately preceding node, and the value of the activity time between the two events in question is added to it. In our example, the value of E for event 2 (E_2) is computed as follows:

$$E_1 + t_{12} = E_2$$

Substituting values from the diagram, we have

$$0 + 2 = 2$$

The value of E for event 2 is two days. This means that the earliest time that event 2 can be completed is two days.

Continuing with our example, event 3 has two possible paths: 1–2–3 or 1–3. When this situation arises, the value for E at node 3 (E_3) must be computed both ways and the largest of the values chosen.

Path 1–2–3:

$$E_2 + t_{23} = E_3$$
$$2 + 5 = 7$$

Path 1–3:

$$E_1 + t_{13} = E_3$$
$$0 + 4 = 4$$

Since the two candidate values for the earliest event time, E_3, at node 3 are four and seven, we must select as the value the largest of the two. Recall that this value represents the earliest time that all preceding activities will be completed.

We then proceed to compute the values for E at each of the remaining nodes in the network. There should be no problem in determining that the values for E at nodes 4 and 5 are 10 days and 14 days, respectively.

A problem arises at node 6 in the network. Note that the activity going from node 5 to node 6 is a dummy, with zero time. At this point, one can see the value of the dummy convention in the analytical procedure. Let us compute the two candidate values for E_6.

Candidate 1:

$$E_4 + t_{46} = E_6$$
$$10 + 7 = 17 \text{ days}$$

Candidate 2:

$$E_5 + t_{56} = E_6$$
$$14 + 0 = 14 \text{ days}$$

Since the largest candidate value must be chosen, the value for E_6 is 17 days.

The remainder of the calculating is straightforward. The reader can verify that the total time to complete the illustrative budget schedule is 20 days. These calculations represent the forwards phase of critical-path analysis. One knows through the calculations that the longest path has a value of 20 days but does not know, at this time, which events are on the critical path. To determine the budgeting activities that are on the critical path, one must complete phase two of the computational procedure. This phase is referred to as "backwards" analysis, and it follows essentially the same procedure as before, except that we start from the last node on the network and work backwards toward the beginning.

(ii) Backwards Phase. The next computational step that must be taken is to compute a quantity that represents the latest time that an event can take place without delaying the overall completion of the budgeting process. This term will be called L, for latest event

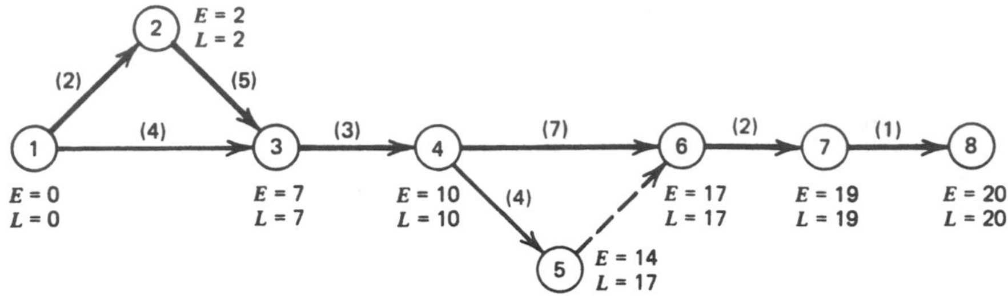

Exhibit 12.9. Critical-path network for budget schedule

time. Instead of starting the computations at the beginning of the network, as in the previous case, we begin at the last node in the network and work backwards. The starting value for the calculation for L is the ending value computed for E of the last node in the network. Therefore, $L_8 = 20$ days.

To compute the L value for each node, we subtract the t value from the L value of the immediately following node. In the case of more than one activity joining at a node, the smallest of the candidate values for L for that node should be chosen. This fact is consistent with the idea that this is the latest allowable time at which the event can occur without delaying the budgeting timetable.

Exhibit 12.9 depicts the network diagram with both the E and the L values entered.

To illustrate the backwards analysis procedure, the value for L at node 7 will be computed:

$$20 - 1 = 19 \text{ days}$$

The interpretation of this value for L_7 is that the latest that we can be at node 7 and still complete the budget within 20 days is the nineteenth day. If, for any reason, we have taken more time, we will do so at the expense of a slippage in the scheduled time of 20 days.

The value for node 6 can be shown to be $L = 17$, since

$$L_7 - t_{67} = L_6$$

$$19 - 2 = 17 \text{ days}$$

The next interesting node is 4, because of the presence of a dummy activity. Because we have two candidates or routes at node 4, we must compute both candidate L values and choose the smallest one for the value for L at node 4.

Candidate 1:

$$L_6 - t_{46} = L_4$$

$$17 - 7 = 10 \text{ days}$$

Candidate 2:

$$L_5 - t_{45} = 4$$

$$17 - 4 = 13 \text{ days}$$

We select the value of 10 days for node 4, since that is the latest time that we must complete that event and still not delay the total completion time for the budgeting process. For the remaining nodes 3, 2, and 1, the respective values for L are seven, two, and zero.

Given the completed values of both E and L for each of the nodes, we are in a position to identify the critical path in our budgeting plan. The critical path is identified in the network as that route going through the events where the E and L values are the same. The interpretation of the critical path is that any increase in the times of those activities on the network will result in additional delays to complete the budgeting process on schedule. Stated another way, on the critical path the activities have no slack time. All events must be completed at the designated times, or else the completion time of the budgeting process will be delayed.

In our example the critical path is the route 1–2–3–4–6–7–8, with a completion time of 20 days. The path is shown in Exhibit 12.9 as a darker line.

The critical path is characterized as having no slack time or float associated with the respective events. All other events on the network have slack time associated with them, so that they could be delayed up to a point and not delay the overall completion of the budget within the target date established by the director.

12.5 CONTROLLING THE BUDGET SCHEDULE WITH THE CRITICAL-PATH METHOD. The budget director of an organization is now in a position to use the information derived from critical-path analysis for decision-making purposes. Recall the comments made previously in this chapter regarding the credibility of the estimates that were the basis for the calculations made. If there is reason to believe that one or more estimates were less than accurate, a sensitivity analysis could be run to explore the ramifications of misestimation(s). It is conceivable that the new solution would yield a rearrangement of the activities that are on the critical path. Furthermore, even if the estimates were accurate, the budget director might be able to shorten the time it would take to complete one or more activities on the critical path. Any such reduction in time would directly contribute to a reduction of the time it would take to complete the budgeting activity.

The director responsible for coordination has another option at his or her disposal. Because attention is focused on the events along the critical path, any change in the precedence relationships could have a substantial effect on the completion time for the overall project. It is conceivable that with some degree of effort, activities could be resequenced so that certain activities are no longer on the critical path. The reader should be advised that in marginal situations, a new route could become the critical path as a result of the change in sequence.

A final area for possible review is based on the traditional concept underlying all critical-path methods. Can resources be taken from non–critical-path activities that possess slack and be deployed on activities that are on the critical path? A mechanism referred to in the literature as *crashing* enables a manager to trade off cost versus time. This aspect of critical-path analysis, although useful, is not an essential aspect of using CPM. The interested reader is once again directed to the Sources and Selected References at the end of this chapter for a more complete presentation of this concept.

12.6 COMPUTER SOFTWARE FOR THE CRITICAL-PATH METHOD. An abundance of software is available to handle both PERT and CPM on both the mainframe and the microcomputer. These packages range from simple to complex in design and can accommodate a wide spectrum of user applications.

Since the complexity of some applications requires a great deal of coordination and recycling within the network, variations have been incorporated in the methodology that has been discussed. As a matter of fact, the whole field of study is referred to as networks and can involve a great deal of mathematical complexity. The budget director need not involve him- or herself in any degree of mathematics. Once the precedence relationships have been determined and the time estimates entered, the director need only have the data entered into a computer program, which, in addition to the necessary calculations, can plot the entire precedence diagram for the network.

The power of the microcomputer enables software ranging in price from \$500 to \$900 to run project networks capable of planning and controling up to 500 tasks. These packages are extremely easy to use and rely on an interactive user interface. Additionally, the reliance on understandable graphics output has added to the usefulness of these programs. Another interesting feature is the ability to define an explicit priority among tasks, which is used in the resource leveling activity. These features add significantly to the functionality and go a long way toward assuring users a realistic representation of their real-world budgeting activity. Variations in reporting formats do not cause a problem because the budget director can select the most meaningful corporate way to represent the final schedule.

12.7 COMPUTER SOFTWARE RESULTS. In this section, we present the computer results of our illustrative budget plan. Exhibit 12.10 presents the CPM chart for the example. Note the inclusion of the starting dates and the finishing dates for each task. Exhibits 12.11 through 12.12 depict a series of useful budget reports created as default reports in the Microsoft Project computer system. Each one is useful for project-control purposes. In our example, they all contain zero values because the budget plan had not been started at the time the reports were prepared. Exhibit 12.11 shows the budget plan's fixed cost, total cost, baseline values, the variance, the actuals, and any remaining costs. Exhibit 12.12 depicts the base calendar template used for the budget planning process. Exhibit 12.13 illustrates the progress of the budgeting activities in terms of the percent of each task that was completed, its cost, and the status of the work.

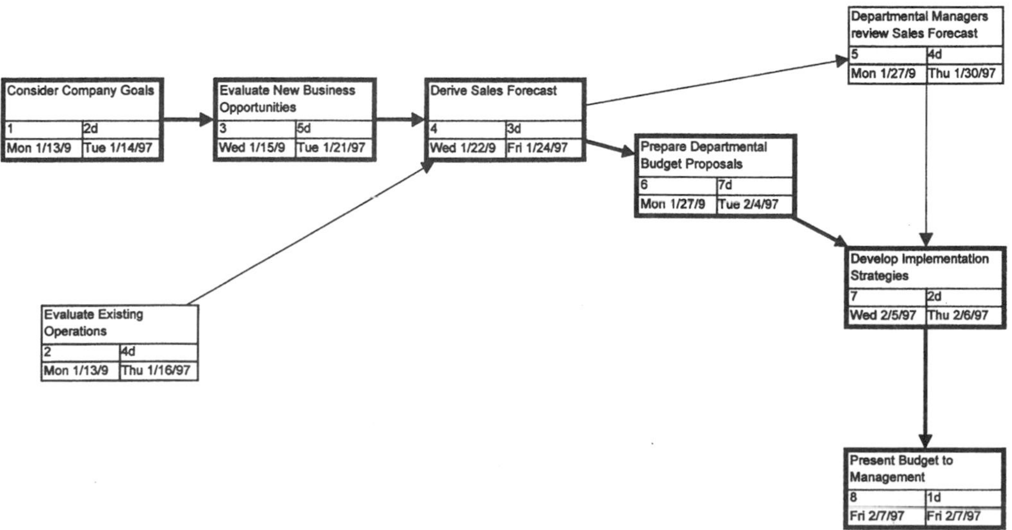

Exhibit 12.10. CPM chart for budget schedule

ID	Task Name	Fixed Cost	Total Cost	Baseline	Variance	Actual	Remaining
1	Consider company goals	$0.00	$0.00	$0.00	$0.00	$0.00	$0.00
2	Evaluate existing operations	$0.00	$0.00	$0.00	$0.00	$0.00	$0.00
3	Evaluate new business opportunities	$0.00	$0.00	$0.00	$0.00	$0.00	$0.00
4	Derive sales forecast	$0.00	$0.00	$0.00	$0.00	$0.00	$0.00
5	Departmental managers review sales forecast	$0.00	$0.00	$0.00	$0.00	$0.00	$0.00
6	Prepare departmental budget proposals	$0.00	$0.00	$0.00	$0.00	$0.00	$0.00
7	Develop implementation strategies	$0.00	$0.00	$0.00	$0.00	$0.00	$0.00
8	Present budget to management	$0.00	$0.00	$0.00	$0.00	$0.00	$0.00
		$0.00	$0.00	$0.00	$0.00	$0.00	$0.00

Exhibit 12.11. Budget report

Base Calendar: Day	Standard Hours
Sunday	Nonworking
Monday	8:00 A.M.–12:00 P.M., 1:00 P.M.–5:00 P.M.
Tuesday	8:00 A.M.–12:00 P.M., 1:00 P.M.–5:00 P.M.
Wednesday	8:00 A.M.–12:00 P.M., 1:00 P.M.–5:00 P.M.
Thursday	8:00 A.M.–12:00 P.M., 1:00 P.M.–5:00 P.M.
Friday	8:00 A.M.–12:00 P.M., 1:00 P.M.–5:00 P.M.
Saturday	Nonworking
Exceptions:	None

Exhibit 12.12. Budget plan template

ID	Task Name	Duration	Start	Finish	% Comp.	Cost	Work
1	Consider company goals	2d	Mon 1/13/97	Tue 1/14/97	0%	$0.00	0h
2	Evaluate existing operations	4d	Mon 1/13/97	Thu 1/16/97	0%	$0.00	0h
3	Evaluate new business opportunities	5d	Wed 1/15/97	Tue 1/21/97	0%	$0.00	0h
4	Derive sales forecast	3d	Wed 1/22/97	Fri 1/24/97	0%	$0.00	0h
5	Department managers review sale	4d	Mon 1/27/97	Thu 1/30/97	0%	$0.00	0h
6	Prepare departmental budget proposals	7d	Mon 1/27/97	Tue 2/4/97	0%	$0.00	0h
7	Develop implementation strategies	2d	Wed 2/5/97	Thu 2/6/97	0%	$0.00	0h
8	Present budget to management	1d	Fri 2/7/97	Fri 2/7/97	0%	$0.00	0h

Exhibit 12.13. Top-level tasks

12.8 SUMMARY. Regardless of the specific approach used by an organization to schedule the budgeting process, the function must still be performed either implicitly by fiat or explicitly, using one or more of the techniques discussed in this chapter. Scheduling is but one side of the coin. Management must ensure that the schedule is being adhered to by the staff. There must be some means for exercising control over the process.

This chapter has identified several of the more readily available techniques for scheduling. At no time should the reader expect that mere quantification in the guise of a procedure is a substitute for common sense. In budgeting, as in most other areas of business, both perspectives have their proper place, and it is hoped that they are not mutually exclusive.

SOURCES AND SUGGESTED REFERENCES

Aronin, Simon, ''Better Forecasting Through Modeling,'' *Folio: The Magazine for Magazine Management,* vol. 19, no. 2, February 1990.

Grady, Robert B., *Practical Software Metrics for Project Management and Process Improvement.* Englewood Cliffs, NJ: Prentice-Hall, 1992.

Lewis, James P., *The Project Manager's Desk Reference.* Chicago: Probus, 1993.

Meredith, J., *The Management of Operations* (4th ed.). New York: John Wiley & Sons, 1992.

Metzger, Lawrence M., ''Using PERT in the Budgeting Process,'' *Journal of Cost Management for the Manufacturing Industry,* vol. 3, no. 4, Winter 1990.

PART 3

PREPARATION OF SPECIFIC BUDGETS

CHAPTER 23
Balance-Sheet Budget

CHAPTER 24
Budgeting for International Operations

CHAPTER 25
Understanding Foreign Exchange Transactions

CHAPTER 26
Budgeting Property and Liability Insurance Requirements

CHAPTER 13

SALES AND MARKETING BUDGET

R. Malcolm Schwartz

PricewaterhouseCoopers L.L.P.

13.1 INTRODUCTION. The sales and marketing budget is an important link with all other budgets. To make this link effective, the budget system should be based on a sound understanding of the vision, culture, and objectives of the organization; on an awareness of the relationships among business processes and with other business functions; on the ability to use external information about competitors, customers, suppliers, and public policy; and on good judgment.

The importance of these factors suggests that the sales and marketing budget process should be discussed broadly and not merely in terms of how related data should be entered, stored, and printed from a computer system. Therefore, this chapter concentrates on the following subjects:

- An overview of the budget process
- Special budgeting problems
- Pertinent tools
- Unique aspects of some industries

13.2 OVERVIEW OF THE BUDGET PROCESS. The sales and marketing budget process links to product, channels of distribution, and profit a group of largely discretionary expenses that focus on customers' acceptance—on the downstream components of the value chain. Most firms try to sell profitably what customers want, that is, what the market will bear. As a result, the sales and marketing budget is a means of integrating the functional plans as well as the process capabilities of an organization. It is important that the budget be controlled because marketing expenses, which are not only largely discretionary but also can be changed dramatically as to priorities and mix, can be misdirected quite easily.

As a result, a budget process should be in place that can be integrated with other plans and that can provide useful analyses to support the judgments of marketing planners.

(a) A Link between Strategic and Other Functional Plans. The sales and marketing budget provides a link between the business strategy and other functional plans. The sales budget defines the level and mix of projected product and service offerings, as well as such support costs as sales organization expense, trade promotion, and education programs. This information generally is developed to be consistent with the organization's overall strategic plan and to provide more detailed information for the planning period covered by the overall budget.

Much sales information traditionally is ''top line'' (that is, it is presented at the top of a profit and loss statement): the identification of short-term activity that it provides links the strategic plan to the budgets of other functions that support achieving the intended operating level. These other budgets include the following:

- *Operations (sourcing, conversion, and physical distribution).* Factors that are affected include inventory and service levels, replenishment techniques, production mix, and lengths of production runs.
- *Research and development (R&D).* Replacing products over their life cycles, anticipating customers' wants and needs and competitors' actions, and taking advantage of technological developments should help to identify priorities for development projects as well as the funding levels.
- *Administration.* A number of these support functions—ranging from clerical activities, such as order entry and customer service, to legal specialists—can be influenced by the sales budget.
- *Capital investment.* The needs for facilities, tooling, and equipment should be coordinated with sales activity.
- *Cash.* Inventory, accounts receivable, and accounts payable all can be affected by the sales budget.

The marketing budget in turn relates in two ways to sales plans. First, it can be driven by sales plans, as when higher volumes can cause greater expenditures for cooperative advertising. Second, it can be used to drive sales plans, as when promotional activities are planned to support sales growth or mix. The overall sales and marketing budget is therefore a means of integrating a number of plans to the strategy of the organization.

Today, many organizations think of this integration in process rather than functional terms. In such cases, plans and budgets may be process focused rather than function focused. A typical framework of processes and the business cycles they encompass might include the following:

- *Customer management.* From offering to selling products and services
- *Product management.* From planning through discontinuing product offerings
- *Supply chain.* From receiving demand signals through delivering products and services, including sourcing and conversion activities
- *Development.* From considering innovations through applying them
- *Support.* All infrastructure activities

Whether a company takes a functional or a process view, the sales and marketing (or customer and product) planning is an important link between strategy and business activities.

(b) Discretionary Expenses. In addition to consideration of product, price, promotion, and volume, the sales and marketing budget deals with a number of expenses that are largely discretionary. Sales budgeting deals with issues such as what products are to be sold, what prices are to be charged, how customer loyalty can be encouraged, and how much volume should result.

The marketing portion of the budget considers what resources are to be used, and in what mix, to move products from the organization to its customers. Major elements of the marketing budget include the following:

- *Selling.* May involve direct selling through various media, an employed sales force, sales representatives, or some combination
- *Sales promotion.* Often includes a combination of price and premium programs, trade shows, store fixtures, coupons, sponsorship, and the like
- *Advertising.* May concentrate on the image of the firm, a product line, or a brand; may be national, regional, local, or customer specific; can use various media
- *Product development.* Some organizations consider this a marketing expense, particularly for short-term efforts; can include new features, packaging changes, new products, and the like
- *Customer service.* Includes both warranty and out-of-warranty support, education, training, complaint handling, and a variety of other services
- *Physical distribution.* Some organizations treat as a marketing expense; might be handled centrally or might be spread through the regions served; other discretionary factors include how goods are shipped and whether the firm elects to use its own resources, distributors, or public warehouses

The marketing budget considers what mix and levels of these elements will be used. Therefore, the budget process should enable analyses that consider trade-offs, priorities, and contingent actions in support of the eventual agreed plan.

(c) Operating Factors. The budgeting process should consider a number of operating factors that shape the expenses planned for sales and marketing.

There are several different ways in which the levels of the various elements of marketing expense can be analyzed and targeted; these include historical trends, standards or benchmarks, and operating factors.

Historical trends can be applied rather simply; for example, if sales are planned to increase by 10%, then advertising can be increased by the same percentage. This approach takes little effort, but it assumes that prior levels of expenses were effective, that there are no benefits from growth, and that similar levels of expense will be needed in the future.

Standards—usually in the form of typical levels of expenses for certain industries—might be available, but because most firms have different objectives and operations, they can be hard to apply. Furthermore, an industry-wide benchmark can be too broad to have useful application. At the least, if benchmarks are used, the underlying practices should be understood and applicable. Standards for marketing expenses are usually more effective for checking if the plan varies from industry practice—and for being able to understand why and the associated risks—than as a means of developing the budget.

When developing the marketing budget, it is probably more useful to analyze the underlying operating factors that drive market performance than to rely on history or on benchmarks. Examples of such drivers include the following:

- Market share
- New account and customer retention rates
- Customer ordering patterns (size, frequency, and mix)
- Value of the customer and value to the customer
- Competitive position
- Impacts of past promotions
- Costs to acquire an account
- Sales call patterns

Exhibit 13.1 shows the impact of these and other factors on sales and marketing costs. By reviewing the factors that are important to the organization and how they relate to

Factor	Impact on Cost: Consumer Product	Impact on Cost: Industrial Product
Increased size of sales force	⇧	⇧
Product purchased more frequently than once per year	⇧	⇩
Higher market share or sales volume	⇩	⇩
Broader geographical coverage	⇩	⇩
Greater number of accounts	⇧	⇧
Marketing effort focused on end user	⇧	⇧
Higher product price	⇧	—
Increased customer service or technical support	—	⇧
Greater amount of distribution through others	⇧	⇧
Greater proportion of orders filled from inventory	⇧	⇧
More competitors	⇧	⇩
Increased importance of the product to the firm	—	⇩

⇧ Tends to increase ratio of marketing cost to sales
⇩ Tend to decrease ratio of marketing cost to sales
— Not significant

Exhibit 13.1. Impact of selected factors on sales and marketing cost

performance, the marketing planner likely will be able to make better recommendations regarding the amount and mix of marketing expense elements. Therefore, the budgeting system should include operating information as well as cost information.

(d) Culture and Management Style. The organizational architecture and the priorities that underlie the sales and marketing budget should fit with management style as well as with other processes. When constructing the sale and marketing budget, and because it is a means of integrating plans throughout the organization and the actions that result, it is important to consider issues of culture and management style. These issues deal with responsibility, authority, accountability, and empowerment; the importance of sole contributors or teams; how decisions get made; and the like. Culture issues also must consider information management—efficiency, cost, integrity, and the like—so that actions can focus on what should be done and not on whose information is correct.

An important culture issue is goal setting. Some executives prefer to hold managers responsible for the actions that they directly control, whereas others want managers to be aware also of the indirect consequences. For example, promotional activity directly affects prices and volumes and might indirectly affect the costs of order entry, credit, and accounts receivable, among other activities. In dealing with these different styles of relating responsibility to the budget structure, two approaches are used, the direct- and the full-cost methods, the concepts of which were discussed in Part II.

The direct-cost method relates to products only those costs that are expressly associated with them; in addition to product costs, these may include elements of the sales and marketing budget, such as promotional expense, cooperative advertising programs, and the like. The full-cost method relates all costs to products by allocating indirect cost elements; as a result, product profitability can be measured in the same way that business profitability is measured. The direct-cost method is often supported today by activity-based costing principles.

In the direct-cost method, which is simpler from a performance management viewpoint, product performance is measured in terms of contribution to business overhead and profit.

Whichever costing method is used, the sales and marketing budget system should be coordinated with other systems. For example, the chart of accounts should be used effectively. With proper planning, subaccounts can be established for products, salespersons, customer classifications, promotional programs, and other categories that are useful for planning and control. Just as expenses can be related to the accounting system, operating factors can be related to other parts of the management information system.

(e) Incremental Planning and Analysis. Assuming that the sales and marketing budget is used to integrate other plans and budgets, and that the revenue and expense information is built up from operating factors, another major system feature is to allow for incremental planning. Depending on the business and industry, planning increments might include geographic regions, channels of distribution, classes of customers, and product lines.

When plans are developed incrementally, adjustments can be more focused during the review process. Key steps in budgeting incrementally include the following:

- Identify the increments.
- Analyze the related operating factors.
- Develop the sales and marketing plan for each increment.

- Extend each increment to revenues and expense.
- Sum the increments to form a base budget.
- Review the base budget for consistency with the organization's strategy, for profit, for an assessment of competitive actions, and for overall affordability.
- Adjust the base budget as needed and at the level of the individual increments.
- Test the adjusted base budget for profit sensitivity to different levels of expense.

Finally, when the optimal incremental programs have been budgeted, and at levels that should generate desired profits, the budget can be approved and a road map will have been provided for sales and marketing efforts. This approach enables the linking of ''top-down'' and ''bottom-up'' budgeting, focused at the sales and marketing decisions. Exhibit 13.2 provides an overview of this process.

13.3 SPECIAL BUDGETING PROBLEMS. Because marketing expenditures are so discretionary and can be combined in so many different ways, it can be difficult to develop meaningful levels of expense for each element of cost. During the budgeted period, it can also be difficult to control expense levels and to adapt them to changing circumstances. This section reviews some of the more general aspects of these problems as they relate to the major cost elements.

(a) Pricing Adjustments. Planned pricing and any adjustments need to be budgeted if future revenues are to be attained and controlled.

Prices are usually developed both in relationship to costs and in response to competition. For products that have leading positions in the market, prices might be based on value to the customer.

New products can be difficult to price. At the time of initial market entry, prices are sometimes set close to cost to achieve desired volume and market share. After these goals are attained, prices might be adjusted. During the same period—as volume is growing—product costs could be declining; as a result, prices could be kept stable and profits would increase.

When prices are declining, it may be necessary to plan additional discounts. These usually can be better controlled in many companies' systems than outright price reductions because they can be recorded and tracked as expenses. Some companies overcome this limitation by tracking both standard and realized prices.

For any product for which a price change is planned, it is useful to control this by budgeting at the base price and then showing for each period in the budget the pricing adjustments that are to be made.

(b) Selling Expense. Selling expense includes a number of cost elements, such as salary, commissions, training, and salespersons' expenses. These costs often are associated with different sales forces for regions, classes of customers, or groups of products. Selling expense should be budgeted incrementally in ways that enable future analyses, for example:

- Organizations with large in-store sales forces might want to budget and report selling expense by department, by transaction, by day, and by time of day; data such as these enable correlating store staffing with service levels.
- Organizations whose sales forces cover wide geographical areas might want to compare the times to call on customers in urban and rural areas.

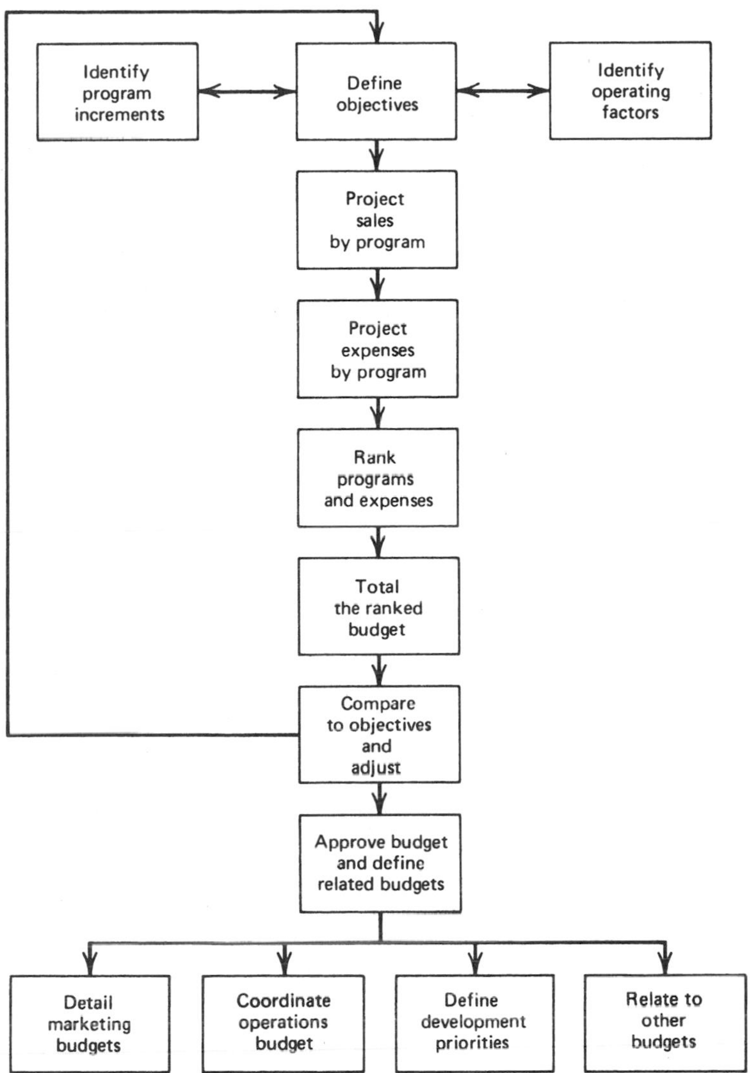

Exhibit 13.2. Approach to incremental budgeting

- Mail-order firms usually want to evaluate selling expense geographically (zip codes are often used) and by the source of the sale (which could be from a specific list of names, from particular advertising copy, or from a media placement).

The kinds of monitoring analyses that will be used should be identified as the budget is being assembled so that techniques for reporting and control can be established.

(c) Sales Promotion Expense. Too often, sales promotions are undertaken to increase sales without sufficient attention to planning and controls. Lack of control can be found with sales personnel as well as with customers, as seen in the following examples:

- The internal auditor for a household products firm found that some promotional fixtures never had been placed in stores, and yet sales representatives were receiving commissions approved by the sales manager.
- When a mail-order firm revised its customer list programs, it found that one customer had made a number of minor changes in his name and address to obtain more than $10,000 worth of free promotional merchandise.

Because there are few industry standards for sales promotion expense, each firm needs to use its own track record to determine what is effective. Records should be kept and incorporated into budgets and controls for the relationships among volume, product, media, and promotional devices. Later promotions can be correlated to benchmarks that are developed, and variances can be analyzed, as misredemption or promotional losses, as examples.

In addition to incremental planning and control of merchandise, the expenses for premiums and coupons and other elements of sales promotion also should be planned and controlled incrementally, for example:

- Trade shows and exhibits often are planned and controlled for each instance, and analyzed in relationship to sales activity generated.
- Samples and giveaways are usually controlled by salespersons, to evaluate any unusual rates of usage.
- Fixtures often are controlled as if they were inventory, and might need accountability by both salesperson and customer.

(d) Advertising Budget. Advertising often appears to be discretionary to management and can become one of the first elements of expense to be reduced in bad times. Therefore, it is important to be able to assess the effectiveness of advertising. Copy, timing, media, and placement can be important factors. The budget should be assembled so that advertising expense and sales activity can be correlated. Similarly, tests of geographical coverage, copy, and the like need to be controlled.

Control can be exercised by having the advertising organization develop standards (examples can include recall, impact, or sales percentages) for effectiveness, and then conduct tests regularly to measure that impact. Advertising expenditures by product are often published (e.g., in *Advertising Age*), so that an organization's expenditures can also be compared to these external benchmarks.

Dealer cooperative advertising presents another problem in planning and control that can influence both the design of a budget system and the process of budgeting. Cooperative claims should be verified by tearsheets for print advertising and by invoices for television and radio. As a consequence, a subsystem is needed, by dealer, in regard to claimable amounts, claims pending, and claims approved and paid. The claimable amounts, which are usually based on purchases of a given product or products for a specified period, should be tracked to establish the potential expense, although actual claims paid might be less.

Even with the use of benchmarks and analyses to explain what advertising is important and why, it still remains a discretionary expense. Occasionally, when management attempts to reduce advertising expense, it finds that commitments already have been made for future expenditures. Therefore, the budget system and the resulting controls should incorporate plans for the timing and amount of commitments as well as expenditures.

(e) Product Development Costs. Marketing management uses product development to procure new styles of packaging, new features, and the like. Such procurements can be internal, or items might be purchased from suppliers. In any case, development efforts and their associated costs are best controlled by project. A product-development project subsystem can be used to link the R&D budget with the marketing expense budget.

(f) Customer Service Expenses. The influence of consumer price and value sensitivities, and the needs for differentiation in the marketplace, have caused warranty and other service programs to be expanded. Recalls and replacements have become more common. More staff is being used to answer consumers' questions, and more information is available, in return, to shape product and marketing plans.

As a result, new methods are being used to plan and control customer service expenses. Warranty expenses have usually been planned as a percentage of sales, but today more attention is being given to relating warranty expense to particular products and their sources. Recall expenses can be projected from total quality management (TQM) programs, and from the statistical process control activities that tend to follow. Replacement expenses can be estimated from failure rate percentages related to the product and developed in the quality control laboratory.

Comparative trends of expenses on these elements of cost should be monitored and should be used to:

- Adjust the budget
- Provide reserves on actual performance
- Focus development activities
- Direct quality assurance actions

(g) Physical Distribution. Physical distribution involves market-responsive trade-offs between service and cost. Service levels should be planned and performance monitored. Often, service can provide an important competitive advantage when price, product features, and the like are not highly differentiable among competitors.

Higher levels of inventory usually accompany better service, and with the annual costs to carry inventory sometimes approaching 25% of inventory value, it is important to ensure that service is worth the cost. In many cases, service can be improved with the same or a reduced inventory level by planning and controlling where the inventory is located across the overall supply chain and for what product, by improving demand communications (using point-of-sale, or POS, information, for example), and by synchronizing the sourcing, conversion, and delivery activities.

As a consequence, the sales and marketing system should be linked to the inventory-control system, and through it, to manufacturing and purchasing. Marketing information is needed by product and location; service as well as cost data should be planned, reported, and analyzed. A system of this sort provides the performance benchmarks related to objectives that can help to resolve the usual conflicts about inventory among marketing, finance, and operating managers.

13.4 PERTINENT TOOLS.

There are a number of techniques that are helpful in budgeting and controlling sales and marketing expense, including the following:

- Product life-cycle analysis
- Marginal analysis
- Break-even analysis
- Forecasting techniques
- Sensitivity techniques
- Bracket budgeting
- Pricing techniques
- Performance tests

This section discusses some of the key features of these techniques.

(a) Analysis of Product Life Cycles. Each phase of a product's life cycle presents different budgeting concerns, ranging from early investment requirements and inventory to "fill the pipeline" to later issues of price and of product discontinuance. Methods must be established in advance to determine when a product is moving from one phase to another so that:

- Strategies and budgets can be adjusted
- Agreement can be reached on whether to extend the product's life
- Planning guidelines can be set on removing the product from the market

A product life cycle is usually longer than the budget period, so a product plan should be developed that relates to a series of budgets. The product plan should include information on the competitive environment because:

- Little competition might relate to the introductory phase
- New competitors might indicate the beginning of the growth phase
- A variety of differentiated products often shows the maturity phase
- Identical competitive products may point to the decline phase

The technique of monitoring products' life cycles can help to direct development efforts for differentiating and improving products and thus for extending their lives.

(b) Marginal Analysis. Marginal analysis, which has been discussed previously, can be helpful for cost allocation. Different geographical or sales categories can be tested so that incremental revenue less incremental cost derived from the last unit sold in each area is equal. To illustrate marginal analysis, an advertising budget can be assigned to two categories, and then $1.00 can be transferred from the first to the second; if profit increases, then the transfer is worthwhile and should be continued until no change in profit occurs.

(c) Break-Even Analysis. Break-even analysis, which was discussed in Chapters 5 and 7, requires knowledge of fixed and variable costs and of contributions for individual products. With these data, the break-even point can be calculated. The result of such an analysis might indicate that increasing the sales of selected products will help to cover fixed costs; if so, the sales and marketing budget should focus on efforts to support that objective.

(d) Forecasting Techniques. Most firms forecast by extending historical data for themselves, for competitors, and/or for the overall industry. Some companies incorporate economic data, or have determined that there are leading indicators that help in forecasting sales, such as new home starts for heavy appliances or marriage rates for tableware. Economic data can be obtained from government publications, trade journals, industry associations, consulting firms, and banks; computer programs can be used to test historical correlations.

Many firms rely heavily on internal data for forecasting sales. By using regression analysis or other statistical techniques, a series of internal and external factors can be selected and tested to determine if they help to predict sales. Often, firms rely on simpler statistical techniques, such as moving averages.

Of course, because forecasts are never precise, it is best to rely on actual demand signals for operational and tactical actions. For planning, however, some form of forecasting usually will be needed. To deal with the uncertainty of forecasts, it is useful to consider a range of possible outcomes, with related assumptions, impacts, and probabilities of occurrence.

(e) Sensitivity Analysis. Sensitivity analysis can be used, for example, to simulate best, likely, and worst cases before they occur. Relationships must first be understood between the conditions that are to be tested and their effects on sales, costs, and profits; these conditions could include changes in the following:

- The market, such as overall demand or competitive share
- The economy, such as monetary or fiscal policies or local business conditions
- The environment, including changes in life style or demographic shifts

Sensitivity analysis is often coupled with probability techniques to answer ''what if'' questions. A firm might want to know the impact of interest rates on cash flow—for example, at 5% interest a particular project is profitable, but at 12% interest it is not. The project can be analyzed for a series of interest rates, and a probability can be assigned to each one. An overall expected benefit thus can be determined, as illustrated in Exhibit 13.3.

(f) Bracket Budgeting. Bracket budgeting is a form of built-in contingency planning. Expenses are developed at higher and lower levels (plus or minus 10%, for example) than the base budget, and sales that are likely to result are then forecast. At a later date, if sales were to rise and management should act to maintain the higher level, the likely impact on expenses would already be understood.

If the sales budget were not achieved, the bracket budget gives management a sense of the profit impact, and a contingency plan can be installed quickly. A more detailed discussion of this subject is found in Chapter 28.

(g) Tactical and Strategic Pricing Techniques. Various techniques are used for tactical pricing, which is usually practiced in times of static market conditions and growing demand. These include cost-based pricing, reaction to competitors, and penetration pricing.

Cost-based pricing rests on sound knowledge of all costs as well as effective management of costs that are allocated among products. Reaction to competitive moves has been used by smaller firms who must respond—often by charging less—to industry leaders.

The Sensitivity Analysis[a]

Year	Cash Flow	5%	6%	8%	10%
1	$10,000	$9,524	$9,434	$9,259	$9,091
2	10,000	9,070	8,900	8,573	8,264
3	8,000	6,910	6,717	6,350	6,010
4	7,000	5,759	5,545	5,145	4,781
5	5,000	3,918	3,737	3,403	3,105
Total cash in		$35,181	$34,333	$32,730	$31,251
Cash out		(33,000)	(33,000)	(33,000)	(33,000)
Net present value		$2,181	$1,333	$ (270)	$ (1,749)

Conclusion: If interest rates approach 8%, do not do the project.
What is management's judgment on the likelihood?

The Expected Benefit Analysis

	Probability by Interest Rate				Adjusted
Year	5%	6%	8%	10%	Net Present Value
1	80%	20%	—	—	$9,506
2	80%	20%	—	—	9,036
3	—	50%	30%	20%	6,466
4	—	50%	30%	20%	5,272
5	—	50%	30%	20%	3,511
Estimated cash in					$33,791
Cash out					(33,000)
Net present value					$ 791

Conclusion: If management's judgment about interest rates is correct, do the project.

[a] Using present value technique.

Exhibit 13.3. Example of sensitivity analysis

Penetration pricing occurs when a firm consciously reduces its usual profit objective to increase market share or to emphasize profitable aftermarket sales (selling razors to sell blades, as an example).

Strategic pricing is appropriate with slow-growing economies, changing demand levels, and stiff competition. This technique often relates to value as perceived by the customer. For example, reformulating a product by removing an additive that did not have broad appeal could enable a price reduction with a concomitant sales gain. Strategic pricing can also relate to the pace of technological change or to the uniqueness of the product.

- For a market in which technology is expected to change in five years, product durability could be designed to that period and price reduced accordingly.
- Unique product or service features—or the level of technical support—might enable product differentiation and value-added pricing; alternatively, store-branded products can be priced lower because they use available capacity and require less marketing expense.

In any regard, the pricing techniques that are used can influence the structure of the sales and marketing budget as well as the related systems and reports. Emphasis on cost-based pricing, for example, requires more complete cost portrayals, more emphasis of cost differentiation by product, and sensible rules for allocating fixed costs; activity-based costing is a useful supportive approach.

(h) Testing Actual Performance. Whatever specialized techniques are used for planning and evaluation, the system should have the ability to provide feedback. Plans to increase or decrease expense should be tested in controlled situations to measure the impact on sales.

For example, results of a market test should be compared to plan, and the budget system should be adapted accordingly. The capability of analyzing controlled changes will enable the extrapolating of results to later budget periods.

13.5 UNIQUE ASPECTS OF SOME INDUSTRIES.

Just as each firm is distinctive, so many industries have different characteristics that cause different approaches to sales and marketing budgeting. This section identifies some features of selected industries—namely, consumer packaged goods, industrial products, retailing, and banking—to illustrate some of the differences. These four industries were selected to illustrate differences resulting from products or services, from customers, and from method of distribution.

(a) Consumer Packaged-Goods Firms. Budgets for this type of firm often begin with stated goals for market share. Strategies for product, distribution, price, copy, media, promotion, special programs, and volume are formed to reach these goals. Costs are assigned to each strategy and, along with expected volume, are compared to profit objectives. Expense levels are generally determined by a combination of experience and test marketing; external standards are rarely used to determine expense levels, but benchmarks are often used to test the reality and risk in the plan.

The budget usually links other functional plans. Marketing efforts are geared to the profit objective. The manufacturing plan provides cost information that must be assumed by marketing management. The product manager (in the marketing organization) often controls the R&D budget. Because plans are linked and the overall effort is market driven, the marketing plan often includes a section that identifies where and how the budget should be changed if conditions warrant.

Selling efforts are often important and the sales force can be large. Pressure therefore can be created to price low, to provide substantial promotional activity, and to structure large incentive compensation programs. The trade (the direct customer) also can come to expect continuing promotions, cooperative allowances, and the like. The budget system enables management to plan and evaluate these activities and to make sure that they really are productive.

(b) Industrial Products Firms. The sales force is the key element in the selling of industrial products; hence, the budget should be geared to provide the mix of expenses that will best support that selling effort. Underlying policies are important, such as warranty, prepaid freight, and trade-in allowance. These are often developed more to fit the company objectives than to imitate competitors' policies. Costs generally are influenced by the policies that are set. This individualized approach precludes the use of external standards to set expense levels, so an internal data base is important. Again, benchmarking and analyzing best practices are increasing in use.

Sales forecasts also are usually based on internal data. Firms with long order lead-in times can analyze their backlogs or, in some cases, the progress against completion of large jobs. Share of market information is seldom used because share tends to remain stable or is less meaningful. Most sales projections involve collecting and interpreting historical and competitive data.

The budget is usually linked with the purchasing and manufacturing plans. Occasionally, too little attention is given to linkages with service and applications engineering budgets. Sales personnel can overpromise service or product adaptability, and the support functions have difficulty in delivering what was promised; effective planning and control, coupled with procedural guidelines, can prevent problems of this sort.

(c) Retailing. Whereas the focus for consumer packaged goods is on the market and for industrial products is on the selling effort, for retail the budgeting focuses on the merchandise—what to sell and how it is to be sold. Key factors include fashion trends, the cycle of selling seasons, and the pressure to move inventory.

Forecasts are often quite detailed, in some cases down to item by store. Forecasts are coordinated between buyers of merchandise and store managers—the first reflects fashion trends and the second relates the merchandise to local conditions. Expenses are usually projected by store and sometimes by department. Various trade associations publish extensive data on expenses by merchandise category, by store size, and by volume. Pricing involves target and historic markups by product line, adjusted for inventory movement and promotional activity.

The budget is closely linked to buying activities. Usually, a buyer can commit only up to an inventory limit (called an ''open to buy''), so merchandise must be sold to enable future merchandise to be bought. Open to buy is carefully planned and monitored. The expense budget is controlled by store management; if sales are low, steps usually are taken to reduce advertising expense or the sales force.

(d) Banking. Bank budgeting focuses on budgeting the differential between the costs to obtain and the costs to lend funds. Key elements of the budget include projecting availability of funds, interest rates, loan demand, deposit demand, and operating expenses.

Economics information and knowledge of the business environment are important factors in budgeting. In banking, sales information is in terms of the amount and types of loans, the interest rates that pertain, the timing of repayment, and likely loan losses.

Sophisticated forecasting and control techniques are used in regard to economic conditions, interest rates, loan demand, and consumer needs. Banks' marketing departments use research techniques (those that are traditionally used by consumer products firms) to evaluate new financial services products.

13.6 SUMMARY. The sales and marketing budget is a key integrative device in many industries. It relates the firm's strategy to operating plans for various functions. It is a means with which to deal with a mass of external and internal data. It should link a number of subsystems for controlling elements of marketing expense and for evaluating the strategy for a product over its life cycle. Therefore, developing and maintaining a sales and marketing budget system requires a broad understanding of the overall business and its strategy and needs.

SOURCES AND SUGGESTED REFERENCES

Ahadiat, Nasrollah, ''Sales Forecasting and Cash Budgeting for Automotive Dealerships,'' *Journal of Business Forecasting,* vol. 11, no. 11, Fall 1992.

Andris, A., Murali K. Mantrala, Sinha Prabhakant, and Zoltners, ''Impact of Resource Allocation Rules on Marketing Investment-Level Decisions and Profitability,'' *Journal of Marketing Research,* vol. 29, no. 2, May 1992.

Anonymous, ''Budgeting for the Agency Sales Force,'' *Agency Sales Magazine,* vol. 20, no. 5, May 1990.

Anonymous, ''The Road to Upfront: Beverages,'' *Mediaweek,* vol. 3, no. 20, May 17, 1993.

Anonymous, ''Sound Budgeting Can Help Control Costs and Increase Profits; Five Basic Ways to Budget for Your Advertising Needs,'' *Profit-Building Strategies for Business Owners,* vol. 22, no. 4, April 1992.

Anonymous, ''You Said It: How Do You Balance Your Sales Budget?'' *Sales & Marketing Management,* vol. 144, no. 11, September 1992.

Anonymous, ''1993 Sales Manager's Budget Planner,'' *Sales & Marketing Management,* vol. 145, no. 7, June 28, 1993.

Book, Joel, ''Building a Marketing Info System,'' *Agri Marketing,* vol. 29, no. 6, June 1991.

Calvin, Robert J., ''Budgeting Prizes and Profits,'' *Small Business Reports,* vol. 18, no. 7, July 1993.

Chatterjee, et al. ''A Communication Response Model for a Mature Industrial Product: Application and Implications,'' *Journal of Marketing Research,* vol. 29, no. 2, May 1992.

Donath, Bob, ''Busting Budget Bean Counters,'' *Marketing News,* vol. 26, no. 18, August 31, 1992.

Doyle, Peter, and John Saunders, ''Multiproduct Advertising Budgeting,'' *Marketing Science,* vol. 9, no. 2, Spring 1990.

Falvey, Jack, ''The Battle of the Budget,'' *Sales & Marketing Management,* vol. 143, no. 14, November 1991.

Fleming, Mary M. K., and Barbara Jizba, ''Promotion Budgeting and Control in the Fast Food Industry,'' *International Journal of Advertising,* vol. 12, no. 1, 1993.

Frank, Howard A., and Gerasimos A. Gianakis, ''Raising the Bridge Using Time Series Forecasting Models,'' *Public Productivity & Management Review,* vol. 14, no. 2, Winter 1990.

Howell, Keith A., ''Lowe's Companies' Statistical Approach to Sales Forecasting,'' *Corporate Controller,* vol. 3, no. 5, May/June 1991.

Hudson, Phillip F., ''What Would You Do?'' *Bank Marketing,* vol. 25, no. 9, September 1993.

Hung, C. L., and Douglas C. West. ''Advertising Budgeting Methods in Canada, the UK and the USA,'' *International Journal of Advertising,* vol. 10, no. 3, 1991.

Krueger, Joseph, ''Developing a Marketing Budget,'' *Target Marketing,* vol. 19, no. 10, October 1996, pp. 118–122.

Lamons, Bob, ''Let's Demand Enough Money to Do the Job,'' *Marketing News,* vol. 27, no. 8, April 12, 1993.

Lynch, James E., and Graham J. Hooley, ''Increasing Sophistication in Advertising Budget Setting,'' *Journal of Advertising Research,* vol. 10, no. 1, February/March 1990.

O'Neal, Jason, ''Budgeting with Trend Projection,'' *CFO: The Magazine for Senior Financial Executives,* vol. 7, no. 8, August 1991.

Pollare, Frank L., ''Marketing Public Relations: Surviving the Budgeting Game,'' *Public Relations Journal,* vol. 46, no. 3, March 1990.

Shawkey, Bruce, ''Building a High-Performance Budget,'' *Credit Union Management,* vol. 15, no. 8, August 1992.

Symons, Paula, ''MCIFs Supply Budget Support,'' *Credit Union Management,* vol. 15, no. 8, August 1992.

Turner, James, ''Budgeting Crunch Requires Creative Solutions,'' *Bank Marketing,* vol. 23, no. 9, September 1991.

Walther, George R. *Upside-Down Marketing.* New York: McGraw-Hill, 1994.

CHAPTER 14

MANUFACTURING BUDGET

C. Eugene Moore

C. Eugene Moore & Associates

14.1 INTRODUCTION. Our objective in this chapter is to review the concepts used in preparing the operations/manufacturing budget, to discuss some of the problems encountered in preparation, and to suggest techniques that the manager should employ in building that budget into a full business plan and profit program *pro forma.* Nothing that exists when you start this process this time should be the same when you finish it. You must plan deliberate change unrelated to history to be successful.

In consulting specialized reference material, readers normally assume that the information is technical and therefore free of an author's bias. This assumption is false. The dynamics of a manufacturing organization make preparation of budgets much more than a sterile planning exercise as the concepts and techniques set forth, all founded in personal experience, are the basis of the recommended approach.

Other aspects of budgeting have been reviewed in previous sections, but their successful assimilation into a total budget depends on the decisions made by managers in the manufacturing organization. The planned action budget methods that will build on management decisions for planned, deliberate change constitute the general assumption throughout this entire section, if you have the will to manage.

Does it work? Yes! In fact, you cannot accomplish the expectations of your associates if you do not follow this concept. The Association for Manufacturing Excellence (AME) has held more than 50 seminars, describing that as many companies engaging in such deliberate changes produced total reductions of more than 30% of total cost of goods sold. It is the approach that is different as explained below.

Peter Drucker stated that ''What distinguishes the truly productive [manager] from the merely competent one is rarely knowledge or effort, let alone talent. The men who are truly productive are men who focus their knowledge, their intelligence, and their efforts on a big, truly worthwhile goal—men who set out to create something [different].

In their acceptance speeches, Nobel prize winners usually say, ''What started me on the work that led to this achievement was a chance remark by a teacher who said: 'Why don't you try something where the results would really make a difference?' . . . This is a very different question from the ones asked in the managerial organization when it does 'long-range planning' or allocates resources. There, one tries to minimize the possible loss. In innovation, one has to maximize the possible results.''

If you believe that your job as a manager is to sit in judgment, you will inevitably veto change. It is always ''impractical.'' You must be a participant in the changes, and when you are, you will see that it takes as much energy and ingenuity to do what we already do just a little better, as it takes to do something entirely different.

A large container manufacturer had elaborate modern accounting systems and monthly budget reports. These had been installed by a major public accounting firm. The manufacturer suffered losses in one division, while the second division, having the major market share in its product line, was steadily declining in annual profit. By virtue of its major market share, the profitable division had held an umbrella over its competitors' costs for years by raising prices to cover the changes in its own operating costs. Suddenly, the second division's declining profit margin slipped, and the total result became a loss.

Management demanded changes, and we decided that none of the existing practices in the better division was sacred and that change was required immediately. We were determined that no activity or element of cost would continue without an organized effort to improve both it and the profits. Deliberate changes were made in the next two years in the more profitable division. These provided sustenance to the crippled division and "saved the company." (These are the recent words of the company chairman.) The results of the deliberate changes were as follows:

- Fixed costs were reduced in six months by reducing floor space by 750,000 square feet for the same volume of production.
- Nonproductive assets were retired and unused property sold.
- The production process was physically re-arranged to provide efficient direct in-line feeding during the process, and indirect costs of transportation were reduced by 50% in an eight-month period on 73 million metal package caps per day.
- Specifications for quality were reviewed and quantified along with the introduction of statistical methods for inspection, thus eliminating 500 employees engaged in visual and manual inspections.
- Manufacturing staff functions were reorganized to reduce personnel by 30%.
- Maintenance organization changes improved "up" time in major processes; output increased.
- The company went from loss to profit in the first year of these changes—and onward to phenomenal growth and profitability.
- The costs to achieve these goals aggregated $2.5 million. These were committed in two increments. The first million was recovered in eight months and the balance within six months of completion (a 14-month process).

Usually, management relates each new budget to those of prior years, without considering the assumptions or real opportunities for changes in plant, methods, personnel, and so on. Some opportunities to do this had existed for years prior to the program, but sliding into the loss column was the event that triggered the change.

Must such drastic events occur before managers re-examine their current practices?

This chapter highlights that all present practices must be reviewed and become the subject of intense scrutiny during budget preparation and that significant changes in margins between revenue and costs can be deliberately changed by management actions.

In another situation—that of a major New England machinery builder—we engaged all members of the manufacturing organization, all functions and departments, in the preparation of new budgets for the following year. We examined the actual requirements of all departments. Some received larger allowances for necessary services to be performed, functions were transferred for lower-cost delivery of the same service, and many items of non–value-added costs and services were discontinued. The first year an 18% reduction in all manufacturing expenses occurred. This was followed in the second year by an additional 15% reduction. These reductions occurred while the output increased 25%, new products were introduced, and delivery service to customers improved. The managers learned to manage costs where they are caused.

Thus, we can see that building the manufacturing budget is the most exciting and creative manufacturing management task. During this period, there are fewer side glances from your peers or your boss that imply, "Why are you tampering with a going operation?" Budget building seems to be the one time when it is proper to take off the wraps and consider some change.

Having completed such rigorous planning in the past would have signaled the organization to "settle down"—to carry on with the work and breathe a sigh of relief that we could now get back to normal. We have all done this. However, this cannot be the approach, not now in the world of "KAISEN."

We must become aware of the competitive forces throughout the world that requires *continuous improvement*: quarterly, monthly, and daily. This concept was originally introduced to Japan by Dr. Edwards Deming, in his 14 points. It was also used by Taiichi Ohno of Toyota and adopted by the Japanese Industrial Engineering Society, as explained by Masaaki Imai in his book *Kaisen: The Key to Japan's Competitive Success.*[1] He has helped manufacturing firms transfer technology between the United States and Japan for 40 years.

The annual rhythmic plan for programming changes in U.S. industrial organizations is a thing of the past. It is well, then, at the outset of this process, that we recognize that it will always be a continuous, never-ending policy, not a program. To get started in this new process, we should be aware of new realities in our environment.

There is a complete discontinuity with past in objectives, techniques, and considerations of direct labor, materials supply, inventories, product design, and process planning, as well as how we want to account for those activities we direct.

First, a budget with regular performance reports does not guarantee a profit. Profit can occur only when actual operating management decisions accomplish beneficial change, not budgets. Many billion-dollar companies regularly go to bankruptcy proceedings with budgets in hand.

Second, most "staff" groups have elaborate mission statements and promise benefits. Seventeen layers of such management at the Ford Motor Company were undone when Mr. Peterson decided to become profitable and he removed them to produce the vigorous successfully competitive company of today (1992).

Third, the direct labor content is usually less than 10% of the price the user pays for the product, with most companies now employing three to four people in various non–value-added jobs for everyone labeled as a direct worker. The real problem here is that, as evidenced from personnel evaluation system failures, most managers do not know and/or do not tell salaried people what the real work task is and what performance will constitute success or failure. The failure of salaried employees to be productive is that

---

[1] Masaaki Imai, *Kaisen: The Key to Japan's Competitive Success* (New York: McGraw-Hill, 1987).

managers do not intend, or do not know how, to have them be gainfully employed or become value-added employees.

Fourth, doing what we are now produces poor results. It may be wise to forget "our way."

Fifth, current results in return on investment, profits, and the consumption of net worth (undistributed surplus) justify a complete review of our operational and organizational styles that have become so traditional.

Sixth, in the 50 plus years since World War II, all international trade and commerce was influenced by the Cold War—East versus West—and we missed the actual growth and development of new trading areas, partners, and opportunities being thrust on the United States by rapid communication and spread of knowledge and information. We are less the masters of the directions of that commerce than we were earlier. We have to earn our way in competitive situations today.

In addition to those enumerated environmental changes, significant techniques have developed in major functional program areas of industrial organizations, which have major impact on the amounts and kinds of expenditures to be budgeted.

A company receives revenue/income from sales of the product and spends money to buy processing equipment, materials to use, and labor to perform conversion activities. Accountants decided at the turn of the century that industrial engineers could identify the value-added work in micromotions; and they decided that all other manufacturing activities should therefore be related to the purest value-creating activities—those micromotions. They lump all the capital and overhead expense costs and then distribute them proportionately to each micromotion to account for and develop cost/pricing programs and management control reports.

(a) Concepts of Direct Labor Have Changed. The transfer of most cut, shape, form, and other conversion operations to mechanical and electronically controlled multiperation equipment, along with the increasing assignments of people to groups of tasks rather than to a series of a few (or one) micromotions has changed the traditional measurement and control of people and tasks, and capital equipment use.

(b) The Economic Criteria about Purchased Materials Have Changed. The important differences between cost-management systems (CMS) and traditional practices include the following:

- Continual improvement and the elimination of non–value-added costs
- Activity-based accounting (cost drivers selected)
- Externally driven targets including target cost
- Improved traceability of information to management reporting objectives

We now know that accounting techniques influence behavior. Studies by the U.S. Air Force have shown that 75% of the cost-reduction programs submitted focus on direct labor (touch labor) rather than the many other larger potential areas such as making knowledge workers more productive, improving supplier costs and performance, design for manufacture, improved processes, and so forth, as illustrated in Exhibit 14.1.

Expressed another way, management must learn where costs are caused or occur and then arrange the accounting to reflect those places and activities, so that the management

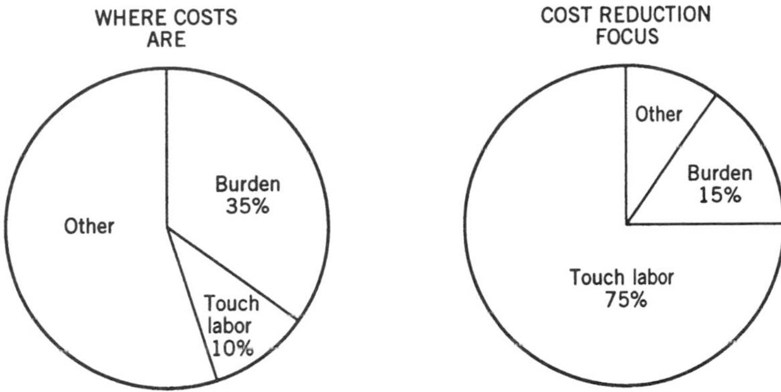

Exhibit 14.1. Where costs are—cost reduction focus

reports and control relate directly to them. The ineffective activities and employees performing non–value-added tasks or duties must be identified.

Following is a formula for manufacturing-cycle efficiency (MCE), which clearly shows non–value-added operations.

$$\text{MCE} = \frac{\text{Processing time}}{\text{Processing time} + \text{Wait} + \text{Move} + \text{Handle} + \text{Waste} + \text{Set-up}}$$

The MCE should equal 1.00 (processing time only). It now equals approximately 0.20 (20%).

To prepare a budget or financial plan in this competitive era without attacks on such basic functional areas is to ignore the real management task of a manager. There are usually conflicts in planning and implementing the programs on which the budget is based.

The different functions necessarily compete for a portion of the existing gross margin above direct costs, to expand or aggrandize their services. The request for growth of each is rationalized as being in the highest interest of either improving the revenue or lowering costs. These conflicting suborganizational goals require that the manufacturing manager make many trade-off decisions in preparing the complete operating plan and budget, as the container manufacturer did in the preceding example. The idea of trade-offs and techniques will be discussed throughout the chapter.

The manufacturing budget is the most significant part of the total business plan because:

- The cost of goods manufactured ranges from 50% to 75% and up of the corporate revenue dollars.
- It establishes the planned production rate that governs the expected revenue and deals with the problem of capacity.
- It establishes the level of services that the functional specialists will supply to the factory-direct conversion operations, thereby setting the overhead costs and rates.
- It contains the plans for acquiring the materials to supply the planned production rates for conversion to your product. Therefore, it acts as a throttle for the level of working capital required in raw materials, work-in-process, and finished goods inventories.

- A company must develop a pricing strategy independent of cost. At the outset, some business plans call for operations for a period without absorbing the total cost.

New products or plants anticipate learning curves, increasing sales, high initial development costs, and the like, recognizing that the marketplace could not support pricing at full absorption. In competitive periods, this also occurs with a going operation. This situation usually requires the kind of changes being discussed earlier.

Frequently, though, there are many products in the same factory, most of which in reality have quite different needs but draw disproportionate or averaged allocated overhead amounts. Standard line products get upgraded and volume shifts occur. Just-in-time (JIT), quality, and automated processes also skew uniform overhead applications in price planning. Your budgeting process should include exhaustive reviews of across-the-board allocations made for easier accounting and so on. More accurate product cost information will lead to better strategic market decisions as well as decisions in investments for hardware and software.

14.2 CONCEPTS. In preparing the manufacturing budget, many decisions have to be made: why each activity is necessary and when, and by what means the various costs are to be met. It is here that the intention of the manager is stated, the action plan is outlined, and the control points selected to monitor those action plans. Scheduled deliveries, dependability, and vendors' product innovation are all currently more important than current price or ritualistic requests for periodic quotations on price and delivery in former times. For example, IBM recently reduced the number of suppliers to their Lexington, Kentucky, location from 5,000 to approximately 500 in a period of two years.

Many times, such programs to reduce the number of vendors raise the invoice price of materials. However, more precision in quality, deliveries, inventory policy, and arrangements mean a lowered net cost to the purchaser. These factors are nowhere to be seen in any current operations statements without extensive deductive accounting research outside the normal report routines. However, these arrangements have been adopted as amazing profit improvers, as evidenced by many published reports of improvements by many companies, for example, members of the Association for Manufacturing Excellence.

Most concepts of inventory have changed since the performance of the Toyota production system was described by Shigeo Shingo, Ohno's protegé, and discovered in the United States on Japanese/English bookshelves by C. Eugene Moore, Romeyn Everdall, APICS, AMA, AME, and major consulting firms. The initial program thrust by APICS, however, was a false start in that everyone conceived the program was a material supply program called "Kanban" (Japanese for "ticket"), now called JIT.

Instead, careful analysis showed that it was a complete analysis; a program of mechanical and industrial engineering to precisely orchestrate supplier delivery, quality, process equipment, materials handling, and a trained employee program to eliminate every waste activity in the conversion of the processing of material into the product. Taiichi Ohno listed the following seven wastes to be eliminated:

1. Waste of overproduction
2. Waste of waiting and setup
3. Waste of transportation and storage
4. Waste of excess processing itself

5. Waste of stocks (inventories)
6. Waste of motion
7. Waste of making defective products

It is obvious from the above that every existing expense account would be affected by changes under the programs to eliminate these seven wastes using current allocation accounting systems. Under the circumstances, budgeting specific plans would be difficult for operation management. This was becoming a significant management communication problem. Frequently, financial investments in hardware or software were disallowed because of the confusion in tracking results using traditional accounting reports.

Similar problems exist in identifying changes when using more complicated automated processes that make many similar cost changes in processing.

14.3 CHANGING TO A COST-MANAGEMENT SYSTEM. These phenomena demonstrated an increasing need for a systematic study to define the role of cost management in such an advanced manufacturing environment.

In early 1986, Computer-Aided Manufacturing–International, Inc. (CAM-I) formed a consortium of progressive industrial organizations, professional accounting firms, and government agencies to define the role of cost management in the new environment. The goal of the coalition was to provide an international forum in which cost-management experts could share ideas and experiences and provide a mechanism for consolidating the knowledge of practices that have proven successful in this new environment. In 1987, the outlines of the new cost-management systems concept were presented, and activity-based accounting and activity-based management programs were outlined.

The initial report, written by James A. Brimson, project director, outlined failures of the existing cost-accounting systems as follows. (These are obviously explanations as to why existing accounting systems have failed to support changes you may have already tried.) Reviewing them may point out management areas for improvement.

- They are plagued by high overhead rates due to inadequately traced costs.
- They do not isolate the costs of unnecessary activities, which add unnecessary cost, rather than customer-perceived value, to product.
- They do not penalize overproduction; the philosophy of overhead absorption through allocation of overhead cost based on production volumes, in fact, encourages excess inventories.
- They do not adequately identify and report the cost of quality deficiencies in products or processes.
- They focus on controlling the production process while significant costs that determine the design and development phases of a product's life cycle are inadequately identified.
- They do not support the justification of new investments in advanced manufacturing technology and fail to monitor the benefits identified.
- They employ performance measurements that often conflict with strategic manufacturing objectives.
- They cannot adequately evaluate the importance of nonfinancial measures such as quality, throughput, flexibility, and so forth.

(a) Collaboration: A Key Concept. The manufacturing budget should present a plan for the coordination of a specified amount of direct production activity and of the specialized services to be supplied in the conversion operation. The following functions should be provided for regardless of whether each function has a manager:

- Product engineering or design for manufacturing
- Materials management (production and inventory control)
- Manufacturing engineering (processes)
- Industrial engineering (fitting people, accessories, and plant layout)
- Plant engineering (maintenance of physical plant and equipment)
- Quality control (training, support to achieve production design and performance expectation)
- Stores and shipping
- Physical distribution

During the planning for such changes, these groups must be led into an intense collaboration with highly mutual goals. In order to meet the organizational requirements, the following must occur:

- Each member must know his or her accountability and yet assume the responsibility for the whole task.
- Each member must recognize the effect of trade-offs in value-added costs and beneficial services for the several activities planned. Do the service at the least net cost.
- There must be open and direct communication and a freedom from fear of being ''wrong'' or ''difficult'' within the group during the preparation and planning.

(b) Budget Does Not Guarantee Profit. A second concept has importance in the preparation of the manufacturing budget: A budget does not a profit make. Simultaneous functional changes must occur, that is, tooling, training, vendors, design engineering, planning, and scheduling. A company typically has the budget performance it deserves. That remains true despite capable, conscientious individual or group efforts that could change the results with more innovative planning.

Manufacturing managers tend to think of auto manufacturers as successful and well managed, but serious challenges to their management skills appeared in the mid-1980's and remain in 1998. Their management styles and strategies require continuous change and eternal vigilance to stay competitive. Design for manufacturing, research in new materials, and more efficient processes are the constant concerns to maintain and regain market share. Of the 20 firms listed in the ''Fortune 500'' (1998) their 10 year (1987–1997) median EPS, Earnings per share was 6% while the median for all listed companies was 8% for the same period.

Managers explain failure to meet budgeted goals with the following reasons:

- Sales forecasts too high
- Bad cash management
- Expanded too quickly
- Not enough capital

- Good product design, but it did not sell
- Unexpected quality problems
- Too much competition
- Obsolete production methods
- Fell behind in technology

These reasons are the same answers given annually to explain poor budget performance in many companies today.

No matter how successful or certain a company seems, most have to regroup and seriously adjust their internal management. Worldwide industrial activity spurred by such extensive communication is too dynamic for companies to rest. Richard Foster, managing director of McKinsey and Company, demonstrates this in *Innovation: the Attackers Advantage.*[2] His studies caused him to observe "companies that were leaders in their field see their fortunes suddenly disappear. Do leading companies in fact not have the natural advantages they are supposed to, or are their natural advantages outweighed by other inherent disadvantages? I think the latter is the case . . . and that these disadvantages result from technological change."

"Technological change is the reason why only one company out of three manages to cover its cost of raising money most of the time. It is why most companies manage to achieve what Bob Waterman and Tom Peters have defined as "excellent" financial performance in any one year out of twenty, and then immediately drop back into the great middle ground of average financial performance; why even the best companies, by anyone's definition of excellence, retain their superior competitive performance for only three to four years."

You may not assume that tomorrow will be like today. Even so, managements feel that innovation is more risky than defending their position, when they find they are behind.

Successful companies make the opposite assumptions; they assume change is going to occur; there are patterns that are discernible and will come more swiftly than is desired. This is because they understand the dynamics of their competition.

Who is responsible when conditions such as these or those of our container manufacturers arise? Neither the customers nor the work force that carried out the orders is. *Management* has to accept responsibility for poor understanding, poor decisions in these areas, and a lack of good action plans.

In his book, *ROI–Practical Theory and Innovative Applications*, Robert Peters notes rather poor performance for many companies in terms of constant dollars.[3] Because budgets are usually synonymous with profit plans in management's thinking, we should review this idea.

Peters states in the preface of his book:

> The Income and Expense statements which attempt to match costs against revenues have been the traditional measures of financial performance. In recent decades, however, two evolutionary changes in the environment of business have eroded their value. First, a combination of technical and social advances has increasingly substituted capital for labor in manufacturing. Second, profit itself, as normally reported has become a product of many artificial

[2] Richard Foster, *Innovation the Attackers Advantage* (New York: Summit Books, 1988), 29*ff.*

[3] Robert Peters, *ROI—Practical Theory and Innovative Applications* (New York: AMACom, 1979).

and transient influences due to latitude in the areas of depreciation, taxes, and capital share values manipulations.

Peters suggests that a better standard should be devised for measuring financial results[4]: "The increasing dominance of capital or cash flows in terms of both investment and a return can provide a more incisive basis for metering business progress, giving support for cost management system (CMS) (activity-based accounting).

There are also some external factors involved in tracing budgets to earnings statements, as all assumptions are not clearly stated in budget documents.

Frequently, inflation and deflation in the economy are not accounted for. We have controlled inflation (1996–present) along with long-term interest rates but short-term rates minus inflation have been rising sharply over the past year (1997–1998). However, Bob Norton of Fortune shows in the Fortune 500, April 1998, that "real rates are higher than they have been since the recession, meaning that the Fed has in effect been tightening monetary policy even as it appeared to sit tight."

Second, many changes have occurred in general asset and balance sheet accounting practices and in the disposition of the profits from the budgeting processes. Ben C. Ball, a former vice-president of corporate planning, a professor at Massachusetts Institute of Technology (MIT), and now a consultant prepared an analysis and expressed concern for these manipulations. It appears to him that the executives assume they are using shareholders' resources [equity] efficiently if the company's performance (return on equity) and earnings are good and shareholders do not rebel. They assume the stock market automatically penalizes those that invest resources poorly. In short, the stock market performance and company performance are inexorably linked.

A close examination he did initially of 50 of the largest, mature, publicly held U.S. companies, 1970–84 shows just that (HBR, July, Aug 1987 by conversation 6, '98 he states "little change in practice"). He continued, "Many profits never found their way to shareholders either as dividends or as higher stock value. Over time, in half the companies a large portion of retained earnings simply disappeared. Traditionally, systems are not designed to track the profits to Wall Street or to see whether it arrives there."

Ball's article "The Mysterious Disappearance of Retained Earnings" states that the shareholders are deprived of their share of this important wealth of the company. Remembering that the budget is a management tool and is actually a plan for the micro-management of the uses of resources to produce a gain or profit, we should be aware of what and where they are. This will be important, as the rapid growth of technology will be increasingly classified as intellectual capital. It could easily become the largest part of future assets.

With capital tools being substituted for manual labor as an operating policy, the concomitant need to use technology and to modernize facilities demands more re-investment capital. Internally generated capital can come only from an excess of revenues over costs. Thus, new cost-management systems must prevail.

Although budgets are a familiar management technique, they must be developed and applied in a more creative way than they have in the past in our large, too-well-bureaucratized institutions, in which plans are usually a substitute for decisions and actions.

During a recent visit with a client, the chief executive officer (CEO) recounted the current malaise of rising costs of materials, labor contracts, and so on. He said, "Well,

---

[4] Peters, pp. v-vi.

the others have the same problems; they'll be facing it the same way, we'll raise prices to cover those changes in costs.''

Global competition and rising real productivity in Asian/Pacific Rim countries now remove this alternative management course of action. The United States cannot assume minimum competition. Since inflation is not acceptable, it increases the need to reconsider the cost of existing functions and style of management when preparing the budget.

It is well to remember that pricing is a marketing responsibility not a ''cost pass-through.''

George Sorter, professor of accounting at the Graduate School of Business, New York University, believes that the emphasis on accounting practice is misplaced. In *The New York Times,* he criticized the new second edition of *Handbook of Modern Accounting,*[5] because it placed primary emphasis on only one line of the statement—profit. ''Can anyone seriously believe,'' he asked, ''that all that has happened to a complex company during an eventful year can adequately be captured by a single bottom line figure?''

Although activity-based accounting/management has yet to be accepted, it is the better tool/information.

(c) Bold Analysis Crucial. When approached on the basis of a bold analysis of things as they are, the process of preparing the manufacturing budget assumes a third critical conceptual dimension. The preparation process becomes an opportunity to create new common objectives among the various manufacturing functions. Analysis may also help eliminate the intense concentration on minute aspects of your problem and the current emphasis on specialists' tasks. Marshall McLuhan calls this the ''strength of western man.'' He remarks that ''the specialist is one who never makes small mistakes while moving towards the grand fallacy.'' Little did he know that he was describing most budgeting processes today. Changing emphasis and finding higher mutual interest for value added to all products from all the specialists' functional programs is of prime importance in putting the manufacturing budget together.

The rewarding fact is that the presence of a budget process is evidence that someone is at least thinking about what is ''expected to be,'' which may appear to be good management. However, the wiser planners have identified and outlined the proper balance of interaction and services, calling for the simultaneous developments of production, tooling, acquiring capital tools, work pace, plant layout, and so forth. They recognize that trade-offs are required to ensure more margin. They also recognize that they can organize their manufacturing for lower costs in four key areas: (1) product design; (2) conversion process design (methods); (3) scheduling (to control throughput rate); and (4) utilization of managers, specialists, and supervisors.

The current management programs that encourage highly developed department objectives should be abandoned in favor of a more collective operations program. This could change ''what is expected'' to ''what ought to be.''

A good manufacturing budget depends on the quality of management imagination and bold plans for breakthrough change based on dissatisfaction with things as they are. This means that managers should acquire new knowledge and improve forecast accuracy. This would create a more proper balance of relationships, better levels of service, and an efficacious budget. The technique is to apply a value-added test to all the factors in the

---

[5] Sidney Davidson and Roman Weil, eds., *Handbook of Modern Accounting,* 2nd ed. (New York: McGraw-Hill, 1984).

MCE formula discussed earlier and review management decisions regarding all elements in the capacity-planning chart.

14.4 PROBLEMS IN PREPARING THE MANUFACTURING BUDGET. Usually, the approach in preparing the manufacturing budget is to avoid any changes from the recent past. Change is viewed as creating risk. In addition, if there may be some windfalls to be realized in the next periods, changes are minimized to provide a little insurance in the future period. A third reason is that a new approach may promise changes that managers believe they cannot control. It seems safer not to change. That approach too often keeps the organization in most factories trapped in programs of diminishing total productivity, as was our container manufacturer and the machinery builder.

There is evidence in business circles of a style called ''new management.'' Harold Wolf, professor of the Sloan Institute at MIT, said in one interview with me earlier:

> While old management concerns itself with efficiency in the production process and the direct work force, the ''new management'' seeks the optimum use of all resources along with flexibility rather than rigidity in job descriptions and lines of authority.

This implies more collaboration among managers. He continued,

> Recognize that new management doesn't have anything to do with age, education, or technology. Success will depend on the manager's comfort in the presence of risk and his tolerance for ambiguity and uncertainty in the pursuit of high mutual interest in common output and cost objectives.

Innovation and higher risk in new budget plans can provide more planned profit.

(a) What Ought to Be. A significant challenge in the budgeting process is to make that process entrepreneurial in character as it moves from ''what is expected,'' which relates to the present, to describing ''what ought to be'' when innovation occurs.

The assessment of what ought to be should come from (1) more analysis, (2) more planning, (3) more frequent injections of ''what if'' questions, and (4) ongoing discussions among the functional managers about what further coordinated programs will increase revenue and lower costs. And decisions to throw off non–value-added activities.

''The operating executive who is forever looking for a single accounting formula or approach on which to base all his decisions should recognize this is futile,'' notes Robert Peters. Instead, investigative effort must be concentrated on areas in which costs are caused or found.

In practice, more than one resource (capacity, manpower, or machinery) will probably be a limitation, so managers must combine and weigh the results and make trade-offs as their judgment dictates. As George Sorter asked when criticizing most accountants' approach during his lectures at the University of Chicago, ''Is profit now more important than other strategic goals—the longer product life expected, expanded markets, new facilities, or shorter delivery cycles?''

Few of these goals can be accomplished in a single budget year; thus, a proper time frame should be established for any changes. This is suggested by Banks and Wheelwright in the *Harvard Business Review,* and is more correct in the 1990s.

> Pressure for shorter term profits can seriously impede the achievement of long range goals. . . . S/L trade-offs are now more obvious than they used to be. Through the expansion and development of formal strategic planning process during the past decade, top managers have become more aware of where the corporations could be going, deviations . . . are more noticeable and the consequences . . . can be more significant as companies continue to grow in size and complexity. Managers receive greater authority and responsibility, and [their] decisions made to favor the short run over strategic goals . . . may have some serious financial consequences.[6]

Faster-paced securities markets, public relations programs, and necessary reassurances to old stockholders in newly conglomerated corporations all increase demands for short-term results. These are not usually expressed in terms of constant dollars or with considerations of the effect of inflation. This is coupled with the realization, too, that short-range forecasts are frequently less accurate than long-range trends.

Banks and Wheelwright indicate the following areas in which these trade-offs occur and in which substantial progress may be deterred by management decision. They suggest that we reconsider during the budget preparation:

- The postponement of capital investment (prolonging lower productivity or higher cost methods)
- Deferring operating expenses in product development or capital facility maintenance
- Reducing operating expenses by reductions in the work force affecting customer service or labor relations
- Reducing inventories with more elegant scheduling to enhance deliveries and service to markets
- Reducing training of employees, impairing quality service or output efficiency
- Other operating changes affecting product mix, delivery, pricing policies, and so forth

Why do such things happen? Unfortunately, when division or plant managers decide to favor short-term profits over long-term strategic goals, they have likely been influenced by two considerations. The first, and perhaps more influential, is the manner in which their performance is measured by the corporation. The second is a combination of the lack of balance between the short- and long-range plans as emphasized in corporate communications on the one hand and the general management culture of the company on the other.

These trade-offs can be properly balanced when the procedure of recording "what is expected" is changed to detailed budget building, which outlines the programs, actions, and organizational changes, along with objectives that are realistic and attainable and yet reflect a change to "what ought to be."

The company's philosophy of operations, its style of management, and the culture of the management group all limit the specific budget programs to whatever extent the management culture in any company limits realism in planning changes. To the extent that realism is limited, a budget becomes less meaningful.

As Thomas Pallante, comptroller of Owens–Illinois Company in Toledo, suggests, "The budgeting process becomes the use of activities-based planning rather than one of applying measurements and yardsticks. [The question to be asked is] What activity is

---

[6] R. L. Banks and S. C. Wheelwright, Operations vs. Strategy: Trading Tomorrow for Today, *Harvard Business Review,* May–June 1979.

necessary to produce these goods efficiently?'' Programs that become budget-approved items or that are eliminated as trade-offs to achieve higher mutual benefit among functions are examples of what he calls ''activities-based planning.''

When time has run out and some or any numbers have to be supplied, it is too late to ''make the budget'' (meaning achieve a planned result). In such a situation, random events, poor forecasts, and overlooked problems will conspire against good performance.

Dennis Hiese, corporate operations comptroller of Texas Instruments, said in a seminar discussion that ''the budget preparation process'' [referring primarily to zero-based budgeting] ''should be a mechanism to facilitate trading off operating expenses against strategic expenses.''

Each manufacturing budget assumes a level of output; each usually sets the revenue. These output data become the basic multiplier for the direct unit costs and require some minimum levels of services from the direct specialists. Beyond that, we cannot overlook the fact that unavoidable cost levels result from such factors as the specific process design (the technology of the conversion processes), machinery layout, handling, and product performance specifications. Further, a level of employment is required to man those processes. Costs can change only when management decides these elements change.

To give a more entrepreneurial character to the budget, the manager must step back and look realistically at the present situation. The current difficulties and crises seem to leave an imprint, making it impossible to perceive how different the general relationships of processes and costs could be.

Three probable reasons for this effect may be noted: (1) The manufacturing manager may feel that approval for change sizeable enough to affect costs rests with someone ''up there''; (2) he or she may also say, ''If I change much of this operation, I admit that I haven't been right up until now''; and (3) there may be a lack of top management perspective about who creates costs and how and where the costs functionally occur.

Unfortunately, feeling justified in the present mode of operation, the manager sees the future as a continuation of the exact same matrix of events. He or she has difficulty perceiving a mechanism to develop the future as anything except a straight-line extrapolation of the present, which forecasts disaster.

14.5 THREE SOLUTIONS. There are three ways to avoid such straitjacket thinking: (1) zero-based budgeting, which is usually initiated by corporate dictum; (2) simple, forceful orders to reduce cost by X%; and (3) a ''planned action'' budget to ensure revenue levels and manage costs, describing what ought to be in detailed programs for improvements in product design, process or method designs, scheduling operations, and utilizing people.

Zero-based budgeting is discussed in detail in Chapter 27 and represents an approach to breaking away from this ''imprint'' or cause-and-effect chain. Specifically, zero-based budgeting assumes as this author does that no present cost is approved and that every item and dollar of cost must be justified as it enters the spending plan of the budget. Usually, this is not possible because of mixed responsibility for several fixed costs buried and allocated along with administrative items, and the CEO will not participate in starting from ground zero. Most adaptations of the zero-based budgeting programs start with the executive targeting a percentage of current costs—usually 50% or more—as a basic starting point. The challenge is to determine whether current practices offer opportunities for significant changes. Many such ''closed or untouchable areas'' present the largest amounts of cost available and amenable to change.

That program has some advantage over the second format, in which top management dictates a cut of some percentage and refuses to participate in any of the strategic decision making necessary to accomplish this order.

The third program, which seems more beneficial to the company, is to reconsider the necessity for existing activities, to support management programs for such activities as manufacturing research, and to determine the possibility of abandoning many of the expenses currently being incurred. This describes the planned action budget. It can establish more realistic goals; it necessarily produces more planned, deliberate change and demonstrates more professional management.

What is the technique for preparing a planned action budget? The technique requires explanation in some detail.

14.6 TECHNIQUE. As noted, a manufacturing budget should not be an accounting document. It should be a management control tool that outlines future action and estimates the expected costs that will be incurred in producing a product at some assumed level of output. It must reflect both strategies and tactics.

A planned action budget, the preferred type, describes what ought to be by outlining and establishing standards for the following:

- What will be shipped?
- When that will happen?
- What materials, labor, and supplies are needed?
- How much time will be used by whom and when?
- Who does what and what is expected of each person?

Most budgets are compiled by accounting after a CEO says, "Next year will be ____ % of this year." He may add that "sales will be up (or down)." Then, present ratios are applied by accountants and the extrapolated budget is published.

The budget should be a map for making a profit that balances expected output from the factory (which is revenue) with the following:

- The levels of services mandated by management (all value-added service)
- The amount of inventory changes planned (Consider JIT work-in-process scheduled time by product and "common to all design concepts.")
- The levels of employment (direct, indirect, salaried, and management) (Does everyone have "real work" to do?)
- Capital acquisitions to be made in the period (usually one year)

The first management decisions to be made go to manufacturing basics. They include concrete judgments on the following:

- The design of the product to be shipped and the quality specifications for it
- The arrangement of production facilities
- The schedule for all parts manufacturing and continuous processes
- How to organize and utilize employees

Costs could be substantially changed as those very decisions are changed.

The ideal technique is to practice planning and decision making, not to improve on accounting technology. The budget should be conceived realistically, in dissatisfaction with the status quo. Finally, it should include specific plans, not hoped-for change.

14.7 DETERMINING PRODUCTION REQUIREMENTS. An initial task faces managers who are trying to determine production requirements to set the activity level. They should first develop a master schedule of confirmed, month-by-month revenues. The schedule should be set down in terms of the units the company sells, not in dollar terms. Only the U.S. Treasury manufacturers dollar bills. Your plant makes assemblies, kits, or product units from specific materials, with trained labor and allocated other costs per unit.

When expressed as shipped units, the master schedule becomes a confirmed total operating plan. It may not be exactly as the sales force stated if inventory usage or building are considered or your plant capacity is overutilized or underutilized. The most common mistake is for company management to be unaware that there are these other considerations.

Capacity, too much optimism, limitations in working capital, and late or incomplete product development are frequent limitations; therefore, manufacturing managers should learn how to review sales forecasts when starting a budget.

The budgets require consideration of many of the following elements:

- The market requirements as perceived by marketing and programs planned on a timely basis to fill that need
- The availability of product design, time phased to support shipments in that period (this includes tool-up, test, and market) (Time should be shorter with simultaneous design, process, and tool planning.)
- The availability of material to be acquired for that shipment plan (Use JIT, stock-where-used, etc.)
- Establishment of a parts or materials replenishment plan to continue the shipping revenue plan materials requirement planning (MRP) and elegant shop floor control.
- A distribution plan to meet the sales demand, including transport mode and time required; schedule and plan to capacity that has been demonstrated.
- Capacity to manufacture products in terms of tools, people, and process time
- Control of facilities programs that support the changes in capacity called for by the new schedule
- A program balancing receivables, payables, and JIT inventory levels to set the working capital levels

If you cannot identify the preceeding items or be assured of reasonable control, the projected shipments and revenue may not occur. Then, the levels of expense and employment planned and the programs started would be excessive for the lower rate of shipments. Also, planned profit could not occur even if managers remained cost conscious.

The way to reconcile these various factors in a shipping rate and revenue plan is to adopt a master scheduling routine for the core of your production items that can be planned. The master schedule routine should contain the following sequence of events:

- *Step 1.* Determine the core of product offerings that can be planned.
- *Step 2.* Obtain sales history and forecast.

- *Step 3.* Schedule new and/or revised product appearance in revenue schedule.
- *Step 4.* Determine inventory changes necessary to accomplish schedules.
- *Step 5.* Establish ''real'' shop capacity.
- *Step 6.* Publish master schedule and report progress.

14.8 STEP 1: DEVELOPING THE PLANNABLE CORE. Such intense interest in planning to make specific shipments of specific products could possibly produce a malaise in the reader. Managers might comment that ''our business is so different, we cannot project or forecast around this.'' Under these circumstances, managers will have the tendency to gloss over or generalize the revenue program into dollars too early in budget preparation.

All companies are faced with this phenomenon. Experience shows, however, that every company can develop a ''plannable core.'' The best evidence is that some companies' revenues may vary more than 10% to 15% a year without identifying where the sales changes occurred. Identifying those items leads to finding constant and variable products that constitute the plannable core.

In most companies, inventories at strategic points in the process or as finished goods provide hedges against planning or forecasting errors. An increase in inventory, however, increases direct-cost factory activity and working capital requirements.

The materials-management section and manufacturing or industrial engineering departments should be able to supply information about and identify the plannable core. Do not be deceived into creating too general a program for future shipments. The shipments are made up of specific products and selected and customer options. A few examples are given below.

In one case, a major replacement auto battery manufacturer had 12 geographically distributed facilities with a number of stock-keeping units in inventory equal to the unshippable unit orders on hand. One-million units were mismatched with demand. With a manufacturing list of 9,958 items, it was soon determined that 200 or fewer were the equivalent of more than 90% of sales. These were most frequently on the stock-out list. Inventory-planning profiles of this plannable core for seasonal and geographic distributions reduced inventories by several million dollars, and immeasurably improved service came when management considered this information that had been there all the time.

A similar example involved a major truck manufacturer. The total finished inventory in house, plus dealers' stocks, which they financed, and major subassembly parts in process were examined and found to be equivalent to more than 1-1/2 years of sales. Analysis of actual purchased truck configurations by major features, which helped to identify the plannable core, reduced all inventories by approximately $25 million and improved factory efficiency and planning.

In both instances, a new approach to existing information produced a better understanding of the plannable core, smoothed production, and improved budget performance. A portable oil derrick manufacturer accepted this same challenge to find a plannable portion of his business. He discovered that approximately 76% could be predicted. Many more examples exist.

14.9 STEP 2: OBTAINING SALES HISTORY AND FORECAST. The plannable core is a basis for a master schedule (in units) that merges and time phases the mutual interests of sales, product-design program, and actual shop capacity into a budget revenue program. The sales information to be supplied should include both history and forecasts. Since marketing expectations drive the whole budgeting process, the forecast should undergo constant scrutiny by operations people, too.

Customer (sales) orders are all converted into shop manufacturing orders. The best information available about actual sales history by product configuration is usually in the production-planning (materials-management) section. When materials management analyzes these data for the sales function, a more accurate story of anticipated sales will emerge. Field sales personnel provide their superior information on product trends, customers, new product needs, product problems, competitive products, quantity, and so forth. In this manner, a superior forecast of sales is accomplished, and "extra" safety stock used to cover low forecast accuracy can be reduced.

The manufacturing department can accept only the marketing or sales functions' final estimates of market demands and the sales program established to meet them. However, manufacturing should be aware of the problems of forecasting sales.

Operating sections require more information than forecasts usually provide if the operating people do not participate in incorporating that forecast into a master schedule. Problems occur or are created for budget performance if the operating department fails to ask sufficently detailed questions during the forecasting process to get the information it needs to plan production levels of various factory processes or departments.

Forecasting accuracy is a basic ingredient in manufacturing budget preparation. The attitudes of manufacturers about and during the process of forecast development are important; all available techniques should be explored to select those most suitable for use.

Copulsky's *Practical Sales Forecasting* (now out of print) approaches the problems of managerial attitude in a humorous way.[7] The following are some paraphrased questions and answers from the book:

Question: Who should not forecast?

Answer: Anyone who believes the future is only a straight-line extrapolation of the past. Recognize that changes occurring are an important element in forecasting. Remember, it is never possible to step twice into the same river.

Question: Who else should not forecast?

Answer: The man who substitutes arithmetic for sense. Alfred North Whitehead, a philosopher, said there is no more common error than to assume that because prolonged and accurate calculations have been made, the applicability of the result of some fact of nature is absolutely certain.

Question: Who *else* should not forecast?

Answer: The man who thinks he has the only magic formula. Inventories are provided in anticipation of that forecast of use or demand.

The various techniques of forecasting are described adequately in the July–August 1971 *Harvard Business Review*.[8] The best uses of each, the kinds of data required, and their dependability are charted for easy review. The list of techniques included follows as a reminder of how wide the range of possible approaches is.

---

[7] William Copulsky, *Practical Sales Forecasting* (New York: AMACom, 1987).

[8] *Harvard Business Review*, July–August 1971, pp. 45–47.

Qualitative Methods

1. Delphi
2. Market research
3. Panel consensus
4. Visionary forecast
5. Historic analogy

Times Series Analysis and Projection

6. Moving average
7. Exponential smoothing
8. Box–Jenkins
9. X-11
10. Trend projection

Causal Methods

11. Regression model
12. Econometric model
13. "Intention to buy" survey
14. Input–output model
15. Economic input–output
16. Diffusion index
17. Leading indicator
18. Life-cycle analysis

A multimethod index approach has recently been tried with excellent results in consumer goods forecasting. It was developed by Bernard T. Smith and is described in his book *Focus Forecasting.*[9]

14.10 STEP 3: SCHEDULING NEW AND REVISED PRODUCT APPEARANCE. The next step in preparation of the master schedule is time phasing the new product design or revisions program. Some companies have many of their major items in a state of flux or design change at a given time, thus limiting shipments. Manufacturing budget planning should provide answers to such questions as: What kind of an effect is this product design going to have on schedules, output, and revenue? When does the new product come on? Does it have an impact?

The master schedule requires a definition of the product represented by the plannable core and forecast items in the form of complete bills of material or parts lists. This is a primary requirement from the product-design section. These lists must be maintained in up-to-date form to avoid continuation of the manufacture of obsolete items. These bills of material describe what the factory will make.

[9] Bernard T. Smith, *Focus Forecasting, Computer Technique for Inventory Control* (New York: Van Nostrand Reinhold, 1978).

Many good budget revenue plans fail because product designs are not available on time. Frequently, management's control of the product design program is so minimal that safety time factors are not included to cover the premature and infant design failures for the new product that is to be shipped in a given period. The production of revenue is also delayed. Operations management has the principal responsibility for delivery of these designs—or proof of concepts, preliminary production runs, and initial production output—in time to accomplish the sales forecast and marketing program and to fulfill revenue budgets.

Obviously, operations managers have to keep product-design managers in the same master schedule relating to the budget if the income plans are to be realized. Techniques used for project control or design include the critical-path method (CPM), program evaluation and review technique (PERT), and others.

14.11 STEP 4: DETERMINING REQUIRED INVENTORY LEVELS. The fourth step in the master schedule routine is the determination of required inventory levels for the budget plan. Once the shipping rate has been established from the forecast, the actual production plan and shop manufacturing orders should be planned to accomplish levels of inventory that support the expected level of shipments. If the forecast, as edited, represents an increase in the rate of shipment, time may be required for the appearance of additional raw or purchased materials and for higher levels of manufacturing to occur. Such change would be supported by consumption of present inventories at a faster-than-normal rate, which would produce a stock-out, or a time of increased levels of work in process could be planned.

Companies invest in inventory when anticipating the receipt of customer orders to shorten delivery offerings or enhance sales by providing instant availability to satisfy consumer requirements.

Care must be taken in the scheduling of raw materials' arrivals and in managing in-process manufacturing time. Further, there must be ample time for finished goods to reach distribution points and for matching the regular, programmed supply to customers if budgeted revenue is to accumulate at the point of distribution.

In preparing the budget, the operations manager must require that the materials management function develop plans that allow time for the manufacturing to take place by the standard methods on which the expense levels are to be predicated.

(a) Definitions and General Information. A review of inventory definitions and general information follows.

Manufacturing inventories are of three kinds: raw materials, work in process, and finished goods.

1. *Raw materials* include all purchased materials to be used in manufacturing but on which no conversion labor has been expended. No distinction is made in the raw materials inventory between direct materials and indirect materials. In many instances, the same materials may be used for either purpose. A distinction is made between direct materials and indirect materials only when they are requisitioned from the raw materials storeroom.
2. *Work in process* includes all costs—material, labor, and burden—that have been expended in the manufacturing process on products not yet complete. The work-in-process inventory is usually broken down into material in process, labor in process, and burden in process. Refer to MCE, discussed earlier.

3. *Finished goods* include all manufactured products that are complete and ready for shipment to the customer. No distinction is made in the finished goods inventory as to material cost, labor cost, and burden cost.

Finished goods inventories transferred to sales control and not used by manufacturing to create revenue are excluded in these manufacturing budget considerations. However, if the manufacturing manager is responsible for the total logistics function, these inventories are also considered in the planning activities.

In many companies, no distinction is made between raw materials, work in process and finished goods. In their place, the general ledger carries three different inventory accounts: materials inventory, labor inventory, and burden inventory. The triple inventory is known as a four-wall inventory system. All materials are charged to materials inventory upon receipt. Direct labor expended is charged to labor inventory. Burden applied is charged to burden inventory. When shipment is made, each inventory is relieved of its *pro rata* share of the product cost. This is the poorest cost control.

(b) Setting Inventory Level. Setting a company inventory level is very difficult because sales, operations, and finance all have different goals and interests in that inventory. This occurs because the top manager judges the performance of each functional head by different criteria. These are the wastes as identified earlier by Taiichi Ohno.

A basic conflict occurs when operations managers want to build and use inventory as a way of carrying them over an excessive number of changeovers. Finance managers want to operate with the least investment. They know that every plan for an increase in inventory to handle the irregular sales demands has a negative aspect as far as maximizing the return on investment is concerned. Sales expects all sizes, colors, and models in order to make dollar sales and quotas competitive.

There exists a plannable core that satisfies the best interests of these three functions. We have demonstrated how such a core can be identified. The ''important few'' (basics) and popular optional add-ons can be immediately distinguished from the ''trivial many'' in terms of frequency and quantity of orders when the actual sales are examined more objectively and in detail, using a classic A-B-C analysis.

Finally, the phasing out of present product designs and preliminary buildup to ship new models requires special attention. Temporary growth in inventory *and* shop activity accompanies these changes.

Understanding that this basic conflict is present in establishing inventory levels enhances the development of higher mutual interests in the preparation of master schedules for shipping product and setting inventory levels.

When most firms put budgets together in dollars, they lose all opportunity for meaningful materials control and management. The final dollar extension is appropriate, but backing into specific material needs from dollars rather than from identifiable product units is the reason top management is frequently not in control of inventory.

14.12 STEP 5: ESTABLISHING REAL DEMONSTRATED SHOP CAPACITY. Two questions should be answered here: Have you identified the level of resources required for the master schedule, the basis of your planned-action budget? Is there capacity available, or can it be made available?

The final element required to prepare the master schedule is the consideration of actual shop capacity. In planning for an output, historical reality should supersede standard figures or theoretical capacities in estimating shipment of product, which produces the revenue.

Let us first dispose of the accounting and cost-allocation concerns and then return to the problems that operations people have in ensuring the expected shipments of goods.

The accounting manager must select a basis for allocating a wide variety of ongoing time-committed costs and costs associated with depletion of asset values such as depreciation. Those allocations are policy decisions on how to spread all indirect costs back into production units for pricing and so forth.

The manufacturing manager is concerned with actually producing the units. In the budget-planning process, other questions relate to how much we can produce now, whether it is enough, and what is required to increase output. A variety of alternative combinations of capacity and operating patterns is usually possible. However, to quote Horngren's *Cost Accounting: A Managerial Emphasis:* "To most people the term 'capacity' implies a constraint in upper limit. This view is commonly held in industry."[10] This suggests that the manager who is planning the budget must test the realism of currently held views of upper limits on capacity.

Horngren also states that "although the term capacity is usually applied to plant and equipment, it is equally applicable to all other resources . . . [such as] . . . manpower, material supply level, [and] executive time or working capital for a higher operating level." Horngren notes further that subcontracting, overtime premiums, or premiums for material may ease these limitations but with an uneconomical result: "Then the upper limit [must be] specified by management for current [budget] planning and control purposes."

There are three general conditions to be noted in considering capacity versus demand. First, where there is a variable demand but the average level is always lower than the maximum capacity, it becomes relatively easy to plan. The second condition would exist when the variable average requirement is about equal to the average capacity. There will be peak periods when the demand will be greater than capacity and periods when it will be lower. This situation needs very close planning to avoid delivery problems.

The third situation, one frequently not recognized by management, occurs when the demand is variable but the average requirements are always greater than the total capacity. It must be recognized that even good planning cannot prevent the delivery problems in this situation.

If there is a constant backlog, the lack of capacity may be limiting actual sales. However, if the backlog has continued to grow, you are making an unconscious decision to limit sales. The failure to increase capacity by improving the use of present resources or additions to plant and equipment should be at least a conscious choice of top management. It is the manufacturing manager's responsibility to define his or her position in this matter in each budget period.

(a) Real Factory Capacity (Demonstrated). Recognizing real factory capacity requires the broadest possible analysis of current demands as defined in the early steps of master scheduling. Also crucial is the utilization of existing plant equipment and human resources in satisfying that demand.

In the planned-action budget, it is important to consider capacity as representing practical, attainable output capacity. Such capacity may be further defined as the maximum level at which the plant or department would operate efficiently from year to year.

It is assumed that there is an existing capacity with historical records of output or a projected statement of proposed output in the *pro forma* program for a new or infant plant. Capacity should be reviewed and expressed in relation to the plannable core units of output

[10] Charles T. Horngren, *Cost Accounting: A Managerial Emphasis* (Parasmus: Practice Hall, 1967).

being forecast—or in appropriate subsets of items or parts used in the final configuration of the predicted product shipments (assemblies, kits, or sets).

One must also distinguish between two other basic elements: (1) continuous-process operations, in which distillation, refinement of basic materials, or automatic processing of materials or parts takes place; and (2) batch processing, batch machining, or assemblies in which other human-controlled operations take place.

It should be noted that many operations managers, when they have some of each type of operation, set some capacities in line with expected output from the continuous operations and some from their batch processes. Although it is slightly more complicated in considering utilization of the factory or several production units, control points are more appropriate and control reports more meaningful if both batch and continuous operations are recognized at planning time. In either instance, the standard volume should be established.

Having suggested that realism in assessing capacity requires a review of several years' historic performance and engineering projection, the current budget year's expected output is computed as a percentage of the long-term level for convenience. This percentage is sometimes called the *index volume.* This technique assists in maintaining a reference point when longer-range capital additions and expansion programs are tied with annual tactical planning.

Realism and the assessment of attainability are both value judgments and provide the keys to successful budget programs. In assessing capacity, operating managers have rates of activities in mind. Too frequently, they apply these to the total lapsed time of the budget period, assuming that they should plan for *ideal* conditions. This is not the best way to plan, since ideal and controlled standard conditions seldom prevail for a whole year.

The average situation is not usually ideal. Manufacturing processes are not going on a full 100% of the lapsed calendar period for which we plan. Anything less than 100% continuous conversion activity is a limitation on the capacity of the enterprise.

Benjamin W. Niebel's charted savings from methods engineering and time studies,[11] examining the disposition of each worker's total time has been adapted as a tool to consider how capacity is affected by unmanaged situations and events. The chart, "Capacity Planning Guide," which is shown in Exhibit 14.2, describes total lapsed (available) clock or calendar time and the uses thereof.

In assessing capacity, the total elapsed time of the budget period contains a minimum-work time content. This is work created by management-directed specifications, designs, technology, processes, and so on. The remainder is the portion of total lapsed time that is ineffective. This reduces capacity. We find that this ineffective time is actually prescribed by the design of ineffective methods and/or management shortcomings, such as weak supervision, failure to train operators, scheduling errors, and nonstandard materials. This ineffective time is management's opportunity to affect capacity directly by improving methods or overcoming management shortcomings. Further, the manager can introduce processes of leadership that address the problems of employee shortcomings in lack of training or job disinterest.

(b) Ideal and Controlled Standard Performance. The graphs shown in Exhibit 14.2 may be used as a map to guide planning for those conditions that preclude ideal or controlled standard performance. They may also stimulate review of those conditions under which added cost in one circumstance could provide a benefit in another. Such a trade-off can either contribute to revenue or change costs beneficially.

---

[11] Benjamin W. Niebel, *Motion and Time Study* (Homewood, IL: Richard D. Irwin, 1972), p. 5.

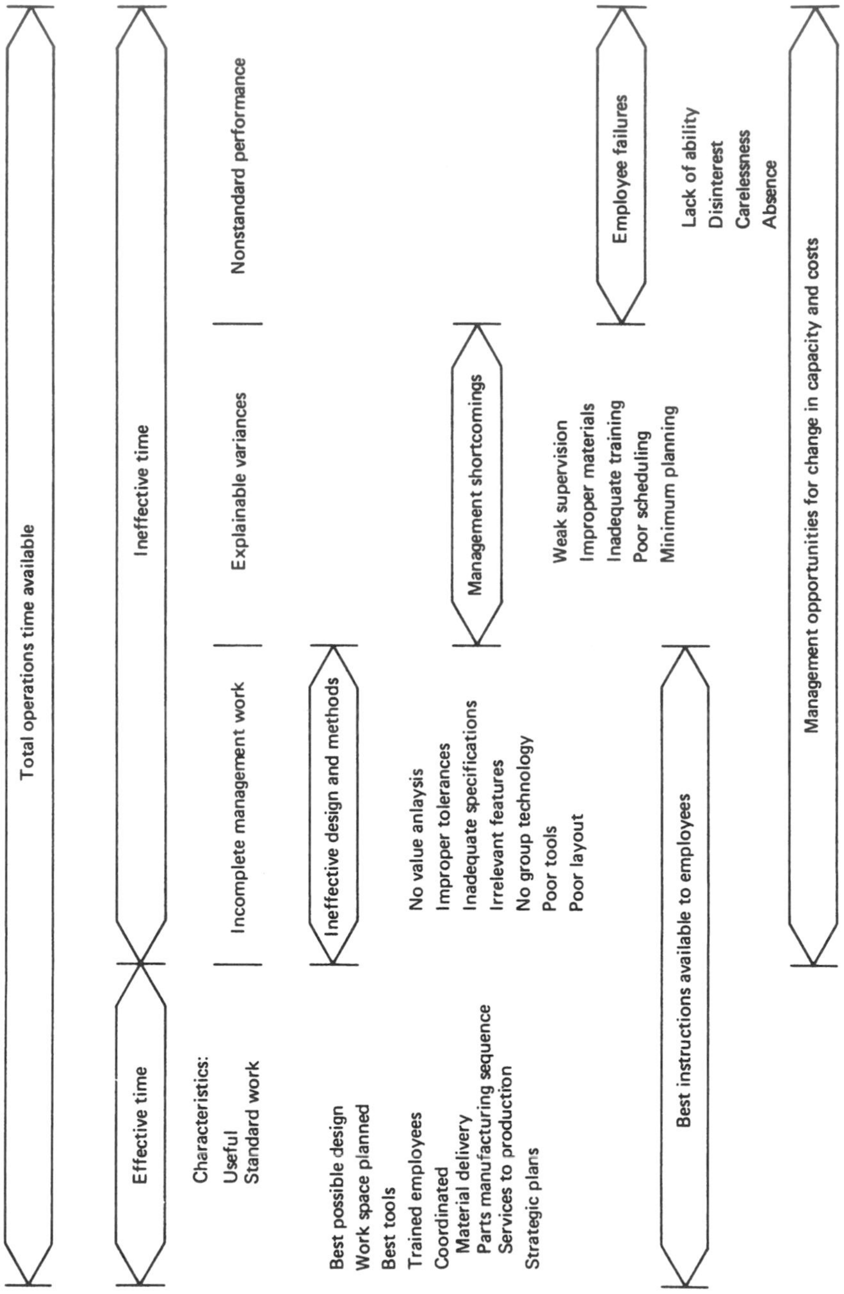

Total operations time available

Effective time

Ineffective time

Characteristics:

Useful
Standard work

Incomplete management work

Explainable variances

Nonstandard performance

Best possible design
Work space planned
Best tools
Trained employees
Coordinated
Material delivery
Parts manufacturing sequence
Services to production
Strategic plans

Ineffective design and methods

No value anlaysis
Improper tolerances
Inadequate specifications
Irrelevant features
No group technology
Poor tools
Poor layout

Management shortcomings

Weak supervision
Improper materials
Inadequate training
Poor scheduling
Minimum planning

Employee failures

Lack of ability
Disinterest
Carelessness
Absence

Best instructions available to employees

Management opportunities for change in capacity and costs

Exhibit 14.2. Capacity-planning guide

The formula for budgeting successful operations is simple: revenue minus cost equals profits. Either increase revenues at the same cost level or lower costs to improve unit profits.

In considering capacity on a realistic basis, we should start by reviewing the activities that affect capacity in order to determine what ought to be and what can be planned for the budget period.

The graphs of lapsed-time utilization in Exhibit 14.3 show an example of changes in actual capacity created by a new capital tooling in a machinery builders' plant. The graphs also demonstrate the effect of current ineffective time used, as shown in Exhibit 14.2.

In considering a family of parts to be manufactured by a numeric-controlled (NC) lathe, a machinery company reported the current total time (Exhibit 14.3*a*). It became apparent that true comparisons of current methods with the new machine would be erroneous unless slack or ineffective time relative to management practices were removed in the comparison. Note the possible recovery from management actions without the new machine, a reduction from 644 minutes to 417 minutes, or 167 minutes. The new method contributes additional time and therefore more capacity, as shown in Exhibit 14.3*c*.

(c) Reducing Ineffective Time. Most failures in budget performance come about because assumptions made during the budget-preparation process were not valid or clear. Very commonly, estimates of overall capacity will be faulty.

For such reasons, manufacturing managements are required to plan for support of efforts to reduce ineffective time. Methods of approach to the problem include value analysis, tolerance control, master scheduling (previously discussed), and employee training. These trade offs add to costs temporarily but lead to major improvements in the amount of effective time spent. They are briefly described below. Each technique deserves additional study.

(i) Value Analysis Reduces Minimum Work Content. The impact on value analysis as a management-directed program to reduce standard materials or manufacturing time and/or programs to improve ineffective methods cannot be minimized in considering budget capacity and costs. A few comments here about each should sharpen budget planning in your operating group.

Value analysis and value engineering are important because the design of a product commits the productive system to specific processing methods. Therefore, the greatest opportunity for cost savings or impact on output capacity occurs during the initial design phase. Once the manufacturing process is under way, however, cost reductions may be possible through *redesign* or changes in the processing methods, selections of components, and materials. Value engineering and value analysis are useful techniques because engineering changes affect adaptations of materials (raw, in-process, and finished), manufacturing processes, time-phase plan, and operation sequence. All of these factors have broad economic impact and define in detail what is to be made.

(ii) Value Engineering Defined. Briefly, *value engineering* is the systematic identification of the function of a part or a product, the establishment of a value for that function, and the testing of it to ensure that the required function is provided at the lowest total alternative cost method. Its purpose is to make certain that every element of cost—such as labor, materials, supplies, styling, service, repair, and warranty—contribute proportionately to the function of the product. The fundamental objectives are (1) to provide better value in delivered products and (2) to improve the company's competitive position.

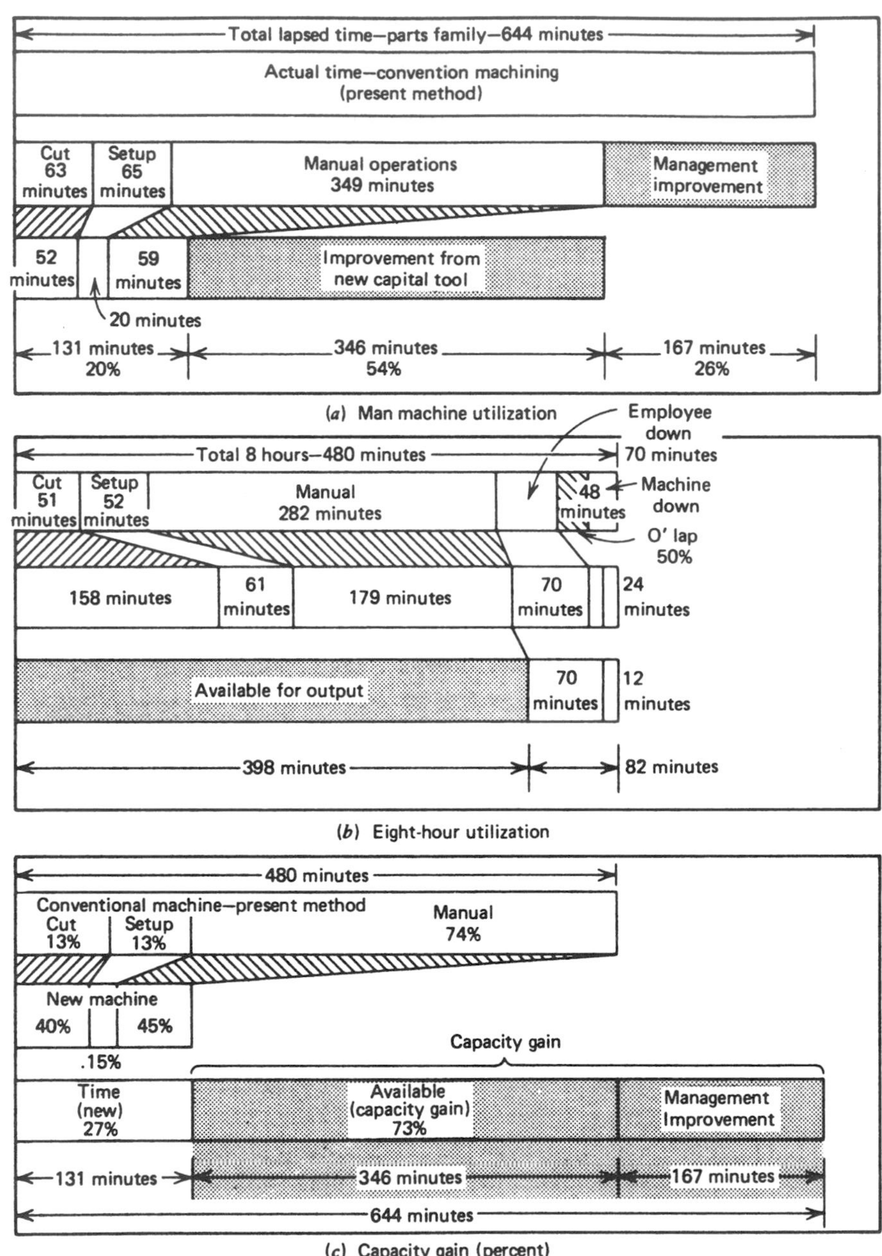

Exhibit 14.3. Lapsed-time utilization

In practice, value engineering includes a series of trade-off decisions intended to improve the product for a given cost and to provide the same or better performance at lower cost without reducing quality or reliability. Value analysis and value engineering must be considered the most effective tools of management because they are planned, deliberate change. Arthur Spinanger, in his *Increasing Profit Through Deliberate Methods Change,* stated that deliberate change is quite different from cost improvement. Improvement techniques frequently resemble efficiency or budget-cutting strategies that encounter psychological resistance from management and labor alike. This is particularly true if the operation is well run and the improvements are difficult to achieve. However, the ''How can the methods of work be changed?'' approach is often much better received, and its advocates claim it has greater potential savings. This approach takes the following point of view:

- Perfection is no barrier to change. This implies that if further improvement to an existing work method is nearly impossible, there is probably a different and superior method that may be feasible.
- Every dollar of cost should contribute its share of the profit. Because each dollar that is invested in anything is done so with the idea of making a profit, the investment should not be made if it does not have this result.
- The savings potential is the full existing cost. This attitude does not consider any item of cost as necessary. An example is the procedure of using a liner in a carton to package shampoo. The liner was omitted first, and next the carton. The shampoo sold better unpackaged. In another example, a storage tank roof involved high maintenance costs, but on examination it was determined that neither evaporation into the air nor dilution through rainfall significantly affected the tank's contents; thus there was no need for a roof, and it was eliminated.

Many value-engineering programs can be adapted to individual needs.

14.13 STEP 6: PUBLISHING THE MASTER SCHEDULE. The sixth and final step in the scenario that ends in a master schedule is to publish the end product. Subsequently, that involves measuring progress. In this phase, the work that went into the earlier steps reaches the payoff stage.

In the program thus far, you have reviewed and considered/made the following:

- Performance improvements in the shop
- Set forth significant changes in ineffective time spent
- Clarified product specifications and processes for quality/cost changes
- Considered value analysis opportunities
- Summarized the changes in ''demonstrated capacity'' forecasted by those changes

New schedules can now be planned to meet the forecasted customer demands as interpreted by the sales/marketing function. The materials supply function should assess, advise, and set-up the master schedule as the categorical imperative for the whole economic enterprise.

If the estimate of the new ''demonstrated capacity'' is not equal to the needs as determined by the sales/marketing program, subcontracting or outright purchase of finished goods must be undertaken. The program, for alternative manufacturing sources, is not part of a manufacturing budget being discussed here.

The following question can be asked as your planned-action budget takes final form for publication to your managers: Do you really have a master schedule? If you can answer the following subsidiary questions logically and sensibly, you are ready for publication of the planned-action budget:

- Are the short- and long-range objectives of the sales operations and of finance the same, and are the same criteria used for judging the performance of each in your division?
- On what criteria is each function judged?
- Can order and mutual interest be developed into a single master schedule?
- Do you know why a master schedule should be expressed in units?
- Is sales information required? What is the difference in need between actual and forecast sales information? What is the value of 10% improvement in forecast accuracy? Does it affect inventory? Does it affect working capital requirements?
- Do schedules for new and revised products affect the master schedules and therefore the revenue?
- Can you define explicitly by parts, lists, or bills of material the units in the master schedule?
- Do engineering changes alter the product defined in the master schedule?
- Do you have control of the changes, their quality, quantity, timing, and urgency?
- Do such changes affect actual product output? How?
- What is the real capacity of the plant? Can you track this with daily booking and shipping reports? (This is discussed later in the chapter.)
- Where do you get standard hour content for guidelines?

14.14 A TOTAL QUALITY PROGRAM—THE OTHER ALTERNATIVE. We have demonstrated the way in which the initial product concept (design) management can impact total cost before (frequently called ''inept'') manufacturing operations even start making the product. We have in most instances ''designed in'' or failed to manage the details of design, processes, and training that cause the costs before manufacturing takes over.

Deming said at the outset that 85% to 90% of the problems in quality were caused by management. In going through endless quality circle group programs, statistical quality control, and employee training exercises, we realize what it takes to correct that management problem. Management of each functional group must—at the start of manufacturing one, some, or all products—control the designs, processes, training of employees, purchases, and plan for quality of the end-product at a part and detail level.

In thousands of daily forays into shop problems with incorrect materials, configuration conformity, or product performance, we find it was uncertainty, error, or lack of vision before the manufacture that were the roots of the quality problems being reviewed. This most significant array of costs can be planned out of the operation. That is what Deming means. A total quality control program produces those savings. They never appear in accounts because they are avoided by management.

Other areas for review in restructuring the ineffective time are tolerance control, process control, and quality specifications. These management alternatives all have concomitant costs that should be considered when preparing manufacturing budgets and outlining what ought to be.

In any manufacturing company, three separate groups are constantly concerned with the problems of determining the magnitude of the tolerances—in dimensions, appearance, or performance—and ultimately what is to be done about manufacturing situations in which the shop does not meet the prescribed specifications and/or tolerances. They are the product-design group, the manufacturing engineering group, and quality control. These three groups do not usually use the same techniques for analyzing tolerance relationships, for example, particularly product design and manufacturing engineering; when problems develop in which the three groups must join forces communication is usually poor and bureaucracy and "turf protection" set in.

In considering mechanical tolerances, for example, managers argue over the correctness of tolerance buildup and calculation. If the calculations from one design engineer are fairly involved, it becomes almost impossible for that person to take another through the maze without losing contact if the second party is not familiar with this whole series of calculations.

What is the problem? In this instance, the techniques of tolerance analysis constitute the problem. Therefore, a common language and communication skills must be developed if these three groups are to talk about tolerances and configurations.

There are well-developed systems for the consideration of mechanical tolerances. One such program was developed by Oliver R. Wade and is explained in a book called *Tolerance Control in Design and Manufacturing*. A second system was described in a section of the U.S.A. Standard Drafting Practices, *Dimensioning and Tolerancing for Engineering Drawings,* published by the American Society of Mechanical Engineers.[12] A third computerized program has been developed and is available from General Motors Production Engineering Center, Detroit, Michigan. This program provides optimum tolerance plans for each component involved in an assembly, thereby forecasting successful combination of fits.

When tolerances change, costs and capacity also change. The effect is demonstrated in Exhibits 14.4 and 14.5, prepared by Dorian Shanin of V. P. Rath and Strong, Boston, a noted authority in quality, and reliability.

It should be clear from these graphs that unnecessary requirements build in total cost of greater magnitude in percentage than efficiency and employee attention can possibly recover for any given design.

All of the following 17 costs are associated with tighter-than-necessary specifications and tolerances that affect capacity and are not easily identified in allocated costs and charts and forecasts:

1. Better-than-necessary manufacturing equipment (higher capital cost)
2. Better-than-necessary tool tolerances (more frequent changes and setups)
3. Better-than-necessary gauges and/or test equipment (more initial cost)
4. Better-than-necessary gauge-checking equipment (higher capital cost)
5. More frequent calibration checking (lost time)
6. Shorter-than-possible tool life (more changes in setup)
7. More inspection planning than needed (more nonproduction time)
8. More frequent process-control checks (more nonproductive time)
9. More frequent process shutdowns (more nonproductive time-loss capacity)
10. More expensive components (higher-cost product as standard)
11. Larger sample sizes for product acceptance (more nonproductive labor)
12. Complete inspection in place of sampling (more nonproductive labor)

[12] *Dimensioning and Tolerancing for Engineering Drawings* (New York: American Society of Mechanical Engineers, 1980).

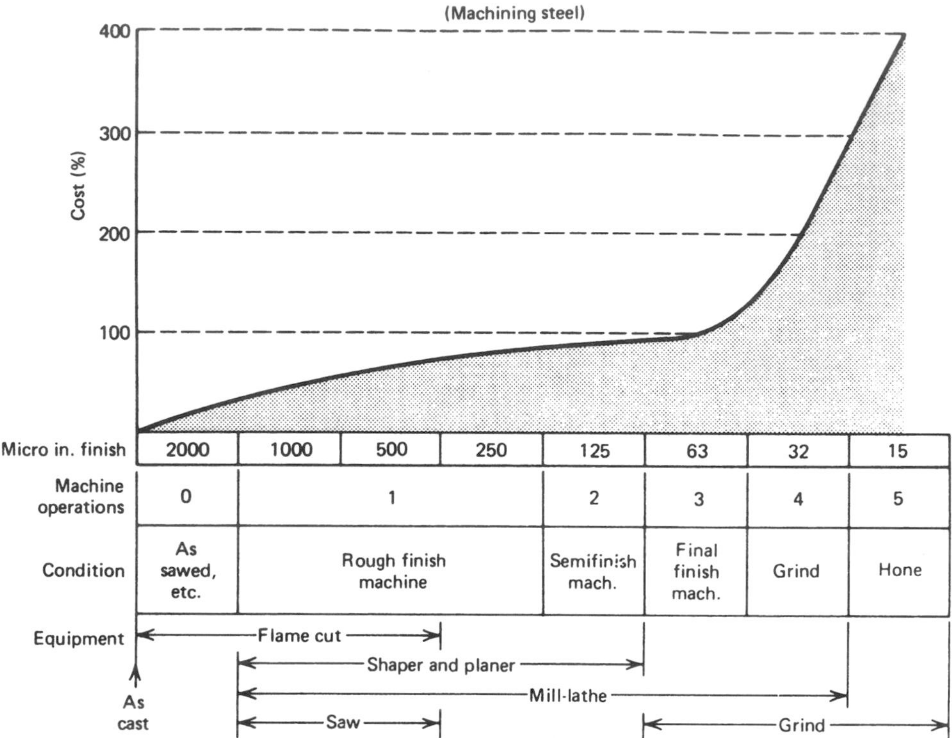

Exhibit 14.4. Relative cost of manufacturing due to tolerance: machine finish tolerances

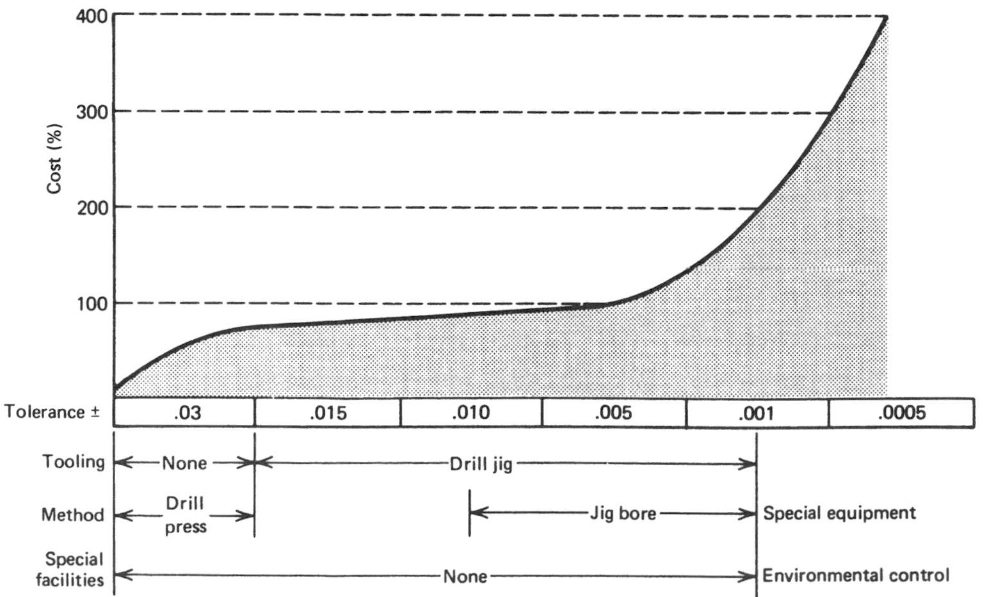

Exhibit 14.5. Relative cost of manufacturing due to tolerance: hole-location tolerances

13. More internal scrap, rework, and extra processing
14. More material review time consumed (more nonproductive management time)
15. More corrective-action time consumed (more nonproductive management time)
16. More written corrective-action reports for customers (potential loss of sales)
17. More less-than-effective specification changes made (more confusion in future)

In considering making changes in manufacturing costs during budget preparation, one should review any recent major manufacturing losses attributable to quality problems. Questions may arise. Is there a common ground of understanding between your design engineers and your manufacturing people? Do you understand how the absence of direction to accomplish uniform thinking in product design, manufacturing, and quality control could generate significant cost and/or delivery problems and surprises for you at some time in the future?

(a) Cost Changes and Capacity Increase. Further opportunities for planning cost changes and capacity increases on a slightly longer-range basis rest in the instructions to product-design engineers and manufacturing engineers to develop multiple uses for the same part, or groups of parts with the same processes, which differ only in size. Have you given every opportunity to the development of parts grouping for maximum application of more productive tools and machinery?

Group technology is the term applied to planning for clusters of parts that are similar in configuration and that use the same general process flow. Frequently, opportunities may exist to arrange factories within factories for such groups of parts that increase machine and manpower utilization and that add capacity in output terms.

The heart of every problem for operations management is the number of items to be manufactured. The capacity of a plant for one part, one size, one shape, and one color is quite different if the same plant has to process 65,000 different parts with varying configurations. Capacity, then, is directly related to the breadth of the product line, which can be altered to some degree by operations managers by their directing product design into simplifications and by applying group technology.

Factory supervisors play a major role in capacity planning by the daily direction of the work force in job assignment. During budget planning, consider programs that improve their job instruction and assignment practices.

The set-up or get-ready time required to make products in all factory processes is accompanied by lost time. There are probably records at your company that document the lost time that has occurred in the past. They should be reviewed to indicate how or to what extent the theoretical capacity was reduced by this non–value-added activity.

Taiichi Ohno developed a program called ''SMED'' (single minute exchange die). Using the concept, American manufacturers have reduced setups by 75%. With current budgets at 25% to 30% of total direct labor in most companies, this is a real cost reducer. One hundred or more companies have reported to AME 70% to 90% reductions of set-up actual times.

In the production set-up time, which is controlled by line managers, the items of lost time or ineffective time include the following:

- Maintenance/repair requirements that shut down machines
- Rework time spent on the productive machine because of either employee errors or engineering changes

- Cleanup operations to maintain the equipment
- Extra time caused by nonstandard methods, parts shortages, materials shortages, nonstandard materials, and so forth
- Experimental and developmental parts manufacturing
- Vendor error rework
- Training time for operator improvement

Capacity is reduced by all of the preceding items. However, even with perfect planning for every movement of material and with superb motivation of the work force, you still should consider two basic pieces of data for capacity planning. First, although the employee has an attendance requirement of 1,900 to 2,000 hours per year, under the most favorable circumstances, he or she will produce not much more than 1,340 to 1,400 standard hours per year that can go into inventory because the employee is not expected to be, nor is he or she able to be, productive during that entire clock time. The reasons for such lost time will be discussed in a later section on determining direct labor costs.

Second, it is commonly agreed that machines can be loaded or expected to perform, or have an uptime, of not more than 90%. It is reasonable that 50% of the employee's downtime will not occur during the downtime of the machine in the same scheduled period.

Further, total capacity for shipments may be seriously limited by only one obscure process or machine. An intensive search must be made for such bottlenecks, in which additional equipment, a new machine, or a new plant may be the solution.

It might seem that all of these considerations for changing capacity through better management of existing plant and equipment are minor and subordinate to purchasing new capital equipment. The concern is not justified. Universally, opportunities exist for the application of existing modern machinery for increased output and for the further development of ''undreamed of'' machinery. However, the capacity of each newly acquired machine is subject to the same reductions by poor management in actual output capacity, as has been outlined in the time chart and highlighted by the charted examples on the purchase of an NC lathe shown previously in lapsed-time utilization (Exhibit 14.3). The effective utilization of such capital acquisition still remains an operating problem that cannot be bought off.

(b) Capital Tools. Capital budgeting is discussed in Chapter 19. These comments may help during budget planning when considering capital acquisitions.

Comprehensive analyses of productivity in the United States suggest that the correlation is highest between productivity figures and the level of capital tool investment. In America, the consideration of processes is synonymous in management's mind with productivity. Whereas the only current measure of productivity is man-hours per unit of output, we recognize that very few products are made entirely by the hands of workers. It is a combination of the worker's hands, their minds, their energy, the management of the employers, and the wise selection of tools or machinery that will reduce the man-hour content and improve productivity. Carl H. Madden, chief economist of the U.S. Chamber of Commerce, said that ''people ought to know that productivity has less to do with working harder or longer than it has with working smarter.'' He continued:

> Productivity comes from know-how. It's surprising enough that people don't know this. It's even more surprising that some government officials and business executives make productivity sound like a repressive campaign for law and order.

Direct labor is not the problem of productivity today. Poor specifications, unnecessary operations, and non–value-added tasks, all authorized or directed to workers to occur by management, subtract from true productivity.

The capacity of your plant or plants is limited only by the thoroughness of your investigation of these several opportunities for change and the development of programs to reduce ineffective time and improve the selection of capital equipment.

Frequently, special-purpose machinery or groups of machines that serve a majority of parts or products and their historical output level are not properly identified with regard to their effect on total output capacity in the plant. Activity-based accounting will greatly assist.

(c) Capacity in Continuous Processes. The capacity of a continuous process may be affected at several points. The process-improvement opportunities chart shown in Exhibits 14.6 illustrates an imaginary composite process and suggests points in the process for control and/or cost change. These points also indicate where capacity is limited or could be altered for the budget's planned output.

Finally, it is also important in assessing capacity in either continuous or batch process to consider idle facilities that cannot be used for the sales level forecasted or that may be too costly to use in production. The continuing fixed costs for these facilities must be accounted for in budgets, while the capacity is not to be used in assessing capacity versus master schedule.

A special note: These expenses for idle plant facilities should never be included in overhead costs that are listed as inventory expense.

14.15 INVENTORY AND REPLENISHMENT.

Two final, yet basically important, factors remain to be reviewed: inventory and replenishment. The two have elements in common, but they should not be confused. *Inventory* is normally considered as the level of raw, work-in-process, and finished goods, whereas *replenishment* is the scheme used to maintain that level.

Again, a series of questions represents the shortest road to determining the actual role of inventory and replenishment in your planned-action budget—and of course in its predecessor, the master schedule:

- Do you understand the *need* as opposed to the rationale for any given level of inventory as distinguished from a replenishment or maintenance of level program?
- Have you adopted MRP, or do you maintain a re-order point system? What manpower planning program do you use in relation to the master schedule? How have you directly related the machinery and equipment or plant capacity with the master schedule?
- Assuming that a computer is available, do you conceive re-order points systems as average requirements planning? Can adjustments in order points levels change the availability for all parts in the list for assembly use?
- If economic order quantities are applied to re-order points, do shortages in assembly of all the different items improve? Why or why not?
- What is the product structure approach to establishing the discrete requirements for a master schedule?
- Does your inventory management program "net out" the requirements? The diagram shown in Exhibit 14.7 outlines this question.

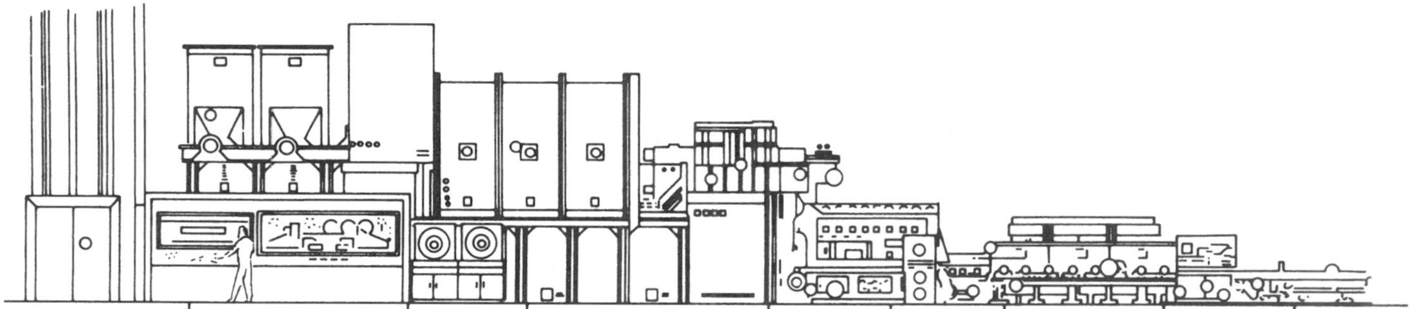

Incoming material	Primary process	Inspect	Secondary process	Inspect	Unitize	Package unit identify	Shipping package	Distribution
Control Quantity Contamination Losses Meter in	Control Input Handling Additional material Ambiance Time Temperature Pressure Atmosphere	Measure	Control Correction Additional material Handling Amblance Time Temperature Pressure Atmosphere		Control Cut Fold Mold Cure Portion	Materials		First package Storage Shipping

Exhibit 14.6. Process-improvement opportunities

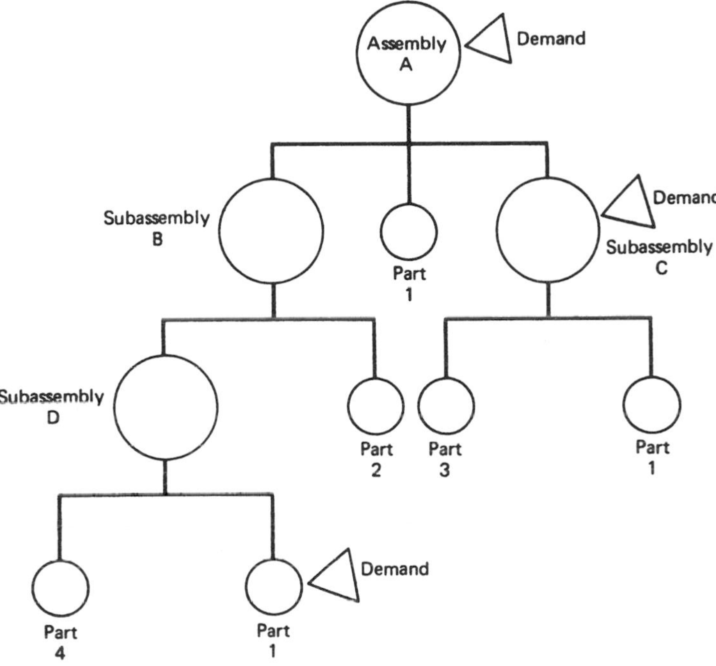

Exhibit 14.7. Product structure approach to material requirements

In connection with Exhibit 14.7 two subquestions should be asked. The first—What are the planning requirements for part number 1 from the diagram?

From demand for product A	2
From demand for assembly C	1
From demand for part 1	1

The second—What are inventory requirements for part number 1 from Exhibit 14.7? Review the differences between planning requirements and inventory requirements. Do your inventory control personnel distinguish between the planning requirements and the numbers they would have in inventory? Review your processes for netting out. The key to this technique is deciding units you really need to store as stock-keeping units. Those that you do not need as stock-keeping units are not required to be kept in inventory as both subassemblies and parts.

It may be sufficient to advise operations or manufacturing managers that there is currently a struggle in materials management about how to handle changes in requirements. The reader would do well to investigate the two schools of thought regarding the handling of such changes. Briefly explained, there are two ways to handle changes in demand. One is to compute only the total net change in demand for parts or materials quantity. The earlier approach was to totally regenerate the new demand, using it as the requirement and abandoning the first forecast. Inventory planning is more immediately satisfied without interpretation when a net change system is used. Materials managers are primarily responsible for this, but in a frequently changing demand, inventory levels could rise faster with regeneration than with the net change program.

The following are some additional questions on inventory management, recognizing that orders to make parts change factory activity:

- Do product structure and discrete planning and scheduling require a structured bill of material (BOM)? Can your computer manipulate a BOM?
- What activities do engineering changes affect in your factory? Materials (raw, in process, and finished), manufacturing specifications, time-phase plan, operations sequence, direct labor performance, direct material usage—whose job is it to control the changes?
- Who knows most about the changes to complete the revision?
- Who should control the introduction of an accepted engineering change?
- Are changes up to date in your plant? How far do they lag behind the planning schedule?
- Do engineering changes affect inventory and replenishment?
- Have you identified the gross annual usage of the parts and classified them into A, B, and C for economic value? (There is a further classification for each part or material into 30, 60, and 90 days average process time required.)
- Must all items be replenished in your program or ordered for use on the same procedural basis? Why not?
- Who does the service parts planning and provisions?

Still other questions should be asked as you move toward publication of the budget. Following are some that can be used in considering the planned output level and the capacity to produce that level:

- Do you have to expend ''nonstandard'' hours and activities to achieve the projected levels? This affects all overhead allocations, usually equivalent to 60% of total cost of goods sold (CGS).
- Are supplies of materials available at the projected levels? What effect will these requirements have on prices paid, or what is the cost impact?
- Where is the bottleneck in the output?
- Are there changes in capacity required for the budget level? Are they labor or capital tool intensive?
- Is the planned level of sufficiently long-range duration to invest in capital-intensive solutions to the problems?
- Can you list the five indirect cost changes most important in the achievement of the budget level of output?
- What is the situation in your plant regarding the expected production per direct labor worker and machine uptime?
- What is the interference factor between the two? Is it the same in each department and on each type of machine?
- What limitations are created by the levels of job skills in the work force? Have you identified these areas in your plant? When assemblymen or skilled persons in smaller special classifications are required, and training is long term or impossible, they could be computed to be capacity limitations, as are machines.

- In addition, can you inquire of your operating people if there are any special building facilities, such as pits, high-ceiling requirements, space, ventilation, and dust-free or environmental spaces, that have a maximum throughput capacity and therefore become limiting in any way? Have you identified these areas in your plant?
- Have you identified families of parts or specific parts whose volume has grown so large or so small that the original equipment or tooling is inappropriate?
- Have you identified specific parts for which a specific patented or special process has been developed that makes your process outmoded?
- Have you considered acquiring the new technology or abandoning the manufacture of your parts by your outmoded process to make that same capacity available for some other items?
- Have you identified the appropriate limits for more vertical integration in your processes?
- Have you identified the areas to reduce your vertical integration?
- What kinds of parts or processes could most economically be subcontracted to expand your plant capacity?
- Have you decided consciously to maintain your division as a cash cow?
- Does your 18-month capital-budget program provide an increase of capacity or simply a reduction in cost? Are you thereby reducing the operation rather than growing?
- What special organization skills are required for growth?
- Have you identified the single unit process change or the investment required to increase capacity?
- Have you ever considered a complete rearrangement and/or minor building modifications as solutions to your plant-capacity problems?

14.16 MORE ON THE MANUFACTURING BUDGET. The topics that remain to be discussed in this chapter are determining raw materials, determining other (indirect) materials, determining direct labor, and determining manufacturing overhead costs.

These topics imply that "what ought to be" in these areas can be defined with some assurance as predictable standard amounts of raw materials, other indirect materials, and direct-labor costs of conversion. The manufacturing overhead costs are a conglomeration of all the administrative activities that assist that conversion to shippable product. The principal questions in each of the four areas are how much is necessary, and how can that be decided?

14.17 DETERMINING RAW-MATERIAL REQUIREMENTS. *Raw materials* are defined herein as those materials acquired for conversion into the product. They could be finished goods, purchased for subsequent assembly, or materials used in vertically integrated manufacturing from refinement of minerals and ores into secondary fabrication and product sales.

The kinds of materials are those selected by the product-design engineer during the design or description of the product. He or she may also authorize substitutes at the time of design.

Manufacturing engineering should indicate the standard materials and their quality and should estimate the usable or sellable yield from the quantity of materials purchased. Every process has some loss in the conversion activity, either by chemical or physical change or by unavoidable production of unusable items.

In addition, during many processes, the unit of control may be changed from pounds to formed units. For example, billets are changed to skelp and then to cut and threaded pipe lengths. The factors used for such conversions in units of measure must be carefully selected to ensure that management has control. The addition of extra amounts of ground particles or fines of materials into mixtures may change the yield; if their inclusion is at all discretionary, then management is not setting proper raw-materials standards.

Historical records may be a clue to usage per unit; however, they should be reviewed to match current technology and process-control capabilities in order to issue valid standards.

The amount provided over the standard direct quantity used for each unit in the schedule is determined by the consumption quantity expected, the amount to cover the usage during the standard replenishment time, plus the safety stock, per policy. This quantity total should then be adjusted by two considerations: (1) forecast accuracy and (2) the commodity character of the materials and the company policy regarding its ownership and costing.

Let us review each of these items and their impact on the budget.

(a) Forecast Accuracy. Most schedules call for a safety-stock base, which should preclude the inventory's reaching the ''zero balance available.'' Most managers think that this is all the safety stock that they have. They are frequently puzzled in trying to reconcile inventory turns with this level of safety stock.

Manufacturing companies, as differentiated from packers, distributors, and so on, have to time phase the receipt of raw materials to include queuing time for batch processing and for several levels of the process into assemblies, kits, or apparatuses.

Most items have some minimum process times. Frequently, subsection managers respond to exacting requirements for ''on-time'' completion by using inventories as a hedge, to avoid criticism. For example, purchasing has material arrive some time before actual requisitions, for withdrawal will show up vendor failures, and each successive factory operation will plan for their anticipated failures by requesting early delivery—''just to be sure.'' Their fudge factors in many different activities throughout the company create impossible scheduling plans, build in work-in-process time, and increase materials for that time period.

The inventory categories affected by policies that are set by managers but usually not evaluated as management-authorized investment levels include:

- *Finished goods.* Safety stock, cycle stock, ''leveling'' stock
- *Assembly.* Work-in-process time
- *Component or parts inventory.* Cycle stock (lot sizing)
- *Fabrication.* Work-in-process time
- *Raw material.* Safety stock or time, cycle stock (lot sizing), commodity ''leveling'' stock

Experiment with your own figures—compute 15% of the value of all those fudge factors outlined above. What percentage improvement in the forecast accuracy would eliminate some of these? What amount of your present inventory would it be?

The focus of such necessary and uncharted acquisitions of material are suggested in the following questions:

- Do you stock finished goods or assemble to order?
- Is there a distribution network that you supply and own?

- Do you have short or long assembly cycles? Are they timed?
- Have you identified the length of fabrication or machining or, in the case of food products, bacterial incubation waiting periods?
- What is your raw material and purchased parts stocking policy?
- Does the number of product lines change raw-material requirements?
- Is there a significant amount of spare part sales for which you inventory? Has the service level policy changed?

A target level for your inventory in all these areas should be set at the time of budget preparation, to ensure that anticipated direct and indirect costs of ownership are included.

(b) Special Commodity Characteristics. The commodity characteristics of the materials you use and the policies that you have consciously or unknowingly authorized affect the levels of inventory, the production rates, and the indirect costs for those inventories.

You should first determine if the volume of materials that your firm uses is a significant factor in the supply–demand curve for that commodity. If you estimate that your demand affects the market, you must next decide if you are going to time the purchases to "even" the price fluctuation or not.

If you have sufficient volume, you could plan and maneuver your purchases to increase values on those materials you already own. If your quantities are not significant, you could select a policy to hedge against price increases. In some instances, this increases earnings on inventories as differentiated from standard-cost values used in budgets and pricing.

Manufacturing engineering sets standards for the production units, using master schedule requirements and prior usage experience as a basis. Purchasing responsibility is to set the standard prices to be paid in the budget period. Wise managers expect and budget for, however, both price and usage variances from standard. At the conclusion of this chapter, a few ideas will be advanced to assist manufacturing managers with the problems of variances from planned cost.

14.18 DETERMINING OTHER INDIRECT-MATERIAL COSTS.

Indirect or other materials are the materials used and consumed during the manufacturing operations that do not become part of the product. They are also items that are difficult to identify with a specific unit of shipped product.

The chart of accounts furnished by your accountant or suggested in other sections of this book provides more specific definitions of the items.

The budgets for and the control of the usage of these items depend mostly on the exercise of judgment, based on historical consumption and specific control procedures.

These indirect costs are usually proportionally lower than other costs, although some materials are very expensive while others are uncontrolled in their use because of their lower value.

The surest way to tackle the level of total cost for this type item is to apply Paredo's law (80% of the expense is in 20% of the items).

Costs for all materials of this nature should be arranged in descending value based on an annual consumption and reviewed to find the closest association between the highest dollar items and some specific direct production process or operation.

The simulated continuous process shown in Exhibit 14.6 suggests areas in which control of indirect materials and labor could also be applied.

If some other materials are identified with specific parts of the process, the consumption allowance should be related to that specific activity. If this correlation cannot be made, the larger expenditures in this category should be identified by the manufacturing engineer for the process or by the industrial engineer in measuring and describing the employee's job and his or her performance.

In either the continuous-process operations or the employee-paced and -managed tasks, the manufacturing engineering staff should set standards for usage of most other materials consumed and describe the limits of expected yield of the process.

Consumable tools in metal working and items such as catalytic materials in a chemical process may either be measured against units produced or be distributed by time period, for the total units produced in that time. Frequently, tools in the perishable class are a significant expense, which requires subclassification for suitable control. In planning for metal-cutting tools, the consumption pattern must be coordinated among tool engineers, quality-control personnel, and industrial engineers.

To explain, the metal-cutting tool is set in relation to a solid object to be cut. Its location is required to be accurate within a few thousandths of an inch. As the tool wears, the final dimension of the piece being cut would change. At the point at which such change would be in excess of allowable shape and size, the tool must be changed. Improved durability of that tool is the responsibility of the manufacturing engineer; quality control could predict, by statistical method, the optimum point in that process at which to change the tools for uniform parts manufacturing, and the industrial engineer will identify the additional amount of direct labor costs for the operations of making such regular changes. In this manner, trade-offs will occur throughout the manufacturing process between the initial costs of tools, the expected levels of quality, and the standard direct labor for employees.

Annual reviews of consumption patterns should suggest manufacturing research projects for improvement. However, elaborate controls that are more costly than the controllable or recoverable amount of the expense should be noticed and abandoned.

14.19 DETERMINING DIRECT-LABOR COSTS. *Direct labor* is defined as labor used directly in the conversion process.

Standard amounts of such labor for budgeting purposes are set by industrial engineers and can be one of the following:

- Historical amounts by part, by product, or by period, considered by the management as a suitable basis for future control and comparison
- Estimated engineered standards by part or by product from time standards data such as motion time measurement (MTM) (Maynard), work factor (Wolfac), time measurement units (John Schwab), and average elements from internal time studies
- Explicit time studies setting the employee's performance by job, by part, or by product unit

If incentive wages are paid for "extra" performance, please remember that it is impossible to produce more than clock or calendar time allows. The incentive, or extra, performance occurs for only an identifiable portion of the total clock or calendar time. Capacity in the plant is frequently miscalculated because of the assumption that incentive performance will occur for all the calendar or clock time. It cannot be so sustained because of shortcomings of both managers and employees, as was discussed previously.

Considering the several allowances that are usually part of the employee relations policy in nonunion shops, or the specific allowances for nonproduction time granted in most union contracts, the budget plan should estimate that the workers' outputs would be approximately 1,350 to 1,400 standard hours per year into inventory, as stated previously.

We have already observed that actual work of direct labor or production from a continuous process is reduced by planning for the minimum labor by designing the product or selecting the most efficient methods or tools and workplace layout that supports a well-trained employee.

Wishing or hoping for such ideal conditions to exist at the time of budget preparation cannot be translated into budgets showing lower costs, unless the specific plans that change current practices are implemented.

We have indicated that budget time is when the most experimental or new, unfettered thinking can take place. The various experiences of your own staff and their bias in favor of one or another approach to defining this standard and fundamental unit of cost can be best resolved by exploration, learning, and conferring to find the highest level of mutual interest in one approach. There are as many good programs as there are good managers.

In the discussion of capacity, the chart on effective and ineffective time shown in Exhibit 14.2 showed good and useful or standard production time spent by the work force, along with its characteristics. The characteristics of ineffective time spent were also shown.

Aside from the potential for lowered planned costs through the redesign of the product, we all look toward the performance of employees in the system. The desirability of their being motivated to be attentive and efficient, and the techniques to achieve such a climate in your company, are for other authors to discuss. However, there are many popular ideas currently in use. They include incentive wage payment plans and profit-sharing schemes; zero defect programs and quality circles for peer pressure; and suggestion systems, which have minor success.

Daniel Yankelovich, president of a well-known public opinion research firm, says in *Industry Week* that traditional incentives are not well matched to today's work force.[13] He finds that fear, money, work organizations, and reliance on work ethic are being blunted as tools of management and are less effective today. He explains that these are to be replaced (on a trend basis, it appears) by flex-time schedules, health improvement, educational opportunities, and other amenities. The forecast he makes is for developing a sort of cafeteria concept of incentives that provide programs tailored for each individual.

To provide a basis for proceeding to establish direct-labor standards, I have arranged a series of questions that touch on most of the major points on work measurement. I recommend that you proceed by planning a series of meetings, well in advance of budget planning time, to begin the dialogues and select a program that meets the capabilities of your personnel and company circumstance.

The questions are those that the reader can ask his or her staff. They will reveal the depths of understanding of the subject and the new knowledge required to establish a program to be used as a basis of a budget. The effect of teams, usually synergistic, is not measurable (specific) at this time.

(a) Getting Realism into Direct-Labor Work Standards

- Do you use machine-operating hours as a standard or man-hours as a standard? Which control is most important? Which control produces the most improved cost?
- Do you consider standards absolute? How much variation is expected? What kinds of variation are predictable and therefore explainable?

---

[13] Daniel Yankelovich, *Industry Week,* August 6, 1979, p. 1 and following.

- Are current standards for performance *attainable* in either machine hours or man-hours in your company?
- Do you recognize that maximum time available for useful work is clock time and/or calendar time minus the established nonproductive periods, such as holidays, non-operating shifts, lunch periods, and specific contracted employee release time?
- What is the maximum ''uptime'' for standards expected in your operations?

(b) Measurement

- How do you establish a physical effort for work-standards purposes? What are rating films? What is the objective of time study?
- If you do time study, how does it compare with MTM or work-factor time values? Do the many studies provide equity from job to job?
- What is an adjusted time-study time? Why omit high and low observations?
- What are allowances for personal time and fatigue? Should they be used?
- Is there a difference between work-measurement and incentive-payment plans?
- Is measured day work a superior management tool?
- Is measurement improper if incentive plans are not used?

(c) Wage Incentives

- Are there actual jobs available in your plant in which the additional physical effort that is possible for a person, without injury to his or her health, can make a contribution in the output level?
- Can these operations be carefully identified, and are they consistent enough that they may be measured and wage payment bonus be paid in a meaningful way for increased output?
- Have you examined the places in which individual performance plans cannot be set up or group plans may be applicable? Is the incentive to be paid only for increased pace in highly repetitive direct-labor operations, or do you intend to pay it for improved performance in other indirect output such as quality, reduced waste, reduced machine downtime, and so forth?
- Is the financial incentive an indirect incentive applied on a company-wide or plant-wide basis, or is it directly related to that small group of employees? If such an opportunity exists, can it be monitored and maintained so that, if changes in the work content occur, the program can change?
- Does an incentive-payment plan maintain a sustained physical output for several years?
- Do incentive programs contain restrictions on management?
- Do hourly incentive-payment plans contain seeds of mistrust between employers and employees?
- What are elements of the total cost of an incentive-payment plan for hourly employees? Do they include excess tool consumption, extra quality costs for policing, costs of lower-quality output, excess machine-maintenance costs, extra expense tool cost, inventory write-offs due to improper counts, shop clerical personnel, additional time-

standards personnel, extra record costs related to information-systems requirements, loss of absentee control, and loss of employee interest in interpersonal relationships with the members of management and technical staff?

14.20 ESTABLISHING THE MANUFACTURING OVERHEAD FUNCTIONS AND SERVICES. Having determined from the master schedule the operating range of various processes in your company, and having considered the programs affecting the effective and ineffective time used, it is necessary to relate the fixed, variable, and other incremental costs associated with the product. We will review here the definition of fixed, or burden, costs, along with some other terminology.

(a) Definitions

(i) Variable Costs. Variable costs are production and distribution costs required to place an additional unit of product in the hands of the customer. These include all costs that vary in direct proportion to sales volume—for example, direct labor and material.

Most manufacturing managers do not understand allocated costs (overhead distribution), in order to glean information about changes occurring: how, where, why? Activity-based accounting was developed because current accounting methods do not relate a cost to the reason or locus of the occurrence. You must understand it now to use and adapt the new way successfully.

(ii) Fixed Costs. *Period costs* are those costs incurred as a function of time rather than volume—for example, administrative salaries.

Programmed costs are those incurred as a result of specific decisions, without direct relation to either sales volume or the passage of time. Examples include research and development (R&D) expenditures, advertising, and the company picnic.

Normal burden rate denotes an average or expected burden rate that is determined in a number of ways. The method is predominant in industry today. It provides for a consistent application of manufacturing burden to the inventory. The rate is based on studies that are made periodically by accounting and manufacturing personnel. It can be based on history and judgment if the historic capacity method is used, or it can result from a more scientific analysis from an industrial engineering study outlining the practical capacity.

The use of the normal rate has the effect of leveling the peaks and valleys of spending and production volume. As such, it is the most acceptable means of arriving at a proper inventory valuation and hence the estimated profits from month to month. Usually, it permits a more prompt method of preparing financial statements and is the most inexpensive clerical method to use.

Unabsorbed burden denotes the difference between the amount of manufacturing expense carried to inventory with product manufactured in the period (by use of normal burden rates) and the actual amount spent for manufacturing expenses during that same period. Unabsorbed burden may consist of *underabsorbed burden* if production is below normal expectations in the period or of *overabsorbed burden* if production into inventory is greater than expectations used as a basis for "normal."

Underabsorbed burden occurs when the actual amount of manufacturing burden expense is in excess of the amount carried to inventory by the normal burden rates. This generally occurs when:

- A company experiences considerable fluctuation during a year in its production because of seasonal variations in product demand.
- Unusual expenses are incurred that were not anticipated when normal burden rates were established.
- A manufacturing plant is geared to produce much more than the sales demand.
- Even in instances where the production level is equal, differences in spending will fluctuate. This, in turn, will distort the inventory valuation and produce entirely unacceptable valuations.
- No provisions are made for the expensing of unused plant capacity during low productive periods. Instead, these costs are carried to inventory by means of overstated manufacturing burden rates. This is not accepted accounting practice, nor is it economically sound. Profits are considerably distorted (overstated), and both potential and active investors are misled.

(b) Levels of Overhead. The levels of overhead that should be budgeted are the most significant part of costs. The levels of these costs on the budget are the most direct reflection of the experience, expectations, and "style" of top management. They are all nontechnical and nonscientific management terms. This is because the levels of these costs are influenced the most by a series of value judgments made by the managers about the level of services the direct conversion activity requires to optimize its performance.

A review was made of the functional basis for costs in many companies relating to the price paid by the consumer for the product. It is shown in Exhibit 14.8. These data were collected by interview and participation in 50 company-management programs and were extrapolated from published statements of an equal or greater number.

If your technical staff has been effective, the 10% standard direct labor represents the probable minimum conversion labor content for present products and/or processes in hours. (This has been converted into dollars for budget purposes.)

Since the owners have invested capital, they are certainly entitled to some rent on their money (profit). As these two elements are each approximately 10%, the remaining 80% of costs are incurred as a result of decisions about how operations people run the company.

	Average Grocery and Household Products	Average Fork Truck Manufacturing	Estimated Drugs
Director labor[a]	$0.09	$0.10	$0.09
Direct material[a]	0.25	0.30	0.3175
Plant overhead expense[a]	0.25	0.30	
Work cost and distribution[a]	$0.59	$0.70	$0.4025
Selling expense			
General expense	$0.26	$0.21	$0.4225
Administrative			
Subtotal	$0.90	$0.91	$0.825
Taxes and profit	$0.10	$0.09	$0.175
	$1.00	$1.00	$1.00

[a] Per sales dollar.

Exhibit 14.8. Concept of managed costs (from approximately 100 corporate statements)

The following are examples of typical questions frequently asked about these functional cost areas:

- What product design review has taken place to reflect the cost benefit of each element of the product or the features offered to the customers?
- What are we doing to be assured that we are using the most effective tools and methods?
- What new, beneficially planned quality and maintenance programs are in process of installation?

In answering these questions, managers create and mandate the cost levels. Therefore, they can do away with costs just as easily, recognizing that the costs are a result of their style of management and determining what they want to control and how.

As the process starts, it must be realized that there should also be a continuity of the top management objective all the way down to the bottom. Integrity is required at every level, because the fudging and hedging that normally alter those top management objectives expressed on the way "down" reduce the credibility of the budget as a real management working plan. Each manager, without control, includes some protection against the "real" expectation, and such actions dilute the realism of subsequent performance reports. It is important, therefore, to start from the right point in order to plan for and achieve better levels of cost.

All overhead of staff departments is based on the work load or volume of items the departments expect to handle. This work load is usually related to the current levels, altered by indications that the future is up or down. This is a sound rationalization, but the planned work expands as the specialization's technology grows.

The manufacturing manager's principal objective to meet or achieve planned costs places the responsibility to forestall such proliferation on his or her own shoulders. These specialists would have a lower work load if the number of items they handle were reduced. A corrective goal for manufacturing managers and their staffs therefore is to simplify the number and variety of items to consider, thereby reducing the number of overhead transactions required per sales dollar.

Maintenance of fixed assets, long-range contracts, capital borrowings, and so forth preclude an opportunity to start over from ground zero. I am reminded of earlier training in planning fixed and semivariable expenses, which had been overlooked in decisions to expand at all costs and/or raise prices to cover inflationary costs.

A suggested approach is simply to recognize that your company's future could be very seriously upset by a variety of random events. Assume, therefore, what some dire circumstance might be; for example, a process failure upsets a whole product line's sales, a prolonged labor dispute occurs, or there is an interruption in the supplies of vital materials. Assume that the extent of that major interruption in revenue will require a six-month shutdown, with an expectation of the resumption of minimum production at the end of six to eight months. Since some kinds of contracted and fixed expenses would continue, identify them. What basic management activities and operations or maintenance programs would have to be continued?

Obviously, such a dramatic change would forecast for some managers that the company would cease to exist, but with reasonably good management it should not be so. (If the purpose of your enterprise is perpetual, as provided for in its charter, is the management less capable in its own life span?)

Wisdom dictates in this exercise that managers faced with planning would be able to proceed without prejudice in the following four major steps:

1. Identify those continuing, fixed, and sunk costs for taxes, insurance, depreciation, maintenance of assets, and so forth.
2. Identify incremental expenses required and timing for the first or minimum unit(s) of output.
3. Plan the direct-cost elements—materials and conversion labor.
4. Determine when and how many additional units of output would require additional management support and overhead costs. It would be well here to try to determine the sensitivity of production rates to various overhead activities or programs.

Inquisitive managers engaging in this process probably now perceive the emergence of management style and sense levels of costs associated with that style—the things they feel they would want to do or are now doing.

The most graphic example of such a complicated concept of style may be seen in the costs of having five daily reports containing information that is considered basic to all operating managers. The example indicates the information required and the ways to get it. The five reports are:

1. Manufacturing managers must know the demand for their output related to their current active production. This is usually available from a daily booking and shipping report, which shows the value of orders received and the value of orders shipped. It usually includes a running total, showing a sales and shipments balance due or indicates backlog that is growing or diminishing. This tells manufacturing managers that they are running ahead or behind the current demand.
2. The operating manager usually has some force report or personnel report showing the direct labor or indicating that the work force is present and equal to, greater than, or less than the requirements of the order board.
3. Daily production usually posts actual output to the schedule. Note: Two kinds of interruption affect production after the proper number of people are present—machine breakdown and quality problems.
4. A maintenance report of production equipment should be available every morning, showing the continuing, chronic production-equipment problems not yet solved and any new, acute, or unusual equipment failure in the past 24 hours.
5. Quality failures in production are usually reported to satisfy accounting procedures, but manufacturing managers should also know daily the continuing chronic failures of materials and parts or production operations and any acute failures that reduced production in the last 24 hours.

These five reports are basic operations management information. These reports can be compiled on a daily basis, even in a larger plant, from telephone calls to a secretary or clerk. On the other hand, they can consist of thousands of details manipulated by the most extensive computers with concomitant costs incurred in all of the following areas:

- Computer rental
- Data collection (leased wire, if any)

- Data-processing personnel
- Program rental costs
- Program personnel
- Program maintenance
- Direct labor reporting collection time allowed or consumed
- Indirect labor reporting collection time allowed or consumed
- Timekeepers
- Production-control information programs
- Scheduling and dispatching time used for information and work-in-process reporting
- Administration analysis time
- Report-preparation time
- Printing and paper costs

Computer costs are soaring in most companies, along with administrative costs that are incurred indirectly in support of computer uses. The following questions can be used as guides in your discussion to determine the appropriate levels for the direct associated costs and those administrative cost elements indirectly associated with your management style:

- Do you know the total management information cost per dollar of sales? Note: Since the information requirements determine the administrative transactions, does the information available have a potential recovery greater than the cost to get it?
- Could you establish what would be a desirable level of per sales dollar for information cost? For how much of this information requirement are government regulations responsible?
- Is the preparation of that information organized for your own administrative and control use?
- Since most budgets start with a sales figure or are related to dollars of revenue, what items of cost are hidden in the change from gross to net sales? Is this discounting of the sales value of goods produced budgeted?
- Do you maintain control reports on the elements of this discounting of gross sales, which include warranty, replacement, service, and sales policy adjustment of factory losses, errors, and defects? What is the percentage of gross sales?

These items are examples of the kinds of costs incurred as a result of management style and of several directives issued to the manufacturing staff, which incur cost because "the boss says he needs this." The vast distance from minimum production in earlier times to present levels in most companies has allowed for these costs of style to become permanent costs in planning budgets.

In proposing a budget of revenue and cost, the presentation fosters the assumption that all of the expenses listed are in appropriate balance. The presentation also represents hundreds of decisions that have been made by the operations managers about the efficacy of existing or authorized personnel programs, relationships, and output plans. (They are therefore minimum levels of expected cost, although they appear to be upper limits.)

Without an edict to start from scratch in implementing zero-base budgeting programs or without the understanding that the manufacturing budget is presenting a suitable total program with its parts having been tested against this total production requirement with all costs at their developed minimum level, we are simply setting up a series of traffic lights, advising stop, caution, or go for various existing activities. Under these circumstances, we have not presented a plan for optimum long- and short-range operating results.

(c) Manufacturing Research. There are many times and circumstances when good planning and forecasting cannot be done with the information available. New knowledge and an understanding of new, untried techniques or machinery are frequently necessary to improve the quality of planning. For these reasons, manufacturing research is every bit as valuable to a company as research for a new product. It is urged that manufacturing managers support at least one manufacturing research project in each budget year.

(d) Review Questions for Overhead Budgets. The following questions are included to guide the reader in conferring with functional heads of industrial engineering, quality control, plant engineering, and production control in developing the new action plans for change that will point the way to lowered levels of expected cost:

- Have you established work simplification as a technique in your industrial engineering programs?
- Does the industrial engineering department maintain a running record of the net effect of standards changes versus or related to the current year's master schedules of parts requirements?
- What is the three-year trend of your products' standard hour content?
- Do you receive quarterly reports? Does the industrial engineering department furnish cost–benefit summaries of their operations?
- Does the industrial engineering department use a total cost concept, including indirect labor, scrap, lost time, and so forth, in developing methods and establishing standards?
- Does the industrial engineer participate in the consideration of new parts or product designs and engineering changes? Are they supported in making suggestions to change the design?
- Does the industrial engineering department regularly engage in the control of tolerances for manufacturing and engineering?
- Does the industrial engineering department ensure that tolerances in "form" are used for flatness, roundness, straightness, and so forth, as defined in the terms of the American National Standards Institute Standards?
- Does the industrial engineer propagate the selection of the most economical tolerance plans with design engineering?
- Has the industrial engineering department eliminated unnecessary extra paperwork by using standard operating descriptions in preparing routines for manufacture of similar parts?
- Are the industrial engineers aware of working capital requirements being established when they select an economic lot size for setup purposes?
- Is the lot size determination more appropriate if done by materials control and scheduling? Does the industrial engineering department conceive its job as being one of the economists for the company?

- Do industrial engineers participate in the quality-control planning of the parts manufacture? Do they understand the full implication of cost for quality-control activities, or has the professionalism of quality control superceded real economic considerations?
- Do the industrial engineers constantly review what place layouts are needed to maintain motion-efficient and safe conditions?
- Do industrial engineers consider the time and cost implications of working safely, or is there a conflict of interest between prescribed methods and employee welfare for the benefit of the lowest standard time?
- Does the incentive payment plan work at cross-purposes with employee safety?
- Has the industrial engineering department developed clear job descriptions that outline the specific skill requirements for each job?
- Have they provided training outlines to enable the personnel in shop departments to train employees in the specific skills that they have allocated?
- Is there a tendency to create too many classifications? How frequently do you use "all-around" machinists' classifications or "all-around" assemblymen? Have you considered the advantages that fewer classifications can bring? Is there a significant cost savings in having many job descriptions, or does this tend to limit assignments, increase conflict, and encumber promotions, transfers, and development of employees?
- Do industrial engineering personnel get opportunities to become shop supervisors and managers?
- Do industrial engineers participate in variance analysis and in regular operations meetings?
- Do industrial engineering standards provide adequate programs for machine maintenance? Has the maintenance department been advised of the requirements in standards for service to machinery and equipment? Does this affect capacity?
- Has the industrial engineering department identified all routine maintenance jobs and established work measurement data for the elements of those routine maintenance jobs, along with the elements of the work in both routine and special repair work?
- Have the chronic variances been identified and basic process changes planned to avoid them?

14.21 QUALITY CONTROL ECONOMICS REVIEW QUESTIONS. Quality control enters the productive system at levels in every function—at the executive level in determining what the product-line general configuration and quality should be; at the operating level in ensuring product conformance to specifications; and at the customer-contact level in quality assurance, so that they get what they thought they were buying.

Perhaps you should ask yourself these questions: Is the quality level of the product accurately evoking the desired corporate image? Are the existing products consistent with the long-range plans and with research? Have you recently decided, as a high-cost manufacturer, to enter a low-cost, competitive quality market with another product? Has this had any impact on your company's reputation? Has it changed the customers who have been buying the higher-quality products from you? Has the reverse been true? Have you been a manufacturer of lower-quality competitive goods, moving into a high-quality prestige market? Have you programmed the market learning trend in this change in your image? Have you established the right atmosphere for quality?

You should recognize that the folowing items can affect attitudes of the employees regarding quality:

- Are your restrooms and locker rooms clean, well lighted, well painted, and equipped with soap, towels, and so forth, or are they dirty and poorly lit and badly in need of painting?
- Is your shop area clean, well lighted, painted and neat, with an orderly flow of material, or do you permit a dirty shop, poor lighting, and confusion in material flow? Is your maintenance of equipment excellent, average, or nonexistent?
- Are your drawings clear and concise, well dimensioned, and most usually not the cause for quality problems, or are they vague, poorly dimensioned, incomplete in detail, and frequently the cause for quality problems? Do your quality and inspection personnel have final approval? Are they respected, well paid, and adequate, or do they have virtually no say, are poorly trained, or are practically nonexistent?

Are the following work elements part of your total quality control system?

- Do you have a plan and administration program for the total quality control system?
- Do you appraise the total quality control system to relate its adequacy to the customer's reliability needs?
- Are the quality data available and sufficient to be included in bid proposals?
- Have you compared the implied customer reliability and quality requirements with the available physical program and with your product?
- Have you considered reliability?
- Have you established appearance standards by both quantitative and qualitative means?
- Have you determined in your industrial engineering measurement programs the location of quality changes, the kind and amount of change possible, procedures to be followed, characteristics to be measured, equipment to be used, and forms and records to be kept?
- Have you planned for testing of your product performance?
- Do you have any program for the design of measurement or test equipment
- Do you have a program for maintaining the calibration of inspection in test equipment?
- Do you train inspection and test personnel?
- Do you distribute quality information to vendors and subcontractors?
- Do you inspect incoming and subcontracted material?
- Do you conduct vendor evaluation?
- Do you frequently instruct workers to use questionable material or frequently require that the shop remanufacture products from the outside from subcontractors?

In summary, does your environment indicate that you are really interested in quality or that it is a temporary campaign program, not worthy of long-range intentions?

14.22 PLANT ENGINEERING BUILDINGS AND EQUIPMENT MAINTENANCE REVIEW QUESTIONS. A further way to improve cost performance is to improve the maintenance function. Maintenance has historically been viewed as low-level work, trailing most other operating functions in importance—a necessary evil to be tolerated. This downgrading is unfortunate, since the maintenance function, if properly run, can greatly enhance the operation of the production system. Nevertheless, an efficient maintenance operation is the exception rather than the rule. As a result, maintenance problems abound.

The following questions indicate symptoms of maintenance neglect:

- Do you have excessive machine breakdowns?
- Do you have frequent emergency work?
- Is there a domination of the maintenance operations by production personnel?
- Is there a lack of equipment-replacement programs?
- Is there sufficient spare equipment for sensitive operations?
- Do you have sufficient preventive maintenance outlined?
- Do you have a planned selection for maintenance supervisors and managers, and have you maintained training courses necessary to keep them at a level commensurate with the skill requirements of new machinery and equipment that you have been purchasing?
- Are there regular training programs for personnel going into the maintenance department? Are they as adequate as those for personnel going into the production operation?
- Does the maintenance department have appropriate shop facilities in which to complete its work?
- Do you recognize that there is an opportunity for reducing unnecessary work through preventive action, better methods, and improved tools in maintenance?
- Have you any correlation, recently developed, that gives you an indication of the labor productivity changes when better planning, scheduling, and performance evaluation of maintenance programs occurs?
- Have you drawn any correlation recently between excess costs, such as overtime, machine downtime, and materials and supplies wasted, and poor maintenance of machinery and equipment?
- Have you ever received a report that an operator's performance or an industrial engineering standard will have an impact on the continued good operation of the machine? Have you ever noted or been asked to referee any conflict between a method or tooling job sequence outline and the plant engineer because of its impact on the machinery and equipment?
- Have you ever considered the probabilities of component breakdown in any of your machines based on your maintenance records so that you could establish a preventive maintenance program?

14.23 FLOOR AND WORK-IN-PROCESS CONTROL REVIEW QUESTIONS.

The following measures of scheduling performance on the shop floor should be checked:

- Has the mean production order completion rate been improving?
- Has the average number of days a job is finished behind schedule increased or decreased?
- Has the percentage utilization of men and machines increased or decreased in recent history?

- Have the characteristics of the process waiting or queuing increased? Do you know what caused them?

Improvements in the scheduling system would be reflected in any or all of the following measures:

- How many jobs, shop orders, or work orders are in the shop now?
- How many do you finish per day, per week, per month, by department?
- Does any product part require more than 30 days of continuous actual manufacturing time?
- Why should a product be in manufacturing in the shop for longer than three months?
- Do you believe that less work and process on the floor improves efficiency more than a complicated scheduling apparatus?
- When dispatching work in the shop, is it related to specific demand for scheduled periods? Could materials requirement planning help?
- Why not use a time period and level of part in the BOM as the schedule priority and thus eliminate factory dates, complicated schemes, and so forth?
- How would a plant-within-a-plant help improve scheduling?[14]
- What is short-interval scheduling? How can it help in a job shop? What is the proper application? (As a scheduling approach, it is severe but has some benefit. As a cost reducer its effect is temporary [6 to 12 months] and disastrous to morale. Study long-range effects carefully.)
- What are all of the transactions required to get a part order? These activities cause work in the production-control department. You, as a manager, can affect the volume by managing other areas.

In measuring performance as suggested in the preceding questions, the results could be summarized with the following questions:

- Have the trends minimized inventories in all classes?
- Has factory utilization actually increased?
- Have we accomplished more uptime for machines?
- Have we more standard hours per direct-labor worker per year?
- Has customer service really improved? How?
- Is direct-labor performance stable, or do we have many production crises?
- Do we have high performance against standard costs?
- What percentage variance do we have to costs—not to direct labor?
- Is it easy to change schedules to accommodate customer requirements, engineering changes, and so forth, or is it difficult?
- Do we have control of our standard methods?
- Do inventory levels provide response to customers' delivery requirements?

[14] See Wickham Skinner, "The Focused Factory," *Harvard Business Review*, May–June 1974, pp. 113–121.

- Have backlogs grown? What is our prediction ability? *Note:* You are in trouble when the actual total inventory exceeds the target by more than 15%, when A items are over the target at all, and when B items are more than 10% over the target.

You are in trouble when the percentage of the parts delivered to the shop for assembly have more than a 7% to 8% shortage. You are in trouble when any percentage of short list items is a surprise. You are in double trouble when surprises are the direct responsibility of production control and inventory control. You are in trouble when scheduled changes are more than a minor inconvenience for shortages of parts and materials.

You are in trouble when you cannot identify a problem as an A, B, or C part and cannot correct the chronic poor supply performance. You are in trouble when the obsolete inventory is greater than one tenth of 1% of the total. You are in trouble when credit balances appear on the inventory records. You are in trouble when you have not identified decontrol items and have used the three-bin system plan.

It should be noted that many decisions in material and inventory control affect various standard performance indexes and measures. Do you know which ones they are? Are you satisfied with the decisions and the methods in making the decisions?

14.24 SUMMARY. This discourse has suggested the early, middle, and final steps in considering what costs should be in preparing a planned action budget. Any form for the budget that satisfies the user and is capable of reporting progress is acceptable.

When the manager has outlined programs and has investigated their expected change in various cost, planned revenue, and inventory accounts, there is the final reality that variances from that plan will occur. They will occur both in prices paid above standard and in labor, materials, and supplies used in achieving the budget shipments.

The major elements of the planned-action budget presented are not new when considered individually, since many techniques discussed have been used for years. The key impact will come from the simultaneous consideration by all operating sections of the company and their probable combined effect on the company statements.

The budget must contain the following elements in order to monitor or report variances from the plan:

- Proper cost standards and flexible budget system construction, so that manufacturing line supervisors will be able to understand the expectation and the actual variance (It should include necessary operating formulas as well as written definitions required for understanding.)
- Placement of each variance in an appropriate group according to type or technical category that is understood by the manufacturing management group.
- Variance and account codes related directly to the proper organizational function or unit that is accountable for the results, in line with the concepts of the basic organizational structure of the company

James Wall, consultant, Union Special Machine Company, discussed variance reporting as follows:

> Cost variances relating to standard cost and flexible budget systems can be separated and reported in four groups so that they will be more understandable to supervision and top

management: processing product, conversion costs, price of material, and cost adjustment. Variances so grouped can be generally described as follows:

- *Processing product.* This group is concerned with the yield, gains, and losses resulting directly from processing products through in-process inventory in the various forms of product, at standard unit value and eventually at standard cost value. This group is sometimes called *operating variances.*
- *Conversion costs.* This group, composed of producers' (direct) labor and all other manufacturing overhead, is concerned with those variations which result in gains or losses from standard conversion cost and should never enter inventory but are written off currently or in line with existing accounting practices.
- *Price material.* This group is concerned with the price variation resulting from the comparison of actual to standard prices for raw and related materials, purchased parts, etc.
- *Cost adjustments.* This group is concerned with those variations which are the result of management policy or accounting decisions and, for the most part, are not the result of operations.

For purposes of definition and for assignment of accountability to management, the first two groups of variances are the result of plant operations and can be related to the processing of products and the general activity of production. The last two groups are the responsibility of functional and top management, rather than plant operations.

The pyramid principle of reporting requires the following:

- Reporting of costs to the level of management that is responsible for cost control and is accountable for taking management action to either improve costs or maintain a continuing performance level.
- The condensing of operation information so that only essential data are presented to each higher level of management (in line with the former organization structure).
- Issuance of one series of control reports for each level of management; additional copies may be provided to others for information purposes, but only one should be directed to each level for purposes of control.

Planned-action budgets are merely management tools and not *management* itself. A successful plan for control of operations requires certain actions and support by management. This means describing what performance ought to be, supporting changes, and providing the proper ''climate'' for improvement in the continuous struggle to achieve a reasonable level of proficiency.

This is not an impossible task, but ''one-shot programs'' and constant directions for erratic short-term changes tend to undermine effective operating control. Continuous improvement is required to compete.

A program of intense study has been recommended for determining what your plant is now doing in order to measure the distance it must move to achieve what ought to be. The effort may appear to be too much for preparation of a budget. The justification for such a complete analysis rests in the disappearing margins of profitability and the growing shortage of internally generated capital for the rejuvenation of our aging manufacturing plants.

It has always been surprising, however, to realize that most companies faced with actual losses can find the organization, energy, and reasons to suddenly take the steps to change from loss to profit. The same opportunities have been available during all of the declining margin years.

The attitudes of the manager have changed. That is all it takes—a real dissatisfaction with things as they are and a willingness to regroup, to question openly what is going on, and to tackle the problem. Such programs usually contain the same elements of review inherent in the planned-action budget approach that has been outlined. I have used these programs in several companies with success, as indicated at the beginning of this chapter. Without such programs being used, margins will continue to decline or prices will be raised to cover these management-created costs.

Finally, when considering new plans, new products, and new approaches, we frequently gamble on the person who is doing the job. We cannot rely solely on statistics, which may be against a proposal, nor can we use them only in defense of the status quo. We put our reputations on the block in committing to proceed with a plan that we have recommended. When we have done a good job of planning and forecasting, we want the boss to take our word. The final test for you now is, was your plan that well prepared? Did it have the winning combination for competition?

SOURCES AND SUGGESTED REFERENCES

Aalbregtse, R. John, John A. Hejka, and K. Princeton, "TQM: How Do You Do It?," *Automation,* vol. 38, no. 8, August 1991.

Aggarwal, Raj, "Justifying Investments in Flexible Manufacturing Technology: Adding Strategic Analysis to Capital Budgeting Under Uncertainty," *Managerial Finance,* vol. 17, nos. 2 and 3, 1991.

Brausch, John M., "Selling ABC," *Management Accounting,* vol. 73, no. 8, February 1992.

Brimson, Jim, and Robin Fraser, "The Key Features of ABB," *Management Accounting* (UK), vol. 69, no. 1, January 1991.

Brownell, Peter, and Kenneth A. Merchant, "The Budgetary and Performance Influences of Product Standardization and Manufacturing Process Automation," *Journal of Accounting Research,* vol. 28, no. 2, Autumn 1990.

Fallone, Paul, and Carmelo Giaccotto, "An Application of the Box–Jenkins Methodology to Capital Budgeting," *Managerial Finance,* vol. 17, nos. 2 and 3, 1991.

Haas, Elizabeth A., "Breakthrough Manufacturing," *Harvard Business Review,* March–April 1987.

Hayes, Robert H., and Ramchandran Jaikumar, "Manufacturing's Crisis: New Technologies, Obsolete Organizations," *Harvard Business Review,* vol. 66, no. 5, September–October 1988.

Hayes, Robert H., and Ramchandran Jaikumar, "Requirements for Successful Implementation of New Manufacturing Technologies," *Journal of Engineering & Technology Management* (Netherlands), vol. 7, nos. 3 and 4, March 1991.

Howery, Kenneth C., and Earl D. Bennett, "How Lockheed Implemented CIM," *Management Accounting,* vol. 73, no. 6, December 1991.

Kakati, M., and U. R. Dhar, "Investment Justification in Flexible Manufacturing Systems," *Engineering Costs & Production Economics,* vol. 21, no. 3, July 1991.

King, Alfred M., "Selling ABC," *Management Accounting,* vol. 73, no. 8, February 1992.

Kulatilaka, Nalin, "Valuing the Flexibility of Flexible Manufacturing Systems," *IEEE Transactions on Engineering Management,* vol. 35, no. 4, November 1988.

Lander, Gerald H., and Mohamed E. Bayou, "Does ROI Apply to Robotic Factories," *Management Accounting,* vol. 73, no. 11, May 1992.

Morrow, Michael, and Tim Connolly, "The Emergence of Activity-Based Budgeting," *Management Accounting* (UK), vol. 69, no. 2, February 1991.

Penzer, Erika, "Making a Federal Case for Quality," *Incentive,* vol. 165, no. 8, August 1991.

Reichheld, Frederick F., and W. Earl Sasser, Jr., "Zero Defections: Quality Comes to Services," *Harvard Business Review,* vol. 68, no. 5, September–October 1990.

Roth, Harold P., and A. Faye Borthick, "ABC Assumptions?," *Management Accounting,* vol. 73, no. 5, November 1991.

Sharp, Douglas, and Linda F. Christensen, ''A New View of Activity-Based Costing,'' *Management Accounting,* vol. 73, no. 3, September 1991.

Swann, K., and W. D. O'Keefe, ''Advanced Manufacturing Technology: Investment Decision Process—Part I,'' *Management Decision* (UK), vol. 28, no. 1, 1990.

Turney, Peter B. B., ''Activity-Based Management,'' *Management Accounting,* vol. 73, no. 7, January 1992.

Uchitelle, Louis. ''The New Faces of U.S. Manufacturing.'' *The New York Times,* July 3, 1994, pp. 3-1, 3-6.

CHAPTER 15

RESEARCH AND DEVELOPMENT BUDGET

Maurice I. Zeldman

Emzee Associates

15.1 THE RELATIONSHIP OF RESEARCH AND DEVELOPMENT AND ENGINEERING TO THE TOTAL BUDGETING PROCESS. To understand the relationship of research and development (R&D) and engineering to the total budgeting process, the difference between those functions and other corporate functions will be examined.

Research and development, unlike any other department, deals in the company's future profits and growth. Corporate growth can be internal, obtained from the products or processes produced by R&D and refined by engineering, or can be attained through acquisition. Strong modern companies involved in high- or medium-technology areas look toward both of these routes for growth.

Other departments of the company—marketing, manufacturing, service, quality assurance, quality control, electronic data processing, purchasing, and so forth—are involved in *today's* profit. These groups produce, test, and sell yesterday's R&D or engineering products or processes. This fact is often overlooked by financial people concerned with today's profit. Research and development is an investment in the future. Statistical data gathered from many sources show an interesting relationship between profits and sales. The data assumes a free market. Monopoly situations or government-regulated industries fall into a different category. Typical sales and profit curves for industrial products and some consumer products are shown in Exhibit 15.1.

The relationship between profits and sales may vary from industry to industry, but generally the profit margin peaks in the middle of the growth period and decreases past this point even though sales continue to grow.

It is obvious from Exhibit 15.1 that a corporation will go out of business without new product sales when current products become obsolete. In industries in which life cycles are short, this phenomenon is more easily observed (i.e., electronics and other high-technology industries). The question that a corporation must ask is, ''What is the right level of R&D funding for healthy corporate growth?''

This question is part of the corporate strategic budget plan. The answer is based on the following:

- Product life cycles
- The level of technology in the industry

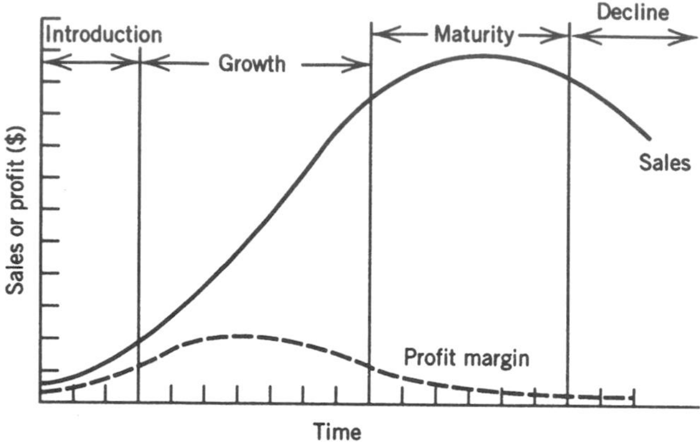

Exhibit 15.1. Typical product or process life-cycle curves

- The position that the company wants to attain in its industry segment—what the competition is doing
- The risk involved in development
- The marketing risk

(a) Product Life Cycles. Every industry has characteristic life cycles. For example, in electronics, life cycles range from one to three years; in chemicals, they range from 10 years to many decades; in pharmaceuticals, they range from several years to 40 years; in mining machinery, the product is often used in the field for up to 40 years; in the iron and steel industry, the life cycle of an alloy can be hundreds of years. Each industry involved in profitable product sales can determine when a product is at the end of its useful life. This occurs when the profit margin can no longer support the investment. When a company can use the funds more efficiently elsewhere, the product is no longer viable.

(b) Level of Technology in Industry. Each industry has technological leaders. The innovative companies set an industry's technological pace. Those companies that do not keep pace lose market share. In old industries, or under conditions in which a company is the last remaining producer of an obsolete product line (e.g., the only buggy-whip manufacturer left in the business), the need for technological innovation does not exist. For all other corporations, not keeping pace with competition technologically can put the company out of business. One method for establishing the technical level for an industry in question is to examine relevant industry statistics.

Statistics for each industry can be obtained by reviewing 10k reports[1] of specific companies. By doing this, a company can determine which of the competitors it wants to use as models. Occasionally, a specific set of statistical data is obscured by conglomerate corporations. If this is the case, the data can be projected from known data.

To show the variation in R&D spending from industry to industry, review the informa-

[1] 10k reports for a company are obtained from a stockbroker or by writing the company directly.

Industry	1988 Average R&D Budget (% of Sales)	R&D Spending R&D Budget (% of Profit)	Average R&D Budget ($/Employee)
Aerospace	4.4	86.7	4,354.3
Appliances	2.0	35.0	1,642.1
Automotive	3.5	54.6	4,919.7
Building materials and construction	1.8	18.6	2,232.4
Chemicals	3.7	31.8	6,208.8
Computers	11.1	93.7	10,987.8
Conglomerates	3.0	36.0	3,382.3
Containers and packaging	1.1	23.2	1,045.2
Drugs and medical products	9.5	46.7	11,766.2
Electrical	2.4	24.6	2,134.0
Electronics	4.4	57.7	3,561.6
Food and beverages	0.7	9.4	852.4
General manufacturing	1.9	20	1,796.6
Instruments	6.0	122.5	5,129.1
Leisure products	5.0	50.9	5,247.4
Microelectronics	9.6	123.6	7,080.1
Metals and mining	1.2	31.7	1,644.9
Office equipment	1.9	22.3	1,779.4
Oil and gas	0.6	10.7	3,151.6
Paper	1.0	10.3	1,604.0
Personal care products	2.7	38.2	4,154.8
Service industries	1.3	31.8	1,049.9
Special machinery[a]	3.0	76.1	3,276.6
Steel	0.7	56.0	981.0
Telecommunications	5.5	55.9	5,794.5
Textiles	0.8	26.2	651.5
Tools (machine and hand)	2.0	37.6	1,875.5
Software services	9.3	72.3	10,771.6
All-industry average	3.4	41.7	4,465.1

[a] Farm machinery and material handling.

Exhibit 15.2. Examples of R&D spending

tion presented in Exhibit 15.2. Keep in mind that these data are *average* for an industry. A specific company will have variations from the average, and as a matter of fact, these variations are often the result of the corporation's strategy.

(c) Position That a Company Wants to Attain. From the information shown in Exhibit 15.2, it is obvious that each corporation can use statistical data as budgetary guides for scaling its R&D. Combining these guides with corporate strategic considerations, and based on its competitive position in an industry, a corporation can form an R&D policy. In some industries, being second in the marketplace with a superior product makes sense. In others, being second is a guarantee of failure. Product life cycles and technological level combine in some industries (e.g., electronics) to force self-imposed product obsolescence. In other industries (e.g., construction equipment), these factors are less important, and production and service factors weigh more heavily.

Corporate strategic considerations are generally not based on industry averages but on specific competitors. By assembling data from 10k reports and stockholder reports for specific competitors, a company can determine what investment competition is making in technology. Then, based on the company's long-range internal growth goals, the level of technological spending can be set. This level considers all or some of the following:

- The long-range company position in the industry
- Overtaking specific competitors
- Maintaining market share
- A lead or lag position technologically
- Growth in specific market segments
- Quality or value relative to competition
- Technological diversification plans
- New markets for existing technology

The concept is to set or find the existing corporate R&D datum, to reference it against specific competitors, and then to determine the effect of technological spending on corporate growth relative to these competitors.

In companies that are conglomerates, setting the technological policy is difficult. It must be a multilevel policy, segmented by different markets and technologies. Most conglomerate companies divide themselves internally by industry groupings. These groupings are generally divisions of the large company. Each division will have different technological goals based on its competitors; a single ''coherent'' technological growth policy is not possible for a conglomerate.

(d) Risk Involved in Development. Risk is a double-edged sword. There are financial risks involved in every new technological venture, but there are also risks in not pursuing technology. Companies have gone out of business by not keeping level with their competition.

Risk analysis requires sound input data. The data are gathered by the major departments of a company and include the following:

- Development costs (technological)
- Sales projections (marketing)
- Fabrication costs (manufacturing)
- Capital-equipment costs (manufacturing)
- Cash-flow requirements (finance)

Based on the industry's product life cycles, annual forecasts must be made for each of the items cited. These forecasts can range from 3 years for one full life cycle to 10 years or more. Optimistic, pessimistic, and likely cash flows for all balance sheet items are then developed, and probability factors are assigned to each. Technological risk, when integrated with market risk, requires a corporate policy for screening and evaluating ideas. Our goal is to minimize this risk without stifling internal growth.

15.2 PROBLEMS IN ESTABLISHING RESEARCH AND DEVELOPMENT AND ENGINEERING OBJECTIVES. Before technical objectives can be established, corporate objectives must be set. Corporate or group objectives set a clear path for business development. If the path is not defined, technological developments can run counter to desired company growth. Large companies have recognized this need for many years. Small companies, unfortunately, often leave the objectives unspecified. Unspecified objectives can result in technological failure. Without a clear company position and direction, a company defeats itself. Thus, the first step in technical planning is to obtain or set, if need be, the company's objectives. The chief executive officer (CEO) should be consulted in this matter. The second step is development of coherent technological objectives for the following:

- Basic research (if any)
- Development of new products or processes
- Maintenance of existing products, processes, or activities
- Defensive activities in response to competitive thrusts or regulatory requirements

Long-range and short-range objectives can be developed. Long-range objectives are generally in the R&D domain, and short-range objectives in the engineering department's domain.

(a) Basic Requirements of an Objective. All objectives, corporate or technological, have basic requirements. These requirements can be stated as follows:

- Objectives should be realistic; that is, they should be achievable and understandable. A little stretch in a corporate position is within the realm of possibility. Too much stretch in attempting to get a corporation from one level to another in too short a time can be demoralizing or outright defeating. Understanding the corporate position, its finances, its technological level, and its ability to withstand adverse conditions leads to setting realistic objectives. Once set, objectives must be clearly communicated. Tasks, goals, or activities that are not understood cannot be achieved.
- Objectives should be measurable in one or all of the following categories:
  Schedule. The accomplishment of given tasks in a given period. The closer a task is to the "state of the art," the more difficult a schedule projection becomes. This is one of the areas of technological risk.
  Fiscal. A budget is a special fiscal measurement of finances versus time and accomplishments. Other fiscal measurements include sales, profits, and expenditures.
  Quantity. This is an easy measurement if the initial planning is realistic. Quantity measurements include volume, product mix, market share, growth, and productivity. Some quantity measurements are easy to measure and others are difficult.
  Quality. This is a more difficult measurement. It may take years to determine the quality of a new technology or the effect on customers. Of course, quality control "go–no-go" measurements are easier to specify and measure.
- Objectives should be desirable. Corporations and technological groups can set objectives that are not worth achieving—the tendency to re-invent the wheel. Yesterday's projects recur often in industry, because they are easily scheduled and because the results and timing are clearly predictable. Of course, the funds expended on these projects will not be returned. Each project or corporate goal should be able to stand on its own merits.
- Objectives must be assignable. Activities, tasks, or specified results are accomplished

by an individual or a group. If an objective is specified, but it is not possible to say *who* will do the work or be responsible for getting the work done, it is clear that the work will not get done. Corporate objectives relating to new product or process internal growth requirements are in the R&D or engineering departments' domain. Naturally, the entire corporate structure is required to accomplish a successful objective, but one individual or department must have clear responsibility and authority if the objective is to be successful.

Many modern corporations use management by objectives (MBO) to control corporate growth and accomplishments. If MBO is used, the objectives should be negotiated. This negotiation is accomplished among senior managers and the people responsible for the work. Without the negotiation process, used to retain realism in the MBO process, management by edict results. Unfortunately, edicts are not necessarily realistic.

(b) Using Corporate Objectives to Develop Research and Development Budgets. Many corporations are apprehensive about internal growth. The reasons are clear: The mortality of new product or process ideas is high. For this reason, most large and some small corporations have a screening system designed to lessen the risk. Prescreening and business analysis, outlined in another part of the chapter, remove the ideas that do not meet corporate objectives. The remaining ideas that enter technological departments have the following statistical mortality ratios:

- On an average (all-industry average), one out of every three ideas that enters technology will be successful. The funding associated with development of successful products is an average of 28% of the total cost associated with getting products into the marketplace. This 28% covers the cost for all developments and their subsequent elimination in favor of the successful product.
- On an average (all-industry average), one out of every two ideas that enters the marketplace is successful. The funding associated with commercializing the successful product is 60% of the total cost. This cost covers all product entries. Thus, although marketing risks are lower, commercialization costs are higher.
- The remaining 12% of the costs associated with a successful product is used to do the screening and business analysis. This analysis eliminates 90% of the raw ideas evaluated by a company.
- Companies that do not screen their products have a small chance of financial success. Screening concepts are outlined in a succeeding section of the chapter.

(c) Long- and Short-Range Technological Objectives. Long-range corporate technological objectives are based on the position that a company wants to achieve in 3 to 10 years. In the food industry, three years is generally considered a long-range plan. In power generation and energy-related industries, 10-year and longer-range plans are often developed.

Long-range plans of an industry segment look forward to problems and advantages to be faced by that industry. Competitive threats, incursions from other technologies, material shortages, market shifts, growth of existing technologies and markets, internal growth, acquisitions, profitability, inflation, and sales growth are examples of long-range planning considerations. Research and development uses the corporate long-range plan to screen ideas. Ideas that pass through screening and business analysis become development projects or areas for basic research. These projects eventually lead to future sales, profits, and internal growth.

The preceding outline does not imply that R&D cannot contribute to ongoing current products or processes. Of course it does. However, the primary thrust of R&D is the future. Too many industries dissipate their R&D funds on product maintenance. By so doing, these industries block the progress of their company.

The mechanical watch and clock industry, an old industry, did not invest in basic research or new product development to the extent that it should have. When the electronics industry replaced the pendulum with an accurate quartz crystal oscillator, and the escapement and gear train with electronic counters, it was able to build a more accurate, more rugged watch at a lower cost. The development of liquid crystal readouts clinched the future. The mechanical watch, except to collectors and antique dealers, was doomed. If the watch industry had invested in true development, it might have made its own product obsolete and remained a competitive force in the business world.

Engineering departments work on shorter-range projects. Their efforts are generally concentrated on new developments slated for production and on product line maintenance. In some companies, R&D and engineering are combined. These companies are in intermediate- to low-technology areas. In high-technology areas, R&D and engineering are separate departments. Engineering does the bulk of the product maintenance, which keeps products or processes current, and application activities. Some engineering departments work on long-range activities, but the primary thrust of engineering is short range.

Historically, the total annual technical budget for most U.S. companies is divided into three major segments: research and exploration, development (applied research), and technological sustaining funds (product or process).

(i) Research and Exploration. This segment is used to do exploratory investigations, assorted studies, and basic research. Basic research is generally a funded activity performed outside the company by special research organizations. There are exceptions to this rule, but most U.S. companies are uncomfortable with in-company research.

In basic research, unlike applied research or development, the technology is not known; thus, the studies cannot be scheduled. These studies can be likened to chartering an explorer to go into unknown territory. The explorer may have a mission to find land suitable for a farm community in the wilderness. Setting off on the mission, he does not know what type of terrain or hostile environment he will face. Basic research is similar. It can be controlled financially in a staircase manner but not with a schedule, or, by definition, it would not be basic research. Staircase control issues a given quantity of money for a given period. If the researcher and the company feel that progress is being made, additional funds and time are alloted to the problem. This process continues until either a successful technology is developed or agreement is reached that the task must be abandoned.

Because basic research cannot be scheduled and results cannot be predicted, most corporations minimize the budget for this function. History shows that the technological growth of an industry is directly related to basic research. Without a continuing investment in this area by the government and corporations, the United States has fallen behind other industrial countries. Historically, funds allocated to basic research in the United States have been gradually reduced each year since the end of World War II. This is not true for other industrial countries and evolving Third World countries.

(ii) Development. In development, the technologies are known. Some technologies are in rapid flux, and the state of the art is shifting rapidly. In others, the technology is

stable and often old art. Product and process development uses a mixture of these technologies, but all projects can be scheduled using the normal planning tools (program evaluation and review technique [PERT], GANTT, critical-path method [CMP], etc.)

When the development activity is close to the state of the art, the scheduled time and budget are more risky. When the development activity is a combination of new and old art, the risks are reduced.

An example of a project with old and new technology is the development of the atomic submarine. The nuclear energy system was new technology, which at that time was the leading edge of the state of the art. Hull design and the crew's quarters were older art. The new art faced the question of how small an atomic pile could be made and still operate, or how much shielding was necessary for the safety of the crew. When these areas were estimated, statistics and probability theory were applied to the time estimates. For other areas, routine estimating techniques were acceptable. Combinations of old and new technology in product or process developments account for the development risks. These risks are the potential cause of developmental failures.

In any event, when the technology is known, development costs and time are estimable. Schedules and budgets can be prepared, and project-control techniques can be applied. It is for this reason that industry concentrates its resources on development. The ratio of development to research is approximately 6:1. New products and processes are the output of development. These developments are the generators of future profit and internal corporate growth.

Development funds can be used defensively to react to competitive threats that might affect a company's market share. Analysis of competitive products or processes, shifts in technology, and monitoring the technological aspects of the marketplace are areas that use parts of the development budget.

(iii) Technological Sustaining Funds. Funds expended in this segment are used to keep existing products from becoming obsolete or for product or process application activities. The bulk of these funds is spent in engineering. The activities include the following:

- Minor modification of the product or process through improvements and/or correction
- Scrap reduction
- Productivity improvement
- Value analysis and cost improvement
- Application studies for interface with other products
- Liaison with production
- Documentation
- Liaison with marketing
- Analysis of technological customer needs

(d) Technological Budget-Segmentation Ratios. In most companies in the United States, budgetary funds are segmented among the technological areas as follows:

Research and exploration	0%–10%
Development	20%–35%
Sustaining	55%–80%

When a company is close to the edge of the state of the art in its technology, it will,

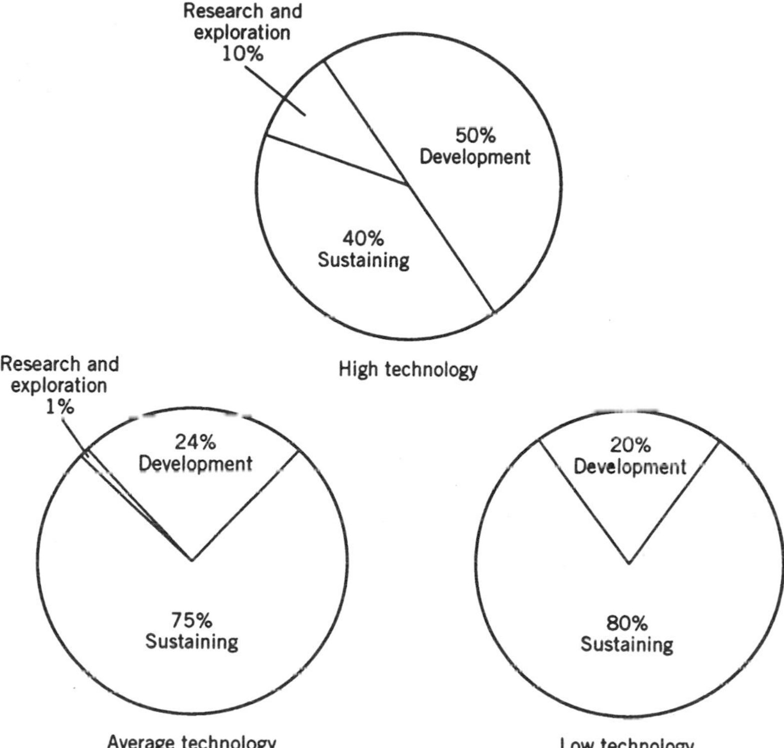

Exhibit 15.3. Budget segmentations

as a result of the environment, spend more money in new technology areas. Research and development departments will be large, and engineering departments either completely submerged in R&D or of equal status.

Companies with older technology will spend small percentages of their funds in R&D and major percentages in engineering. In those companies, R&D is either a nonexistent department or it is submerged in the engineering department.

Three budget segmentations are shown in Exhibit 15.3. One is for high-technology companies involved in such industries as electronics, instruments, pharmaceuticals, and specialty chemicals; another is for low-technology companies involved in such industries as heavy machinery and paper; and the third is for average-technology companies involved in such industries as leisure products and automotive products.

15.3 DEVELOPING A TECHNOLOGICAL BUDGET. To develop the technological budget for either R&D or engineering, it is necessary to use a selectivity principle. Scarcity of technical personnel, equipment, and facilities requires some approach to optimization of these rare and costly areas. Improved engineering and R&D productivity will result.

The general concepts required for project selection include the following:

- Project screening
- Setting project priorities and evaluating finances
- Risk analysis and final project selection

Once these steps have been taken, a budget can be assembled using zero-based concepts. The technique is to assign a priority one first, two next, and so on, until a predetermined level is reached. This predetermined level can be obtained historically from head count and other considerations or by analysis of successful competitors' funding.

A word of caution—it is impossible or inefficient to attempt to control 100% of all development project budgets and schedules. One hundred percent control is a poor use of management time; it eventually throttles creativity. A degree of technical freedom is essential to morale and productivity in technical departments. This does not mean that 100% of the budget cannot be accounted for. Hundreds of little projects and intermediate-sized projects can be funded and accounted for. It is desirable and good management to control 20% of the projects that account for 80% of the budget. This selectivity principle, the 80/20 rule, was developed by Vilfredo Pareto. In studying the wealth distribution of Europeans, Pareto discovered that 80% of the wealth of a country was vested in the hands of 20% of the population. Understanding this truncated or skewed distribution permits its application to many activities. It leads to effective management by exception.

Pareto's Law can be applied to cost reduction. It is senseless to worry about a large number of such low-cost items as nuts, screws, and bolts in an assembly. Good cost-reduction efforts concentrate on the 20% of the parts that accounts for 80% of the cost. (We are using 80/20 as an example—90/10, or 70/30 are possible.)

A budget based on screening and funding the few large projects that account for approximately 80% of the total development costs can be well planned. The remaining 20% is spread over studies, small projects, fire-fighting activities, and so forth. At the end of the year, all costs are accounted for. Small and intermediate projects can be used for manpower leveling. The peaks and valleys associated with manpower needs can be minimized. Exploratory studies can lead to future large development projects. It is a good idea to perform a Pareto analysis in your company to find the distribution.

(a) Project Screening. Once corporate objectives have been outlined, a clear technological path can be established. A project, process, or product can then be subjected to a screen. The screen must include technological, manufacturing, marketing, financial, and other considerations needed to keep the company in a healthy condition relative to its competition. In some industries, one or more of these areas may be overriding. It is therefore necessary to develop a screen that is peculiar to your company. This is accomplished by variable weight for the critical factors. Some of the factors used by companies are shown in Exhibit 15.4.

A screening sheet developed for the preliminary assessment of a power transmission company's raw product ideas is shown in Exhibit 15.5. In this sheet, the factors of importance to the company have been given greater weight factors. These factors were developed by each department head through negotiation with the CEO of the company. They emphasize corporate objectives in the screening process. Not all of the factors outlined in Exhibit 15.4 were considered important for this company. When the projects are screened, each department considers the agreed-to factors and decides whether they represent an excellent (2 ×) weight, a good (1 ×) weight, or a poor (0) weight. By multiplying the opportunity assessment by the importance factor, the department can arrive at a relative score. When all departments have acted, the total scores are compared and negotiated, and a minimum level is agreed upon.

In this screening activity, each department has a veto right if the product is deemed to be unacceptable. For example, if finance cannot show sufficient profitability in initial

Technical
Regulatory requirements (Occupational Safety and Health Administration, Food and Drug Administration, Environmental Protection Agency, etc.)
Likelihood of technical success, risk
Customer's requirements
Development cost
Development time
In-house skills, availability, and capability
Resources and facilities required for development
Patent potential
Historic technological corporate strengths
Project fit with ongoing projects
Cost reduction

Manufacturing or Operations
Capital requirements
Existing facility, availability, capability, and needs
Raw-material availability
Regulatory influences resulting from new manufacturing processes
Manufacturing safety
Manufacturability of the new product
Quality considerations
Productivity variance of the new product

Financial
Profitability and return on investment
Net present worth
Internal rate of return
Profitability index (capital considerations)
Payback period

Financial (cont)
Risk
Asset utilization
Cash flow

Marketing and Sales
Customer needs
Compatibility with other products or processes
Size of potential market
Corporate image leverage in the marketplace
Ability to market the product
Market trends and product growth potential
Market share and trends
Market risk
Pricing strategy and competitors' pricing
Product-line fit
Domestic and international markets
Stocking attractiveness
Effect on current customers
Sales force, increases or decreases

Legal
Warranties
Liabilities
Regulatory compliance
Patents/trademarks/copyrights
Unified commercial code considerations
Contractual commitments

Strategic
Meets long-range objectives
Meets short-range objectives
Timing needs, seasonal/contract/competitive considerations
Overall corporate image

Exhibit 15.4. Factors used to screen products

considerations, legal is convinced that there are liability problems, manufacturing is sure of construction safety difficulties, or technology is concerned about product safety, the product will not be pursued even if the screening score is very high. Naturally, these objections must be verified in order to keep the screening activity from becoming a political process.

On the screening sheet, veto factors are asterisked. Zero score for those factors automatically eliminates the project from development consideration. Thus, to pass through the screen, a product must attain a score above minimum and must not have zero for any of the veto factors.

A word of caution—the screening sheet is a preliminary estimate. Any product that passes through the initial screen will be subjected to a more detailed financial study. This financial study requires sales forecasts, production-cost estimates, and all of the data associated with the preparation of a product or process for the marketplace. The effort to truly evaluate a candidate project is time consuming. It requires a large amount of input

Project: Departmental Considerations	Importance Multiplier	Opinion Factor[a] E 2 ×	G 1 ×	P 0	Total Score
Financial Profitability[b]	3				[b]
Burden absorption	2				
Payback period	1				
Risk	2				
Cash flow requirements	3				
Technical Regulatory requirements[b]	3				[b]
Likelihood of success	3				
Development cost	2				
Effect on corporate projects	1				
In-house skills utilization	2				
Manufacturing Manufacturing safety[b]	3				[b]
Capital requirements	3				
Facility utilization	2				
Raw material availability	2				
Manufacturability	1				
Marketing and Sales Market risk[b]	3				[b]
Customer needs	2				
Marketability	2				
Market size	2				
Effects on customers	2				
Legal and Strategic Warranties and liabilities[b]	3				[b]
Patent potential	2				
Contractual commitment	3				
Corporate image	2				
Seasonal requirements	1				
Total[c]					

[a] E = excellent, G = good, P = poor.
[b] Zero score in these factors vetoes the project.
[c] Minimum acceptable score without veto is 70.

Exhibit 15.5. Project-screening sheet

data. Getting the data is the problem. The evaluation, although mildly complicated, can be computerized or organized in a way that reduces the evaluation to a set of predetermined calculations. A typical filled-out screening sheet is shown in Exhibit 15.6. In Exhibit 15.6, the corporate level of 70, negotiated with the CEO, has been met. When scores are close to 70, the project should be reviewed critically. The score itself is not a priority-ranking system.

Once the financial analysis is complete, additional concepts will be screened out. The few survivors represent real opportunities for future corporate technological development.

(b) Setting Project Priorities and Evaluating Finances. After projects have been screened, the high-cost projects are subjected to financial analysis. This is an intelligent use of Pareto's Law. It is too costly and inefficient to subject all projects to a financial screen, but 20% of the projects that account for 80% of the technical budget must be evaluated. The only exception to this rule are projects involving the Environmental Protection Agency (EPA), Occupational Safety and Health Administration (OSHA), Food and Drug Administration (FDA), or other government agency requirements that are mandated by law. These projects must be done if a company is to remain in business. Other mandated projects may develop from competitive threats.

The basic theory that is followed in setting priorities is, in order:

1. All mandated projects
2. The most financially sound projects. These projects are judged on the basis of one of the following: net present value (NPV), also known as net present worth; internal rate of return (IRR); or profitability index (PI). These indexes will be described in greater detail in this section and are discussed in later chapters. Simple payback period considerations, once used exclusively by industry, are no longer considered valid, since they do not take into account the time value of money.
3. Research and exploration projects. These projects cannot be planned or scheduled, but they represent technological opportunities for future growth potential. Many corporations simply set a fixed percentage of the budget for this function. These projects can be used as fill-in work for scientists or engineers. They tend to level manpower and create an atmosphere of technological freedom for the staff. In so doing, the gain in motivational involvement often carries into the other projects.
4. Sustaining projects. Although this is the largest segment of the engineering and R&D budget, it is the easiest to fund. Based on current products, processes, and technological interfaces, a fixed percentage of sales can be set aside for this function.

Financial decisions are based on the time value of money and on risk analysis. Older techniques involving payback period are not currently used. Definitions of payback period, NPV, IRR, and PI are given on the following pages.

(i) Definitions. *Payback period* is defined as the number of years it takes a firm to recover its original investment from net returns before depreciation but after taxes. Unfortunately, the time value of money is not considered.

Net present value is a discounted cash-flow technique. The technique is implemented by finding the present value of the cash in any period and discounting it at the cost of

Project: Copier Departmental Considerations	Importance Multiplier	Opinion Factors[a] E 2 ×	 G 1 ×	 P 0	Total Score
Financial Profitability[b]	3	√			6[b]
Burden absorption	2	√			4
Payback period	1		√		1
Risk	2		√		2
Cash-flow requirements	3		√		3
Technical Regulatory requirements[b]	3	√			6[b]
Likelihood of success	3	√			6
Development cost	2		√		2
Effect on corporate projects	1			√	0
In-house skills utilization	2		√		2
Manufacturing Manufacturing safety[b]	3	√			6[b]
Capital requirements	3		√		3
Facility utilization	2		√		2
Raw material availability	2			√	0
Manufacturability	1	√			2
Marketing and Sales Market risk[b]	3		√		3[b]
Customer needs	2	√			4
Marketability	2		√		2
Market size	2	√			4
Effects on customers	2	√			4
Legal and Strategic Warranties and liabilities[b]	3		√		3[b]
Patent potential	2		√	√	0
Contractual commitment	3		√		3
Corporate image	2	√			4
Seasonal requirements	1	√			2
Total[c]					74

[a] E = excellent, G = good, P = poor.
[b] Zero score in these factors vetoes the project.
[c] Minimum acceptable score without veto is 70.

Exhibit 15.6. Completed project-screening sheet

capital. Each period's present value is summed for the investment, and then the initial cost outlay of the investment is subtracted. If the NPV is positive, the project should be accepted. If projects are mutually exclusive, that is, that only one can be funded, then the one with the highest NPV is accepted.

$$NPV = \left[\frac{R_1}{(1 + k)^1} + \frac{R_2}{(1 + k)^2} + \cdots \frac{R_n}{(1 + k)^n}\right] - C$$

where R = cash flow for the period, k = cost of capital, and C = cost outlay.

In *internal rate of return,* the interest rate is found for the specific condition in which the sum of the present value is equal to the cost outlay for the project. An interest rate, sometimes referred to as the *hurdle rate,* is used. Corporations often use a hurdle rate that reflects the cost of capital and historic criteria. In this method, which involves trial-and-error procedures or a computer program, all projects should be selected above the hurdle rate. If projects are mutually exclusive, select the project with the highest IRR.

$$C = \left[\frac{R_1}{(1 + r)^1} + \frac{R_2}{(1 + r)^2} + \cdots \frac{R_n}{(1 + r)^n}\right]$$

where r = IRR.

The *profitability index,* sometimes referred to as the *benefit–cost ratio,* is calculated by dividing the sum of the present value for the project or investment by the required investment outlay. If projects are mutually exclusive, choose the highest PI.

$$PI = \frac{\left[\frac{R_1}{(1 + k)^1} + \frac{R_2}{(1 + k)^2} + \cdots \frac{R_n}{(1 + k)^n}\right]}{\text{cost}}$$

where cost = investment outlay. When the outlay occurs over more than one year, the cost includes the present value of future outlays.

A graphic example of NPV is as follows: Assume that a series of investments in all aspects of a product development have been outlined for seven years. These include R&D, engineering, plant equipment tooling, cost of sales, and other expenses. Also assume that sales, amortization, royalties, and cash inflows are estimated for the same period. Then, after income tax and nontax capital inflows and outflows for the period have been established, all cash flows for the product can be calculated and annualized. These data can be organized by filling out the worksheet provided in Exhibit 15.7.

The present value (PV) of cash flows in the future can be obtained by applying a compound interest factor appropriate to the period to each of the annualized results calculated in line 25 of Exhibit 15.7. These factors are obtained from the following equation:

$$PV \text{ (factor)} = \frac{1}{(1 + i)^n}$$

where i = interest rate based on the company's cost of capital and n = the time period in future years when the investment cash flow is being examined.

Client:								
Project: IRR: %	Amount (in $1,000s) Fiscal Year							
Cash Outflow								
1. R&D expense								
2. Market introduction and launching costs								
3. Plant equipment and tooling expense								
4. Cost of sales								
5. Incremental operating expenses								
6. Other								
7. Cash-outflow total (1 through 6)								
Cash Inflow								
8. Sales								
9. Amortized expenses and royalties								
10. Other								
11. Cash inflow total (8 through 10)								
Before-Tax Cash Flow (No Capital)								
12. Line 11 minus line 7								
After-Tax Cash Flow (No Capital)								
13. Income tax at 48%								
14. Line 12 minus line 13								
Capital Expenditures Outflow								
15. Changes in capital								
16. Plant equipment and tools capital changes								
17. Working-capital increases								
18. Total capital (15 through 17)								
19. Line 14 minus line 18								
Capital and Other Inflow								
20. Working-capital decreases								
21. Residual net assets at end of project								
22. Depreciation								
23. Income tax credit								
24. Sum lines 20 to 23								
Net Cash Flow In–Out								
25. Line 19 plus line 24								

Exhibit 15.7. Emzee Associates worksheet

Applying this equation to n time periods at various interest rates generates Exhibit 15.8.

For example, $1 million of income eight years from today at an interest rate of 20% is worth $232,600 today. This figure is obtained by multiplying $1 million by the PV factor for 20% in eight years ($1,000,000 × 0.2326 = $232,600). The interest rate is based on your company's cost of capital and some risk factors. The techniques for evaluating cost of capital are discussed in a later section.

If we assume that a product was evaluated using the annualized worksheet in Exhibit

n (years)	5%	10%	15%	20%	30%	40%
1	0.9524	0.9091	0.8696	0.8333	0.7692	0.7143
2	0.9070	0.8264	0.7561	0.6944	0.5917	0.5102
3	0.8638	0.7513	0.6575	0.5787	0.4552	0.3644
4	0.8227	0.6830	0.5718	0.4823	0.3501	0.2603
5	0.7835	0.6209	0.4972	0.4019	0.2693	0.1859
6	0.7462	0.5645	0.4323	0.3349	0.2072	0.1328
7	0.7106	0.5132	0.3759	0.2791	0.1594	0.0949
8	0.6768	0.4665	0.3269	0.2326	0.1226	0.0678

Exhibit 15.8. $(1/1 + i)^n$ Present-value factor

15.8, and that the data start one year from today, then the possible cash flows that might show on line 25 are:

Dollars (in 1,000s)						
(400)	(250)	100	300	600	1,000	400

The values shown in parentheses are negative values. Is this project sound if the cost of capital is 20%?

The vector diagram shown in Exhibit 15.9 will be used to describe the calculation. It is, of course, possible to get special-purpose calculators or computer programs to do this calculation today, but our purpose is understanding. Once you are familiar with the process, the actual calculation of net present worth (NPW), or NPV, is very easy. The problem is getting the background data. These data involve forecasts of R&D, engineering, manufacturing, marketing, and finance in order to evaluate the project realistically.

The investments in Exhibit 15.9 are laid out at their appropriate time interval and are shown as vectors. All cash outflows are plotted negatively; all cash inflows are plotted positively. Simple addition of these vectors assumes that the interest rate cost of capital is zero. In this example, we will have assumed an interest rate of 20%. For 20%, the PV factors are obtained from Exhibit 15.8. They are shown at the bottom of the graph. Multiplying the money for the period by its PV factor yields the PV or discounted cash flow of the period. If these vectors are added, the result is called net present worth, or net present value. This is done on the origin of the graph. In our example, the NPW is $383,320 positive; thus, the investment is excellent. If the NPW were negative, the return would be less than 20%. Since it is positive, the return is more than 20%.

If a higher cost of capital were used in the example, the NPW would be smaller. Eventually, a point would be reached at which NPW = 0. At this point, the cost of capital is given a special name, internal rate of return. For this example, the IRR = 38.53%.

All of the time-value-of-money methods (NPW, IRR, and PI) are useful for ranking projects. Assuming that the project has passed through the screen, financial analysis can be used to rank projects of first priority, then second, and so forth. Where projects are mutually exclusive, these rankings can be used to select the optimum use of funds.

(c) Risk Analysis and Final Project Selection. Before final project selection, it is often important to determine the project risk. Risk analysis can be done scientifically, or

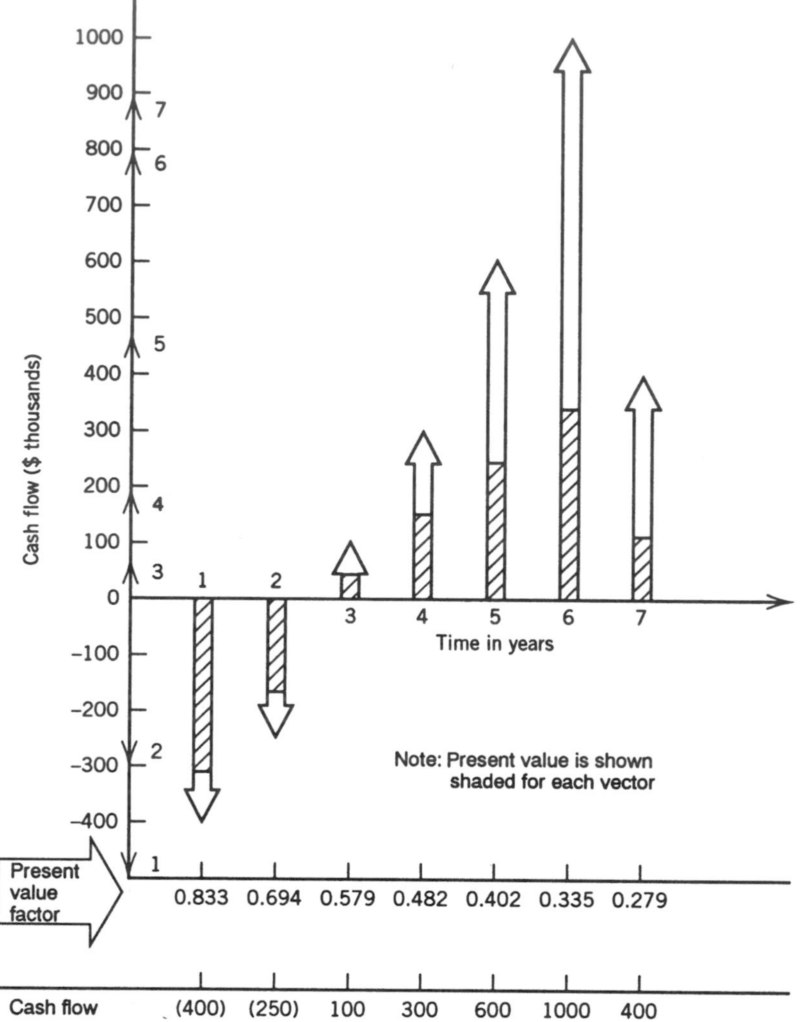

Exhibit 15.9. Net present worth calculation

it can be based on experience. When experience is used to evaluate risk, a variable cost-of-capital technique is common. When scientific methods are used, either Monte Carlo or sensitivity analysis can be employed. It is obvious, however, that a single calculation of NPW is only as good as the input data. These data involve projections of all cash flows into the future. It must be obvious that the chance of accuracy in a single calculation is small. Risk analysis brings credibility to the evaluation.

When experience is used to assess the project risk, different cost-of-capital rates are employed. The *cost of capital* is normally the discount rate used in capital budgeting. This rate varies from industry to industry. Average cost of capital includes a debt-to-equity ratio. For example, assume a 20% debt, a 16.5% cost of equity (net worth), and a 9% cost of debt. The average cost of capital is (20% × 9%) + (80% × 16.5%) = 15%.

One method for normalizing risk is to apply different discount rates to different projects.

Higher-risk projects are given a higher discount rate. Conversely, lower-risk projects are given a lower discount rate. These data can be obtained historically by product line or by industry segment.

Thus, low-risk projects might use a 15% cost of capital, intermediate-risk projects might use 18%, and high-risk projects might use 25%. These factors must be determined by experienced analysts. Even so, the technique has limited appeal.

A more scientific risk analysis is based on a multiple estimate—Monte Carlo analysis, which uses statistical information—or on a sensitivity analysis.

(i) Monte Carlo Analysis. The principles are simple. For each cash flow of Exhibit 15.7, three or more estimates are obtained. These cost estimates shape the annual characteristic curve of the cash flow for that activity. Optimistic, pessimistic, and most likely estimates are normal input data. The problem is bounded by these estimates, some of which are cross-coupled (e.g., sales and manufacturing cost). When one is specified, the other is also specified within some known relationship.

It is possible to do an NPW calculation for all optimistic and all pessimistic conditions, but these data would not be valuable since they are unlikely events. An alternate approach is to divide the data into regions, say 1 to 5, and then to use random number generators for each cash-flow curve. This is shown symbolically in Exhibit 15.10. Cross-coupling is also shown. Once the curves are specified and the data have been zoned, it is possible to generate random numbers for each activity by year and then to calculate NPW for that data. Repeating the process 100 or 1,000 times will yield a range of NPW values that are likely to occur. Computer programs for this process are available. Again, the problem is in getting the input data, not in the actual calculation. The calculation, although cumbersome, is reduced to a routine.

An alternative approach is to do the single NPW calculation with the best data available. Then perturbations or shifts of the data are impressed on the calculation. Some of these data shifts will be insignificant to the NPW; others will alter the NPW significantly. This is a sensitivity analysis. It helps a financial analyst determine areas that should be carefully re-estimated or controlled during project evolution.

Monte Carlo and sensitivity analysis can be applied to all of the financial analysis tools (IRR, NPW, and PI). They demonstrate the strength or weakness in a project. Obviously, projects that run into the poor category easily should be avoided. Final project selection can be guided by profit impact and risk.

(d) Relationship of Budget and Schedule. Technical budgets, both engineering and R&D, are developed from project manpower and material needs. When these needs are correlated with the scheduled activities on a time base, a dollar-versus-time project budget can be developed. The normal techniques involved in scheduling are PERT and a newer form of bar chart called mechanized GANTT. In both methods, a critical path is developed for the project. If PERT is used, a bar chart must still be developed to display the project's real-time manpower and material needs.

To illustrate the budgeting process, we will examine a simple project for the design development fabrication assembly and test of a developmental unit. Budget for this project will be constructed using mechanized GANTT planning concepts. The concepts of PERT can be directly converted to mechanized GANTT charts. These concepts involve critical path, slack time, and interface data applied to a time base.

Realistic planning and scheduling concepts require negotiated estimates. We will assume that the data shown in Exhibit 15.11, the input data for planning, were negotiated

Client:

Project: IRR:	Amount (in $1000s) Fiscal Year						
	1	2	3	4	5	6	7
Cash Outflow							
1. R&D expense	$	$					
2. Market introduction and launching costs			$				
3. Plant equipment and tooling expense		$	$				
4. Cost of sales							
5. Incremental operating expenses							
6. Other							
7. Cash outflow total (1 through 6)							Cross–coupling
Cash Inflow							
8. Sales							
9. Amortized expenses							
10. Other							
11. Cash inflow total (8 through 10)							
Before-Tax Cash Flow (No Capital)							
12. Line 11 minus line 7							

Exhibit 15.10. Emzee Associates worksheet

Project: IRR:	Amount (in $1000s) Fiscal Year						
	1	2	3	4	5	6	7
After-Tax Cash Flow (No Capital) 13. Income tax at 48% 14. Line 12 minus line 13							
Capital Expenditures Outflow 15. Changes in Capital 16. Plant equipment and tools capital changes 17. Working capital increases 18. Total capital (15 through 17) 19. Line 14 minus line 18							
Capital and Other Inflow 20. Working capital decreases 21. Residual net assets at end of project 22. Depreciation 23. Income tax credit 24. Sum lines 20 to 23							
Net Cash Flow In–Out 25. Lines 19 plus line 24							

Exhibit 15.10. *(Continued)*

Code	Task	Activity Interface	Span Time (Months)	Manpower Estimate (Man-Months)	Activity Cost	Cost of Materials
A	Design concept	None	3	3E 6D	$15,000	$ 500
B	Design calculations	None	2	4E	$ 8,000	—
C	Design component tests	None	1	2T 1D 1E	$ 6,000	$ 250
D	Design layouts	100% A	3	6D	$ 9,000	—
		100% B				
		100% C				
E	Detail parts	50% D 75%	2	4D	$ 4,000	—
F	Check layout and parts	100% D	1	1 E	$ 2,000	—
		50% E 50%				
		50% F 25%				
G	Purchase components	100% A	3	—		$10,500
H	Fabricate parts	100% E	2	8M	$10,000	$ 3,500
I	Assemble unit	100% G	2	4T 2M	$ 7,500	$ 1,000
		50% H 50%				
J	Test unit	100% I	1	1T 1E	$ 3,250	$ 1,000
Total					$64,750	$16,750
Total project						$81,500

Exhibit 15.11. Task table

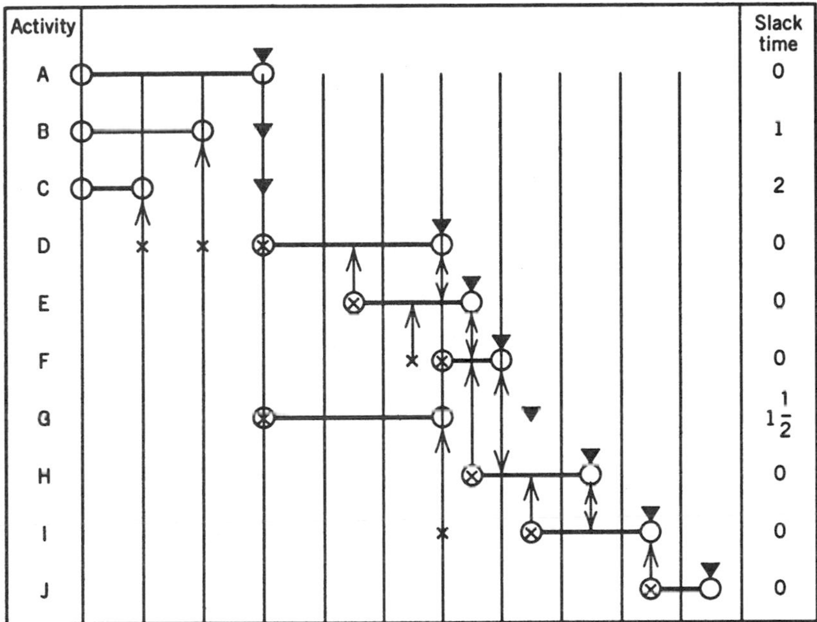

Exhibit 15.12. Project mechanized Gantt chart

with the task leader assigned to each of the coded tasks. This method of getting input data from the people responsible for the work produces commitment and realism in the estimates. If an estimate is too "high," the manager can negotiate it downward. If the task timing or manpower demands are unrealistic, the task leader can negotiate for more time or manpower. With both parties attempting to develop honest input data, the likelihood of a realistic schedule is higher. Schedules that have been established by edict lack commitment and ultimately will fall short of the mark. The manager cannot lose by this negotiation—he or she will gain in the likelihood of project success.

Referring to the data in Exhibit 15.11, task leaders estimated the manpower, span time, and raw materials required to accomplish their task. The project manager developed the interface requirements based on his or her knowledge of the project. Where no interface is shown, activities can be started immediately. Where interfaces are shown, they constrain the dependent activities. The data in this exhibit are used to develop mechanized GANTT schedules, manpower time histograms, and baseline project budgets.

The following symbols are used to develop the mechanized GANTT chart shown in Exhibit 15.12:

- The arrow pointing upward points to the interface constraint.
- The "X" locates a possible constrained activity start. If several X's are located on an activity's plan line, the last X constrains the start of the dependent activity.
- The "O" is used as a start or stop milestone for each activity.
- The line connecting milestones uses real project span time. Thus, a three-month span-time activity would have a milestone at the initial start and another milestone at a

location three months away. The connecting line joins the milestones for the activity's planned duration.

- When 100% is used as an interface, the constrained activity requires that *all* of the constraining activity's work be completed *before* the planned start of that activity (see Exhibit 15.11). When several X constraints exist on a constrained activity line, the last constraining activity dominates. Thus, "100% A" on activity G means that activity G cannot start until activity A is completed. Activity D has three constraints, and the dominant activity in this case is activity A. Thus, activity D cannot start before activity A is completed.
- Where partial constraints are used, they must be followed by a completion constraint requirement. Thus, in activity E, the partial constraint "50% D 75%" means that part drawings can be started when half of the design layouts have been completed. Activity E cannot go beyond its 75% point until *all* of the layouts have been completed. Partial constraints always involve some form of synchronous work between the constraining and constrained activities.
- The arrow pointing downward shows the completion requirement for partial constraints. In Exhibit 15.12, it shows where the end of activity D must meet activity E. Synchronous activities occur between D and E, between E and F, and between H and I.
- The solid triangle denotes the latest time an activity can be completed. It is the same as T_L in a PERT chart. If the triangle is directly over the end milestone, the activity is critical; it has zero slack. If the triangle is displaced from the end milestone, the activity has slack. Slack is developed by multiple constraints. Where several X constraints exist on an activity line, the last one controls the constrained activity start. The other X containing activities have slack equal to the space between this dominant X and the X being considered.

It is possible to use other symbols for the mechanized GANTT chart development, but these were chosen for specific reasons. For example, the "O" is used as a planned milestone start and stop. A solid "O" is used for actual historic start and stop activity milestones. In this way, project control and historic data can be obtained from the same graph. (The solid "O" symbol will be developed further when budget management is discussed.

The data of Exhibit 15.11 are used to develop the project schedule. This mechanized GANTT chart (Exhibit 15.12) shows the interface, span time, critical path, and slack path activities. It is generated using the symbols just described. Once the activities are charted, slack is developed from bottom-up assessment of the multiple interface constraints. If slack cannot be established, the activity is critical. The critical path is A, D, E, F, H, I, S.

A manpower histogram, shown in Exhibit 15.13, is developed by placing the Exhibit 15.11 manpower estimates in time synchronization with the activities displayed in Exhibit 15.12. The histogram developed assumes linear manpower loading. Thus, the designers and the engineer are displayed linearly over the three-month time span of activity A. The high peak in the first week of the program can be eased by using some of the slack associated with activity C. Activities E, H, I, and J start in midmonth. The people assigned to these tasks are shown phased in the manpower histograms in their proper time slots.

To develop the project budget, costs for the skills shown in Exhibit 15.14 are added vertically for each month of the manpower histogram (Exhibit 15.13). In the first week

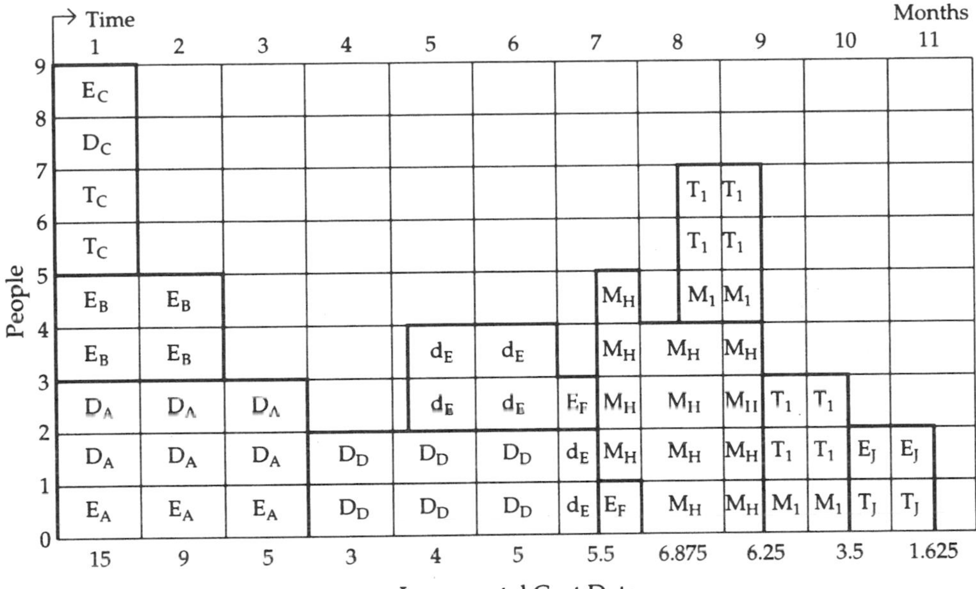

Exhibit 15.13. Manpower histogram

Skill	Code	Cost per Week
Engineer	E	$2,000
Machinist	M	$1,250
Technician	T	$1,250
Designer	D	$1,500
Draftsman	d	$1,000

Exhibit 15.14. Skill cost table

of the project, manpower utilization costs are $15,000. In the next week, they are $9,000, and so forth. Incremental weekly costs are added in this manner to develop the information shown in the incremental row. These costs are then added cumulatively to form the next row of Exhibit 15.15. The project baseline budget is a plot of the labor costs. Material costs from Exhibit 15.11 are synchronized in the correct time frame. When the material and labor budgets are added together, a total budget is obtained. This budget is shown in Exhibit 15.15.

15.4 PREPARING A DEPARTMENTAL BUDGET.

Technical departmental budgets are the summation of all of the project budgets, all R&D allocations, all sustaining engineering, and all contract R&D on engineering activity. The corporation provides all of the funding, with the exception of contract funds.

The total technical department budget reflects an assortment of factors that are used to develop burden rates. These factors include all direct project charges, administrative charges, holidays, vacations, sick leave, positive or negative allocations, fixed expenses, controllable supplies, travel, reproduction, materials, and miscellaneous services.

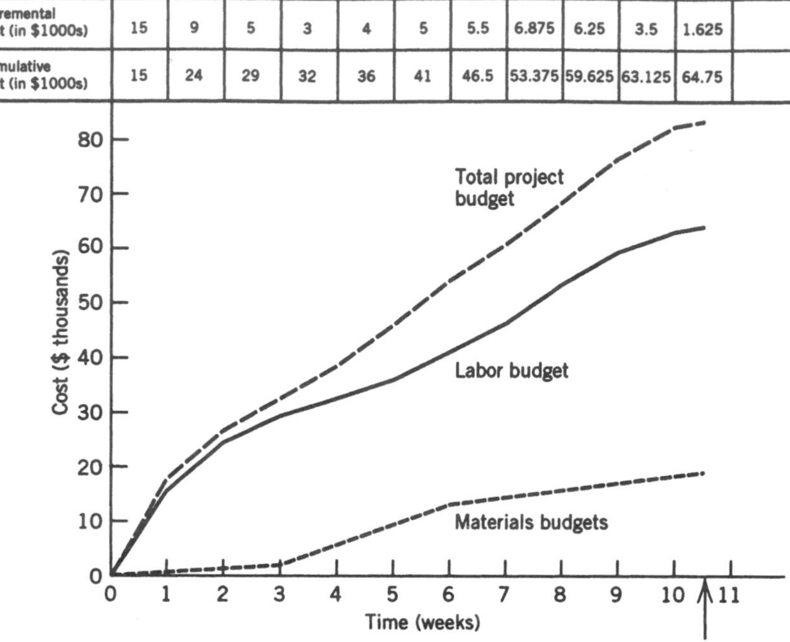

Incremental cost (in $1000s)	15	9	5	3	4	5	5.5	6.875	6.25	3.5	1.625
Cumulative cost (in $1000s)	15	24	29	32	36	41	46.5	53.375	59.625	63.125	64.75

Exhibit 15.15. Total budget

To calculate the direct departmental costs, simply add all of the chargeable project-activity expenses and divide by the chargeable hours. To calculate the burden rate, add administrative overhead, allocations, and service charges to project activity costs and divide by the chargeable hours.

(a) Gross Expenses. Direct chargeable departmental expenses (gross expenses) include the following:

- Labor expenses
  - Salaries
  - Benefits
- Controllable expenses
  - Supplics
  - Travel
  - Reproduction
  - Services
  - Miscellaneous project expenses

Once these expenses have been tabulated for the department, the chargeable hours are calculated.

Chargeable hours generally are assumed to be 2,080 hours per year per person minus the following:

- Holidays
- Sick leave

- Vacations (variable, based on length of service)
- Special, nonchargeable projects or meetings
- Administrative duties for working supervisors

When the chargeable hours have been calculated for each individual, the total departmental hours are calculated—dividing direct departmental expenses by chargeable hours will yield the direct rate.

(b) Burden Rate. Burden is based on nondirect charges. The burdens include the following:

- Interdepartmental allocation costs
- Development overhead costs
- Project administrative expenses
- Secretarial expenses (department)
- Department administrative expenses
- Miscellaneous services and administration expenses for the department

When the burdens have been calculated for the department, they are added to the direct departmental chargeable expenses. This new total is divided by the chargeable hours to determine the burden rate.

These calculations are illustrated in Exhibits 15.16 through 15.18.

There is a major flaw in the concept of burden rate. The flaw develops because the rate is an average for the department. If several major projects are pursued each year, and if *all* of the high-salaried people work on the first priority project and all of the lower-salaried people on the third priority project, the actual project costs are masked. In contract engineering or contract R&D work, the customer for the first project is getting a bargain, but the customer for the third project is obviously overpaying.

Because of this flaw, many departments build project budgets directly from manpower histograms. Actual manpower costs are used in this concept. Burden rates are added to these project budgets to determine the project's ''real'' cost.

Direct Expense	Amount
Salaries	$1,359,990
Employee benefits	339,998
Total labor expense	$1,699,988
Department supplies	$ 58,500
Travel	94,500
Reproduction	27,000
Consultant services	202,500
Project materials	94,500
Miscellaneous expenses	18,000
Total controllable expense	$ 495,000
Total laboratory expense	$2,194,988

Exhibit 15.16. Electrical laboratory annual direct chargeable expenses

Name	Available Hours[a]	Vacation Hours	Special[b] Meetings	Project Administration	Chargeable Project Hours
Walker	1920	120	80	60	1,660
Smith	1920	40	40	—	1,840
Badistella	1920	80	40	—	1,800
Jones	1920	120	80	—	1,720
Pocratsky	1920	160	24	—	1,736
Delmastro	1920	80	24	—	1,816
Hermone	1920	160	120	400	1,240
VanDerBokke	1920	120	60	120	1,620
Devine	1920	80	80	60	1,700
McCarten	1920	120	120	120	1,560
Gupta	1920	120	60	60	1,680
Goldstein	1920	120	24	—	1,776
Total					20,148

[a] 52 weeks × 40 hours/week = 2080 hours annually, minus holidays (10 days/year × 8 hours = 80 hours/year), minus sick leave (10 days/year = 80 hours/year). Total annual hours = 1920.
[b] Company divisional meetings and training meetings (seminars).

Exhibit 15.17. Electrical laboratory chargeable hours

Both of these budgeting methods are in use today. If all projects are paid for by the company, burden rate can be a useful tool, and the actual project cost flaw is of no consequence. However, if development or research contracts are being paid for by a customer, the manpower histogram cost plus burden rate is the most equitable system. At one time, calculating project costs using actual salaries for an entire department was a difficult task. With the advent of the computer, this refinement is easily factored into the budget.

15.5 MANAGING A BUDGET. Traditionally, businesses are managed from budgeted versus actual data, both monthly and cumulative. A typical technical budget is shown in Exhibit 15.19. In this exhibit, the cost centers are individual laboratories or departments that contain the functional skill area. The annual budget column represents each functional laboratory's total for the year. The exhibit also shows the November data. In this budget summary report, each laboratory or department is tracked by comparing its financial performance for the month against the incremental and cumulative year-to-date plan. Some companies plot this data on a chart that shows the total departmental history. Plots of variance are also common.

An individual laboratory's data (electrical laboratory) are broken out in Exhibit 15.20. Salaries, benefits, and so forth, are tracked incrementally and cumulatively for the month and year-to-date.

These monthly reports assist management in controlling a department's expenditures. Most of the traditional tools for tracking technology or construction projects fall short of showing true accomplishment. Overall departmental expenditures can be made on schedule with little or no accomplishment. A more modern technique for tracking projects uses "earned value," a true accomplishment cost. The traditional tools, however, are useful for controlling head count, travel, and supplies. These monthly budgets show potential problem areas. In Exhibit 15.20, the electrical laboratory has used more than its allotted

Laboratory	(1) Chargeable Expenses	(2) Administration and Overhead	(3) Allocated Costs	(4) Total Lab Expenses	(5) Chargeable Hours	(6) Burden Rate[a]	(7) Direct Rate[b]
Electrical	2,194,988	247,500	112,500	2,554,938	20,148	126.8	108.9
Mechanical	2,364,188	202,500	135,000	2,701,638	22,705	119.0	104.1
Model shop	563,625	112,500	67,500	743,625	5,200	143.0	108.4
Chemical and material	1,238,940	180,000	157,500	1,576,440	12,000	131.4	103.2
General engineering	1,464,525	270,000	112,500	1,847,025	13,578	136.0	107.9
Totals for department	7,826,266			9,423,766	73,631	128.0	106.3

Note: All values are in dollars unless specified.

[a] Burden rate is item 4 divided by item 5.
[b] Direct rate is item 1 divided by item 5.

Exhibit 15.18. Burden-rate calculation for technical development department

Laboratory or Department	Amount (in $1,000s)				
	November		Year-to-Date		Annual
	Budget	Actual	Budget	Actual	Budget
Electrical laboratory	212	216	2,295	2,354	2,556
Mechanical laboratory	225	207	2,475	2,457	2,700
Model shop	63	68	675	711	738
Chemical and material	158	185	1,710	1,643	1,575
General engineering	135	171	1,620	1,715	1,845
Total	793	847	8,775	8,880	9,414

Exhibit 15.19. Technical center budget summary report for the period ending November 30, 1992

Expense	Amount (in $1,000s)				
	November		Year-to-Date		Annual
	Budget	Actual	Budget	Actual	Budget
Salaries	126	122	1,206	1,211	1,359
Benefits	32	32	315	333	342
Supplies	5	9	54	68	59
Travel	9	—	81	95	95
Reproduction	5	5	23	18	27
Project materials	5	14	90	113	95
Consultant services	9	5	180	158	203
Miscellaneous expenses	—	—	14	18	18
Total controllable costs	191	187	1,963	2,014	2,198
Fixed costs	32	32	333	342	360
Total expenses	223	219	2,296	2,356	2,558

Exhibit 15.20. Electrical laboratory budget report for the period ending November 30, 1992

travel allowance. By inspecting the November report, one can see that travel is being carefully monitored by the department head.

(a) Earned Value. Earned-value reporting makes use of three pieces of financial data: the two traditional ones, budget and actual costs, and an accomplishment cost, called *earned value.* Inherent in the concept are "work packages," which are used to build the budget. Value is earned when these work packages are completed. The system can work only if the work packages are increments of the total budget that are sufficiently small to be tracked well. If the work packages are 3% of the total budget or smaller, tracking errors will not be significant. If large work packages are used, someone must make an estimate of their percentage complete. This becomes a variable, based on who does the estimate. A poor estimator can destroy the usefulness of the concept. The use of small work packages eliminates the problem.

By counting the completed small work packages and totaling their value, it is possible to obtain the earned value. If one compares earned value with plan or budget, the schedule status can be obtained. By comparing earned value with actual cost, the budgetary status can be developed. Using earned-value reporting for a project, midpoint corrections can be made to keep the project on target. An example and the following definitions will help to clarify the process:

- *Earned value* is the budgeted cost of work performed (BCWP). It is the summation of completed work packages.
- *Plan* or *budget* is the budgeted cost of work scheduled (BCWS). It is initially developed by adding all of the work package costs to time intervals based on planned completion dates.
- *Actual cost of work performed* (ACWP) tracks the actual expenditures of project work packages.
- *Work packages* are the building blocks for establishing earned value. A work package can take many forms. The following categories can be applied:
  - A physical assembly of components—for example, mechanism, electronic printed circuit (PC) boards, the foundation for a building
  - A design and development activity—for example, layout of a foundation, a vehicle suspension design, an experiment, a bacterial culture growth
  - A study—for example, evaluation of an overall project or part of a project, an environmental analysis
- *Selection of natural break points* in a project, and defining these points as work packages, is the standard procedure.

As an example of the earned-value process, let us assume that the contractor has the responsibility for installing individual wall air-conditioning units in a 50-story building. One two-ton unit will cool each floor. The building is under construction; elevators have not been installed. Installation difficulties become more severe as the elevation increases. To simplify the estimate, the contractor has grouped the units into 10-story value categories. The following estimates are given:

Floors	Unit Installation Cost per Floor
1–10	$500
11–20	$550
21–30	$600
31–40	$650
41–50	$700

The contractor has defined a work package as a complete installation consisting of the unit, all electric wires, and the necessary plumbing. There are 50 work packages in the project. (Other definitions could have been used. If 10 installations were defined as a work package, their value would be too big for accurate tracking. Conversely, if lifting the unit was a work package, wiring per floor another, and plumbing another, the total work packages would be too small for efficient reporting.) The contractor's intention is to install five units per week for a total of 10 weeks. We require the completed project in the 10-week time span.

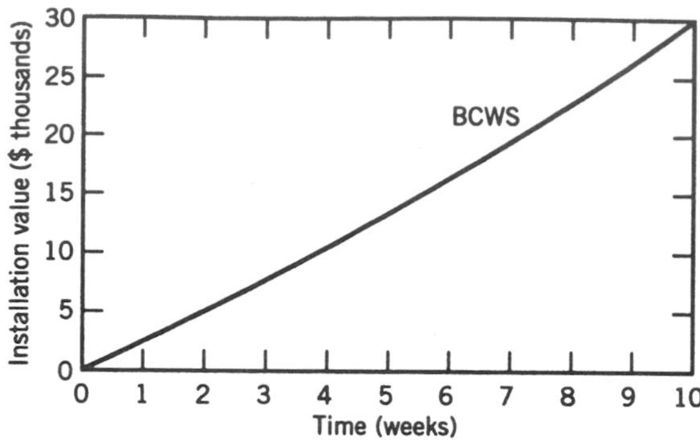

Exhibit 15.21. Baseline budget

The following baseline budget can be developed using the contractor's data:

Week	Installation Value
1	$ 2,500
2	2,500
3	2,750
4	2,750
5	3,000
6	3,000
7	3,250
8	3,250
9	3,500
10	3,500
Total value	$30,000

The baseline budget is plotted in Exhibit 15.21.

Let us assume that the project has been in operation for five weeks with the following data:

Week	Actual Installation	Earned Value	Actual Cost
1	6	$ 3,000	$ 2,950
2	5	2,550	2,500
3	5	2,750	2,750
4	4[a]	2,200	2,450
5	4	2,400	2,400
Total	14	$12,900	$13,050

[a] A teamster strike delayed shipments; overtime was scheduled.

Exhibit 15.22 shows the budget status, which is obtained by plotting the data against the baseline.

At present, this project is one fifth of a week late and $60 over budget. These data are obtained by comparing earned value against plan for the schedule and earned value against actual for the budget.

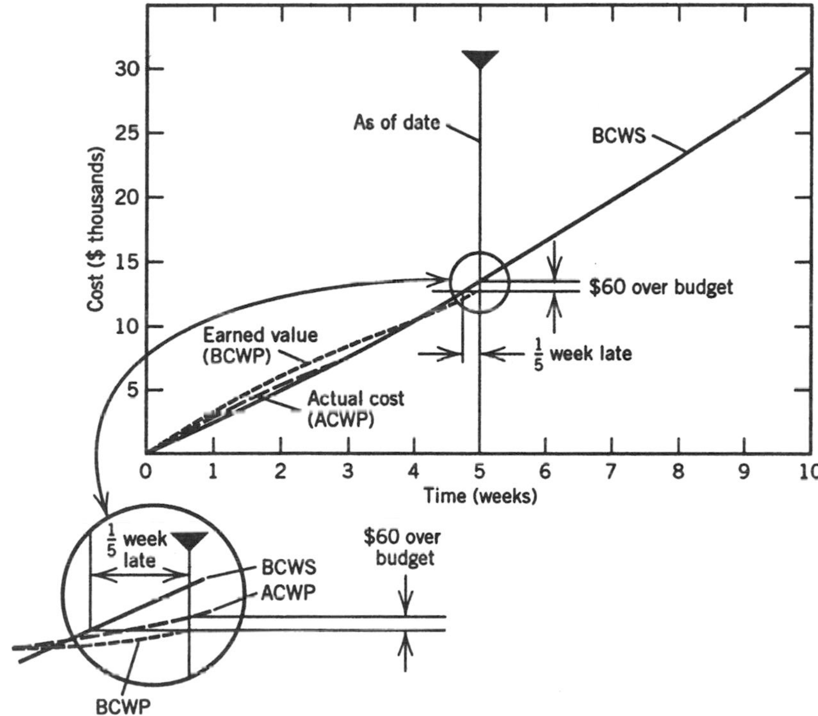

Exhibit 15.22. Budget status

Earned value is a powerful tool. It permits a finance or technical group to monitor accomplishment. In development activities, work packages are defined as tasks or subtasks. The estimate, obtained from manpower histograms and materials, is developed at the beginning of the program. Work packages are then defined as subtasks or groups of tasks, and the baseline budget is generated. As tasks are completed, the value is earned and the development program is tracked.

(b) Budget Tracking. The major advantage of an earned-value tracking system is an outsider's ability to assess real progress without getting involved in the details of day-to-day project management. Project managers can, therefore, evaluate deliveries when the supplier is on a critical path. Department managers can monitor projects without getting into the day-to-day planning and control charts. The earned-value system permits budget management with the knowledge of real accomplishment. Exhibits 15.23 through 15.25 are used as examples.

In Exhibit 15.23, traditional reporting of plan versus actual would assume that this project is in severe difficulty because actual expenditures have been consistently over budget. In reality, the project is in excellent condition. It is ahead of schedule and under budget. In Exhibit 15.24, traditional reporting of plan versus actual would assume that this project is in excellent condition since actual expenditures are below budget. In reality, there is nothing good about this project. It is behind schedule and over budget.

Exhibit 15.25 represents a mixed project. The project is behind schedule, but more value has been earned than money spent. The project manager can schedule overtime with the surplus funds to get this project back on schedule.

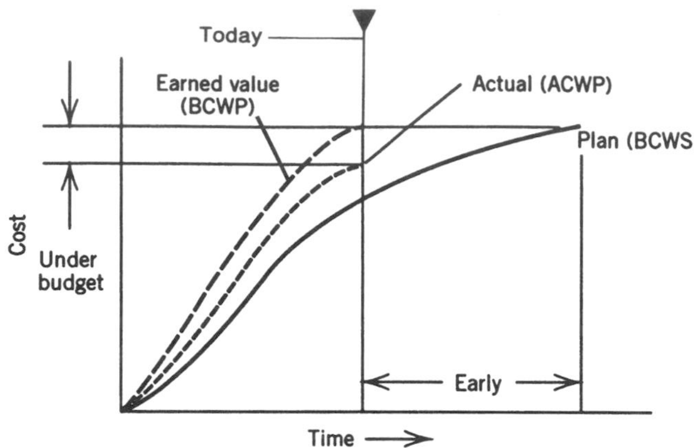

Exhibit 15.23. Traditional reporting of plan versus actual

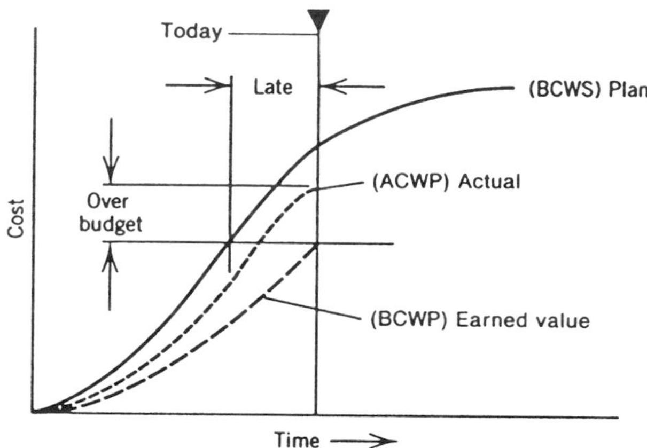

Exhibit 15.24. Traditional reporting of plan versus actual

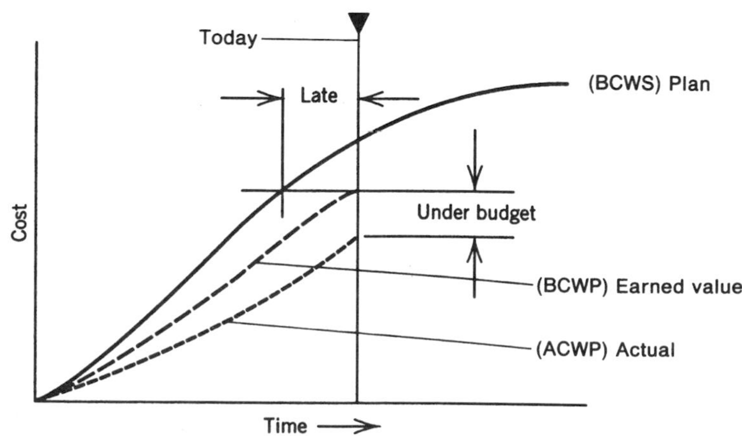

Exhibit 15.25. Mixed project

15.6 COORDINATING PROJECT BUDGETS.

Projects often involve activities for several functional departments. Coordinating the budget across departmental lines is the responsibility of the project manager. In functional organizations, this can be a difficult task, since people assigned to the project do not necessarily report to the project manager. Data can be slow in transmission. The project manager may not be able to get the functional people to work a sufficient amount of time for project success. Some departments may overcharge; others may be too busy to work on the project.

For this reason, companies have gone to other organizational forms. In the project organization, all people who work on a project report to the project manager. In a matrix organization, the project personnel report to two bosses. Responsibility for schedule and budget are the domain of the project manager; responsibility for technology is the domain of the functional manager. Dual reporting gives the project manager the control needed to get the job done, and it gives the functional manager the pooled specialists needed to ensure quality developments.

(a) Organizational Effects on Data Reports.

Exhibit 15.26 outlines the department's major project budgets. The laboratory assigned the development task is coded by number. For example, the electrical laboratory is assigned project number 101, the development of an opto-electronic screen for safeguarding punch press operators' hands. Part of the work will be carried out by the mechanical laboratory, which is responsible for structure, and part by the general engineering laboratory, which is responsible for automation. The model shop will build the physical unit. The electrical laboratory will carry the major burden of design of optics, electronics, and fail-safe circuitry.

In a functional organization, one of the electrical laboratory's engineers would be assigned the project engineering task. In a project organization, people would be pulled out of their individual laboratories for the project duration. A project manager would lead the task until it is completed, and all people would work for him or her. In a matrix

	Projects and Code			
Department	Opto-Electronics #101	Forming Machine #309	Cable Maker #207	Automation #406
Electrical laboratory	$427,500	$ 85,500	$139,500	$ 180,000
Mechanical laboratory	22,500	292,500	427,500	157,500
Model shop	67,500	247,500	202,500	112,500
Chemical and materials	—	922,500	67,500	9,000
General engineering	90,000	382,500	112,500	562,500
Total project budget	$607,500	$1,930,500	$949,500	$1,021,500

Assignment Code		Annual Summary	
Electrical laboratory	100	Major projects total	$4,509,000
Mechanical laboratory	200	Allocated projects	1,822,500
Chemical and materials	300	Sustaining projects	1,206,000
General engineering	400	Miscellaneous projects	1,885,500
Department total			$9,423,000

Exhibit 15.26. Major project budgets for 1992

organization, a project manager assigned from a project-management group would be responsible for the budget and the schedule. The R&D laboratory manager would supply people to work on the project from their normal work area and would be responsible for technology and quality. The people working on the project would have two bosses, each controlling different aspects of their work.

Financial data reporting is most difficult in the functional organization. If projects are to succeed, synchronous data reports from all of the laboratories, from purchasing, and from the model shop are essential. As organizations become larger, this requirement becomes harder to achieve.

The matrix organization requires accurate data, but the demands for reporting are more easily met, since the project manager has a proper balance of authority and responsibility. He or she can cut across all lines to get the data.

The project organization has the easiest reporting system, since all personnel, supplies, and equipment are in the domain of the project manager.

SOURCES AND SUGGESTED REFERENCES

Averch, Harvey A., ''The Political Economy of R&D Taxonomies,'' *Research Policy,* vol. 20, no. 3, June 1991.

Brockhoff, Klaus, ''A Simulation Model of R&D Budgeting,'' *R&D Management* (UK), vol. 19, no. 3, July 1989.

Cook, Thomas J., and Ronald J. Rizzuto, ''Capital Budgeting Practices for R&D: A Survey and Analysis of Business Week's R&D Scoreboard,'' *Engineering Economist,* vol. 34, no. 4, Summer 1989.

Drtina, Ralph E., and Robert L. Porter, ''Controlling R&D Spending,'' *Management Accounting,* vol. 72, no. 11, May 1991.

Magaziner, Ira, and Mark Patinkin, *The Silent War,* Vintage Books, 1990.

Nix, Paul E., and Richard M. Peters, ''Accounting for R&D Expenditures,'' *Research–Technology Management,* vol. 31, no. 1, January–February 1988.

Peters, Blair, and Judy Peters, ''Research Budgets up Overall: Staffing Levels Flat,'' *Marketing News,* vol. 30, no. 11, May 20, 1996, pp. 22, 24.

Pouliot, Janine S., ''High-Tech Budgeting,'' *Management Accounting,* vol. 72, no. 11, May 1991.

Proctor, Charles, ''Top 100 R&D Spenders: Dog Days for R&D,'' *Electronic Business,* vol. 17, no. 15, August 5, 1991.

Thackray, John, ''America's Shifting R&D Focus,'' *Management Today* (UK), July 1987.

Titus, George J., and Matthew J. Liberatore, ''Auditing R&D Planning,'' *IEEE Transactions on Engineering Management,* vol. 38, no. 2, May 1991.

Wilkinson, Alan, ''The Budgeting Process for R&D Laboratories,'' *R&D Management* (UK), vol. 18, no. 2, April 1988.

Zeldman, Maurice, ''Keeping Technical Projects on Target,'' *EMZEE Associates*, Third Edition, 1996.

CHAPTER 16

ADMINISTRATIVE-EXPENSE BUDGET

R. Malcolm Schwartz

PricewaterhouseCoopers L.L.P.

Maria Theresa Mateo

PricewaterhouseCoopers L.L.P.

16.1 INTRODUCTION. The administrative-expense budget is an important link with all other budgets, because it comprises activities that support other budgeted activities, and at the same time it provides some elements of control, and of independent perspective, on those other activities. Therefore, how management views administrative expenses says much about how management governs and leads the overall organization. In this sense, it is important to deal with what administrative expense includes and why it is important, before even beginning to address how it is budgeted. As a consequence, this chapter concentrates on the following subjects:

- The role and scope of the administrative-expense budget
- Methods used for preparing the administrative-expense budget
- Factors that impact the administrative-expense budget
- Unique issues impacting the administrative-expense budget
- Tools and techniques for managing the administrative-expense budget

16.2 ROLE AND SCOPE OF THE ADMINISTRATIVE-EXPENSE BUDGET. The surge of re-engineering and other efforts to improve performance and productivity have increased management focus on administrative expenses. Administrative expenses are somewhat straightforward, but the value of the activities for which administrative expenses are incurred—that is, why administrative expenses are consumed by administrative activities—is not as straightforward. Therefore, the administrative-expense budget is one of the more difficult budgets to manage because it is hard for many people to understand and agree to the value and purpose of administrative expenses. When a company can plan and conduct the activities that consume administrative expenses better than its competitors are able to, the company that is successful in doing so might develop a competitive advantage through such competencies.

(a) Allocating Administrative Expenses from Those Who Incur Them to Those Who Use Them. The difficulty of preparing and managing the administrative-expense budget stems from two factors: (1) the difficulty of allocation, and (2) the discretionary nature of the expenses. A ''fashionable'' company—which has hired the best people, read all the right books, and implemented the academics' and consultants' recommendations—might have empowered its people, established self-directed teams, and pushed accountability into the organization, hence creating many departments, control units, budget units, strategic business units, service centers, and/or profit centers—each having a separate plan, budget, and/or P&L—of the overall administrative-expense budget. Yet, it also might have selectively centralized some core functions that provide economies of scale for the overall organization. To hold individual revenue-producing units—the strategic business units (SBUs) or profit centers—accountable for all activities, however, the organization then might have attempted to assign or allocate these central service organizations (or overheads, as viewed by some SBU leaders). But how should the company allocate the costs, for example, of its corporate-image marketing? Should the largest-revenue SBU shoulder most of the burden? That might be inappropriate if that SBU relies less on the corporate image for achieving its mission than other, smaller units. If that is so, then should the smaller SBUs be assigned a larger share of this cost? If so, the economic effect might be larger than can be tolerated, and steps might have to be taken to affect the corporate-image program, to change the way that costs are assigned, or to discourage new businesses. As can be seen, the dilemma of allocating the costs of the administrative-expense budget can lead management into a vicious circle.

(b) Identifying the Value of Administrative Expenses. The discretionary nature of many of the activities that incur administrative expenses also can bedevil managers, because it is difficult for these activities to ascribe a quantitative value (an output) for the explicitly determined (input) cost budgeted. Managers are not always confident that the correct amounts are being spent. Is a larger legal department, for example, a good thing? For an organization that has incurred large regulatory penalties, or that has been sued for patent infringement, increasing legal expenses might be a good thing, but it might be too late. Therefore, it is often difficult to measure the value of corporate services and the right period of time for budgeting the expenditure compared to the period of time when the benefits will be realized.

The difficulty of measuring value might be attributed to, among other factors, the problem of measuring risk, which often is associated with low-probability occurrences but which can have very high costs per occurrence. Administrative organizations that monitor compliance with governmental or corporate policies on safety, environment, and labor issues are constantly battling for funding and for recognition of their value. Their value becomes apparent only when, for example, companies are faced with lawsuits or a loss of goodwill from their handling of a compliance matter, such as happened with the Exxon Valdez oil spill. Even in hindsight, it still might not be clear what level of additional investment—and, for that matter, what type of additional expenditure—might have mitigated or prevented problems such as this.

One way to deal with this value issue as it relates to the administrative-expense budget is to categorize administrative activities, and the costs that they incur, as serving one of two purposes—efficiency or effectiveness. For example, the purpose of a payroll department is to be efficient. The payroll department strives to process employee paychecks in the most cost-efficient manner. For an area focused on efficiency, the question is, ''How much does it cost the company to do what needs to be done?'' Answering this question is relatively straightforward: Management can conduct a market test, develop unit standards, or purchase available benchmark data to estimate the appropriate cost.

Alternatively, the purpose of another human resources activity—recruiting—is to be effective, not efficient. *Effectiveness* can be defined as the extent to which an activity supports or enables a predetermined objective or target to be met. The recruiting activity strives to identify, hire, and retain high-quality individuals. For an area focused on effectiveness, the question is, ''How do its activities benefit the organization?'' Answering this question is much more difficult than answering the efficiency question because areas that focus on effectiveness usually do not produce a tangible product, and thus there is less relevancy in performing external benchmarks, and there are few external data available. Rather, these areas tend to focus on the company's well-being related to its analysis of risks and objectives, and these areas are not as easily quantifiable. Value can be ascertained by assessing a company's tolerance for risk and how much it is willing to spend to be at a comfortable level of risk.

(c) What Functions Are Included in the Administrative-Expense Budget? The administrative-expense budget can be described by what it does not include: in some ways, this is easier to describe than by starting with what it does include. Typically, activities that touch either the organization's product or the organization's customer are usually considered part of core operations, and their expenses fall into operating, not administrative, expense budgets. These activities typically include customer service, distribution, manufacturing, research and development (R&D), and sales. Marketing and purchasing are usually considered operating expenses but can be found in some organization's administrative-expense budgets.

Thus, everything else (activities not part of the core operations) falls in the administrative-expense budget. These activities often are shared by a number of internal, user organizations. Although organizations more frequently have been taking a process view of their businesses, few companies prepare budgets by process. In most cases, the administrative-expense budget is still prepared on a functional or departmental basis. Exhibit 16.1 lists those areas that are most often part of the administrative-expense budget and identifies whether their purpose is primarily efficiency or effectiveness.

Exhibit 16.1, however, only shows the primary purpose at a high level; for example, within the purchasing function, ordering activities tend to be oriented toward efficiency, but vendor management activities tend to be oriented toward effectiveness. Furthermore, the purpose of an administrative activity can vary from one organization to another, and even for different relationships within an organization. A fast-food company, for example, might want to centralize the purchase of ingredients, to ensure uniformity and to take advantage of scale, and thus might categorize the purchasing department as an administrative expense and might define its purpose as efficiency focused. Conversely, a chain of higher-priced restaurants might purchase locally, to emphasize freshness as well as regional tastes, and therefore might classify the purchasing department as an administrative expense focused more on effectiveness than on efficiency. Organizations also could have the same sizes of administrative-expense budgets, but these budgets might include quite different levels of efficiency and effectiveness. Organizations might have similar levels of performance but a very different levels of administrative costs, as shown in Exhibit 16.2

(d) What Types of Expenses Are Included in the Administrative-Expense Budget? The majority of the administrative expenses typically include costs associated closely with human resources (namely, salary and benefits). There often is a large external-service

Department	Type of Focus	
	Efficiency	Effectiveness
• Finance		
—Accounting	X	
—Fixed assets	X	
—Internal audit		X
—Tax		X
—Treasury		X
• General administration		
—Corporate executives		X
—Internal business development/strategy		X
—Internal consulting		X
—Policies and procedures		X
—Publication services and internal communications	X	
—Risk management		X
—Real estate and facility services	X	
—Secretaries, reproduction, and mailroom	X	
• Human resources		
—Benefits	X	
—Employee–retiree administration	X	
—Payroll	X	
—Recruitment		X
—Training		X
• Insurance and risk management		X
• Information technology (IT)		
—IT development		X
—IT operations	X	
—Telecommunications		X
• Legal		X
• Public relations		
—Community and charitable activities		X
—Government and regulatory relations		X
—Industry, professional, and trade relations		X
—Investor relations	X	
—Media relations		X
• Purchasing	X	

Exhibit 16.1. The primary purposes of typical administrative departments found in the administrative-expense budget

component, as many administrative activities (such as legal, business development, strategy, audit, and data-processing operations and development) are often outsourced. There also might be some capital-asset costs—in the form of depreciation expense, leasehold amortization, and the like—included in the administrative-expense budget, particularly associated with information technology (IT) and real estate. Administrative expenses also can be associated with activities that are not easily understood or that might occur infrequently (such as expenses associated with litigation), and they often cannot be linked to specific products or services. Inasmuch as some administrative costs tend to be discretionary, their value and quality tend to be difficult to measure.

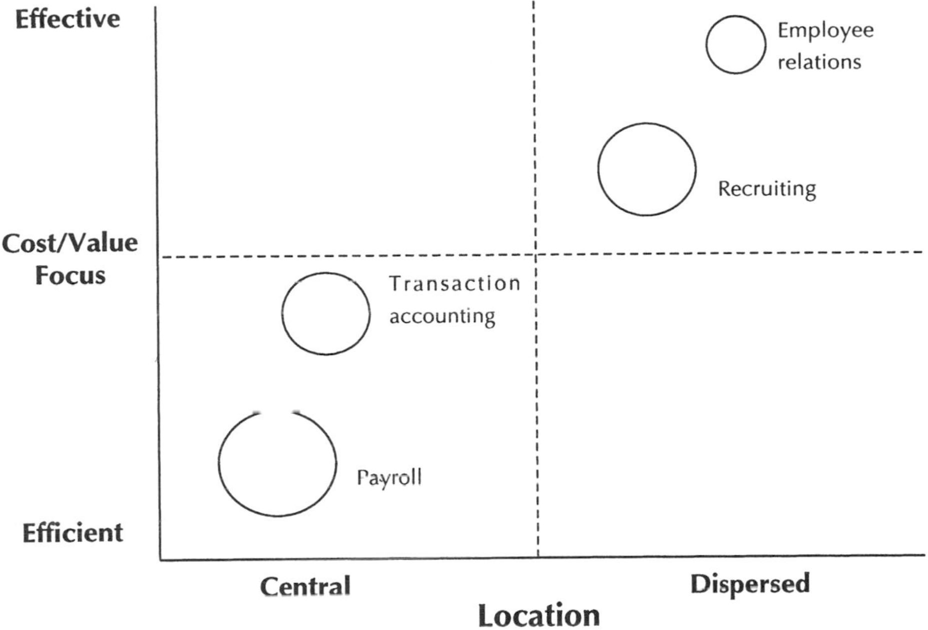

Exhibit 16.2. Levels of administrative costs

In contrast, operating budgets include both physical and human resources costs. Most operating costs are associated with specified and repetitive processes (such as production, sales, and distribution) and can be related to specific products or services. Examples of such operating expenses are raw materials, plant and equipment, and direct labor.

A typical administrative-expense budget, structured for an administrative department, is illustrated in Exhibit 16.3.

16.3 METHODS USED FOR PREPARING THE ADMINISTRATIVE-EXPENSE BUDGET.

After there is agreement on the roles and purposes of the administrative activities, as discussed in the previous section, there are three basic steps to preparing the administrative-expense budget: (1) projecting the level of activity, (2) projecting the level of resources expected to be consumed to support that level of activity, and (3) projecting the factor costs of those resources. Each is discussed below. Also important in preparing the administrative-expense budget is how to gain "buy-in" while maintaining a clear sense of direction. This means combining what are often identified, respectively, as the bottom-up and top-down approaches.

(a) Projecting the Level of Activity. Typically, a first step in preparing the administrative-expense budget is to project the level of services to be provided, and hence to project the level of expenses expected to be incurred to provide that level of services. Companies use a number of different methods to project administrative expenses, and hence to develop a basis for applying costs to administrative activities. This section will discuss briefly the applicability of these methods to the administrative expense budget.

- *Historical basis (or ordinary incremental).* Historical-basis budgeting takes into account the previous year's budget and the actual results. Budgeted levels of activity

Budget Year: 1996
Company Code: 19
Plant: QU
Owner: Alec Mundy
Cost Center: 421 Mail services

Cost Element	Description	Annual
620000	Salaries and wages	$1,956,000
623000	Employee allowances	$11,000
624000	Relocation	$85,000
630000	Other materials and supplies	$504,000
631000	Travel and entertainment	$69,700
634000	Postage	$8,000
640000	Purchased services	$82,000
640015	Maintenance services	$0
641000	Contract labor	$40,000
642000	Professional fees and consult	$6,000
644000	Software	$3,000
	Controllable Totals	**$2,764,700**
621000	Fringe benefits	$731,544
622000	Incentive compensation	$220,050
660000	Depreciation	$400,633
661000	L/T operate lease-equipment	$220,000
670900	Act-office building and overtime	$1,154,687
671803	R&D overhead (admin.)	$402,356
672300	General services	$91,468
	Noncontrollable totals	**$3,200,738**
	Cost center totals	**$5,965,438**

Exhibit 16.3. Typical administrative department expense budget

for the projected period are adjusted, depending on the previous year's results and on the expectations for the projected period. Historical-basis budgeting does not usually consider the nonpeople costs; instead, it drives the budget to the number of people and the rates they are paid and then adds other costs through ratios.

- *Expense/revenue basis.* This method of budgeting determines the amount to be budgeted for the projected period based on some defined relationship between the particular administrative expense under consideration and revenue. For example, human resource departmental expenses, when using this method, might be considered to be equal to about 1% of sales: this ratio might be considered to be valid for future periods. Similar to historical-basis budgeting, this method also is driven by people cost.
- *Zero basis.* Zero-based budgeting is budgeting from the ground up, as though the budget were being prepared for the first time. When using this method, every proposed expenditure comes under review. Though zero-based budgeting requires more work than other forms of budgeting, it forces managers to better justify their outlays. Few firms adopt zero-based budgeting on an annual basis for all departments. When zero-based budgeting is undertaken, it typically is on a less regular basis, and only for a subset of responsibility centers at any one time.

Comparative Factor	Historical Basis	Expense-Revenue Basis	Zero Basis	Activity Basis
Simplicity	Yes	Yes	No	No
Level of effort	No	No	Yes	Yes
Takes a long time	No	No	Yes	Yes
Enables cost management	Yes	Yes	Yes	Yes
Enables cost–benefit analysis	No	Yes	No	Yes
Links cost drivers	No	No	No	Yes
Supports decision making	No	No	Yes	Yes

Exhibit 16.4. A comparison among budgeting methods

- *Activity basis.* Activity-based budgeting focuses on the activities that are projected to be used to support the production and sale of projected products and services, and then on estimating the costs of those activities. Activity-based budgeting can be valuable in the case of indirect—and administrative—costs. There are several ways to develop activity-based costs. In the accounting approach, for example, activity-based budgeting partitions indirect costs into separate but homogeneous activity cost pools. Management then uses cause-and-effect criteria to identify the cost drivers for the separate cost pools. An organization then can apply these drivers to the costs of the services being provided (and, eventually, to the products themselves) in proportion to the volume of activity that a given service consumes. By assigning all resources to an activity, this method is more precise in that it considers more than just people-related costs.

Exhibit 16.4 compares the different methods.

The trade-offs among the various budgeting methods are between effort and value. Clearly, for organizations in which administrative expenses are not very important, simpler methods should be used. However, in many organizations, decisions about administrative expenses are visible and important, so more care might be taken with—and about—the methods used for budgeting such expenses.

In making its choice, an organization also should consider selecting a method that will provide a means to track performance in comparison to the desired outcomes on operational measures. Good budgeting techniques provide an ability to measure value received, and to track performance. Performance measures will vary by activity, and by the importance of any activity to the organization, but most organizations will at the least track (1) profitability; (2) customer satisfaction; (3) innovation; and (4) other internal measures relating to efficiency, quality, and time.

(b) Projecting the Level of Resources Expected to Be Consumed to Support That Level of Activity. A second step in budgeting administrative expenses, once the level of activities is estimated, is to relate resources to activities. For example, processing payroll checks might lead to an estimate of the clerical and supervisory time that is required. The same might be done for each of the administrative activities. Relating resources to be consumed to the level of activity can be accomplished by using any of the methods described in the previous section. The reason for separating the steps in this description of the budgeting process is to suggest that separate analyses of activity levels and of resources consumed should be undertaken. For example, the level of activity might be the same as in the prior year, but the level of resources projected might be less due to the success of re-engineering efforts.

(c) Projecting the Factor Costs of Those Resources. The third step is to project the factor costs that are the unit costs of the resources to be consumed. For example, an increase in the costs of health-care benefits would lead to a higher factor cost for benefits. However, better procedures and training might lead to a lower set of skills to support some activities than in the prior year. Again, this step can be combined with the previous ones, but it is useful to consider it separately; in this way, the budget can be developed separately for the level of activity, for the level of resources consumed by the activity, and for the factor costs (or unit costs) of those resources. Also, projecting factor costs might use other techniques, such as review of economic indicators (projected rates of inflation, for example) or review of changed business circumstances (such as the effects of changes in purchased-service contracts, for example).

(d) Gaining Agreement, Top-Down and Bottom-Up. The process for any of these methods could be top-down, bottom-up, or a hybrid. A typical hybrid approach entails guidelines provided from the top, numbers generated bottom-up and subject to top-level modification, and several iterations before a final budget is submitted. A blending of the top-down and bottom-up approaches is shown in Exhibit 16.5.

The optimal approach for an organization depends on such characteristics as its governance and management styles, the extent of similarity—and of autonomy—among its business units, the competencies in its business units, and so forth. For highly diversified organizations, the optimal approach might be to have limited direction from the top. However, for less diversified organizations, or for organizations that are more operationally oriented (with a number of operating units that are not freestanding, for example), the optimal approach might be to have more direction from the top with regard to budgeting.

16.4 FACTORS THAT IMPACT THE ADMINISTRATIVE-EXPENSE BUDGET.

The characteristics of an organization and its industry not only affect the approach it takes to preparing the administrative-expense budget and the classification of the expenses (efficiency versus effectiveness), but also can affect the size of the administrative-expense budget relative to other costs. Some of the key factors are presented below.

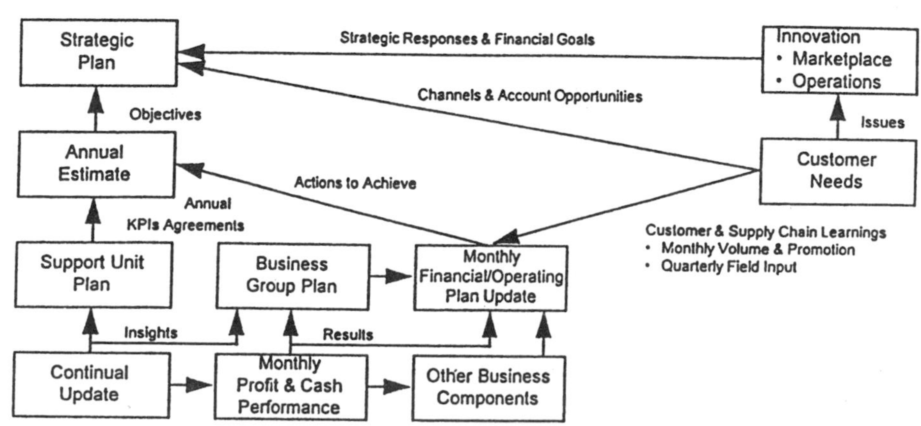

Exhibit 16.5. A comparison of top-down and bottom-up approaches

- Characteristics of the industry
  - *Service or product focus.* Service companies tend to have higher administrative expenses, due to such factors as higher turnover and higher training costs; also, labor reporting tends to be relatively more expensive than production reporting, but the costs tend to be less obvious.
  - *Diversified or simple organization structure.* The diversified structure tends to have higher administrative expenses due to greater needs for coordination.
  - *Cyclical or level volumes.* Uneven flows of work tend to lead to higher administrative expenses, to have in place the resources for the peak periods of activity.
  - *Public or private.* A public organization tends to have higher administrative expenses due to a variety of regulatory and reporting requirements.
  - *Regulated or unregulated.* Regulated industries tend to have higher administrative expenses due to regulatory agency requirements.
- Maturity of the organization and the industry
  - *Startup.* A start-up organization can have higher administrative expenses until it learns how to be efficient and until it becomes stable enough to satisfy investors.
  - *Growing.* A growing organization can have higher administrative expenses because it might not be focused on profits, and it might lose a sense of control on administrative expenses.
  - *Mature.* Mature organizations can have lower administrative expenses, if they have developed a profit focus.
- Organizational structure of company and operating philosophy
  - *Centralized or decentralized.* Decentralized companies tend to have higher administrative expenses because a cost of decentralization often is to have redundant activities.
  - *Level of technology.* The administrative expenses associated with less automated organizations tend to be higher.

16.5 UNIQUE ISSUES IMPACTING THE ADMINISTRATIVE-EXPENSE BUDGET.

Unique issues impact the administrative expense budget. Specifically, how does one quantify the value associated with administrative activities?

Budgeting efficiency-oriented costs is relatively straightforward. One can develop cost—and in some cases, time—standards for such process-oriented activities as payroll, purchasing, and accounts payable, and might choose to use staffing ratios for other activities such as secretarial, investor relations, and telecommunications. These standards can be compared and validated with available benchmarks.

Effectiveness-oriented costs, as discussed earlier, are much more difficult to quantify for such reasons as the following:

- Activities that are oriented toward effectiveness often do not produce a tangible result and often do not produce any result in the same period in which the costs are incurred. For example, legal expenses are best spent to prevent legal problems; if problems do occur, it might be years after the legal effort (to conduct a patent search, for example) was expended. In sum, these activities tend to focus on the company's well-being, which is not easily quantifiable.
- The degree of specialization of these effectiveness-oriented activities tends to be higher than for those administrative activities that are more oriented toward efficiency. It might be difficult for an executive who might have come from a sales background,

for example, to assess the needs and performance of the public affairs department; yet, those activities can help to influence legislators and regulators to understand the organization's point of view, and thus to prevent undesirable regulatory rulings. In the more extreme cases, a lack of understanding can lead to a lack of trust, which can cause inappropriate levels of support for these types of activities over time. Finally, the performance and effectiveness of these types of administrative activities depend much more on the quality of people in place than on the process that is followed.

- The factor costs of the kind of people who support these activities often is much higher than for the more efficiency-oriented activities. Legal, treasury, and business development/strategy personnel are often among the highest-paid staff categories in a company. While the internal costs might be high, the costs of outsourcing these activities by using external groups that provide these services can be even higher.
- These roles often are shaped to, among other factors, prevent—or, if necessary, respond to—high-cost problems that have a low probability of occurring, yet management might fail to assess the value of these risks in a way that supports the budgeting of these activities correctly.
- The environment that drives these effectiveness-oriented costs is not the same as that which drives the other administrative areas or operations areas, and they might be driven by external (technological, governmental, and/or competitive) issues. For example, the costs of recruiting and of corporate advertising might be driven more by how much competitors spend than by the organization's strategy as such.

As noted earlier, the effectiveness orientation can be viewed as the degree to which a predetermined objective or target is to be met, so the value of an activity's effectiveness can be estimated by assessing an organization's tolerance for risk and determining how much it is willing to spend to be at a comfortable level of risk to meet the predetermined objective or target. For example, when considering the legal department, does the organization want to avoid litigation at all costs due to potential damage to its image? Or will some litigation be acceptable, so long as the organization's position is clear and sustainable? Does the organization want all contracts written in an explicit, thorough, and detailed manner because contracting parties are perceived as untrustworthy? Or might the organization accept broader contracts that rely on trust between the contracting parties?

16.6 TOOLS AND TECHNIQUES FOR MANAGING THE ADMINISTRATIVE-EXPENSE BUDGET. There a number of tools and techniques that are useful in managing and controlling administrative expenses. These include the following:

- Budget variance analysis
- Administrative charge-back to the operating units
- Hybrid transfer costing
- Outsourcing alternatives
- Performance measures
- Activity-based costing (ABC)
- Benchmarking

(a) Budget Variance Analysis. Variance analysis provides useful information for making decisions because it helps to provide insights into why the actual results differ from the planned performance. A variance is a performance gap between a benchmark—generally, the budgeted amount—and the actual results, typically as reported in the accounting system for financial information, or in operating systems for nonfinancial information. The most important task in variance analysis is to understand why variances have occurred, and then to use that knowledge to promote learning and continuous improvement, and to enable better planning and better cost management. It is equally important to focus on positive variances as well as negative variances.

(b) Administrative Charge-Back to the Operating Units. Operating groups often are charged for the administrative services to remind profit-center managers that indirect costs exist and that profit-center earnings must be adequate to cover some share of these costs, as well as to provide for a return on invested capital and a fair return to creditors and investors. Organizations who do this believe that it will stimulate profit-center managers to put pressure on administrative managers to control the costs of the services that they provide.

(c) Hybrid Transfer Costing. Operating groups might be charged the budgeted expense instead of the actual expense, with the difference absorbed by the unit incurring the cost. Organizations who use budgeted costs as the basis for charging believe that this helps to motivate the manager of the support department to improve efficiency. During the budget period, the support departments, not the user departments, bear the risk of any unfavorable cost variances because the user departments do not pay for any costs that exceed the budgeted costs.

The decision of whether to allocate budgeted or actual costs affects the level of uncertainty that user departments face. Budgeted costs let the user departments know the costs in advance. Users then are better equipped to determine the amount of the service to request and, if the option exists, whether to use the internal department source or an external vendor.

Some organizations choose to recognize that it might not always be best to impose all of the risks of variances from budgeted amounts completely on the support departments or completely on the user departments.

(d) Outsourcing Alternatives. Exposing administrative-cost centers to competitive forces of the marketplace is another way that some organizations use to force administrative areas to control their expenses. If operating units have a choice of buying services from an external party, then administrative units have the incentive of self-preservation to contain costs. This does, however, pose some risk of suboptimization of the centralized services if some operating units decide to outsource, leaving the remaining operating units with higher costs for these services.

(e) Performance Measures. Performance measures that are linked to compensation help motivate management in the right direction. However, it is critical that an organization's goals are aligned with how its incentive plan is designed. When this technique is used, performance measures that are both financial and nonfinancial measures of effectiveness or efficiency should be considered; they should be monitored on an ongoing and systematic basis.

(f) Activity-Based Costing. Activity-based costing can provide a mechanism for managing administrative expenses. If the administrative and user departments agree to a framework and agree to the level of work, it can provide an actual per-unit basis for charging back the costs with the associated services. However, if the actual usage level is either above or below the targeted level, the actual per-unit charge-back might be different, and management will have to decide how any efficiency gains or losses will be treated.

(g) Benchmarking. Benchmark studies can provide information on the comparative cost efficiency of an organization. Benchmarking is the continual process of comparing products, services, and activities to objective indicators of performance. Benchmarks can be found inside or outside the organization.

16.7 SUMMARY. The administrative-expense budget is an important link with all other budgets because it comprises activities that support other budgeted activities, and at the same time, it provides some elements of control, and of independent perspective, on those other activities. The size of the administrative-expense budget, what it includes, and how it is prepared can be unique to each organization for many reasons. However, the administrative-expense budget primarily reflects how management views its support functions.

SOURCES AND SUGGESTED REFERENCES

Birchard, ''The New Finance,'' *Enterprise,* October 1992.

Boyle (D&T), ''Avoiding Common Pitfalls of Reengineering,'' *Management Accounting.*

Cooper and Kaplan, ''Measure Costs Right: Make The Right Decision,'' *Harvard Business Review*, September–October 1988.

Cooper, Maisel, Morrissey, and Oehm, ''From ABC to ABM,'' *Management Accounting,* November 1992.

Cooper, ''Look Out, Management Accountants,'' *Management Accounting,* May 1996.

Cooper, *When Lean Enterprise Collide.* Boston: Harvard Business School Press, 1995.

———, 1989 ''You Need a New Cost System When. . .,'' *Harvard Business Review,* vol. 67, no. 1.

Cranc and Meyer, ''Focusing on True Costs in a Service Organization,'' *Management Accounting,* February 1993.

Drucker, ''The Information Executives Truly Need,'' *Harvard Business Review*, January–February 1995.

Eccles and Pyburn, ''Creating a Comprehensive System to Measure Performance,'' *Management Accounting,* October 1992.

Ferrara, ''Cost/Management Accounting—The 21st Century Paradigm,'' *Management Accounting,* December 1995.

Gale, ''Quality Profiling: The First Step in Reengineering and Benchmarking,'' *Planning Review,* May–June 1995.

Gunn, Carberry, Frigo, and Behrens, ''Shared Services—Major Companies Are Re-engineering Their Accounting Functions,'' *Management Accounting,* November 1993.

Hart, ''The Power of Internal Guarantees,'' *Harvard Business Review*, January–February 1995.

Housel and Kanevsky, ''A New Methodology for Business Process Auditing,'' *Planning Review,* May–June 1995.

Jacobs, ''Finance Can Lead the Way for Change,'' *Management Accounting,* October 1995.

Jaderstrom, Susan, *Administrative Support Systems & Procedures.* Cincinnati, OH: South-Western Publishing, 1992.

Johnson and Kaplan, *Relevance Lost: The Rise and Fall of Management Accounting.* Boston: Harvard Business School Press, 1987.

Judick, ''Why SG&A Doesn't Always Work,'' *Harvard Business Review*, January–February 1987.

Kaplan and Cooper, ''Get Your Costs Right,'' *Harvard Business Review*, vol. 66, no. 5, 1988.

Kaplan and Norton, ''Using the Balanced Scorecard as a Strategic Management System,'' *Harvard Business Review*, January–February 1996.

Kaplan and Norton, ''Putting the Balanced Scorecard to Work,'' *Harvard Business Review*, September–October 1993.

Kawada and Johnson, ''Strategic Management Accounting—Why and How,'' *Management Accounting,* August 1993.

Keegan and Portik, ''Accounting Will Survive the Coming Century, Won't It?,'' *Management Accounting,* December 1995.

Meeimore and Bell, ''Are We Ready for Fourth-Generation ABC?,'' *Management Accounting,* January 1995.

Pare, ''A New Tool for Managing Costs,'' *Fortune,* June 14, 1993.

Quible, Zane K., *Administrative Office Management.* Englewood Cliffs, NJ: Prentice-Hall, 1995.

Robinson, Glen O., Ernest Gellhorn, and Harold H. Bruff, *The Administrative Process.* West Publishing, 1993.

Shank and Govindarajan, *Strategic Cost Management: The New Tool for Competitive Advantage.* New York: The Free Press, 1993.

———, *Strategic Cost Analysis.* Homewood, IL: Richard D. Irwin, 1989.

———, ''Marking Strategy Explicit in Cost Analysis: A Case Study,'' *Sloan Management Review,* vol. 29, no. 8, 1988.

Simon, Robert, *Lever of Control: How Managers Use Innovative Control Systems to Drive Strategic Renewal.* Boston: Harvard Business School Press, 1995.

Timmons, ''The Jenkins Committee: Where It Missed the Mark,'' *Financial Executive,* May–June 1995.

Vercio, ''What Organization Are You Accounting For?,'' *Management Accounting,* December 1993.

CHAPTER 17

BUDGETING PAYROLL COSTS

Leonard A. Haug, CPP

Digital Equipment Corporation in collaboration with the American Payroll Association

17.1 INTRODUCTION. Finance organizations are placing significant emphasis on reducing transaction processing costs in the payroll function in order to shift resources and business focus to "business partnership" roles. Exhibit 17.1 and 17.2 illustrate this paradigm shift and highlight the need for companies to increase their payroll efficiencies. You will note on the latter exhibit that finance departments are being asked to reduce costs and improve performance. With transactions growing at twice the rate of business growth, and demand for services at a higher rate, this business decision has created pressures on chief financial officers to improve services at lower costs.

Because of the emphasis on reducing labor and costs associated with transaction systems, understanding the costs of such systems has become paramount to the payroll process. Benchmarking payroll costs with those of other companies, both within and outside one's industry, can help management understand the relative degree of opportunity that exists for their company. Consulting firms that provide benchmarking services can often help companies to accelerate the benchmarking process and obtain valuable information on comparative costs and best practices.

Exhibit 17.3 illustrates the varying average cost per transaction for various accounting and related functions. Although the average payroll cost to process a check was estimated, in this comparative benchmark study, to be $2.77, actual costs varied widely among participants. Other cost comparison studies report even higher costs per payment. Payroll expense data are often tracked by cost per payment or annual cost per employee paid, as shared by Digital Equipment Corporation in Exhibit 17.4. Understanding payroll costs and the reasons behind variations in cost from one company to another can help companies improve their cost performance.

The best-practice companies are responding by consolidating multiple decentralized operations and by replacing narrow, "stovepipe" approaches with solutions that address the entire payroll delivery chain. In addition, best-practice companies are emphasizing standardization, simplification, re-engineering, selective automation, effective use of technology, and partial to full outsourcing as ways to improve performance and reduce operating costs. Exhibit 17.5 identifies three implementation stages typical of cost-reduction efforts at successful companies. The primary driver of cost savings appears to be the stage of implementation to which the company has progressed; that is, the higher the implementation stage, the greater the savings.

The Challenge Is Driving a "Paradigm Shift" in the Role of the Finance Function

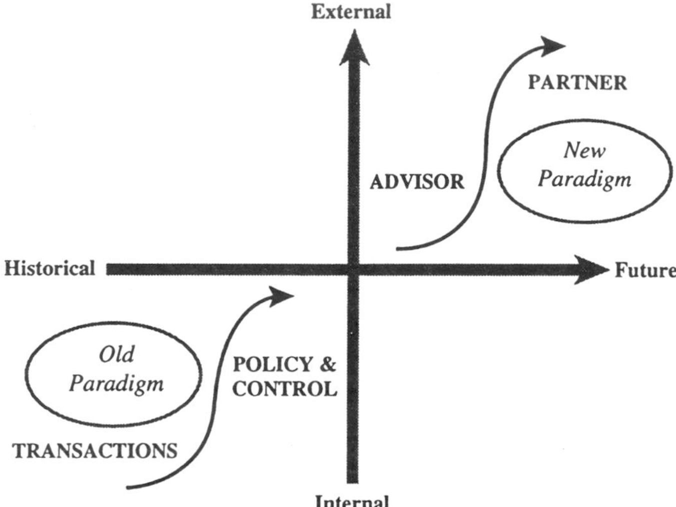

Finance Must Re-prioritize, Re-engineer, and Re-allocate Resources

Exhibit 17.1. Paradigm shifts
Reprinted with permission. © Gunn Partners, Inc.

Finance Is Being Asked to Significantly Reduce Costs at the Same Time It Seeks to Improve Performance

- Transactions are growing at twice the business growth rate
- Internal and external customer demand for service is higher
- Market and regulatory requirements are adding to business complexity
- Finance is being asked to limit or actually reduce costs

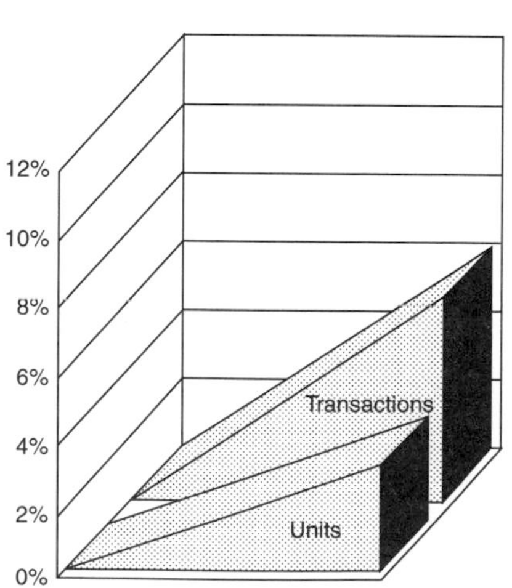

To Satisfy the CEO, Finance Must Deliver More for Less

Exhibit 17.2. Paradigm shift effects
Reprinted with permission. © Gunn Partners, Inc.

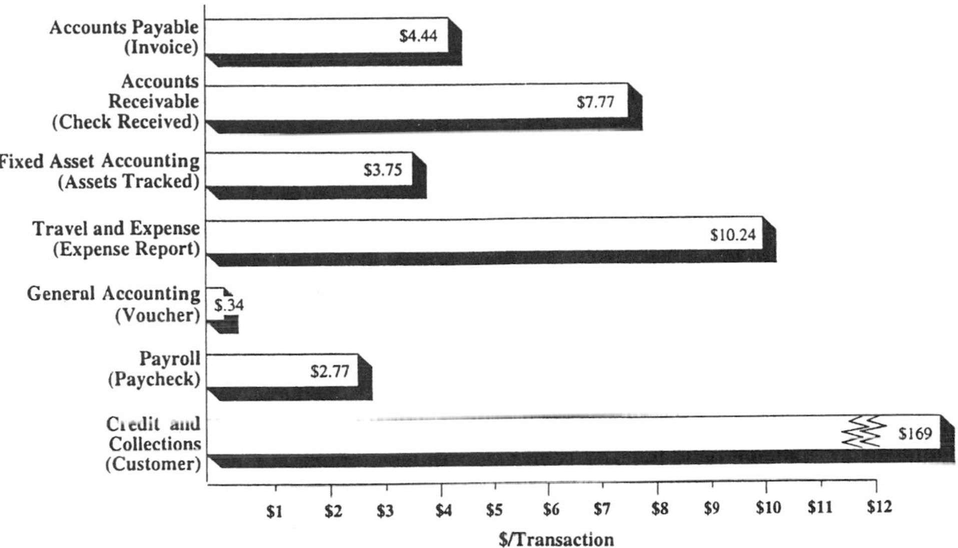

Exhibit 17.3. Average cost per transaction
Reprinted with permission. © 1991, A. T. Kearney, Inc. All rights reserved.

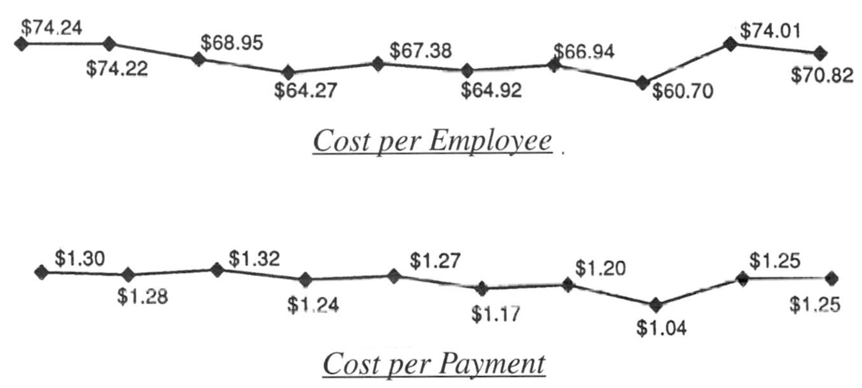

Exhibit 17.4. Payroll cost performance
Reprinted with permission. © Digital Equipment Corporation—U.S. Payroll.

Achievement of cost-effective payroll programs begins with an understanding of the business and its added-value services, customers and suppliers, current costs, and current performance levels. The use of total quality management (TQM) and activity-based costing (ABC) tools provides direction and assistance for understanding the business and for improving core competencies while reducing labor and costs associated with payroll, which ultimately should result in a more cost-effective payroll program.

Whatever your company's current status is, be assured that there are opportunities for higher performance and lower costs. This chapter focuses on helping the reader to achieve these objectives.

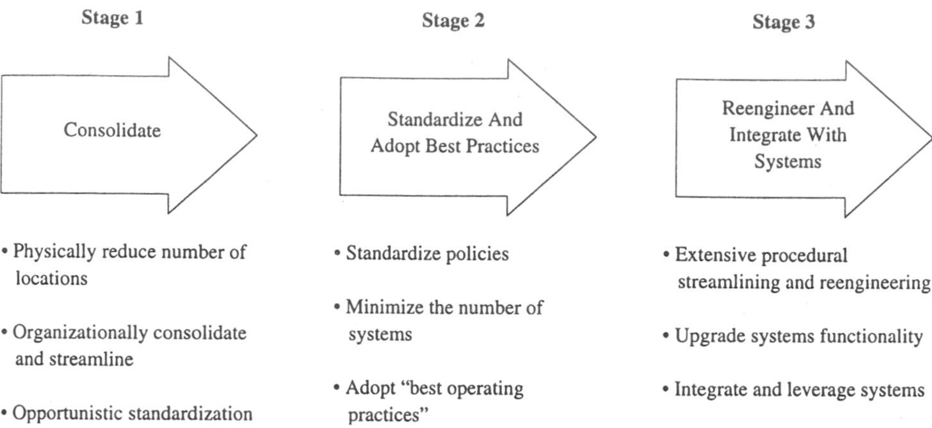

Exhibit 17.5. Stages of implementation

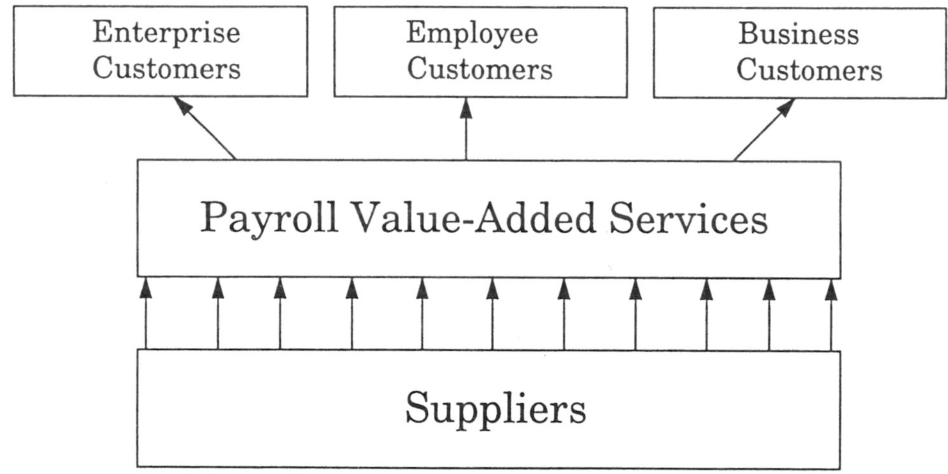

Exhibit 17.6. Supplier/payroll/customer overview

17.2 OVERVIEW OF THE PAYROLL FUNCTION

(a) Payroll Charter and Expectations. *Payroll* is generally defined as a tactical operational organization within accounting, finance, treasury, or human resources chartered with the critical responsibility of producing the company's payroll(s). Company expectations of performance are very high, with zero to little tolerance for anything less than 100% accuracy and timeliness.

(b) Suppliers and Customers. The definition of payroll must begin with the understanding that payroll is not a stand-alone function. Regardless of size, payroll depends on many suppliers, both internal and external, and delivers products and services to many different sets of customers, again both internal and external, as illustrated in Exhibit 17.6.

The definition of payroll from a process and cost perspective, therefore, must extend beyond payroll proper to include overlapping processes and costs incurred by payroll suppliers and customers.

(c) Systems Definition. To understand the function, payroll also must be defined from both a systems and a business perspective.

From a systems perspective, the payroll process is comprised of three components:

INPUT———→GROSS-TO-NET———→OUTPUT

(i) Input. Input includes activities associated with the collection, validation, and approval of information essential to subsequent components of the payroll process. The payroll process begins with input changes made to the employee's record, which may reside on an integrated human resource and payroll system or on a separate human resource system that sends information to payroll for updating to its system.

The input process includes the following generic electronic and/or paper inputs:

- The collection and updating of data to the system, including employee profile and deduction data as well as file maintenance data from within the payroll business
- The creation and/or receipt and storage of reference tables (e.g., tax, insurance, ledger, bank, and site data)
- The receipt and consolidation of time input data, supplementary compensation requests, and pay adjustments and exception payment and data initiated by payroll
- The calculation of vacation accruals and updating of available vacation hours (This process may be done before the pay-calculation process or after, depending on business rules [when an employee is credited with earned vacation hours].)

(ii) Gross-to-Net. Gross-to-net includes activities associated with the calculation of wage, salary, supplementary compensation, and adjustment payments, including the following:

- The calculation of gross pay using master file data and/or timecard, supplementary payment requests, and adjustments collected via the input process
- The calculation of Section 125 pretax deductions (e.g., deductions that are exempt from most federal and/or state and local taxes, such as 401k plans)
- The calculation of taxes to be withheld, including federal income withholding, Social Security and Medicare, state income withholding, and local withholding taxes (as applicable)
- The calculation of single and multiple child support garnishements, tax levies, and other wage attachments in legal-prioritized order
- The calculation (if not precalculated by the originator) of voluntary deductions in company-prioritized order
- The calculation of net pay, which represents the culmination of all of the preceding steps in the pay-calculation process (Some payrolls or types of payments are calculated on a net-to-gross basis and vary from this description.)

(iii) Output. Output includes activities associated with the production and distribution of payments and reports, including the following:

- The creation of paycheck and/or pay deposit statements and applicable bank electronic funds transfer (EFT) file(s)
- The updating of current and historical online payment files and the creation of payroll reports for internal payroll administrative and compliance functions
- The creation of informational output for payroll business customers and suppliers, including earnings extracts for groups such as labor collection and reporting systems (assuming labor allocation is performed outside of payroll), human resources, treasury, insurance providers, and financial institutions
- The creation of payment requests to accounts payable and/or treasury for third-party trade payable checks or EFT payments to taxing agencies, courts, insurance providers, and other recipients, if not directly paid by payroll

(d) Business Definition. From a business perspective, payroll includes the following generic types of activities:

- Data-capture services
- Payment-processing services
- Payroll-delivery services
- Third-party payment and reporting services
- Accounting and reconcillation services
- Customer-support services

(i) Data-Capture Services. Data-capture services include all activities associated with the processing and data entry of all forms and data related to employee record information. Data-capture functions may be a shared and/or integrated function with human resources and/or other organizations. For many companies, time collection is the most labor-intensive activity of all front-end processes. The effort involved depends heavily on company time-reporting policies (who and what is reported) and on the methods of reporting (how time is collected, validated, and processed). Programs with paper timecards and centralized data collection and entry processes represent the most labor-intensive systems and often result in high levels of rework and additional labor costs.

(ii) Payment-Processing Services. As companies increasingly move from fixed compensation programs to variable performance- and incentive-based compensation programs, and as companies consolidate multiple employee disbursement systems into single disbursement systems, the number of supplementary compensation programs with which payroll has to support and interface will continue to increase.

Activities within this service focus on the administration of such programs and require close coordination with each authorizing program office to ensure accurate and timely payment services. The degree of work to perform this function depends not only on volumes but on whether the linkages between originators and payroll are paper or electronic based.

(iii) Payroll-Delivery Services. Delivery services include tasks associated with the preparation and controlled distribution of pay statements from point of production to point of employee receipt. Specific processes will vary, depending on company demographics and method(s) of payment (check or direct deposit), as well as on the number of pay cycles, pay frequencies, and volumes of payments. The method of payment selected, the type of pay production technology used, and the mode of pay statement delivery will determine the overall cost of the function. There are numerous options available for performing this function and lowering overall costs.

(iv) Third-Party Payment and Reporting Services. Third-party payment and reporting services include both mandatory and voluntary activities:

- Tax payment and reporting services

  If not performed in an accurate and timely fashion, tax payment and reporting services may represent one of the highest areas of financial exposure and risk. This function includes activities associated with the monitoring of federal, state, and local tax regulations to ensure ongoing compliance; the authorization and issuance of employee- and company-paid taxes in adherence to tax-payment schedules; and the creation and issuance of customized reports dictated by individual taxing agencies, including calendar year-end wage and tax reporting processes (e.g., W-2s and expatriate reporting).

- Attachment payment and reporting services

  This function includes all activities associated with the receipt, execution, payment, and reporting of various forms of wage attachments related to support orders and federal and state tax levies, as well as civil orders. Due to the lack of standardization regarding withholding, payment, and reporting, this function represents a significant labor effort for most companies. Recent revisions to the Family Support Act making employer-withheld child support mandatory has further increased, in some companies, the workload in this area.

- Voluntary deduction program administration services

  Based on volumes, the number of deductions processed by a payroll organization today often exceeds the number of payments made by ten to one. Therefore, in today's environment, payroll organizations might more appropriately be viewed as "deduction agents" rather than "paymasters." The degree to which this is true will depend on a number of factors, including the number and nature of mandatory and elective deduction programs offered by the company.

  The degree of work and cost involved for payroll will also depend on the role that the payroll organization plays in administering each program. From an overall company perspective, it is important to measure costs for an overall process, regardless of the unit performing a given task. However, the effort for payroll specifically will be smaller in companies in which deduction program ownership lies outside of payroll, for example, with human resources or benefits.

  Conversely, the effort and therefore the cost for payroll will be greater to the degree that the role of payroll extends beyond merely withholding and reporting authorized deductions. For example, payroll costs will be higher if payroll is processing all enrollment, change, and stop forms or performing program compliance reporting functions.

Cost and quality can often be favorably impacted by moving those functions that go beyond deduction agency functions to human resources and/or benefits. With today's technology, benefit enrollment and change processes can often be placed directly with the customer (employee), as discussed later.

(v) Accounting and Reconciliation Services. Accounting and reconciliation services include activities associated with closing the books and reconciling balance sheet accounts, bank accounts, journal entries, labor distribution, employee receivables (tracking and collecting monies due the company), and internal balancing and controls. The number of resources required to perform the function is often an indicator of the quality and efficiency of total payroll operations. Fewer resources and account reconciliations with fewer variances and reconciling items might, for example, point to a well-controlled and clean front-end process, whereas a larger number of resources and a higher number of out-of-balance accounts might indicate an environment with problems.

(vi) Customer-Support Services. Customer-support services include services that provide customers with information, assistance in resolving problems, and support to meet changing system requirements and needs. Although some of these services can be automated, the majority are delivered through direct interaction with customers and suppliers. This value-added service, in many respects, is the most important and challenging of all services provided by the business and may in fact represent one of the most costly of all payroll services.

Performance of this function requires business experts and accessibility to data and information. Communication tools, ad hoc reporting capabilities, structured life cycle expertise (for system development programs), and good record retention and retrieval programs are essential elements for success in this area.

(e) Understanding Your Payroll Is the First Step for Budgeting and Change. Every payroll function will be defined differently and will include different types of responsibilities. An in-depth understanding of the payroll business is needed as a foundation for budgeting and change. Understanding of your payroll function can be enhanced by creating and documenting data and process models, inventories of suppliers and customers, and so on, as illustrated in Exhibit 17.7.

17.3 RELATIONSHIP WITH HUMAN RESOURCE FUNCTION. In most companies, payroll reports through the finance organization. However, there is a trend toward a reporting line within the human resource organization, and there is good reason for this.

Human resources is a major supplier and customer of payroll data, and separate systems and master files represent redundant warehouses, if not repetitive data-entry processes, and offer a significant opportunity for integration. In addition, payroll is primarily an employee function, with significant output information for finance.

Third-party software vendors understand this relationship very well and are leading the way by developing and marketing integrated human resource and payroll software products.

Regardless of reporting lines, finance and human resources must work together to understand total employee administrative processes and must begin to look at payroll and

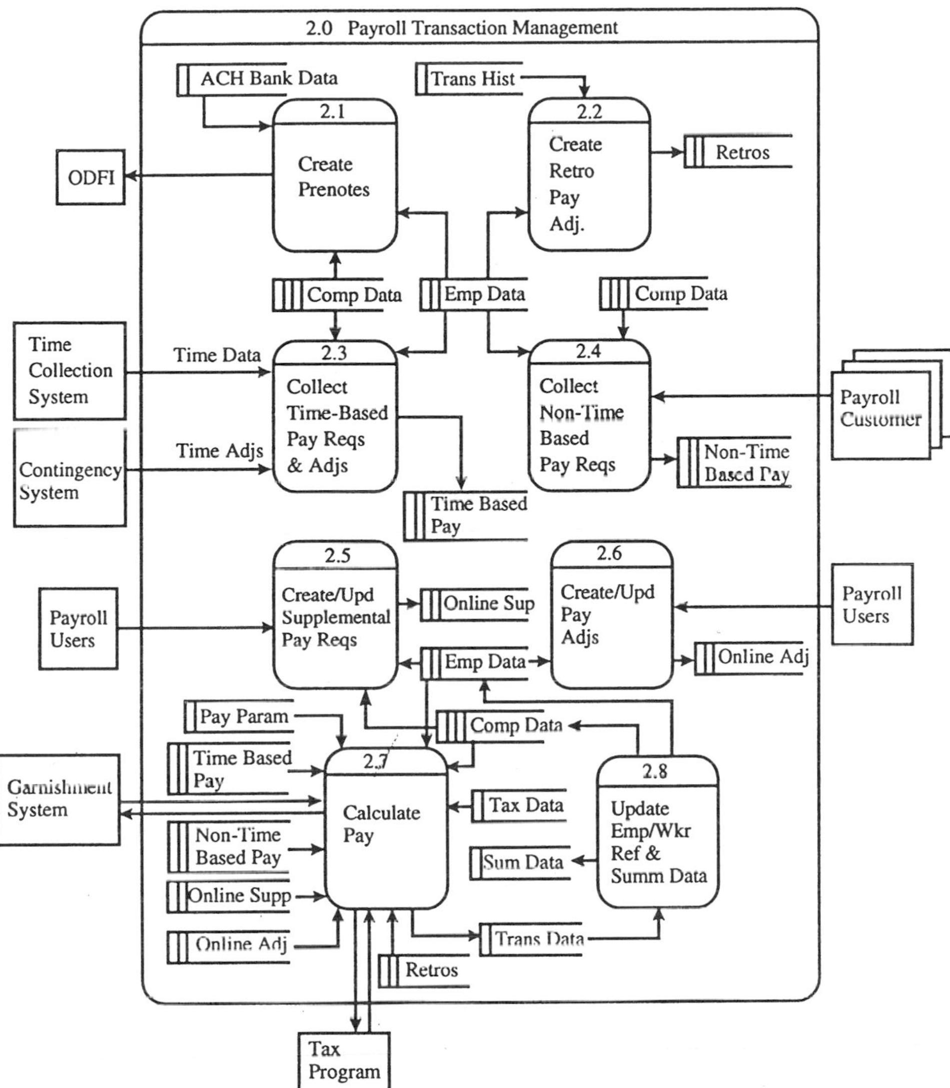

Exhibit 17.7. Payroll process model
Reprinted with permission. © Digital Equipment Corporation—U.S. Payroll.

human resources as part of the same process, not distinct and separate businesses. This approach can offer opportunities for sizable savings.

17.4 MAJOR COMPONENTS OF PAYROLL COSTS. Direct payroll costs will vary greatly depending on the range of activities included in the function. In addition, if the function is outsourced, there will be a different set of cost components from one that is performed in-house. Regardless of how these costs are captured and reported, payroll costs, as in any administrative function, will consist of labor and direct nonlabor costs, as well as indirect or allocated charges and overhead.

In addition to labor-related costs, which normally represent the highest expenditure (as

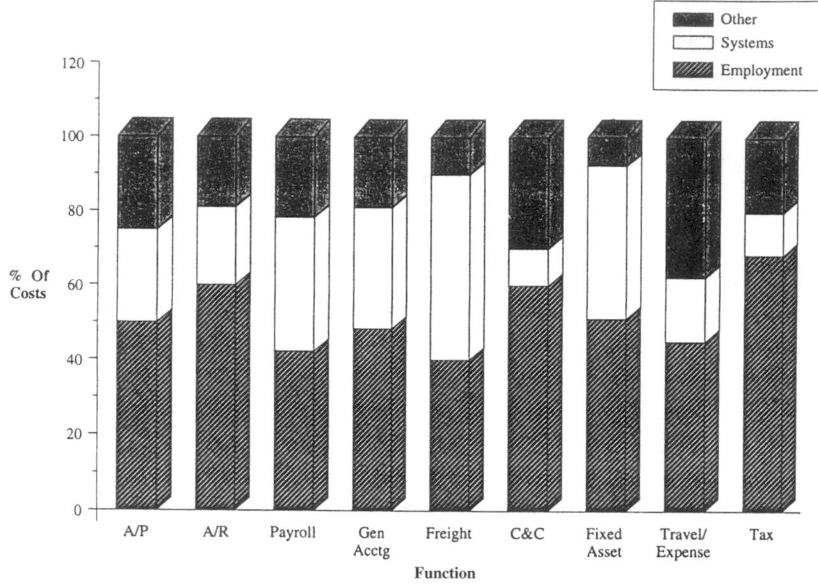

Exhibit 17.8. Cost breakdown by function

illustrated in Exhibit 17.8), major components of payroll costs, in high to low dollar order, normally include systems-related expenses (e.g., hardware, data center, and software application support), and other (direct nonlabor and indirect or allocated charges and overhead) expenses. What is reported as direct versus indirect expenses will vary by company, due to different accounting practices and philosophies, but will include such costs as supplies and forms, third-party production, and delivery-related supplier services and expenses, as well as banking related costs. A more detailed listing of specific payroll cost items appears in Section 17.8 under traditional budgeting approaches.

(a) Understanding Total Costs. It should be noted that payroll component costs may be captured in more than one cost center; only through the identification of all costs can a company fully understand its total payroll cost picture. Finally, ''soft'' costs, though not normally captured and budgeted for, should also be understood, as they may represent significant expense to the company. Examples of soft payroll costs include company labor required to deliver pay statements to employees within each paysite or labor required by employees and supervisors to collect, review, approve, and deliver information to payroll.

(b) Hardware and Data Center Costs. The age and type of the hardware may be a key factor affecting payroll costs. Exhibit 17.9 provides a sample template for estimating annualized hardware-related costs. To calculate payroll-processing costs, one must (1) post the annual depreciation or lease cost of all categories (e.g., mainframe, midrange, and personal computer) of hardware; (2) calculate the percentage of central processing unit (CPU) cycles, input/output, and disk space utilization for the payroll application resident on each hardware platform; (3) add the calculated percentages and divide by the three (essentially, calculate the average of the three percentages); (4) multiply the result of your average calculation in the third step by the annual depreciation or lease cost of

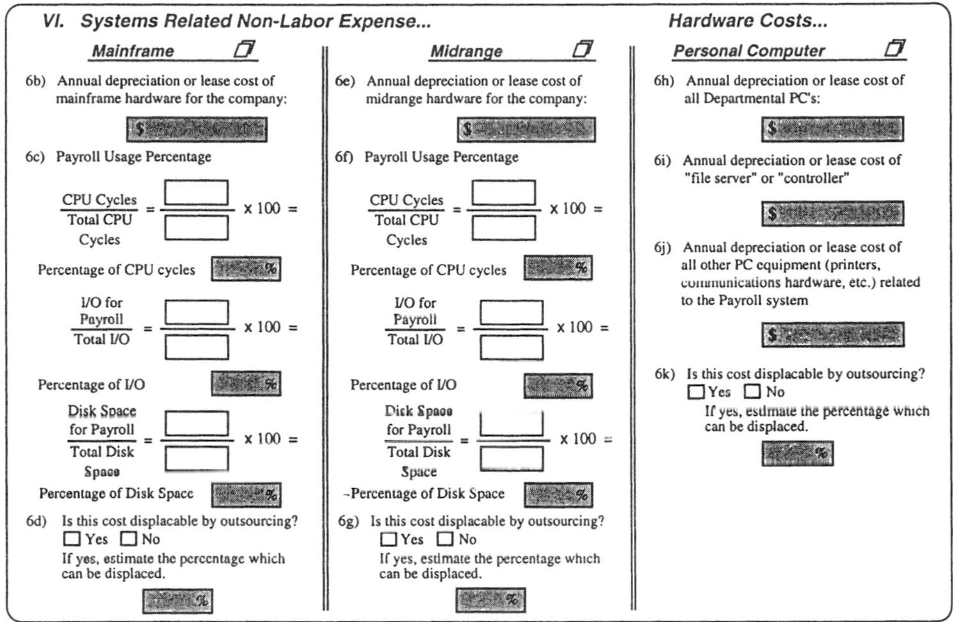

VI. Systems Related Non-Labor Expense... Hardware Costs...

Mainframe

6b) Annual depreciation or lease cost of mainframe hardware for the company: $

6c) Payroll Usage Percentage

CPU Cycles / Total CPU Cycles = ☐ / ☐ x 100 =

Percentage of CPU cycles %

I/O for Payroll / Total I/O = ☐ / ☐ x 100 =

Percentage of I/O %

Disk Space for Payroll / Total Disk Space = ☐ / ☐ x 100 =

Percentage of Disk Space %

6d) Is this cost displacable by outsourcing? ☐ Yes ☐ No

If yes, estimate the percentage which can be displaced. %

Midrange

6e) Annual depreciation or lease cost of midrange hardware for the company: $

6f) Payroll Usage Percentage

CPU Cycles / Total CPU Cycles = ☐ / ☐ x 100 =

Percentage of CPU cycles %

I/O for Payroll / Total I/O = ☐ / ☐ x 100 =

Percentage of I/O %

Disk Space for Payroll / Total Disk Space = ☐ / ☐ x 100 =

Percentage of Disk Space %

6g) Is this cost displacable by outsourcing? ☐ Yes ☐ No

If yes, estimate the percentage which can be displaced. %

Personal Computer

6h) Annual depreciation or lease cost of all Departmental PC's: $

6i) Annual depreciation or lease cost of "file server" or "controller" $

6j) Annual depreciation or lease cost of all other PC equipment (printers, communications hardware, etc.) related to the Payroll system $

6k) Is this cost displacable by outsourcing? ☐ Yes ☐ No

If yes, estimate the percentage which can be displaced. %

Exhibit 17.9. Hardware-related cost estimating
Reprinted with permission. © Coopers & Lybrand L.L.P.

the appropriate hardware category; and (5) add the results of each hardware category for a total hardware cost estimate. It should be emphasized that the result will represent a "quick and dirty" estimate technique. Many companies use a systems cost-allocation methodology for determining hardware-related costs for each application (e.g., payroll). Such methodologies may offer a more accurate estimate of cost.

More often than not, payroll is not supported by dedicated hardware. In today's environment, payroll often utilizes the capacity and expertise resident in a shared service center (SSC). Such use drives standardization and optimizes automated production processes. Costs for such services are often based on standardized cost allocation methodologies provided under a service agreement with rates set on a fiscal-year basis. Whether internally or externally provided, the business should clearly understand the rate structure and performance level provided under such an agreement.

(c) Software and Application Support Costs. Some companies use in-house developed software, whereas others use vendor-acquired software. Each approach involves different kinds of costs. In-house software requires ongoing maintenance support. Software acquired from a third-party vendor requires special investment dollars (usually capitalized) at the time of acquisition and then involves annual license fees. Companies that purchase and then modify third-party software will continue to incur significant ongoing maintenance and enhancement costs as well.

The trend in payroll software is to move from in-house legacy systems, which require significant dollars to maintain and longer time frames to introduce change, onto more flexible and table-driven vendor-acquired products. At the same time, mainframe systems are being replaced with lower cost personal computer (PC)-based architecture.

Please allocate the General Office and field FTEs for each of the labor categories into the Sub–Processes.

General Office:	# of FTEs Supervisor	Clerical	Contractor	Direct Labor / Contractor Costs
Total Number of General Office FTEs	___	___	___	$ ______
Data Capture	___	___	___	$ ______
Payment Processing	___	___	___	$ ______
Payment Production	___	___	___	$ ______
Tax Payments and Reporting	___	___	___	$ ______
Accounting & Reconciliation	___	___	___	$ ______
Customer Support Services	___	___	___	$ ______
Record Retention	___	___	___	$ ______
	___	___	___	______

General Office:	# of FTEs Supervisor	Clerical	Contractor	Direct Labor / Contractor Costs
Total Number of General Office FTEs	___	___	___	$______
Data Capture	___	___	___	$______
Payment Processing	___	___	___	$______
Payment Production	___	___	___	$______
Tax Payments and Reporting	___	___	___	$______
Accounting & Reconciliation	___	___	___	$______
Customer Support Services	___	___	___	$______
Record Retention	___	___	___	$______
Other (non–productive)	___	___	___	$______

Please allocate the FTEs for each of the labor categories:

	# of FTEs	Direct Labor / Contractor Costs
Human Resources	______	$______
Legal	______	$______
Information Systems	______	$______

2. Provide the non–labor and indirect costs for the Payroll process as identified in the scope. Use the following definitions when completing the table.

   Direct Non–Labor cost – Includes all direct, non–labor costs charged to the process.

   Contract Services cost – The outsourcing of all or part of a function to a third party.

   Overhead cost – Costs associated with training, travel, telephone, facilities, office equipment, office supplies, etc.

	1993 Non–Labor Costs
Direct Non–Labor cost	
Contract Services cost	
Overhead cost	
TOTAL	

Exhibit 17.10. Labor resource table
Reprinted with permission. © 3D Consortium. All rights reserved.

(d) Labor-Related Costs. Labor-related costs normally represent the largest single cost component of the payroll function and include labor, overtime, sick, vacation, personal allowance, and fringe benefit allocations. Because labor represents such a large portion of the average payroll budget, companies are well served by understanding and tracking the equivalent headcount required to support each payroll activity. This knowledge, in combination with volumes and anticipated changes in the business, helps to create a more accurate budget. This information is also helpful in identifying opportunities for labor and cost savings. Exhibit 17.10 offers one type of mechanism for capturing headcount and labor-related costs by location and business function.

(e) Supplier Costs. Much of the payroll-related cost will be incurred on behalf of the business by suppliers.

(i) Financial Institutions. Financial institutions that provide payroll services to companies represent important suppliers and should be managed, like any other supplier, under a service agreement and regularly evaluated for performance, including cost of product. Payroll services normally provided by financial institutions include check-processing and reconcilement services, automated clearing house (ACH) direct deposit credit, debit, and prenoting services, as well as an array of other administrative services. The cost of such services may be covered by offsetting balances maintained at the institution or may be based on per-transaction fees with varying rates based on volume. As in any vendor evaluation, requests for proposals (RFPs) should be used to compare services and prices, which can vary significantly from one financial institution to another.

(ii) Federal and State Tax Administration Services. Many companies choose third-party vendors to perform payroll tax payment and reporting functions associated with

federal, state, local, and unemployment tax processes. Companies that select this option gain the expertise of the provider and do not have to maintain in-house resources to perform the function. Historically, the provider has been compensated via access to the funds in advance of scheduled payment due dates; therefore, this may or may not be a budgeted expense. Companies that choose this option retain ultimate liability and relinquish some direct control over the process. The provider is normally liable for errors it makes.

(iii) Forms Providers. Forms, including checks, direct-deposit pay statements, time cards, and W-2s, can represent substantial costs. These costs can be minimized by using laser printers whenever possible or by ordering multiple printed forms under a single purchase order and taking advantage of volume discounts. Stock levels should be sufficient to meet short- to intermediate-term needs but should not be maintained at levels that would represent sizable waste in the event of form revisions.

17.5 CONDITIONS AND FACTORS AFFECTING PAYROLL COSTS.

Many internal and external factors affect payroll costs; some are controllable and others are not. Factors that impact different levels of cost between companies are sometimes referred to as *cost differentiators.*

(a) Differentiators.

Actual payroll costs may vary greatly from one company to another, due to classes of differentiators identified in Exhibit 17.11. Differentiators may cause costs to go up or down.

In some cases, differentiators are largely beyond the control of the business and are often due to the nature of the business or the industry in which the company operates. In other cases, positive or negative differentiators may be the result of company policies or practices. In many instances, these policies and practices can be changed and significant dollars saved in the process.

Differentiators

Features and characteristics of an organization or its practices that distinguish one company from another when attempting to compare efficiency or effectiveness.

- *Questions/concerns you would immediately raise if someone said your "cost per invoice" was 25% below Company B's*
- *If automation is a key driver of cost, and Company A uses a Cray XMP supercomputer and Company B uses an Apple Macintosh, there is clearly a practice difference worth identifying*

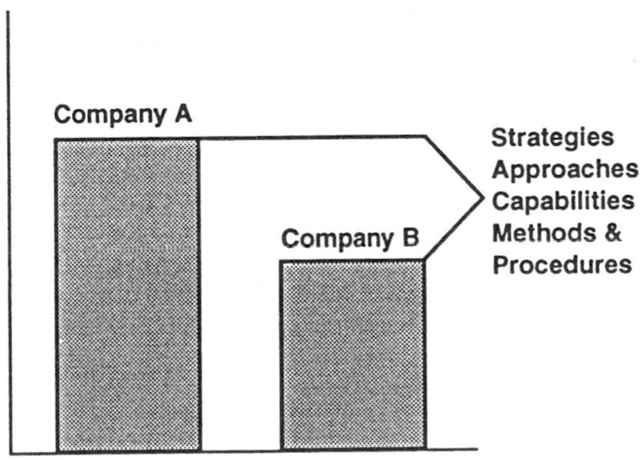

Exhibit 17.11. Classes of differentiators

Examples of differentiators that tend to drive payroll costs up or down include the following:

Category	Higher Costs	Lower Costs
• Employee composition	Heavily hourly	Predominantly exempt
• Labor unions	Present	Absent
• Operations	Decentralized	Centralized
• Pay programs	Multiple	Single
• Pay frequency	More frequent (e.g., weekly)	Less frequent (e.g., biweekly, semi-monthly, etc.)
• Taxing jurisdictions	Larger number	Smaller number
• Earnings categories	Larger number	Smaller number
• Deduction categories	Larger number	Smaller number
• Pay media	Check	Direct deposit
• Time reporting environment	Complex	Simple
• Degree of automation	Low	High
• Use of technology	Low	High
• Human resource and payroll systems	Independent	Integrated
• Controls	Manual	Automated validations
• Payroll skill set focus	Maintenance	Development/change

(b) Work-Load Drivers. In addition, costs are also affected by work-load drivers. Examples of work-load drivers include the following:

- Number of payees
- Number of out-of-cycle payments
- Number of pay adjustments
- Number of paysite locations
- Number of time caputure systems
- Number of time cards processed
- Number of new hires, transfers, terminations, retirees
- Number of child support orders, federal and state levies, civil attachments, and the like
- Number of payroll bank accounts
- Number of direct-deposit accounts offered per employee
- Number of payroll general ledger and subledger accounts

(c) Differentiators and Work-Load Drivers: Key to Understanding Costs. Differentiators and work-load drivers must be fully understood if one is to identify opportunities for improvement and maximize efficiency and effectiveness. As illustrated in Exhibit 17.12, this understanding can be facilitated by categorizing information into types of differentiators and work-load drivers.

Understanding these conditions and factors is the first step toward reaching a high-service, low-cost operation. Factors unique to the industry, as well as historical (and often discretionary) choices made by a company, can have a significant impact on cost of product. It is important to understand these factors as one company compares its costs with those of other companies and sets future spending plans.

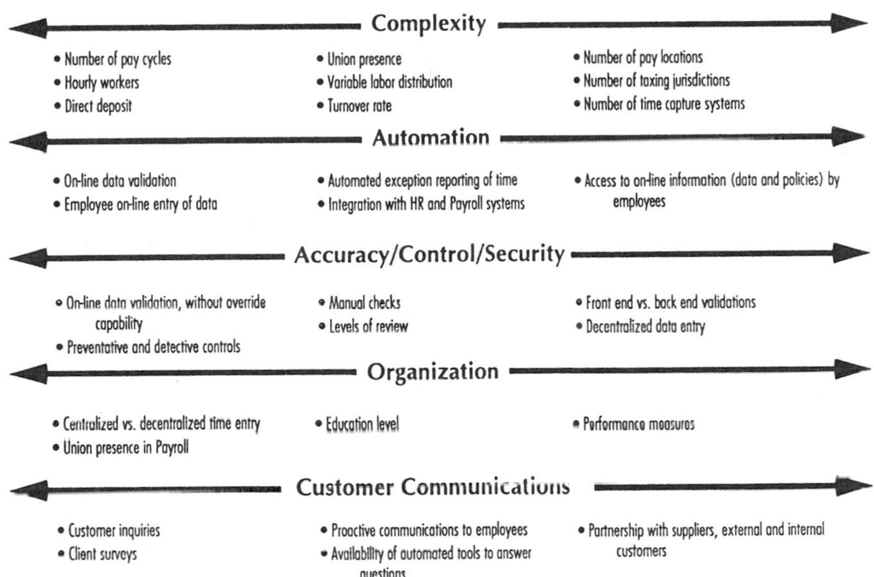

Exhibit 17.12. Types of differentiators and work drivers
Reprinted with permission.

(d) Expanded Explanations. Following are some of the factors that may drive costs up or down.

(i) Company Structure. Paying multiple legal entities significantly impacts costs, especially if each entity has different compensation and benefit programs with different business rules and regulations, pay cycles, and so on. The degree to which these differences can be eliminated will determine whether any cost-saving opportunities exist. At a minimum, each legal entity will require separate tax and accounting processes.

(ii) Decentralized/Centralized Operations. Companies located in multiple states or regions have additional requirements when it comes to delivery of payroll services. Decentralized payroll operations to support each geographic or sub-business unit may involve redundant resources, systems, processes, and overhead expenses. Companies currently operating with multiple-payroll operating units should consider consolidation. Given today's technology and networking capabilities, companies are combining the benefits of consolidated processing with the advantages of distributed input and output capabilities. Operating in a consolidated fashion presents problems only when input and output at the processing location are based on paper.

(iii) Population Supported. The size of the population being paid can drive the cost of the function up, especially in the absence of consolidation, standardization, and automation. However, employee population of and by itself is not the primary driver of expense.

(iv) Tax Compliance and Reporting Requirements. The number of taxing jurisdictions to which the payroll function is subject, at the federal, state, and local levels, certainly

drives cost and potentially represents the highest level of financial exposure and risk. In today's environment, taxing jurisdictions are looking for every dollar they can generate and are quick to impose fines and penalties. Employers cannot afford to underspend in this area. At the same time, there are many opportunities to lower costs in this area, including consolidated tax reporting under a single employer identification number (EIN); utilization of available software vendor products to permit downloading of payroll withheld taxes into customized tax paper and electronic payment and reporting formats; or outsourcing to third-party vendors.

(v) Pay-Frequency Alternatives. Less frequent pay cycles can save dollars. Payroll costs, whether measured via cost of money or cost of operation, can be minimized by selecting the least frequent pay cycle allowable by state law (or bargaining agreement, in the case of unions). The standard and most commonly used pay frequency within the United States is biweekly, followed by semimonthly. Although states do not change pay-frequency laws often, companies should monitor state pay-frequency regulations periodically. For example, the Commonwealth of Massachusetts now permits biweekly pay cycles. Some states also provide exemptions to weekly state pay-frequency laws through partitions and under certain conditions, when formally requested by employers.

(vi) Multiple Pay Programs. Consolidating multiple pay-frequency programs also offers an opportunity for savings. For example, some employers maintain a separate executive payroll. Elimination of multiple pay cycles translates into fewer differences between employee sets (e.g., fewer unique policies, procedures, forms, and processes) and in turn reduces costs of production and administration.

In both of these cases, companies need to understand their demographics and, within the framework of current state legal parameters, evaluate the financial, business, operational, and employee relations pros and cons of each viable option. As is true of other payroll-related decisions, cross-functional considerations are a necessary part of the decision-making process.

(vii) Collective Bargaining Agreements. There is no question that payrolls required to support bargaining units are more costly. The number of bargaining units and the differences between each bargaining agreement determine the degree of cost impact. Although companies may not be able to effect short-term change, the challenge exists to begin to influence administrative changes that provide win-win opportunities. Eliminating costly customized services that provide less value to the customer may provide a starting point for mutually supported change.

(viii) Pay Media. Finance management and decision makers often do not understand that payment via direct deposit offers an opportunity for savings. Check processing is more expensive, especially in low interest periods. Direct-deposit operational savings match and often exceed the loss of float. Companies should complete a comparative cost analysis between the two payment methods. Hard and soft savings statistics often support claims that direct deposit is less expensive. One example of a soft savings is costs saved in employee time away from work for cashing checks. Best-practice companies have high-participation direct-deposit levels and are moving toward electronic pay delivery solutions

Direct Deposit Cost/Savings Analysis

	Cost/Savings	Our Company
I. Initial Investment		
1. Modifications to payroll system	$ _______	$0.00
II. Annual Costs		
2. A. Initial collection of authorization forms and input (includes paper cost for advices)	$ _______	$6,367.20
B. Annual add, stop, change file maintenance	$ _______	$5,068.80
3. Bank service charges @ ____________ per item	$ _______	$67,200.00
4. Direct deposit campaign costs	$ _______	N/A
5. Lost float	$ _______	$218,736.00
6. 20% of investment (item I) (5 year amortization)	$ _______	N/A
TOTAL	**$ _______**	**$207,372.00**
III. Annual Savings		
7. Bank check processing charges @ ______ per item x number of items	$ _______	$353,472.00
8. Bank reconcilement maintenance @ per month	$ _______	$ incl. in #1
9. Bank reconcilement charges @ _______ per item x number of items	$ _______	$ incl. in #1
10. In-house reconcilement costs	$ _______	$1,584.00
11. Check storage and microfilming	$ _______	$ incl. in #1
12. Bank stop-payment charges @ $ ________ per stop x number of items	$ _______	$3,000.00
13. Check reissue costs ________ (cost per reissue x number of reissues)	$ _______	$15,000.00
14. Incremental check forms costs	$ _______	$12,280.80
15. Check distribution and handling costs	$ _______	$528,768.00
16. Check cashing service charge (if applicable)	$ _______	N/A
17. Employee lost time to cash checks (____ hours per employee x average pay per hour x # of employees) NOTE: Some companies prefer to exclude item 16 from analysis due to difficulty in estimating.	$ _______	N/A
TOTAL	**$ _______**	**$914,104.80**
IV. Net Addition to Profits		
A. 1st year	$ _______	**$616,732.80**
B. 2nd through 5th year (if depreciating initial investment)	$ _______	N/A
C. After fifth year (if depreciating initial investment)	$ _______	N/A

Modified from *The Payroll Manager's Guide to Successful Direct Deposit*, Sixth Edition.

Exhibit 17.13. Sample direct-deposit cost savings
Reprinted with permission. © American Payroll Association.

to replace paper pay statements, representing even more savings. Exhibit 17.13 presents one company's projected cost savings achievable via converting to direct deposit. You will see that, in this illustration, savings exceeded costs by $616,732.80. This points out that direct deposit can provide payroll savings to many companies, with the amount of savings directly linked to the percentage of direct participants.

At the same time, when considering the implementation or expansion of direct-deposit programs, employers need to recognize that state pay media laws vary, and in most states employees must voluntarily agree to participate. Regional and nationwide employers cannot, under most current state laws, impose compulsory direct-deposit programs for salary and wage payments.

(ix) Level of Service Provided. It is a traditional mindset within the payroll area that service means doing anything and everything that customers (anyone) ask for. Fortunately, this mindset is being challenged, and services and levels of performance provided are being adjusted and balanced with business need and cost considerations. The customer is being redefined to recognize that the internal customer (employee) is not equivalent to the customer that buys the company's products and services.

Companies are beginning to learn that the focus of internal administrative services should be on core competencies (for example, accuracy and timeliness) and that services and performance levels that go beyond might offer opportunities for cost savings. Companies with high direct-deposit participation levels, for example, may be able to eliminate advance vacation pay options, as employees will have access to their funds while on vacation or away from the work site.

(x) Earnings Programs Offered. Over the years, companies have had a tendency to create new earnings categories "on demand," without giving proper attention to the costs associated with introducing and maintaining each new earnings category—not only for payroll, but for downstream suppliers and customers. Each earnings category, regardless of whether the software can accommodate the addition, involves ongoing administrative costs in the form of specialized processes, forms, policies, and procedures.

In addition, companies are rapidly moving from traditional fixed compensation programs to variable, performance-based programs. With this change, the number of earnings programs is increasing and becoming more complex. For these reasons, best-practice companies are moving to reduce or consolidate the number of earnings categories, to replace (in the case of those with in-house software) hard-coded earnings logic with table-driven menus and to place greater responsibility with business suppliers and customers for calculating such payments and storing historical data.

(xi) Deduction Programs Offered. Payroll has become more of a deduction than a disbursement agent. Though much of this is unavoidable, many best-practice companies are revising their roles in deduction administration and moving to eliminate discretionary deduction programs not essential to the business. Where elective deduction programs are offered, some companies are beginning to pass administrative costs on to employees or providers.

The number of deduction programs that payroll offers and the role that payroll plays in the process will impact cost. For example, if payroll is responsible for processing enrollment and changes to deduction programs, its costs will be higher.

Best-practice companies are also moving toward accountability and entry at the source. For example, the use of voice response systems and client server technology permits employees, supervisors, and/or suppliers (e.g., human resources, benefits, etc.) to initiate or change transactions without the involvement of payroll employees. In turn, payroll can then receive prevalidated data in a format that can be processed automatically.

(xii) Time Collection/Reporting Methodologies. Time collection and reporting processes can be two of the most labor-intensive and error-prone processes in the payroll

supply chain, especially if they are manual (paper based). All processes in the creation, approval, and processing of time data should be fully understood. Companies are beginning to realize that time reporting programs often represent high cost and low value. As a result, best-practice companies are moving from mandatory reporting to exception reporting processes when possible, and reducing and/or eliminating the number of reporting categories.

Companies must begin to ask whether the need for reporting is based on current legal and business requirements or on historical precedent. Unessential time reporting practices should be discontinued and necessary reporting upgraded to smart clocks, voice, or terminal-entered processes available from multiple third-party vendors.

(xiii) Relationships with Other Internal Financial and Accounting Systems. Some organizations perform labor collection and reporting duties as well as other peripheral duties. Each of these functions should be re-examined to determine first whether the function serves a valid business need, and second, if essential, where the function might best be performed. Often, companies find that tasks being performed are no longer needed or that such functions could better be performed elsewhere.

(xiv) Mergers and Acquisitions. In today's rapidly changing business climate, many companies are acquiring new businesses, establishing new business alliances, or looking to divest portions of their existing businesses. These situations ultimately involve decisions regarding the delivery of administrative functions, such as payroll services. Each of these opportunities should be closely examined prior to making any decision. Supporting new compensation and benefit programs that normally accompany acquisitions may represent significant complexity and cost. Added to the complexity is the fact that often such decisions have to be made quickly. The decision to operate under separate payroll systems, migrate to one system, or use a third-party service provider, on a temporary or permanent basis, should all be considered from legal, service, and cost perspectives prior to a final decision.

(xv) Industry- and Company-Unique Pay Practices. Additional practices unique to an industry or company can also drive costs higher and also should be considered. Whenever possible, these practices should be modified or eliminated to maximize service and minimize cost. Reviewing company compensation policies, for example, might identify pay practices that are not legally required and if eliminated would provide financial as well as operational savings. For example, some companies have determined that their overtime pay practices exceed those required by law (e.g., paying overtime for more than eight hours a day versus more than forty hours a week).

17.6 CHOICES AND DECISIONS: OUTSOURCING, ACQUISITION, AND DEVELOPMENT. No solution is permanent, and all companies sooner or later need to make decisions about whether to outsource payroll to a third-party processor, purchase an external software product, invest in the internal development of an in-house application, or manage a variety of these solutions. Many companies are currently evaluating these choices as their current legacy systems are not Year 2000 compliant. Each approach has its pros and cons and should be considered carefully during the budgeting process, as all choices will have financial/non-financial implications.

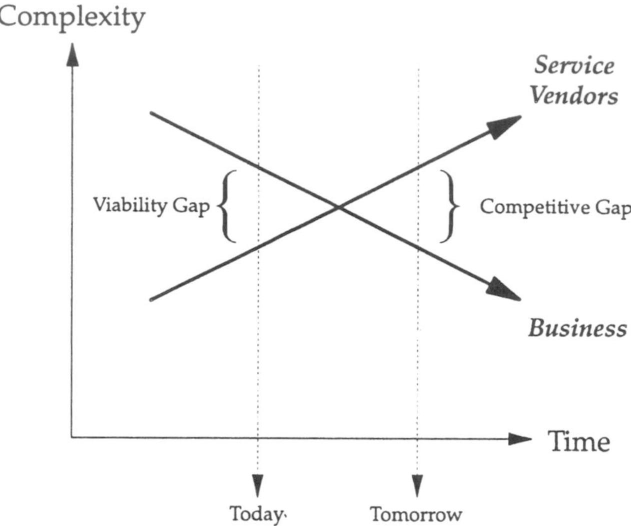

Exhibit 17.14. Service provider potential
Reprinted with permission. © Gunn Partners, Inc.

(a) Outsourcing

(i) Understanding the Pluses and the Minuses. Outsourcing has become an emerging best-in-class practice, especially in areas of benefit administration (e.g., 401k, pension). In payroll, companies are also looking at outsourcing all or portions of the payroll function. Cost is increasingly the motivating factor.

Size of company often determines the viability of outsourcing. The smaller the company, the more likely it is that outsourcing will provide a cost-effective solution. This is true because normally smaller companies have less need for customized solutions. Their needs can be more readily met via an outside service bureau with a generic set of products and services.

However, as depicted in Exhibit 17.14, the gap between what larger companies need and what service providers can deliver at a competitive rate is closing, and some consultants now predict that, within two to three years, service providers will be able to offer viable products and services to this yet untapped market. Experts predict that this will happen as a result of several ''enablers.'' First, as companies are consolidating and re-engineering their internal payroll operations, they are also standardizing and simplifying their internal programs. Second, service providers are combining forces with payroll software vendors and are adopting or developing more flexible and functionally robust software applications.

At the same time, outsourcing, even for medium-sized and smaller companies, should not be viewed as a panacea. All companies that are evaluating the option of outsourcing should consider (1) how complex their needs are; (2) how much customization is anticipated (not only at the time of implementation, but also in the future); and (3) how much control is needed over the vendor's products and services. Unfortunately, companies sometimes discover, after they have outsourced payroll, that their service bureau is unable to support their unique needs for change at an affordable price and within the time frame needed. As in carpentry, companies would do well to ''measure twice and cut once.''

(ii) Rationale. Companies considering outsourcing should clearly understand their rationale for outsourcing and should weigh both direct and indirect potential benefits and risks against the overall strategic objectives of the business. Some valid reasons may include the following:

- *Rate of change.* The business must implement solutions faster than it can develop them internally.
- *Resources.* There is a shortage of dedicated business and/or technical resources and/or equipment.
- *Expertise.* The base knowledge is not available or is eroding.
- *Expense.* The function is too costly to establish or sustain.
- *Exposure.* Company performance in areas of compliance and cost avoidance has been unacceptable.

(iii) Other Considerations—Costs and Benefits. When determining if outsourcing is an effective alternative, consideration should also be given to the not-so-obvious costs and benefits. Some services currently provided to employees may be lost as a result of outsourcing and other services may have to continue to be performed by the company. Decisions on these issues may have both financial and nonfinancial (e.g., employee relations) implications.

The business should also carefully evaluate whether there are low- or no-cost underutilized resources within the company that, if used, would make outsourcing an expensive alternative. Underutilized computer capacity and resources are a prime example.

(iv) Opportunities. Payroll outsourcing traditionally includes the processing of prevalidated input data (company and employee profile data, authorized deduction amounts, and time card input), the gross-to-net (pay calculation) process, and the production of checks and standard payroll-related reports and general ledger interfaces. Supplementary services may be added at additional cost (e.g., the generation and distribution of W-2s, optional employee direct-deposit account(s), tax-filing services, unemployment reporting, etc.).

Even when companies outsource payroll, they will need to continue to maintain human resource and payroll professionals in-house to collect, validate, and process accurate input to the service provider and to act as a liaison to the provider. This is often the most costly portion of the process.

However, outsourcing does not have to be an all-or-nothing proposition. Instead of an all-inclusive package, companies can outsource portions of the function. Some of the specific payroll-related functions that lend themselves to outsourcing include the following:

- Tax administration (the payment and reporting of federal, state, and local income and unemployment payroll taxes)
- Pension payrolls
- Expatriate and/or foreign payrolls
- Subsidiary, division, or decentralized payrolls
- Deduction programs (e.g., U.S. Savings Bonds administration)
- Special employee payroll sets (e.g., hourly employees, executive payrolls, annuity payrolls, etc.)

- Pay statement production and distribution services
- W-2 production and distribution services

(v) Outsourcing Does Not Mean Relinquishing Accountability. Outsourcing does not mean relinquishing accountability for the outsourced function(s). Regardless of the magnitude of outsourcing being considered, companies must realize that outsourcing is often easier than bringing the function back in house. Therefore, the longer-term implications and cost of outsourcing should be carefully considered in the evaluation and vendor selection process.

In considering the outsourcing of payroll, a detailed analysis of company requirements against the service provider's capabilities should be undertaken, including a cost-comparison analysis. If positive, a detailed service agreement should be developed (including performance standards and measurements, fee schedules, software change conditions, contingency plans, cancellation rights, and responsibilities) to ensure that all aspects of the business are covered.

(b) Application Acquisition versus Development

(i) Legacy System—What to Do? In today's environment, larger companies are finding that legacy payroll systems do not meet today's more complex needs. More often than not, companies find themselves in a quandary over whether to continue to invest in their current systems or to purchase an outside vendor package. In either case, the cost of making major modifications to existing software or of purchasing an outside product is an expensive undertaking, often amounting, for medium to large companies, to hundreds of thousands of dollars.

Traditionally, payroll has not been the recipient of corporate investment dollars, and changes have normally been made in a reactive fashion, thereby increasing the complexity of such software and compounding the difficulty and cost of future changes. On the positive side, though, in-house solutions have traditionally been reliable. Their weakness is normally limited functionality and flexibility, along with high maintenance costs. In general, aged systems (those more than ten years old) are not equipped to support the more dynamic environment of today's business needs. Although the acquisition or development of software is a big-ticket item, software limitations, if not addressed, can be more costly or even catastrophic to a company.

(ii) The Decision-Making Process. Unfortunately, decisions are more often forced around a short-term crisis or change in business needs than around a solution arising from a longer-range tactical evaluation and plan. Ideally, this decision should be made only after the following steps have been completed:

- As a basis for planning, the current system should be well documented. Documentation should include business and technical documentation, data and process models, strengths and weaknesses, costs, and the like.
- Current and future business requirements should be inventoried. This process should include the participation of both business customers and suppliers.
- An opportunity evaluation should be completed to identify and justify the need for change. The scope of change and the cost of internal software development should be calculated.

- An RFP should be prepared to define business requirements and then should be sent to selected (prescreened) vendors.

The quality of this work will determine the quality of vendor responses and often the quality of the final decisions made from the process. Quality should be emphasized on the front end, as it will reduce the cost and effort of downstream action items. Access to software products for on-site testing is not always possible but is always preferable before entering into a purchase contract.

(iii) Software Packages Will Require Modification. Once an employer decides to select an outside product, the decision-making process is not over. The purchaser will have to determine how much of the work will be contracted to the vendor and how much of the work will be performed in house. It should be noted that understanding, modifying, testing, and implementing a new software product is a significant effort, often requiring 24 to 36 months to complete, depending on the complexity of the business. Training, communications, and coordination with business suppliers and customers will also require substantial efforts. For these reasons, selection of the vendor and the vendor's product is a very critical step.

There should also be an agreement with the vendor on how much customization will be allowed for the vendor to continue to support the product. In some cases, overcustomization has forced the payroll organization to take ownership of software changes. This can ultimately lead to another legacy system.

(iv) To Purchase or Not to Purchase: A Cross-Functional Decision. Finally, the decision to purchase is not only a finance or payroll and technology decision, but a human resources decision as well. Payroll is a subprocess of the human resource process, regardless of reporting lines. It is inconceivable that human resources or payroll would make an architectural decision of this magnitude without the involvement of its business partner in today's business environment. Such an independent decision might very well cost the company even more money in future years.

In summary, short-term needs of 12 months or less can hardly ever be met via product acquisition. The key is to anticipate and make this investment decision well in advance of the need. This requires that the payroll professional understand the directions of the company, its business customers, and suppliers, and that investment dollars to support this effort be included in the budget.

17.7 ORGANIZATIONAL FACTORS AFFECTING COST

(a) Past Organizational Structures and Perceptions. Traditionally, payroll organizational structures have been formed hierarchically with a manager, supervisor(s), and a staff of accounting and clerical personnel. Until recently, the payroll function has been viewed as a predominantly clerical (transaction-processing) function and has been staffed with hourly or nonexempt employees. As an overhead function that is perceived as simply being a ''check-cutting'' organization, payroll has not always received the resources and investment dollars it has deserved. As a result, its development and contributions to the company have been impeded.

In many companies today, payroll labor (and therefore costs) is greater than it needs to be due to these outdated perceptions.

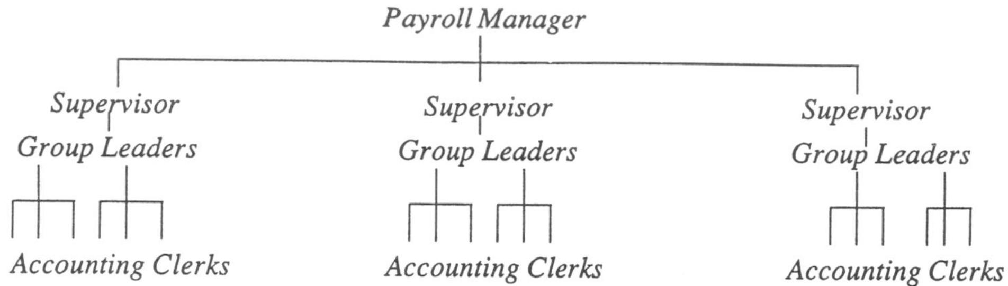

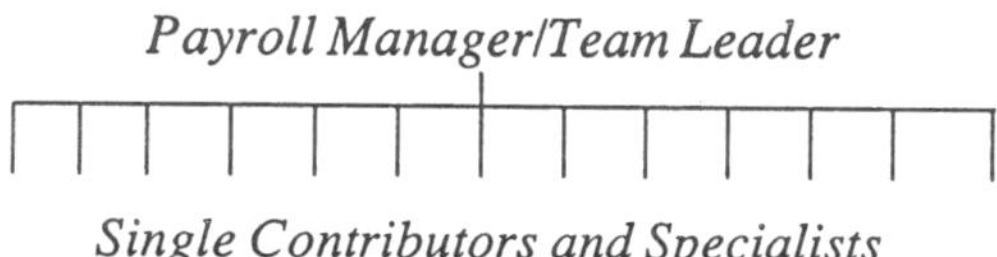

Exhibit 17.15. Organizational structures contrasted
Reprinted with permission. © Digital Equipment Corporation—U.S. Payroll.

(b) Changing Organizational Structures and Perceptions. Fortunately, this is now changing. Today, best-in-class payroll organizations with low cost of products and high levels of customer satisfaction have the following organizational characteristics:

- Payroll departments are more likely to be staffed by professional (exempt) rather than clerical (hourly) jobs. Best-in-class payroll organizations are often staffed with 80% to 90% professionals of 80% to 90% clerical.
- Payroll professionals in these organizations bring with them a higher level of education than in the past. Employees with bachelor's degrees are now more common than those with high school diplomas. Master's degrees and professional certifications (e.g., Certified Payroll Professional [CPP] are increasingly common.
- Outdated organizational structures with multiple reporting levels are being replaced with teams of highly specialized single contributors, as illustrated in Exhibit 17.15.

(c) Coming of Age. The focus of these new payroll organizations and jobs has shifted from status quo and maintenance to change and development and from transaction processing to financial control and accountability. Payroll professionals today have an opportunity to be viewed more as valued business partners and are now in a position to influence decisions and contribute to the success of the enterprise at a level never before possible.

In summary, how the payroll organization is viewed and how it is staffed and organized are key to the company's success. Decisions and actions taken on this matter will ultimately determine payroll and company costs.

17.8 TRADITIONAL AND CONTEMPORARY BUDGETING APPROACHES. Traditional budgeting approaches are based on understanding the business in accordance with established general ledger accounts and the company chart of accounts. Newer approaches focus on understanding the business from the perspective of its value-added services and its cost drivers. Referred to as ABC or activity-based management (ABM), these newer methods force business owners to look more closely at their business. Activity-based costing captures cost by individual value-added service and provides a structure for pricing products and services to business customers. Activity-based costing has become increasingly more important as some companies begin to deliver financial services (including payroll) to their divisions and subsidiaries via shared service centers.

For some time into the future, businesses may have to use both traditional and ABC processes and try to map one to the other. Activity-based costing not only allows companies to understand costs of each component, it also provides the ability to track costs to specific customer sets. Activity-based costing, in turn, lays the groundwork for treating payroll and other overhead functions like the businesses they truly are. The following subsections discuss the differences between these methods.

(a) Line-Item (Traditional) Budgeting Approach. A traditional payroll department budget consists of the following components, with dollars typically based on historical spending patterns adjusted for anticipated changes. In establishing spending levels by account, it is wise to document assumptions for each line item within the budget:

- Labor and benefits
  - Salaries
  - Overtime (seasonal, periodic, conversions)
  - Fringes (employment taxes and benefits)
  - Pension (defined benefit, defined contribution)
  - Perquisites (parking, wellness, dependent care, education, others)
  - Workers' compensation
  - Consultants and contract labor
- Data processing
  - Software-related support expenses
  - Hardware-related expenses
  - Outstanding-related expenses
  - Licenses
  - Equipment rental and leases
  - Supplies
- Travel and entertainment
  - Travel
  - Lodging
  - Meals
  - Car rentals
  - Entertainment
  - Other travel-related costs
- Capital assets and related expenses (capitalized or expensed)
  - Equipment (machinery, transportation, installation, training)
  - Software
  - Furniture and fixtures
  - Leasehold improvements (permanent improvements or upkeep)
  - Maintenance and repairs

  - Depreciation
- Facilities
  - Office space/rent
  - Utilities
  - Maintenance and repairs
  - Storage and archives
- Communications
  - Telephones (line charges, instrument lease, maintenance)
  - Long distance (WATS, inbound 800 numbers, vendor costs)
  - Fax
  - Postage (post office box, stamps, postage meter, W-2s, certified)
  - Couriers (ground and air)
- Reproduction/Printing
  - Forms
  - Check and direct deposit statements
  - Employee communications (memos/stuffers)
  - Supplies (paper/toner/staples)
- Professional Associations and Publications
  - Trade association membership dues (American Payroll Association)
  - Trade and educational conferences
  - Trade publications
- Miscellaneous and Conditional Expenses
  - Audit-related costs
  - Legal and tax compliance-related liabilities and costs
  - ''Corporate Services'' allocations (i.e., mailroom support, human resource support, etc.)
  - Recruitment and relocation costs
  - System conversion and implementation costs
  - Contingencies (crisis management, change management, unknowns)
  - Banking-related costs

(b) Activity-Based Costing (Contemporary) Budgeting Approach. Although the traditional method provides a vehicle for planning and tracking payroll-related expenses, the traditional line-item budgeting approach does not lead to maximum understanding of the business. As highlighted in Exhibit 17.16, ABC helps companies to gain added insight into the cost of current payroll operations. [Please refer to this exhibit again when reading section 17.12(b) on benchmarking].

This knowledge can help the business to focus its attention on opportunities for reducing its costs. It can also provide an opportunity for influencing change in business practices, as well as serve as a pricing structure for allocating costs to business customers (e.g., divisions). As illustrated in Exhibit 17.17, keeping the pricing metric simple facilitates both the administration and the communication of the ABC program. As reflected in the exhibit, costing based on numbers of employees paid and/or numbers of transactions processed is the simplest method. Tracking time and materials and pricing services by using other metrics on a selective basis might be appropriate as well.

Activity-based costing is essential for companies evaluating outsourcing, as it will

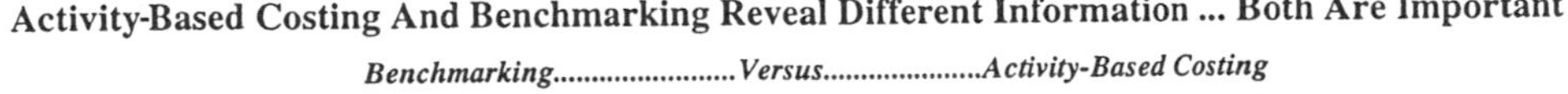

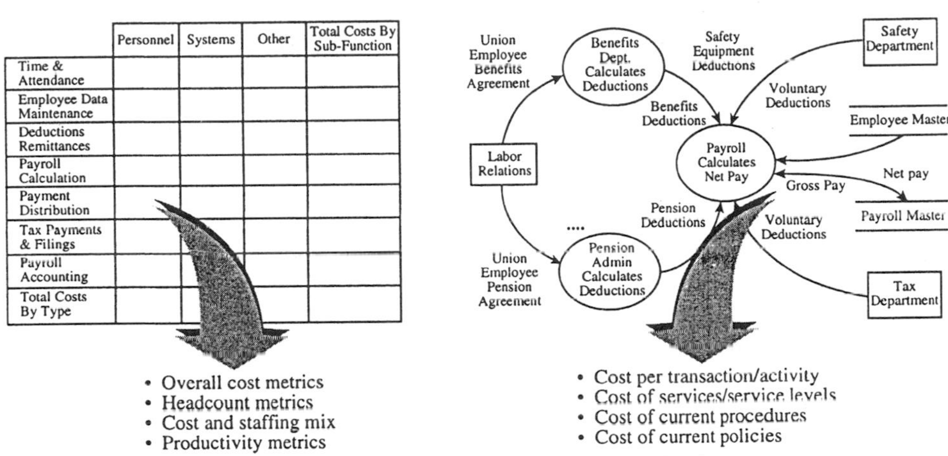

Exhibit 17.16. Benchmarking versus activity-based costing
Reprinted with permission. © Gunn Partners, Inc.

Payroll Added-Value Service	Pricing Metric
✪ Reference management	Number of employees
✪ Salary and wage calculation	Number of employees
✪ Supplementary compensation	Number of employees
✪ Payment delivery	Number of employees
✪ Tax payment and reporting	Number of employees
✪ Deduction administration	Number of employees
✪ Customer support	
→ Employee inquiry	Number of employees
→ Pay adjustment	Number of transactions
→ Customized information	Time and materials
→ Tactical/Strategic support	Time and materials
✪ Accounting	Number of employees

Exhibit 17.17. Payroll service pricing model
Reprinted with permission. © Digital Equipment Corporation—U.S. Payroll.

provide a more accurate means of cost comparison. For a complete discussion on this subject, see Chapter 31.

(c) Both Are Important. In reality, both methods are essential. The first method supports current accounting systems and is not likely to be replaced in the short term. The second method provides the knowledge essential to truly manage the business. It requires additional work to design, implement, and maintain. Because the value of activity-based costing is in the knowledge derived, it does not have to be precise, automated, or repetitive.

A periodic ABC look at the business can provide the necessary information needed. At least initially, companies might want to keep the use of ABC as simple as possible.

17.9 SMART BUDGETING (SPENDING MONEY TO SAVE MONEY)

(a) Investing in Resources Required to Achieve Change. Change (including cost savings) does not come without spending some money. Companies should invest in people, particularly those who can effectively act as catalysts of change (e.g., planning specialists, business systems analysts, data and process model specialists). In addition, support for the development and training of payroll department personnel will pay big dividends over the longer term, as will support for participation in the American Payroll Association's CPP education and certification program. Management should not look at the payroll function as a clerical function but should begin to view it as an important professional organization critical to the success of the enterprise.

(b) Budgeting for Continuous Improvement. A sound budget should include investment dollars for continuous improvement. Investments today can mean success in the future. Waiting to invest until there is a ''real'' problem is one way to ensure that there will be a problem in the future. Too many companies find out too late that making major changes takes time. For example, many companies are scrambling today to modify legacy systems to support the year 2000 complaint.

(c) The Importance of Strategic Planning. Budgeting for payroll is not a single-cycle event with strictly short-term spending implications. A successful budgeting process should be built on a solid long-term business plan that considers the directions and needs of the enterprise.

Many have heard the saying, ''You cannot do anything about yesterday—it's gone—but you can do something about today and tomorrow.'' Proper planning allows payroll to correct problems of the past and anticipate the future, thereby being in a proactive instead of reactive mode of operation.

Those responsible for payroll must always be looking to introduce and develop new models of and approaches to running the payroll function, to be more effective and, most of all, efficient in serving their customers. This is where strategic planning is beneficial. Strategic planning involves identifying and analyzing areas that are both internal and external to your organization. To succeed, the business must focus on the following:

- Its mission statement
- The company's long-range ''strategic'' issues
- Goals and objectives
- Communication

Strategic planning is the key to the success of the payroll department because it allows the business to stay focused on the future objectives. As part of the strategic planning process, the following questions should be asked:

- Where are we now?
- Where are we going in the longer term?
- Where should we be going?
- How will we get there?

Strategic planning will ensure success if focus is maintained on established goals and objectives that are measurable and quantifiable in real time, by evidence of performance, while permitting the business to stay focused on today and tomorrow.

17.10 THINKING BEYOND BORDERS AND STOVEPIPES.

A number of companies are now beginning to think beyond geographic borders and functional stovepipes to reap additional savings.

(a) Consolidating Country Payrolls.

Given today's more sophisticated software, technology, and banking capabilities, many companies are now beginning to consolidate payroll operations at one location and delivering payroll services to employees in multiple countries (United States, Canada, Latin America, and even Europe and Asia Pacific). Companies have realized the benefits of centralizing operations within a geography and are now applying that same concept across borders to eliminate inherent redundancies and reduce operating costs while delivering a more consistent product and service to its international employee population. Within North America, a first step that companies might want to consider is the consolidation of U.S. and Canada payrolls.

(b) Consolidating Company Disbursements Processes.

Companies are also beginning to understand that there are opportunities for consolidation in other disbursement areas, such as accounts payable, employee travel, and business expense. Each of these processes involve similar tasks and require similar types of resources. At the same time, each process may have a different cycle time. Consolidating these processes under a single reporting structure may permit a company to reduce headcount by eliminating redundant management and supervisory levels, sharing resources to cover peaks and valleys of fluctuating workloads, sharing equipment that would otherwise sit idle, and consolidating generic processes such as production control, accounting, and customer service functions. In addition, there may even be an opportunity to eliminate redundant disbursement systems.

These opportunities are available to any company that can free itself from traditional thinking and self-imposed boundaries. The potential benefits are significant.

17.11 INNOVATIVE METHODS FOR RECOVERING COSTS INCURRED.

Although some payroll-related costs are fixed, companies can take a number of avenues to reduce expenses. For example, companies can choose not to offer certain payroll services, or can charge suppliers, business customers, or even employees for certain types of activities. Decisions to use these options will require an evaluation of the financial returns against the legal, business, and employee relations implications. Some examples follow.

(a) Eliminating Elective Deduction Programs.

Many companies are choosing to offer only those deductions required by law and eliminate elective deduction programs. Reducing the number of deduction programs offered can result in both systems and administrative cost savings associated with such programs.

(b) Charging for Child Support Payments.

Most courts permit employers to deduct additional monies from employees' wages for each child support payment made, to cover the administrative costs associated with child support withholding, reporting, and payment processes. Courts designate the authorized amount that employers may withhold on each payment; amounts range from under $1.00 to as much as $5.00 per payment. Given the recent changes to the Family Support Act, which requires all child support payments to be employer withheld, as well as the labor-intensive nature of this work, employer costs can be significant. Court-sanctioned cost-recovery programs can offset some or all of this burden.

(c) Charging for Affidavits. As payroll professionals know, preparing affidavits can be a lengthy and costly process. Affidavits often necessitate the preparation of large amounts of data in customized reporting formats. Some companies have begun to charge attorneys for such requests on a cash on delivery basis. Reception has been good, as this represents a standard practice within the legal profession. Attorneys, in turn, pass these costs onto their clients.

(d) Charging for Copies of W-2s. The Internal Revenue Service (IRS) only requires employers to issue a W-2 once. The IRS permits employers to charge employees for duplicate copies, either of current or prior year W-2s. The current rate that employers can charge, as set by the IRS, is $7.50 per copy. This practice not only can help offset some costs, but can also help to discipline employees to take greater ownership of their personnel record keeping. As an alternative, employers do have the option to refer employees to the IRS for copies of previously issued W-2s.

(e) Charging for Rework. Payroll products and services can only be as good as the quality and timeliness of supplier input. If input is inaccurate and/or late, payroll can incur additional costs in reacting to these situations. Companies are beginning to realize the tremendous costs involved in rework. Adjustments, out-of-cycle payments, stop payments, and W-2 copies all represent avoidable cost. More important, companies are also beginning to realize that suppliers (even employees, supervisors, and managers) should be accountable for accurate and timely input.

In response, employers are beginning to quantify and communicate these costs to the sources of the errors and are implementing mechanisms for charging these sources for such errors. Although cross-charging a business supplier or cost center for incorrect input resulting in payroll rework may represent "internal money," it can change behavioral patterns and, in the longer term, provide real dollar savings to the company. Some companies may even wish to pass certain rework costs directly on to the employee. One example might be to charge the employee who receives, but loses or destroys, a paycheck and then requests an out-of-cycle payment to replace the lost or destroyed check. The administrative effort along with the bank charge can easily exceed $50.

(f) Charging for Check versus Direct-Deposit Transactions. Compulsory direct-deposit programs are prohibited in most states, but companies do have the option of passing on incremental costs to business customers serviced by payroll (e.g., divisions, subsidiaries, business units) who do not choose to support direct-deposit programs offered by the company. Current data collected via a 1995 American Payroll Association pay media survey of U.S. industry suggests that the average savings per payment via direct deposit versus check can be $0.86 or more.

(g) Charging for Nonstandard and Inefficient or Costly Practices. Companies that provide payroll services to internal business units may want to influence more cost-effective behavior changes by establishing an "ideal" baseline cost for services and then charging business customers (e.g., divisions and/or subsidiaries) for incremental services that are unique or inefficient. For example, a business unit that insists on submitting time card data in paper format when electronic reporting tools exist, or requires unique reports that no other customer requires, should be charged a premium for such practices and services. These tactics are not intended to make money, but rather to force business customers to think twice about the level of service they require.

In summary, there are many opportunities to reduce and or recover costs, and it is up to organizations to look for and implement the opportunities that will work within their business environment. In all cases, financial incentives must be quantified and evaluated against the impact on employees and should be assessed for their potential legal implications as well.

17.12 CYCLICAL PAYROLL EXPENSE PATTERNS IMPACTING BUDGETING AND FORECASTING. Although most payroll charges are constant, variations in spending patterns do occur and must be recognized in the budgeting and forecasting process.

Most notable are costs associated with single planned nonrecurring purchases of products or services, or infrequent but repetitive purchases of forms such as pay deposit and check statements or renewals of hardware and software licenses.

Disbursement patterns may also exist and must be considered. For example, some companies may process salary increases or issue large volumes of commission, bonus, or royalty payments during certain periods of the year. As a result, such companies may incur added costs during these time frames.

Labor settlements and bargaining agreement renewals may also drive costs on a cyclical basis.

Finally, payroll spending patterns often peak in the first and fourth quarters of each calendar year, because of annual expenses related to the production, delivery, and administration of W-2s and related wage and tax reporting processes, including expatriate equalization (if applicable).

At the same time, preparations for the beginning of a new tax year affect work load and spending. These closing-out and starting-up activities associated with the tax year can represent significant costs in both labor and material and should be carefully considered in the budgeting process.

As in other areas of payroll, there are a number of opportunities for reducing the stress and cost related to cyclical work load patterns. For example, the use of temporary accounting resources during such times may be a good investment and can negate the need to carry additional full-time resources throughout the year to accommodate work load fluctuations.

In regard to year-end costs, as in all processes, front-end validations of supplier input, including accurate employee address information, can reduce the number of W-2Cs and W-2 reissues, which in turn can lower the amount of rework and costs associated with corrections.

Finally, investments made in timely and complete communications to employees can more than pay for themselves in the form of lower volumes of inquiries.

In summary, budgeting and forecasting cyclical and nonrecurring expenses, along with proper expense tracking processes, can eliminate the element of surprise and contribute to proper cash-flow requirements and spending forecasts.

17.13 USE OF TOTAL QUALITY MANAGEMENT

(a) Overview of Total Quality Management. Total quality management methods and tools are designed to improve business performance and improve customer satisfaction.

Total quality management represents a shift in focus from inward considerations to customer (internal and external) satisfaction.

There are many different TQM methods and tools. No single method or tool can satisfy all needs. Many TQM methods and tools overlap each other and are often used in combination with each other. Total quality management can address multiple goals of productivity, quality, customer satisfaction, and economic benefits, as illustrated in Exhibit 17.18. Exhibit 17.19 emphasizes what TQM is and is not.

- **Productivity**
  - Cost and headcount metrics
  - Cost per product/transactions per employee
- **Quality**
  - Error rates
  - Cycle times
- **Customer satisfaction**
  - Customer surveys
  - Problem resolution reports
- **Economic benefit**
  - Direct contribution
  - Upstream and downstream contribution

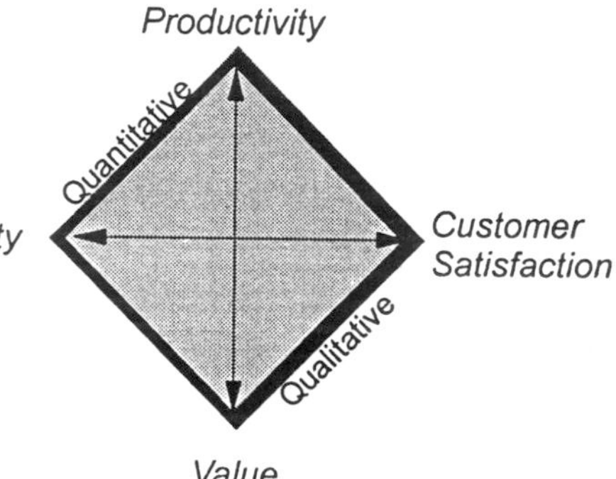

Exhibit 17.18. TQM goals
Reprinted with permission. © Gunn Partners, Inc.

Total Quality Management—A Definition:
Conformance to Standards

What it is . . .	. . . and isn't -
• A new way of thinking, being, acting and doing (change)	• Doing the same things differently
• Error-rate analysis	• Getting it right the first time
• Customer driven	• Internally focused
• Changing the work itself	• Stressing people–work linkages
• Expensive (in the short and even intermediate term)	• Expensive over the long term
• A permanent change in the way work is done (continuous improvement)	• A temporary adjustment

Exhibit 17.19. TQM definition
Reprinted with permission. © Management Resource Group.

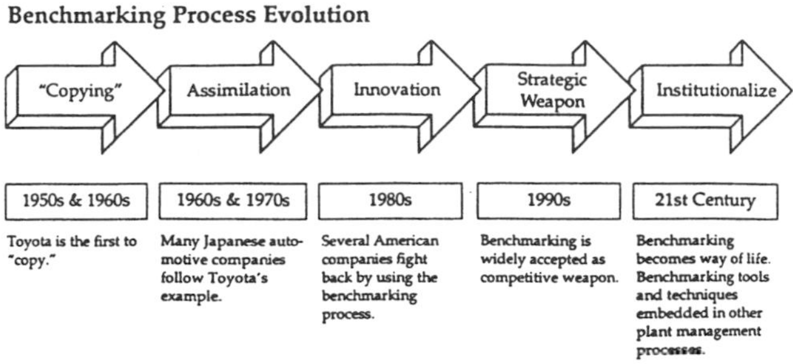

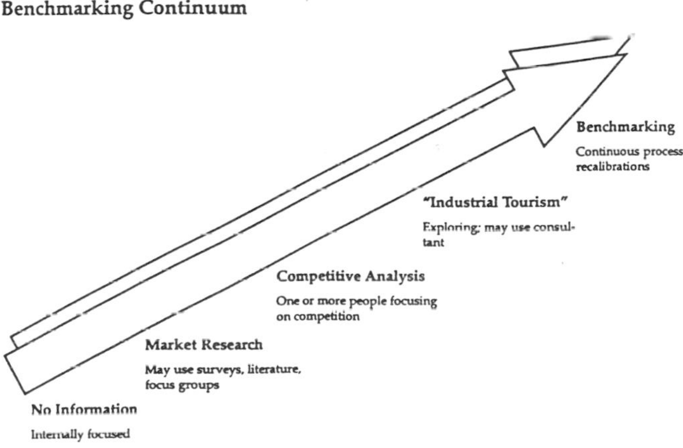

Exhibit 17.20. Benchmarking
Reprinted with permission. © EDS People Systems.

Following are some examples of TQM methods and tools being used by companies today.

(b) Benchmarking. Benchmarking involves learning from others and adopting their best practices to the benefit of your company. Exhibits 17.20 and 17.21 provide a visual history, brief description, and overview of the benchmarking process.

The 12 steps in a typical benchmarking process include the following:

1. Initiate project
2. Identify key processes to be benchmarked
3. Identify customer(s) for benchmarking
4. Select and prepare team
5. Identify type of benchmarking
6. Approach benchmarking partners
7. Collect data
8. Analyze data
9. Communicate findings

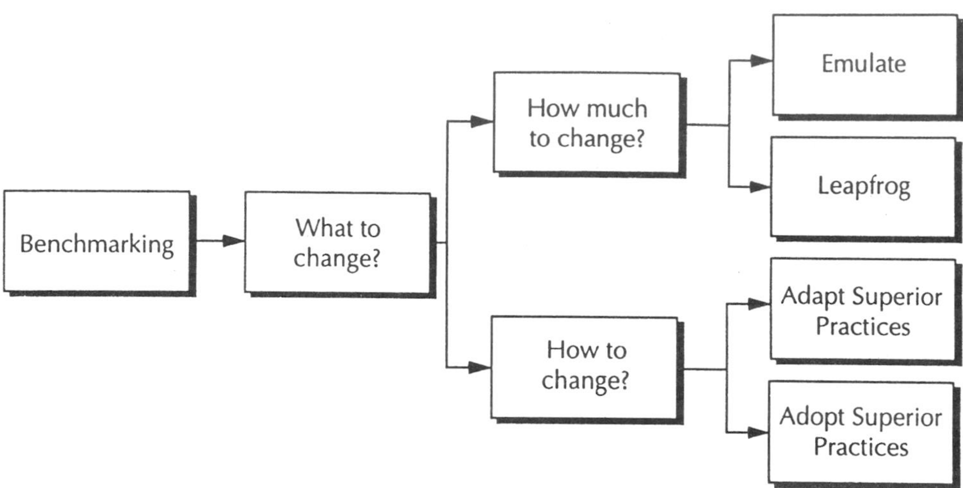

Exhibit 17.21. Benchmarking process

10. Develop action plan
11. Implement and monitor
12. Recalibrate

When undertaking a benchmarking effort, it is important that participants understand their processes and have done their homework and that those who are identified as benchmarking partners be recognized leaders in the areas under comparison. The most successful benchmarking efforts focus on specific areas of interest rather than attempt to benchmark an entire function. For example, a focus on benchmarking payroll time-reporting practices may be more fruitful than attempting to benchmark every aspect of payroll.

Benchmarking can lead to new insights and possibilities that can, in turn, lead to dramatic improvements. Any company that is not taking full advantage of benchmarking risks is losing its competitive edge. Unlike the early days of benchmarking, there are many new ways to keep pace with best-in-class practices. For example, many services and associations, such as the International Benchmarking Clearing House, provide access to benchmarking information never before available at reasonable costs.

(c) Re-engineering. Re-engineering represents an approach that looks at the business from fresh perspectives and evaluates the processes through which products and services are currently delivered to customers. It is not initially about automation, although automation may be a downstream action coming out of the re-engineering process. Re-engineering looks at the business as a total process, from supplier to customer, and in that sense is closely linked with the Six Sigma approach to understanding the business. Re-engineering, in essence, draws upon all the other TQM methods and tools and translates learning into action plans. It addresses whether the work should be done, who should do the work, where the work should be performed, and how the work should be done.

Re-engineering focuses on the business model, especially customers and the products that satisfy customer needs. With regard to each process, activity, and task, the re-engineering process prompts the business to ask the question, "Why?" Why is the business doing this? What is its purpose? What customer is this serving? Asking these fundamental questions is what distinguishes re-engineering from incremental process improvement. Exhibit 17.22 provides an overview of the various phases of the re-engineering cycle.

(d) A delta t. A delta t, developed by Digital Equipment Corporation, provides a simple methodology for mapping current process steps and identifying non–value-added steps, with the focus on reducing total cycle time. Through the use of this tool, the delta (difference or change) between current actual and theoretical process times can be identified and potentially eliminated.

Unlike most mapping tools, A delta t does not require extensive mapping knowledge and, more important, engages those responsible for the process in performing this work. As illustrated in Exhibit 17.23, a number of steps have been eliminated from this time

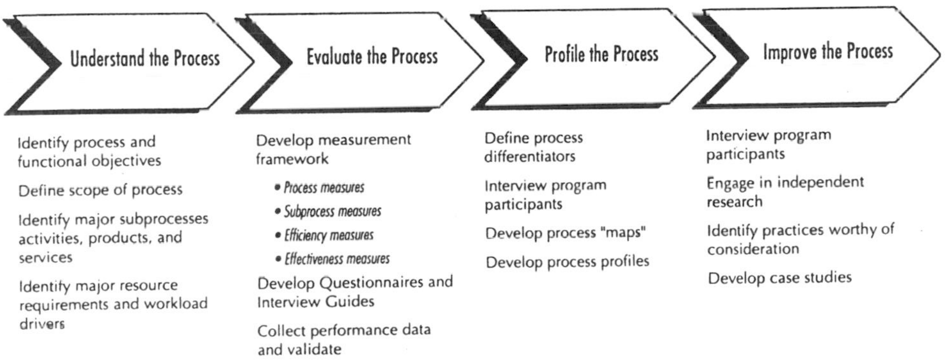

Exhibit 17.22. The re-engineering cycle
Reprinted with permission. © 3D Consortium. All rights reserved.

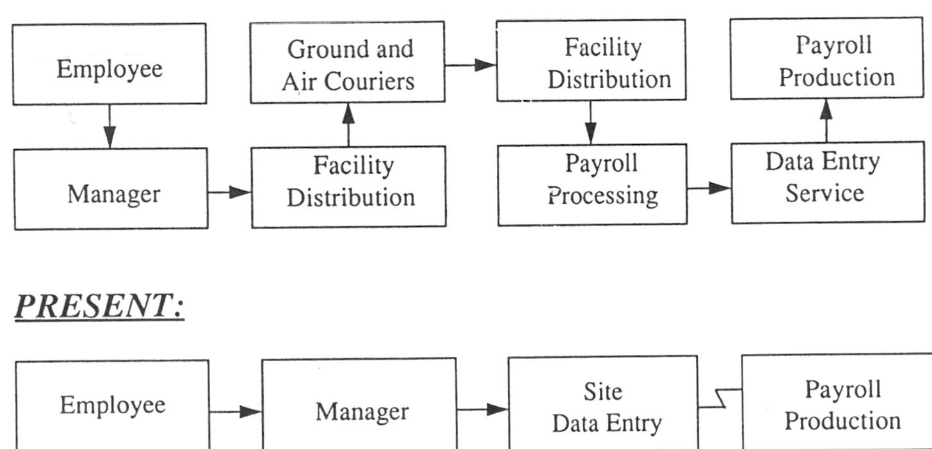

Exhibit 17.23. A delta t reporting
Reprinted with permission. © Digital Equipment Corporation—U.S. Payroll.

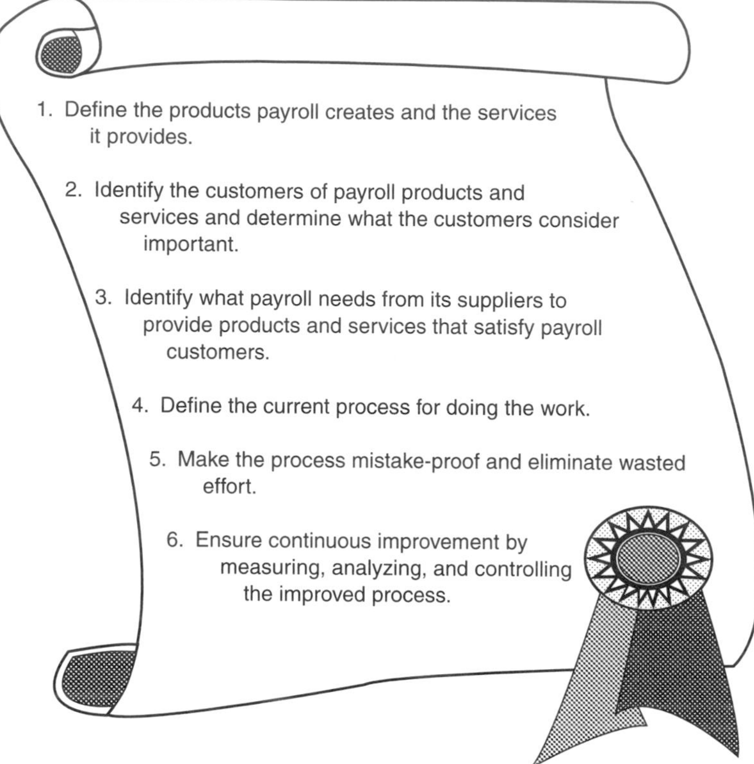

Exhibit 17.24. Six steps of the Six Sigma program
Reprinted with permission. © Motorola, Inc.

reporting process example. A delta t, by reducing the number of steps, often contributes to lower defect levels by eliminating additional opportunities for such defects from the process, which in turn translates into lower costs.

(e) Six Sigma. The Six Sigma program, as designed by Motorola, Inc., focuses on reducing defects and provides both a methodology for measuring defect levels and a system for reaching a level of three defects or fewer per million opportunities. The Six Sigma program is designed around six steps, as outlined in Exhibit 17.24.

Six Sigma was originally created for use in the manufacturing and engineering environment, but it can be applied to any business area. For example, Digital Equipment Corporation has implemented Six Sigma extensively within finance to improve its payroll performance. Digital Equipment Corporation is recognized as a best-in-class payroll organization and has reached levels of three defects or fewer per million opportunities via the Six Sigma program in a number of its payroll products and services. Exhibit 17.25 illustrates the use of the Six Sigma program within the deposit area.

In summary, Six Sigma is a powerful tool for defining and understanding the business from the customer's perspective and for focusing attention and energy on the opportunities for defects that represent the highest payback. It helps businesses to understand the entire pipeline from supplier to customer and provides a statistical tracking mechanism for under-

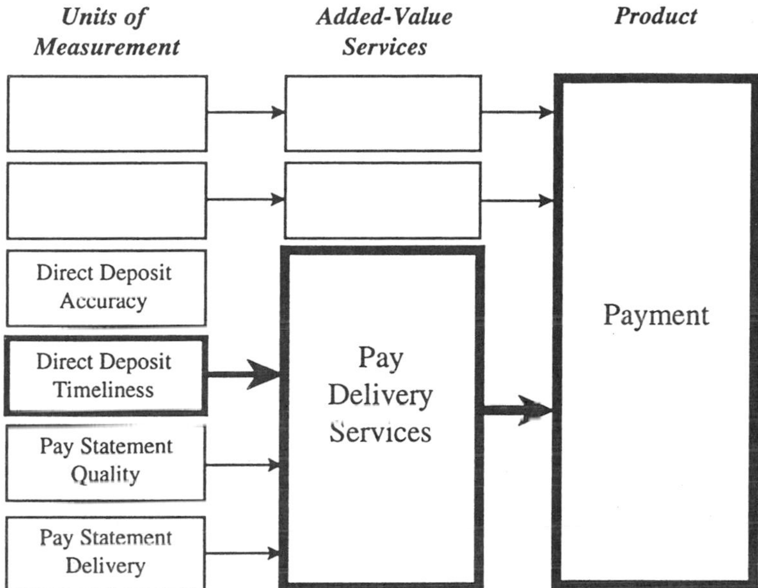

Exhibit 17.25. Digital Equipment Corporation's Six Sigma program
Reprinted with permission. © Digital Equipment Corporation—U.S. Payroll.

standing and tracking performance in areas important to the customer. Those interested in knowing more about the Six Sigma program may wish to contact Motorola, Inc., directly.

(f) Continuous Improvement. Total quality management tools do not deliver a final resolution on any process. They provide a means for catching up or momentarily taking the lead. Ongoing programs geared toward continuous or incremental improvement must always be in place. As quality improves, customers begin to expect higher levels of performance. All of these TQM tools must continue to be used and new ones applied to ensure ongoing success. Motorola, Inc., for example, is setting new goals and designing new programs to reach three defects per billion opportunities. Other companies must continue to raise their sights as well.

Methods and tools are just methods and tools. They can be misused and can become product rather than a process for improvement. If they become an end in themselves, they are not fulfilling the purpose for which they were intended. They can provide valuable information, but learning can be misinterpreted and can lead to erroneous conclusions and incorrect actions if the users of these methods and tools are not careful. At the same time, these risks should not be used as justification for not employing TQM tools.

All methods and tools require investments, first to understand them, and second to apply them correctly. Investments can lead to exciting changes and add to the success of the business, or they can waste valuable time and resources. It is all up to the user. For a further, in-depth discussion on TQM, refer to Chapter 29.

17.14 PUTTING TECHNOLOGY TO WORK. The secret to the successful use of technology is in (1) selecting and applying technology appropriate to the need and (2) the proper training of users. Technology must pay for itself to be justified. The timing and sequencing of technology application is important to maximizing benefits. General capabil-

U.S. Payroll Six Sigma Program

2.5.4 Direct Deposit (Timeliness)

Product: Payments

value-added Service: **Payment Delivery Services**

Customer Expectation:

Immediate access to pay by opening of banking hours on pay day (Thursday)

Measurement of:

Timeliness of weekly employee direct deposit pay delivery to all U.S. financial institutions (including DCU) as measured by notification on non receipt by employee, Receiving Financial Institution, or Originating Depository Financial Institution (Shawmut/Connecticut National Bank.)

Defects:

Late Deposit: Pay not deposited in employee account on opening of banking hours on payday (Thursday). NOTE: Effective Q2FY92, Payroll will begin to utilize a more conservative defect counting procedure. In the past, Payroll has only counted defects as individually reported by customers. In the future, we will begin to count the total number of depositors at a financial institution as individual defects if the problem is determined to be institution–wide even though not all customers may be aware of or impacted by the problem.

Opportunities for Defects: (in chronological order) = X

Entity	**Opportunities**
1. Payroll	X
2. Payroll Systems	X
3. Data Center	X
4. Shawmut/Connecticut National Bank	X
5. Federal Reserve Bank/ACH	X
6. Receiving Financial Institution	X
# Opportunities for Defects	6

Explanation of Defect Opportunities:

1. Payroll fails to begin or complete weekly production on time. Cut-off transmission time to ODFI missed.
2. Payroll Systems software changes result in production related defect(s) impacting direct deposit timeliness.
3. Data Center fails to perform data center services in an accurate and timely fashion in accordance with Service Agreement.
4. ODFI unable to process files in time to deliver to Federal Reserve Bank for Tuesday AM window.
5. Federal Reserve Bank experience operational problems which delay interregional routing and timely distribution to Receiving Financial Institutions.
6. Receiving Financial Institution (including DCU) does not receive transactions or receives but fails to post pay to employee account on time.

Data Source:

Transactions: **Totals page from the final Deposit Statement Files**
Defects: **Bank Problem Logs maintained by Customer Service**

Exhibit 17.25. *(continued)*

Six Sigma-Goal Worksheet

Direct Deposit Timeliness Goal Worksheet

Total Defects Per Million Opportunities (DPMO) as of FY94: .47

DPMO Performance Goal for Fiscal Year 95: ≤.47

Description of Specific Defect Area(s) to be Addressed:

Defect #4: ODFI unable to process files in time to deliver to Federal Reserve Bank for Tuesday AM window

Strategies to Achieve (FY95) DPMO Performance Goal:

1. Work with ODFI to assure that all procedures are documented and contingency plans are in place.

Exhibit 17.25. *(continued)*

ities can be enhanced or limited by the computing environment selected by the business. Specific tools, such as interactive voice response technology, can be used to eliminate manual and paper-based processes.

Following is an inventory of various technologies, along with brief descriptions, benefits, and possible applications within the payroll environment.

(a) Windows. Windows™ software allows the user to access multiple screens on one video display unit (VDU) and permits the user to view, update, and report on multiple applications and options at the same time. With Windows capabilities, the user can increase productivity and better service customers.

In today's environment, when access to information is the key to success, Windows enables the payroll user to increase the amount of data that can be seen simultaneously. Separate application options can be designed to handle different tasks, thereby allowing the user to perform multiple functions at the same time. Because many human resource and payroll systems are separate, Windows can be used to link both systems together on a single screen, thereby obviating the need to log in and out of separate systems. (Windows is a trademark of Microsoft Corporation.)

(b) Desktop Integration. Desktop integration uses a series of software and hardware tools that allow users to access and process information from their desks. These tools permit users to download data from a larger system (mainframe or other host system) to a desktop workstation on a PC platform. The user can work on the data at his or her personal workstation and then upload the changed data back to the host machine. This concept enables the business user to access all the applications and systems right from the desktop. With desktop-integrated tools, the payroll user is able to perform all job functions independently, without time-consuming and complex processes. Full integration of hardware and software can mean much greater productivity.

(c) Client–Server Environment. The client–server environment is a computing environment that provides access to information to different users with varying business needs while sharing the computer resources among multiple users spread across different organizations and locations. The distinguishing characteristic of a client–server environment is the distribution of tasks among multiple processors.

The client–server environment is software rather than hardware driven. It permits central storage of data (on the server) while allowing access to data at remote areas (or client workstations) and offers tremendous opportunities regarding where and how work

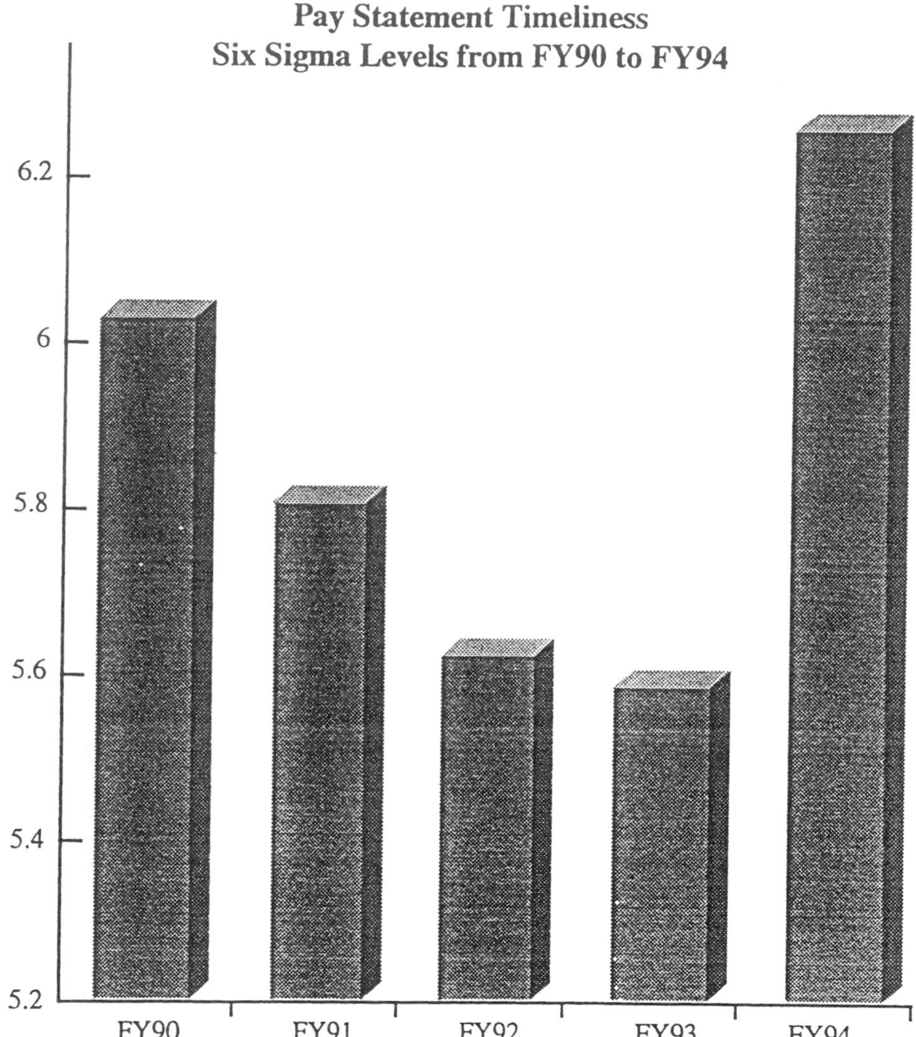

Exhibit 17.25. *(continued)*

is performed. For example, in a client–server environment, local sites may be responsible for entering time card data into a system that resides elsewhere. At the same time, it can permit centralized production of gross-to-net processes for greater efficiency, lower cost, and higher levels of control. On the output side, it can permit local sites to receive pay information for local printing and distribution of pay statements. Client–server environments offer the best of both worlds, and are especially advantageous to businesses with multiple dispersed operating units.

(d) Decision Support System. Decision support systems are data bases of information with preprogrammed access routines or user-defined queries that allow the business to access information in the time and format necessary. This permits the business to have access to up-to-date information without special programming efforts. In essence, decision support systems can automatically access raw data and apply such data to various formulas and analyses to permit users to draw conclusions and take appropriate actions. For example, in the payroll environment, decision support systems can be used to collect and validate supplier feeds to ensure data accuracy prior to the pay calculation process.

(e) Multimedia. Multimedia consists of a series of PC applications that allow a user to access multiple types of data and to research key business issues and create presentations. Multimedia tools are often on a CD-ROM application that can hold up to twenty times more information than can be held on a common 3.5-inch diskette. Multimedia also allows access to information stored on both video and compact cassette tapes. The benefit of multimedia is that it allows access to up-to-date information and speeds up the process of retrieving such information from many sources to produce charts, graphs, and other types of presentations. In the payroll function, some tax law service providers are replacing their paper products, often consisting of five or more volumes, with one CD, thus providing their payroll customers with an easier vehicle to access federal, state, and local payroll tax-related information.

(f) Document Image Processing. Document image processing—the storage and subsequent retrieval of document images in electronic format—is rapidly changing the records management industry. This new technology permits data to be condensed and then recreated in its original format as needed. It is particularly cost effective for high-volume operations, but is steadily becoming affordable for lower-volume users as well. By changing the manner in which historical records and source documents are stored and accessed, companies can eliminate the more labor-intensive processes that most still use to store and retrieve paper documents. Document image processing, once in place, can reduce offsite storage costs and, more importantly, provide immediate access (via integrated desktop systems) to historical records. As a transaction-processing system, there are many applications for the payroll function, including but not limited to W-2s, W-4s, time cards, special payment authorization forms, new hire and termination paperwork, benefit enrollment forms, and so on. Document image-processing service providers are now beginning to make this a financially viable option for more and more companies.

(g) Interactive Voice Response. Interactive voice response (IVR) systems, as illustrated in Exhibit 17.26, derive their name from the use of scripted voice prompts and responses to interact with callers who use a touch-tone telephone to enter requests for simple information or to initiate routine transactions. Unlike many other voice systems, IVR systems have a unique power to communicate directly with other computer systems to access payroll data base information requested by callers. Interactive voice response systems have also kept pace with trends in computing and data base management, and the current generation of systems is very proficient in interfacing to both mainframe systems and network-based systems. The shift, in recent years, has been toward accessing payroll information through a client–server architecture. Because client–server systems can be implemented on different data bases, IVR systems are available with efficient access to the newly designed data base systems.

Interactive voice response systems can handle many of the routine calls directed to a payroll department, resulting in a significant increase in payroll department productivity. In addition, in applications in which employees or supervisors are entering information,

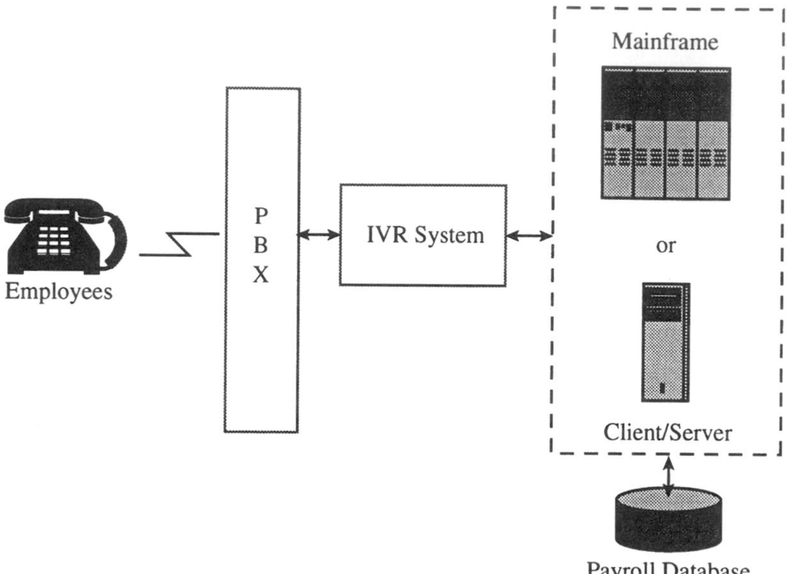

Exhibit 17.26. IVR system interfaces
Reprinted with permission. © TALX Corporation. All rights reserved.

a substantial reduction in errors can be anticipated because IVR systems check each entry as it is made. General paperwork handling and key entry tasks are also reduced when IVR systems are used to collect routine benefit enrollment information.

There are many payroll applications. For example, IVR systems can be used to provide employees with access to current or historical pay information; enroll in, change, or stop direct deposit; or request a copy of their current or historical W-2s, as presented in Exhibit 17.27. The opportunities are almost limitless, and functionality can be customized to the specific needs of the business. The capability can be performed in house or outsourced to a service provider. Interactive voice response systems in combination with automated call directors can provide cost-effective solutions to labor-intensive processes while improving overall customer service levels.

(h) Check-Printing and Forms-Processing Technologies. The most commonly used check-printing technology involves the impact printer, which consists of physical characters that ''impact'' or strike the form through an ink ribbon. Impact printers come in many forms to support low- to high-volume operations and can be rented, leased, or purchased.

Laser printers, a newer technology, use heat and toner to create the print characters. As with impact printers, laser printers can be tailored to meet the unique needs and volumes of a business.

Impact printers cost less to implement and maintain than laser printers but do not allow as much flexibility. The use of laser printing technology is ideally suited for higher-volume businesses that process forms with frequent changes. Laser printing technology can also permit the use of bar-coded zip codes to expedite delivery and obtain lower presorted zip code U.S. Postal Service rates, a savings that could be significant for employers that deliver pay statements to employees' homes via the U.S. Postal Service. Laser paycheck

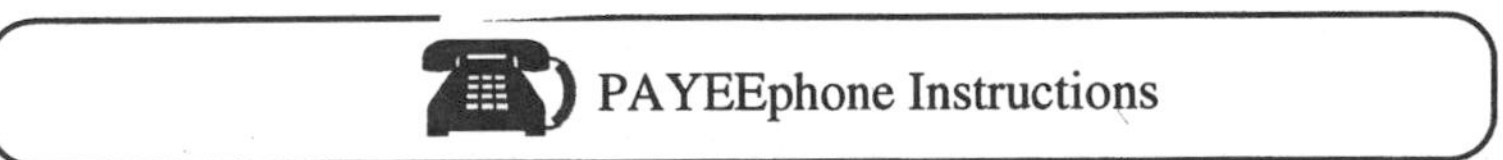

PAYEEphone is the Touch-Tone Phone system that allows you to enroll in Direct Deposit for both Payroll and Employee Expense, allows you to listen to your recent Payroll pay information, and provides you with current year W-2 assistance. This system is available 24 hrs. each day, seven days each week for your convenience.

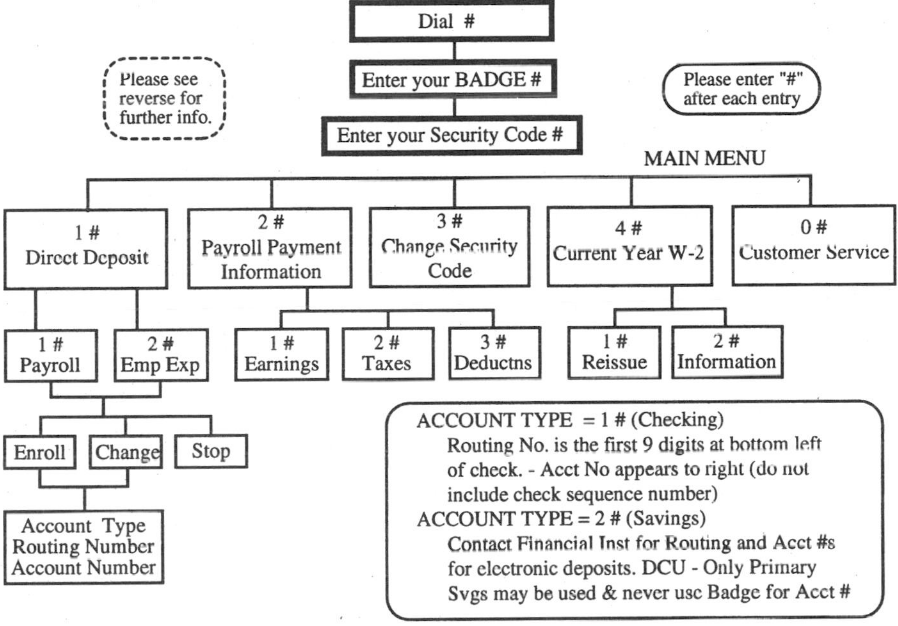

Exhibit 17.27. Payroll IVR system
Reprinted with permission. © Digital Equipment Corporation—U.S. Payroll.

delivery vendor products also exist and permit companies to transmit pay data and print paychecks at remote sites in place of courier delivery services.

One cannot discuss printer technology without also discussing form-construction and form-processing equipment. Forms can consist of single or multipart forms (using carbon or noncarbon). Self-mailer forms can eliminate the need for separate envelopes and insertion processes and can be especially useful in large operations in which pay statements are sent via the U.S. Postal Service to employees' homes. In addition, self-mailers offer greater security. Pressure and heat-sealing form-processing equipment, as with printers, can be rented, leased, or purchased.

Companies wishing to maximize capabilities while minimizing costs should review all printer, forms, and form-processing equipment options in a single evaluation. Companies would be wise to look at these needs across multiple disciplines (e.g., payroll, accounts payable, and other disbursement functions) rather than within a single discipline, such as payroll, and should be careful about purchasing equipment that might be better rented or leased—in today's rapidly changing environment, purchased equipment far too often becomes obsolete prior to full depreciation. In any case, a thorough financial evaluation and return on investment (ROI) should be completed in advance of any decision.

17.15 BUDGETING TASKS AND CALENDAR. Although the budgeting schedule will vary based on each company's unique fiscal calendar, generic tasks to create a sound budget will be similar. Ideally, the process should not begin with budgeting dollars, but with a review of the following:

- Company documents (stated values, goals, directions, etc.)
- Business partner long-range plans and priorities, especially those of finance, human resources, benefits, and compensation
- External conditions and factors that may affect payroll (e.g., changes in federal or state wage or tax laws)
- Payroll charter, long-range plan, and current operational status
- Current and prior-year payroll spending performance and analysis

From these items, which may represent the most time-consuming portion of the process, fiscal-year business priorities can be set and an informed budget created. Confirmation of business priorities should be obtained from decision makers prior to creating the budget or as part of the budget review and approval process.

Next, rates for the coming budget period should be collected from all necessary sources, including but not limited to information surrounding future salary plans, fringe rates, occupancy rates, supplier pricing estimates, and so on, along with estimated volume information essential to the business (e.g., projected company employee population data). Using this information, budgets for individual line items can then be calculated.

Because labor usually represents the single largest cost for payroll functions, the initial focus should be placed on direct labor, fringe, and related labor cost projections. This job is made simpler if the salary planning calendar parallels the fiscal calendar. If it does not, a portion of the budget will be based on the salary plan and a portion on estimated salaries. Assumptions are always a key component of each expense line of the budget. Assumptions must be made and documented regarding anticipated turnover, increases or decreases in headcount, performance ratings, job level reclassifications and promotions, and salary increases, as well as estimated overtime usage.

A similar process should be followed for each expense category within the budget.

The final budget package should include not only the financials but also the text supporting the proposed spending levels. This information will be important later in the year to understand both positive and negative variances and to adjust future spending forecasts.

Building the budget on a month-by-month basis results in a more accurate plan than creating a fiscal year plan and then allocating the dollars by month and quarter. However, this process may take a little longer and may not be justified in some cases. In general, best-practice companies are reducing the number of expense reporting and forecasting cycles.

Time spent on the front end of the budgeting process pays off throughout the year with less time needed to reconcile actuals and understand differences between budgeted and actual dollars. The use of automated budgeting tools also facilitates the preparation and modification of budgets while providing good audit trails. These same tools can be used to translate line-item budget dollars into ABC budgets.

Although budgeting is important to payroll, like other overhead functions, it should not be the primary focus of the business. If done properly, only a small portion of payroll resources and time should be required for developing and managing the payroll budget.

17.16 MANAGEMENT AND LEADERSHIP APPROACHES. A high-performance, low-cost payroll function cannot be achieved overnight and can only be achieved with vision and commitment, and through empowered people. As companies work toward a more efficient and cost-effective program, they should consider the advice of Southwestern Bell Telephone Company:

- *Do What's Right.* That is to say, do not focus on work-force and expense reduction alone, but on quality; do not look to shift costs; wisely challenge top-down directions that are not cost-effective; and, finally, work to achieve an informed decision.
- *Actions Speak Louder Than Words.* Work to create an environment that focuses on the big picture; do not always require "it" to be in writing; and of course, in the process, have fun!
- *View Yourself as a Corporate Trustee.* Clearly understand the required levels of authority; determine who needs to know and understand who really cares; use experienced consultants; and, finally, develop a conservative business case for each project.

As learned by Digital Equipment Corporation's payroll organization in its ongoing evolution to higher payroll quality and lower cost, change cannot be dictated, but must begin from within the organization. The right attitudes are a prerequisite. Visions come before plans and actions. Those who wish to take on change must also accept accountability and risk. There is a logical and sequential order to change. The process must engage business customers and suppliers. When getting started, companies should begin small and build on success. Use structure as a process, not as an end product. Most importantly, invest in the people who are going to make you and your company successful!

17.17 SUMMARY. In summary, budgeting for payroll can be as limited or as limitless as companies want the process to be. Some may view the process as strictly an exercise to create a line-item budget to ensure that anticipated costs can be covered over the coming year. Others will view the budgeting process as something more and will use it as a springboard to better understand the business, its customers, and its suppliers, and as a vehicle to seek out opportunities for improving performance and reducing costs.

Good budgeting can help to facilitate the implementation of business plans, enhance financial controls, and improve the overall decision-making process. Higher quality and lower cost are not mutually exclusive and can be achieved via the budgeting process.

If this chapter can help both sets of users described herein to see the possibilities, then the work put forth in this chapter will have been well worth the effort!

ACKNOWLEDGMENTS. The author would like to acknowledge the following companies and individuals for their contributions and their permission to use exhibits appearing in this document:

- Eileen Anderson, Editor, Paytech, American Payroll Association
- Nancy S. Bishop, Director, Editorial Services, A.T. Kearney, Inc.
- Matthew J. DeLuca, President, Management Resource Group, Inc.
- L. Robert Dillon, Vice President, Duke Engineering and Services, in behalf of the 3D Consortium (Digital Equipment Corporation, Duke Engineering and Services, Inc., and Deloitte & Touche) with the Center for Performance Management

- Robert A. Foster, Managing Associate, Coopers & Lybrand L.L.P.
- James A. Motter, Partner, Gunn Partners, Inc.
- James Owen, Payroll Manager, Meijer, Inc.
- Michael E. Smith, Vice President, TALX Corporation
- Roger A. Smith, CPP, Business Planning Consultant, EDS People Systems
- Joseph L. Urban, Corporate Payroll Manager, Motorola, Inc.

The author would also like to acknowledge the expertise, contributions, and assistance provided by the following companies and individuals in the preparation of this document:

- Kenneth Bourgeois, U.S. Payroll Production Control Staff Accountant, Digital Equipment Corporation
- Robert C. Cunningham, Manager, Compensation Processing and Human Resource Operations and Employee Services, Chevron Corporation
- Andrew E. Jones III, General Manager—Accounts Payable and Payroll, Southwestern Bell Telephone Co.
- Michael D. Jones, Director of Payroll Operations, NYNEX Corporation and President, American Payroll Association
- Mary Lou Koch-Hanners, CPP, Payroll Manager, Ross Products Division, Abbott Laboratories and President, American Payroll Association
- Anna R. Lipofsky, U.S. Payroll TQM Consultant, Digital Equipment Corporation
- Kenneth McGonagill, CPP, Director, Human Resources, Manheim Auctions, Cox Enterprises, Inc.
- William A. Minneman, Midwest Region Manager, The Hunter Group, Inc.
- Pamela Starr Nisetich, U.S. Payroll Senior Business Consultant, Digital Equipment Corporation
- William Price, National Account Manager, Automated Data Processing Inc.
- Michael P. O'Toole, Director, Education Division, American Payroll Association
- Robert Rachlin, Assistant Dean for Business Studies, UCCE, Hofstra University
- Kenneth Sawyer, Vice-President and General Manager, Dun & Bradstreet Software

SOURCES AND SUGGESTED REFERENCES

American Payroll Association, *APA Guide to Payroll Practice and Management.* New York: American Payroll Association, 1995.

American Payroll Association, *Federal Payroll Tax Laws and Regulations.* American Payroll Association, 1995.

American Payroll Association, *The Payroll Manager's Guide to Successful Direct Deposit* (8th ed.). American Payroll Association, 1995.

American Payroll Association, *The Payroll Source.* New York: American Payroll Association, 1995.

American Payroll Association Basic Guide to Payroll. Bureau of Business Practice/Prentice Hall, 1995.

Clermont, Paul, ''Outsourcing Without Guilt,'' *Computerworld.* September 1991.

Gow, Brent, ''Analyze Your Options,'' *Paytech.* July/August 1994, pp. 30–32.

Kotter, John P., and James L. Heskett, *Corporate Culture and Performance.* New York: Free Press, 1992.

Quinn, James Brian, Thomas L. Doorley, and Penny C. Paquette, ''Beyond Products: Services-Based Strategy,'' *Harvard Business Review,* no. 90212, March–April 1990.

Rhinesmith, Stephen H., *A Manager's Guide to Globalization.* Six Skills for Success in a Changing World (2nd ed.). AmerSociety for Training, 1996.

Tagliani, Bob, ''Service Bureau or In-House Payroll Processing?,'' *Paytech*, July–August 1994.

Watson, Gregory H., *The Benchmarking Workbook.* Cambridge, MA: Productivity Press, 1994.

CHAPTER 18

BUDGETING THE PURCHASING DEPARTMENT AND THE PURCHASING PROCESS

Carl Benner
John N. Trush
Thomas F. Norris

PricewaterhouseCoopers L.L.P.

18.1 DESCRIPTION AND DEFINITION OF THE PROCESS APPROACH. Traditionally, management has used the budget as a tool to track, control, and forecast the financial effectiveness of the business. Typically, budgets are prepared in some hierarchical manner by departments and then aggregated along organizational lines to create the business unit's budget. Today, as a result of the use of such techniques as re-engineering and and right-sizing, and the use of cross-functional teams, there is an increased emphasis and need to manage and optimize along a process perspective as well as to use budgeting for control of the individual responsibilities, departments, and functions within the process. (To distinguish the purchasing department from the purchasing process, the term *procurement* will be used herein to identify the process perspective.) To be effective, an organization must control the spending of both the function and the process; in other words, the organization must consider the following:

- Purchasing as defined by the activities of the purchasing department
- Purchasing as defined by the activities of the procurement process

(a) The Purchasing Department. The control of the purchasing departmental budget is a very important piece of the procurement process. The purchasing budget, to begin, will be influenced by the manner in which the business is organized. Many purchasing departments function both centrally and locally. For example, companies might buy key commodities or services centrally through long-term purchasing agreements, but the actual ordering and releasing might be executed locally, at the operating site. Additionally, there might be local purchasing departments that buy items and services such as capital equipment and maintenance for that particular site. Purchasing activities are sometimes intentionally delegated and distributed to other departments. This normally is a function of size, efficiency, and mission, and the level of special competencies required. The following are some examples:

- Advertising, purchased by the marketing department
- Research and development (R&D), purchased by medical doctors or scientific specialists
- Transportation, purchased by the logistics arm of the organization
- Outsourcing of information technology (IT) activities
- Travel and entertainment, purchased by authorized managers

Another common technique used by the purchasing department to delegate authority to the organization is via the procurement card, usually used for low-dollar and high-volume item purchases. This tool has enabled significant cost reductions through the elimination of several activities, such as the requisition, the purchase order (PO), the invoice, the check request, and the check itself. Some leading-edge companies, in support of programs called "JIT II Purchasing," further delegate purchasing by bringing key suppliers on-site and "hooking them up" to the company's information system. The suppliers then actually do the buying/planning of the material or service provided to the company. Whenever purchasing delegates responsibility, it is still responsible for oversight, as well as appropriate purchasing training and education.

The purchasing department also has an important role in providing both strategic and operating assistance to the organization. Strategically, purchasing is an integral partner in all make/buy decisions. Purchasing is involved in developing the budget for materials and services. This is a consistent role among the various business sectors, whether private, public, or nonprofit. A 1990 study by the National Association of Purchasing Managers (NAPM) concluded that the tasks or duties that purchasing managers perform are fairly similar in the private, public, and nonprofit sectors—"Purchasers across these sectors appear to 'speak the same language' and approach their jobs with reasonably the same duties and goals in mind." An article in the December 1996 issue of *Purchasing Today* concludes that manufacturing and service industries are facing similar struggles: "In many cases, service industry purchasers find themselves dealing with issues that manufacturing sector companies have already confronted, such as supplier reduction strategies and cost-price analysis."[1]

Purchasing is the department most involved in the selection and control of suppliers. Purchasing typically establishes the policies and procedures that govern the review, selection, and certification of suppliers. Many purchasing departments have focused on cost elimination through strategic partnerships. Successful partnerships have individually yielded cost reductions of 15% to 45% of the purchasing bill. Because only a handful of partnerships can be resourced and managed, each partnership is highly leverageable and could be worth 3% to 5% of the total annual buy dollars. Advanced organizations are building these targets into their purchasing budgets. A critical mass needs to be developed and dedicated to expand improvement efforts internally and, as appropriate, to extend them to the supplier's suppliers. Care must be taken that reductions are properly resourced and budgeted for implementation.

The purchasing department is well positioned to strongly influence the entire procurement process by its involvement in various supply-chain activities. Purchasing typically is involved in both product and process development, as well as in other technical activities

---

[1] Carolyn Pye, "Service-Industry Speaks Out," *Purchasing Today* 12, no. 12 (December 1996), 24–26.

within the organization. In most organizations, purchasing has continual involvement with operational activities, such as stores, materials handling, production, quality, receiving, and shipping, as well as with administrative activities such as accounts payable and accounts receivable.

Whether purchasing departments function centrally, locally, or in a distributed model, or are in the private, public, or nonprofit sectors, departmental expenses can be identified and budgets combined or separated as needed to manage and control departmental spending.

(b) The Procurement Process. It is more difficult to identify and control the expenses of the procurement process. In many organizations, procurement is not recognized as a process, and therefore the complete set of its elements has not been identified. Additionally, expenses are more difficult to track because they are spread throughout the organization. However, there is a value in expanding the departmental focus of the typical budget process to include the entire procurement process. Particularly, this is responsive to management's need for continuous improvement.

To begin, it is useful to identify the elements of a process and determine the definition of a process. A *process* is a set of linked activities that take an input, transform it, and create an output. Ideally, the transformation that occurs in a process should add value to the input and should create an output that is more useful to, and effective for, the recipient. Exhibit 18.1 describes a process and illustrates the movement from supplier to customer. How does a process add value? Value can be created or added through improved product quality and/or service, reduced cycle time, and reduced cost to the customer. Exhibit 18.2 describes these value metrics in greater detail. The procurement process not only encompasses the internal organization but also includes external customers and suppliers. This process will vary by industry, by business unit, and by the nature of the product or service provided.

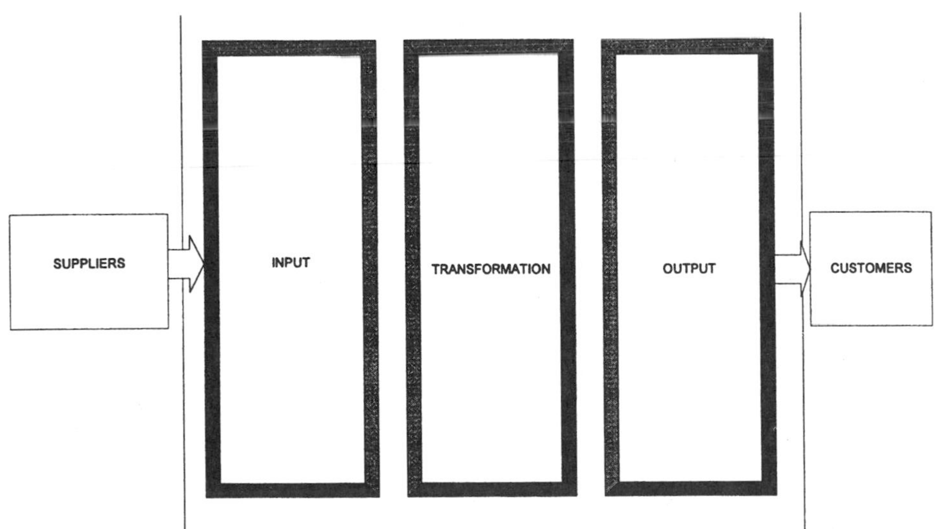

Exhibit 18.1. Illustration of the purchasing process
Reprinted with permission. David K. Carr and Henry J. Johansson, Best Practices in Reengineering (McGraw-Hill, 1995).

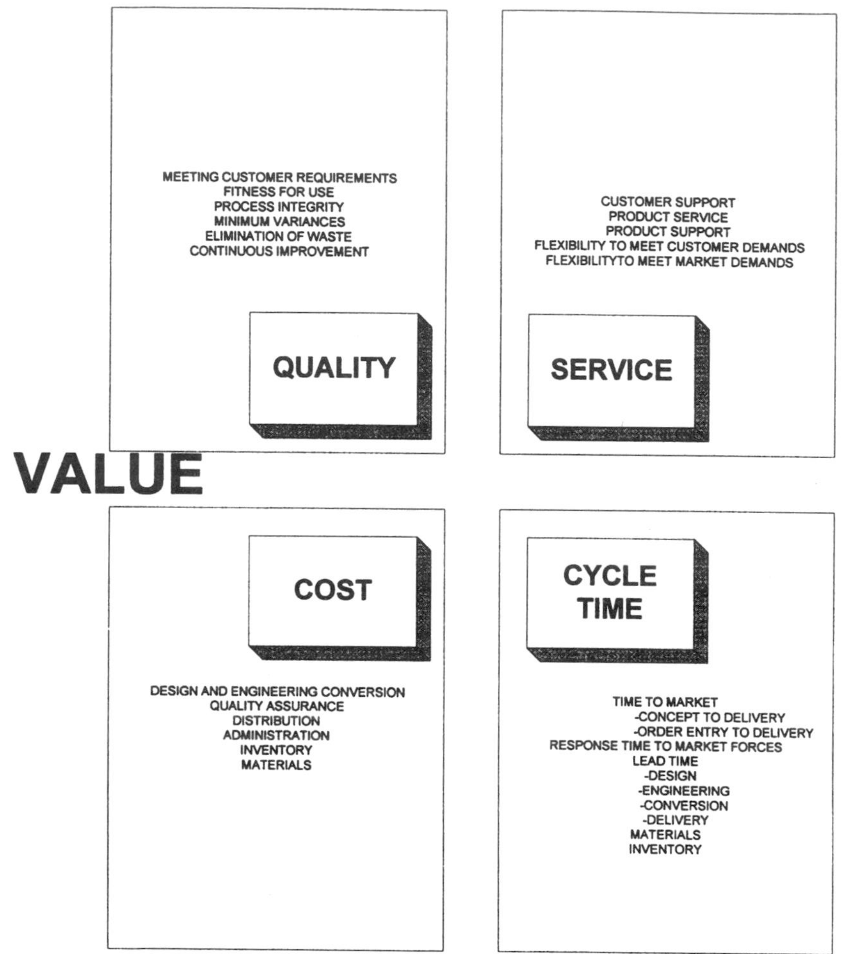

Exhibit 18.2. Metrics for adding value
Reprinted with permission. Henry J. Johansson, Patrick McHugh, John A. Pendlebury, and William A. Wheeler III, *Business Process Engineering,* New York: John Wiley & Sons, 1993.

For most companies, there are two major components of the procurement process, namely:

- The product development subprocess, which encompasses the make/buy selection and includes the following:
  - Marketing
  - Design
  - Manufacturing
  - Costing
  - Engineering
  - Supplier
  - Customer

  - Purchasing
  - Accounting
- The ordering subprocess, which encompasses ordering, delivery, receipt, and payment of the requested goods or services, including the following:
  - Customer or requisitioner
  - Purchasing
  - Supplier
  - Receiving
  - Quality
  - Materials handling
  - Production
  - Customer
  - Accounts payable

(c) Implications of the Process Approach. The primary benefits of a process approach are that it is more holistic, reduces departmental suboptimization, and provides a better identification of the total cost and benefit to the business unit.

The evolution of such techniques as benchmarking, and the use of best practices, has facilitated the ability to establish goals for continuous process improvement. Activity-based costing (ABC) provides the information to understand what is spent, what is done, and what resources are required; it also is a useful tool for segregating value-adding from non–value-adding activities, rather than having to rely only on control through variances based on estimates and averages. Companies are just starting to recognize that the application of ABC to the procurement process is the next tool required.

18.2 ROLE OF PROCESS MEASURES.

A key to managing the procurement process is establishing key performance indicators (KPIs), or process measures. Key performance measures will support the enterprise in meeting its objectives. Key performance indicators establish the visibility to monitor and control the process. Each company will have to establish the appropriate measures for its business. Measures should be both strategic and tactical, and should be focused on the goals of the business.

The importance of this focus is re-inforced in *Reinventing the CFO*. The authors stress that "best practices derive appropriate business measures from business objectives rather than merely from financial reporting line items. These measures ask: Is what we want to achieve good enough? What key performance indicators must we focus on to meet our goals?"[2]

To be effective, measures must be timely and should result in value-added and integrated support of the process. In the case of the procurement process, measures inevitably will involve each supplier's ability to meet the needs of the process and will be established as part of the budget process when the company typically sets business-specific improvement goals.

(a) Supplier Capabilities and Process Requirements. One of the most strategic aspects of the procurement process is the supplier base. The management of this critical asset requires some very difficult decisions both during the budget process and during operations. There are three very different classes of suppliers:

[2] Thomas Walther, Henry J. Johansson, John Dunleavy, and Elizabeth Hjelm, *Reinventing the CFO* (New York: McGraw-Hill, 1997).

1. *Strategic.* A provider with whom an open partnership has been established, and who provides goods or services that are critical to operations, of high value, and essential for competitive advantage
2. *Collaborative.* A provider with whom dealings are continual and trustworthy, and who provides goods or services that are important to operations, of high value, and required but not essential for competitive advantage
3. *Arms-length.* A provider with whom dealings are under market conditions, and from whom purchases are typically at spot or catalog prices, and who provides goods or services that are not of high value and are not essential to the core business

The number of suppliers needed for each class is dependent on a very specific understanding of procurement requirements and on the supplier's ability to meet these requirements. A supplier's classification should be based on its ability to meet specific performance expectations in categories such as the following:

- Production
- Product development
- Cost reduction

The individual category measures will vary by industry and the specific needs of the business. However, the number of suppliers per category should be re-evaluated during the budget process and, once established, be continually reviewed and re-aligned based upon the supplier's performance.

18.3 PROCESS MEASURES.

With an understanding of the industry, the business, process requirements, and supplier's capabilities, specific process improvement goals and process improvement metrics can be established within each of the following categories:

- Production capabilities
- Product development capabilities
- Cost-reduction capabilities

By addressing these measures at the time of budgeting the procurement process, the focus is on both planning and improvement.

(a) Production Capabilities.

Measures also can be established during the budget process to plan and monitor—in other words, to control—each supplier's production capabilities: Such measures include the following:

- *Supplier process reliability.* The ability of the process to constantly produce high-quality product (The processes must run when they are required, at the capable rate, and produce a quality product.)
- *Supplier certification capability and potential.* The ability of the supplier to produce quality output at start-up and throughout the production run, without rework
- *Supplier capacity utilization.* The time the process is actually in operation compared to the total available time the process is available for operation

- *Commodity management.* The right size supplier base as measured by the number of suppliers per materials category
- *Inventory management capability.* The ability to control and manage the days of inventory on hand for the total supply chain based on seasonally adjusted sales
- *Technology.* Measured by the systems used to control production, develop products, and communicate and share information
- *Leveraging purchasing power.* Can be measured as the ability of the customer and the supplier to combine requirements resulting in preferential treatment
- *Reserve capacity.* The amount of production capacity in excess of baseline capacity that is available to support incremental demand for promotions
- *Supplier lead times.* The elapsed time from order placement to actual delivery
- *Service requirements (quantity and timeliness).* Can be measured by the ability to deliver the requested quantities, on time, and as requested, with the required accurate paperwork
- *Quality levels.* Measured internally as incoming and production defects in parts per million and externally by amount of product returns, reclaims, and recalls
- *Continuous improvement capability.* The ability to make improvements year to year based on mutually agreed targets and criteria

These measures provide the necessary information for evaluating supplier's capabilities, identifying areas for improvement, providing the data for measuring performance, and establishing targets for continuous improvement.

(b) Product Development Capabilities. Product development capability is an area that many companies do not formally measure for either budgeting or monitoring purposes. This can be a critical part of the overall business process, and selected measurement often can lead to substantial improvements. Depending on the business needs and goals, some possible areas in which useful measures can be developed are discussed below.

- *Renewal of specifications.* The review and updating of all specifications could identify major opportunities. Cross-functional development teams are useful in this area and should include suppliers.
- *Qualified materials.* It is important to review the requirements for materials specifications and establish performance-based specifications. Overspecifying can limit the supplier's ability to take full advantage of the commodity market because it can create the need for specialty materials or their equivalents.
- *Development process and budgets.* Reviewing opportunities to increase collaborative efforts by sharing technology and best practices could both improve time to market and reduce costs. When these areas are considered, it might lead to the development of a set of mutually agreed measures that will drive the desired cooperative behavior, such as joint
  - Specification development and review, early in the product development cycle
  - Process improvement
  - Product development
  - Cost reduction
- *Number of varieties.* Re-evaluating the need for the number of varieties (such as

flavors, widths, sizes, colors, and the like) might lead to highlighting products or supplies that are very close to each other, and hence might offer opportunities for rationalization.

- *Testing requirements.* Reviewing the need and value of the various customer-specified quality tests might identify areas for cost reduction.
- *Lot-control requirements.* Reviewing the extent to which suppliers are requested to maintain lot control and identification can identify improvement opportunities.
- *Labeling and identification requirements.* Reviewing the extent to which the supplier is required to label, mark, and identify specified information is another possible improvement area.

In summary, it can be seen that procurement budgeting is much more oriented toward operations improvement and control than it is to merely estimating the amount of goods to be procured.

(c) Cost-Reduction Capabilities. Many of the factors that impact product development also impact operational costs and vice versa. Both areas should be reviewed as part of budgeting as both potential cost drivers and appropriate measures should be established. Some possibilities are as follows:

- *Customer requirements and procedures for loading and identification information.* Review all of the requested loading information, such as bills of lading, packing lists, advance shipping notices (ASNs), bar codes, labels, load reports, and the like, and evaluate costs and benefits.
- *Procedures for establishing and communicating forecast information, orders, and changes to the supplier.* Frequent and ultimately changes to quantities, varieties, and delivery dates create the need for excess capacity, and supplier inventories, and are a source of hidden costs. Re-examine the need and the costs avoided by the customer compared to the costs incurred and passed along by the supplier.
- *Communications.* Communications and the supporting technologies are enablers of all improvement opportunities. This is especially true in the area of information technology. Explore opportunities to jointly develop approaches to systems such as the following:
- Management of total supply inventory at the supplier, in-transit, and at the customer, considering:
  - Consignment
  - Automatic replenishment
  - Direct vendor shipments to customers
- Administrative systems, including:
  - Procurement cards
  - Monthly or consolidated invoicing
  - Electronic Data Interchange to share forecasts and transmit orders
  - Electronic funds transfer/automated clearing house (EFT/ACH) for payment
  - Bar coding, to record receipts and track inventories
  - Advance Shipping Notice, to schedule receiving
  - Pay-on-receipt, eliminating invoices

- *Quality information.* Are there opportunities to share certificates of analysis and other quality information?
- *Sharing business plans.* Synchronize business plans, including business development, product development, and process development, with an emphasis on capital expenditures and cost reduction.
- *Sharing technology.* Share both the plans and the current application of various technologies, such as process automation, information automation, and communications automation.
- *Materials and capacity utilization.* Assess opportunities to favorably impact a supplier's cost of underutilized capacity or to share/leverage energy.
- *Sourcing arrangements.* Realign the supplier's shipping locations with the customer's producing plants.
- *Buffer stock requirements.* Variations between the standard and actual plant efficiency and scrap factors have an impact on run-out and replenishment orders placed by the plants. These variations should be mitigated by the plant's run strategy, plant safety stocks, and supplier buffer stocks. There might be an opportunity to improve the effectiveness and cost of how these factors are being used and balanced.
- *Various ways trucks are used, and how material is loaded and unloaded.* Review common routes and evaluate whether there are opportunities for cross-docking, mixed truckloads, or joint scheduling of back hauls. Review the quality and materials-handling characteristics to determine cost-effective ways to load and unload trucks, such as the use of dunnage, re-usable pallets, disposable pallets, and so forth. Evaluate the use of requested containers and their usefulness in production.
- *Purchasing leverage with the suppliers of the supplier.* There might be opportunities to combine volume and increase leverage for commodities, for energy, and for shared capacity with suppliers, or by commonly using such items as maintenance materials and spare parts.
- *Physical assets.* Review and compare the locations, equipment, and information used by both companies. There might be opportunities to share facilities, equipment, offices, communications systems, and/or information systems.
- *Best-practice initiatives.* Evaluate each supplier's (and its supplier's) process improvement initiatives and such enablers as statistical process control (SPC), supplier certification production certification, and International Standards Organization (ISO) certification.

Finally, the sharing and accuracy of cost information should be reviewed and confirmed during the budget process. Understanding costs will have an important bearing on each supplier's cost reduction capabilities. The following are some of the elements required to understand a supplier's costs:

- Breakdown of costs (labor, materials, and overhead)
- Service requirements (quantity and timeliness)
- Cycle times
- Quality levels
- Continuous improvement capabilities

As with product development, cost-reduction capabilities being reviewed at the budget cycle can lead to substantial improvements beyond simply estimating future procurement expenditures.

18.4 CREATING THE PROCUREMENT PROCESS BUDGET.

Today, many companies use a series of performance measures to manage and control the budget processes for procurement. These performance measures either supplement or replace traditional budgets. The steps involved are as follows:

- Defining the process
- Establishing appropriate business goals
- Identifying the requirements of the process
- Relating business goals to the process
- Establishing goals for the process
- Establishing metrics for the process
- Organizing those metrics into a meaningful process budget

Many techniques that support process management are available and in use today, such as the following:

- Business-process re-engineering (BPR) is a widely accepted and proven technique to define process and identify requirements.
- Benchmarking and best-practice techniques can identify opportunities for improvement.
- Activity-based costing and performance metrics can be used to identify and track causes and results.
- Management reporting can be used to organize and present the results.

All of these techniques are directly applicable to procurement. In addition, there are profesional organizations that specialize in procurement. Two of the best are CAPS and NAPM. The Center for Advanced Purchasing Studies is jointly sponsored by Arizona State University and the NAPM. Both are important sources for purchasing benchmarking and performance data, and for the cost of the process, providing data such as the following:

- Purchasing expense per purchasing dollar
- Annual purchasing dollar per purchasing employee (as full-time equivalents, or FTEs)
- Average invoices per employee in the accounts payable function
- Average receipts and inspections per employee involved
- Active suppliers per purchasing employee
- Company purchase dollars per active supplier

Center for Advanced Purchasing Studies provides substantive research data; its mission states that ''CAPS strives to contribute competitive advantages to organizations by providing leading-edge research to support the evolution of strategic purchasing/supply management.'' This includes research that

- Identifies the leading edge of current practice and application
- Identifies the current state of procurement practice
- Benchmarks the current state of the practice

Local experience together with sources like CAPS and NAPM can be used to establish metrics to be used in budgeting. These metrics can be prioritized and further integrated with the strategic and tactical goals of the business units as well as with the key activities of the procurement process. Business-process re-engineering supported with benchmarking and ABC can be used to identify areas for improvement. The goals of the business unit can be used to establish priorities. Together with an understanding of the process, and with the availability and the skill sets of resources and of performance categories, specific targets can be established. These measures, when organized into a process framework, can be used to predict the impact of planned continual improvement, and can provide for the management and control of a process-oriented purchasing/procurement budget.

SOURCES AND SUGGESTED REFERENCES

Carr, David K., and Henry J. Johansson, *Best Practices in Reengineering*. New York: McGraw-Hill, Inc., 1995.

Gumaer, Robert, ''Synchronizing the Supply Chain,'' *APICS* 7, No. 1 (January 1997), 46–48.

Harwick, Tom, ''Optimal Decision-Making for the Supply Chain,'' *APICS* 7, no. 1 (January 1997), 42–44.

Johansson, Henry J., Patrick McHugh, John A. Pendlebury, and William A. Wheeler III, *Business Process Reengineering*. New York: John Wiley & Sons, 1994.

Kaplan, Robert S., *Measures for Manufacturing*, Cambridge, MA: Harvard Business School Press, 1990.

Maskell, Brian H., *Performance Measurement for World Class Manufacturing*. Cambridge, MA, Norwalk, CT: Productivity Press, 1991.

McNair, C. J., William Mosconi, and Thomas Norris, *Beyond the Bottom Line*. Homewood, IL: Dow Jones–Irwin, 1989.

McNair, C. J., William Mosconi, and Thomas Norris, *Meeting the Technology Challenge: Cost Accounting in a JIT Environment*. Montvale, NJ: National Association of Accountants, 1988.

Pye, Carolyn, ''Service-Industry Speaks Out,'' *Purchasing Today*, December 1996.

Walther, Thomas, Henry J. Johansson, John Dunleavy, and Elizabeth Hjelm, *Reinventing the CFO*. New York: McGraw-Hill, 1996.

CHAPTER 19

CAPITAL-INVESTMENT BUDGETING PROCESS

Surendra S. Singhvi

Singhvi & Associates, Inc.

19.1 INTRODUCTION. Capital-investment budgeting is extremely important in a free-enterprise system because capital-investment decisions are generally irreversible, require substantial financial resources, and affect the organization's performance over a long time. Decision makers in the free world are likely to find a severe scarcity of capital resources during the next decade as a result of worldwide inflation, which erodes profits and requires large sums of capital to replace and/or expand existing facilities. Therefore, the organizations that plan and manage capital investments successfully will probably have no difficulties in raising capital resources in the future, except for government constraints, if any.

A *capital investment* (or expenditure) is defined as any project that involves the use of spending power in return for an anticipated flow of future benefits for a long period, generally more than one year. The spending power represents one's cash and credit resources available for a long period, generally more than one year. For example, one acquires the use of a building with 25 years of useful life for an initial cash payment of $5,000 and debt assumption of $45,000 to be paid over 25 years. The capital investment in the project is $50,000, since the amount represents a total use of one's spending power.

As contrasted with a capital investment, any project that uses one's spending power in return for anticipated benefits for a short period, generally less than one year, is defined as an *expense investment* or an *operating investment.* For example, one acquires the use of a building for six months for an initial cash payment of $200 and debt assumption of $1,000 to be paid over the next five months. The use of spending power in the amount of $1,200 in this illustration is not a capital investment, but it is an expense for this period.

A capital investment could represent an increase in fixed assets (plant, property, and equipment), ownership in other businesses, and permanent increase in working capital (current assets less current liabilities).

19.2 REASONS FOR CAPITAL INVESTMENTS. The ultimate reason for making capital investments is to improve or maintain the overall profitability and worth (or value) of the enterprise over the long run. However, the specific reasons for these investment projects could be the following:

- To reduce present and projected costs of labor, energy, transportation, material, and the like
- To increase sales volume by increasing production capacity either internally or externally through acquisition of other enterprises
- To upgrade a product's quality by adding facilities that will produce higher profit per unit sold
- To protect or defend the present level of sales and profits by adding new facilities or replacing present facilities to satisfy governmental requirements or to remain competitive

19.3 CAPITAL-INVESTMENT BUDGETING PROCEDURES. Capital-investment proposals generally do not crop up overnight but require careful and well-thought-out planning within an organization. In capital-intensive businesses, it might be appropriate to classify all capital investments in two categories for budgeting and approval purposes: (1) normal capital investments and (2) special capital investments.

(a) Normal Capital Investments. This category of capital investments includes those projects of routine nature that are required to maintain the present level of operations. Generally, each project does not require a large sum of capital. For example, a minor replacement of equipment, such as a lathe or a forklift truck requiring high repair cost, is classified as a normal capital investment. A minor cost-reduction project also falls in the same category. However, the definition of a minor or major project will vary from one organization to another.

These projects are conceived at the plant or division level during the year for the following year. Each project to be included in the normal capital-investment budget must be justified financially or otherwise by the plant or divisional management. All divisions submit their proposed budget for capital investments for approval by top management and the board of directors. Once the budget is approved, the divisional management is authorized to appropriate funds for the projects included in the budget during the following year. Such approval procedures allow top management to concentrate its efforts in evaluating major, nonroutine types of capital investments and also place more responsibility on divisions for managing their normal type of capital investments. Of course, this system requires top management review and approval when a deviation from the approved budget is anticipated by divisions.

(b) Special Capital Investments. This category of capital investments includes those projects that require relatively large sums of money for expansion, major cost-reduction, or replacement purposes. Since these projects are of a nonroutine nature, they require special planning and approval procedures.

Generally, these projects are conceived at the profit center (or division) level and are discussed in one of the periodic meetings devoted to capital-expenditure planning. Occasionally, a project could be conceived at the top management level and directed to one of the profit centers for further consideration.

For example, a product manager may realize a need for a second pipe plant since the present plant is unable to satisfy the customer demand. Without any engineering work done, the product manager, based on his or her experience, indicates a capital-investment need for approximately $2 million. Since the present plant is successful, the profit center manager approves this project for further study and may appoint a task force committee of individuals representing sales, finance, engineering, and operations. The task force committee may be authorized to spend up to 2% to 3% of the estimated capital-investment amount to define the project's scope and complete some engineering and market research work.

As soon as the task force committee completes the preliminary study on the proposed project, the profit center manager reviews the task force report. If the project, now estimated to cost $2.1 million, is considered promising at this stage, the profit center manager authorizes development of a complete program request, with economic justification, for submission to corporate management for approval. A program request is a document that generally includes the background information on the business or product line, proposed facilities, sales support, critical requirements, and financial justification.

Once the program request is approved by the profit center manager, it is submitted to corporate management for approval. If the investment amount exceeds a predetermined maximum amount, the program request must be submitted to the board of directors for approval. All other projects not requiring approval must be reviewed with the board periodically. If a project is approved, the engineering function will develop more precise estimates of the capital-investment amount based on bids from contractors. If the estimate is in excess of the program request amount by a certain percentage, a supplemental program request must be approved by those who approved the original program request. The profit center manager now can appropriate funds to carry the project to its completion. During construction, if the capital investment estimate exceeds the amount appropriated by a certain percentage, additional approval must be obtained from corporate management.

The time required from the day a project is conceived and the day it is approved by top management would depend upon the nature, size, and urgency of the project. For example, a capital investment to acquire a company could be planned and approved in much shorter time than a capital investment to build a paper mill.

19.4 SEARCH FOR NEW PROJECTS. Search for new capital-investment projects is not limited to any one function or group of managers. New projects could be conceived in numerous ways, such as the following:

- New product or process development as a result of research and development efforts, which will either increase the market share or reduce operating costs
- Modern facilities to remain competitive and to maintain present market share, as suggested by sales people
- Acquisition projects, as suggested by investment bankers or corporate planning people, to increase market share or to diversify in other businesses
- Replacement projects, as suggested by operating people, to reduce increasing maintenance costs
- Expansion of facilities to satisfy growing demand for product, as projected by marketing research people
- Modern computers, as suggested by systems people, to reduce cost or to remain competitive

19.5 INPUT DATA FOR PROJECT EVALUATION. To evaluate a new capital-investment project, the decision maker must have reliable and relevant input data projected over the economic life of the project. This section will identify and discuss the major input data needed for project evaluation.

(a) Cash Outflows

(i) Initial Cash Outflow. The net effect on cash outlay resulting from the decision to invest in a proposed capital investment is defined as the *initial cash outflow*. This cash outflow could take place all at one time, such as in the case of acquiring a computer. Alternatively, this cash outflow could take place over several years, such as in the case of building an oil refinery. In the latter case, one must provide adequate allowance for contingencies while estimating the proposed capital-investment amount.

From an accounting point of view, a portion of the proposed capital investment could be expensed (i.e., shown as current-period cost) and the remaining portion capitalized (i.e., shown as an asset, which is depreciated over its life). Regardless of the accounting treatment, one must consider the total outlay of cash, not only the portion to be capitalized. For example, a pipe mill costs $5 million, and the start-up cost is estimated to be $400,000. Though the firm is likely to capitalize only $5 million and expense $400,000 for accounting and tax purposes, the initial cash outflow for the project is $5.4 million.

The input data related to initial cash outflows for a capital investment must come from the engineering function (internal or external). If the proposed investment relates to a company acquisition, the initial cash outflow or its equivalent must be determined by the finance function based on the fair market value of the company to be acquired.

The initial cash outflow should be projected on an incremental basis. For example, an old machine with an original cost of $10 million and a 10-year useful life is being considered for replacement by Seema & Company after it has been in use for four years. It is estimated that the old machine can be sold for $3 million, and it can be replaced with a modern machine costing $15 million with a six-year useful life. It is also estimated that there would be additional costs related to the new machine, such as transportation, personnel training, and the like, in the magnitude of $3 million, and these costs must be capitalized. The firm uses the straight-line depreciation method, and its marginal tax rate is 40%. In this situation, the initial cash outflow related to the decision to replace is not $18 million but only $13.8 million, as shown in Exhibit 19.1.

Initial cash outflow need not be in terms of actual cash going out of the firm. For example, one buys a building with a fair market value of $4 million, agrees to a 10%

Cash cost of new machine	$15.0
Cash cost of capitalized expenses	3.0
Total cash cost of new machine	18.0
Less salvage value of old machine	(3.0)
Less tax savings on old machine	(1.2)[a]
Incremental initial cash outflow	$13.8

[a] *Note:*

Less Depreciation for four years	(4.0)
Book value of old machine	6.0
Less salvage value	(3.0)
Loss on sale	$ 3.0
Marginal tax rate assumed	40%
Tax savings (credit or refund) as a result of loss	$ 1.2

Exhibit 19.1. Incremental initial cash outflow ($ million)

Period	Sales	Working Capital	Percentage of Sales
1	$105	$22	21.0
2	112	25	22.3
3	115	26	22.6
4	120	28	23.3
5	116	28	24.1
6	123	30	24.4
7	130	31	23.8
8	131	33	25.2
9	127	32	25.2
10	150	36	24.0

Exhibit 19.2. Manoj & Company's sales and working capital ($ million)

down payment, and assumes a mortgage for the remaining $3.6 million. Though this capital investment project physically requires an initial cash outflow of only $400,000, the firm has used up its borrowing capacity to the extent of $3.6 million. Alternatively, the firm could have borrowed $3.6 million from a bank and paid $4 million in cash to acquire the building. Therefore, to evaluate an investment project, one must consider the initial cash outflow in terms of total cash and its equivalent, that is, total spending power.

(ii) Working Capital. There are some capital-investment projects, such as replacement, pollution control, and cost reduction, that are not likely to require any additional working capital (current assets less current liabilities). Conversely, there are projects such as expansion of existing product lines and new product lines that require investment in additional working capital. In some situations, it is also possible that a capital investment could reduce the present investment in working capital.

Regardless of the direction, one must project these changes in working capital related to a proposed capital investment. The ratio analysis can be used in projecting additional working-capital requirements. For example, if working capital as a percentage of sales has been, on an average, 16% for a given line of business over the past three to five years, one can use this percentage in projecting additional working capital related to the proposed investment. If necessary, one could apply ratio analysis to key elements of working capital, such as inventories, trade, receivables, and payables.

Additionally, one can use regression analysis to project working capital. For example, Manoj & Company's sales and working capital data for its major product for the past 10 years are summarized in Exhibit 19.2.

Using a simple regression analysis, one gets the following equation, where y equals working capital and x equals annual sales:

$$y = -9.81 + 0.32(x)$$

By substituting sales value in place of x, one can project working-capital requirements. If sales is forecasted to be $160 million for the 11th period, the projected working capital should be $41 million.

(iii) Normal Capital Expenditures. Projects with long, useful lives generally require some capital expenditures for minor replacement of parts a few years after the initial

investment is made, or the repair expenses could be very high. The engineering and operating people would be in the best position to estimate such cash outflows. If it is difficult to project such cash outflows by specific years, a total estimate for such expenditures over the project's life could be made and an average cash flow per year could be used, with full recognition that the actual amount would be higher than the projected in some years and lower in other years. As a guide rule, the average annual cash outflow for normal capital expenditure should not exceed the average annual depreciation amount.

(b) Cash Inflows

(i) Net Income. Each discretionary capital investment is expected to increase net income over the project's useful life. This could come about in numerous ways, such as the following:

- Increased sales volume
- Increased sales price per unit as a result of improved quality
- Reduced operating and/or nonoperating cost per unit
- Combination of all the preceding factors

A sales forecast related to the proposed capital investment, where relevant, should be prepared by the sales function. Various forecasting techniques are used to predict sales, such as jury of executive opinion, trend analysis, moving average, regression analysis, life-cycle analysis, and the like.

Cost savings, resulting in increased net income, should be forecasted by operating people in conjunction with engineering, purchasing, and finance functions. Cost savings or additional sales revenues should be projected on an incremental basis if the proposed capital investment is discretionary in nature. For example, if Seema & Company decides to replace an old machine with a new machine, as discussed previously, the effect on annual net income on an incremental basis is shown in Exhibit 19.3.

(ii) Noncash Expenses. The net income figure of \$2.4 million shown in Exhibit 19.3 is based on generally accepted accounting principles (GAAP). However, net income does not reflect the true cash inflow from operations, because some of the expenses do not require any cash outflow during a given period. In the illustration of Seema & Company, an increase in depreciation by \$2 million per year is shown, but no check for that amount is given to anyone in that year. For cash-flow purposes, and not for accounting and tax purposes, one can either eliminate depreciation expense and show an incremental cash

Labor and material costs—old machine	$168.0
Less labor and material costs—new machine	162.0
Gross savings	6.0
Less net increase in depreciation	(2.0)
Net increase in taxable income	4.0
Less tax at marginal rate of 40%	(1.6)
Incremental net income	$ 2.4

Exhibit 19.3. Incremental annual net income ($ million)

	Method		
	#1	#2	#3
Gross savings	$6.0	$6.0	$6.0
Less depreciation	(2.0)	—	—
Taxable income	4.0	—	6.0
Less tax at 40%	(1.6)	(1.6)	(2.4)
Net income	2.4	—	3.6
Add depreciation	2.0	—	—
Add tax savings from depreciation	—	—	0.8
Cash inflow	$4.4	$4.4	$4.4

Exhibit 19.4. Depreciation as a source of cash ($ million)

income of $4.4 million by subtracting the tax provision of $1.6 million from the projected gross savings of $6 million or add $2 million depreciation to $2.4 million net income to compute cash inflow from operations of $4.4 million. Therefore, cash flow from operations equals net income plus depreciation plus other noncash expenses (such as amortization). Only in this context is depreciation referred to as a source of cash.

Depreciation is a source of cash only because it reduces one's taxable income and subsequently the tax liability. If net income has been estimated ignoring any depreciation expense, the cash inflow from depreciation will equal the depreciation amount, times the marginal tax rate. In the illustration of Seema & Company, the projected cash inflow as a result of depreciation can be calculated using any one of the three methods shown in Exhibit 19.4.

Depreciation expense can be calculated using any of the following methods: straight line, double declining balance, sum-of-the years digits, and unit of production. Many firms use one method for book reporting to stockholders and another method for tax-calculation purposes. Of course, when a straight-line depreciation method is used for book-reporting purposes, and an accelerated depreciation method is used for tax purposes, a deferred tax liability is recognized. For the purpose of evaluating an investment, one is interested in cash flows and therefore must use either the accelerated depreciation method if elected for tax purposes or the straight-line depreciation method along with recognition of deferred taxes.

(iii) Adjustment for Financing Costs. While making investment decisions, the objective should be to evaluate the project's productivity, disregarding any specific source of financing, that is, equity or dept capital. If investment decisions are kept separate from financing decisions, the projected rate of return on a given project should be compared with the firm's overall cost of capital.

Our objective, therefore, is to forecast net operating profit after tax (NOPAT) related to a given capital investment. This figure equals net income after tax plus interest expense after tax. The illustration in Exhibit 19.5 shows the difference between NOPAT and net income.

(iv) Residual Value. While projecting cash flows of a project, one must estimate the project's residual value (also known as salvage value) at the end of its useful life to the firm. There are several ways to estimate the project's residual value:

	Alternative	
	#1	#2
Sales	$1000	$1000
Cost of sales	(600)	(600)
Interest expense	(100)	—
Profit before tax	300	400
Tax at 40%	(120)	(160)
Net income	$ 180	—
Add interest expense after tax	60	—
NOPAT	$ 240	$ 240

Exhibit 19.5. NOPAT versus net income

Hurdle Rate	Economic Life (Years)				
(%)	5	10	15	20	25
4	822	676	555	456	375
8	681	463	315	215	146
12	567	322	183	104	59
16	476	227	108	51	24
20	402	162	65	26	10

Exhibit 19.6. Present values of $1,000 residual value

- Engineers can estimate the value based on historical experience with a similar facility.
- Suppliers of the facility can assist in estimating such value based on their research, experience, and judgment.
- Financial analysts can estimate the value to be equal to the undepreciated book value.
- In the case of an acquisition of a going business, the residual value can be estimated based on a price-earning ratio analysis.

One need not spend too much time in estimating the project's residual value if the useful life is fairly long and the hurdle rate is relatively high. Exhibit 19.6 shows the present value of $1,000 residual value for various economic lives and hurdle rates. If the estimated residual value is higher or lower than the undepreciated book value of the assets, a tax gain or expense must be recognized.

(c) Tax Implications on Cash Flows. All cash flows must be projected on an aftertax basis using the firm's marginal tax rate, not the average tax rate. In most countries of the free world, governments provide some kind of tax incentives to encourage capital investments.

(d) Economic Life Projection. Since a capital investment is made in anticipation of benefits to be derived for several years, it is necessary that the project's economic or useful life be projected. The economic life of a project could be different from the physical life or depreciation life established by the tax authorities. For example, a coke oven facility in a steel mill complex is estimated to have a physical life of 40 years (assuming minor replacement and reasonable maintenance), and it can be depreciated over 18 years according to the tax laws in the United States. However, the economic life of the coke oven facility could be longer or shorter than 18 years but not more than 40 years. The economic life indicates the duration of an asset beyond which time it would prove to be uneconomical to operate because of excessive repair cost or declining demand for the product the asset produces.

Similar to the residual value projection, the project's economic life can be estimated by engineers and/or suppliers based on their experience and judgment. Otherwise, one could assume the depreciation life of the asset to be equal to the economic life. To be conservative, one could use the shorter of the two lives.

(e) Cash Flows with and without the Proposed Project. Normally, one needs to project only incremental cash flows related to a proposed capital investment. However, there are occasions when a larger investment is made to protect the smaller present investment. The question one should raise is whether the present investment is worth protecting. For example, a firm has a total investment of \$100 million, which earns, on an average, \$15 million per year. The government regulatory agency requires the firm either to invest an additional \$150 million for pollution abatement or to close the operation. On an incremental but defensive basis, the return is \$15 million on \$150 million investment, or 10%. However, on a total investment (present and proposed) basis, the rate of return is only 6%. Cash flows for the business with and without the proposed project should be projected, since such data provides a proper perspective to decision makers.

(f) Sunk Cost Consideration. *Sunk cost* is the money already spent prior to approval of a project. For example, if a consultant is hired to make a feasibility study on a proposed project, his or her recommendation could be negative or positive. The consultant's fee is referred to as sunk cost, and it should not be included in the proposed investment analysis.

(g) Value of Transferred Assets. In a multidivision organization, the excess assets of one division could be sold in the marketplace or transferred to another division for its use. While analyzing an investment project, a fair market value of the asset transferred from another division should be reflected in cash outflows as if the asset transferred were purchased for cash. This is an example where the firm did not pay any cash for the asset transferred from one division to another, but it lost a possible cash inflow by not selling the excess asset to outsiders.

(h) Inflation and Projected Cash Flows. Managements in those countries with relatively small rates of inflation need not recognize the inflation factor. However, some inflation adjustment should be made in capital investments in those countries where the rate of inflation is relatively high. Inflation in a given country does not affect all sectors equally. Because of demand–supply forces and/or price–wage controls, some businesses are affected more by inflation than others. It is therefore recommended that prices and costs be adjusted over the project's life, reflecting specific anticipated inflation rates. For example, the general inflation rate could be 10% per year, but the inflation rate for stainless steel products could be 3% per year. In projecting cash flows for a capital investment in the stainless steel business, one should consider using the 3% inflation rate rather than 10%. General and specific inflation rates are difficult to project for several years in the future. However, one could analyze the history and extrapolate the specific inflation rates, which could be adjusted for known future developments.

Several input data are needed to analyze an investment proposal. One need not spend substantial time in refining all of these data, since some inputs are less sensitive in terms of the project's rate of return than others. By using sensitivity analysis, one can identify the most sensitive input data and refine those data in detail.

19.6 CAPITAL-INVESTMENT BUDGETING CONSIDERATIONS

(a) Business Strategy. Capital-investment budgeting would be effective and rewarding if a firm had developed a comprehensive business strategy. A firm might have a strategy of maintaining a balanced portfolio of business in order to minimize overall risk through product and/or geographic diversification. *Portfolio management* means identification of businesses based on relative market share and market segment growth rate, as shown in Exhibit 19.7. If a proposed capital investment (such as replacement) belongs to a business that has low projected market growth rate, has low market share, and is a net user of cash, top management might reject the project, even with its high rate of return. Several firms employ two "screens"—a strategic screen first, and if a project passes it, an economic evaluation screen.

A firm's business strategy establishes different criteria for different businesses. A cash-constrained steel company may reject an expansion project despite its projected high return, while it may accept another project to reduce its dependence for energy, even though its projected return is below the cutoff rate.

Management must ask strategic questions before approving a project. These strategic considerations, shown below, could favor a less profitable project or reject a more profitable project:

- Are we expanding in areas of our competitive advantages?
- Do we wish to increase our dependence on earnings from this industry?
- Do we wish to remain dependent on imported raw material?
- Why not milk a mature business rather than expand?
- Is the political climate in a foreign country conducive to new or additional investment?

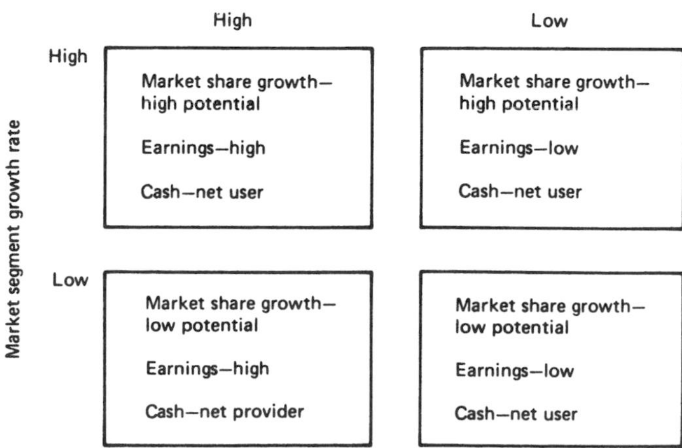

Exhibit 19.7. Business portfolio classification: relative market share

If such considerations give the proposed investment a low priority, there is no reason to collect data and perform a justification analysis.

(b) Postcompletion Audit. One of the major problems in the area of capital investment budgeting is the poor quality of input data used to support an investment proposal. If the profit center manager knows the predetermined hurdle rate for new projects, it is not too difficult to develop the input data, which would generate a rate of return in excess of the hurdle rate.

To overcome this problem to some extent, all major investment projects should be audited by a team of individuals from the profit center involved and corporate staff once the project is in full operation. The objectives of a postcompletion audit of investment projects are:

- It provides information for subsequent decision making and can be used for corrective action if estimates were poor.
- It serves to hold the estimators to continued responsibility. If those who do the estimating know that an audit will be made, they might be more careful in their forecasting than otherwise might be the case.
- Such audits imply that management recognizes the importance of investment decisions and the studies that underline them.

(c) Guidelines for Initiating a Postcompletion Audit

(i) When Should the First Audit Be Performed? The first postcompletion audit should take place as soon as the project in question has had the opportunity to "shake down." The length of the shakedown period will depend on the complexity of the project, the amount of "debugging" required, and the time necessary for operators to reach approximately normal efficiency. Premature audits are not a realistic basis for taking corrective action with respect to either project implementation or future investment decisions. However, if too much time elapses, the opportunity cost of delayed corrective action may be substantial. Since the length of the shakedown period will vary from one project to another, there is ample justification for a reasonably flexible timing policy. The general corporate policy on the matter should be to initiate the first audit as soon as a new project has been debugged and operators have become accustomed to their equipment; in any event, it should occur between one year from the start-up date and five years from the date a project is approved.

Continuing to audit a project after it has been deemed satisfactory is warranted if it is initially predicted that the project's economic performance will change substantially over time or if estimates of the project's life are of critical importance. However, continuing to audit satisfactory projects when estimated cash flow is nearly constant appears to be a poor use of auditing effort.

(ii) Who Should Perform and Review the Audit? Assigning responsibility for the original study and the postcompletion audit to the same people has many advantages. One advantage is that the group doing the audit will know more about the project and the conditions surrounding the justification study than anyone else and, as a result, will do an efficient job of auditing. However, one wonders whether such a group may not be too close to the project to be objective. The requirement that one part of an organization audit

the work of another part can cause serious problems. An alternative approach is that of using a postaudit team made up of the people involved in the justification study and one or more individuals not involved in the original study. Such a group would have a high degree of familiarity with the project audited, and an element of objectivity could be maintained at the same time.

(iii) What Should Be Audited? Decisions must be made as to what projects and what types of information to audit. A comprehensive approach to selecting projects for auditing is to audit all large ones (special capital expenditure) and systematically selected samples of smaller ones (normal capital expenditures). For example, the sample should include projects having relatively large prospective incremental profits. If a selective sampling approach is used in auditing smaller investments, the size of the sample should be adjusted to reach the point where the incremental costs of additional auditing and the incremental benefits therefrom are roughly equal.

It should be made clear that the investment in a project has already been made and is a sunk cost as far as postcompletion audits are concerned. The expenditure of capital funds is usually monitored by a separate procedure that provides the basis for control over expenditures. The reasons for deviations from an investment budget should be determined as soon as detected. There is nothing to gain from delaying this investigation; hence, it ought to precede the postcompletion audit in most cases. Ideally, all of the estimates of operating costs and revenues that were used in justifying a project should be audited. It is preferable to select the elements of particular significance in the original study. It is also desirable to investigate both quantitative and qualitative aspects of a project's performance.

(iv) How Should the Audit Be Planned? Regardless of whether a project is large enough to have its own permanent accounts, the postcompletion audit can be executed more efficiently if it is planned for at the time of the justification study. When this is done, the data in the justification study must be presented in such a way that they can be more readily audited at a future date and so that preliminary plans for the audit can be developed. In regard to interpretation, when actual figures turn out to be different from estimates, the underlying cause should be determined.

Exhibit 19.8 outlines suggested captions to be used in preparing information for the audit report.

1. Title and project number
2. Brief description of the project, with underlying key assumptions
3. Expenditures planned versus amount spent
4. Planned versus actual completion date
5. Planned versus actual payback period
6. Planned versus actual return on investment
7. Explanation of project overruns or underruns of more than 10%
8. Reasons for substantial variations in return on investment
9. Analysis by sales manager if product under sales goal
10. Lessons learned from this project that would help improve performance on future projects of this nature
11. Names of the individuals who developed the information for the original request
12. Names of the individuals who participated in this review

Exhibit 19.8. Suggested format of postcompletion audit report

Criteria	Number of Firms	Percentage of Total
Total dollars spent	24	80
Type of expenditure	12	40
Time since expenditure was made	11	37
Management request	11	37
Other	5	17

Exhibit 19.9. Criteria for selecting projects for postcompletion audit

It should be recognized that a postcompletion audit cannot be made in all instances, and in any event it is not without difficulties of its own. Although audits can be effective in reviewing noninterdependent projects, audits of interdependent projects (expansion, replacement) require the same type of subjective assumptions used for the original capital-investment request.

(d) Empirical Data on Postcompletion Audit. An unpublished survey of 30 large companies indicates that all respondents conduct reviews that compare actual to anticipated performance for fixed-asset expenditures. The criteria for selection of expenditures to be reviewed are shown in Exhibit 19.9.

The minimum dollar amount of projects that are reviewed ranged from $50,000 to $2 million, with $1 million being mentioned by 6 of the 16 companies that indicated a dollar amount. Expenditures that were intended to improve profits (expansion, cost savings, etc.) were mentioned by most companies that indicated the type of expenditure criterion used in selecting the projects for review. Of the 11 companies that used time as a criterion for selection, 7 used one year from the start-up or date of installation.

Of the 17 respondents that reviewed expenditures more than once, 9 indicated a flexible approach that required additional reviews if the initial review was inconclusive in measuring the outcome. Other companies required monthly, quarterly, annual, or longer periods to elapse between reviews at regular predetermined review dates.

The results of the review were prepared by the corporate staff only in 10 companies, by the profit center people only in 10 companies, and by a team of corporate and profit center people in 10 companies. The results of the review were presented to the various levels of management groups such as: board of directors (40%), corporate management (83%), and a management level that approved the project (63%).

Of the 30 companies, 27 mentioned return on investment as one of the three most significant items in reviewing project performance, and 15 companies ranked it as the most significant. This was followed closely by the measuring of profit results achieved. Cash flow was mentioned as the third significant item in reviewing profit performance. Other items mentioned were payback period, investment amount, and technical or strategic achievements.

Of the respondents, 83% project future results at the time a project is reviewed, and most of them combine these forecasts with actual results for overall project reviews. Of the 29 companies in which a change in assumptions is made during the review in either actual results or the original proposal, most of them indicated that the assumptions are changed for future projections of earnings based on actual experience to date. None of the respondents revises the original proposal after it has been approved, except for accounting rule changes such as first-in–first-out (FIFO) to last-in–first-out (LIFO).

The problem areas mentioned previously frequently were difficulty in obtaining actual data that are not available from the accounting system (incremental costs), measuring the effect of changing market conditions as opposed to management actions, and lack of time and interest in the results, including defensiveness of management that sponsored the investment. The benefit mentioned most frequently was that the review procedure improves the forecasting of future proposals.

(e) Request Preparation. The basic responsibility for preparing the request rests with the profit center that initiates the project. This concept is important under the philosophy of profit centers whereby individual managers have specific responsibility for conceiving the idea, proposing it to corporate management, and implementing the proposal that will help in achieving the company's strategic plans.

In a relatively decentralized organization, formal presentations are an essential communication medium among the profit centers, corporate management, and the board of directors. Investment decisions are the most important decisions a company can make. Since these requests are a reflection of management thinking in this vital area, they inevitably represent one basis on which corporate management is going to evaluate the abilities of profit center personnel and on which the board of directors will appraise the abilities of both profit center and corporate management.

A request must therefore be a document that clearly describes in a logical and systematic manner the project being recommended. It must include all key factors, both pros and cons, that need to be evaluated in arriving at a decision and must make clear the reasoning behind management's recommendation. It is also most important that a request be as realistic as possible. If a request is prepared realistically, and the end result looks like a marginal investment, then it is time to take a critical look at the proposal rather than attempting to "window dress" the project to make it appear acceptable.

A request must convey the true flavor of the project, covering both the opportunities and the risks. The proponents of the project must have a thorough understanding of what is involved and must carefully consider all of the alternatives available and their profit implications for stockholders. It is unrealistic to assume that one can always get all of the information one would like to have in reliable form before having to make a decision. Where this is the case, the request must take special care to identify and evaluate the major unknowns and to furnish a measure of the reliability of such factual information as is presented.

There can be no single set of rules that applies equally to all investment projects under consideration. However, a well-prepared request should convince the reader that all of the important factors have been considered. Confidence in a proposal can usually be enhanced by adhering to several guidelines, which are shown in Exhibit 19.10.

(i) Guidelines for Preparing a Request

1. *Consider the knowledge of the reader.* Top management knows far less about the situation described than does profit center management. For a request to be meaningful, it generally needs more explanation than one that might be completely adequate within the particular profit center. Also, technical terms unfamiliar to the readers should be avoided or explained.

2. *Make the story complete.* Top managers do not usually retain copies of requests, and in a large company it is not reasonable to expect them to remember details of a specific project. Essential background information should therefore be repeated in each new presen-

1. Consider the knowledge of the reader
2. Make the story complete
3. Put the story in proper perspective
4. Analyze the alternatives
5. Identify and evaluate all the risks
6. Provide estimates on a comparative basis
7. Evaluate the financial projections
8. Avoid defending a project as absolutely necessary
9. Limit the length of the proposal
10. Be specific

Exhibit 19.10. Guidelines for preparing a request

tation. Also, in a changing situation, what a top manager is currently being told should be reconciled with what he or she was told in previous requests or memorandums. A complete explanation of all major discrepancies, whether favorable or unfavorable, is essential to retaining top management's confidence.

3. *Put the story in proper perspective.* Any major request should be put into proper perspective by describing how the project fits in with the existing business and with overall strategic plans. Is the project being justified as an isolated investment, or is it rather the first step in some more ambitious program? If such a program is needed to make the particular project attractive for the long pull, is the program itself attractive to the company and consistent with the direction in which the company intends to head? How does the proposal of a new position in an area, country, or industry tie in with the company's long-range strategic plans?

4. *Analyze the alternatives.* One of the prerequisites to creating confidence that the project being proposed is the right one is to include in the request an examination of the relative merits and demerits of other alternatives that may be available or the reason why certain alternatives may not be available. Such alternatives might include different ways of getting the same job done, such as the relative cost of a new versus an existing machine, the option of buying versus manufacturing, and the consequences of doing nothing about the situation at this time. Although it may not be feasible to examine all conceivable alternatives in detail, recognition at least should be given to the fact that alternatives do exist or that there are no feasible alternatives.

5. *Identify and evaluate all the risks.* A satisfactory request requires recognition of all of the known political, economic, technological, and other risks involved in the proposed project. In addition to identifying the risks, the sponsor of the project is in the best position to evaluate its seriousness for the company.

6. *Provide estimates on a comparative basis.* While preparing a request, one must always use sales and expenses on a comparative basis. The estimates should attempt to measure the difference between what would occur if the project under consideration were accepted and if it were not accepted. Since every estimate of cash flows involves an implied comparison, it is extremely important that a realistic situation be projected as the one likely to occur if the proposed investment is not undertaken.

7. *Evaluate the financial projections.* The adequacy and accuracy of the financial estimates in the request should be objectively appraised. When precise projections are difficult,

some measure of the possible upside or downside deviations is usually helpful. It is erroneous to assume, while preparing a request, that the future can be directly extrapolated from the past. Although it is necessary to assign numerical values to the projected performance of the project, it is equally important that the narrative describe the profit environment expected for the project both in the near future and in the distant future—perhaps 5 or 10 years out. Particularly for requests involving acquisitions or the introduction of a new product line, it is important that the request include a description of the market conditions and competitive situation expected for the industry as a whole, with particular emphasis on the company's expected position within the industry. One of the difficult financial factors to project is the level of prices that will exist over the life of a project. The underlying assumptions used in arriving at price projections for a request must be very carefully thought out and conservatively arrived at. All of the major assumptions should be set forth in detail in the request, with supporting facts and figures.

8. *Avoid defending a project as absolutely necessary.* Occasionally, the gains from an investment may seem so large that no satisfactory economic justification is provided in the request. For example, a steel company must replace an old mill or abandon the product that the old mill produces. The principal danger to be avoided in analyzing such projects is the assumption that, if only the present necessary investment is made, future cash flows will proceed. If the proposed investment is a borderline case, then what is required is a projection not only of the present investment but also of the necessary additional investments that will be required in the future, thus making it possible to decide whether the whole series of investments will be profitable. Otherwise, one may find gradually rebuilding an unprofitable mill with many small expenditures considered as absolutely necessary.

9. *Limit the length of the proposal.* The length of the presentation should generally be commensurate with the dollar amount involved and the complexity of the project. However, exceptions should be made for projects (1) that propose an investment in a new business, (2) that involve unusually high risk, and (3) that represent a deviation from normal company policy.

10. *Be specific.* Specific figures and information should be used rather than general statements. Use of small summary tables within the narrative is desirable. Adjectives and adverbs, which are subject to wide interpretation, should be eliminated.

(f) Expenditure Control. Successful capital investment budgeting requires an effective control of various investment projects throughout the company. A planner might divide various projects into the following phases in order to communicate to top management the degree of commitment for each project:

- *Inceptive phase.* This phase should include all capital-investment projects that have been conceived throughout the company to reduce costs, to expand sales, to improve quality, and the like. These projects are simply ideas on paper and do not have any engineering and marketing studies to support them.
- *Planning phase.* A project in this phase is investigated by individuals representing various functions within the company. The project's cash flows, based on brief engineering and marketing studies, have been identified over its economic life. The project has been reviewed and approved by the divisional management.
- *Approval phase.* A project with a supporting justification study is submitted to top management for approval. Depending on the capital-expenditure amount involved, the project might be presented to the board of directors for approval. The justification

study should include sales support, financial analysis, engineering estimates, and background on existing business and business plans.

- *Appropriation phase.* Projects in this phase are supported by detailed engineering studies based on firm bids or quotations from contractors. If the detailed engineering studies do not require funds in excess of the approved amount, the project administrator is allowed to appropriate funds. An appropriation request, along with a copy of the detailed engineering study, should be prepared and approved by top management. If the appropriation amount is in excess of a certain percentage over the approved amount, the project must be taken to the same authorities who approved it originally.

A monthly or quarterly report of all projects should be prepared by phases and years of expenditures, as shown in Exhibit 19.11. Such a report controls all projects approved or under consideration by management at all levels. Projects added or deleted from the report can be analyzed, showing the effect on the company's forecasted cash flows.

It might be useful to have another report prepared monthly to control projects in the appropriation phase, where money is spent regularly to complete the project. Exhibit 19.12 shows an illustrative report form to control these expenditures by project. This report places emphasis on actual expenditures, whereas the project status report places emphasis on expenditures forecast. Any overrun for a given project is communicated to top managers every month to enable them to take any corrective action.

Authority for a project approval and appropriation could be delegated at various levels of management, with certain dollar limits for each project. Such delegation of authority expedites the approval and appropriation procedure. One or several members of the auditing function should be assigned the task of reviewing capital-expenditure appropriation requests to determine if procedures are followed.

The approval or appropriation procedures should not be influenced by the method of financing a project. For example, if it is decided that equipment should be leased, the approval and appropriation procedures should be the same as if the equipment were purchased. A financing method should not eliminate the need to justify the acquisition of the proposed equipment.

It would be most beneficial to the company if it can have a capital-expenditure manual spelling out all procedures necessary for approval and all appropriations related to capital expenditures. Such a manual should be regularly updated to reflect the changing circumstances and should be made available to those who get involved in capital budgeting. Noncompliance with the manual should be discouraged, to eliminate inconsistencies and to improve the degree of control.

19.7 SUMMARY. Capital-investment budgeting will remain one of the most important activities and challenges for the organization's success, especially in capital-intensive businesses. Management's first responsibility in this area is to encourage employees to initiate new projects. Second, a system should be established to develop the necessary input data that have a great degree of credibility. This requires consultation with experts within and outside the company, and this process of data gathering should not be short circuited because of ill-conceived deadlines. The input data for a project should be evaluated using modern techniques and a computer. It must be remembered that the modern techniques only supplement, not supplant, management's judgment. In addition to economic justification, management must consider numerous factors, such as business strat-

Reporting Unit ________
For the Quarter Ending ________

Project Number	Project Description	Approved Amount	Approval Date	Appropriation Amount	Estimated Cost		Actual Expenditures			Estimated Expenditures			Estimated Completion Date
					Prior	Current	Prior Year	Year to Date	Total	1998	1999	2000	
	Appropriation Phase												
10	Pulp machine	5.2	1/98	5.3	5.2	5.3	2.0	1.0	3.0	2.0	1.0	0.3	3/00
	Approval Phase												
12	Paper coating	2.6	4/98	—	—	2.6	—	—	—	1.0	1.6	—	12/99
	Planning Phase												
13	Mill expansion	—	—	—	—	3.5	—	—	—	0.5	2.0	1.0	12/00
14	Energy saver	—	—	—	—	0.8	—	—	—	0.1	0.7	—	12/00
	Inceptive Phase												
15	Waste disposal	—	—	—	—	1.5	—	—	—	—	0.2	1.3	12/00
16	Golf course	—	—	—	—	0.4	—	—	—	—	—	0.4	12/00

Exhibit 19.11. Project status report ($ million)

Reporting Unit ________
For the Month Ending ________

Appropriation				Expended			Net	Est.	
Number	Date	Project Description	Appropriation Amount	Month	Year to Date	Total	(Underrun) Overrun	Total Cost	Completion Date
10	2/98	Pulp machine	5.3	0.2	1.0	3.0	—	5.3	3/94

Exhibit 19.12. Capital-expenditures report ($ million)

egy, project risk, availability of funds, nature of financing, effect on reported earnings, confidence in divisional management, and the like.

SOURCES AND SUGGESTED REFERENCES

Aggarwal, Raj, *Capital Budgeting Under Uncertainty.* Englewood Cliffs, NJ: Prentice Hall, 1993.

Agmon, Tamir, ''Capital Budgeting and the Utilization of Full Information: Performance Evaluation and the Exercise of Real Options,'' *Managerial Finance,* vol. 17, nos. 2 and 3, 1991.

Ang, James S., ''Budgeting in a Competitive Environment,'' *Managerial Finance,* vol. 17, nos. 2 and 3, 1991.

Baldwin, Carliss Y., ''How Capital Budgeting Deters Innovation—And What to Do About It,'' *Research–Technology Management,* vol. 34, no. 6, November–December 1991.

Binder, Stephen, ''Facilities Forecasting and Budgeting,'' *Facilities Design & Management,* vol. 7, no. 10, November–December 1988.

Cavinato, Joseph, ''Capital Budgeting: A Winning Strategy,'' *Distribution,* vol. 88, no. 11, November 1989.

Chaney, Paul K., ''Moral Hazard and Capital Budgeting,'' *Journal of Financial Research,* vol. 12, no. 2, Summer 1989.

Cho, Dongsae, ''An Alternative and Practical Theory of Capital Budgeting: Stockholder Wealth Maximization Approach,'' *Mid-Atlantic Journal of Business,* vol. 32, no. 2, June 1996, pp. 93–104.

Cronshaw, Steven F., and Ralph A. Alexander, ''Why Capital Budgeting Techniques Are Suited for Assessing the Utility of Personnel Programs: A Reply to Hunter, Schmidt, and Coggin (1988),'' *Journal of Applied Psychology,* vol. 76, no. 3, June 1991.

Davey, Patrick J., *Managing Capital Investments.* New York: The Conference Board, 1984.

Ferreira, Eurico J., and C. Don Wiggins, ''How Large Companies Have Adjusted Their Capital-Budgeting Decisions for Inflation,'' *Mid-South Business Journal,* vol. 7, no. 2, April 1987.

Ferreira, Eurico J., and LeRoy Brooks, ''Capital Budgeting: A Key Management Challenge,'' *Business,* vol. 38, no. 4, October–November–December 1988.

Freeman, Mark, and Garry Hobbes, ''Capital Budgeting: Theory Versus Practice,'' *Australian Accountant,* vol. 61, no. 8, September 1991.

Frigo, Mark L., ''A Diagnostic Approach to Improve the Capital Budgeting Process,'' *Corporate Controller,* vol. 3, no. 4, March–April 1991.

Gordon, Lawrence A., George E. Pinches, and Frank T. Stockton, ''Sophisticated Methods of Capital Budgeting: An Economics of Internal Organization Approach,'' *Managerial Finance* (UK), vol. 14, nos. 2 and 3, 1988.

Hawley, Delvin D., and R. Phil Malone, ''The Relative Performance of Duration in the Capital Budgeting Selection Process,'' *Engineering Economist,* vol. 35, no. 1, Fall 1989.

Howell, Robert A., and Stephen R. Soucy, ''Capital Investment in the New Manufacturing Environment,'' *Management Accounting,* vol. 69, no. 5, November 1987.

Krinsky, Itzhak, ''Capital Budgeting and Plant Capacity,'' *Engineering Costs & Production Economics,* vol. 21, no. 3, July 1991.

Kumar, P.C., and Trami Lu, ''Capital Budgeting Decisions in Large Scale, Integrated Projects: Case Study of a Mathematical Programming Application,'' *Engineering Economist,* vol. 36, no. 2, Winter 1991.

Mukherjee, Tarun K., and Glenn V. Henderson, ''The Capital Budgeting Process: Theory and Practice,'' *Interfaces,* vol. 17, no. 2, March–April 1987.

Mukherjee, Tarun K., ''Reducing the Uncertainty-Induced Bias in Capital Budgeting Decisions—A Hurdle Rate Approach,'' *Journal of Business Finance & Accounting,* vol. 18, no. 5, September 1991.

Myers, Mary D., Lawrence A. Gordon, and Michelle M. Hamer, ''Postauditing Capital Assets and Firm Performance: An Empirical Investigation,'' *Managerial & Decision Economics,* vol. 12, no. 4, August 1991.

O'Brien, Thomas J., ''Operating Leverage in Cost Reduction Capital Budgeting Proposals: A Rigorous and Practical Approach,'' *Engineering Economist,* vol. 34, no. 4, Summer 1989.

Pike, Richard H., ''The Capital Budgeting Revolution,'' *Management Accounting* (UK), vol. 66, no. 9, October 1988.

Pike, Richard H., ''Do Sophisticated Capital Budgeting Approaches Improve Investment Decision-Making Effectiveness?,'' *Engineering Economist,* vol. 34, no. 2, Winter 1989.

Pruitt, Stephen W., and Lawrence J. Gitman, ''Capital Budgeting Forecast Biases: Evidence from the *Fortune* 500,'' *Financial Management,* vol. 16, no. 1, Spring 1987.

Singhvi, Surendra S., ''Affordability Analysis for Capital Investments,'' *Healthcare Financial Management,* vol. 50, no. 6, June 1996, pp. 68–75.

Singhvi, Surendra S., ''Post-Completion Review for Capital Projects,'' *Planning Review,* vol. 14, no. 3 May 1986, pp. 37–39.

Singhvi, Surendra S., and Hiam Alexander, ''The Gains from Cost/Benefit Analysis,'' *The Small Business Controller,* vol. 9, no. 1, pp. 55–57. Winter 1996.

Smith, Michael F., ''Capital Investment Budgeting,'' *Small Business Reports,* vol. 13, no. 10, December 1988.

Springsteel, Ian, ''The Big Chill?,'' *CFO: The Magazine for Senior Financial Executives,* vol. 12, no. 6, June 1996, p. 15.

Tole, Thomas M., Sam O. McCord, and Charles Edmonds, ''Fluctuating Interest Rates and Capital Budgeting Decisions,'' *National Public Accountant,* vol. 34, no. 10, October 1989.

Wacht, Richard F., ''Capital Investment Analysis for the Small Business,'' *Business,* vol. 39, no. 4, October–December 1989.

Weaver, Samuel C., ''Capital Budgeting,'' *Financial Management,* vol. 18, no. 1, Spring 1989.

White, Bob, ''Capital Budgeting and Project Selection on a Microcomputer,'' *Computers & Industrial Engineering,* vol. 19, nos. 1–4, 1990.

CHAPTER 20

CAPITAL-EXPENDITURE EVALUATION METHODS

Surendra S. Singhvi

Singhvi and Associates, Inc.

20.1 INTRODUCTION. Several methods or techniques are available for evaluating a proposed capital-investment project. Some organizations rely heavily on one technique only, whereas others rely on several techniques in evaluating a project. Also, one finds that some of the techniques are more complex than others. This chapter will present the widely known project evaluation techniques, with their respective merits and demerits, and some empirical evidence on the degree of their usage in the business world.

20.2 TIME VALUE OF MONEY. Before discussing the time-adjusted evaluation techniques, it will be appropriate to review the concept of the time value of money. According to this concept, an investor is entitled to a return (or interest) in proportion to the length of time his or her capital remains invested. Of course, the return on a given amount of capital for a given length of time could be higher or lower, depending upon the degree of risk associated with the project.

Because of the time value of money, a dollar (or a monetary unit) received today is more valuable than a dollar to be received one year from now. For example, if one can invest in a bank at a 5% interest rate compounded annually, the one dollar invested today will grow to \$1.05 one year from now. The difference between what one invests today and what one gets in the future is the *time value of money.*

(a) Compounding. The time value of money is calculated using the concept of compounding. If investors do not withdraw their interest (or return) but allow it to remain invested, they will earn interest on interest; this is called *compounding.* An investor deposits \$1,000 in a bank that pays 5% interest compounded annually. At the end of one year, he or she will have \$1,050 in the bank account. To treat the matter systematically, let us define the following terms:

P = principal amount invested, or present value

i = interest rate

I = interest earned during a period ($I = P \times i$)

A = accumulated amount at the end of the period ($P + I$)

Year	Principal Amount (P)	× (1 + i)	=	Accumulated Amount (A)
1	$1,000	1.05		$1,050
2	$1,050	1.05		$1,103
3	$1,103	1.05		$1,158
4	$1,158	1.05		$1,216
5	$1,216	1.05		$1,277

Exhibit 20.1. Illustration of compounding process

A may be calculated as follows:

$$a = P + I$$
$$= P + Pi$$
$$= P(1 + i)$$

Substituting figures, $A = \$1{,}000\ (1 + .05) = \$1{,}050$.

If an investor leaves the $1,000 on deposit for five years, to what amount will it have grown at the end of that period at an interest rate of 5%? As shown in Exhibit 20.1, the amount after five years would be $1,277.

Note that the accumulated amount at the end of the second year, A_2, is found as:

$$A_2 = P_2\ (1 + i) = P_1\ (1 + i)(1 + i) = P_1\ (1 + i)^2$$

Similarly, A_3, the accumulated amount after three years, is found as:

$$A_3 = P_3\ (1 + i) = A_2\ (1 + i)$$

Since $A_2 = P_1\ (1 + i)^2$

$$A_3 = P_1(1 + i)^2(1 + i)$$
$$= P_1(1 + i)^3$$

In general, the compound amount A_n at the end of any period n, is found as:

$$A_n = P_1\ (1 + i)^n$$

For example, to find the accumulated amount (A) for $1,000 ($P$) invested today at 5% ($i$) interest for five ($n$) years, compounded annually, one needs to solve the following equation:

$$A = \$1{,}000(1 + .05)^5 = \$1{,}277$$

Compound value tables have been constructed by experts for values of $(1 + i)^n$ for wide ranges of i and n. Table 1 in the Appendix is illustrative. Use of the table simply requires finding the factor at the intersection of the rate of interest and the number of

Annuity	Compound Value Factor	Compound Value
$1,000	1.170	$1,170
1,000	1.125	1,125
1,000	1.082	1,082
1,000	1.040	1,040
1,000	1.000	1,000
$5,000		$5,417

Exhibit 20.2. Compound value of an annuity

years applicable. For 5% and five years the number provided by the table is 1.276 (rounding the difference).

Problems of compounding sometimes involve the accumulation of regular equal payments for deposit, all amounts compounding until the end of the final period. For example, an investor plans to save $1,000 at the end of each year for the next five years. How much will he or she accumulate if the interest rate is 4%? The first $1,000 will be invested only four full years, the second $1,000 for three years, the third for two years, the fourth for one year. The fifth investment will have earned no interest. As shown in Exhibit 20.2, the total investment will accumulate $5,417 in the next five years.

One can also obtain $5,417 by adding each of the compound value factors and multiplying by $1,000 (5.417 × $1,000 = $5,417). Table 2 in the Appendix has performed this calculation, and the compound value factor at the intersection of five years and 4% is 5.416 (rounding the difference).

The "rule of 72" is very helpful in compounding problems. Accordingly, the invested money doubles in X years at y% interest rate if X times y equals 72. For example, the invested money doubles in 12 years at a 6% interest rate compounded annually, or in 6 years at a 12% interest rate, or in 9 years at 8% interest, and so on.

(b) Discounting. The discounting concept is the reverse of the compounding concept. The basic question in compounding is: If P dollars are invested today at i rate of interest, how much will be accumulated in n years? The answer is provided by solving for the unknown A, using the following equation:

$$A = P(1 + i)^n$$

The basic question in discounting is: How much should one invest today at compound interest rate i to receive a given amount at the end of n years? Instead of A being the unknown, P is now the unknown, which can be derived by the following equation:

$$P = \frac{A}{(1 + i)^n}$$

The present value (P) is defined as the amount of money necessary to invest today at the assumed interest rate (i) for n years to accumulate the future amount (A). The process of deriving the present value of a future amount using the preceding equation is referred to as *discounting*. For example, how much does an investor have to invest today to accumulate $1,277 at the end of five years if he or she can earn 5% on the money? This is a present value question, and the answer is derived through the discounting process. Substituting the figures in the formula, we derive the present value of $1,000 as follows:

$$P = A \frac{1}{(1 + .05)^5}$$

$$P = \$1{,}277 \frac{1}{1.277}$$

$$P = \$1{,}000$$

Tables have also been constructed by experts to relieve some of the mathematical computations. Table 3 in the Appendix solves the equation $1/(1 + i)^n$ for various combinations of i and n. For five years at 5%, the present value provided by the table is 0.784. The present value amount, $1,000, is derived by multiplying the future amount of $1,277 by the present value factor of 0.784 derived from the table.

(c) Present Value as a Decision-Making Criterion. If investors could earn 5% on their money, would they prefer $100 now or $110.25 in two years? Presumably, they would be indifferent, since they can invest $100 today at 5%, which will accumulate to $110.25 in two years.

What is the most investors are willing to invest today in order to receive $110.25 in two years if their investment opportunity rate is 5%? (What can be earned on alternative investment opportunities is referred to as the *investment opportunity rate of return*). The answer is that investors will be willing to pay up to $100 today, in view of their alternative investment opportunity. If they are required to pay more than $100 to receive $110.25 in two years, they will turn down the offer since they can invest elsewhere and realize more money. In brief, the present value of a future amount represents the most an investor would pay for the investment alternative.

Sometimes problems of discounting involve the *annuity,* which is defined as a series of cash flows of a fixed amount per period for a specified number of periods. Suppose investors are offered the following alternative: a three-year annuity of $1,000 per year or a lump-sum payment today. How large must the lump-sum payment today be to make it equivalent to the annuity if the investment opportunity rate is 10%? The most an investor, whose investment opportunity rate is 10%, is willing to pay for the three-year annuity of $1,000 per year is $2,487. Tables have been constructed by experts to aid in computing the present value of an annuity. Table 4 in the Appendix is illustrative. It shows that the present value of $1 received at the end of years 1, 2, and 3 is 2.487 when discounted at 10%.

20.3 DISCOUNTED CASH-FLOW RATE OF RETURN.

Discounted cash-flow rate of return (DCFRR), also known as *internal rate of return,* is a technique that measures profitability of a project by the timing and amount of its cash flows over the project's economic life. It is the discount or interest rate that equates the present value of cash inflows and cash outflows related to the proposed investment.

Suppose an investor invests $1,000 today and expects to receive $1,277 at the end of five years. Using the discounting process and Table 3 in the Appendix, the present value of $1,277 to be received at the end of five years will be $1,000 if discounted at 5%. Therefore, the DCFRR on this investment is 5%, since at this discount rate the present value of cash outflow equals the present value of cash inflow. In other words, DCFRR is a compound interest rate over the life of the investment project.

Suppose an investor invests $2,487 today and expects to receive $1,000 at the end of each year for three years. Using the discounting process and Table 4 in the Appendix, the present value of $1,000 each year for three years will be $2,487 if discounted at 10%. Therefore, the DCFRR on this investment is 10%, since at this discount rate the present value of cash outflow equals the present value of cash inflow.

It is relatively simple to compute DCFRR when cash outflows take place at time zero and cash inflows are constant in each period over the project's life. For example, the initial cash outflow related to the machine replacement project at Seema & Company, discussed in Chapter 19, is estimated to be $13.8 million, and the annual cash inflow as a result of cost savings is estimated to be $4.4 million over the economic life of six years. To compute DCFRR, we first compute the present value factor by dividing the annual cash inflows into the initial cash outflow:

$$\frac{\$13.8}{\$\ 4.4} = 3.1364$$

Referring to Table 4 in the Appendix for the present value of an annuity of $1, one can read the DCFRR by finding the 3.136 present value factor in the row representing six years. The present value factor of 3.136 lies between 20% and 24%. The precise DCFRR figure can be obtained using the interpolation approach, as shown in Exhibit 20.3.

When a project is expected to have uneven cash inflows from one period to another, one computes DCFRR using a trial-and-error procedure. For example, an investment by Sandeep, Inc., in a printing press requires an initial cash outflow of $10,000. It will generate a cash inflow (net income + depreciation) of $3,000 per year for four years. The estimated salvage value of the press after four years is $4,000 net of tax. Annual cash flows for this investment are summarized in Exhibit 20.4.

To minimize the number of trials to find out the discount rate that would equate the present value of cash inflows to cash outflow, one should compute the average annual cash inflow, which is $4,000 in this example. The present value factor for this project is 2.500 ($10,000 divided by $4,000). Using Table 4 in the Appendix, the DCFRR is close to 20% to 24%. Now one has a starting point for making a first trial for computing DCFRR.

Using 20% and information from Appendix Tables 3 and 4, one finds that the present

		22%	=	3.326		
	x				0.190	
4%		Actual	=	3.136		0.306
		24%	=	3.020		

$$\frac{x}{4} = \frac{0.190}{0.306} \qquad x = \frac{0.190 \times 4}{0.306} = 2.42$$

DCFRR = 22.42%

Exhibit 20.3. Interpolation approach to DCFRR

Period	Cash Outflow	Cash Inflows
0	$10,000	—
1	—	$3,000
2	—	3,000
3	—	3,000
4	—	7,000
Total	$10,000	$16,000

Exhibit 20.4. Investment in printing press

value of the cash inflows is $9,692, which is less than the cash outflow of $10,000, suggesting an actual DCFRR of less than 20%. (The lower the discount or interest rate, the higher the present value of future cash inflows, and vice versa). The second trial using 18% shows that the present value of the cash inflows is $10,134, which is higher than the cash outflows of $10,000, suggesting an actual DCFRR of higher than 18%. Using the interpolation approach, one finds that the actual DCFRR for the project is 18.61%.

(a) Computer and DCFRR. One can use a computer to calculate DCFRR for any number of periods and for varying cash flows in these periods in a matter of minutes. The cost of using computers for this purpose is insignificant compared to the man-hours required for such problems using the trial-and-error procedure. Several software programs are available that can be used to calculate DCFRR, payback period, and net present value for various capital budgeting problems.

One can also use a programmable calculator such as Texas Instrument's Business Analyst model to calculate DCFRR.

(b) Arguments for and against Using DCFRR. As will be shown later in this chapter, the use of DCFRR has increased in the business world. First, it measures benefits over the project's life, reflecting the time value of money. Second, it places emphasis on cash flows rather than on net profits only, and therefore different accounting treatment of depreciation expense does not affect the project's overall profitability. Third, it evaluates a project's cash flows period by period and gives one a rate-of-return figure for the entire project, which is easy to communicate to top management.

However, DCFRR technique has a few drawbacks compared to other techniques. First, the DCFRR technique will provide multiple and false solutions when there are negative cash flows after having positive cash flows for one period or more. For example, Joe Smith received a government subsidy of $425 now toward a capital investment of $1,000 to be made within a year, which will generate cash inflow of $250 per year, beginning the second year. The projected net cash flows with their present values at 35% and 63% are shown in Exhibit 20.5.

Accordingly, Joe Smith has two DCFRRs for his project, but neither one is valid. One way to overcome this problem is to assume that the initial cash inflow of $425 will be reinvested for one year by Joe Smith at some rate, say 10%. Therefore, in one year the initial cash flow of $425 will grow to $468, which should be used to reduce the projected cash outflow of $1,000 one year from now. The DCFRR on the net investment of $532 by Joe Smith is 19.4%.

Year	Cash Inflows (Outflows)	Present Value at 35%	Present Value at 63%
0	$425	$425	$425
1	(1,000)	(741)	(613)
2	250		
3	250	316	188
4	250		
Total	$175	0	$0

Exhibit 20.5. Illustration of multiple DCFRR

Year	Cash Inflow (Outflow)	Present Value at 12%	
		Factor	Amount
0	$<10,000>	1.000	$<10,000>
1	3,000		
2	3,000	2.402	7,206
3	3,000		
4	7,000	0.636	4,452
Total	$6,000		$1,658

Exhibit 20.6. Net present value of printing press investment

Second, the DCFRR technique might accept one of the mutually exclusive projects that might not be accepted if the net present value technique is used to evaluate such projects. Again, this problem arises because of different re-investment assumptions implicit in these techniques. (This point will be illustrated after discussing the net present value technique.) Mutually exclusive projects are those where the acceptance of one project precludes the acceptance of other projects. For example, an oil firm needs additional transport facilities for its products. It can build a pipeline or acquire additional tankers and ship by water. The acceptance of the first project will preclude the acceptance of the latter.

Third, the DCFRR calculations are time consuming if cash flows are uneven and if one does not have access to a computer.

Finally, it is difficult to compare DCFRR with the historical rates of return. The DCFRR measures the return, not for a given year, but over the project's life based on its cash flows. However, the historical rate of return measures the profitability year by year based on actual net income and book investment.

20.4 NET PRESENT VALUE. Net present value (NPV) is a technique that measures the difference between the present value of cash inflows and the present value of cash outflows discounted at the appropriate cost of capital rate. For example, the NPV for the printing press investment by Sandeep, Inc., is calculated in Exhibit 20.6, assuming a 12% cost of capital.

The NPV for this example is $1,658. The NPV amounts can be interpreted as follows:

NPV ($)	DCFRR (%)	Project Recommendation
Zero	Equal to cost of capital	Marginal
Negative	Less than cost of capital	Unacceptable
Positive	More than cost of capital	Acceptable

(a) Arguments for and against Net Present Value. First, the NPV technique is easier to use than the DCFRR, since no trial-and-error procedure is needed. Second, like DCFRR, this technique measures a project's profitability, considering cash flows over its useful life. Third, it assumes that the project's cash inflows will be reinvested at the cost of capital rate and therefore will indicate neither multiple nor false solutions.

The NPV technique could provide a different ranking of the mutually exclusive projects than the DCFRR. Let us consider two situations—size disparity and time disparity. The DCFRR technique favors project A, whereas the NPV technique favors project B in Exhibit 20.7, which compares two projects with equal lives but different investment amounts.

The DCFRR technique favors project C, whereas the NPV technique favors project D in Exhibit 20.8, which compares two projects with equal investment amounts but different lives.

Year	Project A	Project B
0	$(4,000)	$(10,000)
1	—	—
2	—	—
3	—	—
4	$ 8,300	$ 18,100
DCFRR	20%	16%
NPV at 12%	$ 1,280	$ 1,520

Exhibit 20.7. Size disparity and mutually exclusive projects

Year	Project C	Project D
0	$(5,000)	$(5,000)
1	—	—
2	$6,730	—
3	—	—
4	—	—
5	—	—
6	—	$10,965
DCFRR	16%	14%
NPV at 12%	$ 364	$ 560

Exhibit 20.8. Time disparity and mutually exclusive projects

Year	Cash Inflow (Outflow)	Present Value at 12% Factor	Present Value at 12% Amount	
0	$(10,000)	1.000	$(10,000)	
1	3,000			
2	3,000	2.402	7,206	
3	3,000			$11,658
4	7,000	0.636	4,452	

$$\text{Profitability index} = \frac{11{,}658}{10{,}000} = 1.17$$

Exhibit 20.9. Profitability index for printing press

These different rankings of mutually exclusive projects is attributable to the implicit re-investment assumption made in these techniques. The DCFRR technique assumes that cash inflows are reinvested at the DCFRR on the original investment, whereas the NPV technique assumes that cash inflows are re-invested at the cost of capital or at the investment opportunity rate. To reconcile these differences, one should use the re-investment rate (cost of capital or investment opportunity rate) and select the project with the highest terminal value.

It must be pointed out that there are some drawbacks to using the NPV technique. First, the NPV of a project is difficult to communicate to top management and nonfinance people because of its complexity. Second, it is difficult to compare the NPV with historical results prepared by accountants. Finally, an analyst must know the cost of capital or investment opportunity rate prior to analyzing the project; however, such information is not needed for DCFRR calculation.

(b) Profitability Index. *Profitability index* (PI), also known as *present value index* or *benefit–cost ratio,* represents the ratio of the present value of cash inflows to the present value of cash outflows discounted at the appropriate cost of capital rate. For example, the profitability index for the printing press investment is calculated in Exhibit 20.9, assuming a 12% cost of capital. The PI value can be interpreted as follows:

PI Value	NPV ($)	DCFRR (%)	Project Recommendation
1.0	Zero	Equal to cost of capital	Marginal
More than 1.0	Positive	More than cost of capital	Acceptable
Less than 1.0	Negative	Less than cost of capital	Unacceptable

Arguments for and against the PI technique are the same as those discussed previously in connection with the NPV technique, with one exception. The NPV technique expresses results in absolute terms, whereas the PI technique expresses results in relative terms, as illustrated in Exhibit 20.10.

Based on the NPV technique, both projects are equally attractive; however, the PI technique shows that project A is relatively more profitable than project B.

	Project A	Project B
Initial investment	$10,000	$100,000
Present value of cash inflows	$11,658	$101,658
NPV	$ 1,658	$ 1,658
PI	1,658	1,017

Exhibit 20.10. NPV versus PI technique

Year	Investment or Net Assets (Undepreciated Book Value)	Net Operating Profit After Tax	RONA (%)
0	$10,000	—	—
1	8,500	$1,500	16.2
2	7,000	1,500	19.4
3	5,500	1,500	24.0
4	4,000	1,500	31.6
Average	7,000	1,500	21.4

Exhibit 20.11. Return on net assets of printing press investment

20.5 ACCOUNTING RATE OF RETURN. *Accounting rate of return* (ARR) represents the ratio of the average annual net profit to the average investment in the project over its life. There are several variations of this technique, but the one that measures the investment's productivity is called *return on net assets* (RONA). The RONA equals the annual operating profit after tax (net profit plus aftertax interest expense) divided by average net assets (total assets minus current liabilities). For example, the projected RONA for the printing press investment is calculated in Exhibit 20.11.

Compared to 18.6% DCFRR, the project's average RONA is estimated to be 21.4%. It should be noted that the RONA for each year varies from 16.2% to 31.6% because of constant net operating profit and declining net assets. The proposed investment is depreciated on the straight-line method of depreciation, a four-year economic life, and $4,000 residual value assumptions. The average investment can also be calculated by adding initial investment to the residual value and dividing by two.

(a) Arguments for and against Accounting Rate of Return. One of the arguments in favor of using the ARR technique is its simplicity in terms of computation and communication to management. Further, the estimated ARR for a given project is easier to postaudit annually compared to DCFRR since one can calculate a project's ARR for each year, which is not possible with DCFRR.

Several arguments have been made against the use of ARR. First, it ignores the time pattern of income or cash flows. For example, each of the two investment projects with four-year lives and no residual values requires a $1,200 initial cash outlay. Estimated annual operating earnings and cash inflows for these two projects are shown in Exhibit 20.12.

Because the ARR technique ignores the time pattern of benefits, it cannot discriminate between these two projects, whereas the DCFRR technique shows that project A is less attractive than project B. Second, ARR places emphasis on accounting net income instead

Project	Year	Operating Earnings	Depreciation Expense	Taxable Earnings	Aftertax Earnings	Cash Inflows	
A	1	$300	$300	$ 0	$ 0	$ 300	
	2	500	300	200	100	400	
	3	700	300	400	200	500	
	4	900	300	600	300	600	
Total			$1,200		$600	$1,800	16%
B	1	$900	$300	$600	$300	$600	↑
	2	700	300	400	200	500	DCFRR
	3	500	300	200	100	400	↓
	4	300	300	0	0	300	
Total			$1,200		$600	$1,800	21%

$$\text{Accounting rate of return (for either project)} = \frac{600 \div 4}{\frac{1200 + 0}{2}} = \frac{150}{600} = 25\%$$

Exhibit 20.12. Illustration of ARR versus DCFRR

Year	Cash Outflow	Cash Inflow	Cumulative Cash Inflow (Outflow)
0	$10,000	—	$(10,000)
1	—	$3,000	(7,000)
2	—	3,000	(4,000)
3	—	3,000	(1,000)
4	—	7,000	6,000

[a] Payback period in year 4.

Exhibit 20.13. Illustration of payback periods[a]

of cash flows. Since accounting income is based on the generally accepted accounting principles (GAAP) that allow the use of one of the several depreciation methods, net income could be higher or lower depending upon the method of depreciation chosen by a given firm.

It must be noted that ARR is a good estimate of DCFRR when (1) annual net income is constant, (2) there is no significant residual value, and (3) the project's life is less than twice the payback period.

20.6 PAYBACK PERIOD. The payback-period technique determines the number of years required to recover, through the project's cash flow, the capital commitment (i.e., cash outflow). For example, the payback period for the printing press investment is calculated in Exhibit 20.13.

The payback in this illustration occurs in the fourth year and most likely in the first two months of the fourth year. (The project's unrecovered investment balance at the end of the third year is $1,000, and the project is estimated to earn $3,000 during the year, with $4,000 residual value at the end of the fourth year.) If the annual cash inflows are constant and all cash outflows occur at one time, the payback period can be estimated by dividing annual cash inflows into initial cash outflow:

$$\text{Payback period} = \frac{\text{Initial cash outflow}}{\text{Constant annual cash inflow}}$$

(a) Arguments for and against Payback Period. This technique is widely used in the business world for screening projects because it is simple to calculate and communicate. Also, it is an appropriate technique in which a quick return of cash is desired. The technique measures a project's liquidity more than its profitability. Generally, payback period is used as a supplementary or secondary evaluation technique rather than as a primary evaluation technique.

The payback-period technique ignores all cash flows beyond the payback period. For example, two projects shown in Exhibit 20.14 have the same payback period of two years and therefore are equally attractive based on this criterion. However, the DCFRR technique, which considers all cash flows over the project's life, shows that only project B is acceptable.

Another criticism of the payback-period technique is that it ignores the time pattern of cash flows (i.e., time value of money). However, this drawback can be overcome by using a discounted payback period, using the cost of capital rate for discounting purposes. As a result, the discounted payback period will be longer than the simple payback period, as shown in Exhibit 20.15.

Year	Project A	Project B
0	$(10,000)	$(10,000)
1	5,000	5,000
2	5,000	5,000
3	—	5,000
4	—	5,000
Payback period	2 years	2 years
DCFRR	0	35%

Exhibit 20.14. Payback period versus DCFRR

Year	Annual Cash Flows	Cumulative Cash Flows	Annual PV of Cash Flows at 12%	Cumulative PV of Cash Flows
0	$(10,000)	$(10,000)	$(10,000)	$(10,000)
1	5,000	(5,000)	4,465	(5,535)
2	5,000	0	3,985	(1,550)
3	5,000	5,000	3,560	2,010
4	5,000	10,000	3,180	5,190

[a] Simple payback period in year 2. Discounted payback period in year 3.

Exhibit 20.15. Simple versus discounted payback period[a]

(b) Payback Period and DCFRR Approximation. It must be noted that the reciprocal of simple payback period times 100 is also a good estimate of DCFRR when (1) annual cash inflows are constant, (2) there is no significant residual value, and (3) the project's life is more than twice the payback period. For example, a project with a 20-year life and no residual value requires an initial investment of $2,000 and generates $400 each year. The simple payback period is five years (2,000/400), and the reciprocal of the payback period times 100 is 20% (1/5 × 100). The DCFRR for this project is about 19.5%.

20.7 MAPI TECHNIQUE. This technique was developed by the Machinery and Allied Products Institute (MAPI) to evaluate capital replacement projects. This technique measures the urgency of the project today as compared to a year from now. According to this method, the higher the urgency rating, the more important it is to replace the equipment now rather than defer its replacement. The technique has several disadvantages since it involves the use of a group of graphs and assumptions.

20.8 CAPITAL BUDGETING TECHNIQUES IN PRACTICE. Various surveys have been conducted on the effectiveness of capital budgeting techniques in practice.

Based on various surveys, it seems that the more capital-intensive industries prefer the time-adjusted techniques—DCFRR and NPV—and the less capital-intensive industries prefer the payback period technique. Since each of the evaluation techniques has some shortcomings, it is desirable for firms to use more than one technique in evaluating a project. For example, one could use the DCFRR technique, supplemented by the ARR and the payback-period techniques.

20.9 RISK-ANALYSIS TECHNIQUE. The financial evaluation of capital-investment projects is made using one or more of such techniques as payback period, APR, NPV and DCFRR. These techniques are generally used by firms to provide one "most likely" estimate of the project's performance expressed in terms of its payback period, rate of return, or NPV. This approach fails to take into account the extent of the uncertainty or risk associated with the project.

Risk, like beauty, lies in the eyes of the beholder. *Risk* is generally defined as the estimated degree of uncertainty with respect to the realization of expected future returns. The wider the range of expected future returns around the most likely estimate, the more risky the investment. Accordingly, project B is more risky than project A in Exhibit 20.16.

The project risk is defined by many executives as the probability of not achieving a target return. Here, management is concerned only with negative variation. Another definition of project risk relates to variation in returns without regard to the direction of such variation. Finally, some executives define project risk in terms of the payback period.

Project	Return	Probability	Expected Return
A	$1,000	1.00	$1,000
B	500	0.25	125
	1,000	0.50	500
	1,500	0.25	375
		1.00	$1,000

Exhibit 20.16. Illustration of degree of risk

(a) Approaches to Coping with Risk. Project risk has been recognized by businesses of every size and type either formally or intuitively. Various approaches are used by decision makers to cope with the risk or uncertainty associated with a proposed investment. Such approaches include the following:

- Requiring a lower payback period for risky projects than the target payback period for normal-risk projects.
- Raising the hurdle rate for risky projects in relation to the overall cost of capital. For example, if the overall cost of capital is 10%, the hurdle rates for cost saving, expansion, and new business projects could be established at 10%, 15%, and 20%, respectively.
- Reducing the best estimates of future cash inflows for risky projects based on management judgment.
- Using three-level estimates of DCFRR—optimistic, most likely, and pessimistic. A wider range of return indicates more risk for the project than a narrower range. One could assign probabilities to these estimates and calculate an expected rate of return.
- Applying risk analysis using a computer simulation model (Monte Carlo) and the probability concept. This approach will be discussed later in detail.

(b) Definition of Risk Analysis. *Risk-analysis technique* estimates a range of possible results of a proposed investment decision based on the given input data and states the probability that the overall result will be within a specified range. It simulates the effects of the uncertainty surrounding key variables entering into the evaluation on the returns one is likely to achieve.

Risk analysis adds two distinctive features to the conventional one-figure measures of evaluation: first, it quantifies the uncertainty in the factors affecting the outcome of an investment decision, and second, it combines these estimates using a simulation process to produce a description of the risk attached to the proposed investment.

(i) Quantifying Uncertainty. Quantifying uncertainty is the first distinctive feature of risk analysis. Management selects those factors affecting cash flow whose uncertainty is to be quantified, that is, capital investment amount, sales price, volume, working capital, and the like. Judgment must be used in selecting only those factors that have significant effect on the project's future cash flow. The appropriate managers obtain the necessary data for each factor by (1) assigning the highest and lowest possible values for the factor, (2) splitting this range of values into four or five subranges, and (3) estimating the probability of the values lying in each subrange. Using these guidelines, a probability distribution of sales volume is illustrated in Exhibit 20.17.

Probability data should be developed by a group of experts representing various functions such as marketing, engineering, finance, operations, and the like. Each member of the group should assign probabilities based on his or her own background and experience. An average of these individual probabilities would express the group's overall degree of confidence for the occurrence of an event. In some cases, empirical evidence can be used to support the probabilities assigned. For example, the probability of base cost per ton could be assigned using the historical data.

The standard deviation (SD) is a statistical technique to measure deviation from the mean. As a rule, the smaller the SD value, the lower the variation or uncertainty. Based

Sales Volume (Million Tons/Year)	Probability of Sales In a Given Range	Probability of Sales Being Equal to or Less Than Upper Limit of Range Shown
5–10	0.10	0.10
10–15	0.30	0.40
15–20	0.40	0.80
20–25	0.15	0.95
25–30	0.05	1.00
	1.00	

Exhibit 20.17. Illustration of quantifying uncertainty

on the SD and mean values, one can estimate an interval or range showing the degree of confidence one has in such estimation.

Statisticians have shown mathematically that about 68% of sample observations normally lie between + 1 SD from the mean, about 95% of the observations lie between ± 2 SDs, and 98% of the observations lie between ± 2.33 SDs. These values can be found in any standard textbook on statistics.

At the 98% level, the confidence interval for product X with a mean sales of $80 and an SD of $7 would be as follows:

$$\begin{aligned}\text{Confidence interval} &= \text{Sample mean} \pm \text{sample SD} \times 2.33\\ &= \$80 \pm \$7 \times 2.33\\ &= \$63.70 \text{ to } \$96.30\end{aligned}$$

This means that product X sales for any month would be between $63.70 and $96.30, and this estimation should be true 98 out of 100 times.

(ii) Computer Simulation. Simulating the outcome is the second distinctive feature of risk analysis. Simulatin calculations are made by a computer, which simulates the many possible outcomes of an investment decision. During simulation the computer chooses values at random from the probability distribution of each factor affecting the future cash flows. The computer then uses these random values to calculate the cash flow and DCFRR over the project's life. Then it repeats these calculations several times, each time choosing another set of values at random and generating different values of the DCFRR.

(c) An Illustration of Risk Analysis. Normally, the data shown in Exhibit 20.18 are developed for an economic justification study related to a real-life investment proposal. So far no attempt is being made to quantify the degree of risk. Additional data, as shown in Exhibit 20.19, are required on a proposed project in order to apply the risk analysis technique. Basically, Exhibit 20.19 requires the range of values with probability distributions for key variables entering into the cash flow projections. In this example, only six variables with three subranges for each variable have been used; however, the computer program can accommodate additional variables with additional subranges.

Based on 200 trials, the computer estimated a mean DCFRR of 19.4%, with an SD of

Year	Capital Expenditure	Additional Working Capital	Sales	Manufacturing Profit as Percentage of Sales	General Overhead as Percentage of Sales	Residual Value	Depreciation
0	$1,800	—	—	—	—		$ 58
1	406	$ 550	$ 2,500	17.5	8.7		133
2		550	5,000	24.5	8.7		150
3		293	6,333	25.0	8.7		150
4		128	6,917	25.0	8.7		150
5		74	7,250	25.0	8.7		150
6			7,250	25.0	8.7		150
7			7,250	25.0	8.7		150
8			7,250	25.0	8.7		150
9			7,250	25.0	8.7		150
10			7,250	25.0	8.7		150
11			7,250	25.0	8.7		150
12			7,250	25.0	8.7	$1,960	150
Total	$2,206	$1,595	$78,750			$1,960	$1,841

Exhibit 20.18. Input data for proposed pipe plant

0.8%. It can now be inferred that 98 out of 100 times the DCFRR will fall between 17.6% and 21.3%. However, it must be kept in mind that such estimation is valid to the extent that our assumptions are valid.

Exhibit 20.20 shows a risk profile chart prepared by the computer, which indicates returns on the horizontal axis and the probability of achieving these returns on the vertical axis. Point A on the chart can be interpreted as 99% probability that the DCFRR would be 17.6% or higher, point B as 50% probability that the DCFRR would be 19.4% or higher, point C as 16% probability that the DCFRR would be 20.4% or higher, and point D as 1% probability that the DCFRR would be 21.3% or higher.

Similarly, based on 200 trials, the computer estimated a mean payback period of 6.68 years, with an SD of 0.19 years. It can now be inferred that 98 out of 100 times the payback period will fall between 6.24 and 7.12 years.

20.10 SENSITIVITY-ANALYSIS TECHNIQUE. This technique supplements the risk analysis applied to new projects. The objective is to determine the degree of change in terms of the project's DCFRR or NPV if the key variables entering into the financial justification are exposed to unfavorable variances. Effect on the DCFRR of an assumed 10% unfavorable variance in each key variable in Exhibit 20.20 is shown in Exhibit 20.21.

If manufacturing profit as a percentage of sales is off by 10% from the median value, other things being equal, the DCFRR will deteriorate from 19.4% to 16.9%, as shown in Exhibit 20.21. In this example, the most sensitive variable appears to be the manufacturing profit as a percentage of sales. One could have used 15% or 20% unfavorable variance to test the sensitivity of key variables.

Additional sensitivity analysis can be undertaken to see the effect of two or more

Key Variables	Deviation from Median Estimate	Probability
Capital Expenditure		
High	+5%	.15
Median	0	.82
Low	−2%	.03
		1.00
Residual Value		
High	+1%	.10
Median	0	.70
Low	−10%	.20
		1.00
Sales Forecast		
High	+5%	.55
Median	0	.25
Low	−10%	.20
		1.00
Additional Working Capital as Percentage of Sales		
High	+3%	.25
Median	0	.25
Low	−10%	.50
		1.00
General Overhead Percentage of Sales		
High	+3%	.10
Median	0	.30
Low	−2%	.60
		1.00
Manufacturing Profit as Percentage of Sales		
High	+10%	.60
Median	0	.30
Low	−5%	.10
		1.00

Exhibit 20.19. Probability input for risk analysis

variables on the DCFRR. For example, if sales are off by 25% and the manufacturing profit percentage is off by 10%, the resulting DCFRR would be 12.9%.

Based on sensitivity analyses, management can investigate and research thoroughly only those variables that are very sensitive in terms of their effect on DCFRR and need not spend any time on those variables that are least sensitive.

20.11 CRITICAL LOOK AT RISK AND SENSITIVITY ANALYSES. According to some critics, the computerized simulation–based risk analysis as a management tool has not been successful. There are few difficulties inherent in any application of risk analysis in capital investments such as obtaining various assessments of risks and probabilities from individual managers, trading off risk against return in a structured way, and adjusting procedures for evaluating and controlling projects for some of the after effects of risk

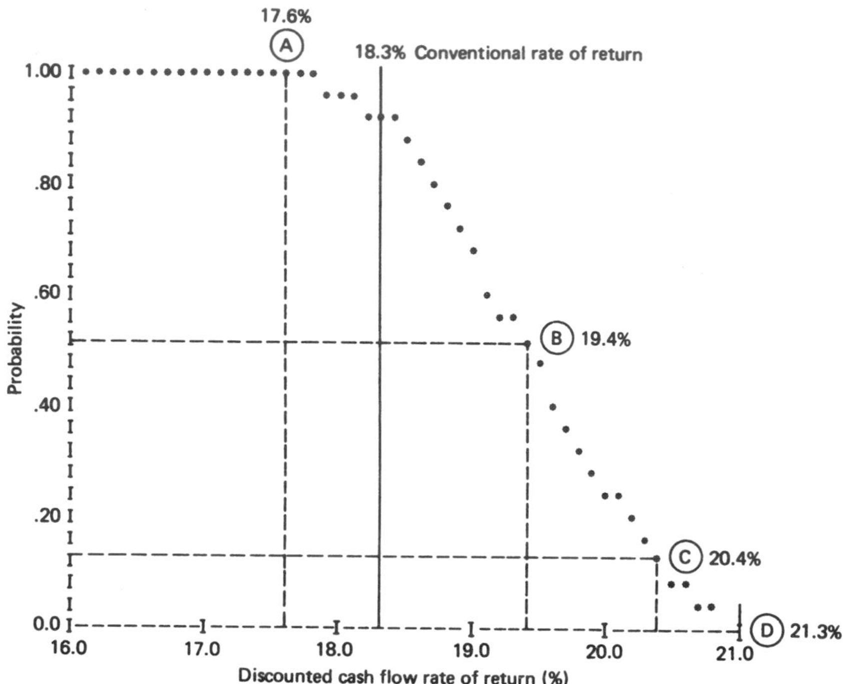

Exhibit 20.20. Risk profile

Original DCFRR	19.4%
Manufacturing profit as percentage of sales	16.9
Sales revenue	17.6
Capital expenditures	18.3
General overhead as percentage of sales	18.5
Working capital	18.6
Residual value	19.3

Exhibit 20.21. Sensitivity analysis

analysis. The degree of success with risk analysis depends on the resolution of several questions, such as:

- How are the managers responsible for using the technique prepared for handling it?
- How are the data generated and put together in model form?
- What role does top management reserve for itself in deciding to install risk analysis?

The key problem in implementing risk analysis seems to be the development of probability input and the selection of relevant variables for which the risk is to be quantified. Like any other technique's successful implementation, top management must support the use of it and the people must be educated about its use. It is possible that an individual manager could misuse the risk analysis technique by using optimistic data and by quantifying irrelevant risks, but these are not the shortcomings of the technique per se. It seems that the risk and sensitivity analyses tools could be used in evaluating major capital investment proposals to provide additional useful information to decision makers that would not be available to them otherwise. It is difficult to accept the fact that the future is uncertain, and therefore no attempt should be made to quantify such uncertainties.

20.12 LEASE-VERSUS-BUY ANALYSIS TECHNIQUES.

Once an investment project has been evaluated and justified based on its rate of return in relation to its risk, the question of financing is considered. A project can be financed either internally or externally. Externally, a firm could raise funds by raising equity or debt capital. Lease financing is a form of debt capital.

Though all leases have financial, operating, and risk characteristics, a division of leases into those that are primarily operating and those that are primarily financial or capital will be useful. The essential characteristic of an *operating lease* is that it can be canceled; that is, the agreement does not involve unavoidable future commitments. An example of this type of lease is the renting of an automobile for a day or a week. *Financial* or *capital leases* are typified by a stream of noncancelable payments. An example of this type of lease is the leasing of an aircraft for eight years.

The similarity of the long-term, noncancelable lease to debt has been noted by various groups. There is a common feeling among financial executives that financial lease agreements carry with them an interest cost that is related to the long-term-borrowing interest rate. Since it is generally recognized and accepted that financial lease obligations carry many of the same burdens as long-term debt, then it must also be recognized that, in any financial lease agreement of which this is true, the lessee (the one who obtains the use of an asset owned by the lessor) is obtaining long-term financing paid for by his or her periodic lease payments.

The lease-versus-buy decision is a financing decision to determine the method of raising funds having the lowest cost once the investment decision to acquire the use of an asset has been made. In the financing decision, the objective is to select the source of financing that has the lowest cost; in the investment decision, the objective is to select the outlet for investments that promises the highest return. In practice, a firm using several sources of financing cannot identify an investment plan with the cost of a particular source of financing; therefore, it is suggested that both the financing decision and the investment decision be treated separately but simultaneously.

The first step in the lease-versus-buy analysis is to determine the cash flows and their time pattern. Next, the cash outflows and inflows are discounted to determine their present value. To calculate the present value, a discount rate that can be applied to all cash flows must be determined.

If a firm buys the asset in question, the tax shield afforded by depreciation and interest payments and the investment tax credit must be considered. Since all cash outflows and inflows are likely to have different time horizons, these flows must be discounted to the zero period so that such flows are on a comparable basis. If a firm desires to acquire the use of a given asset through lease financing, the present value of rental payments and the present value of the tax savings given by the rental expense deduction must be considered.

(a) Discounted Cash Flow Technique.

One of the methods used to analyze a lease-versus-buy problem is the widely known discounted cash flow technique. Using this technique, a discount rate or an interest rate is calculated that equates the present values of cash inflows to the present value of cash outflows associated with the lease or buy decision.

If a firm can raise funds at a cost that is lower than the discount rate calculated for the given lease or buy decision, it should not lease the asset. A summary of the information related to an example of a lease or buy problem is as follows:

Purchase Basis	Lease Basis
Purchase cost—$600,000 Estimated useful life—6 years Tax rate—48% Investment tax credit—4.67% (⅔ of 7%) Straight-line depreciation Estimated residual value—zero	Rental charges for first 3 years—$155,000/year; for next 3 years—$145,000/year Tax rate—48%

The first step in analyzing the problem is to identify relevant cash flows, as shown in Exhibit 20.22. One can estimate these cash flows on a monthly or quarterly basis. For purposes of simplicity, we have calculated these cash flows on a yearly basis.

The next step is to calculate the discount or interest rate, which will equate the present values of cash inflows for six years to the initial cash outflow of $600,000. Using the trial-and-error procedure, one can estimate the discount rate for these cash flows to be 8.6%. Alternatively, one can use a time-sharing computer to estimate the discount rate.

One should remember that the discount rate is computed based on aftertax cash flows. If a firm can raise funds at an aftertax cost that is less than 8.6%, it should not lease the asset in question. In other words, the calculated discount rate of 8.6% becomes the indifference point from the viewpoint of the prospective lessee.

(b) Net Present Value Technique. Some analysts prefer to use the NPV technique to analyze a lease-versus-buy problem. The opportunity cost to raise funds to finance the asset in question is used to calculate present values of cash flows under the purchase basis and the lease basis. Since the objective is to minimize the cost of financing the asset, the alternative giving the lower NPV is selected.

Let us reconsider the previous example. We assume that the firm can raise funds at

	Purchase Basis			Lease Basis	
Period	Purchase Cost	Savings in Tax Payments Due to Depreciation	Investment Tax Credit	Aftertax Rental Savings	Differential Cash Flows
0	$(600,000)	—	—	—	($600,000)
1		$ 48,000	$28,020	$ 80,600	156,620
2		48,000		80,600	128,600
3		48,000		80,600	128,600
4		48,000		75,400	123,400
5		48,000		75,400	123,400
6		48,000		75,400	123,400
Total	$(600,000)	$288,000	$28,020	$468,000	$184,020

Exhibit 20.22. Discounted cash flow technique applied to lease-versus-buy analysis

Lease Basis

Period	Pretax Lease Rentals	Aftertax Lease	Present Value at 4%
1	$155,000	$80,600	$77,537
2	155,000	80,600	74,555
3	155,000	80,600	71,653
4	145,000	75,400	64,467
5	145,000	75,400	61,979
6	145,000	75,400	59,566
Total	$900,000	$468,000	$409,757

Purchase Basis

Period	Depreciation	Tax Savings	Investment Tax Credit	Total Savings	Present Value at 4%
1	$100,000	$48,000	$28,020	$76,020	$73,131
2	100,000	48,000		48,000	44,400
3	100,000	48,000		48,000	42,672
4	100,000	48,000		48,000	41,040
5	100,000	48,000		48,000	39,456
6	100,000	48,000		48,000	37,920
Total	$600,000	$288,000	$28,020	$316,020	$278,619

Present value of initial purchase price	= $600,000
Less present value of tax savings	= 278,619
Net cost	= $321,381
Savings in terms of present value if the asset is purchased rather than leased ($409,757 − $321,381)	= $88,376

Exhibit 20.23. NPV technique applied to lease-versus-buy analysis

4% after tax from alternate sources. The evaluation procedure is shown in Exhibit 20.23. Using a 4% discount rate, the lease plan is not desirable from a financial viewpoint. However, nonfinancial factors could change the decision.

20.13 SUMMARY. This chapter has presented various techniques generally used in evaluating capital investment projects. Empirical data suggest that the use of various techniques vary from one firm to another. However, there is a growing trend among firms to use sophisticated techniques to evaluate capital investments. Some of these techniques are also used in evaluating financing decisions such as lease-versus-buy decisions. Needless to say, there are certain problems in using the risk-analysis technique, but with more education, businessmen will overcome such problems.

SOURCES AND SUGGESTED REFERENCES

Benke, Ralph L., Jr., and Charles P. Baril, "The Lease vs. Purchase Decision," *Management Accounting,* vol. 71, no. 9, March 1990.

Bierman, Harold, "Beyond Cash Flow ROI," *Midland Corporate Finance Journal,* vol. 5, no. 4, Winter 1988.

Brooks, LeRoy D., "Capital Budgeting for Replacements with Unequal Remaining Life," *Managerial Finance,* vol. 17, nos. 2 and 3, 1991.

Butler, J. S., and Barry Schachter, ''The Investment Decision: Estimation Risk and Risk Adjusted Discount Rates,'' *Financial Management,* vol. 18, no. 4, Winter 1989.

Cho, Dongsae, ''An Alternative and Practical Theory of Capital Budgeting: Stockholder Wealth Maximization Approach,'' *Mid-Atlantic Journal of Business,* vol. 32, no. 2, June 1996, pp. 93–104.

Evans, Dorla A., ''Investment Decision Making Under Uncertainty: Potential Environmental/Social Impacts of New Products,'' *Engineering Economist,* vol. 32, no. 4, Summer 1987.

Fields, M. Andrew, ''Effect of the Learning Curve on the Capital Budgeting Process,'' *Managerial Finance,* vol. 17, nos. 2 and 3, 1991.

Frankel, Alan N., ''When It's Not a Capital Idea, Leasing Pays Off,'' *Quality,* vol. 30, no. 4, April 1991.

Frigo, Mark L., ''Holding the Line on Leasing,'' *Corporate Controller,* vol. 3, no. 6, July–August 1991.

Geltner, David, ''Return Risk and Cash Flow Risk with Long-Term Riskless Leases in Commercial Real Estate,'' *AREUEA Journal,* vol. 18, no. 4, Winter 1990.

Giaccotto, Carmelo, ''Cash Flow Modelling and Forecasting in Capital Budgeting Under Uncertainty,'' *Decision Sciences,* vol. 21, no. 4, Fall 1990.

Ho, Simon S. M., and Richard H. Pike, ''Risk Analysis in Capital Budgeting Contexts: Simple or Sophisticated?,'' *Accounting & Business Research,* vol. 21, no. 83, Summer 1991.

Kee, Robert, and Bruce Bublitz, ''The Role of Payback in the Investment Process,'' *Accounting & Business Research* (UK), vol. 18, no. 70, Spring 1988.

Lee, C. Jevons, ''Capital Budgeting Under Uncertainty: The Issue of Optimal Timing,'' *Journal of Business Finance & Accounting* (UK), vol. 15, no. 2, Summer 1988.

Lohmann, Jack R., ''The IRR, NPV and the Fallacy of the Reinvestment Rate Assumptions,'' *Engineering Economist,* vol. 33, no. 4, Summer 1988.

Mathur, Krishan S., ''Risk Analysis in Capital Cost Estimating,'' *Cost Engineering,* vol. 31, no. 8, August 1989.

Meyer, Richard L., Scott Besley, and James R. Longstreet, ''An Examination of Capital Budgeting Decision Alternatives for Mutually Exclusive Investments With Unequal Lives,'' *Journal of Business Finance & Accounting* (UK), vol. 15, no. 3, Autumn 1988.

Miller, Edward M., ''Safety Margins and Capital Budgeting Criteria,'' *Managerial Finance* (UK), vol. 14, nos. 2 and 3, 1988.

Moribayashi, Masaaki, and Chao-Yen Wu, ''A Decision Support System for Capital Budgeting and Allocation,'' *Computers & Industrial Engineering,* vol. 19, nos. 1–4, 1990.

Mukherjee, Tarun K., ''A Survey of Corporate Leasing Analysis,'' *Financial Management,* vol. 20, no. 3, Autumn 1991.

Myers, Stewart C., ''Notes on an Expert System for Capital Budgeting,'' *Financial Management,* vol. 17, no. 3, Autumn 1988.

Norgaard, Richard, and Timothy Killeen, ''Applied Capital Budgeting with Cash Flow Dependencies,'' *Decision Sciences,* vol. 21, no. 3, Summer 1990.

Rachlin, Robert, *Return on Investment Manual: Tools and Applications for Managing Financial Results.* Armonk, NY: M. E. Sharpe, 1997.

Singhvi, Surendra S., ''Affordability Analysis for Capital Investments,'' *Healthcare Financial Management,* vol. 50, no. 6, June 1996, pp. 68–75.

Singhvi, Surendra S., ''Financial Assessments-Use of a Discount Rate in Present Value Analysis,'' *Credit & Financial Management,* vol. 89, no. 2, February 1987, pp. 31–35.

Singhvi, Surendra S., ''How to Evaluate if Sale/Leaseback Transactions are Right for Your Company,'' *Corporate Controller,* vol. 1, no. 6, July–August 1989, pp. 22–26.

Singhvi, Surendra S. and Hiam Alexander, ''The Gains from Cost/Benefit Analysis,'' *The Small Business Controller,* vol. 9, no. 1, Winter 1966, pp. 55–57.

Solis, Rafael, and Manuchehr Shahrokhi, ''LP: An Expert System for Lease Versus Purchase Decision,'' *Managerial Finance* (UK), vol. 15, no. 5, 1989.

Springsteel, Ian, ''The Big Chill?,'' *CFO: The Magazine for Senior Financial Executives,* vol. 12, no. 6, Junc 1996, p. 15.

APPENDIX*

Table 1.
Compound Value of $1

Year	Interest Rate													
	1%	2%	3%	4%	5%	6%	7%	8%	9%	10%	12%	14%	15%	16%
1	1.010	1.020	1.030	1.040	1.050	1.060	1.070	1.080	1.090	1.100	1.120	1.140	1.150	1.160
2	1.020	1.040	1.061	1.082	1.102	1.124	1.145	1.166	1.188	1.210	1.254	1.300	1.322	1.346
3	1.030	1.061	1.093	1.125	1.158	1.191	1.225	1.260	1.295	1.331	1.405	1.482	1.521	1.561
4	1.041	1.082	1.126	1.170	1.216	1.262	1.311	1.360	1.412	1.464	1.574	1.689	1.749	1.811
5	1.051	1.104	1.159	1.217	1.276	1.338	1.403	1.469	1.539	1.611	1.762	1.925	2.011	2.100
6	1.062	1.126	1.194	1.265	1.340	1.419	1.501	1.587	1.677	1.772	1.974	2.195	2.313	2.436
7	1.072	1.149	1.230	1.316	1.407	1.504	1.606	1.714	1.828	1.949	2.211	2.502	2.660	2.826
8	1.083	1.172	1.267	1.369	1.477	1.594	1.718	1.851	1.993	2.144	2.476	2.853	3.059	3.278
9	1.094	1.195	1.305	1.423	1.551	1.689	1.838	1.999	2.172	2.358	2.773	3.252	3.518	3.803
10	1.105	1.219	1.344	1.480	1.629	1.791	1.967	2.159	2.367	2.594	3.106	3.707	4.046	4.411
11	1.116	1.243	1.384	1.539	1.710	1.898	2.105	2.332	2.580	2.853	3.479	4.226	4.652	5.117
12	1.127	1.268	1.426	1.601	1.796	2.012	2.252	2.518	2.813	3.138	3.896	4.818	5.350	5.936
13	1.138	1.294	1.469	1.665	1.886	2.133	2.410	2.720	3.066	3.452	4.363	5.492	6.153	6.886
14	1.149	1.319	1.513	1.732	1.980	2.261	2.579	2.937	3.342	3.797	4.887	6.261	7.076	7.988
15	1.161	1.346	1.558	1.801	2.079	2.397	2.759	3.172	3.642	4.177	5.474	7.138	8.137	9.266
16	1.173	1.373	1.605	1.873	2.183	2.540	2.952	3.426	3.970	4.595	6.130	8.137	9.358	10.748
17	1.184	1.400	1.653	1.948	2.292	2.693	3.159	3.700	4.328	5.054	6.866	9.276	10.761	12.468
18	1.196	1.428	1.702	2.026	2.407	2.854	3.380	3.996	4.717	5.560	7.690	10.575	12.375	14.463
19	1.208	1.457	1.754	2.107	2.527	3.026	3.617	4.316	5.142	6.116	8.613	12.056	14.232	16.777
20	1.220	1.486	1.806	2.191	2.653	3.207	3.870	4.661	5.604	6.728	9.646	13.743	16.367	19.461
25	1.282	1.641	2.094	2.666	3.386	4.292	5.427	6.848	8.623	10.835	17.000	26.462	32.919	40.874
30	1.348	1.811	2.427	3.243	4.322	5.743	7.612	10.063	13.268	17.449	29.960	50.950	66.212	85.850

* For detailed compound value and present value tables, refer to *Financial Compound Interest & Annuity Tables*, published by Financial Publishing Company, 82 Brookline Ave., Boston, MA 02215, 1970, p. 884.

Table 1.
Compound Value of $1 (*continued*)

Year	Interest Rate (*continued*)											
	18%	20%	24%	28%	32%	36%	40%	50%	60%	70%	80%	90%
1	1.180	1.200	1.210	1.280	1.320	1.360	1.400	1.500	1.600	1.700	1.800	1.900
2	1.392	1.440	1.538	1.638	1.742	1.850	1.960	2.250	2.560	2.890	3.240	3.610
3	1.643	1.728	1.907	2.067	2.300	2.515	2.744	3.375	4.096	4.913	5.832	6.859
4	1.939	2.074	2.364	2.684	3.036	3.421	3.842	5.062	6.544	8.352	10.498	13.032
5	2.288	2.488	2.932	3.436	4.007	4.653	5.378	7.594	10.486	14.199	18.896	24.761
6	2.700	2.986	3.635	4.398	5.290	6.328	7.530	11.391	16.777	24.138	34.012	47.046
7	3.185	3.583	4.508	5.629	6.983	8.605	10.541	17.086	26.844	41.034	61.222	89.387
8	3.759	4.300	5.590	7.206	9.217	11.703	14.758	25.629	42.950	69.758	110.200	169.836
9	4.435	5.160	6.931	9.223	12.166	15.917	20.661	38.443	68.720	118.588	198.359	322.688
10	5.234	6.192	8.594	11.806	16.060	21.647	28.925	57.665	109.951	201.599	357.047	613.107
11	6.176	7.430	10.657	15.112	21.199	29.439	40.496	86.498	175.922	342.719	642.684	1164.902
12	7.288	8.916	13.215	19.343	27.983	40.037	56.694	129.746	281.475	582.622	1156.831	2213.314
13	8.599	10.699	16.386	24.759	36.937	54.451	79.372	194.619	450.360	990.457	2082.295	4205.297
14	10.147	12.839	20.319	31.691	48.757	74.053	111.120	291.929	720.576	1683.777	3748.131	7990.065
15	11.974	15.407	25.196	40.565	64.359	100.712	155.568	437.894	1152.921	2862.421	6746.636	15181.122
16	14.129	18.488	31.243	51.923	84.954	136.97	217.795	656.84	1844.7	4866.1	12144.	28844.0
17	16.672	22.186	38.741	66.461	112.14	186.28	304.914	985.26	2951.5	8272.4	21859.	54804.0
18	19.673	26.623	48.039	85.071	148.02	253.34	426.879	1477.9	4722.4	14063.0	39346.	104130.0
19	23.214	31.948	59.568	108.89	195.39	344.54	597.630	2216.8	7555.8	23907.0	70824.	197840.0
20	27.393	38.338	73.864	139.38	257.92	468.57	836.683	3325.3	12089.0	40642.0	127480.	375900.0
25	62.669	95.396	216.542	478.90	1033.6	2180.1	4499.880	25251.	126760.0	577060.0	2408900.	9307600.0
30	143.371	237.376	634.820	164.55	4142.1	10143.	24201.432	191750.	1329200.	8193500.0	45517000.	230470000.0

Table 2.
Compound Value of $1 per period

Year	Interest Rate 1%	2%	3%	4%	5%	6%	7%	8%	9%	10%	12%	14%
1	1.000	1.000	1.000	1.000	1.000	1.000	1.000	1.000	1.000	1.000	1.000	1.000
2	2.010	2.020	2.030	2.040	2.050	2.060	2.070	2.080	2.090	2.100	2.120	2.140
3	2.030	3.060	3.091	3.122	3.152	3.184	3.215	3.246	3.278	3.310	3.374	3.440
4	4.060	4.122	4.184	4.246	4.310	4.375	4.440	4.506	4.573	4.641	4.770	4.921
5	5.101	5.204	5.309	5.416	5.526	5.637	5.751	5.867	5.985	6.105	6.353	6.610
6	6.152	6.308	6.468	6.633	6.802	6.975	7.153	7.336	7.523	7.716	8.115	8.536
7	7.214	7.434	7.662	7.898	8.142	8.394	8.654	8.923	9.200	9.487	10.089	10.730
8	8.286	8.583	8.892	9.214	9.549	9.897	10.260	10.637	11.028	11.436	12.300	13.233
9	9.369	9.755	10.159	10.583	11.027	11.491	11.978	12.488	13.021	13.579	14.776	16.085
10	10.462	10.950	11.464	12.006	12.578	13.181	13.816	14.487	15.193	15.937	17.549	19.337
11	11.567	12.169	12.808	13.486	14.207	14.972	15.784	16.645	17.560	18.531	20.655	23.044
12	12.683	13.412	14.192	15.026	15.917	16.870	17.888	18.977	20.141	21.384	24.133	27.271
13	13.809	14.680	15.618	16.627	17.713	18.882	20.141	21.495	22.953	24.523	28.029	32.089
14	14.947	15.974	17.086	18.292	19.599	21.051	22.550	24.215	26.019	27.975	32.393	37.581
15	16.097	17.293	18.599	20.024	21.579	23.276	25.129	27.152	29.361	31.772	37.280	43.842
16	17.258	18.639	20.157	21.825	23.657	25.673	27.888	30.324	33.003	35.950	42.753	50.980
17	18.430	20.012	21.762	23.698	25.840	28.213	30.840	33.750	36.974	40.545	48.884	59.118
18	19.615	21.412	23.414	25.645	28.132	30.906	33.999	37.450	41.301	45.599	55.750	68.394
19	20.811	22.841	25.117	27.671	30.539	33.760	37.379	41.446	46.018	51.159	63.440	78.969
20	22.019	24.297	26.870	29.778	33.066	36.786	40.995	45.762	51.160	57.275	72.052	91.025
25	28.243	32.030	36.459	41.646	47.727	54.865	63.249	73.106	84.701	98.347	133.334	181.871
30	34.785	40.568	47.575	56.085	66.439	79.058	94.461	113.283	136.308	164.494	241.333	356.787

Table 2.
Compound Value of $1 per period (*continued*)

Year	Interest Rate (*continued*)											
	16%	18%	20%	24%	28%	32%	36%	40%	50%	60%	70%	80%
1	1.000	1.000	1.000	1.000	1.000	1.000	1.000	1.000	1.000	1.000	1.000	1.000
2	2.160	2.180	2.200	2.240	2.280	2.320	2.360	2.400	2.500	2.600	2.700	2.800
3	3.506	3.572	3.640	3.778	3.918	4.062	4.210	4.360	4.750	5.160	5.590	6.040
4	5.066	5.215	5.368	5.684	6.016	6.362	6.725	7.104	8.125	9.256	10.503	11.872
5	6.877	7.154	7.442	8.048	8.700	9.398	10.146	10.846	13.188	15.810	18.855	22.370
6	8.977	9.442	9.930	10.980	12.136	13.406	14.799	16.324	20.781	26.295	33.054	41.265
7	11.414	12.142	12.916	14.615	16.534	18.696	21.126	23.853	32.172	43.073	57.191	75.278
8	14.240	15.327	16.499	19.123	22.163	25.678	29.732	34.395	49.258	69.916	98.225	136.500
9	17.518	19.086	20.799	24.712	29.369	34.895	41.435	49.153	74.887	112.866	167.983	246.699
10	21.321	23.521	25.959	31.643	38.592	47.062	57.352	69.814	113.330	181.585	286.570	445.058
11	25.733	28.755	32.150	40.238	50.399	63.122	78.998	98.739	170.995	291.536	488.170	802.105
12	30.850	34.931	39.580	50.985	65.510	84.320	108.437	139.235	257.493	467.458	830.888	1444.788
13	36.786	42.219	48.497	64.110	84.853	112.303	148.475	195.929	387.239	748.933	1413.510	2601.619
14	43.672	50.818	59.196	80.496	109.612	149.240	202.926	275.300	581.859	1199.293	2403.968	4683.914
15	51.660	60.965	72.035	100.815	141.303	197.997	276.979	386.420	873.788	1919.869	4087.745	8432.045
16	60.925	72.939	87.442	126.011	181.87	262.36	377.69	541.99	1311.7	3072.8	6950.2	15179.0
17	71.673	87.065	105.931	157.253	233.79	347.31	514.66	759.78	1968.5	4917.5	11816.0	27323.0
18	84.141	103.740	128.117	195.994	300.25	459.45	700.94	1064.7	2953.8	7868.9	20089.0	49182.0
19	98.603	123.414	154.740	244.033	385.32	607.47	954.28	1491.6	4431.7	12591.0	34152.0	88528.0
20	115.380	146.628	186.688	303.601	494.21	802.86	1298.8	2089.2	6648.5	20147.0	58059.0	159350.0
25	249.214	342.603	471.981	898.092	1706.8	3226.8	6053.0	11247.0	50500.0	211270.0	824370.0	3011100.0
30	530.312	790.948	1181.882	2640.916	5873.2	12941.0	28172.0	60501.0	383500.0	2215400.0	11705000.0	56896000.0

Table 3.
Present Value of $1

Year	Interest Rate 1%	2%	3%	4%	5%	6%	7%	8%	9%	10%	12%	14%	15%
1	.990	.980	.971	.962	.952	.943	.935	.926	.917	.909	.893	.877	.870
2	.980	.961	.943	.925	.907	.890	.873	.857	.842	.826	.797	.769	.756
3	.971	.942	.915	.889	.864	.840	.816	.794	.772	.751	.712	.675	.658
4	.961	.924	.889	.855	.823	.792	.763	.735	.708	.683	.636	.592	.572
5	.951	.906	.863	.822	.784	.747	.713	.681	.650	.621	.567	.519	.497
6	.942	.888	.838	.790	.746	.705	.666	.630	.596	.564	.507	.456	.432
7	.933	.871	.813	.760	.711	.665	.623	.583	.547	.513	.452	.400	.376
8	.923	.853	.789	.731	.677	.627	.582	.540	.502	.467	.404	.351	.327
9	.914	.837	.766	.703	.645	.592	.544	.500	.460	.424	.361	.308	.284
10	.905	.820	.744	.676	.614	.558	.508	.463	.422	.386	.322	.270	.247
11	.896	.804	.722	.650	.585	.527	.475	.429	.388	.350	.287	.237	.215
12	.887	.788	.701	.625	.557	.497	.444	.397	.356	.319	.257	.208	.187
13	.879	.773	.681	.601	.530	.469	.415	.368	.326	.290	.229	.182	.163
14	.870	.758	.661	.577	.505	.442	.388	.340	.299	.263	.205	.160	.141
15	.861	.743	.642	.555	.481	.417	.362	.315	.275	.239	.183	.140	.123
16	.853	.728	.623	.534	.458	.394	.339	.292	.252	.218	.163	.123	.107
17	.844	.714	.605	.513	.436	.371	.317	.270	.231	.198	.146	.108	.093
18	.836	.700	.587	.494	.416	.350	.296	.250	.212	.180	.130	.095	.081
19	.828	.686	.570	.475	.396	.331	.276	.232	.194	.164	.116	.083	.070
20	.820	.673	.554	.456	.377	.319	.258	.215	.178	.149	.104	.073	.061
25	.780	.610	.478	.375	.295	.233	.184	.146	.116	.092	.059	.038	.030
30	.742	.552	.412	.308	.231	.174	.131	.099	.075	.057	.033	.020	.015

Year	Interest Rate *(continued)* 16%	18%	20%	24%	28%	32%	36%	40%	50%	60%	70%	80%	90%
1	.862	.847	.833	.808	.781	.758	.735	.714	.667	.625	.588	.556	.526
2	.743	.718	.694	.650	.610	.574	.541	.510	.444	.391	.346	.309	.277
3	.641	.609	.579	.524	.477	.435	.398	.364	.296	.244	.204	.171	.146
4	.552	.516	.482	.423	.373	.329	.292	.260	.198	.153	.120	.095	.077
5	.476	.437	.402	.341	.291	.250	.215	.186	.132	.095	.070	.053	.040
6	.410	.370	.335	.275	.227	.189	.158	.133	.088	.060	.041	.029	.021
7	.354	.314	.279	.222	.178	.143	.116	.095	.059	.037	.024	.016	.011
8	.305	.266	.233	.179	.139	.108	.085	.068	.039	.023	.014	.009	.006
9	.263	.226	.194	.144	.108	.082	.063	.048	.026	.015	.008	.005	.003
10	.227	.191	.162	.116	.085	.062	.046	.035	.017	.009	.005	.003	.002
11	.195	.162	.135	.094	.066	.047	.034	.025	.012	.006	.003	.002	.001
12	.168	.137	.112	.076	.052	.036	.025	.018	.008	.004	.002	.001	.001
13	.145	.116	.093	.061	.040	.027	.018	.013	.005	.002	.001	.001	.000
14	.125	.099	.078	.049	.032	.021	.014	.009	.003	.001	.001	.000	.000
15	.108	.084	.065	.040	.025	.016	.010	.006	.002	.001	.000	.000	.000
16	.093	.071	.054	.032	.019	.012	.007	.005	.002	.001	.000	.000	
17	.080	.060	.045	.026	.015	.009	.005	.003	.001	.000	.000		
18	.089	.051	.038	.021	.012	.007	.004	.002	.001	.000	.000		
19	.030	.043	.031	.017	.009	.005	.003	.002	.000	.000			
20	.051	.037	.026	.014	.007	.004	.002	.001	.000	.000			
25	.024	.016	.010	.005	.002	.001	.000	.000					
30	.012	.007	.004	.002	.001	.000	.000						

Table 4.
Present Value of an Annuity of $1

Year	Interest Rate 1%	2%	3%	4%	5%	6%	7%	8%	9%	10%
1	0.990	0.980	0.971	0.962	0.952	0.943	0.935	0.926	0.917	0.909
2	1.970	1.942	1.913	1.886	1.859	1.833	1.808	1.783	1.759	1.736
3	2.941	2.884	2.829	2.775	2.723	2.673	2.624	2.577	2.531	2.487
4	3.902	3.808	3.717	3.630	3.546	3.465	3.387	3.312	3.240	3.170
5	4.853	4.713	4.580	4.452	4.329	4.212	4.100	3.993	3.890	3.791
6	5.795	5.601	5.417	5.242	5.076	4.917	4.766	4.623	4.486	4.355
7	6.728	6.472	6.230	6.002	5.786	5.582	5.389	5.206	5.033	4.868
8	7.652	7.325	7.020	6.733	6.463	6.210	6.971	5.747	5.535	5.335
9	8.566	8.162	7.786	7.435	7.108	6.802	6.515	6.247	5.985	5.759
10	9.471	8.983	8.530	8.111	7.722	7.360	7.024	6.710	6.418	6.145
11	10.368	9.787	9.253	8.760	8.306	7.887	7.499	7.139	6.805	6.495
12	11.255	10.575	9.954	9.385	8.863	8.384	7.943	7.536	7.161	6.814
13	12.134	11.348	10.635	9.986	9.394	8.853	8.358	7.904	7.487	7.103
14	13.004	12.106	11.296	10.563	9.899	9.295	8.745	8.244	7.786	7.367
15	13.865	12.849	11.938	11.118	10.380	9.712	9.108	8.559	8.060	7.606
16	14.718	13.578	12.561	11.652	10.838	10.106	9.447	8.851	8.312	7.824
17	15.562	14.292	13.166	12.166	11.274	10.477	9.763	9.122	8.544	8.022
18	16.398	14.992	13.754	12.659	11.690	10.828	10.059	9.372	8.756	8.201
19	17.226	15.678	14.324	13.134	12.085	11.158	10.336	9.604	8.950	8.365
20	18.046	16.351	14.877	13.590	12.462	11.470	10.594	9.818	9.128	8.514
25	22.023	19.523	17.413	15.622	14.094	12.783	11.654	10.675	9.823	9.077
30	25.808	22.397	19.600	17.292	15.373	13.765	12.409	11.258	10.274	9.427

Year	Interest Rate *(continued)* 12%	14%	16%	18%	20%	24%	28%	32%	36%
1	0.893	0.877	0.862	0.847	0.833	0.806	0.781	0.758	0.735
2	1.690	1.647	1.605	1.566	1.528	1.457	1.392	1.332	1.276
3	2.402	2.322	2.246	2.174	2.106	1.981	1.868	1.766	1.674
4	3.037	2.914	2.798	2.690	2.589	2.404	2.241	2.096	1.966
5	3.605	3.433	3.274	3.127	2.991	2.745	2.532	2.345	2.181
6	4.111	3.889	3.685	3.498	3.326	3.020	2.759	2.534	2.339
7	4.564	4.288	4.039	3.812	3.605	3.242	2.937	2.678	2.455
8	4.968	4.639	4.344	4.078	3.837	3.421	3.076	2.786	2.540
9	5.328	4.946	4.607	4.303	4.031	3.566	3.184	2.868	2.608
10	5.650	5.216	4.833	4.494	4.193	3.682	3.269	2.930	2.650
11	5.988	5.453	5.029	4.656	4.327	3.776	3.335	2.978	2.683
12	6.194	5.660	5.197	4.793	4.439	3.851	3.387	3.013	2.708
13	6.424	5.842	5.342	4.910	4.533	3.912	3.427	3.040	2.727
14	6.628	6.002	5.468	5.008	4.611	3.962	3.459	3.061	2.740
15	6.811	6.142	5.575	5.092	4.675	4.001	3.483	3.076	2.750
16	6.974	6.265	5.669	5.162	4.730	4.033	3.503	3.088	2.758
17	7.120	5.373	5.749	4.222	4.775	4.059	3.518	3.097	2.763
18	7.250	6.467	5.818	5.273	4.812	4.080	3.529	3.104	2.767
19	7.366	6.550	5.877	5.316	4.844	4.097	3.539	3.109	2.770
20	7.469	6.623	5.929	5.353	4.870	4.110	3.546	3.113	2.772
25	7.843	6.873	6.097	5.467	4.948	4.147	3.564	3.122	2.776
30	8.055	7.003	6.177	5.517	4.979	4.160	3.569	3.124	2.778

CHAPTER 21

LEASING

Robert Dale Apgood

Canterbury Group

21.1 INTRODUCTION. The budgetary process in today's business environment requires a dutiful coordination of a business strategic plan carefully supported by a capital budget (primarily a balance-sheet–planning tool) and an operating budget (typically an income-statement–planning tool) (see Exhibit 21.1).

Typically, top management envisions a strategy and subsequently subordinates are required to project a capital plan (assets, liabilities, and equity) that will enable the company to march toward fulfillment of the strategy vision. Accordingly, a capital budget is prepared, complete with all necessary asset, liability, and equity elements. Frequently, however, the company prefers to avoid balance sheet implications by electing to lease assets. Thus, off–balance-sheet financing is selected, the balance sheet impact is minimized, and the operating budget is impacted. To graphically illustrate the financial statement impact, let us examine Exhibit 21.2.

From a budgetary viewpoint, it thus becomes evident that leases must be analyzed carefully, in order that the proper budgets become impacted. Occasionally, leasing transactions may be immaterial for a company, but since the mid-1980s, nearly 33% of all property, plant, and equipment acquired by U.S. companies have been acquired through operating and capital leases.[1]

Thus, the case is made. Budgeting is important and leasing is an increasingly material part thereof.

21.2 OVERVIEW OF THE LEASING PROCESS. A typical lease (usually called a single-inventor lease) involves four parties (Exhibit 21.3).

Simple analysis suggests that, if the lessor retains title to the asset in question, the transaction is a rental or lease. If, however, the lessee eventually ends up with the asset, the lease in question begins to look like some kind of sale from the lessor to the lessee. In budgetary parlance, the transaction is either analyzed as part of the operating budget (if an operating lease) or the capital budget (if a capital lease). Because these two budgets are frequently prepared by different persons, require vastly differing analytical approaches, and dramatically alter balance sheet and income statement presentation, we must become

[1] Annual statistics available from Equipment Leasing Association of America (ELA), Arlington, Virginia.

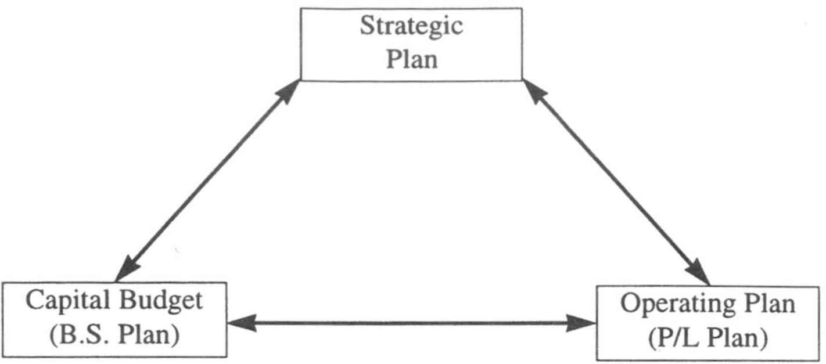

Exhibit 21.1. Coordination of planning tools

	Operating Lease		Capital Lease	
	Balance Sheet	*P/L*	*Balance Sheet*	*P/L*
Lessee	-0-	Rent expense	Fixed asset	Depreciation expense
			Accumulated depreciation:	Interest expense
			Debt:	
			Current	
			Long-term	
Lessor	Fixed asset	Depreciation expense		
	Accumulated depreciation		-0-	Income
	Debt:	Interest expense		
	Current	Rental income	(Simplest of several possible structures)	
	Long-term			

Exhibit 21.2. The impact of leasing in financial statements

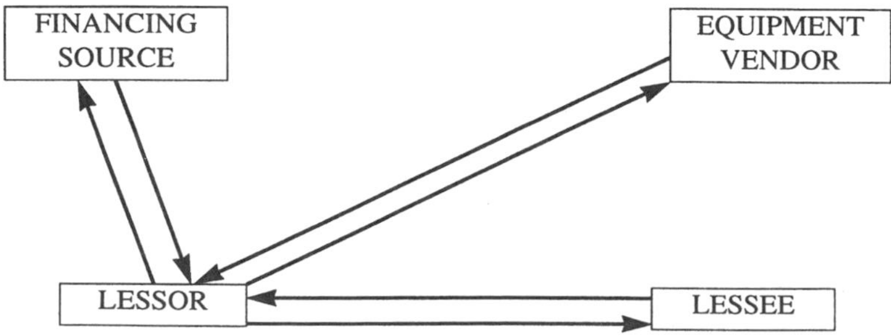

Exhibit 21.3. Typical lease

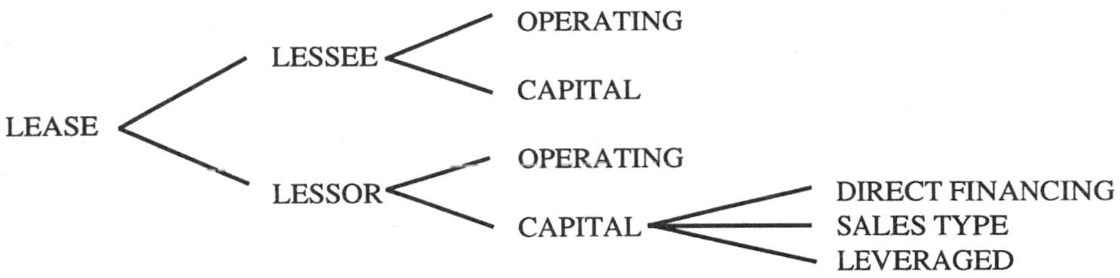

Exhibit 21.4. Lease analysis

Countries Utilizing Form	Countries Utilizing Substance	Rules of Substance Found in:
France	United States	FASB 13, 91, 98, and IAS 17
Italy	United Kingdom	SSAP 21 and IAS 17
Spain	Canada	CICA 3065 and IAS 17
Portugal	Australia	ASAP 21 and IAS 17
Malta	New Zealand	IAS 17
	Holland	IAS 17
	Approximately 50 additional countries	IAS 17

Exhibit 21.5. International lease typology

skilled captains of the leasing ship as it sails the financial waters. Exhibit 21.4 shows the four typical lease analyses.

Internationally, two different approaches have been taken to properly classify leases on financial statements. The first and simplest approach is observed in the geographical region roughly approximated by Southern Europe and is called the "form" approach to leasing. In these countries, if the lease contract stipulates or labels a lease as an operating lease, all analysis is finished. It *is* a rental. Lessor has balance sheet ownership and lessee is a renter. If, in contrast, the lease agreement calls the transaction a capital lease, it *is*. Lessor then accounts for the transaction as a sale and the lessee has balance sheet ownership. How simple and consistent! One party is always an owner and the other a nonowner.

In the United States, however, as in many other countries, it matters not what a lease is called or labeled. Evidence must be gathered, measurements taken, and then the lease classified as either on or off balance sheet for both lessee and lessor. In other words, the substance of a lease dictates its financial statement classification. A short list of countries using each system is displayed in Exhibit 21.5.

As long as both parties to the lease, lessee and lessor, are in the same country, lease treatment will normally be uniform. In the event, however, that a lease becomes binational, intriguing cross-border financial results are possible.

Case One

1. Both the lessee and lessor are in France.
2. The lease document stipulates that the lease is an operating lease—therefore, it is.
3. Lessor assumes balance-sheet ownership and is, therefore, entitled to the related

income-statement deductions for depreciation and interest expenses. Lessor also has balance-sheet ramifications.

4. Lessee may not assume balance-sheet ownership, but rather must account for the lease as a rental.
5. There is one owner and one nonowner.

	Balance Sheet	Income Statement
Lessor	Fixed asset	Depreciation expense
	Accumulated depreciation	Interest expense
	Debt:	Rental income
	Current portion	
	Long-term portion	
Lessee	No impact	Rental expense

Case Two

1. Lessor is an Italian corporation, and lessee is in the United States.
2. The lease document stipulates that the lease is an operating lease. For this lessor, it is.
3. Lessor assumes balance-sheet ownership and takes the related income statement deductions for depreciation and interest expenses as well as all balance-sheet ramifications.
4. Lessee must follow Financial Account Standards Board (FASB) rule 13 (U.S. rules). Let us assume that the present value of the minimum lease payments is greater than 90% of the fair value of the leased asset. According to U.S. rules, the lease is a capital lease, the lessee assumes balance-sheet ownership also (not necessarily legal ownership), and we have a double-dip lease, or, as it is frequently called, a *cross-border tax transfer.*
5. Both lessee and lessor must follow the accounting rules of their countries. Thus, each claims accounting ownership.

	Balance Sheet	Income Statement
Lessor	Fixed asset	Depreciation expense
	Accumulated depreciation	Interest expense
	Debt:	Rental income
	Current portion	
	Long-term portion	
Lessee	Fixed asset	Depreciation expense
	Accumulated depreciation	Interest expense
	Debt:	
	Current portion	
	Long-term portion	

Case Three

1. Lessor is a Spanish corporation, and lessee is in the United States.
2. The lease document stipulates that the lease is a capital lease. For this lessor, it is.
3. Lessor accounts for the lease as a sale. It is no longer on the balance sheet.

4. Lessee must follow FASB 13. Let us assume that the present value of the minimum lease payments is less than 90% of the fair market value of the asset. According to U.S. rules, the lease is an operating lease. The lessee does not have balance sheet ownership and accounts for the transaction as a rental. In this case, neither lessee nor lessor claims balance-sheet ownership. It is off the books for each and rightfully so. Lessee and lessor *must* each follow the generally accepted accounting principles of its own country. In the parlance of the leasing community, this is sometimes called a skinny-dip lease, since neither party has balance-sheet coverage.

	Balance Sheet	Income Statement
Lessor	Nothing. This assumes the asset was sold and the resulting note receivable was also sold.	Income
Lessee	Nothing	Rental expense

21.3 POSSIBLE ADVANTAGES OF LEASING

1. Shifts risk of obsolescence to lessor.
2. Shifts legal ownership and responsibility to lessor.
3. Provides off–balance-sheet financing.
4. Typically paid for from operating budget rather than capital budget.
5. Profitability ratios appear improved.
6. Liquidity ratios appear improved.
7. Solvency ratios appear improved.
8. Tax benefits (depreciation and interest expense) can be shifted to a party better able to utilize them.
9. Lower cash flow up front to obtain asset.
10. Flexibility increases (swaps, upgrades, roll-overs, take-outs, etc.).
11. Inflation hedge (can negotiate longer term and pay with cheaper dollars).
12. Approval can be accelerated.
13. Circumventing capital budget constraints.
14. Delaying sales tax payments (as high as 33% in some European countries).
15. Government reimbursement policies (overhead is frequently a limited or prescribed element for reimbursement; lease payments are not overhead and qualify for reimbursement).
16. Alternative minimum tax (AMT) may dictate no additional purchases.
17. Ownership may be unavailable (satellite usage).
18. Bundling (full-service leases) is facilitated.
19. Excessive usage of equipment by lessee would make ownership unwise.
20. Vendor control (nonperformance of equipment).
21. Finance source diversification.
22. Fewer restrictions (bank covenants).
23. Lower cost (lessor may obtain economies of scale and pass through to lessee).

21.4 POSSIBLE DISADVANTAGES OF LEASING

1 Opportunity to gain from residual value is shifted to lessor.
2. Balance sheet analysis is hindered, as both asset and liability are disclosed only in footnotes.
3. Capital budgeting decisions are disguised and frequently not analyzed.
4. Tax benefits of ownership: depreciation and interest expense are not normally available to minimize cash flows.
5. Reimbursement policies may be hindered (utilities, for example, are often given a targeted return on assets (ROA) approval figure for rates. If leased, the assets are less and the targeted profitability can be reduced—rates lowered).
6. Higher cost (if lessee is not sophisticated in lease negotiations).
7. Lease versus buy analytical techniques are not universally known and applied.
8. Trends or fads may suggest that leasing is wise when it is only current.

21.5 TYPES OF LEASE SOURCES

Lessors

- Financial institutions (banks, savings and loans, finance companies, etc.)
- Captives (vendors and banks)
- Independents

In the United States, independent leasing companies have traditionally held the biggest share of the leasing business.[2] Banks entered the game in a big way in the late 1970s and early 1980s and built large portfolios, many of which were liquidated in the late 1980s and early 1990s as they experienced operating and regulatory difficulties. The current trend in the industry is the awakening and substantial growth of the ''vendor'' sector, who have discovered that leasing can be a tremendous marketing tool for expansion as well as a profit center. Exhibit 21.6 illustrates a third-party lease for a typical independent lease company.

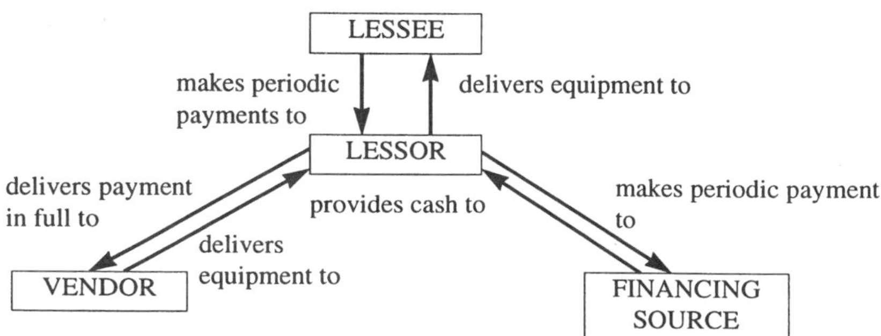

Exhibit 21.6. Typical independent lease company transaction (third-party lease)

[2] ELA statistics.

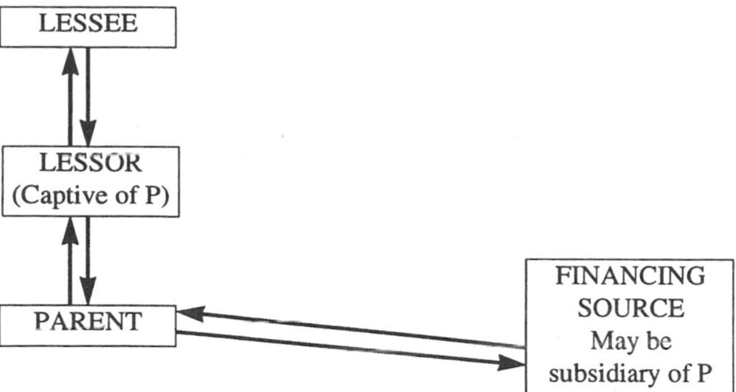

Exhibit 21.7. Typical captive lease transaction

Many entities have joined the leasing game. They include the following:

- *Independent leasing companies.* This is the traditional type of lease provider who originally would lease anything to anyone (Exhibit 21.4). Increased competitive pressure has forced many of these companies to concentrate in niches, such as telecommunications or automobiles. The largest such player is Comdisco, an international participant in Chicago that specialized originally in the used IBM market. Exhibit 21.7 illustrates a typical captive lease transaction
- *Captives.* This is the hot market of the early 1990s. Because they operate under the scrutiny of a parent, they are usually not as nimble and flexible as an independent, but they have tremendous clout because of this same parent relationship (Exhibit 21.5). Examples include GECC (General Electric) and ICC (IBM).
- *Brokers.* During the frothy and profitable ''go-go'' years of the 1980s, many experienced leasing professionals discovered that they could function as financial intermediaries, bringing together the necessary participants, thus functioning as a manager. Brokers come and go, but typically prefer to manage bigger deals, such as jumbo jets and large computer mainframes.
- *Banks.* In the United States, banks entered the leasing game after it was somewhat mature. By way of contrast, banks in Europe and the Middle East were primary developers, and hence currently enjoy a much larger market presence in those geographical regions. Banks in the United States dramatically altered their position in the leasing arena during the last few years because of large credit losses and subsequent government tightening of regulations.
- *Insurance companies.* Two approaches have been taken in this industry. Several large firms, such as Metropolitan Life Insurance, formed leasing subsidiaries and aggressively funded deals. Others are content to purchase large individual leases or portfolios on the secondary market, much like the home mortgage market.
- *Finance companies.* Many of these players jumped into the arena, especially in the area of consumer leasing. Because they already were active here, they expanded their horizon to include operating leases and thereby assumed a risk they were not experienced in—residual risk!
- *Pension funds.* Usually, these funds serve as a reservoir of lease portfolios and pur-

chased leases from others. Needless to say, many questionable and some worthless paper found its way into the hands of these typically inexperienced participants.

- *Lease pools.* Functioning much like a mutual fund, many lease pools sold "shares" in future expected values to wealthy individuals and companies.

21.6 LEASE REPORTING

- FASB 13, 91, 98—Provide criteria for accrual (income statement, balance sheet) reporting
- IRS Revenue Ruling 55-540, Revenue Procedure 75-21—Provide criteria for tax analysis of a lease.
- International Accounting Standard (IAS)—Provides criteria for international lease reporting to the approximately 55 member nations who have adopted it.
- Internal reporting
  - Lease versus buy
  - Internal rate of return
  - Net present value
  - Breakeven
  - Pricing
  - Asset tracking
  - Accounting
  - Tax
  - Billing and collections
  - Portfolio management.

Software providers have developed an abundance of software application packages to assist in lease analysis and reporting.[3]

(a) Basic Terminology. The leasing industry is exceedingly creative, and accordingly a host of synonyms or near-synonyms has been created to describe operating and capital leases. These include the ones listed in Exhibit 21.8.

(b) Technical Analysis. Various national and international bodies have labored extensively to codify leasing rules. In the United States, the Internal Revenue Service (IRS) and FASB have provided mandatory models.

The IRS was the first group in the United States to codify leasing rules, and these still exist. In 1955, Revenue Ruling 55-540 provided initial but very weak "nonguidelines" for lease classifications as either operating or capital. The IRS followed up this initial attempt with an improved but still weak definition of operating and capital in 1975 with Revenue Procedure 75-21. Since then, the IRS has given the lease definition and measurement process little additional attention. Because what it has produced is impractical and insufficient for satisfactory application, the IRS tends to rely on the subsequent and much superior FASB 13 in its deliberations.

The FASB in 1975 issued FASB 13, which became effective in 1977. This is a much

---

[3] Some of the major software dealers are: Decision Systems, Inc., Minneapolis, Minnesota; SSI, Norcross, Georgia; Better Programs, Denver, Colorado; McCue Systems, Inc., Burlingame, California; The LeMans Group, King of Prussia, Pennsylvania.

Operating Lease Synonyms	Capital Lease Synonyms
Operating	Capital
Real	Direct finance
True	Finance
Rental	Installment sales contract
Off balance sheet	Deferred sales contract
Off the books	Open-end lease with a bargain purchase option
Closed-end	$1.00 purchase option
Open-end lease with fair market value purchase option	Nominal purchase option
Tax	Peppercorn (British)
Guideline	Full payout
Nonguideline	Full payoff
Walk away	Sales type
	Nontax
	Secured transaction

Exhibit 21.8. Basic terminology to describe operating and capital leases

tighter document, which provides definitions and measurements for operating and capital lease classifications.

(c) FASB 13. FASB 13 contains the four criteria that must be observed if a lease is to be classified as a capital lease.

(i) Four Tests of Substance

1. Will title pass from lessor to lessee?
2. Does the lease contain a bargain purchase option?
3. Is the lease life greater than or equal to 75% of the economic life?
4. Is the present value of the minimum lease payments greater than or equal to 90% of the fair market value of the equipment?

If the answer to any of these questions is affirmative, the lease is a capital lease. If all four are negative, the lease is an operating lease.

Internationally, all of the previously mentioned lease codification numbers (CICA 3065 in Canada, FASB 13 in the United States, SSAP 21 in England, etc.) are substantially identical and are also substantially identical to IAS 17, issued by the International Accounting Standards Board in London. In other words, once the intricacies of FASB 13 are mastered, all others are virtually identical.

Therefore, these four tests must be carefully examined and mastered if the financial statements are to be properly stated *and* if the budgeting classifications of operating and capital assets are to be proper. An operating lease will be included in the operating ''budget'' and is usually approved by a department head. A capital lease, however, is in the capital budget and is typically approved by someone at a higher corporate level.

(ii) Analysis of the Four Tests. The first test is simple to control. If an operating lease is desired, do not provide for the transfer of title in the lease document. Simply state that

the lease is a closed-end lease or a walk-away lease (i.e., no purchase option is available to the lessee). Conversely, if a capital lease is desired, stipulate how and when title will pass (i.e., after 24 payments, after 60 months, etc.).

The second test is equally easy to control. If an operating lease is desired, avoid the inclusion of a bargain purchase option (BPO) in the lease agreement. If the parties to the lease desire a capital lease, a BPO provision automatically qualifies the lease as a purchase.

The third test is quite easy to control once one term is mastered—*economic life.* As used in the leasing industry, and in contrast to accounting and tax usage, life of an asset in its ''economic'' sense is defined as the expected useful life. Fully deciphered, FASB and the leasing industry define *economic life* as the length of time the asset has usefulness to multiple, subsequent users, not just the present user. Thus, economic life assumes a measure much longer than book life and considerably longer than tax life—a long, long life. Thus, cars usually are given an economic life of 10 to 15 years, mainframe computers 12 to 15 years, and ordinary desks and chairs a life of 15 to 20 years. The budget analyst who is trying to convert a lease into a capital variety is probably wise not to try to qualify it with this third test. Lease lives are virtually always much less than 75% of the economic life. This third test will normally result in a rental situation.

Understanding and manipulating (not meant in its derogatory connotation) the budgetary journey of a lease from operating to capital usually involves a very mundane control of the fourth test—the present value (PV) of cash flows. This can easily be the point of departure at which the budget novice errs, concluding that a lease is operating when in fact it should be capital and vice versa. In short, the forecasted balance sheet and income statement are in danger of being misbudgeted and malforecasted.

To shorten the fourth test, we observe the technical language of FASB 13.

$$(\text{PV})(\text{MLPs}) \geq (90\%)(\text{FMV})$$

If the present value of the minimum lease payments (MLPs) is greater than or equal to 90% of the fair market value (FMV), a capital lease exists. Of course, the result is an operating lease if the 90% line of demarcation is not reached now to understand the implications of the formula.

(iii) Present Value—How? FASB 13 dictates the alternative discounting rates to be utilized by the lessor and lessee.

Discount Rate to Be Utilized by Lessor	Lower of Discount Rate to Be Utilized by Lessee
The lessor must present-value the cash flows using the implicit rate in the lease.	The lessee must use the lower of: 1. The lessor's implicit rate in the lease, if known by the lessee. or 2. The incremental borrowing rate of the lessee.

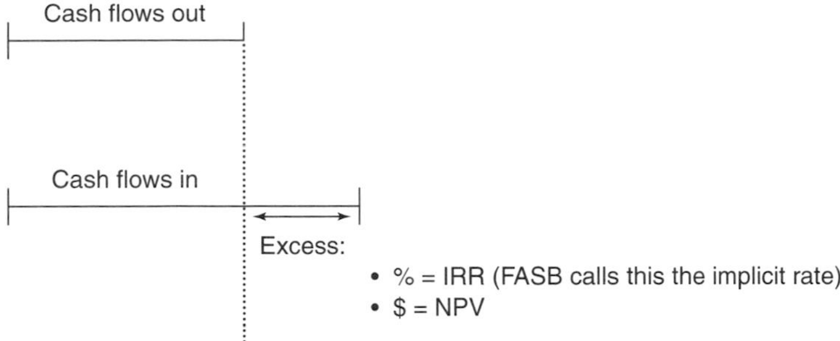

Exhibit 21.9. In–out cash flow in a leasing transaction

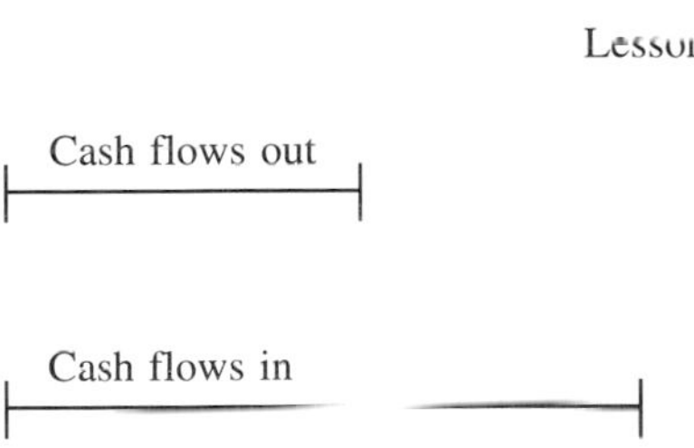

Exhibit 21.10. In–out cash flow in a leasing transaction.

Let us examine why FASB directed that the implicit rate is the only acceptable rate for the lessor. In order to establish its logic, let us pictorially examine the cash flows of the lessor in a leasing transaction (see Exhibits 21.9 and 21.10).

Possible cash flows out for the lessor include the following:

1. Equipment cost (broadly defined as historical cost of the equipment plus freight-in, installation, debugging, etc.)
2. Initial direct costs (referred to in FASB 13 and FASB 91 as IDCs)
   - **A.** Commissions paid by lessor to sales representative to obtain lease
   - **B.** Lawyers' fees paid by lessor to structure document
   - **C.** Credit investigation fees paid by lessor to ascertain creditworthiness of lessee
   - **D.** Other costs

Possible cash flows in for the lessor include the following:

1. Initial (at inception date of lease)
   - **A.** Advance payments
   - **B.** Refundable fees
   - **C.** Nonrefundable fees
2. Periodic (typically occur monthly in U.S. lease transactions but frequently quarterly or semiannually in European deals)

3. Terminal (at the end of the lease term)
   A. Fees (nonrefundable fees, pick-up fees, refurbishing fees, etc.)
   B. Sale (could either be to the lessee or to a third party)
   C. Re-lease (could either be to the lessee or to a third party)
   D. Lessee-guaranteed residual value (which automatically makes the lease a capital lease, as all risk has effectively been removed for the lessor)
   E. Third-party residual insurance (the lessor could buy an insurance policy at lease inception date providing for a stipulated terminal value).

Now let us quickly cast our gaze again at the top of Exhibit 21.10, keeping in mind that we are examining it from the viewpoint of the lessor. It becomes clear that the lessor knows with precision each and every cash flow assumption (interpret this to mean budget or forecast) in the exhibit. Thus, the lessor can indeed calculate the implicit rate in the lease because the lessor knows all the data.

Next, let us remove our lessor hat and replace it with that of the lessee—think like a lessee. Look again at Exhibit 21.10. The lessee rarely knows the equipment cost, never knows the commissions paid, the lawyers' fees, the credit investigation charges, and so on. In other words, the lessee does not know all cash flows out. Likewise, the lessee does not know all cash flows in. Some budgeted (estimated) flows in are known, such as the initial and the periodic flows, but the lessee would only know the terminal budgeted flows if the lessee holds a purchase or renewal option. In conclusion, the lessee would virtually never know all cash flows forecasted in a lease transaction. Thus, lessee could not possibly calculate the implicit rate inherent in the lease. The only other way for the lessee to know (notice FASB 13 did not use the words, ''estimate the implicit rate''—it says ''know it'') the implicit rate would be to ask the lessor for it. Because the implicit rate is also the profitability rate inherent in the lease transaction, no lessor would or could divulge such detail to an outside party. In other words, the lessee normally cannot know the implicit rate. This brings us to the alternative discount rate posited by FASB for use by the lessee—the incremental, pretax, installment, secured, co-terminus borrowing rate—what rate would the lessee have to pay to borrow a like sum for a like period for a like transaction? A strong lessee might, therefore, select prime, whereas a weaker lessee would add several percentage points to the rate.

Lessor and lessee will each present value the budgeted cash flows, but each will use a different rate. If each uses a different rate, one set of cash flows could be above the magic 90% and the other below. Conclusion: It is possible, and indeed desirable, that the sophisticated lessor and lessee may structure the budgeted lease so that each gets the desired result, which could be:

- Single-dip lease—on one set of books only
- Double-dip lease—on both sets of books
- Skinny dip lease—on neither set of books

Enough of rates. Let's move on to MLPs, the second element in the formula of test number four.

(d) Minimum Lease Payments. Financial Account Standard Board rule 13 directs lessors and lessees to present-value the MLPs. Minimum lease payments are not all but just some of the cash flows in the lease—the flows that can be predicted or budgeted with certainty.

Lessor	Lessee
1. Periodic payment in lease (usually monthly payment)	1. Periodic payment in lease (usually monthly payment)
2. Guaranteed residual payment	2. Lessee-guaranteed residual payments
3. Nonrenewal penalties	3. Nonrenewal penalties
4. BUT	4. Fees
Fees, per FASB 91, are to be capitalized by lessor and amortized over the lease life, thus impacting future budget periods	
5. Bargain purchase option	5. Bargain purchase option
6. *But not* executory costs	6. *But not* executory costs
7. Third-party residual insurance on the terminal value of the equipment	

Let's take a brief detour to discuss executory costs, after which we'll return to MLPs. Executory costs are defined in FASB 13 and 91 as cash flows out—operating costs paid by the lessee once a lease is in place. A logical way to picture these appears in Exhibit 21.11; Exhibit 21.12 illustrates how lessee executory costs are calculated.

Now assume:

$$(PV)(\$500) = 92\% \text{ of FV} = \text{Capital lease}$$

Lessee may not desire a budgeted capital transaction, so the two parties negotiate a bundled lease resulting in the $800 monthly budgeted payment being allocated as shown in Exhibit 21.13.

Thus, the (PV)($450) < 90% FMV and the lessee gets an operating lease. Real-world evidence of this exists in the normal lease proposals of Xerox, IBM, and many other companies, wherein they push bundling. They want to provide a machine plus supplies, maintenance, insurance, training, and any other products and/or services.

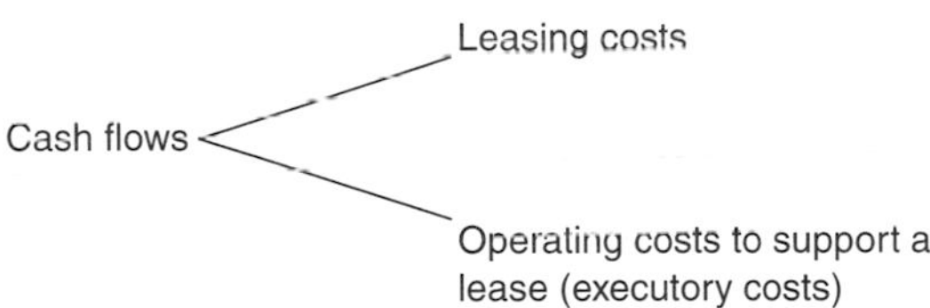

Exhibit 21.11. Executory costs

Net Lease	Full-Service Lease or Bundled Lease
The lease pays only a: 1. Low net monthly payment (assume $500) PLUS 2. Executory (operating) costs (assume $300 per month)	The lessee pays a higher monthly payment to lessor who, in turn, pays the executory costs. New monthly payment would be approximately $500 + $300 = $800.

Exhibit 21.12. Lessee executory costs

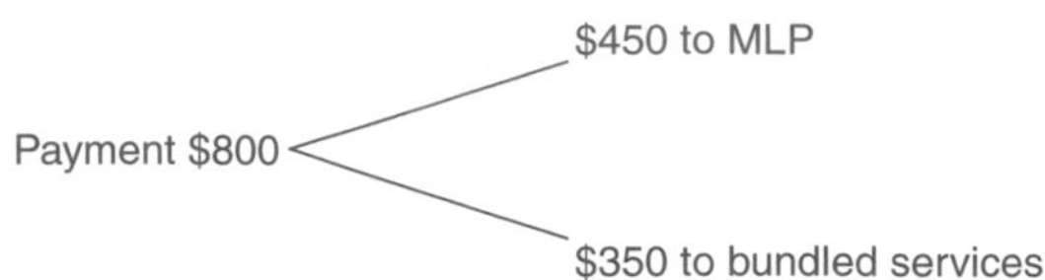

Exhibit 21.13. Bundles lease

If the lessee desires a budgeted capital lease, the agreement can bundle more cash flow into the monthly payment. If, however, the capital budget is all used up, bundle a lease so that less of the cash flow is attributed to the monthly payment and an operating lease is created.

Now, let's return from our detour to the MLP discussion. Notice that FASB directed that executory costs not be included in the MLP to be present-valued. Also, notice that the minimum lease payments listed under lessor and lessee are *not* the same.

The result? If different budgeted cash flows are present-valued, it is possible to:

- Single-dip a lease
- Double-dip a lease
- Skinny-dip a lease

(e) Ninety Percent Rule. In all countries of the world that follow the rules of substance (not form countries), there is general agreement on the 90% rule. However, the lessee and lessor each must measure according to ''known'' information. Thus, the lessor and lessee end up with different comparison bases (90% of the fair market value).

Lessor	Lessee
90% of ''the'' FMV	90% of ''an'' FMV

Because the exact cost of the equipment is known to the lessor, the lessor can indeed make this calculation. The lessee, however, normally will not ''know with precision'' the FMV. Thus, an estimate must suffice. Conceptually, this means that the lessee will rely on one of the following for the FMV:

- Written bid
- Telephone quotation
- Newspaper advertisement
- Price list—wholesale
- Price list—retail
- Estimated cost
- Other

Conclusion: Rarely would the lessor and the lessee take 90% of the same cost.

(f) Retrospect. Once again, let us examine the fourth test of substance.

$$(PV)(MLPs) \geq 90\% \text{ of the FMV}$$

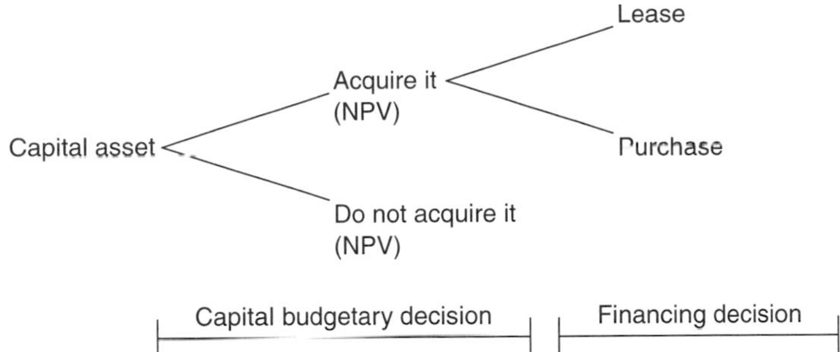

Exhibit 21.14. Lease-versus-purchase analysis

As we have seen, lessor and lessee will utilize different variables for three of the four test components. It is not only possible but probable that each can control the variables to obtain the desired type of lease and thereby shift impact from the operating budget to the capital budget or vice versa.

21.7 LEASE-VERSUS-PURCHASE ANALYSIS. Lease-versus-purchase analysis begins with the assumption that the investment analysis (capital budgeting) decision has been made in favor of acquiring a piece of equipment. The next step requires a financing decision—lease versus-purchase analysis. Exhibit 21.14 illustrates the analysis between lease-versus-purchase lease arrangements.

Mega Corporation recently decided to obtain a computer with a retail value of $400,000. The company can either obtain a loan and purchase the computer, or it can be leased. Mega Corporation is in the 40% tax bracket.

(a) Relevant Inforrnation for Purchase Alternative. A bank loan must be obtained for the purchase price of $400,000 less a down payment of $100,000. The balance ($300,000) is to be financed over 36 months with monthly payments in arrears of $9,680, an implicit borrowing rate of about 10%. Sales tax is 6% and will be paid at the time of purchase. The bank requires a loan origination fee of 2% of the loan proceeds. Each monthly payment is composed of both principal and interest, the latter being tax deductible as follows:

Year 1	$25,939
Year 2	$16,492
Year 3	$ 6,055

Depreciation expense on the computer will be straight line for book purposes and Modified Accelerated Cost Recovery System (MACRS) with a five-year life for tax. The sales tax of $24,000 will be capitalized as part of the computer's depreciable base.

(b) Depreciation Calculation

Weighted average aftertax cost of capital of 12%.

Equipment cost	$400,000
Sales tax	24,000
Depreciable basis	$424,000

Year 1	$84,800	(20%)(424,000)
Year 2	135,680	(32%)(424,000)
Year 3	81,408	(19.2%)(424,000)
Year 4	48,760	(11.5%)(424,000)
Year 5	48,760	(11.5%)(424,000)
Year 6	24,592	(5.8%)(424,000)
	$424,000	

Operating costs (executory cost):

- Repairs and maintenance = $1,000 per month for 72 months
- Insurance = $400 per month for 72 months
- Supplies = $700 per month for 72 months

Preset Value Factors

Type of Flow	Rate	N	Factor
PV annuity	.83%	36 months	31.0093
PV annuity	1%	72 months	51.1504
PV annuity	1%	70 months	50.1685
PV annuity	.83%	72 months	54.0375
PV of 1	12%	3 years	0.7118
PV of 1	12%	2 years	0.7972
PV of 1	12%	1 year	0.8929
PV of 1	12%	4 years	0.6355
PV of 1	12%	5 years	0.5674
PV of 1	12%	6 years	0.5066

HP 12 C keystrokes for loan amortization:
300,000 CHS PV

g end
9,680 PMT
10 g 12 ÷
0 n

12 f amort	25,939	
X ≷ Y	90,221	
RCL PV	209,779	
12 f amort	16,492	
X ≷ Y	99,668	
RCL PV	110,111	
12 f amort	6,055	
X ≷ Y	110,105	
RCL PV	7	(Rounding error)

(c) Leasing Information. The lease would be for six years with monthly payments of $8,250 in advance. The first and last two payments are due at the lease inception date. A lease origination fee of $4,000 must be paid in advance. The lease contains an FMV purchase option, but Mega Corporation does not plan on exercising the option.

Operating costs (executory costs) are as follows:

- Use tax of 6% on each monthly payment = $495
- Insurance = $425 per month
- Repairs and maintenance = $1,000 per month
- Supplies = $600 per month

Present Value of Purchase Alternative

	Cash Flow	x PV Factor	x Tax Factor	= Amount
Initial flows:				
Down payment	$100,000	1	N/A	$100,000
Sales tax	24,000	1	N/A	24,000
	6,000	1	1-0.4	3,600
Periodic flows:	9,680	31.0	N/A	300,080
Terminal flows:				
Repairs and maintenance	1,000	54.04	1-0.4	32,424
Insurance	400	54.04	1-0.4	12,970
Supplies	700	54.04	1-0.4	22,697
Tax shielded by:				
Interest expense				(16,247)
Depreciation expense				(125,176)
Net present value of aftertax cash flows to purchase				$354,348

Present Value of Leasing Alternative

	Cash Flow	x PV Factor	x Tax Factor	= Amount
Initial flows:				
Advance payments (2)	$16,500	1	1-0.4	$9,900
	4,000	1	1-0.4	2,400
Periodic flows:				
Monthly payments (70)	8,250	50.17	1-0.4	248,342
Terminal flows:				
Use tax in advance (2)	990	1	1-0.4	594
Use tax	495	50.17	1-0.4	14,900
Insurance	425	50.17	1-0.4	12,793
Repairs and maintenance	1,000	50.17	1-0.4	30,102
Supplies	600	50.17	1-0.4	18,061
Net present value of aftertax cash flows to lease				$310,001

Calculation of Tax Shielded by Interest Expense

Year	Interest Expense	PV Factor	Tax Factor	Income Tax Shielded
1	$25,939	0.8929	0.4	$9,264
2	16,492	0.7972	0.4	5,259
3	6,055	0.7118	0.4	1,724
	$48,486			$16,247

Calculation of Tax Shielded by Depreciation Expense

Year	Interest Expense	PV Factor	Tax Factor	Income Tax Shielded
1	$84,800	0.8929	0.4	$30,287
2	135,680	0.7972	0.4	43,266
3	81,408	0.7118	0.4	23,178
4	48,760	0.6355	0.4	12,395
5	48,760	0.5674	0.4	11,067
6	24,592	0.5066	0.4	4,983
	$424,000			$125,176

21.8 FINANCIAL ACCOUNTING STANDARDS BOARD RULE 13 CASE ILLUSTRATION

Lease provisions

- Lease term: 60 months
- List price of equipment: $140,000
- Discount to lessor from vendor: $14,000
- First and last two payments due at inception date
- Nonrenewal penalty: $1,500
- Estimated residual value: $19,000
- Monthly payment, net of executory costs: $2,600

(a) Lessor Solution

Step 1: Calculation of Implicit Rate

Keystrokes	Display	Explanation
f REG	0.00	Clears all registers
118,200 CHS g CFo	118,200	Enters initial cash flow
2,600 g CFj	2,600	Enters first cash flow
57 g Nj	57.00	Enters number of times first flow occurs
0 g CFj	0.00	Enters second cash flow
2 g Nj	2.00	Enters number of times second flow occurs
20,500 g CFj	20,500	Enters third cash flow
f IRR	1.16	Answer (the calculated monthly yield)
12X	13.94	IRR (the implicit rate)

Step 2: PV of MLPs

Keystrokes	Display	Explanation
f REG	0.00	Clears all registers
1.16 i	1.16	Enters monthly discount rate
7,800 g CFo	7,800.00	Enters initial cash flow
2,600 g CFj	2,600.00	Enters first cash flow
57 g Nj	57.00	Enters number of times first flow occurs
0 g CFj	0.00	Enters second cash flow
2 g Nj	2.00	Enters number of times second flow occurs
1,500 g CFj	1,500.00	Enters third cash flow
f NPV	116,540.57	Answer (the calculated net present value)

Step 3: Calculation of a Comparison Base

$126,000
x 0.9
$113,400

Conclusion: Capital lease, because the PV of the MLPs is more than 90% of the FMV.

(b) Lessee Solution

Step 1: PV of MLPs

Keystrokes	Display	Explanation
f REG	0.00	Clears all registers
10 g 12 ÷	0.83	Enters monthly discount rate
7,800 g CFo	7,800	Enters initial cash flow
2,600 g CFj	2,600	Enters first cash flow
57 g Nj	57.00	Enters number of times first flow occurs
0 g CFj	0.00	Enters second cash flow
2 g Nj	2.00	Enters number of times second flow occurs
1,500 g CFj	1,500	Enters third cash flow
f NPV	126,301.28	Answer (the calculated present value)

Step 2: Calculation of a Comparison Base

$140,000
x 0.9
$126,000

Conclusion: Capital lease, because the PV of the MLPs is more than 90% of the FMV.

(c) Conclusion. For the lessor, the lease would be classified as a capital lease because (PV)(MLP) $\geq$ (90%)(FMV). But for the lessee, the lease could be either operating or capital, depending on the choice of the PV rate. If the lease is being analyzed near the end of the year and if the lessee has extra cash available in the operating budget, an operating lease could be structured, keeping the deal off the books. If, however, the lessee has cash left in the capital budget, a direct finance lease could be structured, thereby putting the equipment on the books.

It becomes imperative that budget experts, both operating and capital, understand the principles dictated by FASB 13 in order to optimize plans and results.

21.9 NEGOTIATION OF LEASES. How do you negotiate a lease? Many factors must be considered, including, but not limited to:

- Number of periodic payments
- Number of advance payments
- Stub payments (partial initial payments)
- Nonrenewal penalties
- Lease origination fees
- Contingent payments
- Excess usage or "beat up" fees
- Deposits
- Step up, step down, skip payment provisions
- COLA or other escalation provisions
- Tax indemnifications
- Equipment subleasing rights
- Usage restrictions
- Late payment penalties
- Leasehold improvement ownership rights
- Lease assignment rights
- Lessor subrogation rights
- Executory cost provisions (insurance, supplies, repairs, taxes, etc.)
- Warranties on equipment by vendor and/or lessor
- Rollovers, upgrades, early outs, swaps
- Renewal options
- Purchase options
- Residual value insurance
- Equipment inspection provisions
- Equipment maintenance provisions

21.10 SELECTING A LESSOR. Lessor selection demands that the lessee consider the following:

- Financial condition of leasing company
- Flexibility
- Services offered
- Rate commitment
- Turnaround time
- Prior experience with similar equipment
- Geographic presence
- Financing sources
- Ultimate disposition of lease paper

21.11 LEASE-ANALYSIS TECHNIQUES. There are many types of returns which may be calculated for any lease transaction. These measures of performance are usually stated in some form of return on investment. Typical returns would be stated as the internal rate of return for a particular transaction or the ''return'' on a portfolio. The return on a portfolio would be some type of weighted-average calculation. However, all quoted returns are based on cash flows, or, in other words, when cash changes hands. The following are some of the different titles for types of returns:

- Internal Rate of Return
- External Rate of Return
- Modified Rate of Return
- Street Rate or Stream Rate
- Return on Assets
- Return on Equity
- Average Return on Assets
- Yield

Because so many different names may be used, it would be easier to take a particular transaction and view the different types of return calculations from the lessee and lessor perspectives. For this example, the following 11 assumptions will be utilized in developing different yield calculations:

1. Lease term: Four years with the first rental payment due at the end of the first year of the lease. For tax purposes, the lease is considered a true or guideline lease; that is, the lessor will be entitled to the tax benefits of tax depreciation, and the lessee will be entitled to expense the full amount of the payments made to the lessor.
2. At the conclusion of the lease term, the lessee will have the option of purchasing the equipment for its then FMV, renewing the lease for the equipment at its then FMV, or returning the equipment to the lessor and having no further involvement with the particular piece of equipment.
3. The lessor is a calendar year taxpayer in the 35% tax bracket.
4. The annual rental shall be $60,000, and the inception date of the lease transaction is December 31.
5. The purchase price or FMV of the equipment is $200,000.
6. The expected FMV of the equipment at the end of the lease term is $30,000, as estimated by the lessor at the inception of the lease arrangement.
7. The lessor will require a $5,000 refundable security deposit from the lessee. This amount will be held by the lessor throughout the term of the lease and returned to the lessee at the end of the lease term if there is no reason to use it for default reasons. The lessor will not pay the lessee any monies for the use of these funds.
8. A $1,000 nonrefundable commitment fee is to be received by the lessor from the lessee.
9. A $2,500 brokerage fee is to be paid by the lessor to a third party as compensation for its bringing this transaction to the lessor.

10. General and administrative costs have been allocated to the lease along with the initial direct costs of $4,000. First-year general and administrative costs are $3,000 and have a 5% inflation factor built in.
11. Tax benefits are assumed to result fully in tax savings.

The ''interest'' cost to the lessee is the first type of yield calculation to be performed. The lessee ''cost'' is calculated because a lease transaction does not contain a stated interest rate or cost of money, as a lease is a usage transaction and not a money-financing transaction. The lessor is providing the use of equipment and not the lending of money to the lessee to be used for whatever purpose it desires.

From the lessee's perspective, it is gaining the use of $200,000 of equipment for four years and at the end of four years it has a number of options which may be exercised at its discretion. If the lessee returns the equipment to the lessor at the end of the initial lease term, then it would have the use of $200,000 for four years at a cost of $60,000, payments in arrears for the four-year period. The ''interest'' cost of money would be 7.71 percent. If the lessee were to purchase the equipment at the end of the four-year term for the lessor's estimated FMV of $30,000, the ''interest'' cost of money would be 12.29%. If the lessee were to renew the equipment lease at the end of the four-year term, it would not be possible to calculate an ''interest'' cost of money to the lessor, because the terms of the renewal are not yet known, even if the renewal amount of $30,000 were to be known.

Both the 7.71% and 12.29% calculations are pretax. From the perspective of the lessee, any aftertax calculations would be based on a number of assumptions and are really not relevant to an understanding of this transaction.

The remainder of the calculations in this chapter are from the lessor perspective and are done from both a pretax and aftertax perspective. The calculations are numerous and it can readily be seen why confusion often reigns when trying to compare yields in lease transactions. One must understand what elements of cash flow are included when arriving at a particular stated yield and whether the calculation is pretax or aftertax. To fully understand aftertax calculations, one must also understand the leverage or gearing of the lessor and whether the transactions have been funded on a pooled or match-funded basis, the pretax cost of debt to the lessor and whether the rate is fixed throughout the transaction or is adjusted at times throughout the lease term in accordance with some borrowing agreement in place for the lessor. The corporate tax rate and the timing of when taxes are remitted enter into a fine tuning of any calculation, and the desired return on equity contributed funds plays perhaps the most important role of all these variables.

Pretax lessor calculations would be as follows:

1. *Stream or street rate.* This calculation takes into account only the cost of the equipment to the lessor and any noncancelable payment amounts. Because the residual amount is anticipated but not absolutely known (unknown to the lessee), it would be the same as making a $200,000 investment and receiving $60,000 per year in arrears for the use of this invested amount. This would be a return of 7.71% and compares with the same amount as calculated by the lessee previously.
2. *Stream rate including residual.* This calculation includes the expected, but unguaranteed, residual amount of $30,000. When the residual is included in the calculation, then the lessor yield would be 12.29% and would be equivalent to the similar calculation of the lessee as performed previously.

3. *Pretax payback.* Both the stream rate and stream rate with residual calculations would indicate a payback period of 3.33 years. This does not take into account any adjustment for the time value of money. A time-adjusted payback period could be calculated if one were to assume some hurdle rate or cost of funds to the lessor. For purposes of this chapter, this calculation is not performed, but could be readily accomplished if some hurdle rate were to be brought into focus.
4. *An all-inclusive pretax ROA yield.* This amount would include all of the pretax cash flows and would be based on when the cash is expected to change hands. This would take into account all known and expected cash flows to be received by the lessor, but does not take into account the tax benefits to be received and utilized by the lessor. In our example, the cash flows would occur as follows:

Initial or inception:

($200,000)	Equipment cost
(2,500)	Brokerage fee
(4,000)	Initial direct costs
1,000	Nonrefundable fee
5,000	Refundable security deposit
($200,500)	Net outflow at inception

During the term of the transaction:

Three payments of $60,000 per year

At termination:

$60,000	Final payment amount
30,000	Purchase option amount
(5,000)	Security deposit refund
$85,000	Net termination inflow

When taking into account all of these cash flows and the timing of when they would occur, the yield to the lessor is 11.47%. This is close to the 12.29% amount previously calculated, but includes all cash flows. As must be noted, this is a lower value than the stream rate including the residual.

5. *Net pretax yield.* This calculation takes into account all of the cash flows as shown in item 4 with the addition of the general and administrative costs. The following illustration shows the timing of the cash flows and results in a pretax yield to the lessor of 9.25%. The 9.25% value is calculated by determining the internal rate of return for the cash flow amounts for each year of the transaction.

	0	1	2	3	4
Rental payments	0	60,000	60,000	60,000	60,000
Commitment fee	1,000				
Initial direct costs	(4,000)	0	0	0	0
Brokerage fee	(2,500)				
General and administrative (G&A)	0	(3,000)	(3,150)	(3,308)	(3,473)
Residual	0	0	0	0	30,000
Security deposit	(5,000)	0	0	0	(5,000)
Deduct: cost of equipment	(200,000)	0	0	0	0
TOTAL	(200,500)	57,000	56,850	56,692	81,527

fIRR = 9.25

6. *Net aftertax yield.* This calculation takes into account the cash flows included in the previous calculations and then includes the impact of recovering the lessor's investment through tax depreciation. It is seen that this net aftertax yield is 7.00%. Some analysts will arrive at the aftertax yield by multiplying the pretax yield of 9.25% by the reciprocal of the tax rate, or 65%. If this were done (9.25 times 0.65), the resultant yield would be 6.01%. As can be seen when calculating the internal rate of return for the final cash flows, the yield is 7.00%. The difference is due to the timing of the cash flows, which is not taken into account when performing the 6.01% calculation.

	0	1	2	3	4
Rental payments	0	60,000	60,000	60,000	60,000
Commitment fee	1,000	0	0	0	0
Initial direct costs	(4,000)	0	0	0	0
Brokerage fee	(2,500)	0	0	0	0
G&A	0	(3,000)	(3,150)	(3,308)	(3,473)
Depreciation	(40,000)	(64,000)	(38,400)	(23,040)	(34,560)
Residual	0	0	0	0	30,000
Pretax income	(45,500)	(7,000)	18,450	33,652	51,967
Taxes @ 35%	15,925	2,450	(6,458)	(11,778)	(18,188)
A-T income	(29,575)	(4,550)	11,993	21,874	33,779
Add: depreciation	40,000	64,000	38,400	23,040	34,560
Security deposit	5,000	0	0	0	0
Deduct: cost of equipment	(200,000)	0	0	0	0
TOTAL	(184,575)	59,450	50,393	44,914	63,339

7. *Return on equity (ROE).* This final calculation is found by making assumptions as to the method of funding employed by the lessor, which, in this example, assumes that the lessor wishes the lease. Also, the leverage employed by the lessor is 80% debt and 20% equity. The pretax interest cost on borrowed funds is 9% and the tax rate of the lessor throughout the life of the transaction will be 35%. The ROE for the lessor based on the cash flows calculated in 6 and adjusted for the cost of debt and including the repayment of borrowed funds is 11.60%. This amount is found by deducting the aftertax cost of debt from the aftertax cost of capital as calculated in 6.00 or 7.00%. The aftertax cost of debt to the lessor is found by multiplying the pretax cost of debt times the quantity (one minus the tax rate or 0.65) times the 0.8 debt leverage factor. This is found to be 4.68%.

When this amount is deducted from aftertax cost of capital of 7.00%, the cost of equity is determined to be 2.32%. When this is divided by the 0.2 equity leverage factor, the ROE to the lessor is determined as 11.60%.

Net Aftertax Cash Flows				
0	1	2	3	4
(184,575)	59,450	50,393	44,914	63,339

80% Debt = 147,660
20% Equity = 36,915

Year One

147,660 × 0.09 = 13,289 × 0.65 =	8,638 A-T Return on Debt
36,915 × 11.60 =	4,282 A-T Return on Equity
	12,920
.8 × 9(.65) = 4.68	(59,450) CF
.2 × 11.60 = 2.32	46,530
7.00	× .8
	37,224 Debt
	9,306 Equity

Year Two

147,660 − 37,224 = 110,436 × 0.09 = 9.939 × 0.65 =	6,461 A-T Return on Debt
36,915 − 9,306 = 27,609 × 0.1160 =	3,203 A-T Return on Equity
	9,664
	(50,393) CF
	40,729
	× .8
	32,583 Debt
	8,146 Equity

Year Three

110,436 − 32,583 = 77,853 × 0.09 = 7,007 × 0.65 =	4,554 A-T ROD
27,609 − 8,246 = 19,463 × 0.1160 =	2,258 A-T ROE
	6,812
	(44,914) CF
	38,102
	× .8
	30,482 Debt
	7,620 Equity

Year Four

77,853 − 30,482 = 47,371 × 0.09 = 4,263 × 0.65 =	2,771 ROD
[x]	
19,463 − 7,620 = 11,843 × 0.1160 =	1,374 ROE
[y]	4,145
	(63,339) CF
	59,194
	× .8
[x] 16 △ due to rounding.	[x] 47,355 Debt
[y] 4 △ due to rounding.	[y] 11,839 Equity

21.12 LEASE FORM

AGREEMENT NO.________

EQUIPMENT LEASE

LESSOR: ______________________	LESSEE: ______________________
______________________	______________________
(STREET ADDRESS)	(STREET ADDRESS)
______________________	______________________
(CITY, STATE, AND ZIP)	(CITY, STATE, AND ZIP)

Description of Leased Equipment

NEW/USED	QUANTITY	MAKE and DESCRIPTION	SERIAL NO.

EQUIPMENT LOCATION: ☐ SAME AS ABOVE ☐ OTHER: (address)________

LEASE PAYMENT TERMS

<u>MONTHS</u>	<u>AMOUNTS</u>
TOTAL LEASE TERM # ____MONTHS	MONTHLY RENTAL AMOUNT: _____ PLUS USE TAX, IF ANY
ADVANCE RENTALS PAID # ______ MONTHS	TOTAL RENTALS PAID IN ADVANCE: ____________ RENTAL × # PAID

<u>TERMS AND CONDITIONS OF LEASE</u>

LESSEE HEREBY WARRANTS AND REPRESENTS THAT THE EQUIPMENT WILL BE USED FOR BUSINESS PURPOSES, AND NOT FOR PERSONAL, FAMILY, HOUSEHOLD, OR AGRICULTURAL PURPOSES. LESSEE ACKNOWLEDGES THAT LESSOR AND ITS ASSIGNS HAVE RELIED UPON THIS REPRESENTATION IN ENTERING INTO THIS LEASE.

1. LESSEE ACKNOWLEDGES THAT LESSOR IS NOT THE MANUFACTURER OF THE EQUIPMENT, NOR MANUFACTURER'S AGENT AND LESSEE REPRESENTS THAT LESSEE HAS SELECTED THE EQUIPMENT LEASED HEREUNDER BASED UPON LESSEE'S JUDGMENT

THE UNDERSIGNED AGREE TO ALL THE TERMS AND CONDITIONS SET FORTH ABOVE AND ON THE REVERSE SIDE HEREOF, AND IN WITNESS WHEREOF, HEREBY EXECUTES THIS LEASE AND CERTIFIES THAT THE UNDERSIGNED IS DULY AUTHORIZED TO EXECUTE SAME, ON BEHALF OF OR AS THE LESSEE AND THAT HE HAS RECEIVED AN EXECUTED COPY OF THIS LEASE.

(Continued on next pages.)

Executed this _____ day of ________________, 19__.

LESSOR: ____________________ LESSEE: ____________________

BY: ____________________ BY: ____________________
TITLE

TITLE: ____________________ BY: ____________________
TITLE

PRIOR TO HAVING REQUESTED THE LEASE. THE EQUIPMENT LEASED HEREUNDER IS OF A DESIGN, SIZE, FITNESS, AND CAPACITY SELECTED BY LESSEE AND LESSEE IS SATISFIED THAT THE SAME IS SUITABLE AND FIT FOR ITS INTENDED PURPOSES. LESSEE FURTHER AGREES THAT <u>LESSOR HAS MADE AND MAKES NO REPRESENTATIONS OR WARRANTIES OF WHATSOEVER NATURE, DIRECTLY OR INDIRECTLY, EXPRESSED OR IMPLIED, INCLUDING BUT NOT LIMITED TO ANY REPRESENTATIONS OR WARRANTIES WITH RESPECT TO SUITABILITY, DURABILITY, FITNESS FOR USE AND MECHANTABILITY OF ANY SUCH EQUIPMENT, THE PURPOSES AND USES OF THE LESSEE, OR OTHERWISE.</u> LESSEE SPECIFICALLY WAIVES ALL RIGHTS TO MAKE CLAIM AGAINST LESSOR HEREIN FOR BREACH OF ANY WARRANTY OF ANY KIND WHATSOEVER. LESSOR HEREBY PASSES TO LESSEE ALL WARRANTIES, IF ANY, RECEIVED BY LESSOR BY VIRTUE OF ITS OWNERSHIP OF THE EQUIPMENT. LESSOR SHALL NOT BE LIABLE TO LESSEE FOR ANY LOSS, DAMAGE, OR EXPENSE OF ANY KIND OR NATURE CAUSED DIRECTLY OR INDIRECTLY BY ANY EQUIPMENT LEASED HEREUNDER FOR THE USE OF MAINTENANCE THEREOF, OR FOR THE FAILURE OF OPERATIONS THEREOF, OR BY ANY INTERRUPTION OF SERVICE OR LOSS OF USE THEREOF OR FOR ANY LOSS OF BUSINESS OR ANY OTHER DAMAGE WHATSOEVER AND HOWSOEVER CAUSED. NO DEFECT OR UNFITNESS OF THE EQUIPMENT SHALL RELIEVE LESSEE OF THE OBLIGATION TO PAY RENT, OR ANY OTHER OBLIGATION UNDER THIS AGREEMENT OR ITS ASSIGNEE.

1. LEASE: Lessor hereby leases to Lessee and Lessee hereby hires and takes from Lessor the personal property described above and on any attached supplemental ''schedule A'' (hereinafter, with all replacement parts, additions, repairs, and accessories incorporated therein and/or affixed thereto, referred to as ''Equipment'').

2. TERM AND RENT: This Lease is non-cancelable for the term stated above and shall commence upon the Date of Acceptance of the equipment and shall continue for the period specified as the ''term'' stated above. If one or more advance rentals are payable, the total amount of such advance rentals shall be set forth in the Advance Rental Payment(s) section above and shall be due upon acceptance by the Lessor of this lease. Advance rentals, when received by Lessor, shall be applied to the first rent payment for the Equipment and the balance of the advance rental shall be applied to the final rental payment or payments for said Equipment. In no event shall any advance rent or any other rent payments be refunded to Lessee.

3. Equipment is and shall at all times remain, the property of Lessor, and Lessee shall have no right, title, or interest therein, except as herein set forth, and no right to purchase or otherwise acquire title to or ownership of any of the equipment. If Lessor supplies Lessee with labels indicating that the equipment is owned by Lessor, Lessee shall affix such labels to and keep them in a prominent place on the equipment. Lessee hereby authorizes Lessor to insert in this lease the serial numbers and other identification data of equipment when determined by Lessor. Lessor is hereby appointed by Lessee as its true and lawful attorney in respect to being hereby authorized by Lessee, at Lessee's expense, to cause this lease, or any statement or other instrument in respect of this lease showing the interest of Lessor in the equipment, including Uniform Commercial Code Financing Statements, to be filed or recorded and refiled and re-recorded, and grants Lessor the right to execute Lessee's name thereto. Lessee agrees to execute and deliver any statement or instrument requested by Lessor for such purpose, and agrees to pay or reimburse Lessor for any searches, filings, recordings, or stamp fees or taxes arising from the filing or recording any such instrument or statement.

4. Lessee, at Lessee's own cost and expense, shall keep the equipment in good repair, condition, and working order and shall furnish all parts, mechanism, devices, and servicing required therefor and shall not materially alter the equipment without the consent of Lessor.

5. Lessee hereby assumes and shall bear the entire risk of loss for the theft, loss, damage, or destruction of the equipment, from any and every cause whatsoever. No such loss or damage shall impair any obligation of Lessee under this Agreement which shall continue in full force and effect. In the event of such loss or damage and irrespective of, but applying full credit for payment from any insurance coverage, Lessee shall, at its own cost and expense at the option of Lessor: (a) place the same in good repair, condition, and working order; or (b) replace the same with similar equipment of equal value; or (c) pay all the sums due and owing under this Agreement, computed from the date of such loss or damage, in which case this Agreement shall terminate, except for Lessee's duties under paragraph 9, as of the date such payment is received by Lessor.

6. Lessor shall have no tort liability to Lessee related to the equipment, and Lessee shall indemnify, defend, and hold Lessor harmless against any liabilities, claims, actions, and expenses, including court costs and legal expenses incurred by or asserted against Lessor in any way relating to the manufacture, purchase, ownership, delivery, lease, possession, use, operation, condition, return, or other disposition of the equipment by Lessor or Lessee or otherwise related to this lease, including any claim alleging latent or other defect under the doctrine of strict liability or otherwise; any other claim under the doctrine of strict liability; and any claim for patent, trademark, service mark, or copyright infringement. Each party shall give the other notice of any event covered hereby promptly following learning thereof.

7. Lessee shall keep the equipment insured against all risks of loss or damage from every cause whatsoever. Lessee shall maintain (a) actual cash value all risk insurance on the equipment, naming Lessor as *LOSS PAYEE* and (b) single limit public liability and property damage insurance of not less than $300,000 per occurrence,

or such greater or lesser amount as Lessor may from time to time request on notice to Lessee, naming Lessee as Named Insured and Lessor as *ADDITIONAL INSURED* and Lessee shall be liable for all deductible portions of all required insurance. All said insurance shall be in form and amount and with companies satisfactory to Lessor. All insurance for loss or damage shall provide that losses, if any, shall be payable to Lessor, and all such liability insurance shall be in the joint names of Lessor and Lessee. Lessee shall pay the premiums therefor and deliver to Lessor the policies of insurance or duplicates thereof, or other evidence satisfactory to Lessor of such insurance coverage. Each insurer shall agree, by endorsement upon the policy or policies issued by it or by independent instrument furnished to Lessor, that it will give Lessor *10 DAYS* written notice prior to the effective date of any alteration or cancellation of such policy. The proceeds of such insurance payable as a result of loss of or damage to the equipment shall be applied at the option of Lessor, as set out in paragraph 6. Lessee hereby irrevocably appoints Lessor as Lessee's attorney-in-fact to make claim for, receive payment of, and execute and endorse all documents, checks, or drafts received in payment for loss or damage under any said insurance policies. In case of the failure of Lessee to procure or maintain said insurance or to comply with any other provision of this Agreement, Lessor shall have the right but shall not be obligated, to effect such insurance or compliance on behalf of Lessee. In that event, all money spent by and expenses of Lessor shall have the right but shall not be obligated, to effect such insurance or compliance on behalf of Lessee. In that event, all money spent by and expenses of Lessor in effecting such insurance or compliance shall be deemed to be additional rent, and shall be paid by Lessee to Lessor with the next monthly payment of rent.

8. Lessee shall pay directly, or to Lessor, all license fees, registration fees, assessments, and taxes which may now or hereafter be imposed upon the ownership, sale (if authorized), possession, or use of the equipment, excepting only those based on Lessor's income, and shall keep the equipment free and clear of all levies, liens, or encumbrances arising therefrom. Lessee shall make all filings as to and pay when due all property taxes on the equipment, on behalf of Lessor, with all appropriate governmental agencies, except where Lessor is notified by the taxing jurisdiction that Lessor must pay the tax direct, and within not more than 60 days after the due date of such filing to send Lessor a confirmation of such filing. If Lessee fails to pay any said fees, assessments, or taxes, Lessor shall have the right, but not the obligation, to pay the same and such amount, including penalties and costs, which shall be repayable to Lessor with the next installment of rent and if not so paid shall be the same as failure to pay any installment of rent due hereunder. Lessor shall not be responsible for contesting any valuation of or tax imposed on the equipment, but may do so strictly as an accommodation to Lessee and shall not be liable or accountable to Lessee therefor.

9. Time is of the essence in this agreement and no waiver by Lessor of any breach or default shall constitute a waiver of any additional or subsequent breach or default by Lessor nor shall it be a waiver of any of Lessor's rights. If any rental payment shall be unpaid for more than TEN (10) DAYS after the due date thereof. Lessor shall have the right to add and collect a reasonable late charge of *five percent (5%)* or a lesser amount if established by any state or federal statute

applicable thereto, plus interest at the maximum rate permitted by law together with any other expense necessarily incurred by reason of such non-payment and Lessor may exercise any one or more of the remedies set forth in paragraph 12.

10. An event of default shall occur if: (a) Lessee fails to pay when due any installment of rent; (b) Lessee shall fail to perform or observe any covenant, condition, or agreement to be performed or observed by it hereunder; (c) Lessee ceases doing business as a going concern, makes an assignment for the benefit of creditors, admits in writing its inability to pay its debts as they become due, files a voluntary petition in bankruptcy, is adjudicated a bankrupt or an insolvent, files a petition seeking for itself any reorganization, arrangement, composition readjustment, liquidation, dissolution, or similar arrangement under any present or future statute, law, or regulation or files an answer admitting the material allegations of a petition filed against it in any such proceeding, consents to or acquiesces in the appointment of a trustee, receiver, or liquidator of it or all or any substantial part of its assets or properties, or if it or its shareholders shall take any action looking to its dissolution or liquidation; (d) within 60 days after the appointment without Lessee's consent or acquiescence of any trustee, receiver, or liquidator of it or of all or any substantial part of its assets and properties, such appointment shall not be vacated, or (e) Lessee attempts to remove, sell, transfer, encumber, part with possession, or sublet the equipment or any item thereof.

11. Upon Lessee's default, the rights and duties of the parties shall be as set forth in this paragraph: (a) Acceleration: Lessor may revoke Lessee's privilege of paying the total rent installments and, upon Lessor's demand, the portion of the total rent then remaining unpaid plus all other sums due and unpaid shall promptly be paid to Lessor. (b) Retaking: at Lessor's option, Lessor may demand and Lessee must promptly deliver the equipment to Lessor. If Lessee does not so deliver, Lessee shall make the equipment available for retaking and authorizes Lessor, its employees, and nominees to enter the premises of the Lessee and other premises (insofar as Lessee can permit) for the purpose of retaking. Lessor shall not be obligated to give notice or to obtain legal process for retaking. In the event of retaking, Lessee expressly waives all rights to possession and all claims of injuries suffered through or loss caused by retaking. (c) Disposition: Lessor may sell or release the equipment and Lessee agrees to pay any deficiency resulting from the sale or releasing of the equipment. To the extent of Lessee's liability, all proceeds of the sale or releasing, or both, less all expenses incurred in retaking the goods, all expenses incurred in the enforcement of this lease, all damages that Lessor shall have sustained by reason of Lessee's default, including those incurred by obtaining a deficiency judgment and a reasonable attorney fee, shall be credited to Lessee as and when received by Lessor. Sums in excess of Lessee's liability shall belong to Lessor. (d) Unpaid Rent: The provisions of this paragraph shall not prejudice Lessor's right to recover or prove damages for unpaid rent accrued prior to default. Lessor may seek to enforce the terms of this Agreement through any court of competent jurisdiction and Lessor may seek relief other than as specified in this Agreement to the extent such relief is not inconsistent with the terms of this Agreement. Lessee agrees to pay reasonable attorney's fees and court costs incurred by Lessor in the enforcement of the terms of this Agreement. In any instance where Lessee and Lessor have entered into more than one contract,

Lessee's default under any one contract shall be a default under all contracts and Lessor shall be entitled to enforce appropriate remedies for Lessee's default under each such contract.

12. Lessee shall not sell, assign, sublet, pledge, mortgage, or otherwise encumber or suffer a lien upon or against any interest in this agreement or the equipment or remove the equipment from the place of installation set forth herein, unless Lessee obtains the written consent of Lessor which consent shall not be unreasonably withheld. Lessee's interest herein is not assignable or transferable by operation of the law. Lessee agrees not to waive its right to use and possess the equipment in favor of any party other than Lessor and further agrees not to abandon the equipment to any party other than Lessor. Lessor may inspect the equipment during normal business hours and enter the premises where the equipment may be located for such purpose. Lessee shall comply with all laws, regulations, and orders relating to this Agreement and the use, operation, or maintenance of the equipment.

13. All rights of Lessor hereunder and to the equipment may be assigned, pledged, or otherwise disposed of, in whole or in part, without notice to Lessee, but subject to the rights of Lessee hereunder. Lessee shall acknowledge receipt of any notice of assignment in writing and shall thereafter pay any amounts designated in such notice as directed therein. If Lessor assigns this lease or any interest herein, no default by Lessor hereunder or under any other agreement between Lessor and Lessee shall excuse performance by Lessee of any provision hereof. In the event of such default by Lessor, Lessee shall pursue any rights on account thereof solely against Lessor and shall pay the full amount of the assigned rental payments to the assignee. No such assignee shall be obligated to perform any duty, covenant, or condition required to be performed by Lessor under the terms of this lease.

14. This Agreement cannot be canceled or terminated by Lessee on or after the date the equipment is delivered to and accepted by Lessee. If Lessee cancels or terminates this Agreement prior to delivery or acceptance of the equipment, Lessee shall pay to Lessor (a) the value (at cost) of all equipment ordered or purchased by Lessor prior to Lessee's termination or cancellation, (b) all of Lessor's out-of-pocket expenses, and (c) a sum equal to *1%* of the total rents for the lease term as liquidated damages, the exact sum of which would be extremely difficult to determine, to reasonably compensate Lessor for credit review, document preparation, ordering equipment, and other administrative expenses.

15. Upon expiration of the lease term, Lessee will immediately return the equipment in as good a condition as received, less normal wear, tear, and depreciation, to Lessor's branch office which is nearest to the place of installation or to such other reasonable place as is designated by Lessor. The equipment shall be carefully crated, shipped freight prepaid, and properly insured. Should Lessee not return the equipment at the end of the lease term, Lessee shall continue to pay rent to Lessor in the sum and on the due dates set out in this Agreement as a month-to-month lease term until returned by Lessee or demand therefor is made by Lessor.

16. This Lease Agreement consisting of the foregoing and the reverse side hereof, correctly sets forth the entire agreement between Lessor and Lessee. No agree-

ments or understandings shall be binding on either of the parties hereto unless set forth in writing signed by the parties. The term ''Lessee'' as used herein shall mean and include any and all Lessees who sign hereunder, each of whom shall be jointly and severally bound thereby. No representations, warranties, or promises, guarantees, or agreements, oral or written, express or implied, have been made by either party hereto with respect to this lease or the equipment other than set forth herein. No agent or employee of the supplier is authorized to bind Lessor to this or to waive or alter any terms or conditions printed herein or add any provision hereto. This Lease Agreement is binding upon the legal representatives and successors in interest of the Lessee. Lessee shall provide Lessor with such interim or annual financial statements as Lessor may reasonably request. In addition, Lessee warrants that the application, statements, and financial reports submitted by it to the Lessor are material inducements to the granting of this lease and that any material misrepresentations shall constitute a default hereunder. If any portion of this contract is deemed invalid, it shall not affect the balance of this Agreement.

DELIVERY AND ACCEPTANCE NOTICE

The undersigned Lessee hereby acknowledges receipt of the equipment described below or on any attached schedule (the ''Equipment'') fully installed and in good working condition, and Lessee hereby accepts the Equipment after full inspection thereof as satisfactory for all purposes of the above-referenced lease executed by Lessee with the Lessor. Lessee certifies that Lessor has fully and satisfactorily performed all covenants and conditions to be performed by Lessor under the Lease and has delivered the Equipment selected solely by Lessee in accordance with Lessee's directions.

LESSEE AGREES THAT THE LESSOR HAS MADE AND MAKES NO REPRESENTATIONS OR WARRANTIES OF ANY KIND OR NATURE, DIRECTLY OR INDIRECTLY, EXPRESS OR IMPLIED, AS TO ANY MATTER WHATSOEVER, INCLUDING THE SUITABILITY OF SUCH EQUIPMENT, ITS DURABILITY, ITS FITNESS FOR ANY PARTICULAR PURPOSE, ITS MERCHANTABILITY, ITS CONDITION, AND/OR ITS QUALITY, AND AS BETWEEN LESSEE AND LESSOR OR LESSOR'S ASSIGNEE, LESSEE LEASES THE EQUIPMENT ''AS IS'' AND LESSEE AFFIRMS THAT IT HAS NO DEFENSES OR COUNTECLAIMS AGAINST LESSOR IN CONNECTION WITH THE LEASE.

____

(Lessee)

Date Equipment Accepted: ____________ By: ________________________

21.13 SUMMARY. Leasing over the past several decades has become a very complicated topic, one that affects the budgetary process in a multitude of ways. The FASB has specified the treatment of leases on balance sheets, income statements, and cash flow statements. Additionally, internal analysis, such as lease versus purchase, pushes the treatment of leasing well beyond generally accepted accounting principles considerations. In today's international financial milieu, the managerial expert must cross the financial Rubicon and extend the frontiers of leasing, budgeting, and finance well into heretofore uncharted domains.

SOURCES AND SUGGESTED REFERENCES

Allison, ''New Rules Increase Exposure of Lessors to Tax on Rents that Will Not Be Received Until Later,'' *Journal of Taxation,* vol. 64, 1986, p. 8.

Amembal and Halladay, *A Guide to Accounting for Leases,* Publishers Press, 1992.

Carson, Roger L., ''Leasing, Asset Lives and Uncertainty: A Practitioner's Comments,'' *Financial Management,* Summer 1987.

Carter and Wight, ''New Tax Law Makes Major Changes to the Foreign Tax Credit Limitation,'' *Journal of Taxation,* vol. 66, 1987, p. 140.

Delessio and Shenkman, ''Improvement to Leased Property: Maximizing the Tax Benefits Regardless of Who Makes Them,'' *Taxation for Accountants,* vol. 33, 1984, p. 256.

Financial Accounting Standards Board, ''Accounting for Leases,'' *Financial Accounting Standards Board Statement No. 13,* November 1976.

Knight, Ray, and Lee G. Knight, ''True Leases Versus Disguised Installment and Sales/Purchases,'' *The Tax Adviser,* March 1987.

Naughton, ''International Leverage and Facility Leasing in the United States,'' *NYU Institute* of Federal Taxation, vol. 44, chapter 47 (1986).

Rosen, Howard, *Leasing Law in the European Community,* Euromoney Books, 1991.

Shulman and Cox, *Leasing for Profit,* AMA, 1987.

CHAPTER 22

CASH MANAGEMENT AND BUDGETING*

Donniel Schulman
George Adams
PricewaterhouseCoopers L.L.P.

22.1 INTRODUCTION. In an environment of limited economic resources, operating margins must be evaluated in light of the level of resources required to generate those returns. This is the basic principle behind asset management. Asset management applies the same ''time value of money'' concept to evaluate capital investment and the investment of liquid assets required for operations. Cash budgeting encourages a company to examine the use of all corporate assets, including accounts receivable and inventory. By budgeting disbursements and receipts, in addition to expenses and revenue, a company can make better use of financial resources, minimizing net interest expense.

For a business to be viable, sufficient resources must be available to fund the ongoing investment required by operations. A financial manager uses cash forecasting and budgeting to ensure that this is accomplished. The process is very simple. Each of the operating units projects its cash needs into the future based on current operations, adjusting for the impact of current initiatives. Marketing estimates the funds available from customers, and adds inflows from the sale of assets. Combining these estimates into a time-phased schedule indicates the excess or shortfall of and the timing of such occurrences. Management finds a way to smooth out expenditures or marketing boosts sales for a given period to bring the sources and uses into balance. To the extent that the two cannot be balanced, the financial manager must procure additional funds from reserves or outside financing. Should financing be required, the cash-flow forecast becomes a very important tool for the prospective lenders to develop a financing arrangement that will meet the company's needs.

The financial manager must determine the height and timing of surges in cash needs to ensure a source of adequate cash for these periods. It is also important to identify periods of significant surplus to plan for intermediate-term investing. The seasonality of a business normally mandates financing because not all expenses flow directly with volume. Ob-

* The authors would like to thank Jeffrey Greenberg, an Associate with PricewaterhouseCoopers, L.L.P., for conducting the research and development for this material.

viously, to the extent that expenditures can be planned in such a way as to fit the cash availability of the business, the need for outside financing will be diminished. Predicting these events is one of the most difficult aspects of cash budgeting. To meet the above needs of business, this chapter will address in detail the many facets of cash budgeting and forecasting.

22.2 PURPOSE OF CASH BUDGETING. Although the operating budget has been standardized around a 12-month period, cash budgeting applies to three distinct planning horizons. These represent the three primary applications: short-term funding of operations, annual planning for capital investment, and long-term financing of expansion. Each type of cash budgeting employs different techniques and levels of precision. The objectives of the cash budgeting processes can be summarized as the following:

- To provide funds for transactional needs on a daily basis
- To take advantage of opportunities, dictated by rising interest rates, to generate investment income from surplus cash
- To provide increased control over bank relations and reduce transaction costs through centralization
- To mitigate bank compensation
- To improve quality of control of sources of information
- To provide adequate liquidity for corporate growth, especially in times of credit restrictions

Financial managers focus on managing account balances to cover transactional needs within the firm, while maximizing interest returns. It is the cash manager's responsibility to see that receipts and available cash are at least equal to current funding requirements of ongoing transactions. More specifically, the cash manager directs funds from within the banking network collection points to disbursement interest bearing accounts. Payments from customers and funds from lines of credit must be transferred to bank accounts on which payroll and accounts payable draw. The challenge to the financial manager is to minimize transaction costs, maximize float, and consolidate bank accounts to minimize banking administration costs. Cash budgeting in this sense is focused on weekly forecasting, and then optimizing, the level of funds in various disbursement and investment accounts. Greater precision is possible because money can be made on the margins. Timing in particular is critical, because an extra day of float garners significant returns.

Obviously, the risk of poor planning for cash in the short term is that of upsetting employees and suppliers with slow payment. Credibility is difficult to regain. More important, such behavior may prompt outside suppliers to restrict credit. Therefore, mismanagement can impinge upon future attempts at working-capital maximization. The stability of customer receipts and supplier payments, and the accuracy of capital budgeting requirements will determine the ability to accurate forecast cash in the short term. Means of ensuring prompt payment from customers and stretching payment cycles with suppliers to facilitate cash management will be addressed later (see Role of the Financial Manager).

	Short	Time Horizon Intermediate	Long
Time Frame	5–90 days by week	3 to 12 months by month	1–5 years by half year
Applications	Trade Payables	Capital Purchases	Acquisitions
Sources	Customer Payments	Lines of Credit	Long-term Financing
Activity	Optimizing cash (float)	Minimize outside financing	Balance Debt to Equity
Reporting Level	Bank Account	Department/Process	Consolidated Entity
Tools	Operational Forecast	Business Model	Strategic Plan

Generation of investment income, especially in periods of rising interest rates, is an important contribution of many financial managers. This is accomplished by freeing up funds that can be invested in money markets (federal funds, repurchase agreements, and other vehicles) or by reducing the level of non–working assets required by the firm to provide goods or services. Capable cash-flow forecasting and budgeting programs support the purchase of short- and intermediate-term securities and the reduction of corporate lines of credit. It can also help manage funding of corporate subsidiaries. The objective is to reduce the overall cost of capital for the firm and increase the return on assets (ROA).

In the intermediate term, a period from 3 to 18 months out, cash budgeting is concerned with meeting the demands of the capital budget. Because capital funding requires larger individual outlays or financing than operations, the financial manager must plan cash flow carefully to guarantee fulfillment of purchase and financing agreements. Disbursements for capital are more occasional and can be managed on a more ad hoc basis. Timing of capital transactions may be more flexible. Therefore, the financial manager has the opportunity to time transactions and minimize the impact on cash. Looking five or ten years into the future, the financial manager uses the budget process to position the company to accommodate growth. In this framework, cash budgeting supports balance-sheet planning in preparation for expansion. Long-term cash-budgeting strategies help direct the tactics of the shorter and intermediate terms. Monitoring cash long term also provides feedback on the company's performance in relation to its stage of maturity.

22.3 STATEMENT OF CASH FLOW. Essentially, a cash-flow statement can be viewed as a schedule depicting the transfer of funds rather than the exchange of consideration between the company, its suppliers, and its customers. A statement of cash flow approximates the company's financial condition based on cash-accounting methods, eliminating the effects of accruals in the standard accounting process. The cash-flow statement shows the strength of a company's ability to fund operations and growth, distinct from the ability of the company to generate profits (market value) from activity.

(a) Objectives. The cash-flow statement documents the liquidity position of the company at a given point. Cash-flow statements are most useful over time. Other objectives of cash-flow statements include the following:

- To summarize increases and decreases in cash and illustrate how beginning and ending cash balances were affected by operations during the accounting period
- To highlight all sources and uses of cash and near-cash assets to summarize daily cash receipts and disbursements forecasting
- To provide a historical base for developing a cash budget on both monthly and annual bases

(b) Advantages of Cash-Flow Statements. The principal advantages of cash-flow statements include the following:

- Cash-flow statements highlight the timing of cash received and the requirement for disbursement of funds for the period under evaluation. This provides greater insights into the ongoing liquidity and viability of the firm.
- These statements highlight the ability of the operations area of the company to generate a cash stream and identify where cash flow has been used.
- Cash-flow statements provide warning signals so that the firm does not appear to be viable from a balance-sheet perspective but is operationally illiquid.
- Cash-flow statements utilized in a cash budgeting integrate daily cash receipts and disbursement forecasting of funds flow.

(c) Disadvantages of Cash-Flow Statements. The principal disadvantages of cash-flow statements include the following:

- Cash-flow statements do not reflect all significant working-capital transactions. To this extent, dramatic increases in inventory for valid warehousing purposes, such as anticipation of labor problems, are reflected in the cash-flow statement but not readily visible. A cash-flow analysis can be used to assess the impact of the sources and application of funds and how they tie to their respective asset and liability accounts. Therefore, a thorough analysis must view the statement of cash flows and the balance sheet side by side.
- Cash-flow statements may focus on cash flows to the exclusion of other important measurements, such as profits, after real but accrued expenses are deducted. Consequently, it is possible that profits could be overstated by the exclusion of accrued expenses, providing an erroneous view of the cost of goods sold and of net income produced from operations. Therefore, the statement of cash flows should be examined for inconsistencies with the income statement.

22.4 USING THE FINANCIAL ACCOUNTING STANDARDS BOARD 95 FORMAT.

The statement of cash flows was formerly known as the funds statement, statement of source and application of funds, and, most recently, the statement of changes in financial position. The new statement of cash flows, Financial Accounting Standard Board (FASB) 95, reflects where, why, and how much cash was generated or spent and reflects the changes in cash balances from one period to another. Cash flows must be classified into receipts (inflows) and disbursements (outflows) and must be classified as to whether the cash came from operating, investing, or financing activities of the company.

(a) Operating Activities. Operating activities include all transactions and events that are not classified as either investing or financing activities. They involve the generation of cash flows that results from net income activities. These activities are broken down into the following cash inflows and outflows:

(i) Cash Inflows

- Cash receipts from the sale of goods or services
- Collection or sale of accounts and short- and long-term notes receivable arising from these sales
- Cash receipts from return on loans (interest), other debt instruments, and dividends on equity securities
- Others not classified as investing or financing activities and events

(ii) Cash Outflows

- Cash payments to suppliers for purchased inventory
- Cash payments to employees and other suppliers for goods or services
- Cash payments to governmental agencies for taxes due
- Cash payments of interest to lenders and other creditors
- All other expenses classified as operating activities

(b) Investing Activities. Investing activities include lending and collecting on loans and buying and selling debt or equity investments and long-term productive assets. These activities are also broken down into cash inflows and cash outflows.

(i) Cash Inflows

- Cash receipts from the sales of productive assets such as property, plant, and equipment (PPE)
- Cash receipts from the sales of debt or equity instruments of other companies
- Cash receipts from the collection or sales of other entities' debt instruments that were purchased by the company

(ii) Cash Outflows

- Cash disbursements to purchase productive assets such as PPE
- Cash payments for the purchase of debt or equity instruments of other companies
- Disbursements of loans to other entities

(c) Financing Activities. Financing activities include liability and owner's equity capital and result in a return on the owner's investments. It also involves acquiring cash from creditors and repaying amounts borrowed. These activities are also broken down into cash inflows and cash outflows.

(i) Cash Inflows

- Cash receipts from the sales of equity instruments
- The receipt of proceeds from the issuance of such debt instruments as bonds, notes, mortgages, and other short- or long-term borrowings

(ii) Cash Outflows

- Dividend payments or other distributions to stockholders
- The acquisition of capital stock
- The repayment of long-term debt

(d) Direct and Indirect Methods. Using the direct method of statement creation, the financial manager extracts cash-flow information from the source transaction applications to report cash in and out. This method is preferred for its accuracy, but the costs of

Transaction Summary

	Period 1	Period 2	Period 3
Sales to customers	$ 200	$ 250	$ 300
Cost of sales	100	125	150
Purchased from suppliers	50	75	75
Paid to suppliers	0	25	50
Paid other payables	60	73	84
Paid to bank	0	50	100
Collected receivables	40	170	240
Purchased fixed assets	5	10	5
Incurred expenses:			
Warehousing	10	12	15
Selling	40	50	60
General and Administrative	15	15	15
Depreciation	4	4	4
Interest	3	3	3
Taxes	7	10	13

Exhibit 22.1. ABC Distribution Company—transaction summary

Trial Balance

	Opening	Period 1		Period 2		Period 3	
	Balance	Postings	Balance	Postings	Balance	Postings	Balance
Cash	$ 50	$ −20	$ 30	$ 22	$ 52	$ 6	$ 58
Accounts Receivable		160	160	80	240	60	300
Inventories	500	−50	450	−50	400	−75	325
Fixed Assets	150	1	151	6	157	1	158
Accounts Payable		−70	−70	−77	−147	−52	−199
Loans Payable	−400	0	−400	50	−350	100	−250
Capital Stock	−50		−50		−50		−50
Paid-in Capital	−250		−250		−250		−250
Retained Earnings			0		0		0
Sales		−200	−200	−250	−450	−300	−750
Cost of Sales		100	100	125	225	150	375
Warehousing		10	10	12	22	15	37
Selling Expense		40	40	SO	90	60	150
General Expense		15	15	15	30	15	45
Depreciation		4	4	4	8	4	12
Interest Expense		3	3	3	6	3	9
Taxes		7	7	10	17	13	30
Total	$ 0	$ 0	$ 0	$ 0	$ 0	$ 0	$ 0

Exhibit 22.2. ABC Distribution Company—trial balance

compilation may exceed the benefits. When using the direct method, the financial analyst must provide the reconciliation of net income to net cash flow from operations on a separate schedule.

An alternative, the indirect method, starts with the net income and reports cash flow as items reflected in the income statement adjusted for changes in the balance sheet. The statement of cash flow adjusts net income for expenses that do not use cash, such as depreciation, and sources that do not provide funds, such as amortization of bond premiums. Using the indirect method, the reconciliation of net income to cash can be reported separately or together with the statement. Both approaches are shown below, utilizing the same information laid out in the trial balance.

A summary listing of data for an imaginary distribution company is shown in Exhibit 22.1. A trial balance has been constructed from the operating data and is shown in Exhibit 22.2. It is assumed that the company has just been formed and the initialization transactions are shown along with those for the first three periods. From the trial balance, an income statement and balance sheet have been prepared. These statements are shown in Exhibits 22.3 and 22.4.

Income Statement

	End of 3rd Period
Net Sales	$ 750
Cost of Sales	375
Gross Margin	375
Operating Expenses	244
Operating Income	131
Interest	9
Taxes	30
Net Income	$ 92

Exhibit 22.3. ABC Distribution Company—income statement

Balance Sheet

	End of 3rd Period
Assets	
Cash	$ 58
Accounts receivable	300
Inventories	325
Fixed assets	158
Total	841
Liabilities and capital	
Accounts payable	199
Loans payable	250
Capital stock	50
Paid in capital	250
Retained earnings	92
Total	$ 841

Exhibit 22.4. ABC Distribution Company—balance sheet

Consolidated Statement of Cash Flows
Increase (Decrease) in Cash and Cash Equivalents

	From Inception	Three Periods
Cash flow from operating activities:		
Cash received from customers	$ 450	$ 450
Cash paid to suppliers and employees	772	−272
Net cash provided by operating activities	322	178
Cash flow from investing activities:		
Capital expenditures	−170	−20
Net cash provided by investing activities	170	−20
Cash flow from financing activities:		
Net borrowings	250	−150
Proceeds from issuance of capital stock	300	
Net cash provided by financing activities	550	−150
Net increase in cash and cash equivalents	58	8
Cash and cash equivalents at beginning of period	0	50
Cash and cash equivalents at end of period	$ 58	$ 58
Reconciliation of net income to net cash provided by operating activities:		
Cash flow from operating activities:		
Net income	$ 92	$ 92
Adjustments to reconcile net income to net cash:		
Depreciation	12	12
Changes in assets and liabilities:		
Accounts receivable	−300	−300
Inventory	−325	175
Accounts payable	199	199
Total adjustments	−414	86
Net cash provided by operating activities	$ −322	$ 178

Exhibit 22.5. ABC Distribution Company—consolidated statement of cash flows

Using this information, it is possible to generate examples of both the direct and indirect statement methods, which are shown in Exhibits 22.5 and 22.6. Both of these formats are workable. The indirect method is easier because it flows from financial data, which is stored in the company's general ledger. The direct method, on the other hand, is simpler descriptively but requires that the company track information in a parallel format. It is not a difficult exercise, however; if clarity and simplicity are important for stockholders and the like, it will be well worth the effort to capture and store the information.

For internal reporting and forecasting purposes other formats are often used. Exhibit 22.7 shows a format that is simple and straightforward. Further, a short, descriptive form, which might be used in a monthly reporting commentary, is shown in Exhibit 22.8.

All of these formats provide equivalent information. For internal purposes, the design depends on management's focus and the company's system capabilities. It should be sufficiently detailed to allow for proper forecasting and adequately clear to be understood by nonaccountants. Following that guideline and carefully developing your forecasting

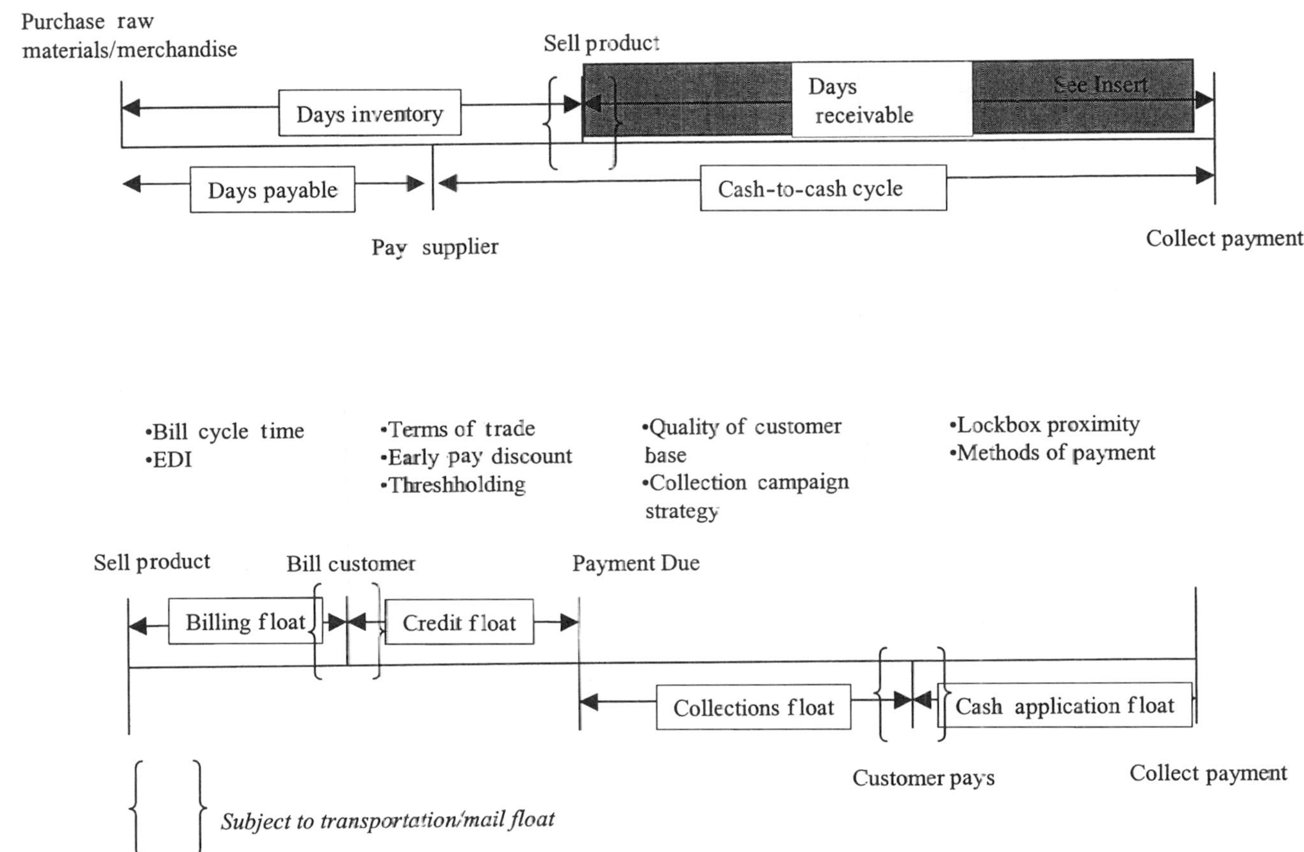

Exhibit 22.6. Days receivable magnification

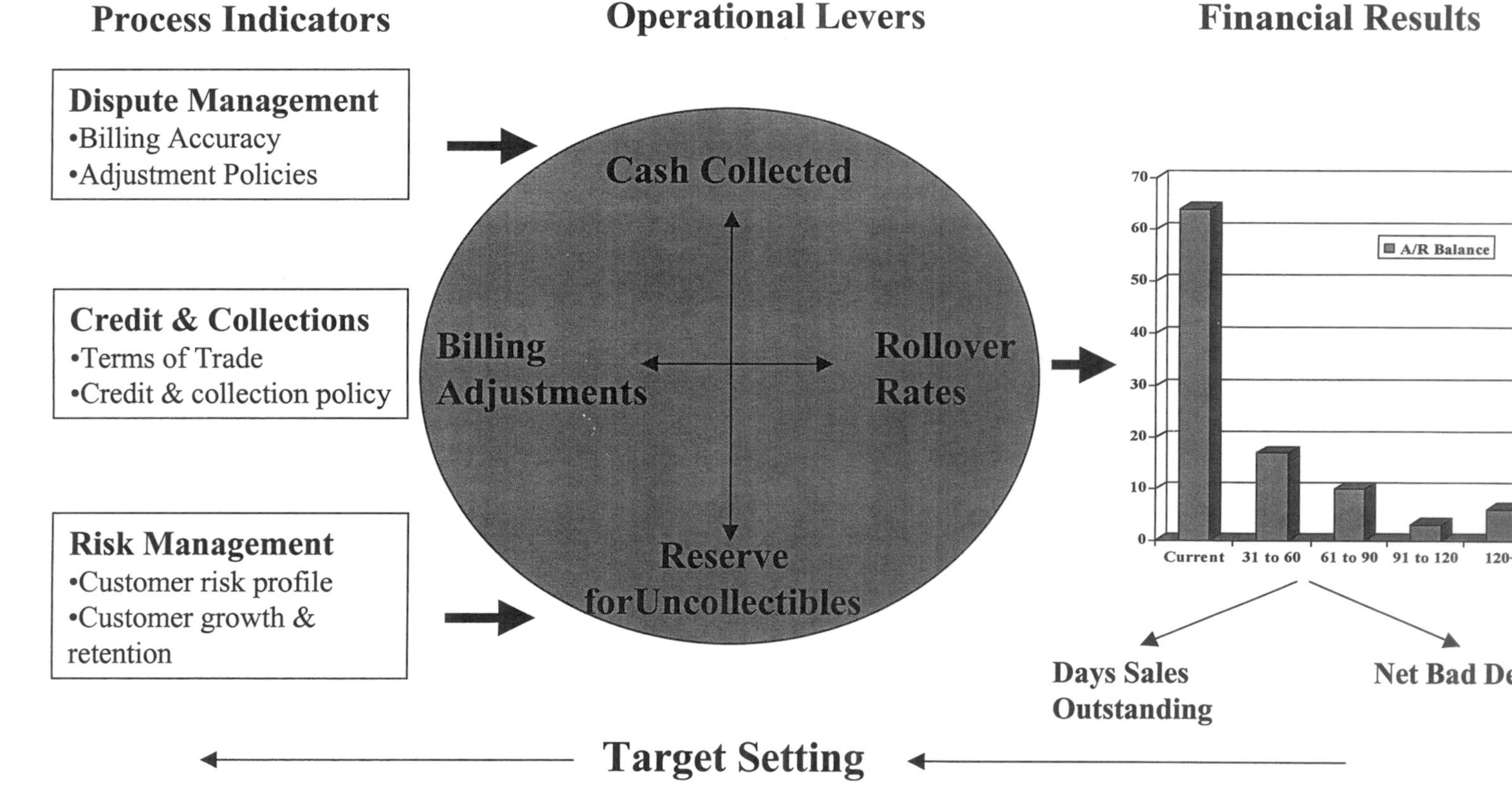

Exhibit 22.7. Performance measure framework

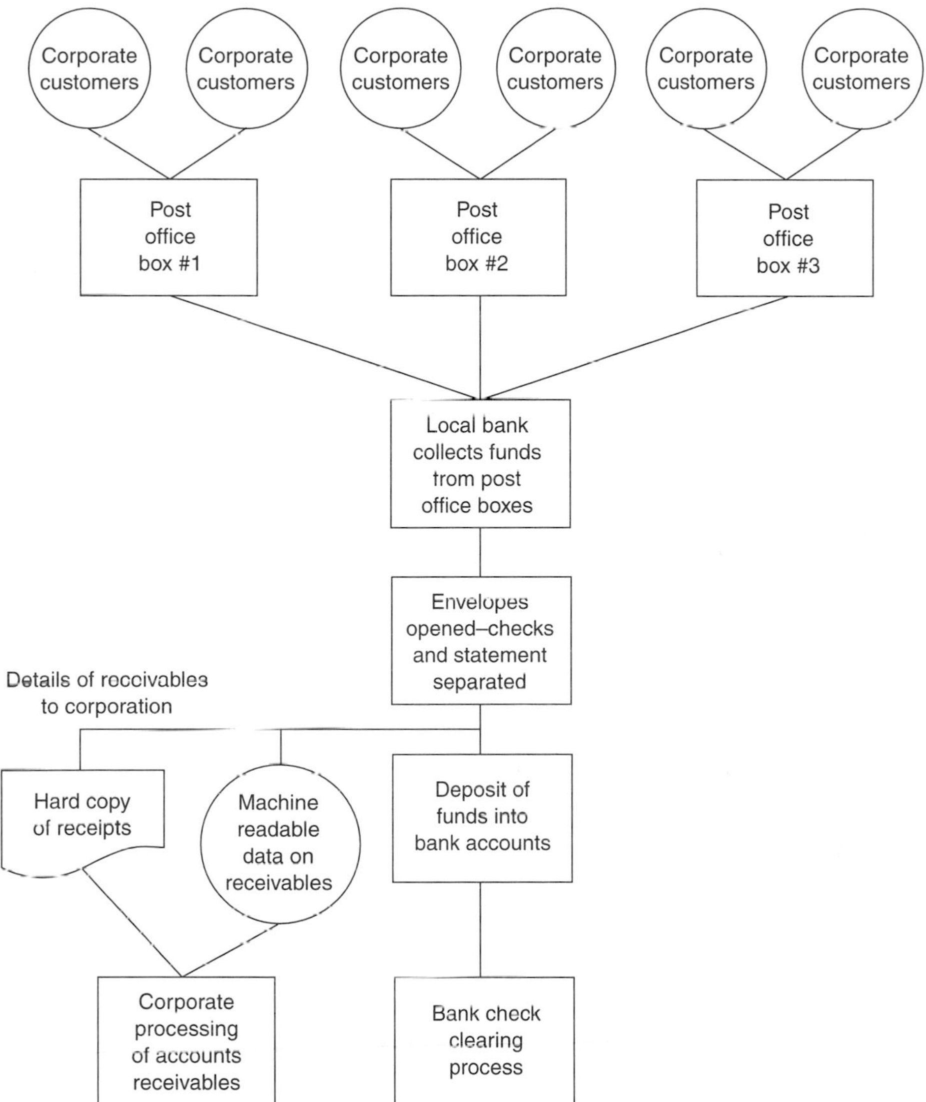

Exhibit 22.8. Overview of lockbox system processing

program will ensure that the company's cash-flow position is clearly understood and properly considered in the overall management of the business.

The prudent financial manager utilizes cash-flow statements to illustrate different perspectives of the corporation's financial health and well-being. These statements are the financial manager's foundation for cash budgeting. On the one hand, funds-flow analysis provides a broader-based view of the working-capital condition and future requirements of the company, although it does not demonstrate accurately the liquidity and viability of the day-to-day operations. On the other hand, cash-flow analysis provides perspective into the short-term liquidity of the corporation, the ability of the company to pay current debts, the buffer for future activity in the area of expansion, and level of insulation against business downturns.

The use of the cash-flow statement is a logical extension of the cash manager's function of preparing daily, weekly, and monthly cash-flow forecasts, utilizing cash receipts and disbursements forecasting methods. Utilization of both cash- and funds-flow analysis will provide a balance to financial management. These analyses are essential ingredients in implementing corporate cash-management programs.

22.5 DEVELOPING A CASH BUDGET. The scheduling of sources and uses of funds is required to properly forecast cash requirements. Budgeted expenditures for the business can be met only if the necessary funds are available to cover the requirements in a timely and efficient manner. Timing of these needs will point out the needs for cash and will then indicate whether cash will be generated internally or financed from outside sources. These requirements must be met if the business is to succeed.

The starting point for cash budgeting is a review of the income statement and balance sheet, prepared for the annual budget. These figures must be adjusted to a cash basis, to indicate when payments will be made rather than when the expense is incurred. Much of the confusion with regard to cash budgeting results from the use of cash accounting rather than the accrual methods normally used for financial reporting. The key distinction between the two is in the timing of the recognition of transactions. Revenue and expense are recognized at the time that the commitment to transact is made. Receipts and disbursements are recognized at the time that the funds are transferred from one party to the other. Once determined, the cash items are laid out in a weekly or monthly forecast.

The resultant differences between forecasted cash inflows and outflows will indicate the cash surplus or the shortfall. The financing requirements or investment opportunities for the company become apparent, and the timing of these cash needs is then made clear to the financial officer. Growth is possible only if funding is available when needed to seize an opportunity when it arises. Therefore, cash forecasting provides structure to support the growth of any business.

Time-phased budgeting of revenue and expenses is the first step in forecasting cash flows. However, because the regular budgeting fails to incorporate business practices and industry dynamics that affect a company's ability to translate sales to receipts expenses to expenditures, additional adjustments must be made.

Sales are often subject to trade credit terms, billing discrepancies, and bad debt. Similarly, purchases can be subject to the same devices. The financial manager must demonstrate the impact of these practices on cash flow and earnings. The effectiveness of credit and collections will directly impact the company's ability to project cash position based on business projections. The faster a company can convert sales to cash (conversion rate), the lower the reserves necessary to fund operations. Put another way, the faster the conversions rate the greater the relative contribution of internal financing (i.e., from revenue) over outside financing. The more stable a company's conversion rate, the closer the relationship between the cash and operating budgets.

22.6 IMPACT OF ECONOMIC INDICATORS AND INDUSTRY TRENDS. To develop a plan for the company's business, management must formulate a workable business strategy, which reflects the expectations for the company during the coming year. These projections are tempered not only by the plans and expectations of management, but also by the impact of trends in the general economy, industry, and marketplace. The inflation rate, the real growth rate for the economy, and the prevailing interest rates will have an impact on the cash budget.

(a) Interest. Interest rates determine the relative value of today's dollar in tomorrow's market. The willingness of a cash manager to retain cash reserves is dictated by the rate of inflation. In times of high interest rates, cash-budgeting accuracy significantly improves net income by minimizing capital requirements and thus the cost of capital. When interest rates are low, the timing of transactions is less critical, diminishing the financial impact of the cash budget.

Perhaps more important to planning than the absolute interest rate is the rate of change. Projections as to changes in interest rates help the cash manager make investment decisions. Under conditions of rapidly rising or falling rates, a cash manager may accelerate or delay financing (or delay or speed-up investment). Dynamic cash planning models include provisions for such interest rate scenarios.

(b) Inflation. The rate of inflation significantly affects the cost of goods purchased, operating expenses in general, and the selling price of your products or services. Forecasting of inflation rates over the period is helpful to determine tolerable levels of surplus cash. Whereas interest rates may influence a company to invest in financial markets, inflation may encourage a company to invest in raw materials or other inventory. These investments come at the expense of cash.

Projection of inflation is commonly practiced, and forecasts of rates are readily available with evaluations and projections for one to two years. They can be found in business newspapers, trade organization reports, and newsletters, and can be obtained in more detail from banking institutions and economists. It is always a continuing battle for companies to keep expenses below the inflation rate and to achieve growth in sales that exceeds the inflation rate while maintaining real margins at least as good as in the previous year.

(c) Market and Industry Factors. Ordinarily, the accuracy of the cash budget fluctuates with that of the operating budget. As such, the validity of the cash budget is dependent on the realization of market and industry assumptions from the operating budget. Market factors such as the substitutability of goods and substitutability of inputs determine the impact budgeting for inflation. Other factors such as the stage of the market and the company's growth strategy also impact the cash budget. The interaction of these factors determines the required accuracy and flexibility of the cash budget.

Changes in cash position are directed correlated to profits. The ability of a company to protect its margins, and thus maintain steady cash surpluses, is dependent upon the company's ability to pass on higher prices to its customers. To the degree that inputs such as raw materials and labor are replaceable, the company will be able to keep price increases under control. Planning for expenditures can be more reliable. In the alternative, if suppliers raise prices, profits and cash reserves will suffer. To offset cost increases, the company has to raise the prices of its own products or services. The outcome of this is subject to the same principle of substitution. The ratio between the substitutability of a company's inputs to its outputs determines the degree to which inflation concerns the cash budget.

The stage of the market will also shape the cash management strategy reflected in the cash budget. In the early stages of a new market, undisciplined companies will invest surplus cash in market development. The company risks expending its cash surplus too quickly. Alternatively, young industries or companies preparing for growth may choose to have more cash on hand to increase flexibility. Being able to self-finance acquisitions or internal business development rather than minimizing cash requirements is the focus. In either case, the financial manager is responsible for maintaining spending in accordance with the original budget.

22.7 ROLE OF THE FINANCIAL MANAGER. The financial budgeting process represents the planning function within the corporate manager's responsibility. The budgeting process needs to consider not only the flow of funds generally throughout the system but also the specific movement of cash within the company (i.e., among various bank accounts), to provide for immediate and short-term needs. This budgeting process establishes guidelines to be used during the coming period to control the accumulation and utilization of company assets. The challenge is to determine the financial impact of business-process changes. However, by tracking significant ratios, the financial manager can gauge the economic impact of alternatives and use the budgeting process to help the organization prioritize.

The operational aspect of budgeting is represented by the cash-management function within a firm. The cash manager is responsible for the day-to-day liquidity of the firm and for managing assets in the short term. He or she is responsible for managing and monitoring the established cash- and funds-flow budget and for managing overall bank relationships. In this regard, the corporate cash manager is responsible for providing sufficient flexibility to take advantage of marketplace opportunities while ensuring adequate corporate liquidity. Additionally, the corporate cash manager may adjust or move the asset base of the corporation to increase overall return on assets or reduce borrowing costs. Whereas the budgeting process is forward thinking, day-to-day cash management represents the execution of budgeting plans with the flexibility to react to changing financial conditions.

Of increasing importance to the financial manager is the concept of performance measurement. In the area of cash-flow and funds-flow forecasting and control, as well as in cash-management operations, measurement of results needs to be augmented incorporating measurements of cash utilization.

(a) Influencing the Business through Performance Measurement. While operations managers understand the importance of cash to the business, they often fail to recognize the impact of various business practices have on cash. To improve cash performance, the financial manager then must develop intermediate measures that obviate that impact. To begin, the financial manager should explain the relationships between business activities and their corresponding cash transactions. Exhibits 22.6 and 22.7 illustrate the impact on collection process and performance measurement.

Each of the components of cash is the domain of different business functions. The financial manager has the ability to focus attention on float by integrating measures of these items into the review process. The degree to which there is variability in any of these float components, the accuracy of cash budgeting suffers. The role of financial manager, then, is twofold. First, the financial manager must heighten awareness of the cash impact of business procedures by translating overall measures into comprehensible and actionable components for operations. Next, the financial manager must institutionalize cash-maximizing practices through policy to reduce variability and improve cash forecasting.

Taking the industry and market factors into consideration, the financial manager first works with operations to identify areas that can alleviate working-capital demands and facilitate cash flow. Once that area is identified, the relationship between cash flow and the business activity (transaction) is measured and then monitored over time. This provides feedback to operations and enables them to evaluate the processes and make improvements not only in efficiency but also in cash return. For example, a manager for a company with a fragmented supplier base realizes that increasing liabilities to suppliers (extending payment) would ease cash demands without hurting productivity (or relationships). Therefore, the manager works with purchasing and accounts payable to incorporate a days-payable-outstanding measure into their review process. This heightened attention encourages purchasing to work for better terms and supports accounts payable in holding payment until required. As time goes by, the standard terms are adjusted and funds are stably flowing to suppliers later. To clarify these effects, a further discussion of float follows.

Float can be either collection or disbursement float. *Collection float* is defined as customer liabilities for delivered goods not available as cash. Collection float consists of monies tied up in billing, terms of trade, or collections of past-due balances. Collection float is frequently measured as days sales outstanding (DSO), the number of days revenue is in the process between billing and cash application. Days sales outstanding approximates the number of days a company requires to collect on customer balances. Aggregate calculations based on total accounts receivable and total sales can be used to derive DSO. Alternatively, collection float can be measured by taking a representative sample of receivables for a period and averaging the number of days required from the transaction date to the time that funds are available from the banking system.

Disbursement float may be defined as funds that are liabilities to the corporation (such as accounts payable) that have been issued by the company for payment but that have not yet been transferred from the corporate bank account. Consequently, these funds are still available for corporate use. Disbursement float may be quantified by taking a sampling to determine the number of days it has taken a check issued and placed in the mail to clear from the corporation's drawee bank.

The principal elements in float quantification include the following:

- Mail transmission time, for either the receipt of funds or the disbursement of funds
- Credit terms, which is the payment delay granted in the sales contract
- Internal processing time, which is the time required by a company to receive payments, open them, process them through their internal accounting system, and make deposits to the bank for collection
- Availability, which refers to the amount of time it takes the bank to collect the item from the drawee bank

These four combined elements constitute the overall float-days factor, which needs to be applied to the average daily receipts or disbursements in order to define a benchmark for the dollar value of items trapped within the corporate collection and disbursement system.

A specific example of collection float is:

Monthly collections	$10 million per month
Mail transmission time	2 days per item
Credit terms	15 days from receipt
Processing time	0.7 days per item
Mail transmission time	2 days per item
Availability time	1.2 days per item
Total collection float	21 days
Average daily collections (30 days)	$333,334
Total float	$7,000,014

Using this example as a benchmark, modifications made in the cash management system through specific techniques affect different parts of the total float. Consequently, an improvement in any component can decrease the amount of funds required for operations. Interfacing the cash-management functions and the budgeting approach is essential to providing the correct benchmark measurements to enable the corporation to monitor its performance in the coming year.

(b) Business Modeling. Business modeling is an effective means of communicating the effects changes in procedure have on cash position. Business modeling in this sense refers specifically to demonstrating the relationships between cash-flow and income statements. The accelerated conversion of revenue into cash, and a stable and efficient procurement and inventory-management program can improve cash flow and support strategic investment and financing decisions. Short-term modeling takes the form of integrating commitments from customers and suppliers into a weekly or daily cash forecast to improve banking efficiency. Integrated systems or EIS tools that combine data from accounts payable and accounts receivable systems feed short-term modeling.

In the intermediate term, business modeling establishes dynamic targets for the "budget" or one year horizon. The mechanism enables the financial manager to effectively embed the operational importance of cash flow into targets and influence operational policies and decisions. A critical component of business modeling involves the building of linkage to key components of the cash-to-cash cycle. Policies with regard to extending customer credit, adjusting customer bills, and pursuing past-due balances are reflected in changes to DSO. This is used to project cash receipts based on sales projections. The relationships between procedures (i.e., credit and risk policy) to the operational levels (i.e., level of net bad debt), and ultimately to cash (i.e., DSO), must be a focal point of the cash budgeting process.

In modeling the cash-flow impact of the revenue cycle, projecting time to collection based on historical DSO is key. Understanding cash-flow improvement from the revenue cycle requires the determination of cash receipts and the corresponding noncash relief (bad debt, billing adjustments as a percent of revenue). Projected changes in the risk profile of the customer base, effectiveness of collection programs, billing cycles and accuracy, and other process indicators drive different scenarios of cash. By linking experience levels and policy/customer-base direction, noncash relief forecasts can be updated.

The mechanism through which cash from sales is projected is DSO which is a reflection of rollover rates. Rollover is the percentage of balances within each accounts receivable age category that remains uncollected. By estimating the accounts receivable profile relative to sales revenue, DSO changes can be estimated incorporating changes in the cash-to-cash cycles occur (terms of trade, new collection programs, improved cash application, etc.). Adjusting DSO reveals levels of noncash relief and cash receipts necessary to achieve targets. Through modeling the impact on cash, the financial manager can influence the operations. The same process can be open to link procurement and inventory requirements to sales projections and build the linkage to days payable outstanding and inventory on hand.

22.8 CASH-MANAGEMENT TECHNIQUES.

A sophisticated cash management process will attempt to increase cash for investment, decrease service fees, and decrease administration time.

The evolution of cash-management techniques has been stimulated by the financial marketplace, which has required development and implementation of innovative approaches to managing cash positions. The cash-management services utilized by corporations today fall within the following five major areas:

1. Credit services
2. Collection services
3. Concentration systems design
4. Disbursement techniques
5. Audit control and information services

Credit services can be defined as those services that manage the company's exposure to bad debt. Through improved credit services, a company can become more adept at forecasting adjustments to cash inflow.

Collection services can be defined as those services that accelerate the receipt of funds to the corporation and make funds available. Specific examples of these services would include lockbox services, pre-authorized checks, and techniques such as concentration banking.

Concentration systems design refers to the analysis of specific collection points within a cash-management system that identifies the optimum number of concentration points and takes into account the credit and noncredit services required by a corporation. Traditionally, concentration design would also include the analysis of money center banks or concentration banks and the role they play in an overall cash-management system.

Disbursement techniques are those that increase the dollars not yet paid. Services would include zero-balance accounts and remote or controlled disbursing techniques.

Audit control and information services are those that provide information regarding money, enabling the cash manager to better control the daily position in movement of funds. Specific examples of these kinds of services would include account reconcilement services, forecasting, and management information recording.

To understand a company's opportunities for improvement, one should consider the following:

- Minimizing the number of banks
- Utilizing sweep accounts that automatically invest excess cash
- Maintaining zero-balance accounts (ZBAs) to segregate disbursements
- Using lockboxes located based on customer dispersion
- Establishing short-term lines of credit
- Using commitment registers with dating of expected receipts
- Using electronic data interchange (EDI) for billing and monitoring funds transfers
- Setting up on-line access to bank accounts
- Automating daily polling of bank accounts
- Netting for all transactions with internal business partners

(a) Credit Services. On-line access to credit bureaus and behavior scoring can help control the sales to cash conversion.

(b) Collection Services. An important strategy utilized by cash managers today is to accelerate the receipt and deposits of funds in order to reduce outstanding float in accounts receivable. The specific services available include lockbox services, pre-authorized checks, and pre-authorized debits.

(i) Electronic Data Interchange—Electronic Billing. Electronic data interchange impacts many aspects of the collection cycle. Electronic billing reduces the free payment days associated with the mail delay required by paper invoicing. It also facilitates the processes of posting adjustments. This practice is also being adopted to reduce costs of processing transactions (i.e., producing and distributing invoices).

(ii) Electronic Funds Transfer. Electronic funds transfer (EFT) reduces the free payment days associated with the mail delay used by customers mailing in payments. This practice is also being adopted to reduce costs of cash application.

(iii) Lockbox Services. Lockbox services represent the oldest and the most widely used of the cash management services. They are extremely useful in reducing the amount of collection float in a corporate collection system. The objective of a lockbox is to provide a mail-intercept point to reduce the mail float that occurs when the payor places a receipt of payment into the mail. Exhibit 22.8 is a graphic illustration of the lockbox processing system. The basic concept is, rather than mailing a payment direct to the company, it goes directly to a bank-controlled post office box. The bank collects and processes the items quickly and deposits the checks directly to the customer's account for collection. An additional dimension is that multiple lockbox location points can be to eliminate mail time.

An occasional review of lockbox systems is required because the payor profile changes over time and because sophisticated payors occasionally misdirect mail to gain additional disbursement float. In addition, changes in customers' accounts payable functions, as the result of shared-services consolidation or mergers change the proximity of some locations. Banks traditionally charge on a per-item basis for providing the lockbox service. The net result of lockboxes is to reduce mail-collection float time and eliminate internal processing time per item received.

(iv) Alternate Payment Methods. Other means of collecting customer payments such as the acceptance of credit cards and direct debiting of customer bank accounts can also improve collections float. Credit card programs are similar to factoring in that the receivable is sold to the customer's bank at a 2% to 3% discount. Direct debiting includes the electronic payment benefits of EFT and increases the control over the timing of customer payments.

(c) Concentration Systems Design. Establishing concentration systems is an important consideration in cash-management programs. Although generalizing about concentration systems applicable for industries or types of companies is not practical because of indigenous business requirements, review of specific considerations can be helpful in identifying company characteristics. Concentration systems design should be viewed from two major perspectives: (1) establishing the structure for the concentration system and (2) funds mobilization from concentration points.

(i) Structuring the Concentration System. Utilization of collection and disbursement systems alone may not achieve optimum results in the cash management and control

area within the financial manager's responsibilities. Designing a rational and intelligent approach to concentration systems is required in addition to using specific techniques. Specific designs applicable to a corporation will depend on the corporate philosophy regarding centralization of receipts and disbursements.

Major areas requiring consideration include the following:

- Degree of financial autonomy provided to company divisions
- Geographic dispersion of locations
- The total number of divisions to be controlled
- Service reliability of banks in the areas involved

The simplest approach to concentration systems design is a single-node approach, which is easiest for the cash manager and which eliminates intermediate banks and control problems. Limiting regional concentration banks is an important consideration for increasing control both in the budgeting area for field divisions and for the concentration system. Benefits from limiting concentration bank involvement include the following:

- Reduction in cash management staff requirements for control and support
- Reduction in the number of lockbox and depository banks
- Reduction in requirements for establishing multiple credit line
- Increase in budgetary control

(ii) Funds Mobilization. Following the concentration system architecture, the evaluation of collection patterns is an important consideration in determining how funds should be moved to concentration points. *Wire transfer services* are among the major techniques used for funds movement. The purpose of wire transfer services is to move collected funds and make them available on the same day to a receiving party. The primary advantage of using wire transfer services is that funds may be moved from one location to another quickly and without the loss of valued funds for one day. Wire transfer services have been increasing in use dramatically over the past few years for the following reasons:

- Increasing value of funds resulting in a decreased break-even point for wire transfer services
- Improved management of bank target balances directly related to the need to increase the return on assets within the corporation
- Increased need to cover transactional requirements

Traditionally, wire transfer services have been used for high-dollar and low-volume types of transfer; however, as interest rates rise, the break-even point for wire transfers declines significantly.

There are essentially two wire transfer systems available for the movement of funds: the Federal Reserve wire transfer system and the bank wire transfer system. The essential difference between the two is the form in which settlement is made at the receiving location. In the Federal Reserve system, account balances are changed within the Federal Reserve bank at the close of business on the day of the transfer. Utilizing the bank wire system, correspondent bank balances are modified to account for the transfers. From a practical point of view for the cash manager and financial manager of a corporation, there is no difference whether the bank uses one transfer system or another, since the net result to the user is the transfer of funds on the same day with no difference in cost.

(d) Disbursement Techniques. The objective of disbursement-control techniques is to extend the clearing time or settlement time of checks issued by the company in payment for obligations. Centralization of payables is an important consideration to the corporation utilizing these techniques because it enables the cash manager to centrally control disbursements made and to track their clearance accurately. Early disbursements can be as wasteful and uneconomical for a company as incurring late-payment charges from discount deadlines. For example, by paying an invoice in the amount of $25,000 in 15 days rather than taking the full 60 days, the company loses an investment income of approximately $184.93, assuming the funds can be invested at 9%. Specific disbursement services most often used in cash management include zero-balance accounts, payable through drafts, and remote (uncontrolled) disbursement.

(i) Zero-Balance Accounts. Zero-balance accounts are disbursement accounts linked to a master disbursement account. Checks can be written against these subsidiary accounts and presented for payment to the banks, with the understanding that they will be funded by the master account.

Exhibit 22.9 is an overview of zero-balance accounting services. The purpose of the service is to allow autonomy of various corporate functions for disbursement of checks to the local suppliers while maintaining a centralized control over the dollar disbursements. Major benefits derived by the company from zero-balance accounts include the following:

- Centralized cash management control over funds disbursed
- Decentralized autonomy of disbursements
- Reduced or eliminated interest accounts
- Float extension through issuance of decentralized disbursements

(e) Audit Control and Management Information Services. Use of audit and control techniques has been growing in order to increase control over the cash-flow budget and cash-management control areas. Specific services most often utilized include cash-management information services, account-reconcilement services, and data-transmission services. The integration of transaction systems to provide short-term cash forecasts can also facilitate cash management and budgeting.

(i) Cash-Management Information Services. Corporations and banks are increasingly demanding better cash-management information. The type of information required by cash managers to monitor and measure against the cash-flow and funds-flow budget techniques includes up-to-date information on collected and available balances as well as detailed information on debits and credits from prior days' activities. To meet these information needs, money center banks have developed extensive cash-management information services based on wide networks of telecommunication devices, which are available to corporations as additional noncredit services.

Exhibit 22.10 illustrates the services included in many of the cash-management information services offered today. Many of these services can be customized to provide better

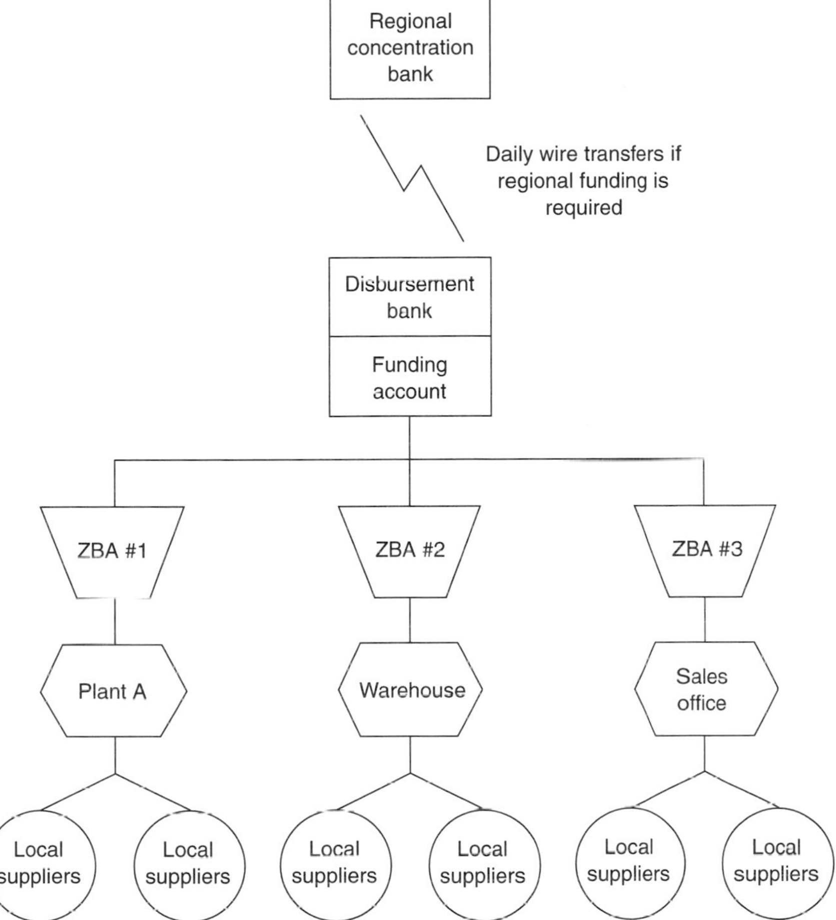

Exhibit 22.9. Zero-balance disbursement flow, Alpha Corporation

and more specific tracking of cash budgeting and funds-flow budgeting data, as were developed earlier in the chapter. The services are categorized in three principal areas:

1. Deposit reporting services, which provide nationwide reporting of deposit information made by subsidiaries and usually interface with the bank's internal computing systems. They provide automated depository transfer checks.
2. Balance-reporting services, which provide a multilevel access to balance information on both detail and summary level for the corporation on a daily basis.
3. Investment and control services, which tend to be more customized, providing the corporation with access to forecasting money market funds and providing information directly to banks regarding the movement of funds.

Most often, national and international time-sharing services are utilized to provide these services to corporations.

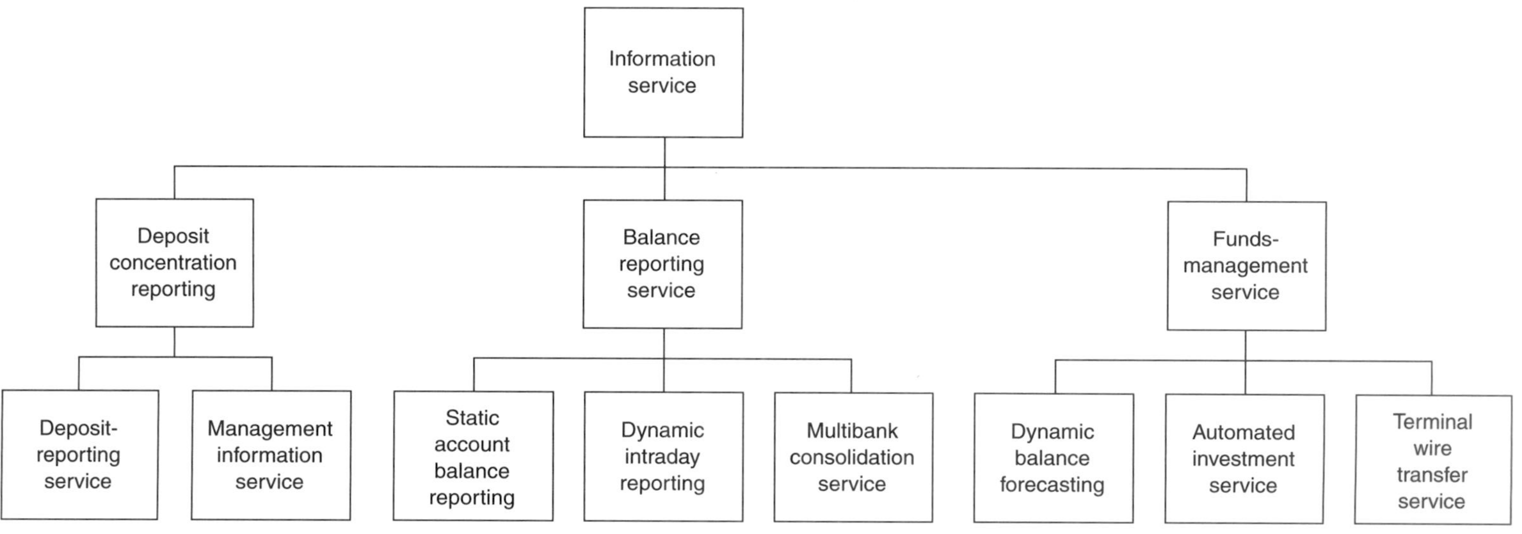

Exhibit 22.10. Cash-management information services

(ii) Account Reconcilement Services. Another service often used to facilitate control and reduce internal work is the automated account reconcilement service. The object of this service is to provide, under a full or partial account reconcilement to the corporation, a full listing of checks issued and dates cleared, which are automatically compared by the bank's file as checks were presented. Using this service, internal controls can be increased and costs reduced (See Exhibit 22.11).

Overall, a company's ability to develop and maintain a sophisticated cash management process will depend on the level of systems/processes embedded within the business environment. Advanced cash management techniques emphasize centralized and efficient functions, minimal banking relationships, risk policies, and integrated systems. The Cash Management Performance Grid reflected in Exhibit 22.11 demonstrates the various levels of cash management performance that companies should rank their cash management operations. Moving up the grid from minimal to best performance should be a key component of better executing an effective cash management strategy.

22.9 TYPES OF FINANCING

(a) Short-Term. Short-term financing generally represents a revolving credit line. Three types of short-term financing follow in Exhibits 22.12 through 22.14.

(i) Trade Financing. Trade financing is a credit line based on the forecasted needs of the business for a given period of time, generally a year. It is not tied to specific assets, but requires certain financial parameters to be kept and a specific payment schedule to be met. Annual cleanup is generally required. Cleanup is a period of time, usually a month, when no loan is outstanding. In addition to the rate of interest paid, compensating balances will probably be required. This is the bank's way of enhancing their return and should be considered in the equation when comparing this source of financing with other sources.

(ii) Asset-Based Financing. Asset-based financing is a credit line based on assets of the company, usually inventory and receivables, and usually advances a percentage of these assets up to the limit of the line of credit. Typically, this could be a credit line made up of a combination of 80% of eligible receivables and 50% of inventory. Maximum limits of each could be stipulated and, in any case, no advances above the line of credit would be made. This type of loan also requires cleanup and compensating balances. This type of financing is particularly useful in a seasonal business, where peak needs for inventory financing may be significant before the sales begin to generate cash for payment.

(iii) Factoring. Factoring is a method of borrowing in which a third party (factor) advances a portion of the accounts receivable. In some cases, the factor advances to the company then the company collects the receivables and repays the factor. In other agreements, the third party buys the receivables at a discounted value and collects from your customers, retaining the margin as their profit.

Generally, this type of financing is more expensive than asset-based financing and is used most often where inventory lead times are short and sales are highly seasonal and often sold with dating arrangements. The company must accept heavy involvement of the factor in company credit decisions.

(b) Long-Term. Long-term financing is more likely to be a fixed loan, which is payable in installments over a specific term with interest rates prescribed for the life of the loan.

Systems/Process	Minimal	Adequate	Best
Establish and maintain cash-control mechanisms	Cash-control procedures in place.	Segregation of duties with strong cash control procedures.	Eliminate cash handling function and/or segregate function.
	Proliferation of cash-control points based on historic usage.	Minimum number of points for cash handling.	Minimize or outsource points for cash collection handling.
	All transactions settled in cash between companies.	Periodic cash settlements between companies.	Policies minimize intergroup cash transactions.
Reconcile bank statements and match cash	Banking relationships organised locally by business units (BUs).	Banking arrangement set-up by each group of companies.	Minimum number on banking relationships.
	Periodic reconciliation of unmatched cash.	Daily reconciliation of cash receipts to identify unmatched cash.	Establish close relationship with customers to eliminate cause of unmatched cash.
	Ad hoc bank reconciliations with documented procedures.	Manual periodic reconciliation bank completed and signed off. Follow up on outstanding items on exception basis within agreed time scales.	Reconciliations are automated and completed and signed off daily. Action taken on all reconciling times within predefined timescales.
	Petty cash used for all local purchases and re-imbursed as incurred.	Impress control over petty cash.	Maximize use of alternatives to petty cash (e.g., company credit cards).
Report and manage cash balances	Independent management of cash resources by business units.	Periodic consolidation of cash balance e.g., monthly.	Consolidated use of cash balances on a daily basis.
	Treasury function managed independently by BUs within policy constraints.	Central Treasury function takes lead in obtaining information on cash requirements from BUs.	Treasury management function is centralized with close relationships with BUs.
	Monthly review by Treasurer of risk position.	Monthly review by FD based on current position and exposure to risks.	Treasury management committee setting guidelines on risk and regularly monitoring.
Forecast cash requirements	Information available to support periodic forecasts requested from BUs on a regular basis.	Annual 5-year forecast, 12 months produced quarterly, weekly forecast 3 months out, and daily forecasts 4 weeks out.	Annual 5-year forecast, rolling 12-months forecast produced monthly, with weekly forecasts 3 months out and daily forecast 4 weeks out.
	Manual analysis of short-term commitments, liabilities from BU returns. Ad hoc/annual estimates.	Systems reports used as the basis for determining commitments, liabilities etc.	Systems provides integrate position on all recorded commitments and liabilities.

Exhibit 22.11. Cash-management performance grid

Consolidated Statement of Cash Flows
Increase (Decrease) in Cash and Cash Equivalents

	From Inception	Three Periods
Cash flow from operating activities:		
Net income	$ 92	$ 92
Adjustments to reconcile net income to net cash:		
Depreciation	12	12
Changes in assets and liabilities:		
Accounts receivable	−300	−300
Inventory	−325	175
Accounts payable	199	199
Total adjustments	−414	86
Net cash provided by operating activities	−322	78
Cash flow from investing activities:		
Capital expenditures	−170	20
Net cash provided by investing activities	−170	−20
Cash flow from financing activities:		
Net borrowings	250	−150
Proceeds from issuance of capital stock	300	
Net cash provided by financing activities	550	−150
Net increase in cash and cash equivalents	58	5
Cash and cash equivalents at beginning of period	0	50
Cash and cash equivalents at end of period	$ 58	$ 58

Exhibit 22.12. ABC Distribution Company—consolidated statement of cash flows

Internal Cash-Flow Schedule

	From Inception		Three Periods
Profit before interest and tax		$ 131	$ 131
Changes in working capital:			
Accounts receivable		300	−300
Inventories		−325	175
Accounts payable		199	199
	−426	74	
	−295	205	
Capital expenditures		−170	−20
Depreciation		12	12
Interest		−9	−9
Taxes		−30	−30
		−197	−47
		−492	158
Capital stock		300	
		−192	158
Loans		250	−150
Increase (decrease) in cash		$ 58	$ 8

Exhibit 22.13. ABC Distribution Company—internal cash-flow schedule

Internal Cash-Flow Commentary Summary

	From Inception	Three Periods
Cash received from:		
Accounts receivable	$ 450	$ 450
Capital stock	300	
Bank loans	400	
Total cash receipts	1,150	450
Cash used for:		
Suppliers	575	75
Other payables	197	197
Bank loan reductions	150	150
Capital expenditures	170	20
Total cash disbursements	1,092	442
Increase (decrease) in cash	$ 58	$ 8

Exhibit 22.14. ABC Distribution Company—internal cash-flow commentary summary

Term loans are generally used to spread the cash needs for expansion over a longer period to eliminate peaks and valleys in cash flow and ensure an adequate, reliable supply capital to the business.

22.10 SUMMARY. Over the years, the importance of cash flow and the balance sheet has become more visible as companies have sought to deliver shareholder value across all segments of the business. The increased importance of cash and the continually changing level of cash management techniques have also changed the profile of the financial manager today.

The financial manager today needs to be able to operate along three distinct planning horizons: short-term funding of operations, annual planning for capital investment, and long-term financing of expansion. Additionally, the cash manager needs to balance the need for functional expertise to deal with new technology and cash management techniques, with need for strategic perspective to influence operational policies and impact growth.

From cash budgeting to business modeling the cash manager is operating on a varied horizon of sophistication. In this environment, preparing a statement of cash flow, improving the cash-to-cash cycle by influencing DSO policies, and implementing a new set of cash management techniques are all key roles of today's financial manager.

The importance of the cash budget is a natural output of the financial manager's need to meet the cash flow needs of the business.

SOURCES AND SUGGESTED REFERENCES

Bort, Richard, *Corporate Cash Management Handbook.* Boston, MA: Warren, Gorham & Lamont, 1994.

Briscoe, Carl G., II, and Arlene F. Perkins, ''Automating the Cash Management Transaction Processing Cycle,'' *Journal of Cash Management,* vol. 11, no. 2, March–April 1991.

Checkley, Keith, *Cash Is King: A Practical Guide to Strategic Cash Management.* New York: Pitman Publishing, 1994.

Coopers & Lybrand L.L.P., Revenue Assurance Management Benchmarking Study, 1997.

Gamble, Richard H., ''Global Cash Management: Strategies for Netting and Reinvoicing,'' *Controller Magazine,* February 1997.

Gamble, Richard H., ''Converting Days to Dollars,'' *Controller Magazine,* May 1997.

Giovacchini, Paula, ''High Performance Collections: Six A/R Breakthroughs,'' *Corporate Cash Flow,* July 1995.

Kaplan, Robert S., *The Balanced Scorecard.* Boston: Harvard University Press, 1997.

King, Alfred M., *Total Cash Forecasting, Managing, and Improving Cash Flow.* New York: McGraw-Hill, 1994.

Loscalzo, William, *Cash Flow Forecasting.* New York: McGraw-Hill, 1995.

Malburg, Christopher R., *The Cash Management Handbook.* Englewood Cliffs, NJ: Prentice-Hall, 1992.

Mattson, Kyle, Men Hackbart, and James R. Ramsey, ''State and Corporate Cash Management: A Comparison,'' *Public Budgeting & Finance,* vol. 10, no. 4, Winter 1990.

Mavrotis, Basil P., *Cashflow, Credit & Collection.* Chicago: Probus, 1994.

Prose, Leonard, ''The Importance of Good Cash Management,'' *Agency Sales Magazine,* vol. 20, no. 5, May 1990.

Prueitt, George C., and Chan S. Park, ''Monitoring Project Performance With Post-Audit Information: Cash Flow Control Charts,'' *Engineering Economist,* vol. 36, no. 4, Summer 1991.

Rachlin, Robert, *Total Business Budgeting: A Step-by-Step Guide With Forms.* New York: John Wiley & Sons, 1991.

Sagner, James S., *Cashflow Reengineering: How to Optimize the Cashflow Timeline and Improve Financial Efficiency.* New York: AMACOM, 1997.

CHAPTER 23

BALANCE-SHEET BUDGET

James E. Kristy

23.1 INTRODUCTION. Budgeting is most often thought of as having to do with the planning and control of revenues and expense, that is, managing the day-to-day operations of a business or other organization. The primary goal of a business, as Peter Drucker says, is "to create customers" with the right product and price and to skillfully manage costs so as to make a profit. Profit and loss budgets therefore get the most attention because that is where the action is.

As a consequence, in many businesses the balance sheet is like a stepchild left to his own devices on the theory that, if the household is run efficiently, he will somehow grow straight and strong. Also, if I may stretch the simile a bit further, he only gets attention when he gets sick or fails to do his chores.

Thus, many firms that are dedicated to an operating budget pay scant attention to the balance sheet and more or less let the assets and liabilities fall where they may. Many a neglected balance sheet grows strong anyway, but it is always at the cost of some profit and of the incurring of extra risk. The balance-sheet budget is a logical supplement to an operating budget, and its benefits, though less apparent, are more profound and lasting.

23.2 PURPOSE OF THE BALANCE-SHEET BUDGET. The purpose of the balance-sheet budget is to help management plan a mix of assets, liabilities, and equity that will:

- Permit an uninhibited operation of the business with the least investment.
- Maintain enough reserve strength to cushion economic shocks.
- Provide a capability for exploiting unforeseen opportunities.

The key word in balance sheet budgeting is *proportion.* The same quality that provides grace in art and strength in architecture lends effectiveness to the balance sheet. The size of a balance sheet account only has meaning when it is related to some other balance sheet or income account—or group of accounts. Unlike the profit and loss statement where more means better, the best balance sheet is one with optimum ratios rather than numbers.

23.3 DEFINITION. A *balance-sheet budget* is a systematic plan or forecast of future assets, liabilities, and equity. A typical arrangement of these balance-sheet accounts are shown in Exhibit 23.1. The need for such a plan arises because of the timing differences between business expenditures and income. Like an architect's plan for the construction of a building, it lays out in financial terms the resources (assets) needed to establish or carry on the business. The budget goes further, however, in that it also specifies where the money comes from (liabilities and equity) to acquire the necessary assets.

Assets
Current assets
  Cash and short-term investments
  Accounts receivable
  Inventories
  Prepaid expenses
Investments
Property, plant, and equipment
  Less accumulated depreciation
Intangible and miscellaneous assets

Liabilities and Equity
Current liabilities
  Notes payable
  Accounts payable
  Income tax payable
  Accrued liabilities
Current portion of long-term debt
Long-term debt
Deferred credits and other liabilities
Minority interest
Stockholders' equity
  Preferred and common stock
  Capital surplus
  Retained earnings

Exhibit 23.1. A typical arrangement of balance sheet accounts

23.4 RESPONSIBILITY FOR THE BUDGET. Used most effectively, the balance-sheet budget is a method not only for estimating and planning but also for controlling a company's various resources. Once the budget is agreed to, it becomes a standard against which future performance can be measured. For the budget to be fully effective, the responsibility for managing each item on the balance sheet should be assigned to a specific person or department as shown in Exhibit 23.2.

(a) Financial Assets. The financial assets—cash, short-term investments, and receivables—are normally the province of the chief financial officer (CFO). However, because the purpose of accounts receivable is to help market the company's products, it follows that the marketing department has a special interest in the firm's credit policy. The interest may be a little too special to permit complete control by the marketing people, but the best budget will allow them some say-so over receivables policy and hold them partly responsible for credit costs—the cost of money, credit administration, and bad debts.

There are many ways of handling this dual (finance and marketing) control over accounts receivable. Some considerations are:

- Salespeople should know the rudiments of credit approval, enough so that they can prescreen their prospective customers and be aware of those who are not likely to be approved.
- Credit investigation and approval is a speciality best done by credit professionals. In approving credit today, there is much less stress on ''character'' than there was in J. P. Morgan's day—people have not changed much, but it is harder, given modern

	Board of Directors	CEO	Finance	Marketing	Production	Administration
Assets						
Cash			Ⓟ[a]			
Short-term investments			Ⓟ			
Accounts receivable			Ⓟ	◯		
Inventory			◯	◯	Ⓟ	
Fixed assets	◯	Ⓟ	◯	◯	◯	◯
Liabilities						
Notes payable		Ⓟ	◯			
Accounts payable			Ⓟ		◯	
Taxes payable		◯	Ⓟ			
Long-term debt	◯	Ⓟ	◯			
Equity	Ⓟ	◯	◯			

[a] Ⓟ indicates primary responsibility.

Exhibit 23.2. Balance-sheet budget responsibility

communications, to deceive. The emphasis has shifted to "capacity," which is measured by an analysis of a company's financial strength.

- The collection of past-due accounts works well as a joint effort of marketing and finance. The following steps should be taken:
  - The initial step in collection should be a friendly, but impersonal, notice that payment has not been received. A good many past-due payments are the result of misunderstandings, errors, and disputes that could be the fault of either party.
  - The second stage of collection—from, say, 10 to 30 days past due—is often best left to the salesperson handling the account. The advantages are that it provides a friendly approach that can often be combined with a further sales effort; it offers a more direct means (than working through the credit department) of resolving disputes and adjustments; and, should his or her efforts fail, it softens the salesperson to a harder collection effort by the credit department.
  - If stronger means of collection are required, marketing should leave the field to finance. Salespeople would only be in the way, and there is no point in associating salespeople with disagreeable, but necessary, pressures on the customer.

(b) Inventory Levels. Inventory levels are usually managed by the chief production officer in a manufacturing company or the purchasing officer in a retail organization. However, there is often an important influence, it not authority, from the marketing managers.

Moreover, the CFO has an implied responsibility to see that the cash tied up in inventory is yielding the highest return. The purpose of inventory is to uncouple production and sales so that temporary stops and spurts of activity in one will not affect the other.[1] Production is most efficient when it is a smooth and continuous flow. Customers, however,

[1] John D. Martin et al., *Basic Financial Management* (Englewood Cliffs, NJ: Prentice-Hall, 1979), p. 231.

could not care less. They want their goods when they want them, and delivery delays very often jeopardize a sale.

Decision models for inventory control, such as the Economic Order Quantity (EOQ) model,[2] are in fairly widespread use. Generally, their purpose is to find the right balance between the cost of carrying inventory—tied-up money, storage, insurance, and obsolescence—and the cost of replenishing stock.

(c) Fixed Assets. The fixed assets of a firm are usually controlled at the point of purchase by a capital-expenditures policy. Typically, the manager or department that will use the asset proposes its purchase, and a capital-investment committee consisting of the chief executive officer (CEO), the CFO, and other executives or directors passes on the proposal.

(d) Liabilities. The management of a company's liabilities is concentrated in the general staff nucleus. As expected, the CFO plays an important role—sometimes primary, sometimes secondary—in the day-to-day management of all liabilities and shareholder affairs. The chief executive is also active in nearly all debt equity management. Even if he or she has little training or interest in finance, the company's commercial and investment bankers generally insist on considerable personal involvement.

(e) Accounts Payable. Accounts payable are usually handled automatically by the controller's department. The purchase of goods on credit carries an implicit promise to pay on a particular day. Although trade credit is notoriously flexible, the complacence of suppliers should not be taken as a sign that they are uncaring about prompt payment. Occasionally, there are stories of companies that deliberately pay their accounts late so as to earn more interest on their cash balances. Such policies are, in a word, dumb. The monetary gains—measured in hundredths of a percentage point per day—are so far from the potential cost attending a loss of trust as to brand such policies as misguided, at best.

When a company is unable, as opposed to unwilling, to pay trade creditors on time, the finance department may be aided by the purchasing department in obtaining extensions or in setting priorities of payment. There may be a hundred items of supply, the lack of any one of which being enough to shut down a production line. The more nearly that condition exists, the more influence the production department should have in managing accounts payable.

(f) Notes Payable. Notes payable to banks, and any long-term credit arrangements, are frequently covered by loan agreements that, among other things, require the maintenance of certain balance-sheet ratios. Typical examples of requirements are a debt–equity ratio less than 1.00, or a current ratio greater than 1.50. The management of such ratios—an unwieldy job at best—falls to the CFO. Lenders of large sums, however, will insist upon the close involvement of the CEO, and although they may listen to the explanations of the CFO, they like to talk right into the horse's ear.

(g) Corporate Taxes. The management of corporate taxes increases in importance and complexity with each passing year. One may now obtain a Master's degree in taxation (for example, from the fully accredited Golden Gate University, San Francisco), and the

---

[2] Roger D. Eck, *Operations Research for Business* (Belmont, CA: Wadsworth Publishing, 1976), p. 347.

title "Vice-President, Taxes" is no longer rare. Such a post is normally under the CFO; however, the expectation today is that the CEO will be actively ratifying taxation strategies, if not actually directing them. The switch, for example, from a first-in–first-out (FIFO) to a last-in–first-out (LIFO) valuation of inventory can have far-reaching effects not only on the cash flow of a corporation but also on the reported earnings, which in turn affects the cost of equity capital.

(h) Capital Structure. The management of a corporation's capital structure (long-term debt plus equity) generally requires the personal direction of the CEO. The task of finding the optimal mix of semipermanent funds—that is, the combination that will maximize stockholders' return—is very difficult. (Perhaps the classic, and still pertinent, book on this subject is Solomon's *The Theory of Financial Management.*[3]) It requires the aid, on the one hand, of a CFO familiar with the concepts of leverage and the cost of capital and the mature judgment, on the other hand, of a board of directors as to the outlook for the economy, interest rates, and equity financing. In smaller firms, in which the deeply personal and hidden motives of shareholders have more sway, it requires a CEO who not only knows the right thing to do but is able to persuade others to it.

The American economy in the 1970s, 1980s, and 1990s witnessed the usual cycles of high growth and recession that are endemic to capitalism (or "market economy," if you prefer).

When times are good, investors are enthused, and as stories of success follow one another, capital flows into new investments. Unfortunately, we have no way of knowing when the amount of new investment is sufficient—we only know when there is too much. Overinvestment drives down dollar profits and devastates percentage returns, setting the stage for recession. This cycle is about as predictable as the flu and at least as unpleasant.

When a recession does occur, those firms with the weakest demand for their products or services and/or the weakest balance sheets are unsentimentally weeded out until supply and demand is once again in harmony and the seeds of new growth can once again take root.

Perhaps the only thing surprising about the business cycle is the way people tend to ignore it—stretching themselves too thin in times of prosperity, and deploring the lack of bank support just when the economy turns sour and they need borrowed money the most. The renascent timidity of investors and bankers is forseeable, even if the economic downturns to which they respond are not.

Two principles should guide senior executives in their capital-structure decisions. First, the more debt a company has, the more dependent it is on future cash flows. The requirement to pay interest and principal is implacable, while the stream of future profits ebbs and flows. Adjust the debt–equity mix, therefore, to the uncertainty of future earnings, and keep a liquidity reserve to see you through the dry spells that are almost certain to come.

That great teacher, *experience*, who likes to give the test first and the lesson afterward, repeats this instruction for business newcomers every five to ten years or so: The way you make money with borrowed funds is the same way you lose it; borrowed money multiplies both profits and losses.

---

[3] Ezra Solomon, *The Theory of Financial Management* (New York: Columbia University Press, 1963).

Compounding the "normal" business cycle is a new era of manufacturing ushered in by the Japanese who have leapfrogged the mass-production system with their "lean-production" methods. While these revolutionary changes have been going on for a decade, many U.S. firms have been slow to react. That company of companies, General Motors, sailed into the rough seas and dropped $2 billion before noticing the water crashing over the deck.[4]

A second guideline is to earn an adequate return on assets (ROA). The penalty for having a skimpy ROA is not limited to the agitated reaction of a faceless horde of shareholders. Their annoyance can unsettle a shareholders' meeting, but they rarely act in concert enough to do something really disgusting such as getting rid of senior executives. A worse problem is that we have entered an era of leveraged buyouts and unfriendly takeovers. Those companies whose assets are earning less than they would if sold to somebody else are enticing corporate raiders. A low ROA betokens change—in managers, products, and marketing. It is true that many business problems resolve themselves while waiting for us to act, but not this one.

23.5 TYPES OF FINANCIAL BUDGETS.

There are three principal categories of budgets, sometimes referred to as *financial budgets* or *financial plans* to distinguish them from the more detailed operating budgets.

(a) Profit Budget.

If we accept the premise that the primary purpose of a business enterprise is to create customers and thereby earn a profit, then it is clear that the profit budget is the compass by which it steers. In its simplest form, business has two functions: (1) make a product or provide a service and (2) sell it. All employees and all activities of a firm support one or the other or both of these functions. The profit budget sets forth the anticipated revenues (a self-set goal within a frame of reasonable expectations) and the expense of producing the products, selling them, managing the business, and financing it.

The profit budget is compiled from estimates by each of the several operating departments. Once approved by management, it returns to those departments in the form of an operating budget—a detailed plan for their activities.

(b) Cash Budget.

The cash budget is a schedule of cash receipts and disbursements. Its initial objective is to take a weekly or monthly reading of expected cash balances so as to determine the amount and timing of any new financing that may be needed.

Final approval of a cash budget may depend in part on the company's bank or other financing source. In the typical business, there is a rhythm to the ebb and flow of cash and a gradual accumulation from profits. However, the development of the profit budget—particularly those parts dealing with long-range goals, product mix strategies, and the economic outlook—will also give rise to cash needs for new capital assets. Perhaps a larger manufacturing plant will be necessary to meet production goals; special equipment may be needed to produce a new product; or plans might include opening a sales and service center in Europe.

Such capital investments likewise affect the balance sheet, sometimes profoundly. Moreover, once begun, they may be difficult or impossible to stop and in ways large and small forever alter the company's circumstances.

For example, the Singer (sewing machine) Company's capital budgeting decision to manufacture computer systems was found later to have been a serious mistake. Undoing

[4] Donald Woutat, *Los Angeles Times,* May 30, 1992, p. 1.

it in the mid-1970s wiped out in one fell swoop three quarters of the retained earnings patiently accumulated by the company over 125 years.

Decisions, therefore, regarding such crucial proposals are usually made with the careful consideration of a capital investment committee, which normally includes representatives from general management, finance, the board of directors, and, when appropriate, marketing, production, and other specialities.

(c) Balance-Sheet Budget. The balance-sheet budget has a format similar to the other two—major balance-sheet items are listed month by month. This budget will reflect the levels of current and fixed assets needed to support the expected sales. Most current and long-term liabilities will also be affected over time by changes in the sales volume, and the line showing retained earnings will change each month by the amount of the profit or loss and dividends declared. The object of this budget is to ensure that month-by-month liquidity is adequate and that the leverage is controlled. It helps to include as supplementary line items the basic ratios that measure these important financial characteristics.

22.6 PREPARING FINANCIAL BUDGETS.

The budget process is now widely established in the large public corporations, most medium-sized firms, and a good many smaller ones. Companies whose own volition may not incline them to a budget system are often persuaded to it by their bankers, who find budgeting to be a valuable passageway leading from the "art of lending" to the "science of lending."

Bringing a budget to a point at which the time and effort spent in creating it is matched by its usefulness requires seasoning. It will take the typical firm from two to five years to make all of the parts fit, to accustom employees to the disciplined thought process and paperwork required, to condition senior management to using a budget as the basis of a reward system, and to harden by exposure the determination needed to make any complex system of rules work. When first seen by middle managers, a budget may seem to be another way of tightening control over their activities. In fact, it more sharply defines the goals to be achieved but expands the influence of middle managers in setting the goals and finding the best means to reach them. The steps in preparing financial budgets are shown in Exhibit 23.3.

It is one thing to work for a company with a budget in place and quite another to be involved in creating a budget system from the ground up. Here are some guidelines for the latter task.

(a) Budget System Checklist

Information Needed

1. Past sales figures in dollars *and* units by
   - a. Product
   - b. Territory
   - c. Distribution (such as dealer sales and direct sales)
2. Industry sales figures
   - a. Domestic production
   - b. Imports
   - c. Generic competitors[5] (who satisfy the same needs with other types of products, as, for example, makers of mopeds or jogging equipment might for bicycle customers)

[5] Philip Kotler, *Marketing Management* (Englewood Cliffs, NJ: Prentice-Hall, 1976) p. 25.

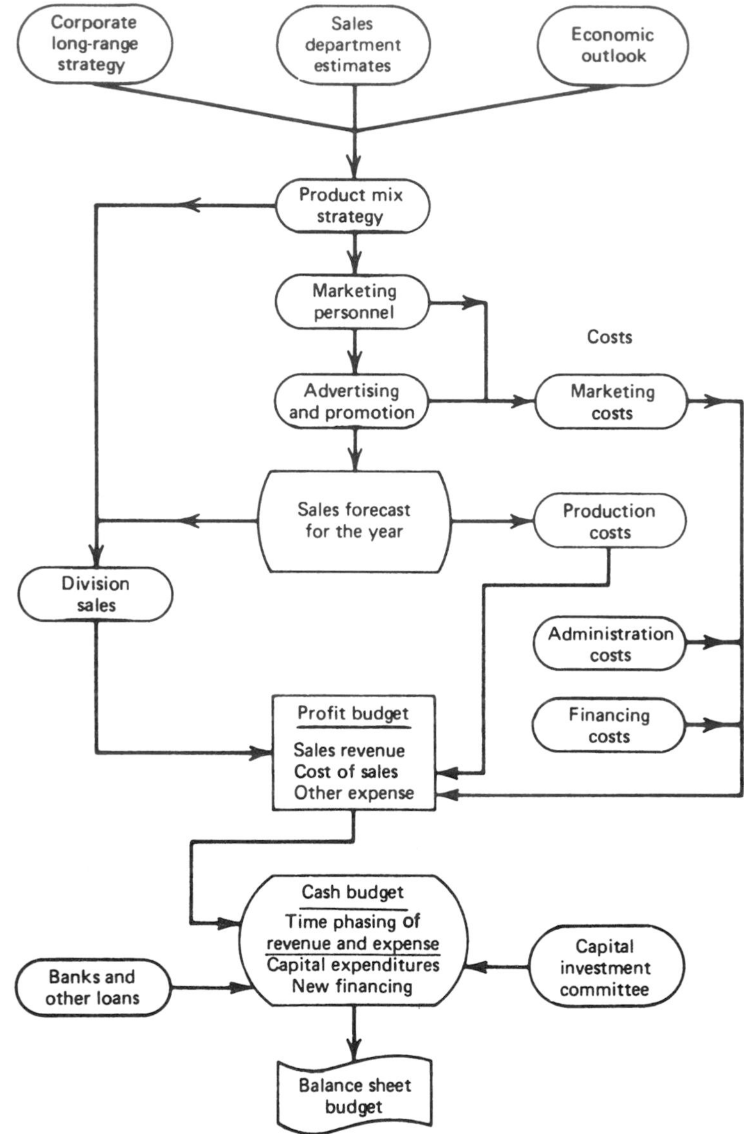

Exhibit 23.3. Steps in preparing the financial budget

3. Economic forecasts
4. Estimates of the potential market for any new product or new group of customers
5. Expenses
   a. Cost of goods sold
   b. Marketing, administration, and other expense
6. New capital equipment needs
   a. Production equipment
   b. Data processing, communications, and general office equipment
   c. Warehouse space, materials handling equipment, and vehicles
7. External financing requirements

Chronology

1. Set corporate sales and profit goals.
2. Prepare standard forms and write instructions for the various budgets.
3. Get ground-floor estimates of
   a. Future sales to existing customers
   b. Personnel requirements, by department throughout the company
   c. Lists of new equipment needed
   d. Existing lines of credit
4. Prepare the required budgets.
   a. Sales and profit budget
   b. Production budget
      - Materials budget
      - Direct labor budget
      - Manufacturing overhead budget
   c. Marketing expense budget
      - Sales personnel budget (salespersons and their managers)
      - Sales administration budget
      - Advertising and promotion budget
      - Distribution budget (including warehousing and delivery equipment expense)
      - Service and parts budget
   d. Research and development budget
   e. Administration budget (including the CEO's and the finance department)
   f. Capital-investment budget
   g. Cash budget (including financing costs)
   h. Balance-sheet budget
      - Accounts receivable budget
      - Inventory budgets: raw materials, work in process, finished goods (units and dollars), and manufacturing supplies
      - Fixed-asset budget
5. Assemble the subbudgets and prepare the financial plan or master budget.
6. Review the master budget and negotiate necessary changes with affected departments.
7. Redo the subbudgets based on the final version of the master budget.
8. Reproduce and distribute the master and subsidiary budgets.
9. Each ensuing month get actual performance figures and identify variances.
10. Conduct monthly management reviews of performance compared to budget.

As time passes, the need may arise to change the master budget. Most companies will redo their fiscal year's budget at least once during the period. Some firms—and it helps to have automated the budgeting process—prepare a full year's budget each month, continuously inputting current information. There is a danger, however, in overbudgeting—in amassing such a quantity of detail that the chain linking the effect and cause of problems becomes too long for use in day-to-day management.[6]

23.7 PREPARING THE BALANCE-SHEET BUDGET. The only way to learn to prepare a balance-sheet budget is to do it. A handbook such as this will remind you of the information needed and the steps to take and thus save you a great deal of time. However,

[6] J. Fred Weston and Eugene F. Brigham, *Managerial Finance* (Hinsdale, Il: The Dryden Press, 1978), p. 121.

PROJECTION OF
FINANCIAL STATEMENTS

SUBMITTED BY American Skate Company

ACTUAL PROJECTIONS ☞

		SPREAD IN HUNDREDS ☐ / SPREAD IN THOUSANDS ☑ — DATE / PERIOD	12-31-79 Year	Jan	Feb	Mar	Apr	
PROFIT and LOSS	1	NET SALES	4 358	437	479	523	501	1
	2	Less: Materials Used	1 651	186	204	223	214	2
	3	Direct Labor	507	51	56	61	59	3
	4	Other Manufacturing Expense	595	60	66	72	69	4
	5	Depreciation	32	3	3	4	3	5
	6	COST OF GOODS SOLD	2 985	300	329	360	345	6
	7	GROSS PROFIT	1 373	137	150	163	156	7
	8	Less: Sales Expense	436	37	41	42	42	8
	9	General Administrative Expense	606	57	58	59	59	9
	10							10
	11	OPERATING PROFIT	331	43	51	62	55	11
	12	Less: Other Expense or Income (Net)						12
	13	Income Tax Provision	133	17	20	25	22	13
	14							14
	15	NET PROFIT	198	26	31	37	33	15
CASH PROJECTIONS	16	CASH BALANCE (Opening) (Incl securities)		138	157	43	46	16
	17	Plus RECEIPTS: Receivable Collections		421	246	450	492	17
	18							18
	19	Fixed Asset Financing			24			19
	20	Bank Loan Proceeds		24	10	22		20
	21	Total		583	528	515	538	21
	22	Less: DISBURSEMENTS: Trade Payables–Mtls		191	213	202	188	22
	23	Direct Labor		61	59	54	50	23
	24	Other M'fg Expense		69	69	66	61	24
	25	Sales Gen'l and Adm. Exp.		94	99	101	101	25
	26	Fixed Asset Additions		5	39	5	5	26
	27	Income Taxes				26	33	27
	28							28
	29	Dividends or Withdrawals				8		29
	30	Payments on long-term debt		6	6	7	7	30
	31	Bank Loan Repayment					10	31
	32	Total		426	485	469	455	32
	33	CASH BALANCE (Closing)		157	43	46	83	33
BALANCE SHEET	34	ASSETS: Cash	48	57	43	46	83	34
	35	Marketable Securities	90	100				35
	36	Receivables (Net)	536	552	785	858	867	36
	37	Inventory (Net)	875	916	914	856	786	37
	38	Prepaid Expenses	49	50	51	51	52	38
	39	CURRENT ASSETS	1 598	1 675	1 793	1 811	1 788	39
	40	Fixed Assets (Net)	372	374	410	411	413	40
	41							41
	42	Other Tangible Assets	128	128	128	128	128	42
	43							43
	44	Deferred Charges	38	38	38	38	38	44
	45	TOTAL ASSETS	2 136	2 215	2 369	2 388	2 367	45
	46	LIABILITIES: Notes Payable–Banks	312	336	437	459	449	46
	47	Trade Payables	304	322	305	280	254	47
	48	Income Tax	26	42	61	58	46	48
	49							49
	50	Current Portion-LTD	72	72	84	84	84	50
	51	Accruals and Other	41	41	42	43	43	51
	52	CURRENT LIABILITIES	755	813	929	924	876	52
	53	Long-Term Debt	217	211	217	210	203	53
	54	Deferred Taxes	71	72	73	75	76	54
	55							55
	56	CAPITAL STOCK } Net Worth for	245	245	245	245	245	56
	57	SURPLUS } Partnership or Individual	848	874	905	934	967	57
	58	TOTAL LIABILITIES AND NET WORTH	2 136	2 215	2 369	2 388	2 367	58
	59	WORKING CAPITAL	843	862	864	887	912	59

Exhibit 23.4. American Skate Company—projection of financial statements

FOLD HERE - COMMENTS AND SUGGESTIONS ON REVERSE

May	Jun	Jul	Aug	Sept		Oct	Nov	Dec	Year		
458	414	370	425	468	1	512	447	196	5 230		1
196	177	159	183	201	2	221	193	85	2 242		2
54	49	44	50	55	3	60	53	23	615		3
63	56	50	59	65	4	72	61	25	718		4
3	4	3	3	4	5	3	4	4	41		5
316	286	256	295	325	6	356	311	137	3 616		6
142	128	114	130	143	7	156	136	59	1 614		7
44	43	43	45	45	8	46	48	47	523		8
60	60	61	62	62	9	63	63	64	728		9
					10						10
38	25	10	23	36	11	47	25	(52)	363		11
					12						12
15	10	4	9	14	13	19	10	(20)	145		13
					14						14
23	15	6	14	22	15	28	15	(32)	218		15
83	175	191	189	158	16	87	179	247	138		16
516	488	445	401	386	17	438	482	492	5 257		17
					18						18
					19	96			120		19
			8	21	20	21			197		20
599	663	636	598	565	21	642	661	739	5 712		21
172	175	188	200	196	22	138	183	226	2 272		22
45	47	54	56	56	23	36	44	66	628		23
56	53	58	65	66	24	53	45	62	723		24
104	103	104	107	107	25	109	111	111	1 251		25
5	6	5	5	5	26	120	5	6	211		26
	33			33	27			33	158		27
					28						28
	12			8	29			12	40		29
7	7	7	7	7	30	7	11	11	90		30
35	36	31			31		15	123	250		31
424	472	447	440	478	32	463	414	650	5 623		32
175	191	189	158	87	33	179	247	89	89		33
85	61	49	58	57	34	59	57	39			34
90	130	140	100	30	35	120	190	50			35
809	735	660	684	766	36	840	805	509			36
757	765	836	851	744	37	742	704	965			37
53	54	55	55	56	38	57	58	59			38
1 794	1 745	1 740	1 748	1 653	39	1 818	1 814	1 622			39
415	417	419	421	422	40	539	540	542			40
					41						41
128	128	128	128	128	42	128	128	128			42
					43						43
38	38	38	38	38	44	38	38	38			44
2 375	2 328	2 325	2 335	2 241	45	2 523	2 520	2 330			45
414	378	347	355	376	46	397	382	259			46
265	280	306	291	187	47	311	310	352			47
60	36	40	48	28	48	46	55	3			48
					49						49
84	84	84	84	84	50	132	132	132			50
44	45	44	45	46	51	47	46	45			51
867	823	821	823	721	52	933	925	791			52
196	189	182	175	168	53	209	198	187			53
77	78	78	79	80	54	81	82	81			54
					55						55
245	245	245	245	245	56	245	245	245			56
990	993	999	1 013	1 027	57	1 055	1 070	1 026			57
2 375	2 328	2 325	2 335	2 241	58	2 523	2 520	2 330			58
927	922	919	925	932	59	885	889	831			59

Exhibit 23.4. *(Continued)*

our minds are not accustomed to thinking in the slow plodding way that budgets are built. Mistakes are reducible but inevitable. The personal computer (PC) with electronic spreadsheet (such as Lotus 1-2-3 or Excel) is a near-perfect tool for this task. If such equipment is unavailable or you are *still* computer illiterate, do the work with a No. 2 pencil. In the past, I have done or reviewed hundreds of budgets and cannot recall a single one that was completed without wearing out an eraser or two.

Throughout this chapter, examples are used from a fictional manufacturing firm, the American Skate Company, a maker of roller skates. All three of its financial budgets—income, cash, and balance sheet—are shown complete in Exhibit 23.4. In addition to a discussion of the balance-sheet budget in general terms, a step-by-step explanation will be given of how the cash budget and balance-sheet budget were constructed. (The derivation of the income budget is not discussed, having been covered in earlier chapters.) There are also chapters on cash budgeting, but that activity is so closely linked with balance-sheet budgeting that an explanation of one without the other would be like a treatise on effective parenting without mention of the child.

A stock printed form will be used for this example. It can be reproduced on Lotus by someone with moderate skill. There are also several software programs for the PC that offer ready-made formats for budgeting. The complexity, sophistication, ease of use, and price of these programs varies widely. The best way to find a good one is the way you would find a dentist in a new town—referral by someone who likes you.

If your budgeting is a prelude to applying for a bank loan, ask your banker's opinion of planning formats. Most commercial loan officers are well engaged in computer forecasting, and using their format might add to your convenience and lessen their resistance.

One feature to look for in a budget package is the simultaneous development of all three financial budgets—income, balance sheet, and cash flow. For example, when a number on the cash budget is changed, the cash line on the balance sheet should be automatically adjusted also. It helps to have a complete view of the financial consequences of the budgeting process in a single format.

(a) Cash and Short-Term Investments. If the balance sheet budget is prepared without an accompanying cash budget, cash—the first item on the balance sheet—is the last line item to be completed. It becomes, in effect, the ''plug'' figure that makes the balance sheet balance. The usual procedure is to work out all the other items (as will be discussed) and then to drop in the balancing cash figures. Excesses and shortfalls of cash that are revealed are interplayed with the short-term investment or bank loan accounts to adjust the cash balances to the desirable figure.

If the cash budget is prepared beforehand, the cash balances are already known and are simply transferred to the balance sheet budget.

(b) Accounts Receivable. Accounts receivable balances are highly correlated to the company's sales, rising and falling in unison with these revenues at some time later. One of the simplest ways of forecasting accounts receivable is to begin by calculating the company's average collection period from the most recent balance sheet:

$$\text{Average collection period} = \frac{\text{Accounts receivable}}{\text{Sales for the year}} \times 365$$

The average collection period (also referred to as days sales outstanding) is then applied to each month's forecasted sales to determine the receivable balance.

Where there is a pronounced seasonality to sales, as in the case of the American Skate Company (notice the low point in December in Exhibit 23.4), a more accurate average is obtained using just the fourth quarter (Q4) 1979 sales figures:

Q4–1979	Sales (thousands)
October	$427
November	372
December	164
Total	$963

Because we are using the sales of only one quarter, the multiplier in our formula is the number of days in the quarter:

$$\text{Average collection period} = \frac{\$536}{\$963} \times 92 = 51 \text{ days}$$

Therefore, the accounts receivable forecast each month were the current month's sales plus 21/30ths of the previous month's sales. The method is illustrated in Exhibit 23.5. Once the receivable balances are known, the receivable collections can be computed. They will equal the current sales (minus an increase or plus a decrease) in the receivable balance. The resulting balances, line 3, and collections, line 7, are then transferred to Exhibit 23.4, lines 36 and 17.

Another popular method of estimating accounts receivable balances is to note what percentage of a month's sales is collected in each subsequent month and to forecast the uncollected balances on the same basis. The American Skate Company found the following pattern:

	Accounts Receivable	
Typical Month	Paid During Month	Owing at End of Month
Current month	5%	95%
One month later	45	50
Two months later	25	25
Three months later	25	0

Now, to forecast the accounts receivable balance on, say, March 31, 1980, the percentages are applied to March and previous months' sales:

Month	Sales (thousands)
March	$523 × 0.95 = $497
February	479 × 0.50 = 240
January	437 × 0.25 = 109
Total	$846

The two methods of forecasting produce slightly different results. The second method is more reflective of the way money really is collected, but it requires more estimates (the

American Skate Company
Projection of Accounts Receivable
$000s

	1980 →	JAN	FEB	MAR	APR	MAY	JUN	JUL	AUG	SEP	OCT	NOV	DEC	TOTAL
1	Sales [a]	437	479	523	501	458	414	370	425	468	512	447	196	5230
2	21/30 of prev mo	115	306	335	366	351	321	290	259	298	328	358	313	
3	Total [b]	552	785	858	867	809	735	660	684	766	840	805	509	
4														
5	Change in A/R balance	16	233	73	9	(58)	(74)	(75)	24	82	74	(35)	(296)	(27)
6	Collections:													
7	Line 1 - Line 5 [c]	421	246	450	492	516	488	445	401	386	438	482	492	5257
8														
9														
10	References:													
11	[a] From Exh. 17–4, L1													
12	[b] To " , L36													
13	[c] To " , L17													
14														
15														
16														
17														
18														
19														
20														
21														
22														
23														
24														
25														
26														
27														
28														
29														
30														
31														

Exhibit 23.5. American Skate Company—projection of accounts receivable

percentages) and additional work. To reflect the real world, the collection percentages would spread out more like nine months than three, tripling the work but improving the results very little. My own preference is the first method (using the average collection period) because it is a little easier and faster. Besides, the more refinements one makes of estimates, the less chance one leaves for errors to cancel out one another.

That is not as facetious as it sounds. There are many factors that influence customers to pay their bills: their cash on hand; the pressure from other creditors; opportunities to earn a discount by paying promptly or to earn interest by not; and their attitude toward the creditor company, its representatives, and its products. Most important is the way *their* cash flows and that of *their* customers and their customers' customers, and so on. Like the images reflected in interfacing mirrors, the influences on the collection of receivables are an endless series of circumstances that can never be fully known, much less foretold.

(c) Inventories. In general there are five factors that influence the amount of inventory a company will seek to have on hand: (1) level of sales, (2) length of the production process, (3) availability of raw materials, (4) durability of finished goods, and (5) distribution methods.

(i) Level of Sales. In most companies the relationship of inventory to sales is relatively constant. The number of times inventory is "turned over" in a year may vary widely from one industry to another and moderately between firms in the same industry, but in the same company over time the variance is usually slight. A useful measure of inventory turnover is the days sales in inventory (DSI) ratio:

$$\text{DSI} = \frac{\text{Inventory}}{\text{Period cost of sales}} \times \text{Days in the period}$$

An example of the calculation using figures from the American Skate Company December 31, 1979, balance sheet (Exhibit 23.4) is as follows (dollars are in thousands):

$$\frac{\text{(Line 37)}\ \$875}{\text{(Line 6)}\ \$2{,}985} \times 365 = 107\ \text{days}$$

Because of seasonal fluctuations, a more accurate figure is obtained using figures from only the fourth quarter of the year:

Month	Cost of Sales (thousands)
October 1979	$290
November	255
December	113
Total	$658

$$\text{DSI} = \frac{\$875}{\$658} \times 92 = 122\ \text{days}$$

As this figure is approximately four months, one simple method of planning inventory levels is to add the latest four months' cost of sales. Thus, the inventory for January 1980 would be planned at $958 ($658 + $300).

Unlike accounts receivable, however, which relate to *past* sales, inventory is there to service *future* sales. So a better planning technique is the calculation of future DSI. Using the beginning inventory and the cost of sales for Q1–1980 we find (dollars in thousands)

$$\text{Future DSI} = \frac{\$875}{\$300 + 329 + 360} \times 91 = 81 \text{ days}$$

If this method were to be used, the assumption that 81 days' inventory is adequate should be tested by computing the future DSI for known periods in the past, particularly those that included unforeseen sales fluctuations or for which inventory shortages are remembered. A future DSI of 81 days means that inventory at the end of each month is equal to the next two months' cost of sales plus 20/30ths of the third months. Using our example:

Month	Cost of Sales (thousands)
February 1980	$329
March	360
April × ⅔	230
Desired inventory at 1-31-80	$919

As mentioned previously, the main function of inventory is to uncouple production activities from sales activities, so that if someone in manufacturing catches a cold, it will not cause a sneeze in marketing. The trade-offs for having an abundance of inventory are the people, space, and money thus used and the increased risk of loss from obsolescense. Moreover, every dollar in inventory is one less dollar in the checking account, one less available to pay expenses or make other profitable investments.

(ii) Length of Production Process. A company that manufactures electronic testing equipment is apt to require an average DSI of 120 days or more because of the complexity of the production process and the many tests needed for quality control. A meat packer, on the other hand, would need a gas mask to count inventory if the DSI went much beyond two weeks.[7] The inventory budgeting of wholesalers or retailers who want to uncouple their purchasing and sales activities is much less complicated than that of manufacturers, who must maintain slack between their raw material purchasing and production process, as well as the sales of finished goods.

(iii) Availability of Raw Materials. By definition, all manufacturers have a raw material inventory. *Raw* refers to the fact that it has not yet entered the production process. A completely finished and tested cathode ray tube may be the raw material of a computer

[7] Composite financial data on more than 300 lines of business can be found in *Annual Statement Studies,* published by Robert Morris Associates.

equipment manufacturer.[8] Determining the size of this inventory is a study unique to each individual firm. The following are some of the factors to be considered:

- Purchase period—order processing and delivery time
- Future demand in relation to the suppliers' capacity
- Payment requirements—terms of sale and availability of credit
- Outlook for prices
- Possible labor disruptions
- Other, nonbusiness, hindrance to supply lines

Just-in-time (JIT) inventory management has gained a respectable audience in the United States after being pioneered by the Japanese industrial juggernaut. As the name implies, its purpose is to reduce manufacturers' stocks or raw materials by having suppliers make more timely deliveries, thereby making the whole process more efficient.

The demand by large manufacturers for delivery times and quantities that suit *their* convenience rather than the suppliers' seems to have stimulated some efficiencies such as shortening set-up times for manufacturing runs and forcing greater coordination between production and shipping.

If, however, we look behind the apparent benefits of JIT we see the same old struggle (described below) that characterizes virtually all chains of distribution: The effort to place the burden and expense of inventory with someone else. It appears that in many cases the benefits of JIT to the customer simply become a greater burden to the supplier who must increase his own inventories to ensure the prompt deliveries now required. Moreover, the closer we tie the customer and supplier the more each shares the other's mistakes and misfortunes if and when they occur.

(iv) Durability of Finished Goods. With respect to finished goods, durability means not only resistance to wear and decay but also the whims of fashion, style changes, and technical innovations. The manufacturer of hammers, saws, and screwdrivers has few problems with durability.[9] The same could be said for makers of wristwatches until the electronic model was developed.

(v) Distribution Methods. There is an axiom in marketing management that the best location for inventory is the one nearest the final customer. Typically, that would mean with the dealer or retailer who sells to the end user. However, the financial burden and risks attending inventories are not welcomed with open arms. The automobile industry employs floor-plan financing and enthusiastic persuasion to keep dealer lots choked with new models. Magazine and book publishers practice a form of consignment with their liberal ''returns'' policies. It is perhaps fitting that the principal inventory burden is usually borne by the manufacturers, for they have the most to gain of all members of the distribution chain. With some notable exceptions, middlemen exist at the sufferance of the manufacturer; if the middle ground gets fertile enough, a vertical marketing system soon emerges.

---

[8] *See* footnote 1, p. 232.

[9] *See* footnote 6, p. 190.

(vi) Illustration of a Comprehensive Inventory Budget. A comprehensive inventory budget would take into account the five factors that have been enumerated. This can be illustrated with the American Skate Company case.

Studies by the company's engineers showed that the average length of the production process was 15 days, including the averaging in of weekends and a factor for holidays. The average value of goods in the production cycle was 81% of their final total cost. No dramatic changes were anticipated for the coming year, although the firm was constantly on the lookout for new production equipment that would increase efficiency.

There were some concerns about the availability of raw materials. The bulk of the purchases were of raw polyurethane, steel and nylon bearings, and leather. Although these items, except for some of the metal bearings, were available locally and on relatively short notice, the company made it a practice to keep a month's supply on hand. The raw materials used were normally about 62% of total cost of sales. No changes in the supply pattern were foreseen for 1980. In the forecast of sales and cost of goods sold, an assumption was made that inflation would account for an 8% increase in dollar sales and a slightly higher increase in the cost of sales.

As to the durability of the finished goods, American Skate had few problems, of course, with breakage and spoilage. But the public's fancy for skating products was another matter. The demand for skateboards had reached its peak in the mid-1970s and had declined slowly but steadily the remainder of the decade. The sales lost in that area, however, were more than offset by a spurt in the sales of shoe skates with the new polyurethane wheels. In fact, 1978 witnessed a modest fad for shoe skates, with much of the demand coming from new, adult customers who favored the high end of the line. (It is one thing to buy skates for your nephew, but another when they are for yourself.)

Sales to this new market segment held steady in 1979, which was taken by some members of American Skate's management to mean that the honeymoon for expensive shoe skates was now or soon to be ended. Moreover, there were a number of new competitor manufacturers gearing up for this uncertain market. (Some of these became original equipment manufacturers customers of American Skate.) During 1979 the finished goods inventory had averaged 50 days' sales, and the consensus of management was that it should be targeted for 45 days in 1980.

Then too, there had been discussions about the state of the economy. Most economists had branded 1979 a recession year, and when subsequent statistics failed to ratify their opinion, many of them said we had had a small dip and would soon have another—and later some even said three dips—in the year's economy (a tactic that *Barron's* promptly labeled the "ice cream cone" method of forecasting). To compound the confusion, the company's senior managers had not themselves seen any signs of the elusive recession other than what the media said. It was decided that the company should have a prompt budget review if and when there was a verified change in the economy but for the present make no adjustments for that possibility. The discussion ended with a quote attributed to G. B. Shaw that if all the economists were laid end to end, they would not reach a conclusion.[10]

As to methods of distribution, American Skate used a variety of marketing channels.[11] Sales were made to wholesalers, direct to large retailers, original equipment manufacturers, and, if the order were large enough, to skating rinks. This diversity of distribution channels

[10] *Modern Quotations* (New York: Penguin Books, 1971, 211:73).

[11] *See* footnote 5, p. 276.

resulted in a strong resistance by the wholesalers to stocking large inventories, and there seemed to be little the company could do to shift some of its finished goods closer to the end user.

After all factors were considered, the company set the following three standards as a basis for its 1980 inventory budget:

1. Finished goods inventory at the end of January should equal the next 50 days' sales and gradually decline to 45 days' sales by December 31.
2. Work-in-process inventory represented the goods in the production pipeline. That figure stood at $133,000 and varied little. Although production would be sped up or slowed according to the pattern of sales, the amount of goods in a semifinished state remained the same. The company was operating at 75% of capacity and would need no major additional facilities to handle 1980 production.
3. Raw materials inventory at month's end should be sufficient to produce the goods expected to be sold in the third month forward.

Once the standards were agreed to, the final inventory budget was constructed, as illustrated in Exhibit 23.6.

Having made an inventory budget, the company was able to schedule production. The production in any given month will be

$$\text{Goods sold} \pm \text{Change in finished goods inventory} = \text{Goods manufactured}$$

In some companies the management of production is more critical than the management of inventory, and the formula becomes

$$\text{Goods manufactured} - \text{Goods sold} = \text{Finished goods inventory change}$$

Almost every situation requires some trade-offs between manufacturing control and inventory control. The advantages of large-scale purchases, steady production flows, and well-stocked shelves are obvious and, unfortunately, often beguiling. What is not so obvious are the great risks and costs that accompany excessive inventory. There is more truth, perhaps, than style in the grim proverb that "inventory is the graveyard of business." Losses may arise from obsolescence, fashion changes, or the lowering of prices by competitors. The costs of carrying inventory include the expense of storage, insurance, shrinkage, and lost opportunity on the money that is tied up.

At American Skate the supply of raw materials was plentiful, the production process uncomplicated, and the labor market—for the time being—stable and adequate. On the other hand, there was concern over the fad factor in current sales. It seemed a time for the company to hold its manufacturing department to strict inventory levels. The resulting production schedule is summarized on line 5, Exhibit 23.7. On line 3 is the cost of goods delivered that month—in other words, the cost of sales. Added to or subtracted from that figure is the budgeted change in finished goods inventory (line 4). For example, the $16,000 increase in February is the difference between the February and January inventories ($585,000 − $569,000), as shown in Exhibit 23.6, line 6.

By using known averages, it was possible to split the cost of goods manufactured (Exhibit 23.7, line 5) into component parts:

	American Skate Company Inventory Budget $000s													
	1980 →	JAN	FEB	MAR	APR	MAY	JUN	JUL	AUG	SEP	OCT	NOV	DEC	TOTAL
1	Sales [a]	437	479	523	501	458	414	370	425	468	512	447	196	5230
2	Cost of Sales [b]	300	329	360	345	316	286	256	295	325	356	311	137	3616
3	Finished Goods Inv:													
4	COS 1 mo forward	329	360	345	316	286	256	295	325	356	311	137	363	
5	COS 2/3 of 2nd mo fwd [c]	240	225	201	178	155	174	187	200	170	73	187	199	
6	FG Inventory at EOM	569	585	546	494	441	430	482	525	526	384	324	562	
7														
8	WIP Inventory	133	133	133	133	133	133	133	133	133	133	133	133	
9														
10	Raw Mtls Inventory [d]	214	196	177	159	183	202	221	193	85	225	247	270	
11														
12	Total, L6, 8 & 10 [e]	916	914	856	786	757	765	836	851	744	742	704	965	
13														
14														
15	References:													
16	[a] From Exh. 17–4, L1													
17	[b] " " , L6													
18	[c] Begins at 20/30 and ends at 15/30 of the 2nd month forward.													
19	[d] .62 x cos, 3rd mo fwd													
20	[e] To Exh. 17–4, L37													
21														
22														
23														
24														
25														
26														
27														
28														
29														
30														
31														

Exhibit 23.6. American Skate Company—inventory budget

	American Skate Company Schedule of Goods Manufactured $000s													
	1980 →	JAN	FEB	MAR	APR	MAY	JUN	JUL	AUG	SEP	OCT	NOV	DEC	TOTAL
1	Sales [a]	437	479	523	501	458	414	370	425	468	512	447	196	5230
2	Production:													
3	Goods Sold [b]	300	329	360	345	316	286	256	295	325	356	311	137	3616
4	Change in FG Inv [c]	50	16	(39)	(52)	(53)	(11)	52	43	1	(142)	(60)	238	43
5	Goods manufactured	350	345	321	293	263	275	308	338	326	214	251	375	3659
6														
7	Dir Labor: .17 × L5 [d]	61	59	54	50	45	47	54	56	56	36	44	66	628
8														
9	Oth mfg exp: .2 × L5	70	69	63	59	52	54	62	68	64	42	49	75	727
10	Pymt: .5 of prev mo	34	35	35	32	30	26	27	31	34	32	21	25	
11	.5 of cur mo	35	34	31	29	26	27	31	34	32	21	24	37	
12	Total L10 & 11 [e]	69	59	66	61	56	53	58	65	66	53	45	62	723
13														
14	Mtls used: .62 × L5	217	214	199	182	163	170	191	210	202	133	156	232	2269
15	Add change in RM Inv [f]	(9)	(8)	(9)	(18)	24	19	19	(28)	(108)	140	22	23	47
16	- Raw mtls purchased	208	196	130	164	187	189	210	182	94	273	178	255	2316
17	Pymts for mtls purch'd:													
18	.5 x L16, 1 mo prev	108	104	98	90	82	93	94	105	91	47	136	89	
19	.5 x L16, 2 mos prev	83	109	104	98	90	82	94	95	105	91	47	137	
20	Total [g]	191	213	202	188	172	175	188	200	196	138	183	226	2272
21														
22	References:													
23	[a] From Exh. 17–4, L1													
24	[b] " " , L6													
25	[c] Calculated from Exh. 17–6, L6													
26	[d] To Exh. 17–4, L23													
27	[e] " " , L24													
28	[f] Calculated from Exh. 17–6, L10													
29	[g] To Exh. 17–4, L22													
30														
31														

Exhibit 23.7. American Skate Company—schedule of goods manufactured

Cost	Percentage	Line
Direct labor	17	7
Other manufacturing expense	20	9
Raw materials	62	14
Depreciation	1	

Remember, these are the costs of goods *manufactured,* not *sold,* during the month. The difference between the two is the change in the level of the finished goods inventory (line 4).

With the breakdown in manufacturing activity, a forecast can be made of the cash payment flows. Most of the goods and services purchased by American Skate called for payment in 30 days, but a few larger suppliers were content to wait 60 days. The average payment period—calculated the same way as the average collection period but using accounts payable and purchases—was 50 days. However, management felt that there had been ill will because of the slow payment of a few bills, and it was decided to shorten the average payment period to 45 days in 1980. There are only two ''legitimate'' reasons for not paying your debts on time: (1) an honest dispute about what is owed and (2) lack of money. Any other delay is purchased with reputation to character; character flaws, once discovered, are not forgotten within the lifetime of the witness.

A schedule for raw material payments is shown in Exhibit 23.7, lines 17 to 20, and the totals also in Exhibit 23.4, line 22.

With respect to direct-labor costs, it was assumed that all payments would be made in the same month they were incurred. Thus, the amounts on line 7 of Exhibit 23.7 were transferred directly to the cash budget (Exhibit 23.4, line 23). Other manufacturing expense (line 9, Exhibit 23.7) would be paid half in the same month, half in the next. The cash effect is shown on line 12, which amounts were transferred to Exhibit 23.4, line 24. Depreciation, a noncash expense, is excluded from the cash budget.

(d) Prepaid Expenses. Prepaid rent, interest, insurance, and various supplies are usually budgeted at a constant amount or increased as sales increase. In the example in Exhibit 23.4, the amounts on line 38 grew 20% during the year, the same as those on line 1.

(e) Fixed Assets. The budgeting of capital expenditures is the subject of other chapters of this handbook and forms a part of every standard work on financial management. There are, besides, a number of books devoted entirely to the topic. In these works, the emphasis typically is on techniques for maximizing return on investment—comparing the costs and benefits of various investment proposals in terms of the time value of money flowing out and in.[12] Here we are concerned with an additional aspect of capital assets—their relation to other accounts on the balance sheet and their effect on a firm's liquidity and leverage positions.

Fixed assets, with one or two exceptions—most notably land—can be viewed as long-term prepaid expenses. They are, in effect, lost costs whose value lies only in their use in producing products that can be sold at a profit. Unlike the fixed assets of an individual—a car and a house, which may be of value to thousands of other persons—the vast

[12] *See* footnote 1, pp. 261–340; *See* footnote 6, pp. 283–340; and Robert Rachlin, *Return on Investment—Strategies for Profit.* (Plainview, NY: Marr Publications, 1976).

majority of business fixed assets have little value beyond their intended first use. The fate of fixed assets is to eat away net worth, either through the orderly process of depreciation or—if a mistake is recognized—through a peremptory write off.

That is not to say that fixed assets should be avoided at all costs. A company needs resources to produce the goods or services it sells. Those resources are a mix of people and capital goods—both are expenses, both are vital. The two have an important difference, however. To a large extent the number of people employed on a job can be varied with the amount of sales. As sales increase, more people are added, and the expense is a *variable* cost. However, when a machine is substituted for labor, this variable cost is exchanged for the *fixed* cost of depreciation. The extent to which capital assets are used in place of labor is referred to as the degree of *operating leverage.* Once the fixed costs have been covered, a high level of operating leverage will produce proportionally higher profits; likewise, proportionally greater losses will occur when revenues drop below the total of fixed costs.[13]

The decision making, then, centers on the best mix and on whether the best is good (profitable) enough. There are, of course, certain capital investments, such as office furniture, that "do not require a return on investment justification, since they are investments essential or necessary to the existence of the business."[14] In fact, it is the failure to understand the *continuing* requirement for new capital goods that causes most errors in fixed asset budgeting.

In the 1950s the concept of cash flow came into prominence. Business people quickly fell in love with the idea of adding depreciation to profits in order to see how much cash there was to play with. If profit was vanilla ice cream, cash flow was a chocolate sundae. What many people overlooked was that the cash generated from depreciation would have to be plowed right back into fixed assets. I wrote about the misleading nature of cash flow in an earlier book:

> In what I call the "non-cash illusion," we are led to think that depreciation (the source of cash) is an act independent of adding fixed assets (a use of cash). In fact, it is easily observed that 90% of the time a typical business will add more in fixed assets than the amount of depreciation in any given year.
>
> Plants and equipment must be replenished, just as inventory is. To say that funds from depreciation do not have to be spent on new fixed assets is as deceptive as saying that cash received from a sale does not have to be spent to buy new merchandise.[15]

As a general rule, net fixed assets will increase as much as or more than sales do. Many of the capital asset expenditures are foreseen and planned, but some—like a suddenly leaking roof—are not. The balance-sheet budget, therefore, should make allowance for the unforeseen requirements.

Meanwhile, back at American Skate, the capital-investment committee approved two large expenditures for 1980. One was for automotive equipment at an expected cost of $34,000. Delivery was scheduled for February. The other was for some plastic injection and transfer molding equipment to be installed in October at a cost of $115,000. There

---

[13] Leopold A. Bernstein, *Financial Statement Analysis* (Homewood, IL: Richard D. Irwin 1974), p. 526.

[14] *See* footnote 14, p. 40.

[15] James E. Kristy, *Analyzing Financial Statements: Quick and Clean,* 5th ed., (Buena Park, CA: Books on Business, 1991), p. 44.

were no other large investments anticipated, but the committee also budgeted an amount (unallocated to any specific operating department) for contingencies based on the levels of unplanned expenses in the past three years, adjusted for inflation and growth. The results appear in Exhibit 23.8. The financing of the new additions—whether it be from internally generated funds, borrowed money, or lease financing—will be covered in a discussion on liability budgeting.

The company uses accelerated methods of depreciation for most of its capitalized assets. The average estimated useful lives are:

Buildings and related equipment	30 years
Machinery and equipment	15 years
Furniture and fixtures	10 years
Automotive equipment	5 years

Ordinary maintenance and repair costs are charged to earnings, but major renewals or improvements are capitalized. The net fixed assets shown on line 7 of Exhibit 23.8 was transferred to Exhibit 23.4, line 40, while the additions on lines 3 and 4 were reflected also on line 26, Exhibit 23.4.

(i) Inflation and Replacement Costs of Fixed Assets. The problem of replacing capital equipment in an era of moderate inflation has been honored in hundreds of acticles and speeches. I hesitate adding to the rhetoric, except for the undue pessimism that characterizes most of the talk. We all know that inflation is a terrible blight because that message is drilled into us daily. Yet the history of the world is inflation. Whether it has been the effect of man's progress, a contributory cause, or neither is not all that clear. What is clear is that today's average American bears this economic cross in a comfort and security known only to the upper class back when a dollar was really a dollar.

The principal effect of inflation is a shifting of wealth—generally from lenders to borrowers—and the trouble is that it is an unorderly shift and, in the minds of many, an unjust one. It is the scramble to be on the winning side of inflation that causes dislocations and risks.

It is these dislocations—a quick rise in interest rates, the rapid movement of capital into and out of gold, and so forth—that are the main concerns for business, not the fact that capital equipment will cost more dollars. Businesses seldom have trouble raising their own prices in a general inflation unless they have boxed themselves in with long-term contracts. What's more, it is not uncommon to see a business use the everything-costs-more mentality as an excuse to gain a little ground on the field of profit. (To use a homely example, I recently bought a replacement part for a major appliance. I had previously replaced the same part five years before to the month. In that time the price of the part had exactly doubled. That is a compounded rate increase of 15% per year, far greater than the five-year inflation rate.)

The task of someday replacing equipment at inflated prices is not unlike that of an individual planning to buy a house at some future date. The new house will probably cost more, the mortgage company will probably lend more, and the buyer will probably be earning more. If the business manages its leverage and liquidity so that equity and cash keep pace with the inflation (and the company's growth), the problem of replacing equipment will not be any greater than if there were no inflation.

The other concern for business under inflation is that the return on shareholders' equity be increased to compensate for the lost purchasing power of their investment. Lenders of

American Skate Company
Budget of Fixed Assets
$000s

	1980 →	JAN	FEB	MAR	APR	MAY	JUN	JUL	AUG	SEP	OCT	NOV	DEC	TOTAL
1	Net Fixed Assets, EOM [a]	372	374	410	411	413	415	417	419	421	422	539	540	372
2														
3	Additions: Known [b]		34								115			149
4	Unknown [b]	5	5	5	5	5	6	5	5	5	5	5	6	62
5	Less: Depreciation [c]	3	3	4	3	3	4	3	3	4	3	4	4	41
6														
7	Net Fixed Assets, EOM [d]	374	410	411	413	415	417	419	421	422	539	540	542	542
8														
9														
10	References:													
11	[a] From Exh. 17–4, L40, 12–31–79													
12	[b] To Exh. 17–4, L26													
13	[c] From Exh. 17–4, L5													
14	[d] To Exh. 17–4, L40													
15														
16														
17														
18														
19														
20														
21														
22														
23														
24														
25														
26														
27														
28														
29														
30														
31														

Exhibit 23.8. American Skate Company—budget of fixed assets

money anticipate inflation with higher interest charges. Investors must be given the same relief or they will give up being investors in favor of being lenders. Also, the company that earns more for its investors will be able to retain more earnings and thus help satisfy the need for increased equity to finance fixed asset replacements.

(f) Other Assets. The budgeting of assets other than current and fixed is almost entirely a matter for each particular company. Whether the assets are investments, long-term receivables, goodwill, deposits, or deferred charges, the circumstances surrounding them are so varied that generalizations are useless. In our American Skate example, the other tangible assets and deferred charges (Exhibit 23.4, lines 42 and 44) were carried unchanged through 1980.

(g) Notes Payable—Banks and Others. The budgeting of notes payable will depend largely on the terms of the credits. The purpose of short-term notes is to finance temporary needs—seasonal increases in receivables and inventory are the classic ones. Nowadays, many ''short-term'' loans are really revolving, or ''evergreen,'' credits, sometimes supported with an assignment of receivables or other viable assets and with repayment planned from profits, a new issue of stock, or a long-term debt issue. Perhaps the ideal arrangement is a working capital line of credit, which means that within the limits of the line the company borrows and repays to suit itself, so long as specified indicators of liquidity (e.g., current ratio), leverage (debt–equity), and profit (return on investment) are satisfactory. Such loans are interfaced with the cash account, and the two are budgeted to traverse the peaks and valleys of cash needs with the least inconvenience and cost.

A company should strive to keep some loan availability in reserve for life's little surprises. In addition, the expanding firm will have ever increasing needs for debt, so that while loans in particular are being paid off, loans in general are usually expanding. The prime prerequisites to obtaining new financing are (1) an outlook for profits and (2) a satisfactory leverage position.

(i) Outlook for Profits. The outlook for profits comprises far fewer elements than the resulting profits. That is, there are so many factors that influence resulting profits, we are unable—even with the most powerful computers—to reckon them all. That is just the tip of the iceberg. Identifying all of the influencing factors is an even greater challenge. Thus, a bank or insurance company faced with a decision to lend its money to a particular company will generally concentrate on six elements. These are listed in the most common order of importance, as follows:

1. *Past earnings.* A steady upward trend is ideal, but caution: points are deducted for ''creative accounting.''
2. *Past sales and present marketing position.* Lenders feel (or are) helpless in advising how to move the stuff out of the warehouse, so they attach much importance to marketing ability.
3. *Demand for the product.* Again, steadiness is the key; anything dependent on the public's whim or fashion arouses doubt.
4. *Foreseeable changes in competition.* New companies or products entering the field also create uncertainty.
5. *Outlook for the economy.*
6. *Company's ability to control costs and pass along price increases.*

(ii) Leverage. *Leverage* refers to the mix of debt and equity used by a company to acquire its assets. As the term is defined, more leverage means more debt. Business professionals love leverage because if they can borrow money at 15% and earn a return of 20% on the way they invest it, they get to keep the excess—and the more the better. Lenders, however, hate leverage because more leverage means greater risk. Leverage multiplies losses as well as profits, and creditors who never share in a company's profits *do* share—or, rather, bear—its losses, once they have eaten away all of the equity.

Since there are always more people willing to borrow money than to lend it, companies must be mindful, in their balance sheet budgeting, of maintaining a leverage position agreeable to present and future lenders. Exactly where that position lies cannot be said with certainty because it is a matter of each lender's judgment. Of course, if a company goes bankrupt, we can say it should have had a little less leverage than it had. Later, in discussing balance-sheet ratios, a guideline will be given for an acceptable amount of leverage.

The American Skate Company had a $750,000 line of credit with its bank, whereby the company could borrow up to 70% of its accounts receivable plus 15% of the total inventories. No assignment of these assets was made to the bank, but the company did execute a negative pledge, agreeing not to assign them to anyone else, and each month an aging of receivables and description of the inventories—certified by two company officers—was given the bank. The line of credit was renewed each year on April 30. The company agreed to maintain compensating balances equal to 15% of the average outstanding loan.

The company's budget strategy was to minimize this revolving loan because of the high interest cost (prime + 3%), while stretching out existing long-term debt, which then had more favorable rates. The first step in budgeting the bank loan was to calculate availability and budget a decline that seemed feasible in the loan balance. The existing long-term debt was budgeted according to terms, and new financing was planned only for the new capital investments, using the cheapest financing known to be available. The results are depicted in Exhibit 23.9.

The amounts for long-term debt (lines 20 and 21) were transferred to Exhibit 23.4, lines 50 and 53. At the same time, the cash effect of new financing and monthly payments (lines 17 and 18) was likewise reflected in Exhibit 23.4, lines 19 and 30.

After all of the other balance sheet items are budgeted, the monthly cash position is computed, as well as the leverage ratio. Adjustments to financing, if any, are then considered. This interactive process is one of the things computers do best. Given the desired and minimum levels of cash and the desired and maximum levels of leverage, a computer can be programmed to provide the optimal loan position. Optimal, that is, from the standpoint of the borrowing company. There are still the lenders to be convinced, but if the right guidelines are used, the resulting budget will satisfy them, too.

(h) Trade Payables. One can hardly exaggerate the usefulness of trade credit, both to the buyer and to the seller. The convenience alone is enough to recommend it. But there is much more. To the buyer it is the cheapest and most easily obtained credit—the first and sometimes the only form of credit to the fledgling business; a prime source of funds to the rapidly growing firm; and a significant form of financing for most established businesses (e.g., nearly $4 billion for Sears Roebuck and Company).[16] Trade credit can

[16] *See* Sears December 31, 1989, annual report.

	American Skate Company Loan Budget $000s													
	1980 →	JAN	FEB	MAR	APR	MAY	JUN	JUL	AUG	SEP	OCT	NOV	DEC	TOTAL
1	Notes Payable - Banks													
2	Availability:													
3	.7 × Accts Rec [a]	386	550	601	607	566	514	462	479	536	588	564	356	
4	.15 × Inventory [b]	139	138	128	115	109	113	125	129	111	100	108	135	
5	Total	525	688	729	722	675	627	587	608	647	688	672	491	
6														
7	Loan balance													
8	.65 × Line 5 [c]	341	447	474	469	439	408	382	395	421	447	437	319	
9	Less: planned reduct	5	10	15	20	25	30	35	40	45	50	55	60	
10	Adj balance [d]	336	437	459	449	414	378	347	355	376	397	382	259	
11	Net loan or (pymts) [e]	24	101	22	(10)	(35)	(36)	(31)	8	21	21	(15)	(123)	(53)
12														
13	Long-term debt													
14	Bal BOM, Current	[f] 72	72	84	84	84	84	84	84	84	84	132	132	72
15	Non-current	[g] 217	211	217	210	203	196	189	182	175	168	209	198	217
16	Total	289	283	301	294	287	280	273	266	259	252	341	330	289
17	Plus: New financing [h]		24								96			120
18	Less: Payments [i]	6	6	7	7	7	7	7	7	7	7	11	11	90
19	EOM Balance:													
20	Current [j]	72	84	84	84	84	84	84	84	84	132	132	132	132
21	Non-current [k]	211	217	210	203	196	189	182	175	168	209	198	187	187
22	Total	283	301	294	287	280	273	266	259	252	341	330	319	319
23														
24	References:													
25	[a] Calculated from Exh. 17–4, L36.			[h] To Exh. 17–4, L19										
26	[b] " " " , L37			[i] To " , L30										
27	[c] Avg loan/availability in 1979			[j] To " , L50										
28	[d] To Exh. 17–4, L46			[k] To " , L53										
29	[e] To " , L20 & 31													
30	[f] From " , L50 at 12-31-79.													
31	[g] " " , L53 at 12-31-79.													

Exhibit 23.9. American Skate Company—loan budget

be overdone, and when that happens it makes news. For every overextended firm that declares bankruptcy, however, there are hundreds that have been saved from that fate by pliant trade creditors. For the sellers, trade credit multiplies the customers and gives them a host of outlets. In addition, it often serves to smooth out the production cycle and to shift inventory nearer the consumer.

Some business professionals, sad to say, take advantage of creditor complacence by deliberately withholding payment beyond terms or paying a supplier in Miami with a check drawn on a bank in Yakima. Those who are so tempted are risking something dear to gain something cheap. To the chiseler such little gains are soon forgotten in the sweep of daily events, but the "chiselee," like the mild-mannered elephant who has been kicked, always remembers.

In managing trade payables, my advice would be to pay all bills about a week early. Such prepayment is unusual and quite likely to earn you a favored spot in your supplier's heart, if not on his or her customer list. There are many unspoken ways that the supplier can return the favor: with prompt deliveries when suppliers are short, with the freshest merchandise, with customer referrals, with advance notice of price increases, and so on. In a contrary manner can the deadbeat be disfavored.

Of course, if you do not have the money to pay promptly, you do not have the money. If you are caught in that situation, that is the most effective thing to tell a bill collector—"I don't have the money." It will at least shorten those time-consuming and fretful collection calls. If your delinquency is due to the pressures of expansion, you might point out to your supplier that he or she will deservedly share in the increased business. If it is due to losses, try to avoid the collection calls and concentrate on the cause of the problem. Silence buys a little time.

The budgeting and management of accounts payable are tricky because payables cut horizontally through all of the operating income budgets. Every major department will generate payables—including sales and administration—yet their purchases are governed by an expense budget, not a cash budget. If a cash shortfall arises, it may be necessary to impose additional restrictions on expenditures. Allocating cash to operating departments is a difficult task, for the pressures on department managers are already great, and their appeals for more money can be touching (e.g., "If I don't get that wire, the line will shut down!"). It is good practice to disclose company cash problems to department managers, at least the upper levels. Such confidence brings out the best in people, in terms of both loyalty and resourcefulness. Besides, they will learn of the problem from suppliers soon enough, anyway, and the rumors that spring up are likely to be far worse than the truth.

To obtain payables figures for the balance sheet budget, it is necessary to estimate a normal payment cycle. Even a modest-sized company can have a thousand vendors with a couple of dozen different payment terms. An average payment period can be calculated using the following formula:

$$\text{Average payment period} = \frac{\text{Accounts payable}}{\text{Annual credit expenses}} \times 365$$

However, getting a figure for the total expenses put through the accounts payable account is not always easy. Expenses are often mixed in with payments for hard assets and prepaid expenses.

What we are trying to do here is synchronize the three financial budgets—income, cash, and balance sheet. All items of expense on the income budget (except depreciation and other noncash expenses) must be time-phased to the cash budget. Any purchases or expenses not paid in the same month must necessarily be added to the accounts payable balance. Thus, every expense must be reflected either in the cash payments or accounts payable for that month.

Another method of estimating payables is to divide them into broad categories and estimate payment cycles for each. An example of this is given in the American Skate Company case.

You will recall that in 1979 American Skate paid for its purchases in an average of 50 days and decided to bring that figure down to 45 days by the end of 1980. The schedule for raw materials payments is summarized in Exhibit 23.7, line 20. It was assumed that direct labor would be paid the same month; the schedule for other manufacturing expense is shown in Exhibit 23.7, line 12. The sales expenses and general and administrative expenses (Exhibit 23.4, lines 8 and 9), which include salaries, were estimated to be paid one half in the same month they are incurred and one half the following month. The payment schedule for those expenses is shown in Exhibit 23.10.

After comparing the payment schedule on line 9 with the expense schedule on line 4, the CFO decided that the difference was too slight to bother with. So the figures on line 4 were transferred to the cash budget (Exhibit 23.4, line 25), thus saving one step in the process of calculating the accounts payable balances.

That process was to take the accounts payable at the beginning of January, add to it the credit expenses incurred for raw materials purchased and other manufacturing expenses, and subtract the payments on accounts payable during the month. The expenses of sales, administration, and direct labor were excluded from the calculation because they were expected to be incurred and paid in the same month. Here is how it worked.

The figures for the rest of the year are computed in the same fashion—month by month—as shown in the accounts payable budget, Exhibit 23.11.

January 1980	Amount (thousands)	Location
Beginning accounts payable	$304	From Exhibit 23.4 (line 47, at 12-79)
Add: Materials purchased	208	From Exhibit 23.7 (line 16)
Other manufacturing expenses	70	From Exhibit 23.7 (line 9)
Deduct: Payments for materials	(191)	From Exhibit 23.7 (line 20)
Payments for other manufacturing expenses	(69)	From Exhibit 23.7 (line 12)
Ending accounts payable	$322	To Exhibit 23.4 (line 47)

(i) Income Tax Payable. Companies reporting a calendar year must make estimated tax payments on the 15th of April, June, September, and December. To avoid penalties, the payments must total 80% of the actual tax liability or be equal to the tax paid the previous year. Payment of the difference between estimated and actual tax is due March 15 of the year following.[17]

Legislation passed in 1997 fixed the corporate tax (effective 5/7/97) as follows:

[17] Tax laws occasionally change. Consult the current regulations before acting on any specific matter.

American Skate Company Schedule of Payments for Sales and G&A Expenses $000s														
	1980 →	JAN	FEB	MAR	APR	MAY	JUN	JUL	AUG	SEP	OCT	NOV	DEC	TOTAL
1	Expenses from Exh. 17–4:													
2	L8, Sales	37	41	42	42	44	43	43	45	45	46	48	47	523
3	L9, G&A	57	58	59	59	60	60	61	62	62	63	63	64	728
4	Total [a]	94	99	101	101	104	103	104	107	107	109	111	111	1251
5														
6	Payment													
7	.5 3 L4, prev mo	48	47	50	51	51	52	52	52	54	54	55	56	
8	.5 3 L4, curr mo	47	49	50	50	52	51	52	53	53	54	55	55	
9	Total [a]	95	96	100	101	103	103	104	105	107	108	110	111	
10														
11	References:													
12	[a] Line 9 is too close to Line 4 to bother													
13	with. Transfer Line 4 to Exh. 17–4, L25.													
14														
15														
16														
17														
18														
19														
20														
21														
22														
23														
24														
25														
26														
27														
28														
29														
30														
31														

Exhibit 23.10. American Skate Company—schedule of payments for sales and general and administrative expenses

American Skate Company
Accounts Payable Budget
$000s

	1980 →	JAN	FEB	MAR	APR	MAY	JUN	JUL	AUG	SEP	OCT	NOV	DEC	TOTAL
1	Accounts Payable BOM [a]	304	322	305	280	254	265	280	306	291	187	311	310	304
2	Add: Mtls purchased [b]	208	196	180	164	187	189	210	182	94	273	178	255	2316
3	Oth Mfg Expense [c]	70	69	63	59	52	54	62	68	64	42	49	75	727
4	Deduct payments for:													
5	Raw Materials [d]	(191)	(213)	(202)	(188)	(172)	(175)	(188)	(200)	(196)	(138)	(183)	(226)	(2272)
6	Other mfg expense [e]	(69)	(69)	(66)	(61)	(56)	(53)	(58)	(65)	(66)	(53)	(45)	(62)	(723)
7														
8	Accounts Payable EOM [f]	322	305	280	254	265	280	306	291	187	311	310	352	352
9														
10	References:													
11	[a] From Exh. 17–4, L47 at 2-31	79.												
12	[b] " Exh. 17–7, L16													
13	[c] " " , L9													
14	[d] " " , L20													
15	[e] " " , L12													
16	[f] To Exh. 17–4, L47													
17														
18														
19														
20														
21														
22														
23														
24														
25														
26														
27														
28														
29														
30														
31														

Exhibit 23.11. American Skate Company—accounts payable budget

1997

Taxable Income Over	But Not Over	Pay	% on Excess	Not the amount over—
$ 0—$	50,000	$ 0	15%	$ 0
50,000—	75,000	7,500	25	50,000
75,000—	100,000	13,750	34	75,000
100,000—	335,000	22,250	39	100,000
335,000—	10,000,000	113,900	34	335,000
10,000,000—	15,000,000	3,400,000	35	10,000,000
15,000,000	18,333,333	5,150,000	38	15,000,000
18,333,333—	....	6,416,667	35	18,333,333

Taxable income of certain personal service corporations is taxed at a flat rate of 35%.

In preparing their income budget, companies that expect pretax earnings over $100,000 may allocate the savings from the early rates to each month of the year. Alternatively, they may compute the tax on budgeted income, calculate the effective rate, and apply that rate to each month's earnings. American Skate chose to do the latter. Here is the calculation (dollars are in thousands):

1980 operating profit (Exhibit 23.4, line 11)	$363
Less nontaxable income	(9)
	$354
Tax on first $100	$ 22.25
$\frac{0.39}{100} \times \$254$	60.06
Tax	$ 82.31

$$\text{Tax rate} = \frac{\$82.31}{363} = 22.7\%$$

A rate of 22.7% was then applied to each month's operating profit. Thus, January's tax provision on pretax earnings of $43,000 was $9,761 (Exhibit 23.4, lines 11 and 13).

Most corporations defer part of their income tax liability through the use of accelerated depreciation methods, LIFO valuation of inventory, installment sales, or other strategies that result in timing differences between accounting income and taxable income. The result is a savings in immediate tax payments but not (theoretically) in tax expense. Accountants compute the tax liability as if there were no tax-saving devices, and the resulting figure constitutes the firm's income tax expense. The expense is then allocated between income tax payable and deferred taxes.[18]

In its income budget for 1980 American Skate estimated that of the $145,000 tax liability (Exhibit 23.4, line 13), about 7%, or $10,000, would be deferred. Each month when the tax liability was computed, 93% was allocated to income tax payable and the remaining 7% to other deferred liabilities. In January 1980, for example, the income tax provision was $17,000 (Exhibit 23.4, line 13). Of that, $16,000 was added to income tax payable (line 48) and $1,000 to deferred taxes (line 54). An income tax budget illustrating the interplay between provision, payment, current liability, and deferred liability is given in Exhibit 23.12. From this schedule the amounts are obtained for Exhibit 23.4, the balance sheet budget (lines 48 and 54), and the cash budget (line 27).

---

[18] Paul H. Walgenbach, Norman E. Dittrich, and Ernest I. Hanson, *Principles of Accounting* (New York: Harcourt Brace Jovanovich, 1976); p. 470.

	American Skate Company Income Tax Budget $000s													
	1980 →	JAN	FEB	MAR	APR	MAY	JUN	JUL	AUG	SEP	OCT	NOV	DEC	TOTAL
1	Operating Profit [a]	43	51	62	55	38	25	10	23	36	47	25	(52)	363
2	Tax Provision [b]	17	20	25	22	15	10	4	9	14	19	10	(20)	145
3														
4	Inc Tax Pay-BOM [c]	26	42	61	58	46	60	36	40	48	28	46	55	26
5	Plus: Cur tax .93 × L2	16	19	23	21	14	9	5	8	13	18	9	(19)	135
6	Less: Tax payments [d]			(26)	(33)		(33)			(33)			(33)	(158)
7	Inc Tax Pay-EOM [e]	42	61	58	46	60	36	40	48	28	46	55	3	3
8														
9	Deferred Taxes .07 × L2	1	1	2	1	1	1		1	1	1	1	(1)	10
10	Deferred Taxes-EOM [f]	72	73	75	76	77	78	78	79	80	81	82	81	
11														
12														
13	References:													
14	[a] From 19–4, L11													
15	[b] To Exh. 17–4, L13													
16	[c] From Exh. 17–4, L48 at 12-31-79													
17	[d] To Exh. 17–4, L27													
18	[e] To " , L48													
19	[f] To " , L54													
20														
21														
22														
23														
24														
25														
26														
27														
28														
29														
30														
31														

Exhibit 23.12. American Skate Company—income tax budget

(j) Accruals and Other Liabilities. Accrued liabilities—also known as accrued expenses—arise because costs that are incurred in one period are not paid until a later period or entered in a payable account. For example, most companies at the end of a month will owe employees some part of their wages. Besides, there is vacation pay, real and personal property taxes, and possible warranty expenses that are best spread throughout the year.[19] The total of these accounting liabilities is generally not significant, nor will it vary much in the typical company. Here are ways in which these amounts may be budgeted:

- Unchanged throughout the year
- As a percentage of sales or total operating expense
- As a percentage of the number of employees or total payroll expense

Other liabilities—for example, customer deposits, dividends payable, and deferred income—are allocated between current and long-term liabilities and budgeted according to their nature. The result for American Skate is shown in Exhibit 23.4, line 51.

(k) Equity Accounts. The long-range strategies of most businesses are based on the objective of increasing sales in order to increase profits—in a word, *growth,* both in revenues and in earnings. As a company expands, it needs more equity to (1) finance the additional receivables, inventory, and other assets, and (2) to provide a leverage base upon which additional borrowed money can be obtained, also for expansion. Nearly all companies meet some of their increased equity needs with earnings retained in the business. At times the growth in retained earnings will match that of sales, assets, and debt, and expansion proceeds almost unnoticed. More often the elements grow disproportionately and adjustments become necessary. Just how these adjustments are made will affect the stability and strength of the company.[20]

A firm whose growth in sales and assets is outpacing that of equity can choose among a number of tactics to avoid an imbalance:

- *Limit sales growth.* This tactic has a strong following among outside lenders and inside managers whose position or personality causes them to see the risks accompanying growth more sharply than the rewards. In theory it works fine. When demand for the company's products is excessive, the firm can raise prices, cheapen quality, tighten credit standards, cut sales expense, and so on, until just the right growth level is reached. In practice, it works very poorly. Product demand is as elusive as it is precious, and in most companies the money, effort, pressure, and prayers expended to get sales is so great that the idea of deliberately limiting them will not even be comprehended.
- *Keep dividends low.* This works very well when the growth rate is high. If investors understand anything at all, it is making hay while the sun shines. Of course, shareholders who forego dividends expect to be rewarded with higher market prices for their shares, and every time shares trade hands it introduces a stockholder to whom past market price increases mean nothing—one who is concerned only with performance from this time forward.

[19] *Id.,* p. 333.
[20] Jules I. Bogen, ed., *Financial Handbook,* 4th ed., (New York: Ronald, 1964); p. 15.30.

- *Sell more stock.* It is unusual if a successful company does not resort to this tactic sooner or later—more often than not, unwillingly, for shareholders do not like their pie cut into more pieces, even when promised a larger pie. Besides, the process is made tedious by regulatory agencies and expensive by underwriters. These drawbacks will be lessened or magnified by a high or low price earnings multiple on the stock in question. Nevertheless, most companies do—and all should—prepare for the eventuality by setting a limit to the financial leverage they will permit[21]—beyond which they will seek more equity money.
- *Increase financial leverage.* There are two critical elements in determining the amount of leverage a company will employ—the attitude of management and the attitude of creditors. Management may be reluctant to sell more stock because of how that might affect its control or influence in the business. Yet, to borrow instead means to incur greater risk. In the larger corporations management control is little affected by increasing the outstanding stock. The ownership is so widespread and diffused that adding a few more shareholders will not shift the balance of control. Then, too, salaried managers tend to place more value on stability than on high growth. The result is that the strongest companies—ones that have the most say-so about their leverage—are usually more conservative in that regard than the smaller firms. Those companies with one, two, or a handful of stockholders usually have less access to additional equity money and, besides, are often more willing to risk higher leverage because of their direct benefit from the rewards.

Nevertheless, the attitude of lenders and other creditors is often the decisive factor. They see leverage as risk, and each places in the file—or in a corner of his or her mind—a leverage point beyond which they will begin to shy away from a particular company. Usually, a firm will have to guess where that point is, for lenders who complain ominously when leverage is too high generally say nothing when it is too low.[22] Guidelines for the best level of leverage are discussed in the section on financial ratios.

In the case of the American Skate Company, ownership was spread among 20 shareholders, but majority control resided in five persons, all related. There had been no stock issued for several years, and the dividend policy tended to be influenced more by the personal needs of the family owners than by anything else. With the recent revival in demand for roller skate products, the need for more equity was recognized; a dividend totaling $40,000 had remained unchanged for the past three years, even though a greater amount was permitted by existing loan agreements. Management felt that leverage, though moderate in relation to most other companies in the industry, was still too high, and it was decided to continue the same dividend rate in 1980. The cash payments are shown in Exhibit 23.4, line 29.

The equity budget summarizing the effect of profits and dividends on retained earnings (''surplus'' on the form used here) is shown in Exhibit 23.13. With the transferring of retained earnings (EOM, line 4) to Exhibit 23.4, line 57, the balance sheet budget was complete except for the balancing cash (and marketable securities) figures.

(l) The Balancing Cash Figure. The final steps proceeded as follows:

1. The total of cash and marketable securities at December 31, 1979, was $138. (All dollars in this section are in thousands.) That became the cash balance—opening

[21] *See* footnote 1, p. 468.

[22] *See* footnote 6, p. 687.

American Skate Company
Equity Budget
$000s

	1980 →	JAN	FEB	MAR	APR	MAY	JUN	JUL	AUG	SEP	OCT	NOV	DEC	TOTAL
1	Retained Earnings-BOM	[a] 848	874	905	934	967	990	993	999	1013	1027	1055	1070	848
2	Plus: Net Profit [b]	26	31	37	33	23	15	6	14	22	28	15	(32)	218
3	Less: Dividends [c]			(8)			(12)			(8)			(12)	(40)
4	Retained Earn-EOM [d]	874	905	934	967	990	993	999	1013	1027	1055	1070	1026	1026
5														
6	Plus: Capital Stock [e]	245	245	245	245	245	245	245	245	245	245	245	245	245
7	Total Equity	1119	1150	1179	1212	1235	1238	1244	1258	1272	1300	1315	1271	1271
8														
9														
10	References:													
11	[a] From Exh. 17–4, L57 at 12-31-79													
12	[b] " " , L15													
13	[c] To Exh. 17–4, L29													
14	[d] To " , L57													
15	[e] From Exh. 17–4, L56													
16														
17														
18														
19														
20														
21														
22														
23														
24														
25														
26														
27														
28														
29														
30														
31														

Exhibit 23.13. American Skate Company—equity budget

(Exhibit 23.4, line 16) for January; it was added to receipts and totaled on line 21: $583.

2. The disbursements added up to $426 (line 32).
3. $583 − $426 = $157, the cash balance—closing on line 33 and the cash balance—opening for February.
4. The $157 was apportioned between cash (line 34) and marketable securities (line 35) by calculating the compensating balance required by the bank and rounding the marketable securities portion down to even $10s. 15% × $336 (line 46) = $50.40

	First Cut	Adjusted
Cash	$ 50.40	$ 57
Marketable securities	106.60	100
Total	$157.00	$157

5. The last step was to foot the balance sheet and try to figure out why it did not balance. Actually, the reader has been spared that last agony by having the balanced version. Of the hundreds of budgets I have prepared or reviewed, however, I cannot recall one that was done without some error the first time. Of course, those budgets done by computer are often errorless, because all the dues are paid in the programming and debugging process.
6. This form C117 also has a line (59) for working capital, which is current assets (line 39) minus current liabilities (line 52).
7. The process is then repeated month by month throughout the year.

23.8 ADEQUATE CASH.

The first test of a balance-sheet budget and/or cash budget is the sufficiency of cash. Businesses are operated for profit, but they are operated on cash. The income budget is not complete unless it is supported by a feasible balance sheet budget. It is possible for a company to go bankrupt while making a profit—a legitimate profit. (It happened to an appliance dealer whose trade-in sale was so successful that all of his cash became tied up in slow-moving used appliances.) Short of that problem, there is a lot of mischief and costly inconvenience that a firm can bring on itself by running out of cash.

If a cash shortfall appears in any part of the budget, this is the time to plan a remedy for it. Ways to consider include the following:

- *Borrowing from the bank.* If it can be repaid within the annual cycle, the bank loan is an ideal arrangement for both parties, and the balance-sheet budget will go a long way in selling the bank on the idea.
- *Reducing receivables, inventory, or other assets.* These items seem to have a natural propensity to expand—even when everything else is static—so an occasional trimming is beneficial.
- *Cutting costs.* There are always some expenses that can be deferred without great impairment to the business. How often, do you suppose, is lengthy deliberation about the replacement of departing employees used to save a few dollars under the guise of personnel prudence?

- *Raising prices.* Where this fits—if it fits at all—in a firm's list of options depends pretty much on the competition, both direct and indirect (from substitute products) and sometimes on government and social factors.
- *Leaning on trade creditors and others.* This should be done only reluctantly, for it is impossible to foresee the harm it may cause. Other obligations that might be deferred are management bonuses or major stockholder loans. Even utility bills, tax payments, and bank payments have some ''give'' in them, but this is last resort stuff.

23.9 FINANCIAL RATIOS. Once the cash shortfalls are provided for, the financial budgets should be further tested for liquidity, leverage, and profitability. At least five ratios should be employed. Ratio analysis adds dimension to the budgets, for it is the harmony between assets, liabilities, and equity, the proportion of the accounts one to another, and the balance of cash flows that determine the financial capabilities of a firm.

There are two problems connected with the use of ratios. One is their proliferation. In my research, I have uncovered more than 150 different financial ratios in use today. The good ones you can count on the fingers of both hands. Most of the others are deficient in some way; that is, they tell you the same story as the good ratios but in a roundabout manner, or they give you a figure that is of no practical use. An example is the ratio of current liabilities to net worth. It says nothing about liquidity because it omits current assets; it gives a misleading picture of leverage because it leaves out the long-term liabilities. Using it to measure financial condition gives haphazard results, at best. It is a little like gauging the gas in your car's tank by counting the miles since the last fill-up.

The second problem is finding standards by which you can judge whether a ratio is good or bad. The way that most financial authors solve this problem—assuming they do not just announce that there are no standards—is to cite industry averages as the standards of acceptance:

> Each year a considerable effort is mounted to compile financial statistics and classify them according to industry. Robert Morris Associates gathers financial data from their member banks on over 300 lines of business, and has published ''Annual Statement Studies'' for nearly sixty years. Dun & Bradstreet computes ''14 Key Business Ratios'' annually for each of 124 industries. And many industry associations do likewise for their own groups.
>
> Industry averages can be instructive and sometimes heartening to a firm in much the same way as average salary studies are to individuals. But they must be used with discretion. If the average ROI [return on investment] for department stores is 7%, it does not mean that a store earning 9% is doing well. It means, rather, that department stores taken together are not doing so hot.
>
> A company should never model itself on industry averages or the ratios of other firms. The differences in assets and liabilities, management skills and location, product appeal and price, reputation and luck . . . and a hundred other variables . . . severely limit a comparison. Besides, success in a competitive marketplace is the prize of those who best turn their *unique* capabilities to useful account. Banks illustrate the point. They are virtually alike in products, services, safety, and interest charged and paid. They compete best with their unique resources—people and locations.[23]

There is, I think, a better solution than industry averages: arbitrary standards. While working in financial management nearly three decades, and teaching the subject to college

[23] *See* footnote 15, p. 15.

and postgraduate students as well as thousands of executives in public and private seminars, I developed a set of standards, which are presented here, that have served me well in business and, if I can trust the comments of my readers, hundreds of other companies throughout the industry list. Some of the standards are well known—they are established in the literature of finance, and their importance has been verified by statistical studies. Other standards may be unfamiliar, for having found none in my research, I supplied them from my own empirical observations. The standards presented are universal and apply to most types of commercial enterprises. (Exceptions are banks and other lenders, utilities, and transportation companies.)

The ratios and standards are presented along with a description of the financial characteristics that they measure: (1) liquidity, (2) leverage, and (3) profitability.

(a) Liquidity. *Liquidity* refers to a firm's ability to pay its debts on time. The sale of its products and the collection of receivables bring cash into a firm each day, while the payment of salaries, expenses, and accounts payable take it out. The amount to be paid out is known more or less in advance, but the cash inflow is less predictable. Thus, the need arises for a reservoir of cash, so that obligations may be met despite the daily ebb and flow of receipts. A company's liquidity position bears a closer watch than its leverage or even its profitability because the dynamics of liquidity are more urgent and pressing. Although a firm can operate with losses for months or even years, the missing of one payroll is apt to close it down forever. The amount of cash flowing in and out of a typical company each year will be three to four times its total equity and may be 20 times the amount of cash normally kept on hand. Unless that rapid flow is minded and regulated, liquidity can go to the dogs while you are off on a two-week vacation.

To avoid problems, a company should measure its liquidity with three different ratios. The first is the relationship of current assets to current liabilities, known as the *current ratio.* It has been widely used as a measure of liquidity for about a hundred years and is the oldest of the financial ratios.

Ratio 1	Formula	American Skate (12-31-79)
Current ratio	$\frac{\text{Current Assets}}{\text{Current liabilities}}$	$\frac{\$1{,}598}{\$755} = 2.12$
Standard: 2.00 to 1		

''Standard'' here means standard of excellence. Thus, we would say that American Skate, with a 2.12 to 1, has an excellent current ratio.

This is one measure of liquidity, but we should look at two others to get a complete picture. Current assets comprise three principal elements—cash, accounts receivable, and inventory. Each has a different proximity to cash and therefore lends a different weight to liquidity. Shortly after the current ratio was conceived, it was found that when a company's current assets are composed primarily of inventory, its liquidity position is not as good as one with a more even spread of the three elements. After the current ratio was developed, the *quick ratio*—known also as the *acid test*—came into use as a second test of liquidity.

Ratio 2	Formula	American Skate (12-31-79)
Quick ratio	$\dfrac{\text{Cash + mkt. sec. + accts. rec.}}{\text{Current liabilities}}$	$\dfrac{\$674}{\$755} = 0.89$
Standard: 1.00 to 1		

At 0.89, I would characterize American Skate's quick ratio as good, which gives one "excellent" and one "good" indicator of liquidity.

The third ratio is one that is still not in widespread use. When I first began applying it in the late 1960s, there was no established name for it. I called it the *liquidity ratio,* but as it has gradually come into use, another name—better, I think—is emerging: *cash ratio.* The cash ratio is a refinement of the quick ratio, as the latter is of the current ratio.

Ratio 3	Formula	American Skate (12-31-79)
Cash ratio	$\dfrac{\text{Cash + marketable securities}}{\text{Current liabilities}}$	$\dfrac{\$138}{\$755} = 0.18$
Standard: 0.40 to 1		

I would call American Skate's cash ratio "fair minus" or "poor plus." Although the standards given for the current and quick ratios are well established among financial analysts, the standard for the cash ratio is my own—one that I have used for more than 10 years and have found well-serving:

> The cash ratio deserves special attention in marginal cases, for it is perhaps the single best leading indicator of business failure. A company approaching insolvency finds it all but impossible to maintain good cash balances. Occasionally a strong company will post a low cash ratio, relying on available bank lines to meet current needs rather than an inventory of cash; however, the inherent strength of such a firm should be evident in the other ratios.
>
> The cash ratio has also a close correlation to promptness in making trade payments. The typical firm will begin to show some trade delinquency when the cash ratio declines to about the 0.20 level.[24]

Taking the three ratios together, we might describe the American Skate Company's liquidity position as "good." The cash ratio needs improving, but there is no great urgency about it. The company has an established bank line going into 1980, and its current ratio reveals excellent support among the less liquid, but still current, assets. Not to correct the cash ratio, however, would be shortsighted. The humor in the epigram that "banks only lend to those with no need to borrow" hides the truth that banks draw a sharp distinction between "growth" loans and "bail-out" loans. Lenders have little desire to hand their money to a company that cannot manage its own.

(b) Leverage. *Financial leverage* refers to the relationship between a company's debt and its equity funds—the funds contributed to the business by creditors as compared to

[24] *See* footnote 15, p. 9.

shareholders. The British refer to it as ''gearing.''[25] By leveraging its equity (that is, borrowing on it), a company can multiply its return (both positive and negative) on investment.

Entrepreneurs concentrate on the extra profits that leverage brings and creditors on the extra risks, and the two often pretend not to understand each other's position. An interesting study made of the 1975 financial statements of more than 2,000 industrial firms revealed almost no correlation at all between leverage and profitability. (The Spearman rank correlation coefficient of the profit–equity and debt–equity ratios was −.12.[26]) This would seem to indicate that the chances of leverage—as used in business today—helping or hurting a company are pretty evenly matched.

There are several ratios used to measure a company's leverage position. The one I prefer, the *asset ratio,* shows the dollars of assets for each dollar of creditor money.

Ratio 4	Formula	American Skate (12-31-79)
Asset ratio	$\frac{\text{Total assets}}{\text{Total liabilities}}$	$\frac{\$2,136}{\$1,043} = 2.05$
Standard: 2.75 to 1		

When talking leverage with bankers, you will more often find them referring to the ''debt to worth (equity)'' or the ''worth to debt'' ratios rather than to the asset ratio. However, the three ratios all tell the same story and are mathematically linked. The following table shows the equivalent standards:

		As the Ratio Decreases	
Ratio	Standard	Leverage	Risk/Return
Asset ratio	2.75 to 1	Increases	Increases
Debt to worth	0.57 to 1	Decreases	Decreases
Worth to debt	1.75 to 1	Increases	Increases

The standard for the asset ratio, like that for the cash ratio, is my own, although most persons concerned with business borrowing or lending will recognize its appropriateness. The amount of leverage a creditor will tolerate is not only an individual opinion but one blown this way and that by the winds of confidence and fear. Since World War II, business conditions within and among developed countries have stabilized, and we find more and more leverage employed. International conflict, recession, inflation, and other destabilizing forces tend to make creditors tighten their standards.

As for American Skate Company, its leverage position is ''good minus.'' Should its asset ratio drop below 2.00 (the limit prescribed in its bank loan agreement), it can expect its bank to nick it for another point over prime or perhaps tighten the borrowing formula. If the ratio got in the vicinity of 1.50, the bank would likely introduce American Skate to a commercial finance company and politely suggest that the loan be transferred out of the bank.

[25] *Dictionary of Economics* (New York: Penguin Books, 1972), s. v. ''gearing.''

[26] George Foster, *Financial Statement Analysis* (Englewood Cliffs, NJ: Prentice-Hall, 1978), p. 182.

(c) Profitability. Profit in business is the result of many factors. We do not even know them all. Of those we know, we can measure only a small percentage. Of those we can measure, we can control but a minority. Moreover, the influence of each factor is constantly shifting, as with the most important element: demand for the company's products or services. Another important profit factor is the effectiveness of management. Yet each manager differs from another, and each one changes in a small way every day.

Nevertheless, although we have much to learn about predicting future profits, we have pretty good information about evaluating current earnings. Also, all of the many factors involved can be combined and measured in a single scale, the fifth ratio.

Ratio 5	Formula	American Skate (12-31-79)
Return on equity (ROE)	$\frac{\text{Profit}}{\text{Equity}}$	$\frac{\$198}{\$1,093} = 18.1\%$
Standard: 14%*		

* For convenience, the ending equity is used in this calculation.

Although I do not find it worth the trouble, a truer ROE would use an average equity: (beginning equity + ending equity)/2. A corresponding standard would be 15%.

The standard proposed here is higher than those I have published in the past (10% in 1970, 12% in 1977) because of the double-digit inflation accompanying us into the 1980s. Inflation affects ROE in two ways. First, investors ask for higher yields to compensate for the loss of purchasing power. Second, inflation means a higher replacement cost for capital assets, which requires a faster accumulation of profits just to stay at the same production levels.

The return on equity that an individual company strives for is determined by both theoretical and practical factors. Theoretical factors influencing expected ROE are:

- The basic rent for money, which is the investor's reward for postponing the use of his or her money and letting someone else use it. Historically, this has been about 3%.
- The expected rate of inflation, which is difficult to judge if we observe that the inflation rate during much of this century was between 1% and 2%, whereas in 1979 it reached 13%. The average inflation rate in the 1990s is expected to be 5% to 6%.
- The risk of loss, the premium for which, among established companies, has averaged about 6% as measured by the difference in the yields of AAA corporate bonds and the respective company's common stock.[27]

The ROE goal a company sets for itself will also be influenced by *practical considerations* unique to it. These include the following:

- How difficult it is for competitors to enter the same business. Companies requiring heavy capital investment, long lead times, or limited natural resources will be able to achieve higher returns than those in industries that are easy to enter.

[27] Douglas A. Hayes and W. Scott Bauman, *Investments,* 3rd ed., (New York: Collier MacMillan, 1976), pp. 343–347.

- How unique its products or services are. If competitors can be held at bay with patients, licenses, copyrights, or trademarks, or outdistanced with new products, new models, or new features, a firm can aim for a higher-than-average yield.
- Unexpected changes in demand or supply. These often affect a company's ROE temporarily. Since shortages tend to be followed by gluts, a company should be wary of making long-term commitments to grasp short-lived opportunities.

In the case of American Skate, the 18.1% ROE was rather pleasing to its stockholders, and they recognized that the public's current fancy for roller skates might lessen in the near future. This, plus increased production and marketing aggressiveness by competitors, led management to think that the current rate of return could not be sustained.

A summary of the ratios discussed appears in Exhibit 23.14. In addition, American Skate's ratios were calculated for each month's end of 1980 from the financial budgets, and those results are shown in Exhibit 23.15.

The projection of financial ratios revealed a general weakening in the balance sheet in the first quarter, especially February. Although Q1 profits account for 43% of the year's

Ratio	Standard	What It Measures
Current ratio (CUR)	2.00	Liquidity
Quick ratio (QR)	1.00	Liquidity
Cash ratio (CAR)	0.40	Liquidity
Asset ratio (AR)	2.75	Leverage
Return on equity (ROE)	0.14	Profitability

Exhibit 23.14. Summary of financial ratios

Month End	CUR[a] (2.00)	QR (1.00)	CAR (0.40)	AR (2.75)	ROE[b] (0.14)
December 1979	2.12	0.89	0.18	2.05	0.18
January 1980	2.06	0.87	0.19	2.02	
February	1.93	0.89	0.05	1.94	
March	1.96	0.98	0.05	1.98	
April	2.04	1.08	0.09	2.05	
May	2.07	1.13	0.20	2.08	
June	2.12	1.13	0.23	2.14	
July	2.12	1.03	0.23	2.15	
August	2.12	1.02	0.19	2.17	
September	2.29	1.18	0.12	2.31	
October	1.95	1.09	0.19	2.06	
November	1.96	1.14	0.27	2.09	
December	2.05	0.76	0.11	2.20	0.17

[a] Standards are in parentheses.

[b] $\frac{\text{Net profit for the year}}{\text{Year-end equity}}$

Exhibit 23.15. American Skate Company projected financial ratios for 1980

total, they are accompanied by a distinct drop in the liquidity and leverage positions. Liquidity dips again in December but not to the same extent. That these declines are seasonal does not mean they should be ignored, any more than you would ignore dressing warmly in winter just because the cold weather was seasonal.

Among the steps the company might take to improve its interim financial condition is to postpone the February acquisition of automotive equipment (Exhibit 23.4, lines 19 and 26) until, say, April. Of course, there may be compelling reasons for making the purchase in February, but probably not. That small action alone would raise the February ratios a few percentage points:

- CUR from 1.93 to 1.97
- QR from 0.89 to 0.91
- CAR from 0.05 to 0.06
- AR from 1.94 to 1.96

Another reconsideration should be the planned reduction in the bank loan, a total of $60,000 (Exhibit 23.9, line 9). While the attempt to reduce costly borrowing is understandable, it is more important to avoid weak liquidity positions. As Murphy's Law warns us, it is often when we are most vulnerable that fate chooses to trifle with us. Leaving out the reduction would change December 1980 ratios as follows:

- CUR from 2.05 to 1.98
- QR from 0.76 to 0.77
- CAR from 0.11 to 0.18
- AR from 2.20 to 2.14
- ROE from 0.17 to 0.17

Even greater improvement can be made, however, in overall bank loan tactics. The company has regularly borrowed 65% of its available bank line, in effect ignoring seasonal cash needs in favor of a consistent and conservative borrowing pattern. This is a mistake. The purpose of the revolving credit is to meet seasonal as well as growth needs, and the company should smooth out its liquidity position by varying the percentage of available credit it uses each month. A month-end cash level equal to 20% of current liabilities is necessary in most companies to avoid any slowness in payment to creditors or drawing on uncollected funds during the month.

There is also a psychology of cash. People and companies with too little cash often speak of others as having too much cash, while those they thus accuse say nothing. Large cash holdings seem to command a certain respect and a reputation for power, strength, and brains. That this reputation is not deserved is not so important as the advantages one may make of it. Operating with a zero bank balance is no crime, but it is no great honor, either. To be in that position as a result of chance or inadequate planning is understandable. To get into it deliberately may be a sign of extravagant cleverness.

23.10 ANALYZING CHANGES IN THE BALANCE SHEET. The balance sheet gives us a picture of the physical assets and financial resources a company has on a particular day. It is these that create the products for future sales and profits. When we speak of a company's financial strength or financial capabilities, we mean its potential for generating future income. Most physical assets are like prepaid expenses—their value lies only in their ability to produce a stream of revenues. By looking at past profits and a current balance sheet, we can impute future earnings.

In addition to the picture drawn from a balance sheet, we can gain knowledge by analyzing the changes in the balance sheet from one period to another. The income statement is, in effect, an analysis of a single balance-sheet account—retained earnings.

Changes in the other accounts are revealed in the *statement of cash flows,* formerly called by other names: statement of changes; sources and uses of funds; source and application of cash; and, in pre-M.B.A. days, when simplicity was still a virtue, the "where-got, where-gone" statement.

Balance sheets are changed, of course, by the dynamics, or activities, of a business. Cash flows out in all directions—for raw materials, salaries, equipment, and so forth—and flows in as a result of sales, loans, and shareholder investments. This flow of cash is subject to a thousand changing forces, but it does acquire a certain inertia, which results in trends, or at least tendencies. The revelation and the control of these trends constitute the basis of balance sheet budgeting.

The analysis of cash flows gained prominence in the prosperous 1960s. In 1988, the Financial Accounting Standards Board (FASB)—the policy-making arm of the American Institute of Certified Public Accountants (AICPA)—prescribed its present form and use. The balance sheet, income statement, and statement of cash flows make up the three major financial statements.

Exhibits 23.16 and 23.17 are from the September 30, 1979, annual report of Rockwell International. The changes in the balance sheet from September 30, 1978, to September 30, 1979, are reflected in the statement of changes in the column headed "1979."

Unfortunately, the format adopted by the accounting profession is unnecessarily complicated and unwieldy. It is difficult for an accountant to prepare and more difficult for the nonaccountant to read and understand. As a result, what was once hailed as a breakthrough in financial analysis has, by its convoluted form, given little comfort to investors or use to managers.

As an illustration, we might wonder how the net fixed assets (property) of Rockwell has changed during the year. Given the two years' figures in Exhibit 23.16, we can compute the change: \$1,044.3 − \$910.4 = \$133.9 (millions) increase. But to obtain that amount from Exhibit 23.17 is all but impossible.

Property additions	\$275.8 (millions)
Less: Depreciation of property	(125.7)
Depreciation from discontinued operations	(5.2)
Proceeds from disposition	(63.9)
of property and businesses	68.9
Plus: Acquisition of business	\$149.9

This is about as close as we can come. We can see from the balance sheet that long-term debt declined \$32 million (\$431.0 − \$463.0) during the year, which is a significant change in view of the \$592.1 increase in total assets. Yet, it is impossible to find that figure on

Assets	September 30	1979	1978
		(In millions)	
Current assets			
Cash (including time deposits and certificates of deposit. 1979, $584.2 million; 1978, $371.4 million)		**$ 633.6**	$ 452.2
Receivables		**1,060.1**	986.4
Inventories		**1,092.6**	937.5
Prepaid expenses and other current assets		**31.8**	34.0
Total current assets		**2,818.1**	2,410.1
Investments		**156.9**	111.3
Property—At cost			
Land		**58.2**	56.6
Improvements to land and leaseholds		**72.2**	63.4
Buildings		**441.0**	403.5
Machinery and equipment		**1,200.0**	1,094.0
Furniture, fixtures and office equipment		**126.6**	117.2
Construction in progress		**132.5**	106.8
Total		**2,030.5**	1,841.5
Less accumulated depreciation		**986.2**	931.1
Net property		**1,044.3**	910.4
Other assets		**108.3**	103.7
Total		**$4,127.6**	$3,535.5

Liabilities		
Current liabilities		
Short-term debt	**$ 132.7**	$ 51.5
Accounts payable-trade	**447.9**	389.7
Advance payments from customers	**228.5**	177.2
Accrued payroll	**167.6**	131.6
Accrued retirement plan costs	**169.0**	144.2
Accrued income taxes	**114.3**	81.9
Deferred income taxes	**434.0**	329.9
Other current liabilities	**338.3**	333.1
Total current liabilities	**2,032.3**	1,639.1
Long-term debt	**431.0**	463.0
Other liabilities		
Deferred income taxes	**107.4**	63.6
Minority interests in subsidiaries	**17.7**	15.2
Total other liabilities	**125.1**	78.8
Stockholders' equity		
Capital stock:		
Preferred stock, without par value:		
Series A (entitled in liquidation to $53.0 million)	**1.3**	1.9
Series B (entitled in liquidation to $36.9 million)	**0.9**	1.1
Common stock, $1 par value	**35.8**	34.5
Additional capital	**266.3**	251.0
Retained earnings	**1,234.9**	1,066.1
Total stockholders' equity	**1,539.2**	1,354.6
Total	**$4,127.6**	$3.535.5

Exhibit 23.16. Consolidated balance sheet

Years ended September 30	1979	1978
Resources provided	(In millions)	
Income from continuing operations	**$261.1**	$212.8
Add (deduct) items not requiring use of working capital:		
Depreciation of property	**125.7**	116.3
Gain on dispositions of property and businesses	(24.8)	(11.9)
Deferred income taxes	**40.6**	(4.7)
Equity in income of unconsolidated subsidiaries and affiliates	(4.1)	(5.6)
Other	**7.1**	(3.1)
Total from continuing operations	**405.6**	303.8
Loss from discontinued operations	—	(36.2)
Add items not requiring use of working capital:		
Loss on dispositions	**20.0**	
Other, including depreciation of property	**5.2**	9.4
Total from (applied to) discontinued operations	**25.2**	(26.8)
Total from operations	**430.8**	277.0
Proceeds from dispositions of discontinued businesses	**101.9**	
Proceeds from dispositions of property and businesses	**63.9**	63.0
Issuance of common stock	**21.0**	10.7
Working capital of businesses purchased	**14.8**	
Decreases in investments	**2.4**	55.6
Long-term borrowings	**1.5**	12.0
Other	**9.0**	6.1
Resources provided	**645.3**	424.4
Resources applied		
Property additions	**275.8**	218.9
Cash dividends	**92.3**	80.9
Working capital of businesses sold	**77.6**	
Acquisition of businesses	**68.9**	
Increases in investments	**45.8**	5.4
Reduction in long-term debt	**42.1**	78.3
Other	**28.0**	22.8
Resources applied	**630.5**	406.3
Increase in working capital	**$ 14.8**	$ 18.1
Changes within working capital		
Increases (decreases) in current assets:		
Cash	**$181.4**	$ (24.5)
Receivables	**73.7**	69.2
Inventories	**155.1**	74.3
Prepaid expenses and other current assets	(2.2)	2.7
Increase in current assets	**408.0**	121.7
Increases (decreases) in current liabilities:		
Short-term debt	**81.2**	71.0
Accounts payable-trade	**58.2**	5.4
Advance payments from customers	**51.3**	37.5
Accrued payroll	**36.0**	9.3
Accrued retirement plan costs	**24.8**	38.3
Accrued income taxes	**32.4**	(7.5)
Deferred income taxes	**104.1**	132.4
Other current liabilities	**5.2**	(40.8)
Increase in current liabilities	**393.2**	103.6
Increase in working capital	**$ 14.8**	$ 18.1

Exhibit 23.17. Statement of consolidated changes in financial position

the statement of changes or even to compute it from the information given. A solution to the problem is already apparent—simply compute the changes between the two balance sheets.

An example of that simpler approach is shown in Exhibit 23.18 created the *delta flow statement* a few years ago as a tool to highlight the changes in major balance sheet items. This format groups the balance sheet changes so that the relation of long- and short-term sources and uses of cash can be seen at a glance.

> The *Delta Flow Statement* shows the changes between one year-end and the next. It begins with the profits and dividends (Lines 1 and 2) for the year, which together amount to the change in the Retained Earnings account. The rest of the items are simply the present balance sheet amounts minus the same figures from the year before. Normally a company that is growing, or at least keeping pace with inflation, will have positive changes in all of the Delta Flow items.
>
> The things to look for are (1) negative changes, (2) large changes plus or minus, and (3) the change in the mix of long term sources and uses of cash (summarized on Lines 10 and 19, and netted on Line 26).[28]

The delta flow statement for the 1979 Rockwell figures is shown in Exhibit 23.18. It can be seen that there was a good buildup of equity during the year (line 4) but only a negligible increase in deferred obligations (line 9). There was an unusual rise in current liabilities (line 14). A more complete breakdown of that increase can be found in Exhibit 23.17, the bottom section. There was a normal increase in current assets other than cash (line 23), and cash itself took a significant leap, as shown on line 25.

As a guideline, the long-term sources (line 10) should cover the change in noncurrent assets (line 19) plus about half of the change in current assets (line 23). In the case of Rockwell it does not, and the result is a drop in liquidity as measured by the current and quick ratios. It is offset, however, by the big increase in cash balances. The maintenance of a good cash ratio to mitigate an only fair current ratio shows good balance sheet management. Nearly all of the cash—except that needed to meet compensating balance requirements—is in short-term investments, earning interest. When you read in the Rockwell annual report that the "weighted average interest rates for all short-term borrowings were 21.1% in both 1979 and 1978,"[29] you begin to appreciate the degree of management and care employed. The temptation to apply, say, $500 million of that cash to outstanding loans must be very great. If we assume about a 5% differential between what is earned on short-term investments and what is paid on the most expensive loans, the compan could save nearly $3,000 an hour in interest costs—days, nights, and holidays! Prudence has its price, but the lessons of experience tell us to pay it.

There is one remaining element in balance sheet budgeting that is critical yet difficult to cover in a handbook such as this. That is an awareness of each item of the balance sheet—the meaning behind what the figures say. You cannot take the measure of an asset by its accounting value any more than you can take the measure of a person by weighing him or her. The accounts receivable include amounts that will never be paid; inventories

---

[28] *See* footnote 15, p. 20.

[29] See Rockwell's September 30, 1979, annual report.

By JEK

Company Rockwell International Corporation   Date 2-20-80

Instructions: Show changes in the balance sheet from one period to the next. Increases are shown as (+) amounts, decreases as (−) or in brackets ( ).

☐ Thousands
☑ Millions

		Date	9-30-79					
		Period	Year					
	SOURCES OF CASH							
1	Net Income		$ 261	1	$		$	
2	Less Dividends		(92	3)				
3	Other Capital Accounts		15	8				
4	**NET WORTH**		184	6				
5	Long Term Debt		(32	0)				
6	Deferred Liabilities		43	8				
7	Minority Interest		2	5				
8	Other							
9	**DEFERRED OBLIGATIONS**		14	3				
10	**LONG TERM SOURCES** Lines 4 plus 9		198	9				
11	Accounts Payable		52	8				
12	Notes Payable		81	2				
13	Other		259	2				
14	**CURRENT LIABILITIES**		393	2				
15	**TOTAL SOURCES OF CASH** Lines 10 plus 14		592	1				
	USES OF CASH							
16	Net Fixed Assets		133	9				
17	Intangibles							
18	Other Slow Assets		50	2				
19	**NON-CURRENT ASSETS**		184	1				
20	Accounts Receivable		73	7				
21	Inventories		155	1				
22	Other		(2	2)				
23	**CURRENT ASSETS**		226	6				
24	**TOTAL USES OF CASH** Lines 19 plus 23		410	7				
25	Cash Increase (Decrease) Lines 15 minus 24		181	4				
26	Working Capital Increase Lines 10 minus 19		14	8				

The items listed as Sources or Uses of Cash normally increase as a company grows. If an item is a negative amount, that is, the balance sheet amount declined from one year to the next, instead of being a source of cash it will be a use and vice versa.

Exhibit 23.18. Delta flow statement

list items that do not exist or that lie broken in the corner of a warehouse; machinery with a zero book value hums away, still producing goods. It is only when assets are observed "in action" that the full value of balance sheet budgeting can be realized.

SOURCES AND SUGGESTED REFERENCES

Campbell, Terry, and Jeff Madura, "Forecasting Financial Budgets with Monte Carlo Simulation," *Journal of Accounting and EDP,* vol. 5, no. 1, Spring 1989.

Oppedahl, Richard A., "Working Capital Management," *South Dakota Business Review,* vol. 49, no. 2, December 1990.

CHAPTER 24

BUDGETING FOR INTERNATIONAL OPERATIONS

George Cassidy

SC Management Services Corporation

Gert Schumann

24.1 INTRODUCTION. There is still a wide variety of practice with regard to administration of international operations. However, a developing trend appears to be to organize a group of foreign corporate subsidiaries and affiliates under a holding company or international division which is located in the home country of the parent group. Depending on the number of foreign units, complexity of operations, or amount of parent investment, one or more regional companies or advisory groups may intervene in this organization. However, these are ancillary to the ''thrust'' of the overall organization (see Exhibit 24.1).

The majority of the chapter describes the various budget documents, their contents, and the review and other procedures which would comprise a complete budget cycle for the international business of ''Bigco, Inc.'' The process of drawing budgets for international operations is somewhat dependent on the organizational structure of the branch, division, corporation, or some other entity for which it is prepared. However, certain general observations are applicable to the process in any circumstances and can be grouped into three phases: top to bottom qualitative review, operating and capital budgets, and regional group budget reviews.

During the 1990s, two elements have developed that have tended to encourage centralization of the budgeting process for international operations, at least among the larger multinational groups. The first of these is the increasing understanding and availability of derivative instruments to manage financial (foreign exchange, interest rate, credit) and operational (commodity, sovereign risk) risks associated with international business. The second is the growth of regional treasury and shared service centers for European, Asian, and Latin American operations. These centers achieve economies of scale for the largest multinationals, by concentrating on accounting, finance, human resources, and other staff activities for regional activities.

The imminent economic an monetary union (EMU) within Europe will result in radical changes to the international budgeting process. The currencies of 11 European countries will be subsumed into one monetary unit—the euro—on January 1, 1999. In succeed-

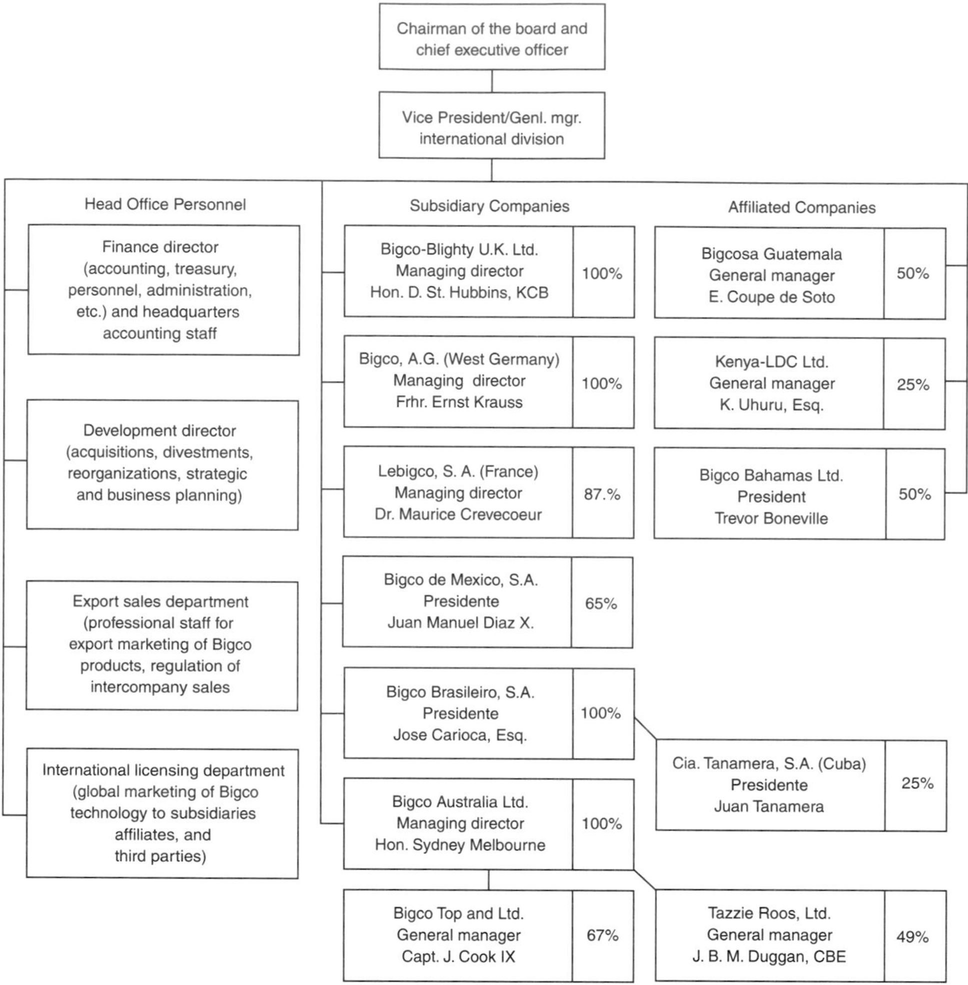

Exhibit 24.1. BIGCO, Inc., organization chart for the international business as of December 31, 19XX

ing rounds of economic and monetary convergence, it is probable that virtually all European Organization for Economic Cooperation and Development (OECD) economies will become part of the Euro bloc. Although the euro will continue to fluctuate against other currencies, such as the dollar and yen, foreign exchange considerations for the Euro-bloc countries will be eliminated.

24.2 "TOP-TO-BOTTOM" QUALITATIVE REVIEW. A qualitative and strategic analysis should precede any detailed ''number crunching,'' and should be administered on a ''top-to-bottom'' basis. By assigning strategic objectives to individual operations, and advising critical issues to be addressed, the general management of the international business ensures a uniform approach despite language, social, or cultural differences among the members of the international group.

The review should be disseminated by the international general management group, upward to the top level of corporate management, and downward to operating management of foreign units in the form of a strategic direction paper (SDP). Typically, the contents of an SDP would be as described in the section of the chapter which is devoted to that document.

There should be only a few numbers in the SDP, and as far as possible they should relate to aggregate objectives of the international business: return on investment (ROI), strategic growth expectations, cash to be returned to the parent group during the next fiscal year, and so on. Such commitments to the parent group should be made in its own currency and so expressed in the SDP.

24.3 OPERATING AND CAPITAL BUDGETS. The SDP should be followed by a quantitative budget of operating and capital expenditure requirements. This phase of the budgeting process should normally flow from "bottom to top," within SDP guidelines in basically the same manner as is employed for budgeting of domestic operations.

The operating results of international units are subject to variation on account of a number of significant, uncontrollable, and largely unpredictable factors (e.g., exchange rate developments, political risks) which are superimposed on the normal economic and business cycles. Because of this phenomenon, detailed multi-year forecasts of international results are increasingly being considered as "exercises in futility."

In the authors' experience, detailed operating budgets ought to be restricted to the fiscal year immediately following the one in which the budget is prepared. Any quantitative data prepared for succeeding years should include only major categories of financial data (e.g., sales, operating expenses and income, and financial charges) without detail and should be considered as indicative only. Management of foreign units should be encouraged to reconsider the outlook for operations each year without imposing the artificial constraint of comparison with prior budgets.

Operating budgets and subsequent periodic reports, which compare performance with budget, should be expressed in both the home currency of the parent group and the local currency of each of the foreign units. Such "twin currency" budgets and reports should not only be maintained within the international business, but also circulated to corporate management to enhance awareness of the unique nature of international business. That is, operating variances in foreign units may arise not only from price and volume factors, but also from distortions arising from currency exchange rates.

Capital expenditure budgets pose a different case. Determination of the capital needs required to maintain, or to expand, the business are an integral part of the strategic outlook for international operations. Therefore, "solid" forecasts of capital project requirements should be extended as far as possible into the future and, certainly, not for less than three fiscal years following the one in which the budget is prepared.

24.4 REGIONAL/GROUP BUDGET REVIEWS. After copies of individual operating budgets have been provided to the parent company, but before distribution of the consolidated budget document to corporate management, a review of the submissions should be scheduled between local management of the foreign units and the general management of the international business. This would ideally be a plenary session; however, in instances in which groups of companies are widely separated (e.g., Pacific Rim, Latin America, and Europe) and are only slightly integrated, a series of regional reviews is an adequate substitute.

During these reviews, representatives (usually, the managing and financial directors or their equivalents) of each foreign unit present and justify their budget figures. They explain what additional economic, political, and operational premises they have added to the "base case" stated in the SDP in arriving at their company forecasts.

To the extent that the SDP goals for the international business are not satisfied by the budget presentations, general management of the business should then counsel with its local counterparts and jointly agree on appropriate adjustments to satisfy these objectives. Curtailment or delay of capital projects, tighter control of working capital, and additional evaluation of financing costs and alternatives are examples of alterations and improvements to budgets which might result from such exchanges of views.

24.5 PUBLICATION OF INTEGRATED PLANNING DOCUMENT. The *integrated planning document (IPD)* is the culmination of the budgeting and planning process. An IPD is produced for each foreign unit and region, as well as for the consolidated international business. The latter document is distributed to corporate management as the basis against which the actions and results of the business are to be judged during the succeeding year. The components of the IPD consume, refine, and expand on all the preceding steps in the process. They are:

- A qualitatively oriented, multi-year *strategic plan* for operations in narrative form and incorporating only a few critical figures concerning development of these operations during the next three to five years
- A quantitative *operating budget* for the next fiscal year (the profit plan)
- The *capital-expenditure budget* for at least three years, in as much detail as possible, indicating the resources required by the operation to attain its stated objectives

The IPD is the annual report to management of the international business, and each of its units, concerning: (1) its present position in the market, (2) options and strategy for development of activities, (3) the status of various programs and projects in process, (4) financial details of results achieved during the present year and expectations for the succeeding year, and (5) the productive resources employed and expected to be needed during the next several years to achieve and implement all the other aspects.

24.6 STRATEGIC DIRECTION PAPER. The SDP is prepared for each budget cycle, by the general management of the international business, to establish the framework of strategic goals within which the individual foreign units must work to compile their tactical budgets of operations and capital expenditure programs. The proper time for promulgation of the SDP is approximately six to eight months before the start of the fiscal year for which the budget is being prepared.

(a) Ten-Year Mission: Statement of Objectives—Bigco, Inc. Periodic restatement and gradual refinement of the strategic mission for the international business is a valuable discipline for the general management of that business. It also provides guidelines for local management in the conduct of their daily operations, which tactically support achievement of long-range objectives. Typically, some of the objectives the international business might include in such a "mission statement" would be the following:

- Development of goals for (e.g., accounting and cash flow) return on parent capital invested would be established at appropriate levels (higher than domestic counterpart operations) to compensate for economic, sovereign, and exchange risks involved in international operations.

- Maintain profitability and other financial and operating criteria of local operations in the top rank of local industry in the host country
- If opportunities exist for vertical product integration, use of Bigco components by the foreign units will be practically maximized (incremental group profit from such integration should, for management purposes, be attributable to the international business)
- Create strong, local management teams to implement the strategy and take necessary actions to achieve this with minimum use of expatriates
- In a mature organization, build on what is ''in place,'' without recourse to the parent for either direct or indirect financial support
- Develop abilities and strategies of the export sales and international licensing departments, to maximize activities consistent with the supply of products and marketable technology available from the parent company for this purpose

(b) Assessments: Looking Both Back and Forward. It is helpful, in observing the development of long-range plans and general strategic objectives over a number of years, to document the events and achievements affecting these plans and one's progress during each year. For this purpose, the SDP should include an ''assessment'' worksheet.

The assessment, which is completed for each level of the business (global, regional, national, or by company) begins with the evaluation and specific operating strategy of the preceding budget, documents actions taken and events affecting during the budget year, and is completed with the revised assessment and strategy for the next budget year. A suggested form of this worksheet, to be incorporated into the SDP, is shown in Exhibit 24.2.

Without such visible evidence of progress toward one's objectives (or otherwise), both general and local management run the risks of losing their perspective in the midst of many distracting and, sometimes, conflicting circumstances which arise in the course of daily operations.

The assessments worksheet, properly filled up with concise descriptions of objectives for each of the international operations and actions and events affecting them, provides an invaluable budgeting/planning tool for keeping on track. It allocates available resources to the units and businesses with the most positive long-range outlook.

(c) Enumeration of "Critical Issues." The SDP begins the process of identifying and enumerating critical issues for the international business. This process should be expanded and refined by local management, and culminate in a comprehensive listing of such issues in the IPD.

A ''critical issue'' is strategic, not tactical. Such considerations as market position, competition, and so on are ''nonstarters'' in this particular category. Valid critical issues might include, although they are certainly not limited to: host country infrastructure (economic, political, etc.), basic strengths or weakness in the unit's organization or resources, and similar core concerns with long-term and/or radical implications for the future of the business. The critical issues of Bigco are indicated in Exhibit 24.3.

(d) Optional "Investment Strategy Matrix." The probable future course of development of the individual units within the organization, and of the allocation of resources within the international business, may be recapitulated within the SDP in an investment

Last Year's Strategic Plan	Current Year's Developments	This Year's Strategic Plan
Europe		
Assessment and strategy of these European operations are closely tied to the continued availability of critical components from the parent company's stampings plant in Peoria.	The parent company has taken the decision to curtail production of Peoria stampings, in view of its decision to enter a joint manufacturing venture for these with a South Korean firm.	Assessment is that continued European operations can only be supported to the extent that U.S.-source stampings continue to be available from the parent company's Peoria plant.
Without these integrative benefits, profitability outlook for European operations is probably not sufficient to justify continued employment of the present level of parent investment by Bigco.	Although cost is reduced in primary markets, the economics of shipment from South Korea to Europe are such that the profit increment from integration is eliminated.	Strategy is to allocate Peoria stampings to the highest profit business in Europe, curtailing or closing operations as necessary. Repatriations (dividends, trade accounts) to be maximized from marginal operations which are not immediately salable.
United Kingdom		
Assessment is that the BB Ltd. operation is dependent on government contract business for 85% of sales and 92% of profits. Diversification of product offerings and markets is needed.	Three large department store accounts have been obtained on a long-term contract basis, with very favorable profit margins. BB Ltd. is now the fourth largest producer of consumer products in this market.	Assessment is that BB Ltd. has successfully implemented the shift in markets, with corresponding increases in profitability and customer base. The medium- to long-term outlook for the company is markedly improved with expectation for continued favorable developments.
Strategy is to introduce Bigco consumer products in this market at the earliest possible moment, coupled with a "draw back" from some low margin government business.	After declining to tender for three Post Office contracts, the relative shares of sales and profit attributable to government business have declined to 55 and 48% respectively.	Strategy is to construct a new assembly line at Rutledge (close to primary markets) sufficient for projected growth through the end of this year. Any additional expansion to be contingent on profit and cash-flow developments.
	The company proposes to expand the Wapping and Rutledge facilities, with the addition of new assembly lines, to accommodate projected three year growth in new product lines.	Supplies of U.S.-source stampings will be increased by 10% during the next year, consistent with forecast production levels. These should be available without damage to other business because of loss of major accounts at Lebigco, Paris.

Exhibit 24.2. BIGCO, Inc., international business strategic plan for the fiscal year 19XX, assessments and strategies

Global Issues
○ Currency exchange rates
○ Growing protectionism and nationalism
○ Environmental considerations
○ Disposition of debts owing from less developed to developed countries
Europe
○ Creation of single European Market in Western Europe as of 1993
○ Opening of Eastern European markets
○ Achieving compliance with ISO-9000 quality control programs
○ Apparently decreasing global competitiveness of European-source manufactured goods
Great Britain
○ Bigco Blighty plants need heavy investments to meet environmental and competitive standards
○ Potentially high degree of integration with U.S. parent company product lines
Germany
○ Modern plants and highly productive work force
○ Geographic and cultural gateway to Eastern European markets
○ Little or no integrative benefit with parent company because of product lines
France
○ Effects of single European Market integration
○ Lebigco plants are too small for local market and need heavy capital investment
○ Lessening integration with U.S. parent company plants decreases global profitability
○ Weak middle management structure poses problems with successorship
Latin America–Africa
○ Hyperinflation burdens basically weak economies
○ Frequently unstable political environments
○ Capital controls restrict repatriations of funds
Australia
○ Integration, profit, and growth potential possibly increased by U.S.–South Korean venture
○ Long-term inflation and labor inefficiencies inhibit Pacific Rim competitiveness
○ National overcapacity in principal lines of Bigco business

Exhibit 24.3. BIGCO, Inc., international business strategic plan for the fiscal year 19XX, statement of critical issues

strategy matrix, whereby each of these units receives an assignment to one of the following (or similarly intended) ''investment strategy'' categories:

- ''Maintain investment,'' because the assessment of circumstances and critical issues affecting the unit are favorable on balance, and the specified strategy for it is being implemented on a timely basis (or attractive alternatives to the previous strategy are available)
- ''Status to be evaluated,'' because certain strategic factors are impeding progress of the unit toward its objectives and no feasible alternatives are readily apparent
- ''Divest or close,'' when all alternative paths to progress have been explored to a ''dead end''

It is generally advisable to compile such a matrix at the basic level of activity, that is, the individual plant, mill, or factory. Such discrete analysis will often allow excision of a part of the unit's operation and expedite restoration of the remainder to satisfactory performance.

24.7 DISTRIBUTION OF STRATEGIC DIRECTION PAPER/RECEIPT OF DRAFT INTEGRATED PLANNING DOCUMENT. Not less than six months before the beginning of the budget fiscal year, the SPD is distributed, by general management of the international business, to both corporate and local management.

(a) Corporate Review of Strategic Direction Paper: "Feedback" to Group. The general management of the parent company should review the SDP for the international business within a month, and advise international management of its acceptance of, or exception to, the proposed direction of the business for the following year.

In a well-developed international organization, administering various foreign subsidiary and affiliate corporations, the principal interface between the international business and the corporation will probably be involved with the amount of cash to be received by the corporation, and associated foreign and domestic tax planning. In this respect, the ability to develop the business with available resources "in place," while providing an acceptable cash return, the international business relates to the parent company in the same way as the parent does to its own shareholders and their representatives, the directors.

It is at this point that the corporation should advise international management of any special tax or financial circumstances affecting the amount or category of funds to be received as "foreign-source income" (a specially defined term for U.S. parent companies) during the following fiscal year in the form of dividends, royalties, income from export sales, and interest if applicable. Timely advice from corporate management will ensure that these circumstances and the parent company's expectations for cash return can be incorporated into budget reviews and, ultimately, into the IPD for the budget year.

(b) Receipt of Draft Budgets/Integrated Planning Documents. Approximately four months before the beginning of the budget fiscal year, management of the international business should be in possession of all the draft IPDs prepared by local management. These draft submissions are complete in all respects (as detailed in the section devoted to the IPD).

The financial director and his or her staff then prepare a consolidated draft IPD, to determine how closely the initial plans of the foreign units approach the consolidated profit plan and strategy goals for the business. At this point, international group management develops proposals to deal with such exceptions as excessive capital expenditures or operating expense; these proposals will be among the bases for discussion at the forthcoming budget reviews.

(c) Exchange Rates Established with Draft Integrated Planning Documents. Local management of the foreign units submit draft IPDs denominated in both the local and the home currency of the parent company. The exchange-rate forecasts are generally projected not only for the profit plan fiscal year, but also for the strategic portion (two or more following years) of the IPD. The local manager includes with the draft IPD submission his or her remarks, indicating the bases on which the exchange-rate forecasts are developed, and any professional or other expert sources who may have been consulted in the course of compiling them.

The exchange-rate forecasts should, of course, be checked by the group financial director, and any exceptional situations (e.g., managers of two units in the same country reporting different currency forecasts) should be adjusted. However, the local management is generally closer to the situation with respect to their own currency and has the better "feel" for developments which might affect it during the profit or strategic plan period.

The local forecast also represents commitment, by local management, to certain performance levels in the parent company's currency. For all these reasons, downward-imposed changes to currency forecasts should be handled with care and circumspection.

A few of the larger multinational groups are now in a position to reverse the upward flow of assumptions regarding exchange-rate developments. These companies aggregate regional or global "per-currency" exposures—as well as other financial and operational exposures—and hedge them, using derivatives and other financial instruments. In such cases, the jobs of exchange rate forecasting and managing the effects of exchange rates on earnings are removed from local management, who receive "guaranteed" exchange rate for their cross currency transactions during the budget year. Even in such cases, however, local management is charged with identifying the exposures that have to be managed by the regional or global financial services group.

(d) Procedure Embraces Only Controlled Units. Circulation of the SDP should be limited to subsidiaries or otherwise controlled companies, and the requirement to prepare an IPD submission should be restricted likewise. Inclusion of affiliated units in the procedure will almost certainly vitiate its effectiveness, as well as creating a risk of disseminating critical strategic information into the hands of competitive, or otherwise unfriendly, local interests.

Management of the international business has to accept that this abridgment of the process' scope and effectiveness is an inevitable by-product of "low profile" international investment. Dissatisfaction with results achieved through this avenue has created some "draw back" from international investment by relative newcomers (who tended to practice it) and reinforced the philosophy of old-line international companies generally to maintain a controlling position in all their foreign units, except where local restrictions made this illegal or impractical.

24.8 BUDGET-REVIEW PROCEDURE.

A general review, or a series of regional reviews, of the draft IPDs should be scheduled by management of the international business, to take place about three months before the beginning of the profit plan fiscal year. In the hypothetical case of Bigco, reviews would probably be scheduled for Europe, Latin America, and Australia.

The review takes the form of a "round table" discussion. The vice-president, finance director, and development director represent the parent company with local units represented by their senior operating and financial managers.

It may be ordinarily advisable to select a review site within the operating region, in order to minimize associated travel time and expense. However, at frequent intervals, it is probably advisable, for purposes of "visibility" and to create a corporate empathy with international personnel, to schedule a general budget and planning review at the corporate headquarters of the parent company. As a complement to such visits, local managers should be encouraged to make presentations to corporate general management and to the directors regarding their business.

In any event, the basic matter of the review comprises a presentation of the profit and strategic plans for each foreign unit by the managing and financial directors of that unit. This is followed by a general discussion among the review participants, in which the presenters will be called on to expand upon, refine, and in some cases (when regional reductions in capital or operating expenditures are indicated) defend the following:

- The underlying assumptions which have been superimposed on the ''base case'' of the SDP, in developing the unit's IPD
- The forecast profit plan results and expected, subsequent strategic plans for development, and the amount and allocation of resources required to achieve these
- Specifically, for the capital program proposed for each unit, the timing of such investments, and how forecast returns will be achieved

During these reviews, management of the international business will allocate necessary ''headquarters adjustments'' to the IPDs of individual units, to conform the consolidated results with the objectives agreed with the parent company. The review is, obviously, the most unstructured part of the budgeting and planning process. As such, it is impossible to provide a ''script'' for the proceedings. However, it is important for the success of the review that adequate time be provided for the presentation, analysis, and discussion of each of the units' IPDs. In our experience, this allocation is only nominally related to the size of the unit involved, and it will generally be necessary to allocate at least two clear hours for even the smallest of them. Larger and more complex companies, with multiple plants and/or lines of business, may require a long, full day of presentation and discussion to ensure adequate coverage.

24.9 INTEGRATED PLANNING DOCUMENT. The IPD, in its final form, should be submitted by individual foreign units to international group management about two months before the beginning of the profit plan fiscal year. The consolidated form of the document will be provided to corporate general management approximately one month later.

(a) Purposes of the Integrated Planning Document. The annual IPD compels the management of each component of the international business to (1) re-assess where his or her operation stands, particularly in relation to its competition in the market(s) served, (2) given his or her present position, to develop a ''base case'' and several alternative options for progress, (3) to apprise international and corporate management of expected financial results which will result from pursuit of the strategy and to define the economic environment in which these will occur, and (4) to determine the human, financial, technical, and other resources which will be required to implement such programs.

(b) Elements of the Document. The first section of the IPD is devoted to a statement of the unit's, or business's *strategic plan.* This qualitative document contains, in final form, many of the issues and considerations initiated months ago in the SDP:

- An assessment of the *present position* of the unit in terms of its markets, competition, economic environment, and available resources leading to a statement of opportunities, threats, strengths, and weaknesses in the present circumstances
- The *strategic statement,* which specifies how the unit will proceed to capitalize on positive factors in its present situation, and to eliminate or neutralize unfavorable exposures
- The *critical issues* that need to be faced and resolved in order to implement such strategy
- A description of the *necessary programs and resources* to implement the strategy, with discrete analysis of results expected from each and, if requirements exceed the

unit's expected ability to satisfy them, an analysis of how the "shortfall" will be covered

Most of the factors of the strategic statement are common to budgeting and planning procedures for both domestic and foreign operations. However, they assume a special importance and often require further development for the international business, because of the unique factors involved (exchange rates, sovereign risks) and also because allocation of resources is more difficult across borders and among corporations than with the homogenous operations of the parent's domestic businesses. Guidelines for a typical strategic plan presentation of one of Bigco's foreign units are included in Exhibit 24.4.

The second major document comprehended within the IPD is the unit's *profit plan.* In the profit plan, results expected to be achieved from implementing the unit's strategy during the next fiscal year are set forth in the customary detail involved with the parent company's management accounting system. The contingencies and any other developments which might affect these results are included in a narrative section of the plan. Also, selected income, asset, and liability accounts are carried forward for several more periods to document expected growth of profits and operations. However, the emphasis of the profit plan document is strongly placed on interpretation and presentation of results for the succeeding fiscal year. In the "typical" corporate organization of Bigco, which reports according to the foreign company, product-line data is included for the profit plan year where more than one product is involved.

The forms used for preparation of next year's profit plan are generally the same as those employed in the parent company's regular management reports. However, they are prepared in both the local currency of the reporting unit and the home currency of the parent, in order to provide proper frames of reference for (1) accuracy of currency forecast developments, and (2) comparisons of results achieved against counterparts in the local economy. However, there are two important summary forms that are included with the profit plan: (1) The *financial summary* of critical accounts, which are displayed on both a historical and forecast basis for the full term of the unit's strategic plan, as shown in Exhibit 24.5 (note that the financial summary is expanded to include estimates of required hourly and salaried personnel for the plan); and (2) the *summary of economic indexes,* both historical and forecast, which give rise to the results in the strategic plan and profit plan, as contained in Exhibit 24.6.

The last major section of the IPD comprises the *capital budget* of the unit, in detail for the profit plan fiscal year and incorporating major projects (level of significance to be optionally established) for at least the next two years. Management of the foreign operations should be encouraged to segregate the projects in the following (or similar) categories:

- *Income-maintaining projects,* which are necessary for the continued successful operation of the business (i.e., capitalized repairs or replacement of broken or deficient equipment essential to the unit's core business)
- *Income-producing projects,* together with an estimate of the incremental benefit of the project to the unit's operating income defined (for purposes of this document), as income before financial charges, taxes, and special items
- *Leased items* contained in the first two categories, with a statement of annual leasing cost and equivalent purchase cost

Strategic Position	
Market position:	Discuss how your situation has changed since the last strategic plan, or what is expected to change. Please include a statement of the impact of these factors on your present strategy.
Competitive position:	Provide the competitive ranking of your organization with your top three or four competitors in market(s) and product line(s) served. Explain the reason for the rankings, and the implications for your operations in each area of comparison. Also, state what you understand to be the strategies of your principal competitors in each area.
Critical Issues	
Statement:	State the critical issues for your operation, as developed from the strategic direction paper provided you for that purpose, as amended and expanded on the occasion of the budget review procedure. Comment on the changes and expansions between: (1) last year's IPD and (2) the SDP, giving the reasons and expected consequences.
Strategy	
Mission statement:	Provide a ''mission statement'' for your unit, indicating the strategic direction of the operation during the next 5 to 10 years, according to your strategic position, investment programs, and so on. Highlight any changes and the reasons therefore.
Programs	
For each critical issue, there should be at least one program response designed to bring about change and to implement your strategic direction:	
Identification:	Identify the program(s) that you have developed in response to each of the critical issues contained in your IPD.
Implementation:	State, or show in tabular form, the objective of the program, who will be responsible for implementing it, the major components of what needs to be done, the resources (both internal and external) needed for carrying it out, and the time table for completion.
Expectations:	Provide the specific expected operating and financial results to be achieved from each program. Also, provide the range (optimistic/pessimistic) of possible results and the conditions under which the extremes of the range might be expected to occur.
Risk assessment:	Based on the major assumptions which had to be made for your profit projections, discuss the likelihood of the assumption happening as planned. What will be the likely result if the outcome is missed?
Contingency plans:	For each essential assumption in your plan (e.g., cost and price developments, volume level of production), state what contingency plans you have developed to achieve minimum financial and operating objectives (as contained in the profit plan) in the event of unfavorable developments.

Exhibit 24.4. BIGCO, Inc., integrated planning document suggested format of the strategic plan for the fiscal years 19X0 through 19X1

Each of the major items (according to the chosen level of significance) is then prioritized and a brief discussion of each such item is included in the capital budget, justifying the indicated order of priorities and commenting (with quantification of results, wherever possible) on the probable effects of deletion or delay of the project.

Filing of an approved capital budget via the IPD should not provide management of

	Last Year Actual	This Year Estimated	Profit Plan	Strategic Plan Forecast			
				Year 2	Year 3	Year 4	Year 5
Sales/Profits							
Net sales	—	—	—	—	—	—	—
Operating income[a]	—	—	—	—	—	—	—
Net aftertax	—	—	—	—	—	—	—
Assets/Year-End							
Receivables	—	—	—	—	—	—	—
Inventories	—	—	—	—	—	—	—
Net PPE[b]	—	—	—	—	—	—	—
Total	—	—	—	—	—	—	—
Capital expenditure	—	—	—	—	—	—	—
Depreciation		—	—	—	—	—	—
Ratios							
ROI (corp. formula)	—	—	—	—	—	—	—
Turnover ratios							
Receivables	—	—	—	—	—	—	—
Inventories	—	—	—	—	—	—	—
Op. Inc./Sales	—	—	—	—	—	—	—
Manpower							
Hourly	—	—	—	—	—	—	—
Salaried	—	—	—	—	—	—	—

[a] Income before financial charges, taxes, and special items.
[b] Plant, property, and equipment.

Exhibit 24.5. BIGCO, Inc., profit plan company/division ——, financial summary ($million)

	Last Year Actual	This Year Estimated	Profit Plan	Strategic Plan Forecast			
				Year 2	Year 3	Year 4	Year 5
GNP growth (%)	—	—	—	—	—	—	—
CPI change (%)	—	—	—	—	—	—	—
Industrial production growth (%)	—	—	—	—	—	—	—
Consumption growth	—	—	—	—	—	—	—
Imports growth (%)	—	—	—	—	—	—	—
Exports growth (%)	—	—	—	—	—	—	—
Unemployment (%)	—	—	—	—	—	—	—
Wage increase (%) (incl. fringes)	—	—	—	—	—	—	—
Domestic prime rate (%)	—	—	—	—	—	—	—
Exchange rates							
U.S.$/L.C.	—	—	—	—	—	—	—
L.C./US$	—	—	—	—	—	—	—

Exhibit 24.6. BIGCO, Inc., profit plan company/division ——, economic indexes–assumptions

the local unit with blanket authority to undertake the projected expenditures. An optional level of local spending authority should be established consistent with the authorities and ability of each local manager, and a second for the general management of the international business. Approved capital items outside these authority levels, and any significant non-budgeted projects, should be referred to corporate general management and/or the board of directors, in accordance with existing delegation of authority procedures for domestic operations.

24.10 MONTHLY REPORTING PROCEDURES. The flesh and muscle of the budget process is added to the bare bones of the IPD, with a consistent and meaningful reporting package, to be received and reviewed in depth on a monthly basis. It is not as important to receive this report within days or hours after the end of an accounting period as it is to have on hand adequate and accurate information to determine performance of local units versus their profit and strategic plan's commitments.

(a) The Manager's Letter (Report). The heart of such a reporting package is a meaningful manager's letter which explains the activities for the period, identifying and explaining significant variances (in either or both currencies) from both budget expectations and past experience. The manager's letter is the critical element in continuing communication between the parent company and the local business; it is therefore essential that it be written in, or translated into, clear and understandable commercial English and that the author (when necessary, the translator also) have an appreciation of accounting standards in the home country of the parent company, and the effects of foreign-exchange translation on the local currency statements for his or her unit. Comments on each of these factors should be regularly included in the content of the manager's letter.

(b) "Twin Currency" Income Statement. In addition to the dollar-based (or other home currency) income statement needed for consolidated corporate accounts, the monthly reporting package should include a statement of income (current period and year to date) for the reporting unit, which is denominated in both its local currency and in the home currency of the parent company.

This statement should compare results in both currencies to the profit plan section of the IPD and to last year's experience, to the extent such comparison is not required by the ordinary management accounts of the parent company for its domestic operations. A sample form of the statement is shown in Exhibit 24.7.

Such "twin currency" reports should be circulated to corporate general management, together with appropriate explanatory notes. Without an understanding of the vagaries of the foreign-exchange market, it is difficult for general management to understand how above-average performance in the local market can produce apparently dismal results in the home currency, or vice versa. Periodic exposure to, and education concerning, local currency versus home currency performance is essential to proper evaluation of not only the efficiency of local and group management, but (since exchange exposure is an inevitable corollary of foreign direct investment) also the parent company's appetite for expansion of foreign operations.

(c) Variance Analysis: Operating versus Financial. A valuable tool for earnings analysis should be a monthly "worksheet" that segregates budget-versus-actual differences into the principal components of operating (price, volume, cost, labor and material usage, and value added in inventory) and financial (foreign exchange) variances. Ideally,

	U.S. $thousand						£thousand					
	This Month			Year to Date			This Month			Year to Date		
	Actual	Budget	Last Year	Actual	Budget	Last Year	Actual	Budget	Last Year	Actual	Budget	Last Year
Net sales	—	—	—	—	—	—	—	—	—	—	—	—
Cost of sales	—	—	—	—	—	—	—	—	—	—	—	—
Gross profit	—	—	—	—	—	—	—	—	—	—	—	—
Selling expense	—	—	—	—	—	—	—	—	—	—	—	—
Admin. Expense	—	—	—	—	—	—	—	—	—	—	—	—
General expense	—	—	—	—	—	—	—	—	—	—	—	—
Operating profit	—	—	—	—	—	—	—	—	—	—	—	—
Financial chges.	—	—	—	—	—	—	—	—	—	—	—	—
Forex P/(L)[a]	—	—	—	—	—	—	—	—	—	—	—	—
Other (inc.)/exp.	—	—	—	—	—	—	—	—	—	—	—	—
Pretax income	═	═	═	═	═	═	═	═	═	═	═	═

[a] Foreign exchange P/(L) relating to translation of foreign currency accounts into home currency of the parent group of vice versa for the operating unit.

Exhibit 24.7. BIGCO–BLIGHTY, Ltd. comparative income statement (LC vs. US$) for the period ended ——, 19XX

	Current Month		Production (Units) Year to Date		
Sales Variance	Budget	Last Year	Budget	Last Year	Actual Budget Last Year Explanation
Price	—	—	—	—	(Actual price-budget/last year price) × (production)
Volume	—	—	—	—	(Actual production-budget/last year production) × (added sales value per budget)
(A) Subtotal	—	—	—	—	
Mfg. variance					
Material:					
Cost	—	—	—	—	(Budget/last year cost-actual cost) × (consumption)
Usage	—	—	—	—	Balance of material variance.
Labor	—	—	—	—	Budget-actual costs
Other conversion	—	—	—	—	Budget-actual costs
Invty change	—	—	—	—	(Value added to work in process and finished goods per budget) − (actual value added).
(B) Subtotal	—	—	—	—	
Gross profit var.	—	—	—	—	(A) + (B)
Operating expense	—	—	—	—	(Budget) − (actual expenses)
Forex variance	—	—	—	—	(Sum of all local currency variances) × (actual average exchange rate for the period-budget rate)
Other (inc.)/exp.	—	—	—	—	(Budget) − (actual (income) and expenses).
(C) Pretax varnce	—	—	—	—	

Exhibit 24.8. BIGCO, Inc., international business monthly operating and financial report variance analysis worksheet ($thousand)

such a worksheet would also address the categories of selling, administrative, and general expense, as well as various categories of nonoperating items.

Such a worksheet pinpoints the contribution of operating and financial factors to the apparent overall profitability of the local units. It also provides the means with which to determine whether the unit is efficiently countering negative financial factors with improved operating efficiencies and, conversely, whether poor and inefficient operating performance is being cloaked by developments in the foreign exchange and local financial markets. A typical form of such a variance worksheet is shown in Exhibit 24.8.

In cases in which the budget exchange rate has been guaranteed to local operations by the parent company, this analysis will be performed at the regional or corporate financial center. The local variance reports will be translated at the guaranteed exchange rate and will only highlight operational variances.

(d) Full-Year Estimate: Actual and Forecast. The final major component of the monthly report by local units to operating management should be the *full-year estimate.*

This report, which can be in any form suitable to the parent company, adds the forecast results for the balance of the profit plan fiscal year to the actual results achieved (year to date) to provide a continuously updated forecast of expected results for the year. Notable variances versus budget or last year's actual results should be justified by a narrative accompaniment to the full year estimate, to the extent they are not already satisfactorily dealt with elsewhere in the monthly report.

(e) "Shareholder Relations" with General Management. The wealth of material that is received from foreign units in the monthly reporting package is essential to the management of the international business in administering its subsidiary companies around the world. However, the extent and format of some of the material would make it superfluous, perhaps unintelligible to general management, which may be neither financially nor internationally oriented.

It has been noted earlier that the relationship of the international business to the parent company is analogous to the parent's relation with its own shareholders. In order to communicate adequately and effectively the state of the international business upward, an abridged and refined monthly report, also called an exercise in "shareholder relations," will have to be developed.

In such a report, figures of critical interest to management (e.g., actual sales and income, and variances from budget and historical levels), as well as pertinent information and analysis should be condensed into one page for each foreign subsidiary. Available information regarding affiliated companies should be incorporated to the extent it is regularly available on a reliable basis. The report should also include a full set of consolidated financial statements (including cash flow) for the international business.

Management of the international business may also find it advisable, even valuable, to publish an annual report of its results and activities. The annual document should follow the same general format as the monthly reports to management, but with expanded items of information regarding the business and each of its operations.

(f) Desirability of Graphic Data. The widespread availability of computer-based graph systems provides an opportunity for enhancing reports to management which should not be overlooked. More complete and quicker comprehension of statistical information can be achieved with a few well-selected and designed graphs than with pages of dense text.

Almost any account balance or ratio can be presented in the perspective of budget expectations and historical experience. What is or is not included will be largely a matter of the type of business, and the preferences of general and international management. However, a core presentation of sales, profit before financial charges, special items, and taxes (operating profit), and return on investment should probably be included if the decision is made to use graphic material in periodic reports to general management. Another useful graphic presentation would be the monthly progression of each unit's full year estimates of sales and profits versus the comparable budgets for these figures.

24.11 BUDGETING FOR HEADQUARTERS OPERATIONS.

In an increasing number of corporate organizations, the decision has been taken to hand over control of all three phases of international corporate activity to the "international division" or other form of central international management. These, in addition to investment in foreign operations, comprise licensing of the parent company's technology and exports of its products, either to foreign units of the company or to third parties. Usually, each of these functions is performed by a specialized group within the corporate organization of the parent company and, if they are organized within the international business, it is necessary to include their strategic and profit plans in the budget cycle.

Although the matters with which they deal can be complex and technically oriented, the objective of these headquarters businesses is to sell as much as they can of product, technology, or whatever may be the center of their interest. Except for a relatively few companies which have made a systematic commitment to export development, the export sales group often has the level of its activity fixed by the amount of products which the parent group has available for sale after satisfying all domestic requirements.

Therefore, the principal thrust of the budgets for headquarters unit (including the general management of the international business) is more involved with cost control than with revenue creation. In this context, it is usually not necessary to have as broad-gauged a review and development procedure for these departments, or to consider as many ''critical issues,'' as with the foreign operations.

24.12 ALTERNATIVE ORGANIZATIONS OF INTERNATIONAL BUSINESS. The budgeting process will be influenced by the parent company's choice of organizational structure, although many of the basic procedures and documents enumerated and explained herein are readily adaptable to international businesses oriented according to regions or product lines. A choice of one of these alternative structures is dependent on a number of factors involving the size and relationship of the foreign operations to the parent company:

- The percentage of parent company sales, profits, and shareholders funds which are invested in international business—a relatively small commitment (i.e., less than the lesser of 10% or $10 million) may not warrant a specialized, central, international management structure
- A corollary of the above is the percentage of ownership or control exercised by the parent company in its foreign units—if most or all investments are by way of a minority position, there is little need or incentive to establish an administrative superstructure
- The degree of technical support or other interrelation between the operations of the parent and its foreign operations—in relatively ''high-tech'' organizations, the need for vertical access to technology exceeds the need for international skills; from this, product oriented organization ensues

As a general observation in any of these organizational structures, consolidation of licensing and export sales with investment management is right out of the picture. Also, any structure other than the international division or central management, with its network of subsidiaries and affiliates, will tend to increase ''overhead'' associated with the international business. The special skills of the central management team (particularly the financial) will have to be replicated for each product line and/or region on which the parent company wishes to confer independence of operation.

Although the basic budgeting cycle would vary relatively little, product line and/or regional structures tend to multiply the number of documents required to be processed by corporate general management. This is another hidden cost of decentralized organization, which needs to be weighed against the technical or operating benefits expected to be derived therefrom.

SOURCES AND SUGGESTED REFERENCES

Buckley, Adrian, ''Evaluating Overseas Projects,'' *Accountancy* (UK), vol. 99, no. 1125, May 1987.

Goddard, Scott, ''Political Risk in International Capital Budgeting,'' *Managerial Finance* (UK), vol. 16, no. 2, 1990.

Holland, John, ''Capital Budgeting for International Business: A Framework for Analysis,'' *Managerial Finance* (UK), vol. 16, no. 2, 1990.

Madura, Jeff, Geraldo M. Vasconcellos, and Richard J. Kish, ''A Valuation Model for International Acquisitions,'' *Management Decision,* vol. 29, no. 4, 1991.

Mannino, Paul V., and Ken Milani, ''Budgeting for an International Business,'' *Management Accounting,* vol. 73, no. 8, February 1992.

CHAPTER 25

UNDERSTANDING FOREIGN EXCHANGE TRANSACTIONS

Françoise Soares-Kemp

Bank of New York

25.1 FOREIGN EXCHANGE RATES.

As multinational companies become involved with payables and receivables denominated in many different currencies, product and service shipments across national borders, and subsidiaries operating in different political jurisdictions, they face an additional set of problems than the firm with a purely domestic operation. The basic issues—budget control, cash management, intracompany transfers, and capital budgeting—face all multinational companies. These companies have responded by becoming increasingly sophisticated in international finance and foreign exchange. This chapter attempts to give a summary description of these topics.

(a) Exchange Rate.

The *exchange rate* is the price for which a currency can be bought or sold in terms of another currency. Most of the time the value of the exchange rate is decided by free market forces, but occasionally there is central bank intervention in an attempt to ensure that currencies do not depreciate or appreciate excessively.

(i) Spot Rate.

A *spot foreign exchange deal* is one made for settlement in two working days. Under normal conditions, a spot deal done on Monday is settled on Wednesday.

A *working day* is defined as one in which both banks are open for business in both settlement countries; except that if the deal is done against the U.S. dollar, if the first of the two days is a holiday in the United States, but not in the other settlement country, that day is also counted as a working day. *Direct quotation* of foreign exchange rates takes the form of variable amounts of domestic currency against a fixed amount of foreign currency. *Indirect quotation,* conversely, takes the form of fixed amounts of domestic currency against varying amounts of foreign currency. In the United States, both types of quotations are used. For domestic business, as well as on the commodity exchanges, U.S. terms are used, that is, direct quotation (e.g., DM 1 = US $0.6800). For international business and increasingly for domestic business too, U.S. banks use European terms or reciprocal indirect quotation (e.g., US $1 = DM 1.4706). Whatever system is used, when two cross-border interests wish to transact foreign currency business, one of them will have to apply an indirect quotation when dealing in the other's currency.

A foreign exchange rate is called a *cross-rate* when the national currency is not party to the transaction. A Paris bank buying or selling Deutschemarks against the U.S. dollar is using a cross-rate. A New York bank buying or selling Deutschemarks against French francs is also using a cross-rate.

Example: Customer wants to buy DM 10,000,000 against French francs. Because usually all currencies are quoted against the dollar, we have to work it out with the respective dollar rates, which at the moment may be:

$$\$/DM = 1.4750 - 1.4760$$

$$\$/FF = 5.1280 - 5.1305$$

We get our selling rate for DM against French francs with this calculation:

$$\$/DM = 1.4750 - 1.4760$$

divided by

$$\$/FF = 5.1280 - 5.1305$$

$$\frac{\text{Sell Ffr } 5.1305}{\text{Buy DM } 1.4750} = \text{Ffr } 3.4783$$

(b) Forward Operations. A *forward exchange contract* is an agreement between a bank and another party to exchange one currency for another at some future date. The rate at which the exchange is to be made, the delivery date, and the amounts involved are fixed at the time of agreement. Such a contract is distinguished from a foreign exchange futures contract in that a *futures contract* is a contract between two parties for the exchange of a certain amount of foreign currency at a future date, with the date and the amount usually standardized.

Theoretically, the forward (or futures) price for a currency can be identical to the spot price. Almost always, however, the forward (futures) price in practice is either higher (premium) or lower (discount) than the spot price. Suppose a quoted currency is more expensive in the future than it is now in terms of the base currency; the quoted currency is thus said to be at a premium in the forward market, relative to the base currency. Conversely, the base currency may be said to stand at a discount relative to the quoted currency.

Taking the U.S. dollar as the base currency and the French franc as the quoted currency, we have a spot rate of US $1 = FF 5.1120. The dollar buys fewer French francs in one year than it does today and thus the dollar is at a discount to the French franc. Conversely, the French franc is at a premium to the U.S. dollar.

The size of the dollar discount or French franc premium is the difference between 5.1300 and 5.1120, that is, 1.80 centimes. This is normally quoted as 180 points. To arrive at the forward price, the French franc premium or dollar discount must be subtracted from the spot. The spot rate might be quoted as 5.1300/50 and the one-year discount at 180/130. In other words, if the trader is buying U.S. dollars forward, he or she will charge a discount of 180 points, but if he or she is selling, he or she will give away only a 130-point discount.

A price of 180/130 indicates a premium for the quoted currency (the French franc) in the forward market and a discount for the base currency (the U.S. dollar). However, a price of 130/180 would indicate a discount for the quoted and a premium for the base. In summary,

$$\text{High/Low} = \text{Subtract points}$$

$$\text{Low/High} = \text{Add points}$$

The use of points in forward quotations is convenient because the points tend to move much less quickly than the spots, and because it is the points that are relevant in the forward and swap markets.

The forward swap points (discount or premium) always tend to be equal to the interest differential in the Euromarket. When the markets are not disturbed by monetary or political unrest, the bulk of activity in the forward market originates from money market activities and (to a lesser extent) commercial operations. Interest rate levels in the Euromarket for the various currencies will be the determinant of forward points or swap points.

(c) Swap Operations. In general, a *swap* is an exchange of one currency for another on one day matched by a reverse exchange on a later day. Swaps have two basic uses:

1. To switch a deal from one currency to another, and back again, on a hedged basis
2. To move a given currency deal forward or backward in time

The formula to derive swap (or forward) points is:

$$\text{Swap points} = \text{Spot rate} \times (\text{Currency interest rate} - \text{U.S. interest rate}) \times \text{No. of days/365}$$

Example:

$$\frac{\text{12 months}}{\text{U.S. interest rate}} = \frac{\text{Bid}}{6.75} - \frac{\text{Offer}}{7.00}$$

$$\text{French interest rate} = 6.50 - 6.75$$

$$\text{Swap points} = 1.5300 \times (0.25) \times \frac{365}{365}$$

$$\text{Swap points} = \text{129 points premium for the French franc}$$

The forward premium (or discount) on a currency relative to the dollar, expressed as a percentage of the spot rate, will tend to (about) equal the differential between interest rates available in that currency and dollar interest rates.

(d) Derivatives Operations. *Derivatives* is a term usually applied to futures, options, and interest rate and currency swaps. These are markets that are "derived" from other markets. They are all additional instruments to be used by a multinational for hedging and, when appropriate, for profit. To hedge is to reduce risk. A hedger transfers risk by temporarily offsetting a position in a cash market with a related position in a futures market.

Options have become a very useful tool in foreign exchange markets. They allow us the luxury of a one-way bet. We can bet that a rate will go up and make a profit from that—but if it comes down, we don't lose. They are particularly useful for hedging cash flows when we feel uncertain about the future. They can also be used to take leveraged positions.

A *currency option* is an agreement between two parties. One party grants the other the right to buy or sell a currency under certain conditions. The counterparty pays a premium for the privilege of being able to buy or sell the instrument without committing to do so. There are two basic types of options: puts and calls. A *call option* gives the buyer the right to buy or ''call'' a specified amount of the underlying currency at the specified price during a specified period. The price at which the instrument may be bought is the *exercise price,* or the *strike price.* The last day on which the option may be called or exercised is called the *expiry date,* or the *maturity date.* A *put option* gives the buyer the right to sell or put to the writer a specified amount of the underlying currency at the strike price until the expiry date. Under an American option, the holder of the option has the right to exercise at any time before maturity. Under a European option, the holder may exercise it only at the time of expiration.

The growth of options contracts since the early 1980s has stimulated the development of new products and techniques for managing foreign exchange assets and liabilities. One recent development combines the features of the forward contract and option contract. Terms such as ''break forward,'' ''participating forward,'' or ''FOX'' (forward with option exit) refer to forward contracts with an option to break out of the contract at a future date. In this case, the forward exchange rate includes an option premium for the right to break the forward contract. The incentive for such a contract comes from the desire of customers to have the insurance provided by a forward contract when the exchange rate moves against them and yet not to lose the potential for profit available with favorable exchange rate movements. The break-forward contract has several good features that do not exist with an option. For one thing, an option requires an up-front premium payment. Corporate treasurers may not have a budget for option premiums or may not have management approval for using options. The break-forward hides the option premium in the forward rate. Because the price at which the forward contract is broken is fixed in advance, the break-forward may be treated as a simple forward contract for tax and accounting purposes, whether the contract is broken or not.

One of the more difficult problems in hedging foreign exchange risk arises in bidding on contracts. The bidder submits a proposal to perform some task to a firm or government agency seeking to award a contract to the successful bidder. As there may be many other bidders, the bidding firms face the foreign exchange risk associated with the contract only if they, in fact, are awarded the contract. Suppose a particular bidder assesses only a 20% chance of winning the contract. Should it buy a forward contract or option today to hedge the foreign exchange risk it faces in the event it is the successful bidder? If substantial foreign exchange risk is involved for the successful bidder, then both the bidders and the contract awarder face a dilemma. The bids will not be as competitive with the outstanding foreign exchange risk as they would be if the exchange rate uncertainty were hedged.

One approach to this problem is the ''Scout'' contract. Midland Bank developed the Scout (share currency option under tender) as an option that is sold to the contract awarder, which then sells it to the successful bidder. The awarding agency now receives more competitive and, perhaps, a greater number of bids, because the bidders know that the foreign exchange hedge is arranged.

Over time, we are seeing a proliferation of new financial market products aimed at dealing with future transactions involving foreign exchange. If there is a corporate interest in customizing an option or forward arrangement to a specific type of transaction, an innovative bank will step in and offer a product.

(e) Forecasting and Foreign Exchange Risk. International business involves foreign exchange risk, because the value of transactions in different currencies will be sensitive to exchange rate changes. The appropriate strategy for the corporate treasurer and the individual speculator is at least partly determined by expectations of the future path of the exchange rate. As a result, exchange rate forecasts are an important part of the decision-making process of international investors.

One problem we encounter when trying to evaluate the effect of exchange rate changes on a multinational company arises in determining the appropriate concept of exposure to foreign exchange risk. Understanding exchange exposure is complicated by the multiplicity of definitions and interpretations of what constitutes foreign exchange risk for the company. For example, anticipated foreign exchange rate movements represent no risk, as they can be embodied in the corporate budget. (As an example, most of the impact of the devaluation of the Mexican peso can be anticipated and reflected in the company budget.) However, unanticipated currency changes are a source of risk, because they cannot be incorporated into the budgeting process.

The distinction between economic and financial risk is also important in understanding foreign exchange exposures. *Economic risk or exposure* is the danger that budgeted business expenses could become uncompetitive because the real purchasing power of a currency has risen to a point where competitors with costs in other currencies could gain a significant advantage.

All other exposure or risk is financial and can lead to losses realized in cash or unrealized losses, which show up in companies' balance sheets. Economic exposure management is part of the wider subjective corporate planning task, which includes estimating future cash flows over an arbitrary time horizon, using economic analysis. The finance and budgeting, marketing, production, and sourcing departments must all be involved in this process. These departments must all take a hard look at whether a sustained real rise, or drop, of a currency against the currencies of competitors will—adversely or positively affect the company's competitive costs and, therefore, its sales, profit margins, and market share, which in turn will reduce or increase the return on the capital and revenue investment previously sunk in its present commercial activity. This forces the corporation to focus continuously on the specific nature of the business of each individual overseas subsidiary and allows no sweeping generalizations.

Furthermore, focusing on economic exposure is consistent with the overall corporate goal of maximizing cash flows or profits over time. In considering strategies for hedging budgeted cash flows, a company's options include changing foreign currency product prices and entering into foreign exchange contracts.

An exchange rate change will affect the U.S. company's dollar-denominated cash flows through two channels. First, changes in the foreign exchange rate will affect the dollar value of all relevant foreign currency denominated cash flows directly. For example, for a U.S. dollar-based company, the dollar value of future sales denominated in a foreign currency will decline when that currency depreciates against the U.S. dollar. Secondly, actions taken in response to changes in the exchange rate can affect the foreign currency value of these cash flows. These actions could take the form of changes in sales volume or sales prices. Foreign currency values of future sales would increase if (1) prices are raised to compensate for depreciation of the currency or (2) sales rise because of increased competitive advantage in the foreign market. In these instances, there is an automatic hedging mechanism which partially or totally eliminates the exposure. The combined impact of these two factors determines the ultimate overall impact of exchange rate changes on the dollar-denominated value of cash flows. When the two effects do not offset each other, the affected flows are said to be "exposed" to the particular foreign currency involved.

Forward market hedges are appropriate only when foreign currency prices cannot be changed immediately following a change in the exchange rate between the particular currency and the dollar. The forward market hedge thus provides protection against losses that occur between the time of the exchange rate change and the compensating price changes.

Prices changing to compensate for exchange rate changes is also a big marketing issue, and pricing policy considers many factors in addition to exchange rate movements. Volatility of exchange rate movements is another major consideration in pricing changes. If a depreciation currency begins to appreciate after prices have increased, the market share for that product could be threatened (or enhanced). Thus, exchange-rate changes are financial in nature and frequently bear little relation in the short term to the local business environment. Trying to change prices as fast as exchange rates change is not advisable, and, in reality, raising prices that quickly is impossible. Forward market hedges can provide protection against losses while pricing decisions are evaluated and implemented. The ideal hedge considers the time each entity needs to effect these changes; only in this way can the maturity of the hedge be structured to maximize its benefits.

Having defined economic exchange exposure or risk, we can go on to identify others. *Transaction exchange exposure or risk* refers to gains and losses that arise from the settlement of transactions whose terms are stated in a foreign currency. Foreign-exchange transactions may include the following:

- Purchasing or selling on credit goods or services in foreign currencies
- Borrowing or lending funds denominated in foreign currencies
- Being a party to an unperformed forward foreign exchange contract
- Acquiring assets or incurring liabilities denominated in foreign currencies.

Translation exposure (risk), often referred to as *accounting* or *FASB* (Financial Accounting Standards Board) *exposure (risk),* arises from the need to report consolidated worldwide operations according to predetermined accounting rules. Assets, liabilities, revenues, and expenses originally measured to a foreign currency must be restated in terms of a home currency to be consolidated with home currency accounts.

Whether a company focuses on accounting or economic exposure, stock market analysts seem to focus on the economic consequences of foreign exchange rate changes. Apparently this market reaction has been triggered by concerns over fluctuating exchange rates, volatile inflation rates, taxation of foreign source earnings, and the widespread political instability that has given rise to these conditions. An integral part of a company's attempts to adjust to this volatile financial environment is the increased emphasis it places on forecasting foreign exchange rate movements. Volumes of literature discuss the causes of these movements. To summarize, the main factors that make currencies move and influence the demand and supply of each currency in the market are:

- Relative price levels
- Relative inflation rates
- Relative interest rates
- Relative changes in money supply
- Investment or portfolio preferences of big international investors
- Bandwagon effect (if a currency seems to be on the way up, speculators may exaggerate the trend by buying in the hope of a quick profit)
- Intervention by central banks
- Political changes and stability

Regression analysis models are at the basis of many forecasting services, but the most impressive results have recently been obtained by market analysts called "chartists," who simply track price movements. Finally, some forecasters concentrate on so-called psychology gleaned from the attitudes and statements of people with the greatest direct influence on the supply and demand of currencies, such as the monetary authorities of the major reserve currencies and those responsible for administering huge portfolios such as mutual funds and pension funds.

All three methods can be used simultaneously, and this way the many aspects of foreign exchange forecasting are all addressed. It has already been concluded, after years of effort, that accurate forecasting is probably impossible. All companies' foreign exchange managers are unavoidably in the business of forecasting, but they should restrict their efforts in this endeavor to the greatest extent possible. The following organizations provide some form of foreign exchange advisory service:

- Morgan Guaranty Trust Company
- Citibank
- MMS
- IDEA

The ability to anticipate and prepare for events is critical to a company's remaining competitive in today's world.

25.2 IMPACT OF FOREIGN EXCHANGE ON OPERATING EXPOSURE MANAGEMENT. An unexpected change in foreign exchange rates affects a company's levels, depending on the time horizon under review. The goal of operating exposure management is to anticipate and influence the effect of unexpected changes in foreign exchange rates on a firm's future cash flows—rather than just keeping one's fingers crossed!

To illustrate the impact of operating exposure, here is an example: Parfumeries S.A. is the wholly owned French subsidiary of Perfumes U.S.A., a U.S.-based multi-national firm. The required rate of return after taxes to Perfumes U.S.A. is 20% from Parfumeries S.A.

Parfumeries S.A. manufactures in France from French material and labor. Fifty percent of production is sold in France and the other half is sold in the European Union. All sales are invoiced in French francs, and accounts receivable are equal to 25% of annual sales.

In this example, we assume that on January 1, 1996, before any business has begun, the French franc unexpectedly drops 20% in value, from FF 5.13/$ to FF 6.1550/$.

Parfumeries S.A.
Beginning Balance Sheet and Expected Cash Flows

Balance Sheet, December 31, 1995

Cash	FF 2,000,000	A/P	1,000,000
A/R	4,000,000	S/T Bank Loan	2,000,000
Inv.	3,000,000	L/T Debt	2,000,000
Net P&E	5,000,000	Comm. St.	2,000,000
		Ret. Earn.	7,000,000
Total	FF 14,000,000		
		Total	FF 14,000,000

Case 1. *Expected Cash Flow, No Devaluation, 1996*

Sales (500,000 units @ FF 25/unit)	FF 12,500,000
Direct costs (500,000 units @ FF 20/unit)	10,000,000
Cash operating fixed expenses	1,500,000
Depreciation	250,000
Pretax profit	FF 750,000
Income tax expense (50%)	375,000
Profit after tax	FF 375,000
Add back depreciation	625,000
Cash flow from operation in FF	FF 1,000,000

Existing exchange rate: FF 5.13 = $1.00

Cash flow from operations in U.S. dollars = $195,000

Cash flow from operations in francs = FF 1,000,000

New exchange rate: FF. 6.1550 = $1

Cash flow from operations in U.S. dollars = $162,500

Parfumeries S.A. has experienced a shortfall of US $32,500 in its French franc cash flow.

However, we now assume that sales in France double following the devaluation, because French-made perfume is now more competitive with foreign imports. Furthermore, export volume doubles. The sales price is kept constant in French franc terms because management of Parfumeries S.A. has not had any change in its local French operating costs.

Case 2. *Expected Cash Flow, Volume Increases*

Sales (1,000,000 units @ 41 FF 25/unit)	FF 25,000,000
Direct costs (1,000,000 units @ FF 20/unit)	20,000,000
Cash operations final expenses	1,500,000
Depreciation	250,000
Pretax profit	FF 3,250,000
Income tax expense (50%)	1,625,000

Profit after tax	FF 1,625,000
Add back depreciation	250,000
Cash flow from operations in FF	FF 1,875,000

New exchange rate: FF 6.1550 = US $1.00

Cash flow from operations in U.S. dollars = $305,000

Projected cash flows for five years:

Year	*Item*	*Francs*	*Dollars @ FF 6.1550*
1	Cash flow from operations	FF 1,875,000	
	less new investment in working capital	− 4,000,000	
		FF −2,125,000	$−345,000
2	Cash flow from operations	1,875,000	305,000
3	Cash flow from operations	1,875,000	305,000
4	Cash flow from operations	1,875,000	305,000
5	Cash flow from operations	1,875,000	305,000
	Incremental working-capital recapture	4,000,000	650,000

Case 3. *Expected Cash Flow, Sales Price Increase*

Sales (500,000 @ FF 30/unit)	FF 15,000,000
Direct costs (500,000 @ 20/unit)	10,000,000
Cash operating final expenses	1,500,000
Depreciation	250,000
Pretax profit	FF 3,250,000
Income tax expense (50%)	1,625,000
Profit after tax	FF 1,625,000
Add back depreciation	250,000
Cash flow from operations in FF	FF 1,875,000

New exchange rate: FF 6.1550 = $1.00

Cash flow from operations in U.S. dollars = $305,000

Projected cash flows for five years:

Year	*Item*	*Francs*	*Dollars @ FF 6.1550*
1	Cash flow from operations	FF 1,875,000	
	less new investment in working capital	−600,000	
		FF 1,275,000	$207,000
2	Cash flow from operations	1,875,000	305,000
3	Cash flow from operations	1,875,000	305,000
4	Cash flow from operations	1,875,000	305,000
5	Cash flow from operations	1,875,000	305,000
	Incremental working capital recaptured last year	600,000	97,500

The key to this improvement is in the operating leverage. If costs are incurred in francs and do not increase after a devaluation, an increase in the sales price will lead to sharply higher profits.

If a company's operations are well diversified internationally, management is prepositioned both to recognize disequilibrium when it occurs and to react to maintain competitiveness and profitability.

In summary, multinational companies must obtain information in a form valid for internal evaluation and control of their subsidiaries. Comparison of results with operating budgets is the dominant criterion for performance evaluation of foreign subsidiaries. Performance relative to budget in an international context involves decisions about which exchange rate to use in the budgeting process and which to use in the assessment of results. Use of a forecasted exchange rate in budgeting and the end-of-period actual rate in assessment is most common.

SOURCES AND SUGGESTED REFERENCES

Choi, Frederick D. S., "International Data Sources for Empirical Research in Financial Management," *Financial Management,* Summer 1988, pp. 80–98.

Holland, John, *International Financial Management.* New York and Oxford, U.K.: Basil Blackwell, 1986.

Lessard, Donald R., "Global Competition and Corporate Finance in 1990's," *Journal of Applied Corporate Finance,* vol. 3, no. 4, Winter 1991, pp. 59–72.

Lessard, Donald R., and David Sharp, "Measuring the Performance of Operations Subject to Fluctuating Exchange Rates," *Midland Corporate Finance Journal,* Fall 1984, pp. 18–30.

Mueller, Gerhard G., Helen Gernon, and Gary Meek, *Accounting: An International Perspective.* Homewood, IL: Richard D. Irwin, 1993.

Shapiro, Alan C., "The Evaluation and Control of Foreign Affiliates," *Midland Corporate Finance Journal,* Spring 1984, pp. 13–25.

Walmsley, Julian, *A Dictionary of International Finance.* New York: John Wiley & Sons, 1998.

Walmsley, Julian, *The Foreign Exchange and Money Markets Guide.* New York: John Wiley & Sons, 1992.

Walmsley, Julian, *Global Investing.* London: Macmillan, 1991.

Weetman, Pauline, and Sidney J. Gray, "International Financial Analysis and Comparative Corporate Performance: The Impact of U.K. vs. U.S. Accounting Principles on Earnings," *Journal of International Financial Management and Accounting,* vol. 2, nos. 2 and 3, Summer & Autumn 1990, pp. 111–130.

CHAPTER 26

BUDGETING PROPERTY AND LIABILITY INSURANCE REQUIREMENTS

Ronald K. Tucker

Hagedorn & Company

Vicki L. Tucker

Good Samaritan Hospital

26.1 INTRODUCTION. Very often, budgeting property and liability insurance expenditures is thought of as a simple purchase with little or few variables. Basically, one buys a policy to protect against an unpredictable loss and should it occur, the firm will be made whole. Largely, this is true but there are many variables. Understanding the role of property and liability insurance in the budgeting process requires attention and management of these variables. Unpredictable expenses can ruin the collective efforts of the entire firm in the accomplishment of their financial plan or mission objectives. Inappropriate attention to detail may also ruin the careers of those responsible for understanding the implications of the property and liability protection.

The purpose of this chapter is to assist the budget process through a brief and elementary discussion of financial plans. Usually, the purchase of property and liability insurance is relegated to the financial manager. Often, the person responsible for this program is not trained in all or some of the aspects necessary to purchase insurance such as: the risk management process, the types of insurance available, insurance mechanisms, the roles of insurance/risk consultants, the role of insurance brokers/agents, the role of other service providers, quantitative models for informed decisions, how to identify risks and values, property and casualty coverages, and/or managing insurer insolvencies.

Obviously, a full discussion of each of these subjects requires more time than allocated in this chapter. A brief discussion, however, is possible to assist in forming a decision format with some basis of understanding. Any person responsible for the financial well-being of the assets and revenues of their firm will need much technical and professional assistance in order to maximize the decision-making process. This assistance is usually found through counsel with insurance brokers, agents and consultants, accountants, and attorneys. Each brings a unique perspective to the problem, and the energy created by this team is critical to the proper allocation of limited resources for each firm.

A review with leading financial executives suggested this chapter be written with emphasis on the choices, processes, and variables present in the purchase of property and casualty coverages. Almost all had a strong accounting background and focused on the inadequacy of their accounting experience to help understand the demands of the risk management elements of their jobs. This chapter will render assistance to persons in similar situations.

This analysis summarizes the principal insurance coverages and programs available and purchased by most middle-market buyers as the center of their risk-management program. Self-insurance alternatives are not usually considered until the firm accumulates earnings that are large enough to sustain significant losses and still not seriously diminish the value of the enterprise.

Common terms are defined as follows:

- *Middle-market firms.* Generally, firms under $500 million in gross sales producing net incomes of $10 million or less.
- *Self-insurance.* Absorption of some risk on behalf of the firm. Insurance above a retention (deductible) is purchased. There is a finance plan, which also involves risk financing and loss prevention/reduction, in the risk retention/deductible area.
- *Twenty-four-hour coverage.* A concept of combined efforts in various areas of medical reimbursement. The three most common casualty coverages are workers' compensation (medical component), no-fault automobile coverage, and employee health plan (sickness and accident). Twenty-four-hour coverage attempts to manage medical exposures more economically. As of this writing, this coverage is available in a few states.
- *Third-party administrator* (TPA): An outside vendor (usually a claims administrator) hired to help administer the self-insurance portion (retention/deductible) of a risk-management program.

What does this mean to effective budgeting? Budgeting of property and liability losses, coverages, and ultimate costs are not static. Many premiums are not flat charges, but variable costs depending on sales, payroll, units, employees, values, or other fluctuating variables. A budgeter must be aware of these variables in order to plan effectively.

In addition, property and casualty losses cost much more than the actual loss and involve asset replacement or indemnification of injured third parties. This hidden cost of loss resembles an iceberg: The cost of the actual loss is the visible iceberg, and the less identifiable costs are buried beneath the water. The hidden costs are usually three to four times the actual loss cost—a truly significant amount.

26.2 ROLE RISK MANAGEMENT PLAYS IN THE BUDGETING PROCESS. The overall purpose of any risk-transfer system is the preservation of physical assets from their value reduction due to fortuitous physical losses. Any decrease in asset value reduces equity or net worth and organizational value for the owners.

All business ventures expect some accidental physical losses. The role of risk management in the budgeting process is to identify the risk possibility of losses and treat them in the most economical and desirable way to minimize adverse effects on the organization. Simply put, losses diminish the organization's worth and ability to produce positive revenues.

Identification of risk exposures is the first step in the risk-management process. An outline of the risk-management process follows:

- Identification of exposure—What and where could it happen?
- Evaluation of risk—If it happens, how much could it hurt?
- Risk control—What can I do to prevent, eliminate, reduce, or transfer losses?
- Risk financing—We expect some losses. How should we pay for them?

Usually, most firms use insurance as a risk treatment solution (transfer). Risk transfer trades the cost of premium for the assumption of risk by an insurance carrier. Firms that are large enough to absorb the majority of their losses from current revenues are candidates for sophisticated financing techniques such as captive insurance companies, pooling arrangements, or self-funded programs. Because most firms purchase insurance to transfer their risk, we will focus primarily on insurance and its importance to the budget process.

Projecting insurance cost and the effect of losses on profits is a most important element. Insurance costs are not always ''flat'' charges, but vary depending on fluctuations in exposure bases. Examples are workers' compensation cost, which vary directly with changes in payroll; or product and general liability, which vary directly with net sales and other variables.

Understanding these charges will prevent embarrassment with superiors or further diminution of profits from operations. The more important issue is the purchasing of insurance and understanding premium variables so that accurate costs may be anticipated and budgeted.

26.3 TYPES OF INSURANCE MECHANISMS.

In order to understand the purchase of insurance, this brief introduction to the types of property and casualty organizations, which exist principally in the United States, follows. These are direct writers; agency/brokerage carriers; self-funded arrangements such as: captives, risk retention groups, and self-insurance.

(a) Direct Writers. Direct writers are insurance carriers evidenced principally by their distribution system. Their product is offered directly by company sales persons who can only offer *their* employer's products and services. Examples of such carriers are Nationwide and Allstate.

(b) Agency/Brokerage Carriers. Agency/brokerage carriers are also principally identified by their distribution system. These insurance companies distribute their product through independent agents or brokers who usually represent several companies in their local offices. These insurance companies can take several different forms such as stock, mutual, or reciprocal. We will avoid a discussion of these as this would carry us beyond the purpose of this chapter.

An agent is differentiated from a broker in several ways. An agent is a legal representative of an insurance carrier and functions under contract on behalf of the insurance company. A broker has no legal authority to act on behalf of the carrier. Practically, brokers and agents act as advisors and counselors to their insureds. There may be no apparent difference to the buyer, but specific checking with your representative is always advisable.

(c) Self-Funded Plans. Self-funded plans are modified self-insurance financing techniques usually most appropriate to very large buyers. Statistically, as a firm grows, the predictability of their actual losses gets more accurate. Specifically, some casualty losses with high frequency and small cost per claim are excellent candidates for self-funding. Examples are workers' compensation, general liability, and automobile losses for large clients.

As the firm grows, and their casualty losses become predictable, their smaller losses can be more effectively paid as a direct expense rather than an insurance premium. The reason is that a property or casualty insurance premium, at best, will return only 60% to 65% in claims benefits to policyholders. Therefore, payment of these type of losses are really a financing issue rather than a transfer issue.

There are a myriad of plans to better finance losses for larger firms such as retrospective rating plans, deductible plans, captive insurance companies, and fronted programs. Computing these alternatives requires estimating the largest individual loss or the total amount of accumulated losses, which can be absorbed by the firm's ''worst case'' and form the basis of a modified self-insurance or self-funding finance plan.

26.4 ROLE OF INSURANCE/RISK CONSULTANTS.

An insurance or risk consultant can be a very valuable asset to a buyer. Insurance agents/brokers generally perform consulting functions to some extent during their brokering process. If the agent/broker is going to perform these functions, generally there will be no charge for the services as an agent/broker is generally rewarded by commissions built into the price of the insurance premium. If a consultant is used, a fee is generally negotiated depending on the services to be performed.

The benefit of a consultant is to have a completely disinterested third party provide advice and counsel. Generally, there will be a greater attention to details provided by consultants, as their credentials may be superior to most agent/brokers. Reviewing credentials should be an important element in most buyers' decision processes.

Whichever decision is reached, the buyer needs assistance in planning and executing a risk-management program. Unless the buyer is trained in risk management, there is a great need for competent advice to assist individuals and firms in maximizing their risk management budgets.

26.5 USE OF AGENTS/BROKERS.

As previously presented, agents and brokers usually perform the consulting function as part of their brokering process. It is important to be aware of the differences when selecting an agent/broker. A buyer is wise to compare the following characteristics:

- Credentials of salespersons or account executives: Bachelor of Business Administration, Juris Doctor, Master's of Business Administration degrees, and Chartered Property and Causal Underwriter, Chartered Life Underwriter, Associate in Risk Management designations
- Depth of technical support persons and their backgrounds
- Services provided: consulting, actuarial, loss control, claims management, risk management, loss modeling
- Extent of branch office network (i.e., domestic and international)
- Areas of particular expertise: manufacturing, aviation, medical construction, banking, international

- Types of clients: size, industry group, location
- Marketing focus: *Fortune* 500, 100, middle market
- Carriers represented
- Security committee to evaluate carrier's financial stability
- Corporate vision and mission statement

Very often, the choice of a broker is made for some nonbusiness reasons (i.e., friend, relative, college roommate, or golfing acquaintance). Since the product is very complicated, some buyers feel more comfortable with someone they know and trust. All too often, they exchange comfort for poor risk management programs at higher costs. A buyer should be aware of a firm's past decisions and the underlying reasons for making them.

26.6 SELF-INSURANCE ALTERNATIVES. As a firm grows, the likelihood of fortuitous losses becomes more certain. This factor is due to the increase of similar exposure units. Obviously, the larger the pool of similar exposure units, the smaller the outcome variations. This statistical concept has been called the *law of large numbers* and forms the basis for the insurance industry's rate structure and outcome predictability. By combining large groups of similar exposure units, an insurer, with the aid of an actuary, can readily predict the losses for this group.

Large firms begin to accumulate group status and predictability as they grow. This predictability becomes the basis for self-insurance plans. As discussed in the introduction to this chapter, self-insurance suggests a plan of risk financing based on risk/reward scenarios and other factors. Largely, a self-insurance program evolves in several ways beginning with small retentions (deductibles).

Good exposure candidates for self-funding are small predictable losses high in frequency but low in severity. Workers' compensation exposures are excellent candidates, as the most frequent losses tend to be small medical claims with no lost time. A catastrophe exposure exists, but severe large losses are rare in most industries. An industry and individual-loss assessment is urgent before considering even the most basic self-insurance plan.

A key element for any level of self-insurance is the separation of losses from administrative services. An insurance premium contains two elements, losses and expenses (sales, administrative, profit, claims adjustment, taxes licenses, and fees). Generally, a premium allocates approximately 65% to 75% for losses and 35% to 25% for expenses. By separating these elements, the insured controls them and can improve ultimate costs.

The most basic self-insurance plans are known as *retro plans*. Here, the ultimate premium is a result of ultimate losses plus expenses. The firm's worst case scenario is capped at a prenegotiated threshold, with the majority of self-funding in the most predictable small loss area. Often, it takes five to seven years before all losses are paid and ultimate costs determined. This fact is critical to the budget process; proper forecasts of ultimate costs are a must. Retro plans are the more efficient net cost plans but represent significant challenges to budgeters. A list of plans from the least aggressive to the most aggressive self-insurance programs follows:

- Retention, sliding scale dividend, or loss divisor plan
- Incurred loss retro
- Paid–loss retro/deductible plan
- Fronted program
- Captive or self-insurance program

A brief outline of the services needed to administer an aggressive self-insurance program follows. The intent of this analysis is to help management become familiar with the terms and functions of TPAs available to assist in the administration of a self-funded plan.

(a) Actuarial Services An actuary is a very sophisticated statistician who will predict future losses and their impact. Within certain confidence intervals, an actuary can predict future losses by both frequency and severity for years to come. These predictions are based on the analysis of past losses and other key factors pertinent to that particular business environment. This computation is largely the first step in any self-insurance analysis and forms the basis of the financial model to help management make a self-insurance decision.

(b) Claims Administration and Reserving. Any self-insurance program requires an individually administered claims program. The function of a claims administrator is to assess the ultimate liability of a casualty claim (liability or workers' compensation) once it has occurred. The administrator uses the details of the claim and their individual experience in the appropriate jurisdiction to estimate the ultimate costs for each claim. It is important to recognize the full extent of an obligation as soon as possible after its occurrence. These claim ''reserves'' or estimates of obligation to be paid in the future form the basis for many elements of a self-insurance program, the actuarial analysis, the financial analysis, and the budget allocation for future obligations.

(c) Information-Reporting Systems. Providing decision makers with claims and exposure information is a basic element in any risk-management program. If you don't know a problem exists, how can you deal with it? A good information-reporting system is a critical element in managing losses and controlling long-term costs.

(d) Loss Control. Of equal importance to a risk manager, chief financial officer (CFO), or comptroller is the loss-control function. Simply stated, loss control is the process of pre- and postevent procedures to prevent, eliminate, or reduce losses and their financial impact on the firm.

Good loss-control services are a must for both insured *and* self-insured programs. Generally, an insurance company will provide limited loss control services, which are interpreted often by clients to be myopic and punitive in nature. Buyers need positive assistance to control loss costs and are usually more interested in these services offered by TPAs or agents/brokers. The reason for this perception appears to be a focus on loss control from the client's and not the insurance carriers' viewpoint. Although not always the case, TPAs or agent/broker loss-control services should be considered in the risk-management decision process.

(e) Legal Representation. Choosing a competent defense firm is unquestionably important for a self-insurance program. In liability litigation, a competent defense firm can save a business many thousands of unnecessary dollars in defense costs as well as damage awards. ''Without proper legal assistance, the success of our self-insured trust may not be as certain,'' says Ed Vanderloop, Director of Risk Management and Quality Assurance, Ellis Hospital, Schenectady, New York.

When choosing legal representation, some of the discriminating elements are:

- Reputation
- Experience in the type of litigation pertinent to the business represented

- Referrals by colleagues
- Depth of staff
- Qualifications and experience of the attorney assigned to the business
- Communication procedures: frequency and form (written and/or oral)
- Parameters for settlement
- Participation of the defense firm in the risk-management program

(f) Program Administration. Very often, a broker or consultant should be employed to help supervise and oversee the entire administration of the program. Any brokering commissions should be negotiated to eliminate double charges from the transaction. Double charges are commission and administrative fees. A consultant should be used in such situations to completely eliminate any feelings of conflict on the part of the client. This is not to say conflict does exist with a broker; however, an ''arms' length'' agreement will help to eliminate concerns.

26.7 IDENTIFYING THE NEED FOR INSURANCE.

In order to assess the need for insurance versus self-insurance (deductibles, etc.), management must identify how much risk is desirable or appropriate. This process involves a frank assessment by management.

(a) Risk/Reward Scenarios. Using a risk/reward index is one example of a quantitative assessment model useful for comparison of various plans. Simply stated, it is an analysis of out-of-pocket losses expected against the reward anticipated. If the fraction created by this analysis exceeds one, the risk exceeds the reward expectations. Management then has a simple index system to compare different risk scenarios.

Obviously, this is a simple model. It is not intended to be a panacea, but rather a beginning method for analysis of insurance versus no insurance decisions. Also, the calculation of both elements included in this index may involve the use of very sophisticated statistical techniques, which are far beyond the purpose of this chapter. An example of the risk reward index may be helpful.

Situation: A firm is considering changing its deductible for collision losses. The firm has 10 vehicles with a current deductible for each vehicle of \$250 per occurrence. How can the risk reward index be utilized to determine the best alternative? The numbers utilized in this analysis are illustrative only.

1. *Decision:* Will increasing the deductible on the fleet be cost effective?
2. *Statement of Facts:* Ten vehicles with collision deductibles of \$250 per occurrence. Average annual collision loss equals 1.5 collisions/year. Annual premium savings per unit per year:

$$\begin{aligned} \$500 \text{ deductible} &= \$100 \text{ per vehicle} \\ \$1{,}000 \text{ deductible} &= \$140 \text{ per vehicle} \\ \$2{,}500 \text{ deductible} &= \$150 \text{ per vehicle} \end{aligned}$$

3. *Risk Calculation:*

$$\text{Risk} = 1.5 \text{ collisions/year}$$

$$\text{Formula: New deductible} - \text{Old deductible} \times 1.5 = \text{Losses per year}$$

Risk Values after Formula:

$500 deductible = ($500 − $250) × 1.5 = $ 375

$1,000 deductible = ($1,000 − $250) × 1.5 = $1,125

$2,500 deductible = ($2,500 − $250) × 1.5 = $3,375

4. *Reward Calculations:* See Item 2
   Please note: These calculations are *additional* savings over the existing $250 deductibles.

$500 deductible = $100/vehicle × 10 = $1,000

$1,000 deductible = $140/vehicle × 10 = $1,400

$2,500 deductible = $150/vehicle × 10 = $1,500

5. *Risk Reward Indices:*

$500 deductible = $375/1,000 = .375

$1,000 deductible = $1,125/1,400 = .804

$2,500 deductible = $3,375/1,500 = 2.250

The lowest index (0.375) represents the largest gain for the least risk. Depending on management's risk philosophy, the $500 deductible option would offer the best choice for the firm. Many managers will choose higher risk/reward choices. Why? There are as many answers as there are different attitudes.

(b) Qualitative Evaluations. Management philosophies toward risk will play a very large role in any decision process. Some firms are more risk *adverse* than others and would choose a different deductible in the foregoing example. Also, if lowest net premium cost is important, then the $250 deductible option is most attractive to management. Even though the additional deductible expense must be paid at the time of loss, risk takers may be more comfortable with the lowest premium now and take their chances on no losses occurring, less severe losses occurring, or not repairing the damages if the vehicles' operation is only cosmetic. Obviously, there is no correct single answer for everyone.

If management considers *all* elements of long-term cost, the best alternative will involve direct attention to "pre-event" loss-control programs involving prevention, elimination, and reduction techniques as well as "postevent" controls such as the following:

- Superior loss adjusting
- Claims handling
- Medical/occupational rehabilitation
- Subrogation
- Claims review
- Communication techniques

The cost of losses themselves tend to represent only a fraction of their total cost due to unallocated expenses not generally recognized such as the following:

- Production downtime
- Additional expense incurred to correct the situation
- Management and supervisory time to solve problems created by losses
- Loss of customer base through delays and nondelivery of merchandise or services
- Additional resources and time needed to settle losses
- Pain and suffering caused to all involved parties

(c) Earnings Diminution Analysis. Another method of insurance-versus-noninsurance selection by management is the impact on earnings due to losses. Earning diminution is a very accurate yardstick to judge the risk philosophy of management. Putting a quantitative value on foregone earnings due to property and liability losses will quickly focus attention to the real costs of losses and risk treatment plans.

By using risk/reward scenarios, qualitative evaluations, and earnings diminution analysis, a manager can most readily assess the true cost of losses and insurance and how management sees risk. The forgoing suggestions are only a few of the techniques used by management and others in the budget process to identify real cost and select the alternatives most appropriate for the firm.

Once identified, how does a manager select the amount, types, and most efficient insurance products to maximize the firms objectives?

26.8 KEY INSURANCE COVERAGES. It may be helpful to briefly review the primary insurance coverages purchased by most firms. This analysis is not designed to be a complete review of all coverages available or risks to be treated, but only a primary discussion of key coverages.

(a) Property Coverages. All organizations own assets and therefore must protect them from physical loss or damage. In addition, most firms have mortgages or lienholders with financial interest in the preservation of these assets. These debt interests may force the organization to purchase insurance to protect their interest as well as the interest of the business firm.

The most important evaluation when purchasing property coverage is *value*. What is the value of the property? There are many value structures, each serving a different financial need. The following are some of these value structures:

- Replacement or reproduction cost
- Actual cash value
- Book value
- Tax value
- Debt value
- Functional value/production value/earning value
- Real estate/market value
- Appraised value

Although it may appear confusing, the reason for this discussion is to help the purchaser or budgeter be aware of these variables and to ask the proper questions to identify which value system will apply at the time of loss. Choosing an inappropriate value system and protecting the incorrect value may render a completely inappropriate settlement and cause financial harm to the firm.

The next most important element in property insurance is the insuring agreements. What perils (causes of loss) is this property protected against? Most commonly, property is protected by two general coverage principals: named perils coverage or special perils coverage.

Specifically, named perils protect the property from only those perils named specifically and *not* excluded. Simply speaking, special perils protection defines the actual coverage by the policy exclusions (perils not covered). This means everything is covered except that which is excluded. One needs only to be aware of this situation to properly prepare for the purchase of property insurance.

Generally, special perils coverage is preferred because there are more advantages in a broad policy statement with only the exclusions to manage. Perils such as earthquakes, flood, and property usually in transit are always exceptions and should be treated separately. If one analyzes the exclusions and the property *not* covered, a better picture will be available to the budgeter.

The use of deductibles is probably the largest cost element besides value. Property premiums are determined by many variables, but deductibles are one of the larger ones. A good manager should investigate deductibles as a means to maximize premiums as well as a proactive management tool for a successful risk or insurance program.

Business interruption is one of the most misunderstood coverages and causes a significant amount of litigation between insureds and insurance companies. Basically, when an asset is destroyed, a resulting loss of revenue may occur. Most business assets are production assets, which add to the firm's revenues: without them, revenues are reduced. As budgeters and managers, analysis of the impact to revenues is extremely important. Business interruption is the property insurance used to cover these losses. The coverage is really analyzed as a ''time'' function as well as a lost revenue value issue. It is also generally defined by the cost elements in gross revenues as respects continuation or elimination after the loss. It is extremely urgent that a budgeter get assistance in the purchase of this coverage, as it is widely misunderstood but vitally urgent to the firm's financial health. Understanding this coverage is extremely important.

Several terms and conditions are generally encountered in the purchase of property coverages: blanket coverage, co-insurance, and agreed amount clauses. All three forms of property coverages help the insured and weaken the defenses of an insurance carrier. Property insurance is first-party coverage (the insured gets payment) and not usually considered adversarial. There are some defenses built into property coverage to assist the insurer maintain a proper premium base from which to pay losses. The most common idea is co-insurance. Simply stated, an insured may be penalized if he/she does not purchase enough coverages when losses are partial. This method puts ''value'' issues clearly at the door of the insured. To obviate the negative value issues at the time of the loss, insurance carriers commonly allow for exceptions if asked. The use of blanket coverage and agreed-amount clauses are methods that help eliminate value problems at the time of loss. Without enormous detail, a buyer should be aware of these techniques and request their use when buying property coverage.

Larger insureds can utilize other techniques to maximize the purchase of property insurance. Ideas such as dispersion analysis as evidenced by loss limitation proposals, location or aggregate deductibles, and property retros are techniques available should a firm qualify. Generally, however, property insurance is not a very good candidate for self-insurance treatment, as losses are *not* readily predictable and tend to be too volatile by outcome and size to be insured. A good broker, carrier, or consultant is a must to maximize options.

(b) Casualty Coverages. These coverages are identified by payments being made on behalf of the insured to a third party. The coverages are termed *liability* protection and typically include general liability, product liability, employee benefits liability, auto liability, fiduciary liability, umbrella liability, and workers' compensation. This coverage protects the firm from claims made against it by third parties alleging damages to themselves or their property. This coverage also includes defense of the firm and payment of any judgment up to the limits of liability purchased.

Purchasing the property liability limits is extremely important to any firm. Receiving a judgment in excess of policy limits could easily bankrupt a firm. The purchase of adequate limits has been the subject of a great deal of debate and has evolved into many theories proclaiming the correct answer. A wise buyer will seek assistance from many counselors in this area. The correct answer is the one most suitable to the firm from an expense, security, and risk attitude perspective.

A buyer should be aware of the variables in the policies confronting them. Most insurance language has been standardized through the Insurance Services Office (ISO). Insurance Services Office is an organization supported by the insurance companies, which conducts policy research for rate and form standardization for its member companies. The purpose for its formation was basically economic in nature. There are many thousands of insurance carriers who cannot afford to conduct individual statistical gatherings for rate-making or policy wording and testing. Very often, they did not have the resources or personnel needed for these functions. Therefore, they pool resources in ISO to perform these functions for the member companies.

It is important that policies be reviewed. It is a reasonable certainty that ISO forms are acceptable, as the wording is standard. Like most insurance policies, the coverages are granted and defined by the exclusions. It is urgent that all exclusions be checked and any uncertainty be addressed in writing by the broker, consultant, or insurer. There are several liability forms, which are not standardized.

Fiduciary and employee benefits liability are examples of two such nonstandard forms. Also, workers' compensation is not necessarily an adversarial coverage such as liability. Workers' compensation is heavily controlled by state regulatory authorities. Since the coverage is statutory in nature, both coverages and rates are heavily controlled. Workers' compensation is basically no-fault protection for the employee and his or her family. The coverage provides for on-the-job medical protection as well as reimbursement for lost-time wages due to employment injuries. Coverage disputes are usually settled by a nonlitigious review board thereby eliminating the right for an employee to sue his employer. Several states have an adversarial system presently, but the majority do not. It is wise to seek competent advice for the firm's situation.

Currently, the insurance market pricing is extremely competitive and may offer the best bargaining power for the firm. It is usually beneficial to shop for all insurance coverages, but the firm's casualty coverage may be the most important. A large firm has a good opportunity for self-insurance options due to the nature of casualty losses. Generally, losses are numerous and are small in severity. However, notoriety has been given the exceptional single large loss costing millions of dollars. These losses are not the norm.

Casualty premiums are usually a function of limits purchased, actual exposure and operations, type of coverage, and geographic area of operations. Specific cost drivers will be discussed separately later in this chapter. Casualty coverages tend to cost more in direct relation to the size of the firm. Casualty coverages are also good candidates for deductibles or self-insured retentions as a tool for modified self-insurance options. Also, premium payments may be made on an interval basis without interest charges.

(c) Crime Coverage. The entire issue of crime protection is often overlooked by many insurance purchasers, but can be an area of severe losses. Identification of the types of crimes that may affect the firm's net worth are generally divided into employer and third-party crimes. The insurance industry distinguishes crimes further by the type of property taken (i.e., cash versus inventory). Another breakdown is usually where the crime occurs as well as the circumstances (i.e., robbery of money on or off premises versus burglary of merchandise or *money on premises only*). Each scenario is different and requires specific insurance treatment. Seeking expert counsel is a must in this area.

The largest premium variables are limits purchased, protection, and area of the firm's operation. Managing these variables can be a real challenge. It is also imperative to understand the definitions and exclusions of crime policies, as each is very specifically defined. Some of the largest losses have been linked to crime perils, and protection against these occurrences is a must.

(d) Directors and Officers Liability. Directors and officers liability (D&O) coverage pays damages to third-part claimants against ''wrongful acts'' by the directors and officers. This coverage indemnifies the corporation and its directors and officers against such suits. The ''wrongful acts,'' which is defined very broadly implies a violation of a duty causing damages. Acts of the board, which cause physical injuries to persons or damage to property is covered by the general liability policy of the firm and not the D&O policy. There are many other damages that may be caused by director's decisions, such as the following:

- Discrimination
- Loss of pension or profit-sharing profits under ERISA statutes
- A decision causing the firm to lose earnings or value
- A decision violating human rights
- Use of corporate resources for the personal gain of a director(s)
- A myriad of other breaches of the duties of loyalty, reasonable care, and obedience

As always, competent advice is needed to secure the proper coverage for the firm. Directors and officers liability is a particular specialty and requires special understanding and research on behalf of the buyer or advisor.

There are many variables in the purchase of D&O coverage such as nonstandardized policy forms, deductibles per director as well as per occurrence, percentage deductibles per director, corporate reimbursement deductibles, coordination with corporate bylaws, specific exclusions, different policy definitions of ''wrongful acts,'' and other acts or decisions of a board or individual officer. These variables and others will have a different impact on both premium and coverage availability in the event of a D&O lawsuit.

In addition, special care is needed, as a mistake will affect the most influential persons in the organization who are usually the most powerful. Many careers can be altered forever by a mistake in a firm's D&O coverage. A more detailed analysis of this volatile coverage is beyond the purpose of this analysis but is highly recommended for anyone responsible for purchasing D&O protection.

With a brief discussion of some appropriate coverages, it may be opportune to determine how to purchase insurance, how premiums are determined and carriers rated, how to use the risk-management process, and what this means to the budget function.

(e) Fiduciary/Pension Trust Liability. In addition to D&O needs, diligent attention to two more areas producing substantial litigation activity is necessary. These areas are fiduciary/pension trust liability and employment practices liability. Fiduciary liability has been created by ERISA statutes for employee benefit plans. Employment practices have been created by collective litigation from injured victims.

Fiduciary liability creates responsibility for anyone managing or investing funds for any employee benefit plan. What constitutes an employee benefit plan? Generally, any program established or maintained by an employer or employee/organization for the purpose of providing benefits to employees or beneficiaries are usually considered employee benefit plans. Examples include pension, profit sharing, health, 401k/403b, sick pay, vacation pay, or severance pay plans.

One can become a fiduciary in several ways; you, or your position, may be identified as the fiduciary. You, or your position, may manage plan assets or may have discretionary responsibility for plan administration.

What are the responsibilities of a fiduciary?

- You must conduct all activities for the sole benefit of plan participants.
- You must exercise the care and diligence of a prudent person familiar with the administration of similar plans.
- You must be sure plan investments are diversified to minimize large losses to plan participants.
- You must act in a manner consistent with the legal documents of the plan, or if these documents are confusing, you must act in compliance with the ERISA statutes.

Although these requirements may appear confusing and conflicting, their enforcement is sure and reinforced by the courts in most jurisdictions, fiduciary/pension trust liability insurance is an inexpensive solution to this morass. The coverage is readily available and moderately priced. Budgeting this coverage into a firm's risk treatment plan may save the career of an uninformed CFO or comptroller. A fiduciary can be individually named in a suit even if they have delegated fiduciary duties to a third party, insurance carrier, or bank.

(f) Employment Practices Liability. Another liability created by recent litigation is employment practices liability (EPL). Many societal factors have contributed to these challenges such as corporate downsizing, discrimination challenges, wrongful termination challenges, sexual harassment, invasion of privacy, defamation, emotional distress, and mental anguish.

The alleged victims are demanding damages from employed individuals, directors and officers, and the corporate entity itself. Some courts have allowed punitive damages in addition to compensatory and special damages. Any person or organization is vulnerable to attack.

Once again, insurance coverage known as EPL is readily available. The coverage forms are not standard and have been evolving for several years. Deductibles, retentions, claims made forms, and policy warrants are the current arenas for this protection. A wise buyer will require their insurance representative to make a thorough market survey and coverage review or comparison for management's consideration.

Very often, EPL can be added to a firms D&O policy for a nominal charge. When accomplished in this format, the D&O aggregate limit is generally shared which may prove unacceptable to management. If this solution is limiting, the purchase of additional limits may be a solution. A budgeter should consult with their risk management representative for a complete evaluation of needs and costs.

26.9 IDENTIFYING YOUR OWN RISKS. From a planning standpoint, every risk that goes unidentified has the potential to cause an unexpected loss and reduce earnings without ever being treated. An unplanned loss can ruin a successful budget and reduce the collective efforts of the entire firm.

The past indicates the future. Past experiences are an excellent place to begin test assumptions about loss patterns. This is an appropriate technique for casualty losses, but not generally acceptable for losses from property perils such as fire, earthquakes, windstorms, and flood. The reasons for this range from the highly *fortuitous* nature of property perils to the catastrophic nature of floods and earthquakes. The more unpredictable the loss, the more difficult to predict the likely outcomes. ''So,'' one says, ''what aspects can a buyer control and how does one choose the proper limits, perils, and prices?'' The following brief discussion will try to assist with the proper thought process.

Property is divided into two distinct categories: (1) real property and (2) personal property. Real property usually applies to buildings and other property permanently attached to the building or pertaining to the service of same. One should check their property coverage for an exact definition. Personal property usually applies to all other property owned, which is not real property. Often, property coverage is written on a replacement cost basis for real property, but an actual cash value (ACV) basis on personal property representing a depreciated value may be substantially lower.

Real-property values are usually determined from a replacement or functional replacement value. This should not be compared with book value, assessed value, going concern value, or any other value system in vogue. The safest method of determining property values is by purchasing an appraisal from a reputable insurance appraisal firm. There are many good firms that can determine replacement cost, actual cash value, and functional replacement cost and defend their findings to an insurer, public adjuster, or court. A broker will sometimes provide this service, but will usually disclaim the values as they are not generally a licensed appraiser.

Should a buyer wish to appraise their own property, some appraisal firms sell guides to assist the amateur. Depending on budget constraints, this may offer the only alternative to choosing proper values. Contents values, however, are a bit trickier.

There are too many variables in choosing values for business and personal property to be considered in this presentation; however, a brief analysis is possible. Replacement cost is the cost for like, kind, and quality of the property to be replaced. A buyer should begin with an inventory of all physical assets and update this inventory as property is added and deleted. Usually, a firm does not keep a running inventory of personal property and can only estimate personal values from their balance sheet. Unfortunately, the balance-sheet values may be extremely inaccurate, as the original cost may be a far cry from current replacement cost. In addition, physical assets are depreciated, which may prove to further exacerbate the problem. Once again, a professional appraisal is available as a tool to assist the budgeter.

Estimating the cost of raw materials, goods in process, and finished goods inventories are a bit easier as the balance sheet and generally accepted accounting principles (GAAP) rules help to keep inventory values at a consistent value basis. Often, the accounting procedures for inventory including the tax ramifications are at odds with each other regarding insurance values. Using a last-in–first-out (LIFO) or first-in–first-out (FIFO) system may alter values considerably during high inflationary periods. The selling price of finished goods may also be insured. This covers the gross margin as well as the actual cost of the product. It is important for a budgeter to know which value system is best for their firm and to then make an educated decision. Since premium is a direct function of values insured, higher limits means more expense. An alternative to selling price coverage may be accomplished with proper business-interruption protection. A brief discussion follows.

> Business interruption protection is designed to protect the firm from loss of certain revenues resulting from a property loss to a firm's production facilities. There are many different business interruption forms and an analysis of their specific terms and conditions is beyond the purpose of this chapter. A budgeter would serve their firm well by assuring a complete understanding of business interruption coverage and limits.
>
> Business interruption forms define gross earnings as: "The reduction in gross earnings less non-continuing expenses." Simply stated, this statement translates to continuing expenses and gross profit lost for the time it takes to restore the operations to capacity. Business interruption is then a function of two (2) variables, production value, and the time for restoration. Any analysis of proper limits must involve a complete study of these two variables as well as the exact policy terms and conditions.

Another coverage that may be appropriate for the firm is extra expense coverages. In easier terms, extra expenses are costs necessary to allow a firm to continue operations after a property loss to production facilities. An example might be helpful: A service organization suffers a huge flood, which shuts down its office building for 13 days. Management sets up facilities for customer service in another location. Extra expense would provide funds for the extra cost of telephone, movers, advertising to notify clients, and overtime wages needed to set up the temporary facilities as long as the loss was caused by an insured peril. In this specific case, the firm needed extra expense coverage for flood perils.

Choosing the proper limits for both business interruption and extra expense is aided by the use of worksheets designed to assist the firm in calculating their exposure. A budgeter should consult the firm's broker or carrier for advice and details. There are also other factors to consider when analyzing business interruption exposures such as insured perils, manufacturing processes, contingent business interruption, disaster planning, alternative locations, construction economy, cost of capital, sales cycles, and modern building codes, which all have an effect on a budgeter's buying decisions. The last area of value assessment for property coverages is the area of irreplaceable or very old equipment. Often, production equipment outlasts its book value. Also, the industry does not change substantially to warrant reinvestment: The old equipment still produces efficiently. If there is no active used equipment market and/or the technology is very specialized, how does one restore or replace the damaged equipment?

Management must plan for the replacement and ascertain specific appraised values on this type of equipment. Machinery appraisers like jewelry appraisers are skilled in the valuation of such equipment. Value may still not solve the dilemma of availability. Maybe this equipment must be operated in a secure environment to be certain it cannot be lost in a catastrophe act. Clearly, risk management or loss prevention techniques may be more valuable than insuring to the proper value. Possibly the only answer is to upgrade equipment when a loss occurs. With this scenario, the budgeter may find a severe shortfall between the appraised value and the replacement cost for modern equipment. If this could be the case, it is wise to know before the loss occurs. Having to replace equipment before its time can certainly ruin a firm's capital budget and may severely impair its revenue stream as well. Such scenarios can easily cost a budgeter's job in the process.

26.10 HOW CAN ONE BUDGET FOR CASUALTY PREMIUMS? Choosing the best casualty program is a subject of a great deal of analysis and controversy. The proper limits, perils, exclusions, conditions, and rating program requires a discussion far in excess of time available herein. As a buyer, professional help is a must to evaluate all the variables. As a budgeter, casualty coverages are variable expenses, and understanding the premium cost drivers is a must for the budgeting process.

Basically, premiums for workers compensation and general liability coverages vary directly with payroll and sales. It is important for a budgeter to know the rates applicable per unit of variation (payroll/sales) to project ultimate premiums. The estimated annual premium is exactly that, an estimate. At the beginning of the policy period, estimates for payrolls and sales are used to calculate the policy premium. At the end of the policy period, an audit is conducted and the premium is recomputed based on the actual exposures. Obviously, this can cause great fluctuations in the premium charged and wonderful surprises for the uninformed. Frequently, this audit feature can be used as a capital source when the firm is growing.

Specifically, the firm can understate their expected sales and payroll to minimize the estimated premiums and use the *saved* premium to help fund the firm's growth. The bill for this growth must be paid later and could cause great distress for the firms' future earnings and tax implications. This method of funds management has been used effectively by many firms, but only lasts as long as the insurance carrier remains unwary (usually one year). This method also has great limitations in the areas of cost allocation and financial management and is not recommended as a substitute for good capital management.

Another feature of casualty variables is the audit limitations is both payroll and sales. In other words, not all sales and payroll data are counted. Often, there are limits on maximum payroll chargeable per person and complete elimination of certain payroll classes, drivers, driver's helpers, executive officers, clerical workers, and draftsmen. These features are prevalent in general liability, and some are applicable to workers' compensation. A wise budgeter must know how their casualty program coverages are priced and the rating rules applicable.

As the firm grows, very often, casualty premiums are driven by losses and in programs generally termed ''loss sensitive.'' The plans are largely variations on ''retro'' plans, where losses and administrative charges are separated and the loss element drives the ultimate premium costs. These type of plans are most prevalent in workers' compensation coverages but may be combined with liability and automobile coverages for the larger firms. Generally, these plans maximize administrative costs, cash flow, benefits, and loss-control features such as elimination and reduction techniques.

From the position of budgeting, the ultimate net costs of these programs are not determined until each loss is ultimately settled. This may take five to eight years before the ultimate costs are absolutely finite.

Obviously, this is an extreme impediment to accurate budgeting. Attention to proper loss reserving will help estimate ultimate costs and relate them to the proper revenue periods. The reserve, when calculated by a credible and recognized expert, may be used as an identified cost element in the current revenue period. For complete analysis, the firm should consult proper accounting and tax expertise.

The remainder of the property and casualty insurance products purchased by the firm are flat charge premiums with no variation except the amount purchased, perils, and actual exposure to loss. It should be noted that most insurers will apportion the annual premium into installments if requested. Usually, these installments are available for no interest charge or a small administrative service charge. If the carrier refuses to provide installments, the premium may be financed by finance companies at competitive interest rates. In addition, this financing does not impair the firm's credit as the debt is entirely secured by the equity in the policy represented in the unearned premium. As such, the finance agreements are not entered as current liabilities. One should consult proper accounting advice for a complete explanation of this feature. The foregoing discussion has been attempted as a "how to" purchase analysis of property and casualty coverages. It is only an outline and requires further study before competent budgeting decisions can be made for each firm. Although brief in nature, no such treatise would be complete without a brief discussion of the carriers or insurance companies.

Property and casualty carriers continue to be regulated on a state level through a federal exemption granted under the McCarren Ferguson Act. This federal document continues to grant state authority for regulation of carriers, rates, forms, and the proper conduct of this business. The reasons for this federal exemption are many, and this act is under constant attack for repeal. To date, state jurisdiction remains.

As anyone can see, having 50 separate regulatory bodies may cause some confusion and create some gaps in the administration of this industry due to unequal tax bases, talent availability, and legislative prioritization. All regulation attempts to balance the issues of insurer solvency and unfairly discriminatory rates. If the rates are too high, the carriers may be solvent, but the taxpayer is gouged. If the rates are too low, the taxpayer has an immediate benefit in lower premiums, but a long-term problem in insurer solvency. Since carriers are regulated by the states, solvency is also state regulated. In order to help a buyer understand the solvency issue, a brief discussion of the types of insurers may be helpful. An insurance company may operate in a state under many legal definitions admitted, licensed, nonadmitted, alien, and foreign. The most common types are admitted and nonadmitted insurers. Both are licensed by the state to conduct business, but their status and legal definitions are different.

(a) Admitted Carrier. *Admitted carrier* is the most desirable status from a consumer standpoint for the following reasons:

- There is a larger policyholder surplus requirement making it more secure to pay losses.

- An insolvency of an admitted carrier gives a policyholder access to state insolvency funds to pay losses incurred.
- The state regulatory body spends more time analyzing the financial health of an admitted carrier. This provides an early warning mechanism for policyholders to allow for choosing another company.

(b) Nonadmitted Carrier. A nonadmitted carrier may be a very secure company, but choose to operate on this legal basis for many reasons. Generally, policyholders of nonadmitted insurers do *not* have the protection of state insolvency funds to help secure their policies. Also, a carrier may have substantially less policyholder surplus required to operate and transact business. The carrier may choose to operate on this basis to avoid regulation for forms and rates. Therefore, a buyer must be more aware of the terms and conditions of their policies when dealing with a nonadmitted carrier.

Very often, a buyer must also pay a user fee, known as a *surplus lines tax* to use a nonadmitted carrier thereby raising the price of the coverage. Why, then, would a buyer use a surplus lines carrier? The primary reasons are as follows:

- Unique coverage needs not readily available in the traditional market such as errors and omissions, hazardous liability protection (blasting, scaffolding, etc.), or high-limit situations such as re-insurance or excess umbrella capacity limits over $50 million
- More competitive terms for both form and rate
- Unique needs such as financial guarantee coverages or substandard risks (vacant buildings or high-crime-area property).

It is always wise for a buyer to consider *all* alternatives as long as they have identified the risks inherent in each alternative described above. In order to rate insurance carriers, a buyer may gain access to some available resources to assist:

- A. M. Best's rating guides
- Moody's insurance rating guides
- The insurance department in the appropriate state
- A broker or consultant
- Other policyholder in the same carrier

Frequently, the large brokers maintain security committees who analyze insurance companies and report to their branch offices. This is clearly a feature that is highly desirable and valuable to the policyholder. Many buyers choose their broker on such capabilities and expertise, not merely on premium cost. A wise buyer analyzes *value* and not only price. In addition, the broker maintaining such a function may create an additional obligation to a client and increase additional benefit to help further secure the contrast.

There really is no absolute guarantee to a policyholder that benefits will be payable at the time of a loss. Features such as those mentioned above help increase the policyholder's chances of a positive financial outcome; but surely they are not a guarantee. Insurance carriers are businesses, and their rates are a function of competition, economies, management, and regulation. A wise buyer tries to manage these variables using the tools of proper information, professional representation, and careful monitoring of their insurer's economic health.

26.11 SUMMARY. The purpose of this chapter is to assist persons responsible for the risk-management function in their firm and to apply it to the budgeting process. Only through the understanding of the choices, process, and variables in the purchase of property and casualty coverages can a manager truly help his or her firm. The risks are great and the stakes are high for imprudent or improper decisions.

The most important and overriding element to proper budgeting is the gathering of credible information from professional sources. In property and casualty coverages, the team is usually composed of legal, accounting, and professional insurance advice from an agent, broker, or consultant. Understanding the meaning of some of the coverages is always helpful. Understanding the premium variables, deductible applicability, the hidden cost of losses, and asset valuation is a must for any budget. Without this understanding, there are too many variables and too much fluctuation in costs.

The chapter discussed some of the following variables:

- The risk-management process
- Available insurance mechanisms
- Role of insurance/risk consultants
- Role of brokers/agents
- Other TPA and service providers
- One quantitative model: risk/reward index
- Identification of risk/values
- Property and casualty coverages and
- Managing insurance insolvencies

If this analysis is to be successful, it must be used. Although property and casualty is usually a small expense item as a percentage of gross sales, the impact to asset preservation and conservation as well as maintaining revenues is extremely critical. If a firm's resources of production are destroyed, the firm's ability to generate revenues may also be hampered. Depending on the severity of this destruction, the firm may perish or at least be weakened.

Risk and budgeting managers must avoid this outcome or be a possible party to the detriment of the firm's solvency.

SOURCES AND SUGGESTED REFERENCES

Arnold, A. S., *General Insurance Principles.* Malvern, PA: American Institute for Property & Liability Underwriters, 1983

Bayne, David C., *The Philosophy of Corporate Control: A Treatise on the Law of Fiduciary Duty.* Chicago, IL: Loyola University Press, 1986.

Bieber, Robert M., "The Making of a Risk Manager, Part I and Part II," *Risk Management,* September–October 1987.

Brodsky, Edward, and Patricia M. Adamski, *Law of Corporate Officers and Directors: Rights, Duties and Liabilities.* Deerfield, IL: Callaghan & Co., 1989.

Commercial Law and Practice Service, *Directors & Officers Liability Update.* Harrisburg, PA: Pennsylvania Bar Institute, 1988.

Glad, Paul E. B., ''Interpretation of Business Interruption Contracts,'' *The Risk Report,* vol. 8, no. 7, March 1986.

Greenwald, Judy, ''Fiduciary Duties in Flux,'' *Business Insurance,* May 25, 1992.

Head, George, ''Truth in Insurance Contracts,'' *The National Underwriter,* October 16, 1989.

Rafter, Robert J., ''After Busy 10 Years, Fiduciary Responsibility Shifts to Participants,'' *Pension World,* April 1992.

Scher, William B., Jr., ''Are Insurance Agents Employees or Independent Contractors?,'' *Life Association News,* May 1992.

Welling, Brad, ''Director Liability: Understanding the Risks,'' *ABA Banking Journal,* 1992.

Williams, Arthur C. Jr., and Richard M. Heins. *Management and Insurance* (5th ed), Malvern, PA: American Institute for Property & Liability Underwriters, 1985.

PART 4

BUDGETING APPLICATIONS

CHAPTER 27

ZERO-BASED BUDGETING

Peter A. Pyhrr

Magnetic Ticket & Label Corp.

27.1 INTRODUCTION. Zero-based budgeting (ZBB) is nothing conceptually new, is not a budgeting process, and is not "reinventing the wheel." It is, however, a management approach, and it can be a key decision-making tool for the chief executive officer (CEO).

The term *zero-based budgeting* was launched into vogue by former President Jimmy Carter, who installed the process while governor of Georgia and who attempted to install it throughout the federal government. However, the process was developed in industry, at Texas Instruments, and is currently being used by industrial companies. There are several key characteristics about the process in its application to date:

- The decision to implement ZBB is usually made by the CEO or other key operating managers, not by the vice-president of finance or the controller.
- It is being used by companies noted for their good management. ("Good management is always looking for better decision-making tools.")
- The process is difficult, requires a great deal of effort to implement effectively, and may be perceived as a threat by many managers. It has failed in a few organizations and is no panacea, yet most companies have found that the benefits far outweigh the costs of implementation.

Those organizations that have had the most success with ZBB have learned that it is not a "budgeting" process but a management approach.

The chief beneficiaries of the zero-based management approach are the CEO and top-level managers with profit and loss responsibilities. The purposes of this chapter are to focus on the problems of top management with the traditional management, planning, and budgeting systems; to explain the zero-based approach; and to identify the potential benefits (and problems) that the approach might offer.

27.2 PROBLEMS WITH TRADITIONAL TECHNIQUES. Top-level executives are faced with the difficult tasks of management and decision making in a complex and dynamic environment. Managers must often face conflicting demands, typified by the demand for growth that often requires a significant allocation of today's funds for tomorrow's new product or market versus the requirement to produce this year's profit. Managers are continuously besieged for funds for diverse activities such as research, marketing, maintenance, and data processing, for which they must play Solomon in determining how the baby will be divided. The individual executive is not an expert in each of the specialties competing for funds, yet he or she must make the ultimate funding allocation decisions. The environment is becoming more complex, with increased government regulation, increasing worldwide competition, rapidly changing technology, and increasing difficulty in raising prices. The only constant seems to be the continual rise in costs.

Although the business climate is continually evolving, the management tools available to top management have remained basically static. The traditional tools, especially planning and budgeting, have not evolved at the same pace in order to provide top managers with an effective tool for managing their business.

Under the traditional planning and budgeting procedures, management's attention is focused primarily on planned changes from the previous year's expenditure level. This is usually referred to as *incremental budgeting.* Although considerable thought goes into the development of these plans, it is primarily the year-over-year increment that receives the most critical and analytical attention by senior management. Thus, in many cases, the "base" to which the increment is added is treated as though it were already authorized and required little additional review or evaluation.

This traditional incremental approach often creates several typical problems for top management:

1. Budgeting requests exceed funding availability, often forcing management to recycle the process. The incremental approach usually aggravates this problem. Since managers know their initial budget requests will be slashed, they usually inflate these requests. (Managers who turn in low requests on the initial budget submission quickly learn that they will often receive a cut—often in similar proportion to managers who inflate their initial budget requests.)
2. Difficulty in translating long-term objectives into action plans (and budgets). Long-term projections are often wish lists and economic forecasts, although specific projects must be funded to achieve growth. New projects, however, are often the first items cut from the budget request when funding requests exceed funding availability.
3. Key problems and decision areas are not highlighted.
4. Alternatives are not identified. One set of numbers is submitted without an identification of alternative means of performing the function or alternative funding levels (especially lower levels).
5. Difficulty to adjust budgets and operations readily to changing situations, since work loads are not clearly identified (except direct manufacturing costs that are controlled by standard costing systems), nor are priorities established throughout the organization.
6. Trade-offs among long-term goals and programs, operating needs, and profits are not clearly identified. Projects and priorities are not clearly identified, and new development funds are often the first to be cut when the "cut 10%" dictate is given.

Top managers will readily nod their heads in agreement to these problems, but then ask what alternatives they have. The zero-based management approach is a major alternative and can be a significant tool enabling top management to focus on key problems, alternatives, and priorities throughout the organization.

27.3 ZERO-BASED APPROACH. Zero-based budgeting is nothing conceptually new. It is a logical process, combining many elements of good management. The key elements of ZBB include (1) identification of objectives, (2) evaluation of alternative means of accomplishing each activity, (3) evaluation of alternative funding levels (elimination, lower levels, current level, and increased levels), (4) evaluation of work load and performance measures, and (5) establishment of priorities. However, the key word in the statement that ZBB is nothing conceptually new is *conceptually*.

Although the process is nothing conceptually new, it is radically different from the traditional planning and budgeting process generally practiced today. What ZBB does that is different is to recognize that the budgeting process is, in fact, a management process. It also recognizes budgeting as a key decision-making process and a driving force (managers must perform the ZBB analysis in order to get any budget at all).

Thus, ZBB is not a budgeting process in the traditional sense of the word—it is first a management process, second a planning process, and only third a budgeting process. The term *zero-based* does not mean that everybody's position is automatically ''zeroed,'' or that we must re-invent the wheel, which would be entirely unrealistic in a pragmatic world. What it does mean is that we must re-evaluate all activities to see if they should be eliminated, funded at a reduced level, funded at a similar level, or increased. Which of these funding levels—from zero to a significant increase—is appropriate will be determined by the priorities established by top management and by the availability of total funding.

(a) Application of Zero-Based Budgeting. Zero-based budgeting applies to all actionable or discretionary activities, programs, and costs for which we can identify some cost-benefit relationship—even if this relationship is highly subjective. In government, ZBB can be applied to all operations. In industry, it can be applied to all costs except direct labor, material, and fixed overhead, since these costs are normally handled by a standard costing system. Zero-base can therefore be applied to all administrative and staff functions (data processing, financial, supervision, legal), technical and manufacturing indirect costs (research and development [R&D], laboratory, engineering, maintenance, quality control, production planning), and commercial functions (sales, marketing, purchasing, traffic).

These manufacturing indirect and overhead costs to which ZBB directly applies may make up only a fraction of the total budget of a heavy manufacturing operation, but they represent activities that are usually the most difficult to plan and control, and they offer management the greatest lever to use in affecting profits. Consider these three areas of activity that are subject to ZBB analysis and how resource allocation could affect them as well as the entire organization:

1. Marketing and R&D programs determine the future course of an organization. If development funds are not adequate, or if marketing support is not sufficient to handle expected sales volume, long-term plans for growth may not be achieved.
2. Funding for R&D, capital, industrial engineering, production planning, and so forth can directly affect manufacturing technology and heavily influence direct manufacturing costs.
3. Arbitrary cost reductions in the service and support functions without a full understanding of the consequences can create severe problems, with the cost savings proving minor compared to the resulting production problems and increased direct manufacturing costs.

Zero-based addresses those areas where management has a difficult time evaluating efficiency and effectiveness, because budget variances are not necessarily good indicators of performance. In a pure manufacturing environment, it makes sense to evaluate a manager on the basis of actual versus budgeted costs. If the budget for production of a million widgets is $3 million, and if a manager has produced a million widgets for $2.8 million, he or she is usually credited with having done a good job if the widgets are up to specification. But if a manager were told to spend $3 million on research and development and came back a year later having spent only $2.8 million, one would be hard put to say whether or not the manager had done a good job. The distinction is that the first manager produced something tangible; there should be no question as to whether or not a million acceptable widgets were actually produced. However, given the very tenuous connection between dollars going into the research and development pipeline and the value coming out, it is impossible to say whether the second manager ''produced'' the right amount of R&D. Obviously, if one does not know how costs affect output, it is not possible to measure outputs by measuring costs. This problem is compounded for the CEO who has this problem with R&D, advertising, data processing, maintenance, and numerous other specialties for which he or she is not an expert.

27.4 ZERO-BASED BUDGETING PROCEDURES. The zero-based approach requires each organization to evaluate and review all programs and activities (current as well as new) systematically, to review activities on a basis of output or performance as well as cost, to emphasize manager decision making first, number-oriented budgets second, and to increase analysis. However, it should be stressed that zero-base is an approach, not a fixed procedure or set of forms to be applied uniformly from one organization to the next. The mechanics and management approach has differed significantly among the organizations that have adopted zero-base, and the process must be adapted to fit the specific needs of each user.

Although the specifics differ among organizations, there are four basic steps to the zero-based approach that must be addressed by each organization:

1. Identify ''decision units.''
2. Analyze each decision unit in a ''decision package.''
3. Evaluate and rank all decision packages to develop the budget request and profit and loss statement.
4. Prepare the detailed operating budgets reflecting those decision packages approved in the budget.

(a) Defining Decision Units. Zero-based budgeting attempts to focus management's attention on evaluating activities and making decisions. Therefore, the ''meaningful elements'' of each organization must be defined so that they can be isolated for analysis and decision making. For the sake of terminology, these meaningful elements have been termed ''decision units.''

For those organizations with a detailed cost center structure, the decision unit may correspond to the cost center. In some cases the cost center manager may wish to identify separately different functions or operations within the cost center if they are significant in size and require separate analysis. For example, a single cost center for the controller's office might be divided into general accounting, financial analysis, cost accounting, and credit and collection. Decision units might also be projects (R&D, management information systems [MIS], engineering), services provided or received (data processing charged to each major user), objects of expense (advertising by product and market, legal or consulting fees), or capital projects.

27.5 DECISION PACKAGE. The decision package is the building block of the ZBB process. It provides a description and evaluation of each decision unit for management review and decision making. The decision package form is designed to produce an evaluation of each decision unit that will describe the following:

- Purpose or objective
- Description of actions (What are we going to do, and how are we going to do it?)
- Costs and benefits
- Work-load and performance measures
- Alternative means of accomplishing objectives
- Various levels of effort (What benefits do we get for various levels of funding?)

The key to developing decision packages is the formulation of meaningful alternatives. The following are types of alternatives that should be considered in developing decision packages:

- *Alternative methods of accomplishing the objective or performing the operation.* Managers should identify and evaluate all meaningful alternatives and choose the one they consider best. If an alternative to the current method of doing business is chosen, the recommended way should be shown in the decision package, with the current way shown as the alternative not recommended.
- *Different levels of effort of performing the operation.* Once the best method of accomplishing the operation has been chosen from among the various alternative methods evaluated, a manager must identify alternative levels of effort and funding to perform that operation. Managers must establish a minimum level of effort, which must be below the current level of operation, and then identify additional levels or increments of separate decision packages. These incremental levels above the minimum might bring the operation up to its current level and to several multiples of the current level of effort.

A *decision package* is defined as one incremental level in a decision unit. Thus, there may be several decision packages for each decision unit, as shown in Exhibit 27.1. In evaluating each level, managers are evaluating the incremental benefit they get for incre-

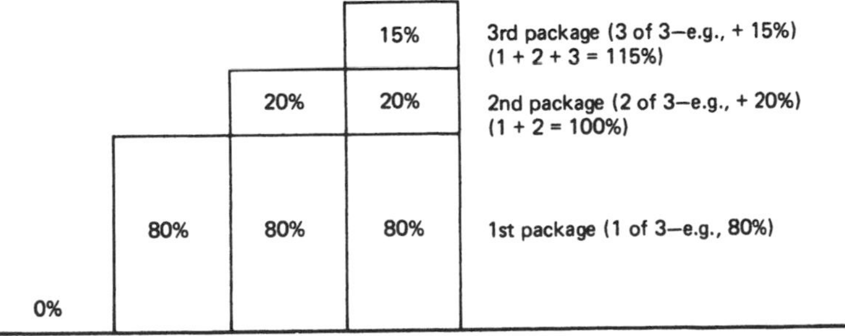

Exhibit 27.1. Graphic representation of levels of effort (descision packages) for each decision unit

mental expenditures. For example, looking at level 2 in Exhibit 27.1, managers will be evaluating the additional benefit they get from spending an additional 20%, or $20,000 (not the 100% total). It is these incremental levels that get ranked. By identifying a minimum level of effort, plus additional increments as separate decision packages, each manager thus presents several alternatives for top management decision making:

- *Elimination.* Eliminate the operation if no decision packages are approved.
- *Reduced level.* Reduce the level of funding if only the minimum-level decision package is approved.
- *Current level.* Maintain the same level of effort if the minimum level and the one or two incremental levels (bringing the operation from the minimum level to the current level of effort) are approved. (Note: The current level of effort refers only to the level of output or performance, sometimes called *maintenance level.* However, even at the current level of effort, managers may have changed their method of operation and made operating improvements, so that the current level of effort may be accomplished at a reduced cost.)
- *Increased levels.* Increase the levels of funding and performance if one or more increments above the current level are approved.

Identifying and evaluating the minimum level of effort is the most difficult element in the zero-based approach—especially identifying a minimum level that is usually 70% to 80% of current and may be much less for some discretionary activities such as advertising. Maintenance is not worried about being eliminated, but the maintenance manager will be extremely concerned about identifying a lower level of effort. If the requirement for a minimum level is so difficult, why does ZBB emphasize this requirement?

There are two fundamental reasons for defining a minimum level. First, the minimum level forces managers to make an in-depth evaluation of their operations. This requirement of identifying a minimum below the current level of effort forces managers to consider alternatives, identify what is most important (all things are not equal), and quantify workload and performance measures to justify their conclusions. If only one level were required, reflecting the total funding desired, managers in mandatory functions such as maintenance could avoid an in-depth analysis and would normally recommend continuing past practices.

Second, top management needs the option of elimination and reduction if funds are to be reallocated, and elimination is viable only in a limited number of programs. If only one level of effort were analyzed (probably reflecting the funding level desired by each manager), top management would be forced to make a yes or no decision on the funding request, thus funding at the requested level, eliminating the program, making arbitrary reductions, or recycling the budget process if requests exceeded funding availability.

The minimum level of effort is the most difficult level to identify, since there is no magic number (i.e., 75% of the current level) that would be meaningful to all operations. The minimum level must be identified by each manager for his or her operations. The minimum level must be below the current level of effort and should attempt to identify that critical level of effort, below which the operation would be discontinued because it loses its viability of effectiveness. There are several considerations that can aid managers in defining the minimum level of effort:

1. The minimum level may not completely achieve the total objective of the operation. (Even the additional levels of effort recommended may not completely achieve the objective because of realistic budget and/or achievement levels.)

2. The minimum level should address itself to the most critical population being served or should attack the most serious problem areas.
3. The minimum level may merely reduce the amount of service (or number of services) provided.
4. The minimum level may reflect operating improvements, organizational changes, or improvements in efficiency that result in cost reductions.
5. Combinations of considerations 1 through 4.

By identifying the minimum level, each manager is not necessarily recommending that his or her operation be funded at the minimum level but is merely identifying that alternative to top management. If a manager identifies several levels of effort, he or she is recommending that all levels be funded.

The operating manager responsible for the decision unit normally does the analysis of the unit, since he or she is the most knowledgeable about its operation and will be responsible for carrying it out. However, this analysis will be reviewed by higher management levels and the financial staff. Thus, we can get the analysis work load spread among many managers, yet we have the review and ranking process that will allow top managers to play their normal devil's advocate role and require decision package revisions where appropriate.

(a) Example Decision Package Analysis and Forms. The following example of materials handling (which is the decision unit) is an actual decision package analysis taken from a specialty steel mill. The following description provides the highlights of the analysis, which is translated into the completed decision package forms shown in Exhibit 27.2 (levels 1 and 2 are shown, with each level described on a two-page form):
Situation: Centralized materials-handling department, handling from raw material stores through all production phases to finished goods inventory.

Different Ways of Performing the Same Function: Recommended alternative is to maintain current organization with multiple shift coverage using forklift trucks and palletized production loads. Alternatives not recommended are (1) returning materials-handling function to individual production departments and (2) combining function with work stores department (which has a separate materials-handling function).

Different Levels of Effort for Performing This Function:

1. Materials handling (1 of 4)—cost $590,000; 25 people. Twenty vehicle operators using forklifts; two dispatchers and two head persons to provide minimal service in moving output from three shifts by reducing frequency of service and elimination of some shift coverage. This level would increase average work-in-process inventory 12% because of some additional queuing on first and second shifts and by eliminating the third shift in the cold mill by queuing all materials for the third shift by the end of the second shift. This will require some limited movement of material by production personnel on third shift.
2. Materials handling (2 of 4): cost $81,000; 4 people (levels 1 + 2 = $671,000). Add four vehicle operators to provide additional second-shift materials-handling service for the bar mills, annealing and pickling department in the hot mill building. Provide added frequency of shop mule service from two to four routes per day, and

DECISION PACKAGE — Page 1 of ____

(1) PACKAGE NAME	(2) DEPARTMENT		(3) PREPARED BY	(4) DATE	(5) RANK
MATERIALS HANDLING – (1 of 4)	409	Materials Handling	J. JONES	7/28/78	

(6) PURPOSE/OBJECTIVE

Provide materials handling from raw materials stores thru all production departments to finished goods inventory.

(7) DESCRIPTION OF ACTIONS (OPERATIONS) FOR THIS LEVEL

Twenty vehicle operators using forklifts; two dispatchers and two head men to provide minimal service to move output from three shifts by reducing frequency of service and elimination of some shift coverage. This level would increase average WIP inventory 12% due to some additional queuing on first and second shifts, and by eliminating the third shift in the Cold Mill by queuing all materials for the third shift by the end of the second shift. This will require some limited movement of material by production personnel on third shift. Handling for maintenance and reclamation would be reduced from scheduled to an on call basis, which would require an additional queuing of material and some additional work space or palletizing for the additional storage required.
Shop mule service reduced from 4 to 2 routes per day.

Staffing: 21 vehicle operators, 2 dispatchers, 2 head men

(8) CHANGES/IMPROVEMENTS FROM CURRENT OPERATIONS (CAPITAL EQUIPMENT)

- Cold Mill – elimination of third shift
- Hot Mill – reduced frequency but maintaining 3 shift coverage
- Roll & Grind – reduced frequency of service
- Maintenance and Reclamation – reduced from scheduled to on-call basis
- Shop mule service reduced from 4 to 2 routes per day

(9) WORKLOAD/PERFORMANCE MEASURES	1977	1978	1979	(10) RESOURCES REQUIRED	1977 Actual	1978 Budget	1978 Revised	1979 Proposed
Production pounds/year (mil.)	9.8	10.1	12.6	Positions – this level				25
Average daily work-in-process (lbs.)	8,580	8,700	9,700	– cumulative	27	29	29	25
Metered fork lift hours per vehicle	1038	1045	1185	Expense – this level				590.0
Number of fork lift trucks	11	11	9	– cumulative	621	671	671	590.0
				% of Prior Year		108	100	88
				Capital				0

Exhibit 27.2. Decision package analysis forms

improve service to the hot mill on first shift. Add third shift coverage to the cold strip mill.

3. Materials handling (3 of 4): cost \$56,100; 2 people (levels 1 + 2 + 3 = \$727,100). Add one vehicle operator and one head person to provide full service in the hot mill and hot mill service areas on first shift. Provide full service to all departments on first-shift basis. Provide work direction for materials-handling functions on third shift.
4. Materials handling (4 of 4): cost \$106,200; 2 people (levels 1 + 2 + 3 + 4 = \$833,300). Add two vehicle operators to increase frequency of service to the roll grind and shipping departments, plus purchase of \$60,000 of skids and hoppers.

In reviewing this example, you should note several factors:

- Only one alternative was proposed, with the other alternatives listed with the reason for rejection. Top management might challenge the reasoning or ask why other alternatives that they might identify were not considered.
- The minimum level is 88% of the 1978 revised estimate of current year's costs—yet in previous sections minimum levels of 70% to 80% of current were discussed. However, if you look at the work-load measures, you will see that production pounds per year (in millions) has increased from 10.1 to 12.6 (a 25% increase); normal

DECISION PACKAGE — Page 2 of ____

(1) PACKAGE NAME	(2) DEPARTMENT		(3) PREPARED BY	(4) DATE	(5) RANK
MATERIALS HANDLING – BASE LEVEL (1 of 4)	409	Materials Handling	J. JONES	7/28/78	

(11) CONSEQUENCES OF ELIMINATING THIS PACKAGE

Disapproval of this package will require this function to be de-centralized and absorbed into individual production departments and will be done at a 15–20% increased cost to the Division.

(12) OTHER LEVELS OF EFFORT IDENTIFIED

2 of 4 $81.0K Add 4 Veh. Operators to support Hot Mills and restore third shift coverage to Cold Strip Mill

3 of 4 $56.1K Add 1 Veh. Operator & 1 headman to provide support for Hot Mill and Maintenance dispatching

4 of 4 $106.2 Add 2 Veh. Operators to increase frequency of service to Roll Grind and shipping departments

(13) ALTERNATIVE MEANS OF ACCOMPLISHING THIS PACKAGE

1. Return the Material Handling function to the individual production departments. This was rejected due to productivity declines, loss of flexibility within the division, and higher costs. The material handling was decentralized until 1975, with the current structure producing a 15% savings when this function was centralized.

2. Combine this function with Work Stores. This alternative was rejected due to potential bargaining unit problems and decreases in flexibility because of contract negotiated work rules in the stores area.

func. #	exp. #	(14) DETAIL EXPENDITURES	1977 Revised	1978 Proposed
		Salaries (Hourly)		342.8
		Wage Premium		17.7
		Total Labor		360.5
		Fringes		180.9
		Propane Fuel		28.6
		Maintenance		20.0
		Total		590.0

Exhibit 27.2. *(Continued)*

inflation might have accounted for an additional 6% to 8% increase in costs. The production work load was a planning assumption used by all departments, and it is not meaningful in this example to cut to 88% as a minimum by reducing the amount of materials handled. There may be some examples where there might be a reasonable alternative not to handle all material or provide all the prior services.

- The narrative and data sections combine to give a complete picture of the operation. Even traditional reviews to evaluate items of expense are augmented by narrative sections and the work-load and performance measures, which can raise many red flags for the expense analysis.

Top management might be very pleased to reduce these materials handling costs to a minimum, but the decision package also describes the negative consequences of such actions. The final determination as to the number of decision packages that will be funded will be determined in the ranking process.

27.6 RANKING PROCESS. The ranking process attempts to provide management with a technique for allocating its limited resources by answering (1) What objectives should we attempt to achieve? and (2) How much should we spend in this attempt?

Management can attempt to answer these questions by taking the decision packages identified and listing (ranking) them in order of decreasing benefit to the organization, as shown in Exhibit 27.3. Management could then identify the benefits to be gained at each expenditure level and the consequences of not approving additional packages ranked below

DECISION PACKAGE Page 1 of ____

(1) PACKAGE NAME	(2) DEPARTMENT		(3) PREPARED BY	(4) DATE	(5) RANK
MATERIALS HANDLING – (2 of 4)	409	Materials Handling	J. JONES	7/28/78	

(6) PURPOSE/OBJECTIVE

Provide materials handling from raw materials stores thru all production departments to finished goods inventory.

(7) DESCRIPTION OF ACTIONS (OPERATIONS) FOR THIS LEVEL

Add four Vehicle Operators to provide additional second shift material handling service for the Bar Mills, Annealing and Pickling Department in the Hot Mill building. This will free the dispatch truck to move released material from Hot Mill Hold area and speed production flow. Provide added frequency of shop mule service from 2 to 4 routes per day, and improve service to the Hot Mill on first shift. Add third shift coverage to the Cold Strip Mill.

Staff: Add 4 Veh. Operators

(8) CHANGES/IMPROVEMENTS FROM CURRENT OPERATIONS (CAPITAL EQUIPMENT)

Hot Mills – Reduced frequency and some additional WIP (5%).
Maintenance & Reclamation provided on on-call basis only.

(9) WORKLOAD/PERFORMANCE MEASURES	1976	1977	1978	(10) RESOURCE REQUIRED	1976 Actual	1977 Revised	1977 Revised	1978 Proposed
Production pounds/year (mil.)	9.8	10.1	12.6	Positions – this level				4
Average daily work-in-process (lbs.)	8,580	8,700	9,300	– cumulative	27	29	29	29
Metered fork lift hours per vehicle	1038	1045	1150	Expense – this level				81.0
Number of fork lift trucks	11	11	11	– cumulative	621	671	671	671.0
				% of Prior Year		108	100	100.0
				Capital				5

Exhibit 27.2. *(Continued)*

the expenditure level. The total request, or traditional budget, would be the sum of all decision packages proposed. However, management now would have the option of funding all packages, no packages, or any number of packages. Regardless of the number of packages funded, top managers can assure themselves that they are funding the most important packages—current or new.

The ranking process establishes priorities among the functions as described in the decision packages. If a company wanted to severely limit its ranking, it could have only those managers preparing packages rank their own packages. However, this approach is obviously unsatisfactory, since it does not offer top management and the CEO any opportunity to trade off expenditures among cost centers or other, larger divisions of the company. The burden would be on division managers to establish trade-offs among industrial engineering, production planning, and maintenance, as well as sales and administrative functions.

At the other extreme, a single ranking of decision packages could be required for an entire company. This ranking would be made by top management. Although this single ranking would identify the best allocation of resources, ranking and judging the high volume of packages created by describing all the discrete activities of a large company would impose a ponderous—if not impossible—burden on top management. One realistic compromise (depending primarily on organizational size) might be to stop the formal ranking process at some intermediate organizational level—for example, at the level of the plant manager or profit center. Many companies solve the dilemma by grouping cost centers or profit and loss units together naturally, according to kinds of activity, and producing consolidated rankings for each grouping. Top management will use these rankings to analyze the trade-offs among profit centers and specifically to compare the marginal benefits of funding additional decision packages against the organization's profit needs.

DECISION PACKAGE Page 2 of ____

(1) PACKAGE NAME	(2) DEPARTMENT		(3) PREPARED BY	(4) DATE	(5) RANK
MATERIALS HANDLING – (2 of 4)	409	Materials Handling	J. JONES	7/28/78	

(11) CONSEQUENCES OF ELIMINATING THIS PACKAGE

Will result in some production departments providing their own materials handling (Zero-incremental cost); but excess WIP inventories and less efficient production activity could result. Delayed shipments could cause a shift delay in movement in Hot Mill.

(12) OTHER LEVELS OF EFFORT IDENTIFIED

(1 of 4) $590.0 Minimum materials handling coverage for the Mill reducing frequency and shift coverage; 25 people

(3 of 4) $56.1K Add 1 Veh. Operator & 1 headman to provide support for Hot Mill and Maintenance dispatching

(4 of 4) $106.2 Add 2 Veh. Operators to increase frequency of service to Holl Grind and shipping departments

(13) ALTERNATIVE MEANS OF ACCOMPLISHING THIS PACKAGE

1. Return the Material Handling function to the individual production departments. This was rejected due to productivity declines, loss of flexibility within the division, and higher costs. The material handling was decentralized until 1975, with the current structure producing a 15% savings when this function was centralized.

2. Combine this function with Work Stores. This alternative was rejected due to potential bargaining unit problems and decreases in flexibility because of contract negotiated work rules in the stores area.

func. #	exp. #	(14) DETAIL EXPENDITURES	1977 Revised	1978 Proposed
		Salaries (Hourly)		38.1
		Wage Premium		12.2
		Total Labor		50.3
		Fringes		20.4
		Propane Fuel		2.3
		Maintenance		8.0
		Total		81.0

Exhibit 27.2. *(Continued)*

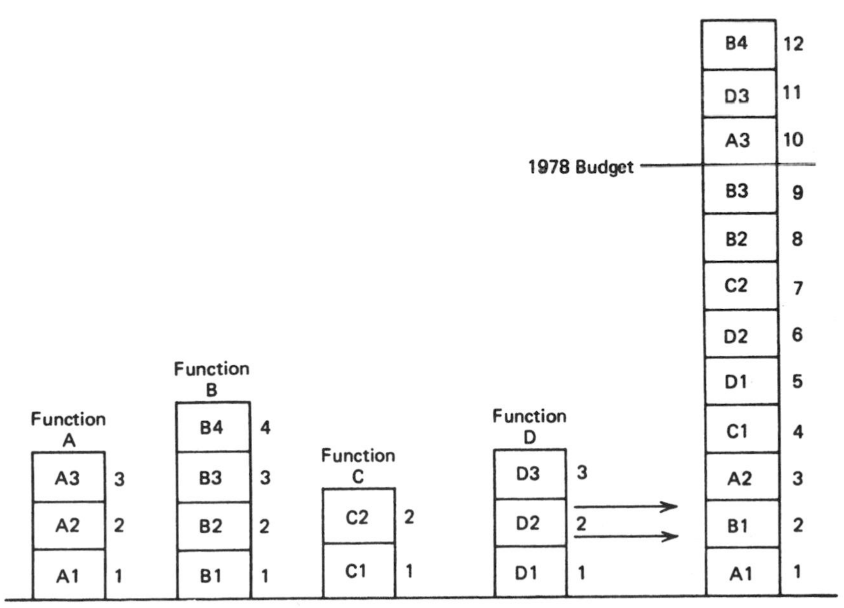

Exhibit 27.3. The ranking process

Decision Unit	FY'78 Estimate	Base Pkg.	Pkg. 2	Pkg. 3	Pkg. 4	Pkg. 5	Total Request
145A Supervise air melt	$ 277	$ 234	$ 56	$ 39	$ 36	$	$ 365
146A Supervise vac melt	281	260	39	35	—		334
147A Supervise hot mills	567	565	36	78	—		679
168A Supervise manufacturing service area	203	178	36	36	17		267
190A Supervise cold strip mill	289	308	39	15	—		362
409A Material handling	686	590	81	56	105		832
409B Vehicle operators	106	63	50	27	27		167
409C Grounds maintenance	207	187	42	25	27		281
409D Garage vehicle repair	330	377	56	35	36		504
409E Utility labor pool	15	7	7	—	—		14
409F Department supervision	104	92	34	31	—		157
446A Shop floor control	284	203	92	21	—		316
446B Work stores	293	255	63	70	—		388
454A Mill process engineering	641	517	172	78	66		833
454B Mill process engineering —other	43	46	83	—	—		129
461A Mill management	199	130	46	—	—		176
Total	$4,525	$4,012	$ 932	$ 546	$ 314		$5,804
Cumulative		4,012	4,944	5,490	5,804		
Cumulative %		88.7%	109.3%	121.3%	128.3%		

Exhibit 27.4. Decision unit summary for steel mill operations

Continuing with the steel mill example in which materials handling is only one out of 16 decision units, the mill manager had to make a single ranking of 52 decision packages encompassing all 16 decision units within the mill. Exhibit 27.4 shows the matrix of all 16 decision units within the mill, which have from 2 to 4 levels of effort for each decision unit. The resulting ranking is shown in Exhibit 27.5.

27.7 COMPLETING THE PROFIT AND LOSS. With the decision packages ranked in order of priority, management can continually revise budgets by revising the cutoff level on any or all rankings—that is, it can fund package numbers 1 through 41 but not package numbers 42 through 52. This ensures that the highest-priority decision packages have been funded. Of course, this means that some of the new high-priority programs have been funded by eliminating or reducing lower-priority, ongoing programs rather than by reducing profits.

Top management and the CEO complete the profit and loss by taking sales and other income; less direct labor, material, and fixed overhead; less some number of decision packages. This is graphically shown in Exhibit 27.6. Top management can make a direct trade of decision packages in various rankings versus profit. To aid top management focus, decision packages and rankings may be segregated to show operating activities, strategic and long-range development programs, and capital (showing cash and depreciation expense). Top management must now make the very difficult decisions on funding allocations. The zero-based approach has systematically laid out the alternatives and priorities, not to make the decision process easier, but to make it better.

DECISION PACKAGE RANKING

(1) RANK	(2) PACKAGE NAME	(3) 1978 PROPOSED		(4) 1979 CUMULATIVE		
		Positions	Expense (excl. cap.)	Positions	Expense (excl. cap.)	% of 1978 Revised
1	Supervise Air Melt Shop, Material Reclaim & Weighroom (1 of 4)	7	235	7	235	5
2	Supervise ESR, Vac Arc Remelting, VIM & EB Melt (1 of 3)	8	260	15	495	11
3	Supervise & Operate Hot Mills and Forging (1 of 3)	18	566	33	1061	23
4	Supervise & Operate Cold Strip Mill (1 of 3)	10	309	43	1370	30
5	Supervise & Operate Manufacturing Service (1 of 4)	6	179	49	1549	34
6	M.P. E. Std. Practice Control & Trouble Shooting (1 of 1)	17	518	66	2067	45
7	Mill Management (1 of 2)	3	130	69	2197	48
8	Material Handling (1 of 4)	25	591	94	2788	61
9	Garage Vehicle Repair (1 of 4)	8	378	102	3166	69
10	Yard Departmental Supervision (1 of 3)	3	92	105	3258	71
11	Supervise Air Melt, Material Reclaim & Weighroom (2 of 4)	3	50	108	3314	73
12	Supervise ESR, Vac Arc Remelting, VIM & EB Melt (2 of 3)	2	39	110	3353	73
13	Supervise & Operate Hot Mills & Forging (2 of 3)	2	36	112	3389	74
14	Supervise & Operate Cold Strip Mill (2 of 3)	2	39	114	3428	75
15	Supervise & Operate Manufacturing Area (2 of 4)	2	36	116	3464	76
16	Shop Floor Control (1 of 3)	7	204	123	3668	80
17	M. P. E. Statistical Process Control & Process Optimization (2 of 1)	6	172	129	3840	84
18	Shop Floor Control (2 of 3)	4	92	133	3932	86
19	Grounds Maintenance (1 of 4)	7	178	140	4110	90
ORGANIZATION BEING RANKED MILL PRODUCTS		PREPARED BY MILL MANAGER		DATE 7/29/78	Page 1 of 3	

(1) RANK	(2) PACKAGE NAME	(3) 1978 PROPOSED		(4) 1979 CUMULATIVE		
		Positions	Expense (excl. cap.)	Positions	Expense (excl. cap.)	% of 1978 Revised
20	Work Stores (1 of 3)	10	255	150	4365	96
21	Vehicle Operator (1 of 4)	3	63	153	4428	97
22	Material Handling (2 of 4)	4	81	157	4509	99
23	Garage Vehicle Repair (2 of 4)	2	56	159	4565	100
24	Division Utility Labor Pool (1 of 2)	8	7	167	4572	100
25	Yard Departmental Supervision (2 of 3)	2	34	169	4606	101
26	Material Handling (3 of 4)	3	56	172	4662	103
27	Grounds Maintenance (2 of 4)	2	42	174	4704	103
28	Grounds Maintenance (3 of 4)	2	25	176	4729	104
29	Work Stores (2 of 3)	4	63	180	4792	105
30	Supervise ESR, Vac Arc Remelting, VIM & EB Melting (3 of 3)	2	35	182	4827	106
31	Supervise & Operate Manufacturing Service Area (3 of 4)	2	36	184	4863	107
32	Vehicle Operator (2 of 4)	2	50	186	4913	108
33	Garage Vehicle Repair (3 of 4)	2	35	188	4948	108
34	Vehicle Operator (3 of 4)	2	27	190	4975	109
35	Supervise & Operate Hot Mills & Forging (3 of 3)	3	78	193	5053	111
36	Supervise & Operate Cold Strip Mill (3 of 3)	2	15	195	5068	111
37	M.P.E. (other than Mill Service) (1 of 1)	2	46	197	5114	112
38	Division Utility Labor Pool (2 of 2)	8	7	205	5121	112
ORGANIZATION BEING RANKED MILL PRODUCTS		PREPARED BY MILL MANAGER		DATE 7/29/78	Page 2 of 3	

Exhibit 27.5. Decision package ranking

DECISION PACKAGE RANKING

(1) RANK	(2) PACKAGE NAME	(3) 1978 PROPOSED		(4) 1979 CUMULATIVE		
		Positions	Expense (excl. cap.)	Positions	Expense (excl. cap.)	% of 1978 Revised
39	Supervise Air Melt, Reclaim & Weighroom (3 of 4)	2	39	207	5160	113
40	Mill Management (2 of 2)	2	46	209	5206	114
41	M.P.E. – Eng. Relief on Conversion Coverage (3 of 1)	3	78	212	5284	116
42	Supervise & Operate Mfgr. Services Area (4 of 4)	2	17	214	5301	116
43	Grounds Maintenance (4 of 4)	2	27	216	5328	117
44	Material Handling (4 of 4)	3	106	219	5434	119
45	Yard Departmental Supervision (3 of 3)	2	31	221	5465	120
46	Supervise Air Melt, Reclaim & Weighroom (4 of 4)	2	36	223	5501	121
47	M.P.E. (2 of 1)	2	83	226	5584	122
48	Vehicle Operators (4 of 4)	2	27	228	5611	123
49	Garage Vehicle Repair (4 of 4)	2	36	230	5647	124
50	M.P.E. (Off-shift Coverage) (4 of 1)	3	66	233	5713	125
51	Shop Floor Control (3 of 3)	2	21	235	5734	126
52	Work Stores (3 of 3)	3	70	238	5804	127

ORGANIZATION BEING RANKED	PREPARED BY	DATE	Page 3 of 3
MILL PRODUCTS	MILL MANAGER	7/29/78	

Exhibit 27.5. *(Continued)*

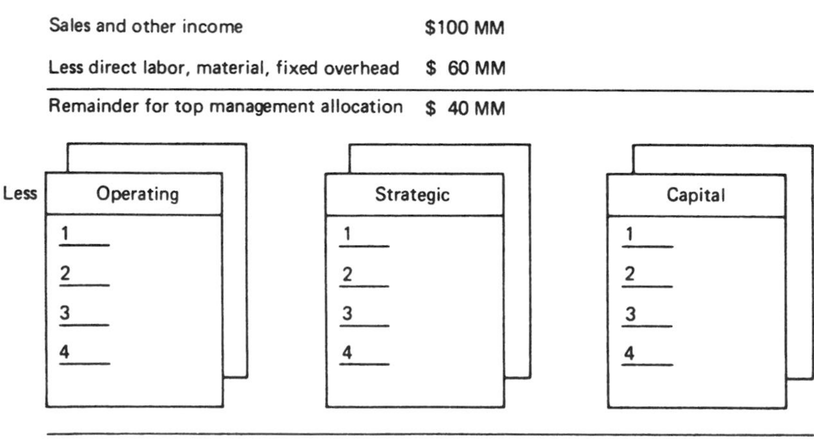

Exhibit 27.6. Top-management decision making

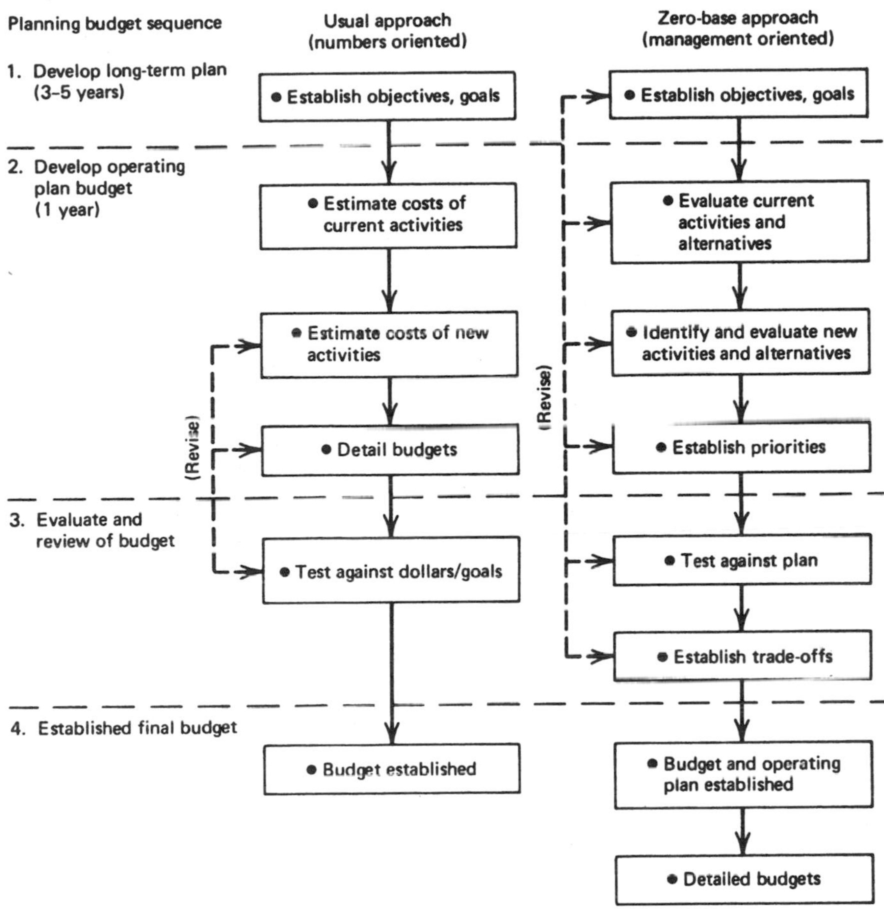

Exhibit 27.7. Traditional versus zero-based budgeting

27.8 PREPARING DETAILED BUDGETS.

After the CEO has made the final funding decisions and established the division and corporate profit and loss, the approved decision packages are handed back to each manager for preparation of the detailed budget. The approved decision packages identified not only approved budget and manpower levels but also the accomplishments that were expected from each manager. Each manager then prepared his or her detail budgets, showing detailed expense accounts by month, which may be fed into the computer for monthly reporting purposes.

(a) Traditional versus Zero-Based Budgeting. Exhibit 27.7 depicts traditional and zero-based budgeting as they flow through each of these stages. To simplify the comparison, let us assume that each process is preceded by a long-term plan. Then, during the initial stages of the operating plan and budget, both processes develop sales forecasts from which the costs of direct labor, material, and overhead are calculated using standard costing procedures.

Up until this stage, both standard and zero-based procedures are similar; however, they now part company. Under the traditional method, each operating manager's (or financial staff's) next step is normally to estimate the cost of continuing current activities. This cost is usually not challenged in depth and is considered as a fixed base for the following year's operating plan. Managers then focus their time on developing costs for new activities proposed for the upcoming year. (This procedure is sometimes reversed if an entire organization must reduce its budget, with managers asked what they must do to cut X% of their budget. However, the same basic problems still apply, except that the increment focused upon is down instead of up.) In many organizations, each manager's request for new costs is often combined with a cost estimate for continuing current operations. The manager then provides to higher levels of management a detailed budget combining all proposed costs, which is usually accompanied by a narrative highlighting the new programs as well as next year's anticipated operations. These detailed budgets are then presented to top management.

Top management is now in the unhappy position of attempting to evaluate the detailed budgets and to reconcile them against the organization's goals and objectives. As all too frequently happens, budget requests exceed funding availability. When a budget is rejected, it is normally returned to the budget unit, where the budget development process is repeated and a revised detailed budget is prepared. Evaluation is not an easy task. Managers often are unable to determine whether appropriate actions have been planned or budgeted to achieve established goals. They must test the detailed budgets against dollar goals and typically find that alternatives and lower levels of expense, and their consequences, are not identified.

Under zero-based budgeting, current activities and alternatives are evaluated at the same time as new programs are identified and considered. Operating managers establish their priorities and thereby identify the trade-offs between expenditure levels and operating needs. New activities can be ranked higher than current ones, and thus new programs can be funded within existing funding levels. Top management makes the final evaluation and funding decisions on the basis of the decision package and the ranking analysis.

Using ZBB, top management can readily test the budget against the operating plan, since it is looking at an evaluation in terms of priorities rather than in terms of numbers. It can identify trade-offs, determine the consequences of alternative expenditure levels, and, based on its evaluation, come up with a new and better set of allocations for the upcoming budget year. From its analysis of decision packages, management gets not only a budget but an operating plan, and the budget is a product of operating decisions. (All too often, companies make budget decisions first, and these decisions become a rigid framework within which line managers must make their operating plans.)

(b) Additional Applications. Top managers have two additional key benefits that they can derive from the zero-based approach: (1) ability to react effectively to changing situations and (2) ability to focus on strategic development efforts in a program matrix.

(i) Changing Situations. The environment seems to be getting more and more unpredictable, and the sales and other projections made by management at the beginning of the planning and budgeting cycle versus the actual situation are sometimes very different by the time the budget cycle is complete—and even more at variance during the operating year. Some companies try to counteract this problem by building contingency plans.

The zero-based approach, however, is a built-in contingency plan, based on the decision packages and priorities. If sales or other assumptions change, or if actuals differ from budget, one can quickly take the following four steps:

1. Adjust direct labor, material, and fixed overhead budgets based on the standard costing system.
2. Identify on an exception basis those decision packages directly affected by the change—usually a small percentage of the packages (e.g., if sales change, maintenance and quality control packages will be modified, but accounting and research will not be affected).
3. Modify rankings, if required, for changes in priorities or ranking of new or expanded programs.
4. Add or delete decision packages in priority order.

This process can be done rapidly even in large organizations because decision packages and rankings can be modified on an exception basis—the entire process does not have to be recycled. These revisions can be made during the planning and budgeting process as planning assumptions change or during the operating year as actuals differ from plan (reflecting, of course, that once midway through the year, the decision package costs that can be affected will be reduced accordingly).

(ii) Strategic Development. As discussed in Chapter 2, strategic planning is one of the most difficult tasks facing top management. It deals with futures and many uncertainties and cuts across organizational lines; these programs are often among the first to be cut, because they are new and are easier to cut than operations such as maintenance. Many organizations have three- to five-year projections showing sales and profit growth, yet their five-year plan becomes a six-year plan when the final "cut 5%" eliminates or severely reduces many of those development programs required to achieve growth. The responsibility for strategic development rests heavily with top management and should be a major focus during the planning and budgeting review.

The zero-based approach offers top management a vehicle to use in translating long-term plans into action plans and budgets by way of the decision package and ranking. Decision packages may be prepared for the research, marketing, engineering, manufacturing, and capital requirements of each strategic plan. These decision packages can then be ranked by major program or objective (rather than by organization). Top management can then focus on these strategic development plans, ensure a coordinated approach (e.g., the research department's setting a high priority on the program while marketing eliminates its efforts), and determine the funding trade-offs among elements of the strategic program, among strategic programs, and among strategic/operating/profit needs (as shown in Exhibit 27.6).

27.9 SUMMARY. The zero-based approach is not a panacea and is not without its problems. The major problem is that many managers feel threatened by a process that evaluates the effectiveness of their programs. The zero-based process also requires a great deal of effective administration, communication, and training of managers who will be involved in the analysis. Managers may also have problems in identifying appropriate decision units, developing adequate data to produce an effective analysis, determining the minimum level of effort, ranking dissimilar programs, and handling large volumes of packages. For many programs, work-load and performance measures may be lacking or the program's impact may not be well defined so that the analysis will be less than perfect. Therefore, zero-based budgeting should be looked upon as a longer-term management development process rather than a one-year cure-all.

If done properly, the zero-based approach is not subject to the gamesmanship one might anticipate. The traditional budget approach offers maximum opportunity for gamesmanship because current operations are seldom evaluated, and many discreet decisions are never explicitly identified and get "buried in the numbers." However, the zero-based approach removes the umbrella covering current operations and requires managers to identify operating decisions clearly. In ZBB, the most obvious forms of gamesmanship would be to avoid identifying reasonable alternatives, to include the pet projects within the minimum-level package, and to rank high priority programs low in order to obtain additional funding. However, if the decision packages are formatted to display the alternatives considered, the work-load and performance data, the descriptions of actions, and enough cost data so that discretionary items cannot be built into the cost estimate, it becomes very obvious when such gamesmanship is attempted. Also, because the entire ranking of decision packages must be displayed, it is very easy to challenge a high-priority item that received a low ranking or a low-priority item that received a high ranking.

The problems in implementing ZBB are not to be minimized. The specific needs, problems, and capabilities of each organization must be considered in adapting the approach. Although most of the basic concepts of the approach have been maintained, the specifics of administration, formats, and procedures have been different for each organization that has adopted the approach. Zero-based budgeting can be applied on an intensive basis throughout all levels of an organization, only to selected programs, or only at major program levels rather than involving all operating managers. The strategy of implementing the zero-based approach must be developed for each organization, depending on its specific needs and capabilities.

Top management must play a major role in implementation. Because the process is difficult, managers must stand behind it, understand it, and use it. Finally, managers must be willing to make the tough decisions and trade-offs that the process requires.

SOURCES AND SUGGESTED REFERENCES

Anonymous, "Zero-Base Budgeting: Making Optimal Use of Resources," *Small Business Report,* vol. 13, no. 4, April 1988.

Becwar, Gregory E., and Jack L. Armitage, "Zero-Base Budgeting: Is It Really Dead?," *Ohio CPA Journal,* vol. 48, no. 4, Winter 1989.

Chew, Andrew S. C., "A Practical Guide to Zero-Based Budgeting," *Singapore Accountant,* vol. 3, no. 12, December 1987.

Duffy, Michael F., "ZBB, MBO, PPB and Their Effectiveness Within the Planning/Marketing Process," *Strategic Management Journal* (UK), vol. 10, no. 2, March–April 1989.

Foskett, D. J., and Lynne Brindley, "Zero-Base Budgeting: The Aston Experience," *Library Management,* vol. 12, no. 4, 1991.

Hayes, Randall B., and William R. Cron, "Changes in Task Uncertainty Induced by Zero-Base Budgeting: Using the Thompson and Hirst Models to Predict Dysfunctional Behaviour," *Abacus* (Australia), vol. 24, no. 2, September 1988.

Morden, Anthony R., "Zero-Base Budgeting: A Potential Revisited," *Management Accounting* (UK), vol. 64, no. 9, October 1986.

Pyhrr, Peter A., *Zero-Base Budgeting: A Practical Management Tool for Evaluating Expenses.* New York: John Wiley & Sons, 1973.

Schulze, William C., ''Zero-Based Budgeting as a Planning and Budgeting Tool for Information Systems,'' *Journal of Information Management,* vol. 9, no. 1, Spring 1988.

Shinn, Linda J., and Sue M. Sturgeon, ''Budgeting from Ground Zero,'' *Association Management,* vol. 42, no. 9, September 1990.

Small Business Report, ''Zero-Base Budgeting: Making Optimal Use of Resources,'' *Small Business Report,* vol. 13, no. 4, April 1988.

Stangler, Kevin J., ''Modified Approach to Zero-Base Budgeting,'' *Interpreter,* vol. 47, February 1988.

Wise, David, ''Better Budgeting for Better Results: The Role of Zero-Base Budgets,'' *Management Accounting* (UK), vol. 66, no. 5, May 1988.

CHAPTER 28

BRACKET BUDGETING

Michael W. Curran*

Decision Sciences Corporation

28.1 INTRODUCTION. Annual budgeting is a way of life in most organization . Planning and control, the two phases of operational budgeting, receive considerable attention at all levels of management. All too often, however, the actual profit differs significantly from the target. This difference is generally attributed to the vagaries of modern business, and rightly so. But this is simply an admission that conventional budgeting is often incapable of coping with business realities.

The reason for this deficiency is fundamental. With conventional budgeting, the forecast of each element in the budget must ultimately be represented as a single number, even though management may know beforehand that thousands of other values are possible. If there are more than a few such elements, the number of possible ways in which they can combine and their effects cascade to the bottom line defies analysis. Bracket budgeting, an analytical procedure that complements conventional budgeting techniques, overcomes this serious inadequacy. This relatively new methodology is a synergistic combination of basic concepts in modeling, simulation, and heuristics that gives management an unequaled understanding of the future.

It must be emphasized that the personal computer plays an integral and indispensable role in bracket budgeting. This means, of course, that it must be programmed to perform the myriad calculations required. Although bracket budgeting can be successfully employed by any manager, development of the necessary computer programs requires substantial technical expertise. The purpose here is to explain the general theory of bracket budgeting and how it is applied by management. Technical issues underlying the theory are discussed only in terms of their practical interpretation and application. No attempt is made to adequately cover this complex subject.

28.2 APPLICATION OF BRACKET BUDGETING. The profit or cost center is the basic level of application of bracket budgeting. (Hereafter, profit and cost centers will often be referred to as "budget centers," with the bottom line of the cost center considered as negative profit.) The scope of the budget center depends upon such factors as the size of the company, its organizational characteristics, and the manner in which budgetary responsibilities are defined. A small firm may consist of a single budget center. In larger organizations, each division may be composed of numerous budget centers such as production departments, sales branches, or product lines. Since bracket budgeting is merely an adjunct of conventional budgeting, its wholesale application throughout an entire company or division is not required; only those budget centers that can benefit from the technique should employ it. The determining factors are uncertainty, complexity, controllability, and commitment. Each of these must be in evidence to a significant degree for a budget center to implement and utilize bracket budgeting successfully.

A budget center is a candidate for bracket budgeting if any possible variance from its targeted bottom line would, in management's eyes, constitute a significant change in the bottom line of the operational unit of which it is a part. In other words, the degree of uncertainty about its bottom-line performance must be substantial enough to cause concern at higher levels of management. In companies organized by divisions, this criterion tends to eliminate from consideration a number of budget centers in each division and, in some cases, entire divisions.

Assuming that the budget center demonstrates the requisite degree of uncertainty, it must then be shown to possess significant complexity. In this sense, *complexity* means that there is a significant number of elements in the budget and that the ways in which they interact to produce changes in the bottom line are not patently obvious. Complexity should not be confused with size. Many budget centers that are large insofar as their bottom lines are concerned are rather simple in operation. On the other hand, many small budget centers are quite complex.

Next, there is the matter of controllability. If the nature of the budget center is such that management has a very limited range of decision options with which to influence bottom-line results, there is little point in applying bracket budgeting. The principal benefit of the technique lies in its ability to identify potential problems and opportunities related to future bottom-line performance. If management cannot then change the probable course of events by exercising its influence over those critical elements of the business which account for these potentialities, the major benefit of bracket budgeting is obviated.

Finally, and perhaps most important, there must be a genuine commitment by the budget center's management to apply and aggressively exploit the capabilities afforded by bracket budgeting. More than lip service is needed. Management must attach the utmost importance to the planning process and recognize that its benefits result from diligence, not default.

28.3 PREMISES TO PROFITS? "Profit planning and budgetary control," a phrase in common use, implicitly differentiates between the terms *profit plan* and *budget.* The profit plan, an antecedent of the budget, is management's assessment of the coming fiscal year, along with a planned course of action to attain acceptable financial performance for that period. The degree of formalization of the profit plan varies according to the needs and attitudes of management. Generally, the larger and more complex the business, the more formal the profit plan. In some cases, it may simply be a verbal consensus on the most critical components; in other cases, it may receive much attention in all stages of its development. Elaborate details may be injected regarding industry and market share trends, advertising, key accounts, production, distribution, and so forth. Page after page of supporting narrative may be included to explain the overall thrust of the plan and its various intricacies.

In simplest terms, however, the profit plan is a set of premises upon which management charts a course of action for the coming fiscal year. The budget is the quantification of the profit plan into accounting formats. Of principal concern here is the *pro forma* income statement and its supporting detail. In essence then, the budgeted bottom line on the income statement is a fairly accurate estimate of the actual bottom line—*if* the set of premises (the profit plan) is essentially valid *or if* "compensating factors" occur. Herein lies the problem.

A firm's track record with budgeting usually reflects the complexity of its business and the uncertainty conditions under which it must operate. An organization with few products or services operating in a relatively stable environment tends to have little difficulty in forecasting profit within an acceptable margin of error. On the other hand, a firm offering a multitude of products or services under volatile conditions is more apt to experience a large variance from forecast. This is particularly true of individual budget centers within such an organization. In a budget center where a significant profit variance is possible, the value of budgeting is called into question. What can management hope to accomplish? This question is appropriate to both the planning and control phases of operational budgeting.

With regard to budgetary control, consider the case of a budget center experiencing a substantially unfavorable year-to-date profit variance. Management carefully reviews the operation and, as a result, decides to do something differently. In other words, it changes tactics. What, exactly, is its reason for doing this? One is tempted to say that the purpose is to achieve the annual profit target. In fact, however, this is not the basic objective. Consciously or otherwise, management is attempting to improve its chances, or probability, that actual profit will be at least as much as the target. As it turns out of course, increasing this probability increases profit—even if the target is not reached. Recognition of this subtle but important difference leads to the conclusion that conventional budgeting falls far short of management's objective. There is no mechanism to measure, monitor and manage this probability throughout the budgeting period. More important, potential profit problems and opportunities that influence this probability cannot be identified and ranked in order of decision priority so that management can take early and appropriate action to improve the odds for success.

Similar shortcomings are apparent in the annual planning phase. What chance is there of attaining next year's profit target? Is it close to 75% or nearer to 10%? (Managers are often shocked to learn it is inordinately low or high.) What factors, ranked in order of importance, account for this low or high probability? Which of these factors can something be done about now to improve the chance of success? Practically speaking, what is the lowest potential profit next year? The highest? Will this proposed marketing plan increase the probability of reaching the annual profit target? By how much? With bracket budgeting, critical questions such as these can be adequately answered to avoid surprises later.

28.4 DEVELOPING A TACTICAL BUDGETING MODEL. Once it is determined that bracket budgeting should be implemented in a budget center, a tactical budgeting model must be developed. Prior to actually developing the model, a careful examination is made of the budget and its supporting detail. Wherever possible, significant line items in the budget are analyzed in terms of their basic elements. Thus, sales may be stated by product and, if appropriate, each product considered in terms of unit demand and selling price per unit. In some cases this may be further refined to major customers or some other subcategory. Once these basic elements are identified, they are used to develop a tactical budgeting model, which is generally a series of simple equations showing how the elements combine to produce the bottom line.

Effective use of bracket budgeting largely depends upon the complexity of the tactical budgeting model. Strange as it may seem, the more time devoted to developing this model, the less useful it probably will be. The reason is quite simple. Spending a considerable amount of time attempting to make the model as realistic as possible inevitably leads to a level of complexity that the budget center manager will find neither necessary nor understandable. The objective here is not to make mathematicians out of managers but to provide them with a fairly simple and highly useful model.

It must be remembered that this model will be used in tactical budgeting, an area of application where the period being forecasted does not extend years into the future as it does in strategic budgeting problems. This permits the inclusion of many simplifying assumptions, assumptions that would not hold water if the model were to be used in a capital investment analysis, for example. Unlimited production capacity and products having no market elasticity are good examples of simplifying assumptions that can very often be made in developing a tactical budgeting model. In those few cases in which such an assumption would be inappropriate for whatever reason, the model can be expanded to describe the situation adequately. Again, however, these exceptions should be treated as simply as possible. If developing a tactical budgeting model requires more than a few hours or days, there is every likelihood that it will be more complex than is necessary or desirable. And that would be a serious error indeed.

One technique often used to simplify development of a tactical budgeting model deserves special mention. It is particularly helpful in developing a model of a budget center having a substantial number of products: from a hundred up into the thousands. Almost a century ago, Vilfredo Pareto observed that a small number of people accounted for a large portion of total wealth. This phenomenon of a relatively small percentage of a population accounting for a very large portion of a characteristic of the population can be found in innumerable situations and is referred to as ''Pareto's Law'' or the ''80/20 rule.'' Pareto's Law is well known to most managers but exploited by few. It frequently manifests itself in a budget center having a very large number of products: a relatively small number of them will account for a very large portion of the bottom line. The best measure of a product's contribution to the bottom line is its gross profit, in dollars. Those relatively few products that are important can be readily identified by a stratified-cumulative gross profit analysis, as is later demonstrated. The number of elements in the tactical budgeting model can therefore be drastically reduced by enumerating only the important products and accounting for the remainder in just two elements—''sales of all other products'' and ''cost of goods sold of all other products,'' for example.

(a) Identifying the Critical Elements. A principal feature of conventional budgeting is its ability to analyze past performance—last month or year-to-date, for example. Bracket budgeting also tracks actual performance, albeit in a much different way. However, bracket budgeting's primary focus is on the future—next year during annual profit planning and next month or next quarter in the budgetary control phase.

In the budgetary control application, bracket budgeting enables management to challenge tactics in order to determine whether there is a high probability they will lead to the desired result—achieving targeted profit for the next quarter, for example. If current tactics are demonstrated to be unequal to the task, bracket budgeting highlights those areas that deserve attention. With these hot spots identified and ranked, management then concentrates its effort where it is needed most—in developing one or more alternate methods of achieving the goal. Bracket budgeting is re-employed to test these alternatives and management then implements that alternative which maximizes the chance for success. In many organizations, applying this concept on a monthly rather than a quarterly basis would be ineffective; an appreciable part of the month will have gone by before any benefits would be realized from a change in tactics.

Once the budget center's basic elements are identified and a tactical budgeting model is developed, the next quarter's budget is analyzed to determine each element's impact and critical variance. Each element, in turn, is set at a value that is 1% more favorable than its target (while all other elements are held at their respective targets) and the resultant change in the budget center's bottom line is determined. This change is called that element's 1% impact. Since all elements are varied each in turn by this same percentage, their impacts can be compared. Management then specifies the maximum percentage change from the profit target that it is willing to accept as attributable to any one element. In most budget centers, 2% works quite nicely. This cutoff value, along with the impact, is then used to determine the critical variance of each element.

For example, if the profit target is $100,000 and the 2% figure is used, then the cutoff value at the bottom line is $2,000. If a given element's 1% impact is $250, the critical variance for that element is 8%, as is found by dividing 2,000 by 250. Looking at it another way, for every 1% variance from target on this element, the bottom line is changed by $250. Thus, an 8% variance would change the bottom line by $2,000. However, that is the cutoff value stipulated by management; therefore, the critical variance for the element must be 8%. Management generally finds it more helpful if critical variances are expressed in units rather than percentages. For example, if a sales element has a target of 3,000 gallons and a critical variance of 3%, the critical variance would be expressed as 90 gallons.

If, for the next quarter, it is conceivable that the variance of any given element can exceed its critical variance either favorably or unfavorably, then that element is classified as a critical element. Pareto's Law predicts there will be relatively few. In actual practice, a budget center typically has between 10 and 20 critical elements—regardless of the budget center's size or complexity. Thus, management's attention can be sharply focused on those relatively few elements of the business that play such vital roles in its bottom-line performance.

(i) Fishing Supplies Company. Fishing Supplies Company, a hypothetical budget center, may be thought of as a small firm or as a profit center in a larger corporation. The management team consists of a general manager (Gene), a marketing manager (Mary), a production manager (Paul), and a controller (Carl). Fishing Supplies is just about to complete the fifth month of its current fiscal year. The budget for its upcoming third quarter is shown in Exhibit 28.1. (Since any example must necessarily be brief, much fault can

Sales		$500,000
Cost of goods sold		360,000
Gross profit		$140,000
Operating expenses		
Commissions	$45,000	
Advertising	9,000	
Other selling expenses	6,000	
Administrative expenses	32,000	
Total operating expenses		92,000
Net operating income		$48,000
Other income	$3,000	
Other expense	1,000	2,000
Net income before taxes		$50,000

Exhibit 28.1. Fishing Supplies Company's third-quarter budget

be found with this one. Undoubtedly, the real world is not as simple as suggested here, but this lack of reality in no way impairs a serious treatment of the bracket budgeting methodology.)

Carl took the first step in developing the tactical budgeting model by preparing an analysis of the third-quarter budget in terms of gross profit, both before and after fixed costs. The results are depicted in Exhibit 28.2. The management team feels that exclusion of the fixed portion of cost of goods sold from gross profit more faithfully represents the bottom-line contributions of the products. (Gross profit before fixed costs will hereafter be referred to simply as ''gross profit.'') In effect, Carl treated these data as if Fishing Supplies were operating under a direct costing system. It needs to be pointed out, however, that bracket budgeting requires no specific method of costing; it operates equally well with standard, direct, activity based, and other types of accounting systems.

Next, Carl prepared Exhibit 28.3 showing the sales, variable cost, and gross profit for each of the six product lines. He identified the importance of each product line by indicating its rank according to the magnitude of its budgeted gross profit in the third quarter. Carl was not surprised to see that lures are the largest contributor to Fishing Supplies' bottom-line and bait buckets the smallest. After reviewing this information, he was able to quickly prepare the stratified-cumulative gross profit analysis shown in Exhibit 28.4. Carl simply listed the product lines in descending order of gross profit, indicating the percentage each accounts for of the total gross profit and, in the last column, the cumulative percentage. The Pareto effect is quite obvious here; half of the products account for 89.3% of total gross profit. Since Fishing Supplies does not have that many products to start with, the management team decided to include all of them as individual elements in the tactical budgeting model.

Sales	$500,000
Cost of goods sold (variable costs only)	270,000
Gross profit (before fixed costs)	$230,000
Cost of goods sold (fixed factory overhead)	90,000
Gross profit (after fixed costs)	$140,000

Exhibit 28.2. Fishing Supplies Company's third-quarter budget—gross profit before and after fixed costs

Product Line	Sales	Variable Cost	Gross Profit[a]	Rank
Rods	$ 26,404	$ 14,028	$ 12,376	4
Reels	135,999	95,046	40,953	3
Lures	190,402	97,691	92,711	1
Bait buckets	12,012	6,258	5,754	6
Minnow traps	19,596	13,156	6,440	5
Tackle boxes	115,587	43,821	71,766	2
Total	$500,000	$270,000	$230,000	

[a] Before fixed costs.

Exhibit 28.3. Fishing Supplies Company's third-quarter budget—gross profit (before fixed costs) by product line

Product Line	Rank	Gross Profit[a]	Percentage of Total	Cumulative Percentage
Lures	1	$ 92,711	40.3	40.3
Tackle boxes	2	71,766	31.2	71.5
Reels	3	40,953	17.8	89.3
Rods	4	12,376	5.4	94.7
Minnow traps	5	6,440	2.8	97.5
Bait buckets	6	5,754	2.5	100.0
Total		$230,000	100.0	

[a] Before fixed costs.

Exhibit 28.4. Fishing Supplies Company's third-quarter budget—gross profit (before fixed costs) by product line, using stratified–cumulative analysis

Product Line	Sales	Variable Cost	Unit Sales	Selling Price per Unit	Variable Cost per Unit
Rods	$ 26,404	$ 14,028	2,800 ea.	$ 9.43	$ 5.01
Reels	135,999	95,046	7,300 ea.	18.63	13.02
Lures	190,402	97,691	8,300 doz.	22.94	11.77
Bait buckets	12,012	6,258	2,100 ea.	5.72	2.98
Minnow traps	19,596	13,156	4,600 ea.	4.26	2.86
Tackle boxes	115,587	43,821	8,100 ea.	14.27	5.41
Total	$500,000	$270,000			

Exhibit 28.5. Fishing Supplies Company's third-quarter budget—unit sales with unit selling prices and unit variable costs

After Gene, Mary, and Paul reviewed all this information, Carl prepared Exhibit 28.5 showing the third-quarter budgeted unit sales, unit selling prices, and unit variable costs for all six product lines. Upon meeting and discussing all of these analyses, the management team developed a simple tactical budgeting model. Its elements are described in Exhibit 28.6 and their logical relationships to the bottom line are given in Exhibit 28.7. The model consists of 25 elements, 19 of which pertain to sales and cost of goods sold. Because commissions are a variable expense, they are stated as a percentage of sales, the element upon which they depend.

The model was then used to analyze the third-quarter budget and to calculate the impact and critical variance of each element. The results are given in Exhibit 28.8. Reviewing the data for just one of the elements will clarify the very important concepts of impact and critical variance. The unit sales of reels was favorably varied by 1% from its target of 7,300 units, in effect making it 7,373 units, while all other elements were held at their respective targets. The model then calculated the bottom line and found it to be $50,287 rather than the $50,000 target. Thus, selling 73 additional reels would increase the bottom line by $287, the element's 1% impact as shown in Exhibit 28.8. This is verified rather easily by noting that the element's unit selling price of $18.63 yields an additional $1,359.99 in sales when multiplied by the 73 additional units, and its unit variable cost of $13.02 results in an additional $950.46 in cost of goods sold when multiplied by the

Element	Description of Element	Unit
E1	Rods—unit sales	ea.
E2	Rods—selling price	$/ea.
E3	Rods—variable cost	$/ea.
E4	Reels—unit sales	ea.
E5	Reels—selling price	$/ea.
E6	Reels—variable cost	$/ea.
E7	Lures—unit sales	doz.
E8	Lures—selling price	$/doz.
E9	Lures—variable cost	$/doz.
E10	Bait buckets—unit sales	ea.
E11	Bait buckets—selling price	$/ea.
E12	Bait buckets—variable cost	$/ea.
E13	Minnow traps—unit sales	ea.
E14	Minnow traps—selling price	$/ea.
E15	Minnow traps—variable cost	$/ea.
E16	Tackle boxes—unit sales	ea.
E17	Tackle boxes—selling price	$/ea.
E18	Tackle boxes—variable cost	$/ea.
E19	Fixed factory overhead	$
E20	Commissions (% of sales)	%
E21	Advertising	$
E22	Other selling expenses	$
E23	Administrative expenses	$
E24	Other income	$
E25	Other expense	$

Exhibit 28.6. Fishing Supplies Company—elements of tactical budgeting model

Sales = (E1 × E2) + (E4 × E5) + (E7 × E8) + (E10 × E11) + (E13 × E14)
+ (E16 × E17)
Variable costs = (E1 × E3) + (E4 × E6) + (E7 × E9) + (E10 × E12) + (E13 × E15)
+ (E16 × E18)
Total cost of goods sold = Variable costs + E19
Gross profit = Sales − Total cost of goods sold
Commissions = 0.01 × E20 × Sales
Total operating expenses = Commissions + E21 + E22 + E23
Net operating income = Gross profit − Total operating expenses
Net income before taxes = Net operating income + E24 − E25

Exhibit 28.7. Fishing Supplies Company—tactical budgeting model

same 73 units. Thus, the difference between the $1,359.99 addiitonal sales and the $950.46 additional cost is $409.53 additional gross profit.

Commissions would have to be paid on these additional sales, a fact considered by the model. (Like all the other elements, commissions was held at its target value, but that value is a rate, not dollars. Thus, the model will reduce any additional sales by the appropriate amount of commissions to reflect the correct net effect at the bottom line.) At the rate

Description of Element	Unit	Target	One Percent Impact ($)	Critical Variance
Rods—unit sales	ea.	2,800	100	280
Rods—selling price	$/ea.	9.43	240	0.39
Rods—variable cost	$/ea.	5.01	140	0.36
Reels—unit sales[a]	ea.	7,300	287	254
Reels—selling price[a]	$/ea.	18.63	1,238	0.15
Reels—variable cost[a]	$/ea.	13.02	950	0.14
Lures—unit sales[a]	doz.	8,300	756	110
Lures—selling price[a]	$/doz.	22.94	1,733	0.13
Lures—variable cost	$/doz.	11.77	977	0.12
Bait buckets—unit sales	ea.	2,100	47	449
Bait buckets—selling price	$/ea.	5.72	109	0.52
Bait buckets—variable cost	$/ea.	2.98	63	0.48
Minnow traps—unit sales	ea.	4,600	47	984
Minnow traps—selling price	$/ea.	4.26	178	0.24
Minnow traps—variable cost	$/ea.	2.86	132	0.22
Tackle boxes—unit sales[a]	ea.	8,100	614	132
Tackle boxes—selling price[a]	$/ea.	14.27	1,052	0.14
Tackle boxes—variable cost[a]	$/ea.	5.41	438	0.12
Fixed factory overhead[a]	$	90,000	900	1,000
Commissions (% of sales)	%	9.0	450	0.2
Advertising	$	9,000	90	1,000
Other selling expenses	$	6,000	60	1,000
Administrative expenses[a]	$	32,000	320	1,000
Other income	$	3,000	30	1,000
Other expense	$	1,000	10	1,000

[a] Critical element.

Exhibit 28.8. Fishing Supplies Company's third-quarter budget—impact and critical variance analysis

of 9% there would be an additional commission cost of $122.40 on the additional $1,359.99 of sales. Subtracting this $122.40 from the $409.53 additional gross profit previously calculated leaves $287.13 which, to the nearest dollar, is the 1% impact for the unit sales of reels shown in Exhibit 28.8.

Now, since a 1% change in the unit sales of reels would result in a $287 change in the bottom line, then for the bottom line to swing by as much as the cutoff value of 2% (which is $1,000), the unit sales of reels would have to vary by 3.48%, as is found by dividing $1,000 by the $287.13 impact figure. Therefore, the critical variance is 3.48% or, as is found by multiplying 7,300 by 3.48%, 254 units. This is the critical variance for the unit sales of reels as shown in the exhibit.

Upon reviewing the information in Exhibit 28.8, Fishing Supplies' management identified 10 critical elements. Each of these is noted in the exhibit. As an example, the unit sales of reels was deemed critical since, according to Mary, its third-quarter performance could easily vary from target by more than 254 units, its critical variance. Conversely, Paul stated that the maximum potential fluctuation in the variable cost of rods is less than its critical variance of $0.36 per unit. That explains why this particular element is not critical. Commissions is not a critical element since management rightfully expects its actual value to be identical to its target, which is expressed as a rate rather than as dollars.

(b) Scientific Guessing. If uncertainty is to be dealt with effectively, it must be measured. The bottom line target reposes in a two-dimensional world: dollars and the chance of achieving those dollars. (In this sense, *achieving* means an actual value at least as favorable as the target.) Managers are aware of this second dimension but, lacking a yardstick to measure it, they are forced to deal with it in a qualitative, often disastrous, fashion. The uncertainty associated with the bottom line target results from the uncertainties of the critical elements above it on the budgeted income statement. If the number of such elements is more than a few, as is usually the case, the human mind finds itself incapable of adequately evaluating their concurrent potential effects on the bottom line.

However, this is exactly what conventional budgeting asks management to do. Bracket budgeting, on the other hand, breaks the problem down into its component parts. Management is asked to assess the uncertainty of each critical element. Then, with the use of the tactical budgeting model and a personal computer, bracket budgeting puts all of these individual uncertainties together in such a way that the uncertainty related to the bottom line can be determined and presented to management for decision-making purposes.

A critical element's uncertainty may be assessed in a number of ways. Most of these, however, require a basic understanding of probability theory and statistics, technical knowledge that all managers cannot be presumed to have. There is one simple, but effective, measure: the range. The manager determines the range by specifying the highest value that the element's actual can assume, the lowest value that the element's actual can assume, and the probability that the element's actual value will be at least as favorable as its target. By measuring uncertainty with the range, the manager ''brackets'' the element's ultimate true value, a process analogous to skeet shooting—high scores are achieved with a shotgun, not a rifle.

The lowest and highest estimates in the range have no importance per se; they merely serve as boundaries. The greater the uncertainty, of course, the farther apart these boundaries and the broader the range. The element's target is also a boundary in that it divides the range into two parts, favorable and unfavorable. (If the target is infeasible, then the entire range is either favorable or unfavorable.) The probability factor is simply management's confidence that the element's actual value will materialize anywhere in the favorable part of the range. For that reason, this probability is often called the *confidence factor.* The confidence factor's complement is the risk. For example, if a confidence factor of 75% is specified for a given element, then the chance of unfavorable performance (i.e., risk) is 25%.

By assessing each critical element in this manner, management can better articulate its perception of the future—certainly much better than by mentally wrestling with all the elements simultaneously. This approach also has the advantage of putting the target into perspective. Assuming it is attainable, the target is but one point in a spectrum of feasible points. Unfortunately, the target is often referred to as the ''best estimate.'' This implies that there is at least a 50% chance that the actual will be at least as favorable as the target. Although this may indeed be true, it can be misleading in that it says nothing about how far the actual might be from that target, in either direction. A range is much more practical than a target or average figure—imagine a person who cannot swim, about to wade across a river, being told the average depth is three feet! Also, ranging tends to minimize the differences between bullish and bearish managers; the capability of looking at an element in terms of its potential extremes begs for a realistic assessment of its uncertainty.

When specifying a critical element's range, management takes into account all foreseeable circumstances. Ideally, the lowest estimate should be determined in such a manner that there is slightly less than a 1% chance of the actual going beyond that boundary of the range. The highest estimate should be determined in similar fashion. In essence then, the chance that the actual will fall within the range is better than 98% or, for all practical purposes, 100%.

In qualitative terms, the lowest and highest estimates should each be far enough out to capture the extremely improbable, but not the slightly absurd. When first faced with making a judgment of this type, some managers are uneasy about the procedure since it involves "a lot" of guesswork. But that is precisely why conventional budgeting comes up short in many cases; working solely with targets involves only a little guesswork. So little, in fact, that the potential variability of the bottom line cannot be adequately ascertained. There is nothing wrong with guessing, as long as proper recognition is given to inherent error. After all, Nobel prizes have resulted from shrewd scientific guessing. A ranging error in bracket budgeting has far less import than a comparable percentage error in the target if the target is the only measure of future performance. In terms of informational enrichment, the target often suffers in abject poverty. The range, no matter how subjective it is, has much more informational reliability than any single point from within it, including the target.

(i) Fishing Supplies Company. One month from now, Fishing Supplies' third quarter will begin. Four months from now, no one will be able to do anything about it. Potential problems must be uncovered now before they become realities later. Management cannot afford to wait until the middle of the quarter for a report showing the actuals for the first month of that quarter. (That is like steering a car along an interstate highway by watching nothing other than the white line in the rearview mirror.)

Yesterday morning the management team reviewed the third-quarter budget, considering all currently available information and under the assumption that business will be conducted according to the tactics originally outlined in the profit plan. The greatest portion of this meeting was devoted to establishing ranges for the critical elements. Two targets were found to be infeasible since they fell outside of their respective ranges. However, the managers did not establish new targets for these elements. Instead of rebudgeting, they merely reassessed the reasonableness of the original targets by stating ranges. No time was spent ranging the noncritical elements. The forecast of each of these was "frozen" at its target, unless management believed another value was a better estimate; then the element was frozen at that value instead of its target.

The data developed during yesterday morning's meeting are given in Exhibit 28.9. By having this opportunity to "tell it like it is," Fishing Supplies' managers have come to grips head on with the problem of uncertainty. It is evident that they know much more about the current status of each critical element than they could possibly convey in any single-value forecast. This informational reservoir has previously gone untapped at Fishing Supplies—untapped, at least, by any reliable method.

Mary stated that, under the poorest conditions she could imagine, sales of reels would not fall below 6,500 units. On the other hand, she could not envision demand rising above 8,000 units. (This assessment spans 1,501 possibilities, one of which is the target of 7,300 units.) Furthermore, she was rather confident that the actual value would be at least as

Description of Element	Original Target	Confidence Factor	Lowest Estimate	Highest Estimate	Frozen Value
Rods—unit sales	2,800				2,600
Rods—selling price	9.43				9.58
Rods—variable cost	5.01				5.05
Reels—unit sales	7,300	75%	6,500	8,000	
Reels—selling price	18.63	0%	18.05	18.55	
Reels—variable cost	13.02	80%	12.75	13.10	
Lures—unit sales	8,300	40%	7,500	8,700	
Lures—selling price	22.94	75%	22.65	23.25	
Lures—variable cost	11.77				11.75
Bait buckets—unit sales	2,100				2,100
Bait buckets—selling price	5.72				5.72
Bait buckets—variable cost	2.98				2.98
Minnow traps—unit sales	4,600				3,900
Minnow traps—selling price	4.26				4.35
Minnow traps—variable cost	2.86				2.90
Tackle boxes—unit sales	8,100	20%	4,700	8,600	
Tackle boxes—selling price	14.27	50%	13.70	14.70	
Tackle boxes—variable cost	5.41	60%	5.30	5.55	
Fixed factory overhead	90,000	60%	87,000	93,000	
Commissions (% of sales)	9.0				9.0
Advertising	9,000				8,200
Other selling expenses	6,000				5,400
Administrative expenses	32,000	100%	30,000	31,500	
Other income	3,000				3,400
Other expense	1,000				1,000
Net income before taxes	50,000	?'	?	?	

Exhibit 28.9. Fishing Supplies Company—management's assessment of third quarter, based on original plan

favorable as the target, believing that there were three out of four chances this would occur. She therefore specified a confidence factor of 75%. The target for the selling price of reels was deemed infeasible, in an unfavorable way. Conversely, the target for administrative expenses was judged infeasible, in a favorable way.

Last week, Mary met with one of Fishing Supplies' major customers. During the course of conversation, she learned that the customer was experiencing considerable shifts in sales activity, including a dramatic reduction in the demand for tackle boxes. In fact, at the current rate of sales, the customer had enough in inventory for the next five months. Unfortunately, Mary had no way of predicting this when she prepared the annual profit plan; the third-quarter budget assumed continued high demand for tackle boxes from this major customer. (One of those premises just turned sour!) This is the primary reason why Mary's range for the unit sales of tackle boxes was so unfavorable compared to its target.

Although some of these ranges are rather broad, compared to many budget centers in the real world, Fishing Supplies' uncertainties are mild indeed. For that reason, and primarily because of the simplistic nature of this example, it is not difficult to see that Fishing Supplies' third-quarter pretax income target is in jeopardy. But what is the most urgent problem and how important is it? Even in this simple example, that question is not so easily answered. Considering only the unfavorable end points of the ranges, the lowest possible third-quarter pretax income is $3,224. Similarly, considering only the favorable end points, the highest pretax income is $74,489. However, the chance of the future unfolding close to either of these extremes is ridiculously small; these theoretical income limits are thus useless for all practical purposes.

(c) Tapping the Power of the Personal Computer. Even with the few ranges in Fishing Supplies' case, there is an astronomical number of ways for the elements to combine to produce third-quarter pretax income. Not one of these combinations is important since the chance of it actually occurring is extremely small. What is important is the manner in which they compare with one another in what is known as the *income profile.* There is no need to consider each and every combination to determine the income profile, any more than it is necessary for a pharmaceutical company to inspect millions of tablets to reliably determine the quality of a given production run. Indeed, the quality can be determined by scientifically sampling a very small number of tablets.

In Fishing Supplies' case, a personal computer scientifically sampled relatively few combinations to develop a highly reliable income profile. In each sample, the computer selected a value from within the range of each of the 10 critical elements. (Any value contained in a range was available for selection, although all values did not have the same chance of being selected.) The computer then used these 10 values, along with the 15 frozen values of the noncritical elements, to compute the pretax income for that particular sample. This procedure was repeated many times over to develop the income profile. In any one of these samples, the value selected from within one range was in no way related to the value selected from within any other range, any more than in the "real world" the unit sales of reels is related to the variable cost of bait buckets. Thus, one sample might have reflected a high demand for reels and a low variable cost for bait buckets, whereas the next sample might have been the reverse of this, or any other possible combination of these two elements. In any case, the computer did nothing more than what management said was feasible. For example, considering unit sales of reels in any one sample, the computer selected one of the 1,501 possibilities that lie within its range. Furthermore, for each sample, there was a 25% chance of the computer's selecting a value less than the 7,300 target.

The computer sampled a total of 1,000 possibilities. In effect, it prepared 1,000 income statements of the third quarter, remembering the pretax income in each case. This number of samples is in excess of the reliability called for in this problem but the computer required just a few seconds to complete the task. After completing the sampling process, the computer sorted the pretax income figures into an array of descending values. As a result, the top-most value was $63,128 and the bottom-most $18,863. In other words, in the 1,000 samples, the computer did not find a value either less than $18,863 or greater than $63,128. Thus, for all practical purposes, the odds are greater than 1,000 to 1 against the actual third-quarter pretax income falling outside of these two values. For this reason, these values are referred to as the *practical income limits.*

Having been told that the target is $50,000 pretax income, the computer then searched the ranked array, starting at the top-most (largest) value. It continued searching down the array until it found the first value that was less than the $50,000 target. This occurred at the 278th position from the top. The value located there was just a few dollars less than the target. This means that 277 (or 27.7%) of the 1,000 values were at least as large as the target. Therefore, the computer reported that Fishing Supplies has a 28% chance of achieving its third-quarter pretax income goal. Conversely, since 723 of the 1,000 values were less than the target, the chance of an unfavorable result (i.e., the risk) is 72%.

The chance that actual pretax income will be at least as much as any given figure in the ranked array can be similarly determined. For example, the 900th value from the top was $30,362 pretax. Thus, there is a 90% chance that the actual will be at least $30,362. Printing all of these 1,000 pretax income figures on a report is unnecessary. The computer merely selects representative values and displays them in tabular or graphical form.

(i) Potential Problems and Opportunities. Finally, the computer examined all of the critical elements in Fishing Supplies' budget to determine the relative proportion that each accounts for of all potential income problems and opportunities. (This can be accomplished with a heuristic which jointly considers the element's importance to the bottom line, the magnitudes of its potential favorable and unfavorable variances as specified by its range, and management's confidence that the element's actual value will be at least as favorable as its target.) The noncritical elements were evaluated as a group in a different, but comparable, fashion. The results of these analyses are given in Exhibit 28.10.

NET INCOME BEFORE TAXES			PROBABILITY OF ACHIEVING TARGET
LOWEST $18,863	TARGET $50,000	HIGHEST $63,128	28%

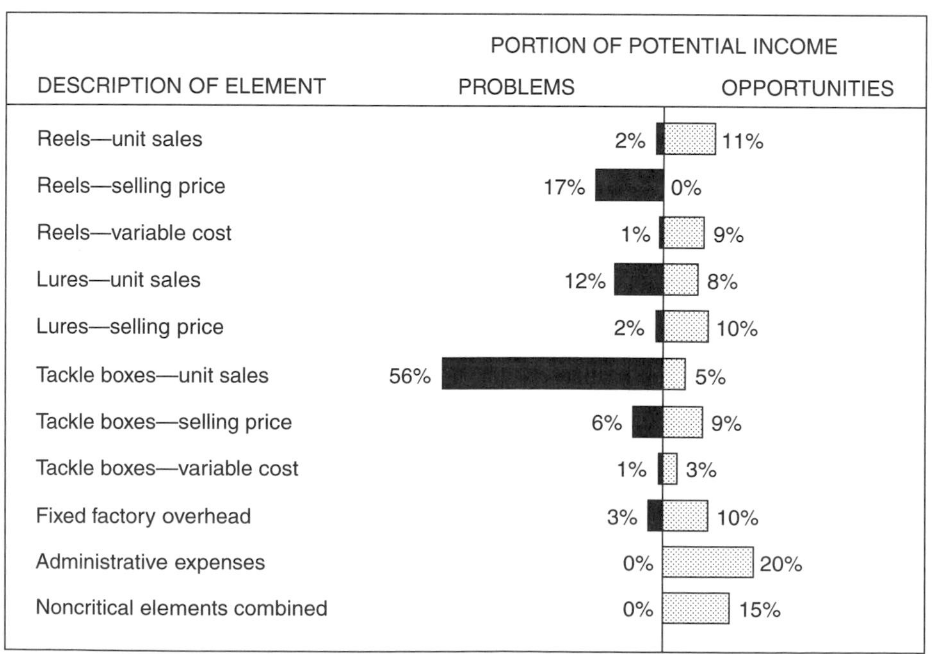

Exhibit 28.10. Fishing Supplies Company—results of computer simulation of third quarter, based on original plan

As could have been expected from Pareto's Law, a relatively small number of elements accounts for the greatest portion of Fishing Supplies' potential income problems. Unit sales of tackle boxes accounts for 56%, the selling price of reels 17%, and unit sales of lures 12%. Thus, 85% of all potential income problems in the third quarter can be attributed to these three elements alone. None of the three contributes any significant potential income opportunity since, as can be noted from their ranges, little or no favorable variances from their targets are possible. Administrative expenses presents no potential income problems since, according to its range, no unfavorable variance is foreseen. All things considered, Fishing Supplies is heading into a troublesome third quarter. There is only one way to improve the prognosis—change tactics. Having recognized this after reviewing these results late yesterday morning, the managers decided to continue their meeting into the afternoon.

(d) A Plan Is Nothing—Planning Is Everything. Right now, the management team at Fishing Supplies has a better chance of winning a coin toss than of meeting its third-quarter pretax income goal. Some tactical replanning is clearly in order. The purpose of yesterday afternoon's meeting was to develop an alternative plan to improve the odds for success. Naturally, attention was immediately trained on the most important potential income problem: unit sales of tackle boxes. After the four managers explored several options that proved unpromising, Mary hit on an idea. For some time, Fishing Supplies recognized a need to introduce tackle boxes into the Dallas market. This was carefully reviewed when this year's profit plan was developed. As a result, the introduction of tackle boxes into the Dallas market was scheduled for the fourth quarter this year. That would give the production department an opportunity to build the necessary increase in inventory during the slack season, the third quarter.

Mary's proposal is to move the target date ahead three months and to open up this new market in the third quarter rather than the fourth. This action would not simply displace sales from one quarter to another since strong demand for the product can reasonably be expected to continue throughout the remainder of the year. Assuming this alternative is implemented, Mary stated that third-quarter sales of tackle boxes will be between 7,200 and 11,600 units. Whereas she previously had said there was only a 20% chance of achieving the target of 8,100 units, she now believes there are about 8 chances out of 10 that a favorable sales variance will occur on this product. However, third-quarter advertising expenses are expected to be $1,600 higher and other selling expenses $500 higher than their frozen values in Exhibit 28.9.

Paul voiced concern as soon as he heard that sales could increase by as much as 3,000 units over the original range, stating that production did not have enough inventory to meet this much demand and that customer service would deteriorate as a result. Everyone agreed this could not be tolerated, especially when opening up a new market. At that point Carl suggested building inventory during the first several weeks of the quarter by manufacturing the product on an overtime basis. This seemed feasible, so Paul re-assessed the variable cost of tackle boxes to reflect this additional labor. He concluded that, spread over all units of the product, the variable cost in the third quarter would be somewhere between $5.50 and $5.80 per unit. This would make his $5.41 target unfavorably infeasible, but this alternative plan must be judged on the basis of what is best for the entire budget center: Will it improve the odds of reaching the bottom line goal?

The revised values of the four elements affected by this proposed change in tactics are

Description of Element	Original Target	Confidence Factor	Lowest Estimate	Highest Estimate	Frozen Value
Tackle boxes—unit sales	8,100	80%	7,200	11,600	
Tackle boxes—variable cost	5.41	0%	5.50	5.80	
Advertising	9,000				9,800
Other selling expenses	6,000				5,900
Net income before taxes	50,000	?	?	?	

Exhibit 28.11. Fishing Supplies Company—management's assessment of third quarter, based on introducing tackle boxes into Dallas market

NET INCOME BEFORE TAXES			PROBABILITY OF ACHIEVING TARGET
LOWEST $32,930	TARGET $50,000	HIGHEST $81,530	56%

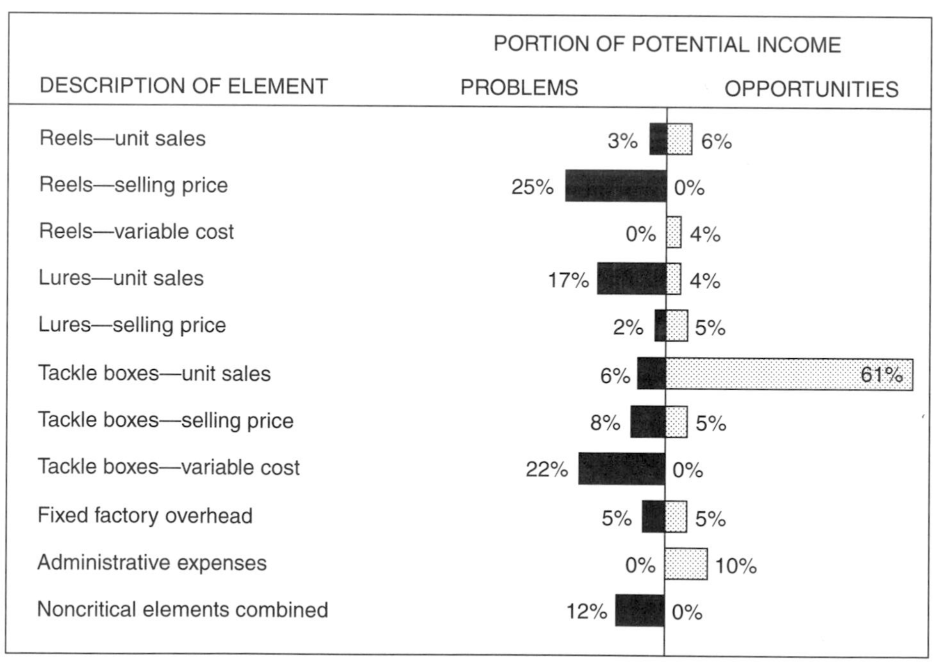

Exhibit 28.12. Fishing Supplies Company—results of computer simulation of third quarter, based on introducing tackle boxes into Dallas market

shown in Exhibit 28.11. The assessments of all other elements remain unchanged. Using these new data, the computer again simulated the third quarter, but on the assumption that management would implement this alternative plan. One thousand samples were again taken. The results are given in Exhibit 28.12.

The chance of achieving the third-quarter pretax income goal is now 56% and, as is evident from the increases in the lowest and highest pretax figures, the entire income profile has shifted upward. The potential income problem associated with unit sales of tackle boxes is significantly less than it was before. In fact, this element now represents the largest potential income opportunity. As had been expected, the variable cost of tackle boxes rose on the problem list; of all remaining potential income problems, 22% can be attributed to this element alone. The unfavorable reassessments of advertising and other sales expenses are also apparent in the shifting of the noncritical elements into the problem column. Obviously, however, all of these unfavorable changes are more than offset by the improvement in unit sales of tackle boxes.

Upon studying the results shown in Exhibit 28.12, the management team decided to investigate the advisability of increasing the selling price of reels, the top remaining potential problem. Gene noted from Exhibit 28.8 that the 1% impact for the selling price of reels is $1,238 whereas the 1% impact for their unit sales is $287. Since the ratio of these two impacts is about 4.3 to 1, this means that the bottom line churn from a 1% increase in the product's selling price is 4.3 times greater than that due to a 1% increase (or decrease) in its unit sales. Roughly speaking, this means that management can increase selling price by 1%, lose as much as 4.3% in unit sales, and still stay even at the bottom line.

Carl reminded everyone that such a conclusion is correct only if the relatively small effect of the joint change in both price and demand is ignored. (The bottom-line effect of this joint change becomes significant for larger changes in price. For example, it would be incorrect to use the ratio of 4.3 to 1 to conclude that management can increase the selling price by 10%, lose as much as 43% in unit sales, and still stay even at the bottom line.) Since Gene and Mary were contemplating a price increase of 10%, Carl used a joint effects formula to quickly determine that 30.1% is the maximum decrease in demand that could be tolerated without eroding the bottom line.

Mary was delighted to learn this because she had already estimated that a 10% price increase on reels would result in a maximum decrease of 12% in unit sales. In fact, she felt that the decrease could be as low as 4%.

The management team therefore decided to evaluate this alternative. The previous range for the selling price of reels was revised to show a 10% price increase of $1.86 per reel; thus, the previous lowest and highest estimates were each increased by this amount. This resulted in a lowest estimate that was greater than the target, thus making the confidence factor 100% on the selling price of reels. To reduce the previous range for unit sales of reels, Mary reduced the previous lowest estimate by 12%, making it 5,720 units; similarly, she reduced the previous highest estimate by 4%, making it 7,680 units. She then felt there would only be 1 chance in 10 of having a favorable variance in unit sales on this product.

These two new ranges pertaining to the alternative of increasing the selling price of reels are given in Exhibit 28.13. One thousand samples were taken based upon the second alternative plan—introduce tackle boxes into Dallas *and* raise the selling price of reels. The results of the computer simulation are shown in Exhibit 28.14.

Obviously, these results indicate that a 10% increase in the selling price of reels should be implemented as soon as possible since, all things considered, the probability of Fishing Supplies achieving its targeted bottom line is increased to an enviable 93%. The income profiles of the original and two alternative plans are graphically compared in Exhibit 28.15. After the management team reviewed these results early this morning, all agreed that the alternative plan must be adopted. Mary prepared a formal announcement of the impending changes for the field sales force and then everyone moved into high gear for

Description of Element	Original Target	Confidence Factor	Lowest Estimate	Highest Estimate	Frozen Value
Reels—unit sales	7,300	10%	5,720	7,680	
Reels—selling price	18.63	100%	19.91	20.41	
Net income before taxes	50,000	?	?	?	

Exhibit 28.13. Fishing Supplies Company—management's assessment of third quarter, based on introducing tackle boxes into Dallas market and increasing the selling price of reels

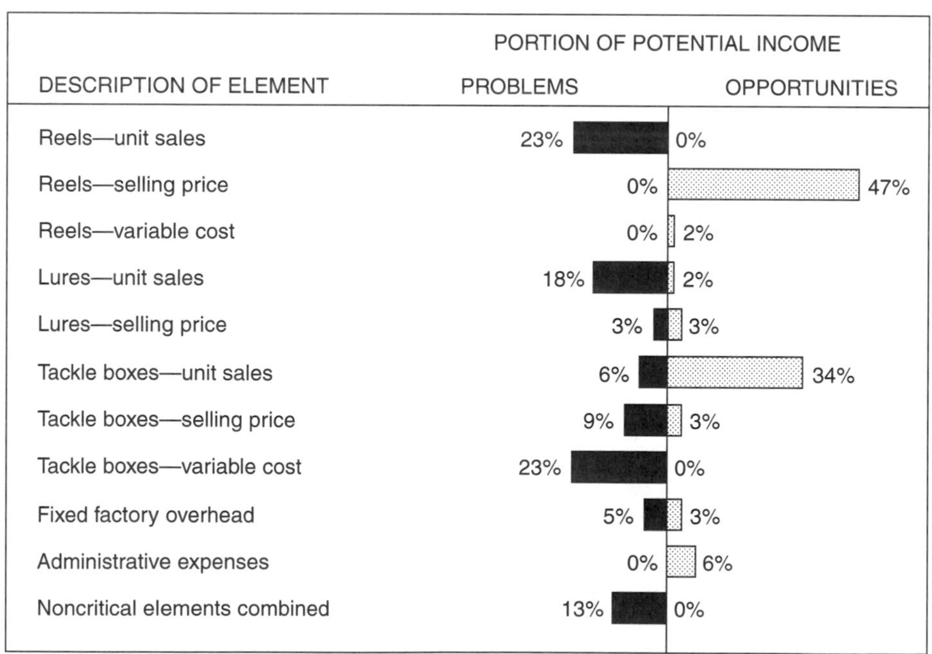

Exhibit 28.14. Fishing Supplies Company—results of computer simulation of third quarter, based on introducing tackle boxes into Dallas market and increasing the selling price of reels

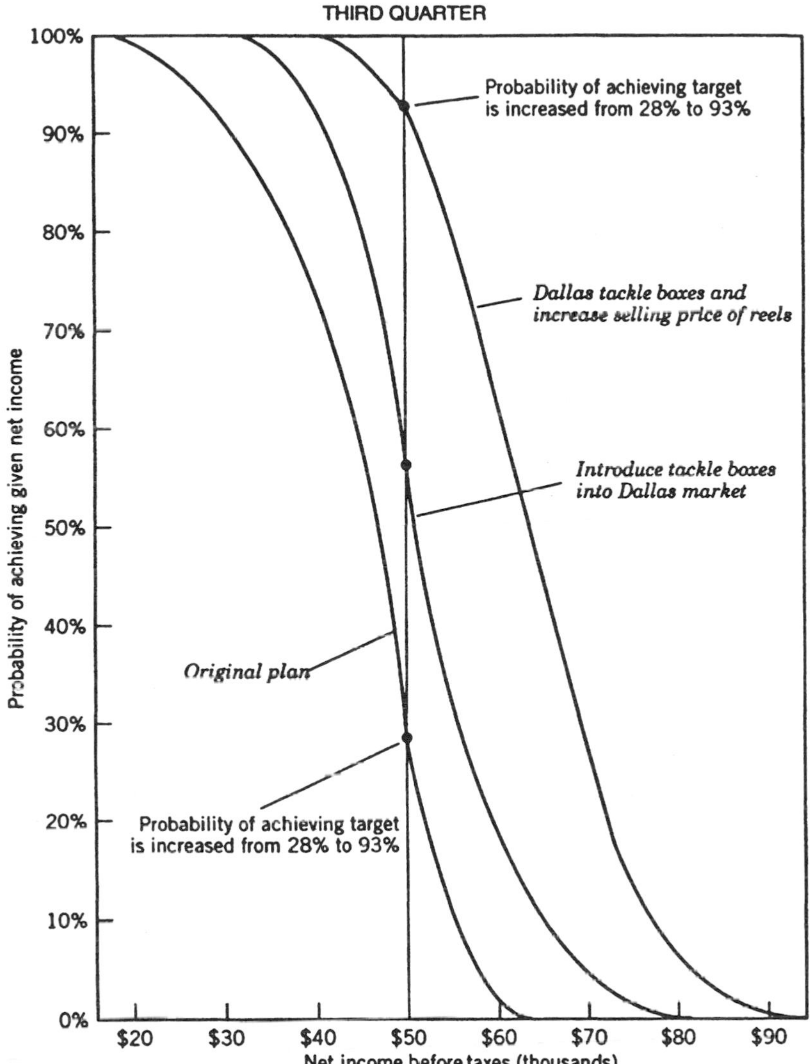

Exhibit 28.15. Fishing Supplies Company—income profiles of third quarter

introducing tackle boxes into the Dallas market and increasing the selling price of reels. By concentrating on the residual problems indicated in Exhibit 28.14 they might well have been able to develop another alternative to further improve the odds for success. For brevity's sake, however, it is assumed that no other options were available.

(e) Tracking and Feedback Mechanism. Fishing Supplies' third quarter came to an end about 10 days ago. Today the management team is reviewing the results summarized in Exhibit 28.16. The actual pretax income of $54,803 exceeded the target by nearly 10%. The income forecast of $62,264 was determined by the tactical budgeting model using the data shown in the forecast column of the exhibit. (The forecast column reflects introducing tackle boxes into the Dallas market and increasing the selling price of reels.) The difference between the forecast and actual pretax income is shown in the last column as

Description of Element	Unit	Original Target	Forecast	Actual	Error at Bottom Line
Rods—unit sales	ea.	2,800	2,600	2,561	$ 143+
Rods—selling price	$/ea.	9.43	9.58	9.47	260+
Rods—variable cost	$/ea.	5.01	5.05	5.02	78−
Reels—unit sales	ea.	7,300	6,829	6,574	1,376+
Reels—selling price	$/ea.	18.63	20.16	20.33	1,056−
Reels—variable cost	$/ea.	13.02	12.95	12.86	615−
Lures—unit sales	doz.	8,300	8,190	8,024	1,522+
Lures—selling price	$/doz.	22.94	22.99	22.95	298+
Lures—variable cost	$/doz.	11.77	11.75	11.79	328+
Bait buckets—unit sales	ea.	2,100	2,100	1,935	367+
Bait buckets—selling price	$/ea.	5.72	5.72	5.67	96+
Bait buckets—variable cost	$/ea.	2.98	2.98	3.04	126+
Minnow traps—unit sales	ea.	4,600	3,900	3,764	144+
Minnow traps—selling price	$/ea.	4.26	4.35	4.31	142+
Minnow traps—variable cost	$/ea.	2.86	2.90	2.89	39−
Tackle boxes—unit sales	ea.	8,100	8,995	8,879	849+
Tackle boxes—selling price	$/ea.	14.27	14.25	14.03	1,801+
Tackle boxes—variable cost	$/ea.	5.41	5.65	5.78	1,169+
Fixed factory overhead	$	90,000	89,800	89,603	197−
Commissions (% of sales)	%	9.0	9.0	9.0	0
Advertising	$	9,000	9,800	9,855	55+
Other selling expenses	$	6,000	5,900	6,294	394+
Administrative expenses	$	32,000	30,750	30,778	28+
Other income	$	3,000	3,400	3,512	112−
Other expense	$	1,000	1,000	1,473	473+
Error due to joint effects					13−
Net income before taxes	$	50,000	62,264	54,803	$ 7,461+

Exhibit 28.16. Fishing Supplies Company—tracking data on third quarter

$7,461+, signifying that the forecasted income overestimated the actual bottom line by $7,461. In turn, this $7,461 overestimate is traced back to individual elements. (All figures shown in the "Error at Bottom Line" column are pretax income dollars. Plus signs denote overestimates and minus signs underestimates.)

The forecast figure given for each noncritical element is simply the value at which management froze that element for the simulation. In the case of a critical element, the forecast value shown is the weighted average of the element's range. In other words, if an infinite number of values were scientifically sampled from within the range, the average of those values would be identical to what is labeled as the element's forecast value in Exhibit 28.16. This figure may also be thought of as the range's center of gravity. By comparing it to the element's actual value, it can be quickly determined whether the manager who prepared the range was optimistic or pessimistic about the element's performance.

For example, the forecast for sales of tackle boxes was 8,995 units. This is 116 units greater than the actual of 8,879. Thus, Mary was somewhat optimistic about third-quarter unit sales of the product. (Perhaps the Dallas market was not quite as large as anticipated.) This overestimate of 116 units of tackle boxes was traced all the way to the bottom line and, in effect, was found to have overestimated pretax income by the $849 figure shown. Conversely, the selling price of reels was underestimated, which in turn underestimated pretax income by $1,056.

By monitoring this tracking information quarter by quarter, managers can identify any bias that might be consistently present in the range estimates of any critical element. Such undue optimism or pessimism may then be tempered by adjustments in the future ranges for that element. By identifying those elements that contributed large errors in the forecast of the bottom line, management can give them the additional attention they deserve when they are ranged in future quarters. This is particularly helpful to new managers who are trying to get a better grip on their operations.

28.5 BRACKET BUDGETING IN ANNUAL PLANNING.

The traditional approach to annual profit planning generally involves preparation of a ''realistic'' budget. But what is realistic? In the marketing function it may mean a pretax goal that management is 50% confident of achieving. In the financial area it may mean a target that has a 75% chance of attainment. If ''realistic'' means a 50% confidence factor, then it would seem that all elements in the budget should be targeted at the 50% confidence level. However, this rarely results in what is expected; the probability of meeting the targeted bottom line may be substantially lower or higher than 50%. If all elements are targeted at the 75% confidence level, the resultant pretax target would have nearly a 100% chance of attainability and correspondingly would probably not represent an acceptable level of performance. Thus, management must grapple with the problem of balancing the planned profit with the chance of attaining that profit. If the latter is not measured in critical budget centers, top management is flying blind. Measuring this uncertainty not only results in a clearer and more realistic portrayal of the coming fiscal year, it also provides for more effective communication among the members of the management team.

The application of bracket budgeting in annual planning is similar to its use in budgetary control. The primary purposes are to maximize the odds of achieving an acceptable profit and to identify potential profit problems and opportunities. Instead of dealing with quarterly figures, however, the elements' proposed annual targets are evaluated. By addressing the annual planning problem in this manner, management can easily test many different alternatives, thus eliminating the need to prepare two or more budgets before the final version is approved. This tends to streamline the planning process and reduce managerial frustration.

28.6 CONSOLIDATING INCOME STATEMENTS.

Although its application is selective at the budget center level, bracket budgeting may be used to present a unified picture of an entire division by linking together its budget centers, including those operating with conventional budgeting only. Likewise, a composite of the entire company may be obtained by chaining together all of its divisions and corporate overhead departments, even though some of those units may not be using bracket budgeting.

Exhibit 28.17 demonstrates the manner in which such a consolidation is made. In this example, the Fun Time Company, a hypothetical corporation, consists of 11 critical budget centers. Next year's income profile of each was used as input for a computer simulation of corporate earnings per share. As a result, it was determined that there is a 72% chance that next year's earnings per share will be at least as much as the $1.27 target. As is also noted, three profit centers collectively account for 68% of all potential corporate earnings problems next fiscal year. If management wishes to be more confident with its forecast, the appropriate figure can readily be found in the earnings per share profile (not shown).

ANNUAL EARNINGS PER SHARE			PROBABILITY OF ACHIEVING TARGET
LOWEST	TARGET	HIGHEST	
$1.10	$1.27	$1.45	72%

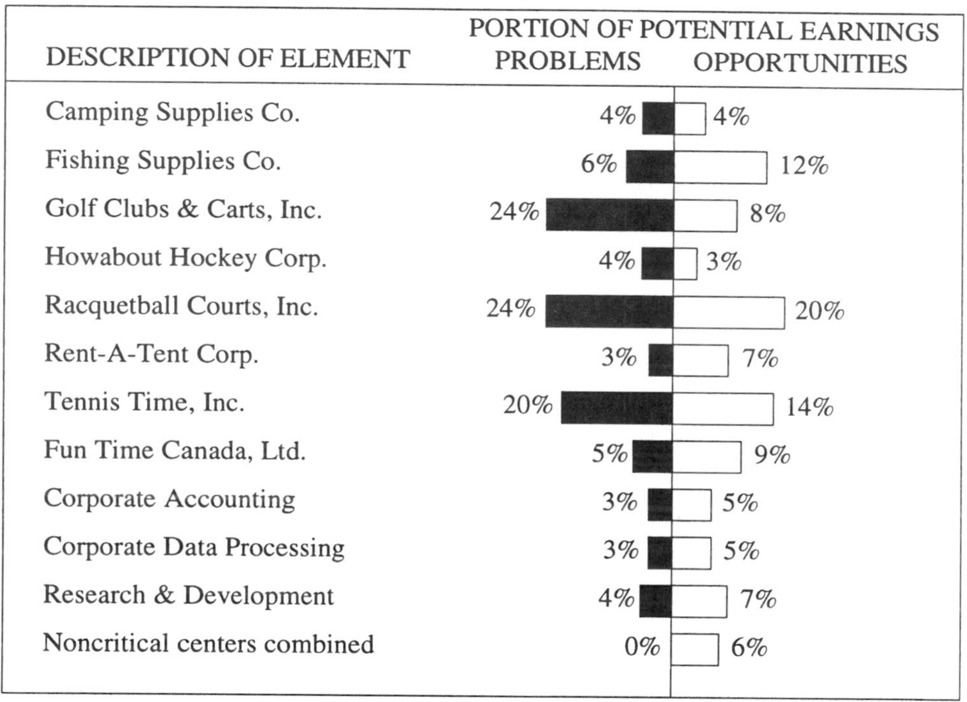

Exhibit 28.17. The Fun Time Company—results of computer simulation of next fiscal year

For example, management can be 90% confident that next year's earnings will be at least $1.22 per share.

28.7 SUMMARY OF BENEFITS. When it is properly implemented and applied, bracket budgeting:

- Recognizes the unique nature of any given business. The tactical budgeting model is tailored to the specific needs of management.
- Is an early warning system. Potential earnings problems and opportunities are identified well in advance. In other words, management can act rather than react.
- Enables management to establish a list of decision priorities to influence future earnings performance.
- Minimizes the amount of information presented to management for decision making. The more complex the business (e.g., many products, varying gross profit percentages), the more beneficial it is.

- Complements, not replaces or alters, conventional methods of budgeting.
- Integrates easily with all costing methods—standard, direct, activity based, and so forth.
- Capitalizes not only on what management knows about the future but also on what management knows it does not know.
- Has tutorial feedback mechanisms to assist managers in refining their future inputs. This is particularly helpful to newly appointed managers who have significant bottom line responsibilities.
- Allows tactical budgeting models to be developed very rapidly, many times within a matter of hours. Consequently, for the few times that they require changes, models can be revised in minimal time.
- Requires no understanding of higher mathematics or computer programming to be used effectively.

28.8 SUMMARY. In some firms, the application of bracket budgeting would be equivalent to killing a fly with an elephant gun. In others, the sole use of conventional budgeting is not unlike trying to kill an elephant with a fly swatter. For businesses in which major uncertainties can play havoc with the bottom line, bracket budgeting provides management with the means to cope effectively with the problems that such uncertainties pose and with little more effort than is currently exerted.

SOURCES AND SUGGESTED READINGS

''Automation No Panacea for Estimating Problems,'' *Architects' Office Management & Administration Report,* vol. 89-9, 1989, pp. 8–9.

''Computer-Assisted Estimating System Yields Odds on Problems and Profits,'' *Engineering News-Record,* vol. 196, no. 4, January 22, 1976, pp. 32A,32D.

Curran, K. M., ''Range Estimating: User Friendly Risk Analysis,'' *Proceedings,* First Congress on Computing in Civil Engineering, American Society of Civil Engineers, 1994.

Curran, K. M., and W. P. Rowland, ''Range Estimating in Value Engineering,'' *Transactions,* American Association of Cost Engineers, 1991, pp. G.3.1–G.3.5.

Curran, M. W., ''Range Estimating: Betting on the Bottom Line,'' *St. Louis Computing,* vol. 8, no. 3, August 1990, pp. 13–14.

Curran, M. W., ''Range Estimating Reduces Iatrogenic Risk,'' *Transactions,* American Association of Cost Engineers, 1990, pp. K.3.1–K.3.3.

Curran, M. W., ''Range Estimating: User Friendly Risk Analysis,'' *Proceedings,* Project Management Institute, 1989, pp. 64–71.

Curran, M. W., ''Range Estimating: Contingencies with Confidence,'' *Transactions,* American Association of Cost Engineers, 1989, pp. B.7.1–B.7.4.

Curran, M. W., ''Range Estimating,'' *Cost Engineering,* vol. 31, no. 3, March 1989, pp. 18–26.

Curran, M. W., ''Range Estimating: Reasoning with Risk,'' *Transactions,* American Association of Cost Engineers, 1988, pp. N.3.1–N.3.9.

Curran, M. W., ''Range Estimating: Conquerng the Cost Overrun,'' *DE Technology,* vol. 49, no. 3, March 1988, pp. 10–14.

Curran, M. W., ''Range Estimatingon Your PC,'' *Constructor,* vol. 68, no. 8, August 1986, pp. 30–32.

Curran, M. W., ''Using PCs to Avoid Construction Cost Overruns,'' *Baltimore Business Journal,* vol. 4, no. 5, July 14-20, 1986, p. 11B.

Curran, M. W., "Range Estimating Operating & Manufacturing Costs," *Transactions,* American Association of Cost Engineers, 1986, pp. F.1.1–F.1.8.

Curran, M. W., "Range Estimating Takes Gamble out of Building," *St. Louis Business Journal,* vol. 6, no. 21, February 17-23, 1986, p. 20C.

Curran, M. W., "Range Estimating for Plaudits and Profits," *Gateway Engineer,* vol. 65, no. 10, November 1985, pp. 10–12.

Curran, M. W., "Range Estimating and Profits," *Washington U. Construction Management Center News Letter,* vol. 1, no. 3, Fall-Winter 1985, pp. 1,3.

Curran, M. W., "Range Estimating—Coping with Uncertainty," *Transactions,* American Association of Cost Engineers, 1976, pp. 366–372.

Curran, M. W., "Range Estimating and Uncertainty," *Proceedings, Engineering News-Record* Cost Technology Conference, 1975, pp. 25–38.

Curran, M. W., "How Bracket Budgeting Helps Managers Cope with Uncertainty," Part 2, *Management Review*, vol. 64, no. 5, May 1975, pp. 16–24.

Curran, M. W., "How Bracket Budgeting Helps Managers Cope with Uncertainty," Part 1, *Management Review*, vol. 64, no. 4, April 1975, pp. 4–15.

Curran, M. W., "A Scientific Approach to Bidding: Range Estimating," *Constructor*, vol. 57, no. 1, January 1975, pp. 17–33.

Dickinson, C. H., and C. R. Hendrix, "Risk and Opportunity Analysis using Range Estimating Program," internal report of STEARNS CATALYTIC CORP., Charlotte, NC, 1979.

Doris, V. K., "Estimators Evaluate Automation," *Engineering News-Record,* vol. 223, no. 11, 1989, pp. 32–34.

"Engineers Can Reduce Risks in Estimating," *Midwest Engineer,* vol. 39, no. 5, January 1987, pp. 15–16.

Frassoni, di A., "Quando L'incertezza e il Nemico da Battere," *Espansione,* no. 140, January 1982, pp. 42–47.

Harris-Stewart, C., "Method Reduces Bid Risk," *Engineering News-Record,* vol. 221, no. 5, 1988, pp. 23,26.

Hertz, D. B., "Risk Analysis in Capital Investment," *Harvard Business Review,* vol. 57, no. 5, September–October 1979, pp. 169–182.

"Improving the Accuracy of Early Cost Estimates for Federal Construction Projects," Building Research Board, National Research Council, National Academies of Science & Engineering, National Academy Press, Washington, DC, 1990.

"Improving Your Odds in the Business Gamble," *Office Products,* vol. 132, no. 11, December 1, 1970, pp. 24–28.

Konieczynski, R. D., and D. J. Aleman, "Range Estimating Solves Tunnel Machine Builder's Estimating Problem," internal report of Atlas Copco Jarva Inc., Solon, OH, 1982.

Lewis, L., "Range Estimating," *Advanced Management Journal,* vol. 45, Spring 1981.

Lewis, L., "Range Estimating–Managing Uncertainty," AACE (American Association of Cost Engineers) Bulletin, November–December 1977, pp. 205–207.

"Management of Project Risks and Uncertainties," report by Construction Industry Institute, University of Texas, Austin, TX, 1989.

"Modern Management Systems: A Construction Industry Cost Effectiveness Project Report," The Business Roundtable, New York, NY, Report A-6, November 1982, pp. 2,12,15,16,18,34.

"New Estimating Technique Uses Probability Analysis," *Contractor,* vol. 35, no. 11, November 1988, pp. 8–9.

Poliski, I., "Improving the Odds in the Business Gamble," *Business Automation,* vol. 17, no. 8 August 1970, pp. 30–34.

"Quantifying Error Improves Estimates," *St. Louis Construction News & Review,* vol. 10, no. 4, April 19, 1978, p. 17.

"Range Estimating Gains Support," *Engineering News-Record,* vol. 213, no. 12, September 20, 1984, p. 106.

''Range Estimating Provides an Edge in Running the Race Against Risk,'' *Engineering News-Record,* vol. 198, no. 25, June 23, 1977, pp. 94–99.

''Risk Management in Capital Projects,'' report by Construction Industry Institute, University of Texas, Austin, TX, 1988.

True, N. F., and R. A. Barry, ''Contemporary Estimating,'' report by Sargent & Lundy Engineers, Chicago IL., presented at the American Power Conference, Chicago, IL., April 22–24, 1985.

Weaver, M. R., ''Improved Estimating Practices using Range Estimating Decision Technology,'' M.S.C.E. thesis, University of Maryland, Baltimore, MD, 1989.

Welker, H. J., ''Range Estimating as a Project Management Tool,'' *Engineering and Contract Record,* June 1978, pp. 26–27.

Welker, H. J., ''Range Estimating: An Owner's Experience,'' *Constructor,* vol. 59, no. 8, August 1997, pp. 20–22.

CHAPTER 29

BUDGETING FOR TOTAL QUALITY MANAGEMENT

Ronald A. Follett

RF Group, Inc.

29.1 INTRODUCTION. The purpose of this chapter is to provide a basic foundation for an understanding of total quality management (TQM) and the model for the development of a budgeting system which reflects implementation and maintenance costs and tracks benefits.

Total quality management came on the scene more than a decade ago as the great elixir for a struggling industrial atmosphere. Most of the known, and many other not-so-well-known, experts got into the game and developed books and programs for every need. For those who fit TQM to their business and worked at it, the results were reflected in growth and profits for the business. The initial successes within the industrial environment prompted other types of organizations to get into TQM and adapt the programs to their functions and infrastructure. Soon, schools, hospitals, government, nonprofit service organizations, and others were working their continuous improvement activities with their empowered employee teams. Through all of this, though, little had been developed or implemented related to the budgeting impacts on the organization. This chapter puts this into perspective.

(a) Brief History of Total Quality Management. Although the TQM acronym is relatively new, the principles and concepts have been around and in practice much longer. Dr. Joseph Juran, many years ago, noted in his *Quality Manual:*

> A key dimension of the management *process* is the establishment and maintenance of a work *climate* that encourages and makes it possible for *workers* to behave in ways that contribute to effective individuals and organizational performance. Only management can create the conditions which enable workers to control the process over which they preside and participate with management in projects that seek to achieve breakthrough to new quality levels.[1]

That is what TQM is really all about: empowering employees to improve the process and creating a culture that encourages error-free performance. The exact chronology of TQM is probably less important than the factors that combined to cause it to come on the scene. Key among these factors are two major changes in the international and domestic industry

[1] Juran, J. M., *Quality Control Handbook,* 4th ed. (New York: McGraw Hill, 1988).

environment: (1) the end of the Cold War, with the result that a major part of industry found that its primary customer was no longer the U.S. government, and (2) the recognition that quality of products and quality of management performance were essential for the new customer base (the public consumer).

(b) Why Total Quality Management Was Developed. During that period of time, many publications and spokespersons expounded the values of excellence: *In Search of Excellence,* by Tom Peters[2]; *Quality is Free,* by Philip Crosby[3]; and *Iacocca,* by Lee Iacocca[4]; as well as books more specifically related to quality by Deming, Juran, Feigenbaum, and others less well known. This proliferation of information and insight, combined with visible support by the United States demonstrated with its announcement of the Malcolm Baldrige Award for Quality Excellence, demanded a ''program.'' This program became known as TQM.

(c) TQM the Acronym. One of the confusing areas of the business culture is the use of acronyms and their meaning. For the purpose of simplicity within this chapter, *TQM* means total quality management (continuous improvement of the management process toward the goal of perfection). If we consider that the management process consists of strategic activities and operational activities (implementation of strategies), TQM focuses primarily on the operational activities.

It is also worth noting that TQM is today's acronym. Other acronyms that existed in the past addressed many of the same issues and techniques (total quality control, quality circles, self-managed teams), and there will be new ones in the future. However, the principles remain the same, and the goal continues to be essential to success.

(d) How Total Quality Management Relates to the Budgeting System. In many ways, the relationship of TQM to the budgeting system is introduced in Chapter 31 on activity-based budgeting, particularly Section 31.2, ''Traditional Budgeting Does Not Support Excellence.'' Total quality management is about creating excellence. Total quality management deals with the development of operating processes, review and continuous improvement of these processes (by utilization of employee-empowered teams), and identification of cost reductions and waste. A major factor in the identification of waste and potential cost reduction is the budget and its related dollar distribution. One of the tools TQM also uses to measure continuous improvement looks very similar to the ''actual vs. budget'' performance reports used in financial tracking.

(e) Key Individual Contributors to Total Quality Management. A chronological review of TQM begins with F. W. Taylor.

(i) Taylor. Taylor really had a negative impact on what has ultimately developed into what we now call TQM. In the early 1900s, he developed and implemented the management control system, which separated the planning function from the execution functions. This resulted in the creation of the specialist and the proliferation of organizations. Although many good things came out of this movement, responsibility and accountability

[2] Tom Peters, *In Search of Excellence* (Harper Row, 1982).

[3] Philip Crosby, *Quality Is Free: The Art of Making Quality Certain* (New York: McGraw-Hill, 1979).

[4] Lee Iacocca, *Iacocca* (New York: Banton, 1984).

for problems were lost by this decentralization. This approach is in direct contrast to TQM, which emphasizes employee responsibility and accountability for problem identification and resolution.

(ii) Deming. Dr. W. Edwards Deming had been on the quality scene for a number of years; however, his prominence developed in the 1950s, when he went to Japan to support the U.S. occupation program. His contribution became critical to all future quality practices. Although his philosophies and total contribution were far reaching, the basics rely on two concepts: Define the process and measure the performance, with emphasis on statistical process control.

(iii) Juran. Dr. Joseph Juran was also involved in the support of the U.S. occupation force, and provided additional concepts that have become key to TQM and other quality programs. One of Juran's contributions has been *The Quality Handbook,* which is essentially the bible for quality. However, his major contribution to the TQM philosophy was insight into the application of teams in the management of quality, and the concept of customer needs and satisfaction in the definition of quality.

(iv) Crosby. Unlike Juran and Deming, Philip Crosby came along after the Japan quality revolution, but Crosby has also had his impact on the quality culture throughout the U.S. environment. He is probably best known for his Quality College, which was established to educate and train industry in quality concepts. The training includes concepts from Juran and Deming and is further supplemented by two major areas of emphasis: utilization of quality motivation and a cultural set that requires performance perfection and rejects a ''good-enough'' philosophy.

(v) Others. Several other individuals and organizations have also contributed to the TQM culture. The basic elements expounded in all of the various quality definitions emphasize the following:

- Utilize employee-empowered teams
- Define and measure the process
- Create a culture that drives continuous improvement to excellence

(vi) Summary of Inputs. All of the identified quality ''gurus'' summarized their quality programs by listing a number of points. Although each listing was different in context, they all essentially emphasize the same basic issues:

- Build a management commitment to continuous improvement for the future
- Create empowerment and teamwork
- Continuously measure the process quality indicators
- Continuously emphasize excellence as the only goal
- Expand training in quality skills

All of their program elements focus on the three basic elements of culture, process, and people, which are the basis of any effective TQM program.

29.2 DEFINITIONS AND CONCEPTS

(a) Unique Language. The language of TQM is not unique in its words, but in their definition and implications within the environment and culture. The following defines some of the common terms used in TQM:

- *TQM.* A system designed to involve all employees in the improvement of the work process. Total quality management involves all employees in improving work effectiveness and output, focuses on customer needs, emphasizes improvement of every company process, and concentrates on process, not end result.
- *Standard.* Perfection; no-fault performance
- *Quality.* Meeting customer requirements and expectations. These requirements generally take on the parameters of timeliness/schedule, performance within resource allocation (manpower and dollar budget), and customer satisfaction.
- *Product.* Any output item or information provided to or used by others
- *Customer.* The receiver of any output or product
- *Empowerment.* Allocation of accountability and responsibility for decisions and changes
- *Core processes.* Processes that are essential to the operation's attaining its goals and objectives
- *Teams.* Employee groups selected and empowered for resolution of a specific issue or problem. Three types of teams are generally formed in the TQM environment: problem-solving teams (selected for a specific problem), task teams (selected to accomplish a specific task), and standing teams (requires specific knowledge in area of involvement).

(b) Defining the Elements. As noted earlier in this chapter, key individual contributors (Juran, Deming, Crosby) stressed three common elements within each of their quality process definitions: culture, process, and people.

- *Culture.* The working environment of the organization, starting with the management message. The end product is not an element of TQM, but is an indicator of the final process output step.
- *Process.* The continuous series of steps or activities by which anything is done
- *People.* The employees, who are the most important resource and provide members for the empowered teams

(c) Understanding the Elements. Although there are only three significant elements, understanding them is critical to a successful TQM program or process. They are further significant to the budgeting process because this is where the expense (investment) occurs, and where the waste and cost reduction are identified.

The *culture* is the environment, the work ethic, the standards, the expectations, and the clear message that exists within the organization for its people. In a TQM program, this culture must clearly state and reinforce the requirement for perfection as the ultimate goal. This must be reinforced by the rewards and recognition program as well as by the performance example of management. It must be clear that continuous improvement in every action and activity is everyone's responsibility.

The *process* of performing any activity is a series of discrete steps or actions that link together to provide an outcome. The approach that TQM utilizes in analyzing these processes is to look separately at each step's inputs and outputs. The aim is to assure perfection at each step in the process. It follows that if each step in the process is done to perfection, the process will be perfect. The concept that requires effort and diligence is the definition of each step in the process.

The *people* are the medium that holds it all together and makes it all happen. The people need to be a part of the changing culture.

- They are the active team members who solve the problems.
- They search for continuous improvement opportunities.
- They define and evaluate the processes.
- They are experts in the execution of the process; that is what they do.
- They want to be the best they can be and to be respected for it.

(d) Benchmarking Relationship to Budgeting and Total Quality Management. A *benchmark,* in its original context, was a reference point used to establish the attitude or base position in a topographical survey. The term has since migrated into business, where it has come to signify a reference point or standard for a process or operation performance. Benchmarking is the continuous, ongoing process of measuring performance against these benchmarks. These benchmarks or standards are key in the development of a budget, because they define the anticipated or planned parameters of operation and resource needs. Development of the budget within the TQM environment drives ''budgeting for perfection'' based on benchmarks for error-free performance. The difference in dollars between the perfection budget and the operating budget identifies the cost of poor quality and the opportunity for improvement.

(e) Core Processes. Knowing and understanding the core processes is essential to defining the operation and identifying opportunities for improvement and cost saving. The *core processes* define activities critical to the daily operation. Although they generally fall into five basic functional categories (the market, the product, the delivery system, the resource base [financial and manpower], and the planning), they diagram the specific implementation processes defined in the mission and the strategic plan. Exhibit 29.1 illustrates the core process family tree by listing the critical functions and the corresponding core processes.

(f) New Paradigms. Industry and organizations are often based on one paradigm: ''That's the way we have always done it.'' To successfully implement TQM and an aggressive budget, the paradigms must be put on the shelf. The new paradigms should be:

- Operational problems can best be recognized and solved by the employees involved in the process, not management.
- Continuous improvement is the responsibility of all employees.
- Self-empowered employee teams are an effective problem-solving tool.

Mission/Vision	
Critical Functions	Core Processes
Market	Market definition
	Market analysis
	Sales strategy
	Advertising and public relations
Product	Product definition
	Product development
	Product control
	Services (internal and external)
Delivery System	Resource needs
	Direct needs
	Support needs
	Capital needs
Resource Base	Financial
	Manpower
	Obtain
	Manage
	Develop
Planning	Past performance review
	Growth goals
	Resource availability and needs
	Organizational inputs

Exhibit 29.1. Core process family tree

- Processes must be measured if consistency in performance is to be attained.
- Excellence is the only acceptable goal.

29.3 APPLYING QUALITY CONCEPTS

(a) Product versus Process. The application of quality concepts to a product rather than a process differs considerably. However, from a wider viewpoint, there are similarities. Because TQM is focused on the process, it is important to understand how basic quality concepts apply.

- Product quality is based on performance as measured against end product performance standards.
- Process quality is based on the outputs of each step as measured against a defined benchmark for that step.

The marked difference is that product quality is measured on the end item, whereas the process is measured against the established benchmarks for each of the individual steps. This is true whether the end item is a hard item or a service product output. Those of us involved in the product manufacturing industry are all aware of the process control charts present on the factory floor; those charts graphically indicate the results of that step in the process as measured against upper and lower control limits. This is generally referred to as *total quality control.* When these methods are applied to a management process, it

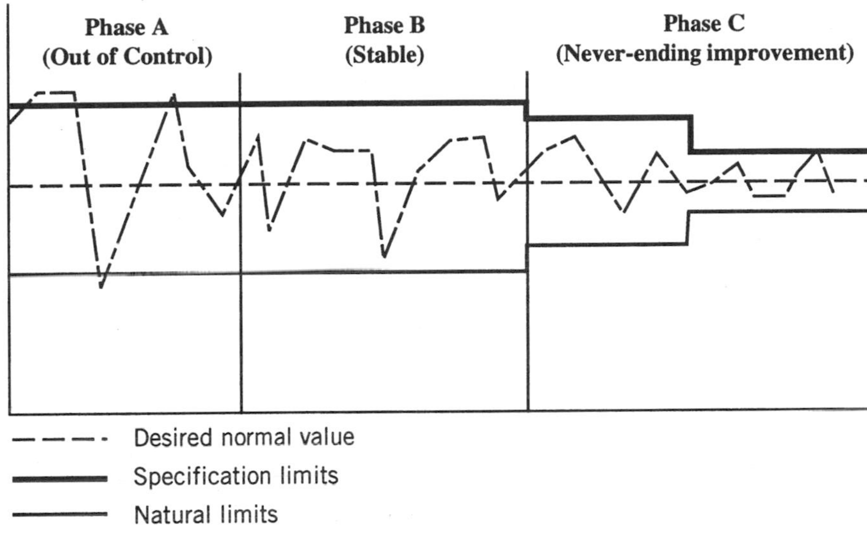

Exhibit 29.2. Process control chart

becomes TQM. We are also aware that product quality generally refers to the resultant end product of a factory process. However, very few, if any, have ever seen similar process control charts for operational processes such as purchasing, the planning process, service performance, or other operational processes. These operational process controls are the ones that TQM measures and identifies as opportunities for improvement and cost savings. An example of a process control chart is shown in Exhibit 29.2.

(b) Manufacturing versus Nonmanufacturing Processes. Manufacturing processes are generally considered to define the movement of a product through assembly, test, and shipment. These process steps tend to be tangible, with a product that can be viewed as it progresses. Other characteristics of the manufacturing process are that it tends to be very machine intensive, with people in a support role. Manufacturing is also a repetitive process in which a product that is designed is repeatedly produced in some defined volume.

The product of a nonmanufacturing process generally is less tangible, such as advice, counsel, service, or products that develop through a natural process that does not involve people. Nonmanufacturing by its nature is defined in its entirety by a series of steps, and is almost totally people intensive. See Exhibit 29.3 for an example of the purchasing function. The basic differences in characteristics are:

- The nonmanufacturing processes are not repetitive in detail.
- They tend not to be machine intensive, but rather people intensive.
- The output is generally unique to a specific situation.

29.4 FOCUSING ON THE CUSTOMER

(a) How to Identify the Customer. To address the issue of the customer, it is first necessary to clearly identify and define that entity. The generic definition used is the end

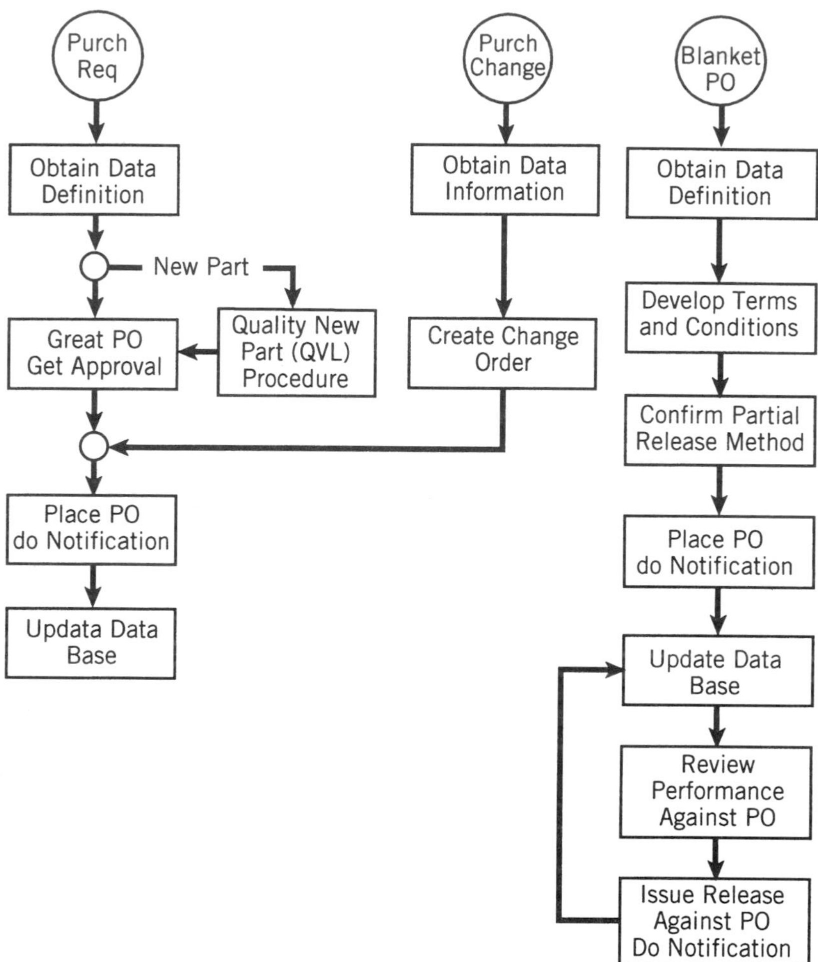

Exhibit 29.3. Flowchart

user of the product. The customer within the end-product environment is the person or function to which the end product is delivered. The customer within the process-sensitive environment is the next person or function in the process. One way to simplify this definition is to isolate a particular function or step in the process and determine the inputs to and the outputs from that entity. The inputs are provided by suppliers and the outputs are provided to customers, as shown in Exhibit 29.4.

(b) How to Understand Customer Expectations. The best answer to this question is to ask the customer. Several tools and techniques can be used to obtain this information:

- Direct interface with agreed-to and documented output
- Regular review of this output with the customer

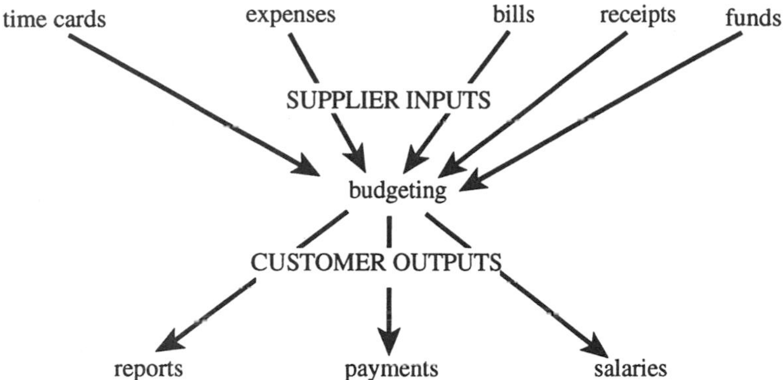

Exhibit 29.4. Customer–supplier relationship

- Periodic customer survey
- Mutual definition of benchmarks
- Evaluation of customer complaints and returns

The emphasis should be on the effort to obtain information.

(c) Use of Benchmarking to Understand Customer Expectations. By definition, benchmarks are derived from the best, world-class performance. The customer determines whether performance is the best by acceptance or rejection of it. Therefore, the benchmarks are customer driven and describe customer expectations and acceptance.

29.5 TOTAL QUALITY MANAGEMENT MODEL

(a) Basis for the Model. The following three assumptions form the basis of this model and its related implementation plan:

1. It is essential for management to understand, accept, and support the program.
2. Total quality management is not an automatic fit in all operations. The program must be made to fit the industry and the specific organization.
3. The program must be adapted to identified policies, processes, and problem areas.

(b) Characteristics of the Model

(i) Audit. The first activity necessary in implementation of the TQM program is the audit. This involves two distinct types of review and analysis, one that is used to evaluate the human elements of the organization and another that is used to evaluate performance and business stability of the organization.

The employee audit involves a series of interviews with a cross-section of the employee and management base. There are several reasons for this activity, but the major goal is to determine the personality of the organization. Properly executed, it will identify the following:

- Leadership goals as related to commitment to continuous improvement
- Skills, attitudes, and commitment of key personnel

Personnel attributes:
  Name
  Education (primary, secondary, other)
  Work experience (last three positions or last ten years)
  Related skills
Organizational attributes
  Position in the organization
  Reports to/number of reports
  Primary involvement
Goals and plans
  Personal goals
  Plans within the organization/company
  Present activities in support of goals (education, skills training, etc.)
What items or issues prevent excellence in performance?
  What is being done on individual basis?
  What organizational changes would you make?
  What policies and procedures should be changed?
General comments regarding position, organization, personnel interfaces, etc.

Exhibit 29.5. Employee audit checklist

- Evaluation of "right people in correct position"
- Current status and depth of planning efforts
- Identification of issues that prevent people from performing their jobs

The interviews and the resultant audit report should focus on who they are, what they do, how they do it, and what opportunities for improvement exist. Exhibit 29.5 is an example of an employee audit checklist and should be addressed in the interview.

The business audit involves the review and analysis of business characteristics and the effectiveness of the organization. This involves three types of business indicators: financial, organizational, and performance against industry benchmarks. Examples of these audit items are listed Exhibit 29.6. This audit provides critical information on organizational effectiveness and ability to take on the challenges of a TQM program.

(ii) Total Quality Management Program Management. The TQM program management for a specific operation is established outside of the normal management structure. It is essential that this not become another management program, but that it be identified from its inception as an employee empowerment action. Therefore, management of the program is by a steering committee with membership from all employee levels. The chairperson is the TQM coordinator and becomes the primary interface to management and the outside world. The steering committee has the responsibility of defining the mission statement for the program, defining the policies and procedures for operation, and managing the overall TQM program.

(iii) Mission/Vision Statement. The mission/vision statement establishes a focus for the program and also provides a visible indicator on which the organization can focus. The mission/vision statement essentially defines the organization's focus on excellence. It is brief, inspiring, clear, and challenging, is about excellence, and provides a constant challenge.

Financial indicators
- Income
- Budgeting and management of financial resources
- Cash flow
- Outstanding financial liabilities

Organizational
- Management levels
- Levels of authority
- Accountability delegation
- Communication

Performance
- Schedule conformance
- Budget performance
- Customer satisfaction
- Other strategic goals

Exhibit 29.6. Business audit items

(iv) The Infrastructure. A key part of the continuous improvement process is the empowered employee teams. These are groups of employees that analyze, evaluate, and develop solutions for the problems that impede perfectly performing processes. These teams are selected by the steering committee based on their involvement and knowledge of the process. They are selected from all levels of the employee strata and are given the power to work as a team in resolving the issues and developing a solution.

(v) Core Processes. Total quality management is about continuous improvement of the operational processes; therefore, it is necessary that those processes be identified. The most important processes are those that define the essential or *core* activities of the organization. These are generally identified in the critical goals reflected in the strategic plan and are classified as the core processes. From this base, the initial opportunities are selected for empowered employee teams to develop improvements.

- *Developing core processes*

  The determination and definition of the core processes are initiated with an analysis of the mission and goals of the organization, which are developed as part of the strategic plan activity. The strategic plan will define the product, the market, and the strategy.

  In developing the core processes, it is necessary to work the sequence from the top down. It starts with the mission statement, which defines the reason for existence and the vision of future goals. If this does not exist, it must be created. Evaluation and review of the mission and visions will allow the organization to define the product, the market, the delivery system, the resources (financial and manpower), and the planning process. In each of these critical functional categories, there are a number of activities and processes that must occur to support the mission and vision. These processes provide the listing which, when prioritized, identifies the core processes.
- *Determination of core processes*

  The *core processes* are defined as those activities critical to the success of the strategy implementation. Although this process of determining the core processes sounds easy, experience has demonstrated that it is one of the more difficult activities. The major reason seems to be that people and organizations do not often try to think about what they actually do for a living. One of the more effective methods seems to be the combination of brainstorming and workshop session with key employees. Exhibit 29.7 illustrates examples of core processes by types of industry.

- *Mapping the process* (see Exhibit 29.3)

  Mapping of the core processes will result in a pictorial representation (process flowchart) of the steps involved. Accurately accomplishing this generally involves interviews and brainstorming sessions with the people who actively participate in the process. As each step is developed, four parameters must evolve: what is done, who does it, how it is done, and when it is done.

(vi) Benchmarking. The benchmarking of each core process is an essential part of the TQM model, in that it defines the numerical goal for that process activity based on the performance of top-of-the-class operation, or the best process capability. The benchmark establishes the standard of performance for excellence, creates the baseline against which the process improvements will be measured, and becomes the barometer of success, as shown in Exhibits 29.8 and 29.9.

Industry	Core processes
Manufacturing	Design product
	Market and sell
	Procure materials and services
	Provide competent staff
	Manage financial solvency
	Plan for future
Construction	Estimate jobs
	Buy out materials and services
	Manage projects
	Provide competent manpower
	Manage financial solvency
	Plan for future
Health care	Determine population market
	Educate market
	Service market
	Support regulations (state and federal)
	Provide competent staff
	Maintain financial solvency
	Plan for future

Exhibit 29.7. Examples of core processes

Competition
Process capability studies
Previous performance
Industry studies

Exhibit 29.8. Sources of benchmarks

Industry	Process	Benchmarks
Manufacturing	Product design	Time to market Conformance to product cost
	Marketing/sales	Cost of sales % of market
	Procurement	Materials cost vs. goal Materials availability to manufacturing
Construction	Job estimating	Capture rate Estimate vs. budget vs. completion cost
	Buy out of materials	Availability vs. need Cost vs. budget
	Project management	Scope (number of jobs) % completion to budget and schedule
Health care	Service the market	Cost per client % market serviced Customer satisfaction index

Exhibit 29.9. Examples of benchmarks

(vii) Continuous Improvement. The continuous improvement activity is the ongoing process of identifying areas for improvement (reaching for the benchmark), evaluating, modifying, and changing the processes. Within the TQM environment, the continuous improvement process involves:

- Identifying opportunities for improvement
- Selecting and establishing self-empowerment teams
- Evaluating information and data
- Developing solutions and a schedule of plans for improvement
- Implementing the changes and measuring resultant performance

This entire activity is coordinated by the steering committee and conducted in conformance with the policies and procedures.

(viii) Performance Measurement. The performance measurement activity is the ongoing activity of determining actual process performance. This measurement is indexed not only to the benchmarks, but also to previous performance, to ensure that changes are creating positive gains. The other important purpose of the process measurement is to provide positive reinforcement and demonstration of the TQM process. The importance of this activity cannot be overemphasized.

(ix) Performance Reporting. As with any good program, it is essential that activities and progress be reported to the organization and the employees on a regular basis. Many pieces of information can be reported; however, at a minimum, continuous update should be provided on the following:

- Active projects
- Teams and participants

- Schedule of activities
- Copies of proceedings
- Policies and procedures
- Numerical charting and reporting of improvement numerics
- Future opportunities for improvement

In addition to the text reports and information, a number of visual charting techniques are useful in communicating process performance and improvements, as shown in Exhibit 29.10.

29.6 PHASES OF IMPLEMENTATION.

Total quality management is not a process that occurs instantly. The time-consuming part of the program is changing the mindset of the participants and the culture of the company. Experience has shown that from initiation to integration will probably take two years. However, by utilizing the model defined in this chapter, progress and improvement will be occurring during that entire time. To better define the implementation, we have identified six separate phases.

(a) Phase I—Preparation.

If TQM is to be effective and successful, the organization and its management must be ready to accept it and must be organizationally structured to implement it. The purpose of the preparation phase is to evaluate and align the company for this TQM implementation. Three separate, but linked, activities occur during the preparation phase, which essentially includes items (i) through (vi) in the model.

1. *Awareness* presentations are focused on providing senior management and employees with an understanding of quality concepts, principles, and commitment. Although this first phase really occurs prior to actual implementation, it is a critical decision point where management decides to commit to involvement. It also provides an opportunity to establish initial baselines of the operation.
2. *Audits* are conducted to evaluate the organization, people, and processes used to manage the company and to help establish basic core processes and benchmarks.
3. *Alignment* and adjustments within the operation may be needed to ensure compatibility and effectiveness with the program.

(b) Phase II—Initial Implementation.

Once the organization and its management are properly prepared, the implementation is planned and initiated. This is the beginning of the activities which become the repetitive continuous improvement process and involves items (vii) through (ix) of the model. Phase II has one major goal—to demonstrate the tools and techniques that will take the organization toward excellence. The following activities occur during this phase:

- Employees are trained.
- Cross-functional teams are built.
- Problem-solving techniques are demonstrated.
- Visibility into organization occurs (who does what).
- New communication loops between groups grow.
- Meeting effectiveness and reporting are developed.

Balance Sheet
(based on construction company core activities)

Activity	Benchmark	Performance	
		Plan	Actual
Estimate	Estimate vs. completion cost	90%	75%
	Material cost vs. budget	100%	80%
	Capture rate	60%	70%
Management	Change order acceptance		
	> $100,000 impact	< 45 days	52 days
	< $100,000 impact	< 30 days	28 days
	< $50,000 impact	< 15days	17 days
	< $10,000 impact	< 5 days	7 days
	performance to schedule (% of all jobs)		
	weekly performance	± 10%	18%
	completion performance	100%	75%
	performance to budget (% of all jobs)		
	weekly performance	± 15%	20%
	completion performance	100%	60%
Customer Satisfaction			
	based on job completion survey	95%	98%
	based on contract litigation	1%	1/2%

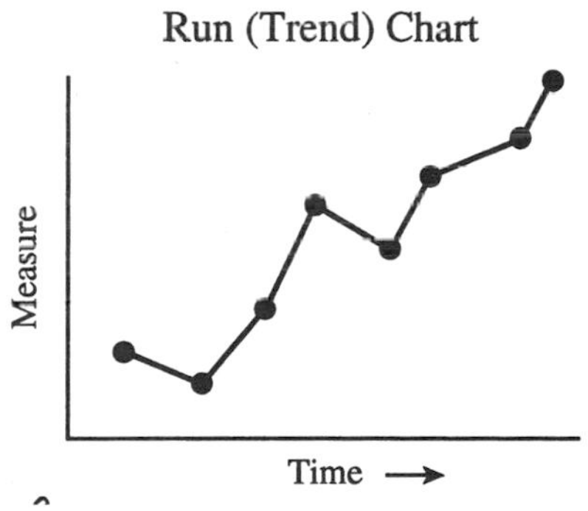

Run (Trend) Chart

Measure

Time →

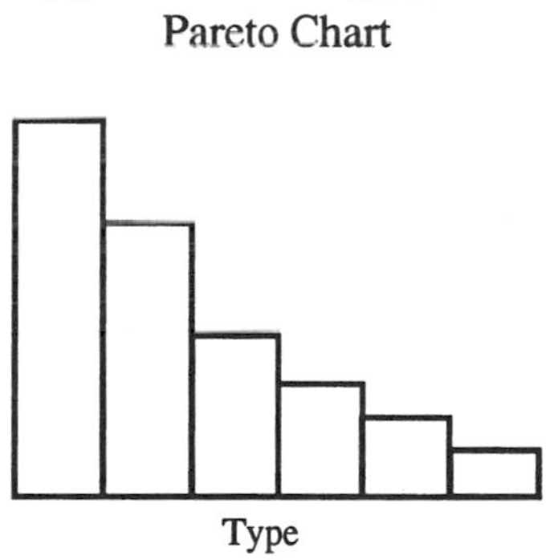

Pareto Chart

Type

Exhibit 29.10. Visual charting

- Process deviation analysis and root cause analysis are introduced.

This phase normally requires outside assistance, but it is the first step in developing acceptance and credibility within the organization and the employees.

(c) Phase III—Transition. At this point in the implementation, the basics of empowerment, process development, and evaluation and problem solving have been demonstrated. The level of credibility and acceptance has risen, but there are still many skeptics. It is necessary for the organization to take charge and make quality a part of everyone's job and performance goals. During this phase, credibility and acceptance become critical. This phase includes all of the activities of phase II, but there are significant differences.

- The steering committee takes over control of the program.
  - Training
  - Solution implementation
  - Team discipline
  - Measurement and evaluation
  - Employee motivation
- Policies and procedures for TQM are modified and expanded.
- Activity must result in considerable growth in credibility, acceptance, employee involvement, and positive management reinforcement.

Management and the steering committee need to be cautious with their involvement. They must have a role of guiding, not directing. They must be sure they truly understand the process. They should call on some outside assistance in auditing and critiquing progress and outputs.

(d) Phase IV—Growth. The goal of this phase is to spread the problem solving, employee empowerment, and culture change through the organization. The new activities occurring deal with the continued change in the way management thinks and works in the process of doing their jobs.

- A high level of visibility for communication and public relations
- A high level of employee involvement
- Many documented successes
- A problem identification system that reflects process variation
- A defined system of process control and measurement
- A policy with related benchmarks

At this point, TQM and its measured outputs should be solidly in the management culture of the organization and acceptance should be high.

(e) Phase V—Internal Institutionalization. The goal is simply to make TQM total and complete across the organization. This has occurred when employee empowerment and problem-solving techniques are in place and natural, and when the numerical output of the measurement system becomes a management tool by which success is gauged. The new activities that become a part of this phase are as follows:

- Define and document all critical processes.
- Define aggressive benchmarks for all critical processes.
- Develop and utilize a measurement and reporting system for all critical processes.
- Define a TQM function in management.

The activities in this phase are to assure the permanence and staying power of TQM.

(f) Phase VI—External Institutionalization. As the organization takes control of its internal processes, it becomes obvious that external influences continue to affect the search for excellence. The goal of this phase is to develop a program that supports and interfaces with these outside influences. The program to be developed must have a degree of similarity to and synergism with the one the organization has implemented. Therefore, it is obvious that the model followed in development of the organization's successful and in-place TQM program is appropriate, because it will naturally be compatible and has already been tested.

29.7 BUDGETING FOR TOTAL QUALITY MANAGEMENT.

All smart managers know that poor quality costs money in lost customers and profits. However, quality improvement and TQM are not free. It does not make sense to address continuous quality improvement unless it will have a positive effect on the bottom line. The budgeting-for-quality activity provides a clear picture of the costs of TQM and points to the areas of profit and cost savings.

(a) Management Commitment.

Management's commitment to TQM involves more than a decision to introduce a new program. It involves an open and active commitment to employee empowerment, culture change, and the financial support necessary to sustain the efforts. The commitment also involves a proactive change in the strategic plan to include TQM as a management tool.

Experience has shown that TQM programs have not been successful with internally initiated and directed programs. Implicit in this is the expense of a consultant or consulting organization. The major reason for this is that organizations have difficulty in creating the self assessment and culture change without outside help. The amount of effort involved for the consultant and the duration of tenure will vary, depending on the needs and desires of the management staff. The details of the management commitment and approximate costs are tabulated in Exhibit 29.11. They essentially track phases I and II of Exhibit 29.6.

Awareness and planning activities (see Exhibit 29.11) include those needed for the staff to attain a basic knowledge of TQM, possible support needed, and the development of an initial plan and budget. Those total costs are cash expenses plus the cost of committed employee hours directly involved in the program (man-hours per person or mh/person).

The scheduled time span of this activity should be approximately three months, with the costs spread evenly over that period.

(b) Manpower and Time Commitment.

The manpower and time commitment becomes more intense as the program implementation occurs. The primary reason for this

Activity	Cash Expenses/Manpower	
Awareness education	$3,000 to $5,000	40 mh/person
Books		
Seminars		
Direct presentation		
Management training (consultant)	$2,000	16 mh/person
Employee audit (10% to 15% of employees)	$2,000 to $3,000	1 mh/person
Infrastructure	$2,000 to $3,000	24 mh/person
Organization		
Policies and procedures		
Core process development and benchmarking	$5,000	24 mh/person

Exhibit 29.11. Awareness and planning costs

Activity	Cash Expenses/Manpower	
Team selection and training	$2,000	16 mh/person
Team meetings (continuous improvement) assume five teams	$5,000 to $6,000	15 mh/person
Solution implementation	$1,000	8 mh/person
Employee motivation	$2,000	

Exhibit 29.12. Implementation costs

Activity	Cash Expenses/Manpower	
Continued training and motivation		16 mh/person
Team meetings (eight teams/yr)		15 mh/person
Solution implementation	$5,000/yr	8 mh/person
Employee motivation	$2,000/yr	
Consultant audit and assistance	$5,000/yr	

Exhibit 29.13. Sustaining costs

is that the employees are brought in and become the major resource of the program. Initial implementation of the program involves activities (see Exhibits 29.12 and 29.13 that introduce the program to the employees and begin to involve them in the continuous improvement process. The consulting activity is still very much involved in process, because implementation is most difficult and requires an ongoing learning process and continuous reinforcement of the culture changes necessary. The consultant will be directly involved in the problem-solving teams during the first cycle and then will proceed to detach during the transition phase to a point where it assumes the role of an advisor only. These activities and events are those related in phases II and III of Exhibit 29.6. Those costs again reflect cash and manpower commitments with an even spread over a period of three to four months.

(c) Maintenance Cost Commitment. The initial costs of the TQM program are incurred during the initial phases, which tend to occur over the first six months of the program. However, there are no free lunches—as with any worthwhile effort, there are ongoing maintenance costs, primarily for the manpower commitment and the cost of positive reinforcement. The efforts and costs related essentially address the items in phases III, IV, V, and VI and will become a part of the regular operating budget.

(d) Impact on the Budgeting Process. The manpower and cash estimates previously identified provide a scope of the commitment necessary in the implementation of a TQM program. In addition, it is necessary that the organization recognize the time span necessary for solid implementation. The impact on the expense budget is the management commitment over the first three months, the manpower commitment over the next three to four months, and the ongoing maintenance commitment as a built-in operating expense within the operating budget (see Exhibit 29.14). This obviously implies that initial funding will be an out-of-budget expense. However, the ongoing budget expense after the implementation phase is very predictable and controllable. It is the expense of involving new employees on new teams, the motivation, and the periodic need for outside assistance.

Management commitment	$18,000	Over 4 mos
Manpower commitment*	$11,000	Over 4 mos
Maintenance commitment*	$12,000	Per annum

* Manpower and cost commitments are related to the organization and its size.

Exhibit 29.14. Budget impact summary

Organization	Team Goal	Result
Construction	Improve performance to budget and schedule	Performance to budget and schedule from 40% to 60% resulted in $300,000 added annual profit
Brokerage company	Reduce turnaround on reports	Reduce turnaround from 7 to 3 days
Construction	Reduce equipment downtime	Developed maintenance program and reduced average down time from 16 hr per mo to 2 hr per mo
Manufacturing	On time, in budget procurement	Purchasing system improved; on time from 60% to 90%, in budget from 40% to 80%
Health-care service	Improve vendor communication	Reduced forms from 3 to 1 Developed mutually acceptable standards of performance
Construction	Small tool replacement costs 2% of total revenue	Instituted tool control system which reduced cost to 1% ($50,000 savings)

Exhibit 29.15. Examples of TQM impact

29.8 RETURN ON INVESTMENT

(a) Assessment of Impact on Bottom Line. The impact on the bottom line is more difficult to identify, because it generally involves cost avoidance or reductions in operating expenses as well as the effect of new opportunities for revenue. Part of the reason that this is difficult to quantify is the fact that organizations and companies do not generally have a good measure of their detailed operating costs within the processes. However, when this level of measurement has been put in place, it has been demonstrated that the bottom-line impact has more than offset TQM program costs. There are many examples of bottom-line improvements which were the result of TQM-type programs that used employee-empowered teams to improve process efficiency and effectiveness (see Exhibit 29.15).

Many of these operational improvements are included within factors utilized in the budgeting process, such as productivity, efficiency, or general and administrative (G&A) items, that translate into dollars and reflect directly to the bottom line. However, an analysis of these budgeting factors can provide a baseline from which cost savings and cost avoidance can be measured. Some examples of these subtle savings are as follows:

- Missing a schedule causes additional manpower costs, facilities cost, administrative support, and possible utility and occupancy costs. All of these are generally accounted for in the budgeting process by including them in the standard factors or in (often accepted) overruns.

- A budget overrun obviously has a direct impact on profitability, which can additionally have an impact on competitiveness and ability to obtain business.
- Equipment downtime not only impacts the productivity and efficiency factors, but can affect manpower allocation, schedules, and eventually budget overruns.
- Although materials cost is typically the smaller part of product or service costs, the impact of materials cost variances and availability is felt across all the other product cost areas.
- The ever-present paperwork and its need to grow are accepted as part of company growth; however, experience shows that there is seldom a plan to throw out the old, obsolete, and unnecessary. Paperwork takes time to generate and review, and time is money.

The examples in Exhibit 29.15 show some of the changes and improvements that resulted in cost reductions and efficiencies in daily operations, and the savings that may result.

(b) Risks and Pitfalls. As with anything new and threatening, there are several risks. This is particularly true with a change that occurs within the cultural environment and that affects the "comfort zone." Total quality management requires scrutiny and evaluation of everything being done, and strongly says that the status quo is not acceptable. This upsets the balance and results in an immediate defensive reaction by those involved. The development of, and linkage to, a TQM budget is an essential step to tie the unknown to a known. The other necessary action is to recognize and address known risks and pitfalls. Although there are several classic risks and pitfalls that all programs have exhibited, continuous evaluation and review must be an active part of the implementation and maintenance plan. The following are typical problems:

- *Expectation.* We live in a world in which instant gratification is not soon enough. Total quality management will not result in immediate, recognizable financial returns. Effective and stable integration of a TQM philosophy will take two years or more. People are reluctant to accept a change to their normal lifestyles, and that is what TQM does.
- *Control.* It is absolutely necessary that program and employee control be defined and planned, particularly during the initial phases of the program. Although TQM involves employee involvement, the level of empowerment must be defined and planned. There are several areas that should not be included in open employee empowerment. Generally, areas of open involvement should be limited to operational processes. Those tasks related to mission development, strategic planning, budget, organization, and manpower planning and evaluation, should be left to management and staff.
- *Commitment.* Once the decision has been made to implement and support a TQM program, management must be diligent in their commitment toward its success. This requires visible, open support and recognition of the people and the ultimate results. Lack of commitment is the number one cause of failure of most programs.
- *Linkage to budget.* "Good for You" programs do not survive if they are not linked to traditional operational values. Therefore, creating a budget that integrates TQM provides a level of understanding and acceptance into the existing culture. This level

of acceptance, comfort, and understanding is essential for success. Without this linkage, it becomes someone else's program that is a threat to others' position and control.

This list contains the basic pitfalls and risks. There will be others peculiar to each specific situation, but they will essentially be a subset of those noted.

29.9 INDUSTRY EXAMPLES AND STRATEGIES

(a) Manufacturing. The ABC Manufacturing Company provides products to the consumer market for use in telecommunications applications. This company had been very successful for eight years with total annual revenue of $60 million. However, their flagship products were no longer the latest technology, and new products were continually late to market. In addition, ABC was having difficulty being competitive due to an inefficient and costly manufacturing operation. Management made a strategic decision to implement TQM and assigned three members of the senior staff to implement a program.

The following are the parameters of the program developed:

Budget for first two years	$150,000
Total employment to be involved	400
First year	200
Second year	200
Source of training	Outside consultant
Measure of success	Improved employee attitude
	Reduced manufacturing costs
	Improved productivity
	Improved scheduling and performance to schedule

Twenty-five employees were initially trained, who were formed into the steering committee (ten members) and three problem teams of five each. The following is a summary of a problem evaluated by one of the teams. One problem identified was the large materials premium costs:

Audit input (annual)	Gross income	$60,000,000
	Gross margin	30%
	Product cost (70%)	$42,000,000
	Materials cost (30% of product cost)	$12,600,000
	Material needing premium (5%)	$630,000
	Average premium (50%)	$315,000

Therefore, there was an opportunity to reduce premium costs on materials by $315,000. The team made two changes in the materials release and procurement process that reduced the premium costs by 50%, with an annual savings of approximately $160,000. The two changes involved are as follows:

- Creation of a proactive system of identifying material lead times
- Clear identification of long lead items on the materials lists

The other two initial problems identified were as follows:

- Product-to-market time
- Manufacturing repair cost and reduction in process defects

The total projected savings from these three problems and the related process improvements were in excess of $500,000.

(b) Construction Industry. The Do Good Construction Company is a subcontractor in the commercial building portion of the construction industry. Its areas of involvement are structural fireproofing, facade design, and construction and internal drywall installation. This company has an employee core of 80 people and utilizes union manpower for direct construction labor. The company is 15 years old and into the second generation of ownership. Recent gross revenue has been flat at $30 million for the last three years. The new generation of management has determined that there is considerable waste which must be eliminated. As a result, a three-person executive committee has enlisted a consultant to assist in the development of a plan.

The following are the parameters of the program proposed:

Budget for first year	$30,000
Budget reserve for next two years	$30,000
Total employees to be involved	80
First year	50
Next two years	30 (nonresident in home office area)
Source of training and assistance	Outside consultant
Measure of success	Improved employee attitude
	Reduced operating costs
	Improved competitiveness

Twenty-one people were initially trained and formed into the steering committee (five members) and three problem teams of five each. One of the problems addressed by a team was that of excessive downtime of the equipment used in spray-coating fireproofing on the structures and in coating materials utilized on facades.

The following is a summary of the problem details:

Average spray system usage	2 full-time
Manpower involved per system	4-person team
Hourly rate	$30
Average equipment down time	6 hours per week (1 unit)
Sum of down-time cost	$120 per hour (1 unit)
	= $1,440 (2 units, 1 week)
Annually	$75,000

This identified an opportunity of $75,000 in cost reduction for this portion of the business. The team made three changes in the utilization of this equipment and associated manpower, which reduced initial downtime to two hours per week and to zero downtime after six months. These changes resulted in a saving to the company of more than $50,000 in the first year. The changes made were:

- Weekly preventative maintenance program
- Formal on-the-job training for operators
- Major maintenance recall to the shop

The other two problems identified were:

- Proper documentation of change orders
- Control and maintenance of small tools (value of less than $500)

The total identified annual cost savings from these three problems was $150,000.

(c) Health-Care Industry. Northwest Home Care is a nonprofit organization that services the elder clients of a specific geographic area that has approximately 9,000 potential clients. This organization has 150 highly motivated, well-qualified employees, one-half of whom are directly involved in planning and managing the necessary client services. These services are procured from outside suppliers. Ninety percent of Northwest's revenue comes from state and federal reimbursement (at a standard rate) for its services. An internal audit found that actual client cost was $220 per month and state/federal reimbursement rate was $200. An internal committee was formed to look into the problem, and they came to the following conclusions:

- Procedures were lacking, and those that did exist were inadequate.
- Client tracking was very primitive.
- Employee training was lacking in the task management and administrative areas.
- Client managers were overloaded.
- Vendor communication was lacking.
- There was little or no understanding of the total process and, with the exception of the financial area, no performance tracking.

In addition to some specific short-term administrative changes, the committee recommended that a TQM program be initiated, and strongly suggested that the identified area of revenue be addressed as a problem area.

The following are the parameters of the program proposed:

Total employees to be involved	150
First year	90
Second year	60
Source of training and assistance	Outside consultant
Measure of success	Employee expertise in management
	Revenue differential reduction
	Process development
	Performance tracking
	Client satisfaction

(*Note:* The outside consultant used was available from a nonprofit service group which provided service at a special low rate for other nonprofits).

Thirty people were trained in the initial phase and formed into the steering committee (eight members), and four problem solving teams of five each. One of the problems addressed by a team was the billing process and the collection of data to support it.

A summary of the problem details follows:

Total revenue	\$8,000,000
Federal and state reimbursement (90%)	\$7,200,000
Active clients	3,000
Average reimbursement per client	\$200 per month
Average cost of services per client	\$220 per month

The audit of this information indicated that growth was not possible without additional outside funding. It further showed that the 10% differential was an unacceptable problem. The team made three basic changes which immediately resulted in a reduction of \$18 per month, and recommended changes which would result in an additional \$2 per month. As a result, the costs would be in control.

- Create an accurate client-tracking system which would assure that client services were accurately billed to the state. The present system was not a real-time system based on daily inputs.
- Develop a vendor reporting system for providing accurate numbers on services provided, and develop an audit path for that input.
- Create a statistical performance-tracking system on major vendors.

These changes immediately pointed out that the billing was inconsistent, and generally understated state billing versus vendor invoicing.

Additional needs were:

- Improved client manager training
- Better definition of service requirements to the vendors, to eliminate unnecessary tasks and reduce charges
- Identification and definition of key or core processes

The ultimate result of these changes was a more cost-effective, higher-quality service, as well as a more efficient operation.

These three examples of TQM implementation and the resulting changes are based on actual cases (numbers and names changed). They are intended to show the types of problems and activities that develop in a TQM program implementation, and that, although the changes may appear small on the surface, they become significant in the overall picture.

29.10 SUMMARY. Once management has made the decision to implement TQM, they have made a commitment to change the way the operation will do business in the future. They will develop and encourage employee empowerment, visibly support the concepts and elements of TQM, and boost credibility by adding TQM into their strategy and its supporting budgets. The critical steps involved in developing a TQM organization are as follows:

- Audit the organization and business elements to establish a baseline.
- Evaluate the industry and competition to determine appropriate operating benchmarks.

- Scope the proposed TQM program, with its parameters and implementation schedule.
- Develop the budget to support necessary actions and activities.
- Organize and activate the program and measure the gains.

Phil Crosby wrote *Quality Is Free,* but that is really not a correct assessment of the picture. Good quality actually adds to the bottom line, and often can mean the difference between success and failure.

SOURCES AND SUGGESTED REFERENCES

Adair, Charlene B., *Breakthrough Process Redesign: New Pathways to Customer Value.* New York: AMACOM, 1994.

Baldrige Winners on World-Class Quality. The Conference Board Report No. 990. New York: Conference Board, 1992.

Barry, Thomas J., *Management Excellence Through Quality.* Milwaukee, WJ: ASQC Quality Press, 1992.

Berry, Thomas H., *Managing the Total Quality Transformation.* New York: McGraw-Hill, 1991.

Bogan, Christopher E., and Michael J. English, *Benchmarking for Best Practices: Winning Through Innovation Adaption.* New York: McGraw-Hill, 1994.

Brancato, Carolyn Key, *New Corporate Performance Measures: A Research Report.* New York: Conference Board, 1995.

Brocka, Bruce, *Quality Management: Implementing the Best Ideas of the Masters.* Homewood, IL: Business One Irwin, 1992.

Bruno, Gerard, *The Process Analysis Workbook for Government: How to Achieve More With Less.* Milwaukee, WI: ASQC Quality Press, 1995.

Carter, Carla C., *Human Resources Management and the Total Quality Imperative.* New York: AMACOM, 1994.

Cortada, James W., *TQM for Sales and Marketing Management.* New York: McGraw-Hill, 1993.

Creating a Customer-Focused Organization. The Conference Board Report No. 1030. New York: Conference Board, 1993.

Creech, Bill, *The Five Pillars of TQM: How to Make Total Quality Management Work for You.* New York: Truman Talley Books/Dutton, 1995.

Crosby, Philip, *Let's Talk Quality.* New York: McGraw-Hill, 1990.

Crosby, Philip, *Quality is Free: The Art of Making Quality Certain.* New York: McGraw-Hill, 1979.

Crosby, Philip, *Quality Without Tears: The Art of Hassle-Free Management.* New York: McGraw-Hill, 1984.

Deming, W. Edwards, *Out of the Crisis.* Cambridge, MA: Massachusetts Institute of Technology, Center for Advanced Engineering Study, 1986.

Deming, W. Edwards, *Quality, Productivity and Competitive Position.* Cambridge, MA: Massachusetts Institute of Technology, Center for Advanced Engineering Study, 1982.

Gevirtz, Charles D., *Developing New Products With TQM.* New York: McGraw-Hill, 1994.

Hiam, Alexander, *Does Quality Work? A Review of Relevant Studies.* The Conference Board No. 1043. New York: Conference Board, 1993.

Hoffherr, Glen D., *Breakthrough Thinking in Total Quality Management.* Englewood Cliffs, NJ: PTR Prentice Hall, 1994.

Johnson, Richard S., *TQM: Leadership for the Quality Transformation.* ASQC Total Quality Management Series, vol. 1. Milwaukee, WI: ASQC Quality Press, 1993.

Johnson, Richard S., *TQM: Management Processes for Quality Operations.* ASQC Total Quality Management Series, vol. 2. MIlawaukee, WJ: ASQC Quality Press, 1993.

Juran, J. M., *Juran's Quality Control Handbook* (4th ed.) New York: McGraw-Hill, 1988.

Katzenbach, Jon R., and Douglas K. Smith, *The Wisdom of Teams.* Boston, MA: Harvard Business School Press, 1993.

Levine, David I., *Reinventing the Workplace: How Business and Employees Can Both Win.* Washington, DC: Brookings Institution, 1995.

Linneman, Robert E., *Marketing Planning in a Total Quality Environment.* New York: Haworth Press, 1995.

Mahoney, Francis Xavier, *The TQM Trilogy: Using ISO 9000. The Deming Prize and the Baldridge Award to Establish a System for Total Quality Management.* New York: AMACOM, 1994.

Maintaining the Total Quality Advantage. The Conference Board Report No. 979. New York: Conference Board, 1991.

Managing Globally: Key Perspectives. The Conference Board Report No. 972. New York: Conference Board, 1991.

Milakovich, Michael E., "Total Quality Management for Public Sector Productivity Improvement," *Public Productivity & Management Review,* vol. 14, no. 1, Fall 1990.

Miller, William C., *Quantum Quality: Quality Improvement Through Innovation, Learning, and Creativity.* White Plains, NY: Quality Resources, 1993.

Organizational Transformation in Health Care: A Work in Progress (1st ed.). San Francisco: Jossey-Bass Publishers, 1994.

Petrone, Joe, *Building the High Performance Sales Force.* New York: AMACOM, 1994.

Pfau, Bruce N., *Innovative Reward and Recognition Strategies in TQM.* The Conference Board Report No. 1051. New York: Conference Board, 1993.

Profiting From Total Quality. The Conference Board Report No. 1048, New York: Conference Board, 1993.

The Quality Roadmap: How to Get Your Company on the Quality Track—And Keep It There. New York: AMACOM, 1994.

Rabbitt, John T., *The ISO 9000 Book: A Global Competitor's Guide to Compliance and Certification* (2d ed.). White Plains, NY: Quality Resources, 1994.

Roberts, Harry V., *Quality Is Personal: A Foundation for Total Quality Management.* New York: Free Press, 1993.

Rust, R., Zahorik, A., and T. Keiningham, *Return on Quality.* Chicago: Probus, 1994.

Sashkin, Marshall, *Putting Total Quality Management to Work: What TQM Means, How to Use It and How to Sustain It Over the Long Run.* San Francisco: Berrett-Koehler, 1993.

Schmidt, Warren H., *TQManager: A Practical Guide for Managing in a Total Quality Organization.* San Francisco: Jossey-Bass, 1993.

Schonberger, Richard, *Total Quality Management Cuts a Broad Swath Through Manufacturing and Beyond.* American Management Briefing: Managing a Dynamic Organization. New York: AMA Membership Publications Division, 1993.

Snyder, Neil H., *Vision Values, and Courage: Leadership for Quality Management.* New York: Free Press, 1994.

Spendolini, Michael, *The Benchmarking Book.* New York: AMACOM, 1994.

Taylor, Paul, "Benchmark Is Set by Clear Winners in Product Groups," *The Financial Times,* June 27, 1994, p. 9.

Tenner, Arthur R., and Irving J. DeToro, *Total Quality Management: Three Steps to Continuous Improvement.* Reading, MA: Addison-Wesley, 1992.

Total Quality Management for Law Firms. New York: Practising Law Institute, 1992.

Total Quality Management in Higher Education. New directions for institutional research no. 71. San Francisco: Jossey-Bass, 1991.

Watson, Gregory H. *The Benchmarking Workbook: Adapting Best Practices for Performance Improvement.* Cambridge, MA: Productivity Press, 1994.

CHAPTER 30

PROGRAM BUDGETING: PLANNING, PROGRAMMING, BUDGETING

William B. Iwaskow

30.1 INTRODUCTION. As noted in the previous chapters, budgeting has evolved into a major integrating tool for planning and control. It can bridge the gap between strategic planning, long- and medium-range planning, and current actions. Without an adequate union, planning can be out of touch with the constraints of scarce resources, and budgeting can be divorced from the direction of plans and programs.

This chapter provides a broad, comprehensive approach to integrating planning and budgeting, called *program budgeting* (PB), which is another designation for planning, programming, and budgeting. This approach represents a significant stage in the continuing evolution of planning and budgetary techniques and the general technology of management decision making.

The PB integration is basically accomplished by the use of strategic output-oriented programs that are based on goals, purposes, and objectives. Providing output-oriented budget information with a long-range perspective to allocate resources more effectively in PB's basic objective. The output-oriented program expenditures are later translated into traditional line-item appropriation budget requests. A budget based on PB concepts is a statement of policy for a planning period and a means for implementing it. Because of the output orientation of PB, designating it as "output budgeting" might be more descriptive, as it has in the United Kingdom.

Program budgeting was introduced into the U.S. Department of Defense (DOD) in 1961 with considerable publicity because of its revolutionary approach to government planning and budgeting techniques. By 1968, its utilization became epidemic in the federal government as well as in various state and local governments. Both public and private sectors have since utilized the concepts and lessons of PB, sometimes under different labels and forms.

Program budgeting applies not only to government but also to industry and nonprofit organizations. The concepts of PB have origins in both the private and public sectors. This chapter will address the concepts, background, requirements, and lessons of PB.

30.2 DESCRIPTION OF PROGRAM BUDGETING. Program budgeting does not have a standardized definition because of its encompassing nature. Its many aspects include concepts; a system and process; a technique and format; and, in some cases, almost a management philosophy. Essentially, it is a management decision-making system that ties together strategic and long-range planning with conventional budgeting and supporting analysis so that an organization can most effectively assign resources to achieve both its

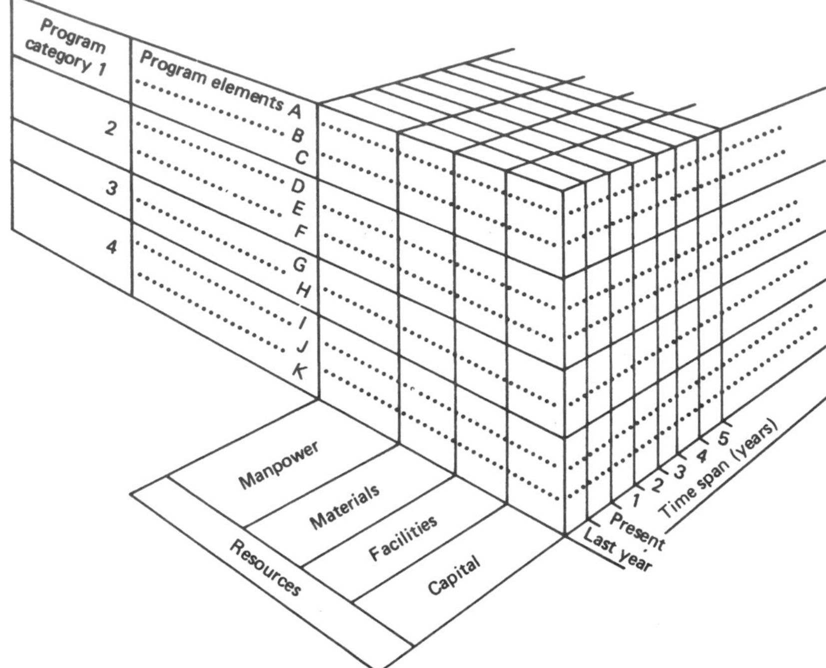

Exhibit 30.1. Program, resources, and time matrix

short- and long-range objectives. It utilizes a planning and budgeting process in an output-oriented program format, which is oriented to its objectives to facilitate developing and evaluating alternatives and making decisions. This process ultimately leads to an allocation of resources over a planning period. This is then a basis for constructing a budget, which supports the goals, strategies, and decisions.

Under PB, a program contains a specified combination of resources or manpower, materials, facilities (including equipment), and capital, which operate together to achieve a set of common objectives within a planning period. A program resource matrix extended over time in a program hierarchy is shown in Exhibit 30.1. The matrix shows an allocation of resources to various programs over time. The development, structuring, and hierarchy of programs will be explained in a subsequent section.

(a) Concepts. The functions of management can be summarized as planning, implementation, and control. Program budgeting is one of the most comprehensive decision-making systems designed to accommodate and integrate these multiple management functions. It integrates all of the organization's planning activities (from conceptual to partially implemented stages) and budgeting into a total system. It relates and integrates into one conceptual framework all plans (strategic, long-range, medium-range, projects, etc.) and budgets, objectives and costs, key activities and operations, organizational units, resource allocations, analysis and measurements, including reengineering studies, controls and results. Great emphasis is continually placed on the analysis of alternatives (including the effectiveness of existing programs) and on estimating the cost of accomplishing objectives and fulfilling purposes and needs.

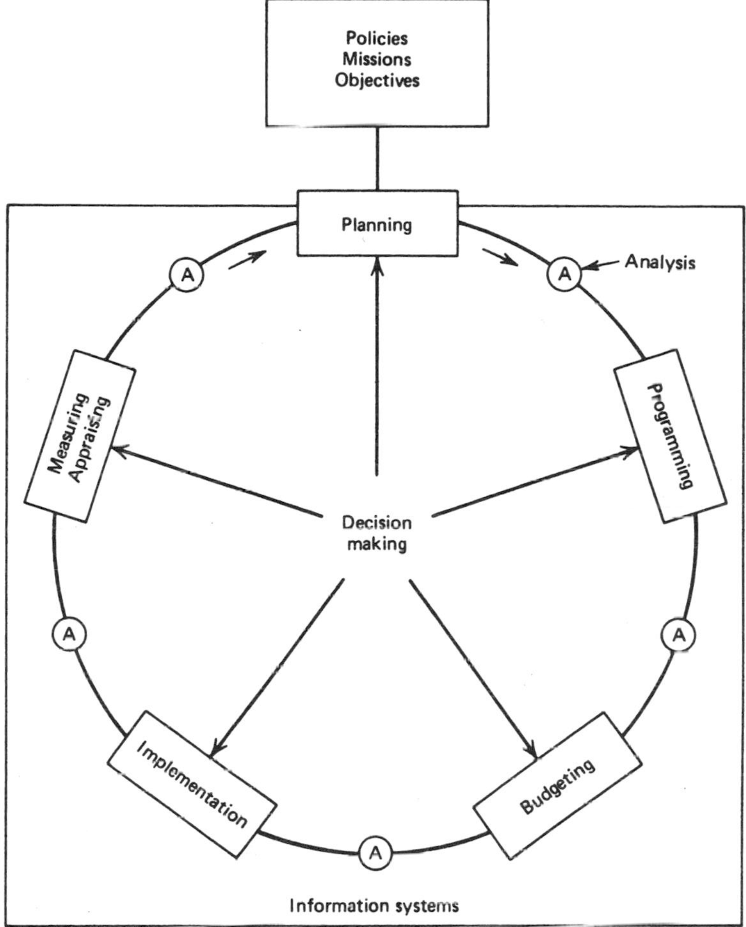

Exhibit 30.2. Program budgeting process cycle

A schema of a PB process cycle is shown in Exhibit 30.2 in the process context of management requirements and decision making.

The schema shows an organization's policies, missions, and objectives serving as the basis for the cycle, with various key decision-making and analysis checkpoint intervals operating within the existing information systems. The planning–programming–budgeting steps have separate interlocking and interactive time intervals, with different requirements in increasing detail.

From the standpoint that budgeting has already evolved to a significant extent as a major integrating tool for planning and control, there is a bit of PB in every budget system. Traditionally, however, most budget systems have been primarily structured for the implementation of ongoing activities and the attendant spending control. There are many differences between traditional budgeting and PB.

To begin with, the flow of decisions is generally different in a PB system than in one utilizing traditional line budgeting. In the later, especially when outside a planning context, the flow of budgetary decisions is primarily upward, with an aggregative information flow.

In PB, however, the budget is a means of implementing the long-range plans, and the decision making is primarily downward and disaggregative to the information data base.

Traditional budgeting has also generally emphasized the current means or objects of work achievement and the attendant efficiency with appropriate controls, whereas PB is also concerned with the purpose of the work. Program budgeting requires that budgetary decisions be made by emphasizing output categories such as goals, objectives, purposes, and products or services instead of inputs such as salaries, materials, and facilities.

Traditional budgetary approaches have also generally taken a retrospective focus in measuring what was done with current means in estimating the next budget year. In contrast, PB is more prospective, with its focus on the future impacts of current major decisions or choices. *The PB focus rests on the premise that more resources are wasted in implementing wrong decisions efficiently than in implementing right decisions inefficiency.* The system aims at the major issues facing an organization and incorporates policy, goals, objectives, and strategy directly into the budget process.

A budget in a PB system is initially decided in a planning framework, with the expenditures expressed in an output-oriented program structure. It is then translated into a traditional line-item appropriation form by means of a ''crosswalk,'' as shown in the schema in Exhibit 30.3. The schema shows the basic and smallest program entities, or *program elements,* extended over a planning period and aggregated into the more encompassing program categories. It also shows their respective connections to a traditional line budget for year 1. (The different types of program groupings are discussed in the section on program hierarchy.)

This crosswalk reconciliation, or cross-classification, allows data to be converted from a PB planning framework in year 1 (by moving to the left) into a traditional line budget, which generally represents a management and control framework. It also allows data to

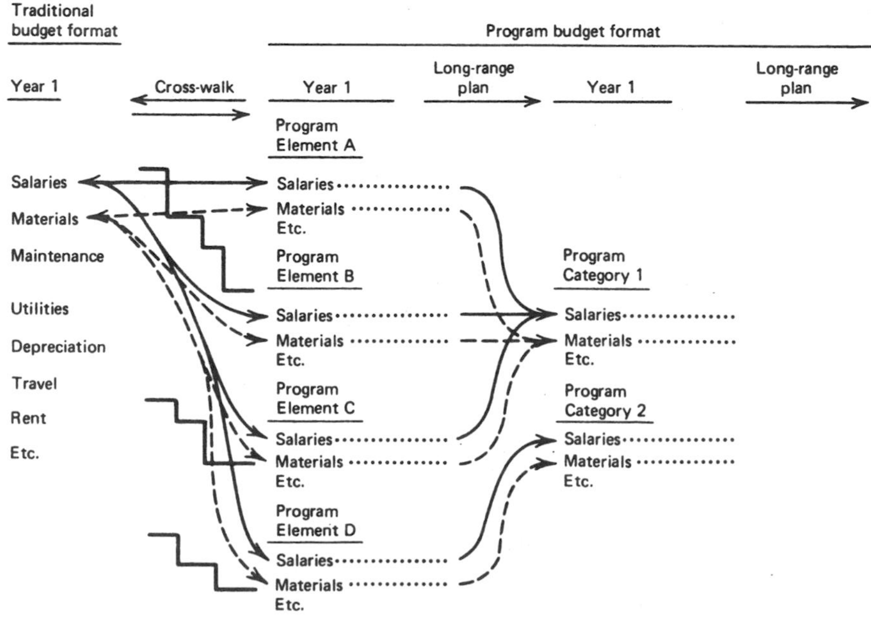

Exhibit 30.3. Schema of a crosswalk

move in both directions and is constructed only for the budget year. Although PB gives a major role to planning in the construction of a budget, it also embraces the control functions of budgeting with provisions such as a crosswalk. This is elaborated upon further under the section on crosswalk.

The novelty of PB is not with the various ingredients just indicated. Each of them is familiar, reflecting past and current practices to some degree. What is novel is the combination of a number of these ingredients into a comprehensive package and system with an output focus. Program budgeting gives a coherence to the various ingredients that were not consciously or sufficiently related previously.

The PB approach is a significant shift from traditional budgeting, especially in government. Industry's "profit center" approach of relating product or service line revenues to costs has many similarities to PB, but the comprehensiveness and completeness is often limited in the budgeting, planning, or analysis phases.

(b) Managerial Needs. Program budgeting came into being for some of the same reasons that other management techniques developed, such as management by objectives; strategic planning, zero-based, flexible, and bracket budgeting; cost accounting; and so forth. Managerial tools need to be updated and new ones developed. Solutions must be found for problems arising from technology, diversification, growth, size, government regulations, economic conditions, international interplay, general complexity, or new needs.

Many executives are swamped with studies, information, and rapidly changing events. They are inclined to believe, however, that a relatively small number of their decisions dealing with strategies and policy ultimately determines 80% to 90% of their success or failure, in the context of Pareto's Law, or the "80/20 rule." Strategic planning allows the isolation of a small number of decision areas that can have a big impact. Program budgeting is of particular interest as a management decision-making tool since it links the broad strategic planning process to the detail-oriented budget process, which at least provides a semblance of rational direction and control in organizations of overwhelming size or complexity. A PB system is one of the few strategic management tools that can help manage large, diverse organizations and bring top management and policy makers into the total decision-making process, from planning to the primary budgetary areas, in a comprehensive and disciplined fashion.

Unfortunately, new management approaches are sometimes taken literally in a cookbook fashion and are regarded as panaceas rather than as guiding concepts. In any case, they will continue to be sought after as a means of overcoming many of the perennial shortcomings of budget and planning systems, which include the following:

- A generally dim focus of budgets on strategic or key decision areas
- Gaps between planning and financial management
- Lack of comprehensive, integrated, multipurpose data systems
- Piecemeal departmental plans and budgets lacking comprehensive, organization-wide perspective and linkage
- Limited coping with uncertainty and changes in the world, including global interplay
- Limited time horizon and perspective of budgets to provide the full cost implications of current decisions
- Limited examination of alternatives and lack of sufficient relationship of benefits to costs or effectiveness

- Arbitrary budget allocations (or cuts) resulting from an inability to judge the relative worth of a multitude of budget requests

(c) What Program Budgeting Is Not. Program budgeting does not reduce decision making to a formula that eliminates the need for judgment and intuition. Its function is to provide a comprehensive framework and system within which effective decisions can be made.

Program budgeting is not a new accounting system, and it does not necessarily require changes in an existing accounting system to accommodate its output program classifications. It is not a management information system, although the availability of one in good form is beneficial.

Program budgeting is not a plan for reorganization to fit its output program structure. However, an organization structured to its purposes and goals would be considered ideal.

Program budgeting is not a mathematical model or a computerized form of management. It does not depend on the use of computers or complicated mathematics.

30.3 HISTORY. Program budgeting has origins in both U.S. industry and the federal government. Its approaches were initially utilized by industry in the 1920s, with analyses utilized by Bell Laboratories and a system introduced by the DuPont Company into General Motors. In the early 1940s, the federal government started a wartime materials-control system that utilized many of the principles of PB in its concept. Although the term *program* had occasionally appeared in some government documents prior to the 1940s, it had no connection with the concepts described here.

There also are a number of other antecedent paths from both the private and the public sectors that converged in the 1950s to develop PB. They include the growing sophistication of macroeconomic analyses and modeling; the use of microeconomics for appraising public projects; the increased use of government economic analyses for formulating fiscal policy; refinements in scientific management and decision-making techniques; improved information-handling technologies and computers; the increased use of analytic tools such as systems analysis and operations research, especially in the U.S. Department of Defense; and the continuing improvement of planning and budgeting techniques.

The most extensive use of PB ever embarked upon was by the U.S. federal government. The scope and scale of its application has never been matched by any other budgetary technique for a single organizational entity (other than the traditional line-item approach). Program budgeting became an official budget approach utilized throughout the federal government by the mid-1960s, which was well documented. It is presented here in considerable detail, therefore, and in much of its original nomenclature.

(a) Industry. Bell Laboratories employed a systems analysis in the 1920s that included some economic, political, and social considerations, but it was primarily hardware oriented.

DuPont used a form of program budgeting around 1915 and introduced a similar concept to General Motors in the early 1920s, when the company made its major investment in GM. Since then, the automobile industry has utilized many PB concepts through its long-time concern with the following:

- Planning models into the future
- Identifying clear objectives (models and price classes)

- Establishing programs to achieve objectives
- Allocating resources to program potentials
- Utilizing forecasts, studies, and analyses

Over the years, many private and public organizations in fact have been using various concepts of PB, under categories such as strategic planning and project management. However, most companies treat their management systems as proprietary matters and do not allow general publication. A few companies, such as General Electric (in the research and development [R&D] area) and John Hancock Insurance, have published their experience with PB approaches. The strategic planning at GE, which was developed in concert with the McKinsey management consulting organization, utilized strategic business units (SBUs). They had many similarities to the strategic program groupings of PB.

(b) Federal Government. Over the past 70 years, the federal government has made three basic alterations to its budgeting approaches.

Between 1921 and 1949, emphasis was on the expenditure control of cost inputs such as salaries, rent, materials, and so forth, which is generally characterized as a line-item type of budgeting. The connections of these items to goals, objectives, or results were very limited; the primary focus was on accountability.

Between 1949 and the early 1960s, "performance-type" budgeting, emphasizing efficiency, was implemented. In 1949, the Hoover Commission recommended that the entire budgetary concept be refashioned into a budget based on functions, activities, and projects. Its focus was work–cost measurement and managerial efficiency. That is, cost and production goals were established and then compared to actual performance. Limited attention was paid to whether the chosen goals addressed public needs or whether they were effective.

Between 1965 and the present, additional attention has been paid to strategic and long-range planning and the effective allocation of limited resources among varying public needs, along with efficiency. An across-the-board application of PB in the federal government started in 1965, after a news conference held by President Johnson formally launched it. At that news conference on August 25, 1965, President Johnson announced "a very new and very revolutionary system of planning and programming and budgeting throughout the vast government—so that through the tools of modern management the full promise of a finer life can be brought to every American at the lowest possible cost."[1]

The federal government PB antecedents, however, go back to World War II in the controlling of critical materials and to Department of Defense: analyses in the mid-1950s.

(i) World War II. During World War II, a shortage of critical materials necessitated a wartime materials control system. It was essentially the first type of program budget utilized in the government. It translated major U.S. goals (combat and civilian) into specific programs for allocating materials, crossed organizational lines (land, sea, air), extended the budget time frames a number of years out, and examined alternatives through systematic analyses. This approach fell into disuse after the war.

(ii) Rand Corporation. In 1953, the Rand Corporation, a not-for-profit "think tank" specializing in military-type planning and research, proposed a program budget format to

[1] "Transcript of the President's News Conference on Foreign & Domestic Affairs," *New York Times,* August 26, 1965.

the Air Force for weapon systems. Rand had already been performing systems analyses for weapons, taking into account such nontraditional considerations as social, political, and economic factors. The proposal was never acted upon until Rand published some studies on the subject that came to the attention of the Kennedy Administration.

(iii) Kennedy Administration. In 1961, under the direction of Defense Secretary Robert McNamara, PB was introduced into the DOD. Before that time, there was almost a complete separation between military planning and budgeting in DOD, resulting in unbalanced forces not readily deployable for combat duties. Moreover, the branches of the armed services (Army, Navy, Air Force) were each vying for control over different weapons systems without an overall coordinated defense policy. Although each had been conducting long-range planning and using systems analysis and operations research in allocating funds, these studies were essentially conducted independently of each other's activities. In fact, they were not always concerned with the same war possibilities.

(iv) Johnson Administration. Program Budgeting worked so well for the DOD that it was officially established throughout the federal government in 1965 by Lyndon B. Johnson in response to the growing complexity of budget requests and to the need to better allocate resources across the spectrum of the nation's needs. By 1967, the Bureau of the Budget (BOB) which administered PB, had implemented it in 21 federal agencies. It was found to be particularly helpful in foreign aid planning and in defining the Peace Corps missions. It was beginning to be recognized as the greatest advance in the art of government since the introduction of a competency basis into the Civil Service a hundred years before. Bureaucracies generally perform poorly in innovating or generating effective forward motion; their best performance is limited to routine tasks. Program Budgeting had the potential to correct this old defect.

In 1968, the federal government also financed the introduction of PB (for a year) in five states, five cities, and five counties under a "5-5-5 Program."

(v) Nixon Administration. In 1970, under President Nixon, the BOB was renamed the Office of Management and Budget (OMB), emphasizing efficiency, effectiveness, and realism in response to the fiscal pressures brought on by the Vietnam War.

In 1971, the OMB indicated that it was no longer necessary to submit a budget under the rigid PB format. Efficiency, again, became the primary concern. The OMB's instructions did not eliminate the utilization of the PB concepts but only the rigid format that had evolved. It was sometimes characterized as a management by objective (MBO) approach or an attenuated PB. Some of the PB-type requirements were maintained for special situations. That is, multi-year costing beyond the budget year was required for special OMB requests or whenever legislation was needed for resource authorization; cost–benefit analysis was necessary whenever something different or novel was advanced into the budget. Another favorable sign was the retention of the PB units in the various federal agencies for continuing analysis and strategy development. Moreover, President Nixon's message on the fiscal 1972 budget stressed the need to emphasize outputs, long-range planning, and the allocation of resources instead of a view limited to cost activities.

Program budgeting had led many federal agencies to re-appraise their missions and functions. In addition, an increased use of cost–benefit and cost-effectiveness analysis, and a greater concern and involvement with goals and objectives, generally remained.

Thus, many of the aspects of PB continued, as well as its spirit, although the concepts were presented differently.

(vi) Carter Administration. President Carter introduced zero-based budgeting (ZBB) to the federal government in the mid-1970s, following his experience with it as the governor of Georgia. Zero-based budgeting was, among other things, an organizational departure from PB in that it developed budgets from the ''bottom up'' rather than PB's ''top-down'' approach. This hierarchical direction distinction is fading in budgeting and planning systems with the growing horizontal, global type of organizations in the twenty-first century era of global capitalism.

In a short time, ZBB became unweildly and was disbanded due to its burdensome requirement as essentially a 100% annual review system and its inability to easily integrate into long-range planning.

(vii) Federal Phase-Out. Some of the reasons, therefore, that the official PB format was phased out of the federal government include the following:

- The availability of funds became tight with the Vietnam conflict, and the emphasis reversed to the old standbys of budgeting: control and accountability.
- President Nixon's management style emphasized shorter-range performance by the agencies in meeting agreed-to objectives. This course was supported under the constrained resources situation and by the fact that many of the public welfare programs of the Johnson Administration were expensive and not meeting expectations.
- Policy development was being concentrated within President Nixon's office through the Domestic and National Security Councils. In effect, increased layers of authority were placed between the budgeters and the top policy makers. The PB system that had been developed was geared to develop a great deal of policy at the agency level.
- President Nixon was trying to reorganize many of the agencies into decision-making entities along many of the developing PB program lines, which to a degree subordinated the need for a PB structure.
- The special PB plans and analyses were essentially designed for and used by the executive branch and were not appropriately incorporated into the operational flow of data to Congress, with its various committee requirements and politics.
- The routines became burdensome, with too much paperwork and time consumption.
- Linking the PB analytic process, particularly the policy analysis, to the budget process was difficult and generally was resisted. Also, too many issues were raised in regard to the scarce analytic capabilities, and many times they were not relevant.
- Gaps in coordination and compatibility between the special PB and regular budget staffs caused problems.
- The PB format was basically the one developed by the DOD, with insufficient consideration given to the individual needs of civilian agencies or to the status of their existing information systems. More tailoring was necessary with a much lesser emphasis on format and procedures.
- President Carter's introduction of ZBB and its lack of success gave further impetus to the bureaucratic and legislative entities to ease back to the old, comfortable, politically more manipulative standby: line-item budgeting.

Some caution is offered regarding a possible negative evaluation of PB's basic merits based solely on its experience in the federal government. It is important to make the evaluation with the perspective that the federal government is very complex and one of the largest fiscal units in the world, with its spending having a value of more than 20% of the country's gross national product (GNP). In the years PB was formally utilized, the annual federal spending was $300 billion in magnitude. In addition, the entire decision-making process operated within a highly complex governmental apparatus containing several conflicting layers of decision makers within a traditional, fragmented, and intensely political legislative environment.

In short, the federal phase-out was attributable to many factors that do not negate PB's basic concepts, validity, or contributions. Program budgeting never truly became a tool for both the executive and the legislative branches. It is only when people use a management system that it can have vitality. Also, to have expected PB to perform miracles was unrealistic. There is no magic in PB, as there is none in any management system or technique. Even under the most favorable of circumstances, PB can only organize and improve the data for decision making and management. It does not make decisions! It only provides a long-range perspective regarding the consequences of budgetary decisions.

(c) Utilization Overview. Program budgeting has been tried in whole and in piecemeal and has been modified and incorporated into the decision-making processes of many areas outside the federal government. It has taken many different forms, different emphases, and even different names over the years. Many school districts in the United States have termed their version of PB *educational resources management system;* in the United Kingdom, the term is sometimes referred to as *output budgeting*. The different names and modifications, in fact, present difficulties in tracking and evaluating PB. Perhaps some of the changes in designation reflect a disassociation with the federal government approach or an increasing management sophistication in not adopting novel techniques literally.

The system has also been introduced in industry and in various states, counties, cities, school districts, universities, libraries, and not-for-profit institutions in the United States as well as in several foreign countries. California, in particular, has had numerous successes. The results appear to be mixed, however, and the system seems least successful where PB's application was rigid and not tailored to individual needs or insufficiently integrated into political environments.

Cynical economists and budgetary analysts have felt that for the public and government sectors, in particular, with their inherent significant political dynamics, only the line-item type of budgeting is feasible. They feel the bureaucrats and politicians do not want to relinquish their easier control of allocating resources via the line-item approach or discipline themselves in reviewing the consequences of their budgetary decisions.

Some of the disappointments reflect unusually high initial expectations or an overselling of the management tool in relation to the human and institutional realities and the multiple demands of a budgetary process. Budgeting, for example, with its control orientation, is geared to demanding routines and deadlines, which can clash with the varied PB analysis and timing requirements. Many organizations also have encountered difficulties in trying to identify their objectives and in relating activities to them in program terms. Many assumed that programs would define themselves through some "black-box" magic formula of strict rote technique. There generally appears to have been an excessive preoccupation with technique and format rather than the development of disciplined thinking about what an organization is and what it should be producing with its budget allocations, the basic concept of PB. More than a thousand years ago, an Oriental philosopher, Lao-tse, advised: "Govern a great nation as you would cook a small fish. Do not overdo it."

It is interesting to note, however, that the beginnings of PB in Europe appear to have been somewhat smoother than in the United States. Although there have also been difficulties, generally the approach has been slower and more cautious. More attention has been paid to understanding the concept and to preparing for potential difficulties.

Although the utilization of PB has taken many forms and its efficacy varies, interest continues as organizations grow in size, scope, and complexity, with inadequate management tools for coping with change and the allocation of limited resources.

30.4 FRAMEWORK OF PROGRAM BUDGETING. A major aim of PB is to convert the annual routine of preparing a budget into a conscious appraisal and formulation of an organization's goals by providing a long-range perspective. A PB framework requires the fusion of strategic and long-range planning with budgeting processes through the use of various structural, analytical, and informational elements.

A generalized PB system does not exist. In applying PB to an organization, managers must tailor it to the organization's particular context and needs. There are several key processes and elements, however, that are common to most PB systems.

(a) Process Phases. Program budgeting operates within three basic interlocking and interactive process phases in its annual cycle: *planning, programming,* and *budgeting.* They have separate time allotments, with reviews and key decision checkpoints at each juncture, providing progressively more detailed views. A schema of a PB process cycle was shown in Exhibit 30.2 in the context of management requirements and decision making.

The planning phase should provide ample time for identifying and studying challenges, objectives, and alternatives, and for resolving the basic strategy and program structure. The programming phase should provide time for the assembly and review of detailed planning forecasts (inputs and related outputs in a program structure). The budgeting phase should provide sufficient time to translate the previous efforts into a traditional line-item budget.

The progressively more detailed views are likely to involve different kinds and magnitudes of change or direction. The planning phase may trigger significant changes, and the programming phase generally results in some adjustments of the plans. Although the budgeting phase may still bring more significant light to bear, it generally only modifies earlier decisions. All of the phases, however, are expected by design to trigger major changes if required by further information or analysis.

(i) Planning Phase. The planning phase deals with the development of missions, goals, objectives, and alternatives and with the strategies and general resource allocations for achieving them over a long-range time frame expressed in a basic program structure. A basic program structure classification should be developed or updated in this phase.

The planning phase can be viewed and conducted sequentially. Strategic planning is the first consideration. This means planning for an entity as a whole, not merely adding up the separate plans of the respective parts without a common and guiding thread. When dealing with a company as a whole in industry, this strategic planning is sometimes referred to as *corporate planning.*

Strategic planning is basically concerned with the long-term destiny of an organization. It is the guiding light. Whatever the organization's size, its destiny will generally depend upon two, three, or four key decisions. If they are right, the organization will be well positioned to take advantage of most opportunities or to solve most problems that come along. If they are wrong, it may not just mean having the wrong foot on the playing field, but playing the wrong sport in the wrong stadium. The result can be a serious deterioration in, or the demise of, an organization.

Strategic planning consists of identifying what those few decisions are and getting them right. Although strategic planning is deceptively simple, this does not mean that it is easy. Difficulties arise because the decisions are pivotal, with big impacts, and they depend largely on judgment and intuition in an uncertain future. A strategic plan should summarize in very broad terms and quantification what the key decision makers believe the organization should look like in the next 5 to 10 years, together with a realistic statement as to how it will be done. Apart from the instrinsic value of the strategic plan, a sense of consensus and cohesion in an organization generally follows its development, with more members pulling in the same direction and at the same speed. This is especially so if the planning process was interactive up and down the line. If an organization is big and diverse, the major component entities should also develop supporting strategic plans, which, of course, must ultimately be governed by the organization's overall requirements and program structure.

In all cases, the initial broad focus of strategic planning generates the major options and aids in decisions on the missions, objectives, policies, and major PB program groupings and on the general acquisition, use, and disposition of resources necessary to attain the objectives. This must be done in the realistic context of an organization's status quo and critical issues. This then serves as a basis for the more detailed planning and quantification of the planning phase, which is sometimes referred to as *long-range planning*. It generally represents further translation toward implementation and is sometimes not much more than additional long-range details of the chosen options.

The long-range planning, then, as distinguished from strategic planning, moves closer to the planning of current operations and of all the units of an organization. This further planning could include completing the PB program structure hierarchy, additional analysis of alternatives, data development, inclusion of more organizational units, further operational and functional area considerations, re-engineering studies, and generally more details. In industry, it might also include product and market planning, finance and manpower planning, and R&D and manufacturing planning; these would be expressed within the chosen program structure, with their respective resource allocations.

The major considerations for the various kinds of planning can begin with the taking of a situational inventory. This is done by identifying and studying the critical issues or challenges facing an organization or planning unit that revolve around its competition, major problems, needs, threats, opportunities, strengths, and weaknesses. Various alternatives and strategies are then generated in response to the issues. This process also serves as a creative stimulus by exposing the decision makers to situations demanding solutions. The evaluations and directions that result are measured against the existing goals and objectives in order to confirm, change, or update them as well as the strategic responses. The strategic responses are then expressed in output-oriented programs, with estimates and data that are not detailed. Again, strategic planning would have the most general data, whereas long-range planning would start to provide more details and forecasts to fit into current operations.

The next significant level of detail would be accomplished in the next phase—programming. In some planning systems this activity could still be regarded as being in the planning phase, as part of the long-range planning mentioned previously, and would involve the assembly and review of long-range plans in further forecast detail. This distinction is not critical, as long as a planning system's process and data provide a comprehensive decision-making base in increasing detail and in a program structure for building a connected, supportive, and consistent budget. In many cases, however, the details of the long-range plans are too limited or disconnected for easy conversion to a budget. The programming phase, in particular, addresses such deficiencies.

The planning and programming phases as described here, therefore, are essentially parts of the same activity, differing primarily in planning detail. The major strategic considerations, however, should be resolved in the planning phase. The key decision makers should be integrally involved in both phases and should review the results before moving to the budgeting phase.

(ii) Programming Phase. The term *programming* can possibly be a bit confusing in PB jargon and should be differentiated from the term *program.* The creation of the major PB program groupings is generally handled in the planning phase, with the term *program* indicating an output-oriented strategic classification. Probably, the programming phase could have more appropriately been designed as "multi-year forecasting."

Programming primarily deals with the more detailed application of resources (manpower, materials, facilities, and equipment) and schedules to the plans and programs. That is, it is the programming of resource expenditures (capital planning) for the programs in significant detail for incorporation into a budget. It is the level of detail after planning that bridges the gap to budgeting and reflects all of the strategic decisions and projected expenditures in a program format for a planning period. In a sense, it represents a multi-year budget in a program format.

Objectives should be well defined by the programming phase, but they should still be challenged. The attention should now be focused on translating the preferred alternatives for implementation and the deployment of resources. Quantification data in considerable detail are necessary at this stage because the budgeting consequences of the approved programs should be anticipated. Assembly of the various multi-year financial forecasts of the planning period is completed in this phase according to all the program groupings, with the resources allocated within financial capabilities. The crosswalks are also completed in this phase. The multi-year forecasts need only be in a program structure format. It is not necessary that they also be in a regular line-item format. Only the budget year is translated into a line-item format, as will be discussed later.

After the programming phase is completed and approved, preparation commences on the budget or the annual profit plan, as it is often called in industry. The first year of the multi-year forecasts in the PB format is now fully translated into a regular line-item budget format through the crosswalks (described later). Such details significantly facilitate the preparation of the budget with a soundly conceived foundation regarding the likely future requirements. It is expected that much of the annual budget debate can take place in the programming phase and can result in the basic budget assumptions, guidelines, and decisions.

(iii) Budgeting Phase. In the budgeting phase, final allocations of resources and more detailed reviews are made in a traditional line-item format to accomplish and control the approved programs for the first year of the plan. They are based on the latest information, the crosswalk translations, and the basic budget decisions made in the programming phase. Here, again, there should still be an allowance for decisions that may be necessary to modify program choices, but, obviously, at this late stage, changes must be judiciously applied. If the budget changes are significant, the multi-year forecasts of the programming phase should be recast promptly in order to balance inputs and outputs and to view the ramifications to allow for possible strategic adjustments.

(iv) Key Elements. There are commonalities in all PB systems. This include various key *structural, analytical,* and *informational elements* in the process leading to a budget. Although there is some overlap among them, and although they are balanced differently in some PB systems, they are presented here as separate entities for clarity and emphasis. They include various key activities and components that should take a written form for proper communication and reference.

Throughout this chapter, considerable reference is made to the federal PB terminology because of its vast influence on all systems. A separate section titled ''Federal Program Budgeting Format'' is provided later, more fully describing the components.

(v) Program Structure. A program structure is the basic framework of PB. An output-oriented program structure should be established in the planning phase and should be based on a translation of an organization's fundamental missions, goals, objectives, or purposes. The translation establishes the strategic program classifications in a program hierarchy. The hierarchy ranges from the largest program category classification to the basic and smallest constituents, termed *program elements.* Each program should represent activities and resources with a common purpose that will produce the same outputs.

The program groupings, however, will not likely conform to an existing organizational structure, and they need not be so constructed. In the early evaluation stages, the programs can preliminarily overlap the existing organizational structure in the deployment of resources. The program structure should provide insights into an organization's objectives, as well as its priorities, according to the allocations made with the programs. The possible overlaps can be resolved in the later stages of the planning phase or in the programming phase.

The basic considerations in developing a PB program structure are provided also later in the section on program structuring because of the special significance of this aspect.

A program structure analysis should contain the program choices made, the alternatives considered, and the rationale and broad strategies upon which the programs are built, including the attendant long-range goals and anticipated program accomplishments. The calculations supporting the chosen program groupings should also be included, with as much history along the basic program structure lines as is feasible. This analysis can be part of the strategic and long-range plans and can represent a part of their basis. In the federal PB terminology, this type of analysis would be a basis for a ''program memorandum (PM).'' It could also be characterized as a kind of strategic position paper.

(vi) Issues Analysis. A continual conducting of key studies is necessary to provide an analytic foundation for decisions made in a PB system. These studies include the identification and review of critical issues and challenges facing an organization that must be made

periodically and injected into a PB cycle for strategic consideration, addition, confirmation, or rejection. This can be part of the strategic planning and its periodic updating. This activity has been referred to as an *issues analysis.* In the federal PB format, it was termed *special studies,* which are basically of two kinds. Some were carried out for the purpose of resolving issues in the budget year, whereas others had time frames that extended beyond the budget year in order to serve the development of future recommendations and actions. Without these analytic inputs, the process of planning, programming, and budgeting can become overly procedural, with limited vitality and substance. They can deteriorate into an exercise in numerology without interactive analytic inputs on the key issues. In the context of more current management lexicon, some of these studies could include or be part of *re-engineering-type audits/studies.*

(vii) Strategic and Long-Range Plans. The strategic and long-range plans may be completed and considered as one unit or be separate, but connected, entities. As indicated previously, this distinction is not critical. It depends a great deal on the characteristics of an organization and its current planning system and needs. It is certainly critical, however, that a strategic plan be developed for the basic organizational direction and program structure.

A *strategic plan* should deploy the major resources of an organization. It summarizes an organization's future direction, objectives, and rationale for the chosen program groupings, with their broadly estimated resources, costs, and returns. A strategic plan can be largely qualitative and should serve as a good basis for developing more planning details. It should not require extensive revision every year and should only consist of a few pages as the foundation of the various plans. Separate subordinate strategic plans may also be necessary for the major entities of large or diverse organizations. The federal government PB *program memoranda* (PM) had many similarities to strategic plans.

Related *long-range plans,* which support the strategic plan and provide additional definition of current operations, program groupings, organizational units, functional areas, objectives, strategy, and financial details, should be developed and updated each year. This serves as a basis for more detailed multi-year comprehensive forecasts in a program format for ultimate conversion to a budget. In PB, these details are represented in multi-year program forecasts.

(viii) Multi-Year Program Forecasts. Detailed long-range forecasts of inputs and outputs resulting from the strategic and long-range planning that includes the budget year should be developed in a program format along with as much history as is feasible. In the federal PB terminology, this forecast had also been called a multi-year *program and financial plan* (PFP). These forecasts show the probable impact of current decisions on future revenues and expenditures for all the programs from the broad program category level to the narrower program element level. Although these forecasts were in considerable detail, they were less detailed than a budget and were the result of completing the programming phase. They provided all the pertinent data related to the outputs, costs, capital, and financing of the programs in sufficient enough detail for the traditional budget preparations.

In short, these multi-year forecasts were the basic quantitative and comprehensive statistical planning documentation of PB. It relates the quantitative measures of the program

	Program Category I						
	History	Budget Year 1	Year 2	Year 3	Year 4	Year 5	Total Costs
Expense Outlay							
Salaries		$15,000					
Materials		10,000					
Maintenance		3,000					
Utilities		2,000					
Depreciation		2,000					
Travel		5,000					
Rent		7,000					
Total expense		$44,000					
Capital Outlay							
Buildings		$3,000					
Property		1,000					
Equipment		5,000					
Fixed capital		9,000					
Working capital		4,000					
Total capital		$13,000					
Select output							
Indicators and benefits							

Exhibit 30.4. Outline of a multi-year program and financial plan ($thousand)

outputs to the respective operating and capital expenditures. It is generally a statistical tabulation, covering a planning period, as outlined in Exhibit 30.4 at a program category level. Expenditures are indicated only for the budget year for purposes of simplicity.

In industry, these forecasts could include profit and loss, cash flow, and capital expenditure statements or tabulations. The outputs would include the sales of key related product or service areas, with their respective profits and returns.

In nonindustry organizations where the outputs cannot be measured in monetary terms, it is also necessary to conceive of output indicators in addition to a program structure. This is necessary to measuring in physical terms the outputs of the various programs. The output measure chosen should be the most important quantitative performance indicator of a program. For example, for an on-the-job training program, it could be the number of workers trained; for a health program, it could be lowered disease incidence; for highway construction, it could be the number of lane miles built or reduced traffic accidents per mile; and so forth.

New circumstances or thinking may dictate significant changes in the budgeting and this, in turn, may require a timely rebalancing of the multi-year forecasts to evaluate the impacts on the basic thrust of the plans.

A multi-year forecast will also generally have an accompanying crosswalk (or reconciliation tabulation), cross-referencing a PB program format to the existing appropriation and fund accounts for the first year of the planning period. The purpose of the reconciliation is to ensure that the budget submissions are consistent with the intent of the program decisions and that they can be implemented through the existing budget structure.

Traditional Cost Categories		Crosswalk ⇄	PB Format		
Account No.	Account	Totals	Program Category 1	Program Category 2	Program Category 3
100	Salaries	$ 25,000	$15,000	$ 5,000	$ 5,000
200	Materials	50,000	10,000	35,000	5,000
300	Maintenance	5,000	3,000	1,000	1,000
400	Utilities	5,000	2,000	2,000	1,000
500	Depreciation	10,000	2,000	7,000	1,000
600	Travel	15,000	5,000	5,000	5,000
700	Rent	60,000	7,000	50,000	3,000
Etc.	Etc.	—	—	—	—
	Operating expense outlay	$170,000	$44,000	$105,000	$21,000
1100	Buildings	20,000	3,000	12,000	5,000
1200	Property	10,000	1,000	7,000	2,000
1300	Equipment	15,000	5,000	9,000	1,000
1400	Fixed capital outlay	$ 45,000	$ 9,000	$ 28,000	$ 8,000
1500	Working capital outlay	15,000	4,000	8,000	3,000
	Total capital	$ 60,000	$13,000	$ 36,000	$ 11,000

Exhibit 30.5. Sample expenditure crosswalk: year 1

(ix) Crosswalk. If a program structure differs from an existing budget structure, as is very likely, then a crosswalk reconciliation, or cross-classification, must be established to connect them and to transform the first year of a PB format into a line-item budget. By the use of a crosswalk, the information from the existing data base can first be allocated and programmed into the strategic program groupings more appropriate to policy making and later regrouped for implementation and control.

The crosswalk allows the movement of data between planning and budgeting. The approach can be an elaborate one, utilizing an extensive reconciliation between a PB budget coding and a regular budget appropriations coding and the use of a computer. It also can be a simple tabular and manual cross-classification in a two-dimensional array with a less elaborate reconciliation, especially used for initial purposes as shown in Exhibit 30.5. It need only be constructed for the budget year.

Exhibit 30.5 shows an expenditure crosswalk tabulation for year 1, or the budget year, for three program categories. A reconciliation could even be carried down to a program element level. (Distinctions between the levels in a program hierarchy will be discussed later.) However, this is very much a circumstantial decision in which judgment must be applied for particular needs and merits. Certainly, some kind of cross-reference must be maintained to construct and explain, if necessary, the building of the larger program categories from their basic program elements and resource allocations. Most budget submissions would not likely include crosswalks at a detail level below that of a program category, the largest program grouping used.

The crosswalk tabulation indicates how each traditional line item and its account numbers (shown in rows) are allocated and cross-classified to the various program categories (columns) for the budget year through the same crosswalk totals. Also note that program category 1 ties back to the multi-year program forecast tabulation shown in Exhibit 30.4.

The PB format does not eliminate the need for the more traditional formats dealing with administrative, operational, organizational, and performance requirements. The system is not intended or designed to increase the efficiency in the performance of daily operations or to improve the administrative control of the expenditure funds. It primarily ties planning, analysis, and budgeting together. It is necessary, however, that the various budgetary formats used be connected to a PB format by a crosswalk.

(x) Change Analysis. Change may be characterized as the lifeblood of PB. The handling of change keeps a PB system alive and lively. It is especially necessary to determine periodically the need for strategic redirections. Provisions should be established in the annual planning and budgeting processes for necessary revisions. This should include at least a definite review period in the planning phase and flexible procedures and time allowances through the budgeting phase for ad hoc situations. It is difficult to schedule exact times throughout the year because of the ever-present uncertainties and the interlocking and interacting nature of the PB phases that provoke change. For certain, the major issues should always be resolved before considering the dependent ones, and flexibility must be available. In PB terminology, these revisions, particularly major ones, have sometimes been referred to as *change proposals.*

The changes may be the result of shifts in significant external and internal factors or assumptions. In industry, for example, significant changes could come from new information dealing with technology, competition, customers, or pricing; from shifts in the general economy or political or social climate; from more detailed analyses of resource requirements or outcomes; and so forth. A proposal for change, therefore, might cover a new product, service, or approach; a revision of an existing program or its cancellation; and so on. It would include the quantitative ramifications, the rationale, and all the relevant information. This could serve as a basis for redoing the multi-year program forecasts or could stand alone as an interim revision for further reflection and later incorporation. Such considerations, as well as a format, depend on the particular circumstances of an organization.

A change analysis should contain at least an outline of the major considerations and information, including summary quantification impacts.

(xi) Annual Calendar. An annual PB cycle must be established, with regular intervals for the planning, programming, and budgeting phases. This is to allow sufficient time for analysis and decision making at all levels of management.

An annual PB cycle should provide a year-round process of addressing program objectives, performance, and costs with a disciplined approach to change. It should also allow sufficient time for the program-oriented data to be translated into the budgeting phase with the required control details. Appropriate checkpoints should be included in order to ensure that all the essential steps are taken and that current reviews, revisions, and recommendations are given consideration at appropriate times in the cycle. A typical federal annual PB cycle is shown in Exhibit 30.6.

(xii) Systematic Analysis. An outstanding feature of PB is the emphasis on analysis throughout all its phases. Systematic analyses must be performed to clarify the conceptual framework in which decisions are made, to define possible alternative objectives, and to explore the cost and effectiveness of alternative courses of action. The system itself is an

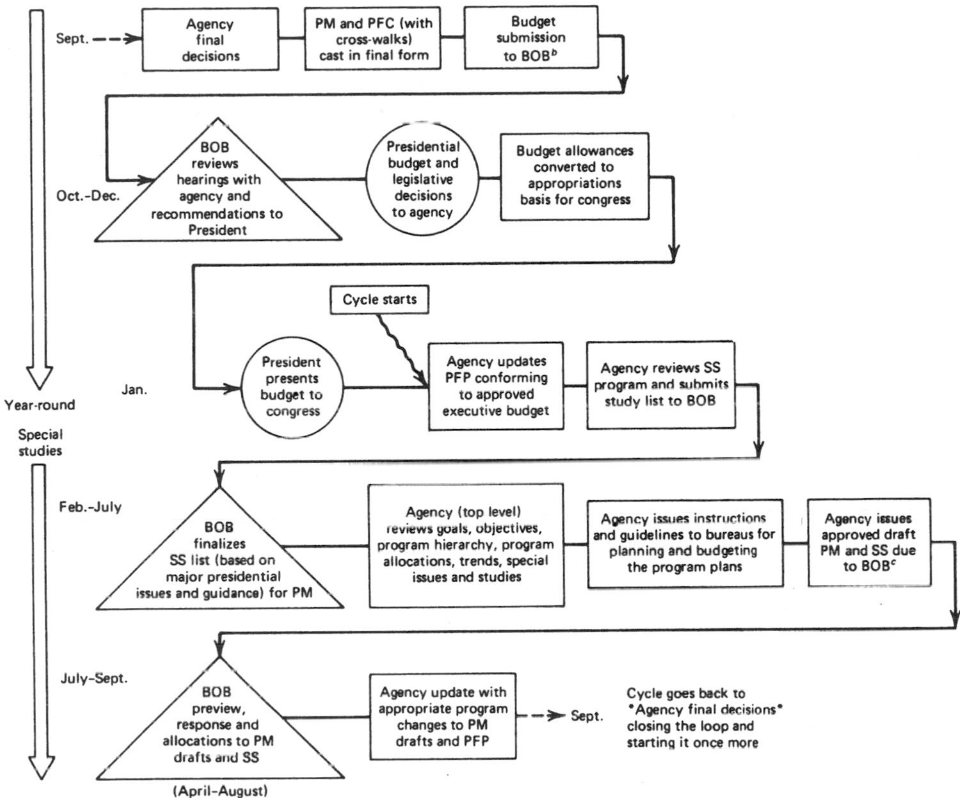

Exhibit 30.6. Typical annual PB cycle for a federal government agency

analytical tool. Because of the importance of analysis to PB, this topic is covered in greater depth in the section on types of analysis.

(xiii) Information Systems. Program budgeting should derive its information primarily from existing management records and practices. The existing data base and accounting systems should provide information (or be adapted) to the planning, programming, and budgeting phases in a program structure hierarchy. It should allow the basic forecasting, implementation, and analysis, as well as the progress reporting and control with updating procedures. The basic requirements need not be difficult to set up. Various considerations for setting up a PB system are provided in the section on installation considerations.

(b) Federal Program Budgeting Format. Combinations of the various PB elements can, of course, take many forms. More specifically, the format that was developed in the federal government is of greatest interest because of its wide use, publicity, and extensive scope as follows.

(i) Documents. Three kinds of federal PB documents were generated annually along with the traditional budget addressing various qualitative and quantitative considerations.

Program memoranda (PM) were provided by each federal agency, containing its program structure recommendations to fit its objectives for the forthcoming period. These objectives were required to be defined in quantifiable and measurable terms, to allow for meaningful program analysis and implementation. The PM was basically a strategic decision document. It essentially is a strategic plan in which a program structure analysis is also included.

The PM was expected to be a brief written document explaining the program issues, the rationale of alternative program groupings recommended or rejected, and their costs and effectiveness. It was also to include the results of special studies, which are described subsequently. The PM encouraged policy debate among decision makers in the executive branch and communicated the final policy.

Aspects of ZBB are also in a PM because it includes a defense and review of total expenditures proposed for a program, rather than just indicating the changes from previous appropriations. The government instructions pointed out that as much attention should be paid to reducing and modifying obsolete and low-priority programs as to expanding others and introducing new ones. However, the government ultimately retreated from a full embracing of ZBB. It gravitated somewhere between incremental budgeting and a zero-based review of all programs.

The multi-year PFP summarized in tabular form the data from each agency that were pertinent to its program outputs, costs, and financing for the past two years, the budget year, and four additional years. The time span could be longer for special situations, such as for timber production or water resource projects.

The PFP was the result of the programming phase and was meant to be a record of the consequences of the current year's decisions. The data of the PM, on the other hand, did not have to be so confined and could reflect on consequences outside the budget year decisions.

The outputs enumerated in the PFP were the measurable end products or services that were produced by the individual program elements. For example, a health program might use mortality data; an on-the-job training program could cite the increase in the income of the workers trained.

The PFP also included tables on the financial requirements for all the major program groupings, down to the smallest program element. The financial data included total program costs, which encompassed program-oriented R&D and all related operating costs and capital investments. Each program element was assigned a program budget code based on the regular appropriation code in order to provide a crosswalk reconciliation. This crosswalk was a tabulation in the PFP and made it possible to translate the program costs back into conventional budget requests through the existing organizational structure. This was necessary since the President was required to recommend his budget to the Congress in an established appropriations structure and also to monitor the consistency of the budget submission with the program decisions. The crosswalk did not have to show a reconciliation down to a program element level but only to the major program groupings, the program categories.

Special studies (SS) provided the basic data and analytic foundation for the program decisions of the PM regarding the program choices and rejection of alternatives. They usually covered specific aspects of programs. They showed the costs and benefits of prior programs and compared alternative program mixes.

These analyses were for decision-making purposes and considered economic opportunity and marginal costs in addition to regular budget-type costs. The costs in the PFP, however, were more limited and in a regular budgetary mode. The PFP constituted a link between the mixed bag of analytical costs covered in both the SS and the PM to the regular budget financing needed to implement the programs.

In addition, the SS served as a vehicle for general policy issue analyses in which the major issues were identified, analyzed, and then incorporated into the budget. There was no fixed length or format for SS. It was performed and issued year round to support an agency's strategic directions or upon request from the BOB. It was not part of the final submitted budget package. Yearly, the BOB and the agencies jointly agreed to a list of program issues requiring detailed analysis. Some of them were for resolving issues in the budget and others were for future actions.

The basic quality of the various PB documents were judged on some of the following criteria: For the PM, it was the concentration of major policy decisions and the identification of major alternatives; for the PFP, it was the accuracy of cost and output estimates; and for the SS, it was the usefulness of the information and the identified alternatives for achieving the program objectives.

(ii) Final Federal Submission. Program budgeting became the third way in which each federal agency was required to display its annual budget. Each agency was required to identify the major objectives it was pursuing and to display its budgetary data in the following terms:

- Appropriations for control of expenditures (line item traditional cost format)
- Activity for management efficiency (''performance'' format)
- Program budgeting format, which included the PM and PFP as integral parts of the traditional budget submissions and reviews

(iii) Annual Federal Cycle. The federal PB cycle was an annual comprehensive process of addressing program objectives, performance, and costs by systematically bringing planning, analysis, and budgeting together. It provided checkpoints to ensure that essential steps were taken and that current reviews, revisions, and recommendations were given consideration at appropriate times in the budget process. Throughout the process it utilized the basic PB documents: the PM, PFP, and SS.

Each federal agency had latitude for tailored modifications in the cycle as long as they met the BOB's basic legal and legislative schedule requirements. Each agency head was expected to receive recommendations from his or her principal managers on all the major program issues. It was the responsibility of each agency head to ensure that line managers at appropriate levels participated in the cycle.

An outline of a typical annual PB cycle utilizing the various PB process steps for the federal agencies is shown in Exhibit 30.6 within a year around special studies activities. The cycle shown is basically for an established PB system. It breaks into the cycle in the September activities to highlight the beginning context of the cycle that starts in January. The cycle begins in January with an updated multi-year program and financial plan conforming to the approved executive budget soon after the President's submission of the Administration's budget to Congress the same month. This is the basis for the various planning activities that proceed through August. Also in August are the programming activities that are reflected in the updating and program changes of the PFP before the start of the September budgeting activities. The budgeting activities of the cycle go from

September through January and end with the President's budget presentation for the next fiscal year. There is some overlap or combination of PB process activities in some of the checkpoint intervals. This is to be expected, with the interlocking and interactive nature of the PB to provide the most timely and comprehensive decision-oriented data.

30.5 PROGRAM STRUCTURING.

Program structuring is a vital ingredient of PB that transforms an organization's existing cost structure into strategic output-oriented information. It arranges an organization's activities into a hierarchy of strategic program groupings with common outputs and objectives. It is a way of organizing information to show how much is spent or should be spent for an organization's various purposes, irrespective of its existing organizational structure. As indicated previously, the SBUs employed in the GE/McKinsey strategic planning technique have many similarities to the strategic program groupings of PB. The term *profit center,* utilized in industry, also has many similarities.

The following are a number of key considerations to be aware of in developing and structuring PB programs for both private and public sector organizations.

(a) No Set Formula.

There is no set formula for creating programs or a program structure. There are as many ways of conceiving programs as there are of organizing activities.

The possibilities for regrouping activities are almost endless, and different program grouping schemes may be necessary for different organizational needs and circumstances. Rigidity and inflexibility should be avoided. A test of satisfactory program structure is its utility in facilitating and clarifying an organization's current decision-making processes for strategically allocating resources.

Programs in a planning development stage need not be mutually exclusive because an organization's objectives may require some overlapping structures between business, geographic, and functional areas. This can help in evaluating programs, in making trade-offs, and ultimately in choosing a final program and in resolving the budget.

(b) Traditional versus Program Budgeting Format.

Examples that vividly differentiate a PB program structure from one of traditional budgeting with a more limited output orientation are as follows:

Possible Program Structures	
Traditional Structure	PB Structure
Coast Guard	*Coast Guard*
Vessel operations	Search and rescue
Aviation operations	Aids to navigation
Repair and supply facilities	Law enforcement
Forest Service	*Forest Service*
Forest protection	Timber production
Range improvements	Outdoor recreation
Land acquisition	Natural beauty
Access roads	Wildlife

The PB program structure clearly emphasizes the purposes and objectives of the Coast Guard and Forest Service, whereas the traditional structure emphasizes the methods or means used.

A PB program structure can provide a better framework for strategic decision making and resource allocations between the various activities. This factor does not negate the need for other kinds of budgeting structures which can be more helpful in dealing with operations, performance, and efficiency. Different views can provide an additional basis for sound decision making and controls.

(c) Program Hierarchy. Program structuring involves defining a hierarchy of programs. The concept of a program hierarchy presents the logic of moving from defined objectives into programs and operating activities in meaningful implementation terms. In PB terminology, they can range from the largest aggregation of activities, *program categories* (which address the broad objectives or missions); to intermediate categories, *program subcategories* or *program packages;* to the smallest program units, *program elements.* The designation distinctions between these category levels are not important. It is important to have meaningful hierarchical program groupings to assist in choosing among program alternatives and for making fund allocations across the program spectrum of an organization.

Probably, the missions of an organization, particularly the market missions in industry that assume a "purposes" tone and that relate to encompassing (or the highest) levels of an organization's activities, can best help define the broad program categories.

A program element is the smallest program unit that is self-contained. In the industry sense, it might be termed a *profit center* or *key product area.* It is a complete, identifiable, self-contained activity or decision unit such as a system, a product, or a service that contributes to an organization's purpose and objectives. It serves as a building block of a program structure.

All major costs, facilities, major equipment, manpower, and other resources directly related to the programs must be identified (see Exhibit 30.1 for a matrix view).

(d) Program Development. Programs can be generated by focusing on broad objectives related to purposes, by separating costs into generic activities, by separating means from ends, by considering current strategic requirements, by breaking a major area into its primary components, and so forth. A creative approach could utilize many of these approaches concurrently, with a choice ultimately being made according to an organization's particular circumstances and needs.

A hierarchy of programs can be constructed from two directions, that is, from smaller units into larger ones or from purposeful generic umbrellas broken down into smaller units. The main approach is the latter. The upper levels of major programs should focus primarily on outputs, whereas the lower levels can focus more on means to achieving objectives. The development process is iterative and very subjective to an organization and circumstances.

(e) Classification Schemes. There is a variety of classification schemes that can be utilized for creating program categories. The groupings should all focus on objectives and purposes and can cover a wide range, such as customers, markets, age–sex–type groups, geography, primary function, product, or service lines.

(i) Industry. A hypothetical conglomerate industrial organization could include plant and toiletry products with the following possible program hierarchy:

Industry Program Hierarchy		
Plant Products	**Toiletry Products**	
1. *Fertilizer*	1. *Hair care*	
a. Industrial	a. Cleansing	
b. Home and garden	b. Coloring	
or	or	or
Chemical types	• Shampoo	• Consumer
	• Dyes, tints	• Institutional
2. *Pesticides*	2. *Mouth care*	
a. Industrial	a. Cleaning	
b. Home and garden	b. Deodorizing	
or	or	or
Destruction	• Toothpaste	• Consumer
means:	• Mouthwash	• Institutional
• Mechanical	3. Skin care	
• Chemical		
• Biological		

(ii) Federal Government. A segment of program hierarchies from two federal agencies are as follows:

Federal Program Hierarchy	
Department of Health, Education & Welfare (February 1968)	**Department of Labor (May 1968)**
Education	*Manpower Development Assistance*
1. Basic skills department	1. Training
a. General population	a. On-the-job
b. Economically disadvantaged	b. Institutional (classroom)
c. Handicapped	2. Special manpower program
Health	a. Experimental projects
1. Development of health resources	3. Work programs
a. Increasing knowledge	a. Neighborhood youth corps
• Heart disease	b. Community employment
• Cancer	c. Work incentive program
b. Providing facilities/equipment	*Employment Assistance*
2. Prevention/control health problems	1. Employment market information
a. Disease control	2. Job development/placement
3. Health services provision	a. Assistance
a. Aged	b. Agricultural
b. Poor	c. Veterans
c. Indians	3. Employability assistance
d. Children and mothers	4. Civil rights compliance

It can be seen that a variety of program classifications can be established for the programs described here, and they could all be valid in accommodating various organizational needs. It is interesting to note the scope that PB took in the DOD with about 10 program categories and more than 800 program elements.

(f) Problems. There are several problems in establishing a PB program structure that should be taken into consideration. These include the following:

- Increased paperwork and manpower time, and possible increased costs to do the work. For example, superimposing a program structure onto a conventional accounting system will require a reconciliation through a crosswalk.
- Power struggles with program delineation. Since program delineations may be arbitrary and may not respect organizational lines, struggles to retain budgetary control may ensue.
- Confusion with cost allocations. Differences are bound to occur regarding the apportionment of costs that cut across jurisdictional lines.

Although there are formidable problems to consider in structuring programs, they can be managed if one anticipates them. The payoff can be improved results and viability.

30.6 TYPES OF ANALYSIS. The cornerstone of PB is the systematic identification and analysis of alternatives, which are examined in relation to benefits and costs. As mentioned earlier, some of the current management jargon in this genre would include re-engineering audits/studies. Buzzwords such as *cost–benefit,* however, became strongly identified with PB in its heyday at the Pentagon and are still very much a part of the lexicon. The distinctions between the various types of applicable analyses, however, are not always clear.

Three basic types of analysis have been associated with PB: (1) *systems analysis;* (2) *cost–benefit* and *cost-effectiveness* analysis, which are similar terms and are sometimes used synonymously; and (3) *operations research.* These types are sometimes used interchangeably because of the overlap among them. In a sense, they represent an analytical hierarchy, with the differentiating factors being the degree of problem scope, complexity, and uncertainty. Reviewing the similarities and differences between these analyses should shed some light on their key elements and applications.

The approach of all of these analyses to solving problems is the scientific method: analysis, synthesis, and verification. All of them are a form of systems analysis in that they all relate to inputs and outputs within defined boundaries. They all break a given area or system into its component inputs and outputs, which collectively serve as a model.

(a) Systems Analysis. A systems analysis has the broadest orientation and is generally concerned with broad or ill-structured problems (bordering on policy, goals, and strategy) having choices that cannot be reduced solely to an economic basis.

Systems analysis has been characterized as a way to a solution, or as ''quantitative common sense.'' This means, of course, that for very complex problems dealing with the future, particularly those dealing with strategy or significant political, social, or public factors, a solution is generally not obvious in a quantitative sense. In such cases, a systems analysis aids a decision maker in creating alternatives and in selecting one. It provides a comprehensive summary of all the relevant information. It is more concerned with widening the range of alternatives or creating sensible objectives rather than with selecting the best one from a limited given range. It attempts to ensure the achievement of a larger objective more effectively rather than solely focusing on optimizing a few component parts. Its premise is that it is better to be roughly right rather than exactly wrong. It seeks to avoid gross error. In this sense, it is a rough kind of grand optimum for a broad set of circumstances.

(i) Limited Mathematics. Systems analysis involves applying broad concepts to situations having a significant number of uncontrolled and unpredictable factors. The extensive use of mathematical statistical techniques in such cases is limited. One can deal with uncertainty through the use of scenario alternatives, sensitivity tests, and the use of quantitative ranges. The calculations generally utilized are relatively uncomplicated in the context of the broad basic concepts of macroeconomics, where informed judgment still plays the bigger role. Although systems analysis uses calculations, it puts less emphasis on them relative to the other types of analysis.

Breaking up a complex management system into a conceptually oriented framework of smaller component systems or subsystems, such as in PB, with various inputs and outputs, is a form of systems analysis. It is not some arcane, heavily computerized or mathematically oriented form of analysis. Strategic and long-range planning in industry are forms of systems analysis, as is an analysis of strategic weapons systems in the military.

(ii) Iterative Process. As with strategic or long-range planning, the analytic process is highly iterative in the mold of the scientific method and in trial and error. A sequence of the process could be defining the problem (or opportunity), selecting objectives, designing alternatives, collecting data, building models, evaluating costs attendant to benefits, testing for sensitivity, reviewing original premises against the forecast results, re-examining the objectives, designing new alternatives, reformulating the problem, determining new or modified objectives, and so on to a solution (or strategy).

(b) Cost–Benefit and Cost-Effectiveness Analysis. Every systems analysis must reach the point, after getting past the grand objectives and strategies, of evaluating the costs, benefits, or effectiveness of specific alternatives or subsystems for achieving specified objectives. At this juncture, the broad qualitative policy issues are either minimized or well defined. The analyses of such alternatives has generally been termed cost–benefit or cost-effectiveness analysis. Apparently, because these analyses frequently receive the most attention, the entire analysis, including the systems analysis portion, receives the cost–benefit or cost-effectiveness label.

Both types of analysis require the measurement of inputs and outputs for a given alternative and measure costs in monetary terms. Their distinction lies basically on the output side. In cost–benefit analysis the outputs can be computed in monetary terms, whereas in cost-effectiveness analysis the outputs can be quantified only in physical units. Some problems may have combinations of both kinds of analysis.

(i) Different Evaluation Values. A cost–benefit analysis is quite common in industry where, for example, major new capital projects require extensive cost–benefit calculations, including profit and loss, breakeven, cash flow, payouts, return-on-investment, discounted rates of return (internal rate of return, net present value), and cost–benefit ratio analyses. However, this technique has evolved to the point where it is now capable of handling broader problems than those traditionally found in business. In situations where monetary values are only a part of the total value, or where important quantitative value factors cannot be expressed in monetary terms, a combination cost–benefit and cost-effectiveness analysis is helpful.

In government, educational, and various nonprofit institutions, many of the major decisions reflect social benefits and costs and political considerations. The cost-effectiveness approach is used primarily in such cases, with the outputs measured in physical outputs. The benefits in such cases may include workers trained, disease reduced, fatalities prevented, junk yards beautified, billboards removed, youths trained, and so on.

When the costs or benefits cannot be well quantified, one has to fall back on a systems-analysis mode. When costs can be quantified, but not benefits or effectiveness, one is then faced with a hybrid structure. The approach to utility theory used in Bayesian decision theory, statistics, and economics can be helpful in such cases. The utility (satisfaction, value, worth) preferences of people can be represented in numerically useful ways, with probability distributions or degrees of "yes" or "no" for policy decisions. Such approaches have significant implications for welfare and ethics economics.

The cost–benefit and cost-effectiveness types of analysis provide a method by which many of the major relationships in a problem capable of being reduced to a quantitative basis are so translated, thereby leaving the decision maker with a better basis for applying judgment and intuition to the remainder.

In its collective utilization, PB including that of the federal government, has probably put more people to work trying to learn how to do analyses of social systems than any other management effort in history.

(ii) Basic Approaches. A cost–benefit and cost-effectiveness analysis can be approached from a few basic points of view: the cost is constrained or fixed, and the solution is the maximum benefit or effectiveness; the level of benefit or effectiveness is fixed, and the solution is the option with the lowest cost. Also, in the case of cost–benefit analysis, and dealing strictly in monetary terms, a solution may be to maximize net benefits (benefits minus costs). Generally, however, all of these analyses are constrained by the limited resources of a budget.

In reaching a decision, the risk and returns should be evaluated on both a quantity and a ratio basis. The various measurements may include cost–benefit or cost-effectiveness ratios, net present values, internal rates of return, and the like. Of course, intuition and judgment are also important in considering the relevance of the qualitative factors and sometimes the primary basis after the number crunching.

(iii) Cost–Benefit Example. A cost–benefit analysis may mix quantitative and nonmonetary-oriented data in order to enable choosing among alternatives. An example of this would be the following: An industrial corporation has decided to put up a new combination headquarters–research building next to its primary manufacturing facilities. The facilities for research and administration had previously been rented. A simplified cost–benefit

structure is shown in the following table, which highlights the various cost and benefit considerations for five alternatives:

	Owned Facility			Rented Facility	
	Alternatives				
	1	2	3	4	5
Benefits					
New product sales					
Improved existing product sales					
Enhanced company image					
Improved morale and productivity					
Savings (rental removal)					
Tax benefits					
Better communications, cross-fertilization					
Reduced turnover					
Reduced staff travel time					
Increased new products introductions					
Percentage increase in manufacturing efficiency					
Higher-caliber technical staff attraction					
Increased customer service and contact					
Government contract enhancement					
Increased patent production					
Improved university relationships					
Improved team spirit					
Cost					
Capital investment					
Operating cost					
Depreciation					
Salaries					
Maintenance					
Rental					
Equipment					
Other					

A complete cost–benefit analysis could also take into account appropriate time spans and additional financial considerations, including cost–benefit ratios, cash flow, internal rates of return or net present values, payouts, returns on investment, and so on.

(iv) Industry Applications. Although the cost–benefit and cost-effectiveness approach has largely been utilized by government and not-for-profit institutions (e.g., educational institutions, libraries) to deal with social and political factors, it has been relatively unused by profit-making organizations in its complete context. As nonmonetary factors become more important to industry decision making, undoubtedly the broader aspects of these analyses will be increasingly utilized. Such analyses already have many existing useful applications for preparing budgets in nonrevenue departments, such as personnel, finance, and public relations. Generally, those budgets are approached on a limited incremental basis from year to year or requirements are injected into the department. In both approaches, the potential results are not adequately measured against costs.

The emphasis in preparing budgets for nonrevenue departments should be on identifying, and if possible, measuring the derived benefits or effectiveness against the costs and on determining whether greater advantage might not be obtained by shifting the directions (or even aborting some) in which the available funds are spent. Obviously, there are aspects of ZBB to this approach. All of this encourages economics in the large sense rather than in the small, as with incremental budgeting. In addition, these types of analysis provide a mechanism for establishing a comprehensive dialogue between the involved parties to discuss policy issues of a department in the concrete terms of constructing a budget.

(c) Operations Research. Operations research involves the application of sophisticated applied mathematics and scientific methods to problems in order to provide optimum solutions. The term was coined during World War II. The beginnings of systems analysis appear to be the successful operations research that was employed during World War II to handle military problems of defense and logistics. It initially dealt with military operations, such as preferred bomb mixes for different bombing missions, and gravitated into the broader considerations of strategic weapons systems. The label that is generally preferred for the broader type of problems, though, is systems analysis.

(i) Characteristics. Operations research is concerned primarily with efficiency and far less with the construction of choices, as contrasted with systems analysis. It tries to select an optimum solution from a predetermined set of alternatives and in a sense is a form of cost–benefit or cost-effectiveness analysis in which the numerical results have a high reliability in decision making. It generally deals with the optimization of smaller subsystems in which the data are assumed to be sufficiently accurate to allow sophisticated and detailed calculations within a range of statistical validity.

Operations research emphasizes applied mathematical techniques for discrete problems or for those that are better defined, narrower, or subject to constraints. Such problems are sufficiently defined so that they can be adequately described by a mathematical model in which the element of calculation is dominant; therefore, in a sense, the mathematics substitutes for the need for judgment. The mathematics includes linear and dynamic programming, queueing theory, decision theory, Monte Carlo techniques, search theory, inventory theory, control theory, and the like. The assumption is, again, that the empirical data are sufficiently accurate for the sophisticated calculations. In such cases, of course, the computer can be extremely helpful and fast.

Good examples of operations research–oriented analyses deal with materials and inventory management in industry or the military and with the routing and scheduling of transportation-related activites (trucking, airlines, rail, etc.).

(d) Comparison of the Analyses. There are similarities between systems analysis, operations research, and cost–benefit and cost-effectiveness analysis, because they all employ the scientific method to problem solving and because there is some overlap. At the extremes, however, systems analysis is more complex and less neat and quantitative. Although they are all quantitatively oriented, systems analysis tends to include a much large proportion of nonquantitative elements influencing the outcomes. In the cases of developing a new consumer or industrial product, designing a new weapons system, or developing an urban renewal plan, a systems analysis could be employed, and although operations research or a cost–benefit or cost-effectiveness analysis could be a part, they would likely have a more limited role. Again, a systems analysis is more concerned with avoiding strategic gross error and focuses on providing a wider range of choices or on designing a new solution. If there is an optimum with a systems analysis it is with the large scope (in the grand sense) rather than with the small.

Although the differences between systems analysis, cost–benefit and cost-effectiveness analysis, and operations research are not absolutely clear, an analogy that has been used points to the differences that exist between strategy and tactics.

(e) Modeling. All of the analyses that have been described utilize models as a simplifying mechanism to simulate the behavior of the real world. A *model* is essentially a simplified representation of an operation that contains only those aspects of primary importance to the problem under study. Although models generally take the form of a set of equations, they can be cast in several different quantitative and qualitative forms. They may vary from objects to verbal pictures to precise mathematical formulas.

Pro forma balance sheets, profit and loss statements, and breakeven charts are good examples of quantitative models simulating the financial processes of an organization. An accounting system is also a model; it is a simplified representation on paper, in the form of accounts and ledgers, of the flow of goods and services through a business enterprise.

There are also many nonquantitative types of models that must be employed, because all situations cannot be easily or fully translated into a neat quantitative framework or equation. These models are frequently utilized in strategic planning, systems analysis, or policy development, and they mostly rely on the informed judgment of experts on the issues. They include the following:

- *Scenarios.* A future is described under a possible chain of events in order to discuss policy options.
- *Delphi technique.* Experts forecast and interact indirectly on the future through a questionnaire. This is particularly useful in single-discipline situations.
- *Gaming.* A role-playing approach for simulating the interactions of people in the real world. This is particularly useful in situations requiring multidisciplines.

(i) Two Types. Models may be characterized as one of two general types: deterministic or probabilistic. The distinction is not so important in actually constructing a model as it is in utilizing the appropriate mathematics for a set of circumstances.

A deterministic model is used to represent operations or processes in which the degree of predictability is very high and the circumstances can be significantly controlled. Many operations research models fall into this category with the mathematics largely dictating the decision.

A probabilistic model is used to represent situations that have many uncertainties, the interactions of which are difficult to relate and control, with the ultimate consequences thus being extremely difficult to predict. Systems analysis and planning models generally fall into this category, as does PB as a model. Most of the submodels of PB tend to be probabilistic.

(ii) New Emphasis. There is very little that is new about modeling techniques, as they date back to ancient times. What is new is the emphasis in all kinds of organizations, government through industry, on developing larger comprehensive conceptual frameworks, as in PB, that will:

- Better elucidate the various relationships
- Better cope with the greater recognition of the existing uncertainties
- Better quantify outcomes
- More clearly demonstrate the consequences of various decisions

(ii) Handling Uncertainty. Through the manipulation of a model, one can demonstrate the influences of various kinds of uncertainty. For example, in the government, uncertainty can range from unpredictable congressional or citizenry attitudes to ally or enemy reactions. In business, uncertainty may result from new technology, energy crises, competitive reactions to pricing, product shifts in customer or consumer attitudes and demand, changes in interest rates, or the availability of capital, inflation, recession, and so on.

In such cases, a sensitivity analysis can be performed, using a model to determine the relative sensitivity of the significant variable factors to the outcomes. *Sensitivity analysis* is nothing more than a measuring of the degree to which costs or benefits may change with varying assumptions. Such an analysis in industry could include changes in profitability under varying levels of pricing, product mix, sales volume, cost, and capital. The model facilitates this kind of analysis, uncovering the important relationships so that appropriate actions may be taken.

(iv) The Acid Test. The acid test for determining the value of a model does not rest with the model's complexity or mathematical elegance but with its ability to provide insights into the problems raised and the solutions required and to predict the likely outcomes with sufficient accuracy. And, of course, in the end to facilitate sound decision making.

(f) Overview of Analyses. Program budgeting is concerned primarily with the methodology of systems analysis and cost–benefit and cost-effectiveness analysis rather than with that of operations research because many of the significant factors elude sophisticated quantification. However, the benefits of operations research can be substantial when the quantitative approach is appropriately utilized in total or in part. Operations research correctly applied can provide firm and reliable answers rather than just uncovering additional remedies of unknown or unverifiable success potential.

Systems analysis utilizes the scientific method, but it is more an art than a science. It generally is an approach to complex problems of choice under conditions of significant uncertainty, and its focus is with uncovering remedies. There is no single methodology that can be employed. Doing it helps decision makers recognize that one is managing a total and complex system with many relationships that cannot be managed by brushfire fighting or a mathematical formula. It helps focus on the importance of a central role and direction in managerial decision making, particularly in the strategic considerations.

Analysis is an aid, but not a replacement, for the decision maker. It sharpens intuition and judgment, stimulating the right questions and putting them in a logical array of priorities. How much of a budget should be allocated among competing programs in an organization is a decision problem that must finally depend on judgment, intuition, and faith in large part along side the numbers and forecasts.

Program budgeting can be viewed as a model of an organization's overall input–output process. It, therefore, is itself an analytical tool, because it generates objectives and alternatives, summarizes the costs and benefits, draws out the criteria, and provides a decision-oriented array in a distilled form.

30.7 INSTALLATION CONSIDERATIONS.

The framework, program structuring, and analytical aspects of PB have been covered in the previous sections. There are additional aspects to be taken into account when installing a complete, modified, or partial utilization of PB in an organization. They involve information and accounting systems, assessing and organizing, and tailoring and staffing. In many organizations, a PB installation will be more a process of consolidating and systematizing the ingredients already in place.

(a) Information System.

A critical ingredient of PB is data. An inadequate information system can be a major constraint to PB's operating effectively. A PB system may require restructuring data from existing systems, modifying some of the existing systems, or developing new supporting systems.

Many of the required information sources, reporting subsystems, and processing capabilities already exist in most large or up-to-date organizations. One may employ expedient stopgap approaches to get a PB system started, but, in all cases, the primary effort is with strategic and long-range planning rather than with the mechanical manipulation of data.

(i) Role in Program Budgeting.

Program budgeting is not a management information system. In some instances management information systems were undertaken as a substitute for major PB features. However, PB is not synonymous with the installation of a new computer system or related techniques for making management data more readily available. It is not the sole, or even the prime reason, for an organization to undertake company-wide information systems improvement programs. Even though a good management information system is very useful to PB operations, alone it lacks the planning emphasis, program structuring, and alternative analysis that are so vital to PB. Increasing the amount of hardware, firepower, and automatic processing does not provide these key PB elements. If an organization has the sophistication to consider a better link between its planning and budgeting systems, it very likely has the existing data systems adequately set up to utilize or readily adapt to PB techniques.

(ii) Program Budgeting Matrix.

The existing information system should allow the construction of a resources and cost matrix in a program format. It should allow displays and summaries by program, cost, organizational unit, function, or resource category in sufficient detail and validity to make decisions. Of course, if any of the existing systems are inadequate, they should be improved or eliminated, irrespective of installing a PB system.

(iii) Management's Needs.

Most management information system accomplishments have been in the areas of mechanization or computerization of record keeping and other routine operational activities and with middle management–type problems. They have been structured primarily for control and do not sufficiently serve the multiple needs of all levels of management; particularly in the areas of information and analytical support for the planning and policy decision making of the PB type. With the widespread availability of minicomputers and microcomputers and more sophisticated software programs, there is increasing potential for building dynamic, multifactor models for analysis and resource allocation.

(b) Accounting System. It is unnecessary to change an existing accounting or reporting system to conform to a program structure; in fact, it maybe undesirable. A PB program structure is not a static framework to be maintained despite significant external and internal changes or new strategic insights. The basis of PB is a periodic re-examination of program results in order to evaluate and restructure programs and objectives. A PB system and structure, like all planning systems, must be dynamically oriented to be valuable. Since programs and objectives are subject to change, it would be very disruptive to parallel changes each time with the accounting and reporting systems. Moreover, it would be equally chaotic to make organizational changes based solely on a program structure. If an organization is comfortable and knowledgeable with its existing accounting system, and it can be used, PB can be more smoothly introduced.

(i) Cost Aggregation. The existing accounting system must allow data to be consolidated into the large aggregative program categories from a program element level. Both direct and indirect costs must be in proper form and appropriately coded. The adjustment of the data should be kept to a minimum when accumulated into the larger categories. Methods should be developed to eliminate arbitrary allocations of indirect costs in the beginning. Moreover, the system should permit a summation of detailed cost elements from all cost elements to responsible organizational units (indicating the magnitude of the work load and resources each program requires). Also, appropriate coding or initial tracking for a crosswalk should be developed for transforming a PB format into an existing budget format.

(c) Assessment and Organization. Before organizing a PB system, it is helpful to take an inventory of the existing decision-making processes, including an assessment of the analytical capabilities and data system operations and support. The following sampling of questions could be included:

- What are the objectives and key issues of the organization? Strengths and weaknesses? Threats? Opportunities?
- Who makes the strategic decisions? The chief executive officer? The board of directors? Individuals? A committee? At what level?
- Who brings the strategic issues to the decision makers, and how? What is the size and experience of the analytical staff?
- What are the external influences and constraints in the general managerial processes, and how are they handled?
- What special studies, policy issues, analyses, and data are considered? Who prepares and analyzes them? How far into the future are these studies and forecasts generally made? How are benefits measured? Are the current data valid and up to date? Can history be reconstructed? What kinds of forecasts or projections are generally made from the data base? Where and how are data collected, processed, and displayed?
- What controls, measurements, and appraisals exist to indicate actual costs, benefits, and accountability?
- What kind of planning exists? How is it coordinated for different programs and resources?
- How is the budget prepared? On what basis? What are the accounting systems utilized?

- What is the timetable for the key decision making in the organization? Is there a regular schedule or cycle for planning and budgeting? For capital requests? For new ventures?

(i) Alternatives. The following are some of the alternatives to be considered in applying PB in an organization:

- Integrate it into the existing managerial and financial systems.
- Superimpose it over the existing systems.
- Implement it company-wide.
- Implement it on a select organizational basis.
- Do it piecemeal; for example, do program structuring without extensive analysis.

(ii) Tailoring. All questions and alternatives such as those given should be addressed in order to tailor a PB approach to an organization. The installation can be a crash effort, a methodical piecemeal approach, or something in between. The success of a chosen approach depends on a realistic evaluation of the various considerations and on the leadership and active participation of top management, not just on their approval. The key decision makers should fully understand the need for a PB-type system and that, though it facilitates strategic decision making, it does not make decisions. They must also encourage the use of analysis. Good judgment is improved only when operating on the basis of good data and analysis. The final decisions must still finally reflect the judgment and intuition of the decision makers in determining the important goals and objectives to pursue.

The existing systems should be utilized as much as possible initially. Practicality and flexibility should be employed in introducing a PB system. Choices are available between across-the-board and step-by-step approaches regarding the parts of the organization covered and the parts or scope of the methodology applied.

Some clashes can be anticipated between organizational jurisdictions with possible overlapping PB program structures in the unresolved planning stages, as well as with the time-consuming analysis requirements conflicting with demanding budget schedules. These possible adversities can be minimized with preplanning, timely communication, and flexible approaches.

One premise is certain—the pace of PB implementation should match the capacity of the organization and its parts to absorb it. If the organization is large, parts of it may adjust to PB at different rates and levels of sophistication. If the approach is not tailored, the utilization of PB can be jettisoned before it really starts, possibly for the wrong reasons.

(d) Staffing. Most major private and public sector organizations already have the staff expertise and capability to consider and implement a PB approach without personnel additions. In many instances there are special groups to perform capital projects analysis, venture analyses, acquisitions, make-or-buy analyses, and so on. The central PB coordination in a large organization can be managed by a corporate long-range planning group or a corporate financial group. If the organization is large enough to have divisions, a PB planning coordinator should probably be designated in each division to facilitate the process and gain the necessary commitment. Reporting to a division head is preferable. In addition, the active support and involvement of the head of the organization is essential. To be effective, PB requires strong leadership and interest at the top, especially for the extensive analysis of alternatives. The strategic decision making that PB involves, however, should not be delegated to analysts. The analysts should primarily facilitate the process and fully analyze the ramifications of the chosen options and decisions.

There are three ways in which a PB staff can be acquired:

1. It can be recruited from the outside.
2. The existing staff can be oriented and trained for the new approaches.
3. A combination of 1 and 2 can be used.

Because of PB's emphasis on analysis, it requires individuals who have had significant experience with analytical approaches or some related training or education. Planning and financial analysis experience provides a good foundation.

These requirements are not necessarily met by new elaborate personnel recruiting, education, or training efforts. Generally, what is primarily needed is some orientation and redirection of existing personnel. However, organizations should also consider the prospects of some staff additions and the costs and time associated with installing a PB approach.

(i) Staff Characteristics. A PB system is interdisciplinary in nature and therefore must draw upon many types of specialists or properly experienced generalists. No single academic discipline is *de rigueur,* although it is very helpful for one to have studied a quantitatively oriented subject.

The ideal staff member would have a good knowledge of macroeconomics, microeconomics, mathematics, statistics, engineering, computers, or finance. Experience in budgeting, planning, financial analysis, project management, marketing, or management processes in general is also very helpful. Some line experience, moreover, can be helpful in taking practical approaches. The person should be creative, curious, flexible, courageous, communicative, and results-oriented and should have integrity. Obviously, the ideal individual would have the potential to become an executive within the organization. In addition, it is preferable that the individual have a practical working knowledge of the areas in which the work will be involved. This should be gained within a short time, if the individual does not start on such a basis. Usually, analysis cannot be applied in some sort of pure fashion with significant effectiveness without some working insight or experience.

The entire staff, however, need not have all the ideal characteristics mentioned. A group can be built around one or two solid staff specialists. The others can be trained through the involved cross-disciplinary processes of PB. An interesting statistic is that the federal government built up a cadre of about 1,200 individuals who were essentially dedicated full time to PB activities.

Realistically, the expectation of instant results should be viewed with askance. The development of analytical skills for PB, which essentially entails a wide and complex form of analysis, must have a gestation period. The entire organization and the information system are similarly involved with a complex learning process that requires time. An overzealous effort can be counterproductive.

30.8 SUMMARY. It is through budgetary decisions that an organization's policy is put into effect. Budgeting is increasingly being regarded as the cutting edge of planning and policy development. Strategic and long-range plans that disregard the realities of budgetary needs and resource constraints become exercises of limited value. Budgeting has traditionally been primarily associated with financial data rather than with the policy making and planning that lie behind the numbers.

Historically, budgetary data were presented in terms of administrative units, cost object classes, or line-item details. Budget determinations were generally restricted to how things should be done or the means used, with very limited consideration given to whether they should be undertaken at all. How effective the existing organizational goals and activities or programs are in satisfying fundamental purposes and needs is at the heart of program budgeting.

Also, the future costs of decisions in the budget process are frequently ignored or not well considered, and the search for more effective ways of achieving goals through the expenditures is limited. Formal planning and the analysis of alternatives in many instances have a limited effect on budget decisions, particularly the ones in government. Program budgeting was designed to overcome many of these shortcomings.

Whether a budget system is of the PB type or not, it should be made a part of a comprehensive planning program. In a sense, budgeting disciplines the entire planning process. It is a major operational fault not to tie a planning system and budgeting process together. An integration link ensures a satisfactory degree of coordination among the various operating areas of an organization. The integration relationships can range from loose to tight, and PB has much to offer in any case. The right formula should be tailored to fit a particular organization and should be one that encourages creativity and develops strategic thinking and interactions along with the necessary controls. In striking a proper balance, one should consider an organization's size, stability, structure, scope, resources, management style, function, business, and needs.

Program budgeting is not only a linking system for planning and budgeting but also a strategic decision-making system for allocating resources. The PB system provides the key decision makers with the relevant data, both past and future, appropriately structured into a goal-, purpose-, and objective-oriented format and analyzed into a decision-making mode. Intuition and judgment then act upon these data. These elements, in concert, then allow management to make better decisions regarding the strategic allocation of resources.

Program budgeting has three distinct process phases, which interlock, interact, and are progressively more detailed—*planning, programming,* and *budgeting.* Programming is the intermediate connecting phase for making comprehensive and detailed resource and cost allocations in a program format for translating strategic and long-range planning into a proper form to serve budget preparations. The assembly of detailed input–output forecasts for the planning period is completed in the programming phase, ending in a tabular fashion similar to a multi-year budget in a program format. A cross-walk reconciliation connects the first year of the plan in the program format to an existing budget format for translation into a traditional line budget for control and implementation.

A PB system embraces three basic kinds of elements in its framework: *structural, analytical,* and *informational.* The structural program framework is used to process and classify data for ultimately making strategic budgetary decisions. It emphasizes the long-range perspective in an output-oriented program format. The structural hierarchy of programs makes a logical progression in meaningful terms from stated objectives to operating activities. The analytical processes, primarily system analysis and cost–benefit and cost-effectiveness analysis, emphasize a systematic examination of alternative courses of action and their implications, resulting in sharpened intuition and judgment. The informational portion provides the data from which objectives can be specified, analyses made, and progress reported and controlled. In order to keep a PB system alive and lively, it must also provide for disciplined change and analyses of key issues. Periodic updating is also one of the important PB keys.

The PB system has probably put more people to work trying to learn how to do analysis of social systems than any other management effort in history. In its early utilization it took on an aura of magic with the cost–benefit analysis mystique, but it relies heavily on intuition and judgment along with a great deal of hard work and simple arithmetic.

Like many new managerial techniques, PB was initiated with a great deal of publicity, exaggerated expectations, and much overselling. Many organizations have had the desire to install a functioning PB system instantly. It was often assumed that devising such a format was the only or the primary task and that its accomplishment had some automatic qualities for developing strategic programs. New management information systems, accounting systems, organization charts, or the generous use of the term *program* in traditional budget systems are not in themselves PB. They cannot provide the vital analytical program structuring or future perspective improvements for decision making.

The costs, time, paperwork, staffing, and organizational impact of installing PB can be significant for some organizations. Most, particularly those that are up to date or large, should not have any special problems if they tailor their approach.

Originally, it was thought that a complete PB system must be installed at the outset. However, it appears that a piecemeal approach is feasible; that is, partial applications of either organizational units or PB methodology are possible. Whichever approach is chosen, an essential ingredient to effectiveness is strong leadership at the top, especially for the required analysis of alternatives at key stages in its cycle.

The pace and the efficacy of adopting PB have varied, but interest in it and its concepts continues as organizations grow in size, scope, and complexity, with the need to better allocate resources. Because of the many changes in the PB designation, there is difficulty in tracking its utilization and efficacy. It is likely that the changes reflect a disassociation with the mixed federal government experience or increased management sophistication in not taking new techniques literally.

Even in the federal government, however, it is generally acknowledged that PB was a significant step forward in its budgetary, planning, and decision-making practices. The bureaucracy was challenged, and on a continuing basis there is a greater consciousness about balancing problems, objectives, programs and alternatives, and benefits and costs. Moreover, there generally is a greater emphasis on the long-range considerations of decisions. Many budget areas are now forecast beyond one year.

The concepts, approaches and spirit of PB endure, therefore, albeit under other labels and forms. No other budgetary approach has provided the futurity and comprehensiveness for resource allocations, especially for public sector organizations.

It generally appears that, even in those cases where the complete application of PB has been less than successful, there are residual benefits such as the following:

- It helps strategic and long-range planning find an expression in the budget process.
- The use of cost–benefit analysis (including re-engineering audits/studies) generally increases the analytic proficiency and the employment of analysis for alternatives. That is, analysis is better perceived and utilized as an integral part of decision making.
- The PB process helps to better define an organization's missions, goals, objectives, and strategies. It facilitates the rethinking of roles for an organization and its personnel.

While PB history is a great teacher, many are destined to repeat the lessons. It is clear that more and more we need to think of budgets longer than one year and the consequences, especially as we enter the twenty-first century. Information, ideas, technology, and money flow easily and quickly across borders, and businesses and jobs go where they can best be performed. Global economic forces are making cataclysmic, fast-pased changes. They have a variety of threats, instabilities, and opportunities that must be addressed in shorter time frames with ever-greater consequences. This demands more from public and private organizations as they redefine their goals and roles and allocate their resources. Futurity and its importance in budgets and current decision making grows. Program budgeting is a strategic tool that can provide guidance through these uncharted and opportunistic seas. The traditional line-item budget cannot serve all of these critical needs.

Even if an organization has initially focused only on the important PB element of defining goals and objectives for program structuring, this would be a major management activity by itself. Defining goals, as Peter Drucker has urged, is a vital initial management activity in shaping the strategic direction of an organization:

> It is not possible to be effective unless one first decides what one wants to accomplish. It is not possible to manage, in other words, unless one first has a goal. It is not even possible to design the structure of an organization unless one knows what it is supposed to be doing and how to measure whether it is doing it. In fact, it is never possible to give a final answer to the question, ''What is our business?'' Any answer becomes obsolete within a short period. The question has to be thought through again and again.
>
> But if no answer at all is forthcoming, if objectives are not clearly set, resources will be splintered and wasted. There will be no way to measure the results. If the organization has not determined what its objectives are, it cannot determine what effectiveness it has and whether it is obtaining results or not.[2]

Program budgeting addresses the challenges of goal setting and change and matches them to an organization's resources and capabilities for effectiveness through an integrated planning and budgeting process in a program format. Its concepts have many applications for planning and budgeting systems. Management must continually explore advances in decision-making technology, such as PB, for potential use. A greater measure of success is likely for those who explore, plan, and manage change.

SOURCES AND SUGGESTED REFERENCES

Babunakis, Michael, *Budget Reform for Government.* Quorum Books, 1982.

Cutt, James, *A Planning, Programming and Budgeting Manual-Resource Allocation in Public Sector Economics*, Praeger, New York, 1974.

Frank, Howard A., *Budgetary Forcasting in Local Government: New Tools and Techniques.* Quorum Books, 1993.

Greider, William, *One Word Ready or Not: The Manic Logic of Global Capitalism.* New York: Simon & Schuster, 1997.

Korb, Lawrence J., ''Ordeal of PPBS in the Pentagon,'' *Bureaucrat,* vol. 17, no. 3, Fall 1988.

Levy, Michael E., ''Planning–Programming–Budgeting: Government's New Tool for Improving Efficiency,'' *Conference Board Record,* vol. 4, May 1967.

[2] Peter F. Drucker, *The Age of Discontinuity: Guidelines to Our Changing Society.* (New York: Harper & Row, 1968), pp. 190–191.

Lyden, Fremon J., and Miller, E.G., *Planning-Programming-Budgeting: A Systems Approach to Management,* Markham, Chicago, IL 1968.

Novick, David, *Program Budgeting: Program Analysis and The Federal Budget.* Cambridge, MA: Harvard University Press, 1965.

Novick, David, "The Origin and History of Program Budgeting," *California Management Review,* vol. 11, Fall 1968.

Reich, Robert B., *The Work of Nations: Preparing Ourselves for 21st-Century Capitalism.* Alfred A. Knopf, 1991.

Shreeves, Edward, *Guide to Budget Allocation for Information.* American Library Association, 1991

Trumpeter, Margo C. and Richard S. Rounds, *Basic Budgeting for Librarians.* American Library Association, 1985.

Turnbull, Augustus B., *Government Budgeting and PPBS: A Programmed Introduction.* Reading, PA: Addison-Wesley, 1970.

U.S. General Accounting Office, *Glossary For Systems Analysis and Planning–Programming–Budgeting.* Washington, DC: U.S. Government Printing Office, 1969.

U.S. Congress, Joint Economic Committee, "The PPB System: A Compendium of Papers," *The Analysis and Evaluation of Public Expenditures,* vol. 91, 1969.

U.S. Congress, Joint Economic Committee, "Progress and Potentials," (hearings and report), *The Planning–Programming–Budgeting System,* vol. 90, 1967.

Wildavsicy, Aaron A., *Budgeting: A Comparative Theory of Budgeting Processes.* Transaction Books, 1986.

CHAPTER 31

ACTIVITY-BASED BUDGETING*

James A. Brimson

IPM, Inc.

John J. Antos

Value Creation Group, Inc.

31.1 INTRODUCTION. The purposes of this chapter are to discuss problems with traditional budgeting, define activity-based budgeting (ABB), and discuss the ABB process.

A budget is a financial expression of a plan. Traditional budgeting focuses on planning resources for an organizational unit. Each year, managers look at history and any significant changes and create an annual budget. The budgeting process starts with the senior executive's announcing budget goals. These may consist of revenue and profit goals as well as goals for new services.

Many managers respond by looking at last year's numbers and increasing their budget for the year based on inflation and/or the amount of the increase in revenues (see Exhibit 31.1). For example, if revenues increase 10%, then the various department managers might increase the budgets for their departments by 10%.

The problem with this approach is that last year's inefficiencies are incorporated into this year's budget. Often, little attention is paid to improvements in each department. Finally, little incentive is incorporated into the budgeting process for continuous improvement. Changing workload for each department often is not considered.

Senior managers, during budgeting, often make arbitrary cuts across the board. A potentially negative consequence is that the better-managed departments may have already cut the majority of waste and now may have to cut into necessary resources. Instead, other, less-efficient departments should make more radical reductions to bring them to the same level of efficiency as the better-managed departments.

Budgets in this environment often become wrestling matches in which those who are

---

* This material has been adapted from James A. Brimson and John J. Antos, *Activity-Based Management for Service Industries, Government Entities, and Not-for-Profit Organizations* (New York: John Wiley & Sons, 1994).

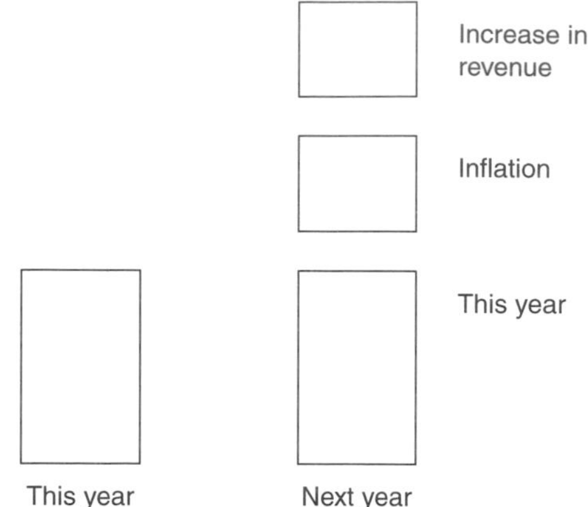

Exhibit 31.1. Manager's response to next year's forecast

the best presenters are given larger budgets. The theory goes that the best at presenting the reasons for the larger budget deserves the larger budget.

Once the budget is agreed on, it is often cast in concrete for the year.

31.2 TRADITIONAL BUDGETING DOES NOT SUPPORT EXCELLENCE. First, the budgeting process should highlight cost reduction and the elimination of wasteful activities and tasks. Traditional budgeting does not make visible what the organization does. Instead, managers look at their history of spending and simply increase last year's budget and/or actuals based on inflation and/or increases in revenue.

Second, budgeting should be a formal mechanism for reducing work load to the minimal level to support enterprise objectives. Excess workload due to poor structuring of activities and business process drives up cost and does not improve customer satisfaction. The budgeting process itself should give insight into how to reduce work load and how to set work-load reduction goals.

Third, budgeting should consider all costs as variable; yet budgeting often formalizes the laissez-faire attitude toward occupancy and equipment costs. Most are familiar with the concept of fixed and variable costs. The problem with this classification is a psychological one. The term *fixed costs* seems to imply that these costs cannot be eliminated because they are fixed. Yet we all know that buildings and equipment can be put to alternative use, sold, demolished, or leased. Many assets are often dedicated to specific activities. By making these assets more flexible, the total capital base of an enterprise can be lowered. Even property taxes and property insurance can be reduced. A budget based on variable and fixed costs often focuses attention on the variable costs and implies that the fixed costs are not controllable.

A better classification would be utilized and unutilized capacity. This classification simply shows that some assets are being used and some are not. It does not present the psychological barrier to change that the term *fixed costs* does. Unutilized capacity can be saved for future growth, eliminated, used for other purposes, or consolidated with another division.

An important goal of budgeting should be to improve each process on a continuous basis. Traditional budgeting, as it is commonly practiced, seems to focus on simply repeating history. Activity budgeting sets improvement targets by activity/business process.

Thus, this approach is something everyone can understand and use to work toward improvement. However, traditional budgeting sets goals like "reduce costs" by a specific percentage, without giving employees insights on how to achieve those targets.

Activity budgeting works to synchronize activities and thus improve business processes. Traditional budgeting may take the approach of "every department for itself." Managers pay lip service to coordinating between departments; however, managers will almost certainly respond in a way that will maximize their own department's performance. The inevitable consequence is to lower the performance of the organization as a whole.

Activity budgeting sets business process improvement goals, which requires the joint efforts of employees from a variety of departments. Because the goal is to improve the business process, old barriers between departments begin to crumble.

Traditional budgeting does not formally consider external and internal suppliers and customers. However, activity budgeting requires asking the internal and external suppliers and customers to describe their needs and their respective work-load requirements.

Too often, the focus in traditional budgeting is to control the result. For example, consider the organization that closes its financial books in 4 to 15 days. Each month managers focus on information that is 34 to 45 days old.

It makes more sense to control the *process,* rather than to try to control the *result* through financial statements. The Japanese have unsophisticated accounting systems compared to U.S. companies of a similar size. If the secret was a more sophisticated accounting system, then U.S. companies should be superior. Yet that is not necessarily the case.

Activity budgeting and activity management focus on controlling the process. Only by controlling the process can results improve.

In a similar vein, traditional budgeting tends to focus on the effects rather than the causes. For example, it often requires a long time to hire new employees or introduce a new service. In reality, organizations should focus on the causes of these long lead times. In Japan, managers come to meetings asking their peers for suggestions to solve their problems. In the United States, our individualistic attitudes often make managers consider a request for help as a sign of weakness. Managers therefore make up excuses to explain the reasons they were over budget, rather than concentrating their efforts on how to improve operations.

Because activity budgeting focuses on the root cause of problems, everyone can work to identify how to reduce or eliminate them. Only by eliminating the "root cause" of the problem can the cost be permanently eliminated.

Activity budgeting requires that customers be asked for their requirements. Only by asking the customer can an organization understand whether it has properly applied resources to meet the customer's needs (e.g., do the patrons of the U.S. Postal Service want two- to three-day delivery, or do they want consistent delivery within some stated time period?). By asking the customer, the work load connected with the activities necessary to please the customer can better be determined.

Activity budgeting focuses on output, not on input. It focuses on what work is done, how the work is performed, and how much work is done. The required resources are only a consequence of the activities. The problem with traditional budgeting is that it lacks ownership. Even if the department manager "owns" the budget, seldom do the individual employees in that department own the budget. Activity budgeting asks each person to look at the activities he or she performs and set performance targets for those activities in the context of customer requirements and organizational objectives.

Activity budgeting allows people to be empowered to manage their activities properly.

If something is wrong, if there is a better way to perform the activity or business process, or if a quality issue arises, the employee(s) who performs the activity or business process should make the necessary improvements or corrections without requiring management approval. (This assumes that the employee is not changing the service or the quality provided to the customer, and is improving the service or business process at a lower cost.)

Senior management needs to remember that people will not work themselves out of a job. People will contribute ideas to improve operations only if they understand that improvement in value-added activities allows the transfer of resources to growth-enabling activities.

Under activity budgeting, mistakes are acceptable, but repetition of mistakes is unacceptable. An executive told Sam Walton of a $10 million mistake and submitted his resignation. Walton told the executive he couldn't resign because the company had just spent $10 million training him. People need to know they can make mistakes, but they must learn from those mistakes and not repeat them.

Activity budgeting uses a common language—the language of the activities or business processes that everyone is performing. Traditional budgeting uses terms that only the accountants are familiar with. This Tower of Babel makes communication more difficult and encourages specialization at the expense of cooperation.

Activity budgeting looks for consistency of the output. This means that the activity should be performed in a consistent way over time. Continuous improvement must be encouraged, but the activity should only be performed in accordance with current best practice. Success depends on finding the best possible way to perform an activity or business process and consistently looking for ways to improve it, while performing the activity/business process in a consistent manner.

Activity budgeting requires setting activity or business process targets as the minimum level of performance rather than the absolute level. These activity or business process targets should identify the minimum level of performance necessary to support organizational objectives. Managers should not try to exceed these minimum levels. Instead, they should look at ways to reduce waste and non–value-added portions of various activities.

31.3 ACTIVITY-BASED BUDGETING DEFINITIONS.

Activity-based budgeting is the process of planning and controlling the expected activities of the organization to derive a cost-effective budget that meets forecast workload and agreed strategic goals.

Activity-based budgeting is a quantitative expression of the expected activities of the organization, reflecting management forecast of workload and financial and nonfinancial requirements to meet agreed strategic goals and planned changes to improve performance.

The three key elements of ABB include the following:

1. Type of work to be done
2. Quantity of work to be done
3. Cost of work to be done

(a) Principles of Activity-Based Budgeting.

Activity-based budgeting must reflect what is done, that is, the activities or business processes, not cost elements. Resources required (cost elements) must be derived from the expected activities or business processes and workload. *Workload* is simply the number of units of an activity that are required.

For example, in the human resource department, the work load for the activity ''hire employees'' might be to hire 25 employees. The cost elements to perform that activity might be the wages and benefits of the recruiter, travel, advertising, testing, supplies, and occupancy costs for the space occupied by the recruiter and for interviewing. If a hiring freeze occurs, then the work load for this activity would be zero.

Budgets must be based on the future work load in order to meet:

- Customer requirements
- Organizational/departmental goals and strategies
- New/changed services and service mix
- Changes in business processes
- Improvements in efficiency and effectiveness
- Quality, flexibility, and cycle-time goals
- Changes in service levels

The final budget must reflect the changes in resource cost levels and foreign exchange fluctuations. However, it is better to initially budget using constant cost and foreign exchange rates to facilitate comparisons, and then to add inflation and foreign exchange adjustments at the conclusion of the budgeting process.

As part of the activity budgeting process, it is important to highlight continuous improvement. Each department should identify the activities or business processes to be improved, the amount of improvement, and how it plans to achieve its improvement targets.

(b) Requirements for Successful Activity-Based Budgeting. The organization must be committed to excellence. If the organization does not have this commitment, then resources will be wasted on data-analysis activities that will never be implemented. Changing is not easy. It is easier to study the problem than to make the difficult decisions required to improve.

(c) Process Management Approach. The organization must use a process management approach to improvement. This requires defining each activity as part of a repeatable, robust business process that can be continuously improved and the variability removed. Activities defined this way can use various techniques to decrease time, improve quality, and reduce the cost of those activities.

Process management is crucial to excellence, because high levels of performance are possible only when activities are done to best practices, the unused capacity is minimal, the best practices are continually made better, and the activities are executed perfectly. Activity definitions must support process management. Activities must be in the form of verb plus a noun. There must be a physical output. Two-stage definitions of drivers are usually not adequate. For example, the activity ''pay employee'' is compatible with process management. To define an activity as ''supplies handling'' and the output measure as the ''number of service production runs'' would not be compatible activity definitions. Two-stage activity definitions might be used in assigning costs to a service, but it does not help in improving operations. A better way to define this sample activity would be ''move supplies,'' with the output measure defined as the ''number of moves.''

One of the first steps that an activity manager may have to take is to review activity definitions to make sure that they are compatible with a process approach.

Cultural Barriers	Actions
Departmental structure often interferes with departments interacting, in order to minimize total enterprise cost.	Change information systems so the organization can see total cost of business processes rather than just the costs in a specific department.
Policies and procedures provide guidelines for employee behavior. These were often set up to ensure consistency and to make it easy for employees to handle specific situations.	Empower employees to handle various situations to ensure customer satisfaction. Use policies to set general guidelines and train, support, and empower employees to satisfy the customer.
Suggestion programs usually require the approval of management to implement change. This slows the change process.	Suggestion programs are only for changes to the service or for capital requests. Changes to efficiency should be made by employees without management approval.
Measurement systems tend to focus on the department level.	Abolish micromanagement. Give managers/employees the tools, authority, and responsibility to do their jobs. Make them responsible for outputs and a budget level of resources to do their work.
Specialization assumes that lowest cost is achievable through economies of scale.	Today flexibility is critical. People must be cross-trained for a variety of tasks. First, as slack or heavy periods occur, employees can help out in other departments. Second, they need to understand how what they do affects other departments and how what other departments do affects them.

Exhibit 31.2. Cultural barriers

(d) Culture Encourages Sustaining Benefits. The organization culture should encourage sustaining benefits. These benefits should not be something that lasts for only a short while, after which everyone goes back to the old way. These benefits should change the way the people in the organization think and act. Often this means changing the way the employees are compensated, so that they share in the productivity improvement.

Organizations must overcome the cultural barriers shown in Exhibit 31.2. Next to these barriers are actions the organization must take in order to overcome these cultural barriers.

(e) Commitment to Excellence. Many organizations take a short-term approach to improving operations. Costs are easy to control—simply stop spending money. This approach is similar to a crash diet. The problem with crash diets is that the dieter usually regains what he or she lost and often gains even more weight. If an organization is committed to excellence, then its goal is to change the way it does business. This is similar to changing eating habits. For example, organizations must start compensating people based on business-process performance rather than the traditional actual versus budget of cost elements that most organizations have historically used.

31.4 ACTIVITY-BASED BUDGETING PROCESS.

The ABB process begins with the customer. The organization must determine who the customer is and what the customer wants. It must look to its competitors. Competition consists of both direct competitors and alternate services that might compete with the organization's services.

Then, the organization must develop a strategy to meet customer needs. A restaurant must decide whether to be a five-star restaurant, with crystal and linen tablecloths, or to provide good food in a clean environment with less sophisticated decor but with good value to the customer.

Next, the organization should forecast work load. Management and sales determine what sales levels will be, and managers need to estimate their work loads as a result of these sales levels. Often, the sales forecast includes new services and new markets, as well as any changes in strategy.

Planning guidelines must be articulated to each manager to establish the specific activity-level targets within a business process context. Eventually, every activity manager should have targets for improving his or her respective value-added activities and eliminating non–value-added activities.

Next, interdepartmental projects should be identified. Because these projects will affect the work load, as well as the activities in several departments, they must be coordinated and done prior to each manager improving his or her own activities.

At this point in the budgeting process, specific activity-level projects can be identified. These are projects to improve operations at the individual activity level. However, improvement should always be within organizational objectives, a business-process context, and a customer satisfaction context.

Activity-based investment analysis consists of defining improvement projects, evaluating those projects, and then using committees to select projects that will meet the organization's goals and meet customers' needs.

The final step is to determine the activities and work load for the coming year.

31.5 LINKING STRATEGY AND BUDGETING.

One of the problems with traditional budgeting is that a clear link between the enterprise's strategy and budgeting often does not exist. Therefore, operating managers do not know how to incorporate strategy into their budgets.

(a) Principles of Strategic Management.

There are a variety of seminars and books available on the subject of strategic management. This chapter does not discuss those techniques, but simply assumes that a strategic plan exists. The role of senior management is to set performance targets based on the strategic plans. The performance targets might be for sales, number of new services and/or markets, cycle time, cost, quality, or customer service levels. The role of the activity manager is to achieve or exceed those targets.

Strategic objectives and performance targets must be translated into activity-level targets. Activity managers must ensure that service requirements are a direct derivative of customer needs.

The translation process starts with customer requirements and an analysis of competitive strategies. Then strategic objectives are set. The price for services allowable by the market are determined and time, quality, and cost targets are determined. Then these targets are translated into activity-level targets.

There are several important strategic management tools to assist with this process. The key ones include the following:

- Customer surveys
- Core competency analysis
- Benchmarking

- Quality function deployment
- Reverse engineering

(b) Customer Surveys. One of the first steps in the strategic management process is to perform a customer survey. The customer survey can be done in person, by telephone, or by direct mail. The survey asks a variety of questions, but the focus is on the factors that are important to the customer, a ranking of those factors by the customer, and, finally, the customer's perception of the organization's performance regarding those factors.

Based on this survey, the organization needs to start with the factors most important to the customer and determine whether it is satisfying the customer on those factors of performance. Activity or business process and investment preference must be given to those activities or business processes that the customer feels are most important. Especially in the case where satisfaction levels are not satisfactory to the customer, the organization needs to change, improve, or increase resources and effectiveness of those activities or business processes.

For example, if an organization determines that it needs to allow nurses to spend more time with patients and less time doing paperwork, then it could create an activity budget in the following way:

For the activity ''complete medical charts'':

Total Cost	Salaries	Depreciation	Supplies	Phone	Occupancy
$24,410	22,000	400	900	150	960

The assumptions are that a person would be hired to ''complete medical charts.'' The employee's salary and benefits would be $22,000 per year. Depreciation on his or her desk and computer would be $400. Supplies connected with filling out the charts are estimated to be $900. Because this person would be communicating with other departments, a phone would be necessary for interhospital calls. The fully loaded cost of hospital space (including depreciation, heat, electricity, building maintenance, and janitorial cost based on the number of square feet occupied) equals $960.

Hiring this person will enable 10 nurses to spend 10% of their time comforting, informing, and answering questions for patients. A nurse earns $36,000 annually, including benefits.

For the activity ''communicate with patients:''

Total Cost	Salaries	Depreciation	Supplies	Phone	Occupancy
$46,320	36,000	1,000	2,000	320	7,000

The following assumptions were made. Annual salaries and benefits for 10 nurses at $36,000 per nurse equals $360,000. Because they will spend 10% of their time on this activity, the salary portion of this activity cost equals $36,000. There would be some depreciation on the desk for the portion of time performing this activity. Some educational literature would be given to the patients, which would total approximately $2,000. Nurses would need a phone line for tracking down answers to patient questions, and a reasonable percentage of the total phone cost was estimated at $320. Because the nurses spent some time sitting at a desk for this activity, 10% of their total occupancy costs was apportioned, which amounted to $7,000.

Now senior management can look at the customer survey and performance as it relates to nurses communicating and comforting patients—a high-priority item in the eyes of the customer. Then they can determine if it is worth spending a total of $70,730 ($24,410 plus $46,320) to improve customer satisfaction in this area.

(c) Core Competency Analysis. An organization starts by asking what activities or business processes are critical to its industry. These activities or business processes become the *core competencies* of that industry. Then the organizations can ask themselves which activities or business processes they perform well. They need to compare themselves with external benchmarks and determine where there is a core competency gap. Then the organizations can set budget targets in terms of cost, quality, and time.

Industry	Core Competency
Banking	Accuracy, fast turnaround, full service
Insurance	Low rates, knowledgeable representatives, fast claims handling
Hospitals	Friendly nurses, full service, high success rate
Airlines	On-time, convenient departures, reasonable fares
Fast food	Quality, service, cleanliness
Internal Revenue Service (IRS)	Rules that are easy to comply with, fairness, easy access
Fund raisers	Good cause, large percentage of funds directly to cause

An auto dealer decided that a core competency of the repair shop was to provide quality repairs the first time. A further analysis revealed an opportunity to improve performance by conducting auto repair training seminars for the mechanics. Four seminars for 20 mechanics who earn $14 per hour were planned. Each seminar was to be five hours long with $500 in training supplies. A consultant will charge $3,000 per training session. For the activity "train mechanics":

Total Cost	Salaries	Supplies	Phone	Consultant
$18,100	5,600	500	0	12,000

(d) Benchmarking. The benchmarking process compares performance to other organizations, either internally or externally. Benchmarks may measure the following:

- Activities
- Business processes
- Time
- New service introduction
- Customer service
- Quality
- Cost

Comparisons should be made, where possible, across divisions, with competitors, and with the best organizations in the world. For example, one telephone company can process a request for new phone service within 43 seconds. This is a speed few other organizations can duplicate and would serve as a great benchmark for the activity ''process new customers' credit requests.''

One association felt it was important to answer the phone after only two rings. This would be a high-quality service to the members, and would avoid lost sales of books and seminars because people tired of waiting for someone to answer the phone. The association's operators were currently answering the phone on the third or fourth ring. It decided to increase the number of telephone operators by three. Telephone operators could be hired for $18,000 per year. They would need a desk, a personal computer (PC), a phone, and supplies for order taking. Fully loaded occupancy costs were running $10 per square foot. Each operator would need 64 square feet of space.

For the activity ''answer phones'':

Total cost	Salaries	Depreciation	Supplies	Phone	Occupancy
$60,120	54,000	2,000	1,200	1,000	1,920

(e) Activity Function Deployment. Activity function deployment (AFD) is a concept similar to Quality Function Development that originated in the quality field, and is applicable to activity budgeting. In AFD, the organization compares the customers' requirements with the activities or business processes necessary to meet those requirements. For each activity or business process, a comparison is also made with the competition to determine how the organization is doing against the competition. Also, a correlation is made between activities to show which activities have a strong positive or strong negative correlation with meeting customer requirements. Some activities will have no correlation with each other. Finally, a correlation is made between various activities and customer requirements. Thus, the organization can determine which activities are critical to greatest customer satisfaction. Customer requirements are ranked as part of this analysis.

Although a complete explanation of this technique can be found in a number of quality books and seminars, a simple example will be discussed here. An airline is looking to increase market share by better satisfying its customers. Using AFD, the airline determines that quick turnaround time is important in order to have on-time departures. One way to improve in this area is to have two jetbridges to load passengers instead of only one. There are two activities—''move jetbridge'' and ''maintain jetbridge''—connected with this second jetbridge.

The airline determines that 10 percent of a ticketing agent's time is needed to handle this second jetbridge. A ticketing agent earns $32,000 per year. Two hundred ticketing agents will be affected. This means that salaries with benefits dedicated to the activity ''move jetbridge'' would be $640,000 (200 × 10% × $32,000). An additional 100 jetbridges would have to be purchased, at the rate of $10,000 per jetbridge. Therefore, the depreciation on $1,000,000 (100 × $10,000) using a five-year life would be $200,000 per year. The annual cost of maintenance labor is $100,000 on these jetbridges and is $50,000 on maintenance parts. Occupancy costs are $20,000 for the maintenance space needed for these jetbridges.

For the activities "move jetbridge" and "maintain jetbridge":

Activity	Activity Cost	Salaries	Depreciation	Parts	Occupancy
Move jetbridge	640,000	640,000			
Maintain jetbridge	370,000	100,000	200,000	50,000	20,000
Total cost	1,010,000	740,000	200,000	50,000	20,000

(f) Reverse Engineering. Reverse engineering involves studying a competitor's services. At first glance, one would think that reverse engineering is a concept that applies only to products. However, applying reverse engineering to a service and seeing how competitors perform the service is a very useful tool.

For example, consider a company that has a regulatory affairs department that must file with the Food and Drug Administration (FDA) to get regulatory approval. The company's managers studied the competitor's process of filing for regulatory approval. The objective was to determine how to perform the process more effectively.

Using reverse engineering principles, they started by asking the customer, in this case the FDA, the testing requirements in order to get this new product approved. Then, based on the FDA comments, they improved how they designed their products and their testing procedures in order to get approval more quickly.

For the activity, "improve the FDA approval process," the following activity costs are determined: Regulatory personnel with salaries of $50,000 will spend 10% of their time on this project. They will have travel costs amounting to $3,000. Supplies are expected to run $600. A seminar on this topic will cost $1,700. A 10% share of their office occupancy cost is running $2,000 per year.

For the activity "improve FDA approval process":

Total Cost	Salaries	Travel	Supplies	Seminar	Occupancy
$12,300	5,000	3,000	600	1,700	2,000

31.6 TRANSLATE STRATEGY TO ACTIVITIES.

Strategy must be translated to an activity level to identify necessary changes. An example of a translating procedure follows:

Steps	Example
Define mission statement with enterprise goals	Dominate the market and diversify where advantage can be applied
Establish critical success factors	Grow market share; increase new service sales as percent of total sales
Establish service targets	Increase market share: Service 1 by 7%; Service 2 by 8%; discontinue Service 3
Establish service-level targets	Service 1: increase sales 5%; decrease cost 8%; deliver in 2 hours

(a) Identify Activity Targets by Bill of Activities. The next step is to identify activity targets for each service.

For example: the mission might be to dominate the consumer loan business in Dallas; the critical success factor might be to grow market share; the service target might be to grow auto loan revenue by 7%; and the service level targets might be to increase auto loan sales by 5% and decrease cost by 8%.

Bill of Activities

Activity Description	Cost/ Output $	Units of Output	Cost of Service $	Target Activity Reduction (%)	($)	Target Cost of Service ($)
Take application	100	1	100	⟨5⟩	⟨5⟩	95
Order reports	50	3	150	⟨10⟩	⟨15⟩	135
Review loans	200	1	200	⟨7⟩	⟨14⟩	186
Complete paperwork	25	4	100	⟨30⟩	⟨30⟩	70
Disburse funds	250	1	250			250
Totals			800	⟨8⟩	⟨64⟩	736

This table shows that the employees have established cost reduction targets for four of the five activities. The total reduction of $64 is an 8% reduction from last year's bill of activity cost.

Once these strategic management tools are employed, then cost, time, and quality targets can be set by the employees for each activity. The following is an example of cost, time, and quality targets.

(b) Strategic Management Tools and Targets

Tool	Activity	Cost	Time	Quality
Customer survey	Communicate with patients	C: 46,320 T: 40,000	C: 10 minutes T: 30 minutes	C: 80% satisfaction T: 90%
Core competency	Train mechanics	C: 18,100 T: 22,000	C: 20 hours T: 24 hours	C: 9% redos T: 5% redos
Bench marking	Answer phone	C: 60,120 T:	C: 4 rings T: 2 rings	C: T:
QFD	Move and maintain jetbridge	C: 1,010,000 T: 900,000	C: 45 minutes T: 30 minutes	C: 85% T: 90% on time
Reverse engineering	Obtain FDA approval	C: 12,300 T: 10,000	C: 5 years T: 2 years	C: 75% T: 80% approval

C = current; T = target.

(c) Match Resource to Goals. Next, match resources to goals. Goals should be set to be achievable. Resources should be oriented toward goals. Identify improvements to business processes as well as activities.

31.7 DETERMINE WORK LOAD.

There are three major steps in determining activity or business process work load. These include the following:

1. Forecast service-determined activities or business processes.
2. Forecast non–service-related activities or business processes.
3. Forecast special projects.

(a) Work Load of Service-Determined Activities or Business Processes.

The first step in forecasting total organization work load is to forecast work load for service-determined activities:

- Identify activities for new services.
- Identify planned changes to services.
- Create/update a bill of activities for each service line.
- Forecast services by service lines rather than individual services, in most cases.
- Explode bill of activities to determine activity quantity for each service line.

(b) Explode Bill of Activities.

To explode a bill of activities, simply list each service line and the forecasted quantity of that service line. List the units of each activity used by each service line. Then, multiply units of service times the units of each activity to calculate the activity quantity volume by service. Then, sum the total activity quantities.

Service	Units of Service	Bill of Activity Units required for Each Service	Activity Quantities
Mortgages	5,000	Order report 3	15,000
Auto loans	1,800	Order report 1	1,800
Personal loans	1,000	Order report 1	1,000
		Total reports	17,800

(c) Work Load for Non–Service-Related Activities.

The second step is to forecast work load of non–service-related activities. Non–service-related activities are those performed by support departments such as MIS human resources, security, and accounting.

Activity Class	Activity Measures
General management	Number of employees
Financial reporting	Number of financial reports
Corporate advertising	Number of TV advertisements
	Number of promotions
Marketing	Number of trade shows
	Number of market surveys
Research	Number of new services
Facilities	Number of square feet

(d) Work Load for Special Projects. The third step is to forecast work load for special projects. Examples of special projects include the following:

- Install activity-based management.
- Install activity-based budgeting.
- Install new computer system.
- Expand office.

Then, the organization needs to set up a calendar for each special project, with the activities and tasks listed by time period.

31.8 ACTIVITY-BASED BUDGETING CALENDAR

Brief senior management	*					
Select team	**					
Select departments/services		**				
Review activity definitions			****			
Review strategic plan				****		
Explode bill of activities					****	
Start improvement projects						***

Each * equals a week

31.9 CREATE PLANNING GUIDELINES. An organization should identify activity or business process-level projects with the goal of continuous improvement. Look at the budgeted work load and divide it into mandatory, discretionary, and optional units for each activity or business process. This split helps to decide what portion of value-added activities to eliminate. For example, an organization might determine that it needs only one quote to purchase supplies. The work load to obtain quotes is the minimum mandatory work. Discretionary work occurs when the purchasing agent believes a lower price is obtainable through two quotes. For optional work, the agent feels better by getting three or four quotes, some of which are from noncertified vendors.

31.10 IDENTIFY INTERDEPARTMENTAL PROJECTS. The organization should look at its business processes to eliminate duplicate activities and synchronize the remaining ones. Consider the following business process to ‘‘procure supplies.’’

(a) Activity-Based Budget for Procuring Supplies

Activity		Labor	Technology	Facility	Utilities	Supplies	Travel	Other	Total
LY	PQ	89088		7827	1293	1075	4000	162	103445
TY									
LY	IP	101479		8915	1472	1225	4000	175	117266
TY									
LY	AP	108404	190299	9524	1573	1308	4000	187	315295
TY									
LY	SS	29211		2568	424	353	5562	50	38168
TY									
LY	MA	65545		5871	938	578	200	111	73243
TY									

PQ = prepare quotes; IP = issue purchase order; AP = administer p.o.; SS = source supplies; MA = manage area; LY = last year; TY = this year.

After reviewing last year's total costs for each activity, the next step is to calculate last year's unit cost for each activity. For example, the activity "prepare quotes" cost $103,445. Last year, 2,000 quotes were prepared. By dividing annual quotes into total cost, the unit cost for this activity is $51.72 per quote.

Activities	Work Load Measures	Volume	Total Cost $	Unit Cost $	Target Cost $
Prepare quotes	Quotes	2,000	103,445	51.72	50.00
Issue purchase order (PO)	PO	5,679	117,265	20.65	19.65
Administer PO	PO	5,679	315,295	55.52	53.00
Source supplies	New suppliers	100	38,167	381.68	375.00
Manage area	Staff	28	72,243	2,580	2,200

(b) Activity Based Budgeting Example of Target Cost. The organization has set a target of $50 per quote. This is a reduction of $1.72 from last year's cost of $51.72 per quote. The improvement process for 2,000 quotes at $1.72 per quote results in a savings of $3,440. Managers feel that they can reduce supplies by $440 by keeping more information on the computer and less on paper. Travel could be reduced $1,000 by having more vendors come to the organization's offices. Because quotes will be kept on the computer, there will be a reduction in the filing activity, saving $2,000 for part-time employee wages and benefits.

(c) Creative Thinking Approaches. Continuous improvement requires innovative approaches to streamlining the way an activity is done. Although creativity is a very personal trait, studies have shown that certain environments and methods are better suited to drawing out creative ideas. Some of the more effective methods are:

1. Challenging assumptions about:
    - People
    - Supplies
    - Business processes
    - Location
    - Capital
    - Automation
    - Activities
2. Viewing activities or business processes based on new assumptions
3. Perceiving patterns from other:
    - Divisions
    - Offices
    - Services
    - Departments
4. Making connections with other organizations
5. Establishing networks between suppliers, suppliers' suppliers, you, customers, and end users
6. Exploiting failures (e.g., the glue for Post-It notes was too weak)
7. Performing activity or business process backward and from the middle
8. Using idea triggers (e.g., a new idea for each of Baskin & Robbins 31 flavors)
9. Creating superheroes
10. Imagining you are the service, activity, or business process

(d) Brainstorming. Brainstorming techniques are fairly common today. They consist of the following:

- Suspending judgment until all ideas are on the table
- Emphasizing quantity of ideas without worrying about quality
- Stimulating a freewheeling session, with wild ideas encouraged
- Involving people from throughout the organization
- Reminding people that wild ideas often will fertilize the thinking process

(e) Storyboarding. Storyboarding is a creativity tool that consists of using colored index cards to show business processes, activities, and tasks. The first step is to define the department mission statement. For a hotel, the department mission for the maids might be "to keep rooms clean in order to delight customers at a minimum cost."

Activities

	Stock Cart	Clean Rooms	Empty Carts
T	Stack towels	Empty trash	Dispose garbage
A	Stack linens	Change bedsheets	Separate linens/towels
S	Stack toiletries	Clean bathroom	Store cart/vacuum
K	Stack stationery	Restock toiletries	
S	Stack cleaning supplies	Replace towels	
		Dust room	
		Vacuum room	
		Refill stationery	

(f) Value Management. Value management is an organized way of thinking. It is an objective appraisal of functions performed by services and procedures. The focus is on necessary functions for the lowest cost. It increases reliability and productivity. Costs are decreased. Value management challenges everything an organization does.

It starts by gathering information such as:

- The purpose and use of each service
- The operating and performance issues
- The physical and environmental requirements

For example, fresh fish must be kept cold. Jewelry must be kept in a secure environment. What types of support requirements are there? What problems exist? Which and how many liaison personnel are required? What are the economic issues?

These requirements are translated into required functionality of the service. Begin by determining the worth of each portion of the service. Then calculate the value improvement potential. What part of the service does the customer want? Which parts add cost? Which part is the customer willing to pay for?

Begin using creativity. Ask the customers to value different features. Ask suppliers for ideas. Use cross-functional teams and brainstorming. Use reverse engineering techniques and look at the competitor's services. Benchmark in other industries. Find the best customer service, warehousing, and order fulfillment organization. Eliminate part of the service. How can the organization create more commonality of services and support services as well as common reports and forms?

Evaluate whether it would be better to buy a portion of the service from outside (e.g., catering/training/maintenance for airlines; check processing and MIS for banks; body work for car dealers; janitorial, engineering, waste collection for cities) or to perform those services and support services in-house. Analyze customer trade-off of cost and features. Calculate value versus cost to produce various portions of the service. Eliminate functions, procedures, and reports. Simplify procedures, business processes, and functions. Use alternate supplies, specifications, and methods. Shorten the service operation cycle with cross-training of departments.

(g) Task-Level Analysis. Sometimes, it is useful to analyze the tasks of an activity in order to determine the improvement potential. For example, the activity "pay vendor invoice" has the following tasks:

Task	Total	Non–Value-Added	Value-Added	Best Practice
Receive PO	.50	.50		
Locate receiver (R)	.50	.50		
Get vendor invoice (I)	.50	.50		
Match PO, R, I	2.00	2.00		
Enter data	4.50		4.50	2.00
Determine errors	2.50	2.50		
Expedite payment	1.25	1.25		
Make payment: computer	3.00		3.00	2.75
Make payment: manual	1.00	1.00		
Document file	3.00	1.50	1.50	1.25
	18.75	9.75	9.00	6.00

31.11 IMPROVEMENT PROCESS.

The improvement process starts with creative thinking to determine solutions. An investment proposal is then prepared. Management selects the projects that have the highest priority in meeting customer needs. The solution is implemented and incorporated into the activity budget.

(a) Ranking Budget Requests. After all the budget requests have been made, they are ranked. One convenient way to rank them is through a rating system in which management looks at the budget requests in comparison with the customer needs. Another useful tool is to classify them according to whether they support the current level of service or whether they are at the minimum or intermediate. "Current" implies that this is the cost of activities as they are presently performed. "Minimum" implies that this is the minimum level of service for an activity. "Intermediate" implies that this is not a final solution.

(b) Impact of Projects. Then the organization should look at the impact of these projects in terms of the change in work load, but also in terms of the changes in activity or business process cost.

31.12 FINALIZING THE BUDGET.

Budget proposals are created for the most promising projects. They should be reviewed and the highest-priority projects selected. An implementation plan should be conceived. An activity impact report should be generated to include its cost impact, assuming no inflation or foreign currency issues. This allows for comparisons with previous activity or business-process performance. Finally, inflation and foreign currency should be incorporated into the budget.

(a) Budget Review Panels. Budget review panels should consist of cross-functional teams whose purpose is to question and review the budget. A review panel might consist of the directors, support departments such as human resources, administration, quality, finance, and operations.

(b) Budgeting Options. An organization has two options for activity budgeting. First, budget and report by activities. Second, budget by activities and convert the activity budget into a traditional cost element budget. In this second approach, the organization plans on an activity or business process basis. Managers would use activity costs per unit to determine cost elements. Then they would summarize by cost elements. This second approach is only temporary until the organization better understands how to manage by activities, and usually lasts for only a year.

(c) Steps in Implementing

Activities/Tasks	Months 1 2 3 4
Train and educate	**
Perform strategic analysis	****
Forecast work load	******
Establish planning guidelines	****
Propose interdepartmental improvement	****
Propose activity improvement	********
Select improvement options	*******
Finalize budget	***

Each * equals one week.

(d) Initial Project. A steering group of three to five members should be created. A series of panels with five to six members from different departments should be created to discuss cross-departmental issues. Each budgeting unit should have a budgeting manager, which could be someone other than the department manager. There would be 10 to 20 budgeting units per in-house coordinator or per consultant.

31.13 PERFORMANCE REPORTING. Remember that the most effective reports are those that do not have to be made. Therefore, introduce proactive control rather than reactive cost monitoring wherever possible. Activity-based budgeting encourages this approach.

Emphasis should be made to control the process so that output is consistent. Also, make sure resources can be shifted when work load varies—work load seldom stays the same throughout the year. Plan and budget for using those slack times to improve the organization.

(a) Data Capture. There are three methods for data capture within an ongoing system. First, there are *dedicated resources.* Set up cost centers and define work-load measures at the activity or business process level. Second, there are *shared resources,* in which an organization does time reporting by activity. Third, use a *surrogate* in which actual outputs are used at a standard activity cost. Actual costs would be compared to total department earned cost in this approach. Total actual cost could also be compared to best practices earned value.

(b) Activity-Based Budget Report

Department Total			Activity Analysis			
Expense	Budget $	Actual $	Issue Purchase Order	Certify Vendor	Expedite Order	Other
Wages	180,000	180,000				
Supplies	40,000	38,000				
Space	30,000	30,000				
Equipment	18,000	18,000				
Travel	22,000	20,000				
Other	10,000	8,000				
Total	200,000	194,000				

Output Measure	Total	Number of Purchase Order	Number of Certification	Number of Orders	
Charge rate		$50	$2,000	$10	$9,000
Budgeted volume		3,000	20	100	1
Budgeted value	200,000	$150,000	$40,000	$1,000	$9,000
Actual volume		2,700	18	90	1
Earned value*	181,000	$135,000	$36,000	$900	$9,100
Earned-value variance	13,000				

*Charge rate times actual volume.

In this example, the organization budgeted the activity "issue purchase orders" at $50 per purchase order. It budgeted 3,000 purchase orders. This yielded a budgeted value for the "issue purchase order" activity of $150,000. The same activity budgeting process was followed for the remaining activities, including an "other" or miscellaneous category of activities. This yielded a total activity budget for this department of $200,000, which was backflushed into expense categories.

The actual expenses for the period were $194,000. Compared to the original budget of $200,000, this looks very good. However, when the earned value is calculated, the department is shown to have an earned value variance of $13,000. Earned value is calculated for each activity by multiplying the actual volume for each activity by that activity's charge rate. For the "issue purchase order" activity, the actual volume of 2,700 purchase orders when multiplied by the charge rate of $50 yields $135,000. The same calculation is made for all activities and the answers added for each department. This earned value total of $181,000 is compared to actual expenses of $194,000 to yield an earned value variance of a negative $13,000. This is a different picture than simply comparing actual ($194,000) with budget ($200,000), which yielded a favorable variance of $6,000. Managers can now use this as a planning tool as well as a means to operate the organization more efficiently.

(c) Business-Process Reporting. In business-process reporting, activity cost could be shown for each department, as well as for each business process that delivers a service. This is an exercise for organizations that are more advanced in ABB techniques.

31.14 SUMMARY. Activity-based budgeting gives managers the tools they need to make better decisions about running their organization. This budgeting technique spends most of the time on improvement rather than filling out forms, which is often the case with traditional budgeting. This technique gives managers a method to improve activities as well as business processes.

SOURCES AND SUGGESTED REFERENCES

Antos, John J., ''Activity-Based Management for Service, Not-for-Profit, and Government Organizations,'' *Journal of Cost Management,* vol. 6, no. 2, 1992.

Brimson, James A., and John J. Antos, *Activity-Based Management.* New York: John Wiley & Sons, 1994.

Brimson, James A., *Activity Accounting,* New York: John Wiley & Sons, 1991.

Brimson, James A., *Activity-Based Investment Management.* New York: American Management Association, 1989.

Brimson, James A., and John J. Antos, *Driving Value Using Activity-Based Budgeting.* New York: John Wiley & Sons, 1999.

CHAPTER 32

COMPUTER APPLICATIONS IN BUDGETING

Donald R. Moscato
Thomas Pollina

Iona College

32.1 VALUE OF COMPUTERS IN THE BUDGETING PROCESS. In earlier chapters, numerous types of budgets that an organization utilizes were presented. Regardless of the size or complexity of any budget, they all have one thing in common: They all require considerable "number crunching." In the past, it was this aspect of the budgeting process that was always considered to be the most laborious as well as the most susceptible to error. The acceptance of the computer has virtually eliminated the need for manual, tedious calculations and the inevitable errors that traditionally accompany such methods. No longer is it necessary to spend precious hours revising budgets because you must change one number. A well-designed budget model can be updated in its entirety in a matter of seconds, and the new version will be free of calculation errors. In this way, the manager can run as many scenarios as is necessary before the final budget is selected. Exploring multiple scenarios has proven to be indispensible in an organization's budgeting process.

In attempting to explain computers the traditional approach is to discuss input, processing, and output. This same approach could also be used to describe the budgeting process. As an example, we can consider the production budget. In order to derive a production budget specific information is needed (input) including a sales budget and an inventory budget. Given this input, the controller would manipulate the numbers (processing) and eventually arrive at a completed production budget (output). When we look at computing and budgeting in this light, we can conclude that the computer is a natural for the budgeting process. This is even more true if the controller wanted to use a statistical technique-like regression analysis to generate a forecast for the sales budget.

In a word, the value of the computer in the budgeting process is its *efficiency:* efficient in its accuracy since costly errors are avoided; efficient in its speed—information is provided on a timely basis; and efficient in its response to feedback. Budgets can be adjusted quickly as more information becomes available.

32.2 HOW TO CHOOSE A COMPUTER SYSTEM. In the budgeting application it is vitally important to have a clear idea of the present and future requirements before selecting both the hardware and software. The people responsible for the preparation of the various budgets are the best people to render this judgment. How integrated will the budgets be? What level of detail will each have? Will the budgeting applications be linked to any of the other information systems within the organization? These are but three of the types of questions that must be addressed adequately if proper system scoping and sizing is to occur.

(a) System Portability. With the reality of the ubiquitous microcomputer, organizations are discovering that their budgeting applications must be capable of running on a varied assortment of computing platforms. There might be versions on mainframes (micros) as well as on portable laptop computers. The latter for use on the road as well as at the budget analyst's home. Careful attention has to be given to the budgeting system's flexibility to adapt to how people do business and not the other way around.

A final dimension of portability is the ability of the system to be able to interface within a multisite environment to other data bases and applications. Having this ability will minimize the need to rely on inefficient and/or manual bridges, which could destroy very rapidly the quality of life for the person who must share vital corporate information in a timely manner.

(b) Training and Support. Regardless of the computing system used in the budgeting process it is imperative that adequate consideration be given to the enormous hidden costs inherent in both user training and client support. The actual cost of acquisition of the hardware can range from $1,000 to well over $1 million. The cost of software starts at a somewhat lower price, but can rise to the million dollar level. Differences in systems' costs are a function of system size, speed of processing, and the degree of complexity of the application. In general, these costs are visible and are usually included as a part of the acquisition team's analysis. The place where problems occur is in the underestimation of the steepness of the costs associated with the learning curve required to bring the staff of the organization up to speed. All software applications have a learning curve. Some applications allow a slow, steady increase in client skills. Other systems need an extended period of time for costly formal training and an even longer time frame for the user to become functionally literate in the software. You must ask how many people and at what times will training be needed? What will be the impact of upgrades and new releases? How much retraining will be necessary?

In concluding this section, it is wise to point out that the traditional approach in a mainframe environment was to choose the hardware first and then the software. However, in the microcomputer setting it is generally considered more prudent to set the application needs first, select the appropriate software, and, finally, choose the hardware platform.

32.3 CHOOSING AN EFFECTIVE SOFTWARE SYSTEM.

Once the decision is made to implement the company's budgeting system on a computer, careful attention should be given to the fundamental approach that is to be followed. In this section, we will focus on the major features inherent in the four major options: spreadsheet software, financial modeling software, expert systems/artificial intelligence software, and in-house developed systems.

(a) Spreadsheet Software. It could be argued that budgeting was one of the earliest business applications of the spreadsheet. This application was transformed from the manual mode to the row/column format of the spreadsheet structure. The inherent two-dimensional nature of the application is a perfect technical fit for the spreadsheet. Frequent "what if" analyses were run using a base case along with the well-accepted best- and worst-case scenarios. Some spreadsheet packages soon included some advanced sensitivity analysis features or else the analyst could purchase system add-on packages, which gave the basic spreadsheet systems a form of upgrade via a "brain transplant."

Although millions of spreadsheet packages were sold, they were not without critics. Various limitations of the spreadsheet approach were pointed out. They included an inability to represent higher forms of data dimensionality typically present in many financial applications as well as an inability to be tied to large corporate data bases via a common command language. Other critics cited the limitation of the lack of a genuine risk analysis capability, which made it impossible to introduce probabilities into the budgeting process.

Even with these criticisms proponents of the spreadsheet approach probably make up the most frequently used approach to budgeting today. Businesses of all sizes can use spreadsheets and know that someone in their organization will have the technical capability to prepare a budget using one of the many systems available.

(b) Financial Modeling Software. These systems were born on the mainframe during the 1970s, and many were downsized for the microcomputer environment. The budget model logic is formulated using equations that have the ability to traverse several time periods. Often, these languages are extremely powerful and use higher-level modeling capabilities such as the ability to solve simultaneous equations, backward "what if" analysis, as well as optimization and extensive forecasting routines coupled to sophisticated multidimensional data bases. The sheer size and complexity of these systems on the mainframe often necessitates a support group and can prove difficult for a budget analyst to master with only limited or occasional use.

The micro versions of these systems contain abbreviated functionality, but have the advantage of being able to interface with their mainframe counterparts. Another advantage of modeling systems is that the risk-analysis capability allows the budget analyst to formulate probabilistic models, which add a whole new dimension to the budgeting process. Cost, training, and system complexity are other important factors to consider before committing to a financial planning and modeling system package. Exhibit 32.1 depicts the structure of a typical system.

(c) Expert System/Artificial Intelligence Software. Each time a budgeting model is created there is a reliance on choosing the appropriate variables, estimating their values, and establishing the correct organizational relationships. Although the general structure of all budgeting models may be similar, each organization puts its own "twist" on the process. However, there are definite linkages and similarities among the various budgets used by organizations.

The uniqueness of each organization's budgeting process as well as the infant stage of expert system/artificial intelligence has contributed to the paucity of applications in this area. Nevertheless, the potential for applications in the various budgeting areas warrants a brief discussion in this section.

The general field of research referred to as artificial intelligence is an attempt to replicate human intelligent actions by the use of the computer. In order for this to happen, a computer must be supplied with a compendium of knowledge in one form or another. This knowledge base is then manipulated by a series of rules based on practice. These rules are of varying degrees of formality and precision. Often, they are merely "rules of thumb" or guidelines. The union of the rules to the knowledge base results in solutions to a given problem, which in our case would be the preparation of the budget.

An expert system in budgeting would involve the assemblage of a group of individuals

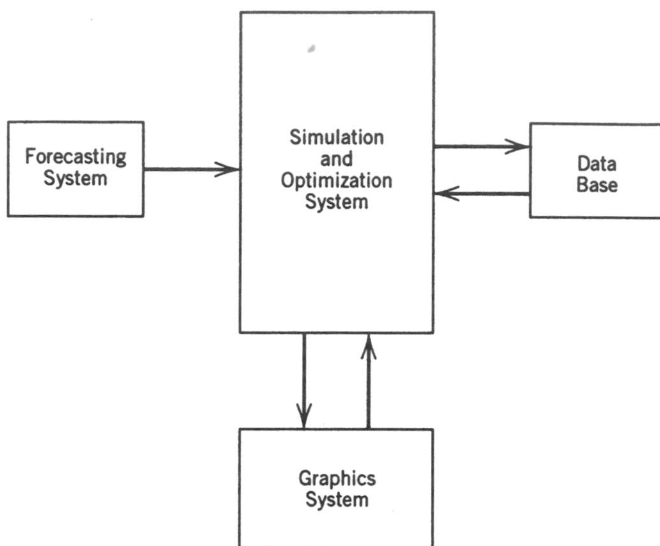

Exhibit 32.1. Financial modeling system functionality

or experts. These people would actively construct a working base of accumulated corporate knowledge surrounding the elements of the budgeting process (e.g., capital budgeting, for a particular organization). Careful construction of the knowledge base is critical to the success of this project. Current accounting practice as well as corporate policy directives would have to be scrutinized and added to the system. Any existing decision rules used by management would also be added. Personnel involved in this extraction and synthesis process are most important. They are referred to as *knowledge engineers* because their skills involve both extraction of information as well as synthesis of rules and relationships.

At this point in the process, it is necessary to have an inference engine, which is a software system that uses either a forward or backward chaining process that functions as the system evaluator. The purpose of this capability is to map out and document the proposed "solution" to the budgeting task at hand.

Throughout the process of developing the expert system for budgeting the analyst must interact with the system via an interface which is called the *system shell.* Emphasis is placed on giving the budget developer a degree of transparency to the actual software programming of the system.

The tasks required to develop a fully integrated corporate budgeting system using artificial intelligence/expert system are monumental. Researchers are taking the approach that subsystem design is the most feasible way to proceed. Once a commercially successful system is implemented, its proprietary nature would limit its public exposure. Each and every person who develops a sophisticated budgeting application, which must be used and communicated to many other people, might look forward to the day when expert systems approaches are used routinely in practice. Unfortunately, much work remains to be done in this area before that can happen.

(d) In-House Developed Systems. The alternative to a custom-developed budgeting system using either of the methods discussed previously in this section is the "off-the-shelf" version. In this "plug-and-run" option the budget manager must find an existing budgeting system that fits exactly his/her organizational needs. There are several comprehensive reporting and control systems that contain several accounting modules, but the challenge is more pronounced to create a general purpose budget model(s), which covers the many different types of budgeting applications discussed in this volume. In most cases, an organization selects a particular budget application and either starts from the beginning and converts the existing manual system to one that is computer based or purchases a general purpose model and makes the necessary changes to customize it to fit their unique corporate needs. The best choice to make depends on many factors, but some of the more significant ones are the presence of in-house modeling expertise, time, system complexity, system idiosyncracies, and system availability for your corporate hardware platform or system configuration. In any event, you can always expect to have to do a significant amount of tailoring before any outside developed software system is successfully implemented. The fact that some of these systems are available as templates to spreadsheet packages simplifies the process to some extent.

32.4 MICROCOMPUTER OVERVIEW AND NEEDS ASSESSMENT.

There are several factors that dominate the microcomputer environment. In this section, we discuss the four major ones: software, memory, speed, and peripherals. Each one is important in its own right.

(a) Software. Before choosing the actual computer, the first thing to discuss with the manager is what specific applications will be run on the computer. This discussion covers not only the immediate applications, but also focuses on possible future applications. Because we are most interested in budgeting, we should also consider possible extensions to consolidations, spreadsheet analysis, and graphics capability. This is very important since the required memory and speed desired stem from the applications selected.

(b) Memory. Once the software requirements have been decided, then the question of memory must be addressed. This decision deals with primary memory or what is commonly known as random access memory (RAM). Any data stored in RAM can be accessed virtually instantaneously. It does not require a search as when the data is stored in secondary memory. Secondary memory includes diskettes, hard disks, removable disks, tapes, and the like. The larger the RAM, the greater the speed in accomplishing computer tasks. As programs have become increasingly sophisticated, the amount of RAM needed to run them has increased sharply. For example, programs, data bases, and spreadsheets developed for Microsoft's Windows 95 Office when transferred to the Office 97 platform require significantly more memory. Of course, the more RAM, the greater will be the system cost. However, since the cost of increased RAM has been dropping significantly for quite some time, it is usually a prudent idea to use a multiple of the amount of RAM that your current needs justify. There is also another reason to have abundant RAM in your system. Cache programs convert unused RAM into a storage area for frequently used data. The effect of this is greatly increased speed of the computer application.

(c) Speed. The speed of a microcomputer is determined, for the most part, by its microprocessor chip. Early personal computers (PCs) used relatively slow processor chips compared to those available today. New generations of chips appear every eighteen months. This phenomenon causes the user to decide whether to purchase an upgrade chip or to trade in the entire system for an entirely new model. It is important to realize that speed is usually perceived as a relative concept. The micro model builder who has a significant amount of "number crunching" to do can become quite perturbed if the wait time extends beyond several minutes. The power user rapidly extends the limits of the hardware in many applications.

(d) Peripherals. Most people concentrate on the hardware processor and software, but it is also important to consider the range of supporting equipment and operating environment that you will be using. There is a wide range of printing options, starting at the top with color printers and laser printers to rather crude draft copy dot matrix printers. Since these devices could cost several thousand dollars alone a careful assessment of the frequency, printing speed in pages per minute (ppm), and quality of printed output must be done.

The video display or system monitor is another important choice that must be made. What size screen? Today, a 17-inch screen is often found in an office environment, while a 15-inch screen is normal for the home computer. What should the resolution be for your needs? Will you be doing much with graphics? Is there a need for video?

Once these questions are answered, a decision must be made regarding the need for a communications capability, the need for a local area network, a graphics plotter, a fax capability (Will you be using the internet?), and some provision for backup and security. It is easy to see that the cost of many of these peripherals could easily rival the cost of the software and processor. Another factor often overlooked is the impact of the system on the space requirements of your office and the need for space in which to place any new computer-related furniture.

We can conclude this section by pointing out that the microcomputer selection decision is further complicated by the rapidly changing technology. No sooner have you unpacked and installed your system configuration than you receive in the mail the announcement of a new, improved version. Unfortunately, this has been a characteristic of the industry since its inception. As long as your system continues to contribute toward your productivity, you must continually evaluate the new technology and balance the costs of migrating to a new environment against the perceived improvement in your productivity.

32.5 BUDGETING APPLICATIONS AND THEIR RELATIONSHIP TO OTHER CORPORATE SYSTEMS.

In this section the specific elements of several computer-based applications to budgeting are demonstrated. Care is given to providing system linkages to other organizational entities that are critical to a successful corporate-wide budgeting operation.

(a) Master Budget. A master budget is a network of individual budgets. Exhibit 32.2 clearly illustrates the relationships.

There are two key points that should be made: (1) all of the individual budgets are either directly or indirectly dependent upon the sales budget, and (2) any individual budget is related to one or more of the other budgets.

Why is this significant? Its importance lies in the fact that, as numbers are changed in the sales budget, all of the other individual budgets will have to be adjusted accordingly. Second, if we adjust any of the budgets other than sales there will be a change in at least one of the other budgets. In the best of cases, this fact causes a significant amount of work in adjusting a budget. In the worst of situations, this can cause errors in the budget because of omissions and incorrect calculations.

A carefully constructed budget model can eliminate these problems. As an illustration,

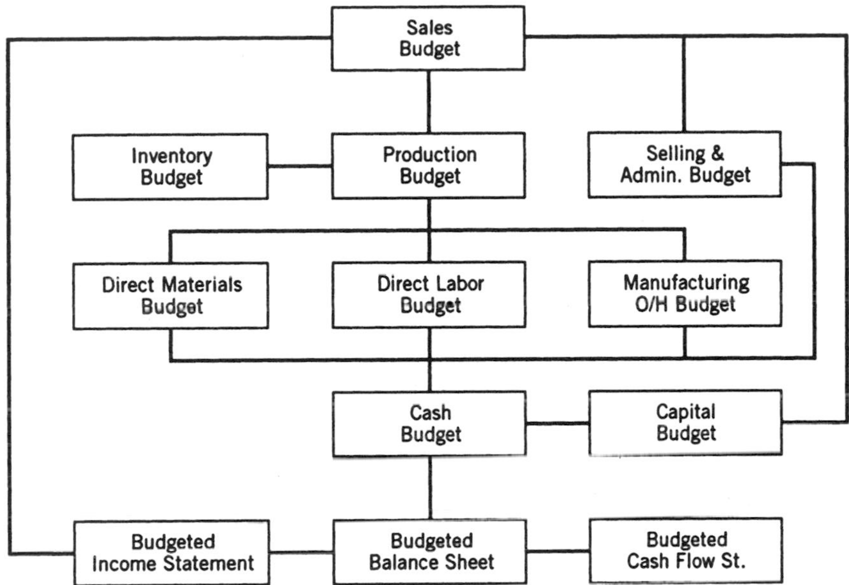

Exhibit 32.2. The master budget

consider the following scenario. Since the sales budget is the engine that drives the entire master budget, we must develop a sales forecast for the coming budget period. This forecast will be used to develop the sales budget. A sales forecast is dependent on many factors, including, but not limited to, the following factors:

- Prior sales history
- Pricing policy
- Back orders
- Economic conditions (general and industry)
- Planned advertising

In forecasting the sales for future years, these factors as well as others can be considered. We might choose to use the statistical forecasting tools such as regression, trend, and correlation analysis. The developers of the various spreadsheet and modeling systems have provided the end users with the means to use these statistical tools. Lotus Corporation's 1-2-3 has built in functions that enable the modeler to compute compound growth rates, standard deviations, variances, minimum and maximum values, internal rates of return, net present value, and net future value.

Once a sales forecast has been developed, a sales budget would be prepared. Exhibit 32.3 depicts a sales budget along with a simplified production and direct labor budget.

This sales budget was prepared using Lotus 1-2-3 with an add-in program to enhance printing. A complete sales budget would also show expected cash collections. However, since our purpose is to show how the computer may be used in the budgeting process we have chosen to omit this element. Note also the presentation of the production and direct labor budgets.

A	B	C	D	E	F
XYZ CORPORATION					
SALES BUDGET					
YEAR ENDING 12/31/19X1					
	Year	*1st Qtr*	*2nd Qtr*	*3rd Qtr*	*4th Qtr*
Forecasted Sales in Unit	5,200	1,100	1,200	1,500	1,400
Selling Price	20	20	20	20	20
Total Sales	104,000	22,000	24,000	30,000	28,000
XYZ CORPORATION					
PRODUCTION BUDGET					
YEAR ENDING 12/31/19X1					
	Year	*1st Qtr*	*2nd Qtr*	*3rd Qtr*	*4th Qtr*
Expected Unit Sales	5,200	1,100	1,200	1,500	1,400
Desired Ending Inventory	125	100	150	175	125
Total Required	5,325	1,200	1,350	1,675	1,525
Beginning Inventory	75	75	100	150	175
Units to be Produced	5,250	1,125	1,250	1,525	1,350
XYZ CORPORATION					
PRODUCTION BUDGET					
YEAR ENDING 12/31/19X1					
	Year	*1st Qtr*	*2nd Qtr*	*3rd Qtr*	*4th Qtr*
Units to be Produced	5,250	1,125	1,250	1,525	1,350
D/L Hours Per Unit	3	3	3	3	3
Total Hours Required	15,750	3,375	3,750	4,575	4,050
D/L Cost per Hour	11	11	11	11	11
Total D/L Cost	173,250	37,125	41,250	50,325	44,550

Exhibit 32.3. Sales, production, and direct-labor budgets

As mentioned previously, all of the individual budgets in the master budget are interrelated. In preparing a manual budget, if the forecasted unit sales for the first quarter were changed from 1,100 to some other number, then the number of units to be produced for the first quarter would change. This would also necessitate a change in the direct labor budget. By using a spreadsheet program, once the forecasted sales in units was changed, the entire master budget would be updated automatically. In order to accomplish this, all

XYZ COMPANY
QUARTERLY BUDGET (STATIC)
QUARTER ENDING 3/31/____

	Budget
Units Produced	10,000
Variable Costs:	
Direct Material	$18,000
Direct Labor	43,000
Other Variable Costs	12,000
Total Variable Costs	$73,000

XYZ COMPANY
BUDGET PERFORMANCE REPORT
QUARTER ENDING 3/31/____

	Budget	Actual	Variance
Units Produced	10,000	9,000	(1,000)
Variable Costs:			
Direct Material	$18,000	$16,500	$1,500
Direct Labor	43,000	41,000	2,000
Other Variable Costs	12,000	11,000	1,000
Total Variable Costs	$73,000	$68,500	$4,500

Exhibit 32.4. Static budget and performance report

entries that depend upon another entry are referenced to that entry. For example, cell C21 references cell C7, and C38 references C27. In effect, when C7 is changed, C21 is changed automatically, which in turn updates cell C27, which automatically changes cell C38. This is a very powerful feature of the spreadsheet model.

(b) Flexible Budgets. In the preceding section the budgets in the illustration were all geared to a single level of activity. Performance would be measured against this single level of activity. This type of budget is said to be static. A flexible budget is an alternative. It is not limited to a single activity level. Rather, it is developed for a range of activity. Let us compare the two budget models.

A static budget for the XYZ Company is presented in Exhibit 32.4 along with the related budget performance report. This budget addresses only one activity level: 10,000 units. This budget is meaningful only if the company attains its exact budgeted production level. The same is true for the budget performance report. The variances provided in the performance report are meaningless. This is true because we budgeted for a level of 10,000 units but the company was only able to operate at a level of 9,000. It is not possible to determine if we are over or under budget with respect to costs. If we had a budget at the 9,000 activity level then the variances are meaningful. The static budget simply tells us that we did not meet our production budget of 10,000 units but fails to tell us anything about our costs. It may even be concluded erroneously that the company operated at a 4,500 favorable variance (the budgeted costs exceeded the actual costs.) Recognizing this

XYZ COMPANY
QUARTERLY BUDGET (FLEXIBLE)
QUARTER ENDING 3/31/____

	Cost Per Unit	Range of Production		
		8,000	9,000	10,000
Variable Costs:				
Direct Material	1.80	$14,400	$16,200	$18,000
Direct Labor	4.30	34,400	38,700	43,000
Other Variable Costs	1.20	9,600	10,800	12,000
Total Variable Costs		$58,400	$65,700	$73,000

XYZ COMPANY
BUDGET PERFORMANCE REPORT
QUARTER ENDING 3/31/____

	Budget	Actual	Variance
Units Produced	9,000		
Variable Costs:			
Direct Material	$16,200	$16,500	$ (300)
Direct Labor	38,700	41,000	(2,300)
Other Variable Costs	10,800	11,000	(200)
Total Variable Costs	$65,700	$68,500	$(2,800)

Exhibit 32.5. Flexible budget and performance report

flaw in the static budget model, management accountants developed the flexible budgeting concept.

In developing a flexible budget the following information is necessary: (1) a relevant range over which an activity is expected to fluctuate, and (2) an understanding of cost behavior over this relevant range. This usually includes a separation of fixed and variable costs.

Exhibit 32.5 depicts a spreadsheet model of a flexible budget and its related budget performance report. A close examination reveals that the company was operating over budget by $2,800.

It is clear that this type of budget analysis is tailor made for spreadsheet packages. The row by column format is obvious in both the budget and performance reports. Also all calculations were made automatically and without error by the computer. In the flexible budget, the analyst need only enter the levels of activity (8,000, 9,000, and 10,000) and the unit prices for variable costs (direct materials, 1.80; direct labor, 4.30; and other variable costs, 1.20). The budget model made all of the calculations including the totals. Notice that the budget performance report was tied directly into the model. The only variables that needed to be entered were the units produced and the actual costs. Once the data are entered, the model uses a conditional branch capability to select the appropriate budget amounts and then calculates the variances.

(c) Fixed versus Variable Cost in the Budget Model. In the previous section, it was stressed how necessary it was to understand how costs would behave if we were to develop

	A	B	C	D	E
1					
2		Prior Year's Results			
3					
4		Units		Monthly	
5		Produced		Cost	
6	January	27,000		$ 51,000	
7	February	31,000		55,000	
8	March	29,000		54,000	
9	April	33,000		57,000	
10	May	41,000		65,000	
11	June	51,000		73,000	
12	July	60,000		98,000	
13	August	82,000		105,000	
14	September	92,000		111,000	
15	October	70,000		100,000	
16	November	32,000		56,000	
17	December	24,000		48,000	
18					
19					
20	Minimum Value	24,000		$ 48,000	
21					
22	Maximum Value	92,000		$ 111,000	
23					
24	Difference	68,000		$ 63,000	
25					
26	Variable Cost Per Unit	0.93			
27					
28					
29	Total Cost	$ 111,000			
30	Variable Cost	$ 85,235			
31					
32	Fixed Cost	$ 25,765			
33	Total Cost =	$ 25,765 +			0.93 Units Produced
34					

Exhibit 32.6. Fixed and variable cost model

an accurate spreadsheet budget model. While some costs are clearly fixed, and others are clearly variable, we encounter some costs that have both a fixed and variable component. To be able to accurately predict and then to budget these costs we must be able to separate them into their two components—fixed and variable.

For example, a company's maintenance cost will generally increase with increased production (the variable portion). However, even with zero production there would still be some costs incurred (fixed portion). One way to identify what portion is fixed and what portion is variable is to use the high–low method in the form of a spreadsheet model. This is illustrated in Exhibit 32.6.

The top portion of the spreadsheet model, the rectangle (range) defined by cells A1 through E18 represents the historical results for the prior year. These entries are made up of labels and values. They can be considered the input to the model. The second half of the model (cells A19 through E34) are computational, except for the obvious label locations. An explanation of these various computational cells follows:

Cell	Contents	Explanation
B20	@Min(B6..B17)	Finds the minimum value in the range B6 to B17
D20	@Min(D6..D17)	Finds the minimum value in the range D6 to D17
B22	@Max(B6..B17)	Finds the maximum value in the range B6 to B17
D22	@Max(D6..D17)	Finds the maximum value in the range D6 to D17
B24	+B22-B20	Subtracts cell B20 from B22
D24	+D22-D20	Subtracts cell D20 from D22
B26	+D24/B24	Divides cell D24 by B24
B29	+D22	Selects the amount in cell D22
B30	+B26*B22	Multiplies the V/C per unit by the number of units produced
B32	+B29-B30	Subtracts contents of B30 from B29
B35	+B32	Selects the amount in cell B32
D35	+B26	Selects the amount in cell B26

This model has developed the appropriate cost function, and it is presented in row 35. This function allows the budget analyst to determine the cost at various levels of activity. At a zero level of activity, the company incurs a cost of $25,765. For each added unit of production it can be seen that production costs would increase by $0.93.

(d) Capital Budgeting Model. Capital budgeting addresses the area of long-term investment decisions. Since the concepts of capital budgeting are discussed elsewhere in this volume, we will confine our coverage to the development of a spreadsheet model. Spreadsheet packages are ideally suited to assist in the development of discounted cash flow–net present value (DCF–NPV) capital budgeting models. Built-in functions are able to calculate the NPV of various cash flows. They can also calculate the exact internal rate of return (IRR). This frees the analyst from having to use complicated tables and formulas. A simple capital budgeting model in spreadsheet form is presented in Exhibit 32.7.

A company is considering investing in a new piece of equipment. It can be purchased outright for $200,000. At the end of the third year it will require an overhaul at a cost of $15,000. The equipment's useful life is estimated to be five years. In exchange for these cash outflows the company will realize savings in materials ($23,000 per year), labor ($19,000 per year), and in other costs ($11,000 per year.) In addition, at the end of the equipment's life, it can be sold for $20,000. For the sake of simplicity, all tax considerations have been eliminated from the model.

Our model lists the various cash flows (outflows as negative numbers and inflows as positive numbers) and assumes that such cash flows occur at the end of the year. The area of the spreadsheet model defined by the range D6 to I16 is used to enter these cash flows. The budget analyst determines the discount rate and enters the rate in cell B1. The model calculates the present value of each row (initial investment, salvage value, etc.) by the use of the spreadsheet's built-in functions for sum, and the NPV is calculated. The model indicates that the investment will yield an amount in excess of 9 percent. Based on this result or further sensitivity analysis, the company can decide if they want to acquire the piece of equipment.

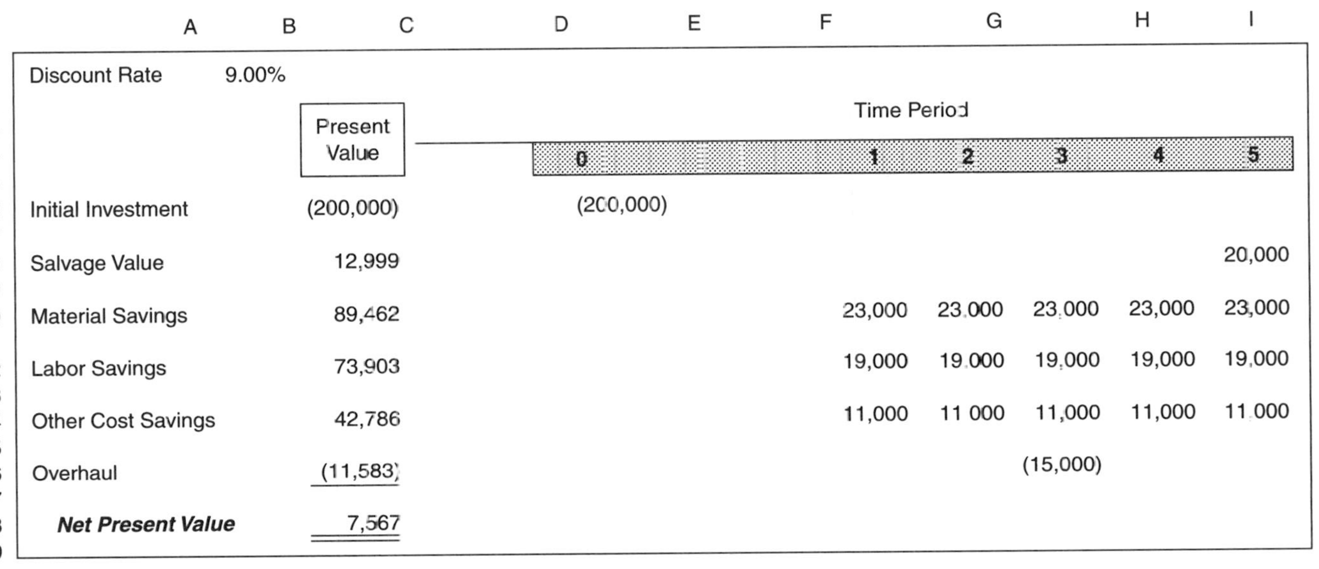

	A	B	C	D	E	F	G	H	I
1	Discount Rate	9.00%							
2						Time Period			
3			Present Value						
4				0		1	2	3	4	5
5									
6	Initial Investment		(200,000)	(200,000)					
7									
8	Salvage Value		12,999						20,000
9									
10	Material Savings		89,462			23,000	23,000	23,000	23,000	23,000
11									
12	Labor Savings		73,903			19,000	19,000	19,000	19,000	19,000
13									
14	Other Cost Savings		42,786			11,000	11 000	11,000	11,000	11.000
15									
16	Overhaul		(11,583)					(15,000)		
17									
18	***Net Present Value***		7,567						
19									

Exhibit 32.7. Capital budgeting spreadsheet model

It should be clear from the previous several budgeting model examples how valuable the computer has become to the budgeting processes of most organizations.

32.6 MICRO-TO-MAINFRAME LINK. Earlier in this chapter it was emphasized how the typical budgeting application is a prime example of an integrated information systems application. It is not reasonable to expect the budget analyst to have custodial authority over all of the data elements that constitute the various budget reports. This assumption is amplified when the applications are implemented on a microcomputer system platform. The key task is to have rapid access to the appropriate information resources so that all of the relevant information can be culled from the various organizational sources and entered into the budget application. If the data reside on a mainframe, and the application is needed on a microcomputer, then the appropriate data base must be downloaded.

Once the organizational difficulties have been resolved it is then necessary to find the technical solution to the problem of two computer platforms (mainframe and micro), which operate with two different data formats. There are various avenues that could be chosen to create a bridge between the two environments so that data can be moved expeditiously between them. Although the topic is too complicated to discuss in detail in this setting, the budget analyst can make use of either one or more of the following approaches: terminal emulation, file transfer, cooperative processing, or virtual disks. There is a clear trade-off of availability, cost, and simplicity of operation that must be made in the decision to implement a micro-to-mainframe link.

Many organizations are recognizing that the prime role for the mainframe can be one of a central data repository and as a central switch, which is capable of distributing relevant sections of an overall data base to the appropriate organizational entities on a timely basis. Issues of security, integrity of the data, and timeliness are solved through a cooperative sharing of the corporate data resource. The initial period of microcomputer use featured stand-alone machines doing relatively independent and/or unsophisticated applications. This period soon gave way to micros, which had to be linked to the mainframe. Using local area networks, client–server computing, the Internet, and corporate intranets, there has been an endlessly evolving array of platforms for positioning corporate data for the budgeting application.

The organizational benefits to the budgeting function are significant. Timely, accurate data is derived from existing repositories and rapidly made available to the various departments, which are tied together electronically. This situation allows for better communication across organizational lines and faster preparation and dissemination of important budget information.

32.7 IMPLEMENTING THE SYSTEM. The implementation of a computer-based budgeting system should not be any different from that of any other system of its type. The nature of the application is such that it has the characteristics of both operational and planning systems. Operational systems tend to be data intensive and time dependent and rely on available historical data for input and analysis. The need to interface with other organizational operating systems is present. Planning systems tend to incorporate future-based projections and rely on multiple "what if" scenarios, which are rooted inextricably to well-crafted assumptions. In the vernacular of information systems developers, budget applications have both characteristics of management information systems (MIS) and decision support systems (DSS).

Once the system has been developed and tested to the satisfaction of all concerned there should be a period whereby some degree of concurrent processing of the old system and the new system takes place. The risks associated with a "drop in" conversion and no parallel operation might not be worth taking since budgeting has traditionally been a high profile application. Budgeting exists in a highly charged political environment, and the last thing that is needed is to have validation and/or training errors in the system. The system should be tested thoroughly and sufficient documentation provided to all users so that everyone can come up to speed in time for the first computer-based budgeting cycle.

After the initial budgeting module has been validated and implemented successfully, the organization can begin phasing in the other critical modules until the entire formal budgeting system has been installed. Eventually, modifications will have to be made as new requirements are discovered. With proper implementation and thorough documentation and training the system can undergo a painless evolution to new versions.

One final recommendation is in order. It is best to start the computerization of the budgeting activity with a well-defined subsystem that makes use of well-understood modeling methodologies. Once experience has been gained with the existing system and some time has elapsed it might then be appropriate to enhance the underlying methodology if the perceived gain from increased sophistication is deemed worth the effort that it takes to incorporate the new technologies.

32.8 SUMMARY. In this chapter we have concentrated on the key issues of designing, selecting, and implementing a computer-based budgeting system. Emphasis was placed on the various interrelationships among the modules of a budgeting system and the various system's options, which could be used in their development. Once experience is gained on the earlier system components, a more expansionary profile could be taken. This might include forecasting, more extensive sensitivity analysis, and perhaps even risk analysis. In any event, the budgeting application is a natural for implementation in a computer environment.

CHAPTER 33

FUZZY LOGIC APPLIED TO BUDGETING: AN INTUITIVE APPROACH TO COPING WITH UNCERTAINTY

Donald R. Moscato

Iona College

33.1 CURRENT BUDGETING ENVIRONMENT. One of the most ubiquitous tasks in organizations is the preparation of the operating budget. It is a tool to make concrete the operating plan for the coming year. Budgeting has undergone an evolution from the manual method of preparation to the spreadsheet format of today.

Most budgeting logic is fairly well understood. Managers know the key business drivers. The challenge is to estimate the values of these key variables. The method the manager uses to derive these estimates is the focus of fuzzy number modeling.

The current state of budgeting makes use of best case, worst case, and most likely operations scenarios. From this exercise in sensitivity analysis, the decision maker must settle on a final set of estimates which becomes the foundation of the operating budget. Fuzzy number modeling can improve budgeting effectiveness and efficiency.

33.2 POTENTIAL OF FUZZY LOGIC IN BUDGETING. In the mid-1960s researchers led by Lofti Zadeh developed an extension of set theory known as *fuzzy sets*. Fuzzy logic can be thought of as approximate reasoning. Since so much of business is characterized by vague statements of belief, confidence, or feeling, our analytical tools are more accurate when they are adapted to this reality.

Fuzzy modeling recognizes the inherent imprecision of management communications in the decision-making process. Traditional tools of analysis require a precision that creates arbitrary future estimates with no allowance for variability.

Fuzzy sets and fuzzy logic have many practical applications: refocusing cameras, automotive antilock brake systems, intelligent appliances, and business machines. Chips that were designed with traditional logic circuits have been augmented to include fuzzy logic analytical reasoning capability. Applications, as well as research, have been wide ranging in the defense business and across continents.

Fuzzy logic found its way into business modeling applications as soon as spreadsheet modeling systems could handle the methodology of fuzzy numbers and their requisite operators.

33.3 NEED FOR INNOVATIVE THINKING. Business decision makers use both intuitive and analytical resources to make critical decisions. Some managers are comfortable with spreadsheets and others shy away from "managing by the numbers." Whether intuitive or analytical, most people would concede that graphical representations are more appealing than a simple column or table of numbers. Both spreadsheets and graphs assume that the numbers or graphs represent what is really believed as being a true representation of a manager's confidence level in the thing being measured. Today's spreadsheet tools assume that the use of numbers in the cells properly depict the underlying uncertainty of the events and things that are being measured.

Fuzzy modeling attempts to measure, in a more meaningful and accurate way, the underlying uncertainty present in most business decision making. This chapter illustrates the application of fuzzy modeling concepts to the operational budgeting activity. The vehicle that will be used is the spreadsheet format. Millions of analysts are familiar with the basic format of the spreadsheet, and it has become a *de facto* form of business communication. Fuzzy modeling combines the familiarity and discipline of spreadsheet modeling with the intuitive expressiveness of today's manager. This combination can be a dynamic and innovative way to think about budgeting.

33.4 LIMITATIONS OF CURRENT APPROACHES. Current approaches rely almost exclusively on single value estimates. The implication of this approach is that any uncertainty surrounding the business must either be suppressed, or else several alternative estimates must be run through the budgeting logic. Each scenario introduces possible values of key variables. The decision maker must select a set of plausible values and see how their inclusion in the budget affects the results. After this process is finished a priority must be developed regarding the scenarios in order to help the decision maker resolve the inherent uncertainty surrounding the estimates. Alternatively, the decision maker could run just a single budget scenario and wrestle with the uncertainty in her head without the aid of trying out other plausible scenarios. In either case, uncertainty must be addressed either explicitly in the model or implicitly in the analyst's head.

Analysts use risk analysis to address the issue of capturing uncertainty. In this approach, the decision maker estimates a probability distribution for each input variable that is not treated as being certain. The shape of the probability distribution reflects the likelihood of that variable's values occurring. Software for the microcomputer such as @Risk® and Crystal Ball® can be used to build budgeting models using risk analysis. Inherent in this approach is the idea of randomness surrounding the uncertain input values.

Regardless of which spreadsheet-based approach used to prepare your budget, the decision maker must find an effective and comfortable way to capture the uncertainty present in the estimation process. The fuzzy modeling approach is presented as an alternative to the limitations of the traditional methods of dealing with capturing a decision maker's confidence level with numbers used in the budget model.

33.5 BASIC ELEMENTS OF FUZZY MODELING. A good starting-off point in understanding the basic concepts is to relate them to familiar surroundings, namely spreadsheet modeling using Lotus 1-2-3® or Microsoft's Excel®. In both of these modeling systems, a number is represented as a single value which is used throughout the model. In our framework, this is called a *crisp number.* What would happen if the decision maker was not sure of a particular estimate? For example, he might say that sales will be around one hundred units. He is a little unclear about its eventual value. In this case we can introduce the notion of a *fuzzy* or vague number. This fuzziness is due to a general feeling or

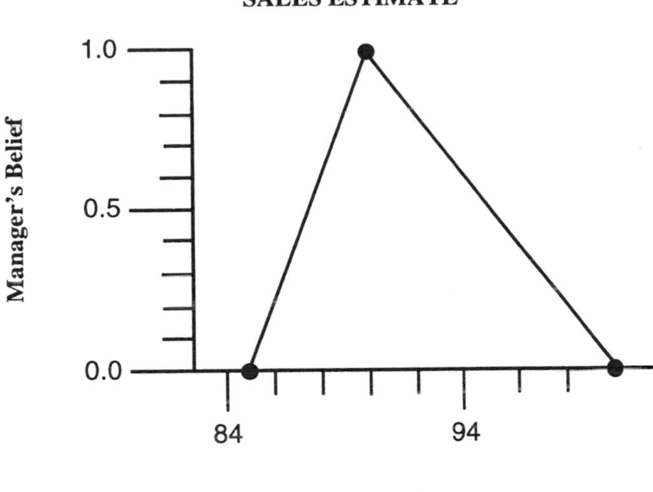

Exhibit 33.1. Triangular belief graph

uncertainty about a given estimate. Rather than representing this belief with a single value, we can introduce a set of points over a plausible range. Each point represents a specific value along with a degree of belief in that particular value's occurring. These numbers are approximate values tempered by one's degree of belief. The more uncertain one is, the wider is the range. The less belief in a value, the lower will be the belief value. This belief measure is how confidence level in a value is represented.

We represent a fuzzy number as a set of points expressed as coordinates. Each possible value has a paired degree of belief. For example, let's say that a scale of zero to one (0.0 to 1.0) is used to depict the strength of belief in a particular value occurring. Next year's sales estimate is required for the budget. Your best thinking states that the actual sales should be between 85 and 100 units. Your strongest belief is that 90 units will be sold. You can assign this value (90 units) a belief of 1.0. Since both 85 and 100 are possible but not very likely, you assign them both a belief of 0.0.

The visual representation of a belief system is defined by the concept of a membership function in fuzzy modeling. This can be presented graphically by a belief graph (Exhibit 33.1).

The X (horizontal) axis represents the range of possible sales in units. The Y (vertical) axis depicts the degree of belief in possible values. This belief graph has three points: the highest belief or confidence (a sales value of 90 units), the maximum value of belief (1.0), and the minimum value of belief (0.0). Any value in this range can represent the degree of belief in a given value's occurring.

To illustrate further how to represent a belief system we can use this sales estimate example to express several different perceptions.

In the first case (Exhibit 33.2), we have a belief graph that looks like a church steeple. This graph expresses much confidence in the sales estimate of 90. Confidence drops off rapidly on either side of 90.

If a manager was very confident in a range of values around 90, the belief graph would

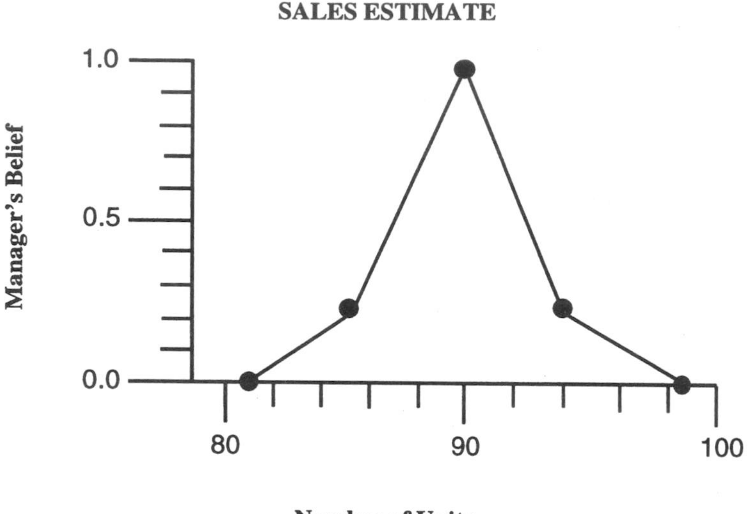

Exhibit 33.2. Steeple belief graph

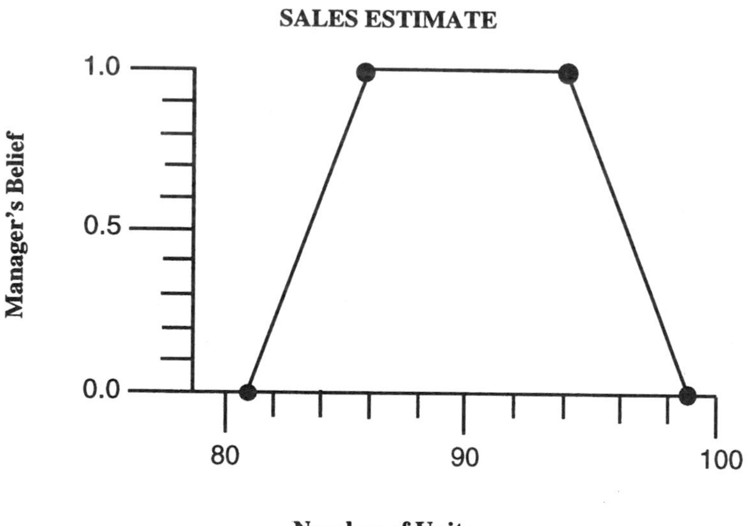

Exhibit 33.3. Trapezoid belief graph

have a trapezoid shape (Exhibit 33.3). The range or width of the plateau would follow the belief or confidence in a wider range of values occurring.

Many times estimates are characterized by vague language. "We should offer around fifty thousand dollars for the equipment bid" would be an example. This type of feeling is often captured with a tent-shaped belief graph. Exhibit 33.4 has five coordinate points. The middle three have beliefs of 0.75, 1.0, and 0.75. In this way, we can communicate the vague or fuzzy statement "around" with a specifically tailored belief graph.

If the manager believes that two values have the highest confidence within a range,

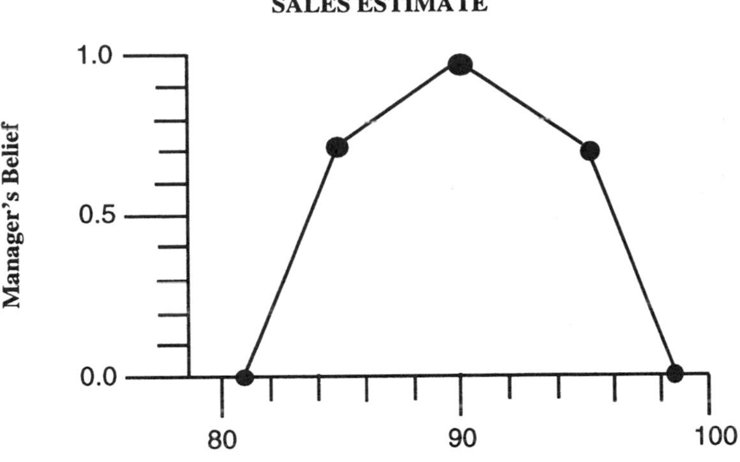

Exhibit 33.4. Tent-shaped belief graph

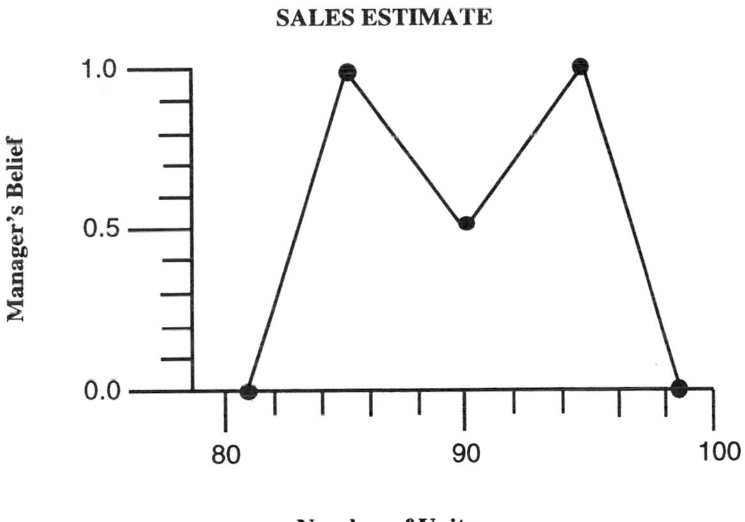

Exhibit 33.5. Twin-peaked belief graph

the belief graph would have two peaks. In Exhibit 33.5, the two values 85 and 95 are illustrated as having the highest belief measures. The sales estimate 90 has only a 0.5 degree of confidence.

In the last two variations of belief graphs, the graphs are cropped or cut off at a sales estimate of 96. Exhibit 33.6 has a highest degree of belief of 1.0 for a range of values. Exhibit 33.7 has a lower degree of confidence expressed for the same range of values; only 0.75. However, both graphs communicate a reasonable degree of belief over a wide range of values.

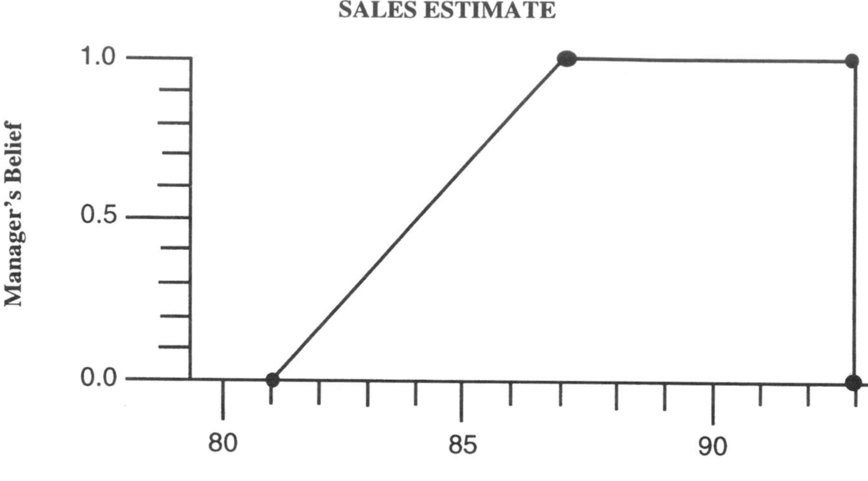

Exhibit 33.6. Modified belief graph (belief of 1.0 at maximum)

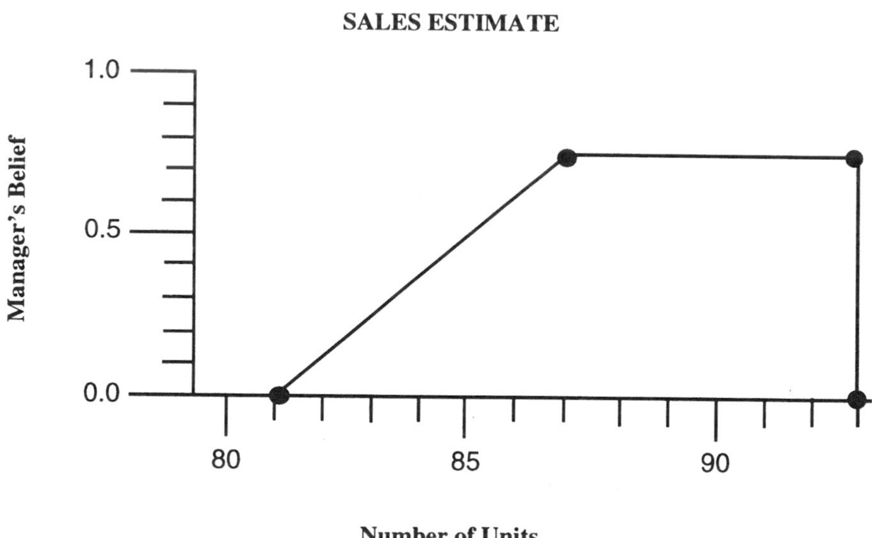

Exhibit 33.7. Modified belief graph (belief of 0.75 at maximum)

Exhibits 33.1 through 33.7 characterize the manager's feelings or degree of confidence that certain values can occur for sales. Estimates, no longer represented as certainty, can be portrayed consistent with the manager's true belief system. The shape of the graph can be tailored to one's expressed feelings.

Once the belief graphs have been defined for the selected key business drivers, you can then simulate the budget and compute the resulting target variables as you did under Lotus 1-2-3 or Excel. The major difference is that, instead of an answer expressed as a crisp certain number, your results will be expressed as a fuzzy number. This resultant fuzzy number has its own belief graph which is also derived with a series of coordinate points. Each point represents a value for the target variable along with its associated confidence level. The important point to appreciate is that the degrees of belief of the input assumptions are logically carried through to the degrees of belief of the criterion variables. You now have a measure of confidence in the eventual outcome variables, which is, after all, the reason you constructed the spreadsheet model in the first place.

When the fuzzy numbers are printed in a spreadsheet cell they are depicted as a single number. The single number that is printed in the cell is called the *centroid value* of the fuzzy number. It can be thought of as the center of gravity or the critical mass of the fuzzy number. All calculations in the spreadsheet model are done using the rules of fuzzy number arithmetic, which have been validated over 30 years of research.

33.6 EXAMPLE OF FUZZY LOGIC MODELING IN THE OPERATING BUDGET APPLICATION. An operating budget for a condominium demonstrates fuzzy modeling in budgeting. The general manager developed the operating budget using his best estimates. However, he believes that there is greater uncertainty surrounding some factors than with others. There is a very high confidence for the revenue side, so he will concentrate on the expense side. This area is made up of six cost categories: building maintenance, grounds maintenance, pool maintenance, utilities, general and administrative, and planned capital expenses. He has decided that his estimates for building maintenance, grounds maintenance, and pool maintenance are fairly certain. He wants to explore the ramifications of uncertainty to a selected group of variables. The greatest degree of uncertainty is present in the sewer, water, electricity, telephone, insurance, and painting estimates.

All spreadsheets in this chapter were created in FUZICAL®, a product of FUZIWARE, Inc. According to the vendor, it is the world's first fuzzy number modeling tool. All models were run in a Microsoft Windows® environment. The spreadsheet for the operating budget appears in Exhibit 33.8. In the traditional budgeting process, the manager expects expenses to total $531,980, which matches expected revenue. What are the implications of uncertainty surrounding some of the key assumptions?

Since the manager feels less comfortable with several of the variables, he will employ fuzzy numbers to express his belief system.

Sewer estimate	Low	$38,160	0.0
	Best	$42,400	1.0
	High	$46,640	0.0
Water estimate	Low	$34,800	0.0
	Best	$38,700	1.0
	High	$42,500	0.0
Electricity estimate	Low	$36,000	0.0
	Best	$40,000	1.0
	High	$44,000	0.0
Telephone estimate	Low	$6,750	0.0
	Best	$7,500	1.0
	High	$8,250	0.0
Insurance estimate	Low	$135,000	0.0
	Best	$150,000	1.0
	High	$165,000	0.0

199X Operating Budget

REVENUES	
Regular Residential Dues	$515,550
Restaurant Lease	$12,180
Late Payment Interest	$500
Late Payment Charges	$1,000
Interest Income	$250
Miscellaneous	2,500
TOTAL REVENUES	$531,980
OPERATING EXPENSES	
BUILDING MAINTENANCE	
Locksmith	$200
Electrical	$2,000
Plumbing	$1,800
Supplies & Equipment	$8,000
HVAC	$1,000
Interior Pest Control	$3,500
Termite Treatment Bond	$600
Elevator Maintenance	$12,000
Fire Protection System	$8,000
TOTAL BUILDING MAINT.	$37,100
GROUNDS MAINTENANCE	
Supplies	$2,500
Signage	$500
Parking Lot	$1,200
Repairs	$1,500
Bulldozing	$3,000
TOTAL GROUNDS MAINT.	$8,700
POOL MAINTENANCE	
Chemicals	$7,500
Supplies	$500
Equipment Maint. & Rep.	$5,000
TOTAL POOL MAINT.	$13,000
UTILITIES	
Electricity	$40,000
Sewer	$42,400
Water	$38,650
Trash Removal	$6,700
Cable TV	$14,400
Telephone Equip. Maint.	$7,500
TOTAL UTILITIES	$149,650
GENERAL & ADMINISTRATIVE	
Management Services	$97,850
Bank Charges	$200
Postage	$2,500
Office Supplies & Dupl.	$1,750
Office Telephone	$700
Insurance	$150,000
Legal Services	$5,000
Audit Expense	$5,500
Other Prof. Services	$1,200
Annual Meeting Expense	$500
Board Travel	$3,000
Board Meeting Expense	$3,500
Tax & Licenses	$500
Bad Debt Expense	$4,000
Pager Service	$1,200
Other	$250
TOTAL G & A	$277,650
General Capital Reserves	$4,405
Restaurant Property Tax	$2,750
HOA Personal Prop. Tax	$975
Contingency Reserves	$16,750
TOTAL OTHER EXPENSE	$24,880
TOTAL OPERATING EXP.	$510,980
PLANNED CAPITAL EXPENSES	
Pool Furniture	$3,000
Landscape	$3,000
Exterior Painting	$15,000
TOTAL CAPITAL EXPENSES	$21,000
TOTAL OPERATING AND CAPITAL EXPENSES	$531,980

Exhibit 33.8. Traditional spreadsheet operating budget

Painting estimate	Low	$13,500	0.0
	Best	$15,000	1.0
	High	$16,500	0.0

Each three-point estimate results in a belief graph. Exhibits 33.9 to 33.12 illustrate the manager's belief graphs for electricity, water, telephone, and painting. Each graph has

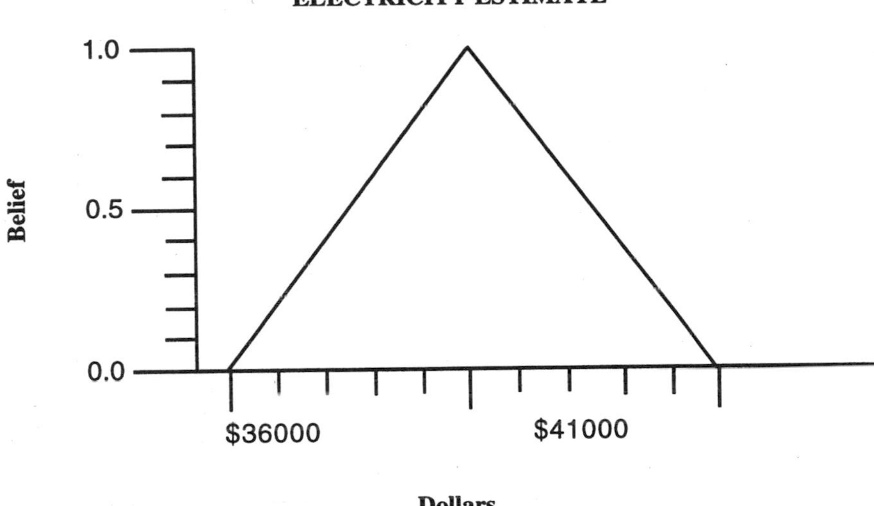

Exhibit 33.9. Manager's belief graph for electricity estimate

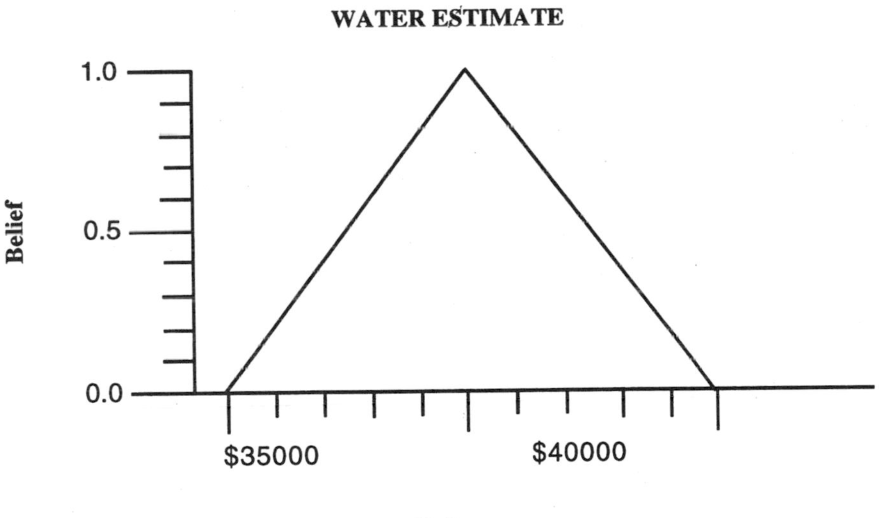

Exhibit 33.10. Manager's belief graph for water estimate

a belief scale from 0 to 1. Values close to 1 represent the greatest belief. The horizontal axes depict the scales of the estimated variables. Note the symmetric nature of each estimate.

Exhibit 33.13 depicts the spreadsheet model with the entries in Column E for the belief graphs' centroid values. For example, the centroid value for the insurance estimate is $150,000.

In this first budget spreadsheet, each selected input variable has a belief graph associated with it. These graphs are all symmetric around the best estimate value. Note that aside from the graphs there is no change in the results. This is due to the fact that the centroid

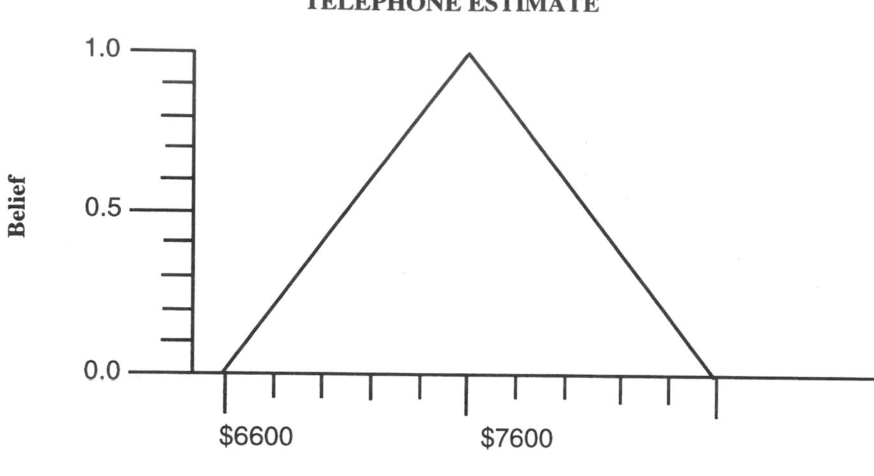

Exhibit 33.11. Manager's belief graph for telephone estimate

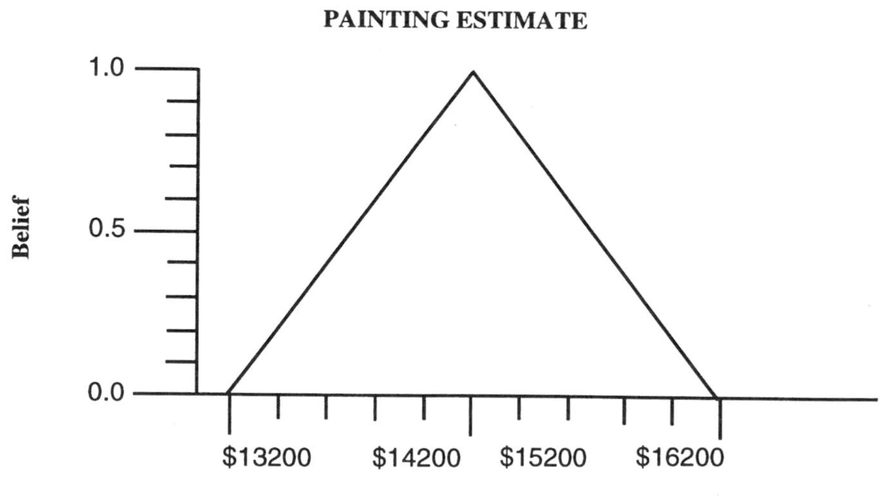

Exhibit 33.12. Manager's belief graph for painting estimate

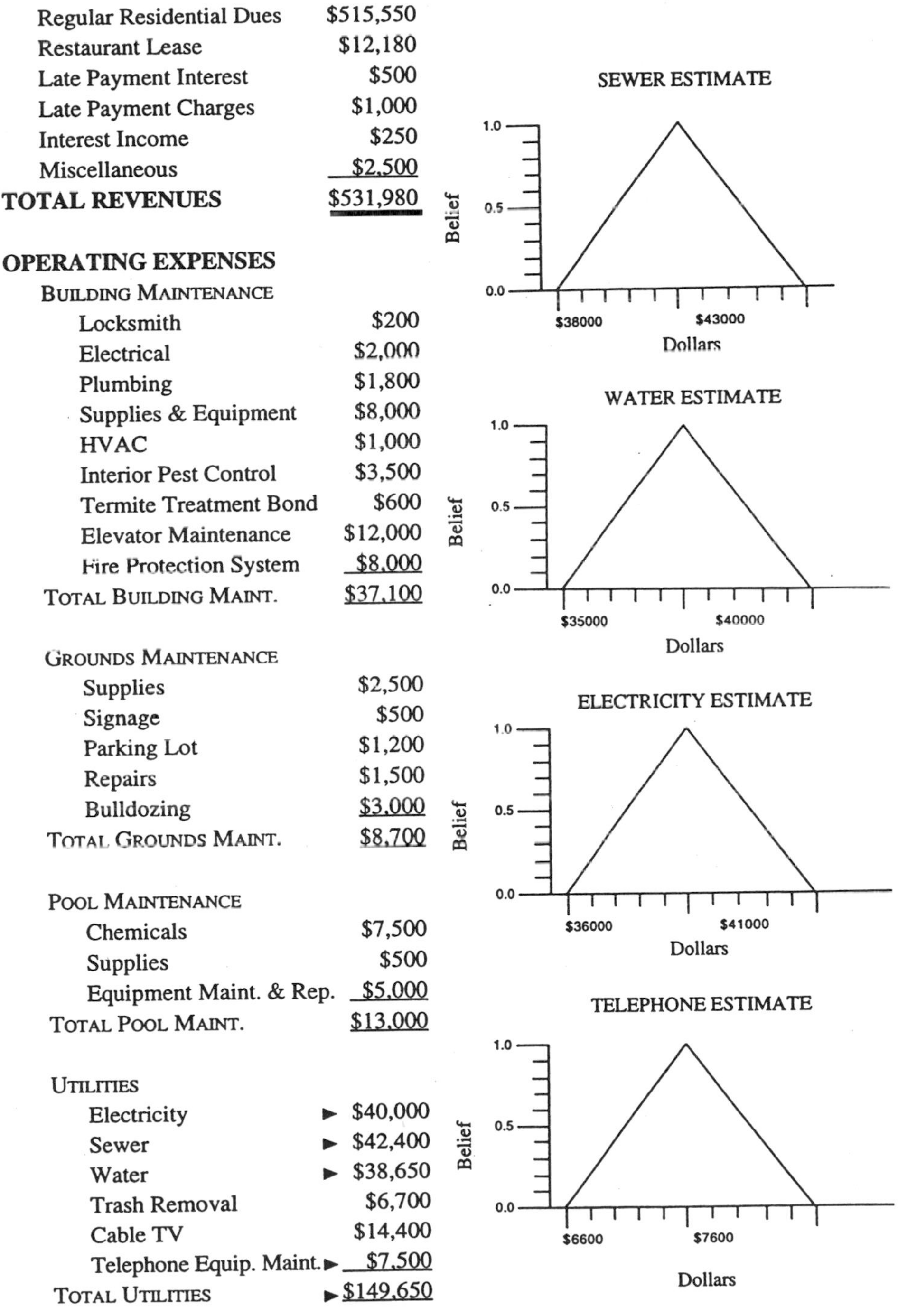

199X Operating Budget

REVENUES

Regular Residential Dues	$515,550
Restaurant Lease	$12,180
Late Payment Interest	$500
Late Payment Charges	$1,000
Interest Income	$250
Miscellaneous	$2,500
TOTAL REVENUES	$531,980

OPERATING EXPENSES

BUILDING MAINTENANCE	
Locksmith	$200
Electrical	$2,000
Plumbing	$1,800
Supplies & Equipment	$8,000
HVAC	$1,000
Interior Pest Control	$3,500
Termite Treatment Bond	$600
Elevator Maintenance	$12,000
Fire Protection System	$8,000
TOTAL BUILDING MAINT.	$37,100
GROUNDS MAINTENANCE	
Supplies	$2,500
Signage	$500
Parking Lot	$1,200
Repairs	$1,500
Bulldozing	$3,000
TOTAL GROUNDS MAINT.	$8,700
POOL MAINTENANCE	
Chemicals	$7,500
Supplies	$500
Equipment Maint. & Rep.	$5,000
TOTAL POOL MAINT.	$13,000
UTILITIES	
Electricity	► $40,000
Sewer	► $42,400
Water	► $38,650
Trash Removal	$6,700
Cable TV	$14,400
Telephone Equip. Maint.	► $7,500
TOTAL UTILITIES	► $149,650

Exhibit 33.13. Fuzzy number spreadsheet for initial budget

199X Operating Budget

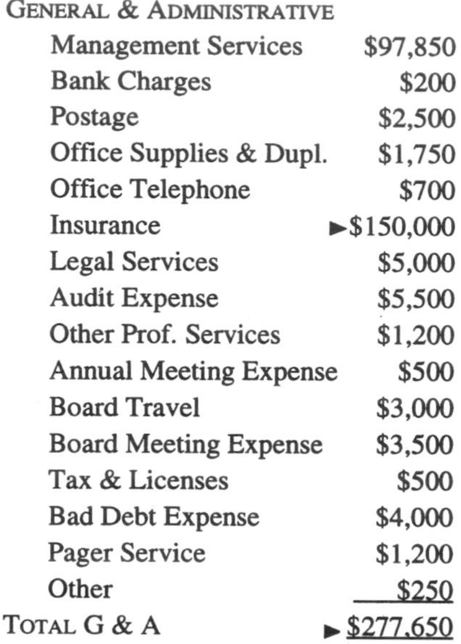

GENERAL & ADMINISTRATIVE	
Management Services	$97,850
Bank Charges	$200
Postage	$2,500
Office Supplies & Dupl.	$1,750
Office Telephone	$700
Insurance	►$150,000
Legal Services	$5,000
Audit Expense	$5,500
Other Prof. Services	$1,200
Annual Meeting Expense	$500
Board Travel	$3,000
Board Meeting Expense	$3,500
Tax & Licenses	$500
Bad Debt Expense	$4,000
Pager Service	$1,200
Other	$250
TOTAL G & A	► $277,650

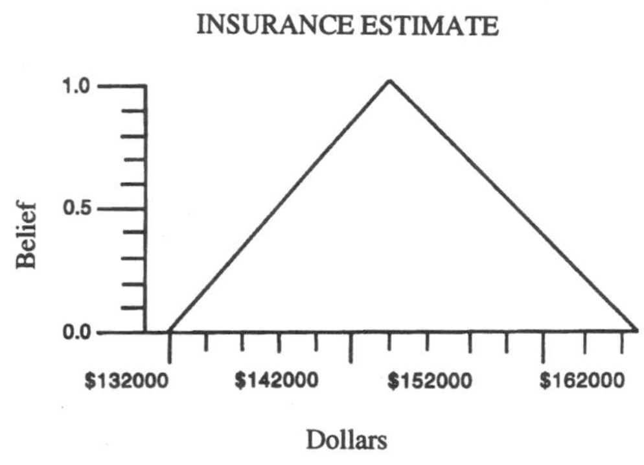

General Capital Reserves	$4,405
Restaurant Property Tax	$2,750
HOA Personal Prop. Tax	$975
Contingency Reserves	$16,750
TOTAL OTHER EXPENSE	$24,880

TOTAL OPERATING EXP. ► $510,980

PLANNED CAPITAL EXPENSES

Pool Furniture	$3,000
Landscape	$3,000
Exterior Painting	►$15,000

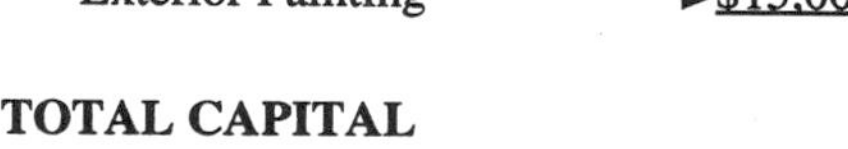

TOTAL CAPITAL EXPENSES ► $21,000

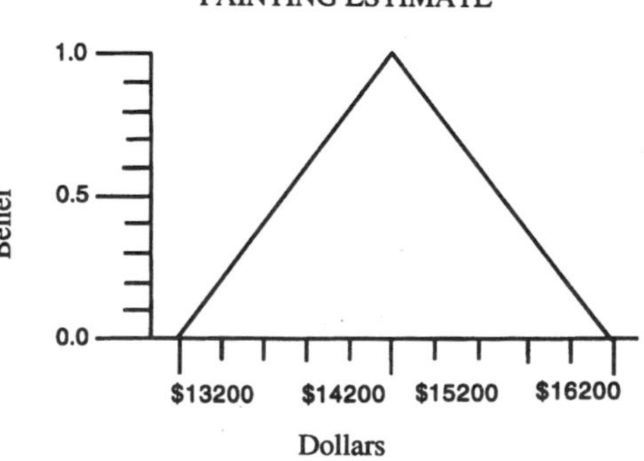

TOTAL OPERATING AND CAPITAL EXPENSES ► $531,980

Exhibit 33.13. *(Continued)*

values are the same as the original crisp estimates from Exhibit 33.8. We will use this spreadsheet as our starting point.

The general manager reviews his estimates and adjusts the belief graph to reflect his degree of confidence in each key variable. The adjusted belief estimates are as follows:

Sewer estimate	Low	$38,160	0.0
	Best	$42,400	1.0
	High	$46,640	0.0
Water estimate	Low	$34,800	0.0
	Best	$39,986	1.0
	High	$42,510	0.0
Electricity estimate	Low	$36,000	0.0
	Best	$40,000	1.0
	High	$44,000	0.0
Telephone estimate	Low	$6,750	0.0
	Best	$7,500	1.0
	High	$8,250	0.0
Insurance estimate	Low	$135,000	0.0
	Best	$159,936	1.0
	High	$165,000	0.0
Painting estimate	Low	$13,500	0.0
	Best	$15,000	1.0
	High	$16,500	0.0

Changes were made only to the belief graphs for water and insurance. The estimates for the other variables in the budget were still acceptable. The results of the new assumptions on the budget are seen in Exhibit 33.14.

The general manager is most interested in the final belief graph, the total operating and capital expenses. The centroid value for this critical variable is $536,887, which is greater than his revenue estimate of $531,980. This analysis means that there is a very strong belief that, with this set of belief assumptions for the input variables, there will be a negative result for the year. Upon closer review, he notes that this imbalance was due to a change in the total operating expense section. The capital expense section was not adversely impacted by the changes.

After reviewing these results with one of his subordinates who pointed out the possibility of an increase in the sewer rates next year by the municipal agency, the general manager felt he had to make one more revision of the budget. In order to account for this increased uncertainty, a new belief graph was constructed to reflect the current assessment of the plausible increase.

Sewer estimate	Low	$38,160	0.0
	Best	$46,552	1.0
	High	$46,552	1.0

He reran the budget with the modified sewer estimate. Exhibit 33.15 shows the results.

A review of the model results shows that the total operating expenses belief graph has changed to reflect the impact of the new input assumption. Its centroid value is now

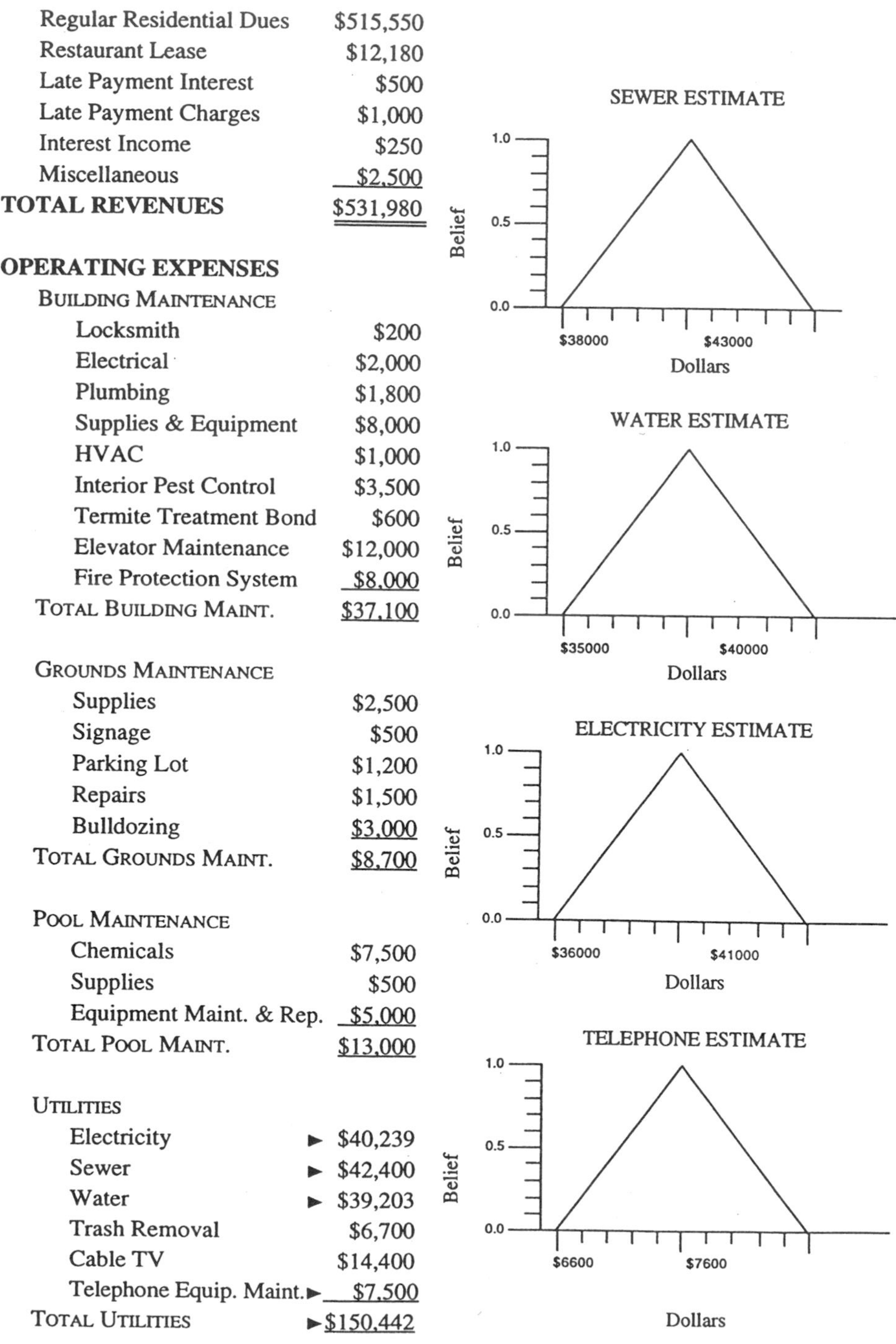

199X Operating Budget

REVENUES	
Regular Residential Dues	$515,550
Restaurant Lease	$12,180
Late Payment Interest	$500
Late Payment Charges	$1,000
Interest Income	$250
Miscellaneous	$2,500
TOTAL REVENUES	$531,980
OPERATING EXPENSES	
BUILDING MAINTENANCE	
Locksmith	$200
Electrical	$2,000
Plumbing	$1,800
Supplies & Equipment	$8,000
HVAC	$1,000
Interior Pest Control	$3,500
Termite Treatment Bond	$600
Elevator Maintenance	$12,000
Fire Protection System	$8,000
TOTAL BUILDING MAINT.	$37,100
GROUNDS MAINTENANCE	
Supplies	$2,500
Signage	$500
Parking Lot	$1,200
Repairs	$1,500
Bulldozing	$3,000
TOTAL GROUNDS MAINT.	$8,700
POOL MAINTENANCE	
Chemicals	$7,500
Supplies	$500
Equipment Maint. & Rep.	$5,000
TOTAL POOL MAINT.	$13,000
UTILITIES	
Electricity	► $40,239
Sewer	► $42,400
Water	► $39,203
Trash Removal	$6,700
Cable TV	$14,400
Telephone Equip. Maint.	► $7,500
TOTAL UTILITIES	► $150,442

Exhibit 33.14. Modified fuzzy number spreadsheet for budget

199X Operating Budget

GENERAL & ADMINISTRATIVE	
Management Services	$97,850
Bank Charges	$200
Postage	$2,500
Office Supplies & Dupl.	$1,750
Office Telephone	$700
Insurance	►$154,116
Legal Services	$5,000
Audit Expense	$5,500
Other Prof. Services	$1,200
Annual Meeting Expense	$500
Board Travel	$3,000
Board Meeting Expense	$3,500
Tax & Licenses	$500
Bad Debt Expense	$4,000
Pager Service	$1,200
Other	$250
TOTAL G & A	►$281,766
General Capital Reserves	$4,405
Restaurant Property Tax	$2,750
HOA Personal Prop. Tax	$975
Contingency Reserves	$16,750
TOTAL OTHER EXPENSE	$24,880
TOTAL OPERATING EXP.	►$515,887
PLANNED CAPITAL EXPENSES	
Pool Furniture	$3,000
Landscape	$3,000
Exterior Painting	►$15,000
TOTAL CAPITAL EXPENSES	►$21,000
TOTAL OPERATING AND CAPITAL EXPENSES	►$536,887

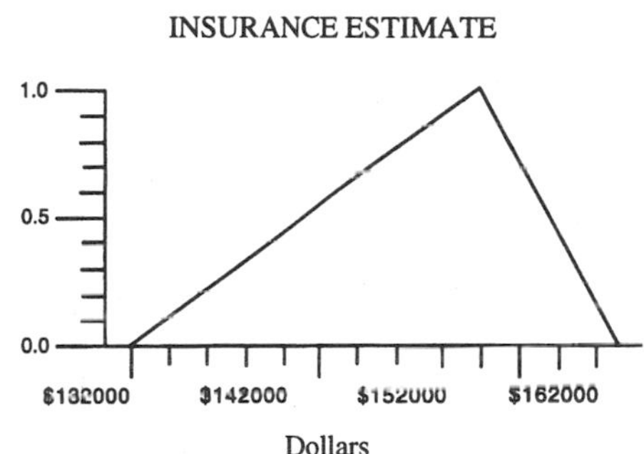

PAINTING ESTIMATE

Belief

1.0

0.5

0.0

$13200 $14200 $15200 $16200

Dollars

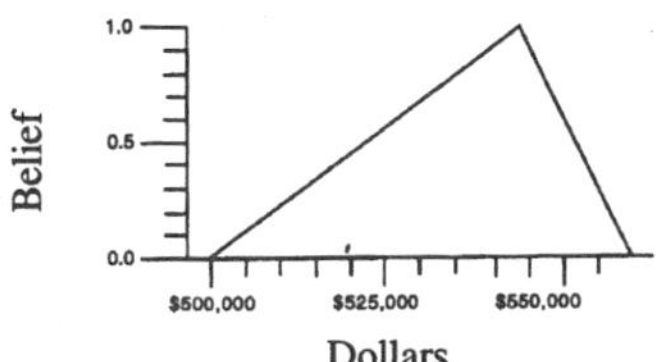

Exhibit 33.14. *(Continued)*

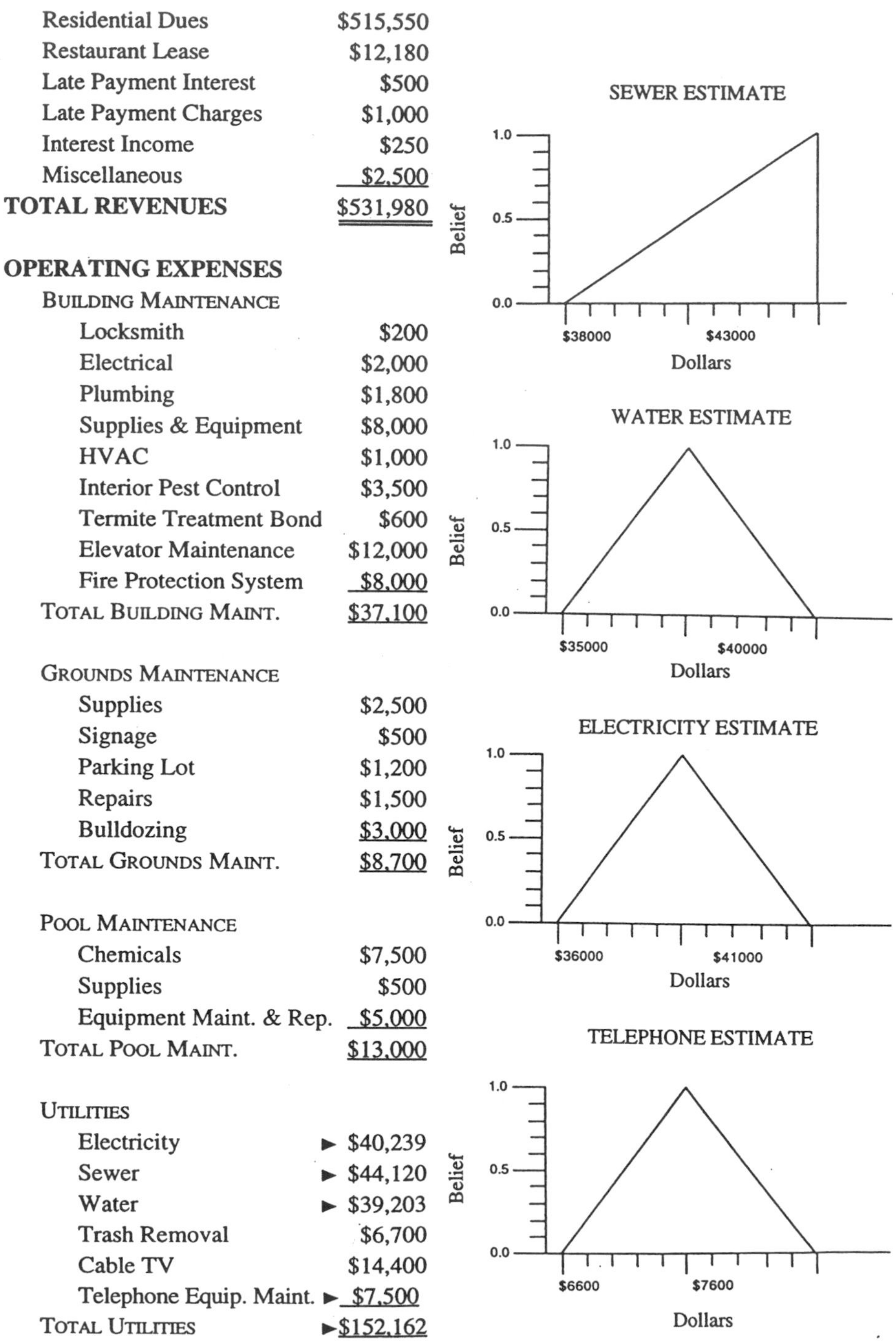

199X Operating Budget

REVENUES

Residential Dues	$515,550
Restaurant Lease	$12,180
Late Payment Interest	$500
Late Payment Charges	$1,000
Interest Income	$250
Miscellaneous	$2,500
TOTAL REVENUES	$531,980

OPERATING EXPENSES

BUILDING MAINTENANCE	
Locksmith	$200
Electrical	$2,000
Plumbing	$1,800
Supplies & Equipment	$8,000
HVAC	$1,000
Interior Pest Control	$3,500
Termite Treatment Bond	$600
Elevator Maintenance	$12,000
Fire Protection System	$8,000
TOTAL BUILDING MAINT.	$37,100
GROUNDS MAINTENANCE	
Supplies	$2,500
Signage	$500
Parking Lot	$1,200
Repairs	$1,500
Bulldozing	$3,000
TOTAL GROUNDS MAINT.	$8,700
POOL MAINTENANCE	
Chemicals	$7,500
Supplies	$500
Equipment Maint. & Rep.	$5,000
TOTAL POOL MAINT.	$13,000
UTILITIES	
Electricity	► $40,239
Sewer	► $44,120
Water	► $39,203
Trash Removal	$6,700
Cable TV	$14,400
Telephone Equip. Maint.	► $7,500
TOTAL UTILITIES	►$152,162

Exhibit 33.15. Final fuzzy number spreadsheet for budget

199X Operating Budget

GENERAL & ADMINISTRATIVE	
Management Services	$97,850
Bank Charges	$200
Postage	$2,500
Office Supplies & Dupl.	$1,750
Office Telephone	$700
Insurance	►$154,116
Legal Services	$5,000
Audit Expense	$5,500
Other Prof. Services	$1,200
Annual Meeting Expense	$500
Board Travel	$3,000
Board Meeting Expense	$3,500
Tax & Licenses	$500
Bad Debt Expense	$4,000
Pager Service	$1,200
Other	$250
TOTAL G & A	►$281,766
General Capital Reserves	$4,405
Restaurant Property Tax	$2,750
HOA Personal Prop. Tax	$975
Contingency Reserves	$16,750
TOTAL OTHER EXPENSE	$24,880
TOTAL OPERATING EXP.	►$517,607
PLANNED CAPITAL EXPENSES	
Pool Furniture	$3,000
Landscape	$3,000
Exterior Painting	►$15,000
TOTAL CAPITAL EXPENSES	►$21,000
TOTAL OPERATING AND CAPITAL EXPENSES	►$538,607

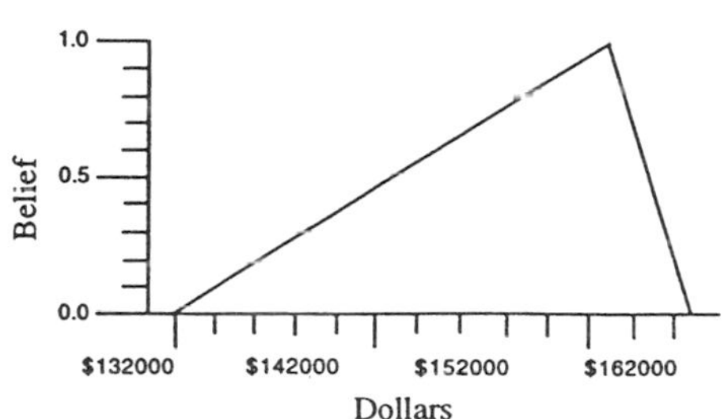

PAINTING ESTIMATE
1.0
0.5
0.0
Belief
$13200
$14200
$15200
$16200
Dollars

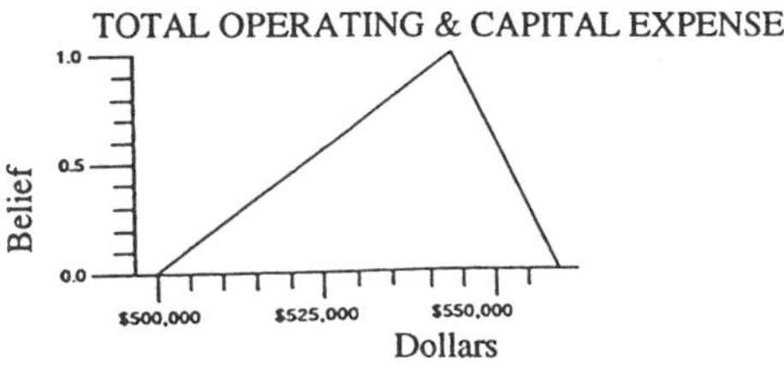

Exhibit 33.15. *(Continued)*

$517,607, approximately a $2,000 increase. Since he is finished with the analysis of the expense side, he will now have to explore alternative ways of bringing his expenses in line with his limited revenues. That process is beyond the scope of this chapter.

The general manager has utilized fuzzy number modeling to better understand the implications of uncertainty of the key business driver variables in his operating budget. He would continue to alter his belief graphs to explore any additional changes in his assumptions until he was content with the final analysis.

33.7 FUTURE ISSUES. It would be unrealistic to expect a new tool like fuzzy modeling to be accepted into mainstream budgeting without experiencing the traditional learning curve. Just as with traditional spreadsheet modeling of budgets with Lotus 1-2-3 and Excel, it will take a period of time before mainstream corporate business becomes comfortable with fuzzy numbers. Perhaps the front-line innovators can use the tool informally to develop their budgets. As the number of beneficial applications of fuzzy logic get publicized, the general level of comfort with the tool will increase.

There will always be the tension between the analytical and intuitive camps when it comes to decision-making areas like budgeting. Fuzzy number techniques can be used to bridge this gap. The use of belief graphs recognizes that there is a wealth of knowledge in the intuitive mind of the decision maker. It is a vehicle to convey her confidence level with the estimates that are used in the budget. It is a methodology to unite, in a synergistic way, both the intuitive and analytical approaches to decision making. This is precisely its unique contribution to budgeting.

SOURCES AND SUGGESTED REFERENCES

Burnette, David, ''MATLIB Adopts Fuzzy Logic Approach,'' *Advanced Systems,* March 1995.

FUZIWARE®, Inc., *FUZICALC User's Guide Ver. 1.5,* FUZIWARE®, Inc., 1994.

Kosko, Bart, *Fuzzy Thinking: The New Science of Fuzzy Logic.* New York: Hyperion, 1994.

McNeil, Daniel, and P. Freiberger, *Fuzzy Logic: The Discovery of a Revolutionary Computer Technology.* New York: Simon and Schuster, 1993.

Von Altrock, Constantin, *Fuzzy Logic and NeuroFuzzy Applications in Business & Finance.* PTR Prentice-Hall, 1997.

Yager, Ronald, S. Ovchinnikov, R. Tong, and H. T. Nguyen, eds., *Fuzzy Sets and Applications: Selected Papers of Lofti Zadeh.* New York: John Wiley & Sons, 1987.

CHAPTER 34

BEHAVIORAL ASPECTS OF BUDGETING

Gyan Chandra

Miami University (Ohio)

34.1 INTRODUCTION. *The Wall Street Journal* carried the following article on its front page recently:

> Budget Seeks to Raise U.S. Living Standards And Reduce Inequality
>
> With the nation at peace and the economy expanding, President Clinton's new budget gives him a chance to attack some underlying, long-run economic problems: a disappointingly slow rise of living standards and a widening gap between the well-off and the poor.[1]

The article emphasizes two points. First, budgeting is a very useful exercise in fiscal management. Even the mighty federal government uses it and has a separate office in charge of collecting data and preparing the annual budget that the President presents to the Congress. Second, the act of balancing resources with the demands on those resources is very difficult. That is where budgeting plays an important role.

One hears about budgets and budgeting every day both in business and in government circles. Both governments and businesses use them. One of the major 1996 general election campaign issues raised by both the Republican and Democratic parties was the need to run the nation's government on a balanced budget basis. There is even talk of a constitutional amendment that will mandate balanced budgets for the government.

Budgets are an expression of management's plans and expectations about the future. They institutionalize organization goals. Budgets make everyone aware of the resources, the demands on those resources, and the limitations. Budgetary limitations are faced by corporate managers all the time. Budgets affect programs and people and their behavior. They involve people at every step of the game and thus impact and are impacted by human behavior.

The purpose of this chapter is to review and learn about the interaction between budgets and people. We will proceed with a review of the relevant literature in management, social psychology, organizational behavior, and other related areas and draw lessons for budgeting. A considerable amount of research has been conducted in the last 60 years or

[1] David Wessel, "Budget Seeks to Raise U.S. Living Standards and Reduce Inequality," *The Wall Street Journal,* February 7, 1997, p. A1.

so on different questions dealing with the behavioral aspects of budgeting. Although it will not be possible to deal with all of the issues in one chapter, an attempt will be made to review the major ones here. A detailed list of readings is provided at the end of the chapter for pursuing the subject in depth.

(a) Objectives of Budgeting. A *budget* is a quantitative plan of action covering a period, normally a year or so, and is prepared for an organization as a whole or for its subunits, and *budgeting* is the process of preparing and implementing a budget. It is now universally considered as a necessary management tool. *Management* means managing limited resources to attain specific goals with efficiency and making decisions about the uncertain future. Successful managers try to attain the organization objectives with the given amount of resources by planning and performing effectively. Their other principal functions include organizing, decision making, staffing, communicating, motivating, leading, controlling, and evaluating performance. Today's managers operate in a complex economic, social, political, and technological environment that is largely beyond their control. The markets are now global, and the environment is all high tech. In fact, social scientists call it the information age. The rate of technological change is dazzling, and the competition is absolutely fierce. And yet successful managers continue to expand the economic horizons by their skillful management of business affairs every day and are taking corporations to greater heights.

Social scientists have perceived the role of a business organization/firm in a variety of ways. In the old days, a firm was considered simply a way of organizing business activities for profit. It was a convenient way of assembling land, labor, capital, and entrepreneurial skills for a common objective—profit for the investors. With the passage of time, the role of the firm expanded. It is now considered as a way to carry out economic activity for social good, to provide goods and services to the consumers, to provide employment to the populace, and to provide a reasonable return on investment to the investors. The role of the firm continues to evolve. With the advent of high technology, the modern firm is increasingly viewed as a *technology delivery system* to the society.

Management uses budgets as an instrument to carry out its plans and policies through the lower echelons of an organization. Budgets serve several *objectives:* planning and coordinating activities, communicating and authorizing goals and actions, motivating people, implementing plans, and controlling and evaluating performance. Whether the organization is a profit-oriented firm or a not-for-profit organization, a small corporation or a large multinational conglomerate, budgets are universally used to carry out management plans and are increasingly used as an instrument to motivate people.

(b) Stages in Budgeting. To accomplish the objectives of budgeting, a budget generally moves through four stages: setting goals, implementing plans, evaluating incentives, and monitoring progress. Each stage involves people—the *budgeter or budgeteer* (one who prepares the budget or, as is the practice in many organizations, the budget committee) and the *budgetee* (for whom and for whose department the budget is prepared). To the extent the budget committee and its members are cognizant of human behavior, they succeed. To begin with, the goals are set and a budget is prepared (computer software can help) and sold, that is, gaining willing acceptance from the participants. Selling of the budget requires knowing the participants, reasonableness of the goals, avoidance of surprises, clarity of priorities, and willingness to negotiate. These steps ensure participation, commitment, and goal congruency. Second, plans have to be implemented through effective communication and by ensuring cooperation and coordination among all parties.

Third, an incentive system is designed to motivate people and favorably influence their level of aspirations and anxiety in a positive manner. Finally, progress is monitored at the appropriate levels of authority.

(c) Budgeting Approaches. There are at least three types of budgets: *imposed or authoritative budgets, consultative budgets,* and *participative budgets.* As the term implies an *imposed or authoritative budget* is a plan handed down by the top management or the budget committee of an organization to the middle and lower-level management. It is also known as the ''top-down'' approach since all the decisions are made by the top management without consulting the lower echelons of an organization. The approach has some obvious advantages. It is a less expensive approach and saves time since not too many people are involved in budget preparation. Another advantage of the approach is the broad (company-wide) perspective it brings to budgeting, as the top management is less likely to suffer from narrow departmental considerations and politics.

Imposed budgets also have some serious flaws. Such budgets are an antithesis of divisionalization and delegation principles. People closer to work have a better feel of the situation and hence could be more realistic in preparing budgets than are people several layers away from the scene. Second, because of the lack of involvement in setting quantitative plans for the future, the lower-level management does not always feel totally committed to the top-management goals and policies. The budgetary goals are often taken as the goals of the top management and not of all the members of the organization. Such budgets fail to motivate employees. *Stretch budgets* are often used to motivate employees (associates). Here, the management tries to push the organization to its limits. Each succeeding year sets targets higher than the previous year's targets. Some successful corporations like General Electric and Boeing have followed such budgeting.

In *consultative budgets,* top managers ask their subordinates to discuss their ideas and goals, but no joint decisions are made. The senior management solicits ideas from the junior management, but the final budgets are those of the senior management. Consultative budgets are an improvement over the imposed budgets, as the junior management is led to believe that it has a say in the budgets. A variation of the approach is known as *pseudoconsultation/participation* wherein the junior managers are given the impression that their input will be used in the final budgets although the top management has no such intentions. Such budgets often give rise to employee frustration and demoralization.

The third type of budget is called *participative budgets* because all levels of management are involved in developing them. Generally, the information emanates from the lower levels of management and reaches the top. For that reason, this approach is also known as ''bottom-up'' approach. The principal advantage of the approach lies in the attainability of the budgetary goals. Because the budgets are prepared on the basis of information provided by the people affected by the budgets, people feel concerned and involved. They develop a sense of commitment that is lacking in the imposed budgets. Participative budgets are also more realistic as they are based on the information provided by the people who are close to the scene of action where things are happening.

The participative budgets are not completely free from problems. They are expensive and time consuming. The old adage that work and expenses grow with the number of people involved holds true here. Participation involves people, and they all want to feel important by participating in the budgeting process and thus adding to the time and resources spent on preparing budgets. Additionally, managers at lower levels may take a rather narrow view of their activities and ignore the effect of their activities on other departments or divisions of the firm. Finally, in their desire to protect their pet projects and look successful at the end (as people like to be achievers rather than losers), the participants may be prompted to inflate or deflate their estimates (build slacks and cushions). Rather than containing realistic estimates, budgets may end up being based on figures as managers wish to see them rather than as they *should* see them.

Negotiated budgets are essentially an extension of participative budgets. Under this approach, budgets are prepared by a process of give and take that may not produce plans liked by everyone but that are the best under the circumstances. The top management sets the broad goals and the constraints, and the lower- and middle-level managers arrive at the final figures through active participation. If either level of management does not feel satisfied with the other's expectations or plans, negotiations proceed to hammer out a consensus. No doubt such an approach could take time, and several rounds of negotiations may have to take place before the master budget is finalized.

34.2 BEHAVIORAL ASSUMPTIONS. Budgets represent corporate quantitative plans of the people, prepared by the people, and prepared for the people. Those plans cannot accomplish much by themselves. It is how they influence people's behavior that distinguishes successful budgets from unsuccessful ones. In carrying out their activities, the accountants and budgeters utilize a frame of reference that is essentially their view of the nature of the firm and its participants. It follows, therefore, that they should operate with an understanding of human behavior and how people behave given certain incentives and rewards. Their model of the firm and operation should have some implicit or explicit assumptions about human behavior in an organizational setting. The relationship of individuals with their peers and others at work has been a fascinating subject of research for sociologists, psychologists, and other behavioral scientists for a long time. Numerous social psychologists have contributed to our understanding in this area. What follows is a review of some of the major contributions in the field.[2]

(a) Traditional View of Human Behavior. The traditional view of human behavior is based on what is considered as the classical economic theory of the firm and organizational behavior. The names of Henry Fayol, Frederick Taylor, Frank and Lilian Gilbreth, and Henry Gantt are most prominent among those who are associated with the traditional view. This view is based on the premise that the principal objective of a firm is profit maximization, and all business activities should be directed toward that goal. This goal could be divided into subgoals, and the latter are assumed to be of additive nature. If every segment of a firm attempts to maximize its profit, the profit of the firm as a whole would also be maximized (shades of Adam Smith's Principles of Economics).

Another premise of the traditional view is that human beings are primarily economic and are motivated primarily by economic forces. The traditionalists assume that people are inefficient and wasteful. They are lazy and do not want to work unless forced by the economic needs. Since work is unpleasant and leisure is pleasant, the employer has to devise ways to get work done in time and within the estimated cost. Henry Fayol described how management should be carried out in the fourteen *universal principles of management.* They included division of work, authority, discipline, unit of command, unity of direction,

[2] A very good overview of the issues discussed in this section can be found in Edwin A. Caplan, "Behavioral Assumptions of Management Accounting," *The Accounting Review,* vol. 41, no. 3, July 1966, pp. 496–509.

subordination of individual interest to the general interest, remuneration, centralization, scaler chain, order, equity, stability and tenure of personnel, initiative, and *esprit de corps.*[3] Frederick Taylor and his followers of the *scientific management* school focused their attention on the measurement and structure of work itself. People were considered as rational, economic beings and mere extensions of the machines they worked on. It was argued that they would act in their own best interest and ultimately in the best interest of the firm, if the workers understood correct work procedures and were assured of a fair reward. Accordingly, time and motion studies were conducted to devise efficient ways of doing work.[4]

The third premise of the traditional view deals with the behavior of management itself. The essence of management control is authority. The flow of authority is downward. The role of a manager is to maximize profit of the firm, and in order to do that, he or she should control wasteful and lazy behavior of the employees. The role of the accounting and budgeting system is to provide information that helps managers in controlling subordinates by pinpointing inadequate and unsatisfactory performance.

(b) Budgeting and the Traditional Management Environment. The traditional view of human behavior is characterized by authoritative management, and, as discussed earlier, budgets are imposed from the top. It is somewhat akin to military lines of command. If the traditional behavioral assumptions were to hold true, budgets would be a grand success. However, the experience shows that when budgets are imposed, the employees responsible for implementing budgets behave *dysfunctionally*. Dysfunctional behavior is defined as a situation wherein the subordinates' conduct does not optimize the performance of the firm or when the goals of subunits do not mesh with the goals of the firm. The actions of the subordinates are in divergence with the overall interests of the organization. Dysfunctional behavior could lead to *goal incongruence,* a condition that results when the goals of the subunits are not in accord with those of the firm. As long as employees are evaluated and rewarded only for achieving their narrow departmental goals, goal incongruency is likely to occur. Employees have a tendency to protect their personal and departmental interests first and then the long-run interests of the firm as a whole.

Another aspect of dysfunctional behavior is *gamesmanship, manipulation, and falsification of information* by the employees. Given the pressure on the subordinates to meet the budgets, they devise their own ways to beat the system. For example, when production exceeds budget target, they report less than the actual production for at least two reasons. One, in the future when the actual output is below the budget, they could use the unreported past output to make up for the shortage. Past excess production serves as a cushion for the future. Second, they are afraid of reporting excess production, as that level could become the standard in future.[5] Centrally planned economies like that of the former USSR and other East European countries provided good illustrations of such a phenomenon. A variation of the abuse can be traced in the tendency to average income (smoothing income) out in the corporate world. The budget participants have learned that a steady upward trend in corporate income is generally viewed more favorably than the fluctuating income.

Finally, the authoritarian management style tends to encourage *short-run performance*

[3] Robert Kreitner, *Management,* 3rd ed. (Boston, MA: Houghton Mifflin, 1986), p. 51.

[4] *Id.*, pp. 50–57.

[5] Mohamed Onsi, "Factor Analysis of Behavioral Variables Affecting Budgetary Slack," *The Accounting Review,* vol. 48, no. 3, July 1973, pp. 535–548.

over the long-run performance. In their eagerness to meet the budgets, managers develop a myopic view of the firm's future. In a budget-constrained environment, managers are often evaluated on the basis of their budgetary performance. Consciously or unconsciously, the emphasis shifts from long-run profitability and effectiveness to immediate performance. Such an environment could discourage paying attention to the critical success factors of business—like customer service, employee training, and product innovation—and foster tension and mistrust among subordinates and managers.[6]

(c) Modern View of Human Behavior. The modern view of human behavior is an amalgam of diverse theories and assumptions relating to organizational behavior, economics, and other social disciplines. The long list of social scientists who have contributed to our understanding of the modern organizational behavior and management practices includes, among others, Chester Barnard, Richard Cyert, Frederick Herzberg, James March, Abraham Maslow, Douglas McGregor, Herbert Simon, and Victor Vroom. The modern view of human behavior essentially started with the writings of Barnard and gained much popularity with the research of Cyert, March, and Simon. Their ideas are premised on the decision-making model of the firm.

Under the modern view, organizations are simply coalitions of individuals who join hands and pool their resources to accomplish certain common goals. As such, organizations do not have *goals.* They are legal fictions and are mindless. Only individuals have goals. The commonly understood organization goals are really the goals of the dominant members of the coalition running an organization. They change with the changes in socio-economic environment and the desires and capabilities of the participants. Today's organizations are a *complex* amalgam of people and resources and can hardly have a single goal like profit maximization. They are likely to operate with multiple goals like earning a reasonable return on investment, maintaining a market share, achieving leadership in research and development, developing a reputation for customer service, maintaining name recognition in the marketplace, and so on.

People join an organization and stay in it as long as they feel their participation will help them attain their own personal goals. As a result, the participants tend to emphasize the attainment of local (subunit) and personal goals more than the organization-wide goals, and if the two sets of goals do not mesh with each other, goal incongruency arises. It follows that organization goals are not always additive, and the maximization of subunit profits does not always lead to maximization of profit of the firm. In fact, survival of the organization becomes the first priority. If the organization survives, the participants then have an opportunity to attain their own goals. It seems that earning a satisfactory or reasonable return on investment rather than maximizing profit is a more realistic goal in today's economy.

In contrast to the traditional view of human behavior, the modern view is that people are motivated by a wide variety of sociopsychological needs and drives in addition to their economic needs. The relative strength of these needs and drives varies from person to person and from time to time. People have limited knowledge of the uncertain environment they face and are not always rational and consistent in their priorities and preferences. They join an organization with the assumption that the membership will help them in meeting their personal needs. The intensity of their efforts in an organization is a function

[6] Anthony G. Hopwood, ''Leadership Climate and the Use of Accounting Data in Performance Evaluation,'' *The Accounting Review,* vol. 49, no. 3, July 1974, pp. 485–495.

of how they perceive the operation of the reward system in that organization. Whether they gain when the organization gains (gain sharing) has become a frequently asked question. The higher and faster the reward for the efforts, the more intensive are the efforts of the participants, as higher and faster rewards could lead them to meet their personal needs more fully and promptly. However, the reward is not always economic. It could be in sociopsychological terms also. Because people's needs are diverse, so should be the reward structure.

Management style is another area where the modern view of organizational behavior differs from the traditional view. The traditional view holds the authority of the management as given, and it can be imposed on the subordinates (or associates, as most firms like to call them), and the responsibility is assumed by the subordinates. In contrast, the modern view recognizes the fact that the responsibility is assigned from above, and the authority is accepted from below. The management's function is to *make decisions and influence* the behavior of others who will either implement those decisions or will be affected by those decisions. Management's responsibility is to create a conducive environment in which subordinates feel they are part of the system, and when they work to attain the organization goals they are also attaining their own personal goals. Realization of self-interest is, probably, the most effective inducement. Successful managers attempt to work out a fine balance between the inducement they offer to the subordinates (associates) and the contribution expected of them. Because of goal complexity and the balancing of inducement and effort, *management control* has acquired added significance in the modern firm. Budgets have been used by management to influence and motivate employee behavior. Budgets communicate and provide feedback to help the managers and employees attain their personal goals. One view is that the budget staff and the accountants are no longer the passive spectators they used to be. They are active participants in the budgeting process.

34.3 HUMAN MOTIVATION.

The word *motivation* originated from the Latin word *movere,* meaning to move or to drive (i.e., a need or desire that causes a person to act). It refers to the psychological process that gives human behavior a direction and purpose. Four theories or groups of theories about human motivation have received much coverage in recent years: needs hierarchy theory, two-factor theory, expectancy theory, and X, Y, and Z theories. These theories are premised on the foundation of a constructive reward (compensation system) in an organization. The four theories or theory groups are briefly reviewed below.

(a) Needs Hierarchy Theory.

In 1943, Maslow, a psychologist, proposed that all human needs can be grouped in a hierarchy of five levels: physiological needs, safety (security) needs, love (social) needs, esteem needs, and self-actualization needs. Since human beings are perpetually wanting animals, as soon as one need is satisfied, they feel the next need. The five needs essentially form a pyramid. At the bottom of the pyramid are the most basic physiological needs of food and shelter. They enable a person to survive. Once those needs are satisfied, the person gets concerned about his or her safety from the elements and other threats. At the third level of hierarchy Maslow stacked up social needs—the need for love, belonging, and friendship. A person satisfied with the social needs enters the fourth stage of self-esteem needs. Much of self-esteem comes from self-confidence, status, and respect from peers. The final and the highest level of needs is characterized as self-actualization or self-realization needs. These needs relate to creativity, continued self-development, and self-realization of one's true potential. People at that level have warmth and sympathy for others. They are open and trusting, and could be rather unconventional in their ways. As managers, these people would be willing to try new ways of doing things because they feel secure within themselves.[7]

Although Maslow's theory of human needs has been questioned for its rigid hierarchy and the very idea of arranging needs into levels, it does have some important implications for today's management process. It is difficult to imagine that people move from one level of needs to the next level only when one type of needs is fully satisfied. People feel most of those needs somewhat concurrently. Nevertheless, the important lesson managers can learn is that satisfied needs cannot motivate people and may even lead them to complacency. For instance, a poorly paid individual could be motivated to work harder for more money, but the well-paid worker may not be. Likewise, one unemployment benefit scheme could fulfill the safety needs of an individual, but the second unemployment benefit scheme will not motivate a fully employed worker to work any harder (shades of diminishing returns). Effective management requires the manager to anticipate employees' emerging needs and devise ways to motivate them while satisfying their needs.

(b) Two-Factor Theory. Frederick Herzberg's studies showed that two groups of factors—hygiene and satisfier—affect human behavior. *Hygiene factors* relate to the job environment. They include working conditions, base pay, organization policies, interpersonal relationships, and supervisors' behavior. A poor job environment inhibits employees' performance. But the improvement in environment by itself cannot motivate employees. It only creates the potential for improvement. The *satisfier factors* relate to job content and how employees feel about their job and work. They include achievement, recognition, responsibility, and perceived opportunity for growth. Presence of poor satisfier factors retards employee satisfaction and their performance. Satisfier factors can motivate employees to higher levels of performance, provided the hygiene factors are also present.[8]

(c) Expectancy Theory. Victor Vroom explained human behavior in terms of an individual's goals, expectations of achieving those goals (outcomes), and the utility he or she places on those outcomes in the form of satisfying his or her personal needs. The theory assumes that individuals can rationally determine which outcomes they prefer and will make a realistic estimate (probability) of the outcomes.[9]

The expectancy theory uses two terms: expectancy and valence. *Expectancy* refers to the person's perception of the probability that certain outcomes will occur due to his or her particular behavior, and *valence* refers to the value or utility of those outcomes to that person. Valences could be of intrinsic or extrinsic nature. Intrinsic valence is the satisfaction one derives from the work itself or from successfully completing a task. The latter generates self-esteem and confidence in the person. The extrinsic valence comes from the outside world. These are rewards and recognitions received in the form of bonuses, promotions, increased pay, and so forth. Motivation, under the theory, is simply a mathematical function of expectancy and valence. Motivation requires the presence of both

---

[7] A. H. Maslow, "A Theory of Human Motivation," *Psychological Review,* vol. 50, no. 3, July 1943, pp. 370–396; and Kreitner, *op cit,* pp. 381–391.

[8] Frederick Herzberg, "One More Time: How Do You Motivate Employees?," *Harvard Business Review,* vol. 46, no. 1, January–February 1968, pp. 53–62.

[9] Victor Vroom, *Work and Motivation.* New York: John Wiley & Sons, 1964; and R. Wayne Mondy, Arthur Sharplin, Robert E. Holmes, and Edwin B. Flippo, *Management Concepts and Practices.* 3rd ed. (Boston, MA: Allyn & Bacon, 1986), pp. 282–302.

factors at a high level. For instance, if a manager has a high expectancy of receiving a promotion and places a high value on it, he or she will be highly motivated to work hard. However, if a manager has low expectancy of receiving a promotion but values it highly, he or she will have low motivation. The other extreme will be when a manager has low expectancy of receiving a promotion and places a low value on it, so that he or she will be hardly motivated to work for the promotion. To be effective, an employee is most motivated when he or she has high level of expectancy and a reasonable probability of achieving the goal.

What is important in the expectancy theory is the perception of the employees (associates) and not of the managers. People are motivated by their own expectations and how they perceive the reward. The effectiveness of the managers depends on how well they understand employees' perception of their expectations and valences. Such perceptions vary from employee to employee, and knowing what inspires each individual employee is a formidable challenge that managers face if they desire to motivate the employees.

Additionally, managers should make sure that employees are well trained in the jobs they are assigned to perform, that rewards are carefully selected to meet employee needs, and that employees understand the reward system and have confidence in the fair and equitable administration of rewards to them. From the employees' point of view, the theory can work only if the employees have a desire for the reward. They should believe that their efforts can lead to good performance and that different levels of performance can lead to differences in the reward.

(d) X, Y, and Z Theories. Douglas McGregor and others have stressed the need for understanding the relationship between motivation and management philosophies. He characterized the practices of management based on traditional assumptions of human behavior as *theory X.*[10]

Under the traditional model of organizational behavior, it is assumed that human beings dislike work, are motivated solely by their economic needs, and believe that authority is usually imposed from the top. One form of imposing such an authority can be found in the practice of imposed budgets. In contrast to theory X, McGregor characterized theory Y with the democratic and participative management environment. *Theory Y* is identified with the modern view of human behavior. This theory assumes that people like work and are willing to assume responsibility and make commitments if the rewards are commensurate with the expected effort.[11] Employees can be motivated to work for organizational goals if their higher order needs can be correctly perceived and satisfied. Managers can be very effective if they can create an accomplishment-oriented environment at the place of work. *Participation* is of key importance in the success of a modern complex organization.

A recent entry in the field of motivation and management philosophies is labeled as *theory Z.* This theory is essentially based on the Japanese style of corporate management. William Ouchi observed that the Japanese corporate environment is characterized by a high degree of mutual responsibility, consideration, and loyalty between the employees and their organizations. The oft-quoted Japanese practice of lifetime employment has fostered a strong sense of loyalty and commitment among the workers. To the extent possible, employee layoffs are avoided in Japan and the employees are expected to develop

---

[10] Douglas McGregor, *The Human Side of Enterprise.* New York: McGraw-Hill, 1960; and Mondy et al., pp. 281–284.

[11] See Douglas McGregor, p. 49.

a feeling of being part of the corporate family. The Japanese companies are also known for *collective decision making* and *total care of their employees.* Consequently, they experience low absenteeism and employee turnover, and have high employee morale. These and many other such practices have created a massive cadre of highly motivated and dedicated managers and workers in Japan. This theory also emphasizes success through commitment, mutual respect, and participation. The well-publicized idea of *quality circles* is but one example of the many successful management practices in Japan.[12]

34.4 BUDGETS AND MOTIVATION.

Budgeting as it affects the motivation of managers and subordinates has received much attention of the researchers in the last three decades or so. The modern theorists have emphasized *participation* of the employees in the budgeting process to increase its effectiveness. They have reached this conclusion on the basis of observing human behavior in a variety of working conditions.[13]

(a) Budgets as Pressure Devices.

One of the most popular impressions about budgets is that they can be used to pressure employees to produce more or meet the ever-rising targets. Managers have been known to use budgets to blame employees for not working hard enough and, hence, not reaching their true potential. The traditional behavioral assumptions imply that if each employee maximizes output and minimizes costs, the firm as a whole will be able to attain its objective of profit maximization or earning the target profit. This often leads managers to think first of setting targets (imposed budgets) and then of enforcing them rigidly. If the targets are not met, the subordinates are to be blamed for the failure. The reward and, especially, the punishment are meted out on the basis of meeting the budgets, and little effort is made to understand the reasons for failure.

In one of the most widely quoted studies of manufacturing plants, Chris Argyris found that the foremen and the workers felt that the budgets were used as pressure devices. Management essentially assumed that the workers were lazy and inefficient and that they lacked self-motivation. Managers had to motivate them, and the finance people (budget staff) believed that budgets would be able to help in motivating the employees.[14] Such feelings do not remain hidden for long. They travel through the organization and reach all levels of the workplace. Once the workers learn, they get irritated and feel alienated from the management.

The management exerts pressure in a variety of ways, ranging from pep talk and red-marking the missed targets to threats and reprimands. What happens when the pressure continues? There is a limit to the degree of pressure one can stand. Workers absorb it initially and then start looking for others with similar experience. They start forming support groups as a defensive device. Once the process starts, it does not end even after the original cause is removed. The groups continue to exist even when the management attempts to eliminate the budget-caused tension by introducing participative budgeting. The employees become suspicious of company moves and wonder whether the management will not devise new ways of putting pressure on them.

---

[12] William G. Ouchi, *Theory Z: How American Business Can Meet the Japanese Challenge.* Reading, MA: Addison-Wesley, 1981; and Mondy et al., pp. 300–304.

[13] Chris Argyris, *The Impact of Budgets on People* (New York: Financial Executives Research Foundation, 1952); and Chris Argyris, ''Human Problems with Budgets,'' *Harvard Business Review,* vol. 31, no. 1, January–February, 1953, pp. 97–110, for many of the comments made in this section of the chapter.

[14] Chris Argyris, ''Human Problems with Budgets,'' p. 98.

How unproductive the budgetary pressure can become can be imagined by the fact that the process does not stop at the workers' level. Caught between the employees and the management, the supervisors also start feeling the ill effects of the budgetary pressure. Argyris observed the supervisors handle the pressure in a number of ways. First, interdepartmental strife may occur as the supervisors try to blame each other for the missed targets. Second, the supervisors may internalize the pressure and become tense. Unfortunately, the problem does not end here. Constant tension creates frustration in the supervisors, which spills over on their work and employees. They may no longer operate efficiently, and the output declines. In short, budgets become counterproductive.

(b) Role Conflict. Conflict between the operating personnel and the budget staff is another disturbing effect of the budget pressure. When budgets are used as a pressure device, conflict between line and staff people is almost inevitable. Budget staff and the operating personnel work under different bosses, and their performance is often evaluated by different people and different standards. They all desire to succeed, but one party's success often becomes the cause of the other party's failure. For instance, if a budget supervisor finds an error or shortfall in a particular production department, he or she is unlikely to go to the production supervisor directly for at least two reasons. For one, such direct communication may not be permitted by the company personnel policy. The two groups of people often communicate through a circuitous route. In addition, and more importantly, the budget supervisor gets no credit for sharing his or her finding with the factory supervisor directly. The budget supervisor's success lies in bringing the error to the notice of his or her boss, who then takes it up with his or her superiors, and so on up the company hierarchy. Once the information has traveled through the budget staff and to the top management, it travels down through the production personnel. Finding errors may win some points for the budget staff but causes much serious damage to the operating supervisor's morale and efficiency. The process illustrates how production and budget people start operating at cross-purposes.

Two additional factors can cause conflicts between the budget staff and operating personnel. First, in its pursuit of discovering errors, budget staff often develops an obsession of it. Second, it often becomes very defensive about its work. Rather than explaining the problem, it reacts negatively to any inquiries. It starts hiding under the maze of technical details. It blames the operating personnel for not understanding the budgeting process and criticizes them for the latter's ignorance.

A major ill consequence of the budgetary pressure is the creation of a *myopic* view among different operating people affected by the budgets. Since the operating supervisors are evaluated on the basis of success in meeting their separate budgets, they often operate unconcerned about the effects of their actions on the other departments and the company as a whole. The pursuit of narrow goals by each operating supervisor does not necessarily optimize performance of the whole company.

The top management has a major role to play if the conflicts between the budget staff and the operating people are to be resolved. Senior managers should understand the problems budgeting creates. Since the interdepartmental and staff-line conflicts are almost inevitable, the best management can do is to control the conflicts. It has to create an environment for all to operate harmoniously. Budgets can be an extension of management's leadership. Effort should be made by both the staff and line personnel to understand the budgets and each other's point of view. Their outlook toward budgets should change. It cannot happen on its own. It is an *educational process* of learning and letting others learn. All levels of management, budget staff, and the operating supervisors should learn about the budgeting process and how it affects human behavior before budgeting is introduced in an organization. Additionally, supervisors should undergo *training* in human relations. Such a training should be focused on the understanding of the underlying problems and not just on the superficial difficulties. The budget staff should also learn about the implications of budgets, on the workers (associates), the effect of pressure on people impacted by the budgets, and the effect of success and failure on employees (associates) and their families.

34.5 BUDGETS AND PARTICIPATION.

Participation by all levels of management in preparing budgets has been generally recommended as a way of resolving many of the problems created by budgets. Support for participation can be found in all of the motivation theories. Budgeting offers an excellent opportunity to the top management to involve the subordinates (associates) in the affairs of a firm. In the following pages an attempt will be made to discuss several important aspects of participation, the careful consideration of which could contribute much to the success of budgets and budgeting.

(a) Nature of Participation.

Participation means the involvement of all levels of management and key employees in developing budgets. It is a process of joint decision making in which top management and the subordinates (associates), especially the middle-level and lower-level managers, freely discuss budget goals and expectations and reach a consensus (the Japanese style). In a participative system, both groups, the top management and the subordinates, understand that the proposals from the top management only form a basis of discussion and do not constitute the final decision. These are not dictates to be followed. Also, participation does not mean that the two groups will always be in complete agreement or that suggestions will always be accepted. It simply means that decisions will not be made unilaterally by the top management as is often done in the traditional environment. There will be full consultation with the subordinates before the higher-ups make a final decision. All genuine, reasonable, and experience-based input of the subordinates, no matter how different it is from the top echelon's expectations, will be seriously considered. Consideration does not mean just lip service or pretense. It means the subordinates' input will be incorporated in the budget to foster trust and openness among the employees. However, consideration does not also mean abdication of authority by the top management. The top management does retain the veto power when the subordinates' participation is frivolous and unreasonable. In a true participatory system, the subordinates become *associates,* and many successful corporations now address their employees that way. It has fused a sense of pride in the employees and fostered a team spirit.

Participation of subordinates can be successful only if it is true and sincere. True participation takes place when the subordinates do not feel inhibited and there is a give and take between the concerned parties. It also implies involvement of subordinates in substantial matters and not the creation of a facade. *Pseudoparticipation* is never a success and is soon recognized for what it is by the participants.[15] Pseudoparticipation leads to half-hearted acceptance and creates trouble later when the budget targets are not met.

In a true participatory system, preparation of budgets starts from the bottom of the hierarchy and moves upward. As the budget preparation moves up and down, it may go through a number of changes. When changes are suggested, they have to be justified, and that minimizes unnecessary changes.

---

[15] *Id.,* p. 108.

(b) Significance of Participation. Participation works because it requires joint decision making in which all levels of management provide input in the decision. When people participate in decision making, they *internalize* the goals. They see those goals as their own goals. They perceive the goals as reasonable because the participants were themselves involved in setting them. The process provides intrinsic motivation to the participants. Participation is also an effective way of building trust among the employees.

The process of goal internalization ultimately results in a higher level of motivation among employees. As Exhibit 34.1 shows, individuals develop their goals through a complex process. To begin with, they bring to an organization their own personal, moral, social, and cultural values, which are part of an individual's upbringing and social life. These values are influenced by the socioeconomic and the legal and political environments. Individuals also have their personal needs and ambitions in life. When individuals join an organization, they bring those needs and ambitions with them and try to match them with the corporate goals and other influences. The solid lines in Exhibit 34.1 establish that relationship.

Exhibit 34.1 also shows that an individual's goals are affected by the organization culture and the style of management leadership. Other influences—for example, the report and reward systems—also have an effect on the goal internalization. The interaction between these variables is denoted by the broken lines. In brief, an individual's goals in an organization are shaped by an interaction of four factors: individual needs, individual ambitions, corporate goals, and operating conditions. The intensity of these factors helps

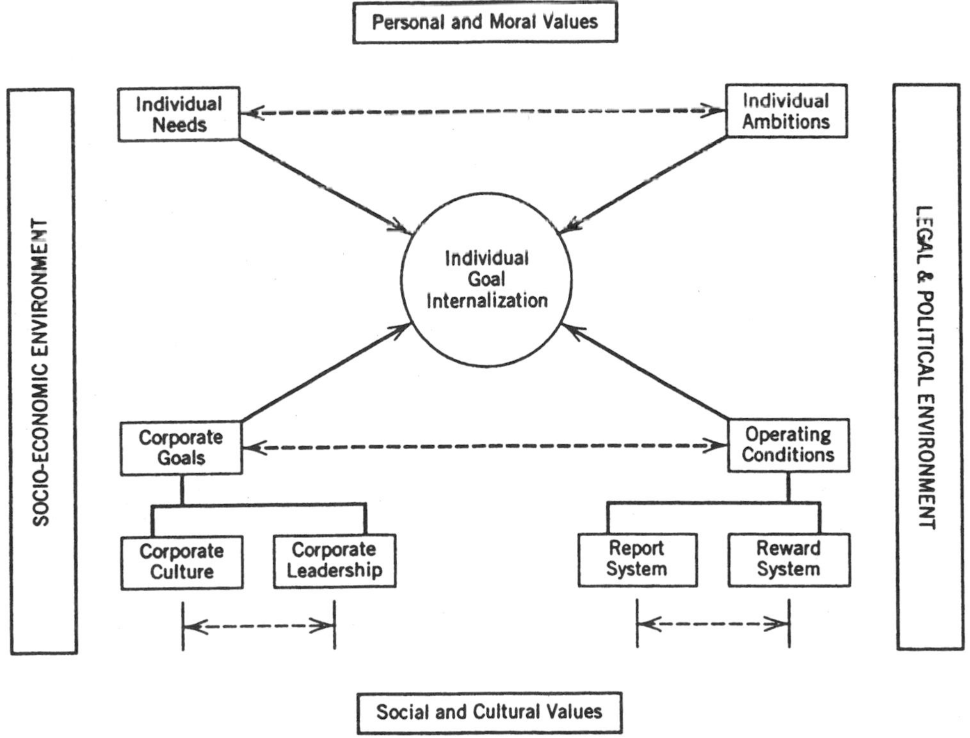

Exhibit 34.1 Individual goal internalization

form an individual's goals at work and the extent of his or her internalizing them. When individuals participate in the budget preparation, they go through the entire process.

Participation in budgeting raises employee morale and commitment at the place of work. Employees develop a stake in the success of budgets and tend to work more efficiently. It creates a ''we'' feeling in the organization and checks the schism of ''them'' versus ''us.'' Participation also encourages *cooperation* among the employees and makes them partners in the undertaking. Being a participant on an equal basis makes them feel important and gives the feeling that what they do matters. The participating employees also experience *job enlargement* and *empowerment,* which gives them self-esteem and satisfaction and creates a positive attitude toward the firm.

(c) Group Dynamics. Participation by itself cannot affect performance. It influences productivity through a complex process called *group dynamics.* Group dynamics is the study of interacting forces within a small human group, that is, how an individual's behavior is affected by the group.

People belong to different groups, including family, church, social, work, and so forth and these groups shape an individual's conduct within that group. At the place of work, individuals interact with their superiors, subordinates, and colleagues. Their performance very much depends on the values and attitudes of these groups and how committed that individual is to these groups. Human beings have a strong urge to ''belong'' and ''connect,'' and this urge attracts an individual to different groups. Their membership, which in most cases is informal, depends on their conformance with the group norms, their acceptance of the group values, the strength and cohesiveness of the group, and their own personality.

Participation in preparing budgets leads managers and subordinates to interact with each other, which increases group cohesiveness and morale. In a cohesive group where members value their membership, they are likely to accept the group norms. If participation increases group cohesiveness and if cohesiveness is rewarded for good performance, participation may lead to higher performance. In a way, participation self-perpetuates the wholesome environment that makes it work. It creates a virtuous circle, where success begets success.[16]

(d) Organization Culture and Leadership. Organization culture refers to the collection of shared values and beliefs that gives a feeling of community to the organization members. To be effective, participation has to fit in the organization culture and leadership style of the management. In an open and progressive organization where there is mutual trust and communication, participation will flourish. However, in an organization characterized by heavy-handedness of the top management and undemocratic ways of doing things, the seeds of participation can be planted but will have difficulty germinating and growing. Likewise, if the lower management is not used to working independently, participation would fail because the subordinates (associates) are conditioned to accepting the dictates of the top management.

Leadership is the process of developing a voluntary following for a common goal. Different managers have different leadership styles. There are aggressive managers, and

[16] Selwyn W. Becker and David Green, Jr., ''Budgeting and Employee Behavior,'' *The Journal of Business,* vol. 35, no. 4, October 1962, pp. 392–402; and Gordon Shillinglaw, *Managerial Cost Accounting,* 4th ed. (Homewood, IL: Richard D. Irwin, 1977), pp. 639–656.

there are weak managers. Both extremes could create problems in an organization. If the managers are not well trained in human relations, their behavior could discourage subordinates (associates) from coming forward with suggestions and taking initiative. Such managers, obviously, need training in winning trust and confidence of their subordinates. The overly aggressive managers can sometimes create the environment of *rejection* among the subordinates. Many of the subordinates may not be able to handle it and may feel discouraged from participating in the future. Effective participation requires a conducive environment where the subordinates do not come out of a budget session with a feeling of rejection. They should have the satisfaction of contributing something important in the preparation of the final budget.

While the overly aggressive managers have difficulty getting the subordinates to participate, the weak managers could also be equally unproductive. In the latter case, nothing could ever become final, and the participative system could degenerate into producing "rubber budgets." Employees soon learn that as long as a suggestion could be justified, it will be accepted and incorporated in the budget.

(e) Standards and Aspirations. Participation affects participants' aspiration levels differently in different situations. *Aspiration level* is the level of performance a person sets for himself for a familiar task. Common sense tells that "reasonably unattainable" standards are helpful because they raise the aspiration level of the employees.[17] Reasonable standards are easily internalized by the employees and lead to recognition and reward. The virtuous cycle is broken when the standards are unreasonably tight or too loose. In the case of standards that are difficult to attain with reasonable effort, the employees even get discouraged from making a normal effort. Because they cannot attain the standards with reasonable effort, the employees lose interest in working for them. Where the reward structure is strictly tied to the budgetary performance, it often leads to budgeting gamesmanship and cushioning to provide covers. Similarly, mediocre standards can also adversely affect employees' aspirations. There is no challenge in such standards. The level of aspirations and performance declines when the standards set for a person are below his or her personal goal. The lesson here is that the standards should be reasonable and challenging enough to get the best out of the employees. Senior managers must recognize the fine line between reasonable and unreasonable levels of performance.

The aspiration levels set by the management generally differ, from and in many cases exceed, those set by the employees (associates) themselves. Stedry ran experiments to see how actual achievements of the employees are related to budget and aspiration levels. He found that where the successful budget performance was rewarded and the failure penalized, performance was significantly influenced by the type of budget, the conditions of administration, and the way aspiration levels were set.[18] In another study, Bart found superior performance resulting when the attitudes of senior managers were consistent with the product managers' reward system.[19]

---

[17] Andrew C. Stedry, *Budget Control and Cost Behavior* (Englewood Cliffs, NJ: Prentice-Hall, 1960), for some of the ideas discussed in this section.

[18] See Andrew C. Stedry; and Nicholas Dopuch, Jacob G. Birnberg, and Joel Demski, *Cost Accounting: Accounting Data for Management's Decisions.* 2nd ed. (New York: Harcourt Brace Jovanovich, 1974), pp. 307–310.

[19] Christopher K. Bart, "Budgeting Gamesmanship," *Academy of Management Executive.* vol. 2, no 4, November 1988, pp. 285–294.

(f) Participation and Slack. Budgetary slack (other commonly used terms are padding, cushion, slush fund, hedge, flexibility, cookie jar, kitty, secret reserve, war chest, and contingency fund/reserve[20]) could be another side effect of the participative process in budgeting. *Slack* is the amount of resources budgeted versus what is really needed to do the task in a proper manner. Even in a participative system, the managers are likely to resort to padding as it offers a cushion for covering errors and shortfalls later. Slack gives flexibility to the managers. For instance, revenues may be underestimated and costs may be overestimated intentionally. Some slack is almost unavoidable—when rewards are too closely linked with performance—and may even be helpful in attaining the budgetary goals. When managers' performance is evaluated on the basis of their budget performance, they are able to attain their personal goals—for example, higher salaries, bonuses, and promotion—more readily if a reasonable amount of slack is present. The positive effect of meeting the budgets and personal goals generally outweighs the cost of inefficiency caused by slack.

A limited amount of slack is almost intentional and useful as it can help managers mitigate the budget pressure. But an unreasonable amount could be very costly to the firm and should be checked. A pragmatic approach lies in reviewing the budgets by the top management at some critical points. This way the top management could control unreasonable padding and still expect the subordinates to pursue reasonable goals of the organization.[21] Another approach is to reduce the inducement for padding. By de-emphasizing rewards based on budgetary performance, senior managers can reduce the temptation to pad.

(g) Performance Reports and Rewards. The importance of timely reporting and feedback in the success of budgets cannot be overemphasized. A firm should have an open, accurate, and understandable system of communicating performance of the managers by their responsibility. Such a system is known as *responsibility accounting.* Performance reports prepared under the system of responsibility accounting provide feedback to both the top management and the subordinates. They enable the management to adapt to the changing situation and take corrective actions on a timely basis. The subordinates also benefit from them because timely communication minimizes surprises. Performance reporting does not mean reporting only the unfavorable results. Reports on the favorable results are just as important for planning the future.

Responsibility accounting is an indispensable part of the budgeting system in a firm. A firm is generally divided into several responsibility units/centers under the control of separate managers. Each responsibility unit manager will usually have budgeted goals and resources to accomplish them. The budgeted goals are then broken down into operational targets by the period. Thus, the budget for each unit indicates what is expected of each unit in any given period. At the end of each period, reports are prepared comparing actual results with the budget targets (computation of variances). Because these reports are prepared by the area of responsibility and not by activity or product, they help in identifying people responsible for the variances.

The conflict between sales and production people presents an interesting situation here. The former often push rush orders as long as the production people are willing to produce

[20] Id.

[21] See Michael Schiff and Arie Y. Lewin, "The Impact of People on Budgets," *The Accounting Review,* vol. 45, no. 2, April 1970, pp. 259–268; and Mohamed Onsi, pp. 535–548.

without charging extra for filling such orders. The latter do not like such emergencies all the time, and the situation creates conflicts and irritation between the two. Such conflicts can be easily avoided by charging rush orders the extra cost of producing the goods and also pointing out the reasons for cost variances. Both steps, the extra charge and the assigning of variances, will have the effect of making the future rush orders more acceptable to the production people and reducing the avoidable rush orders. Responsibility accounting can thus play a very positive role in budgeting.[22]

The performance reports under the responsibility accounting system should emphasize the principle of *controllability* of the items therein. When the budgeted and actual results are reported, they report only what the concerned manager at that level could control. Costs beyond the control of the manager will hardly serve any purpose if included in the report. Removal of uncontrollable items removes unnecessary clutter from the reports and helps management focus attention on relevant items. Reports by themselves cannot control costs. They help control costs by influencing the behavior of the people who are responsible for incurring those costs. The performance reports should be designed to serve the needs of management in this area.

There is, however, one danger in overemphasizing controllability of activities in performance reports. It may lead to compartmentalizing of responsibility on the part of subordinates (associates). The lower-level managers may start acting in a dysfunctional manner and ignore the overall or global interests of the firm. The performance reports thus contain powerful messages both to the top management and to the subordinates and can influence the latter's behavior. Therefore, such reports should be prepared with human sensitivity in mind.

One method of using performance reports effectively is to apply the principle of *management by exception.* This principle implies that management can be effective only if it is selective and attention is devoted to significant matters. By drawing management attention to every variance, the performance reports will lose their effectiveness. Thus, only significant and large variances are brought to management attention. This not only protects the effectiveness of the top management but also provides some flexibility to the subordinates. The subordinates also learn to look at the big picture and devote their time and energy where it matters.

The performance reports should not only clearly *communicate* but also *explain* what they purport to convey. Since most businesses have computerized their performance reporting, a word of caution could be added here. The computer printouts could be very cold, unintelligible, and frightening. Just because the budget/accounting staff understands the computer language and the accounting jargon does not mean everyone else also understands them. It is in everyone's best interest that only the relevant part of the computer printout be presented to the person concerned and that it be accompanied by proper explanation. The lesson is, where possible, make the reports *user friendly.* The purpose of the reports should be to help plan the future and not to blame and penalize people.

Effective participation presupposes recognition and rewarding of good performance. When the budgetees meet their budgets, they should receive prompt and fair recognition. The rewards should be equitably distributed and yet recognize differences in performance. If everyone receives the same reward for working at different levels of effort, there will be no incentive to work hard. Modern behavioral theories suggest that the concepts of

[22] See Raymond Villers, "Control and Freedom in a Decentralized Company," *Harvard Business Review.* vol. 32, no. 2, March–April 1954, pp. 89–96.

positive reinforcement and *gain sharing* be followed in evaluating employees' performance. Efforts leading to positive reinforcement tend to repeat. Punishment of budgetary shortfalls cannot change things, but the recognition of successful efforts may lead to their repetition. In fact, too much focus on failures makes the subordinates too cautious and thwarts their initiative.

(h) Role of Budget Staff. The budget and the accounting staff members play a very crucial role in the participative budgeting system, especially now when the data accumulation and processing are computerized and Internet and Intranet have become part of business vocabulary. The budget staff's role is that of collecting information and coordinating budgets. Budget people simply report budget performance to the top management. However, they are often perceived by the operating personnel as if they are paid for finding faults with them and are thus considered adversaries. The budget people do not enforce budgets and still receive much criticism for budget failures from the line people. It is not unnatural for people to find scapegoats for their failures, and the budget staff is as good a scapegoat as the operating personnel can find.

The members of the budget staff need not be defensive about their role. Hiding behind the numbers or using accounting jargons does not help. Likewise, saying they are simply following top management's wishes does not help either. They should approach their role in a more careful manner and project their image as facilitators rather than number crunchers. They should take steps to change their image. The strategy of explaining their work and the reports they prepare can help. Good communication with the line managers can also increase the budget staff's effectiveness. They should emphasize that their role is to facilitate the task of operating people and not to find faults.

The members of the budget staff should exhibit the utmost amount of *patience* in their work. After all, they have to act as the first line of salesmen for budgets. They are the ones who coordinate the budgets. Finally, the budget people should try to simplify the worksheets and computer printouts they use and make them more intelligible to the operating people. Much can be said about standardizing the forms and data-inputting procedures the budget people use for collecting information. The budget office should collect only the information for which it has some perceivable need and not simply to look busy or keep others busy. Likewise, it should produce only the reports that facilitate the work of operating managers, not merely to justify its own existence.

34.6 BEHAVIORAL LESSONS OF BUDGETING

1. Budgets serve a variety of purposes in business, including planning of future, coordinating disparate goals, and motivating the employees (associates).
2. Maximization of profit at the subunit level does not always lead to profit maximization for the organization as a whole in the absence of goal congruency.
3. Budgets involve people at every level, and the people side of budgeting should not be ignored.
4. The traditional behavioral views—for example, the principal objective of the firm is profit maximization, goals are additive, people are motivated primarily by economic forces, and so on—are not very relevant in the modern setting.
5. The modern views of behavioral organization are that people have a variety of needs and motivations; they join an organization to meet their needs; the organization does not have goals, only the dominant group in the coalition has goals; and so forth. A single goal like profit maximization is difficult to establish and accomplish.

Multiple goals such as satisfactory return on investment, market share, leadership in research and development, customer service, and so forth, are more realistic goals in the present world.

6. Under the modern behavioral view, authority cannot be imposed. It is accepted from below.
7. People join an organization to meet their needs. Management's responsibility is to create an environment in which work should meet the needs of both the employees (associates) and the organization.
8. Imposed budgets create pressure on employees, and they resent it. The pressure leads to strife between departments and between staff and line personnel. Ultimately, morale and productivity suffer.
9. Modern management theories recommend that budgeting should involve people—those who will be directly impacted by the budgets.
10. Participation at all levels of management in budgeting helps resolve problems created by the budgets. Participation works because it helps participants better internalize the budget goals.
11. The success of participation depends on a variety of factors, including the nature of participation (real versus pseudo), organization culture and management leadership, group dynamics, performance report, and reward system.
12. De emphasizing the link between rewards and budgetary performance can reduce the temptation for padding (cushioning) and budgetary stress.
13. Members of the budget staff play an important role in the success of budgets. They should attempt to win the trust and confidence of operating people by explaining and communicating their work in a clear and effective manner.
14. Educating about the role of budgets can help smooth relations and reduce irritation between budget staff and other members of an organization. Budget staff should be sensitive to human needs and aspirations.

34.7 SUMMARY. Today's economy is characterized by rapid technological changes, globalization of markets, shorter product cycles, deregulation, and intense competition. Recent developments like the total quality management and continuous improvement, activity-based management, balanced-score card, and just-in-time and computer-integrated manufacturing systems are revolutionizing the way management has to approach problems today. Business success and, in fact, its very survival depend on excellence. Budgeting has acquired even a more important role in today's economic environment. Budgets are universally used as instruments to convey management goals and expectations. They impact people and are impacted by people. Their role in motivating employees has also been generally recognized.

This chapter discussed both the traditional and modern behavioral assumptions as they affect budgeting. Budgets are known to create stress and are resented for that reason. Research shows that the system of participative budgets and removal of the underlying causes of stress can help resolve many of the problems budgets create in an organization. Participation works because the managers and their subordinates (associates) are able to internalize the budget goals better because the goals are jointly set. Goal internalization leads to higher morale and efficiency. De-emphasizing the linking of rewards with budgetary performance and educating about the role of budgets can go a long way in the lowering of budgeting stress. The important lesson of the chapter is that the people aspect of budgets (and budgeting) cannot be ignored if the management wants budgets to succeed in a modern complex organization.

SOURCES AND SUGGESTED REFERENCES

Atkinson, Anthony A., Rajiv D. Banker, Robert S. Kaplan, and Mark S. Young, *Management Accounting.* 2nd ed. Upper Saddle River, NJ: Prentice-Hall, 1997.

Berret, M.E., and L.B. Fraser III, ''Conflicting Roles in Budgeting for Operations,'' *Harvard Business Review,* vol. 55, no. 4, July–August 1977, pp. 137–146.

Brownell, Peter, and Morris McInnes, ''Budgetary Participation, Motivation, and Managerial Performance,'' *The Accounting Review,* vol. 61, no. 4, October 1986, pp. 587–600.

Burton, Alan, ''Shareholder Value Budgeting,'' *Management Accounting* (London), vol. 74, no. 6, June 1996, pp. 26–27.

Chalos, Peter, and Susan Haka, ''Participative Budgeting and Managerial Performance,'' *Decision Sciences,* vol. 20, no. 2, Spring 1989, pp. 334–347.

Chandra, Gyan, and Surendra S. Singhvi, *Budgeting for Profit.* Oxford, OH: Planning Executives Institute, 1973.

Collins, Frank, Paul Muntey, and Don Wo Finn, ''The Budgeting Games People Play,'' *The Accounting Review,* vol. 62, no. 1, January 1987, pp. 29–49.

Cyert, Richard M., and James G. March, *A Behavioral Theory of the Firm.* Englewood Cliffs, NJ: Prentice-Hall, 1992.

Drtina, Ralph, Steve Hoeger, and John Schaub, ''Continuous Budgeting at the HON Company,'' *Management Accounting,* vol. 77, no. 7, January 1996, pp. 20–24.

Duston, Richard, and Hubert Keasler Jr., ''Off-the-Shelf Software Creates Custom Reports,'' *Management Accounting,* vol. 77, no. 8, February 1996, pp. 48–54.

Ferguson, Dennis H., and Florence Berger, ''The Human Side of Budgeting,'' *Cornell Hotel & Restaurant Administration Quarterly,* vol. 27, no. 2, August 1986, pp. 86–90.

Freeman, Eva, ''Turn Your Budgeting Operation into a Profit Center,'' *Datamation,* vol. 43, no. 1, January 1997, pp. 90–93.

Hirst, Mark K., ''The Effects of Setting Budget Goals and Task Uncertainty on Performance: A Theoretical Analysis,'' *The Accounting Review,* vol. 62, no. 4, October 1987, pp. 774–784.

Horngren, Charles T., George Foster, and Srikant M. Datar, *Cost Accounting: A Managerial Emphasis,* 9th ed. Upper Saddle River, NJ: Prentice Hall, 1997.

Johnson, H. Thomas, and Robert S. Kaplan, *Relevance Lost: The Rise and Fall of Management Accounting.* Boston, MA: Harvard Business School Press, 1991.

Kaplan, Robert S. and David P. Norton, ''Knowing the Score,'' *Financial Executive,* vol. 12, no. 6, November–December, 1996, pp. 30–33.

Merchant, Kenneth A., and Jean-Francois Manzoni, ''The Achievability of Budget Targets in Profit Centers: A Field Study,'' *The Accounting Review,* vol. 64, no. 3, July 1989, pp. 539–558.

Moseley, Owen B., ''Sources of Human Relations Problems in Budgeting,'' *Managerial Planning,* vol. 28, no. 1, July–August 1979, pp. 36–38.

Munter, Paul, Frank Collins, and Don Finn, *Game Play in Budgeting.* Oxford, OH: Planning Executives Institute, 1983.

Rusth, Douglas B., ''The Budgeting Process in a Multinational Firm,'' *Multinational Business Review,* vol. 2, no. 2, Fall 1994, pp. 59–63.

Schmidt, Jeffrey A., ''Is It Time to Replace Traditional Budgeting?,'' *Journal of Accountancy,* vol. 174, no. 4, October 1992, pp. 103–107.

Shank, John K., and Vijay, Govindarajan, ''Strategic Cost Management and the Value Chain,'' *Journal of Cost Management,* vol. 5, no. 4, Winter 1992, pp. 5–21.

Sollenberger, Harold M., ''The Five Phases of Budgeting; the Basic Budget Process Has Evolved into a Sophisticated Planning Tool,'' *Credit Union Executive,* vol. 29, no. 4, Winter 1989, pp. 30–35.

Stewart, Thomas A., ''Why Budgets Are Bad for Business,'' *Fortune,* vol. 121, no. 13, June 4, 1990, pp. 179–190.

Welsch, G. A., R. W. Hilton, and P. N. Gordon, *Budgeting: Profit Planning and Control.* 5th ed. Englewood Cliffs, NJ: Prentice-Hall, 1988.

PART 5

INDUSTRY BUDGETS

CHAPTER 35

BUDGETING IN NONPROFIT ORGANIZATIONS

Richard S. Wasch*

35.1 INTRODUCTION. The nonprofit service segment of our society has undergone explosive growth in the past two decades. This segment is now large enough that it is often referred to as the "third sector" of society—neither public (governmental) nor private (traditional profit-seeking businesses). Peter F. Drucker believes that "service institutions have grown so big, that they may now employ more people than federal, state and local government put together."[1]

This nonprofit sector of our society is so important that we can no longer neglect its effectiveness and productivity in providing services. These organizations are as limited by a scarcity of available resources as any other part of the economy. As Lane Adams, the executive vice-president of the American Cancer Society states, "while business has been under pressure to become more socially conscious the so-called social agencies have been under pressure to become more businesslike."[2]

This chapter explains how nonprofit service organizations can plan and budget their limited resources in a more "businesslike" manner. It is divided into the following four sections:

1. The nonprofit sector
2. Nonprofit budgeting characteristics
3. The nonprofit budget process
4. Tools for use in nonprofit budgeting

35.2 NONPROFIT SECTOR. Nonprofit organizations cover a large spectrum of social concerns. They include hospitals, museums, universities, libraries, foundations, industry or trade associations, chambers of commerce, professional associations and councils, civic groups, religious groups, public interest lobbies, social service organizations, international

---

*Additional contributors to this chapter include John R. Birkofer and Clifford L. Kramer.

[1] Peter F. Drucker, "Managing the Third Sector," *The Wall Street Journal,* October 3, 1978.

[2] Lane Adams, "The Vital Connection: The Voluntary Sector and Free Enterprise," address before the Graduate School of Management, College of Business, Brigham Young University, April 12, 1978. (Printed by the American Cancer Society.)

Externally Oriented Organizations
Health and medical care
Education
Culture
Social services
Foundations
Member-Oriented Organizations
Professional societies
Trade, business, and commercial associations
Labor unions
Agricultural organizations and cooperatives
Athletic and avocational associations
Fraternal organizations
Organizations Not Easily Classified
Religious groups
Public interest groups
Research institutions

Exhibit 35.1. Major classes of nonprofit organizations

assistance groups, symphony orchestras, health associations, fraternal organizations, athletic associations, clubs of almost every description, and any number of special pleaders for every conceivable cause. The *Encyclopedia of Associations* lists more than 1,200 pages of active associations, almost all of which are classified as nonprofit organizations. The Internal Revenue Service (IRS) reports that more than 650,000 nonprofit organizations file annually (and this does not include all nonprofit organizations).[3]

(a) Classification of Nonprofit Organizations. A private nonprofit organization generally falls into one of two categories, depending on whether the services provided are directed *externally*—toward members of society—or directed *internally*—toward its own membership. Exhibit 35.1 classifies nonprofit organizations in this way.[4]

(i) Externally Oriented Organizations. Externally oriented organizations include many of the larger and more visible nonprofit organizations, such as hospitals, universities, museums, performing arts societies, voluntary service agencies, and public interest groups. Economically, they constitute the most important part of the nonprofit environment. Since they often provide specifiable services to individual "clients" in society, they may also be termed *client-oriented* organizations. This orientation helps in planning and pricing activities, since they can identify and assess values for individual services they provide, just as businesses identify products and price them based on market conditions.

(ii) Member-Oriented Organizations. Member-oriented organizations form the other major nonprofit group. These organizations are numerous, but they do not have the same

[3] Burton A. Weisbrod, *The Voluntary Nonprofit Sector* (Lexington, MA: Lexington Books, Heath, 1977), p. 20.

[4] This classification excludes all government organizations on the federal, state, or local level. The budgeting problems and methods of these organizations have special characteristics. Several basic references on government accounting and budgeting are listed in the Sources and Suggested References to this chapter.

economic significance as the first group. Nevertheless, they are often large and complex and require the same managerial skills and attention to performance as other nonprofit organizations.

The distinction between these two classes is not always a clear one. A religious organization, for example, usually attempts to promote the spiritual well-being both of its own members and of society. It is similarly difficult to place a public interest group into either category since the causes it promotes may in part be aimed at more general social ends and in part at satisfying the needs or desires of its membership. A research institution might logically belong to the group of organizations that renders services to society as a whole. Its services, however, are so nonspecific and have such a long-term payoff that it is difficult to classify it in this manner.

(b) Size of Nonprofit Organizations. The exact economic size of the nonprofit sector can be assessed in various ways. One study, based on a sample of tax forms submitted to the IRS by nonprofit organizations, estimated that the 1973 revenue sources of the nonprofit sector amounted to about $531 billion and that its assets totaled $580 billion at the end of that year.[5]

A more conservative estimate may be derived using national income statistics. As recorded in the gross national product, the actual contribution of the voluntary sector is smaller than the study above indicates for two principal reasons:

1. The total revenue figure double-counts funds transferred between different nonprofit organizations. For example, Blue Cross–Blue Shield revenues are passed on to hospitals as payment for services performed, where they again get recorded as revenues.
2. Many sources of revenues (such as grants, contributions, and membership fees) do not represent an exchange of funds for specific goods and services provided. This means that gross national product (GNP) statistics exclude them.

National income statistics include four categories of organizations that are private and predominantly nonprofit in character. These are health, education, social services, and membership organizations. Since only a few nonprofit organizations exist in other categories, these four taken together reasonably approximate the size of the nonprofit sector.

Exhibit 35.2 provides information on the size of the nonprofit sector relative to the rest of the U.S. economy in 1977. Exhibit 35.3 shows how the relative size of the nonprofit sector in the economy changed over the period 1952 to 1977.

For the period that these figures portray, the following conclusions can be drawn:

- The public's consumption of the types of services that nonprofit organizations provide has been increasing more rapidly than consumption in the economy as a whole.
- Nonprofit organizations have expanded to meet this need even more rapidly than public or profit-making organizations. This can be seen most clearly by comparing the increase in nonprofit income or employment to the corresponding increase in total consumption of medical and other services.
- The nonprofit sector, almost inconspicuous in 1952, is now a very sizable factor in

[5] Burton A. Weisbrod, pp. 20–27.

	Income[a] ($ million)	Employee Compensation ($ million)	Employment (thousands of employees)
Nonprofit Services			
Health	$ 69,425	$ 53,998	$ 4,128
Education	11,903	11,491	915
Membership organizations	12,830	12,888	1,317
Social services	6,792	6,736	775
Total nonprofit services	$ 100,950	$ 85,113	$ 7,135
National totals	$1,554,770	$1,153,444	$ 79,508
Nonprofit percentage of national total	6.5%	7.4%	9.0%

Source: Survey of Current Business, United States Department of Commerce, July 1978.
[a] *Income,* as presented here, follows the definition of the Department of Commerce. It excludes capital consumption allowances and indirect business taxes, so does not correspond exactly to GNP.

Exhibit 35.2. The nonprofit sector in 1977

	1952	1960	1970	1977
Nonprofit sector as a percentage of National economy based on:				
Income	2.9	4.1	5.3	6.5
Employee compensation	2.8	3.7	5.4	7.4
Employment	3.8	5.3	7.6	9.0
Consumption expenditures—on medical care, education, religion, and welfare activities (percentage of national economy)	7.8	9.3	10.7	12.6

Source: Survey of Current Business, United States Department of Commerce, various years.

Exhibit 35.3. Growth of the nonprofit sector in the U.S. economy: 1952–1977

the economy. Its income exceeds $100 billion, and it employs nearly one tenth of the labor force.

- These trends appear to be continuing.

35.3 NONPROFIT BUDGETING CHARACTERISTICS.

Certain characteristics of the nonprofit sector tend to increase the frustrations—or challenges—involved in budgeting for nonprofit organizations. Exhibit 35.4 lists and briefly explains nine of these characteristics, which are discussed at greater length in this section.

(a) Budget Planning. Every organization needs to make basic decisions about how it will allocate its resources. The mechanism of the market, however, tends to simplify this task for profit-oriented organizations. When for-profit organizations formulate long-term plans and prepare the annual budget, they allocate funds toward departments or product lines that are more profitable and away from those that are less so. As far as the profit-oriented organization is concerned, there is a fairly objective external mechanism—the marketplace—which helps determine goals and the deployment of resources.

Nonprofit organizations lack the essential motive to earn a profit and must give priority

1. *Budget planning.*
   The lack of a profit measure increases the need for the nonprofit organization to formulate its priorities prior to budget development.
2. *Revenue budgeting*
   Nonprofit organizations have special difficulties in the recognition and budgeting of revenues.
3. *Expense budgeting*
   In preparing and using expense budgets, nonprofit organizations often find it difficult to match expenses incurred in delivery of services to those revenues that support these services.
4. *Measuring effectiveness and control*
   Most nonprofit organizations have difficulty measuring their effectiveness in meeting budgeted service levels.
5. *Budget adaptability*
   Nonprofit budgets are often difficult to modify once they are established. From year to year, budget allocations tend to be determined on an incremental basis.
6. *Budget participants*
   The nonprofit budgeting process involves participants who have widely varying backgrounds and objectives.
7. *Nonprofit organization structure*
   Nonprofit organization structures often impede the development of an effective budgeting system.
8. *Nonprofit accounting practice*
   Nonprofit financial accounting regulations and practice may reduce the usefulness of budget information.
9. *External reporting requirements*
   Reporting requirements to external parties often influence the internal budgeting practices of nonprofit organizations.

Exhibit 35.4. Nonprofit budgeting characteristics

to more diffuse objectives. They also lack profit as an ongoing measure of their effectiveness in achieving their objectives. Therefore, the nonprofit organization must find an alternative method to quantify its success, control its operations, evaluate individual performances, and make resource allocation decisions.

The nonprofit organization requires an explicit planning mechanism for setting goals, determining resource allocation patterns, and deciding what program services will be provided. These plans should be formulated prior to the development of the annual budget. In practice, however, this often does not happen so that the budget becomes the principal resource allocation tool by default. In such a situation the budget is more likely to be a result of interdepartmental politics instead of reflecting priorities of the organization as a whole.

(b) Revenue Budgeting. In developing the budget, nonprofit organizations often have unusual difficulties in budgeting revenues. This is primarily because so many revenues do not result directly from the organization's rendering of services to individuals. Even client-oriented institutions such as hospitals and universities may have fees for services or tuition rates artificially set at a fixed level throughout the year, despite the fact that they might incur significant unbudgeted costs in providing these services.

(i) Endowment Earnings. Endowment earnings, one major form of revenue, tend to fluctuate from year to year depending on the markets for stocks and bonds. A nonprofit

organization may record its yearly income on investments of endowment funds as part of its operating revenues. Some controversy exists, however, over just how to measure this income. The alternative measurements are as follows:[6]

- Report only investment income as an operating inflow. Exclude all gains or losses on holdings, whether realized or not.
- Report investment income plus realized gains or losses.
- Report investment income and all gains or losses, realized or unrealized.
- Report a prudent percentage of average market value of the endowment portfolio as an operating inflow. This last approach is known as the *total return concept* of reporting endowment income and was developed in part because it tends to smooth out fluctuations in endowment earnings.

The total return approach has generated much controversy. Its proponents argue that long-term appreciation of invested capital should be counted as part of the endowment principal and should be made available to the organization as operating revenue. Opponents of the concept attack it as providing too subjective a measure of income and for ignoring the fact that, with inflation, the nominal value of the invested principal must appreciate just to maintain its value in real terms. Currently, the American Institute of Certified Public Accountants (AICPA) does not support the total return approach, but some institutions—especially colleges and universities—have used it.

(ii) Grants and Contracts. Grants and contracts obtained from the federal government, foundations, or other third parties often raise dilemmas for budgeters: Will they come through? When? For how long a period of time? Which expenses will/will not be covered? Organizations such as hospitals who depend on third-party reimbursement of their expenses face similar uncertainties and must always keep abreast of reimbursement regulations, which are subject to frequent change.

(iii) Fund Raising. Nonprofit organizations may boost their revenues through fund-raising efforts or membership drives. They face uncertainty, though, about what new gains can be made and whether past fund-raising successes can be maintained. A distinction is often made between ''hard'' revenue sources—which are likely to continue from year to year—and ''soft'' revenue sources—which result from one-time promotional efforts and may not be renewable. The higher the proportion of soft revenue sources in an organization's budget, the greater the risks that it will not be achieved.

(c) Expense Budgeting. The problems of estimating expenses are usually more manageable than budgeting revenue. It is also generally easier to record and classify expenses when they are actually incurred. Many times, however, it is virtually impossible to match expenses incurred in providing a program service, or in operating a department, to any specific revenue sources. A membership organization, for example, may collect its revenues in the form of yearly dues and allocate them much later to various programs. In such a case, it is impossible to tell whether a specific program has a worth to members that

[6] Robert N. Anthony and Regina E. Herzlinger, *Management Control in Nonprofit Organizations* (Homewood, IL: Richard D. Irwin, 1975), pp. 129–135; 237–242.

justifies the funds allocated to it. The budget still serves as a tool for controlling the program's expenditures, but not for evaluating its effectiveness in meeting members' needs.

(d) Measuring Effectiveness and Control. Most nonprofit organizations provide services, not tangible products. This presents both operating and measurement or control difficulties. The problem of developing measures of effectiveness in providing services is particularly difficult for most nonprofit organizations.

(i) Service Timing. One principal operating problem arises from the fact that a service must be provided at a specific time. It cannot be inventoried as "finished goods." There is no buffer between supply of a service and demand for it. If a bed is available in a hospital and qualified nurses and physicians are on hand, it must be used that day, or the hospital loses the opportunity to provide that service and collect the associated revenue. This creates constant difficulties in short-term scheduling and longer-term capacity planning.

(ii) Labor-Intensive Services. Another operating difficulty for nonprofit organizations is that most services are labor intensive. The labor input required may also vary significantly from one time that a service is performed to the next. This makes service work more difficult to schedule and control than machine-paced operations.

(iii) Service Measurement. The measurement of services is perhaps an even more fundamental problem. Many services are difficult to quantify. How much service, for example, does a physician render to a patient? How much knowledge does a professor transfer to the student who listens to a lecture? Measuring and controlling the quality of services rendered is also difficult, especially when professional effort is involved. Frequently, standards of quality simply do not exist. Efficiency measurements are similarly difficult to obtain. Frequently, organizations use service output measurements that are based directly on the labor put into providing services. The value of such measures in conveying information about efficiency is very limited.

Profit-making service organizations face many of the same difficulties. Market forces, however, do compel them to define their target customers and services more carefully and to develop efficiency measures. Client-oriented nonprofit organizations (such as hospitals or performing arts organizations) often have a similar ability to identify specific services that they can deliver to individual clients and then to measure the costs of each unit of service that is provided. Nonprofit organizations that seek to advance the general interests of their members or specific causes, however, may find it very difficult to identify and control their services.

(iv) Multiple Service Measures. Multiple service measures are often needed, and they are likely not to be expressed in financial terms. A profit-oriented business can often quite easily measure a department's return on investment. A hospital, on the other hand, usually needs to develop multiple statistics that measure patient care, utilization of facilities, and hospital personnel time. Furthermore, it will need to use these statistics differently from one department to another.

(e) Budget Adaptability. Nonprofit budgets often are not easily adapted to changing circumstances during the course of a year. One reason for this is that many nonprofit organizations—especially member-oriented ones—do not undergo significant variations in the level of service they provide over the course of a year. Another reason is that their cost structure often contains many costs that are considered "fixed." A university, for example, will not usually cancel classes or lay off professors once the academic year is under way. It may take years, in fact, for it to change its faculty staffing significantly. Other costs may be fixed because of the requirements of outside funding sources. In many respects, however, this lack of adaptability is due to prevailing attitudes in nonprofit organizations. Many organizations are simply not used to the idea of modifying budget allocations once they are established and are not yet willing to consider adopting flexible budgeting techniques that permit them to adjust for variations in activity levels.

In the same way, budget allocations shift very little from year to year in many nonprofit organizations. Commonly, they practice "incremental" budgeting—they take last year's allocations and tack on a fixed percentage to arrive at the new year's expenditure levels for each department or program. This method is simple, avoids political strains, and works well enough if revenue sources are increasing. More recently, however, its inefficiencies as a resource allocation device have become clearer. Moreover, changes in the growth of revenue sources for many nonprofit organizations (including universities and cultural organizations) have forced them recently to begin making more fundamental budget allocation decisions.

(f) Budget Participants. Preparation of the budget tends to involve just about anyone of importance who is associated with a nonprofit organization. This usually includes the top administrators of the organization, the heads of departments or programs, and the trustees or board members. It may also include community representatives, funding sources, and regulatory agencies. These external parties have different backgrounds and often have different expectations concerning the budget.

A nonprofit organization has this high level of external participation principally as a result of its "public responsibility." This responsibility is vastly different from that of a profit-making organization.

In a profit-making organization, the main responsibility is to the consumers and investors. Profits provide the feedback on how well the organization is fulfilling these responsibilities. Although there is an obligation to justify its performance to government regulators and to groups representing interested members of society, these responsibilities are secondary.

A nonprofit organization does not need to face investors who expect a good return on their investment. Instead, it must respond directly to external influences provided by trustees, funding agencies, foundations, organization members, interested groups, and government regulators at the federal, state, and local levels. These external parties often have conflicting goals and can therefore make it difficult to manage the organization and plan its future.

Internal budget participants may also have different objectives. This difference is especially evident when the organization includes professionals.

Professional concerns for the quality of service often tend to override issues of cost. Hospitals, for example, have often been torn between tightening budgets and the demands of their doctors for the newest diagnostic equipment.

Financial managers of nonprofit organizations often have a different background from that of others in the organization and may set financial priorities that are at variance with the interests of the professionals. Even if the organization has a clear statement of financial objectives, the budget will often be a result of compromises made between various conflicting internal parties.

(g) Nonprofit Organization Structure. The structure of a nonprofit organization may hinder its efforts to establish an effective budgeting system. One major reason for this may be the absence of a reliable responsibility structure. A responsibility system of budgeting divides the organization into effective work units, assigns individual responsibility for each activity of the unit, and classifies costs as controllable or noncontrollable by that unit. The structure corresponds to the way the organization attacks its work on a day-to-day basis. It duplicates the formal chain of authority and is used as a tool for managers to control that part of the organization for which they are directly responsible. This is just as established a concept for the nonprofit organization as it is for the profit-oriented one.

Many nonprofit organizations have recognized that, although responsibility budgeting is a good tool for controlling expenditures (inputs), it does not provide adequate control over the services rendered by the organization (outputs). This recognition has fostered thinking in terms of "programs." Accurate program information can be of great value to an organization in both its planning and budgeting procedures.

The idea of a program structure is relatively recent (first tried on a large scale in the 1960s by the federal government) and has not always been a success. The program structure aligns itself with either the types of services the organization renders or the classes of individuals who benefit from its services. It has great potential as a tool for planning and analysis but can be very difficult to implement. A university, for example, can easily set up a responsibility structure based on its existing departments (English, history, chemistry, etc.). However, it may be harder to classify its outputs and specify who is benefiting from its educational services.

Nonprofit organizations have not often organized along program lines, nor have they thought in that way. Their accounting systems therefore do not usually support program concepts. As a result, program costs are difficult to quantify and record on a consistent basis from year to year. In practice, then, for most nonprofit organizations the responsibility structure prevails in matters of resource allocation.

Ideally, for a program structure to be successful, the following situation should prevail: (1) program and responsibility structure should coincide; (2) programs and program goals should be clearly specified; and (3) program costs should be easy to identify and record. Furthermore, measures of performance should be in place as part of the budgeting process to monitor progress against established goals. This happy state of affairs currently does not exist in most nonprofit organizations. Many of them, however, are having increasing success in introducing program thinking into the prebudget planning phase.

(h) Nonprofit Accounting Practices and the Budget. In comparing financial accounting practices in the nonprofit sector to those prevailing in the private sector, several major differences in the method stand out. Many of these differences in accounting methods may significantly affect their budgeting procedures.

(i) Fund Accounting. Nonprofit organizations typically establish multiple self-balancing funds, which group resources that are similarly restricted in terms of specified activities or objectives. This procedure, known as *fund accounting,* is not seen in business. Its use arose in the nonprofit world because of the idea that these organizations were "stewards" of funds entrusted to them to carry out specific socially useful activities. In an extreme

form, fund accounting may dictate the use of a separate fund for each gift or grant to the organization, with separate accounting made of the use of resources residing in the fund. Most of the published guidelines, however, favor using some variant of the following classification scheme:

- *Current unrestricted funds.* Available for daily operations, with no externally imposed restrictions on use
- *Current restricted funds.* Available for operational use, but only for donor-specified purposes[7]
- *Endowment funds.* Donated funds whose principal is to be maintained perpetually by the organization. The organization, however, may use income from investment of this principal for general operating purposes or for specific purposes as established by the donor.
- *Plant and equipment funds.* Set aside to maintain and replace the organization's long-term assets and to provide for any needed debt servicing associated with them.

Fund accounting is commonly practiced in all areas of the nonprofit sector and is often a legal requirement. An organization that uses it will report a separate balance sheet and a separate statement of activity (akin to the income statement for businesses) for each fund.

Fund accounting requirements tend to complicate the budgeting process. In many nonprofit organizations, a single transaction may have to be classified in four different ways: by funding source, by function or program, by responsibility center, and by natural object of expense. The budget must also be prepared along these same lines. For example, an overall program budget may be divided into the responsibility centers working on the program and further classified by the natural object of expenditure. If a single program is supported by resources from two separate funds, the budget also reflects the percentage of funding from each major fund.

The head of a responsibility center is therefore not only concerned with meeting the responsibility budget but also forced to consider whether the responsibility center is furthering both the program purposes of the organization and the purposes of the original donors of funds.

(ii) Cash versus Accrual Basis Accounting. Many nonprofit organizations use the cash basis of accounting for revenues and expenses or a ''modified accrual'' method, where cash basis books are converted to accrual at year's end. The accrual basis of accounting is generally recommended by the accounting profession and is used almost exclusively in financial reporting by private enterprises.

A cash-based accounting system records actual cash receipts and disbursements, but not payables or receivables. The limitations of this method regarding its ability to report on the worth and solvency of an organization, or on its efficiency in rendering services, are by now widely understood in the nonprofit field. Virtually all of the applicable accounting

[7] An organization's board of directors may at times decide to set aside unrestricted current funds for specified purposes. These so-called designated funds may be treated internally as if they were restricted. For purposes of financial reporting, though, they are ''unrestricted,'' because there is no legal obligation to external parties concerning their use.

guidelines recommend use of the accrual method wherever possible. They do, however, permit use of cash basis accounting for smaller organizations that lack the expertise or resources to keep their books on an accrual basis, provided that this does not result in material differences from what accrual methods would have reported.[8]

Despite accounting guidelines, many nonprofit organizations do not use full accrual accounting. In this case, budget data may be inadequate. Budget reports will convey no knowledge of receivables due or commitments to pay for goods and services already received. Depending on the net effect of accrual adjustments, a cash basis statement could be significantly over or under budget when restated on the accrual basis.

(iii) Other Accounting Issues. In addition to the accounting issues specifically identified, there are other lesser issues that may have an effect upon budget development and planning. We mention these accounting issues only briefly because they are either unique to the nonprofit environment or are treated differently from the way they would otherwise be treated in a for-profit environment.

Many nonprofit organizations that use accrual basis accounting nevertheless do not record "expenses" in the same manner as commercial businesses but instead record "expenditures." An expense measures the amount of goods and services used or consumed during an accounting period; an expenditure measures goods and services acquired during a period and records them as belonging to that period whether or not that is when they are actually used.[9] (Note, however, that an expenditure does recognize the organization's obligation to pay for goods or services once it contracts for them. In this way, it is superior to cash-based accounting, which does not recognize payables.)

Accounting and reporting guidelines vary regarding expenditures and expenses.[10] This reflects the uncertainty that exists in the field about which of the two should be used. Those who prefer the expenditure concept often point out that nonprofit organizations are accountable to external parties who provide funds to be spent in a specific manner and for specific purposes. Others prefer the expense concept because it provides a truer accounting picture of when resources are actually used by the organization and because it makes nonprofit statements comparable to those of private sector businesses.

Some nonprofit organizations, notably colleges and universities, do not depreciate their fixed assets, on the ground that their operating statements should "disclose resources received and expended rather than net income realized."[11] Instead, they keep track of expired capital costs through separate records that do not enter the financial statements.

---

[8] In addition, some nonprofit organizations use a modified accrual approach, recording some types of transactions on a cash basis and others on an accrual basis. In such systems the less predictable inflows and outflows tend to be those that are recorded on the cash basis. State and local governments provide examples of this method of recording financial transactions.

[9] Robert N. Anthony, *Financial Accounting in Nonbusiness Organizations: An Exploratory Study of Conceptual Issues,* Research reports, Financial Accounting Standards Board (FASB), 1978, pp. 78–80.

[10] The AICPA's *Hospital Audit Guide* uses the expense concept, as does its recent statement of position for nonprofit organizations not covered by other AICPA guides. On the other hand, its audit guide for voluntary health and welfare organizations uses the terms expense and expenditure interchangeably without defining either one. In the educational sector, the National Association of Colleges and University Business Officers' *College and University Business Administration* uses the expenditure concept.

[11] National Association of College and University Business Officers, *College and University Business Administration,* 3rd ed. (Washington, DC, 1974), p. 179.

The AICPA disagrees with this practice, arguing that omitting depreciation understates the true costs of an organization's services.

A final area of difference concerns donated goods and services. These transactions are virtually unique to the nonprofit world. Most accounting guidelines recommend that donated goods and services be valued and reported only if the following three conditions apply:

1. The services performed are part of the organization's normal functions and would otherwise be performed by paid personnel.
2. The organization has control over the services being provided.
3. The value of the services can be measured clearly.

(i) External Reporting Requirements and the Budget. Besides creating a need for fund accounting, external funding parties influence the way a nonprofit organization budgets and accounts for its costs. In general these parties establish reporting principles that the recipient nonprofit organization must fulfill as a precondition to obtaining funding, or being reimbursed for costs incurred. These principles vary from one funding source to another, although the Office of Management and Budget (OMB) has helped by issuing standard regulations governing federal grants to most nonprofit organizations.

(i) Reimbursement Procedures. The major budget issue for the recipient organization is to get reimbursed for all of its grant or contract-related costs and not have to cover any unexpected costs out of its own general funds. This means that it will find it to its interest to do the following:

- Minimize any grant-related costs that are not ''allowable'' for reimbursement under the funding party's rules.
- Account for—and charge to the funding party—as many indirect and administrative costs as can be fairly attributed to the grant.
- Prevent cost overruns on grant projects.
- Find ways to charge to the project the costs of winding down a grant project after the cut-off date, thereby absorbing as little as possible through general funds.

Besides controlling individual grant costs in this manner, an organization that receives grants from several sources will be wise to determine which indirect costs are allowed under which grant and to charge them accordingly. Most nonprofit organizations know this; nevertheless, because of inattention or poor budgeting and accounting, they still often have to pay for unbudgeted grant or contract-related expenses.

(ii) Functional Accounting. Partly because of the limitations of fund accounting, nonprofit organizations are increasingly being asked to report their expenses on a functional, or program, basis, as opposed to reporting by natural object classifications or by fund groupings. The AICPA *Audit Guide for Voluntary Health and Welfare Organizations,* issued in 1974, was the first to recommend this. The AICPA's *Statement of Position on Accounting Principles and Reporting Practices for Certain Nonprofit Organizations* states the following:

> The statement of activity should present costs separately for each significant program and supporting activity. Program activities are those directly related to the purposes for which the organization exists. Supporting activities do not relate directly to the purposes for which the organization exists. Fund raising, membership development, and unalocated management and general expense are three examples of supporting activities that should be reported separately.[12]

This requirement for functional expense reporting constitutes an improvement in reporting practices for two reasons. First, it begins to focus the nonprofit financial reports more on what the end results are of an organization's use of its funds rather than on keeping track of where the funds came from. This makes it easier to tell how well the organization is achieving its stated objectives. Second, it forces the organization to think in terms of programs, to collect cost information accordingly, and possibly to begin to manage itself internally along program lines.

(iii) Encumbrance Reporting. Some organizations record their contractual commitments to pay for goods and services often well before they are actually delivered and a business obligation to pay is incurred. In government-related entities, it may even be illegal to use these unexpended, but "encumbered," funds for other purposes, even though they may be temporarily lying idle. These organizations may also be required to report encumbered funds separately on their financial reports.

Accounting guidelines in the private nonprofit sector now uniformly recommend against the external reporting of encumbrances. Many of these organizations, however, still use encumbrances for internal purposes.[13]

35.4 NONPROFIT BUDGET PROCESS. We will now discuss in more detail how a nonprofit organization can establish a budget process that works. This process as presented here will cover the following five phases:

1. Long-range planning
2. Program planning
3. Budget planning
4. Budget development
5. Budget control

Exhibit 35.5 shows how these phases connect with one another and what the key activities of each are and suggests how frequently they should be carried out.

We wish to make four comments about this model before discussing it further. First, it is just a model. It is meant to further the exposition of the budget process and to stimulate the reader's thinking.

Second, as a formal process, it tends to apply best to larger nonprofit organizations. Most of the ideas it expresses, however, can be used to great advantage by smaller organizations in a less formal manner. We will discuss these applications at various points.

Third, it explains the planning process that precedes actual budget development. Plan-

---

[12] American Institute of Certified Public Accountants (AICPA), Accounting Standards Division, *Statement of Position: Accounting Principles and Reporting Practices for Certain Nonprofit Organizations,* December 31, 1978, pp. 29–30.

[13] *Id.,* p. 10.

	Phase				
	1 Long-Range Planning	2 Program Planning	3 Budget Planning	4 Budget Development	5 Budget Control
Key activities	1. Define major objectives. 2. Identify strategies for achieving objectives. 3. Initiate program planning process.	1. Analyze program alternatives. 2. Select desired programs. 3. Develop plan to implement programs.	1. Translate programs into budget terms. 2. Establish responsibility accounting structures. 3. Develop measurement tools. 4. Prepare budget guidelines. 5. Assign budget responsibilities.	1. Estimate revenues for the organization. 2. Prepare budgets by responsibility center. 3. Prepare initial consolidated budget. 4. Review and revise budget. 5. Obtain budget approval.	1. Issue budget control reports. 2. Review reports and analyze variances. 3. Revise budgets and activities if necessary.
Frequency	Every 3–5 years	1–3 years	Revise annually	Annually	Monthly

Exhibit 35.5. The nonprofit budget process

ning is a necessity for nonprofit organizations. Many do not do it and consequently suffer when they try to budget and control their operations.

Finally, the model specifies how to plan, develop, and apply an internal operating budget only. We will later briefly discuss special issues in cash and capital budgeting that affect many nonprofit organizations.

(a) Phase 1: Long-Range Planning. In long-range planning, the organization defines (or redefines) its statement of purpose, establishes objectives to be reached over the following years, and identifies possible paths (or strategies) that may meet these objectives. Long-range planning is widely accepted in business. It is also important to a nonprofit organization, for the following reasons:

- Its goals are social ones and relatively complex and difficult to quantify compared with those of business.
- Its resources are commonly limited and relatively difficult to expand. This makes it important for it to set priorities.
- It is subject to strong external constraints and must determine how to be effective despite this fact.

Long-range plans should cover a 5- to 10-year period for larger organizations. Smaller organizations, such as theater groups, should at least be able to look beyond the current year's activities. Long-range plans should not be changed so often that confusion results concerning the organization's direction. How plans should be modified frequently enough to keep the organization effective in a shifting environment. The organization's top administrators and board of directors should formulate these objectives and plans. Staff may help in assessing environmental conditions and in identifying possible strategies to follow, but the decisions have to be made at the highest level of management. The process itself should be informal enough to encourage creativity but should be aimed at achieving some formal written objectives that can guide the program planning phase that follows.

The key activities in this phase are described in the following paragraphs.

(i) Defining Major Objectives. If the organization does not have a statement of purpose, it should formulate one. If there is an existing statement of purpose but it seems outdated, then it should be revised. Such a statement will tend to be philosophical and full of ideals but will already often begin to convey some practical information about the organization.

For example, a museum may need to make the fundamental decision to be either primarily a cultural repository or an instrument for community education. Similarly, a church may focus its interest on its members' spiritual lives or on serving the community. Both organizations may make this basic choice in a statement of purpose and may direct their ensuing day-to-day activities accordingly.

Once the statement of purpose is clearly established, more specific long-term objectives that are consistent with this purpose should be defined. If a museum decides that its purpose is educational, it still needs to decide what it will teach and to whom. It also needs to set priorities among objectives: How much of its resources, for example, is it willing to allocate away from its curatorial collections toward educational services?

(ii) Identifying Strategies for Achieving Objectives. The next step is to devise ways to achieve objectives. There may be many such strategies, some more feasible than others.

The art history museum seeking to expand its educational programs to the community can do several things. It can set up adult education classes at night, join in a consortium with other museums or with universities, establish branch centers to make its collection more accessible, hold exhibitions having special topical interest, have its staff make visits to community centers or schools, or do some combination of all these. The purpose at this stage is a creative one—to think of alternatives and not to assess them in depth. This detailed analysis comes in the program planning phase.

(iii) Initiating the Program Planning Process. As objectives are being formulated, and some strategies for achieving them identified, the organization should be establishing a program planning group. This group should include key policy makers such as the organization's director, financial officers, and key departmental supervisors. Staff may be added to assist in collection and analysis of information. The group's role will be to take the statements of purpose and objectives developed in the long-range planning phase and to translate these into programs.

The dividing line between long-range planning and program planning may be indistinct. Small organizations may do both together and may never use a formal program planning group. Strategies may be developed in either phase. Findings in the program planning phase may even cause a need to rethink objectives developed during long-range planning. Both phases are necessary, however, since they complement each other—one sets objectives, and the other devises action plans to meet them.

(b) Phase 2: Program Planning

(i) Analyzing Program Alternatives. The program planners should begin by turning each possible strategy defined in long-range planning into specific actions. This initial step need not be too concerned with problems of financing. Instead, the following questions should be asked for each strategy: What organizational functions does it involve? What groups does it reach? What objective(s) does it fulfill? The planners should also ensure that, as a whole, the strategies being considered cover all of the organization's objectives and activities.

Several alternative strategies will probably exist to meet each objective at this point. Program planners will therefore need to analyze individual strategies to determine which one meets the stated objective at least cost to the organization. Cost–benefit analysis may be useful at this point. This is a well-known technique. It is subject to abuse in the nonprofit environment, however, and the following four points should be noted:[14]

1. Before using cost–benefit analysis, make sure that your goals are clearly specified and that your strategies are aimed at achieving your goals. If you are "fighting" cancer, determine whether that means finding a cure for a specific type of cancer, improving techniques for diagnosing it, identifying potential carcinogens, or educating the public about its dangers. Then make sure that the programs you are evaluating are fighting cancer in the way you want them to.
2. Related to the preceding point, do not compare cost–benefit figures for two programs or strategies that are really aimed at different objectives.

[14] Robert N. Anthony, and Regina E. Herzlinger, pp. 186–203.

3. Be skeptical of benefit calculations that are highly quantitative. Nonprofit organizations often provide services whose benefits are not highly visible or very immediate. It makes little sense to try to quantify them. On the other hand, be sure that you have a good grasp of what these intangible benefits are, even when they do not make it into the cost–benefit equation.
4. Allow for a good margin of error in any cost–benefit result obtained. Benefits will almost always be imprecisely estimated. Costs can often be determined more accurately; therefore, if two proposals with similar benefits have significantly different costs, it may be safe to go with the cheaper one. Even so, do not decide solely on the basis of the analysis.

(ii) Selecting Desired Programs. Cost–benefit analysis, if done properly, tells which strategies will meet the desired objectives and at what cost. It will eliminate certain alternatives as being economically infeasible. It is only one input to the decision-making process, however.

The program planners must ask several other questions before deciding. First, are there resources available to the organization to undertake the suggested program? If not, then the objective must be modified or an alternative strategy chosen, which, while it achieves the objective incompletely, is less costly. Another question is: What are the risks involved? An opera company may be rendering an important service to the community by presenting a lavish production of Wagner's Ring Cycle, and the analysis may show that if it receives good reviews, it is likely to do well at the box office. If it does not succeed, though, can the company withstand the financial consequences? The planners must also consider environmental constraints: Will regulators approve a hospital's plan to open an intensive burn care center, if one already exists in the city? Finally, planners should consider whether a new program is a good "fit" for the organization. For example, should a professional society, a farmer's cooperative, or a mountaineering club accede to the requests of many of its members that it take up a lobbying presence in Washington?

(iii) Developing a Plan to Implement Programs. Once the desired strategies are selected through the program planning process, they need to be fleshed out into specific program plans.

A program plan should address the following nine questions, at a minimum:

1. What objectives does it help achieve?
2. What are its expected benefits to society?
3. What are the estimated costs of the program?
4. How long will this program take to accomplish?
5. What persons and organizational functions will be involved or affected?
6. What is the time-phased action plan for accomplishing the project's purposes?
7. Are there key checkpoints to track progress or other methods of control?
8. Where will funding come from? Will the program generate any revenues to pay for itself? Does it use restricted or unrestricted funds?
9. What are the risks or uncertainties involved in carrying out the program? Are there contingency plans?

These plans will probably circulate through the organization and require some rethinking. Once a consensus is obtained on them, they are ready to be introduced into the budget planning process.

(iv) Ongoing Programs versus New Programs. The program planning process just described applies to the establishment of new programs and does not need to be carried out every year. Rather, it should be done every few years or whenever an organization is engaged in a re-examination of its long-term objectives.

There is a need, however, to review ongoing programs on a more frequent basis. An older program may have outgrown its purposes or lost the support of its constitutency. Anthony and Herzlinger suggest ''zero-based review'' as a possible way to catch this.[15] In this system, every program comes up for review periodically—perhaps every five years. This review considers ways to restructure the program, to improve its efficiency, or perhaps to merge it with other programs. It may even question its continued existence. Although this is a good technique for revitalizing programs, it is likely to incur the resistance of managers responsible for the program and may be difficult to implement. (This, by the way, is *not* zero-based budgeting, since it does not involve a budget, has more limited purposes, and is much less time consuming.)

(v) Program Planning in Smaller Organizations. Many smaller organizations do not have the resources to carry on formal program planning, but neither do they have the need to do so. A small theater group's objectives may be dictated entirely by its director. A community service clinic may have just two programs—one for each of its funding sources. In general a smaller nonprofit organization is more likely to be structured along program lines than its larger colleagues and will change its program offerings much more readily if circumstances warrant. It does not need formal program planning.

Because it lives on a day-to-day, hand-to-mouth existence, however, the smaller organization does need the larger perspective that thinking about programs can bring. Even the most modest theater troupe should do the following:

- Set its objectives down on paper.
- Identify its present program offerings (e.g., an experimental theater series, a summer classical repertory offering).
- Identify potential new offerings.
- Plan ways of obtaining resources to keep its present programs and expand into new areas.

It should, in other words, begin to think beyond its survival in the current year. For this organization, program thinking is still important, even if formal program planning is not.

(c) Phase 3: Budget Planning

(i) Translating Programs into Budget Terms. The result of formal program planning is a program structure Exhibit 35.6 shows part of a sample program structure for a university, with the objective being a degree program in business administration. Another program structure, developed by a mental health clinic, identified its five major program

[15] *Id.*, p. 213.

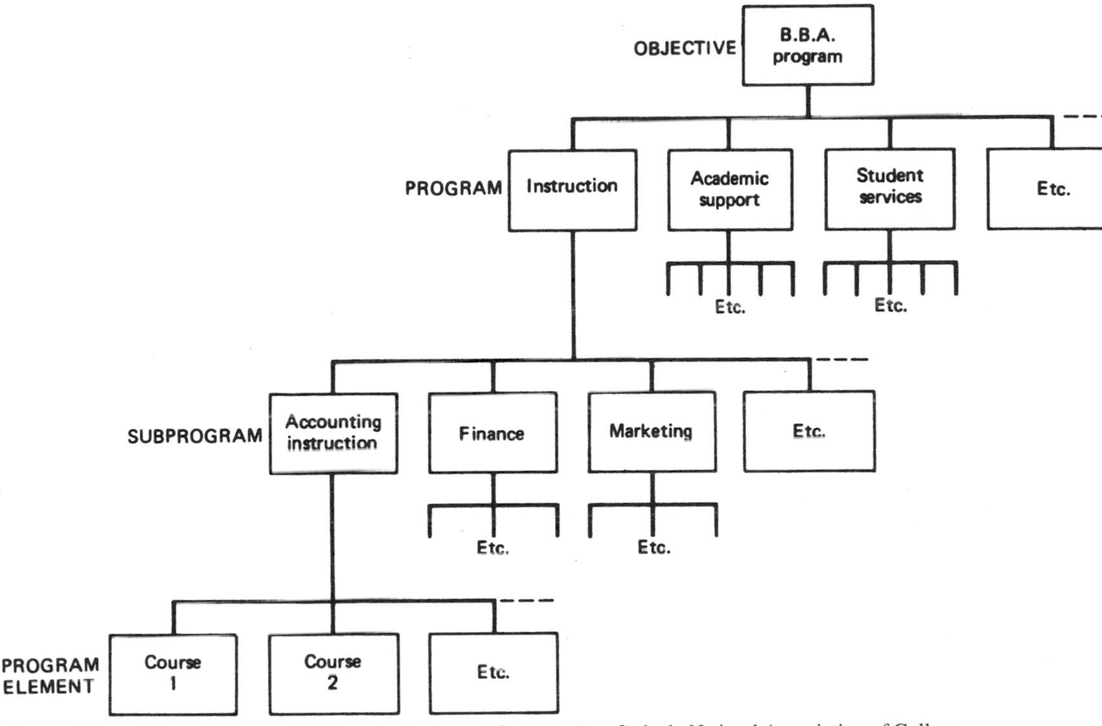

Source: Adapted from *College and University Business Administration*, 2nd ed., National Association of College and University Business Officers, 1974.

Exhibit 35.6. Part of a sample program structure at a university

categories as clinical services, community services, retardation and rehabilitation services, training, and research. Within these categories, it established a structure containing 26 programs.[16]

Many nonprofit organizations have devised meaningful program structures. Fewer of them have actually translated them into budget terms. There are two major reasons for this: (1) program plans and budgets are devised for different purposes—one for planning and the other for operating control; and (2) program structures often conflict with existing responsibilities and thus are difficult to express in budget terms.

The first reason is easier to overcome. Program plans are devised with a longer time frame in mind than the one-year horizon of budgets. They contain less detail about costs and revenues and do not provide an operating plan for managers. This only means, though, that program plans require some translation into specific dollar terms to become useful inputs to annual budgets.

The second reason is more fundamental. The program structure, which is focused on outputs, often cuts across traditional departmental lines of responsibility. This actually constitutes a major strength of the program concept, since it causes the organization to give priority in its considerations to the services it is providing. Organizations such as

[16] Roderick K. Macleod, "Program Budgeting Works in Nonprofit Institutions," *Harvard Business Review,* September–October 1971, p. 52.

universities and hospitals, however, will not shift their organizational structure to match programs. There is often good reason for this. The traditional departmental structure corresponds to the background and training of the organization's staff and to the way they divide up the daily work. Physicians and nurses are trained in specific medical techniques, not in how to conduct inpatient or outpatient services. Professors are trained to teach English or accounting, not to provide student or community program services. Their daily activities follow departmental lines, and so must the budget, if it is to control these activities.

Not all nonprofit organizations face this organizational conflict when applying program methods. The mental health clinic, for example, may be much more able to use program budgeting than the university. In general, the smaller the organization and the less pronounced the specialization of its professional staff, the more likely it will be to benefit from program budgeting.

Even if program budgets are not formally used, however, the organization should keep track of how well it is achieving its program objectives. Some possible ways of doing this include (1) maintaining a committee, possibly the original program planning committee, to monitor and report on the organization's program performance; (2) reporting on program revenues, expenses, and performance measures by including these as memo reports for departmental heads; and (3) requiring that department heads report annually on how well they met program objectives in the past year and that they set program related goals for themselves for the next year.

(ii) Establishing Responsibility Accounting Structures. The budget structure follows the organization's daily operating structure. If the organization operates on a program basis, the budget will be a program budget. If the organization is departmental, so is the budget. In some organizations both program and departmental budgets will be prepared.

The accounting system should be able to track revenues and expenses by natural object of classification and department at the least, if the organization is arranged departmentally. This will give a department head the information to control expenses and revenues for the responsibility unit. If the organization has gone through program planning, it should also classify revenues and expenses by program. This is not conceptually difficult but may often be too tedious for a manual accounting system to handle. A computerized general accounting system with a properly designed chart of accounts can on the other hand provide program-based budget reports to any detail level of responsibility necessary.

One nonprofit organization, which coordinated a number of development projects, devised the following coding structure to handle its general accounting needs and provide budgeting and responsibility reporting by program activities:

Type of Transaction	Company	Fund	Sponsor	Account	Program	Dept.
Assets and liabilities	XX	X		XXXXX		
Revenues	XX	X	XX	XXXXX	XXXXX	
Direct expenses	XX	X	XX	XXXXX	XXXXX	
Administrative expenses	XX	X	XX	XXXXX	XXXXX	XXX

The program component itself features a "roll-up" structure, permitting reporting at various levels of the organization, from the lowest level of responsibility up to a summarized report on major program areas for the organization as a whole. Administrative overhead expenses are charged both to the departments incurring them and to an appropriate program activity. As can be seen, this system also handles the necessary fund accounting requirements, using the "fund" field to indicate major AICPA-specified fund groupings and the "sponsor" field to indicate specific donors.[17]

(iii) Developing Measurement Tools. This is an important step. An accounting system that simply records expenditures must be supplemented by both financial and nonfinancial measures that show what the department or program is doing with its resources and what it is accomplishing.

These measures may address either the *efficiency* or the *effectiveness* of a program or department. The former measures are much more common in nonprofit organizations, because they are more easily generated from internal statistics and do not force the organization to measure its outputs. In fact, nonprofit organizations sometimes try to use what are really efficiency measures as indicators of their effectiveness in achieving their purposes.

A university, for example, may sometimes point to its student-faculty ratio as an effectiveness measure indicating the quality of the education it is providing. Since it measures only the college's *inputs* (i.e., its faculty) per student, this ratio is better applied as an efficiency measure. It shows only how many of its resources the university had to expend to "process" a student, without addressing whether or not the student actually did learn anything. The university should try to develop other measures to tell whether it is effective in producing well educated students.

In general, a program may tend to rely more on effectiveness measures, and a department more on efficiency measures—although they should have both. A program-based operation such as a community drug rehabilitation center will want to record such measures as number of persons contacted, number of contacts per person, time per contact, percentage of target clients reached in the community, and frequency of relapse (and need for re-treatment) of persons contacted. These are all measures relating to its effectiveness as a program. The center can translate these measures into financial terms. It should be careful, however, not to lose sight of what makes it an effective program. A cost-per-visit measure, for example, is a good efficiency measure, but only that. If the center blindly tries to reduce this cost statistic, it may find that it is spending too little time with its clients to help them properly. The program should instead try to measure cost per *successful* contact—if it can find a way of doing this. If it cannot, it should keep its financial statistics and effectiveness measurements separate so they can both be clearly understood.

A laboratory department in a hospital provides a different case. Its purpose—to conduct accurate tests for other hospital units—is fairly clearly stated. If it fails to meet this purpose, even briefly, it receives feedback on its effectiveness (or lack of it) from the other departments in the hospital system which are its clients. The laboratory therefore will usually concentrate on developing careful measures of its efficiency, in terms of labor time and resources spent per test.

Whether or not a unit is developing measures of its efficiency or effectiveness, it should be prepared to develop multiple measures if its activities are not homogeneous. A hospital laboratory may have tests that are simple and direct and others that are difficult and lengthy. It should classify them separately and measure them differently. A drug rehabilitation center may find that heavy drug users occupy its attention in different ways than

[17] A number of nonprofit accounting systems now support program (or "functional") budgeting and reporting. A leading example in the health-care field is the American Hospital Association's recommended uniform chart of accounts, described in its *Chart of Accounts for Hospitals* (Chicago, 1976).

lighter users—or that variations may occur according to the type of drug used. Its measurement system should account for this.

(iv) Preparing Budget Guidelines. In this step, two things need to be done. First, directors should communicate general information that department or program heads will need in developing their budgets. One important piece of information concerns their expenditure constraints. If departments will be expected to cut back expenditures 5% from last year, this is when they should know. Other important information concerns major programs that the organization will undertake in the coming year. Even if budgeting is along departmental lines, heads of departments should know how programs will affect them and how much effort they are expected to put into specific programs.

In this step, it is also necessary to prepare a manual of budget policies and procedures or to update the existing manual. (Smaller organizations will want to do this more informally.) This manual should cover the following six matters (adapted from Seawell[18]):

1. Objectives of the budgetary program
2. Definitions of the authority and responsibilities of all personnel engaged in budget preparation
3. Instructions, in full detail, as to the mechanics of budget development and samples of standardized forms to be used
4. Calendar of budgeting activity, with a time schedule for the completion of each stage of the budgeting program
5. Detailed procedures for the review, revision, and approval of all budgets
6. Specification of the budgetary reporting and control systems to be used, including report preparation, analysis, and follow-up

These manuals must be complete, accurate, and easy to use. For this reason, they should be tested by trial runs before being put into use.

(v) Assigning Budget Responsibilities. These responsibilities should be made clear from the top to the bottom of the organization. Exhibit 35.7 shows how these may be assigned, from the governing board down to program or department heads. In addition to a budget committee, there also may be a program planning committee, which, as discussed previously, will monitor the budget to ensure that it is helping the organization meet its program objectives.

It is vital to the budget structure that it be based on responsibility centers. Persons preparing program or department budgets must have operating authority over these units and must be held accountable for the success or failure of these units. This must hold true for each program or department. If it does not, the budget's use as a planning tool diminishes, and its usefulness for control purposes vanishes completely for that unit.

(d) Phase 4: Budget Development

(i) Estimating Revenues for the Organization. In many nonprofit organizations, this step must be accomplished by the chief financial officers before any budgeting begins at

[18] Vann L. Seawell, *Hospital Financial Accounting: Theory and Practice,* (Chicago: Hospital Financial Management Association, 1975), pp. 141–142.

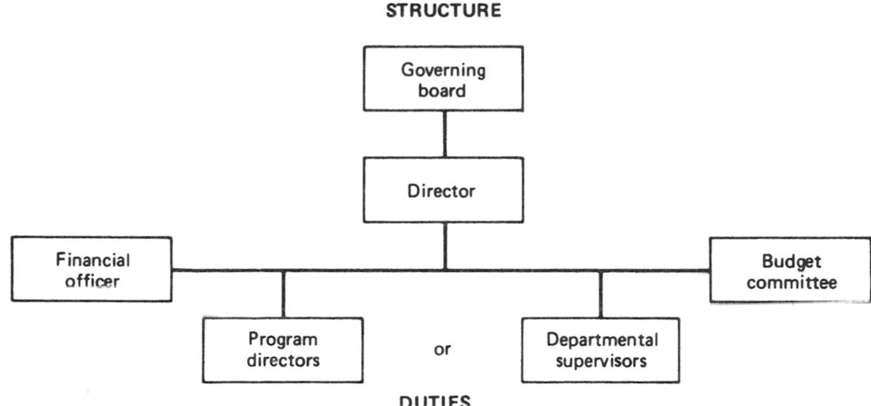

DUTIES

Governing Board
Makes policy decisions affecting the budget (with director)
Ultimate responsibility for budget
Final review authority

Director
Oversees development of budget guidelines
Makes policy decisions affecting the budget (with governing board)
Reviews and approves consolidated budget
Submits budget to governing board

Chief Financial (or Budget) Officer
Coordinates budget development
Issues budget guidelines and manuals
Reviews and consolidates department or program budgets

Program Director or Departmental Supervisor
Prepares detail budgets, in accordance with established procedures and guidelines
Assists in any needed revision to detail budget
Operating responsibility for program or department budget

Exhibit 35.7. Sample budget structure and assignment of duties

the individual unit level. One major reason for this is that many units, whether they are departments or programs, do not fund themselves or only do so partially. For example, university departments are largely funded by tuition revenues and endowment earnings, which are centrally collected. They only partly fund themselves—through grants, for example.

Besides preparing overall revenue estimates, decisions need to be made by upper management concerning issues such as the following: (1) what level of services to provide, (2) what to charge for services rendered, (3) how to obtain other funds needed to support these services, and (4) how to allocate these funds among programs or departments. Even revenue-earning departments, such as direct patient care units in hospitals, will need information of this sort for preparing their own budgets.

It is generally best to have the organization determine its revenues first, on an overall basis, and then to have individual units budget their expenditures to meet these revenues. This gives the units initial direction in preparing the budget. It also avoids the extra iteration that would be needed were the organization to have units prepare their individual expense budgets first and then cause them to be revised because of lack of available funds. Initial revenue estimates should, however, be subject to change based upon responses from unit heads.

Personnel Compensation

1. Breakdown by type of compensation
   Salaries
   Social Security
   Benefits, etc.
2. Breakdown by employee type
   Professional staff
   Skilled support staff
   Clerical staff
   Part-time, voluntary, and other
3. Percentage allocation of employee time
   Across department
   Across program (or function)

Supplies and Other Expenses

1. Supplies used directly in providing client services
2. Other supplies
3. Other expenses

Capital Expenditure Items

Exhibit 35.8. Worksheets for budget purposes

A very small organization, such as a performing arts company, may find it very difficult to project its revenues over the next year. In this case it may estimate different revenue levels on a best-case, worst-case basis and ask its programs to budget and make plans for activity at several different levels. This is sometimes called *step budgeting.*

Other organizations may omit the step of centrally estimating revenues entirely, if they are divided into units that are independent of each other and are responsible for generating all of their own revenue sources and balancing their own budgets. This approach, which some people call putting ''every tub on its own bottom,'' is used by some large universities that are divided into major schools, such as undergraduate education, business, law, medicine, and so on.

(ii) Preparing Budgets by Responsibility Center. The responsibility unit receives from the central budget officers estimates of its level of activity and its expected revenues. The unit may or may not need to supplement this information with its own estimates. For example, a nursing department in a hospital usually receives an estimate of the number of patients it will have to care for in the upcoming year and of the revenues this will generate. It will generally need to add little to these estimates. However, a ballet company that is part of a larger performing arts center may only get notice of the funds it can be expected to receive from the center for purposes of general administration. In addition, it needs to estimate how many productions it will give, how many paying customers it will have, what prices it will charge, and what its revenues from performances will be.

Budgeting expenditures is the next step. The individual unit will want to use budget worksheets in preparing its expenditure estimates. Exhibit 35.8 lists the types of worksheets that might be used. Most nonprofit organizations will require the most detail in regard to personnel expenses, since this usually constitutes the great majority of budgeted costs. Worksheets by type of compensation and type of employee will often be used. If employees tend to divide their time between different departments or programs, a separate worksheet showing how their time is allocated should be drawn up, in conjunction with other units that use the same employee(s).

Supplies should be classified as to whether or not they are used directly in providing client service. Direct expenses can be determined based on the estimated level of client service to be rendered. Examples of this would be food service for hospital patients, tickets for theater patrons, or handout materials to students in a university. Other supplies expenses, and overhead-type costs such as rent and utilities, will necessarily be estimated in a more judgmental fashion or will be based on historical costs. Budget units in a large organization may also be expected to prepare a capital expenditures budget.

When preparing expense budgets, responsibility units need to assess how their costs vary with the level of service they provide. Many of these will be fixed over a large range of activities. Most overhead, and many professional salary costs, are examples of this. Some costs will vary directly with the level of activity. Many costs will remain, however, that are fixed over a short period or for limited changes in activity, but vary if the time frame is longer or the activity changes more pronounced. This often applies to personnel costs. As an example, a hospital may add nursing staff if hospital volume increases by more than 20% but may decide to work existing staff overtime until that point is reached. Universities do not normally hire or fire teaching staff during the course of an academic year, but they may have more leeway to do so at the end of the year. In such cases, it is to the responsibility unit's advantage to know how and when its costs will vary according to its level of activity.

As far as possible, the unit's budget reports should specify the following:

- *Revenues.* By source, type, and, if applicable, accompanied by estimates of the physical units of service (e.g., museum visits, patient care days) that will produce these revenues
- *Expenses.* Salaried expenses, supplies, overhead expenses, and capital expenditure
- *Output measures.* Estimates of the physical units of service that will be provided
- *Unit costs.* Direct costs per unit of service should be estimated and reported. Indirect costs of the responsibility center may also be allocated across the different services provided, to provide a "full-cost" figure for provision of a unit of service. Reviewers should be able to compare these unit costs to the unit prices that are being charged for these services. These price estimates should be obtainable from the revenue side of the budget.

This is an ideal to aim for, not a necessary state of affairs. If outputs are difficult to identify and measure, unit costs cannot be devised. This might indicate the need, however, for further thought on how to measure what the responsibility center is doing.

(iii) Preparing A Consolidated Budget. In this step, the central budget committee or financial officer receives all of the detail responsibility center reports and combines them into a consolidated budget for the organization as a whole. During this consolidation the central budget authority ensures that (1) a proper balance between revenues and expenses is maintained for the organization as a whole, (2) the stated objectives and planned activities of the responsibility centers do not conflict with one another, and (3) the budget is consistent with the organization's long-run strategic and financial objectives.

This can entail a lengthy revision and review process. Exhibit 35.9 reprints a suggested budget calendar for a hospital. Note that about six weeks (May 15 to June 25) are allowed

Date	Participants	Activity
May 1	Administrator, budget officer, and department heads	Specification of general assumptions and objectives; general discussion of budgetary program
May 8	Budget officer and department heads	Discussion of assumptions, departmental objectives, and planning procedures
May 15 to June 15	Budget officer and department heads individually	Projection of departmental plans
June 25	Department heads and budget officer	Submission of initial drafts of departmental budgets
July 1 to July 10	Budget officer and budget committee	Coordination of departmental budgets; review and amendment of the initial drafts
July 15 to July 25	Budget officer and department heads individually	Reprojections of departmental plans
August 1	Department heads and budget officer	Submission of revised drafts of departmental budgets
August 5 to August 10	Budget officer and budget committee	Review and approval of reprojected departmental budgets
August 15	Budget officer	Submission of coordinated budget to administrator
August 20 to August 25	Administrator and budget officer	Review of budget and preparation for presentation to governing board
September 1 to September 15	Administrator, budget officer, and governing board	Presentation and review of budget
September 20	Governing board	Approval of budget
October 1	All hospital personnel	Begin new fiscal year operations under approved budget

Source: L. Vann Seawell, *Hospital Financial Accounting: Theory and Practice.* (Chicago: Hospital Financial Management Association, 1975); p. 143.

Exhibit 35.9. A sample budget calendar for a hospital

for doing the detail work of preparing departmental budgets. However, it is almost two more months (until August 15) until a coordinated budget is finally approved and formally presented to the top administrator! (After that, of course, comes further review by the governing board.)

One issue that may arise at this point is whether or not to allocate organizational overhead expenses to responsibility centers. These are not controllable expenses for heads of these centers and therefore do not need to appear in the budget. Some administrators, however, want to know the full costs of each of their departments—possibly for purposes of pricing. They may therefore decide to allocate these costs in this manner. If this is done, these allocated costs should be listed separately on the budget and should not be used to evaluate the budget performance of heads of responsibility centers.

Another allocation issue concerns ''service centers'' in the organization. Clients of a service center are other responsibility centers in the organization itself. An example would be a data processing facility in a university. In similar instances in business, a service center is allowed to charge other organizational units a transfer price for services rendered and include it as revenue in its own budget. For the responsibility center manager who uses the service, it is considered a controllable cost and included in his or her budget. This is a useful tool in controlling the organization's use of the resources of a service center and can easily be adapted to nonprofit organizations that have such units.

(iv) Reviewing and Revising The Budget. As Exhibit 35.9 indicates, the final consolidated budget still requires approval by the organization's top administrators and finally by the governing board. It is still possible, in a minority of cases, that major budget revisions at the program or departmental level will be needed as a result of these reviews.

(v) Obtaining Final Approval. This is given by the governing board. Once final approval is obtained, everyone should have had his or her proper say in its development and should be ready to carry it out operationally.

(e) Phase 5: Budget Control

(i) Issuing Budget Control Reports. Budgetary control reporting in nonprofit organizations is very similar to what it is in profit-oriented organizations. Heads of responsibility units should normally receive monthly reports on their unit's performance versus budget. These reports should compare monthly and year-to-date actual against budget amounts. Both financial statistics and nonfinancial measures of the unit's activity should be presented.

One line item may appear on a nonprofit budget report that a business would not use. This entry would record *encumbrances,* which are funds committed by the unit for a specific purchase but not yet spent. Encumbrance reporting occurs in organizations that are especially concerned about their accountability for the use of externally provided funds. Encumbrances may be of use when there is a specific amount of cash that must be spent, for whatever reason, in a given period. It is used frequently by government bodies that have this sort of legal restriction. Some hospitals and quite a few universities also use it. If handled properly, it adds a measure of further control over cash disbursements. It is subject to abuse, however. One college library system, for example, systematically reduced the budgets of departments that had funds still encumbered, but not actually expended, at the end of the fiscal year. Many of these funds actually represented normal purchase orders for books that would not be paid for until delivery two or three months later. Moreover, these payments were made by a centralized purchasing group and not by department heads. The proper response to these encumbrances would simply have been to use them to improve the library's cash budgets, instead of penalizing department heads having no control over the actual payments of these funds.

(ii) Reviewing Reports and Analyzing Variances. This step is performed in detail by the head of the responsibility center but also by financial officers and administrators higher up in the organization.

The quality of the initial budget determines the quality of the review of variances that can be performed at this point. A department or program should be able to measure its outputs and the direct costs of providing a unit of output. This permits it to break any variances reported into two parts: (1) that part due to its offering more or less service than what was originally budgeted (called the volume variance) and (2) that part due to either reasons of efficiency or unplanned changes in input prices. In some instances, it may be possible to separate out these efficiency and price variances. Special service units in hospitals, for example, may do this where their work permits the establishment of a system of standard costs and times. In general, however, a nonprofit organization will do well if it can answer the following questions: Are we spending more (or less) than expected because we are doing more (or less) work? Or are there internal reasons for the variance that we need to examine more closely?

(iii) Revising Budgets and Activities. Variance analysis may show that an organization or responsibility center needs to modify its original budget and to cut back (or expand) its previously planned activities. Unit measures and precise budget information continue to be of use at this point, since they help answer this basic question: If we cut back activity X by Y units, how much will it cost in revenues, and how much will it save in expenditures? (An opposite phrasing would apply to an expansion in services.)

Nonprofit budgets are often treated as though they were inflexible once established. In cases in which funds come from endowments or external sources, this is partly true, at least for a given year. Even in these instances, though, the organization has some choice over what services to offer and where to target them. This is especially the case with nonprofit organizations that offer specific client services, which they can vary somewhat and for which they get at least partial payment from the clients themselves. Even a membership organization may be able to obtain the consent of its members in modifying a service it no longer considers useful. The budget, then, should be considered not just as a planning tool but also as a means of identifying needs for change and making the changes in a timely manner.

(f) Afterword: A Note on Cash and Capital Budgeting. Many nonprofit organizations fail to pay much attention to either cash budgeting or capital budgeting, even though both of these tools can benefit them just as much as they benefit businesses. Moreover, cash and capital budgeting procedures are largely transferable from business to the nonprofit environment.

(i) Cash Budgeting. A cash budget should be easy to derive if an organization has done a thorough job in preparing its operating budget. What the treasurer needs to add to this is any necessary information about projected capital purchases, interest payments or

receipts, or other nonoperating transactions that involve inflows or outflows of cash. Cash receipts are generally more difficult than disbursements to predict in the cash budget, since they often come in erratically at nonprofit organizations. For example, grants often arrive long after work on the grant project has commenced, and many grant-related disbursements have already been made. However, universities may receive revenues in the form of tuition at the beginning of a budget period and need to plan how to allocate these funds over the course of a year. Organizations such as hospitals, which are recompensed for specific client services, will need to watch their collections statistics in the same way that businesses watch their accounts receivable. (In fact, because they have many payers of varying reliability, hospitals often face collection difficulties that businesses would not envy.) However, expenses are usually more predictable than revenues, since they go for the most part to salaried employees who are working in fairly stable activities.

(ii) Capital Budgeting. For at least three reasons, nonprofit organizations have difficulties in making rational capital expenditure decisions. The first difficulty is one of evaluation. A nonprofit organization is unable to measure the payoff from a given capital investment alternative in terms of profit but must instead view it in terms of social utility. This is a vague measure and difficult to apply analytically. It also serves as an invitation for groups within society to express their opinions on just what this social utility is. It is not surprising that nonprofit organizations with substantial invested capital—hospitals, for example—face many external pressures and regulatory requirements when they make major capital investment decisions.

The second difficulty concerns their source of funds for capital investments. These organizations do not have equity, and only the largest and most established of them can use debt financing. Consequently, most of them rely on bequests, grants, and fund-raising drives to accumulate the funds needed for capital acquisitions. These fund sources are unpredictable as to timing or amount, their use is often restricted, and they generally cannot be tapped continuously. If they are not available at a given moment, the organization may be forced to abandon or defer expenditures it considers to be of prime importance.

The third difficulty results from traditionally inadequate nonprofit accounting practices for long-term investments. One especially faulty practice was that, until recently, most nonprofit organizations did not record depreciation of long-term assets, either externally or for internal use. As a result, many of them severely underspent on capital maintenance activities, with a resulting decline of their fixed asset base. Universities were prime examples of this, often eventually having to spend badly needed operating funds to repair deteriorating facilities. The use of a separate plant and equipment fund was supposed to have provided a means for nonprofit organizations to maintain their fixed assets. In fact, it often has failed to do so. Plant funds are notorious for being underfunded, since nonprofit organizations often find more urgent uses for their money. Even when the funds are carefully maintained, however, organizations often fail to account for inflation and fund only the historical costs of their fixed assets, not the current replacement costs.

These difficulties all touch on the capital budgeting process to the extent that they affect the validity of the figures involved. It also means that the uncertainty surrounding the capital budget is likely to be higher in a nonprofit organization than in a business. It does not mean, however, that capital budgeting ideas and techniques developed for businesses should not be employed in nonprofit organizations. In fact, the more that they are employed, the better their capital allocation decisions will be.

35.5 TOOLS FOR USE IN NONPROFIT BUDGETING.

This discussion is divided into two parts. The first part concentrates on accounting and budgeting techniques that were developed originally for business but that can be applied usefully by many nonprofit organizations, as well. The second part discusses tools that either were developed for the nonprofit sector or have been used extensively by nonprofit organizations.

All of these techniques are described in greater depth elsewhere in this book. The purpose of this discussion is to indicate what these tools are and how they can be applied to nonprofit organizations. Since many of them are infrequently used by the nonprofit sector, we will also describe the obstacles to their use and ways of overcoming such obstacles.

(a) Tools Borrowed from Business.

The following five tools are the most important to effective nonprofit budgeting:

1. Responsibility center accounting.
2. Variable costing and flexible budgeting.
3. Standards for cost and performance.
4. Work measurement techniques.
5. Time reporting.

(i) Responsibility Center Accounting.

This is the most fundamental of all budgeting tools. No budget will work unless individuals are assigned the responsibility for preparing and managing individual portions of the budget. Our earlier description of the nonprofit budgeting process would be worthless without responsibility accounting.

Nevertheless, many nonprofit organizations do not have well-developed responsibility centers, and they develop a budget for the organization as a whole that is based largely on guesswork. In some cases, the reason for this may be a conventional attitude that a nonprofit organization does not need to plan its use of financial resources in the way that a business does. A more fundamental reason is that, in many nonprofit organizations, relationships are not defined clearly, and responsibilities are not assigned in a definite manner.

These obstacles can be overcome to a great extent by a program planning process that identifies what the organization's services are and that permits the assignment of responsibilities for carrying out these services. Normally, if different services can be identified and tracked separately, there will be a corresponding improvement in the organization's ability to plan the use of its resources. In general, as nonprofit organizations grow, they see a greater need for responsibility center accounting. Hospitals, for example, accept this concept without much ado.

Nonprofit organizations can often make use of the business concepts of expense centers, revenue centers, and even profit centers on occasion. A university's admissions office, for example, may be an expense center because it has no direct sources of revenue but incurs expenses in processing applications that can be directly measured and controlled. The fund-raising arm of the university might be a revenue center, in a manner analogous to a corporation's marketing department. The university may also decide to run certain of its activities, such as its bookstore or athletic events, at a profit. These functions may then be evaluated as profit centers.

Another useful concept involves "mission centers" and "service centers." Mission centers participate directly in carrying out the organization's program services, whereas service centers principally render service to other responsibility centers in the organization. A data processing facility in a university was used previously as an example. Just as in business, a system of transfer prices can be set up whereby a service center charges mission centers for the services it provides them.

(ii) Variable Costing and Flexible Budgeting. These techniques may be used wherever a nonprofit organization (1) experiences measurable variations in its level of activity and (2) can isolate costs or revenues that vary directly with activity levels. This need not apply to all of the organization but can be used with specific responsibility units. Examples are food service in universities and hospitals, costs of processing applications or other paperwork, patient care revenues in hospital wards, or fees for on-line computer searches in libraries. Many nonprofit organizations can probably use variable-budgeting techniques in at least part of their operations. The major obstacle to their widespread use has probably been a lack of ingenuity in measuring the volume of services being provided and in identifying elements of the cost structure that vary with volume.

(iii) Standards for Cost and Performance. Organizations that develop variable-costing methods may eventually be able to establish standards for costs and for individual performance. Except for larger nonprofit organizations, sophisticated standard cost systems such as those seen in business will probably not emerge. Wherever unit costs of providing a service can be obtained, however (serving a meal, for instance, or processing a form), the current costs can be compared against historical costs of performing the same task.

(iv) Work Measurement. In some repetitive activities, it is possible to go a step further and perform engineering studies of the time it should take to perform an operation. Routine clerical work can often be measured in this way. Hospital associations have used work measurement studies to develop "relative value units" that attempt to compare the resources (both material and labor) that go into one medical operation versus another. A tonsillectomy, for example, may consume only three relative value units, and an appendectomy may use up nine. Many hospitals use these "relative value units" in budgeting their activities.

(v) Time Reporting. Personnel costs form an overwhelming portion of most nonprofit budgets. Very commonly, these costs are due to the services of professionals. These services are costly, and it therefore makes sense that the organization budget the time of these professionals with great care. The time of many professionals, though, is hard to predict, as it is highly variable in nature and divided among a number of tasks. The only way to obtain proper information on how they use their time is through time reporting. Profit-making organizations that use highly paid professionals, such as legal and accounting firms, have all developed time reporting systems. The same can be done with physicians in hospitals, professors in universities, and other professionals elsewhere in the nonprofit sector.

All of the last three tools mentioned—cost and performance standards, work measurement, and time reporting—have met with much resistance in nonprofit organizations because they measure individual performance very explicitly. Professionals especially tend to resist being subjected to measurement methods. This resistance often prevails in the nonprofit environment, where there is no overriding concern about profits or efficiency.

Most nonprofit administrators need to keep their professionals and can only implement budgeting tools to the extent that they can obtain professional support for their efforts.

(b) Tools Used Extensively in Nonprofit Organizations. This section discusses the following tools:

- Programming, planning, and budgeting (PPB)
- Zero-based budgeting (ZBB)

(i) Programming, Planning, and Budgeting. Programming, planning, and budgeting was introduced in the federal government in the 1960s and soon became the mandated budgeting procedure. State and local governments began to use this system, as did some private nonprofit organizations. A voluminous literature sprang up around PPB. Despite all the fanfare, or perhaps because of it, PPB proved very difficult to implement in government, and it was generally discarded by the early 1970s.

Program budgeting systems such as PPB are described in another chapter in this book, so we will not discuss their workings here. Programming, planning, and budgeting basically failed, however, for two reasons: (1) It represented a vast improvement in terms of defining policies and objectives but failed to provide a means by which to translate these into effective operating budgets; and (2) expectations for it were too high. It was supposed by many organizations to provide a ready-made cure for their budgeting ills, without any accompanying need for them to undergo deeper structural changes.

The concepts of program planning and budgeting, however, continue to be of great potential use for nonprofit organizations. The budget process described in this chapter includes PPB phases. The difference is that these phases are no longer viewed as being part of a formal method such as PPB. Rather, they should be developed by each organization to meet its practical needs.

(ii) Zero-Based Budgeting. In many respects, ZBB is the ideological successor to PPB. Like PPB, it has been adopted most readily by government organizations, is a highly formalized process, and is receiving a lot of attention. It has met much resistance when being implemented and can be very time consuming if included as part of the annual budgeting procedure. It has yet to be proved as a workable method.

Zero-based budgeting is currently used most in the governmental, instead of the private, nonprofit sector. Some variant of ZBB—one that is not too time-consuming or tedious—could well help nonprofit organizations solve some of their problems in translating program services into budget terms. An organization with a program structure could use ZBB to identify the costs of providing varying amounts of service in a program area and could thereby judge more precisely the point at which benefits from expanded program services no longer justified the added costs of providing them. An organization with a departmental structure may be able to have its departments break out their program services in the form of separate identifiable ''packages.'' A formal, organization-wide ZBB system may be too much for most nonprofit organizations to handle, however.

SOURCES AND SUGGESTED REFERENCES

Beiner, Stanley C., ''Budgeting in Not-for-Profit Organizations,'' *CMA Magazine* (Canada), vol. 61, no. 6, November–December 1987.

Garner, C. William, *Accounting and Budgeting in Public and Nonprofit Organizations: A Manager's Guide.* San Francisco: Jossey-Bass, 1991.

Gelatt, James P., *Managing Nonprofit Organizations in the 21st Century.* Phoenix: Oryx Press, 1992.

Greenfield, James M., *Fund-Raising: Evaluating and Managing the Fund Development Process.* New York: John Wiley & Sons, 1992.

Hayes, Robert D., and James A. Millar, "Measuring Production Efficiency in a Not-for-Profit Setting," *Accounting Review,* vol. 65, no. 3, July 1990.

Jones, Robert A., "Taking the 'Guesstimates' Out of FTE Budgeting," *Nursing Management,* vol. 20, no. 2, February 1989.

Parry, Mark, Arthur E. Parry, and Paul W. Farris, "Marketing Budgeting in Nonprofit Hospitals," *Journal of Health Care Marketing,* vol. 11, no. 2, June 1991.

Shim, Jae K., Joel G. Siegel, and Abraham J. Simon, *Handbook of Budgeting for Nonprofit Organizations.* Englewood Cliffs, NJ: Prentice-Hall, 1996.

Stevens, Craig R., and Morton L. Sorkin, *Nonprofit Controller's Manual.* Boston, MA: Warren, Gorham & Lamont, 1996.

Vinter, Robert D., *Budgeting for Not-for-Profit Organization.* New York: Free Press, 1984.

Zietlow, John T., "Capital and Operating Budgeting Practices in Pure Nonprofit Organizations," *Financial Accountability & Management* (UK), vol. 5, no. 4, Winter 1989.

CHAPTER 36

BUDGETING IN HIGHER EDUCATION

Frederick J. Turk

President, ARAMARK Campus Services

36.1 INTRODUCTION. Institutions of higher education in the United States include colleges and universities both public and private, large and small, and single and multicampus. There are over 3,400 community colleges, four-year colleges, and universities. The 1980s have been a period of growth for institutions. The 1990s, however, have seen the reversal of fortunes for many institutions. In the public sector, state and local appropriations for higher education have dwindled as the economy has suffered and the tax base has diminished in terms of its contribution to health, education, and welfare programs. In response to decreasing appropriations, many public institutions have had to raise tuition and fees substantially to generate sufficient resources to provide education and support services. Similarly, in the private sector the economic climate has made it more difficult for many students to pay the rapidly increasing tuition costs.

In the 1990s, institutions across the spectrum of higher education are experiencing important changes as a result of many important issues that are influencing their financial condition and their ability to accomplish their academic mission. Costs have continued to escalate. Private institutions in particular have faced the need to increase their student aid (funded by institutional dollars) in order to be competitive in attracting and retaining students. Plant additions and deferred maintenance must be addressed if the institution is to have facilities that attract students. Investment earnings have tended to decline, which has reduced available revenues to support operations. Salaries for faculty and staff continue to escalate rapidly reflecting competitive market conditions.

Because of this cost push, institutions have continued to increase tuition and fees. There has been an increasing backlash of public opinion regarding the continuing increases in tuition. It is clearly no longer acceptable to just pass along cost increases to students in the form of ever higher tuition and fees. As a result, institutions are examining their activities carefully to determine what they can do without. Colleges and universities have followed corporate America by instituting downsizing programs to reduce costs and shift resources to higher priority activities. Many institutions have realized that "they cannot be all things to all people" and have responded accordingly by reducing or eliminating programs so they can concentrate scarce resources on fewer programs of excellence. This is often referred to as *growth by substitution.*

The result is that institutions of higher education are finding it necessary to apply sound management principles and to establish support systems to help college and university leadership to address these issues. One fundamental system that continues to get increasing scrutiny and is going through change is the budget system. This chapter will discuss the budgeting methodologies used by colleges and universities.

36.2 RESOURCE MANAGEMENT—BUDGETING IN CONTEXT.

The management of institutional resources is complex in colleges and universities. There is no ''bottom line'' or ''earnings per share'' that drives management to make decisions about how resources will be used. Rather, the substitute for these drivers is institutional mission, goals, and objectives. The budget is a device that represents how the college or university has decided to use its resources. If prepared properly, it provides the means for accountability to assess results, which is the bottom line for which the institution exists.

(a) Role of Budgeting in Higher Education.

A budget is a comprehensive operating plan expressed in terms of dollars, that reflects institutional goals, objectives, and priorities for a stated period of time. It formally assigns responsibility for organizational activities to an individual who can be held accountable for performance. The budget represents the estimated cost of carrying out planned activities and identifies the planned means of financing these activities.

A budgeting process or system is necessary for any enterprise where needs and wants in terms of resources to carry out activities are unlimited. The inevitable conflict of decision making occurs because in most cases resources are limited. Further, colleges or universities face other constraints and uncertainties, for examples, declining traditional college age student population and reduced earnings of endowment and other funds, which will influence the future availability of resources. The budgeting process helps management examine carefully organizational operations, resolve competing demands, and document how resources will be used. Subsequently, the budget serves as a fundamental control device that highlights for management where positive or negative variances have occurred. Thus, management is able to assess the impact of variances and take appropriate action.

A budgeting process in colleges and universities also serves as a means of communicating policies, priorities, commitments, and needs. The budget communicates the focus of the institution because it reflects the way resources are allocated. In essence, the budget process converts institutional rhetoric to action.

Budgeting is an integral part of the management cycle, which is composed of the following four elements:

1. *Planning.* The process of developing an institutional vision and determining the mission, goals, and objectives that should be employed to accomplish the vision. The fundamental question addressed in the planning process is ''What are we now and what should we be in the future?'' Planning precedes the budget process and provides an essential frame of reference that should be used in budgeting.
2. *Budgeting.* Translates the institution's plan into specific financial terms. The budget represents decisions made by management to apply resources (i.e., people, facilities, and money) to carry out strategies and tactics that will accomplish the goals and objectives contained in the plan.
3. *Operations and control.* The process of actually applying resources according to the budget and performing the activities for which the individual is responsible. Control involves the process of ongoing monitoring by management by comparing actual performance to plan. Such a comparison involves examining the use of all resources (i.e., people, facilities, and finances) and determining if progress is being made versus plan.

4. *Evaluation.* The process of after-the-fact review and assessment at the end of the activity or at the end of a period of time such as a fiscal year. The evaluation process involves examining accomplishments and determining whether activities going forward should be modified. In essence, the process of evaluation provides opportunities for resource reallocation. Since the budget establishes the course that the institution will follow to achieve its mission, goals, and objectives, it is essential that it be prepared carefully and that it be used as a management tool to guide future decision making.

(b) Common Budget Maladies. When looking at the budget process, it is helpful to understand what is considered poor or ineffective budgeting. There are a number of common budget maladies that are problematic for institutions that are attempting to use their resources wisely.

- *Incremental budgeting.* Budgeting is often done incrementally such that last year's approved budget is assumed as the "base budget." In essence this assumption accepts as a given that the institution's academic and support programs will continue as before without change. The emphasis in the budgeting process is devoted to proposed additions or changes in the budget base or new program proposals. With all analysis focused on increments, little or no attention is given to the rest of the budget. Frequently, when adjustments are necessary to reduce the budget because of a cut in the state appropriation or some other expected reduction in revenue, the institution must rely on across-the-board cuts, that is, a fixed percentage cut (10%) for every department. This is because the incremental budgeting process does not lend itself to priority setting that will guide action when unfortunate circumstances occur.
- *Insufficient planning.* Too often, budgets are prepared without the benefit of a strategic plan being in place. The institution is content to balance the budget without looking in the future to understand the implications of short-range budget decisions. Individuals preparing the budget and subsequently reviewing and approving the budget do not have a context within which to make rational decisions regarding the use of resources. As a result, broader institutional goals, objectives, strategies, and tactics get lost in the maze of the many individual needs of the departments submitting budgets. While departmental needs must be paramount in deciding how resources will be used, such local decisions should not be made without considering overall institutional goals and objectives. Variances from institution-wide goals and objectives should be scrutinized carefully in reviewing and approving budgets.
- *Ad hoc process.* The budget process in some institutions operates in an ad hoc fashion. The role and responsibilities of different participants in the budget process are unclear. As a result, there are gaps or overlaps in the responsibilities of preparer, reviewer, advisor, and decision maker. There is lack of communication among the chief players in the budget process. Often there is insufficient discussion occurring, lack of information sharing, priorities and needs are not understood, and in some cases the budget is forced to balance based on erroneous assumptions. The result may be that the governing board is misinformed about the true financial budget results that are expected. In some institutions, budgets are still prepared centrally in the finance function. This lack of participation assures that those affected assume no ownership for the budget and limited responsibility for the results at the end of the year.
- *Noncomprehensive.* The budget considers only unrestricted funds (state appropria

tions in the public sector of higher education) and does not include restricted or plant funds. As a result, the total economic picture of the institution is not considered. Those involved in reviewing and approving the budget never can get a comprehensive view of the financial resources for which the institution is fiscally responsible. Budgeting as practiced by some colleges and universities is cost based with much of the attention directed toward budgeting expenses. Revenues are budgeted last and are often applied as a balancing figure. Under those conditions, there is a risk that the budget is prepared based on revenue assumptions that may not be achievable. As a result, the management of revenues is not given sufficient attention in the budget process.

- *Missing control mechanisms.* Control is a fundamental management process. Some institutions do not effectively use the budget during the year to manage their revenues and expenditures. They do not regularly perform budget analysis by comparing actual to budget and conducting budget reviews with departments. Monthly or quarterly budgets are not prepared nor are projections to year end prepared to give management at all levels a sense of where the institution stands compared to budget.
- *Late budget preparation.* Preparing the budget in May or June (or even in September before the fall enrollment is known) if the fiscal year begins on July 1, is entirely too late to effectively make resource decisions. Institutions determine tuition rates as early as December and make faculty commitments in the late winter or early spring. These and other commitments are made before the budget is prepared in some institutions. Thus, many economically significant commitments are made before the actual budgeting process begins. This removes an important prerogative from management and the governing board in deciding how resources should be used in light of the strategic plan.
- *Little flexibility provided.* The budget process often does not include considering ''what if'' senarios should revenue be less than anticipated or certain costs be higher than expected. Thus, there are no fall-back positions identified that were established as part of the budget process that management could apply during the year to offset these unforeseen circumstances by adjusting the budget.

(c) Characteristics of Effective Budgeting. Budgeting should be a year-round process. The budget preparation phase should be based on a long-range strategic plan that identifies the objectives and priorities of the institution, considers appropriate resource reallocation needs, and provides for a continuous review of strategic direction as resources are applied. The budget should consider all operations and activities for which the institution is fiscally responsible to include operating (unrestricted and restricted) and plant needs.

The budget should fix responsibility for segments of the institution as well as activities to be performed. It is essential that the budget preparation process be participative involving all individuals that will be responsible for execution of planned activities.

The budget calendar should be formally established with key dates identified. The budget should be prepared early, long before the fiscal year begins, and commitments are made to hire faculty, increase salaries and benefits, and raise tuition and fees. By preparing the budget early, there will be enough time for all—preparers, management, and the governing board to review, evaluate, and decide on the appropriate allocation of resources. Since the budget should represent how institutional resources will be applied, it provides the single most important device for the governing board to perform its fiduciary oversite responsibility.

The budget should serve as the fundamental control mechanism used by management and the governing board to assess progress in achieving institutional goals and objectives. To work well, the college or university requires an effective financial accounting system that will record, classify, and summarize economic events in a timely and accurate fashion as compared to the institutional budget. The system should be able to report budget versus actual status so that users responsible for organizational entities and management can determine their financial condition.

(d) Intramural Funding Models. *Intramural funding* is a term used to describe the process by which management and the governing board allocate resources among divisions, schools, and departments of an institution. The intramural funding philosophy applied by an institution is embedded in the budgeting system used by the college or university. It sets the parameters for establishing responsibility for the following budgetary considerations:

- Should certain revenues and expenditures resulting directly from activities of budgetary units be their responsibility completely, partially, or not at all?
- Should certain revenues and expenditures that benefit the institution as a whole be allocated to benefiting budgetary units completely, partially, or not at all?

These budgetary considerations raise certain key issues such as, what revenue should be considered institutional funds and what if any should be retained by the budgetary units. Similarly on the expenditure side, the issue focuses on the issue of what services schools should be charged or credited for.

There are a number of intramural funding models at work in higher education today. Typically, these models are influenced by the unique characteristics of the institution, namely, the type of public or private institution (university, college, or community college), the institutional culture, management style, geographical location (single site or multicampus), age of institution, mission of the institution, and its financial status (healthy or distressed). While there are many variants of intramural funding models in colleges and universities, there are three classes of models that are the fundamental structure upon which all variants are based. The three classes of intramural funding models are as follows:

1. *Cost center model.* This is the traditional intramural funding philosophy that we see applied in most colleges and in many universities. In this model direct costs, which benefit budget units (divisions, schools, academic departments, and administrative and support departments) and are under their control are assigned to that unit. Thus, they will budget for all salaries and benefits of faculty and staff working in the budget unit plus other direct costs incurred such as, supplies, travel, and equipment.

   All revenues are the responsibility of senior management and are therefore budgeted centrally. The exception to this rule is that funds restricted by an outside donor are budgeted for the use of the benefiting budget unit.

   This model creates a budget process that is expenditure driven with little direct concern with revenue that might be generated. There is often substantial competition among units to preserve their base expenditure budget and to gain incremental funds to support inflation and new initiatives. Budget units are expected to live within their budget allocation. There is little incentive to use funds wisely. The incentive is to spend up to your budget or face the risk of losing funds next year because you underspent.

2. *Responsibility center model.* This is an intramural funding philosophy that is applied by many universities. This model is often referred to as "each tub on its own bottom" suggesting that divisions and schools of a university are expected to live within their own means. In this model, all direct costs and self-generated revenues of divisions and schools are attributed to the benefiting entities. All indirect costs and all or some central revenues are allocated equitably to divisions and schools.

   This model establishes clearly defined responsibility centers and requires each center to self-generate sufficient revenue to cover direct and indirect costs. Division heads or deans of schools have the decentralized responsibility to manage their resources effectively and make adjustments to the budget as necessary. The primary advantage of this model is that it provides an incentive to use resources wisely assuming there is an opportunity for rewards that benefit the division, school, and/or management. The disadvantage is that without careful leadership the model encourages those making money to demand access to "operating surplus" for program enhancement and salary increases with no responsibility for supporting the university as a whole. This model does, however, focus attention on those losing money and raises questions about their management performance and whether the university should continue to support the division or school. It may suggest that the division or school must be closed or restructured to come in at breakeven or some tolerable bandwidth of losses the university is willing and able to afford.

   The responsibility center model requires clear definitions as to what are self-generated revenues and the methodologies applied to allocate indirect costs and revenues to the benefiting divisions and schools. Attention must be given to whether the divisions and schools can retain fund balances and whether the excess earnings can be retained totally, partially, or not at all. A further complication that must be addressed relates to situations where there are budgeted deficits. Are funds loaned to help a school or is a grant (subvention) given to the school? If funds are loaned, over what period will they be paid back? If a grant, how long can the university continue to support the division or school? Where do the funds come from to provide for loans or grants to divisions or schools? These questions are important issues that must be addressed in the institutions long-range strategic plan and in their annual budget.

3. *Contribution model.* This is a philosophy that is applied by some colleges and universities. It is a newer approach to budgeting that is designed to support decentralized responsibility for performance but does not hold divisions, schools, or departments accountable for costs and revenues they do not control. They are responsible for their direct costs and their self-generated revenues. No allocations of central indirect costs are made to divisions, schools, or departments. Revenue-producing units are responsible for managing to a "contribution margin" (self-generated revenue less direct cost). The contribution margin, although different for each budget unit, should in the aggregate provide sufficient funds to pay for all central costs.

   The contribution model approach eliminates the need for complicated indirect cost allocation methodologies that are often subject to endless discussion. It focuses on holding the budget manager responsible for the use of resources he or she controls directly and for maximizing revenues that are self-generated. It fixes a contribution margin that is a target of performance built into the budget. The attempt is to encourage improved performance and to thereby ''ratchet up'' performance for every division, school, or department. This performance measure must be linked to the personnel evaluation and reward system if the proper incentive for excellence is to result. The contribution model philosophy in higher education budgeting fosters a culture of continuous improvement, which is essential in being a quality institution.

Each of these intramural funding models has positive and negative features. In developing a budget philosophy, it is necessary to recognize that the budget approach used should provide incentives that encourage management at all levels to use resources wisely to accomplish the mission, goals, and objectives of the division, school, or department as well as the institution as a whole. The system needs to encourage responsible behavior and provide rewards for enhanced revenues and controlled expenditures while providing quality services at planned levels.

(e) Gate-Control Budget Management. The cost structure of colleges and universities is dominated by a large proportion of fixed cost. For example, faculty contracts are issued before the budget year begins, which commits the institution to pay faculty salaries and benefits regardless of the number of students that actually enroll. As a result, it is difficult to reduce budgeted expenditures should actual revenues be less than planned or to wisely use excess revenues should an unexpected windfall occur. To prepare for such uncontrolled situations, it is important to build flexibility into the budget system that will permit management action to reduce or increase costs according to a predetermined plan.

The approach that is often used is called *ABC Budgeting.* In this budget approach, there are three budget scenarios that are developed that take into consideration alternative actions that management might take should revenue projections be less than or greater than originally planned. The three budget scenarios are as follows:

1. *''A'' budget.* The A-level budget assumes a pessimistic view of the financial operations of the institution. It assumes that revenues will be less than what is anticipated (e.g., 5% less) or that unusual or unplanned expenditures will be incurred. The A budget identifies minimum budget requirements by identifying items of expenditure, where cuts will be made should that be necessary. Such proposed cuts should be prioritized to facilitate action if required at a later date.
2. *''B'' budget.* The B-level budget represents the most likely scenario that the institution can expect. This is the detailed budget that is normally expected for the institution. The budget is developed in detail according to responsible budget unit.
3. *''C'' budget.* The C-level budget is an optimistic representation of what would occur should the institution enjoy revenues in excess of plan or expenditures that were less than anticipated. This budget identifies priority items that will be funded should additional budget dollars be available.

The A and C budgets operate off the B budget providing management with predetermined options for action that can be applied with minimal consultation and evaluation. In essence, the system applied focuses on identifying line items in the budget that are ''gate controlled'' such that they are not released or authorized for expenditure until a designated date or the occurrence of an event. The items identified in the A and C budgets are what are called *discretionary fixed costs,* which management can decide to spend or not to spend, as opposed to *committed fixed costs,* which are unavoidable and must occur once the institution opens its doors. By applying these multiple budget scenarios, management is able to better control expenditures through the budget. The budget becomes a ''live'' action system that is used to make adjustments that will effectively direct financial resources to achieve institutional priorities.

(f) Monthly Budgets. Most institutions of higher education prepare an annual budget and do not build up the budget in monthly increments. During the year, they manage their budget by comparing year-to-date actual to the annual budget. As a result, it is difficult to determine budget performance during the year. To compensate for the lack of monthly budgets, institutions recognize *encumbrances* along with actual to arrive at a net budget available. Encumbrances are legal commitments issued by the institution in the form of invoices and contracts. In essence, the financial accounting system is used to determine what remains to be spent as opposed to serving as a warning system that highlights expenditure patterns that are markedly different from that planned originally.

Monthly budgets should be prepared to establish the ability to measure expenditure progress versus the plan for the period. When this approach is used, the financial system can become a true ''control system'' that will identify where action by management is required.

36.3 ANNUAL BUDGETING. The process of budgeting in higher education involves a complex configuration of people, policies and procedures, computer systems, and the political system for determining how resources should be assigned to achieve institutional mission, goals, and objectives. The following sections describe the elements of a budgeting system for higher education. In some cases, forms and illustrations are provided to help the reader understand the flow of the budget process and the information that is required.

(a) Organization for Budgeting. The president (chancellor) is responsible for the preparation of the annual budget, its submission to the board of governors for final approval, and the execution of the budget on a day-to-day basis. He or she is usually assisted in carrying out his or her budget responsibilities by the vice-president for finance and administration, who is the chief budget officer. In some cases, the budget officer reports to the president. On occasion, the chief academic officer will also serve as the institutional budget officer.

The governing board is responsible for the final approval of the budget. The board is also responsible for reviewing performance reports provided by management during the year. With this information, the board can evaluate management performance and assess proposed changes to the budget. All proposed budget revisions that change the programs of the institution or total revenues or expenditures should be submitted through the president for approval by the board.

On occasion, there are committees established to review the budget and provide advice regarding the proposed allocation of resources.

These groups are part of the institution's governance process and may include faculty and/or student budget committees that provide their views regarding priorities for resource allocation. The president might establish an advisory committee that will provide guidance during the preparation, review, approval, and evaluation phases of the budget cycle. Its members should include the senior officers of the institution. Others may be added if deemed necessary. Ultimately, the president of a college or university is responsible for deciding how resources should be assigned and presenting recommendations to the governing board for approval.

Typically, the budget and finance committee of the board has responsibility for reviewing, approving, and monitoring the institution's budget. This board committee is involved at key intervals in the budget cycle.

(b) Budget Flow and Responsibilities. It is important to develop a defined flow of the budget process with the roles of the actors determined and understood by all involved. The following are the major components of the budget process:

- Developing budget assumptions
- Course identification and scheduling
- Budget preparation
- Budget review modification and approval

Exhibit 36.1 provides an overview description of a budget flow that is used by a college or university. The sections that follow describe each of the components in more detail.

(i) Developing Budget Assumptions. The president meets with the advisory committee to begin a dialogue regarding the start of the budgeting process. The purpose of this meeting is to (1) determine what information is necessary for effective budgeting, (2) identify major educational philosophies to be considered when budgeting, and (3) define the approach to be followed in preparing the budget.

The advisory committee members and in particular the budget officer consult with the college or university community for the purpose of obtaining their insights regarding assumptions and special concerns that should be considered during the budget cycle. The members of the academic community might include (1) the faculty senate budget committee, (2) student government, (3) alumni, (4) budget and finance committee of the governing board, (5) and other interested parties.

In preparation for the advisory committee meeting, the president and his budget officer should prepare an agenda that includes the following:

- Environmental changes that are affecting university operations
- Enrollment trends
- Budget-preparation guidelines
- Role of participants in the budget process

The meeting(s) with the advisory committee should result in the following being accomplished:

- Assignments given to committee members to evaluate specific questions or assumptions that must be considered
- Agreement regarding policy guidelines for budgeting
- Agreement as to institutional enrollment projections
- Identification of major assumptions to be used in developing the budget
- Identification of environmental factors and their impact

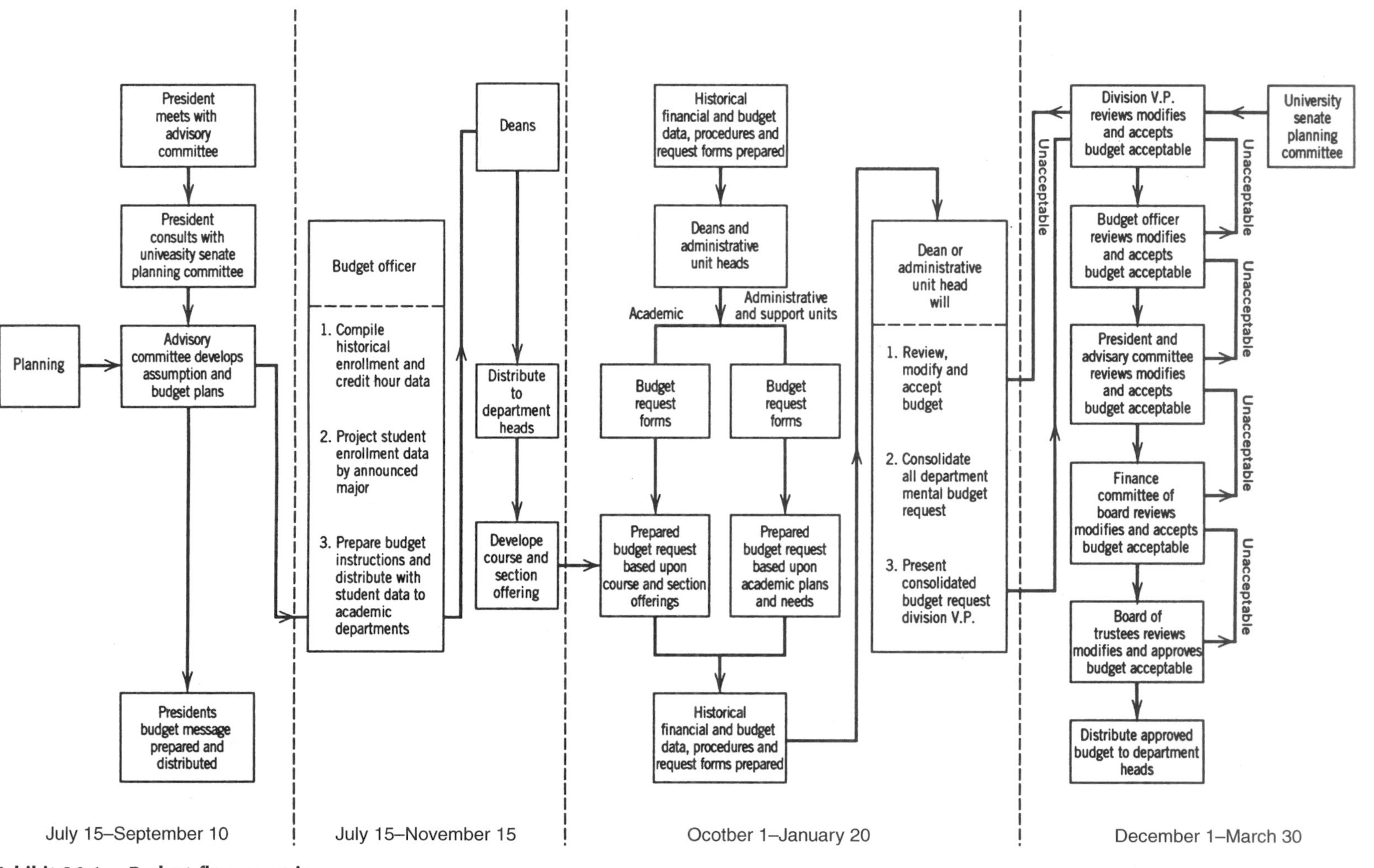

Exhibit 36.1. Budget flow overview

There will be numerous environmental factors that will influence the future of the institution. Environmental factors should be considered if the proposed budget is to reflect the conditions that are likely to influence the college or university in the years ahead. The budget officer should identify the key environmental factors facing the institution and assemble appropriate information that can be used in discussion during the meeting. Examples of environmental factors include the following:

External Factors

- Economic conditions
- High school graduation projections in recruiting areas
- College-going rates in high schools
- Trends of students attending private/public sector
- Financial aid available from government
- Comparative compensation statistics for faculty and staff
- Competitive tuition rates in private/public sector

Internal Factors

- Enrollment and changes in student inquiries and applications
- Changes in attrition rate
- Average class-size statistics
- Average faculty-load statistics
- Trends in student aid awarded

The committee will discuss these and other environmental factors to assess their expected impact on the institution and its budget. The conclusions drawn from this discussion will serve as the basis for comments included in the president's budget message.

The president prepares a budget message to communicate major budget policies, set forth key budget measures, establish the budget timetable, and identify the participants in the budget process. The budget message represents the formal start of the budget process and it sets the tone of the budget preparation exercise for the institution. The message should be short (perhaps three to five pages long) and should include the following four basic elements:

1. Introduction to budgeting—including a description of the accomplishments of the past year, a discussion of the need for the budget process to ensure that resources are applied to accomplish academic quality or other goals, economic factors such as inflation that are facing the institution, and perhaps some reference to financial projections that will frame the budget process this year
2. Overview of budget process—to give the campus an idea of the basic structure for budgeting, the timetable that will be followed, and who the participants will be as the preparation and review process proceeds
3. Anticipated institutional conditions—that should be considered such as the academic program and proposed changes that are being considered, enrollment expectations, and any major changes in the major sources of revenues and uses of funds

4. Key assumptions—that those preparing the budget should consider as they complete their budget requests. Examples might include inflation rates, benefit cost increases, and rates for certain central support functions that are direct charged.

(ii) Course Identification and Scheduling. The budget officer is responsible for compiling historical enrollment and credit-hour information. The registrar assists the budget officer to obtain the historical enrollment information and credit-hour distribution by school and department. The historical information required includes credit hours produced by semester for each course and section given by a department, for the two most recent years.

As part of the budget process, it is necessary to project student enrollment and credit hours. The device used to prepare such a projection is called the *induced course-load matrix* (ICLM). The ICLM is prepared to determine the typical percent distribution of historical enrollment and credit hours for majors taking courses in departments throughout the institution. The ICLM summarizes, by department, the credit hours that a particular major has taken during each of the prior semesters for which data is presented.

A sample ICLM is presented in Exhibit 36.2. This illustration presents the typical credit-hour distribution for all English majors. As shown, all freshmen English majors took 4,663 credit hours, of which 467 credit hours, or 10%, were in the English department. Another 378 credit hours, or 8%, were in the communications department, and so forth. With this information, projections of future enrollment demand can be made if key variables are identified (i.e., enrollment and number of majors). It should be noted that undeclared majors are typically identified as a separate group with their own historical course patterns. Another factor to be considered is the fact that historical patterns last year may change. Projections should be impacted accordingly.

The projections of enrollment and majors come from a number of sources. The registrar's office provides an estimate of the number of students presently enrolled who are anticipated to remain at the institution. The admissions office provides an estimate of the

Matrix
Budget Procedures
Sample Format

	Level of Student									
	Freshman		Sophomore		Junior		Senior		Graduate	
Department	Hrs.	%	Hrs.	%	Hrs.	%	Hrs.	%	Hrs.	%
MAJOR:										
English										
COLLEGE OF										
LIBERAL ARTS										
AND SCIENCES										
Art										
History										
Anthropology	275	6%								
Biology	280	6%								
Communications	378	8%							172	8%
English	467	10%	7,815	18%	1,652	34%	1,650	40%	1,583	78%
TOTAL	4,663	100%	4,341	100%	4,811	100%	4,162	100%	2,158	100%

Exhibit 36.2. Induced course load

number of transfer students by announced major and level. Admissions also projects the number of new freshmen by announced and undeclared major.

It is important for the budget officer to prepare instructions for academic departments to guide them in preparing their budget. The instructions should include items such as the following:

- Description of information provided for each department
- Listing of forms distributed
- Instructions for completing forms
- Discussion of the effect of projected enrollment on schools
- Key budget measures by school
- References to budget procedures that should be reviewed by the dean and department chairpersons

Examples of the forms that may be used to complete course identification and scheduling are as follows:

- *Departmental course and section offering.* This form is provided to academic departments for each semester with historical enrollment and credit hour information provided. This information is given to assist the department head in assigning the total anticipated credit hours for the department to courses and sections that are planned for each semester.
- *Semester faculty assignment plan.* This form is used to schedule the faculty necessary to staff all courses and sections identified on the previous form.
- *Departmental faculty requirements.* This form is used to summarize each semester's faculty assignments. The information provided will help determine how full-time faculty will be used for teaching, research projects, and released time assignments (such as curriculum committee or other assignment) and will help to identify the need for adjunct faculty and their expected assignments.

  It is also important for the budget officer to assemble budget information for at least two years prior to the year being budgeted. The finance office should assist in compiling the historical financial information on revenues and expenditures. This information should be provided on the budget request forms before distribution. The budget officer should also prepare budget instructions for administrative budget units. These instructions should contain most of the same information that was suggested for academic units but tailored to the unique conditions of an administrative function.

(iii) Budget Preparation. The department chairperson or unit head should prepare the departmental budget request for all current operating expenditures of the academic department or unit according to the budget policies and procedures provided earlier. It is necessary to also prepare a request for support services, which may entail communication with the service department to determine the budget cost that should be anticipated.

The preparation of the budget involves completing forms such as the following:

- *Departmental personnel—other.* This form is prepared for nonfaculty personnel in academic departments and for all personnel in administrative support departments.

Staff should be added to or removed from this form according to the needs of the budget unit and the budget resources available. The information provided should include name, title, Social Security number, current salary, and recommended salary.

- *Support service requirements.* This form should list the type of service requested, a description of the service needed, and the name of the individual making the request. It should be sent to the appropriate support service department (e.g., printing, computer services, central stores, building maintenance, requesting a priced quote for the proposed services). With this information returned to the budget unit, the department head can determine the expected cost for that item.
- *Schedule of restricted revenue by source.* This form is used to budget restricted purpose funds received from outside third parties with the requirement that they be used only for the purpose intended. It is necessary to indicate the source of the funds and budget their use this year or indicate that some portion will carry over to future years. A separate form may be used to indicate the budgeted intention to spend restricted funds.
- *Summary departmental budget request.* This form as the title implies is used to summarize the departmental budget request. Besides the salary, miscellaneous income, and other costs of operating the department, operating statistics should be provided in the summary request. Examples include employee count, full-time equivalent faculty, and credit hours produced. Budget measures calculated include average cost per credit hour and average cost per employee.

It is advisable for the department head to prepare a budget cover letter. This letter serves as a vehicle for the department to briefly communicate it goals, objectives, and priorities. It also provides the opportunity to communicate needs and changes included in the request.

As a separate initiative, it is necessary to develop the institutional revenue budget. The budget officer should prepare the revenue estimates for all sources of income. Revenue estimates should include tuition and fees as well as other sources of revenue such as gifts, grants, and endowment income. As school and vice-presidential budget requests are received, the budget officer should review his or her projections as well as any revenue projections appearing on the budget request forms to determine where adjustments may be appropriate.

(iv) Budget Review, Modification, and Approval. The division vice-president is responsible for reviewing the individual requests and a consolidation of the requests for the division that he or she is responsible for. Budget hearings may be held with department heads to answer questions, discuss alternatives to the request, and to agree with or reduce the request. A modified budget may be requested from the department head. This modified request will be reviewed again and after evaluation is accepted.

The budget officer is responsible for reviewing, modifying, and presenting the university summary budget to the president. The budget officer reviews the summary budget with major emphasis placed on determining that the proposed budget is appropriately addressing priorities established by the president in the budget message. The budget officer also focuses on adherence to the key budget measures developed for each school or vice-presidential area and the availability of institutional resources to satisfy the needs identified.

The budget officer with the support of and active participation of the president conducts budget hearings with each vice-presidential area. These hearings focus on the substance of the requests and the rationale that supports the budget requested. The president serves as the final decision maker as to the budget that will be accepted. Naturally, if the institution is a college the scope of budget hearings will involve fewer requests with less complexity that is inherent in a research institution or a university with a variety of professional schools.

The president may decide that the advisory committee should participate in the budget hearings. In this way, the senior officers of the institution will have the opportunity to assist the president in deciding needs and priorities for resource allocation.

The president should submit the final budget to the budget and finance committee of the governing board. It is likely that the president has met with the board earlier to brief them on the budget process and to seek their advice regarding certain major budget assumptions. Further, it is likely that certain budgetary decisions may have been addressed earlier because of the need to take action in announcing key decisions such as tuition and fee rates. Because there is a need to make those decisions in the context of the final or at least almost final budget, it is necessary to have the budget process accelerated so that sufficient information is available to assist the board in making informed decisions.

The president and the budget officer meet with the board to discuss the budget. The president should send the budget to the board with an accompanying budget letter that describes the budget and its key components. It should focus particularly on the key budget assumptions and the major activities that will be carried out to accomplish the institutional mission.

The governing board has the ultimate responsibility for approving the institution's budget. The board must determine that the proposed budget is directing resources to achieve the institution's mission goals and objectives. In performing this responsibility, the board should review the budget to ensure that sufficient resources are available to finance the level of expenditures needed to accomplish the objectives contained in the budget.

After the budget is approved, it is the responsibility of the budget officer to distribute the budget. The budget officer will need to meet with heads of budget units whenever there have been adjustments to the budget.

36.4 SUMMARY. The budget system in higher education involves heavy influence by the community. The formal institutional governance process identifies the key players who need to be involved in the budget-preparation process. The president is the key decision maker responsible for developing a vision for the institution and translating that vision into strategies and tactics, which are reflected in the budget. The governing board has ultimate fiduciary responsibility for deciding how resources will be allocated.

The budget-preparation process should follow a planned process that includes a time schedule that ensures that the budget is completed early enough before the beginning of the year. This will be important to ensure that information is available to support decisions on key actions such as setting tuition and fee policy and salary increments.

It is important that the final approved budget serve as a control mechanism to manage institutional activities during the year. Accordingly, it is important that budget reports are prepared and analyzed regularly to permit corrective action as necessary.

CHAPTER 37

BUDGETING IN THE HEALTH-CARE INDUSTRY*

Christopher S. Spence

Ernst & Young L.L.P.

37.1 OVERVIEW. Budgeting in the health-care industry has become increasingly important in recent years. This is primarily due to the reduced levels of government funding from the Medicare and Medicaid programs and outside pressures for cost containment from private industry and the public. These cost-containment measures have resulted in declining inpatient utilization and have forced hundreds of hospitals and health-care providers out of business across the country. Cost management is one of the keys to the long-term survival of many health-care providers.

Budgeting is the means through which resource allocation decisions are made among the many diverse, yet interdependent activities and programs of the health-care provider. The methods that an organization uses to create the budget will depend on the type and quality of information sources, the availability and sophistication of budgeting staff, and the importance that the organization places on the budgeting function.

Health-care budgeting is generally more complicated than budgeting in other industries. One reason is the lack of a uniform product. Many industries have consistent products that can be readily defined and costed to help develop a reliable budget. However, in health care, there are thousands of different illnesses and treatments. Even for the same illness, treatment patterns can be substantially different for different physicians or providers. Until standardized practice parameters are developed and refined, health care will remain an inexact combination of art and science.

Another difficulty that complicates health-care budgeting is the projection of net revenues. Depending on the location and type of service offered, health-care providers may have dozens of different payors and payment methods. Even with these complications, a high-quality and accurate budget can be created with the correct budgeting tools and methods. This chapter will provide you with the tools and methods to improve and refine your budgeting process.

Health-care budgeting, like that in other industries, is a complex process involving input

---

* The author gratefully acknowledges the following individuals who helped identify budgeting issues and review materials: *Hospital Budgeting:* James Allamian, Ernst & Young (Chicago, IL); *Physician Budgeting:* Kenneth Perlstein, Ernst & Young (Richmond, VA); Robin Hunter Ernst & Young (Boston, MA).

from many sources, extensive discussions, and detailed negotiations over long periods of time. It is also an evolutionary process, which must be modified as better tools and sources of information become available.

While it is unlikely that cost considerations will replace quality as the most important factor in an individual's choice of health-care provider, the cost of services will continue to increase in importance. In situations in which the perceived difference in quality is marginal or difficult to distinguish, individuals, businesses, and payors are beginning to choose the lower-cost health-care provider.

This chapter will concentrate on operations budgeting for two of the major health-care providers—hospitals and physicians. However, many of the concepts and methods that apply to these types of providers also apply to other areas of the health-care industry.

37.2 COST CONTROL.

Until the early 1980s, health-care providers were primarily paid through cost-based reimbursement systems, which allowed providers to expand and improve services without forcing them to closely monitor costs. Due to this and many other factors, both internal and external to the health-care industry, health-care expenses have historically increased rapidly. This rate of increase has been one of the highest of any industry.

(a) Factors Influencing Health-Care Inflation.

This chapter is not intended to give a comprehensive overview of the causes of health-care cost increases. However, it is important to understand some of the different cost pressures on the health-care industry. Some of these cost pressures can be controlled by health-care managers. Other pressures are due to the environment and are difficult or impossible for health-care providers to directly influence.

In addition, it is important to note that many of the *price increases* in the health-care industry are due to cost shifting and not due solely to expense increases. Health-care providers face insufficient payments from many government payors and increasing levels of bad debt from a growing uninsured population. As the percentage of the population that is paying the full price decreases in relation to the total patients, health-care providers must cost shift the shortfalls to the remaining payors. For example, in the State of Connecticut, the average hospital bill, during 1992, included charges that had been increased by 43% to cover government payment shortfalls and levels of uncompensated care.

(i) External Factors.

External factors are due to pressures from outside the health-care provider and generally cannot be controlled. These factors include the following:

- Inflation
- Growth of the population
- Aging of the population
- Historically increased levels of insurance coverage resulting in increased demand for services. This trend is in the process of changing as the cost of health care continues to increase beyond the ability of some individuals and companies to pay.
- Societal health problems that include smoking, poor diet, lack of exercise, poverty, homelessness, AIDS, and drug abuse, among other factors

(ii) Internal Factors.

Internal factors are from within the health-care industry and are more controllable by health-care providers and management. These factors include:

- Increases in technology
- Increases in labor costs
- Inefficient use of current resources
- The practice of defensive medicine

37.3 COST CONTROL IN A COMPETITIVE MARKET.

In the early years of government cost control, much of the government underpayment was shifted to other payors. This cost shifting has become more difficult in recent years due to additional changes in reimbursement by the nongovernment payors and by government regulation. Two of the major elements of the reduced nongovernment payments are the growth of managed care and the emergence of the educated consumer.

(a) Growth of Managed Care. In recent years, there has been an explosive growth of managed-care payors in the form of health maintenance organizations (HMOs) and preferred provider organizations (PPOs). In many parts of the country, managed care payors now represent a larger portion of the nongovernment payors than traditional indemnity insurance. Two of the primary goals of managed-care payors are to improve the quality of the care and to contain costs for their members. The methods used by managed-care payors to contain costs include the following:

- Shifting services to an outpatient setting when medically appropriate
- Minimizing medically unnecessary patient days and inpatient services
- Preparing utilization review information to identify inefficient health-care providers
- Shifting services to more efficient/cost effective providers (preferred providers)

(b) Emergence of the Educated Consumer. In addition to the growth of managed-care initiatives, additional information is being made available to the public concerning the costs and quality of different providers. As the accuracy and reliability of the data increases, individuals and businesses will begin to make more intelligent decisions concerning their health-care services.

All of these cost control measures are increasing the need for health-care providers to monitor and control expense levels to compete effectively with other health-care providers.

37.4 BASICS OF HEALTH-CARE BUDGETING

(a) Meeting the Needs of the Organization's Strategic Plan. One of the primary goals of the budget is to meet and support the goals of the organization's strategic plan. When resources are limited, budgeting provides a framework for setting priorities and making difficult resource allocation decisions. The budget can be an important tool to help achieve the institutional goals and objectives. This purpose needs to be understood by all parties in the budget process including the financial staff who review the budget and the department managers who prepare their requests. Budgetary requests that can be demonstrated to further the stated goals of the organization should be given preference over other requests.

The goals and objectives should consider the following factors:

- Patient care programs
- Quality control and improvement

- Medical education and research programs
- Appropriate staffing and staffing mix levels
- Overall profitability of the organization
- Employee training and development
- Community services and public relations

(b) Developing a Budgeting Timetable. The budgeting process is a time-consuming process and requires a defined, reasonable timetable. Work should be spread over a period of time to avoid unnecessary interference with the normal operations of the organization. It is also important to start the budget process early enough to ensure that there is sufficient time to prepare projections, review and revise the budget, and obtain the necessary approval before the deadlines established by senior management or the board of directors.

(c) Education of Department Managers. There must be an ongoing education process to help managers understand the budgetary information they are required to submit and the standards to which they are held. The budget process will be of limited value if the department managers responsible for preparing the budget requests and for implementing the final budget do not understand the basis for the budget. In addition, this will cause a lack of commitment to the process, and may result in an ineffective budget. Department managers must understand the following:

- The reasons for creating the budget
- The criteria that will be used to evaluate their requests
- The definitions and meanings for the items for which they are providing their requests (i.e., definition of the type of expenses that should be included with each expense item)
- The purpose of the various management reports, which they must monitor and review
- Their responsibility to stay within the budgeted amounts or give reasonable explanations for variances

This education process typically includes memos explaining the different steps in the process, budgetary group meetings, and individual meetings with department managers as required. This process becomes easier as management becomes familiar with the organization's budget process.

Furthermore, an individual's level of motivation toward achievement of an objective and acceptance of the consequences for failure are directly proportional to their involvement in the objective-setting process. If the department manager does not understand the basis of the budget and the factors that are to be used in its development, they will lack involvement with the process. This will reduce the overall quality of the budget as well as its impact on operations.

(d) Current-Year Projections. The starting point for most budgets is providing the department managers with historic information including current-year projections. This information should be provided for each portion of the budget for which they have responsibility. This material is generally provided at the time each section of the budget requests are released to the department managers (i.e., units of service/statistics, staffing and salary, nonsalary expenses). Under traditional budgeting, this information is typically the starting point for the department manager's requests. There are a number of different projection methods that are typically used. These methods will be covered in more detail later in the chapter.

(e) Turnaround Reports. The basis for department manager's budget requests is the turnaround report. This report will typically contain historic information as well as space for the different components of the budget request. It is called a turnaround report because it must be returned to the budget department, after completion, for a review of the requests. This completed report will become part of the basis under which the budget requests are evaluated. Turnaround reports are typically used for units of service (statistics), staffing, and expenses. The various components of revenues, including gross revenue, deductions, allowances, and net revenue can be calculated directly by the financial department.

See Exhibits 37.1 and 37.2 for an example of a nonsalary turnaround report.

(f) Analysis of Budget Requests. An important component of the budget process is the analysis of the department's budgetary requests. The information must be analyzed and compiled for executive management's review. This analysis should include: a review of the explanations given for the budgetary request, a comparison to prior year amounts, a breakdown of the different types of requests (i.e., volume, nonvolume, inflation, new or discontinued programs), and aggregation of different items into overall totals. This process is very important and will play a major role in executive management's review and approval of the final budget.

(g) Budget Committee/Executive Management Review. The budget committee or executive management review will be based on a number of criteria, which include the following:

- How well the budgetary requests meet the strategic plan and goals of the organization
- The level of overall increase in expenses requested and permitted for the organization
- The reduction of certain types of expense items based on the type of category (i.e., reduction of all travel expenses) or because the reason for the request was either missing or incompatible with the overall goals of the provider
- Competitive information related to service units, staffing, expenses, and pricing levels

There are different methods that are normally used to review departmental budget requests. Some health-care providers prefer to use a joint approach centered around a budget review committee with members representing different functional areas of the organization. Areas that are represented generally include: administration, finance, nursing, ancillary, and support services. One benefit to this approach is that it provides a broad experience base for the review function. One drawback to this approach is the length of time that the review function may take as each functional area gives its views on each issue.

If this approach is used, it is important to have a central decision maker. This central decision maker is often the chief operating officer or president of the organization. Without a central decision maker, the different interests in the organization will typically become more involved with ''protecting their turf'' and supporting primarily their own area of responsibility. This will not always be in the organization's best interest.

Another approach involves a joint approach with only the chief financial officer and

1992 Projected Nonsalary Expenses
Based on 6 Months of Actual and 6 Months of Revised Budgeted Information

CCNUM	Name	G/L Number	Description	OCT-ACT	NOV-ACT	DEC-ACT	JAN-ACT	FEB-ACT	MAR-ACT	APR-PRJ	MAY-PRJ	JUN-PRJ	JUL-PRJ	AUG-PRJ	SEP-PRJ	Total
7155	RADIOLOGY—ULTRASOUND	4000	RADIOLOGY FILMS	1,518	1,518	0	1,518	1,587	1,488	1,636	0	1,636	0	1,636	1,541	14,078
		4450	PAPER GOODS/ DISPOSABLES	0	0	0	0	0	0	0	0	0	0	0	0	0
		4600	OFFICE/ADM SUPPLIES	6	18	23	65	131	15	14	18	7	3	28	16	344
		4900	OTHER MINOR EQUIPMENT	0	0	0	0	0	0	25	0	0	0	0	0	25
		5000	OPERATING SUPPLIES GENRL	548	819	353	521	0	1,368	209	781	1,331	17	436	19	6,402
		6250	EQUIP. SERVICE CONTRACTS	20,752	0	0	13,095	1,506	1,506	8,158	0	0	8,158	0	0	53,175
		6660	CONTRCTL SRVCS/ TEMP HELP	0	0	0	0	0	0	0	0	0	0	0	0	0
		8610	DUES/ MEMBERSHIPS	0	0	0	0	0	0	0	0	0	0	0	0	0
		8620	SUBSCRIPTIONS/ PUBLICATIONS	73	0	0	0	0	0	0	0	0	75	0	0	148
		8750	EDUCATIONAL MATERIAL	0	90	380	12	0	0	0	0	26	0	123	55	686
		8800	TRAVEL	0	0	0	0	0	0	0	0	0	0	0	0	0
		8940	FREIGHT IN/OUT BOUND	6	0	5	20	4	33	16	12	10	0	4	2	112
TOTAL	NONSALARY EXPENSES FOR COST CENTER		7155	22,903	2,445	761	15,231	3,228	4,410	10,058	811	3,010	8,253	2,227	1,633	74,970

Exhibit 37.1. Nonsalary turnaround report–Part I

FY 1993 Nonsalary Budget Requests
Report for Department: 7155—Radiology—Ultrasound
Attach the Detailed Explanation Form For All FY 1993 Budget Requests Which Differ from the 1992 Projected/Actual Amount

G/L Number	Description	1991 Actual	1992 Budget	1992 Projected/ Actual	Adjustments To FY 1992 Proj/Actual	Carry Over FY 1992 New Expense	Carry Over FY 1992 Discontinued Expense	FY 1993 New Expense	FY 1993 Discontinued Expense	1993 Budget Request	Requested Spread Method	Variance 1992 Budget vs. 1992 Proj./Act.	Explanation Required?
4000	RADIOLOGY FILMS	14,641	14,875	14,078	____	____	____	____	____	____	____	−797	
4450	PAPER GOODS/DISPOSABLES	0	0	0	____	____	____	____	____	____	____	0	
4600	OFFICE/ADM SUPPLIES	473	481	344	____	____	____	____	____	____	____	−137	
4900	OTHER MINOR EQUIPMENT	25	25	25	____	____	____	____	____	____	____	0	
5000	OPERATING SUPPLIES GENRL	5,648	5,738	6,402	____	____	____	____	____	____	____	664	YES
6250	EQUIP. SERVICE CONTRACTS	35,697	43,960	53,175	____	____	____	____	____	____	____	9,215	YES
6660	CONTRCTL SRVCS/TEMP HELP	0	0	0	____	____	____	____	____	____	____	0	
8610	DUES/MEMBERSHIPS	0	0	0	____	____	____	____	____	____	____	0	
8620	SUBSCRIPTIONS/ PUBLICATIONS	75	75	148	____	____	____	____	____	____	____	73	
8750	EDUCATIONAL MATERIAL	1,054	220	686	____	____	____	____	____	____	____	466	
8800	TRAVEL	0	0	0	____	____	____	____	____	____	____	0	
8940	FREIGHT IN/OUT BOUND	95	97	112	____	____	____	____	____	____	____	15	
TOTAL NONSALARY EXPENSES:		57,708	65,471	74,970								9,499	

APPROVED BY DEPARTMENT'S VICE PRESIDENT ____________

Exhibit 37.2. Nonsalary turnaround report—Part II

chief operating officer. This approach simplifies the process while providing two of the key areas of expertise required. While this approach does not provide the wide experience of the budget committee approach, it includes two of the key perspectives—the financial perspective from the individual responsible for the provider's financial condition and the overview perspective from the individual responsible for the overall well-being of the entire organization. This approach will often eliminate many of the interdepartmental problems concerning the allocation of the available resources.

(h) Monitoring Performance. Another important part of the budget process is variance reporting. This is the mechanism through which the budget department reports to the various managers about the differences between the budgeted and actual amounts. Without periodic variance reporting (typically monthly), department managers will not know how their actual costs compare to the budget. This is an important component to insuring that the budget is enforced and that significant variances are explained and reported to executive management.

(i) Using the Budget to Provide Management Incentives. The value of the budget will be improved if it is used to evaluate a manager's performance. To be effective, deviations from the budget must have a consequence to both the organization and the individual managers within the institution.

At a minimum, budget variance reports should be provided to senior management for the areas for which they have responsibility. In addition, the detailed departmental variance reports and the manager's explanation of variances should be returned to the senior manager responsible for the area for their review. This mechanism provides an additional incentive for the department manager to either stay within the prescribed budget limits or to give a reasonable explanation for any variances.

In addition, some organizations will link management's salary merit increases to compliance with the budget. However, in order for this to be acceptable to management, the budget must be reasonable and sufficiently advanced to allow for certain types of variances, including those caused by volume changes and for factors beyond the manager's control.

(j) Position Review. Typically, the largest component of a health-care provider's expenses are employee expenses for salary and benefits. It is critical to control the growth and changes in staffing levels. In today's dynamic health-care environment, patient volumes can change rapidly. Any changes in staffing levels related to new positions, open positions, or changes in scheduled hours should be reviewed for appropriateness by a position review committee. The position review committee typically includes members of senior management, budgeting, and human resources.

37.5 HOSPITAL BUDGETING

(a) Beginning the Budgeting Process

(i) Gathering Historic Data Typically the starting point for the budget process is the gathering of historic data in departmental and general ledger detail. This information will typically go back for a minimum of two to three years with full monthly detail. The monthly detail is important to check the consistency of the data and to demonstrate any seasonal trends, which are common to the health-care industry. This information typically includes the following:

- Financial information including all expenses and revenues
- Units of service including any intensity measures (i.e., case mix index)
- Staffing information, including a breakdown by job code and type of hours (i.e., base staffing, overtime, nonproductive)

If the hospital has been consistently budgeting, this information should already be available on the current budgeting system.

(ii) Current-Year Projections. The annual budget cycle is usually started with a current-year projection. This projection is distributed to the department managers along with historic information to help develop the department's budgetary request. There are a number of different projection methods that are typically used. These projection methods vary from institution to institution and differ in complexity. The computerized budgeting system in use will have a strong impact on the availability of different projection methods. Some of the typical projection methods are discussed in the following subsections.

(1) Current-Year Budget. Under this method, the current budget is used as the starting point for the new budget projection. This method is one of the simplest but least flexible methods to establish a new budget because it tends to ignore changes in amounts due to actual volume fluctuations and internal and external pressures on the budget. This projection method can be adjusted for these factors, but may cause the projection process to become time consuming and difficult.

While it is recommended that the current year's budget amounts be included with the projected amount for comparison in the turnaround report, this method is not recommended for creating the current-year projection.

(2) Simple Averaging. Using a simple average is one of the easiest but least effective ways to project the current year. Under this method, the actual year-to-date information is simply divided by the number of months that have elapsed. This calculated monthly amount is then multiplied by 12 to project the annualized amount. While this projection is easy to calculate, the information will be lacking the seasonality of health care services and will likely result in substantial under- or overstatement of amounts for the different departments. An example of this calculation would be as follows:

Department	G/L Account	7-Month Amount
230 (5 North)	1200 (Office supplies)	\$700

Simple Average Calculation

$$\$700/7 \text{ months} = \$100/\text{month}$$

$$\text{Annualized amount} = \$100/\text{month} \times 12 \text{ months} = \$1{,}200$$

This calculation would be done for each line item for each department.

(3) Combination of Year-to-Date Actual Plus Budget. Under this method, the year-to-date actual information is combined with the budget information. For example, if seven months of actual information is available, then this amount is combined with the last five

months of the current-year budget. An advantage to this method is that actual information is used for as much time as is available. The remaining months are based on the budgeted amounts and therefore provide a conservative projection to contain expense levels.

It is also important for the department managers to explain any variances between the projected/actual amounts and the full-year budgeted amounts. Under this method, any variances between the projected amounts and budgeted amounts for the year will be due to variances in the year-to-date actual amounts. Any projected amounts that exceed the current year's budget, that are not adequately explained, or are due to inefficiency in the department should be rejected as part of the budget review process. This will permit the budget review function to require explanations for any variations between the projected and the budgeted amounts. These explanations can therefore have an impact on the amounts allowed for the subsequent budget year.

This is one of the more desirable methods because the projection method is relatively straightforward, the projection tends to be conservative, and the work involved to adjust the projection is minimal. However, this method assumes that the current year's budget was correctly allocated to the periods to represent the seasonality of the amounts.

Exhibit 37.3 illustrates an example of a nonsalary current year projection.

(4) Combination of Year-to-Date Actual Plus Inflated Prior Year of Actual. This method involves combining the current year of actual information for the months available plus the prior-year actual information for the remaining periods. This method can be more complicated to project because of the changes that must be made to the prior-year actual amounts.

To provide a reasonable projection, this method requires that the prior-year actual amounts be adjusted to account for inflation, volume, and intensity changes. Because of these variations, different categories of revenues and expenses must be adjusted by different inflation factors. Revenues and allowances need to be adjusted for any changes in rates. This may be difficult if different price changes were used for different services. Expense categories will also need to be adjusted for differences in external inflation factors.

While this method can provide a reasonable projection for the current year, the time involved can be extensive. In addition, it is difficult to require departments to provide explanations for differences between the current year budget and the projection. The departments can simply claim that the differences are due to the projection method and not due to their actual spending.

(iii) Analysis of Current-Year Projections. After the various turnaround reports have been returned with the department's budget requests, the next step is to analyze and summarize the preliminary amounts. This process prepares the detailed information for review by executive management and involves the following types of analysis of the budget requests:

- Comparison of budget requests to the current-year budgeted amount and to prior years of actual information by category and department
- Comparison of any requested variable expenses to the current-year budgeted amount and prior years of actual information, adjusted for volumes and intensity
- Summarization of all amounts into hospital total amounts, by classification and department for review by management

1992 Budget
Budgeted Nonsalary Expenses by Period
Report for Department 6080—Medical I.C.U.

Expense Group	GL/ Number	Description	Oct 91	Nov 91	Dec 91	Jan 92	Feb 92	Mar 92	Apr 92	May 92	Jun 92	Jul 92	Aug 92	Sep 92	Total
Nonsalary Expenses	4100	MED/SURG SUP-NON BILL	198	421	52	69	181	285	86	619	92	341	472	139	2,955
	4600	OFFICE/ADM SUPPLIES	340	1,733	392	421	542	1,067	309	1,349	303	380	486	250	7,572
	4900	OTHER MINOR EQUIPMENT	0	0	0	0	0	0	0	0	0	61	0	0	61
	5000	OPERATING SUPPLIES GENRL	328	463	578	438	636	714	473	411	735	977	1,516	780	8,049
	6200	EQUIPMENT REPAIRS	182	182	182	182	182	182	182	182	182	182	182	177	2,179
	6250	EQUIP. SERVICE CONTRACTS	1,214	1,214	1,214	1,214	1,214	1,214	1,214	1,214	1,214	1,214	1,214	1,214	14,568
	6660	CONTRCTL SRVCS/TEMP HELP	0	4,501	0	1,492	0	0	0	0	0	0	315	1,063	7,371
	7250	DEPRECIATN-PERM FIXTURES	108	108	108	108	108	108	108	110	110	108	109	108	1,301
	7400	DEPRECIATN-EQUIPMENT	4,519	4,519	4,519	4,512	4,512	4,512	4,792	4,791	4,787	4,787	4,787	4,787	55,824
	8620	SUBSCRIPTIONS/PUBLICATNS	28	0	0	70	0	0	0	0	0	0	0	0	98
	8940	FREIGHT IN/OUT BOUND	4	8	16	13	2	6	34	0	10	7	0	17	117
TOTAL FOR EXPENSE GROUP:		Nonsalary Expenses	6,921	13,149	7,061	8,519	7,377	8,088	7,198	8,676	7,433	8,057	9,081	8,535	100,095
TOTAL FOR DEPARTMENT			6,921	13,149	7,061	8,519	7,377	8,088	7,198	8,676	7,433	8,057	9,081	8,535	100,095

Exhibit 37.3. Example of a nonsalary current-year projection

- Summarization of all requested incremental amounts (i.e., volume, new or deleted programs, intensity, etc.) into hospital totals along with the explanations for the request
- Comparison of statistics, revenues, expenses, and staffing to both geographic and size competitors

(b) Units of Service. The projection of units of service is one of the key elements in the budgetary process. Units of service are typically the driving force for changes in both revenues and certain types of expenses. A properly created budget will allow for the expected changes in patient volumes and their expected impact on the budget. The units of service projection has even greater importance if a flexible budget is used to monitor performance. Under a flexible budgeting process, the budget is adjusted for changes in the actual units of service. This will be discussed in more detail under the advanced budgeting section.

Even though units of service can have wide variations from month to month, a review of several years of consistent data will often demonstrate seasonal patterns. In addition to a review of the historical units of service volumes and intensity trends, this projection should consider the following internal and external factors:

- Internal factors
  - Opinions of the medical staff and department heads
  - Planned changes in services offered
  - Changes in measurement techniques (i.e., changing from number of procedures to number of relative value units [RVUs])
  - Other internal factors, including changes in policies
- External Factors
  - Regulatory or accreditation requirements
  - Changes in services offered by competitors
  - Expected changes in the service area demographics including the plans of major employers

(i) Inpatient Routine Units of Service. Inpatient routine units of service typically include patient days and discharges (or admissions) and adjustments for intensity. From these statistics, other useful information can be calculated, including average length of stay and occupancy levels. These statistics are often used as total hospital inpatient statistics because they have an impact on inpatient ancillary units of service. Other total hospital statistics would include adjusted patient days and adjusted or equivalent discharges. Adjusted patient days and adjusted or equivalent discharges are a measure to account for both inpatient and outpatient volumes. This information should be collected by department and by payor if available. The payor information is needed to calculate allowances and payments.

(ii) Ancillary Units of Service. Inpatient and outpatient statistics should be collected separately because of potential differences in average intensities and charges between the areas. Ancillary units of service vary from department to department. These statistics often include tests, procedures, relative value units, and visits. In addition, there will often be multiple statistics for the same department. The statistic used to create the budget should be the one that best represents the *intensity of the service* and projected *revenue.* If one

statistic does not accurately measure both of these measures, then multiple statistics should be collected.

(c) Staffing and Payroll. Health care is a labor-intensive industry. Individuals who are sick require individualized attention. Unlike other industries, technology advances often result in additional staffing to operate and analyze the results of the new and often sophisticated equipment. Newer technologies such as computerized axial tomography (CT) scans or magnetic resonance imaging (MRI) offer more options to the health-care provider rather than simply replacing older imaging methods such as x-rays. Automation and technology advances can help reduce certain types of support services, such as most laboratory services. However, direct patient care is individualized and must be provided by health-care professionals.

Payroll expenses often represent between 45% and 55% of the total expense budget. Once fringe benefits are included, the total staffing related expenses can increase to 50% to 65% of the total expense. Because this represents the single largest portion of the budget, staffing and salary expenses are one of the most important and time-consuming portions of the process. It is also one of the more difficult areas to control and will require considerable monitoring.

(i) Base Staffing and Payroll. The starting point for the payroll budget is the base staffing and payroll projection. Base staffing represents the base authorized hours without any coverage for vacation, holidays, overtime, and the like. These hours will match the hours approved by the hospital's position review committee and are referred to as the authorized hours.

The base staffing can be predicated on either the authorized or the scheduled hours. Scheduled hours represent the hours that the department has actually hired. Because of departmental shortages and overstaffing, these two types of hours will often be different. It is therefore recommended that the base staffing be founded on the authorized and not the actual scheduled hours.

Authorized hours should be used for the budget to force all managers to seek approval for any position changes through the position review function. This will help to minimize staffing increases unless the need can be strongly supported.

These hours should be budgeted with as much detail as possible through the hospital's budgeting system. If possible, staffing should be calculated with full employee detail. If this is not available, the staffing should be calculated using the individual job codes and shifts for each department. The shift information is needed to calculate the incremental expenses for the various shift differentials. This should include any information required to distinguish pay rates including day, evening, and night as well as weekend pay differentials.

(ii) Overtime. The budgeting of overtime is an individual hospital decision. Many hospitals believe that no overtime should be budgeted. If a department is at full staffing, and volumes are close to expected levels, there should be little to no overtime incurred. If a department has vacant positions, then any overtime will be offset by the vacant hours.

Other providers budget for only certain types of overtime, which may include coverage hours for holidays, vacations, sick time, and so on. Overtime can also be budgeted for volume changes through flexible budgeting. If an organization decides to budget for overtime, as much detail as possible should be utilized to determine the appropriate level of overtime staffing.

(iii) Other Budgeted Hours. There are a number of other types of hours that must be reviewed and included in the staffing budget. If the base budget uses authorized hours, only the *incremental* hours should be budgeted. It is also important to consider the various hourly differentials used for each type of hour. For example, holiday time may be paid at 150% of standard. On-call time may be paid at 25% of standard. The types of hours that should be considered include the following:

- Holiday coverage
- Vacation coverage
- Sick coverage
- Weekend coverage
- On-call time
- Call-back time
- Other coverage hours

See Exhibits 37.4 and 37.5 for examples of departmental staffing and salary expense reports.

(iv) Contract Codes. If the organization gives different rates of increase to different employee groups, this information should be included with the employee or job code level of staffing information. This data is differentiated through the use of contract codes and can be used to calculate alternate scenarios for pay increases. This information is typically needed if different employee groups receive different rate increases such as union versus nonunion, or salaried versus nonsalaried employees.

(v) Pay Increases. During payroll budgeting, different scenarios are run to evaluate different employee pay increases for the budget year. This ordinarily occurs after the staffing hour requests have been received and after a baseline (without increases) salary expense budget is run.

During the salary increase analysis staffing hour requests will be evaluated a second time to determine additional cuts based on the overall salary expense projected.

Decisions concerning the pay increase are impacted by the following:

- Wage increases offered by competitors
- Current and expected profitability of the hospital
- Union and other employee negotiations
- General state of the economy including inflation
- Employee staffing shortage areas

There are several ways in which hospitals provide pay increases. The most typical methods are outlined below.

(1) Cost of Living Adjustment. Cost of Living Adjustment (COLA) is the annual increase given to all employees throughout the organization. Occasionally, certain shortage

Budgeted Staffing
Report for Department: 7021—Operating Room

Shift Description	Job Code	Description	Authorized Base Hours FTE	On-Call Hours FTE	Holiday Hours FTE	Vacation/Sick/ Cov Hours FTE	Total FTE	
1 DAYS	1050	NURSING DIRECTOR	1.00	.00	.	.	1.00	
	1070	NURSING SUPERVISOR	1.00	.00	.	.	1.00	
	3100	STAFF NURSE	20.80	.00	.12	.88	21.80	
	3680	PERFUSIONIST-CERTIF.	2.00	.00	.	.12	2.12	
	4030	SURGICAL TECHNICIAN	12.80	.00	.12	.54	13.46	
	5050	UNIT SECRETARY	.20	.00	.	.	.20	
	5070	O.R. SECRETARY	2.00	.00	.	.18	2.18	
	8040	O.R. ATTENDANT	7.40	.00	.03	.31	7.74	
TOTAL FOR: DAYS			47.20	.00	.28	2.03	49.50	
2 EVENINGS	3100	STAFF NURSE	2.40	.00	.17	.08	2.65	
	4030	SURGICAL TECHNICIAN	2.40	.00	.17	.08	2.65	
	5020	CLERK TYPIST	.50	.00	.	.02	.52	
	8040	O.R. ATTENDANT	1.00	.00	.04	.03	1.07	
TOTAL FOR: EVENINGS			6.30	.00	.39	.21	6.90	
TOTAL FOR COST CENTER: OPERATING ROOM				53.50	.00	.67	2.24	56.41

Exhibit 37.4. Departmental staffing budget

1992 Budget
Budgeted Salary Expenses by Period
Report for Department 6016—Float Nursing Personnel

G/L Number	Description	Shift	Jobcode	Description	Oct 91	Nov 91	Dec 91	Jan 92	Feb 92	Mar 92	Apr 92	May 92	Jun 92	Jul 92	Aug 92	Sep 92	Total
135	SUPERVISORS-RN	1	1070	NURSING SUPERVISOR	4,553	4,408	4,553	4,553	4,478	4,781	4,629	4,781	4,629	4,781	4,781	4,624	55,551
*TOTAL JOBCODE 1070					4,553	4,408	4,553	4,553	4,478	4,781	4,629	4,781	4,629	4,781	4,781	4,624	55,551
TOTAL FOR G/L CLASSIFICATION					4,553	4,408	4,553	4,553	4,478	4,781	4,629	4,781	4,629	4,781	4,781	4,624	55,551
300	REGISTERED NURSES	1	3100	STAFF NURSE	11,592	11,229	11,592	11,592	11,184	11,932	11,656	12,043	11,666	12,132	12,149	11,770	140,541
		2	3100	STAFF NURSE	303	294	303	303	291	311	301	311	301	311	318	310	3,657
		5	3100	STAFF NURSE	3,678	3,563	3,678	3,678	3,527	3,775	3,656	3,775	3,689	3,823	3,841	3,719	44,402
*TOTAL JOBCODE 3100					15,573	15,086	15,573	15,573	15,002	16,018	15,613	16,129	15,656	16,266	16,308	15,799	188,600
*TOTAL FOR G/L CLASSIFICATION					15,573	15,086	15,573	15,573	15,002	16,018	15,613	16,129	15,656	16,266	16,308	15,799	188,600
400	LPN	1	4010	L.P.N.	2,555	2,480	2,564	2,564	2,477	2,633	2,555	2,633	2,555	2,633	2,633	2,591	30,872
		2	4010	L.P.N.	416	403	416	416	400	437	423	437	423	437	437	420	5,065
		5	4010	L.P.N.	455	440	455	464	445	475	460	475	460	475	475	459	5,538
*TOTAL JOBCODE 4010					3,426	3,323	3,435	3,444	3,322	3,545	3,438	3,545	3,438	3,545	3,545	3,470	41,475
TOTAL FOR G/L CLASSIFICATION					3,426	3,323	3,435	3,444	3,322	3,545	3,438	3,545	3,438	3,545	3,545	3,470	41,475
500	NURSING AIDES & ORDERLIES	1	8010	NURSE AIDE	275	266	275	275	266	290	281	290	281	290	290	281	3,360
		3	8010	NURSE AIDE	347	336	354	354	340	363	352	363	352	363	363	354	4,241
*TOTAL JOBCODE 8010					622	602	629	629	606	653	633	653	633	653	653	635	7,601
500	NURSING AIDES & ORDERLIES	1	8020	PATIENT ASSISTANT	2,768	3,026	3,005	2,910	2,664	2,866	2,946	2,981	2,822	3,179	3,027	3,070	35,264
*TOTAL JOBCODE 8020					2,768	3,026	3,005	2,910	2,664	2,866	2,946	2,981	2,822	3,179	3,027	3,070	35,264
TOTAL FOR G/L CLASSIFICATION					3,390	3,628	3,634	3,539	3,270	3,519	3,579	3,634	3,455	3,832	3,680	3,705	42,865
TOTAL FOR COST CENTER					26,942	26,445	27,195	27,109	26,072	27,863	27,259	28,089	27,178	28,424	28,314	27,598	328,491

Exhibit 37.5. Salary expense budget

areas, such as nursing or technicians, receive different COLA increases. Because COLA is given to all employees, it does not involve any type of merit evaluation. This increase is determined by the environmental criteria outlined above.

(2) Merit. A merit increase is an individual raise given to an employee based on the quality of their work during the prior review period. Merit increases typically have a minimum and maximum range.

To budget for the merit increase, it is suggested that a global merit increase be budgeted for all employees. If the merit range established by management was from 0% to 3.5%, then an overall merit increase of 2.5% may be budgeted. The advantage to this method is that the department manager has an incentive to give merit increases both above and below the average. Some managers will give all employees the maximum increase. This removes the "merit" from the raise. Under this approach, if a manager gives all employees the maximum increase, then the department will exceed the budgeted salary amount.

(3) Pay Grade and Step. Under the pay grade and step method, an employee group is assigned to a certain pay grade, which will have an established minimum and maximum range for all employees. As employees advance within the same pay grade, their rate of pay is increased by steps to the next level. If the employee has reached the top step in the pay grade, then they will no longer receive a step increase. This form of increase is common in the health-care industry.

This method allows for easier budgeting because each step is defined and can be predetermined. It also helps to control salary expenses because it caps the salary for senior employees who have reached the top step for the pay grade. The top and bottom of the pay grade are often adjusted each year to match the COLA increase. One downside to this form of budgeting is that there is often little merit or incentive to the increase. Often, all employees receive the increase, to the next step, at the time of their review. Therefore, the incentive, through the pay rate review process, to be an exceptional employee is lost. However, many hospitals allow department managers to deny step increases to employees who are deficient or to give multiple increments to employees who are exceptional.

It is also important to have a budgeting system that can calculate this type of increase. If the budgeting system does not have the ability to use the step and grade method, then it will be difficult to determine which employees have reached the top step in their grade and should not receive any additional increases.

(4) Weighted Average Pay Rates. To calculate salary expense, two types of information are required: (1) the staffing hours and (2) the pay rate. These two factors are multiplied together to calculate the salary expense. To calculate payroll, pay rates must be obtained with the same detail as was obtained to project and budget staffing hours. If a staffing hour was budgeted for a certain job code, shift, contract code, and department then a corresponding pay rate must be budgeted for the same job code, shift, contract code, and department. This pay rate will be an aggregation of different employees with different amounts of authorized hours and pay rates. To calculate an accurate salary amount, a weighted average pay rate should be calculated from both the pay rates and the hours for each employee.

A simple example would be:

Employee	Pay Rate	Hours/week	Full-Time Equivalents	Weighted Rate
Jones	$12.00	40	1.0	$12.00
Smith	$14.00	20	.5	7.00
Totals			1.5	$19.00
Weighted Average Rate = $19.00/1.5 = $12.67				

This information should be calculated on a monthly basis to account for individual merit increases, which typically occur on the anniversary hire date of the employee. This can be a time-consuming process if the budgeting system does not have the ability to aggregate the information at this level of detail. This type of budgeting system will need to be interfaced with the hospital's payroll system to obtain the required employee information. If the hospital's current budgeting system does not have the ability to make this type of analysis, then the data processing department could run a data query from the payroll system to calculate the weighted average rates. If this is also not a possibility, then estimates can be made using a spreadsheet program.

(vi) Accrued versus Paid Staffing and Payroll. It is important to remember when budgeting salary expenses, that the amounts will be compared to the salary amounts recorded on the general ledger. Salary expenses on the general ledger will generally be the entire salary expense for the month, including both paid hours and accruals for additional amounts due that have not yet been paid. To perform proper comparison for budget and variance reporting, the budgeted amounts will have to include accruals to match the accruals that are performed monthly for the general ledger. Accrual methods may vary for different institutions. Some organizations accrue based on calendar days, others accrue based on paid days. For example, if employees are paid weekly, then they would receive four pay checks representing 28 days.[1] If the month contains 31 days, and the hospital performs an accrual to account for actual days in the month, an additional accrual of 3 days salary needs to be performed. This could be done by multiplying the actual paid salary expenses by $^{31}/_{28}$ths. The budgeted salary amounts would need to spread by the same method. In this case, it would be spread by the number of days in the month.

(vii) Productive versus Nonproductive Time. If variable or flexible budgeting is performed, then staffing and salary budgets should include levels of productive versus nonproductive time. Productive time represents time actually worked. Nonproductive time includes hours paid but not worked. Nonproductive time would typically include vacation, sick, holiday, and personal time away from work. When calculating work standards to budget hours, it is important to consider the hours actually worked, rather than the hours that are paid.

(d) Fringe Benefits. Fringe benefit projections are typically made with assistance from the personnel department. Personnel will often keep track of many of the items that impact the cost of fringe benefits. Fringe benefits expenses will be based on the following:

[1] This example is based on a calendar days accrual. This accrual will depend on the day employees are paid. There could possibly be five paychecks during the month. In this case, a negative accrual (or reversal of prior period accrual) would need to be performed to reduce the amount to 31 days from the 35 days actually paid.

- The type of benefits offered to employees
- The number of employees that qualify for the benefit
- The cost per benefit per qualified employee

Certain types of fringe benefits such as Federal Insurance Contributions Act (FICA) expenses will be capped once a maximum amount is reached. Some budgeting systems will allow for this type of cap to be calculated. In addition, if a benefit cap is in place, certain benefits such as FICA require the caps to be adjusted for the calendar year rather than the fiscal year.

For all fringe benefits, additional analysis must be done to perform a review of the projected amount. Because fringe benefits are typically calculated as hospital-wide expenses, aggregate projections can be made based on the historical expense and increase levels.

Fringe benefits typically include the following types of expenses:

- FICA (social security and medicare)
- Health-care coverage
- Employee self-insurance (for health services provided by the hospital to employees)
- Dental coverage
- Unemployment insurance (SUI/FUI)
- Life insurance
- Disability insurance
- Pension and retirement
- Workers' compensation
- Tuition reimbursement

(e) Nonsalary Expenses. Nonsalary expenses represent the majority of the items on the budget. Nonsalary budget items are typically very detailed and can vary from small amounts to several million dollars per item. However, the budgeting of nonsalary items is relatively straightforward.

Nonsalary expense are often budgeted with the current-year projection as the starting point. From this amount adjustments are made for factors such as changes in volume, new programs, discontinued programs, administrative cuts, and adjustments for unreasonable projections.

Nonsalary items can be either fixed or variable. Fixed items do not vary with volume changes. Variable items do change with volume changes. Other items can have characteristics of both and are called *semivariable.* As part of the budget request process, departments should identify incremental expenses due to supportable volume changes. Nonsalary expenses include the following types of categories:

- Medical/surgical supplies
- Drugs and pharmaceuticals
- General supplies
- Professional fees
- Interest

- Insurance
- Physician fees
- Travel
- Purchased services
- Utilities
- Depreciation

(f) Revenues and Allowances

(i) Gross Patient Revenues. Gross patient revenues represent the actual charges for services performed. This amount will often differ substantially from the amount actually paid, or the net revenue. Many payors reimburse health-care providers based on their own reimbursement schedule.

(1) Inpatient Routine Revenue. Inpatient routine revenue is the revenue obtained for the room and board charges for inpatient services. The room and board charge is multiplied by the projected number of patient days. If there are multiple types of room charges, each of these amounts would be multiplied by the appropriate type of patient days.

(2) Inpatient Ancillary Revenue. Inpatient ancillary revenue represents revenue generated for support services provided to *inpatients.* This revenue is often calculated by multiplying the department's units of service by an *average* unit price. For many departments there can be dozens to hundreds of different procedures and corresponding prices. For most larger departments, there will often be a relatively consistent mix over time resulting in a fairly stable average revenue per unit of service.

Certain factors should be considered when projecting the average revenue per unit of service. The average revenue can be affected by changes in services offered, case mix (intensity), or technology. If any of these changes are experienced, then the information should be broken out in enough detail to determine the impact of the change. For instance, if a certain group of procedures receives a different price increase than the remainder of the department, then this group should be broken out and individually priced separately from the rest of the department. These two amounts would then be combined to arrive at the total department revenue.

There will often be a different average revenue per unit of service between the inpatient and outpatient areas. This is because of the different types and intensity of services that are often provided between the two areas. It is therefore important to treat the inpatient and outpatient areas as separate projections.

(3) Outpatient Ancillary Revenue. Outpatient ancillary revenue represents revenue generated for support services provided to *outpatients.* Outpatient ancillary revenue is calculated in the same way as inpatient ancillary revenue. However, the average revenue per unit of service will often be different.

(ii) Allowances and Deductions from Revenue. Allowances and deductions represent the difference between what an organization charges for services and what they are actually paid.

There are many types of payments used by different health-care payors. In addition, the payment mechanisms vary based on the type and location of the services. The specific calculation of allowances and deductions from revenue is complex and beyond the scope of this chapter.

(iii) Contractual Allowances. The calculation of allowances requires extensive experience in the different methods of reimbursement. When creating this portion of the budget, the organization's reimbursement specialist should be consulted. However, there are certain concepts that should be applied.

(1) Payor Mix. To determine the allowance, the payor's portion of the total gross revenue must be determined. This information would be obtained for the entire organization as well as any department that receives a different type of reimbursement. If allowances are calculated by department, then full payor mix information must be obtained for all departments.

This information should be obtained with several years of history to determine the most recent activity as well as any projected payor mix changes. Many health-care providers have an increasing portion of their business from government payors including Medicare and Medicaid. Other changes such as a new managed-care contract,[2] should also be considered, if there are any volume change assumptions in the contract.

(2) Payment Method. The next important consideration is the method of payment. Some payors, such as Medicare, pay a fixed amount per discharge.[3] Other payors pay based on detailed charges, types of services, length of stay, or some other criteria. Each individual payor's payment method, with all of the alternatives, must be understood and modeled.

(3) Payor Volumes. The other information required to calculate the payments (and allowances) are the units of service by payor. Similar to the payor's gross revenue, statistics must be collected for any area that impacts the calculated reimbursement.

(iv) Deductions from Revenue. Deductions from revenue typically include bad debts,[4] charity care, employee discounts, and free service. Charity care is often easily determined. The level of charity care will be determined by the provider's policy for providing free care and will also be influenced strongly by the amount of funds available from contributed free bed funds. This amount is easy to budget based on the free-care policies and historical levels of free care.

Bad debts will be influenced by several factors. The primary determinant of bad debts is the amount of self-pay patient charges. The level of bad debt is therefore often calculated as a percent of self-pay gross revenue. For some providers, the level of bad debts exceeds the amount of reported self-pay gross charges. These providers will often budget bad debts as a percent of total gross revenue, total nongovernment gross revenue, or as a percent of gross revenue for a number of different payors.

---

[2] A managed-care contract could also go to a competitor, which could have a negative effect on the patient volumes.

[3] This is very simplified. This fixed amount per discharge is influenced by the DRG (intensity), outliers, pass-through costs, and site of service, among other factors.

[4] Under the most recent audit guidelines for health-care providers, bad debts are included as an expense item. However, for simplicity, bad debts are included with deductions from revenue, as it was historically grouped.

Another factor is the overall state of the economy. During recessionary times, levels of bad debt may increase substantially as workers are laid off or lose health insurance coverage. Levels of bad debt are also influenced by admission screening policies and collection policies and procedures. During the budget process, the business office should be contacted to determine if any policy changes have been made that will impact the levels of expected bad debts.

(v) Net Patient Revenue. To calculate payments or net revenue, the allowances and deductions are subtracted from the gross patient revenue. The calculation of net revenue is an important part of the budget process. If a hospital has had little or no profit from operations, then the calculated net revenue will have a large impact on the level of expense increases permitted.

(vi) Rate Changes. An organization must determine the rate changes required to meet its financial needs within the constraints imposed by the market, third-party payors, regulators, and others. Because gross revenues will impact deductions from revenues and may impact certain operating expenses (i.e., hospital-based physician fees), these components of the preliminary financial projections must also be adjusted in developing the preliminary operating budget.

As payors become increasingly price sensitive, hospitals must have the ability to determine their costs by product lines and by providers. This will be important information in determining pricing levels for different services to bid on managed-care contracts.

Rate changes may be controlled in certain states depending on the existence of a state regulatory agency. Some agencies will prospectively determine the maximum (or minimum) levels that prices may change for the next fiscal year.

In addition, some providers will periodically perform detailed rate analysis. An organization can obtain additional net revenue, while maintaining or reducing the current gross revenue levels by making selective price changes. This discussion is beyond the scope of this chapter, but would include analysis of procedures by payor to determine the optimal price change.

(vii) Other Operating Revenue. Other operating revenue is revenue that is related to the operations of the business, but is not directly obtained from its treatment of patients. Other operating revenue typically includes items such as pharmaceuticals sold to employees, cafeteria income, parking garage income, x-ray silver recovery, etc. Other operating revenue can often be projected on the same basis as gross patient revenues. This would be based on a rate times a projected volume. If there is no measurable volume, or the amount is minimal, then projections could be based on prior year trends.

(viii) Nonoperating Revenue. Nonoperating revenues represent revenues obtained from outside the primary business. This would include items such as interest or gains on investments, real estate income, unrestricted gifts, etc. Nonoperating revenues can fluctuate from year to year to year and do not depend on patient volumes. Because of this, projections are typically based on historic levels.

(g) Other Budget Considerations

(i) Spread Methods. Even with a detailed, accurate budget, monthly reporting will not be relevant unless the amounts are spread correctly. Each department manager should be

allowed to give input to how the total budget amount will be spread to the different budget periods.

(ii) Inflation. Another important consideration, in making projections, is the forecast of inflation. Some organizations allow individual managers to project inflation amounts by expense category. This may lead to excessive inflationary requests that cover up inefficiencies. Other organizations prefer to utilize globally projected inflation. These inflation increases, by type of expense item, are used across the hospital. There are a number of available nationally recognized health-care inflation indices.

(h) Monitoring Performance. It is through monitoring performance that the budget provides management with a tool for controlling hospital operations, evaluating performance, and responding appropriately to unforseen events.

Deviations from the budget can be due to both internal and external factors. Some of the deviations may be caused by internal factors or errors in recording amounts (i.e., charging an item to the wrong expense account). Other deviations can be caused by external factors or unforeseen circumstances that are difficult or impossible to control.

Identifying controllable costs is not a simple matter. Many hospitals tend to designate: (1) all costs, (2) direct costs, or (3) direct variable costs as departmentally controllable. Although these approaches are simple, each have significant problems. For example, assigning all costs grossly overstate controllable costs. Both of the latter two approaches assign some costs that are not controllable and fail to assign other costs that can be influenced by the department head. An effort should be made to identify the costs that the manager can directly control or at least indirectly influence. See discretionary expense under the advanced budgeting section.

(i) Variance Measurement and Reporting. The final portion of the budget process is variance measurement and reporting. This is the process through which actual results are compared to the budget. Without variance reporting, the budget will be of little value if departmental and senior management do not know how their actual results relate to the budget.

This comparison report will typically show the actual and budgeted amounts along with the difference and percent difference between the values. This comparison will often include prior years actual information and may also include a flexed budget. (See the advanced budgeting section for information on flexible budgeting.) In addition, both the current period and year-to-date amounts are presented on the report.

There are several principles that should be considered when utilizing performance reports.

- *Timeliness.* If management is to take corrective action, then the results must be presented in a timely manner.
- *Accuracy.* Management must have confidence in the reported information if they are expected to respond to the results.
- *Detail.* The data presented must be sufficiently detailed to allow the manager to analyze the causes of the variance.
- *Clarity.* Data must be presented in an understandable fashion.
- *Consistency.* Both the actual and budget data must be collected in a consistent manner for comparability.

See Exhibit 37.6 for an example of a departmental profit and loss variance report including operating statistics.

(ii) Management Review. Management action is necessary if the budget is to be used to evaluate actual performance. Because the budget is an important tool to plan for the achievement of objectives, it is important to identify deviations from the plan and to determine the reasons for the variance.

The responsible individual must analyze the reasons for any substantial variances and be required to submit, within a reasonable time period, a report that identifies the following:

- The results of the analysis
- An action plan for correction of the situation or an explanation of why corrective action is not required
- Any changes that are required to the plan itself and the reasons for them

Top-level management must be committed to the entire budget process, which includes requiring action on deviations from the plan. If top-level management does not seem to care whether objectives are met, middle-level managers cannot be expected to commit to the objectives either. If differences between actual and budgeted performance are not perceived to be important, the level of commitment and effort devoted to the development of the budget will not be great. This failure to identify variances, and more importantly to require action on them, is probably the most common cause for the ineffectiveness of existing budget processes.

Most budgets are developed and reported with full general ledger levels of detail. However, all of this information can be confusing to nonfinancial managers. It is important for the managers to concentrate primarily on the areas of high variance. This is often accomplished through the use of exception reporting.

(1) Exception Reporting. Exception reporting involves reporting only those values that exceed certain value or percent thresholds. This exception report is sent along with the standard variance report to highlight areas requiring explanations or review. This will require a budgeting system that will allow reporting based on dollar amount and/or percent thresholds. The most valuable comparisons will show variances that exceed both dollar and percent thresholds at the same time.

(i) Advanced Budgeting. This advanced budgeting section includes several additional methods to budget or review department performance. These advanced budgeting techniques are not suggested for all organizations. Each of these methods will have advantages, but may require increased time, resources, and sophistication for the budgeting function. If these resources are available, then these methods can permit more accurate and meaningful budgeting and actual information comparisons.

(i) Flexible Budgeting. Flexible budgeting is an alternate method of variance reporting. Under this method of variance reporting, the budget is ''flexed'' to adjust for actual changes in service volumes. Revenues and certain types of staffing and expenses are adjusted based on increases or decreases in units of service.

A flexible budget enables management to identify the controllable factors that influence

Ernst & Young General Hospital
Prepared on 03/24/92 at 12:02
Profit and Loss Variance Report (2 years)

Cost Center: 16120 ICU Nov 91–Nov 91					Oct 91–Nov 91			
ACTUAL	BUDGET	Variance	Percent Variance		ACTUAL	BUDGET	Variance	Percent Variance
Inpatient Revenue								
20,930	21,254	−324	−1.5244	1101 I/P MATTHEW THORNTON	27,560	42,646	−15,086	−35.3749
0	2,706	−2,706	−100.0000	1102 I/P HEALTH SOURCE	2,800	5,430	−2,630	−48.4346
14,195	23,164	−8,969	−38.7196	1140 I/P-OTHER COMMERCIAL	36,046	46,479	−10,433	−22.4467
1,850	5,572	−3,722	−66.7983	1145 I/P-OTHER MEDICAID	3,700	11,180	−7,480	−66.9052
0	0	0	0.0000	1146 I/P-WORKMENS COMP	1,850	0	1,850	0.0000
14,411	9,950	4,461	44.8342	1165 I/P-BLUE CROSS OTHER	31,695	19,965	11,730	58.7528
12,990	9,632	3,358	34.8630	1180 I/P-SELF PAY	31,144	19,326	11,818	61.1508
76,946	75,205	1,741	2.3150	1187 I/P-MEDICARE	174,817	150,898	23,919	15.8511
141,322	147,483	−6,161	−4.1774		309,612	295,924	13,688	4.6255
Outpatient Revenue								
160	0	160	0.0000	6301 O/P MATTHEW THORNTON	270	0	270	0.0000
106	0	106	0.0000	6302 O/P HEALTH SOURCE	186	0	186	0.0000
80	0	80	0.0000	6340 O/P-OTHER COMMERCIAL	135	0	135	0.0000
80	0	80	0.0000	6345 O/P-OTHER MEDICAID	200	0	200	0.0000
40	0	40	0.0000	6346 O/P-WORKMENS COMP	40	0	40	0.0000
247	0	247	0.0000	6365 O/P-BLUE CROSS OTHER	268	0	268	0.0000
0	0	0	0.0000	6380 O/P-SELF PAY	25	0	25	0.0000
656	39	617	1,582.0513	6387 O/P-MEDICARE	1,818	78	1,740	2,230.7692
1,369	39	1,330	3,410.2564		2,942	78	2,864	3,671.7949
142,691	147,522	−4,831	−3.2748	GROSS PATIENT REVENUE	312,554	296,002	16,552	5.5919
OPERATING EXPENSES								
4,049	5,795	−1,746	−30.1294	Managerial Salaries	8,201	11,779	−3,578	−30.3761
5,636	12,083	−6,447	−53.3541	Other Salaries	10,877	18,609	−7,732	−41.5511
60,142	58,451	1,691	2.8930	RN Salaries	124,356	118,479	5,877	4.9604
680	0	680	0.0000	LPN Salaries	1,864	0	1,864	0.0000
3,014	0	3,014	0.0000	Earned Time	5,381	0	5,381	0.0000
73,521	76,329	−2,808	−3.6782	TOTAL SALARIES	150,679	148,867	1,812	1.2169

Nonsalary Expenses								
85	81	4	4.9383	37 TELEPHONE EXPENSE	128	81	47	58.0247
1,000	1,000	0	0.0000	270 PHYSICIAN FEES	2,000	2,000	0	0.0000
904	2,881	−1,977	−68.6220	350 M & S SUPPLY-CHARGEABLE	1,354	5,781	−4,427	−76.5784
256	15	241	1,606.6667	360 OFFICE & STATIONERY	372	215	157	73.0233
706	444	262	59.0090	370 FORMS	1,213	713	500	70.1262
3,009	3,035	−26	−0.8567	410 M & S SUPPLY-NON CHARGE	7,794	6,090	1,704	27.9803
0	0	0	0.0000	571 SERVICE CONTRACTS	976	0	976	0.0000
0	0	0	0.0000	580 DEPT PROJECTS	97	0	97	0.0000
30	0	30	0.0000	610 FOOD SUPPLIES	76	0	76	0.0000
6	0	6	0.0000	630 CLEANING SUPPLIES	14	0	14	0.0000
28	29	−1	−3.4483	760 BEEPER EXPENSE	28	58	−30	−51.7241
0	34	−34	−100.0000	890 DUES AND SUBSCRIPTIONS	−281	68	−349	−513.2353
90	56	34	60.7143	910 EDUCATION AND TRAVEL	663	288	375	130.2083
233	416	−183	−43.9904	930 OTHER SUPPLIES & EXPENSE	698	832	−134	−16.1058
11	481	−470	−97.7131	980 MINOR EQUIPMENT	11	962	−951	−98.8565
6,358	8,472	−2,114	−24.9528		15,143	17,088	−1,945	−11.3823
79,879	84,801	−4,922	−5.8037	TOTAL OPERATING EXPENSES	165,822	165,955	−133	−0.0804
62,812	62,721	91	0.1443	GAIN/(LOSS) OPERATIONS	146,732	130,047	16,685	12.8303
Operating Statistics								
Total Admissions								
54	49	5	10.2041	99040 Admissions	109	101	8	7.9208
Total Patient Days								
148	154	−6	−3.8961	99010 Patient days	320	309	11	3.5599
2.74	3.14	−0.40	−12.7946	Average Length of Stay	2.94	3.06	−0.12	−4.0409
4,727	3,878	850	21.9105	Total Paid Hours	8,537	7,882	655	8.3116
15.55	19.68	−4.13	−20.9898	Average Hourly Rate	17.65	18.89	−1.24	−6.5503
955	958	−3	−0.2927	Gross Rev./Adj. Pat Day	968	958	10	1.0290
492	496	−4	−0.7086	Payroll Exp/Adj. Pat Day	466	482	−15	−3.1569
535	551	−16	−2.8996	Total Exp/Adj. Pat Day	513	537	−24	−4.3981
27.62	22.66	4.96	21.9105	Total FTE's	24.53	22.65	1.88	8.3116
0.18	0.15	0.04	25.6690	Total FTE's/Adj. Pat Day	0.08	0.07	0.00	3.6312
2,662	3,369	−707	−20.9898	Payroll Expense/FTE	6,142	6,573	−431	−6.5503

Exhibit 37.6. Departmental profit and loss variance report

budget variances. A flexible budget will help to focus the department manager's attention on the resource inputs and the related costs, which they are responsible for controlling.

If a flexible budget is developed, performance reports will include the flexible budget as compared to actual and fixed (static) budget information. The standard to which managers are held is typically the fixed budget. However, the flexible budget will identify changes in variable expenses and revenues due to changes in volumes compared to the fixed budget.

There are several advantages and disadvantages to flexible budgeting.

Advantages

- Budget can be adjusted to reflect actual activity levels
- Easier to obtain meaningful variance analysis
- Can generate a more enthusiastic acceptance by department managers

Disadvantages

- Requires more time and resources to develop and update
- Requires additional training
- A higher level of sophistication is required on the part of administrative, financial, and operating personnel if the budget is utilized properly

Under *advanced flexible budgeting,* certain types of primary "driver" statistics can be used to project other statistics. Primary driver statistics are typically patient days, discharges, and outpatient volumes. All other statistics (secondary statistics) are derived based on budgeted relationships to the primary statistics. For example, inpatient laboratory tests may be based on a relationship to patient days; outpatient tests on a relationship to outpatient visits. Developing a flexed budget this way allows you to examine budget variances due to treatment inefficiencies.

This form of budgeting should include intensity measures such as case mix index changes. Unexpected increases or decreases in secondary statistics can be caused by changes in intensity as well as practice patterns. It is therefore suggested that driver statistics should only be used to project other statistics where a consistent historic relationship can be demonstrated. If the relationship is weak, then any projections based on a driver statistic will likely result in inaccurate forecasts.

(1) Variable Expenses. Variable expenses are expenses that vary with the department's volume levels. These expenses can be 100% variable and can vary with a one-to-one relationship with changes in volume. Expenses can also be semivariable and vary in an indirect or step fashion with changes in volume. Variable expenses typically include items such as medical and surgical supplies, physician fees, purchased nursing pool expenses, and payroll expense (and associated staffing hours). In addition, many expenses have both a fixed and variable portion. For example, there may be a minimal amount of staffing required, regardless of volume. This would represent the fixed portion of the variable staffing budget.

(2) Fixed Expenses. Fixed expenses are expenses that are not dependent on the volume of the department. These expenses would include items such as depreciation, travel, education, and interest.

(3) Discretionary Expenses. Another category of expense could be defined as discretionary expenses. These are the expense items that the department manager can directly control or at least influence. Compliance with discretionary expenses should be given the most weight when evaluating a manager's performance relative to the budget. The identification of all discretionary expenses can be a difficult process.

Discretionary expenses will include both fixed and variable expense items. This would include fixed items such as travel, education, minor equipment, and consultant fees. It would also include variable expenses such as purchased services and certain types of medical/surgical supplies.

The identification of fixed, variable, and discretionary expenses should be done with input from each of the service areas. They will often have a different perspective than the financial area. If an expense item is identified as fixed, variable, or discretionary, then this designation should be used for the entire organization.

(ii) Variable Staffing. When considering budgeting for variable staffing for a department, several issues should be considered.

- *Size of department.* A small department will often not have the flexibility to adjust staffing with volume changes. In addition, if the salary expense is relatively small, it may not be worth the extra effort to project the variable staffing levels.
- *Seasonal utilization patterns.* If there are little or no seasonal variations in volumes and staffing, there will be little difference between a fixed and flexible budget.
- *General service departments.* If a department's work load is not directly related to patient volumes, then a variable budget will lead to an unrealistic budget.
- *Availability of personnel.* In many cases, it is not possible to use a flexible budget if additional staffing with part-time or temporary help is difficult to obtain.
- *Labor relations.* Some union contracts will impact the organization's ability to provide flexible staffing patterns (especially staffing decreases).

In general, a flexible staffing budget will provide the most benefit for larger, patient care–related departments. These are the departments that will have both the greatest need and ability to change staffing patterns based on patient volumes.

(iii) Fully Costed Departments. The purpose of allocating costs from overhead departments is to reflect the total cost of producing the service. This means that all departments that do not charge patients for their services are allocated to those departments (or services) that are charged. Examples of departments that are not charged to patients include those that provide services to the revenue-producing departments such as housekeeping, laundry, and administration.

The major advantage of allocating costs to the revenue cost centers is that the departmental budgets reflect the full costs of producing each service or procedure. The principal weakness of fully allocated costing is that it may assign costs to departments that are outside the control of the department. Certain types of allocated expenses will be related to the actual usage of the overhead area's resources such as laundry, central supply, or housekeeping. Other overhead departments, such as finance or administration, are beyond the control of the department manager. In addition, if deductions from revenue and allowances are not recorded in the individual departments, then there must be an allocation of these amounts to calculate the department's net revenue along with the direct and indirect costs.

(1) Overhead Expense Allocation. Overhead allocation is the method of allocating costs from nonrevenue producing departments to revenue-producing departments. The purpose of this allocation is to associate all costs, both direct and indirect, with producing a particular service. There are a number of different methods of allocating indirect costs. Several of the most common methods are described briefly below.

- *Direct assignment.* Direct assignment involves directly assigning overhead costs to departments. Although this is simple, there is little science to this method, and it is often of limited accuracy and value.
- *Single step-down.* Step-down allocation involves allocation of overhead costs based on departmental statistics. Under single step-down allocation, once an overhead department's costs are allocated, the department is closed for the purposes of receiving allocations from other departments. As a rough example, if a department uses 20% of the overhead measurement statistic, then they would receive 20% of the overhead departments cost. This method of allocation is the same as the method used to allocate costs for the medicare cost report.
- *Multiple step-down.* Multiple step-down is similar to single step-down except that the step-down is done in multiple iterations until all expenses are allocated. Under this method, a department that has already been allocated can have costs allocated to it, which are then later reallocated to other departments. This method is more time consuming, but more accurate than the single step-down method. It is also less sensitive to the step-down order.

(2) Definition of Statistical Bases. To perform a step-down allocation, statistical bases must be defined as a basis of allocating the overhead costs. Statistics are selected that best represent the revenue producing departments usage of the overhead area. This will often include statistics such as pounds of laundry, housekeeping hours, or square footage. Other statistics are more difficult to define. These would include areas such as finance, administration, plant operation, etc. These areas may be allocated based on statistics such as gross revenue, number of employees, or square feet.

When deciding on the correct allocation statistic, the department manager of the *overhead department* should be consulted. This manager will often have the best understanding of how other departments use its services and can help to select a measurement statistic.

(3) Step-Down Order. If a single step-down allocation is used, the order in which expenses are allocated will have a large impact on the amount of overhead expense received by an revenue-producing department. Departments that have overhead costs allocated to them early in the step-down process will have relatively less expense allocated to them. Departments at the end will receive high levels of allocated expense. In general, it is preferable to allocate departments that utilize smaller amounts of overhead services early in the process and departments that have high utilization of overhead services toward the end of the allocation process.

(iv) Allocation of Deductions and Allowances. An additional consideration in developing a fully costed department is the allocation of deductions and allowances. To deter-

mine the overall profitability of a revenue-producing department, gross revenues, deductions and allowances, and both indirect and indirect costs must be included in the individual department profit and loss (P&L) statement.

Typically, each deduction and allowance is aggregated in single departments or general ledger accounts. To develop a fully costed department, these allowances must be allocated to the individual departments. The starting point for this allocation is the department's budgeted or actual payor mix. Generally, it is too difficult to calculate an individual allowance for a specific department based on the type of services offered. Instead, overall hospital percentages are used to determine the departmental allowance. For example, if the overall Medicare allowance is 28% of gross revenue, then a medicare allowance of 28% of the department's actual or budgeted Medicare revenue would be used to allocate the allowance to the department.

In addition, it is important to be able to allocate the actual allowances in a similar fashion. If actual allowances are not allocated, then the budgeted amount will have little comparative value.

It should also be noted that developing a fully costed budget may be confusing and resisted by department managers. Therefore, if a fully costed budget is developed, additional education of department managers will be required. These departmental managers may also resist this type of budget because many of the allocated amounts are beyond their control. This type of budgeting has the most value when a health-care provider has a need to determine the profitability of different departments or product lines.

(v) Advanced Cost Analysis and Cost Accounting. Advanced cost analysis requires the integration of clinical and financial information at a very detailed level. This type of analysis is difficult and requires advanced information systems that can integrate areas such as medical records information, including case-mix and cost-accounting systems. This type of analysis will become more prevalent in the future as health-care providers become more refined in their cost-analysis ability and as practice parameters are developed and refined. Financial managers alone do not have the expertise required to evaluate the medical appropriateness of various procedures. This type of analysis is beyond the scope of this chapter but would include product line and procedural levels of cost review.

(j) Comparison to Peer Hospitals. Performing comparisons to peer hospitals is important in today's competitive health-care market. This type of comparison should be performed even if separate from the budgeting function. However, this information should be integrated with the budgeting function because it can help to identify areas of inefficiency that require additional management attention and monitoring.

This comparison should include comparisons to both geographic and size competitors. Comparison to *geographic competitors* is important for competitive reasons. It is important to know the hospitals comparative strengths and weakness with respect to other area hospitals. This information can also be helpful for managed-care contracting. Comparisons to *size competitors* will give the most revealing information on comparative costs and efficiencies. Similar-size institutions will often offer similar types of services. Therefore, comparisons can give information on areas that are high priced, high cost, or overstaffed, or identify areas that are low priced, low cost, or understaffed. Most of the public information available is only valid for macromeasures of departments or segments of the hospital such as routine services areas, ancillary services, or general (overhead) services. This information can point-out problem areas that require additional analysis to determine the reason for the differences.

Typical sources of information can include state or federal regulatory agencies, hospital associations, or independent agencies that collect comparative information.

37.6 PHYSICIAN BUDGETING. Budgeting is often a neglected area for physicians, who often work long hours and have limited time to help create and monitor a budget. However, physicians are beginning to feel the same cost-containment pressures that other health-care providers face. In recent years, physicians have experienced reduced payments from commercial payors, HMOs, and government payors. This downward pressure on physician incomes has intensified with the 1992 implementation of Medicare's resource-based relative-value system (RBRVS) for physician reimbursement. Other payors are likely to adopt this system over the next several years.

The principles that apply to physician budgeting are similar to those for other health-care providers. The primary difference between budgeting for physicians and for hospitals is the size of the organization. Most physicians practices do not have the time or sophistication to budget at the level that is required for a hospital. In general, the larger the organization, the more internal controls are needed to monitor and control expenses. However, even solo practitioners and small group practices will benefit from the creation and monitoring of a budget.

All of the areas mentioned under "Basics of Health-Care Budgeting" apply to physician budgeting. In addition, many of the areas under "Hospital Budgeting" will apply to a large multispecialty group practice. These sections in this chapter should be reviewed for additional information as required.

One of the primary difficulties in budgeting for physician practices is the lack of information. Physician business practices typically concentrate on billing activities and related revenues with less emphasis on cost data and statistics.

(a) Physician Budgeting Issues

(i) Budgeting by Department or Specialty. For a large group practice made up of a number of specialties, budgeting should be done by physician specialty or department. This is important because physician compensation is often based on their generated net revenue and portion of expenses. For this analysis to be reliable, both expenses and revenues must be collected with enough detail to differentiate expenses between the various specialties and physicians.

(ii) Physician Compensation. Physicians can be compensated based on a number of different methodologies. The basis of this compensation will have an impact on the budget process. If a physician is paid based on a fixed-salary or minimum-salary guarantee, then the physician compensation is treated as a salary expense. However, if a physician is compensated based on the net profits of the practice, the other expenses and revenues are budgeted first. The physician compensation will be based on the practice's net profit after all expenses are subtracted from the net revenue.

(iii) Cash Accounting and Management. Most types of physician practices are run as for-profit enterprises. Any revenue received that is in excess of expenses is distributed to the partners of the group. Any activity that can help increase revenues or decrease expenses will generate additional profits to the owners of the practice. This is the typical treatment for most partnerships.

Because profits are distributed to the partners, almost all physician practices are accounted for on a cash basis. This is required to match the current expenses paid with the current revenues received. This type of accounting tends to encourage the maximizing of profits in the current year, sometimes at the expense of later periods. This can lead to the underestimation and underfunding of certain types of expenses such as depreciation, maintenance, and pensions. If revenue reserves are not retained by the business, any large purchases can create cash flow problems and will have to be funded through short-term borrowing or reduced income to the physicians. This is one area where physician practices often fail to plan ahead.

(iv) Physician Involvement in the Budgeting Process. Because physicians are the executive managers and often the owners of the business, their involvement in the budget process is critical to its success. Physicians generally do not have the time to be involved in the details of creating a budget. However, they must be involved in the review, approval, and monitoring of the budget for it to be effective.

(v) Comparative Measures. There are not as many comparative measures available for physicians as there are for larger health-care providers. One source of comparative information is the *Medical Group Management Association (MGMA) Cost and Production Survey.* This survey is updated annually and contains expense, revenue, and statistical information by physician specialty. Other sources would include physician specialty societies, the American Medical Association (AMA), the American Hospital Association's (AHA) *Socioeconomic Characteristics of Medical Practice,* and *The Journal of Medical Economics.* This information can serve as a benchmark for comparison purposes. It should also be noted that it is not always preferable to have expenses and expense ratios too far below the averages for a particular specialty. Unusually low expense ratios can indicate that there is insufficient support staff and the physician may be spending too much time performing support functions. If expense levels are found to be especially low, then the operation of the practice should be reviewed to determine if physicians are spending too much time performing functions that could be performed by less costly individuals. In addition, this may indicate that important functions are not being performed at all because of a lack of staff.

(b) Expenses. Physician practice expenses can be broken into three main categories: (1) salaries and fringe benefits, (2) nonsalary expenses, and (3) physician compensation.

(i) Salary and Fringe Benefit Expenses. For physician practices, nonphysician salary expenses will often be a smaller portion of the total expenses than for other health-care providers. This is because the physician provides the majority of the direct patient care. The other staff provides related support functions. It is therefore possible to have some economies of scale in terms of staffing. Many physicians join group practices to obtain the economies of scale for many of the support functions such as reception, billing, nursing, and office management.

Fringe benefits for a physician practice can vary widely based on the size of the practice, profitability, and local norms. Fringe benefits can vary from between 0 and 25% of the salary expense. In addition, there may be a breakdown between physician and nonphysician fringe benefit costs.

Salary expenses and fringe benefits can be budgeted by the methodologies described in Sections 37.5 (c) and (d).[5]

(ii) Nonsalary Expenses. Nonsalary expenses are often not given sufficient attention by physician practices. Certain types of nonsalary expenses often increase faster than inflation if not managed properly. These expenses are described in more detail below. Nonsalary expenses for physicians often include the following types of expenses:

- Medical/surgical supplies
- Malpractice
- Rent
- Billing expense (inhouse or outside agency)
- Software and hardware maintenance and support fees
- Equipment
- Utilities
- Legal and professional fees
- Licenses
- Purchased services
- Dues and publications
- Education and travel
- Pension plan administration
- Laundry
- Phone
- Postage
- Marketing

Certain types of nonsalary expense should receive additional attention by physicians and business office managers. These types of expenses include the following.

- *Equipment.* For equipment purchases, the comparison of lease-versus-purchase terms should be carefully reviewed. For any major purchase/lease, the terms should be reviewed by the practice's accountant or financial advisor. A poor selection of terms can create a large and unnecessary liability for the practice. This can be especially important for practices that utilize expensive technology such as radiology, imaging equipment, or lasers.
- *Supplies.* Both medical and nonmedical supplies are a large expense item for physician practices. This type of expense will often increase at a faster rate than inflation. There are also frequently high increases in pharmaceutical purchases. Significant opportunities exist for practices to reduce these expenses through group purchasing arrangements with other physicians or hospitals and/or through competitive bidding by vendors.
- *Purchased services.* Purchased services for areas such as laboratory testing, radiology

[5] If the physician practice accounting is done on a cash basis, Section 33.5 (vi) will not apply.

services, physical therapy, and locum tenants (temporary replacement for physicians when on vacation, etc.) may be reduced through competitive bidding.

- *Malpractice.* Large group practices may experience economies of scale in purchasing malpractice insurance. However, solo practitioners and small groups should explore group purchase arrangements through professional affiliations. In addition, competitive bids should be received from different sources. Malpractice rates are highly dependent on specialty. However, different insurers may have different experience ratings and will have different pricing, for the same specialty, with similar coverage terms.
- *Computer maintenance.* Computer hardware and software maintenance are often underfunded in physician practices. The costs of paying hardware maintenance should be compared to the costs of repairing or replacing the hardware. The cost of software maintenance should be compared to the cost of repurchasing the software if it becomes damaged or a significant upgrade becomes available.

(iii) Fixed and Variable Expenses. Because many physician compensation arrangements are based on net income after allocation of expenses, the identification of fixed versus variable expenses can be important. Certain expense items vary with patient volumes such as medical supplies, pharmaceuticals, office supplies, and billing expenses. Because this identification may have an impact on the physician's compensation, the doctors in the practice should decide which expenses will be classified as variable. These expenses can then be allocated to the physicians based on the most appropriate statistic such as gross revenue or patient volumes.

(iv) Physician Income. There are a number of ways in which physicians are typically compensated. The majority are paid based on salary plus distribution of excess income. However, there are a number of other methods used to pay physicians, which are outlined below.

(1) Salary. Some physicians are paid based on a fixed annual salary. The projection of this salary amount would be the same as the methods used to project nonphysician salaries. In some situations, physicians are paid an annual salary plus an *incentive payment.* An incentive payment is typically based on the physician meeting or exceeding certain goals established before the start of the payment period. Incentive payments can be based on meeting a certain patient volume or revenue threshold. If a physician meets or exceeds the designated threshold levels, then they receive a bonus in addition to the base salary. During the budget preparation, any potential incentive payments should also be included in the projection.

(2) Base Salary Plus Income Distribution. Income distribution is the most common form of physician compensation. In general terms, any profit is distributed to the partners of the group. There are many different distribution formulas used to determine individual physician compensation. Some groups continue to simply distribute the net profit to each practitioner evenly. This is most likely to occur in a small, homogeneous practice in which there is a single specialty and similar patient volumes. Other groups distribute net profits periodically (often quarterly) after adjusting for individually generated net revenue levels and fixed and variable expenses. Larger multispecialty groups may perform multiple allo-

cations. The first allocation would be to each specialty group. From this first distribution, an additional distribution would be made for each physician within the specialty.

(3) Income Guarantees. Income guarantees are common for new practitioners in a group. Under this method, if the physician's individually generated net profit does not exceed a particular level, then they will receive the guaranteed income amount as a minimum. For example, if a physician had an income guarantee of $100,000, and their individually generated net profit was $80,000, they would receive a payment of $100,000. This income guarantee is subsidized by the other members of the group. However, if the physician generated a net profit of $130,000, then they would receive compensation of $130,000. An income guarantee establishes a minimum compensation. However, it may be as high as the physician is able to generate.

(4) Hourly Employee. Another method that is occasionally used is hourly reimbursement. This method is most frequently used for part time physicians that may be staffing an emergency room or walk-in clinic. These physicians are typically junior physicians that have not yet completed their specialty accreditation.

(v) Revenues. There have recently been some major changes in how physicians are reimbursed. The change that has the largest impact is the creation of Medicare's RBRVS payment methodology, which is expected to redistribute revenue among the physician specialties. This system is intended to promote primary care and the cognitive side of medicine. It is also intended to constrain the procedural part of medicine. This reimbursement system is intended to cause a redistribution of payments from specialists to primary-care physicians. Many individuals contest whether the new system actually fulfills its goals. However, the system is here to stay and will likely be adopted by other payors in the coming years.

(1) Gross Patient Revenues. Gross patient revenues represent the actual charges for services performed for patients. To project gross revenues, several types of information must be collected. The first piece of information required is the units of service. For physicians, units of service are based on CPT-4 codes.[6] These codes represent different types of medical codes assigned to each procedure performed by physicians. The second piece of information required is the charge per procedure.

For a small homogeneous practice, it is generally easy to compile all of the relevant volumes and charges. There will frequently be only a small variation of the different types of procedures performed.

For a large multispecialty group, it may be more difficult to collect the required information. If detailed information is not available or difficult to collect, gross revenues can be projected based on a method similar to that used for hospital revenue budgeting. Gross revenues can be projected by department or specialty based on the average charge. This is calculated by dividing the total revenue by the total units of service (i.e., visits or procedures). It should be noted that because physician reimbursement methods are rapidly changing, projecting revenues without adjusting for changes in types of services or payment methodologies may result in poor revenue projections.

---

[6] Current procedural terminology, 4th edition American Medical Association, 1970.

Physicians often differentiate charges (or billings) from revenues. To most physicians, the actual cash collected represents net revenue. Charges represent what patients are billed.

(2) Allowances and Adjustments to Revenue. There are a number of different types of adjustments to revenue. These adjustments include contractual allowances, bad debts, and professional courtesy write-offs.

A contractual allowance is the difference between what is charged by the physician and what is allowed by the payor. The allowance is based on the payment agreement between the payor and the physician and cannot be billed to the patient.

Almost all physician practices do not calculate allowances at the time of billing. They rely on the payor to pay the correct amount, and then write-off the contractual allowance at the time of payment. Although this is the easiest way to determine the contractual allowance, if the payor is not paying the correct amount, it will not be recognized.

The most precise way to project allowances is based on procedural levels of volumes, payments, and payor mix. However, if this level of detail is not available, then allowances can be projected from historic levels. The prior year amount would be adjusted for any changes in volumes, prices, payor mix, and payor payments.

Bad debt is the portion of patient responsible charges that are not paid by the patient. Bad debt levels can generally be projected from historical experience. However, increases in the amount of self-pay patients can have a significant impact on the amount of bad debt.

Courtesy write-offs are for discounts offered by the physician to the patient. This may include professional discounts or charity care. These levels can also be projected from historical levels and are often minor compared to other types of revenue adjustments.

(3) Nonpatient Revenues. Nonpatient revenues represent income earned from nonpatient care–related activities such as teaching stipends, contracts, interest, or research funding. The treatment of this revenue will depend on the type of compensation that the physician receives. If a physician is paid with a fixed salary, then the additional income is often given to the owners of the practice. If the physician is paid based on some type of income distribution, then the agreement with the other partners must be considered when determining the treatment of this revenue. In some cases, this income will be part of the overall practice income. It may also be treated as income for only the physician performing the work. The treatment of this type of revenue must be reviewed as part of the budget process.

SOURCES AND SUGGESTED REFERENCES

Abernethy, Margaret A., and Johannes U. Stoelwinder, ''Budget Use, Task Uncertainty, System Goal Orientation and Subunit Performance: A Test of the ''Fit'' Hypothesis in Not-for-Profit Hospitals,'' *Accounting, Organizations & Society* (UK), vol. 16, no. 2, 1991.

Bergman, Judson T., and David C. Gordon, ''Developing Capital Investment Guidelines for Acquisitions,'' *Healthcare Financial Management,* vol. 42, no. 5, May 1988.

Chow, Chee W., and Alan H. McNamee, ''Watch for Pitfalls of Discounted Cash Flow Techniques,'' *Healthcare Financial Management,* vol. 45, no. 4, April 1991.

Cook, Donald, ''Strategic Plan Creates a Blueprint for Budgeting,'' *Healthcare Financial Management,* vol. 44, no. 5, May 1990.

Crump, R. S., "Bottom-Line Budgeting Based on Estimated Cash Flow Needs," *Healthcare Financial Management,* April 1992.

Ernst & Whinney, *Introduction to Hospital Budgeting,* Ernst & Young internal information, October 1983.

Ernst & Young, *The Budget Manager (TBM) User Guide Ver. 4.2.* October, 1992.

Francisco, Perry D., "Flexible Budgeting and Variance Analysis," *Nursing Management,* vol. 20, no. 11, November 1989.

Gauss, James W., "The CFO: A Better Paid, Better Prepared Executive," *Healthcare Financial Management,* vol. 43, no. 7, July 1989.

Hauser, Rexford C., Donald E. Edwards, and Judy T. Edwards, "Cash Budgeting: An Underutilized Resource Management Tool in Not-for-Profit Health Care Entities," *Hospital & Health Services Administration,* vol. 36, no. 3, Fall 1991.

Heshmat, S., "The Role of Cost in Hospital Pricing Decisions," *Journal of Hospital Marketing,* 1991.

Hubbard, C.M., "Capital Budgeting and Cost Reimbursement in Investor-Owned and Not-For-Profit Hospitals," *Health Care Management Review,* Summer 1983.

Johnson, Kenneth F., "Developing a Cost Base for Pricing," *Topics in Health Care Financing,* vol. 14, no. 1, Fall 1987.

Kazamek, Thomas J., "Moving to Product Line Budgeting," *Computers in Healthcare,* vol. 9, no. 11, November 1988.

Kerschner, Morley I., and Jeffrey M. Rooney, "Utilizing Cost Accounting Information for Budgeting," *Topics in Health Care Financing,* vol. 13, no. 4, Summer 1987.

Lohrmann, Glenn M., "Flexible Budget System: A Practical Approach to Cost Management," *Healthcare Financial Management,* vol. 43, no. 1, January 1989.

Sorenson, E. L., "Flexible Budgeting—Easier Than You Think," *Healthcare Financial Management,* April 1979.

Ward, William J., *Healthcare Budgeting and Financial Management for Nonfinancial Managers.* Westport, CT: Greenwood Publishing Group, 1994.

CHAPTER **38**

BUDGETING IN THE BIOTECH INDUSTRY*

R. Malcolm Schwartz
Glenn A. White
Robert F. McElroy

PricewaterhouseCoopers L.L.P.

38.1 OVERVIEW. The biotech industry has grown to considerably more than 1,000 public or private companies over the last 20 years. The crowded industry competes for increasingly limited funding; most depend heavily on venture capital, having inadequate cash flows to generate significant interest among typical equity investors. In later stages of successful companies' evolution, equity (IPOs) and debt may be options. Private investments in public entities (PIPEs) are now becoming common for later-stage funding. Nonetheless, $4.7 billion in public and private capital was raised in the 12 months ended June 1994. However, because investors are getting leery and the money flow is decreasing, good management practices—budgeting and planning among them—are very important, for both managing funds and attracting investors.

The industry has been hampered by uneven management, driven by greed to lure new investment and form companies that have little prospect of succeeding, and wracked by product failures. Even those relatively few companies with a more promising new product pipeline are faced with the difficulty of predicting the timing of Food and Drug Administration (FDA) approvals, which exacerbates the challenge of forecasting revenue and income streams. Following FDA approval, they still must face the challenges of physician acceptance and receptivity of the new products. Thus, following approval and introduction, the job of projecting sales volumes is still much more of an art than a science—which is very much counter to the mindset of the average research scientist, who likely has become the company leader.

Once the biotech company has dealth with the problem of projecting sales revenue, the next hurdle is projecting resource requirements and expenses for production operations and support functions. Other industries are somewhat more frequently blessed with some prior history of production capabilities, based on similar products, and thus have some basis for projecting manufacturing operating rates, yields, and costs. In biotech, each

* The authors gratefully acknowledge the invaluable assistance of Charles A. Clerecuzio.

new product is likely to have substantially different production characteristics, making projection of operating rates and costs extremely challenging, to say the least.

Faced with these myriad unknowns and issues, these same biotech companies are faced with the need to develop credible forecasts for their operating plans. These plans are key to being able to prove and justify a need for investment from outside providers of capital.

This chapter discusses some of the key issues that should be addressed and included in the development of a budget for a biotech company. Specific consideration also is given to the different nuances that impact the biotechs based on where their products are in the life cycle. Given the focus on the front, or development, end of the process, a brief discussion on the application of life cycle accounting also is included.

38.2 KEY BUDGETING ISSUES. Given the backdrop of rather extreme uncertainty, biotech manufacturers are nonetheless faced with the same basic need to develop financial plans and budgets as are most of their counterparts in other industries. Forecasts of the expected revenue and expense streams not only support the important task of acquiring financing, but also provide a tool for measuring and managing the operational performance of the enterprise.

Key requirements in the development of the budget include the relatively obvious need to forecast sales (volumes, prices, and the resulting revenue streams); and the subsequent planning for the supporting resource and financial requirements to enable these sales, including capacity, labor, materials, and supplies. However, before reviewing the key elements of budgeting, it is useful to answer some important strategic and tactical questions addressing key operational considerations.

(a) Research and the "Capital Burn Rate." First and foremost, biotech companies depend on the development pipeline. Because the pipeline is key to their survival, they must plan for, manage, and maintain adequate resources to support their development efforts. Especially in the early stages of the life cycle (discussed in further detail in section 34.3), it is critical that the plan be fully developed to support acquisition of adequate capital, and that this capital not be expended too quickly or ineffectively. That is, the early funding must frequently carry the biotech to a defined milestone before further funding can be obtained. This phenomenon is also frequently referred to as *controlling the capital burn rate.* Failure to manage the use and consumption of funds may result in the enterprise running out of financing and, worse yet, financing opportunities, before reaching the point of having a marketable product and the ability to generate its own funding through product sales.

(b) Sales and Marketing Support Levels. As the biotech enterprise initiates commercial operation, the development of a sales force will have to be addressed. To get the right message to the right market takes a more expansive effort than presentations at seminars and conferences by the president and other senior company officers and scientists. However, with a limited product line, an adequate level of both productivity and effectiveness cannot be expected (even) from a dedicated sales force. Therefore, consideration might be given to having products co-marketed by another manufacturer with an established sales force, already calling on the same market and therapeutic area (that is, disease segments such as hypertension, depression, or heart disease) as those for the new biotech's products.

Preceding formal introduction of the product, limited (within limitations imposed by the FDA) marketing and promotional efforts may be initiated, and consideration should be given to this area. Postintroduction, formal marketing and promotion will begin, and messages, literature, and other materials should be planned, created, and available at the point of product launch. Thus, early planning for the funding of these initiatives must be done to ensure that adequate resources are available to execute the plans.

To facilitate the promotional efforts surrounding products, market research should be performed to assess market potential for products, as well as possibly to test different concepts for messages and to develop a better understanding of what will be required to promote the product physically. Again, during budgeting it is important to consider and plan for all potential requirements, so as to allow for resource planning to meet downstream operational requirements.

(c) Production Sourcing. Long before the initiation of commercial production, the biotech company must decide how it plans to produce in order to meet the anticipated market demand. The first question is whether sales volumes are expected to warrant scale-up in any production facility, or if these needs can be met through production in the laboratory. Occasionally, demand for specialized products can be met through the laboratory or pilot facilities; if this route is used, it obviously can simplify the production question, as the operators already know how to produce the product. If larger production capabilities are projected, the next question to be addressed is whether production will be internal, or if contract manufacturers should be considered. The latter alternative, depending on the defined technology, may be quite viable, as there is a significant amount of underutilized capacity at a number of major pharmaceutical manufacturers today. Not only does this provide a relatively ready source of capacity, but these facilities are most likely FDA-approved for production, although specific approval for the new products still must be received.

Once the company decides it is going to manufacture its product internally, it must define and develop new capabilities to meet FDA compliance requirements, as well as the ability to meet cGMPs (current good manufacturing procedures). During the budgeting process, funding must be provided for the planned scale-up and production. If internal resources are not equipped to generate the definition of requirements and costs for this process, consideration should be given to hiring either an external consultant or a new employee to fill this role. In either case, a budget for the expenses associated with this role must be provided.

38.3 CHALLENGES AT STAGES OF THE COMPANY'S LIFE CYCLE.

The budget focus of a typical biotech company evolves as the company transitions through its life cycle. The journey from start-up to a fully integrated pharmaceutical company, expressed as a "life cycle," is pictured in Exhibit 38.1.

Different functional areas, as described in Section 38.4, will become the focus of budget considerations as the company evolves and grows. Managers must carefully direct funding to support the strategic needs of the organization for the current stage, and plan for the needs of future stages.

Each stage of the life cycle carries intrinsic sources of uncertainty that give rise to risks that must be managed. There are costs associated with managing these sources of uncertainty, which must be considered when preparing annual budgets. The management of uncertainty involves deciding on an acceptable level of risk, managing the risks to reduce them to this acceptable level, determining the cost of managing the risks, and budgeting for the risk management in addition to any other contingencies.

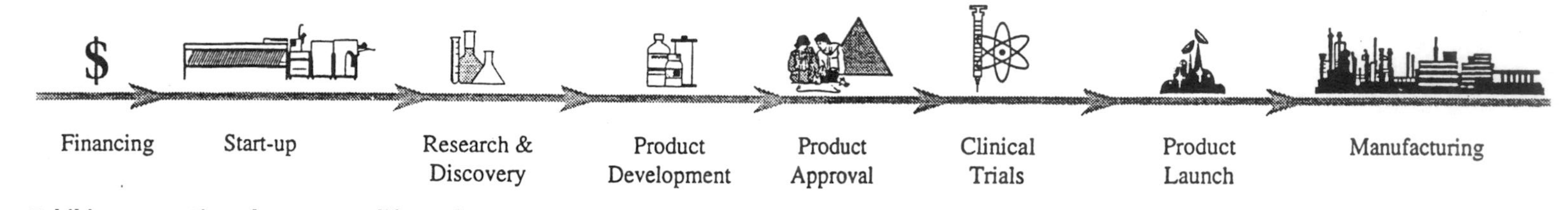

Exhibit 38.1. Biotech company life cycle

(a) Financing and Start-up. The initial stages in the life cycle of a biotechnology company are financing and start-up. Because financing involves raising initial funds that will be deployed through annual budgets beginning during the start-up stage, these stages can be examined together. For a company to move into the start-up stage, the quest for initial financing must have been successful. Today, this means securing a recurring stream of funding, or positioning the company strategically to generate early streams of revenue.

The focus of the company, and the budget, at this stage is to build the organizational foundation of the company and to attract research talent. Laying an organizational foundation does not mean building a large, cumbersome infrastructure or a bureaucratic overhead structure. To the contrary, the company needs to design its business processes so that they can function effectively with a minimal time commitment from the technical staff while limiting the support staff required. This often means early investments in technology, such as information technology, that can allow the company to leverage its human assets. These early foundational investments are more difficult to justify than science and research expenditures, from a budgetary point of view, but if made wisely they can significantly decrease a company's ongoing overhead costs.

Because base salaries at start-up biotechnology companies are often lower than at larger, more established pharmaceutical companies, compensation packages usually include equity or profit-sharing options. This style of compensation carries inherent risk and can be a hurdle in attracting top-notch talent but can also be used to identify people with strong entrepreneurial spirits, which is a desirable quality for anyone involved in a start-up company.

(b) Research and Discovery. The focus of the research and discovery phase in the company life cycle is to maintain a level, uninterrupted funding to allow the company to drive toward discovery of its first potential compound. The source of this funding, and the level of uncertainty it carries, can have a strong effect on annual budget preparation. Funding generated through predictable revenue from operations, such as contract research, carries a greater degree of uncertainty than cash in the bank. The greatest uncertainty during this stage comes simply from the serendipity inherent in the discovery process. This prevents accurate prediction of milestones and breakthroughs. The best way to manage this uncertainty is to design a targeted, focused research initiative. Often, research efforts veer off the main path and follow promising tangents. This causes an unnecessarily high capital burn rate and consumes precious resources. Companies should focus on a specific disease or family of therapies and direct resources in a very targeted manner. Companies developing an enabling technology should target a specific compound or class of compounds for initial prototyping of the technology. Once the technology has been proven, expansion to include other potential product classes can be considered.

The annual budget at this stage should be organized by research project (see Exhibit 38.2). All costs related to a specific project should then be tracked against the budget on a project-by-project basis. This enables both superior focus and budget control, and can provide warnings of projects that are beginning to drift from their targeted focus.

The discovery process can be accelerated through the use of advanced tools, such as combinatorial chemistry, computer-aided drug design, and new techniques and technology. This strategy requires accelerating some capital expenditures and/or technology license payments in order to reduce time-to-market and overall development costs.

	Budget	Actual	Variance
Project Xi.			
Labor:			
Principal Investigator	(1) $100,000	(1) $100,000	0
Senior Scientist(s)	(2) 120,000	(2) 210,000	0
Scientist(s)	(3) 105,000	(2) 70,000	($35,000)
Laboratory Technician(s)	(3) 60,000	(4) 80,000	20,000
Assigned General Lab Labor	35,000	35,000	0
Subtotal Labor	**$420,000**	**$405,000**	**($15,000)**
Materials and Equipment:			
Special Materials	$150,000	$112,000	($38,000)
Special Equipment	250,000	325,000	75,000
Assigned General Materials	100,000	100,000	0
Assigned General Lab Supplies	50,000	65,000	15,000
Assigned General Lab Equipment	85,000	85,000	0
Subtotal Materials and Equipment	**$635,000**	**$687,000**	**$52,000**
Total Project Xi	**$1,055,000**	**$1,092,000**	**$37,000**
Total Projects:			
Labor:			
Principal Investigator	$320,000	$320,000	0
Senior Scientist(s)	384,000	400,000	$16,000
Scientist(s)	340,000	336,000	(4,000)
Laboratory Technician(s)	200,000	192,000	(8,000)
Assigned General Lab Labor	110,000	112,000	2,000
Subtotal Labor	**$1,354,000**	**$1,360,000**	**$6,000**
Materials and Equipment:			
Special Materials	$480,000	$510,000	$30,000
Special Equipment	800,000	790,000	(10,000)
Assigned General Materials	320,000	310,000	(10,000)
Assigned General Lab Supplies	160,000	155,000	(5,000)
Assigned General Lab Equipment	270,000	260,000	(10,000)
Subtotal Materials and Equipment	**$2,030,000**	**$2,025,000**	**($5,000)**
General R&D:			
Unassigned General Lab Labor	$40,000	$38,000	($2,000)
Unassigned General Materials	130,000	140,000	(10,000)
Unassigned General Lab Supplies	100,000	105,000	5,000
Unassigned General Lab Equipment	250,000	280,000	(30,000)
Unassigned R&D General & Admin	325,000	305,000	(20,000)
Subtotal General R&D:	**$845,000**	**$868,000**	**$23,000**
Total R&D	**$4,229,000**	**$4,253,000**	**$24,000**

Exhibit 38.2. Research and development project budget tracking

(c) Product Development. The product development phase focuses on scale-up of the most promising compound(s), and development of a repeatable process for producing these candidate compounds. Standard operating procedures (SOPs) and other process and scale-up documentation are developed to facilitate technology transfer, as well as to provide an auditable trail of the development process. In the past, responsibility for cost of goods sold (COGS) fell upon the manufacturing group. Health-care reform pressures, including requirements for early pharmacoeconomic justifications, have driven attention to COGS further back in the development process. Companies currently focus process development efforts on not only the technical efficiency of the process, but also the cost effectiveness. The sources of uncertainty for this stage in the company's life cycle are the challenges in developing an economical, reproducible process that can supply the market demand, and forecasting a good estimate of that market demand.

Today, in addition to the scale-up hurdles in process development (which are typically more difficult to overcome in biotechnology processes than traditional pharmaceutical processes), the cost effectiveness of the process and pharmacoeconomics of the product must also be considered. These risks can be managed by early investment in market research, and definition of the size and structure of the target market. This will provide the company with the upside potential of developing the lead candidate compound, as well as a basis for developing a cost-effective process and performing pharmacoeconomic studies. These activities also should receive early funding to avoid expensive scale-up development on processes that may later prove not to be economical.

(d) Clinical Trials. The focus of the clinical trials stage of the biotechnology company's life cycle is to conduct the experimentation necessary to collect clinical data on the toxicology, potency, and efficacy of the product, to be used as a basis for FDA approval of the product.

The principal source of uncertainty during this stage is the success or failure of the clinical trials. As a product moves through the various clinical phrases (I, II, and III), the cost commitment increases geometrically. The further into the clinical trial process a product fails, the greater the loss. The best way to manage this risk is to make a greater investment in earlier clinical phases, which will allow more thorough investigation and screening of compounds, and will increase the probability that only high-potential products proceed to the next phase of clinical development. This strategy will assist companies in minimizing phase III surprises. If pharmacoeconomic studies were not conducted during the process development stage, the budget for this stage should be constructed to allow for performance of these studies.

(e) Product Approval. The focus of the product approval stage of the life cycle is preparation and filing of documents for FDA product approval, and for validation of the associated process, facility, and equipment. The assembly of documentation for filing and to support validation activities requires extensive labor resources. This can be mitigated to some degree, for the approval of drugs, through the use of information technology to perform a computer-aided new drug application (CANDA) filing. The labor resources saved, however, must be redeployed to some extent to support the planning and setup of the various systems to support the CANDA.

The source of uncertainty for this stage of the life cycle is FDA approval of the product filing and equipment, facility, and process validations. The best way to address this risk is to budget sufficient funds for well-planned and well-executed FDA filings and validations. The appropriate support resources should be contracted if they are not available in house. This solution may be preferable to hiring the resources, especially for the first product filing. Although contracting will have a higher cost per hour than hiring, contract resources are easily released at the completion of the project; they can also be placed on hold if a delay is encountered, thus not generating any expense during such a holding period.

(f) Product Launch. The primary budgetary focus of the product launch stage of the life cycle is to develop sales and marketing capability and to build sufficient inventory to support the product launch. For companies that choose not to build a sales and marketing function, these activities can be outsourced. In many cases, agreements may already be in place for products that are licensed out.

The chief sources of uncertainty for this life cycle stage are the accuracy of market demand estimates and the ability to deliver product to satisfy that demand. The COGS of biotechnology products, as a percentage of sales, is much greater than for traditional pharmaceutical products. Comparing published fiscal year 1993 results for a group of leading manufacturers, cost of sales within pharmaceuticals is approximately 26%, compared to more than 38% for biotech. Coupled with the highly perishable nature of most biotechnology products, this makes building excessive prelaunch inventory an unwise strategy. A delicate balance must be reached. This concern, further exacerbated by conservative demand estimates, has resulted in early shortages for some new products. The best strategy is still to use relatively conservative estimates and to build a slight excess of prelaunch inventory to hedge the risk of demand being greater than expected. Market demand uncertainty may be somewhat mitigated by clearly defining and researching the target market. Allowances should be made in the budget at this stage for confirmation of the target market.

(g) Manufacturing and Distribution. The final stage in the life cycle is the manufacturing and distribution stage. The focus of the budget during this phase is on capital and labor expenditures to support the development and enhancement of ongoing manufacturing and distribution capabilities. This includes methodologies for forecasting demand (or, preferably, analyzing actual demand), planning capacity expansions, and managing the supply chain.

The major sources of uncertainty for this stage of the life cycle are the accuracy of forecasts; competitive products entering or leaving the market, causing unplanned spikes in the demand pattern; and unexpected process problems that cause sudden shortages in supply. Managing these sources of uncertainty involves improving the accuracy of forecasts or gaining visibility of actual demand; continually collecting market intelligence regarding competitive products, to anticipate spikes in market share and demand; and utilizing advanced analytical techniques and data trending to predict and minimize process problems. Funds for these risk mitigation activities should be provided in the budget, at least as a contingency, to avoid having to ''steal'' money from other budgetary areas.

Exhibit 38.3 summarizes the focus of each stage of the biotech company life cycle, the principal sources of uncertainty, risk management techniques, and budgetary considerations.

38.4 BUDGET FOCUS BY FUNCTION AND AREA.

Currently, most companies in the biotech industry have a functional organization structure, and have not transitioned to a more efficient process-based organization. As a result, budgets are still prepared along functional lines. Even if the company moves to a process orientation, it is still useful to

Lifecycle Phase	Budget Focus	Sources of Uncertainty	Approach
Financing Start-up	Building organization and research capabilities	Acquisition of funding and of R&D talent	Solid business plan, attack empty niche market and obtain significant recurring funding
Research Discovery	Driving discovery and first potential compound	Serendipity of discovery	Target efforts (specific treatments/disease family) and use advanced tools (combinatorial chemistry)
Product Development	Defining process and scaling-up of key compound(s)	Scale-up hurdles, economic process development and market demand	Early funds for scale-up, good market research budget and early process economics
Clinical Trials	Conducting trials to show potency, toxicology, efficacy and bioavailability	Toxicology and therapeutic action results and pharmacoeconomics (emerging)	Allocate greater funds for more comprehensive phase I and II trials to avoid phase III surprises
Product Approval	Filing with FDA for product and facility approval	Regulatory agencies (FDA)	Significant funding to allow complete and well planned/executed NDA filing and facility validation
Product Launch	Building inventory and sales and marketing capabilities	Market size, market share, product demand and delivery lead time	Understand market demand and build sufficient inventory to fully launch product
Manufacturing and Distribution	Using capital and labor to build production and distribution capabilities and cGMP compliance	Competitive products forecasts and demand	Invest early to reduce COGS to strengthen position and concentrate on adding value added customer service

Exhibit 38.3. Summary of the budgeting process by life-cycle phase

consider requirements from the functional perspective. This presents key budget line items in each functional area for a vertically integrated biotech company. This is a "snapshot" budget of ongoing operations, as discussed in Section 38.3. The budget for start-up companies can be very different. For companies with a lesser degree of vertical integration, such as contract research organizations, technology licensers, contract manufacturers, and co-marketers, line items and even entire functional areas may not appear.

(a) Research. Three major cost categories in the research function must be addressed in the budget: labor, materials and supplies, and fixed costs associated with equipment and facilities.

The first and most important cost category is labor. This includes not only scientists and technical personnel, but also research and development (R&D) support staff, such as glassware washers and reagent preparation staff. This often represents the most significant cost category at biotech companies. When budgets are being planned, consideration must be given to anticipated new hires who might be added throughout the year. These new hires may be included in plans to increase staffing due to requirements at different phases of the development cycle. Associated expenses for benefits and employer costs, such as workers' compensation and health insurance, also must be included, as these vary either as a fixed rate per employee or as a percentage of the employees' salaries or wages.

The materials and supplies cost category includes items that will be consumed during or in support of performance of R&D activities. This includes chemical reagents, disposable items (latex gloves, pipettes, and the like), and consumable parts (such as filter cartridges and fractional chromatography tubing).

The third category addresses costs related to expenditures for equipment. Each year new equipment must be purchased to replace used, obsolete, and retired equipment, as well as for expansion of R&D operations. Although anticipated capital expenditures must be included in the capital budget, the operating budget must address the costs related to the operation and depreciation or amortization of these pieces of equipment. Annual maintenance contracts, emergency maintenance, and spare parts are also included in this cost category.

These cost categories, and especially the labor and materials/supplies groups, can be further partitioned by project. Some companies like to capture these costs by project to facilitate their recovery when the company begins to generate revenue, utilizing the life cycle accounting techniques discussed in Section 34.5(a).

(b) Operations. Operational costs are incurred for the production of salable, or trade, materials. Some of the items will be the same as those in the research area, but their accounting treatment will be different. Budget line items for the operations area are typically divided into two broad cost categories: direct costs and indirect costs. Direct costs include all materials consumed in the manufacture of products, including materials and labor. A production unit of finished goods is exploded by means of a bill of materials (BOM), which links from finished goods to work in progress and further back to raw materials (in units or quantities) and labor (man-hours per unit related to the quantity produced); standard costs are then applied.

Indirect costs include all costs that support the manufacturing operations but are not directly consumed in the production process. These costs must be allocated to, absorbed into, or in some other way linked to finished goods produced, to be represented in the COGS or treated as fixed manufacturing overhead and expensed in that way. These indirect costs include such support activities as maintenance, purchasing services, supervision, and materials management. The operations functional area of the budget is unique, in that it is common to see this section of the budget, as well as product projections, calculated in terms of units, quantities, and manhours, which are then converted to dollars.

(c) Selling, General, and Administrative. The sales, general, and administrative section of the budget represents an ''all other expenses'' category for biotechnology companies. This is different from many other industries because many biotechnology companies often do not develop sales and marketing capabilities. Thus, this category tends to be predominantly administrative overhead expenses. The items that typically are included in the general and administrative segment are executive management compensation, accounting and allied business functions, general clerical help, and general support functions such as information technology.

The sales component of this category includes direct and indirect expenses incurred in performing sales and marketing activities. Budget line items included in this cost category are compensation for sales and marketing staff, expense account allocations, product/service promotions, and market research. Compensation for sales and marketing personnel might include complex incentive and bonus packages in addition to base salaries, which introduces a degree of uncertainty into an otherwise straightforward cost category. Even expense account costs are more straightforward because they can be budgeted, on a head-count basis, as the responsibility of the individual salesperson. For most biotechnology products, promotion expenses can be predicted with a relatively high degree of certainty; in today's changing health-care environment, promotion budgets must address service, as well as product, promotions. Market research is also part of the sales and marketing cost category; this includes outsourced services in addition to internal staff compensation and research expenses. Clerical and support staff expenses linked to sales and marketing activities are often broken out as a line item in the sales and marketing cost category, in lieu of being included in the general and administrative cost category.

(d) Facilities and Equipment. Facilities and equipment can be built, leased, or purchased; equipment can likewise be leased or purchased. Each of these options will result in different scenarios for budgetary requirements, specifically related to the magnitude and timing of investment and expense cash flows.

(e) Cash Budget. More so than at larger, more established pharmaceutical companies, biotechnology companies must maintain a delicate balancing act. The company must invest available capital to provide as high a return as possible, to continually extend the life of its capital burn rate, while at the same time keeping enough cash available to satisfy payables in a timely manner (to maintain a good credit rating). This usually involves timed deposits into cash accounts and careful timing of investments. Because these functions are performed by the financial group, that group is in the best position to budget the outward cash flows for the year.

(f) Sales/Revenue Considerations. As the biotech company plans for commercial introduction of its products, the demands of the new health-care market and the managed-care environment in general cause product sales frequently to be tied to the formulary of managed-care providers. Therefore, contracts between manufacturers and these managed-care providers frequently must be initiated to provide the access for sales. These contracts also specify the provision of discount rebates tied to the sales of products. This represents another key item to be planned; simple input of projected sales volumes and prices would overstate actual revenues, as it would fail to recognize these discounts and rebates. A truer assessment of net sales must be achieved by including these items.

38.5 OTHER CONSIDERATIONS AND TOOLS

(a) Life-cycle Accounting. Life-cycle accounting is the accumulation of costs for activities that occur over the entire life cycle of a product, from inception to abandonment by the manufacturer and consumer. Given that a number of products introduced in the biotech industry may be experimental or have a long developmental stage, companies adopting the life cycle accounting approach will benefit, because this treatment considers the full costs from cradle to grave. In addition, because most of the cost of a new product is incurred after the design stage, life cycle costing accounts for 100% of these costs,

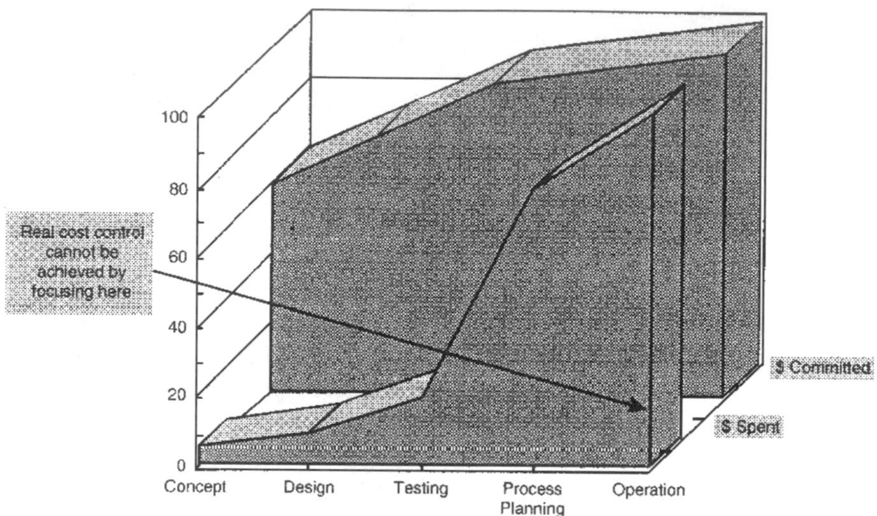

Exhibit 38.4. The concepts of life-cycle costing

including the production, maintenance, and any associated regulatory or environmental expenses. Life-cycle costing also may indicate that a competitive product with high initial costs is a better alternative than one with low acquisition costs but higher operating, maintenance, or regulatory costs. However, it should be noted that all costs throughout a product's life cycle must be considered in order to make a valid comparison of competing products or processes.

Another benefit of life-cycle costing is that it promotes a better matching of revenues and expenses. This is achieved by expensing certain activities based on the total planned number of units to be sold. A distinction, however, is that for management accounting purposes, all costs identified as benefiting the future and directly associated with management's plan are capitalized as incurred. This treatment of capitalizing-as-incurred requires that the expenditures be tied to a future product or program. The accountant or finance person should consider these types of costs (namely, preproduction costs such as R&D, planning, and start-up expenses) when preparing the company's annual budget or strategic plans for a biotech concern. The concepts of life-cycle costing are illustrated Exhibit 38.4. The traditional generally accepted accounting principles (GAAP) model, shown as the ''$ spent'' curve, dictates that project costs be expensed as incurred. The life-cycle model, however, represented by the ''$ committed'' curve, capitalizes items as incurred, for those costs benefiting the future, which can be identified as part of a capital program linked to a future product or management objective.

(b) Technology Accounting. Technology accounting embodies the management accounting concept that technology costs, which include plant, equipment, and information systems, should be treated as direct costs, similar to direct labor and material. Many companies capitalize technology costs and amortize or depreciate them over the estimated useful life of the proposed technology; this method, which links cost to a fixed time period, tends to distort indirect overhead costs (which include amortization of the technology investment), because the fixed period often differs from the product life cycle. An example of this is idle machinery that continues to amortize even though there is little or no production associated with that machinery.

The alternative approach is to amortize the technology costs over planned production runs, thereby matching costs more directly with products manufactured. This is accomplished by calculating a per-unit amortization amount, with the aggregate units identified as those involved in planned production or projected product demand. Those selecting this option should also consider the obsolescence of the asset's technology for the manufacturing process. This methodology also may lead to a different approach to GAAP, as direct production-based amortization replaces a time-based indirect allocation of costs. The financial executive or controller of a biotech firm should consider this alternative approach, because it more accurately spreads technology costs over the product life cycles that the technology supports.

(c) Risk Analysis for Projects. The term *risk* as it relates to a biotech company's capital budgeting decision refers to the uncertainty involved in the potential outcomes of investment decisions and is also known as *strategic risk.* The possibility exists that these outcomes may result in real financial losses, requiring firms to analyze the risk using a variety of methods. These methods can be classified into two major categories, namely:

1. Simple risk adjustment (SRA) methods that rely on achieving a company's desired discount rate or payback period
2. Probabilistic risk-analysis (PRA) techniques that evaluate the uncertainties of critical variables and their probabilities, prior to any decisions made on risk–return/tradeoff. Examples of these include sensitivity analysis, basic probability analysis, Monte Carlo simulation, decision-tree analysis, and capital asset pricing routines. These techniques are used by more sophisticated pharmaceutical companies.

Probabilistic risk-analysis techniques require more rigorous analysis; however, they provide more quantitative information about the risk implied in the prospective project. It is the view of some practitioners that this additional quantitative data allows for greater insight into the nature of the risk and, ultimately, increases shareholder value (see Chapter 11A for further discussions on the subject). Recent surveys conducted on capital budgeting issues indicate that companies have generally transitioned from theoretical discussion to practical use of risk-analysis approaches.

The recent proliferation of financial modeling software has made it easier for companies to use more sophisticated risk-analysis techniques in their evaluation of strategic investments. This is a positive trend, but this increased complexity has, in some cases, unfortunately led to less acceptance of capital projects, thereby reducing the number of investment opportunities presented, which ultimately impacts capital-expenditure levels.

Biotech concerns must begin to develop a portfolio of risk analysis tools, and to use the simple with the sophisticated, in order to enable a more informed decision-making process on capital and strategic investments.

38.6 SUMMARY. With all the complexities and challenges facing biotech companies, operational and financial budgeting may seem a trivial task. Yet, the ability to control one's destiny may lie in effective projection, measurement, and management of internal operations and expenses. As biotechs evolve and mature both in size and commercial focus, increased levels of financial sophistication will be required, both in internal resources and in tools applied. This chapter has presented points of concern and consideration for biotechs (and indeed for other start-up enterprises) so that they may begin with the right questions, and so as to include adequate funding plans for the breadth of resources required to effectively operate their companies.

SOURCES AND SUGGESTED REFERENCES

''Biotech Industry Alive, Proving Naysayers Wrong,'' *Chemical Marketing Reporter,* September 26, 1994, p. 19.

Berliner, Callie, and James A. Brimson, *Cost Management for Today's Advanced Manufacturing.* Boston, MA: Harvard Business School Press, 1988.

Brimson, James A., ''Technology Accounting,'' *Management Accounting,* March 1989, p. 47.

Goldberg, Robert M., ''Health Care Reform and the Future of Biomedical Progress,'' *Journal of American Society of CLU & ChFC,* September 1994, pp. 48–54.

Hamilton, Joan O.C., ''Biotech: An Industry Crowded With Players Faces an Ugly Reckoning,'' *Business Week,* September 26, 1994, pp. 84–92.

Hamilton, Joan O.C., ''Warning: Don't Invest If You Have Heart Problems,'' *Business Week,* September 26, 1994, p. 88.

Ojala, Marydee, ''Business Searching for Biotechnology,'' *Database,* August 1994, pp. 74–76.

Pike, Richard H., ''Do Sophisticated Capital Budgeting Approaches Improve Investment Decision Making Effectiveness?,'' *Engineering Economist,* Winter 1989.

Rotman, David, ''Biotech Sales Flourish, But Cash Remains Scarce,'' *Chemical Week,* September 28, 1994, p. 13.

Simon, S. M. Ho, and Richard Pike, ''Risk Analysis in Capital Budgeting Context: Simple or Sophisticated,'' *Accounting and Business Research,* Summer 1991, pp. 227–237.

Thayer, Ann, ''Biotech Industry Readies for Reform and Renewal,'' *Chemical & Engineering News,* October 3, 1994, p. 17.

INDEX